Frommer's®

China

5th Edition

by Simon Foster, Candice Lee,
Jen Lin-Liu, Beth Reiber,
Tini Tran, Lee Wing-sze, and
Christopher D. Winnan

John Wiley & Sons, Inc.

Published by:
JOHN WILEY & SONS, INC.
111 River St.
Hoboken, NJ 07030-5774

ISBN 978-1-118-09419-8 (paper); ISBN 978-1-118-22352-9 (ebk); ISBN 978-1-118-23677-2 (ebk); ISBN 978-1-118-26179-8 (ebk)

Editors: Jamie Ehrlich and Melinda Quintero
Production Editor: Eric T. Schroeder
Cartographer: Elizabeth Puhl
Photo Editor: Richard Fox
Production by Wiley Indianapolis Composition Services

Front Cover Photo: Naxi-style pagoda reflected in pond with peaks of Jade Dragon Snow Mountain in background, Lijiang, Yunnan Province ©Vetta Stock Photo / iStock Photo.
Back Cover Photo: The shopping area of Nanjing Donglu, Shanghai ©Kevin Foy / Alamy Images.

For information on our other products and services or to obtain technical support, please contact our Customer Care Department within the U.S. at 877/762-2974, outside the U.S. at 317/572-3993 or fax 317/572-4002.

Wiley also publishes its books in a variety of electronic formats. Some content that appears in print may not be available in electronic formats.

Manufactured in the United States of America

5 4 3 2 1

CONTENTS

5 THE NORTHEAST 147

6 ALONG THE YELLOW RIVER 206

7 THE SILK ROUTES 250

8 EASTERN CENTRAL CHINA 336

9 SHANGHAI 427

10 THE SOUTHEAST 489

11 HONG KONG 543

12 THE SOUTHWEST: MOUNTAINS & MINORITIES 594

13 YANGZI & BEYOND 669

14 THE TIBETAN WORLD 740

15 PLANNING YOUR TRIP TO CHINA 786

16 THE CHINESE LANGUAGE 816

17 THE CHINESE MENU 849

LIST OF MAPS

HOW TO CONTACT US

In researching this book, we discovered many wonderful places—hotels, restaurants, shops, and more. We're sure you'll find others. Please tell us about them, so we can share the information with your fellow travelers in upcoming editions. If you were disappointed with a recommendation, we'd love to know that, too. Please write to:

Frommer's China, 5th Edition
John Wiley & Sons, Inc. • 111 River St. • Hoboken, NJ 07030-5774
frommersfeedback@wiley.com

ADVISORY & DISCLAIMER

Travel information can change quickly and unexpectedly, and we strongly advise you to confirm important details locally before traveling, including information on visas, health and safety, traffic and transport, accommodations, shopping, and eating out. We also encourage you to stay alert while traveling and to remain aware of your surroundings. Avoid civil disturbances, and keep a close eye on cameras, purses, wallets, and other valuables.

While we have endeavored to ensure that the information contained within this guide is accurate and up-to-date at the time of publication, we make no representations or warranties with respect to the accuracy or completeness of the contents of this work and specifically disclaim all warranties, including without limitation warranties of fitness for a particular purpose. We accept no responsibility or liability for any inaccuracy or errors or omissions, or for any inconvenience, loss, damage, costs, or expenses of any nature whatsoever incurred or suffered by anyone as a result of any advice or information contained in this guide.

The inclusion of a company, organization, or website in this guide as a service provider and/or potential source of further information does not mean that we endorse them or the information they provide. Be aware that information provided through some websites may be unreliable and can change without notice. Neither the publisher nor author shall be liable for any damages arising herefrom.

ABOUT THE AUTHORS

Simon Foster was born in London and grew up in rural Yorkshire. He started work as a tour leader in the Middle East in 1997 and was then posted to India and China. He has contributed to numerous international guidebooks and magazines, and now lives in sunny southern Taiwan with his wife, daughter, and dog. When he's not writing, Simon leads adventure tours for Bamboo Trails (www.bambootrails.com) and Grasshopper Adventures (www.grasshopperadventures.com) in China, Taiwan, the Philippines, and India.

Candice Lee has lived in Beijing for the past 5 years and has worked as a manager and cooking instructor at Black Sesame Kitchen for 3 years with previous experience working with HIV/AIDS, research, and event managing. She explores, eats, and scrappily finds her way through as many new places as possible (usually by bicycle).

Jen Lin-Liu is the author of *Serve the People: A Stir-Fried Journey Through China* (Harcourt, 2008) and a forthcoming book about the food of the Silk Road (Riverhead Press). She lives in Beijing and has written about food, culture, and travel for a wide range of international publications.

Beth Reiber spent hours pouring over her grandparents' latest *National Geographic* magazines. After living four years in Germany as a university student and then as a freelance travel writer selling to major U.S. newspapers like the *Los Angeles Times* and *Washington Post*, followed by a stint in Tokyo as editor of the *Far East Traveler*, she authored several Frommer's guides, including *Frommer's Japan, Frommer's Tokyo* and *Frommer's Hong Kong*.

Tini Tran has spent nearly two decades as a reporter in the United States and overseas. She is a veteran foreign correspondent who has traveled extensively throughout Asia and parts of the Middle East on assignment, reporting from Pakistan, Afghanistan and Iraq, among other countries. She has been based in China since 2008, most recently working for the Associated Press. She was chosen as a Nieman Fellow at Harvard University from 2006-2007. Prior to that, she served as the Vietnam bureau chief for The AP. Born in Saigon, she returned to her homeland in 1999 to become the first Vietnamese-American allowed to join the foreign press corps.

Lee Wing-sze is a freelance writer, translator, and avid traveler who hails from Hong Kong where she has been witness to the economic and ideologic impact of China on the East-meets-West city since the 1997 handover. Music and basketball are her passion, but her dream is to step foot in every country on the earth, all the while bumping into people of different colors and collecting their compelling life stories.

Christopher D. Winnan's love/hate relationship with the continent currently known as China has lasted more than a decade. Last year he bought a retirement house in Thailand, but even that cannot seem to keep him away from China, and he is currently residing in Dali, Yunnan Province.

FROMMER'S STAR RATINGS, ICONS & ABBREVIATIONS

Every hotel, restaurant, and attraction listing in this guide has been ranked for quality, value, service, amenities, and special features using a **star-rating system.** In country, state, and regional guides, we also rate towns and regions to help you narrow down your choices and budget your time accordingly. Hotels and restaurants are rated on a scale of zero (recommended) to three stars (exceptional). Attractions, shopping, nightlife, towns, and regions are rated according to the following scale: zero stars (recommended), one star (highly recommended), two stars (very highly recommended), and three stars (must-see).

In addition to the star-rating system, we also use **eight feature icons** that point you to the great deals, in-the-know advice, and unique experiences that separate travelers from tourists. Throughout the book, look for:

special finds—those places only insiders know about

fun facts—details that make travelers more informed and their trips more fun

kids—best bets for kids and advice for the whole family

special moments—those experiences that memories are made of

overrated—places or experiences not worth your time or money

insider tips—great ways to save time and money

great values—where to get the best deals

warning—traveler's advisories are usually in effect

The following abbreviations are used for credit cards:

AE American Express | DISC Discover | V Visa

DC Diners Club | MC MasterCard

TRAVEL RESOURCES AT FROMMERS.COM

Frommer's travel resources don't end with this guide. Frommer's website, **www.frommers.com,** has travel information on more than 4,000 destinations. We update features regularly, giving you access to the most current trip-planning information and the best airfare, lodging, and car-rental bargains. You can also listen to podcasts, connect with other Frommers.com members through our active-reader forums, share your travel photos, read blogs from guidebook editors and fellow travelers, and much more.

THE BEST OF CHINA

1

With every new edition of this book, identifying the "best of China" becomes a more and more difficult task. China is such a vast and varied land that you can pick and choose from the diverse range of attractions to suit your interests, timescale, and budget. Broadly speaking though, nature lovers should head west where they will be greeted by some of the most spectacular scenery on the planet, culture vultures should focus on the "cradles of civilization" and traditional imperial sights, while die-hard urbanites will find more than they can handle in Hong Kong and Shanghai.

However, in spite of all of this choice, as this once isolated giant awakens, forces are being unleashed that impact tourism. Devastating pollution, widespread corruption, and the sheer volume of tourists have transformed some of China's best-known sights into overpriced circuses. Fortunately many places within the People's Republic have only recently been opened to visitors, leaving them comparatively untouched and undiscovered. To find the very best that China has to offer, follow the list below.

THE best CHINA EXPERIENCES

- **Exploring the Forbidden City's Forgotten Corners** (Beijing): No one fails to be impressed by the grandeur of the Forbidden City's central axis, which is all most visitors see. But the quieter maze of pavilions, gardens, courtyards, and theaters to either side have the greater charm. See p. 59.
- **Getting Lost in the Lanes Around Beijing's Back Lakes:** No other city in the world has anything quite like the *hutong,* narrow lanes once "as numberless as the hairs on an ox." Now rapidly vanishing, the best-preserved *hutong* are found around a pair of man-made lakes in the city center. This area is almost the last repository of Old Beijing's gritty, low-rise charm, dotted with tiny temples, hole-in-the-wall noodle shops, and quiet courtyard houses whose older residents still wear Mao suits. See the walking tour, "The Back Lakes," on p. 111.
- **Walking on the Great Wall from Jinshanling to Simatai** (Beijing): The Great Wall, winding snakelike through the mountains, was meant to be

walked. This magnificent 3-hour hike follows China's greatest monument through various states of repair, from freshly restored to thoroughly crumbling, over steep peaks and gentle flats, and through patches of wilderness and rugged farmland, with more than two dozen watchtowers along the way. See chapter 4.

- **Strolling Past the Old Russian Architecture in Harbin:** At the heart of the Russian-built city, Zhongyang Dajie's unexpected cupola-topped Art Nouveau mansions are reminders of the 1920s and 1930s, when Harbin was the liveliest stop on this leg of the Trans-Siberian Railroad. See chapter 5.
- **Cycling the City Wall in Xi'an:** The largest city walls in China have been much pierced for modern purposes and can be tackled in a modern way, too, with a breezy, traffic-light-free ride above the rooftops on rented bicycles and tandems. Behold views of remnants of vernacular architecture, clustered around small temples. See chapter 7.
- **Gazing at the Sea of Terra-Cotta Warriors at the Tomb of Qin Shi Huang** (Xi'an): The first sight of the tomb, in a hangarlike building, leaves many visitors stunned and awed. This destination is at the top of almost every visitor's list, and it does not disappoint. See p. 260.
- **Strolling the Old Neighborhoods of Kashgar:** Spending hours watching how citizens of Kashgar live is one of the most rewarding experiences along the Silk Road, but government plans to redevelop most of the old city are already in action and soon this will all be gone. For now the dusty alleys, colorful residential doorways, and mud-brick walls remain as they have for decades, but the diggers are on the move, so get there while you can! See p. 316.
- **Dining on Shanghai's Bund:** The most widely known street in Asia, with its gorgeous colonial buildings that were the banks, hotels, trading firms, and private clubs of foreign taipans (bosses of old Shanghai's trading firms) and adventurers past, deserves to be walked over and over again. After you've seen it by day, come back again at night for a different perspective. See chapter 9.
- **Strolling in Shanghai's French Concession:** This is the most interesting of the colonial districts left in Shanghai, filled with the gorgeous villas, mansions, and apartment houses of the 1920s and 1930s when the French made their mark here. Plenty of Art Deco gems abound, hidden behind years of grime and buried beneath webs of laundry poles, awaiting discovery, so keep your head up. See chapter 9.
- **Riding the Star Ferry** (Hong Kong): The subway between Kowloon and Hong Kong Island may be quicker, but it doesn't hold a candle to the historic Star Ferry, offering one of the most dramatic—and cheapest—5-minute boat rides in the world. The trip is a good reminder that Hong Kong, with its breathtaking skyline, is dominated by water, with one of the world's busiest harbors. See chapter 11.
- **Exploring the Karst Scenery Around Yangshuo:** The cruise down the Li River between Guilin and Yangshuo reveals scenery that is absolutely captivating. Avoid the pricey taxis and motorbike rentals and explore instead in traditional Chinese style, by bicycle. Both the Yulong River and the Jin Bao are still relatively peaceful as they flick lazily through serrated hills like dragon's teeth. See chapter 12.
- **Exploring Lijiang's Old Town:** Built over 800 years ago and partly rebuilt after a massive 1996 earthquake, Lijiang's old town, with its maze of cobblestone streets, gurgling streams, and original and reconstructed traditional Naxi houses, is one of the most atmospheric places in China. Rise before the sun, then watch its golden

rays filter through the gray winding streets, lighting up the dark wooden houses. See chapter 12.

- **Unwinding in a Sichuan Teahouse:** One of the great pleasures of being in Sichuan is drinking tea at a neighborhood teahouse. On any given afternoon at Wangjialou Park, Wenshu Yuan, and Qingyang Gong in Chengdu, for instance, seniors can be found playing mahjong with friends while their caged songbirds sit in nearby trees providing ambient music. As patrons eat watermelon seeds, nuts, dried squid, or beef jerky, attendants appear at regular intervals to refill their cups from copper kettles. For an afternoon of perfect relaxation, stop by and forget about sightseeing for a few hours. See chapter 13.
- **Taking a "Peapod" Boat Tour** (Yangzi River): The best of the Three Gorges cruise excursions, this 2-hour journey through a long, narrow canyon takes passengers to one of the famous suspended coffins of the Ba people and then returns downstream in a fraction of the time. Along the way, howler monkeys may be spotted swinging through the trees, small waterfalls appear from the rocks, and swallows and other small birds flit about. The water in this small tributary is surprisingly clear, and the scenery and silence are thoroughly calming. See chapter 13.

THE best SMALL TOWNS

- **Manzhouli** (Inner Mongolia): A tiny town of 260,000 on the Russian border, lost in a sea of grass, Manzhouli is the East-meets-Wild-West frontier outpost the late David Carradine should have used as the backdrop to the TV series *Kung Fu*. It stands on the edge of the Hulun Buir, an emerald expanse of grassland shot through with radiant patches of wildflowers. See p. 202.
- **Xia He** (Gansu): This delightful monastery town nestles in a mountain valley at an elevation of 2,900m (9,500 ft.). It's divided into two sections, primarily Hui (Muslim) and Han Chinese at its eastern end, changing abruptly to Tibetan as you climb westward to the gorgeous gilded roofs of the vast Labrang Monastery. Tibetan pilgrims make you welcome on the 3km (2-mile) circuit around the monastery's perimeter. Following Tibetan protests, the town was completely closed to foreign visitors until July 2009, but it is now once again open to all-comers. New hotels and a planned airport and rail link mean that Xia He is on the move, so get there before the hordes! See p. 279.
- **Dunhuang** (Gansu): Surrounded by barren deserts, this oasis town beckons with sand dunes, camel treks, and the Buddhist cave art of Mogao. Its tree-lined streets and backpacker cafes give it a laid-back feel that is hard to find elsewhere in China. See p. 291.
- **Yangshuo** (Guangxi): This small town on the Li River, nestled in an ethereal landscape, has enough laid-back charm to be a delightful alternative to popular Guilin. Yangshuo is at the cutting edge of Chinese tourism with some of its best attractions. See p. 604.
- **Dali** (Yunnan): This home of the Bai people, a backpacker's mecca recently gentrified, remains a retreat from the world. You can hike part of the impressive 19-peak Green Mountains (Cang Shan) to the west, sail on the cerulean Er Hai Lake to the east, and take a bike ride into any of the nearby Bai villages. See p. 641.

THE best COUNTRYSIDE TRIPS

- **Eastern Qing Tombs** (Hebei): This rural tomb complex offers more to the visitor than the better-known Ming Tombs, but sees a fraction of the visitors. Though difficult to reach, the effort is rewarded many times over by the Qianlong emperor's breathtakingly beautiful tomb chamber, Yu Ling, and a photo exhibit of the much-maligned dowager empress Cixi. See chapter 4.
- **Changbai Shan** (Jilin): This long-dormant 2,600m-high (8,500-ft.) volcano is home to Tian Chi, a deep, pure, mist-enshrouded crater lake that straddles the China–North Korea border and is sacred to both Koreans and Manchurians. The northern approach to the lake, with its trail that climbs alongside the thundering Changbai Waterfall, is best in the fall. The western approach is ideal in early summer, when its vast fields of vibrant wildflowers are in full bloom. See p. 187.
- **Hulun Buir Grasslands** (Inner Mongolia): Located just outside the remote border town of Manzhouli, the Hulun Buir's grasslands are the most pristine in China. This expanse of gentle emerald hills, perfectly punctuated with small streams and rocky outcrops, is all the more attractive for how difficult it is to reach. See chapter 5.
- **Langmu Si** (Gansu): This Tibetan monastic center is still largely unknown to Chinese tourists, and the tranquil mountain village is reminiscent of Lijiang before it was "discovered." The town is home to two major Tibetan monasteries, housing around 1,000 monks whose chanting of the scriptures may be heard throughout the day. Ramble through narrow ravines and moraine valleys crowded with wildflowers, or take a horse trek up Flower Cap Mountain to obtain stunning views as far as the holy mountain of Amnye Machen. See p. 283.
- **Karakul Lake** (Xinjiang): On the highway between Kashgar and Tashkurgan lies a pristine lake at an altitude of nearly 4,000m (13,120 ft.), surrounded by stark, jagged mountains. Come here for some peace and quiet and a change of scenery from the dusty Uighur towns along the Silk Road. See p. 326.
- **Mile** (Yunnan): While most tourists stick to the confines of the Stine Forest Park, these amazing formations actually stretch for three or four counties all the way down to Mile and beyond. Use the eco resort in the new town as a base and explore what has to be one of the most comfortable climates in the country. See p. 638.
- **Lingyun** (Guangxi): Despite its relatively easy access, the tourist hordes have yet to discover the gorgeous karst scenery of Lingyun, with its natural swimming holes and breath taking mountains and valleys. If you enjoyed Yangshuo and Guilin, then this will really knock your socks off. See p. 625.
- **Around Lijiang** (Yunnan): This area offers a wide variety of countryside experiences, from riding a chairlift up to the glacier park of the magnificent, snowcapped Jade Dragon Snow Mountain, to hiking the sheer-sided Tiger Leaping Gorge while the Yangzi River rages below. See p. 654.
- **The Tea Horse Caravan Trail** (Yunnan): The ancient caravan town of Shaxi has been restored and renovated with great care and attention by a Swiss architecture institute. The old town is a welcome relief from the usual hordes of domestic tourists, with authenticity and history replacing the usual souvenir shops and cafes. See p. 651.
- **Jiuzhaigou** (Sichuan): This national park has dense forest, green meadows, rivers, rapids, ribbon lakes in various shades of blue and green, chalky shoals, and

waterfalls of every kind. Of cultural interest are six Tibetan villages of the original nine from which this valley gets its name. See p. 694.

- **Wulingyuan & Zhangjiajie** (Hunan): This scenic area is made up of three subtropical parklands, with quartzite sandstone peaks and pillars to rival Guilin's scenery. There are plentiful rare plants and insects, swarms of butterflies, a large cave with calcite deposits, and stunning views through bamboo, pine, and oak forests. See p. 733.
- **Amnye Machen** (Qinghai): The route around this holy mountain, for a while believed to be the world's highest, must be clockwise—turning back is sacrilegious. So once you start on the 4- to 8-day trek there's no turning back! But the scenery around the 6,282m (20,605-ft.) peak, and the company of sometimes entire villages of Tibetans, make the trek well worthwhile. See p. 754.
- **Everest Base Camp** (Tibet): Whether by 3-hour drive from the village of New Tingri, or by a 3- to 4-day trek from Old Tingri, the trip to the tented base camp (at 5,150m/16,890 ft.) or to rooms in Rongbuk Monastery (at 4,980m/16,330 ft.) offers unbeatable vistas of the world's toothiest snowcaps set against a startling cobalt sky. See p. 782.

THE best MANSIONS & PALACES

- **The Forbidden City** (Beijing): Preeminent among the surviving complexes of ancient buildings in China, the former residence of the emperors needs far more time than most tours give it. See p. 99.
- **Bishu Shanzhuang** (Chengde): The imperial summer resort and its surrounding Eight Outer Temples form another of the greatest ancient architectural complexes of China, arranged around a green valley. The temples have bizarre borrowings from a number of minority architectural traditions, and both temples and palace have 18th-century replicas of buildings of which the country is most proud. See p. 130.
- **Wang Jia Dayuan** (Hebei): With investment from a Beijing entrepreneur, part of a traditional courtyard mansion that once housed Shanhaiguan's wealthiest burgher has been magnificently restored and is expected to expand farther south. Set in the heart of the old walled town, it also boasts a folk museum crammed with curiosities. Four of the rooms are available for overnight stays, although you'll have to be out before the next day's visitors arrive. See p. 138.
- **Wei Huanggong** (Changchun): Also known as the Puppet Emperor's Palace and best known in the west as the setting for part of Bernardo Bertolucci's film *The Last Emperor,* this impressive palace complex, opened to visitors after an admirable full-scale restoration in 2002, was the residence of Henry Puyi, China's last emperor and subsequently puppet ruler of Japanese-controlled Manchukuo. See p. 178.
- **Wang Jia Dayuan** (Pingyao): It took a century for this vast mansion to grow to 123 courtyards and 1,118 houses; the decorative lattice screens and windows, shaped openings between rooms and courtyards, and undulating walls are exquisite examples of Ming and Qing vernacular architecture. See p. 236.
- **Potala Palace** (Lhasa): A monastery, a palace, and a prison, the Potala symbolizes the fusion of secular and religious power in Tibet in a vast, slab-sided, red-and-white

agglomeration on a hilltop dominating central Lhasa. Despite the modern Chinese developments that surround it, there's still no more haunting sight within China's modern political boundaries, and nothing else that speaks so clearly of the otherness of Tibet. See p. 756.

THE best MUSEUMS

- **The National Museum** (Beijing): After a decade-long effort that cost nearly $400 million, the National Museum—three times the size of the Louvre—impresses with its trove of more than 1 million cultural relics from China's lengthy history. Don't miss the exhibit on Ancient China, which covers in exhaustive detail the prehistoric era through China's final dynasty, the Qing. See p. 108.
- **Shanxi Lishi Bowuguan** (Xi'an): If you can visit only one museum in China, this should be it. An unrivaled collection of treasures, many demonstrating Xi'an's international contacts via the Silk Routes, is more professionally displayed here than almost anywhere else in the mainland, especially since recent renovations. See p. 260.
- **Nanjing Datusha Jinianguan** (Nanjing): The deaths of over 300,000 Chinese, killed over the course of 6 weeks during the 1937 Japanese invasion of Nanjing, are commemorated here. Photographs and artifacts documenting the Japanese onslaught, the atrocities suffered, and the aftermath, are sobering, grisly, and shockingly effective. See p. 397.
- **Shanghai Bowuguan** (Shanghai): China's finest, most modern, and most memorable museum of historic relics has disappointed almost no visitor since it opened in the heart of People's Square. Make it a top priority, and allow a few hours more than you planned on. See p. 466.
- **Tea Horse Road Museum** (Lijiang): The beautiful dioramas here recreate the "Chamagudao" all the way from tropical lowlands into the Tibetan foothills, with English language narration to boot. It's one the best opportunities to get an overall feel for the ancient southern silk road. See p. 660.
- **Hong Kong Museum of History** (Hong Kong): A life-size diorama of a Neolithic settlement, replicas of fishing boats and traditional houses, ethnic clothing, displays of colorful festivals, and whole streets of old shop frontages with their interiors removed piece by piece and rebuilt here, make this the most entertaining museum in China. See p. 570.
- **Sanxing Dui Bowuguan** (Chengdu): An attractive and well-laid-out museum housing items from a group of sacrificial pits, this is one of the most significant finds in 20th-century China. See p. 677.
- **Wang Anting Xiaoxiao Zhanlanguan** (Chengdu): Located in a narrow lane west of the main town square, this small, one-of-a-kind museum contains tens of thousands of Mao pins, Cultural Revolution memorabilia, and vintage photographs. The museum occupies the living room of its devoted proprietor. See p. 679.
- **Tibetan Culture Museum** (Xining): Many people visit this museum purely to examine the world's longest *thangka,* but there are also fascinating medicinal treatises and some wonderful examples of traditional Tibetan dress, all laid-out in state-of-the-art fashion. See p. 746.

THE best TEMPLES

See also Chengde's Bishu Shanzhuang and its Eight Outer Temples, in "The Best Mansions & Palaces," above.

- **Yonghe Gong** (Beijing): After the Qing Yongzheng emperor moved into the Forbidden City, his personal residence was converted into this temple. Several impressive incense burners are scattered throughout the golden-roofed complex, also known as the Lama Temple. A 20m-tall (60-ft.) sandalwood statue of Maitreya, the future Buddha, fills the last building. See p. 106.
- **Temple of Heaven** (Beijing): The circular Hall of Prayer for Good Harvests, one of the finest achievements of Ming architecture, is almost as well known as a symbol of Beijing as the Tian'an Men, but the three-tiered sacrificial altar of plain stone is thought by many to be the most sublime object of beauty in China. See p. 103.
- **Zhengding** (Hebei): Neither the most spectacular nor the best known of temple groups, but within a short walking distance of each other, are some of China's oldest surviving unimproved temple buildings (one of which houses a 30m-high/90-ft. multiarmed bronze of Guanyin), and a collection of ancient pagodas so varied it's almost as if they've been set out specifically to surprise you. See p. 140.
- **Yungang Shiku** (Shanxi): These are the earliest Buddhist caves carved in China. Most were hollowed out over a 65-year period between 460 and 524. Viewed as a whole, they show a movement from Indian and central Asian artistic models to greater reliance on Chinese traditions. See p. 210.
- **Maiji Shan Shiku** (Tianshui): This haystack-shaped mountain of soft red rock, covered in brilliant green foliage, is China's prettiest cave-temple site, and the only one where statuary has been added to the cave walls rather than carved out of them. Views from the stairs and walkways lacing the cliffs are spectacular (including those straight down). See p. 270.
- **Mogao Shiku** (Dunhuang): The biggest, best-preserved, and most significant site of Buddhist statuary and frescoes in all China, with the broadest historical range, the Mogao Caves, in their tranquil desert setting, should be your choice if you can see only one cave site. See p. 294.
- **Longmen Shiku** (**Dragon Gate Grottoes;** Luoyang): The grottoes go well beyond just the identity of a temple, as these caves are considered one of the best sculptural treasure-troves in China. The site comprises a mind-boggling 2,300 caves and niches with more than 2,800 inscriptions and over 100,000 Buddhist statues. See p. 349.
- **Kong Miao** (Qufu): One of China's greatest classical architectural complexes, this spectacular temple in Confucius's hometown is the largest and most magnificent of the hundreds of temples around the country honoring the sage. Greatly enlarged since it was originally built in 478 B.C., it has a series of gates and buildings aligned on a north-south axis and decorated with imperial flourishes like yellow-tiled roofs and dragon-entwined pillars. See p. 372.
- **Songzanlin Monastery** (Yunnan): Ever-changing restrictions on traveling to Tibet make visiting Tibetan regions in other Chinese provinces a more appealing prospect, and Songzanlin provides a wonderful opportunity to see a working monastery in its full glory. See p. 667.

- **Baoding Shan** (Dazu): Artistically among the subtlest and most sophisticated of China's Buddhist grottoes, these Song dynasty caves are situated around a horseshoe-shaped cove, at the center of which is lush forest. See p. 707.
- **Jokhang Temple** (Lhasa): The spiritual heart of Tibetan Buddhism, this temple should be visited twice: once to see the intense devotion of pilgrims circumnavigating it by prostrating themselves repeatedly across cobblestones made slippery by centuries of burning yak-butter lamps, and rubbing their foreheads against the statuary in the dim, smoky interior; and a second time in the afternoon for a closer look at the ancient images they venerate. See p. 763.
- **Sakya Monastery** (**Sajia Si;** Sakya): The massive 35m (115-ft.) windowless gray walls of Lhakhang Chenmo tower above the village and fields on the southern bank of the Trum Chu. Completed in 1274, this monastery fort was largely funded by Kublai Khan, and unlike the older temples of north Sakya, it survived the Cultural Revolution. See p. 779.

THE best MARKETS

- **Panjiayuan Jiuhuo Shichang** (Beijing): A vast outdoor market held on weekends, Panjiayuan teems with what is very likely the world's best selection of things Chinese: row upon row of everything from reproduction Ming furniture to the traditional clothing worn by China's many minorities to Mao memorabilia. Most of the antiques are fakes, although experts have made some surprising finds in the bedlam. See p. 116.
- **Kashgar Sunday Bazaar:** The bazaar is now split in two and not quite what it was, but both parts are well worth visiting, particularly the livestock section. Bearded Uighur men in traditional blue-and-white garb sharpen their knives and trim their sheep, small boys gorge themselves on Hami melons, and Kyrgyz in dark fur hats pick up and drop dozens of lambs to test their weight and meatiness before settling deals with vigorous and protracted handshakes. See p. 321.
- **Khotan Sunday Market:** This is everything the Kashgar Market once was. Jewelers pore over gemstones, blacksmiths busy themselves shoeing horses and repairing farm tools, blanket makers beat cotton balls, rat-poison sellers proudly demonstrate the efficacy of their products—the sights and smells are overwhelming. Don't miss the horse-riding enclosure toward the north side of the melee, where buyers test the road-worthiness of both beast and attached cart, with frequent spectacular tumbles. See p. 330.
- **South Bund Fabric Market** (Shanghai): Bales and bales of fabric (silk, cotton, linen, wool, and cashmere) are sold here at ridiculously low prices. Many stalls have their own in-house tailors who can stitch you a suit, or anything else you want, at rates that are less than half what you'd pay at retail outlets. See p. 475.
- **Yide Road Wholesale Markets** (Guangzhou): With so many markets to choose from in a city whose very raison d'être is commerce, it is difficult to know which one to choose first. This is one of the most colorful. If it was made in China, then there is a very good chance that you will find it around here somewhere. See p. 535.
- **Temple Street Night Market** (Hong Kong): Prices here are outrageous compared to those at China's other markets, but the scene at this nightmarket is very

entertaining, especially the fortunetellers, street-side performers singing Chinese opera, and crowds overflowing the *dai pai dong* (roadside food stalls). See p. 580.

THE best FESTIVALS

For dates and contact information, see also the "China Calendar of Events" on p. 37.

- **Kurban Bairam** (Kashgar): Celebrations are held in Muslim communities across China, but in Kashgar they involve feats of tightrope-walking in the main square and wild dancing outside the Id Kah Mosque. The 4-day festival is held 70 days after the breaking of the fast of Ramadan, on the 10th day of the 12th month (Dhul-Hijjah) in the Islamic calendar. See chapter 2.
- **Miao New Year Festival** (Xi Jiang, Langde): The Miao celebrate many festivals, but one of the biggest blowouts is the occasion of the Miao New Year, usually around December. The celebration features songs, dances, bullfights, and *lusheng* competitions, not to mention Miao women gorgeously bedecked in silver headdresses engaging in various courtship rituals. See chapter 2.
- **Ice & Snow Festival** (Harbin): Not so much a festival as an extended citywide exhibition, Harbin's Ice and Snow Festival runs from December to February every year and is without doubt the northeast's top winter attraction. The festival centers on hundreds of elaborate ice and snow sculptures, frosty reproductions of everything from Tian'an Men to Elvis. See chapter 5.
- **Sanyue Jie** (Dali): This once-religious festival celebrated by the Bai people in mid-April/early May now features 5 days and nights of considerably more secular singing, dancing, wrestling, horse racing, and large-scale trading. This is a rare opportunity to see not only the Bai but a number of Yunnan's other ethnic minorities, gathering in one of the most beautiful and serene settings in the foothills of the Green Mountains (Cang Shan). See chapter 12.
- **Saka Dawa:** Held throughout the Tibetan world, this celebrates the Buddha's passing away and thus attaining nirvana. It's held on the 8th to 15th days of the fourth lunar month, with religious dancing, mass chanting, and "sunning the Buddha"—the public display of giant sanctified silk portraits. See chapter 14.

THE best UP-&-COMING DESTINATIONS

- **Yanbian** (Jilin): A lush, achingly pretty hilly region perched on China's border with North Korea, parts of which have only recently been opened to tourism, Yanbian is home to the largest population of ethnic Koreans outside the peninsula itself. Independent-minded travelers have the opportunity to explore one of the few truly bicultural societies in China. See chapter 5.
- **Pingyao** (Shanxi): Chinese tourists have discovered Pingyao, but the number of Western tourists is still relatively low at what is one of the best-preserved Ming and Qing towns in China. An intact Ming city wall surrounds clusters of elegant high-walled courtyard residences, some of which are also guesthouses. See chapter 6.
- **Yi Xian** (Anhui): Often visited en route to or from Huang Shan, this UNESCO World Heritage county is famous for its Ming and Qing dynasty memorial arches

and residential houses. Structures with ornate brick, stone, and wood carvings provide a peek into China's architectural past. See chapter 8.

- **Lingyun, Poyue, Fengshan & Leye** (Guangxi): It's difficult to reach as yet, but this is what the countryside around Guilin wants to be when it grows up. There are limited facilities, but caves and peaks that will amaze even the most experienced travelers. See chapter 12.

THE best BUYS

Note: Pearls, antiques, jade, jewelry in general, and objets d'art are fakes or are not worth the asking price (usually both). Unless you are an expert or are happy to have a fake, do not buy these things.

- **Factory 798** (Beijing): We were sure that an ad hoc gathering of designers, painters, and sculptors selling avant-garde art in a former military complex wasn't something the regime would tolerate for long. We were wrong. Market rents are now charged, so don't expect to pick up a bargain, but the Dashanzi art district makes for a thoroughly enjoyable afternoon of gallery- and cafe-hopping. See p. 110.
- **Ba Xian An** (Xi'an): There are fakes aplenty, as everywhere else, but this bustling antiques market, fed by continuous new discoveries in the surrounding plain, is too atmospheric to miss. See p. 257.
- **Chen Lu** (Shanxi): Numerous small factories turn out different styles of pottery, and their showrooms have starting prices so low you'll volunteer to pay more. You can also buy original works in the houses of individual artisans. See p. 267.
- **Qipao:** Tailors in Beijing and Shanghai will cut a custom-fit *qipao,* the tight-fitting traditional dress better known by its Cantonese name *cheongsam,* sometimes for hundreds of dollars less than in Hong Kong and the West. A quality tailored dress, lined with silk and finished with handmade buttons, typically costs between $100 and $200. Slightly less fancy versions go for as little as $50. See chapter 9.
- **Dafen Oil Paintings:** Where else can you get an expert artist to paint you and your family into a scene from one of the great masters? And even if you do not fancy yourself inside a Bosch or a Botticelli, there are plenty of contemporary Chinese artists to choose from if you want to invest in some works of art. See p. 540.
- **Jatson School** (Lhasa): High-quality Tibetan handicrafts, including traditional Tibetan clothing, paper, incense, mandala *thangkas,* yak-hide boots, ceramic dolls, door hangings, bags, and cowboy hats, are all made on-site and sold at very fair prices. Your money goes to support poor, orphaned, and disabled Tibetan children. See p. 766.
- **Minority Fabrics & Costumes** (Yunnan & Guizhou): While all of the popular tourist destinations have shops selling silver Miao headdresses, those willing to venture out to the lands of the more obscure minorities will be justly rewarded.
- **Chinese Teas:** Tea is ubiquitous in China, with hundreds of varieties throughout the country. One of the finest is Dragon Well (*longjing cha*), a rare green tea that doesn't come cheap, but is meticulously produced in the mountains surrounding Hangzhou. Get it at the source at the **Dragon Well Tea Plantation** (see p. 486). Also look out for Lapsang Souchong, a delightful, very smoky tea found in **Wuyishan** (see p. 500); Silver Needle tea, a fine white tea once reserved for emperors; flower teas such as jasmine (*molihua cha*); and Pu'er tea, a post-fermented tea found in Yunnan. For more on tea drinking in China, see p. 686.

- **Lhasa Villages Handicrafts** (Lhasa): Finding this little store in the Muslim part of Lhasa is half the fun, and the reward is evident the moment you enter. Quality rugs in traditional and contemporary designs line the walls, painted Tibetan keepsake boxes might catch your eye, and there are a host of smaller items including very cute yak-shaped oven gloves for those who don't want to ship things home. Everything for sale is produced by local villagers as part of a scheme to reinvigorate Tibetan crafts and boost local incomes. See p. 767.

CHINA IN DEPTH

by Simon Foster

2

After 50 years of being closed off to the outside world, China has reopened its doors to outsiders, and the race to see the Middle Kingdom is on. But beyond the Great Wall, Forbidden City, and the Terra-Cotta Warriors, communism, Chairman Mao, human rights issues, the one-child policy, a booming economy, being the factory of the world, and the 2008 Olympics, what can you expect from China? In short, anything and everything; while East Coast and Pearl River Delta cities storm headlong into their skyscraper laden future at a pace inconceivable and unmatchable in the Western world, towns and villages in the west of the country remain unchanged since camel caravans traversed the Silk Road a thousand years ago. Landscapes are startlingly varied and incorporate tropical rainforest, glaciers, fairytale limestone karst towers, loess plateaus, huge river valleys, and gorges along with the world's second biggest desert and its highest mountains. The communities that inhabit these varied landscapes are equally diverse, and though the Han Chinese are predominant throughout most of the country, China's 55 ethnic minorities range from hill tribes in the southwest to Tibetan nomads and Turkic speaking Uighurs in the northwest. On your travels you might meet camel guides, urban fashionistas, goat herders, students, train conductors, and waitresses, each with a story to tell. The fact that they don't speak your language often does little to deter them and, as the world's most populous nation, it is fitting that many travelers' strongest memories of China are of its people. With this geographic and cultural variety comes another bonus for travelers: a culinary diversity that makes China one of the world's great gastronomic destinations. From Beijing Duck to spicy Sichuan, Cantonese *dim sum* to Tibetan *momos,* there's always something new to try, and for those with an open mind and palate there are some dishes that defy belief (ever tried fried scorpion?).

CHINA TODAY

Be not afraid of growing slowly, be only afraid of standing still.

—Chinese proverb

China has come a long, long way in a short span of time, and life is undeniably better for most Chinese than it has ever been. However, this **rapid development** has also exacerbated many of the country's pre-existing problems, and created some new issues along the way. The huge population, gender imbalance, wealth distribution, human rights, territorial disputes, damage to the environment, and the threat posed by respiratory viruses such as SARS, bird flu, and A(H1N1) are just some of the critical issues that need to be addressed in the new China.

In spite of the 2008 world economic crisis and government measures to slow the growth rate, the rapid pace of change in China today is difficult to comprehend and you really do have to go there to understand it. However, not everyone is caught up in the whirlwind and modern China displays greater contrast than anywhere else on the planet. While rich, urban dwellers speed through their high-powered lives in black Audis, stopping to pick up the latest electronic gadgets and designer clothes in shiny new malls, in the countryside, farmers still sporting the blue uniform of the Mao era plow their fields with buffalo and wonder when change might come their way. In spite of programs to try to redress the balance, disparity and inequality look set as fixtures in the Chinese social landscape for the time-being. This disparity has yet to evoke real dissatisfaction—but it's just around the corner and the bright lights of the city beckon many young country dwellers. The government is keen to keep its "iron rice bowl" secure and to this end, in a recent program, incentives such as a new washing machine are offered to those who remain in the countryside. But even if wealth distribution is successful, the larger emerging problem is that as people have more money (and education), they will also want greater social freedom. Social reform looked possible in the early 1980s, but under both Jiang Zemin and now Hu Jintao, it seems farther away than ever. If people don't start to have more social liberties, and soon, they may once again question their social and political rights and rise against the system that is perceived as endemically corrupt and oppressive.

There are still hundreds of thousands of political prisoners in China, and while its human rights record has somewhat limited its international standing in the past, increased wealth is making this increasingly easy for Western governments to ignore. Outwardly, modern China seems to have all the trappings of a free, capitalist society, but don't be lulled into believing that just because there are now Starbucks, five-star hotels, and maglev trains that there isn't oppression: Internally China is still a police state where the media is censored, religions are oppressed, and political principles can land you in prison. This was brought to the world's attention once again in 2010 when human rights activist Liu Xiaobo was awarded the Nobel Peace Prize, but was unable to collect it, or even send a representative to accept it on his behalf, as he was incarcerated in a Chinese jail. The 2011 arrest of prominent artist and outspoken government critic Ai Weiwei, who was involved in the design of the Olympic showpiece Bird's Nest, presents a similarly sad picture of oppression.

Nowhere is this oppression more evident than the peripheral regions of **Tibet** and **Xinjiang.** Both areas have an established history as Chinese tribute regions and are also both predominantly populated by local ethnic groups (the Tibetans and the Muslim Uighurs, respectively). Both regions have long sought independence, and while they are "autonomous" regions of China, the harsh reality is that the Han Chinese are colonizing them, populating the cities with their own people, and extracting minerals and resources. The situation in Tibet has always been fragile at best, and in the lead up to the 2008 Olympics, peaceful protests were met with an armed response and tensions boiled over leaving scores of Han Chinese and Tibetans dead and injured; real numbers have not emerged (and probably never will) due to media blackouts. The situation is still far from resolved and armed troops are an everyday feature on the streets of Lhasa. Cynics would argue that the reason media coverage of the July 2009 Xinjiang riots was more open was because it was principally Han people who were being attacked, and with over 150 dead, these were the heaviest acknowledged street casualties since the Tian'an Men Square Protests in 1989. The Arab world's Jasmine Revolution has further heightened tensions, most readily illustrated by the very visible riot police presence in downtown Ürümqi. Inner Mongolia's protests have thus far remained smaller scale, but the province's superfast economic development has left many Mongolians feeling like strangers in their own land, and this sentiment is beginning to find more of a voice.

Of course, the Chinese have also brought many benefits to these peripheral regions, and doubtless Lhasa, Ürümqi, and Hohhot would not be as developed, wealthy, and well connected as they are now if they were the capitals of independent countries, but separatists argue that this is their decision to make. China is not about to give up these huge, mineral-rich provinces that act as border buffer zones, but neither are the Tibetans, the Uighurs or the Mongolians, which leaves an uneasy stalemate liable to flare up at any time.

Conversely, a decade on, the reacquired territories of **Hong Kong** and **Macau** are being comfortably integrated into modern China, and, following a recent change of leadership, relations with "renegade province" **Taiwan** are also at an all-time high.

Hu Jintao's early departure from the 2009 G8 Summit to deal with the Xinjiang riots recognizes that there are manifold internal issues that need to be dealt with, but, in the wider world, China is finally being recognized as the ascendant power it is and there is more interest in the country than ever. In spite of ongoing trading disputes, particularly with the U.S., China continues to produce and prosper and, in recent years, links have developed with a number of African and South American nations to broaden their trading base. Critics in Europe and the U.S. voice concerns over China's "no conditions" investments in troubled countries like Sudan and Zimbabwe, stating that these contribute to human rights abuses, but the Chinese argue that previous trading partners were doing the same thing before the Chinese arrived and are just unhappy that their roles and profits have been usurped. In world terms, not only has this given developing nations a viable trading alternative, but also a new model for economic development.

Unprecedented development has also dramatically worsened **environmental conditions** to the point that in 2008 China became the world's largest producer of greenhouse gases (although U.S. citizens still produce five times more greenhouse gases per capita). Environmental degradation presents a very real threat to the nation as increasingly frequent dust storms blast through the north of the country, reducing the amount of arable land available to feed China's burgeoning population, while in many cities rivers run black and groundwater is toxic. Though as much driven by economics as conservation, there is now a move toward greater environmental consideration. China has committed to achieving the standards laid out (for developing nations) in the Kyoto Protocol by 2012, and on the ground, measures like the Green Great Wall, which aims to counteract soil erosion in the northwest of the country, are combined with small scale initiatives like seawater flushing toilets and taxes on environmentally damaging products such as disposable chopsticks. However, the country still has a long way to go.

As China has emerged onto the world platform in grand fashion and will doubtless become an increasingly significant international player, it must be remembered that in many respects it is still a developing country and the huge nature of the economic, environmental, political, and, crucially, social problems that face it will continue to test the leadership for many years to come. The long slumbering Chinese dragon has certainly awoken and made its presence known, but it remains to be seen whether it can fly.

LOOKING BACK AT CHINA

A journey of a thousand miles begins with a single step.

—Lao Zi

Given the huge timeline, semi-mythical beginnings, complicated dynastic power struggles, complex modern era, and the sheer size of the country, it isn't surprising that Chinese history can initially seem baffling. Entire volumes have been written about Chinese history and still not covered all of the periods or regions. In this humble book, we've tried to keep it as simple as possible while covering all of the major periods and people, focusing on modern history, and what you're actually likely to see as a visitor.

Pre-History

Legend has it that China was founded by the creator **Panku,** and humans were born of the parasites that infested him. This is certainly a lovely story, but science tells us that the 1926 discovery of skull remains (dubbed **Peking Man**) illustrated that *Homo erectus* in China knew how to use fire and basic stone tools 600,000 years ago. *Homo sapiens* evolved between 500,000 and 200,000 B.C., but it wasn't until 5000 B.C. that the first Chinese society, **Yangshao Culture,** developed. Centered on the Yellow River provinces of Shaanxi and Gansu, Yangshao Culture comprised settled farming communities capable of crafting ceramic and jade wares. **Banpo Neolithic village** (p. 261) and burial ground near Xi'an is the best preserved example of Yangshao Culture and is believed to have been inhabited between 4500 and 3750 B.C.

The Dynastic Age

Aside from the modern period, the bulk of knowledge about Chinese history relates to the dynastic age, and once you have a hold on how this works, the rest begins to fall into place. Essentially dynasties followed bloodlines, and tended to start strong and finish weak, to the point that another dynasty succeeded. The concept of **Divine Mandate** was fundamental to this succession and effectively meant that the emperor was the Son of Heaven and had the right to do pretty much anything he pleased. However, if his actions displeased the gods, a catastrophic event such as a failed harvest, lightning bolt, or invading army would signify that he had lost the Mandate of Heaven, and it was time for a new emperor, or dynasty. This system resulted in an alternating pattern of stable periods of prosperity, development, and expansion, invariably followed by tumultuous times of conflict and uncertainty, and then the cycle would repeat.

FOUNDATION OF THE NATION: THE QIN & THE HAN

Ruthless and driven, **Qin Shi Huang,** "China's first emperor," is one of the most significant players in the whole of Chinese history. After the fractious Warring States Period, Qin Shi Huang emerged victorious and established the brief but brutal **Qin dynasty** (221–206 B.C.). Traditionally seen as a megalomaniac tyrant whose oppressive rule and rebuttal of Confucian ideals far outweighed all of his achievements, there is now a move afoot, at least among Chinese historians, to rescind this view in light of his contribution to the formation of a unified Middle Kingdom. His achievements are unparalleled and include the first version of the Great Wall (p. 122), the Terra-Cotta Warriors (p. 260), and standardized weights and measures.

The enduring **Han dynasty** (206 B.C.–A.D. 220), which still lends its name to China's dominant ethnic group, was a time of consolidation and expansion. The civil service was formalized and exams (based on Confucian texts) were introduced as a means of assessing candidates. There were also great advances in agriculture, textiles, papermaking, and weaponry; the crossbow developed during this time was more accurate and had a longer range than any to date, and this military superiority facilitated the Chinese army's progress as far south as Vietnam. To the west, the Silk Road developed as a trade artery that enabled passage from the capital at **Xianyang** (near Xi'an) all the way to Europe. China's most celebrated historian, **Sima Qian,** lived during the Han dynasty, and his work has enabled future generations to better understand both the Han and those who came before them. However, this knowledge couldn't help the dynasty from repeating the errors of the past, and when the Han dynasty finally came to a close, China was vast, but the imperial coffers were empty. A fractious 4-century period, known as the **Three Kingdoms** (220–581), followed and it wasn't until the **Sui dynasty** (581–618) that China was reunited as a country. The Sui may have been short lived, but this didn't stop them from building one of the world's greatest waterways, the **Grand Canal** (which can still be seen in Suzhou, p. 479, and Hangzhou, p. 482).

THE AGE OF ART: THE TANG & THE SONG

The **glorious Tang dynasty** (618–907) is fondly remembered as China's greatest dynasty, and with good reason. The reconsolidation under the Sui dynasty was definitely progress, but it by no means ensured the reunification of north and south. After 300 years of conflict and uncertainty, the importance of peace, and just getting on with business, is signified by the choice of **Chang'an** (meaning Eternal Peace) as the name for the Tang capital (present day Xi'an). Indeed, the Tang cemented the concept of a united China and the resultant stability brought prosperity, while increased trade and an open-door approach to the outside world ushered in a time of innovation, artistic creativity, and religious tolerance. All of a sudden there was time and money for painting, poetry, and pottery, and when combined with outside influences, this provided the perfect platform for the reinvention of time-honored crafts. But it wasn't all arts and crafts: Territorial expansion was fundamental to the Tang's success and at its peak, Chinese influence was felt from Korea to the Middle East. Equally, trade along the Silk Road and via the southern ports exposed China to outside ideas and religions, and Islam, Nestorianism, and most significantly Buddhism soon found a foothold. Popularity and imperial patronage allowed for the development of some of China's most incredible treasures, including the Buddhist grottoes at Dazu (p. 706), Dunhuang (p. 291), and Luoyang (p. 348). But, glorious as it may have been, a catastrophic loss to the Arabs in the 8th century and a string of weak leaders led to a quiet abdication and the end of the Tang dynasty in 907.

Following the Tang, the **Five Dynasties** (907–960) was yet another dark period that preceded the **Song dynasty** (960–1279), but the first Song emperor, Taizu, quickly consolidated from the new capital in Kaifeng and before long the country was back on track. Once again the arts flourished and the Song dynasty is remembered for landscape painting, poetry, and pottery. It was also a time of great innovation, but

A TRINITY OF teachings

Myth, religion, and philosophy are so intertwined in China that it can be difficult to separate the three. Likewise, the three principal "religions" known as the **Three Teachings** (Buddhism, Confucianism, and Taoism) are inextricably linked and you will often find elements of all three in a single temple. Under Mao the doctrine of the day was undoubtedly socialism, but these days, whilst the Three Teachings are experiencing a renaissance, cynics claim that capitalism and the pursuit of money is the new religion.

Confucianism, based on the life of **Confucius** (Kong Fu Zi; 551–479 B.C.), is arguably a philosophy rather than a religion, but to visit a Confucian temple and see believers worshipping, you'd never know the difference. Kong Fu Zi lived during the Warring States Period, a fractious, uncertain time, and thus it is unsurprising that his belief system focuses on social order. The **Five Confucian Virtues** (benevolence, propriety, righteousness, trustworthiness, and wisdom) form the pillars of the philosophy and such was the importance attributed to his body of work that the Confucian texts remained the standard for imperial civil exams until early in the 20th century. If you're interested in learning more about the great man and his works, a trip to his birthplace and finally resting place at Qufu (p. 369) in Shandong province is worthwhile.

Taoism, China's other native born religion, developed in the same time period as Confucianism under the semi-mythical **Lao Zi,** but could not be more different. Understanding Taoism is a complicated business, but suffice it to say, it focuses on following **the Tao** (or the Way), balancing soft, flowing *yin,* with hard, male *yang* to create harmony. Worldly possessions were seen as contrary to the Way, and many Taoists lived reclusive lives away from the wants and needs of the world.

China's third major religion, **Buddhism,** came from India but quickly found a new home in China; its popularity was aided by its willingness to incorporate pre-existing local deities, a factor that hindered the advancement of the less adaptive Christianity and Islam. Buddhism is based on the life of Siddhartha Gautama, a Nepali prince who relinquished his worldly possessions in search of a higher calling. After spending time as an ascetic wandering the plains of India, the former prince realized that ascetism wasn't the way and finally, in Bodhgaya in northern India, he achieved *nirvana* (enlightenment) under the Bodhi Tree. Reborn as **Sakyamuni** (the Enlightened One) he spent the rest of his days traveling the Indian plains, giving sermons. When Buddhism first reached China in A.D. 67, its form was little different from that practiced in India, but, over time, like so many ideologies before it, it was Sinicized (made Chinese). This transformation is evidenced by the gradual change in appearance of Buddhist iconography in China; early examples featuring slim, Indian looking deities can still be seen in cave art along the Silk Road, but by the Tang dynasty, more rounded, Chinese-looking gods were gracing temples. As well as assimilating local gods into the Buddhist pantheon there was a fundamental belief shift, replacing the individualist Theravada school developed in India, with **Mahayana Buddhism,** a concept far more in keeping with the conformist group nature of Chinese society. In Tibet, Buddhism was fused with aspects of the native shamanist Bon religion to produce Tibetan Buddhism.

The Three Teachings aren't the only religions to be found in China though; there are huge numbers of **Christians** and **Muslims,** although it's difficult to ascertain exact figures because only officially recognized versions are tolerated, meaning that millions practice in secret.

in spite of the invention of both the magnetic compass and gunpowder, the Song failed to exert the military dominance of the Tang, which ultimately led to their downfall.

NORTHERN INVADERS: THE JURCHEN JIN & THE YUAN

In 1126 the Song court was ousted from Kaifeng by the Manchurian Jurchen tribe, who founded their own dynasty, the **Jin** (1115–1234). The Song relocated to Hangzhou and though the arts continued to develop, the Southern Song, as it became known, was hampered and humiliated by hefty payments to the Jin until its demise. Genghis Khan had been busy carving out a huge chunk of Central Asia and his descendants followed suit, making incursions farther and farther into China. In 1279 Genghis's grandson, **Kublai Khan,** founded the **Yuan dynasty** (1279–1368) and established a new capital in Beijing. It wasn't too long before the nomadic Mongols adopted the imperial lifestyle and quickly lost the military might that had driven their success. Losses in both Japan and Southeast Asia contributed to their demise, but ultimately it was trouble on the home front that sealed the fate of the Yuan dynasty. By segregating the Chinese into different social classes, and giving Muslims and Tibetans favored treatment, the Yuan dynasty emperors alienated a huge portion of the populace and a number of secret societies formed with the aim of ousting the outsiders. After a series of foiled plots, eventually a full-blown revolt headed by the rebel leader, Zhu Yuanzhang, instilled the Ming dynasty in 1368.

THE MING DYNASTY (1368–1644)

The Ming dynasty is most famous today for the distinctive pottery produced at the imperial kilns at Jingde Zhen (p. 521); however, their achievements were far more wide ranging. The first Ming emperor, **Hongwu,** established a new capital in Nanjing (you can still see the Ming city wall there to this day; p. 393) and re-established centralized rule. His successor, **Yongle,** moved the imperial seat back to Beijing and began construction of the **Forbidden City** (p. 99). Yongle also sent huge Chinese fleets to explore the world under **Admiral Zheng He.** In seven epic voyages, the Muslim eunuch admiral took the Chinese navy as far as West Africa, and trading routes were established to Malacca (Malaysia) and India's Malabar Coast. Records of the journeys were destroyed following an inauspicious lightning strike on the Forbidden City, and the Ming dynasty suddenly focused inward. Protection against the increasingly powerful northern tribes became a priority and significant improvements were made to the Great Wall under the Ming; most of the brick sections you'll see today (as at Badaling, Mutianyu, and Simatai; p. 122) date from this period. The

THE power OF THE EUNUCH

Only eunuchs were allowed to work as servants inside the imperial palaces in order to ensure the purity of the royal bloodline. However, the eunuchs, who loved nothing more than to eavesdrop and gossip, gradually came to play a greater part in courtly life, and, during the reign of weaker or child emperors, some ruled in all but name. In times of trouble or when it looked like their power might be usurped, the eunuchs weren't shy in administering their own solutions and are thought to have poisoned many of their own, along with the occasional emperor.

latter years of the dynasty saw a string of weak leaders who neglected both the country's defenses and its people. The dynasty ended in a revolt and the last Ming emperor, Chongzhen, fled the Forbidden City and hung himself in Jing Shan Park (p. 108).

THE QING DYNASTY (1644–1911)

The chaos at the end of the Ming dynasty presented the opportunity the increasingly powerful Manchurians had been waiting for. They were quick to capitalize, seized Beijing, and established the Qing dynasty. The early years of the new dynasty are celebrated as a golden age in Chinese history, heralded by the leadership of **Kangxi** (1661–1722), **Yongzheng** (1723–35), and **Qianlong** (1736–95). Kangxi crushed rebellions and expanded the empire to include Mongolia, Tibet, Nepal, and parts of Central Asia, doubling its former size. Closer links with the Tibetan world also led to the construction of the Lama Temple in Beijing (p. 106), while the Manchurians' yearning for the simpler outdoors life of their homeland resulted in the building of the Mountain Retreat in Chengde (p. 129). The Qing dynasty was China's last age as a great imperial empire and the unified country was one of the world's wealthiest nations.

Foreign interest in the wealthy but militarily backward Middle Kingdom grew and a trickle of traders made their way to China looking for a slice of the action. In 1793 Lord Macartney, envoy to the British king, George III, and representative of the **British East India Company,** sought a trading agreement with the Manchurians. His refusal to bow to the Qianlong emperor when they met at Chengde was not a good start. The Qianlong emperor could see no use for foreign goods and refused the British request for an envoy in Beijing, but the East India Company wasn't about to give up and began importing Indian opium into China rather than silver. Before long a significant percentage of the Chinese population was hooked on the drug, demand rose, and the British had the trading leverage to get as much silk and tea as they wanted. This did not sit well with the Qing rulers, and they tried to ban the opium trade, but to little avail. When Lin Zexu, a southern commander, destroyed 20,000 chests of opium in south China, he was seen as a hero, but the British were incensed, and the **First Opium War** (1840–42) ensued. After 2 years of bombardment by the British navy, the Chinese were defeated. The humiliating Treaty of Nanjing forced indemnity payments to the British; gave them trading rights in Guangzhou, Xiamen, Fuzhou, Ningbo, and Shanghai; and ceded to them the small island of Hong Kong. The Chinese hadn't given up, though, and in 1856 they made another stand, which ended with further humiliation 4 years later. This time they had to cede land to the British, French, Germans, Russians, Japanese, and Americans.

Anti-Manchu sentiment, always there, but hidden below the surface, began to reemerge. Of the spate of rebellions against the Qing, the most effective was the million-strong quasi-Christian **Taiping Uprising** (1850–64), which managed to capture large parts of the Chinese heartland. Thirty years later dissatisfaction with foreign influence once again boiled over, and the **Boxer Rebellion** (1899) began. Initially aimed at overthrowing the Qing, once the rebellion had been quashed (ironically with foreign help), the Boxers were then set loose on the streets to rid China once and for all of foreign control, and the German and Japanese ministers were both killed. The cruel, conniving, but politically inept **Empress Dowager Cixi** (1835–1908) and the puppet emperor fled to Xi'an leaving imperial ministers to negotiate yet another peace settlement. Although Cixi held on to the throne until her death in

1908, the dynastic age had been proven time and again to be unable to deal with incursions by modern Western powers, and plans were afoot for a new China, without emperors. A foreign-owned railway line provoked the final rebellion against dynastic China and the last emperor, **Puyi,** was powerless to stop it. In 1911 the provisional Republic of China was founded in **Nanjing** under Dr. Sun Yat-sen (1866–1925).

Modern China

REVOLUTION & THE BATTLE OF IDEOLOGIES

Relief that the dynastic era had come to a close was tempered by continued foreign influence, and the direction and future of the newly formed republic was far from certain. **Sun Yat-sen** was the right man for the job, but, when challenged by the warlord Yuan Shikai, he stepped down rather than invite civil war. When Yuan died a few years later, Sun returned as head of the **Kuomintang (KMT, National People's Party).** In 1923 he nominated **Chiang Kai-shek** (1888–1975) as his successor, and in 1925, Dr. Sun Yat-sen, the "father of modern China," died. His grand memorial stands in Nanjing (p. 389), and Sun is still fondly remembered on both sides of the Taiwan Strait. Under Chiang the military dictatorship of the KMT allowed the privileged to prosper but ignored the needs of the masses, and little was done to rid the country of foreign interference.

Nationalism wasn't the only ideology to emerge after the collapse of dynastic China, and communism, guided by its success in the Russian Revolution, also found a foothold in the new republic. The **Chinese Communist Party (CCP)** was founded in Shanghai in 1921 and counted Zhou Enlai and Mao Zedong among its numbers. Following Russian advice, the CCP and the KMT united in 1923 with the aim of defeating northern warlords who still threatened the stability of the nation. They succeeded, but the alliance did not, and in 1927 Chiang ordered the execution of many of the CCP leaders. Those who survived, including Mao, fled to the mountains of Jiangxi. KMT troops encircled their base in 1934 and it seemed as if the communists were finished. But Mao had other ideas and led 100,000 troops on a 9,656km (6,000-mile) rally, which became known as the **Long March.** Only 10,000 made it all the way to Yan'an in Shaanxi, but the march demonstrated Mao's determination and cemented his position as the leader of the CCP.

The 1919 Treaty of Versailles had granted the Japanese trading rights in China, and they had been eyeing the rest of the country ever since. With the communists and nationalists preoccupied, the Japanese seized the moment, capturing Manchuria in 1931, renaming it Manchukuo and inaugurating the last Qing emperor, Puyi, as its puppet ruler. But Manchuria was just a staging post on the way to full-scale invasion, and in 1937 the Japanese swept into northern China. In spite of another short-lived CCP-KMT alliance, by 1939 the Japanese had captured much of the east coast and the Chinese government was forced to relocate to central Chongqing. By the following year the Japanese controlled Beijing, Shanghai, Nanjing, and Guangzhou, and the CCP-KMT alliance crumbled. As many as 20 million Chinese lost their lives during the Japanese invasion and horrific atrocities were committed during the December 1937 **Rape of Nanjing** (p. 398). The period of Japanese rule was brought to an abrupt halt by the Allied victory in World War II and control of the nation was once again up for grabs. Though the KMT enjoyed U.S. support and control of the cities, it was the communists who had captured the hearts and minds of the rural masses, which catapulted them to victory. Chiang Kai-shek and the remnants of the KMT fled to Taiwan, along with much of the imperial treasure from the Forbidden City. In

Taiwan Chiang founded the **Republic of China (ROC),** from where he planned to eventually retake the mainland.

THE PEOPLE'S REPUBLIC OF CHINA

On October 1, 1949, Mao Zedong declared the foundation of the People's Republic of China, the world's most populous communist state. The nation was in tatters, but there was hope, and the new government set about instituting land redistribution and nationalization. The **Korean War** (1950–53) occupied precious time and funds, but victory bolstered belief in the fledgling government. From the beginning, the party gave the impression of wanting to involve the people in the rule of the country, and Mao's 1957 slogan, "Let a hundred flowers bloom, let a hundred schools of thought contend," was meant to encourage healthy intellectual criticism of the bureaucracy, but resulted in a torrent of direct attacks on the communist system itself. Mao responded with an anti-rightist campaign that branded intellectuals as enemies of socialism and saw half a million people persecuted, sent off to labor camps, and worse. Whether the campaign was a genuine move for freer governance or intended as a trap is still contested. Mao's next grand plan, the 1958 **Great Leap Forward,** aimed to increase both agricultural and industrial productivity with a goal of matching British steel output within 15 years. But the crass plan was flawed from the beginning; the peasantry had only just been granted land, and they were far from happy about collectivizing, and even when they agreed, the panic caused by over-ambitious quotas led to overplanting. The real focus was on industry, though, and farms were neglected. Crops failed 2 years running and the resulting food shortages left millions dead. At the same time, following Khrushchev's historic summit with U.S. President Eisenhower, Sino-Soviet relations faltered and the resulting withdrawal of Russian aid left the economy in ruins. Deng Xiaoping helped get the country back on track, but held fundamentally different views about the direction the country's economic development should take. Deng sought to open up the economy and encourage private enterprise. Mao's reaction was the 1966 **Great Proletarian Cultural Revolution,** which was designed to purge the country of "the four olds"—old culture, customs, habits, and ideas. In Beijing Mao rallied students to form a radical militia, the **Red Guards,** armed them with his *Little Red Book* of thoughts, and set them loose on the country with instructions to destroy all evidence of the four olds. Books, buildings, and businesses were burnt and many of China's greatest treasures were lost forever; only those that were too remote, hidden, or protected under the order of Zhou Enlai survived. Over 15 million people died during the Cultural Revolution and millions more were traumatized. Families and whole communities were torn apart as quotas were established for the reporting and "reeducation" of dissidents. In spite of this, the fact that Mao had managed to instigate these measures only added to his unassailable cult status. However, the dichotomy between people's feelings about Mao and the policies he enacted left a generation who were unable to deal with the reality of what had happened.

In the aftermath of the Cultural Revolution Mao was little seen, and his third wife, **Jiang Qing,** often appeared in his place supported by her radical entourage who became known as the **Gang of Four.** Following the mysterious death of his closest ally, Lin Biao, Mao sought new allies and, while Hua Guofeng was groomed as his successor, the exiled Deng Xiaoping returned to office. There were also some improvements on the international front and **Zhou Enlai,** who had been limiting the worst excesses of Mao's policies since the beginning, helped China gain a U.N. seat

On the People

Nothing and no-one can destroy the Chinese people. They are the oldest civilized people on earth. Their civilization passes through phases, but its basic characteristics remain the same. They yield, they bend to the wind, but they never break.

—Pearl S. Buck

in 1971, and establish trade links with the U.S. after Nixon's 1972 visit. Zhou Enlai died in 1976, and when radicals took away commemorative wreaths placed on the Heroes Monument in Beijing, this sparked a riot. The **Tian'an Men Incident,** as it became known, was blamed on Deng Xiaoping and once again he was deposed from office. With the sudden demise of the moderates, the radicals gained ground, but this was to be short lived. Two months after the Tangshan earthquake hit Hebei, Chairman Mao died, and the Gang of Four had lost their leader. Shortly after Mao's death the Gang of Four were arrested, but it wasn't until 1981 that they were tried and sentenced to 20 years in prison apiece. Jiang Qing killed herself and the others died in jail. The Gang of Four was ostensibly blamed for the worst extremes of the Cultural Revolution, a factor that helped to keep the Mao cult alive long after his death. Ultimately, the legacy of Mao the myth triumphed over Mao the man, and even today his image can be found adorning many a rural living room and city square.

THE REFORM ERA

Following Mao's death, Deng Xiaoping finally ascended and his **Four Transformations** (agriculture, industry, defense, and science) presented the platform for China's economic modernization. Deng's policies were based on economic liberalization in order to encourage foreign investment and internal entrepreneurship. Agricultural collectives were disbanded and farmers were free to sell any surplus on the open market. Focus shifted away from traditional heavy industry and many state-owned businesses were privatized. **Special Economic Zones,** such as Shenzhen (p. 538), were established and quickly attracted overseas investment. These measures, combined with China's huge population and low wages, provided the springboard for China's launch onto the world trade scene and it quickly became, quite literally, the factory of the world.

TIAN'AN MEN SQUARE PROTEST (1989)

Economic reform and social reform did not go hand in hand, though. While the 1980s outwardly presented a more liberal face as shown by the appointment of moderate Hu Yaobang as General Secretary and then Party Chairman, his forced resignation and the party's response to the 1989 Tian'an Men Square protests answered any question there may have been about how much freedom of speech the government would tolerate.

Following Hu Yaobang's death in April 1989, protests erupted in Tian'an Men Square, and in spite of the imposition of Martial Law in May, by June 1989 over a million people had gathered. The crowd was predominantly comprised of students protesting for social reform, but there were also urban workers, angry at the all-pervasive corruption and privatization that had seen many of them lose their jobs. When

DATELINE: CHINESE HISTORY at a glance

Era	Date	Significant Events & People
Prehistory		Peking Man
Yangshao Culture	**5000–3000 B.C.**	
Three Dynasties	**2100–221 B.C.**	Confucius & Lao Zi
Qin	**221–206 B.C.**	Emperor Qin Shi Huang
		Great Wall & Terra-Cotta Warriors
Han	**206 B.C.–A.D. 220**	Territorial expansion
Three Kingdoms	**A.D. 220–581**	
Sui	**581–618**	Grand Canal
Tang	**618–907**	Poets Li Bai and Du Fu
Song	**960–1279**	Poet Su Dongpo
Yuan	**1279–1368**	Emperor Kublai Khan / Marco Polo visits China
Ming	**1368–1644**	Forbidden City built / Zheng He's epic voyages
Qing	**1644–1911**	Opium Wars / Taiping Uprising / Boxer Rebellion
Republican Period	**1911–1949**	Dr. Sun Yat-sen
		Establishment of CCP
		The Long March
		Japanese invasion & Rape of Nanjing
People's Republic	**1949–1976**	Mao Zedong founds PRC
		Chiang Kai-shek founds ROC (Taiwan)
	1956–57	Hundred Flowers Campaign
	1958	Great Leap Forward
	1966	Cultural Revolution
	1976	Mao Zedong dies
Reform Era	**1976–present**	Deng Xiaoping heads PRC
		Economic Liberalization
		China reopens to foreign visitors
	1979	Introduction of One-Child Policy
	1989	Tian'an Men Square Protest
	1992	Jiang Zemin ascends to power
	1997	Deng Xiaoping dies / British return of Hong Kong
	1999	Portuguese return of Macau
	2001	China joins World Trade Organization
	2002	Hu Jintao & Wen Jiabao head CCP
	2008	Beijing hosts Summer Olympics
		Sichuan earthquake / Tibet protests
	2009	Xinjiang riots
	2010	Shanghai hosts World Expo / Yushu Earthquake
	2012	China to comply with Kyoto Agreement

their demands went unanswered, a thousand plus students went on hunger strike. Fifty thousand PLA (People's Liberation Army) soldiers were sent to Beijing and on June 3rd tanks rumbled into Tian'an Men Square. On June 4th troops fired into the unarmed crowd and hundreds, maybe thousands, were killed, although it seems unlikely any reliable statistics will ever emerge. Foreign journalists who had been covering Mikhail Gorbachev's Beijing visit were witness to much of the violence and although satellite links were closed, the world was given a shocking glimpse into modern China. International condemnation and arms embargoes followed, along with protests around the globe; a candlelit vigil is still held in remembrance every June 4th in Hong Kong's Victoria Park. The protests had also highlighted a gaping divide between the moderates who sympathized with the protesters and the staunch party hardliners in favor of using force to remove them. Even now the June 4th Movement (as it is described in party jargon) is rarely talked about in China, and you should be sensitive about who you discuss it with and where.

THE NEW GUARD: THIRD- & FOURTH-GENERATION CHINESE COMMUNISM

Jiang Zemin, the former Mayor of Shanghai, and who was in no way associated with the response to the Tian'an Men protests, moved up the party ranks to become General Secretary of the CCP. Three years later he was appointed president and he fully took the reins of power when Deng died in 1997. Jiang oversaw the **1997 British return of Hong Kong** and the **1999 Portuguese return of Macau.** He continued the economic liberalization started by Deng, and under Jiang the benefits of 20 years of economic reform began to be seen. While internationally everyone wanted a piece of the Chinese economic pie, relations with Western powers, particularly the U.S., were tested by continued arms embargoes and allegations of nuclear espionage. In 2001 a U.S. spy plane collided with a Chinese fighter jet and crash landed on Hainan Island, China's most southerly province. Although none of the U.S. crew was seriously injured, the Chinese pilot died. The incident came at a crucial time when the Bush administration was deciding whether or not to supply Taiwan with arms, a sensitive enough subject in itself. Tensions were further heightened following the accidental NATO bombing of the Chinese Embassy in Belgrade during the Kosovo Crisis. Thankfully, in the end economics prevailed and late in 2001, China was eventually admitted to the **World Trade Organization.** Following the party conference later that year **Hu Jintao,** the Vice President, was appointed as President with **Wen Jiabao** as his prime minister, and the fourth generation of communist leadership began. This erudite pairing have thus far fared well in trying to achieve their primary objective of "harmonious development" in decidedly discordant times.

THE ARTS IN CHINA

As well as appreciating the arts for their inherent beauty and style, the nature of artistic creativity is also a good indicator of the prevailing social influences of an era, and China is no exception. Thus cave paintings focus on food, fire, and shelter, while the preponderance of Red Art during the early years of communism at the expense of all other forms mirrors its ideological stance. But China's history is so long, the country is so big, and its range of arts is so extensive that getting a hold on "the arts" in China isn't straightforward. Below we have concentrated on bronzes, ceramics, calligraphy, literature, poetry, and painting, but whole books have been written about other artistic forms such as jade and lacquer-work. Examples of all the art listed below can be seen today across the country, but many of the best pieces are to be found in Beijing's **National Museum of China** (p. 108), **the Shanghai Museum** (p. 466), and the **Shanxi** (p. 241) and **Shanxi History** (p. 260) **Museums.**

Bronzes & Ceramics

After cave paintings, the earliest form of artistic expression in China is the decorating of household items and funerary objects. As settled communities began to have more time, and techniques improved through the ages, the objects themselves were elevated to the point where they became the art, and Chinese bronzes and ceramics were admired the world over. Bronzes first emerged in the **Shang dynasty** (1600–1122 B.C.) and ceramics can be traced back to roughly the same time, but it wasn't until more effective glazing techniques were established in the **Han dynasty** (221 B.C.–A.D. 220) that they were prized as artistic creations. The stability of the **Tang dynasty** (618–907) afforded the time, effort, and expertise to further refine techniques and it was during this period that the famous tri-color glaze, which can still be seen in emporiums around the country, was established. China's most famous porcelain dates from the **Ming dynasty** (1368–1644), but the cobalt underglaze produced by the imperial kiln at **Jingde Zhen** (p. 521) was actually developed in the previous **Yuan dynasty** (1279–1368).

Calligraphy, Poetry & Prose

The complex Chinese language is inefficient in many ways and requires students to memorize huge numbers of characters before they can competently read and write. However, the tones, rhyming nature, and pictographic representation of the language all lend themselves to the arts. The written Chinese language is wonderfully alluring and, in spite of the 1956 simplification of its characters, calligraphy in the old style remains popular throughout the country, from the streets to store showrooms. Calligraphy traditionally went hand in hand with poetry, and the latter was a favored mode of expression for the educated elite; academics, philosophers, and politicians often quoted poems in speeches and written communiqués. Poetry also came to represent the internal struggle of individuals torn by conflicting emotions. **Tao Yuanming** (365–427) exemplified this perfectly, on the one hand yearning for political success and power, on the other, content with the simple life of a farmer who enjoys a drink. During the Tang dynasty, the words of two of China's most prominent poets, **Li Bai** (701–762) and **Du Fu** (712–770), again reflected struggle, but this time not of the individual, but rather the dichotomy between the ill-matched social ideals of Taoism and Confucianism. The arts continued to flourish in the Song dynasty, and **Su Dongpo** (1037–1101), one-time governor of Hangzhou, is perhaps the most famous of all Chinese poets, and was also a skilled calligrapher, painter, and politician.

Literature as we know it in the West was initially characterized in China by philosophical works like **Confucius**'s seminal ***Book of Songs*** and **Lao Zi's *Tao Te Ching*** *(The Truth of the Way)*. In the Han dynasty (221 B.C.– A.D. 220), Sima Qian's surprisingly lively tome, *Historical Records,* set the tone for future historical works, but reading remained a scholarly pastime for the elites. In the Ming dynasty (1368–1644) writers began harking back to the formative glory years of China, constructing epic tales such as the *Journey to the West, Outlaws of the Marsh,* and *Romance of the Three Kingdoms,* which remain popular to this day. The world's first printed book may have been published in China in A.D. 868, but it wasn't until the end of the 19th century that the vernacular writing style of **Lu Xun** (1881–1936) and later, **Shen Congwen** (1903–86), really made books accessible to the masses. However, once the communists emerged victorious, literary freedom was suppressed and little of interest was written, although Mao's *Little Red Book* offers a fascinating insight into the socialist doctrine that propelled the Red Guards through the Cultural Revolution. Since the death of the Great Helmsman, restrictions have relaxed a little, but anything even remotely sensitive is instantly banned, meaning many of China's best modern authors are little known inside the Middle Kingdom. For more on modern literature, see "China in Popular Culture: Books, Film & Music," (p. 28).

Painting

Aside from cave paintings and calligraphy, painting in China didn't really develop until the Tang dynasty (618–907). Tang paintings were mostly portraits of the imperial family and courtesans and it wasn't until the Song dynasty (960–1279) that things got interesting with the development of **landscape painting.** Mountains were considered the abode of the gods, and this led to paintings that focused exclusively on the natural world, centuries before anything comparable emerged in Europe. Song dynasty artists wanted to convey the endless expanse of the Chinese landscape and to this end they left large blank spaces on the canvas. In the Yuan (1279–1368) and Ming dynasties (1368–1644), the focus on the natural world continued, but rather than whole landscapes, detailed pictures of plants, flowers, and animals became the subjects of choice. During the Qing dynasty (1644–1911), increasing foreign influence in China also made its way onto the canvas, but the bold brush strokes and traditional subjects chosen by artists like **Xu Peiheng** (1893–1953), who had studied in Europe, illustrated that Chinese artists hadn't completely abandoned their roots. Under Mao, artistic creativity in all shapes and forms was suppressed and many prior works were destroyed, but the big, bold **Red Art** that was churned out as just another part of the party propaganda machine is now enjoying something of a revival.

Since economic liberalization, contemporary **modern art** has moved in manifold directions, heavily influenced by suddenly available outside influences, albeit often paying homage to time-old traditions and subjects; **Wang Qingsong**'s photographic parody of the 10th century *Night Revels* is a prime example. Good places to get a feel for China's modern arts scene are **Beijing's Factory 798** (p. 110) in the trendy Dashanzi district, **Shanghai's Museum of Contemporary Art,** and **Guangzhou's Guangdong Museum of Art.**

ARCHITECTURE IN CHINA

Architecture has a vast history in China, but the concept of building design wasn't really established until the dynastic period when palaces and temples were seen as signs of an emperor's status. Throughout the dynastic age, ever grander edifices were constructed, while older buildings from past rulers were altered, enlarged, or destroyed at the whim of the emperor. This historical trend, common to many of the world's greatest civilizations, has resulted in the destruction of many of China's grandest buildings, but at the same time, it has left some astounding architectural feats created over centuries. The Cultural Revolution and now rapid modernization have further come at the expense of traditional architecture—Beijing's *hutong* (p. 59) and Kashgar's soon-to-be-gone old city (p. 316) are just a couple of examples. Fortunately,

WIND & water

To understand Chinese traditional architecture, it is critical to also have an idea of the prevailing social conditions and mores of the time. **Feng shui** was, and is, a crucial part of architectural design in China and can operate on a room, house, palace, or even city scale. Feng shui literally translates as **wind** and **water** and is intended to allow efficient energy flow without disrupting the cosmos. Some of the most basic feng shui principles are that the north should be protected by a hill (thus Jingshan Park protects the back of the Forbidden City), and there should be water flowing toward the front (to bring prosperity). Small mirrors, which you'll often see above doorways to people's houses, are put there to reflect evil spirits.

many imperial architectural treasures such as Beijing's **Forbidden City** (p. 99) and **Temple of Heaven** (p. 103) have survived and are protected.

Outside of the realm of imperial architecture, protection from the elements was the fundamental purpose of buildings, and much regional architecture was initially purely functional. The wooden **Wind and Rain Bridges** of the Dong (p. 653) allowed villagers to stop for a breather on the way back from the fields no matter what the weather, while **drum towers** served as lookout posts from where the village could be warned of impending attack. In Xinjiang the narrow covered alleys of the old cities weren't just to facilitate modern day travelers getting lost; they also served to confuse would-be attackers, and to keep the blistering sun at bay. Equally the famous **Huizhou style houses** (p. 424), developed by wealthy Anhui merchants, first gained their distinctive horse-head gables to prevent the spread of fire between neighboring houses. One of the most incredible styles of Chinese rural architecture belongs to the Hakka in Guangdong and Fujian, who built **huge roundhouses** capable of housing and protecting up to a thousand people.

Outside influences have also contributed to the history of architecture in China and many are still there to be seen today. **Xi'an's Great Mosque** (p. 258) is a fascinating combination of traditional Islamic design fused with Chinese architectural features. Foreign influence in China during the latter part of the Qing dynasty (1644–1911) was an unwanted distraction that contributed to the downfall of the dynastic age, but the architecture left behind still adds diversity and character to cities around China. **Shanghai's Bund** is the classic example and looks like it has been transported directly from 1900s Liverpool, but there are still remnants of the colonial era in ports from Qingdao to Guangzhou. The **Art Deco period** is also well represented in Shanghai and buildings like the Broadway Mansions and the Park Hotel are worth visiting for fans of architecture, even if you don't stay. Foreign influence continued to be felt once the PRC was founded, and grand Soviet-style monoliths like **Beijing's Great Hall of the People** became the order of the day. Since economic reforms in the 1980s, China has followed Hong Kong's model of reaching for the sky and skyscrapers now dominate many city centers. In the most competitive and richest arenas like Shanghai, the bigger and bolder the design the better, and standing out from the crowd has become increasingly difficult, although the spaceshiplike **Oriental Pearl TV Tower,** the **Jin Mao Tower,** and most recently the **World Financial Center** have managed to achieve this. The 2008 Olympics have presented the most

KNOWING your dragons FROM YOUR PHOENIXES

As Chinese culture becomes more accessible around the world, there are many symbols that are instantly identifiable with the Middle Kingdom, and traveling around China you'll see them cropping up again and again, but the big question is, what do they mean? A **pair of lions** standing outside the entrance of a palace, temple, or even a bank represents status and natural order, and if you look carefully you'll see that the female has a cub beneath her paw, while the male has the world at his feet! **Dragon** and **phoenix** motifs represent the emperor and empress, respectively. **Yellow** is the color of the emperor, and **red** symbolizes luck and prosperity. The number of **stone animals** on roof eaves indicates how important a temple or palace is. The rotund, **laughing Buddha** to be seen in the entrance hall to many temples is Maitreya, a Chinese interpretation of the (skinny) Indian god who has come to represent prosperity.

recent impetus to impress and the **Bird's Nest** and **Water Cube** in Beijing both have to be seen to be believed. Looking to the future, China's buildings will undoubtedly continue to rise upward, but it is hoped that the past and Chinese tradition will also play a part in the architecture of China's tomorrow.

CHINA IN POPULAR CULTURE: BOOKS, FILM & MUSIC

Chinese popular culture was all but blotted out by the Cultural Revolution. Now that it is back on its feet, and people are taking more notice of what happens in China, once mystical and unintelligible Chinese popular culture is being deciphered and becoming more accessible to the rest of the world.

Books

There's enough entertaining reading on China to fill a library, so the following is really just a few pointers to get you started. The classics and poetry are described in the Arts in China (p. 24).

Readable modern novelists easily purchased in translation at home include **Ha Jin,** whose stories tend to be remarkably inconclusive and so all the more true to life, derived from his experiences living in the northeast. *Ocean of Words, Waiting,* and the collection of short stories *The Bridegroom* lift the lids on many things not obvious to the casual visitor. *Soul Mountain,* by **Gao Xingjian,** China's first winner of the Nobel Prize for Literature (although the Chinese populace is kept in ignorance of this), is the tale of a man who embarks on a journey through the wilds of Sichuan and Yunnan in search of his own elusive *ling shan* (soul mountain). *The Republic of Wine,* **Mo Yan**'s graphic satire about a doomed detective investigating a case of gourmand-officials eating human baby tenderloin, is at once entertaining and disturbing. His *Garlic Ballads* is an unsettling epic of family conflict, doomed love, and government corruption in a small town dependent on the garlic market. If you want something a little more lighthearted, but still related to China, **Wei Hui**'s *Shanghai Baby* is an irreverent look at love and lust between a Chinese woman and a foreign man in China's financial capital. For a novel that gives a flavor of old Hong Kong, try Richard Mason's *The World of Suzie Wong,* a romantic story about a love affair between a British wanderer and a local prostitute during the British period.

First-class travel books include **Peter Fleming**'s *News from Tartary,* originally published in 1936, and still one of the best travel books ever written about China. Fleming's perceptive account of a hazardous expedition along the southern Silk Route, from Beijing to northern India, is a masterpiece of dry wit. More recent travel biographies to look out for include **Peter Hessler**'s amusing but insightful books *River Town* and *Oracle Bones: A Journey Between China and the West,* and his latest offering *Country Driving,* and **Simon Winchester**'s *The River at the Center of the World: A Journey Up the Yangtze, and Back in Chinese Time. China Cuckoo,* written by *that's* magazine founder **Mark Kitto,** is an amusing read that lends plenty of insight into the troubles foreigners encounter living and establishing businesses in China. For a unique Chinese perspective on travel though the Middle Kingdom, **Ma Jian**'s *Red Dust: A Path Through China* is a fascinating read.

For good general background reading, there are a few authors and publishers who turn out so much excellent work that you should start by having a look at what they've done recently. **Jonathan Spence** writes the most readable histories of China, not just the weighty *The Search for Modern China,* but gripping and very personal histories such as *The Memory Palace of Matteo Ricci,* on the clever self-marketing of the first Jesuit to be allowed to reside in Beijing; *God's Chinese Son,* on the leader of the Taiping Rebellion who thought he was the younger brother of Jesus Christ; and *The Question of Hu,* on the misfortunes of an early Chinese visitor to Europe.

Dover Publications (http://store.doverpublications.com) reprints handy guides to Chinese history and culture, as well as oddities such as **Robert Van Gulik**'s versions of 18th-century Chinese detective stories featuring a Tang dynasty detective-judge, such as *The Haunted Monastery and the Chinese Maze Murders.* Dover's two-volume reprint of the 1903 edition of *The Travels of Marco Polo* is the only edition to own—more than half is footnotes from famous explorers and geographers trying to make sense of Polo's route, corroborating his observations, or puzzling why he goes so astray, and providing fascinating trivia about China far more interesting than the original account. For a different take on the age of maritime discovery, **Gavin Menzies**'s *1421* is a heavy read, but offers convincing proof that much of the world was discovered by the Chinese admiral Zheng He.

For more recent China watching, anything by the Italian diplomat **Tiziano Terzani** is a good place to start, but *Behind the Forbidden Door* is particularly compelling. While many books do their best to present the country in a favorable light, **Nicholas D. Kristof** and **Sheryl WuDunn** present a very realistic picture in *China Wakes.* Perhaps the most recent author to address the subject realistically is **Gordon C. Chang** in *The Coming Collapse of China.* Conversely **Stefan Halpan**'s *The Beijing Consensus* posits that the greatest threat from China comes from the alternate economic model it presents to developing nations around the world.

These next two recommendations barely mention China, but explain the problems that the country faces more clearly than any other recent writer. *The Breakdown of Nations,* by **Leopold Kohr,** examines why the largest nations always face the largest problems. *Small Is Beautiful,* by **E. F. Schumacher,** focuses on the problems a nation faces when it tries to move from an agrarian to an industrial economy; this book is out of print, but you can probably find a copy online. These are truly enlightening books to have with you as you travel around the world's most populous nation.

Film

Filmmaking began in China during Shanghai's golden years, and with the help of American expertise the city remained at the heart of the Chinese movie industry until the Japanese invasion. Shanghai was exotic and enticing, and this attracted a number of big Hollywood names, including Charlie Chaplin, to the Pearl of the Orient. Early themes were often anti-imperialist, and the first Chinese screen heroine, Ruan Lingyu, shot to fame with *The Goddess* in 1934. Once the Japanese arrived, production came to a standstill and many moviemakers fled to Hong Kong.

Under Mao, filmmaking was restricted to propagandist tales celebrating the virtues of communism, and it wasn't until the early 1980s that the Chinese movie industry finally managed to reestablish itself. The **Fifth Generation** (so-called for the number of generations since 1949) of Chinese film-makers began to explore new directions, but the indirect criticism of the communist system apparent in many of their movies, including **Chen Kaige**'s beautifully shot *Yellow Earth* (1984), incensed the authorities. **Zhang Yimou,** who worked the camera on *Yellow Earth,* tried his hand at directing and turned out to be pretty good at it. His 1986 work, *Red Sorghum,* won critical acclaim and he has gone on to score a number of other instant classics, including *Judou* (1990) and *Raise the Red Lantern* (1991), both of which star screen queen **Gong Li.** Like many other Fifth Generation directors, Zhang then turned his attentions to international audiences, releasing the martial arts epic *Hero* (2002), which stars martial artist **Jet Li.** Filling the gap left by Fifth Generation directors, the **Sixth Generation** rose to the challenge of provoking the authorities once more with urban stories like *Beijing Bicycle* (2001). Films like **Du Haibin**'s *1428,* which offers a gritty look at the aftermath of the Sichuan earthquake, are representative of China's new **"D-Generation"** (D for digital) of moviemakers, and unsurprisingly are banned in China, but have received international acclaim.

Hong Kong had always been more relaxed and liberal than the mainland, and as China was enduring the rigors of the Cultural Revolution, moviemaking continued in the British territory unabated. Hong Kong is the world's third biggest movie producer, and the territory's most famous movie exports are its **kung fu** flicks. Early stories focused on the life of martial arts legend Wong Fei-Hung, but kung fu movies were taken to a whole new level by a certain **Bruce Lee.** Affectionately known as Li Xiaolong (Little Dragon Lee), Lee was the first actor to take Chinese movies to the West, and though the dialogue and plots were simple, the action was spectacular and captivated audiences worldwide. His most famous movie, *Enter the Dragon,* was released shortly after his death in 1973. Lee paved the way for the likes of **Jackie Chan,** who blended comedy with kung fu, and eventually found his way to Hollywood. Spearheaded by Jackie Chan, comedy kung fu has become a genre unto itself, and recent titles following the theme include *Shaolin Soccer* (2001) and *Kung Fu Hustle* (2004). The cinematic shooting style of Chinese martial arts movies now features in many Hollywood productions, and the success of movies like the *Matrix* trilogy (1993–2003) was greatly assisted by the fight scene choreography of **Yuen Woo-Ping.**

As Chinese culture becomes ever more accessible to the outside world, a host of movies aimed at Western audiences, retell classic legends. Most famous of these is **Ang Lee**'s *Crouching Tiger, Hidden Dragon* (2000), and more recent offerings include the swashbuckling *The Forbidden Kingdom* (2008) and *Three Kingdoms* (2008).

Music

TRADITIONAL MUSIC

Unlike in the West, opera in China has long been popular at all levels of society, and this is the medium by which most people were exposed to music, especially since the advent of television. There are countless forms of opera, but **Beijing opera** and the deft mask-changing Sichuan variety are the most famous. Most opera stories are based on the Chinese classics, and feature the same high-pitched singing tones and stilted melodies, which means this isn't for everyone, but you should try to see at least one performance, if only for the acrobatics and incredible make-up.

Aside from opera, various forms of traditional music can be heard in parks throughout the country; Beijing's Temple of Heaven gardens, Xi'an's city wall park, and Hangzhou's lakeside parks are all good places to try. Traditional music can be broadly divided by region and focus on the most prevalent instruments: The north is renowned for its drummers; southern forms often feature strings and flutes *(dizi)*. Other popular instruments you'll come across include the *erhu* (silk string violin), *guqin* (zither), and *pipa* (lute).

ROCK & POP

As the grip of the Mao regime loosened and foreign influence once again snuck its way into the country, a new form of music, inspired by Western and Taiwanese rock, began to be composed in China. Beijing was at the center of this movement, and its undisputed champion was **Cui Jian.** While his love lyrics seemed outwardly innocent enough, there was hidden meaning, and his dull view of communism soon incurred the displeasure of the authorities (which is the least one could expect from a musician known as the Godfather of Chinese Rock). To this day Beijing is the best place to see live rock in China, and new bands like Rustic are springing up all the time, while old favorites such as Cold Blooded Animals and Second Hand Rose continue to play gigs in the city.

At the other end of the spectrum, the catchy and romantic melodies of **Canto-pop,** and now **Mando-pop,** are family-friendly forms that leave teenagers screaming in hordes. Many of the big names still come from Hong Kong and Taiwan and include Aaron Kwok, Faye Wong, Andy Lau, Jay Chou, Jolin, Kenny Kwan, and the band S.H.E. Their music is so ubiquitous you will doubtless know a few songs by default after only a few weeks in China.

EATING & DRINKING IN CHINA

Eating

China is a culinary adventure just waiting to happen, and food is so important to the Chinese that *"Ni chi bao le ma?"* or "Have you eaten yet?" is a standard greeting. As you might expect from a country this large and varied, the food is astoundingly diverse both in the nature of ingredients and their preparation. As you travel through the country, you'll come across all kinds of weird and wonderful dishes, and, armed with a phrasebook and a curious palate, you'll never run short of new things to try. Not only are there hundreds of delicious dishes to sample, exploring the cuisine of the areas you travel through will also afford you some insight into the nature of the region.

Places to eat Chinese food range from opulent banquet halls to hole-in-the-wall canteens and street stalls, but generally the focus is on the food rather than the decor,

QUICK STICKS: a chopstick primer

Kuaizi literally translates as quick (or nimble) sticks, and this way of eating has a history going back thousands of years. Chinese food is so popular throughout the world that chopsticks aren't the novelty they once were in the West. Accepted standard technique is that the bottom stick remains immobile while the upper one is held like a pen to position the food. Sticking your chopsticks vertically into your bowl or passing food with chopsticks should both be avoided, as these actions are associated with funerary rites. When you've finished eating, place both sticks horizontally across the rim of the bowl.

and strip lighting and Formica tables are the norm. Don't let this deter you; if a place is busy, chances are it's worth pulling up a chair. So rid yourself of preconceptions of what Chinese food tastes like at home and tuck in.

CUISINE TYPES

Traditionally, cuisine was defined by the produce available locally and thus the wheat-yielding north of the country made bread and wheat noodles, while rice was the staple in the warmer and wetter south. This division exists to this day, but with improved transport and refrigeration, culinary variety from around the country is available in all of the major cities. In terms of the best food, though, the lower the carbon miles of the ingredients, the better your meal is likely to be. For more details of dishes to be found in individual destinations, consult the Chinese language translations in chapter 17.

SOUTHERN (GUANGDONGCAI) Cantonese food is the most widely exported and thus familiar of all the Chinese cuisines. However, Cantonese food in Canton (Guangzhou) or Hong Kong is very different from what you'll find in your local town. Aside from the scary specialty dishes, Cantonese food typically features lots of super fresh seafood cooked in light, fragrant sauces and one-person *shabao* (rice, vegetable, and meat in sand or clay pots). *Dim sum* (*dian xin* in Mandarin) is a Cantonese breakfast or lunch favorite featuring a huge selection of miniature buns, spring rolls, and dumplings served from trolleys that scuttle around the restaurant. Not only is *dim sum* delicious, it also affords non-Chinese speakers an easy way to have a look at what's on offer before committing.

NORTHERN (BEIFANGCAI) Northern cuisine is typified by the use of salt, garlic, ginger, and onion, and hearty staples of *mantou* (steamed buns), noodles *(mian)*, pancakes *(bing)*, and numerous varieties of *jiaozi* (dumplings usually filled with pork and leek or cabbage), for which **Xi'an** is particularly famous. The highest form of Northern cuisine is the opulent Mandarin style, the food of emperors, and **Beijing Duck** is deservedly its most famous dish.

EASTERN (HUAIYANGCAI) Eastern dishes are often considered the least appealing to foreigners as they feature lots of oil, but if you can get beyond this, you'll find a host of fresh flavors and dishes that feature bamboo, mushrooms, seafood, and river fish. **Shanghainese** *(shanghaicai)* cuisine is at the refined end of the eastern scale and offers lightly cooked minuscule treats akin to *dim sum,* including delicious ***xiaolongbao*** (steamed pork dumplings).

SICHUAN (CHUANCAI) Spicy Sichuan dishes typify western cuisine and pack a punch to rival any Indian or Mexican meal. In both Sichuan and Hunan cooking, the meat, fish, or tofu is merely a vehicle to carry the flavor of the sauce to your palate. At the heart of Sichuan cuisine is the concept of **manifold flavoring,** and the aim is to detect the subtler tastes that emerge from beneath the initial chili hit, though this can be near impossible when your mouth feels like it's on fire. Use of fragrant Sichuan flower peppers *(huajiao)* is also common, especially if you're dining in the province itself, and sends a disarming numbness racing around your mouth. Some of the best known and tastiest Sichuan dishes are *gongbao jiding* (chicken with chili and peanuts), *yuxiang rousi* (fish-flavored pork, though there's no fish in the dish), *mapo doufu* (spicy tofu), and the ubiquitous spicy hotpot *(huoguo)*.

WESTERN & VEGETARIAN FOOD

If you tire of Chinese food, Western-style burger joints and coffee shops serve sandwiches in most towns of any size, and in the culinary capitals of Beijing, Shanghai, and Hong Kong you can take your pick of almost any cuisine in the world. For vegetarians, while there are seemingly countless dishes on many menus, you may well find that your egg fried rice has the odd shrimp or pieces of pork in it, and many dishes are cooked in animal-based fats. The bigger cities have vegetarian restaurants, but in smaller places your best bet will be to head to the local Buddhist temple restaurant, where vegetarian food is guaranteed, or failing that, specify, *"Wo shi fojiao tu"* (I'm a Buddhist) when you order. A Buddhist meal will be prepared without using any meat or meat products, and also strong flavors (such as garlic) that allegedly "excite the senses." In some restaurants, this will just mean not using these ingredients in the specified dishes, while in others, traditional Buddhist dishes will be offered.

The flavor enhancer **monosodium glutamate (MSG)** is commonly used in Chinese cooking, and some people can have an adverse reaction to this. It's best to say, *"Wo bu yao weijing"* (I don't want MSG) when you order.

Drinking

Summers are long and hot in most of China, especially in the arid northwest, and it's vital that you keep hydrated. Fortunately China has plenty of refreshing drinks to quench your thirst. As well as the generic bottled water and soft drink brands,

SHOCKING orders

There are almost as many sayings about what the southern Chinese will eat as there are Cantonese dishes, but my favorite is, "Cantonese people will eat anything on land that isn't a car, anything on water that isn't a boat, and anything in the air that isn't an airplane." A trip to any local southern market will confirm this, but fortunately, it's highly unlikely that specialty dishes such as bat, cat, dog, frog, rat, scorpion, or snake will appear before you, unless you order them, as they tend to be far more expensive than regular dishes. This diversity is due to past famines when people ate whatever they could (and then discovered they had a taste for it), and traditional Chinese medicinal beliefs that state that certain foods are beneficial for particular parts of the body. Dining on dog is purported to keep you warm in the winter whilst eating snake is supposed to increase virility.

Jianlibao, an energy drink, and **Hello C,** a tangy lemon drink, are both worth a try. **Fresh fruit juices** are also widely available, especially in the south.

Green tea *(lu cha)* has 2,000 years of history in China and is still the drink of choice for the Chinese. Almost every traveler and office worker has their own personal thermos they regularly refill and clutch for warmth in the winter months. Hundreds of different varieties of tea are found across the country, some of the most famous being *longjing cha* (Dragon Well Tea), oolong from Taiwan, and Guanyin from Fujian. Flower teas, such as jasmine *(molihua),* are also common and particularly refreshing.

Beer *(pijiu)* is also very popular, and thanks to the German annexation of Qingdao, the pilsner varieties produced by local breweries are pretty decent, and better still, cheap. In Western-style bars you may find the full range of international liquors, but in smaller towns you may have to suffice with *baijiu,* a toxic sorghum-based spirit that furnishes drinkers with horrific hangovers. **Rice wine** *(mijiu)* is a little better, particularly if you invest in a more expensive bottle, and is usually preferable to the Chinese red and white wines on offer. This said, China's taste for wine is growing, and as well as the local Dynasty and Great Wall brands, in bigger cities a decent, if expensive, selection of imported wines can often be found in supermarkets and Western restaurants.

WHEN TO GO

Weather details are given below and these certainly play a part in deciding when to go, but a far bigger factor in your calculations should be the movement of domestic tourists. Three days' paid vacation are given to workers for three major holidays in the year. The dates of these celebrations are carefully chosen so that workers in Chinese companies have 7 continuous days of vacation time (having to work during another weekend to make up the deficit), known as "Golden Weeks." These national holidays were first started by the government for China's National Day in 1999 and were primarily intended to help expand the domestic tourism market, improve the national standard of living, and allow people to make long-distance family visits. During the longer public holidays, Chinese tourists take to the road in the tens or even hundreds of millions, crowding all forms of transportation, booking out hotels, and turning even the quietest tourist sights into seas of humanity. In part as a result of these Golden Weeks, the number of domestic Chinese tourist visits has shot from 280 million in 1990 to a whopping 1.6 billion in 2007, the majority of these being peasants from rural areas. This should give you a clear idea of how crowded many of the "must-see" spots have become. Of course, if you really want to get a feel for the size of China's population, then this is a fine time to travel; otherwise give public holidays a miss.

China now has two Golden Week holidays: the **Spring Festival** (Chinese New Year), and the **National Day** holiday, with 3 days given for the **May Day** holiday.

Peak Travel Seasons

CHINESE NEW YEAR (SPRING FESTIVAL) Like many Chinese festivals, this one operates on the lunar calendar. Solar equivalents for the next 3 years should be January 23rd 2012, February 10th 2013, and January 31st 2014. The effects of this holiday are felt from 2 weeks before the date until 2 weeks after, when anyone who's away from home attempts to get back, including an estimated 150 million migrant workers. Although tens of thousands of extra bus and train services are added, tickets for land transport are very difficult to get, and can command high prices on the black market (official prices also rise on some routes, and on ferries between Hong Kong and the mainland). Air tickets are usually obtainable and may even still be discounted. In the few days immediately around the New Year, traffic on long-distance rail and bus services can be light, but local services may dry up altogether. Most tourist sights stay open, although some shut on the holiday itself or have limited opening hours.

LABOR DAY & NATIONAL DAY In a policy known as "holiday economics," the May 1 and October 1 holidays were expanded to 7 days each (including one weekend). However, these so-called "Golden Weeks" were anything but, and resentment at everyone having to travel at the same time led to the shortening of the May holiday to 3 days in 2008. Regardless of duration, these two holidays mark the beginning and end of the domestic travel season, and the twin peaks of leisure travel, with the remainder of May, early June, and September also busy. Most Chinese avoid traveling in the summer except to cooler high ground or an offshore island, usually on a weekend. If you're traveling independently, and have the flexibility, it's best to arrive at a larger destination before the holiday starts, and move on in the middle or after the end. The disposable income to fund travel is more often found in larger cities, so these tend to become quieter, easier to get around, and less polluted, although key attractions will swarm with out-of-towners. In **Hong Kong** and **Macau,** these are only 1- or 2-day holidays introduced in 1997 and 1999 respectively.

UNIVERSITY HOLIDAYS Exact term dates are rarely announced far in advance, but train tickets can be difficult to obtain as the student populace moves between home and college. Terms run for 18 weeks with 2 weeks of exams, from the beginning of September to just before Spring Festival, and from just after the Spring Festival to the end of June.

LOCAL DIFFICULTIES China's main international trade fair occupies the last 2 weeks of April and October, and drives up hotel prices in **Guangzhou,** where it's held, and as far away as Hong Kong. In the summer, pleasant temperatures in the **Northeast** (slightly cooler than the rest of China) draw students on summer vacation (which makes train tickets hard to acquire), as well as large Chinese tour groups; it may not be the best time for your visit. The northeast's Dalian is also overbooked during the International Fashion Festival in September (see later in this chapter). In 2011, the establishment of **National Tourism Day** on May 19 also makes this a date to avoid heading to any of the country's major attractions. Across China, **midweek travel** is always better than weekend travel, particularly true at destinations easily tackled in a weekend, such as Wutai Shan and Pingyao (see chapter 7). Already tight government-imposed travel restrictions in **Tibet** tend to increase around the Monlam Festival (sometime mid-Jan to mid-Feb), Saka Dawa Festival (mid-May to mid-June), and around the present Dalai Lama's birthday (July 6). The border crossing between Hong Kong and the mainland at **Lo Wu** can take a couple of hours at holiday periods.

Climate

China is the fourth-biggest country in the world, with the second-lowest inland depression (Turpan) and some of its highest peaks (Everest and K2 are both partly in China). Its far northeast shares the same weather patterns as Siberia, and its far southwest the same subtropical climate as northern Thailand.

In the **north,** early spring and late autumn are the best times to travel, both offering warm, dry days and cool, dry evenings. During March and April winds blow away the pollution but sometimes bring sand from the Gobi and topsoil from high ground to the northeast of Beijing, increasingly desiccated by the mismanagement of water resources. The sky can at times turn a vivid yellow.

In the **south,** November to February brings a welcome drop both in temperature and in all-pervasive humidity, although in Hong Kong all public interiors and many private houses are air-conditioned year-round. The southeast coast is subject to occasional typhoons from June to September, which can close down shops, services, schools, offices, and transport for up to 48 hours.

Central China has some of the country's bitterest winters along with searing summer temperatures that give the Yangzi cities of Chongqing, Wuhan, and Nanjing their epithet "The Three Furnaces."

Tibet has springlike temperatures but a blisteringly close sun in the summer, while the dry winters are far milder than most people expect, at least in Lhasa. The **northwest** has perhaps the greatest range of temperatures, with severe summers and winters alike, but it is also largely dry.

Average Temperature (Celsius/Fahrenheit)

	JAN	FEB	MAR	APR	MAY	JUNE	JULY	AUG	SEPT	OCT	NOV	DEC
BEIJING	–3/26	0/32	6/43	13/57	20/68	24/76	26/79	25/77	20/69	13/57	5/41	–1/30
SHANGHAI	4/40	5/42	8/48	15/59	20/68	23/75	28/83	27/82	23/75	18/66	12/55	6/44
HONG KONG	16/62	17/63	19/67	22/73	26/79	28/83	29/85	29/85	28/83	26/79	22/72	18/65
XI'AN	0/32	2/35	8/48	14/57	19/66	25/77	27/80	25/77	19/66	14/57	7/44	1/33
LHASA	–2/28	0/32	3/38	8/47	11/53	15/60	15/60	14/59	13/56	8/48	2/37	–1/30

Average Precipitation (centimeters/inches)

	JAN	FEB	MAR	APR	MAY	JUNE	JULY	AUG	SEPT	OCT	NOV	DEC
BEIJING	0/0.2	0/0.2	0/0.3	1/0.7	3/1.3	7/3.1	22/8.8	17/6.7	5/2.3	1/0.7	1/0.4	0/0.1
SHANGHAI	4/1.8	6/2.4	8/3.3	9/3.7	10/4.1	17/6.8	14/5.7	13/5.4	13/5.4	6/2.7	5/2.1	3/1.5
HONG KONG	2/1.1	4/1.7	7/2.9	13/5.5	28/11.2	39/15.7	36/14.3	37/14.8	29/11.7	11/4.7	3/1.5	2/1
XI'AN	0/0.3	1/0.4	2/0.9	4/1.8	6/2.4	5/2.1	9/3.8	8/3.4	10/4.2	5/2.3	1-Feb	0/0.2
LHASA	0/0.1	1/0.5	0/0.3	0/0.2	2/1	6/2.5	12/4.8	8/3.5	6/2.6	1/0.5	0/0.1	0/0

Holidays

Public holidays and their effects vary widely between mainland China and the two Special Administrative Regions, Hong Kong and Macau.

MAINLAND CHINA

A few years ago the Chinese were finally granted a 2-day weekend. Offices close, but stores, restaurants, post offices, transportation, sights and, in some areas, banks, all operate the same services 7 days a week. Most sights, shops, and restaurants are open on public holidays, but offices and anything government-related take as much time off as they can. Although China switched to the Gregorian calendar in 1911, some public holidays (and many festivals—see below) are based on a lunar cycle, meaning their solar dates vary from year to year and precise dates often aren't given until the last minute. Holidays are **New Year's Day** (Jan 1), **Spring Festival** (Chinese New Year; a weeklong holiday), **Qingming Festival** (Apr 4), **Labor Day** (3 days around May 1), **National Day** (a week from Oct 1). See "Peak Travel Seasons," above, for more details on the major holidays, plus exact dates for coming years.

HONG KONG

Saturday is officially a working day in Hong Kong, although many offices take the day off or only open for reduced hours. Weekend ferry sailings and other transport may vary, particularly on Sunday, when many smaller shops are closed and opening hours for attractions may also be different. Hong Kong gets many British holidays, traditional Chinese holidays, plus modern political ones added after 1997, but in shorter forms. Banks, schools, offices, and government departments are all closed on these dates, as are many museums: **New Year's Day** (Jan 1), **Lunar New Year's Day** (for the mainland Spring Festival, but in Hong Kong the day itself plus two more, and an extra Fri or Mon if one day falls on a Sun), **Ching Ming (Qingming) Festival** (Apr 4 or 5), **Good Friday** (usually early Apr, plus the following Sat and **Easter Monday**), **Labor Day** (May 1), **Buddha's Birthday** (1 day in Apr or May), **Tuen Ng** (Dragon Boat Festival, 1 day in June), **Hong Kong SAR Establishment Day** (July 1), **Mid-Autumn Festival** (1 day in Sept, usually moved to the nearest Fri or Mon to make a long weekend), **National Day** (Oct 1), **Chung Yeung Festival** (1 day in Oct), **Christmas Day** and **Boxing Day** (Dec 25, and the next weekday if the 26th is a Sat or Sun).

MACAU

Macau has the same holidays as Hong Kong except for SAR Establishment Day, but with the following variations: **National Day** is 2 days (Oct 1–2), **All Souls' Day** (Nov 2), **Feast of the Immaculate Conception** (Dec 8), **Macau SAR Establishment Day** (Dec 20), **Winter Solstice** (Dec 22), and **Christmas Eve** and **Christmas Day** (Dec 24–25).

China Calendar of Events

China's festivals follow the traditional lunar calendar, and to increase confusion, some minority calendars operate according to different traditions. For conversion to solar/Gregorian calendar dates, try the website www.mandarintools.com/calendar.html.

The Chinese tourism industry is increasingly inventing festivals to try to boost business. Unless indicated below, be wary of any festival with the word "tourism" in its name, for instance.

For an exhaustive list of events beyond those listed here, check http://events.frommers.com, where you'll find a searchable, up-to-the-minute roster of what's happening in cities all over the world.

JANUARY

Spring Festival (Chun Jie), Chinese New Year, nationwide. This is still the occasion for large lion dances and other celebrations in Hong Kong, Macau, and Chinatowns worldwide, but in mainland China it's mainly a time for returning home to feast. Fireworks are now banned in larger cities. Temple fairs have been revived in Beijing, but are mostly fairly low-key shopping opportunities. But in the countryside there's been a gradual revival of stilt-walking and masked processions. Spring Festival is on the day of the first new moon after January 21, and can be no later than February 20. January 23, 2012, February 10, 2013 and January 31, 2014.

FEBRUARY

Lantern Festival (Deng Jie), nationwide, especially Pingyao, Quanzhou, and Zigong. This festival perhaps reached its peak in the late Qing dynasty, when temples, stores, and other public places were hung with fantastically shaped and decorated lanterns, some with figures animated by ingenious mechanisms involving the flow of sand. People paraded through the streets with lightweight lanterns in the shapes of fish, sheep, and so on, and hung lanterns outside their houses, often decorated with riddles. The festival has remained popular in Taiwan, and has undergone a revival on the mainland in recent years with increasingly elaborate designs featuring in cities across the country. The festival always falls 15 days after Spring Festival.

Monlam Festival, throughout the Tibetan world (including at Xia He and Langmu Si). Monasteries are open to all, and there is religious dancing, the offering of *torma* (butter sculptures), and the "sunning of the Buddha" when a silk painting *(thangka)* is consecrated and becomes the living Buddha in the minds of believers. Typically, the festival culminates in the parading of the Maitreya Buddha through the town. Fourth to 16th days of the first lunar month (from Feb 25, 2012; from Feb 15, 2013). Check dates with **Qinghai Mountaineering Association** (✆ **0971/823-8877**), or any of the Lhasa agencies listed on p. 761.

MARCH

Hong Kong Sevens Rugby Tournament, Hong Kong. Known as "The Sevens," this is one of Hong Kong's most popular and one of Asia's largest sporting events, with more than 20 teams from around the world competing for the Cup Championship. Contact the **Hong Kong Rugby Football Union** at ✆ **852/2504 8311** or www.hkrugby.com/en/hksevens. Fourth weekend in March.

APRIL

Cheung Chau Bun Festival, Hong Kong. This weeklong affair on Cheung Chau island is thought to appease restless ghosts and spirits. Originally held to placate the unfortunate souls of those murdered by pirates, it features a street parade of lions and dragons and Chinese opera, as well as floats with children seemingly suspended in the air, held up by cleverly concealed wires. The end of the festival is heralded by a race up one of three huge bamboo-supported bun towers erected outside the Pak Tai Temple. Competitors wear climbing gear and aim to get their hands on the highest (luckiest) buns! **HKTB** organizes tours of the parade; call ✆ **852/2508 1234.** Usually late April or early May, but the exact date is chosen by divination.

Formula One Racing, Shanghai. Motorsport fans can catch Formula One drivers zooming around a state-of-the-art track in the Shanghai suburb of Anting. Apr 13 to 15, 2012.

Hong Kong International Film Festival, Hong Kong. Over 300 films from more than 50 countries are featured at this 2-week event. For more information, call ✆ **852/2970 3300,** or visit www.hkiff.org.hk. Two weeks in March or April.

Luoyang Peony Festival, Luoyang. Over 300 varieties of China's best peonies, first cultivated in Luoyang 1,400 years ago, are on display at the Wangcheng Park (Wangcheng Gongyuan), which is awash in a riot of colors. Two weeks in late April.

Sanyue Jie (Third Month Fair), Dali. This biggest festival of the Bai people had its origins over 1,000 years ago when Buddhist monks and adherents gathered to celebrate the appearance of Guanyin (the Goddess of Mercy) to the Bai. Today's festival has become more secular as the Bai and other minorities from elsewhere in Yunnan gather in the foothills of the Green Mountains (Cang Shan) for 5 days and nights of singing, dancing, wrestling, horse racing, and large-scale trading. Ask **CITS** for more information on the precise dates (✆ **0872/216-6578**). Fifteenth day of the third lunar month (usually mid-Apr or early May).

Sisters' Meal Festival (Zimeifan Jie), Taijiang, Shidong (Guizhou). Celebrated with *lusheng* (wind-instrument music) dancing and antiphonal singing, this is one of the prime occasions for young Miao men and women to socialize and find marriage partners. Elaborately dressed Miao women prepare packets of berry-stained glutinous rice to present to suitors. For exact dates, check with **CITS** Kaili (✆ **0855/827-0168**). Fifteenth day of the third lunar month (usually Apr).

Tomb-Sweeping Festival (Qingming), nationwide, especially Hong Kong and Macau. Another festival frequently observed in Chinese communities overseas, and celebrated in more rural areas of China and in Hong Kong and Macau, Tomb-Sweeping is a family outing on a free day near the festival date. It's a day to honor ancestors by visiting and tidying their graves and making offerings of snacks and alcohol. April 4 or April 5 annually.

Water-Splashing Festival (Poshui Jie), Jinghong, Xishuangbanna. Extremely popular with Chinese tourists, the festive Dai New Year is ushered in with a large market on the first day, dragon-boat races on the second, and copious amounts of water-splashing on the third. Be prepared to get doused, but take heart because the wetter you are, the more luck you'll have. Mid-April.

Weifang International Kite Festival, Weifang. The kite capital of the world hosts the largest kite-flying gala in China, as hundreds of thousands of kite lovers from around the world arrive for several days of competition and demonstrations. Check out www.weifangkite.com for more details. April 20.

MAY

Western Journey Festival (Xiqian Jie) marks the day in 1764 when the Qianlong emperor forced the Xibo people to move from their homeland in Manchuria to Qapqal County (southwest of Yining). Celebrations are marked by the devouring of a whole sheep cooked with coriander, preserved vegetables, and onions. Wrestling, horse riding, and archery contests evoke the Xibo's warrior ancestry. The festival is held on the 18th day of the fourth lunar month (late May to mid-June).

JUNE

Dragon Boat Festival (Longzhou Jie), Shidong. With over 40,000 celebrants, this Miao minority festival, which bears no relation to the Han Dragon Boat Festival, commemorates the killing of a dragon whose body was divided among several Miao villages. Over the course of 3 days, dragon boat races are held in Shidong, Pingzhai, and Tanglong. For exact dates, check with **CITS** Kaili (✆ **0855/822-2506**). Twenty-fourth to 27th day of the fifth lunar month (usually June or early July).

Dragon Boat Races (Tuen Ng Festival), Hong Kong. Races of long, narrow boats, gaily painted and powered by oarsmen who row to the beat of drums, originated in ancient China, where legend held that Qu Yuan, an imperial adviser, drowned himself in a Hunan river to protest government corruption. His faithful followers, wishing to recover his body, supposedly raced out into the river in boats, beating their paddles on the surface of the water and throwing rice to distract water creatures from his body. There are two different races: The biggest is an international competition with 30 teams, held along the waterfront in Tsim Sha Tsui East; approximately 500 local Hong Kong teams also compete in races held on the days around the international festival. Local races can be seen at Stanley, Aberdeen, Chai Wan, Yau Ma Tei, Tai Po, and outlying islands. Contact **HKTB** at ✆ **852/2508-1234.** Forthcoming festival dates are June 23, 2012 and June 12, 2013. On the **mainland,** the festival is still celebrated at places connected with Qu Yuan, such as Zigui, Yichang, and Changsha. Fifth day of the fifth lunar month.

Saka Dawa festival is held throughout the Tibetan world, celebrating the life of Buddha. *Koras* (circuits) of holy lakes, mountains, and buildings are undertaken by the faithful. See the contact info for the Monlam Festival (Jan), above. Eighth to 15th days of the fourth lunar month. May or June.

JULY

Jyekundo Horse Festival, south of Yushu, Qinghai. Khampa nomads gather for a spectacular 10-day celebration involving racing, exhibitions of equestrian skill, and horse trading. Canceled in 2010 due to the Yushu earthquake, but scheduled to be back in July 2012. Contact **Snowlion Tours** (✆ **0971/816-3350;** www.snowliontours.com), for the latest details.

Lurol Festival, Tongren (Repkong). This marks the Sino-Tibetan peace treaty, signed in A.D. 822, with fertility dances and body piercing in honor of a local mountain deity, and has a pagan feel. Check with **Qinghai Mountaineering Association** (✆ **0971/823-8877**). The 16th day of the sixth lunar month.

AUGUST

Naadam, across Inner Mongolia, including Hohhot (at the racetrack, Saima Chang, and the Hulun Buir Grasslands, outside Manzhouli). The festival features Mongolian wrestling, archery, and horse and camel racing, and occurs when the grasslands turn green. That's usually mid-August, but can be as early as July. Dates differ from place to place, and they don't coincide with (the People's Republic of) Mongolia's Naadam festival, which is tied to their National Day and always occurs from July 11 to July 13. For exact locations and dates contact **Hohhot CITS** (✆ **0471/620-1602**).

Qingdao International Beer Festival, Qingdao. Over a million visitors descend on this seaside resort for its famous annual Bavarian bacchanal, which features everything from beer tasting and drinking contests for adults, to amusement-park rides for kids. Second week of August.

Rozi Heyt (**Rouzi Jie** or **Kaizhai Jie**), nationwide. The biggest festival in the Islamic world, Aid al Fitr marks the end of the month-long Fast of Ramadan, and believers are keen for a feast. Presents are exchanged and alms are given to the poor. In Kazakh and Tajik areas this is often celebrated with a "lamb snatching" competition. A dead lamb is contested by two teams mounted on horses or yaks; the winning team succeeds in spiriting the lamb out of reach of their rivals. The festival is held for 4 days after the first sighting of the new moon in the 10th month (Shawwal) of the Islamic calendar. August 19, 2012, moving backward by about 11 days each year.

SEPTEMBER

Confucius's Birthday, Qufu. China's Great Sage is honored with parades, exhibitions, and musical and dance performances that reenact some of the rites mentioned in the *Analects (Lun Yu)*. If you wish to stay over during this time, book your hotel well in advance as decent accommodations are hard to come by. September 28.

International Fashion Festival, Dalian. China's most famous fashion event is the Dalian Guoji Fuzhuang Jie. The 2-week gathering of mostly Asian garment producers offers an opening parade, a series of glamorous fashion shows held in the city's best hotels, and the sight of leggy models strutting downtown streets. Mid-September.

International Motorcycle Tourism Festival, Yinchuan. People from China and abroad ride/transport their motorcycles to Yinchuan. Motorcycle stunts and contests, exhibitions, and tourism activities (beware the last) make up the core activities. Held sometime in September; check with **CITS** (✆ **0951/671-9792**) for exact details.

International Shaolin Martial Arts Festival, Song Shan. Some patience may be necessary to negotiate the crowds of pugilists and Bruce Lee wannabes who show up to trade fists and demonstrate some truly jaw-dropping, gravity-defying martial arts skills. For details, call **CITS** (✆ **0371/6585-2326**). Second week of September.

Mid-Autumn Festival (Tuanyuan Jie) is celebrated in Hong Kong, Macau, and Chinese communities overseas, but in mainland China the last remnant of the festival is the giving and eating of *yuebing* (moon cakes), circular pies with sweet and extremely fattening fillings. Traditionally it's a time to sit and read poetry under the full moon, but pollution in many areas has made the moon largely invisible. The 15th day of the eighth lunar month (usually Sept).

OCTOBER

Bairam (Gu'erbang Jie), nationwide. Known around the world as Aid al Fitar (the Festival of Sacrifice), this is celebrated by Muslims throughout China. It marks the willingness of the prophet Abraham to sacrifice everything to God, even his son Ishmael. Celebrations in Kashgar involve feats of tightrope-walking in the main square and wild dancing outside the Id Kah Mosque. The 4-day festival is held 70 days after the breaking of the fast of Ramadan, on the 10th day of the 12th month (Dhul-Hijjah) in the Islamic calendar. It falls on October 26, 2012, and October 11, 2013, and annually shifts backward by 11 days.

Tsongkapa's Birthday, throughout the Tibetan world. The birthplace of the founder of the Geluk order of Tibetan Buddhism, **Kumbum** (**Ta'er Si;** south of **Xining**) sees the liveliest festival. Religious dancing, mass chanting, and "sunning the Buddha" can be seen. Check with **Kumbum** (✆ **0971/223-2357**). Twentieth to 26th days of the ninth lunar month (late Oct to early Nov).

NOVEMBER

International Festival of Folk Songs and Folk Arts, Nanning. Many of Guangxi's minorities, including the Zhuang, the Miao, and the Dong, gather for a colorful week of ethnic song and dance performances that some have criticized as being mere "urban reenactments." A visit to a village to see the minorities in their own environment is highly recommended, but if you're short on time, this explosion of song and dance will suffice. Check with **CITS** (✆ **0771/261-2027**). First half of November.

DECEMBER

Ice and Snow Festival, Harbin. Every year, tens of thousands of people travel from as far south as Guangdong and brave freezing cold to see the Ha'erbin Bingxue Jie. The city's streets come alive with elaborate ice sculptures equipped with internal wires that blaze to life at night. Most impressive is the Ice and Snow Palace, a life-size frozen-water mansion with multiple levels. From late December to whenever the ice begins to melt (usually late Feb).

Miao New Year Festival, Xinjiang, Langde (Guizhou). The Miao New Year is celebrated with songs, dances, bullfights, and *lusheng* competitions. For exact dates check with **CITS** Kaili (✆ **0855/827-0168**). End of the 10th lunar month (usually Dec).

THE LAY OF THE LAND

As the world's fourth-largest country, China has huge geographic diversity and holds some of the world's most spectacular landscapes, many of which are little known outside of the Middle Kingdom. However, with over 1.3 billion people, China also has the world's largest population, over half of whom still reside in the countryside, and this mass of people is, and will likely always be, the biggest threat to the country's natural environment and wildlife.

Geography

Broadly speaking, the **west** of the country is characterized by huge mountain ranges and deserts, and as you travel **east** the terrain generally becomes lower, flatter, and more fertile. The bulk of the population resides in cities, towns, and villages in the gentler east of the country, and while there is a host of worthwhile natural attractions here, if you're a fan of the great outdoors, head for the spectacular but sparsely populated western provinces. Much of China's wildlife has been depleted by hunting (especially during past famines), poaching (often for traditional Chinese medicinal purposes), and more recently pollution and logging, and aside from birds, insects, and whatever you see in breeding centers and the like, you'll need to commit to spending serious time in the wild if you are intent on spotting any of the country's rarer species in their natural habitats.

MAJOR GEOGRAPHIC FEATURES & NATURAL ATTRACTIONS

Home of the Himalaya, and towering Qomolangma (known internationally as Mount Everest; 8,844m/29,015ft.; p. 782), much of the **Tibetan Plateau** lies at an altitude of over 4,000m (13,123 ft.). Wild yak and argali sheep are commonly seen roaming the uplands here, but the reclusive and endangered snow leopard is seldom sighted. Many of Asia's great rivers including the **Yangzi,** the **Yellow River,** the **Brahmaputra,** and the **Mekong,** begin their course on the Tibetan Plateau.

At 6,437km (4,000 miles) long, the Yangzi is the third longest river in the world and on its course it has carved dramatic gorges that eventually lead to flood plains, and the giant lakes of Dongting and Poyang, before spilling into the ocean. Pollution and the **Three Gorges Dam Project** (p. 709) have rapidly diminished wildlife in and along China's greatest river; the unique Yangzi river dolphin was last sighted in 2002 and declared functionally extinct in 2006, and the situation for the few remaining Chinese alligators and South China tigers is critical.

The **far northwest** of the country is a vast, desert land that contains China's lowest point, the Turpan Depression, but conversely, is fringed by yet more huge mountains, namely the Tian Shan, and the Pamirs that border Pakistan. This is the part of the country to visit if you want to ride a Bactrian camel through the dunes, but don't expect to see much other wildlife aside from the odd lizard or snake scuttling for cover from the relentless desert sun. The endless grasslands of **northerly Inner Mongolia** (and parts of Sichuan, Yunnan, Tibet, and Xinjiang) offer the chance to experience yurt life and take a horse ride out into the steppe.

Much of the little-visited **northeastern provinces** of Liaoning, Jilin, and Heilongjiang are made up of pristine forest, and this is one of China's best wildlife areas, noted for its birdlife. As well as cranes and herons that can be spotted throughout the summer, you might also catch a glimpse of musk deer, reindeer, or even a bear.

The **southwest** is characterized by mammoth limestone landscapes such as the **Stone Forest** near Kunming (p. 637), and Guangxi's incredibly beautiful sea of **karst pinnacles,** between Guilin (p. 596) and Yangshuo (p. 604). Other notable natural attractions in this region include the impossibly deep and steep Tiger Leaping Gorge in Yunnan (p. 664), and Sichuan's other worldly Jiuzhai Gou (p. 694). Yunnan presents China's greatest floral biodiversity and the southwest is home to the world's largest butterfly, the Atlas Moth Butterfly, which can have a wingspan of up to 20cm (8 in.)! China's most famous animal, the cute and cuddly looking **giant panda,** is to be found in dwindling numbers inhabiting small pockets of land in Sichuan (p. 680), Gansu, and Shaanxi, and endangered golden monkeys still survive in these regions, too.

In spite of rapid development, the **south** (and even Hong Kong) has managed to hold onto some of its wetlands, which are vital for migrating birds. The far south also holds China's best beaches, most of which are to be found on the tropical island of Hainan; but if you're looking for a beach holiday, you're better off heading to Thailand or Vietnam.

Generally speaking, the **center** and **east** of the country has less going on for nature lovers, but there are still places worth seeking out, including Hunan's astounding "lost world" sandstone scenery at Zhang Jia Jie (p. 733), and the holy mountains of Huang Shan (p. 417) in Anhui and Tai Shan (p. 365) in Shandong. In terms of scenery, the Three Gorges (p. 709) are wildly overrated, all the more so since the completion of the environmentally questionable Three Gorges Dam Project. Wildlife is next to non-existent in large parts of the central and eastern regions, but you can still find huge bamboo forests in Anhui, and there's allegedly a yeti-like creature stomping the forests of Hubei.

Environmental Threats

China has effectively gone through an industrial revolution in less than a quarter of the time that such monumental changes took place in the Western world, and the resultant threats to the environment are manifold and great. In spite of increasing awareness and changing government policy, the sheer scale of many of these environmental hazards makes it difficult to have too much hope for the future, and this is an issue that will continue to dominate life in China for decades to come.

China's gargantuan geography means that less than a fifth of its surface area is suitable for farming, and the most pressing environmental challenges facing the country today are the **drought** and **desertification** that are reducing this cultivable land by nearly 15,539 sq. km (6,000 sq. miles) per year. As the northwestern deserts spread, less rainfall is generated and the situation is exacerbated. Desert dust is blown from the arid west across the north of the country, and is responsible for a third of air-borne pollution in these regions. While there's plenty of rain in most of the rest of the country, three-quarters of China's lakes and rivers are polluted, which leaves a quarter of the population without access to clean drinking water. In true Chinese fashion, a grand project dubbed the South North Water Diversion, aims to distribute water from the Yangzi up to the parched Yellow River regions, but many experts question its viability. Recent low water levels along the Yangzi, which have rendered several dams (including Three Gorges Dam) incapable of reaching their hydroelectric capacity, cast further doubt on the project.

China is rich in natural resources and has extensive reserves of coal, oil, gas, iron ore, and precious stones and metals, most of which lie in the north and west of the country. This has aided its unprecedented industrial and economic growth, but has done much damage to its natural environment. Increased power needs mean that China is now a net importer of oil, but the bulk of **air pollution** is caused by coal emissions. Acid rain falls on a third of the country, and increasing private vehicle ownership has also dramatically worsened urban air pollution to the point that in 2007, 16 of the world's 20 most polluted cities were to be found in China. The marine environment has also suffered at the hands of China's energy needs, with the country's worst ever **oil spill** occurring off the coast of Dalian in 2010.

It's not all doom and gloom, though, and China's accord with the Kyoto Protocol and pledge to host a green Olympics was also taken as an assurance that it will adopt a more sustainable approach to development and address the country's long-term environmental problems. The younger generation is far more concerned with the plight of their natural environment than their predecessors, and the current government does seem to be taking note, not least because it is estimated that environmental damage costs up to 10% of China's annual GDP.

Cleaner forms of power are also increasingly used to generate electricity, and while grand hydroelectric schemes such as the Three Gorges Dam Project create as many environmental issues as they solve, wind farms are popping up all over the blowy northwest, and second generation waste-sourced biofuel is being developed apace. However, plans to reduce carbon dioxide emissions by 45% by 2020 rely on China's ambitious nuclear program, which is now under close scrutiny following Japan's 2011 quake and tsunami.

Interest in wildlife and environmental tourism is also providing an economic incentive to protect natural habitats, although, unless carefully managed, tourism may present more threats than it does solutions. National parks and conservation areas are being expanded and better protected, and the work of a few dedicated individuals has brought the plight of endangered animal species, notably the giant panda, into the public eye.

To be sure, there is a long way to go, and much of the environmental damage already done is irreversible, but China has at least caught onto the notion of conservation, and

Sustainable Tourism in China

China still doesn't have much in the way of eco-tourism, and indeed the large-scale domestic tourism market is anything but sustainable. In spite of various designated tourist committee forums on the subject, the best they generally come up with is not to urbanize regions famous for their natural beauty! Some regions however, fare better than others, and the wild and wonderful southwest has attracted attention from UNESCO and the WWF and a handful of eco-friendly tour operators have established themselves in Sichuan and Yunnan: **Overland China** and **Wild China** (see below) are both committed and responsible. Another positive sign is the growing awareness of the younger generation who are increasingly concerned with looking after their natural environs. Also just because there isn't much specifically directed at eco-tourism in China, this doesn't mean you can't do your bit. Basic environmental measures such as not getting your hotel linen washed every day, recycling, and walking and cycling rather than taking motorized transport all help to minimize your impact, while buying locally produced crafts from the artisans themselves helps to support local economies.

is starting to move in the right direction, which is more than can be said for some of the world's more developed nations.

SPECIAL-INTEREST TRIPS & ESCORTED GENERAL-INTEREST TOURS

Since China reopened to foreign tourism in the early 1980s, all foreign tour operators have been required to use official state-registered travel companies as ground handlers. All arrangements in China were usually put together by one of three companies: China International Travel Service (CITS), China Travel Service (CTS), or China Youth Travel Service (CYTS). Controls are now loosening, foreign tour companies are allowed some limited activities in China, and the range of possible Chinese partners has increased, but in effect, CITS and the like are the only companies with nationwide networks of offices, and many foreign tour companies still turn to them. They work out the schedule at the highest possible prices and send the costs to the foreign package company, which then adds its own administration charges and hands the resulting quote to you.

You could get the same price yourself by dealing with CITS (which has many offices overseas) directly. But you can get far better prices by organizing things yourself as you go along so, other than convenience, there's little benefit and a great deal of unnecessary cost to buying a package. Just about any tour operator will offer to tailor an itinerary to your needs, which means it will usually simply pass on the request to one of the state monoliths, and pass the result back to you. The benefit of dealing with a Chinese travel company directly is that you cut out the middleman, but if things go wrong, you will be unlikely to obtain any compensation whatsoever. If you book through a home tour operator, you can expect to obtain refunds and compensation if this becomes appropriate. In general, however, when organized through CITS, rail or air tickets for your next leg are reliably delivered to each hotel as you go. Be cautious when booking directly over the Web with a China-based travel service or "private" tour guide. Check that they are licensed to do business with foreigners, and confirm that there are no hidden costs. If you're set on a tour, start with the list of tour companies below in the following sections, nearly all of which will arrange individual itineraries; or contact the **CNTO** (addresses on p. 814) to find properly registered Chinese agencies who may help you. The **Hong Kong Tourism Board** and the **Macau Government Tourism Office,** in whose territories the tourism industry is well regulated, can point you toward reputable operators and reliable licensed private guides.

Special-Interest Trips

As more and more people travel and become more discerning about what they want from their time away, specialized tours have become increasingly popular. Many of the traditional big players have jumped onto the bandwagon and present their own versions; however, you're better off going through an agency that focuses on just one or two specialties, rather than a jack-of-all-trades. The listings below are recommended. If you're thinking of **taking your kids** on a trip around China, see "Family Travel," p. 807.

ACADEMIC TRIPS & LANGUAGE CLASSES

With **Academic Travel Abroad** (U.S.), groups are typically of 20 to 30 people and tour leaders are Mandarin-speaking Americans, with additional specialty study leaders. The company has been operating tours to China since 1979, and operates educational and cultural tours in China for The Smithsonian (educational, cultural) and National Geographic Expeditions (natural history, soft adventure). For more information, check the website at www.academic-travel.com, but book through individual sponsors. The Smithsonian: ✆ **877/338-8687;** www.smithsonianjourneys.org. National Geographic: ✆ **888/966-8687;** www.nationalgeographicexpeditions.com.

Roadscholar ★ (established by not-for-profit Elderhostel; ✆ **800/454-5768** in the U.S.; www.roadscholar.org) takes groups of around 20 people and tours are developed in cooperation with Chinese educational institutions and excursions and activities supplement the educational theme of each course.

ADVENTURE & WELLNESS TRIPS

Based in Taiwan and established by Simon Foster, the author of this chapter, **Bamboo Trails** ★★ (✆ **0970/782-393** in Taiwan; www.bambootrails.com) offers a unique collection of themed itineraries throughout the Chinese world. Clients are mainly individuals and small groups with a desire to get a different perspective on China. Checking out the Middle Kingdom's best movie locations and a signature bamboo trail are two of the journeys on offer.

Bike Asia ★★ (✆ **0773/882-6521** in China; www.bikeasia.com) is based out of Yangshuo in Guangxi province and is one of the best bike tour operators in the country. Bike Asia's Trail of the Dragon Tour was featured in *National Geographic Adventure* magazine's 25 Best New Trips 2007, and they operate a host of other itineraries in south and southwest China.

Bike China Adventures, Inc. ★, U.S.-based, with an office in China (✆ **800/818-1778** in the U.S., or 01388-2266-575 in China; www.bikechina.com), is still one of the leaders in this field, with great organization and guides. Cycling group sizes are from one to eight participants, who have ranged in age from 18 to 86.

The company is based in Chengdu and tours are accompanied by a bilingual local or foreign guide. More than 50 tours operate both around the company's Sichuan base, and farther afield.

Grasshopper Adventures ★★ (✆ **02/280-0832** in Thailand, 818/921-7101 in the US, 020/8123-8144 in the U.K., and 03/9016-3172 in Australia; www.grasshopperadventures.com) presents an interesting range of small group (maximum 16) adventurous tours across the country led by specialist Australian and European tour leaders with real in-depth knowledge and passion for their destinations. Many itineraries are unique, and as well as cycling (and even unicycling) trips, Grasshopper also operates photography tours in China with personal instruction by pro photographer Ewen Bell, and a maximum group size of 8. Full disclosure: Simon Foster, who wrote this chapter, runs tours for Grasshopper in China and Taiwan.

Mongol Global Tour Co. (✆ **866/225-0577** in the U.S. or 714/220-2579; www.mongolglobaltours.com) offers custom tours for adventurers, gourmet food and wine-lovers, lovers of culture, and more. Their tours offer many sites and experiences not generally offered and can be designed with economy in mind. There are local guides in each city and a national guide accompanies tours of 10 or more people. For specialty groups there is often an international guide as well.

Myths and Mountains ★ (✆ **800/670-6984** in the U.S. or 775/832-5454; www.mythsandmountains.com) is an adventure travel company that specializes in getting inside the culture of a country. Their customized trips focus on the themes of China—the culture and arts, religions and holy sites, ethnic groups and trade routes, and environment and how people have adapted to it. Tours range from the eastern coastal cities and villages all the way west to Yunnan, Tibet and Xinjiang.

Focusing on Sichuan and Yunnan, **Overland China ★★** (✆ **646/233-3362** in the U.S.; www.overlandchina.com) demonstrates how small group tourism can positively impact local communities and environments whilst protecting local culture and crafts. Tours come in two styles: all-inclusive, and semi-inclusive, the latter of which allows travelers more flexibility to amend their itinerary as they travel.

Wild China ★★ (✆ **888/902-8808** in the U.S.; www.wildchina.com) is run by a returnee ABC (American-born Chinese) from Harvard, and presents an enticing array of specialized trips in the Middle Kingdom. Current itineraries include The Silk Road Through Your Lens, a photographic odyssey through Xinjiang, and China for Foodies, a culinary exploration from Beijing to Shanghai via Xi'an, Chengdu and Hangzhou. Great attention is paid to comfort and the site's collection of press articles is particularly encouraging. Wild China was deservedly included in *National Geographic Adventure* magazine's 2009 "Best Adventure Travel Companies on Earth."

FOOD & WINE TRIPS

Many of the big international outfits now offer culinary tours, but the best trips are generally operated by specialized companies such as Mongol Global Tours and Wild China (see above). If budget isn't a parameter, **Artisans of Leisure ★** (✆ **800/214-8144** in the U.S.; www.artisansofleisure.com) runs an 11-day culinary tour that takes guests from Beijing to Hong Kong via Shanghai. The tour incorporates private cooking classes in each city and offers top-of-the-line accommodation options including the Peninsula, Raffles, and the Mandarin Oriental. **Hias Gourmet ★** (www.hiasgourmet.com) is another quality outfit and offers everything from food walks and cooking classes in Beijing to full-blown culinary tours around Pingyao and Dali.

VOLUNTEER & WORKING TRIPS
i-to-i (✆ **0800/011-1156** in the U.K.; www.i-to-i.com) is the original volunteer travel company and offers a whole host of volunteer and working trips around China. For those keen to give something back, this is a great way to do it, and if you don't have the skills needed, you can learn them there. TEFL courses can be done online before you go, and they offer a host of placements and durations (from teaching primary school and university students to conservation placements—a favorite being 2 weeks working on panda conservation near Xi'an).

Escorted General-Interest Tours

Escorted tours are structured group tours with a group leader. The price often includes everything from airfare to hotels, meals, tours, admission costs, and local transportation.

Escorted tours do not usually represent savings, but they do take the hassle out of travel arrangements and allow you to see as much as possible in the time you have. Foreign tour companies are required to work with licensed Chinese ground handlers, although some do book as much as they can directly. But even as markets become freer, most deals will continue to be made with the official state operators, if only for convenience. Please read the brochures with as much skepticism as you would read a Realtor's (one man's "scenic splendor" is another's "heavily polluted") and read the following notes carefully.

Most tour companies peddle the same list of mainstream "must-sees," featuring Beijing, Xi'an, Shanghai, Guilin, and the Yangzi River, with some alternative trips to Tibet, Yunnan Province, or the Silk Routes.

When choosing a tour company for China, you must, of course, consider cost, what's included, the itinerary, the likely age and interests of other tour group members, the physical ability required, and the payment and cancellation policies, as you would for any other destination. But you should also investigate the following:

SHOPPING STOPS These are the bane of any tour in China, designed to line the pockets of tour guides, drivers, and sometimes the ground handling company itself. A stop at the Great Wall may be limited to only an hour so as to allow an hour at a cloisonné factory. In some cases the local government owns the shop in question and makes a regulation requiring all tours to stop there. The better foreign tour operators design their own itineraries and have instituted strict contractual controls to keep these stops to a minimum, but they are often unable to do away with them altogether, and tour guides will introduce extra stops whenever they think they can get away with it. Other companies, particularly those that do not specialize in China, just take the package from the Chinese ground handler, put it together with flights, and pass it on uncritically. At shopping stops, you should never ask or accept your tour guide's advice on what is the "right price." You are shopping at the wrong place to start with, where prices will often be 10 times higher than they should be. Typically your guide, driver, and maybe even the tour leader, will split a 30% commission on sales. The "discount" card you are given marks you for yet higher initial prices and tells the seller to which guide commission is owed. So ask your tour company how many of these stops are included, and simply sit out those you cannot avoid.

GUIDES The ability, honesty and attitude of Chinese guides varies enormously, and while some can be highly informative and responsive to your needs, others follow a set program, repeating the same old spiel, no matter what the question, while hurrying you from shop to shop. Better companies vet their guides and will arrange a national guide who will escort you throughout the entire trip; this is great if you get a decent guide, but can be frustrating if not. Cheaper companies may not use guides at all, or may use different local guides as you reach new destinations. While many of the guides may not be that great, the variety, and possibility of landing the odd good guide, at least adds interest. Many guides will be reticent to discuss politics and you should be careful how you phrase potentially sensitive questions. It is also worth discussing with your operator where your guide will be from; in autonomous regions such as Tibet or Xinjiang it is far better to be escorted by a Tibetan or Uighur respectively, and this also helps to support the local community.

Ask your tour company if it will be sending along a guide or tour manager from your home country to accompany trip members and to supplement local guides. This is worth paying more for, as it ensures a smoother trip all-around, and it helps you get more authoritative information. Otherwise, you're better off bringing background reading from home. Conversely, guides in **Hong Kong** and **Macau** are often extremely knowledgeable and both objective and accurate with their histories.

Abercrombie & Kent ★ (✆ **800/554-7016** in the U.S., ✆ **0845/618-2200** in the U.K.; www.abercrombiekent.com) is one of the longest standing and most highly reputed tour companies in the market, and offers a selection of top-flight group tours in China, along with unlimited tailor-made options. Group tours are composed of up to 16 people for Connoisseur Tours and a maximum of 24 for other tours. As well as bilingual tour leaders and local specialist guides, tours afford direct contact with local artists, archaeologists, and colorful personalities.

The maximum group size with **Adventure Center** (✆ **800/228-8747** in the U.S.; www.adventurecenter.com) is 18 (typically 12) and both foreign and local tour leaders are used. Owned by travel giant TUI, the company offers a range of trip styles from affordable grass-roots-style trips designed for younger participants to more inclusive trips using upgraded accommodations for those wanting to combine adventure and comfort. A vast range of tours are on offer; as well as the classic highlights of China, they offer some interesting itineraries including walks on stretches of the Great Wall, and trips into the Tibetan and Xinjiang hinterlands.

For unbelievable deals, check out **China Spree ★★**, especially their Super Value Tours (✆ **866/652-5656** in the U.S.; www.chinaspree.com). The delightful expert tour guides are fonts of local knowledge and anecdotes, filling you in on life in China past and present. The hotels in each city are impressive and top-of-the-line. The price of the tour includes airfare, most meals (which often include local specialties), local transport, and local tours. The company has gotten many raves for its personalized service and tour guides who go above and beyond—all for the price of what usually would only cover airfare.

One of the few Chinese owned and operated agencies that really understands the needs of foreign travelers, **Choice Travel ★★** (✆ **0531/8855-8979** in China; www.choicetravel.cn) offers prompt, efficient and good value services via a carefully selected group of agencies throughout the country. As well as a decent collection of group tours (which can also run as private departures), Choice can also put together tailor-made and specialized itineraries for interests as diverse as tai chi, tea-picking, and tracing Jewish history in China.

Owned by the same group as budget operators Peregrine and Imaginative Traveler, **Gecko's Adventures** (✆ **03/8601-4444;** www.geckosadventures.com) tours are aimed at a younger crowd (typically 20- to 40-year-olds) with a selling point of using local tour leaders (with Gecko's training). Itineraries stick mainly but not entirely to the highlights, but these are more down-to-earth budget tours using smaller guesthouses, local restaurants, and public transport. Branches are located across Australia and now in the U.K. and the U.S.

General Tours World Traveler's (✆ **800/221-2216** in the U.S.; www.generaltours.com) small-group escorted tours are led by a handpicked team of English-speaking guides. Itineraries are experiential and culture-focused, and as such, shopping stops are kept to a minimum. There's a wide choice, including three different Yangzi cruises and tours covering the highlights of China plus Tibet.

With **Laurus Travel** (✆ **877/507-1177** in the U.S. and Canada, or 604/438-7718 in Canada; www.laurustravel.com) group sizes range from 10 to 20 people and a tour leader accompanies the tour from Canadian departure or from arrival in China. Laurus is a China-only specialist, but itineraries are predominantly mainstream.

Tour groups with **R. Crusoe & Son ★** (✆ **800/585-8555** in the U.S.; www.rcrusoe.com) are kept small and are accompanied by a Hong Kong Chinese and joined by local guides and experts at each stop. Tours include extras such as a visit to an area of the Forbidden City that is usually closed to the public, and a view of Xi'an's Terra-Cotta Warriors at eye level, rather than just from the viewing gallery.

SITA World Tours (✆ **800/421-5643** in the U.S. and Canada; www.sitatours.com) has over 75 years of experience, SITA offers luxury, deluxe, and first class tours throughout China and the Orient, escorted by certified guides that are sensitive to the needs of the discerning traveler. SITA also guarantees its departures so there is never a concern in a tour canceling.

Tauck World Discovery (✆ **800/788-7885** in the U.S.; www.tauck.com) offers a 16-day itinerary in China, which features a 3-night Yangzi River cruise, upscale accommodations, and virtually all expenses included (five on-tour flights, 37 meals, admission to all sites and attractions, and so on).

SUGGESTED ITINERARIES

3

China's vast history, ethnic and cultural diversity, along with the sheer enormity of its territory, presents so many travel possibilities that you could spend your whole life here and still not have seen everything. This said, for most first-time visitors, a few cultural icons and spectacular landscapes deserve immediate attention. **Beijing** and its cornucopia of imperial sights, **Xi'an's Terracotta Warriors,** the bustling contrasts of **Hong Kong** and **Shanghai** (and the surrounding water towns), and the fairytale limestone landscapes of **Guangxi** should be your first priorities. The itineraries below principally focus on these areas, and continue on from one another. If you've already visited the previous places then you might want to explore some of China's more remote destinations. Fans of the great outdoors will get the most from the wild **west** of the country, and **Yunnan, Tibet,** and **Xinjiang** are all incredibly worthwhile destinations, not only for their spectacular landscapes, but also for the hardy and hospitable people who live there. All of the destinations mentioned are served by tour companies (p. 44), but you can also make arrangements yourself as you go along without too much trouble, although the harsher western regions are certainly easier with private transport.

Tip: Avoid the May and October Holidays, and the Chinese New Year at all costs. All forms of transport are booked solid and popular destinations quickly become chaotic. Needless to say, the industry makes the most of this opportunity by hiking prices.

THE REGIONS IN BRIEF

Beijing & Hebei

While there was much talk of getting to the Three Gorges on the Yangzi River before the area's partial disappearance, the real urgency is to see what little is left of old Beijing, with its ancient housing and original Ming dynasty street plan. Thanks to new construction, whole city blocks can vanish at once, sometimes taking ancient, long-forgotten temples with them.

But while Beijing suffers from being communism's showpiece for the outside world and a victim of ersatz modernization, it still has far more to offer than several other Chinese cities put together, including some of China's most extravagant monuments, such as the **Forbidden City.** In

Suggested Itineraries

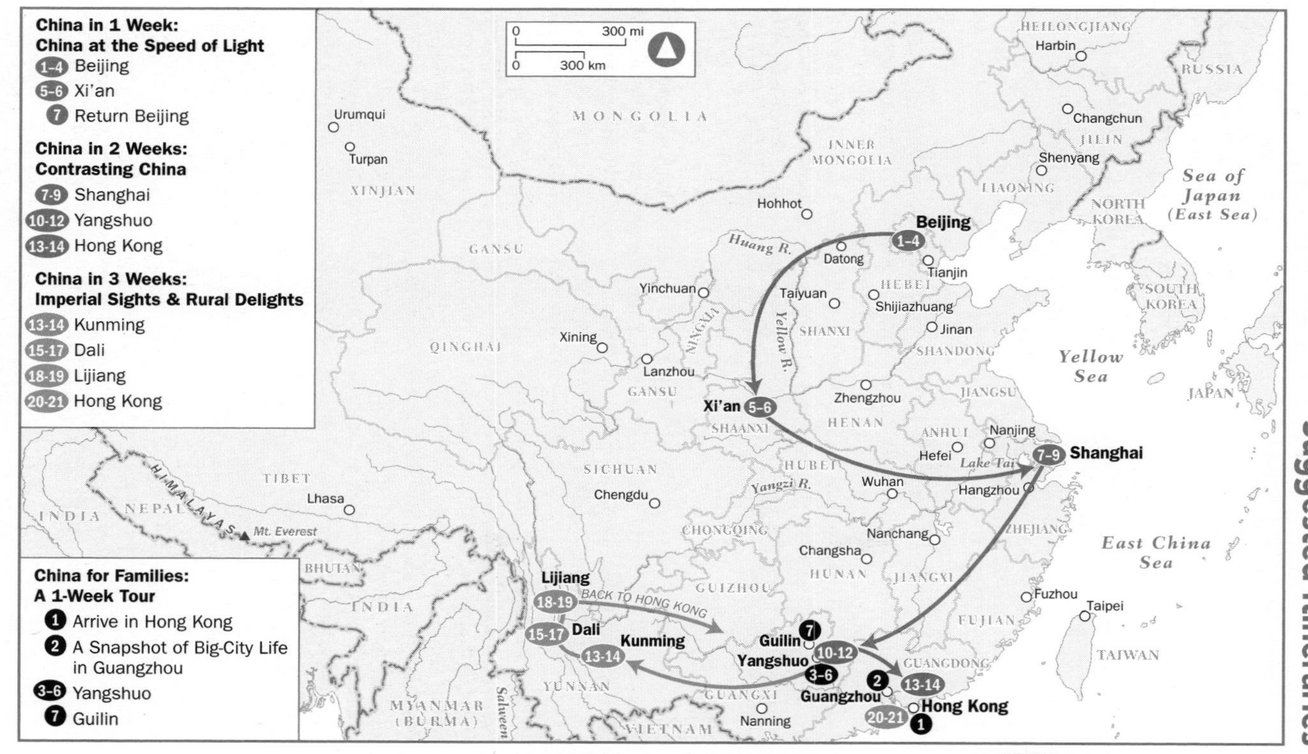

addition, the city has easy access to the surrounding province of **Hebei** with its sinuous sections of the **Great Wall** and vast **tomb complexes.**

The Northeast

Even if the Chinese no longer believe civilization ends at the Great Wall, most tourists still do. The frigid lands to the Northeast, once known as Tartary or Manchuria, represent one of the least-visited and most challenging regions in China, and its last great travel frontier.

Despite industrialization, the provinces of **Liaoning, Jilin,** and **Heilong Jiang,** and the northern section of **Inner Mongolia,** still claim China's largest natural forest, its most pristine grasslands, and one of its most celebrated **lakes (Tian Chi).** You'll also find architectural remnants of the last 350 years—early **Qing palaces and tombs,** incongruous **Russian cupolas,** and eerie structures left over from Japan's wartime occupation.

Around the Yellow River

As covered in this book, this region comprises an area of northern China that includes **Shanxi, Ningxia,** parts of **Shaanxi,** and **Inner Mongolia,** roughly following the central loop of the Yellow River north of Xi'an. One of China's "cradles of civilization," the area is home to most of the country's oldest surviving **timber-frame buildings,** its oldest carved **Buddhist grottoes,** and **Pingyao,** one of its best-preserved **walled cities.**

The Silk Routes

From the ancient former capital of **Xi'an,** famed for the modern rediscovery of the **Terra-Cotta Warriors,** trade routes ran in all directions, but most famously (because they were given a clever name in the 19th c.) west and northwest through **Gansu** and **Xinjiang,** and on to the Middle East. Under the control of Tibetan, Mongol, Indo-European, and Turkic peoples more than of Chinese, these regions are still populated with Uighurs, Tajiks, Kazakhs, Tibetans, and others, some in tiny oasis communities on the rim of the **Taklamakan Desert,** which seem completely remote from China. Indeed, the Uighurs would rather rule themselves, and there has been a resurgence in calls for independence that most recently left over 150 Han Chinese dead after riots in the Xinjiang capital, Ürümqi, in July 2009.

The Silk Routes are littered with alien monuments and tombs, and with magnificent cave-temple sights such as **Dunhuang,** which demonstrate China's import of foreign religions and aesthetics as much as the wealth generated by its exports of silk.

Eastern Central China

Eastern central China, between the Yellow River (Huang He) and the Yangzi River (Chang Jiang), is an area covering the provinces of **Henan, Shandong, Jiangsu,** and **Anhui.** Chinese culture developed and flourished with little outside influence here. **Luoyang** was the capital of nine dynasties, **Kaifeng** capital of six, and **Nanjing** capital of eight. **Qufu,** the hometown of China's most important philosopher, Confucius, is here, as are several of China's holiest mountains, notably **Tai Shan** and **Huang Shan,** as well as that watery equivalent of the Great Wall, the **Grand Canal.**

Shanghai

After 50 years of being overlooked, Shanghai, the Pearl of the Orient, is once again booming and its status as the country's wealthiest city, with the highest per capita incomes, is attracting businesses and workers from around the globe. While the skyscrapers grow taller and ever more eye-catching, the sweep of 19th- and early-20th-century architecture along the **Bund** and the Art Deco masterpieces to be found in the **French Concession** behind it, hark back to the city's last glory days of the 19th century. These contrasting features make Shanghai the mainland's top East-meets-West destination, and it has the restaurants and relaxed and open-minded atmosphere to match. Nearby **Hangzhou** and **Suzhou** offer some of China's most famous scenery.

The Southeast

South of Shanghai and the Yangzi River, the coastal provinces of **Zhejiang, Fujian,** and **Guangdong** have always been China's most outward looking. These areas, which boomed under the relatively open Tang dynasty and were forced to reopen as "treaty ports" by the guns of the first multinationals in the 19th century, are also those most industrialized under the current "reform and opening" policy. Remembering that this is a guide for travelers rather than businesspeople, we have focused on areas of great natural beauty such as **Anji** and **Yandangshan,** rather than "developed" coastal cities. A bit inland, the impoverished pottery-producing province of **Jiangxi** illustrates the two-speed nature of China's growth.

Hong Kong & Macau

Two sets of pencil-slim towers jostle for position on either side of a harbor, close as bristles on a brush. Between them, ponderous oceangoing vessels slide past puttering junks, and century-old ferries waddle and weave across their paths. The mixture of Asia's finest hotels, territory-wide duty-free shopping, incense-filled working temples, rugged and surprisingly remote outlying islands, and fun, historic transport options including the Star Ferry and trams, make this city-state worth flying to Asia to see in its own right. **Macau,** once a provincial backwater, now Asia's gambling capital, still offers a little bit of misplaced Mediterranean, and is a short ferry ride away.

The Southwest

Encompassing the provinces of **Yunnan, Guizhou, Guangxi,** and **Hainan Island,** this region is home to some of China's most spectacular mountain scenery and three of Asia's mightiest rivers, resulting in some of the most breathtaking gorges and lush river valleys in the country.

Even more appealing: This region is easily the most ethnically diverse in China. Twenty-six of China's 56 officially recognized ethnic groups can be found in the southwest, from the Mosu in **Lugu Lake** to the Dai in **Xishuangbanna,** and from the Miao around **Kaili** to the Dong in **San Jiang,** each with different architecture, dress, traditions, and colorful festivals.

The Yangzi River

In addition to shared borders, the landlocked provinces of **Sichuan, Hubei,** and **Hunan** and the municipality of **Chongqing** have in common the world's third-longest river, the Chang Jiang ("Long River," aka Yangzi or Yangtze). The home of five holy Buddhist and/or Daoist mountains, this area contains some of China's most beautiful scenery, particularly in northern Sichuan and northern Hunan.

Sichuan deserves exploration using **Chengdu** as a base, and the Hunan should be explored from **Changsha.** If you're taking the **Three Gorges cruise** (available indefinitely despite what you may have heard), try to at least leave yourself a few days on either end to explore **Chongqing** and **Wuhan.** And a day trip from Chongqing to the Buddhist grottoes at **Dazu** is well worth the time.

The Tibetan World

The Tibetan plateau is roughly the size of western Europe, with an average elevation of over 4,000m (13,123 ft.). Ringed by vast mountain ranges such as the **Kunlun range** to the north and the **Himalayas,** the region offers towering scenic splendors as well as some of the richest minority culture within modern China's borders. **Lhasa,** former seat of the Dalai Lamas, is dominated physically by the vast **Potala Palace,** and emotionally by the fervor of the pilgrims to the **Jokhang Temple.** However, recent discontent and unrest has brought armed Chinese soldiers to the streets of Lhasa. While a trip to the Tibetan Autonomous Region is still to be recommended, neighboring Chinese provinces, particularly **Qinghai,** offer similar scenery and Tibetan culture, and generally speaking, the authorities are less watchful and the atmosphere in both monasteries and on the streets is more relaxed.

CHINA IN 1 WEEK: OR, CHINA AT THE SPEED OF LIGHT

When it comes to travel less is often more, and with only a week in China you are best to confine yourself to just one or two of the principal destinations. **Beijing** and **Xi'an, Beijing** and **Shanghai, Shanghai** and nearby **Suzhou** and **Hangzhou,** or, if you're less keen on culture (or are traveling with your kids), **Hong Kong** and **Yangshuo,** are all viable options. Below is a sample itinerary for Beijing and Xi'an.

Days 1–4: Beijing

Start your time in Beijing with a visit to the **Forbidden City** (p. 99) and make sure you have plenty of time to explore all of its nooks and crannies. The following day head to the **Temple of Heaven** (p. 103) and in the afternoon visit the **Lama Temple** (p. 106), then stroll through the lakes and *hutong* alleys of the **Back Lakes** (p. 111). Dine out over a spectacular view and experience tasty dishes at destination restaurant Capital M ★★★ (p. 85). On the third day, head out early to the **Great Wall** at **Jinshanling** ★★★ or **Simatai** ★★ (p. 123) and take a steep, spectacular hike. By the time you get back to Beijing you will certainly have the appetite for a hearty and delicious Beijing Duck dinner. On day 4 visit the **Summer Palace** (p. 104), the massive **National Museum** (p. 108), or whichever of Beijing's astounding range of attractions appeals, and then take an overnight train to Xi'an.

Days 5–6: Xi'an

Check into your hotel and freshen up before heading out to explore Xi'an's historic sights. Get some insight about what you'll see in the coming days by heading to the first-rate **Shanxi History Museum** ★★★ (p. 260). Later in the day go for a wander through the artist's quarter, maybe looking in on the **Forest of Stelae Museum** ★ (p. 258), or taking a stroll along the **City Wall** ★ (p. 260), which gives a good overview of the city. In the evening dine on dumplings at **De Fa Chang** ★★ (p. 265). Early the following day, head out to the **Terra-Cotta Warriors** ★★★ (p. 260). In the afternoon visit the **Great Mosque** ★ (p. 258) and then as the light fades enjoy an alfresco dinner of kabobs in the Muslim markets. If you have an extra half-day, we also highly recommend **Emperor Jingdi's Mausoleum** ★★ (p. 261).

Day 7: Home Time

Take a morning flight back to Beijing and connect with your international flight home.

CHINA IN 2 WEEKS: CONTRASTING CHINA

An extra week allows visitors to experience some of the incredible contrasts that China has to offer; you'll see imperial sights, ultra-modern cities like Hong Kong and Shanghai, and idyllic Chinese countryside.

Days 7–9: Shanghai

On day 7 make your way down to the **Great Goose Pagoda** (p. 259), and in the afternoon take a flight from Xi'an to **Shanghai.** Speed into town on the maglev and settle into your hotel. In the evening head to **Cloud 9** in the Jin Mao Tower for a cocktail while you gaze out over the city. From here it's not far to **Jade on 36** ★★★ (p. 476), where you enjoy yet more views over dinner.

The following day visit the **Shanghai Museum** ★★★ (p. 469), one of the finest in the country. After exploring the museum, wander around **Yu Garden** (**Yu Yuan;** p. 465), which makes for an interesting afternoon, especially when combined with souvenir shopping in the surrounding bazaar, and then a relaxing pot of green tea in the floating teahouse. In the evening head for a sumptuous dinner at one of the eateries in **Mr. and Mrs. Bund** ★★ (p. 450), and then take a wander along the river. If you have any shoe leather left, cross over and continue your stroll along one of Shanghai's main shopping arteries, **Nanjing Road** (p. 473), where very few places close before 10pm.

On day 9 cross town to the **French Concession** (p. 431), and wander round one of China's best preserved collections of colonial buildings. Enjoy a meal at one of **Xin Tiandi**'s (p. 431) trendy restaurants and after lunch maybe do a spot of shopping at nearby **Huaihai Zhong Lu** (p. 473).

Days 10–12: Yangshuo ★★★

On day 10 fly from Shanghai to Guilin and then transfer to the rural retreat of **Yangshuo.** Spend the next few days taking **boat and bike rides** ★★★ through the stunning scenery to traditional villages and markets, interjected with cultural adventures ranging from tai chi to Chinese cooking classes. Break up your activities with leisurely meals and drinks in Yangshuo's cozy cafes.

Days 13–14: Hong Kong

Finish your trip in one of the world's most captivating cities, Hong Kong. While you're here, make sure you take the **Star Ferry** (p. 552) over to Central, and then take the **Peak Tram** (p. 569) up to **Victoria Peak** (p. 569) for one of the world's great urban vistas. Have a meal on the peak, looking out over it all. Spend the rest of your time in Hong Kong according to what appeals: For some that might mean visiting Hong Kong's famous **markets,** or it may be worth checking out the **Hong Kong History Museum** (p. 570), but for me it would be a boat trip to **Lamma** or **Lantau Islands** (p. 575) for a hike and a swim.

CHINA IN 3 WEEKS: IMPERIAL SIGHTS & RURAL DELIGHTS

If you are fortunate enough to have 3 weeks to spend in China, you can sufficiently explore the side of China that focuses more on its timeless, natural beauty as well as its somewhat more temporary, cultural splendor.

Days 13–14: Kunming

Kunming city center might seem a little threatening after the sublime beauty of Yangshuo, so head up to the **Bamboo Temple** ★ (p. 637), or the **Green Lake area** ★ (p. 633) and spend your first day in the city acclimatizing.

The following day take the train to the **Stone Forest** ★★ (p. 637), or, even better, visit the quieter **Black Pine Stone Forest** (p. 638), which predates the Stone Forest by about 2 million years. Take plenty of supplies in case you decide not to emerge for lunch.

Days 15–17: Dali

Night trains to **Dali** are notoriously difficult to book so grab the earliest bus possible instead and spend the rest of the day exploring the cobbled streets and streams of Dali (p. 641). The next day take the cable car up to the **Cang Shan** (**Green Mountains;** p. 648) and follow the paths as they wind in and out of the surflike clouds. The view from the mountain makes **Er Hai Lake** (p. 648) irresistible, so spend the following day cycling along the shore or visiting some of the islands such as **Jinsuo Dao** (p. 649), filled with caves and caverns. If this all sounds a bit too energetic, weekly markets such as **Shaping** (p. 646) and a host of others are within easy reach and offer the chance to see the local ethnic minorities resplendent in their traditional costumes.

Days 18–19: Lijiang ★★

Hop aboard a Li Jiang bus and after checking into your hotel try some traditional cuisine at **He Shi San Wei Shi Wu** ★ (p. 661). Spend the following day exploring the enchanting old town.

Days 20–21: Hong Kong

Catch a flight back to Kunming and then onward to Hong Kong, one of the world's most captivating cities. See days 13 and 14, above.

CHINA FOR FAMILIES: A 1-WEEK TOUR

China is a great destination for families and you will be warmly received everywhere you go.

Day 1: Arrive in Hong Kong

Depending on how much of the day you have left once you finally touch down at Hong Kong International Airport, head downtown to the **Hong Kong Museum of History** (p. 570). A jaunt aboard the **Star Ferry** (p. 552) across the harbor to Hong Kong Island is still one of the best and certainly one of the most inexpensive experiences that that city has to offer, and it's great for a family. Once on Hong Kong Island take the world's longest escalator and continue up to **Victoria Peak** (p. 569), where a world-class selection of amusements and dining options awaits alongside the fantastic views.

Day 2: A Snapshot of Big-City Life in Guangzhou

Take advantage of the fast, reliable KCR train service and jump on an early morning **Guangzhou express** (p. 527) and arrive in plenty of time for lunch. Head to the striking Canton Tower (p. 533), one of the world's tallest. You can take a ride on the highest Ferris wheel in the world, which rotates around the skyscraper's roof. Catch an early evening sleeper to **Guilin** ★ (p. 596) and see how easy it is to make friends on Chinese public transport.

Day 3: Arrival in Paradise

Avoid the claptrap minibuses and arrange for your **Yangshuo** ★★★ hotel to send a car to fetch you. Spend the first day acclimatizing to **West Street**'s (**Xi Jie**'s; p. 604) laid-back atmosphere and great cafe food. Invest a little time in arranging a few activities for the next few days. That evening take in the local show **"Impression, Sanjie Liu"** (p. 611) and marvel at the magical landscape.

Day 4: The Family That Plays Together . . .

With Yangshuo as your base, prepare to be spoiled with choices for the next few days. Activities include **biking, rafting, climbing,** and **caving,** and the list keeps growing.

Day 5: More Fun in the Great Outdoors

After an early morning swim, followed by a delicious breakfast, take a leisurely bike ride outside of town getting up close and personal with some of the most spectacular scenery China has to offer. Spend the evening souvenir shopping in town before getting a good night's sleep.

Day 6: Venturing Deep into the Dragon's Belly

After all of that great outdoors, it might be time for some great indoors in the form of psychedelic **Silver Cave** (p. 609) just south of town. If the kids enjoy their introduction to speleology, try the recommended **water cave** (p. 627) where they can splash about in primordial ooze to their hearts' content.

Day 7: The Fast Track Home

While the trains are comfortable and efficient, if time is limited, fly back from Guilin to catch your connection flight home. Everybody feels the pangs of sadness as they drive away from those strange geological formations, but don't worry: They have a strange magnetic quality that will likely lure you back.

BEIJING & HEBEI

by Jen Lin-Liu & Candice Lee

The political and cultural capital of the world's most populous country, Beijing offers China's most staggering array of attractions—the Forbidden City, the Temple of Heaven, Tian'an Men Square, and the Great Wall. It's the sheer number of attractions that allows most travelers to look beyond Beijing's ugliness, in comparison to its iconic counterparts of Shanghai and Hong Kong. There is no harbor, no river, just an overflow of concrete and rows of tenements, and its pollution and oppressive grayness are not what anyone would expect at the heart of such an otherwise vivid nation. Yet no other city in the nation attracts more travelers.

4

But grandiose emblems are not the only reason to visit Beijing. Scattered through the city's sprawl are a number of temples, museums, gardens, and other attractions that only grow in charm as they decrease in size. This principle culminates in the *hutong,* narrow lanes that twist through older sections and form an open-air museum where you can happily wander for hours without aim.

Beijing lies 120km (70 miles) west of the Bo Hai (sea), on a sandblasted plain that once separated Han Chinese–dominated territory in the south from the non-Chinese "barbarian" lands to the north. Human settlement in the area dates from the Zhou period (1066 B.C.–221 B.C.), but the first of the four capitals to occupy space here did not appear until A.D. 936, when the Mongolian-speaking Khitan built Yanjing (Capital of Swallows), southern base of power for the Liao Empire (907–1125).

The grid pattern and original walls of what is now Beijing were first laid down in the 13th century, when it was called Khanbalik ("Dadu" in Mandarin) and served as the eastern capital of the Mongolian Empire, referred to in China as the Yuan dynasty (1279–1368). The city was razed, rebuilt, and renamed Beijing by Han Chinese rulers of the subsequent Ming dynasty (1368–1644), who added the Forbidden City and several other of the city's most impressive structures. Manchurian horsemen of the final Qing dynasty (1636–1912) skirted the Great Wall and established themselves in the Forbidden City in 1644. Despite their nomadic origins, Qing leaders found the Chinese system of bureaucratic rule useful in managing their new empire, a strategy mirrored in the relatively few changes they made to the city.

Some of the greatest damage to Beijing has occurred in the last 150 years. Invasions, rebellions, war with Japan, and the struggle between

Communists and Nationalists in the 1930s and 1940s have altered the face of the city more than any events since the 14th century. Particularly severe was the ruin that took place in the decade after the Communist victory in 1949, when Mao, in a desire to put the stamp of his own dynasty on Beijing, leveled the city walls and the old Imperial Way and paved over both.

Present-day Beijing is a vast municipality with a population of roughly 15 million. Economic reform and preparations for the 2008 Olympics accelerated the pace and scale of change and outfitted the city with a semblance of modernity (or at least the Chinese perception of it). Roads that once swarmed with bicycles have been taken over by automobiles. Swaths of *hutong* have been leveled to make way for office towers. And children whose parents hid tapes of Beethoven during the Cultural Revolution now have easy access to DVDs, iPods, double-tall lattes, plastic surgery, and other previously unthinkable bourgeois luxuries.

It is easy, however, to overemphasize the transformations of the past few decades in a city with so many centuries under its belt. To many observers, Beijing has hardly changed at all. The gaze of government looms as large now as it did during the Ming. People fly kites and practice tai chi (*taijiquan*) in the mornings, just as they always have. And perhaps most important, the Great Wall continues to snake along the city's northern border while the Forbidden City gleams at its center.

Beijing shares the same latitude as New York (roughly 40°N) and suffers the same weather: hot, humid summers and bitter winters. Fall, typically mid-September to mid-November, is the nicest season, with mild temperatures and relatively clear skies—by far the best time to visit. Spring brings thoroughly unpleasant sandstorms that blow down from the Mongolian steppe and coat everything in a layer of fine dust. There is little precipitation, and even less of late.

Note: Unless noted otherwise, hours listed in this chapter are the same daily.

ORIENTATION: BEIJING 北京

Getting There & Away

BY PLANE

Beijing's **Capital Airport** (**Shoudu Jichang;** ✆ **010/962-580** for information; domestic ticketing ✆ **010/6601-3336;** international ticketing ✆ **010/6601-6667**) is 25km (16 miles) northeast of the city center. Terminal 3, or T3, which was added in 2008 just before the Olympics, services most international flights and all Air China flights, while Terminal 1 and 2 largely service domestic flights. Double-check your ticket to verify which terminal you are leaving from.

ATM and automatic exchange machines are dispersed throughout the terminals.

Tickets for domestic flights (and international flights) on Chinese airlines are best purchased online via **Ctrip** (http://english.ctrip.com) and **eLong** (www.elong.net), two companies that offer excellent prices on domestic and international tickets. You can book flights online or by phone and pay for tickets in cash upon delivery. You can also pay by credit card (expect a 3%–5% surcharge) after faxing through a credit card authorization form. Both companies have English-speaking agents who can walk you through the booking process. For more personalized service, contact China Ocean International Travel Service, 56 Dong Xing Long Lu ✆ **010/6702-0288;** oceantravelcn@yahoo.com.cn; they will respond to emails in English and offer free delivery around Beijing—ask for Vicky or Richard. Other reliable places to secure domestic

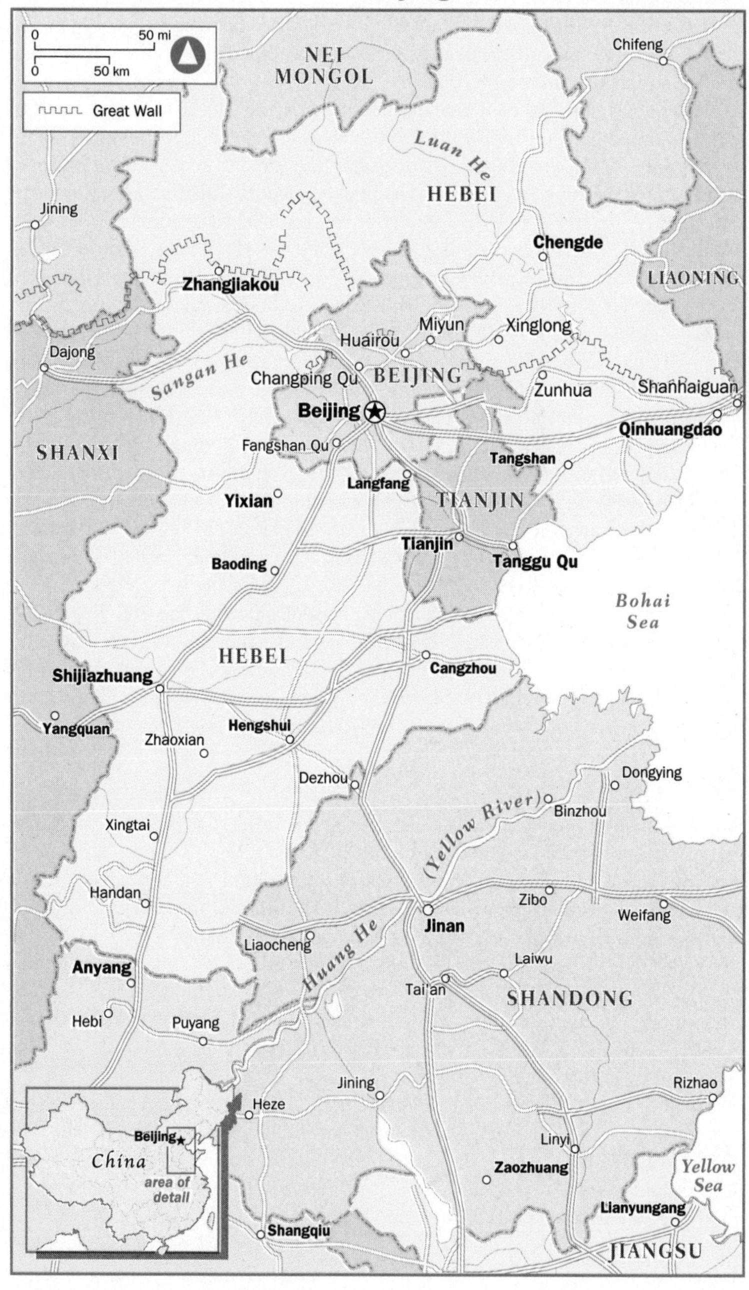
0 50 mi
0 50 km
Great Wall
NEI MONGOL
Chifeng
Luan He
HEBEI
Jining
Chengde
LIAONING
Zhangjiakou
Miyun
Xinglong
Huairou
Dajong
Sangan He
Changping Qu
BEIJING
Zunhua
Shanhaiguan
Beijing
Qinhuangdao
SHANXI
Fangshan Qu
Tangshan
Langfang
Yixian
TIANJIN
Tianjin
Tanggu Qu
Baoding
Bohai Sea
HEBEI
Cangzhou
Shijiazhuang
Yangquan
Zhaoxian
Hengshui
Dezhou
Dongying
(Yellow River)
Binzhou
Xingtai
Handan
Zibo
Jinan
Weifang
Liaocheng
Huang He
Laiwu
Anyang
Tai'an
SHANDONG
Hebi
Puyang
Jining
Rizhao
Heze
Beijing
China
area of detail
Linyi
Zaozhuang
Yellow Sea
Lianyungang
Shangqiu
JIANGSU

tickets include **Airtrans,** C12 Guang Hua Lu, opposite Kerry Centre (✆ **010/6595-2255**), or at the ticketing halls of the Aviation Building (Minhang Dalou; ✆ **010/6656-9988;** fax 010/6656-9333; 24 hr.) at Xi Chang'an Jie 15, just east of the Xidan metro station. Most major international airlines have offices in Beijing; check websites for contact information.

Taxis queue outside the international arrivals gate and take 30 minutes to an hour to reach the city center for ¥80 to ¥100, plus the ¥10 toll, depending on traffic. Bypass any drivers who approach you inside the airport, and head for the rank instead. Insist on using the meter. Air-conditioned **airport shuttle buses,** the cheapest way to get into the city, leave from in front of the domestic arrivals area. The most useful, Line 2, runs 24 hours a day and departs every 10 minutes, 7am to the last arriving flight, for ¥16. Destinations include San Yuan Qiao (near the Hilton and Sheraton hotels), the Dongzhi Men and Dong Si Shi Tiao metro stations, Beijing Railway Station, and the CAAC ticket office in Xi Dan. Lines 1 to 4 all pass through San Yuan Qiao, but only Line 2 lets off passengers at a location convenient for picking up taxis to continue to other destinations. The new Line 5 connects with the university district in the northwest, via Yayun Cun and the North Fourth Ring Road.

The **airport express train** to Dongzhi Men is a mixed blessing. For ¥25, you'll get yourself to downtown Beijing in about 20 minutes. You can use regular metro cards (see "Getting Around," below) for the journey. Unfortunately, the logistics of taking the train can be incredibly annoying. Getting to street level at Dongzhi Men involves a short escalator and then a steep set of stairs (there's an elevator after the escalator but it doesn't take you all the way to street level). Then there's the madness of hailing down a cab around the hordes of public buses just outside the station. Passengers are funneled into the northeast exit of Dongzhi Men and if you want to get to any of the other three corner exits you will have to pay the ¥2 subway fare to walk through the subway station. If you want to switch to the subway, expect more stairs. The express train also stops at **San Yuan Qiao,** a short cab ride away from the hotels on Third Ring.

BY TRAIN

Beijing's two most important railway stations are the Soviet-style Beijing Zhan, southeast of Tian'an Men Square, and the newer Xi Ke Zhan (West Station), between the western Second and Third ring roads. Tickets can be purchased at both stations for any train leaving Beijing up to 4 days in advance. **Round-trip tickets** *(fancheng piao)* to major destinations like Shanghai or Xi'an can be purchased up to 12 days in advance, subject to availability. There are 19 Z (direct) trains connecting with other cities, which depart at night and arrive early the following morning. Cities served are: Changchun, Changsha, Harbin, Hangzhou, Hefei, Nanjing, Shanghai (five trains), Suzhou, Wuhan (four trains), Xi'an, and Yangzhou. Tickets for Z trains may be purchased 20 days in advance.

Satellite ticket offices *(tielu shoupiao chu)* scattered throughout the city charge a negligible ¥5 service fee. One convenient location is 98 Dongsi Shi Tiao ✆ **010/6406-3004** near the Back Lakes area, though a better option is to ask your hotel concierge to book for you. Alternatively, you may also contact a ticket delivery office with no name at ✆ **010/6618-9978;** they will deliver tickets directly to you. Unfortunately, they only speak Mandarin, so ask a friend or concierge to call for you.

Beijing Zhan (**Beijing Railway Station; ✆ 010/5101-9999**) is the easiest to reach of Beijing's two major stations, close to the city center and with its own metro station. The best place to pick up tickets is at the "ticket office for foreigners" inside the soft-berth waiting room on the ground floor of the main hall, in the far left corner (5:30am–11pm). This is the station for trains to Shanghai and cities in the Northeast. Tickets for both versions of the Trans-Siberian, the Russian K19 via Manchuria (Sat 10:56pm) and the Chinese K3 via Mongolia (Wed 7:40am), must be purchased from the CITS international railway ticket office inside the International Hotel (Mon–Fri 8:30am–noon and 1:30–5pm, weekends 9am–noon and 1:30–4pm; ✆ **010/6512-0507;** cuiqing@cits.com.cn), a 10-minute walk north of the station on Jianguo Men Nei Dajie (metro: Dong Dan). Both trains travel to Moscow for ¥2,512 soft sleeper, but only the K3 passes through Mongolia and stops in Ulaan Baatar for ¥845. There is a separate train, the K23, which goes to Ulaan Baatar (Sat 7:40am). The International Hotel is also the nearest spot for picking up the **airport shuttle bus** (see above). CITS also has the train timetables at www.chinatraveldesigner.com.

At the **West Station** (**Xi Ke Zhan; ✆ 010/5182-4233** schedule information), the best ticket outlet is not the main ticket hall but a second office inside the main building, on the second floor to the left of the elevators (signposted in English); this is also where you go to purchase tickets for the Q97 express to Kowloon/Jiulong (daily at 1pm; 24 hr.; ¥738 soft sleeper, ¥465 hard). The West Station is also the starting point for trains to Hanoi, but you have to buy tickets (Thurs and Sun 4:08pm; 34 hr.; ¥2,204 soft sleeper only) at China Railway Travel Service, 1st Floor, Building 20 of Tie You Compound, Bei Feng Wo Lu (9am–4:30pm; ✆ **010/5182-6541**). The nearest airport shuttle stops at the Aviation Building in Xi Dan (see above), reachable by bus no. 52 from the station's east side. The taxi rank is on the second floor. Trains leave from here for Guangzhou, Xi'an, and other points west.

BY BUS

Beijing does not have a central bus station, but rather a series of region-specific stations spread around the outskirts of the city. The airportlike **Lize Qiao Changtu Keyun Zhan** (✆ **010/6347-5092**), on the southwest corner of the Third Ring Road (metro: Gongzhufen, then bus no. 201 to terminus) has air-conditioned services to **Taiyuan** (6:30am–11:20pm, every 20 min. 7am–5pm, less frequent after 5pm; 7 hr.; ¥130–¥171); **Zhengzhou** (only one bus at 5:40pm; 9 hr.; ¥190); and comfortable minibuses to **Shijiazhuang** (8:30am–4:50pm, every 40 min.; 3½ hr.; ¥61). The **Liu Li Qiao Changtu Qiche Keyun Zhan** (✆ **010/8383-1717**), southwest of the Liu Li Qiao bridge, runs luxury buses to Chengde (5:40am–6:40pm; every 20 min.; 3½ hr.; ¥60), Shenyang (three buses daily at 9am, 11:30am, and 9pm; 8 hr.; ¥188). Numerous buses from other cities arrive at the **Dongzhi Men Changtu Qiche Zhan** (✆ **010/6467-3094**), next to the Dongzhi Men metro station, but few are useful to visitors except the occasional Chengde service.

Visitor Information

For the most current information on life in Beijing, particularly nightlife, see listings in the free English-language monthlies *Time Out* (www.timeoutbeijing.com) and the *Beijinger* (www.thebeijinger.com), available in hotel lobbies and at bars in the major drinking districts (see "Beijing After Dark," p. 118). Online, *City Weekend* updates its website (www.cityweekend.com) regularly and *Local Noodles* (www.localnoodles.com) provides user-generated reviews of local restaurants and bars.

The Beijing Tourism Administration (BTA) maintains a **tourist information hot line** (some English spoken) at ✆ **010/12301.** More likely to be of help are the new BTA-managed **Beijing Tourist Information Centers (Beijing Shi Luyou Zixun Fuwu Zhongxin)** located in each district and all marked with aqua-blue signs. The most competent branch is in Chaoyang District, on Gongti Bei Lu across from the City Hotel and next to the KFC (✆ **010/6417-6627;** chaoyang@bta.gov.cn; 9am–5pm). Free simple maps are available at the door, and staff will sometimes make phone calls for you. Ignore their extortionist travel service.

City Layout

Beijing is bordered to the north and west by mountains, the closest of which are occasionally visible through the haze. The city center, known to foreigners in the Qing period (1644–1911) as the Tartar City, was originally surrounded by a complex of walls and gates destroyed in 1958 to make way for the **Second Ring Road (Er Huan).** The city center is organized along a grid with major streets running to the compass points. The Third, Fourth, Fifth, and Sixth ring roads (San Huan, Si Huan, Wu Huan, and Liu Huan respectively) run concentrically ever wider out. At the center of all this is the seldom-referred-to First Ring Road (encircling Tian'an Men Sq.) and **the Forbidden City,** its own internal grid a miniature of the sprawl that surrounds it.

MAJOR STREETS

Streets in Beijing change names like high-school students change identities. Be sure to pick up a city map on arrival (see "Fast Facts: Beijing," p. 66). The best example of this is the city's main east-west artery. **Chang'an Dajie,** which runs between Tian'an Men Square and the Forbidden City, is known (east to west) as Jianguo Men Wai Dajie, Jianguo Men Nei Dajie, Dong (East) Chang'an Dajie, Xi (West) Chang'an Dajie, Fuxing Men Nei Dajie, and Fuxing Men Wai Dajie. **Ping'an Dadao,** a major avenue to the north that runs across the back of Bei Hai Park, has a similar diversity of monikers. Among important north-south streets, **Wangfujing Dajie** (2 long blocks east of the Forbidden City) is the Beijing consumer equivalent of Chicago's Magnificent Mile or London's Oxford Street. **Qian Men Dajie** extends down from the southern end of Tian'an Men Square.

Neighborhoods in Brief

Citywide architectural uniformity means Beijing's neighborhoods are defined more by feel than by appearance. In many cases, but not all, they correspond to districts *(qu).*

Dong Cheng District Dong Cheng (East City) occupies the eastern half of the old, traditional city center. The district features many of Beijing's best sites, including the Temple of Heaven, Tian'an Men Square, the Forbidden City, Wangfujing Dajie, Jing Shan Gongyuan, and Yonghe Gong (the Lama Temple).

Xi Cheng District The western half of the city center is home to Zhong Nan Hai, the off-limits central government compound otherwise known as the new Forbidden City, Bei Hai Gongyuan, and Bai Ta Si (White Dagoba Temple). The district, after having recently incorporated the area south of it, now includes a large Chinese Muslim population.

The Back Lakes (Shicha Hai) & Di'an Men Right in the geographic center of town, just north of the Forbidden City, this area, with its sublime public lakes and well-preserved *hutong,* is where the last fading ghosts of Old (pre-1949) Beijing reside. It's popular among writers, musicians, English-language teachers, and other hipsters in the expatriate community, and their presence has helped spawn a bevy of bars and cafes (see "Beijing After Dark," later in this chapter). Several minor sights here provide excuses for a nice day of wandering (see "Walking Tour: The Back Lakes," p. 111).

Chaoyang District A gargantuan district that encompasses almost all of eastern and northeastern Beijing outside the Second Ring Road, Chaoyang is home to the two main diplomatic areas, the Sanlitun and Chaoyang drinking districts, and the Central Business District (CBD) around the China World Trade Center. This is the richest district in Beijing, the result, according to some, of the district's good feng shui.

Haidian District & Yayun Cun Occupying the northwest, Haidian is the university and high-tech district, optimistically referred to in local media as "China's Silicon Valley." There is hiking in the hills in more distant parts. Yayun Cun, host to most of the Olympic events, is home to Beijing's best new Chinese restaurants.

GETTING AROUND

By Metro

The Beijing metro is the easiest and often fastest way to move around and services many parts of the city. Trains run from 5am to 11pm on two underground lines *(ditie)* and one new light-rail line *(chengtie)*. The most important lines to know include: **Line 1,** which runs east-west past Tian'an Men and the Forbidden City; **Line 2,** or the Loop Line, is a closed circle that roughly follows the path of the Second Ring Road (and the Old City Wall); Line 5 runs north-south, bisecting Line 1 and 2, and extends past the Temple of Heaven. **Line 8** currently connects to Olympic sites and venues and will be extended by early 2012 to the center of town; **Line 10** traces the North and East Third Ring Road and is helpful for navigating to and from the Central Business District; the **Airport Line** runs regularly from Dongzhimen on **Lines 1** and **2** Stations are numbered (see Beijing metro map), signs on platforms tell you which station is the next in each direction, and English announcements are made on trains, so navigation is not difficult.

Tickets cost ¥2 for a ride anywhere with unlimited transfers. The metro card, officially known as the "Municipal Administration and Communication Card" (Shizheng Jiaotong Yikatong, or *Yikatong* for short) can be bought for a ¥40 minimum, including ¥20 for deposit. You can buy and return cards at any station. Single-ride tickets are available from the cashier or from the new electronic ticketing machines that have service in English. See metro map on the inside back cover.

By Taxi

Taxis cost ¥10 for the first 3km (2 miles), then ¥2 per kilometer. Recent gas hikes mean that taxis are adding surcharge of up to ¥2 for trips more than 3km. Green or yellow Hyundai Elantras are roomier and have better air-conditioning. Rates per kilometer jump by 50% after 15km (9 miles). Always insist on using the meter unless negotiating for journeys out of town, in which case be clear about the price beforehand and withhold payment until your return.

By Bus

This is how the vast majority of the city's residents move around, and riding with them is as close (literally shoulder-to-chest) as you can get to understanding the authentic

Beijing. City buses and trolleys (nos. less than 124) charge a flat fare of ¥1 (fares are a mere ¥.40 with a metro card). Longer rides on air-conditioned coaches (nos. 800–900) can start at ¥2 or more. Most buses run between 5am and 11pm (specific times are posted at the stops).

By Bicycle

A bike is the best way to stay in touch with the city between sights, and faster than a taxi when traffic is bad, but you'll have to pay attention to the cars and other riders, both of which pose risks to the unwary. Simple bikes are available for rent at a number of hotels, usually for between ¥10 and ¥30 per day. If you're taking a three-wheel pedicab or rickshaw, make sure to bargain before you hop on as rates vary wildly and are usually exorbitant. Pay no more than ¥30 for short distances.

On Foot

Beijing is no friend of the pedestrian. The city's sights are scattered and most of its roads are broad rivers of unlovely gray with few channels for safe crossing. Use pedestrian underpasses and footbridges wherever available. ***Warning:*** Traffic turning right at lights does not give way to pedestrians, nor does any other traffic unless forced to do so by large groups of people bunching up to cross the road. The only parts of the city where walking is enjoyable are the few remaining *hutong* neighborhoods, where the stroll is the point. Otherwise, use a vehicle.

[Fast FACTS] BEIJING

Banks, Foreign Exchange & ATMs Larger branches of the **Bank of China** typically exchange cash and traveler's checks on weekdays only, from 9am to 5pm, occasionally with a break for lunch (11:30am–1:30pm). Most central is the branch at the bottom of Wangfujing Dajie, next to the Oriental Plaza, with forex and credit card cash advances handled at windows 5 to 11 (until 5pm). Other useful branches include those at Fucheng Men Nei Dajie 410; on Jianguo Men Wai Dajie, west of the Scitech Building; in the Lufthansa Center, next to the Kempinski Hotel; and in Tower 1 of the China World Trade Center. One other bank that offers forex is the **CITIC Industrial Bank** inside the CITIC building (Guoji Dasha) on Jianguo Men Wai Dajie, west of the Friendship Store. Outside the airport, Bank of China **ATMs** accepting international cards include those outside the Wangfujing Dajie branch mentioned above. Others exist farther north on Wangfujing Dajie, outside the Xin (Sun) Dong'an Plaza (24 hr.); on the left just inside the Pacific Century Plaza on Gongti Bei Lu east of Sanlitun (9am–9pm); and adjacent to the Bank of China branch next to the Scitech Building (see above; also 24 hr.). The Citibank HSBC ATMs inside Oriental Plaza are useful. There are also several ATMs at the airport.

Doctors & Dentists For comprehensive care, the best choice is **Beijing United Family Hospital (Hemujia Yiyuan; © 010/5927-7000)** at Jiangtai Lu (2 blocks southeast of the Holiday Inn Lido); it is open 24 hours, staffed with foreign-trained doctors, and has a pharmacy, dental clinic, in- and outpatient care, and ambulance service. Other reputable health-service providers, both with 24-hour ambulance services, are the **International Medical Center** (**© 010/6465-1561**), inside the Lufthansa Center; and the **International SOS Clinic and Alarm Center** (**© 010/6462-9112**), at suite 105, wing 1, Kunsha Building, 16 Xinyuanli.

Embassies & Consulates Beijing has two main embassy areas—one surrounding Ri Tan Gongyuan north of Jianguo Men Wai Dajie, and another in Sanlitun north of Gongti Bei Lu. Embassies are typically open

Monday through Friday from 9am to between 4 and 5pm, with a lunch break from noon to 1:30pm. The **U.S. Embassy** is at 55 An Jia Lou Lu (✆ **010/8531-3000** or, after hours, 010/6532-1910; fax 010/8531-4000). The **Canadian Embassy** is at Dongzhi Men Wai Dajie 19 (✆ **010/5139-4000;** bejing-cs@international.gc.ca). The **British Embassy** consular section is in Ri Tan at Floor 21, North Tower, Kerry Centre, Guanghua Lu 1 (✆ **010/8529-6083,** ext. 3363; fax 010/8529-6081). The **Australian Embassy** is in Sanlitun at Dongzhi Men Wai Dajie 21 (✆ **010/5140-4111;** fax 010/6532-4605). The **New Zealand Embassy** is in Ri Tan at Dong Er Jie 1 (✆ **010/8532-7000;** fax 010/6532-4317).

For onward visas: The **Cambodian Embassy,** in Sanlitun at Dongzhi Men Wai Dajie 9 (✆ **010/6532-2790**), offers 1-month visas for ¥190, processed in 3 days (¥300 for 1 day); the **Laotian Embassy,** in Sanlitun at Dong Si Jie 11 (✆ **010/6532-1224**), charges U.S. citizens ¥400 ($62) and Canadian citizens ¥400 (C$61) for a 30-day visa, processed in 4 days; the **Mongolian Embassy,** in Ri Tan at Xiushui Bei Jie 2 (✆ **010/6532-1203**), charges ¥200 for a 1-month visa processed in 5 days (¥500 for 1 day); and the **Vietnamese Embassy,** in Ri Tan at Guanghua Lu 32 (✆ **010/6532-1155**), charges ¥350 for a single-entry 1-month visa and ¥400 for a 3-month visa, both taking 4 days to process. Obtaining a visa at the **Russian Embassy,** in Sanlitun at Dongzhi Men Bei Zhong Jie 4 (✆ **010/6532-1267** or 010/6532-1991), is notoriously difficult; they claim you must have a "voucher" from a travel agency (not a hotel) in order to be granted a 1-month tourist visa (¥405, 5 days to process; ¥648 for 3-day service, ¥972 for 1-day service; application for express service needs to be submitted before 11am and rate will be slightly higher for U.S. and Australian citizens, though the embassy declines to state a definitive figure). Also, in retaliation for new U.S. immigration policies, U.S. citizens have to fill out an interrogation-style form when applying. If you have problems, contact the Beijing office of **Aeroflot,** first floor the Jinglun Hotel (✆ **010/6500-2412**), for help.

Emergencies For medical emergencies and ambulance service 24 hours a day, call the United Family Health Center emergency number at ✆ **010/5927-7000** or the International SOS Alarm Center (✆ **010/6462-9100**).

Internet Access Internet bars in Beijing are subject to numerous regulations (no one under 18, nonsmoking) and are restricted in number. The best bet for affordable Internet access is any of the city's various **youth hostels;** the cost is usually ¥10 per hour. If you have your own computer, many cafes and hotels in Beijing offer wireless connectivity in public areas. The Wi-Fi at **Café Zarah,** 42 Gulou Dong Dajie (✆ **010/8403-9807**; p. 95), and **The Bookworm,** in back of building 4, Sanlitun Nan Jie (✆ **010/6586-9507**), are reliable.

Maps & Books Maps with Chinese characters, English, and/or Pinyin can be purchased cheaply for ¥5 from vendors near major sights and in hotel lobbies and bookstores. The best selection can be found inside and immediately to the left at the **Wangfujing Bookstore** (9:30am–9pm) at Wangfujing Dajie 218, north of the Oriental Plaza's west entrance. English-language newspapers and magazines can be found at most five-star hotels; a newsdealer on the first floor of the **Kempinski Hotel** at Liangma Qiao Lu 50 is well stocked.

The best selection of English-language books in Beijing can be found at the clearly marked **Foreign Languages Bookstore (Waiwen Shudian;** 9:30am–9:30pm) at Wangfujing Dajie 235, opposite the Xin (Sun) Dong'an Plaza. Look on the left side of the first floor for China-related nonfiction, glossy *hutong* photo books, cookbooks, and the full range of Asiapac's cartoon renditions of Chinese classics. Cheap paperback versions of a huge chunk of the English canon, as well as a number of contemporary works, are sold on the third floor. A more daring collection of fiction is carried by **The Bookworm** (p. 95), which also has a substantial library.

Pharmacies Simple Western remedies are most likely to be found in the lobbies of international five-star hotels and at branches of **Watson's** (on the first floor of Full Link Plaza at Chaoyang Men Wai Dajie 19, 10:30am–9:30pm; in the basement of the Oriental Plaza at the bottom of Wangfujing Dajie 1, 10am–10pm; and in the basement of Sanlitun Village at Sanlitun Bei Lu, SLG33, 10am-10pm). For more specific drugs, try the pharmacies in the Beijing United Family Hospital or the International SOS Clinic (see "Doctors & Dentists," above).

Post Office Numerous post offices are scattered across the city, including one a long block north of the Jianguo Men metro station on the east side of Jianguo Men Bei Dajie (8am–6:30pm), one inside the Landmark Tower (next to the Great Wall Sheraton), one next to the Friendship Store on Jianguo Men Wai Dajie, one on Gongti Bei Lu (opposite the Worker's Stadium), and the EMS Post Office (Beijing Youzheng Sudi Ju) at the corner of Qian Men Dong Dajie and Zhengyi Lu. A **FedEx** office (✆ **800/988-1888** toll-free from a land line, or 400/889-1888 from cell phone with local call charges) is in Oriental Plaza, room 01-05A, No. W1 Office Building. **DHL** has branches in the China World Center and COFCO Plaza, and **UPS-Sinotrans** has a useful branch in the Scitech Building at Jianguo Men Wai Dajie 22.

Visa Extensions The PSB office in Beijing (✆ **010/8402-0101**) is on the south side of the eastern North Second Ring Road, just east of the Lama Temple metro stop (Mon–Sat 8:30am–4:30pm). You will also need your Registration Form of Temporary Residence (your hotel should have a copy) and a certificate of deposit issued by a Chinese bank (ICBC, Bank of China, and so on) proving you have at least US$100/day for the duration of your stay. That is, if you are requesting a 30-day extension, you need to show US$3,000 in a certificate of deposit. Applications take 5 working days to process. Bring your passport and two passport photos (these can be taken at the office for ¥30). Extension fees vary by nationality: U.S. citizens pay ¥940, U.K. citizens ¥469, Canadians and Australians ¥160.

Weather For daily weather forecasts, check *China Daily* or CCTV 9, China Central Television's English channel (broadcast in most hotels).

WHERE TO STAY

No other city in mainland China offers the range of accommodations Beijing does. The high season in Beijing is not well defined, but you should generally expect lower availability and higher rates from mid-May to National Day (Oct 1) and around Chinese New Year (usually late Jan or early Feb). It is usually possible to wrangle discounts of anywhere between 10% and 50% off the rack rate even at these times, although some of the new boutique hotels located in *hutong* courtyards *(siheyuan)* will refuse to bargain except in the dead of winter.

On short visits the best option is to stay within walking distance of the Forbidden City and Tian'an Men Square, on Wangfujing Dajie or nearby. The greatest luxury and highest standards of service can be found in the Chaoyang District. For budget travelers, the obvious choice is the expanding range of comfortable but affordable hostels buried in the labyrinth of *hutong* south and west of Qian Men, with convenient metro and bus access.

Near the Forbidden City & Qian Men

VERY EXPENSIVE

Grand Hyatt (Beijing Dongfang Junyue) ★★ ☺ The Hyatt has an excellent location directly over the Wangfujing metro station, at the foot of the capital's most famous shopping street, and within walking distance of the Forbidden City.

Rooms have the signature Grand Hyatt comfortable modernity, with free broadband Internet access. Well-equipped bathrooms have separate shower cubicles. Kids and adults alike will have fun with the vast un-Hyatt-like swimming pool, buried among mock-tropical decor under a ceiling of electric stars. **Made in China** (p. 85), one of our favorite city restaurants, is one of four dining establishments on site.

Dong Chang'an Jie 1, Dong Cheng Qu (within the Oriental Plaza complex). www.beijing.grand.hyatt.com. ✆ **010/8518-1234.** Fax 010/8518-0000. 782 units. ¥2,100 standard room (summer discounts around ¥1,700), plus 15% service charge. AE, DC, MC, V. Metro: Wangfujing. **Amenities:** 4 restaurants; bar; cafe; airport limousine pickup; fitness center w/latest equipment; Jacuzzi; jogging path; indoor resort-style pool (50m/165 ft.) and children's pool; room service; sauna; solarium. *In room:* A/C, satellite TV, hair dryer, Internet, minibar.

The Peninsula Beijing (Wangfu Bandao Fandian) ★★ Don't let the rather unappealing bathroom-tile exterior deter you: The Peninsula still has major cachet in Beijing, and for good reason. English-speaking service staff are some of the best in the capital, and while rooms are slightly smaller than those at Beijing's newer hotels, they have shiny marble bathrooms, flatscreen televisions, and plush beds. The hotel also has a great location and a terrific spa, managed by an outside group called ESPA. It's well worth a visit for a treatment, which begins with a visit to a well-outfitted sauna, steam room, and relaxation room, and is followed with pampering from an experienced therapist.

Jinyu Hutong 8, Dong Cheng District (at intersection with Dong Dan Bei Dajie). www.peninsula.com. ✆ **010/6512-8899.** Fax 010/6512-9050. 525 units. ¥1,700 standard room (discount rates around ¥1,450); ¥1,900 grand deluxe; ¥2,100 club deluxe, plus 15% service charge. AE, DC, MC, V. Metro: Wangfujing. **Amenities:** 3 restaurants; bar; concierge; executive-level rooms; forex; fully equipped fitness center; indoor pool; room service; sauna; smoke-free rooms. *In room:* A/C, satellite TV/DVD, hair dryer, minibar.

EXPENSIVE

Hilton Beijing Wangfujing (Beijing Wangfujing Xierdun Jiudian) ★★ This hotel is right beside the shopping paradise of Wangfujing, a block away from two major metro stops and within walking distance of the Forbidden City and Tian'an Men Square. Regular rooms here are larger than those at the nearby Regent or Grand Hyatt, and come with amenities (such as free shoe shines and MP3 docking stations) that other five-stars would reserve for suites. Deluxe Plus rooms and suites have sexy black-and-white claw foot tubs inside gigantic shower cubicles, while regular Deluxe rooms come with standard tubs that are rather awkwardly placed in the middle of the room (there's a sliding door if you're shy). For our money, we would skip the suites and book into the Deluxe Plus room; it has bigger windows and the layout—long entranceways from which shoot off walk-in closets and spacious bathrooms—really maximizes space. All rooms are equipped with big, cozy beds, 42-inch flatscreen TVs embedded into light wood paneled walls, and sleek office desks. The breakfast spread is excellent, but avoid the in-house restaurants for lunch and dinner—both serve disappointing, lackluster fare.

8 Wangfujing Dong Jie. www.wangfujing.hilton.com. ✆ **010/5812-8888.** Fax 010/5812-8886. 255 units. ¥1,400–¥2,200 deluxe; ¥2,000–¥2,700 suites; ¥2,500–¥3,200 executive deluxe; ¥3,100–¥4,000 executive suite. AE, DC, MC, V. Metro: Wangfujing or Dongsi. **Amenities:** 2 restaurants; cafe; bar; babysitting; small fitness center with latest equipment; library; glass-enclosed indoor pool (80m/262 ft.); room service; top-notch spa. *In room:* A/C, satellite TV, hair dryer, Internet, minibar, scale.

The Regent (Lijing Fandian) The Regent is sparkly and grand, with an excellent location and fine amenities to boot. But when it comes to getting the most bang

Beijing Hotels & Restaurants

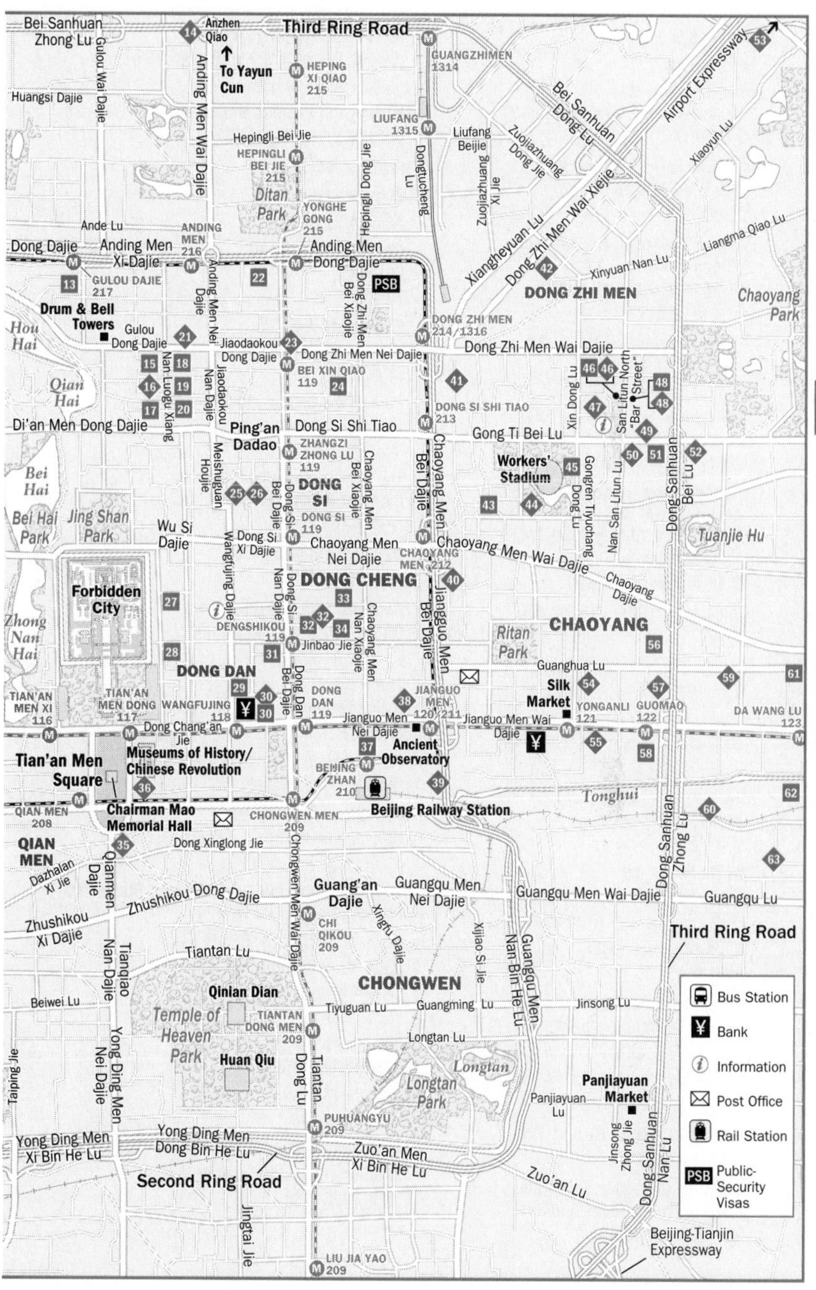

4

BEIJING & HEBEI | Where to Stay

Beijing Hotels & Restaurants Key

HOTELS ■

A.hotel **45**

Aman Beijing **2**
(Beijing Anman Wenhua Jiudian)
安缦酒店

Bamboo Garden Hotel **13**
(Zhu Yuan Binguan)
竹园宾馆

Beijing Downtown Backpackers Accommodation **17**
(Dong Tang Qingnian Lüshe)
东堂青年旅社

Beijing Guxiang 20 Hotel **18**
(Gu Xiang Er Shi)
北京古巷20号商务酒店

City Central Youth Hostel **37**
(Chengshi Qingnian Jiudian)
城市青年酒店

Confucius International Youth Hostel **22**
(Beijing Yong Sheng Xuan Qingnian Jiudia)
北京雍圣轩青年酒店

Courtyard 7 (Qihao Yuan) **15**
七号院

Crowne Plaza Hotel Zhongguancun **3**
北京中关村皇冠假日酒店

Days Inn Forbidden City **28**
(Beijing Xiangjiang Daisi Jiudian)
北京香江戴斯酒店

The Emperor **27**
(Huangjia Yizhan)
皇家驿栈

Du Ge Hotel **19**
(Duge Siheyuan Yishu Jingpin Jiudian)
杜革四合院艺术精品酒店

Feiying Binguan **12**
飞鹰宾馆

Grand Hyatt Beijing **30**
(Beijing Dongfang Junyue)
东方君悦大酒店

The Grand Mercure **11**
北京西单美爵酒店

Grand Millennium Beijing **56**
北京千禧大酒店

Han's Royal Garden Hotel **20**
(Hanzhen Yuan Guoji Jiudian)
涵珍园国际酒店

Hilton Beijing Wangfujing **29**
(Beijing Wangfujing Xierdun Jiudian)
北京王府井希尔顿酒店

Holiday Inn Express Beijing Dongzhimen **24**
北京东直门智选假日酒店

Hotel G **43**

Jingyi Hotel **4**
京仪大酒店

Opposite House **46**
(Yu She)
瑜舍

Park Hyatt **58**
(Beijing Baiyue Jiudian)
北京柏悦酒店

Park Plaza Beijing **32**
(Beijing Li Ting Jiu Dian)
北京丽亭酒店

The Peninsula Beijing **31**
(Wangfu Bandao Fandian)
王府半岛饭店

Red Lantern House **9**
红灯笼客栈

Red Wall Garden Hotel **34**
(Hong Qiang Huayuan Jiudian)
红墙花园酒店

The Regent **32**
(Lijing Fandian)
丽晶酒店

Renaissance Beijing Capital Hotel **62**
北京富力万丽酒店

Ritz-Carlton Beijing **61**
(Beijing Lisi Kaerdun Jiudian)
北京丽思卡尔顿酒店

The Ritz Carlton Beijing Financial Street **10**
(Jinrong Jie Lijia Jiudian)
北京金融街丽思卡尔顿酒店

Saga Youth Hostel **33**
(Shijia Guoji Qingnian Lushe)
实佳国际青年旅社

Shangri-La Beijing Hotel **5**
(Xianggelila Fandian)
香格里拉饭店

Yoyo Hotel **48**
优优客酒店

Zhaolong Qingnian Lüguan **51**
兆龙青年旅馆

4 Where to Stay | BEIJING & HEBEI

RESTAURANTS ◆

Agua **47**

The Aman Grill (at the Aman Resort) **2**
(Yihe Anman)
颐和安缦餐厅

Aria **57**
阿丽雅

Baihe Sushi **1**
(Lily Vegetarian Restaurant)
百合素食

Bei (in the Opposite House hotel) **46**
北餐厅

Beijing Dadong Kaoya Dian **52**
北京大董烤鸭店

Bellagio **44**
(Lu Gang Xiao Zhen)
鹿港小镇

Black Sesame Kitchen **16**
(Heizhima Chufang)
黑芝麻厨房

Capital M **35**
米氏西餐厅

Cepe (in the Ritz-Carlton, Financial Street) **10**
(Yiwei Xuan)
意味轩

Chuan Ban Canting **38**
川办餐厅

Dali Courtyard **21**
(Da Li)
大里院子

Ding Ding Xiang **41**
鼎鼎香

Duck de Chine **50**
全鸭季

Hatsune (Yinquan) **59**
隐泉日本料理

Huajia Yiyuan **23**
花家怡园

Huangcheng Lao Ma **60**
皇城老妈

Jiumen Xiao Chi **7**
九门小吃

Kong Yiji Jiudian **8**
孔乙己酒店

Lan **55**
兰

Lei Garden (next to the Park Plaza hotel) **32**
(Li Yuan)
利苑

Made in China (in the Grand Hyatt hotel) **30**
(Chang An Yi Hao)
长安壹号

Maison Boulud **36**
(Bulu Gong Fa Canting)
布鲁宫 法餐厅

Mare **54**
(Da Pa Shi)
古老海西餐厅

Middle 8th **48**
中8楼

Mosto **47**

Noodle Loft **63**
(Mian Ku Shanxi Shiyi)
面酷山西食艺

Pure Lotus **53**
(Jing Xin Lian)
静心莲

Rumi **49**
入迷

Still Thoughts Vegetarian **25**
(Jingsi Su Shifang)
静思素食坊

Sureño (in the Opposite House hotel) **46**

Susu **26**
苏苏会

Yunnan Jin Kongque Dehong Daiwei Canguan **6**
北京金孔雀德宏傣家风味餐厅

Yotsuba (Si Ye) **42**
四叶

Yunteng Binguan **39**
云腾宾馆

Yuxiang Renjia **40**
渝乡人家

Zhang Sheng Ji Jiudian **14**
张生记酒店

for your buck, it falls short of the Hilton Wangfujing a mere block away, which has bigger rooms and better amenities. The rooms here are still spacious and have an understated elegance with nice Chinese antique accessories. The beige marble bathrooms have free-standing bathtubs and separate shower stalls. The Regent's health club is the best in the Wangfujing area, with multiple workout rooms and a gorgeous 32m (105-ft.) swimming pool that laps along its edges like a tide. Skip dining in the lobby lounge. Sure, it looks impressive, with floor-to-ceiling glass walls, a vaulted atrium, and the modern waterfall centerpiece, but the service is consistently abominable.

99 Jinbao Street. www.regenthotels.com/beijing-hotel-cn-100005/ribjn. ✆ **010/8522-1888.** Fax 010/8522-1818. 448 units. ¥1,650–¥1,850 deluxe; ¥1,700–¥2,000 premium; ¥1,900–¥2,400 executive room; ¥2,300–¥2,800 executive suite, plus 15% service charge. Breakfast not included. AE, DC, MC, V. Metro: Dengshikou. **Amenities:** 4 restaurants; lounge; business center; fitness center; indoor pools; spa. *In room:* A/C, satellite TV, internet, morning newspaper, room-service, computer and fax connections.

MODERATE

The Emperor (Huangjia Yizhan) ★ Down a shady lane right next to the Forbidden City, this four-story boutique hotel offers a fabulous location for tourists and unique rooms. Beds and sofas, built into each room's white walls are streaked with bright textured fabric in a single color of turquoise blue, lime green, or bright orange, giving the rooms a futuristic, stylish feel. While modern, the rooms also pay respect to Chinese culture: Each comes with a Chinese seal that guests can take with them when they leave, and rooms are named after China's various emperors. The rooftop bar and spa have one of the best views in town—guests can gaze straight into the maze of rooms at the Forbidden City. The bar is often filled with expatriates until the early morning hours during the summer, while the spa has a decadent alfresco Jacuzzi.

Qihelou Lu 33. www.theemperorbeijing.cn. ✆ **010/6526-5566.** Fax 010/6523-8786. 55 units. ¥969–¥5,200 superior/deluxe room. Rates include service charge and breakfast. AE, DC, MC, V. Metro: Tian'an Men East. **Amenities:** Restaurant; rooftop bar; concierge; forex; health club; meeting rooms; indoor pool, room service/butler service; all smoke-free rooms; spa. *In room:* A/C, satellite TV, hair dryer, Internet, free minibar.

Park Plaza Beijing (Beijing Li Ting Jiu Dian) ★ Sitting next to its sister hotel The Regent, the Chinese four-star Park Plaza is one notch below in price and grandeur, but it's a good value for business or leisure guests looking for comfortable rooms in a great location without the opulent amenities. Rooms, decorated in wood and beige tones, are a bit cramped but do the job just fine. The hotel is often booked to capacity and is popular with Western business travelers. (Another incentive for staying here: This hotel often overbooks and upgrades its bumped guests to the luxurious Regent next door.)

Jin Bao Jie 97. www.parkplaza.com/beijing-hotel-cn-100005/chnbwan ✆ **010/8522-1999.** Fax 010/8522-1919. 216 units. ¥920–¥1,035 standard room; ¥1,035–¥1,150 suite. ¥1,380–¥1,495, service charge included. Breakfast not included. AE, DC, MC, V. Metro: Dengshikou. **Amenities:** 2 restaurants; bar; babysitting; executive-level rooms; forex; fitness center; smoke-free floor; room service; sauna; smoke-free floor. Breakfast not included. *In room:* A/C, satellite TV, hair dryer, Internet, minibar.

Red Wall Garden Hotel (Hong Qiang Huayuan Jiudian) ★ Cozy and friendly, this intimate courtyard property is a great place to unwind after a day of sightseeing. A small lobby opens into a large wooden patio with plenty of lounge seating and umbrellas. Antique furniture and 1920s rotary phones give rooms a vintage feel, with the exception of the very comfortable modern beds. Upgrade to a duplex for extra room.

Shijia Hutong 41. www.rwghotel.com. © **010/5169-2222.** Fax 010/5219-0221. 40 units. ¥1,880 standard deluxe; ¥2,280 deluxe; ¥2,680 superdeluxe. **Amenities:** 2 restaurants, butler service. *In room:* A/C, Internet.

INEXPENSIVE

Days Inn Forbidden City (Beijing Xiangjiang Daisi Jiudian) ★ A terrific budget choice and a brand familiar to westerners, the Days Inn is just a few minutes' walk in either direction to the Forbidden City and Wangfujing. Rooms are small and don't have much character, but come with all the necessary amenities, including satellite television, a bright, clean bathroom, and Wi-Fi. The staff at reception is fluent in English, something that's hard to come by at other three-star hotels. This is a great value for the neighborhood, where five-star hotels often command triple or quadruple the price of this motel. If you're planning on staying for 3 nights or more, apply for a VIP card for ¥38, which gives you perks like complimentary lunch or an extra night free, depending on how long you stay.

Nanwanzi 1, Nanheyan Dajie. www.daysinn.com. © **010/6512-7788.** Fax 010/6526-0882. 164 units. ¥558–¥1,800 standard to superior rooms. Rates include service charge. AE, DC, MC, V. Metro: Tian'an Men East. **Amenities:** Restaurant; concierge; forex; room service; smoke-free floors. *In room:* A/C, satellite TV, hair dryer, Internet, minibar.

Saga Youth Hostel (Shijia Guoji Qingnian Lushe) ★ Housed in one of Beijing's most famous *hutong,* the Saga is a favorite among savvy backpackers. The decade-old hostel just underwent a long-overdue renovation and looks fresh and lively. The spacious standard rooms on this floor come with their own wet bathrooms (the kind with no divider between the toilet and the shower); some standard rooms have separate sitting areas. The third floor, home to clean and functional dorm rooms, is much more utilitarian hostel in style and decoration. Past visitors have scribbled their thoughts in kaleidoscopic ink and paint on the hallway's white walls. The ratty public bathrooms have thankfully been replaced with clean blue tile, separate cubicles, and

In the Red Lantern District

Southwest of Qian Men, past the mercantile madness of Da Zhalan in the *hutong* that never dreamed of pedicab tour salvation, is where you'll find the **Shanxi Xiang Di'er Binguan** (© **010/6303-4609**)—one of Beijing's most luridly compelling budget hotels. The hotel sits at the north end of Shanxi Xiang (a poorly marked and malodorous lane once at the center of the city's brothel district) and was formerly one of several houses where men of means would go to taste the pleasures of "clouds and rain" prior to 1949. Rooms are arranged on two floors around a central covered courtyard, restored to its original appearance with red columns and walls supporting colorfully painted banisters and roof beams, the latter hung with traditional lanterns. The rooms themselves are tiny and windowless, as befits their original purpose, but they now have air-conditioning, TVs, and bathrooms at ¥150 per night. To reach the hotel from the Hepingmen subway station, walk south on Nan Xinhua Jie for 1km (less than 1 mile), turn left on Zhu Shikou Xi Dajie, then make a left at the second alley, Shanxi Xiang.

showerheads offering decent pressure. The biggest bonus of top-floor accommodations is proximity to the third-floor balcony; the fantastic view west across well-preserved old courtyard houses is a joy, especially at sunrise. There's also a central courtyard on the main floor with cozy patio furniture and sun umbrellas.

Shijia Hutong 9 (west of intersection with Chaoyang Men Nan Xiao Jie). www.sagayouthhostel beijing.cn. ✆ **010/6527-2773.** Fax 010/6524-9098. 34 units, all with in-room shower. ¥230–¥259 twin; ¥65 dorm bed. AE, MC, V. Metro: Dengshikou. **Amenities:** Restaurant; cafe; Internet; self-service kitchen; table soccer; train ticket service. *In room:* A/C, no phone.

Chaoyang District

VERY EXPENSIVE

Opposite House (Yu She) ★★ Located on the Sanlitun bar street, this classy boutique hotel represents how far this once-scummy area (and Beijing as a whole) has come. You won't expect much from the boring glass exterior, but once inside, everything is stylish, from the open atrium lobby featuring Chinese modern art installations to the stainless steel-bottomed pool in the basement. Rooms are decorated in minimalist white with floor-to-ceiling windows and are anchored with pale wood floors. Bathrooms are separated by a glass partition and feature wooden tubs redolent of the Japanese designer Kengo Kuma's ethnic heritage. Hotel staff, in hooded beige vests and appropriately gelled hair, are extremely helpful and courteous. What's also a draw are the food and beverage outlets, including the very popular Mediterranean restaurant **Sureño** (p. 88) and **Bei** (p. 87) for some of the city's finest sushi, plus the twin lounge and nightclub, **Mesh** and **Punk** (p. 121). Great venues plus stylish rooms equals the most happening hotel in town.

Sanlitun Lu 11, the Village, building 1. www.theoppositehouse.com. ✆ **010/6417-6688.** Fax 010/6417-7799. 99 units. ¥1,500–¥6,500 standard plus 15% service charge. AE, DC, MC, V. Metro: Tuanjiehu. Pets allowed (free). **Amenities:** 3 restaurants; 2 bars; forex; fitness center; indoor pool; room service; smoke-free floors; complimentary culture tour; Wi-Fi. *In room:* A/C, satellite TV, hair dryer, Internet, free minibar.

Park Hyatt (Beijing Baiyue Jiudian) ★★ Rising above the area known as the CBD (the Central Business District), this new 66-story hotel impresses with its expansive views of the city, top-notch gym and spa facilities, and unconventional room layouts decorated in beige tones. Most rooms open into an airy bathroom, outfitted with marble tubs next to an open shower, a freestanding his-and-hers sink and mirror, and a sliding door that separates the bathroom from the sleeping quarters beyond. It's sexy, if you're staying with a romantic partner, but inconvenient if you happen to be traveling with your grandmother. There are plenty of fun in-room amenities, including Japanese toilets with bidets and automatic-opening lids, fragrant soaps, and a beautiful collection of complimentary teas. The bar and restaurants here are highly popular among business travelers and expatriates: The 66th-floor China Grill offers delicious, if pricey, steaks and raw seafood, while the 6th-floor-terrace Xiu offers reasonably priced cocktails and live entertainment. If you're looking for a convenient location in the CBD, impressive views, and stylish rooms, this may be it.

Jianguomenwai Dajie 2. http://beijing.park.hyatt.com ✆ **010/8567-1234.** Fax 010/8567-1000. 237 units. ¥2,500–¥3,000 standard/deluxe, plus 15% service charge. AE, DC, MC, V. Metro: Guomao. **Amenities:** 3 restaurants; bar; airport limousine transfers; concierge; forex; fitness center; pool; room service/butler service; spa; Wi-Fi. *In room:* A/C, flatscreen satellite TV, MP3 docking station, hair dryer, minibar.

Ritz-Carlton Beijing (Beijing Lisi Kaerdun Jiudian) ★★ Not to be confused with the *other* Ritz-Carlton on the other side of town, this five-star hotel sits just east of Beijing's CBD (Central Business District) and comes with impressive service and a distinctly old-world, European feel. While rooms have a classic look with flowery throw pillows and dark wood furniture, they're also outfitted with modern technology like iPod docks, flatscreen televisions, and Wi-Fi (but strangely, no DVD players). The gym, spa, and pool are located on the top floor, giving guests great views of the city. The hotel offers stellar restaurants, including Yu, serving Cantonese cuisine and decorated with celadon green ceramics and Buddhist stone sculptures and jade pieces in the private room wing, and Barolo, which offers traditional Italian cuisine with wines by the glass. If you can, try to upgrade to an executive room, which comes with access to the private club room, where a complimentary buffet and drinks are served throughout the day.

Jianguo Rd. 83A. www.ritzcarlton.com/beijing ✆ **010/5908-8888.** Fax 010/5908-8899. 305 units. ¥2,300–¥2,500, ¥3,100–¥2,900 single club room, ¥3,050–¥3,250 double, plus 15% service charge. AE, DC, MC, V. Metro: Dawang Lu. **Amenities:** 3 restaurants; bar; forex; health club and fitness center; free Internet for club rooms; pool; smoke-free floors; spa; Wi-Fi. *In room:* A/C, satellite TV, hair dryer, Internet, minibar.

EXPENSIVE

Grand Millennium Beijing ★ This property provides the amenities of a name-brand five-star hotel without the exorbitant prices. The Millennium boasts a central location in the CBD, views of the iconic CCTV tower, and a luxurious and contemporary feel to it with rooms decorated in a gold, black, and red color scheme. The superior rooms here are large enough for a sitting area, while large windows allow plenty of light. The bathrooms are a highlight, with bathtubs right next to the windows, providing great views while soaking.

Dongsanhuan Zhong Lu 7, Fortune Plaza. www.millenniumhotels.com. ✆ **010/8587-6888.** Fax 010/8587-6999. 521 units. ¥1,600–¥3,200 superior room; ¥1,750–¥3,300 deluxe room; ¥1,900–¥3,700. Breakfast not included. AE, DC, MC, V. Metro: Jintaixizhao. **Amenities:** 2 restaurants; deluxe gym (membership necessary); lap pool; spa; banquet rooms. *In room:* Cable TV, Internet, adaptors and converters.

Hotel G ★ Part of the growing boutique hotel trend in Beijing, Hotel G offers stylish rooms done up in old-fashioned Hollywood glamour. The hotel is in a central location near much of Beijing's nightlife. Rooms have a whimsical touch, with rubber duckies near the tub and toy motorcycles, and come with all the modern technology you'll need, including an iPod dock and flatscreen television. There's no pool, unfortunately, but a cozy gym makes up for it with extensive Technogym workout equipment, and the bar downstairs, Scarlett, features a large cheese bar with selections from Europe and many bargain-priced wines are on the list. The hotel is priced lower than many of its competitors, making it an overall value, especially if you appreciate the irreverent style over the feel of corporate hotel chains.

Gongtixilu A7. www.hotel-g.com. ✆ **010/6552-3600.** Fax 010/6552-3606. 110 units. ¥1,288–¥1,488 standard room, plus 15% service charge. AE, MC, V. Metro: Dongsi Shitiao. **Amenities:** 2 restaurants; fitness center; room service; smoke-free floors; Wi-Fi. *In room:* A/C, satellite TV, MP3 docking station, hair dryer, minibar.

MODERATE

A.hotel This is a modern, minimalist hotel and a cheap alternative to nearby Hotel G or the Opposite House. The dim lighting, black and white curlicue wallpaper, and ambient music in the curved hallways (following the architecture of the Worker's Stadium, where the hotel is located) remind us of a hip bar lounge—soothing and mildly stimulating at the same time. Bathrooms are a bit on the small side, but they come with sleek rain showers. Rooms have big windows and are decorated in neutral tones of beige, cream, and white with maroon accents here and there and chic monochrome photos on the walls. The location is excellent, a quick walk from Sanlitun and literally around the corner from the Worker's Stadium's bars and restaurants, but because the hotel is actually *in* the stadium complex, you may have to deal with the pain of uptight security during soccer matches and concerts. During such times, head straight for the east gate and the hotel should have a staff member waiting at the ready to escort you in past stadium security.

East Gate of Worker's Stadium 6 Tai. www.a-hotel.com.cn. ✆ **010/6586-5858.** Fax 010/6507-8468. 116 units. ¥550–¥800 standard room; ¥1,800 suite. AE, MC, V. Metro: Tuanjiehu or Dongsi Shitiao. **Amenities:** Restaurant. *In room:* A/C, Satellite TV, fridge, hair dryer, Internet, minibar.

Holiday Inn Express Beijing Dongzhimen ★ A terrific location in the Sanlitun area, an excellent price, and amenities to make a traveler's life easier make this new property stand out among the rest. The hotel offers a laundry room on each floor, so you can avoid the usual exorbitant laundry bills associated with hotels; another bonus is a shuttle service to the nearby shopping areas. Rooms are slightly cramped and furnished for utility rather than style, but are comfortable enough given the price. Guests will also be pleased with the complimentary Wi-Fi access and breakfast.

Chunxiu Lu 1. www.holidayinn.com. ✆ **010/6416-9999.** Fax 010/6419-9156. 116 units. ¥498–¥888 standard room. Breakfast included. Kids eat free. AE, MC, DC, V. Metro: Dongzhimen or Dongsi Shitiao. **Amenities:** Restaurant, Wireless Internet. *In room:* A/C, TV, hair dryer, Internet, minibar.

INEXPENSIVE

Yoyo Hotel ★ If you're on a tight budget but aren't willing to sacrifice style, this is a very good option. With an excellent location near the nightlife and restaurants of Sanlitun Bar district, this hip little property is a very discounted version of the ultra-trendy Opposite House (p. 76). All rooms are decorated in brown and tan tones and come with complimentary Wi-Fi, while a few of the featured rooms include cozy rugs and Japanese-style beds that sit close to the ground.

Middle Section of Sanlitun 10F (alley) opposite 3.3 building (off Sanlitun Bar St.). www.yoyohotel.cn. ✆ **010/6417-3388.** Fax 010/6417-8200. 52 units. ¥369–¥399 standard room. AE, MC, DC, V. Metro: Tuanjiehu. **Amenities:** Restaurant. *In room:* A/C, Internet.

Zhaolong Qingnian Luguan Though it's close to the Sanlitun bar area, the Zhaolong is a quiet alternative to the madness of its better-known cousin, Poacher's. Most guests are Chinese backpackers or foreigners conversant in Chinese. Doors close at 1am to discourage revelers. Twins and dorms are simple and clean; neither has an in-room bathroom, but common showers are adequate. Facilities are minimal. Proximity to the East Third Ring Road means convenient bus access to all parts of town.

Gongti Bei Lu 2 (behind Great Dragon Hotel). ✆ **010/6597-2299,** ext. 6111. Fax 010/6597-2288. 60 units. ¥60–¥70 dorm beds; ¥160–¥180 standard room; ¥300 2-bed suite. AE, DC, MC, V. Metro: Tuanjiehu. **Amenities:** Bar; access to indoor pool and sauna for a fee. *In room:* A/C, no phone.

Around the Back Lakes

VERY EXPENSIVE

Du Ge Hotel (Duge Siheyuan Yishu Jingpin Jiudian) ★ ☺ This posh, cozy 10-room boutique hotel sitting right off of the popular alley of Nan Luogu

Xiangis has rooms decorated with a different theme and name, ranging from the "Tibetan Kingdom" to the "Peony Pavilion." Lacquered furniture in bright colors has been custom made and fitted, while fancy touches like crystal chandeliers and antique carpets round out the polished, flashy feel of the rooms. Though definitely grand—it was once part of the home of a Qing dynasty finance minister—the hotel feels a little cramped with a minuscule lobby and small outdoor space that doubles as a bar and restaurant. The hotel is less willing to bargain than other places in the area, but for those who appreciate style and fashion, a stay here will feel worthwhile. One nice touch is two small, intimate rooms designed to give parents relief from their children, or single travelers. Other custom touches include a range of complimentary services, including transfers to and from the airport, use of cellphones and bicycles, and around-the-clock refreshments, coffee, and tea.

Qianyuan'ensi Hutong 26. www.dugecourtyard.com ✆ **010/6406-0686.** Fax 010/6406-0628. 6 units. ¥1,580–¥2,180 standard room/suite, plus 15% service charge. AE, DC, MC, V. Metro: Beixinqiao. **Amenities:** Restaurant; bar; airport transportation; bicycle rentals; cell phone rental; concierge; cooking demos; room service; spa; translator/tour guides; Wi-Fi. *In room:* A/C, satellite TV, hair dryer, Internet, minibar.

Han's Royal Garden Hotel (Hanzhen Yuan Guoji Jiudian) ★★ A collaboration between a wealthy Chinese American and the grandson of a Qing Dynasty chef, this painstakingly restored series of five courtyards has been turned into a luxurious hotel with an emphasis on preserving China's history and culture. The courtyards feature goldfish ponds, hawthorn trees, and stone carvings. Most rooms are decorated comfortably with expensive yet understated dark wood furniture, while the more lavish rooms have been filled with antique Chinese rosewood furniture. The hotel houses an Imperial cuisine restaurant with private rooms on two floors, while a third floor features a stage for the same sort of after-dinner performances that royal families used to indulge in. A basement houses a bar with a stage for dancing and a small spa with Thai, Chinese, and Western massage. The location is fantastic, just off the busy alley of Nan Luogu Xiang, yet on a very quiet, low-key alley where you'd least expect to find such a gem.

Bei Bingmasi Hutong 7. www.hansroyalgarden.com. ✆ **010/8402-5588.** Fax 010/6401-5556. 33 units. ¥1,290 deluxe room, plus 15% service charge; ¥6,800 Rosewood suite, plus 15% service charge. AE, MC, V, DC. Metro: Zhangzizhong Lu. **Amenities:** 2 restaurants; bar; forex; Internet. *In room:* A/C, satellite TV, hair dryer, minibar, Wi-Fi.

EXPENSIVE

Courtyard 7 (Qihao Yuan) ★ Located just off the very popular alley Nan Luogu Xiang, this boutique hotel in a traditional courtyard dwelling offers cozy rooms decorated with Chinese antiques and white curtained windows overlooking one of several central gardens. The hotel has taken an environmental approach in its design—many bricks have been reused from former dwellings and old stone steles with faded engraved calligraphy decorate the outer walls. Rooms come with central air-conditioning and heating, rather than the typical individual cooling and heating units in most buildings in the neighborhood.

Qian Gulou Yuan Hutong 7 (near Nanluoguxiang). www.courtyard7.com. ✆ **010/6406-0777.** Fax 010/8402-6867. 19 units. ¥1,360–¥2,000 standard room/suite, gives discounts over phone. AE, DC, MC, V. Metro: Beixinqiao. **Amenities:** Restaurant; bar; concierge; smoke-free rooms and restaurant. *In room:* A/C, TV, hair dryer, Internet.

MODERATE

Bamboo Garden Hotel (Zhu Yuan Binguan) ★ Said to be the former residence of the infamous Qing dynasty eunuch, Li Lianying, Bamboo Garden was the first major courtyard-style hotel in Beijing and is among the most beautiful. Rooms border three courtyards of rock gardens, clusters of bamboo, and covered corridors. Standard rooms in two multi-story buildings at opposite ends of the complex are decorated with Ming-style furniture and traditional lamps that cast pleasant shadows on the high ceilings. A restaurant looks out over the rear courtyard.

Xiaoshi Qiao Hutong 24 (3rd *hutong* on right walking south from metro stop). www.bbgh.com.cn. ✆ **010/5852-0088.** Fax 010/5852-0066. 60 units. ¥760–¥880 standard room (discounts rare). AE, DC, MC, V. Metro: Gulou. **Amenities:** Restaurant; bar; concierge; forex. *In room:* A/C, satellite TV, fridge.

INEXPENSIVE

Beijing Downtown Backpackers Accommodation (Dong Tang Qingnian Lushe) ★ This is one of the most popular hostels in Beijing, and it's in a fabulous location. They have bargain-basement dorm rooms for ¥75 to ¥90 as well as private singles and standards. The bathroom has that annoying layout with a toilet placed smack in the middle of the shower area, but it is very clean and the folks manning the reception desk speak excellent English.

Nanluoguxiang 85. www.backpackingchina.com. ✆ **010/8400-2429.** Fax 010/6404-9677. 20 units. ¥75–¥90 dorm; ¥160–¥320 standard. Rates include breakfast. No credit cards. Metro: Beixinqiao. **Amenities:** Restaurant; free airport pick-up if you're staying over 4 days (you pay the ¥20 toll fees); bike rental; Internet; laundry service; tours. *In room:* A/C.

Confucius International Youth Hostel (Beijing Yong Sheng Xuan Qingnian Jiudia) ★ This new hostel is right in the thick of things on up-and-coming Wudaoying Hutong, a lively alley that has seen a slew of cafes, restaurants, and boutiques open in the last year. Rooms are basic, but a good size (bigger than at nearby Beijing Downtown Backpackers Accommodation). They come with squeaky-clean tile or faux wood floors and separate wet bathrooms—the kind with no official division between shower and toilet, though there is a shower curtain in place. There's little decor to speak of in-room, just crisp white duvets and plain walls, but the sunshine streaming in during the day and the daily sounds of hutong life make for cozy environs. The hostel itself is a two-story converted courtyard. Public spaces are done in traditional Chinese fashion: Eaves on the central walkway are painted with Chinese scenes or flowers, and wooden beams and pillars have shiny coats of red paint. The best rooms are on the second floor. They may be a bit cramped for taller guests, but the sloping roofs with exposed natural wood beams are a step up from the bare walls and ceilings in first floor rooms. Pick this place and you'll be a stone's throw away from the Lama Temple and the Loop metro line.

Wudaoying Hutong 38. ✆ **010/6402-2082.** 16 units. ¥238 standard room. No credit cards. Metro: Yonghegong Lama Temple. **Amenities:** Restaurant; cafe. *In room:* A/C, TV, Wi-Fi.

West Second Ring & Beyond

VERY EXPENSIVE

Aman Beijing (Beijing Anman Wenhua Jiudian) ★★★ Known as one of the most luxurious resort chains in Asia, the Aman has arrived in Beijing in style. Abutting the Summer Palace on the outskirts of Beijing, the resort is the perfect place to relax and unwind while absorbing many of the historical sites in the area. Traditional courtyard structures that once housed the imperial kitchen of the Summer Palace have been converted into gorgeous, spacious rooms with wood floors, three-story high ceilings, and classic Ming-style furniture. The resort makes good use of its location next to the palace where Qing emperors summered; not only are morning tai-chi classes offered in the Summer Palace, but guests can access the historical site anytime through a private back door entrance. The resort also has a world-class spa, a movie theater, and a Pilates studio. Foodies will enjoy the choice cuts of meat offered at the **Grill** steakhouse (p. 93) and the Japanese kaiseki cuisine restaurant, both of which feature outstanding wine selections from the resident "cellar master."

Gongmenqian Jie 15. www.amanresorts.com/amanatsummerpalace/home.aspx. ✆ **010/5987-9999.** Fax 010/5987-9900. 51 rooms. ¥4,208 guestroom; ¥4,845 courtyard; ¥6,150 suite, plus 15% service charge. AE, DC, MC, V. **Amenities:** 3 restaurants; bar; cinema; concierge; executive-level rooms; forex; health club; indoor pool; room service; smoke-free floors; spa; Wi-Fi. *In room:* A/C, satellite TV, hair dryer, minibar.

EXPENSIVE

Ritz Carlton, Financial Street (Jinrong Jie Lijia Jiudian) ★★ Though this hotel caters to a corporate clientele, the place is decorated with homey touches, as if run by a Chinese version of Martha Stewart. The beds are the comfiest in town, and spacious marble bathrooms come with his and her sinks and televisions anchored in front of the bathtub. The basement health club and spa are top-notch, with a luxurious swimming pool that features a giant television screen on one wall and lounge chairs imbedded in the pool that deliver water jet massages. Upgrading to an executive room gives you access to a 24-hour club lounge that serves a steady stream of delicious bites and drinks throughout the day, plus free Wi-Fi. Be sure to dine in **Cepe** (p. 94), which serves the city's best upscale Italian fare. The only drawback is the location, which isn't particularly central, even though it's an up and coming business district. The hotel is attached to a chic new shopping center.

1 Jinchengfang Dong Jie (next to the National Security Council Building). www.ritzcarlton.com. ✆ **010/6601-6666.** Fax 010/6601-6029. 253 units. ¥4,500–¥5,000 standard room; ¥6,000–¥7,000 suite (discounts up to 60% during the low season, call for discounts), plus 15% service charge. AE, MC, DC, V. Metro: Fuxing Men. **Amenities:** 3 restaurants; bar; babysitting; concierge; executive-level rooms; forex; fitness center; Jacuzzi; indoor pool; room service; sauna; spa. *In room:* A/C, satellite TV, hair dryer, minibar, scale, Wi-Fi.

Shangri-La Beijing Hotel (Xianggelila Fandian) ★★ It looks like a pair of drab office towers from the outside, but the Shangri-La is one of the most well-regarded hotel chains in China. Standard rooms in the older tower are comfortable, but slightly worn—for an extra ¥500, it's worthwhile to upgrade to the Valley Wing, a luxurious tower of new executive rooms decorated in elegant muted beige tones, with access to an indulgent lounge with free breakfast, afternoon cocktails, and canapés. The Chi Spa, one of the most luxurious in the city, offers pricey massages and facials in a calming Tibetan atmosphere. Although off by itself in the northwest, the hotel benefits by having space for a large and lush garden (which includes an outdoor bar and pond), easy access to the Summer Palaces and the Western Hills, and quick routes around Beijing via the third and fourth ring roads.

Zizhu Yuan Lu 29 (northwest corner of Third Ring Rd.). www.shangri-la.com. ✆ **010/6841-2211.** Fax 010/6841-8002. 657 units. ¥1,350–¥1,430 standard room (discounts up to 25% during the low season); ¥1,900 Valley Wing rooms, plus 15% service charge. AE, DC, MC, V. **Amenities:** 3 restaurants; bar; concierge; executive-level rooms; forex; health club with sauna, solarium, exercise room; indoor pool; room service; smoke-free rooms. *In room:* A/C, satellite TV, hair dryer, minibar, Wi-Fi.

MODERATE

Crowne Plaza Hotel Zhongguancun Located in Beijing's Silicon Valley, this well-appointed hotel is a good choice if you're planning some time visiting Beijing's northern attractions like the Summer Palace and the universities. You'll get the amenities and service that come with an international brand—not always a given up in Beijing's north. Wood-paneled rooms are luxurious with very comfortable beds and spacious bathrooms, while staff are professional and courteous.

Zhicun Lu 106. www.crowneplaza.com. ✆ **400/884-0888** or 010/5993-8888. Fax 010/5993-8999. 300 units. ¥1,088 superior room; ¥1,388 deluxe room; ¥1,688 executive king-size; ¥1,688 executive suite, plus 15% service charge; Internet rates are up to 40% off. AE, DC, MC, V. Metro: Zhicunli. **Amenities:** 3 restaurants; ballroom; conference room; pool; Wi-Fi. *In room:* Cable TV, hair dryer, minibar, Wi-Fi and cable Internet (only free in executive rooms).

Jingyi Hotel Though it is Chinese owned and managed, foreign travelers will find this property inviting and stress-free. Though rooms are decorated in a fussy European style popular with Chinese, they feature comfortable beds and a pleasant sitting area; bathrooms come with stylish glass walls. The concierge is very helpful and can speak English and the location, near the universities, attracts a steady following of Chinese and international visitors.

Dazhongsi Dong Lu 9. www.jingyihotel.com. ✆ **010/6216-5588** or 400/181-5588. Fax 010/8212-5267. ¥1,280–¥1,480 standard; ¥1,880 deluxe; ¥2,780 executive, plus 15% service tax; 50%-60% discounts at counter and on Internet. AE, MC, V. Metro: Zhicunli. **Amenities:** 2 restaurants; tea house; conference room; fitness room; pool; spa, ticket office; wireless Internet in lobby. *In room:* Cable TV, fridge, hair dryer, cable Internet.

INEXPENSIVE

Red Lantern House ★ Though technically on the west side of town, this sprawling backpacker's hotel, in a traditional courtyard dwelling, is still quite central to many of Beijing's main sites. Another draw is that it's in a local neighborhood, away from most touristy or expatriate areas, giving it an authentic feel. Rooms vary in size, with the smallest being very small and cramped—be sure to check out the room before you put down your money. However, there is plenty of space in the central garden and in the dining area to laze about and take advantage of the complimentary Wi-Fi. Guests are mostly young and friendly Americans and Europeans. Be sure to specify if you want an en-suite bathroom; otherwise, you'll be using the communal toilets.

Zhengjue Hutong 5, Xinjiekou Nan Dajie. www.redlanternhouse.com. ✆ **010/8328-5771.** Fax 010/8322-9477. 68 units. ¥60–¥70 dorm rooms; ¥200–¥300 private rooms. No credit cards. Metro: Jishuitan or Ping'anli. **Amenities:** 3 restaurants; airport pick-up and drop-off; bike rentals; Internet computers; luggage storage; TV/DVD; Wi-Fi. *In room:* A/C, lockers.

Beijing Station & South

EXPENSIVE

The Grand Mercure ★ Although not among the main clusters of foreign hotels, this hotel is as close to the center of things as any of them, and is quieter and better connected than most. The location—just south of the No. 1 Line's Xi Dan station and north of the Circle Line's Xuanwu Men station—enables guests to get in and out during the worst of rush hour. The medium-size rooms are well appointed, although bathrooms are somewhat cramped.

Xuanwu Men Nei Dajie 6, Xuanwu Qu (just south of Xi Dan metro stop). www.accorhotels.com. ✆ **010/6603-6688.** Fax 010/6603-1488. 296 units. ¥1,105 superior room; ¥1,275 deluxe room

Airport Hotels

Plenty of hotels, all with free shuttle services, are located near the airport. The two top choices are **Langham Place (Langhao Jiudian; ✆ 010/6457-5555;** fax 010/6457-7755; www.beijingairport.langhamplacehotels.com), and the **Hilton Hotel (Xierdun Jiudian; ✆ 010/6458-8888;** fax 010/6458-8889; www.hilton.com), right next to Beijing airport's sparkling Terminal 3, where most international flights arrive and depart. The CITIC Hotel Beijing Airport (Guoduda Fandian) ★ (**✆ 010/6456-5588;** fax 010/6456-1234; www.citichotelbeijing.com) contains large rooms with two queen-size beds for around ¥698 after discount. It has a pleasant resort-style pool complex, and regular shuttles go to the airport (every 30 min. 6:15am–10:45pm) and downtown. A 20-minute drive away from the airport is the new **Traders Upper East Hotel (Shangdong Chengmao Fandian) ★ (✆ 010/5907-8888;** fax 010/5907-8008; www.shangri-la.com), part of the well-respected Shangri-La hotel chain. The hotel has a good restaurant, Wu Li Xiang, offering regional Chinese dishes.

(summer discounts up to 70%), plus 15% service charge. AE, DC, MC, V. Metro: Xi Dan or Xuanwumen. **Amenities:** 2 restaurants; bar; concierge; executive-level rooms; forex; fitness center; indoor pool; room service. *In room:* A/C, satellite TV, hair dryer, Internet, minibar.

Renaissance Beijing Capital Hotel ★ A better value than most five-star hotels, this property is a good option if you're traveling for business and need to stay near the CBD. Rooms are modern and spacious with Chinese accents, while a well-stocked exercise room and long swimming pool will appeal to the fit and healthy. The hotel also features a good Italian restaurant and bar that's often frequented by Italian expats, and the Chinese restaurant Fat Duck is also popular.

Dongsanhuan Zhong Lu 61. www.marriott.com. ✆ **010/5863-8888.** Fax 010/5863-8000. 485 units. ¥1100–¥1600 standard, ¥1750–¥3000 suite. AE, DC, MC, V. Metro: Shuangjing. **Amenities:** 5 restaurants; room service; Wi-Fi. *In room:* A/C, satellite TV, adapters, fridge, hair-dryer, Internet.

MODERATE

City Central Youth Hostel (Chengshi Qingnian Jiudian) ★★ Housed in the old post office building, this newly opened hostel cum hotel has an unbeatable location directly opposite Beijing railway station. The manager was inspired by a visit to the Sydney Central YHA in Australia, and has attempted to create a replica here. Standard rooms on the fifth and sixth floors are minimalist and clean, with none of the sleaze associated with other railway hotels, and at a fraction of the expense. Ask for a room on the north side, facing away from the railway station square. Dorm rooms on the fourth floor have double-glazed windows and comfortable bunk beds, but the squat toilets are a surprise for the less limber.

Beijing Zhan Qian Jie 1, Dong Cheng Qu. www.centralhostel.com. ✆ **010/6525-8066.** Fax 010/6525-9066. ¥288 standard room; from ¥60 dorm beds. Discounts on dorm beds for YHA members. AE, DC, MC, V. Metro: Beijing Zhan. **Amenities:** Bar; bike rental; self-service kitchen; supermarket. *In room:* A/C, TV, Internet.

INEXPENSIVE

Feiying Binguan The Feiying became one of the top budget options in the city after completing a top-to-bottom refurbishment and joining Youth Hostelling International. It's the most "hotel-like" YHA you'll find. Standard rooms are bright and well equipped with slightly hard twin beds; bathrooms have proper tubs. Dorms are also nice with in-room bathrooms and brand-new floors. The hotel's best feature is its location, just east of the Changchun Jie metro and next to several useful bus stops.

Xuanwu Men Xi Dajie 10 (down alley east of Guohua Market). www.yhachina.com. ✆ **010/6317-1116.** Fax 010/6315-1165. 46 units. ¥158–¥488 standard room; ¥60 dorm bed. Discounts for YHA members. No credit cards. Metro: Changchun Jie. **Amenities:** Bar; Internet; self-service kitchen; small convenience store. *In room:* A/C, TV.

WHERE TO EAT

Too many of Beijing's restaurants open and close in any given month to offer an accurate count, but it is difficult to imagine a city with more eateries per square mile, or a more exhaustive variety of Chinese cuisines. The short life span of the average restaurant in Beijing can create headaches (for guidebook writers, in particular), but the upside is a dynamic culinary environment where establishments that manage to stick around have generally earned the right to exist.

Food trends sweep through the city like typhoons. A few years ago it was Cultural Revolution nostalgia dishes, then fish and sweet sauces from Shanghai, and now yuppified cuisine normally served by minorities from Yunnan. Tomorrow it will be something else. See the expatriate periodicals—*Time Out* and the *Beijinger*—for notes on the latest craze.

Proper foreign food is now widely available at generally reasonable prices. Foreign **fast food** and other well-known food and beverage chains, most of them American, blanket the city (that is, if you're desperately hungry and too tired to find anything else). KFC and McDonald's are ubiquitous, and a stable of Délifrance outlets (one each in Xin Dong'an Plaza and the Lufthansa Center) are convenient for breakfast. For cheap sandwiches, there are numerous Subway chains and Schlotzsky's Deli (in the China World Trade Center).

You can buy basic **groceries** and Chinese-style **snacks** at local markets and at the *xiaomaibu* ("little-things-to-buy units") found nearly everywhere. Several fully stocked **supermarkets** and a handful of smaller grocers now carry imported wine and cheese, junk food, Newcastle Brown Ale, and just about anything else you could want, albeit at inflated prices. Supermarkets include one in the basement of the Lufthansa Center, the CRC in the basement of the China World Trade Center, and Oriental Kenzo, above Dongzhi Men metro. April Gourmet, north of Sanlitun bar street, has sliced meats, a decent cheese selection, and a full selection of familiar breakfast cereals; much the same can be found at Jenny Lou's, which has six branches in Beijing; the biggest one is near Chaoyang Park west gate. Among **delis and bakeries,** one of the best is the Kempi Deli (inside the Lufthansa Center) with good crusty-bread sandwiches.

Tour groups and those visiting expat friends tend to get trotted to restaurants with absurd prices and unappetizing food, such as those supposedly specializing in "imperial" cuisine. Fresher, better choices are set out below, but information on the showpiece eateries (Fangshan, Li Family Restaurant) can be found in the expat magazines. For restaurant locations, see the map on p. 70.

Around Wangfujing Dajie

VERY EXPENSIVE

Maison Boulud (Bulu Gong Fa Canting) ★★ FRENCH Ever since New York celebrity chef Daniel Boulud opened his first Eastern outpost just before the

Chinese on the Cheap

Affordable Chinese food is everywhere in Beijing, and not all of the places serving it are an offense to Western hygiene standards. Adequately clean **Chinese fast-food** restaurants include Yonghe Dawang (with KFC-style sign) and Malan noodle outlets (marked with a Chicago Bulls–style graphic). A better option is the **point-to-order food courts** on the top or bottom floor of almost every large shopping center. For late-night dining, a favorite Beijing pastime, try one of the **nightmarkets** at Donghua Men (just off Wangfujing Dajie opposite the Xin Dong'an Plaza) and on Longfu Si Jie (north of Wangfujing Dajie next to the Airlines Ticketing Hall). The famous 24-hour food street on Dongzhi Men Nei Dajie, locally known as **Ghost Street (Gui Jie),** is now much reduced, but dozens of eateries still offer hot pot, *mala longxia* (spicy crayfish), and home-style fare through the lantern-lit night.

2008 Olympics, there's been little reason to go anywhere else in Beijing for French food. Housed in the former pre-1949 American embassy, Boulud's refined food gleams brilliantly amid a landscape of mediocre French restaurants in Beijing—everything at Boulud from the food to wine list to service to atmosphere is top-notch. You'll find updated versions of classic dishes like coq au vin and French twists on contemporary American food like the signature "dB burger"—stuffed with foie gras and stewed short rib meat by executive chef Brian Reimer (Boulud visits Beijing several times a year to keep quality high). All of this comes at a hefty price, but you can expect to pay 25% less here than at Boulud's New York flagship, Daniel, which some would consider a bargain. If that's not enough to lure you, lunch and weekend brunch menus include set meals, which go for around ¥200.

23 Qianmen Dong Da Jie, Chi'en Men 23 (southeast corner of Tian'an Men Sq.). ✆ **010/6559-9200.** www.danielnyc.com/maisonboulud.html. Reservations essential. Meal for 2 ¥1,000–¥1,200. AE, DC, MC, V. 11am–2:30pm and 6–10pm. Metro: Qianmen.

EXPENSIVE

Capital M ★★ INTERNATIONAL With a breathtaking location overlooking Tian'an Men Square, a classy interior, and a tasty international menu, Capital M has quickly become a destination restaurant for literary types, the embassy crowd, and international jetsetters. The Australian owner and face of the restaurant, Michelle Garnaut, hosts frequent cultural events at the restaurant, including an annual Literary Festival every March. Brunch and afternoon tea, with set menus, are particularly popular.

Qianmen Pedestrian Street 2, 3/F. ✆ **010/6702-2727.** www.m-restaurantgroup.com/capitalm. Reservations recommended. Meal for 2 ¥700–¥1,200. AE, DC, MC, V. 11:30am–2:30pm and 6–10:30pm. Metro: Qianmen.

Made in China (Chang An Yi Hao) ★ BEIJING We regularly visit Made in China for its fantastic Peking Duck and its equally enthralling setting—a dining room placed in the middle of an open kitchen, illuminated by the occasional leaping flame from the stove. The Grand Hyatt's showcase restaurant offers traditional northeastern and Beijing dishes including the capital's most palatable *dou zhi* (fermented bean purée), excellent *ma doufu* (mashed soybean), and the ubiquitous *zhajiang mian* (wheat noodles with black bean mince), a dish that has spawned its own chain of restaurants. But the Peking Duck is the highlight—the presentation and flavors are impeccable. There's the odd fusion twist such as foie gras with sesame pancake, and there are excellent plain dishes such as *tong hao* vegetable with rice vinegar and garlic sauce. Quite unexpectedly for a Chinese restaurant, Made in China makes delicious desserts—the pear champagne and passion-fruit sorbet pack a fruity punch. Right next door you'll find the sleek **Red Moon Bar,** perfect for an aperitif.

Dong Chang'an Jie 1, in Grand Hyatt (p. 68). ✆ **010/8518-1234,** ext. 3608. Reservations essential. Meal for 2 ¥600–¥800. AE, DC, MC, V. 11:30am–2:30pm and 5:30–10pm. Metro: Wangfujing.

MODERATE

Lei Garden (Li Yuan) ★★ CANTONESE Up until the recent opening of this Hong Kong chain, pickings were slim for authentic dim sum and Cantonese cuisine. But Lei Garden, regarded as one of Hong Kong's finest restaurants, has brought delicious egg tarts, pan-fried turnip cakes, and shrimp dumplings to the capital. The only drawback is that it's in a sterile office building, but the restaurant makes up for it with stylish booths and attentive service. If you've only got time for one dim sum meal in Beijing, have it here. Book ahead, as it's often packed during the lunch rush.

Jinbao Jie 89, Jinbao Tower 3/F (next to the Regent Hotel). ✆ **010/8522-1212.** Meal for 2 lunch ¥200–¥250, dinner ¥400–¥500. AE, DC, MC, V. 11:30am–2pm and 5:30–9:30pm. Metro: Dengshikou.

Susu ★ VIETNAMESE Deliciously authentic Vietnamese cuisine is offered in a trendy yet traditional courtyard setting at this hot new spot in the *hutongs* near the National Art Museum. Equally pleasant for a casual lunch or dinner, Susu features outdoor dining, excellent pho (soup with rice noodles), and dishes rarely seen outside of Vietnam, like the excellent roasted la vong fish. Good desserts and a varied cocktail list round out the experience.

Qianliang Hutong Xixiang 10. ✆ **010/8400-2699.** Meal for 2 ¥160–¥400. AE, MC, V. 11am–10pm. Metro: Dongsi or Zhangzizhong.

INEXPENSIVE

Still Thoughts Vegetarian (Jingsi Su Shifang) VEGETARIAN This hidden gem is located in the hutongs just north of Wangfujing. It is quite hard to find this unassuming restaurant but well worth the adventure. It's a favorite amongst both local vegetarians and meat eaters. Standout dishes are the cold wheat gluten, the old Beijing shredded "pork" rolls, and the bamboo and sausage dish.

Dafosi Dongjie Jia 18 (continuation north of Meishuguan North St.). ✆ **010/6400-8941.** Reservations recommended. Meal for 2 ¥80–¥120. AE, MC, V. 10am–10pm. Metro: Dongsi.

Chuan Jing Ban Canting ★★ SICHUAN Anyone who has dealt with Chinese officials knows that there is one topic they are all experts on: food. This constantly crowded restaurant occupies the former site of the Qing Imperial examination hall (no traces remain). It is now the headquarters of the Sichuan Provincial Government, and the masses can enjoy the fruits of their rulers' connoisseurship. The spicy *shui zhu yu* consists of sublime, tender fish floating on a bed of crisp bean sprouts, and kids will appreciate the sweet pork with rice crust *(guoba roupian)*. Sichuan standards, such as *mapo doufu* (spicy tofu with chopped meat), are as authentic as the ingredients, which are flown in several times a week. The only evidence you're dining with cadres arrives later in the menu; two pages are dedicated to hard liquor and one to cigarettes.

Gongyuan Tou Tiao 5 (from metro, walk 1 block north along the Second Ring Rd., turn left into Dong Zongbu Hutong, Dong Cheng Qu). ✆ **010/6512-2277.** Meal for 2 ¥50–¥100. No credit cards. 11am–2pm and 5:30–10pm. English menu. Metro: Jianguo Men.

Chaoyang District (North)

VERY EXPENSIVE

Agua ★★ SPANISH For the last few years, Spanish chef Jordi Valles has bounced around several locations in Beijing, and hopefully he's found a permanent home in the trendy Sanlitun district. He's got an infectious energy and can often be found circulating around the dining room to greet guests, explaining the processes behind making his delicious, experimental Spanish tapas. The darkened, classy dining room decorated with a Moorish theme makes a romantic spot for a meal. Tapas are executed flawlessly: Winners include goose liver with red pepper ice cream, suckling pig with apricot puree and baby onions, and a smooth pumpkin soup rumored to be a favorite of Jackie Chan's. The wine list is reasonably priced, with a nice range of by the glass selections from Spain, France, Italy, and the New World.

Sanlitun Beilu 81, Nali Patio 4/F. ✆ **010/5208-6188.** www.agua.com.hk. Reservations essential. Meal for 2 ¥600–¥700. AE, DC, MC, V. Noon–2:30pm and 6–10:30pm. Metro: Tuanjiehu.

Bei ★★ NORTHERN ASIAN Located in the Opposite House hotel in Sanlitun, this contemporary northern Asian restaurant has brought sophistication to this gentrifying neighborhood. It's a good concept—blending the cuisines of Korea, Japan, and China, given the restaurant's location in the heart of China's capital—but the dishes are hit-or-miss. The basement space is decorated with whimsical flying light bulbs, minimalist white tables, and black wooden bucket seats. Some complain that the restaurant is an example of style over substance, but a visit is worthwhile if you like sushi, which is Tokyo-quality in freshness and cut. Sake pairings and creative desserts like fried strawberry *mochi* (sticky rice balls) make this a unique dining experience.

11 Sanlitun Rd., in the basement of the Opposite House (p. 76). ✆ **010/6410-5230.** www.beirestaurant.com. Meal for 2 ¥700–¥800. AE, DC, MC, V. 6–10:15pm. Metro: Tuanjiehu.

Yotsuba (Si Ye) ★★ JAPANESE This tiny restaurant looks like it was plucked up in Tokyo and dropped in the middle of Beijing, what with its traditional Japanese booths and a bar where a Japanese chef (who speaks no Chinese *or* English) works his magic with bare hands and a slender sushi knife. Skip the booths and go directly to the bar, where you can sit and watch the action. This place is made for raw fish aficionados—if you like your food cooked, you're out of luck. But for sushi fans, this is one of the best places to eat or try everything culled fresh out of the sea, including delicious cuts of chu-toro and o-toro (premium tuna) and more exotic items like ark shell, all imported from Dalian, a Chinese coastal city not far from Japan.

Xinyuanli Zhong Jie Building 2. ✆ **010/6467-1837.** Reservations recommended. Meal for 2 ¥400–¥600. AE, DC, MC, V. Tues–Sun 5–10:30pm. Closed Mon. Metro: Liangmaqiao.

EXPENSIVE

Duck de Chine ★ PEKING DUCK This name often draws approving nods when the perennial conversation topic of where to get the best Peking Duck comes up among Beijingers. Decorated with wooden beams, glass windows, and decorative porcelain ducks, the dining room draws wealthy Chinese diaspora for its main attraction—juicy succulent slices of roast duck with thin pancakes and a twist on the traditional sweet flour paste sauce. The menu also features many Hong Kong specialties and a good, if expensive, wine list.

Gongti Beilu, opposite Pacific Century Place South gate, 1949 Hidden City, Courtyard 4. ✆ **010/6501-8881.** www.elite-concepts.com. Meal for 2 ¥700–¥800. AE, MC, V. 11:30am–2:30pm and 5:30–10:30pm. Metro: Tuanjiehu.

Mosto ★★ CONTINENTAL Innovative dishes with a South American flair, a well-curated wine list, and an urbane dining room make this a great choice for a night out on the town. Young 30-something Venezuelan chef Daniel Urdaneta, who is a part owner in the venture, pulses heirloom tomatoes into a gazpacho garnished with chorizo, avocado, and orange caviar and pan-fried codfish with soy and honey to juicy perfection. Lunch is also a good deal with set menus under ¥100.

Sanilitun Lu 81, Nali Patio 3/F. ✆ **010/5208-6030.** www.mostobj.com. Reservations recommended. Meal for 2 ¥800–¥1,000. AE, MC, V. Sun–Thurs noon–2:30pm and 6–10pm; Fri–Sat noon–2:30pm and 6–10:30pm. Metro: Tuanjiehu.

Sureño ★★ MEDITERRANEAN The menu isn't particularly flashy—it's mainly pastas, pizzas, and grilled meats—yet the atmosphere and service make it almost a fine-dining experience (by Beijing standards, at least). Located in the Opposite House hotel, this sunken dining room featuring a small outdoor garden and an open kitchen gets all the basics right, and then some. A delicious citrus butter spread accompanies complimentary warmed flatbread, and a range of tapaslike appetizers can be enjoyed at a leisurely pace before tackling a main entree like the simple yet well-executed rack of lamb and Wagyu tenderloin. The look is contemporary, with warm orange and brown leather seats, and simple unadorned banquettes. Frequented by business travelers on expense account and well-heeled expatriates, this is one of Beijing's more popular upscale restaurants to open in the last year.

11 Sanlitun Rd., in the basement of the Opposite House (p. 76). ✆ **010/6410-5240.** www.surenorestaurant.com. Meal for 2 ¥1,000–¥1,200; Mon–Fri ¥108, ¥138 lunch set meal; Sat and Sun ¥188, ¥298 brunch. AE, DC, MC, V. Mon–Fri noon–10:30pm; Sat 6–10:30pm; Sun noon–10:30pm. Metro: Tuanjiehu.

MODERATE

Beijing Dadong Kaoya Dian ★★ BEIJING No hundred years of history or obscure *hutong* location here, just a crispy-skinned and pleasing roast duck that many say is one of the best in town. The restaurant claims to use a special method to reduce the amount of fat in its birds, although it seems unlikely that duck this flavorful could possibly be good for you. The birds come in either whole (¥198) or half (¥99) portions and are served in slices with a wide assortment of condiments (garlic, green onion, radish). Place the duck on a pancake with plum sauce and your choice of ingredients, and then roll and eat. An excellent plain broth soup, made from the rest of the duck, is included in the price. The English picture menu offers a wide range of other dishes, everything from mustard duck webs to duck tongue in aspic, plus a number of excellent *doufu* (tofu) dishes with thick, tangy sauces. Every meal comes with a free fruit plate and dessert. This is one of the few restaurants in Beijing with a nonsmoking room. A newer second location with the same hours is at 1-2/F Nanxincang International Plaza (southwest corner of Dongsi Shitiao; metro: Dongsi Shitiao; ✆ **010/5169-0329**).

Tuanjiehu Bei Kou 3 (on east side of E. Third Ring Rd., north of Tuanjiehu Park). ✆ **010/6582-2892.** Reservations essential. Meal for 2 (including half-duck) ¥300–¥600. AE, DC, MC, V. 11am–10pm. Metro: Tuanjiehu.

Bellagio (Lu Gang Xiao Zhen) ★ TAIWANESE Taiwanese food, characterized by sweet flavors and subtle use of ginger, is one of the most appealing to Western palates. The clientele of the Gongti branch of this Taiwanese place, stumbling out from Babyface and Angel nightclubs, make for amusing people-watching. The decor is all sleek lines and shimmering beads. Don't miss the braised pork *(lurou),* in which fatty slivers of pork belly are stewed in a delicious soy gravy. *Taiwan dofu bao,* a tofu clay-pot seasoned with shallots, onion, chili, and black beans, is also remarkable, as is the signature dish, *sanbei ji* (chicken reduced in rice wine, sesame oil, and soy sauce). In summer, don't miss the enormous shaved-ice desserts: One serving is enough for four, but gobble it before it comes tumbling down! Other branches are Gongti Xi Lu 6 (south of Gongti 100 bowling center; ✆ **010/6551-3533;** 11am–5am); Jian Guo Lu 87 Beijing Shin Kong Place 6F (metro: Da Wang Lu; ✆ **010/6530-5658;** 11am–10pm); An Hui Bei Li Block 2 Building #4 (✆ **010/6489-4300;** 11am–midnight).

Xiaoyun Lu 35 (opposite Renaissance Hotel). ✆ **010/8451-9988.** Meal for 2 ¥160–¥200. AE, DC, MC, V. Metro: Dongsi Shitiao. 11am–4am.

Pure Lotus (Jing Xin Lian) ★ VEGETARIAN The dimmed restaurant, decorated with prayer wheels and Buddhist statues, offers stylish vegetarian food that wows in taste and presentation. Highlights include the pumpkin soup and the vegetarian dumplings. A monk supposedly owns the restaurant, but we suspect that he's more of a businessman given the relatively high prices. The Metropark Lido Hotel location is a bit of a trek from central Beijing, but offers a stylish, not-to-be-missed setting.

Jiang Tai Lu 6, Metropark Lido Hotel. ✆ **010/6437-6288.** Meal for 2 ¥300–¥600. AE, DC, MC, V. 11am–11pm. Metro: San Yuan Qiao. Another branch at Nongzhan Nanli 12. Tongguan Dasha. ✆ **010/6592-3627.** Meal for 2 ¥400–¥600. AE, MC, V. 11am–11pm. Metro: Tuanjiehu.

Rumi (Lu Gang Xiao Zhen) ★ ☺ PERSIAN Run by a friendly Persian exile, this airy white-walled restaurant located in the trendy Sanlitun bar area offers reasonably priced authentic stews, kebabs, and rice dishes. No liquor is served, but the restaurant lets you bring your own without a corkage fee. An upstairs kid's room makes this a good choice for families.

Gongti Beilu 1A. ✆ **010/8454-3838.** www.rumigrill.com. Meal for 2 ¥200–¥240; buffet lunch Mon–Fri ¥88. AE, DC, MC, V. 11:30am–midnight. Metro: Tuanjiehu.

INEXPENSIVE

Ding Ding Xiang HOT POT This Mongolian-style mutton hot pot restaurant is tremendously and justifiably popular for its signature dipping sauce *(jinpai tiaoliao),* a flavorful sesame sauce so thick they have to dish it out with ice cream scoops. Large plates of fresh sliced lamb *(yangrou)* are surprisingly cheap; other options include beef *(niurou),* spinach *(bocai),* and sliced winter melon *(donggua pian).* Decor is plain, and the place is clean for a local restaurant. Reservations strongly recommended. Other branches (11am–10pm) at bldg. 31 Gan Jia Kou Xiaoqu (✆ **010/8837-1327**); East Gate Plaza at Dong Zhong Jie 9 (✆ **010/6417-9289**); bldg. 7 Guo Xing Jia Yuan, Shou Ti Nan Lu (✆ **010/8835-7775**); and Jian Guo Lu 87 Beijing Shin Kong Place 6/F (✆ **010/6530-5997**).

Dongzhongjie, Yuanjiaguoji Gongyu 2/F. ✆ **010/6417-2546.** http://en.dingdingxiang.com.cn. Reservations highly recommended. Meal for 2 ¥200–¥300. MC, V. 11am–midnight. Metro: Dongsishitiao.

Middle Eight YUNNAN The interior of this eatery, located in an alley behind the Sanlitun bar street, is modern and chic, with food to match. Their extensive stir-fry menu features a large variety of mushroom dishes and a completely separate menu for their array of fruit juices and desserts. This reasonably priced restaurant does not take reservations, so be prepared for a wait if you arrive on a weekend during peak dining hours.

Sanlitun Bei Lu, Dong Sanlitun Building 8. ✆ **010/6413-0629.** Guanghua Lu 9, the Place, South Tower L404A. ✆ **010/6587-1431.** www.middle8th.com. Meal for 2 ¥180–¥220. AE, MC, V. 11am–11pm. Metro: Tuanjiehu, Zhongguancun, or Yong'anli.

Chaoyang District (South)

EXPENSIVE

Aria ★★ MODERN EUROPEAN For years, this restaurant, located in the China World Hotel, has been successful for its location alone—but that changed recently when management hired an inventive chef by the name of Matthew McCool, who trained under Gordon Ramsey in London. Chef McCool has brought innovative and delicious touches to the menu, which features items like Wagyu beef with coffee and foie gras, goat cheese cannelloni, and deconstructed cheesecake with rum strawberries. Despite the wacky combinations, almost everything is a success, plus there's an endless wine list to make this place a real night on the town.

1 Jianguomenwai Dajie, China World Hotel. ✆ **010/6505-2266.** www.shangri-la.com. Meal for 2 ¥1,200–¥2,000. AE, DC, MC, V. Mon–Fri 11:30am–2:30pm; daily 5:30–10pm. Metro: Guomao.

Lan SICHUAN/FUSION This has become *the* place to be seen in Beijing among the trendy set. European Renaissance-style paintings hang on the wall and cabinets hold wacky items like stacks of canned tuna fish and Mao memorabilia. Designed by Phillip Starck, this flagship of a popular chain of Sichuan restaurants serves decent, if overpriced, dishes. Avoid the fusion fare at all costs, and stick to the basics like the kung pao chicken.

4/F, LG Twins Tower, Jianguomenwai Dajie Yi 12. ✆ **010/5109-6012.** www.lan-global.com. Meal for 2 ¥1,000–¥1,200. AE, DC, MC, V. 11am–11pm. Metro: Yong'anli.

MODERATE

Hatsune (Yinquan) ★ JAPANESE Hatsune offers sushi sacrilege via Northern California, with a list of innovative rolls long and elaborate enough to drive serious raw fish traditionalists crazy. But if you're not a purist, nearly every roll is a delight, particularly the 119 Roll—spicy-sweet with bright red tuna inside and out. Avoid the Beijing Roll, a roast duck and special sauce gimmick.

Guanghua Dong Lu, Heqiao Dasha C (4 blocks east of Kerry Centre, opposite Petro China building). ✆ **010/6581-3939.** Meal for 2 ¥300–¥400; Mon–Fri prix-fixe lunch ¥75. AE, DC, MC, V. 11:30am–2:30pm and 5:30–10pm.

Huangcheng Lao Ma HOT POT Upmarket hot pot sounds like a contradiction in terms, but Huangcheng Lao Ma makes it work—and work well. Set inside a huge multi-storied building with a tile-eave facade and relatively pleasant decor, the restaurant is almost constantly packed. The reason is their special ingredient, "Lao Ma's beef," a magical meat that stays tender no matter how long you boil it. Also popular are the large prawns, thrown live into the pot. The traditional broth is eye-watering spicy; order the split *yuanyang* pot with mild *wuyutang* (water world essence) broth in a separate compartment, or risk overheating your tongue.

Dongsanhuan Zhong Lu 24, Building B 2/F. ✆ **010/6779-8801.** Meal for 2 ¥200–¥300. MC, V. 11am–10pm. English menu. Metro:Shuangjing.

Mare (Da Pa Shi) ★★ SPANISH The huge range of tapas, large wine list, and comfortable dining room make us regulars at this elegant restaurant, decorated to look like a lovely Spanish living room. We love the chicken croquettes, mushroom risotto, and deep-fried baby squid. The chocolate molten cake, flanked by small scoops of hazelnut and vanilla ice cream, is our favorite dessert in town.

Guanghua Lu 12, E-Tower. ✆ **010/6595-4178.** Meal for 2 ¥400–¥500. AE, MC, V. Noon–2:30pm and 6–11pm. Metro: Guomao.

Noodle Loft (Mian Ku Shanxi Shiyi) SHANXI Unheard of outside China and rarely found in such stylish surroundings, Shanxi cuisine is noted for its vinegary flavors, liberal use of tomatoes, and large variety of interesting noodles. The Noodle Loft's interior is ultra-modern in orange and gray, with a large open kitchen featuring giant woks and steamers. An English menu makes ordering easy. Highlights include *yi ba zhua* (fried wheat cakes with chives), *qiao mian mao erduo* (cat's ear–shaped pasta stir-fried with chopped meat), and *suancai tudou* (vinegared potato slices).

Guangshun Bei Dajie, Fuma Dasha Building A Floor 2. ✆ **010/6774-9950.** Meal for 2 ¥120–¥200. AE, MC, V. 11am-10pm. Metro: Wangjing.

INEXPENSIVE

Yunteng Binguan YUNNAN Although Yunnan is one of the poorest provinces in China, the Yunnan provincial government (which owns the restaurant) has ingredients flown in several times a week. The decor exudes less warmth than a hospital waiting room, but friendly waitstaff compensate. The signature dish, *guoqiao mixian* (crossing-the-bridge rice noodles) is worth the trip in itself, a delicious blend of ham, chicken, chrysanthemum petals, chives, tofu skin, and a tiny egg, all blended at your table with rice noodles in chicken broth. *Zhusun qiguo Ji* (mushroom and mountain herbs chicken soup) is ideal comfort food, and *zhutong paigu* (spicy stewed pork with mint), has hearty flavors.

Dong Huashi Bei Li Dong Qu 7, Chongwen Qu (follow Jianguo Men Nan Dajie south for 10 min.; on the south side of flyover). ✆ **010/6713-6439.** Meal for 2 ¥160. V. 11:30am–11pm. Metro: Jianguo Men.

Yuxiang Renjia ★ SICHUAN Franchise food in the Chinese capital doesn't carry the same connotations of blandness it does in the United States. Yuxiang Renjia, a constantly crowded chain of restaurants with bright mock-village decor and a talent for producing authentic Sichuan fare, is a case in point. Dishes are slightly heavy on the oil but as flavorful as anything found outside Sichuan itself. The spicy familiar *gongbao jiding* (diced chicken with peanuts and hot peppers) is superb, putting American versions of "kung pao chicken" to shame. They also produce several worthwhile dishes you aren't likely to have tried before, including an interesting smoked duck *(zhangcha ya)* and the "stewed chicken with Grandma's sauce" *(laoganma shao ji)*. Waitstaff sometimes get overwhelmed, and the impressive decor isn't matched by the hygiene.

Chaoyang Men Wai Dajie 20 (on 5th floor of Lianhe Dasha, behind Foreign Ministry Building). ✆ **010/6588-3841.** www.yuxiangrenjia.com (Chinese only). Meal for 2 ¥200. AE, DC, MC, V. 10am–2pm and 5–9:30pm. Metro: Chaoyang Men.

Back Lakes & Dong Cheng

EXPENSIVE

Black Sesame Kitchen (Heizhima Chufang) ★ HOME-STYLE Full disclosure: Jen Lin-Liu, a co-author of this Frommer's edition, is the owner of this cooking school and private kitchen. Located in a residential courtyard just off of the popular alley Nan Luogu Xiang, the kitchen makes home-style Beijing and Sichuan cuisine, with an emphasis on fresh, quality ingredients (the chefs shop daily and stir-fry with non-GM cooking oil, and MSG is banned). The two-room restaurant features a lofty eat-in kitchen where guests can watch all the cooking action, plus a separate lounge for a more relaxed experience. The kitchen's signature dishes include pan-fried pork and pumpkin dumplings, fried shiitake mushrooms seasoned with bamboo shoots and coriander, and cashew kung pao chicken. There's no menu, but diners can inform the kitchen ahead of time if they have any particular dietary preferences or restrictions. The kitchen runs hands-on cooking classes on Thursday and Saturdays, and communal open dinners on Friday evenings seat up to 20 guests; otherwise, you may book classes or dinners daily by private appointment. Be sure to reserve early as the kitchen sometimes books several weeks in advance.

3 Black Sesame Hutong (just off of Nanluoguxiang). ✆ **0/1369-147-4408.** www.blacksesamekitchen.com. Reservations necessary. Meal for 2 ¥600. No credit cards. Open for classes Thurs 11am–1:30pm and Sat 1–4pm; dinner Fri 7–10pm. Also available for private bookings. Metro: Gulou or Beixinqiao.

MODERATE

Dali Courtyard (Da Li) ★★ YUNNAN Romance, romance! Old jazz tunes play in this traditional Chinese courtyard decorated with coal furnaces and Art Deco furniture. There's no menu—the chef serves up a set meal in courses—so it's perfect for couples or small groups who want to try a range of southwestern Chinese dishes. Items include papaya salad, grilled fish, and stir-fried chicken—all fairly light and healthy. The restaurant is perfect for people who don't like the stress of ordering and would prefer to concentrate on the ambience. The food is perfectly fine, but nothing will knock you out of the courtyard.

Gulou Dong Dajie, Xiaojingchang Hutong 67. ✆ **010/8404-1430.** www.dalicourtyard.com. Lunch ¥200; set dinner ¥128–¥320. AE, MC, V. 11am–1:30pm and 5–10pm. Metro: Beixinqiao.

INEXPENSIVE

Huajia Yiyuan HOME-STYLE The chef-owner behind this popular courtyard restaurant claims to have created a new Chinese supercuisine, assembled from the best of the country's regional cooking. Whether Huacai (his name for the cuisine) will ever spread beyond Beijing remains to be seen, but his long menu is one of the city's most impressive. The new restaurant is slightly less raucous than the recently demolished original, but locals still crowd around tables at night to devour heaped plates of spicy crayfish *(mala longxia)* and drink green "good for health" beer. Try the *larou douya juanbing,* a mix of spicy bacon and bean sprouts in pancakes roast duck–style.

Dongzhi Men Nei Dajie 235. ✆ **010/6403-0677.** Meal for 2 ¥300–¥400. AE, MC, V. 10:30am–4am. Metro: Beixinqiao.

Jiumen Xiao Chi (Nine Gate Snacks) ★ ☺ BEIJING The story behind this street snack emporium is almost better than the food: When a neighborhood near Tian'anmen Square was being demolished several years ago, a number of street snack vendors, some of whom made specialties passed down for generations, were forced to move. They relocated to this sprawling space near Houhai Lake, which has become a food court dedicated to Beijing's disappearing snacks. Many of the dishes like tripe soup and fermented soybean drink may not inspire Western appetites, but there are a few less exotic gems, like steamed dumplings and various rice flour pastries. Toy vendors and traditional comedic performances on a stage will keep the kids entertained.

Xiaoyou Hutong 1. ✆ **010/6402-5858.** Meal for 2 ¥100. No credit cards. 10am–10pm. Metro: Jishuitan.

Untraditional Dining in a Traditional Neighborhood

For an area brimming with historic buildings and Chinese culture, the dining options in the Back Lakes are surprisingly limited and some of the best draws are actually international. You might even see the occasional hot dog or bratwurst stand in the hutongs...it's all part of the growing international influence in even the most traditional of neighborhoods. If you're in the area and hunger strikes, there are decent international options, including **Luce** (✆ 010/8402-4417; 138 Jiu Gulou Da Jie) for Italian fare and drinks at reasonable prices in a hip, modern dining space; **Mirch Masala** (✆ 010/6406-4347; 1 Jingyang Hutong; www.masalabj.com) serving fairly authentic Indian cuisine; **Hutong Pizza** (✆ 010/8322-8916; 9 Yindingqiao Hutong) for square-shaped pies with a variety of toppings; **Saveurs de Coree** (✆ 010/5741-5753; 128-1 Xiang Er Hutong; www.saveursdecoree.com.cn) for MSG-free Korean bibimbap and roasted meats; and **Amigo** (✆ 010/8403-3981; 95 Guluo Dong Dajie) for passable burritos and tacos. None of the cuisine is award-winning, but they all make a novel night out on the town.

Kong Yiji Jiudian ★ HUAIYANG This popular restaurant was named for the alcoholic scholar-bum protagonist of a short story by Lu Xun, the father of modern Chinese literature. It offers an enjoyable dining experience, although it is somewhat weighed down by its own popularity. Service is not what it once was. A small bamboo forest leads to a traditional space outfitted with calligraphy scrolls, traditional bookshelves, and other trappings of Chinese scholarship. The menu, written vertically in the old style, features *mizhi luyu,* a whole fish deep-fried then broiled in tin foil with onions in a slightly sweet sauce, and the *youtiao niurou,* savory slices of beef mixed with pieces of fried dough. Nearly everyone orders a small pot of *Dongpo rou,* extremely tender braised fatty pork swimming in savory juice, and a plate of *huixiang dou,* anise-flavored beans. Fans of Lu's story will appreciate the wide selection of *huangjiu,* a sweet "yellow" rice wine aged several years sipped from a special ceramic warming cup.

Desheng Men Nei Dajie (next to the octagonal Teahouse of Family Fu on the northwest bank of Hou Hai). ✆ **010/6618-4917.** No reservations. Meal for 2 ¥200–¥240. AE, DC, MC, V. 10am–2pm and 5–10pm. Metro: Jishuitan.

Western Beijing & Yayun Cun

VERY EXPENSIVE

The Aman Grill (Anman Canting) ★★ STEAKHOUSE Far from the center of town is this gorgeous steakhouse located at the Aman Resort. If you happen to be at Summer Palace or any of Beijing's northwestern tourist sites, this is well worth a visit, especially if you're in the mood for a luxurious, non-Chinese meal. The dining room with high, wooden-beamed ceilings, orchids, and lounge seats decorated with silk pillows feels elegant and subtly Chinese. Beyond the imported T-bone and rib-eye steaks that the restaurant specializes in, the kitchen also makes delicious starters and side dishes, from an enticing pork belly and scallop appetizer lightly seasoned with curry powder to a comforting scalloped bacon and cheese potatoes. A Bible-size wine list with descriptions of all selections completes the fine package.

15 Gongmenqian St., Aman Beijing at the Summer Palace (p. 104). ✆ **010/5987-9999.** Meal for 2 ¥1,200. AE, DC, MC, V. 7–10:30am, noon–2pm, and 4–10pm.

Cepe (Yiwei Xuan) ★★ ITALIAN This restaurant serves the best upscale Italian fare in the city. The waitstaff wear sleek pinstripe suits and are incredibly attentive, zipping over to your table at the merest hint of a frown or inquiring look. This is a place to indulge in a leisurely meal. You must order a pasta dish, as the noodles are freshly made each morning. The decor is contemporary, with an open kitchen housed behind a giant silk screen of a portobello mushroom. There are romantic, semi-private nooks with curtains and leather chaise lounges alongside the back wall. Jazz music and, every now and then, an upbeat Laura Pausini song plays in the background.

Jinchengfang Dong Jie 1 (inside Ritz Carlton, Financial St., p. 81). ✆ **010/6601-6666.** Dinner for 2 ¥600–¥1,500. AE, MC, V. 11:30am–3pm and 6–11pm. Metro: Fuxing Men.

MODERATE

Zhang Sheng Ji Jiudian ★★ HUAIYANG It may lack the ambience of Kong Yiji Jiulou, but this branch of Hangzhou's most successful restaurant delivers more consistent Huaiyang fare. Service is no-fuss, and there's a pleasing amount of space between tables and a high ceiling. For starters, try the flavorful *jiuxiang yugan* (dried fish in wine sauce). The recently added *mati niuliu* (stir-fried beef with broccoli, water chestnuts, and tofu rolls) is excellent, and nearly every table carries the signature *sungan laoya bao* (stewed duck with dried bamboo shoots and ham) which has complex, hearty flavors. You can explore the English picture menu without trepidation; Huaiyang cuisine is delicately spiced, and largely eschews endangered species.

Bei San Huan, Zhejiang Dasha (west of Anzhen Qiao on N. Third Ring Rd.). ✆ **010/6442-0006.** Meal for 2 ¥200. AE, MC, V. 11am–2pm and 5–9pm. Metro: Hepingxiqiao.

INEXPENSIVE

Baihe Sushi (Lily Vegetarian Restaurant) ★★ VEGETARIAN Chinese vegetarian restaurants often get bogged down torturing meaty flavors out of gluten, but at this ultraclean and friendly restaurant you'll find delectable dishes with high-quality ingredients. Start with the hearty *shanyao geng* (yam broth with mushrooms) and the slightly fruity *liangban zi lusun* (purple asparagus salad), followed by *ruyi haitai juan* (vegetarian sushi rolls) and the excellent *huangdi sun shao wanzi* (imperial bamboo shoots and vegetarian meatballs). When in season, their vegetables are sourced from an organic farm west of Beijing, so ask if they have any organic vegetables *(youji shucai)*. Monks dine for free, so you're likely to meet a few.

A23 Caoyuan Hutong, 100m (328 ft.) north of Dongzhimen Bei Xiao Jie. ✆ **010/6405-2082.** Meal for 2 ¥80–¥140. V. 10am–9pm. Metro: Dongzhimen.

Yunnan Jin Kongque Dehong Daiwei Canguan YUNNAN The street north of the Minorities University (Minzu Daxue) was once a claustrophobic *hutong* with Uighur, Korean, and Dai restaurants. Chaps who addressed you as "Hashish" are gone, along with most of the restaurants. But this holy grail of Dai cuisine remains, offering a superb synthesis of Thai and Chinese fare. Mirrors, tiled floors, and predictable bamboo furnishings lend it a sterile feel, but the gracious waitstaff more than compensates. Must-devour dishes include crispy *tudou qiu* (deep-fried potato balls with chili sauce), delectable *boluo fan* (pineapple rice), *zhutong zhurou* (steamed pork with coriander), *zhutong ji* (chicken soup), and *zha xiangjiao* (deep-fried banana) for dessert. Wash it all down with sweet rice wine *(mi jiu)*, served in a bamboo cup.

Minzu Daxue Bei Lu 1 (cross footbridge, head right, take the 1st street on your left). ✆ **010/6893-2030.** Meal for 2 ¥80–¥100. No credit cards. 11am–9:15pm. Bus: 205 or 106 to Weigong Cun from Xi Zhi Men metro.

Cafes & Teahouses

Café Zarah, 42 Gulou Dong Dajie (✆ **010/8403-9807;** www.cafezarah.com) is our favorite independent cafe. It has the best iced lattes in the city, reliable free Wi-Fi, and a cozy space with exposed wood beams and rotating art exhibited on the walls. Curl up with a book at the spacious The Bookworm (Lao Shu Chong)—better yet, there's no need to bring your own book. This Sanlitun fixture has a library of 6,000 English-language titles. They also have free Wi-Fi (Nan Sanlitun Lu Si Lou, behind Pacific Century shopping center, near The Loft; ✆ **010/6586-9507**). **Sculpting in Time (Diaoke Shiguang),** www.sitcoffee.com, which started out as a single, cozy cafe near Peking University, is aiming to become a homegrown version of Starbucks, with many locations around town including the Beijing Institute of Technology, Weigongcun Xi Kou 7, Ligong Daxue Nan Men (✆ **010/6894-6825;** 8am–1am), just to the left of the university's south gate; the Lido area (2B Jiangtai Lu; ✆ **010/5135-8108;** 7:30am–noon) and a new location just east of the National Art Museum on Meishuguan Hou Jie. All serve adequate coffee, sandwiches, and pasta and have Wi-Fi. **The Teahouse of Family Fu (Cha Jia Fu),** located at Hou Hai Nan An, next to Kong Yiji (✆ **010/6657-1588**), is a unique and quiet teahouse, with semiprivate rooms. It's open from 10am to midnight. If you must, there is also **Starbucks,** which arrived at the end of the 1990s and quickly spread to all the places Beijing's wealthy and/or hip congregate, including next to the Friendship Store, in the China World Trade Center, at the Oriental Plaza, and many other locations.

EXPLORING BEIJING

No other city in China, and few other cities in the world, offers so many must-see attractions, or such a likelihood of missed opportunity. It is technically possible to see the big names—the Forbidden City, Temple of Heaven, Summer Palace, and Great Wall—in as little as 3 days, but you'll need at least a week to get any feel for the city. People spend years here and still fail to see everything they should.

Note: Most major sights now charge admission according to the season. The summer high season officially runs from April 1 to October 31 and the winter low season from November 1 to March 31.

Tours

Several companies offer guided group tours of Beijing for English-speakers, but these are overpriced, often incomplete, and best thought of as an emergency measure when time is short. The most popular operators are **BTG Travel** (✆ **010/8563-9959**) and **CITS Travel Service** (✆ **010/6522-2991**), and both have offices scattered through the four- and five-star hotels. City-highlight tours by air-conditioned bus typically cost around ¥300 per person for a half-day and around ¥500 for a full day with a mediocre lunch. Instead, consider the **Chinese Culture Club** (✆ **010/8462-2081;** www.chinesecultureclub.org), which organizes outings, lectures, and film screenings for expatriates with an interest in Chinese culture. Events are often led by prominent lecturers, discussions go well beyond the "5,000 years of history" palaver that CITS will subject you to, and they are constantly on the lookout for new attractions. A smaller operation with a similar philosophy is **Cycle China** (✆ **010/6402-5653;** www.cyclechina.com).

Beijing Attractions

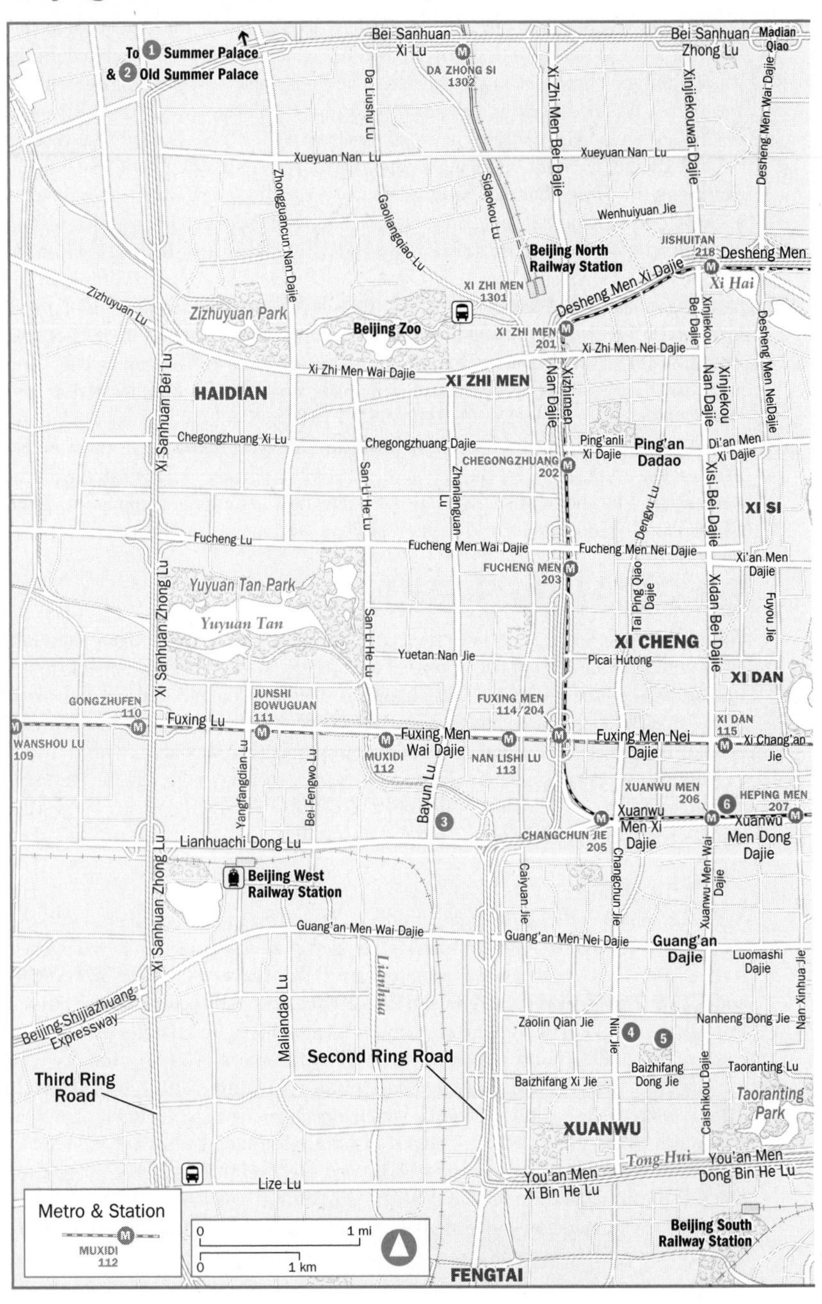

Third Ring Road
Second Ring Road
DONG ZHI MEN
DONG CHENG
DONG SI
DONG DAN
CHAOYANG
CHONGWEN
QIAN MEN
Forbidden City
Tian'an Men Square
Museums of History/ Chinese Revolution
Chairman Mao Memorial Hall
Drum & Bell Towers
Ancient Observatory
Beijing Railway Station
Workers' Stadium
Silk Market
Panjiayuan Market
Temple of Heaven Park
Qinian Dian
Huan Qiu
Ditan Park
Ritan Park
Longtan Park
Chaoyang Park
Jing Shan Park
Bei Hai Park
Tuanjie Hu
To Yayun Cun
Airport Expressway
Beijing-Tianjin Expressway
Bus Station
Bank
Information
Post Office
Rail Station
PSB Public-Security Visas

Beijing Attractions Key

Ancient Observatory **23**
(Gù Guānxiàng Tái)
故观象台

Báiyún Guàn (White Cloud Temple) **3**
白云观

Bei Hăi Park (Bei Hăi Gōngyuán) **8**
北海公园

Chairman Mao's Mausoleum **13**
(Mao Zhŭxi Jìniàn Guăn)
毛主席纪念馆

China National Art Gallery **17**
(Zhōngguó Mĕishùguăn)
中国美术馆

Dōngyuè Miào **24**
东岳庙

Făyuán Sì
(Source of Dharma Temple) **5**
法原寺

Forbidden City (Gù Gōng) **11**
故宫

Former Residence of Lao Shĕ **16**
(Lăo Shĕ Jìnìanguăn)
老舍纪念馆

Great Hall of the People **10**
(Rénmín Dàhùi Táng)
人民大会堂

Gŭdài Jiànzhù Bówùguăn **18**
(Museum of Ancient Architecture)
古代建筑博物馆

Guó Zĭ Jiàn and Kŏng Miáo **20**
国子监和北京孔庙

Jĭng Shān Park (Jĭng Shān Gōngyuán) **9**
景山公园

Míng Chéng Qiáng Gōngyuán **22**
(Míng City Wall Park)
明城墙公园

National Museum of China **15**
(Guójiā Bówùguăn)
国家博物馆

Ox Street Mosque (Niú Jiē Qīngzhēnsì) **4**
牛街清真寺

Prince Gong's Mansion **7**
(Gŏng Wángfŭ Huāyuán)
恭王府花园

Qián Mén **14**
前门

Summer Palace (Yíhé Yuán) **1**
颐和园

South Cathedral (Nán Táng) **6**
南堂

Temple of Heaven (Tiān Tán) **19**
天坛

Tiān'an Mén **12**
(Gate of Heavenly Peace)
天安门

Yōnghé Gōng (Lama Temple) **21**
雍和宫

Yuán Míng Yuán **2**
(Old Summer Palace)
圆明园

OTHER ATTRACTIONS (not on map)

Aòlínpĭkè Gōngyuán
(Olympic Park)
奥林匹克公园

Eastern Qīng Tombs
(Qīng Dōng Líng)
青东陵

Factory 798
(Qījiŭbā Gōngchăng)
798 工场

Great Wall at Mùtiányù
(Mùtiányù Chángchéng)
幕田峪长城

Great Wall at Sīmătái
(Sīmătái Chángchéng)
司马台长城

Jiétái Sì (Temple of the
Ordination Platform)
结台寺

Míng Tombs (Shísāng Líng)
十三陵

Tánzhè Sí
(Temple of the Pool and Wild Mulberry)
潭柘寺

Western Qīng Tombs (Qīng Xī Líng)
青西陵

The Forbidden City (Gu Gong; 故宫)

The universally accepted symbol for the length and grandeur of Chinese civilization is undoubtedly the Great Wall, but the Forbidden City is more immediately impressive. A 720,000-sq.-m (7.75-million-sq.-ft.) complex of red-walled buildings and pavilions topped by a sea of glazed vermilion tile, it dwarfs nearby Tian'an Men Square and is by far the largest and most intricate imperial palace in China. The palace receives more visitors than any other attraction in the country (more than seven million a year, according to the Chinese government), and has been praised in Western travel literature ever since the first Europeans laid eyes on it in the late 1500s. Despite the flood of superlatives and exaggerated statistics that inevitably go into its description, it is impervious to an excess of hype and is large and compelling enough to draw repeat visits from even the most jaded travelers. Make more time for it than you think you'll need.

ESSENTIALS

The palace, most commonly referred to in Chinese as Gu Gong (short for Palace Museum), is on the north side of Tian'an Men Square across Chang'an Dajie (**© 010/6513-2255;** www.dpm.org.cn). It is best approached on foot or via metro (Tian'an Men East), as taxis are not allowed to stop in front. The palace is open from 8:30am to 5pm during summer and from 8:30am to 4:30pm in winter. Regular admission *(men piao)* in summer costs ¥60, dropping to ¥40 in winter; last tickets are sold 1 hour before the doors close. Various exhibition halls and gardens inside the palace charge an additional ¥10. All-inclusive tickets *(lian piao)* have been discontinued, perhaps in an effort to increase revenues (see "The Big Makeover," below), but it's always possible these will be reinstated.

Enter through the Wu Men (Meridian Gate), a short walk north of Chang'an Dajie via Tian'an Men (see below). Ticket counters are clearly marked on either side as you approach. ***Tip:*** If you have a little more time, it is highly recommended that you approach the entrance at Wu Men (Meridian Gate) via Tai Miao to the east, and avoid the gauntlet of touts and souvenir stalls. **Audio tours** in several languages, including English (¥40 plus ¥500 deposit), are available at the gate itself, through the door to the right. Those looking to spend more money can hire **tour guides** with varying degrees of English fluency on the other side of the gate (¥200 for a 1-hr. tour, ¥300 for 1½ hr., ¥400 for 2½ hr.). The tour guide booth also rents **wheelchairs** and **strollers** free of charge, with a ¥500 deposit. ***Note:*** Only the central route through the palace is wheelchair accessible, and steeply so.

BACKGROUND & LAYOUT

Sourcing of materials for the original palace buildings began in 1406, during the reign of the Yongle emperor, and construction was completed in 1420. Much of it was designed by a eunuch from Annam, Nguyen An. Without improvements to the Grand Canal, construction would have been impossible—timber came from as far away as Sichuan, and logs took up to 4 years to reach the capital. The Yuan palace was demolished to make way for the Forbidden City, but the lakes excavated during the Jin (1122–1215) were retained and expanded. Between 1420 and 1923, the palace was home to 24 emperors of the Ming and Qing dynasties. The last was Aisin-Gioro Puyi (see Dongbei, p. 147), who abdicated in 1912 but lived in the palace until 1924.

The Forbidden City is arranged along the compass points, with most major halls opening to the south (the direction associated with imperial rule). Farthest south and

THE BIG makeover

An immense **$75-million renovation of the Forbidden City,** the largest in 90 years, will be completed by 2020. Work has already been completed on the **Wuying Dian (Hall of Valiance and Heroism)** in the southwest corner of the palace, the **Cining Huayuan (Garden of Love and Tranquility)** next to the Taihe Dian, the **Cining Gong (the Palace of Compassion and Tranquility),** and the **Shoukang Gong (the Palace of Longevity and Good Health)**. Plans also call for the construction of new temperature-controlled buildings to house and exhibit what is claimed to be a collection of **930,000 Ming and Qing imperial relics,** most now stored underground.

On the other side of the palace, in the northern section of the Ningshou Gong Huayuan, a remarkable building is undergoing restoration with assistance from the World Cultural Heritage Foundation. Qianlong commissioned the European Jesuit painters in his employ to create large-scale *trompe l'oeil* paintings, which were used in the Forbidden City as well as in the Yuan Ming Yuan (p. 109). **Juanqin Zhai,** an elaborately constructed private opera house, houses the best remaining examples of these paintings, including a stunning image of a wisteria trellis, almost certainly painted by Italian master Castiglione.

in the center is the perfectly symmetrical **outer court,** dominated by the immense ceremonial halls where the emperor conducted official business. Beyond the outer court and on both sides is the **inner court,** a series of smaller buildings and gardens that served as living quarters.

The palace has been ransacked and parts destroyed by fire several times over the centuries, so most of the existing buildings date from the Qing rather than the Ming. Many of the roofs are trimmed in blue or green tile, which some scholars say reminded the Qing's Manchu rulers of the grasslands and fertile fields they had left behind. Only half of the complex is open to visitors (expected to increase to 70% after repairs are completed in 2020; see "The Big Makeover," above), but this still leaves plenty to see.

Tian'an Men (Gate of Heavenly Peace) ★★ This gate is the largest in what was once known as the Imperial City and the most emblematic of Chinese government grandeur. Above the central door, once reserved almost exclusively for the emperor, now hangs the famous **portrait of Mao,** flanked by inscriptions that read: LONG LIVE THE PEOPLE'S REPUBLIC OF CHINA (left) and LONG LIVE THE GREAT UNITY OF THE PEOPLES OF THE WORLD (right). Mao declared the founding of the People's Republic from atop the gate on October 1, 1949. There is no charge to walk through the gate, but tickets are required if you want to ascend to **the upper platform** for worthwhile views of Tian'an Men Square. The ticket office is in the second of two small red shacks, on the left after you pass through. ***Tip:*** If you're traveling in a group of two or more, split up and have one person line up to buy tickets and the other queue to check bags; you'll save yourselves both time and frustration.

North of Tian'an Men Square; ticket office to left as you enter. Admission ¥15. 8am–5pm, last ticket sold at 4:30pm. Mandatory bag storage for ¥2–¥6 behind and to left of ticket booth; cameras allowed.

The Outer Court The intimidating **Wu Men (Meridian Gate),** built in 1420 and last restored in 1801, is the actual entrance to the Forbidden City. The emperor would come here to receive prisoners of war, issue proclamations, and supervise the punishment of troublesome officials. Beyond the gate, across a vast stone-paved courtyard bisected by the balustraded Jin Shui (Golden River), is the **Taihe Men (Gate of Supreme Harmony),** which marks the official beginning of the outer court.

The first of the outer courts' "Three Great Halls" (San Da Dian) is the **Taihe Dian (Hall of Supreme Harmony) ★**. Located beyond the Taihe Men and across an even grander stone courtyard, it is an imposing double-roofed structure mounted atop a three-tiered marble terrace with elaborately carved balustrades. This is the largest wooden hall in China, and the most elaborate and prestigious of the palaces' throne halls; it was therefore rarely used. Emperors came here to mark the new year and winter solstice.

Immediately behind it is the **Zhonghe Dian (Hall of Perfect Harmony),** and farther on lies the **Baohe Dian (Hall of Preserving Harmony).** This last hall, supported by only a few columns, is where the highest levels of imperial examinations were held. At the rear of the hall is a carved marble slab weighing over 200 tons; 20,000 men supposedly spent 28 days dragging it to this position from a mountain roughly 50km (31 miles) away.

The Inner Court Only the emperor, his family, his concubines, and the palace eunuchs (who numbered 1,500 at the end of the Qing dynasty) were allowed in this section, sometimes described as the truly forbidden city. It begins with the **Qianqing Men (Gate of Heavenly Purity),** directly north of the Baohe Dian, beyond which are three palaces designed to mirror the three halls of the outer court.

The first of these is the **Qianqing Gong (Palace of Heavenly Purity),** where the emperors lived until Yongzheng decided to move to another part of the city in the 1720s. Beyond are the rather boring **Jiaotai Dian (Hall of Union),** containing the throne of the empress; and the rather more interesting **Kunning Gong (Palace of Earthly Tranquillity),** a Manchu-style bed chamber where a nervous Puyi (China's last emperor) was expected to spend his wedding night before he fled to more comfortable rooms elsewhere.

At the rear of the inner court is the elaborate **Yu Huayuan (Imperial Garden) ★**, a marvelous scattering of ancient conifers, rockeries, and pavilions said to be largely unchanged since it was built in the Ming dynasty. Puyi's famous British tutor, Reginald Fleming Johnston, lived in the **Yangxin Zhai,** the first building on the west side of the garden (now a tea shop).

From behind the mountain, you can exit the palace through the **Shenwu Men (Gate of Martial Spirit)** and continue on to Jing Shan and/or Bei Hai Park. Those with time to spare, however, should explore less-visited sections on either side of the central path.

Western Axis Most of this area is in a state of heavy disrepair, but a few buildings have been restored and are open to visitors. Most notable is the **Yangxin Dian (Hall of Mental Cultivation),** southwest of the Imperial Garden. The reviled Empress Dowager Cixi, who ruled China for much of the late Qing period, made decisions on behalf of her infant nephew Guangxu from behind a screen in the east room. This is also where emperors lived after Yongzheng moved out of the Qianqing Gong.

Eastern Axis ★ This side tends to be peaceful and quiet even when other sections are teeming. Entrance costs ¥10 and requires purchase of essentially useless over-shoe slippers for ¥2. The most convenient ticket booth is a 5-minute walk southwest of the Qianqing Men, opposite the **Jiulong Bi (Nine Dragon Screen),** a 3.5m-high (12-ft.) wall covered in striking glazed-tile dragons depicted frolicking above a frothing sea.

The Qing dynasty Qianlong emperor (reign 1736–95) abdicated at the age of 85, and this section was built for his retirement, although he never really moved in, continuing to "mentor" his son while living in the Yangxin Dian, a practice later adopted by Empress Dowager Cixi, who also partially took up residence here in 1894. One of the highlights here is the secluded **Ningshou Gong Huayuan ★★★**, behind the Zhenbao Guan (Hall of Jewelry) north of the ticket booth. The Qianlong emperor composed poems and drank from cups of wine he floated in a snakelike water-filled trough carved in the floor of the main pavilion. Qianlong's personal compendium of verse ran to a modest 50,000 poems; he was seldom short of words. East of the garden is the **Changyin Ge,** sometimes called Cixi's Theater, an elaborate three-tiered structure with trapdoors and hidden passageways to allow movement between stages. In the far northeastern corner is the **Zhenfei Jing (Well of the Pearl Concubine),** a narrow hole covered by a large circle of stone, slightly askance. The Pearl Concubine, one of the Guangxu emperor's favorites, was 25 when Cixi had her stuffed down the well as they were fleeing in the aftermath of the Boxer Rebellion. According to most accounts, Cixi was miffed at the girl's insistence that Guangxu stay and take responsibility for the imperial family's support of the Boxers.

Also worth seeing is the **Hall of Clocks (Zhongbiao Guan),** a collection of elaborate timepieces, many of them gifts to the emperors from European envoys. The exhibit costs ¥10 and at press time was temporarily relocated in a hall to the right (east) of the Baohe Dian while the original Hall of Clocks is restored.

Tian'an Men Square (Tian'an Men Guangchang; 天安门广场)

This is the world's largest public square, the size of 90 American football fields (40 hectares/99 acres), with standing room for 300,000. It is surrounded by the Forbidden City to the north, the Great Hall of the People to the west, and the museums of Chinese History and Chinese Revolution to the east. In the center of the square stands the **Monument to the People's Heroes (Renmin Yingxiong Jinian Bei),** a 37m (124-ft.) granite obelisk engraved with scenes from famous uprisings and bearing a central inscription (in Mao's handwriting): THE PEOPLE'S HEROES ARE IMMORTAL.

The area on which the obelisk stands was originally occupied by the **Imperial Way**—a central road that stretched from the Gate of Heavenly Peace south to Qian Men, the still extant main entrance to the Tartar City (see below). This road, lined on either side with imperial government ministries, was the site of the pivotal May Fourth movement (1919), in which thousands of university students gathered to protest the weakness and corruption of China's then Republican government. Mao ordered destruction of the old ministries and paved over the rubble in 1959, replacing them with the vast but largely empty **Great Hall of the People** to the west and the equally vast but unimpressive **museums** to the east, as part of a spate of construction to celebrate 10 years of Communist rule. But the site has remained a magnet for politically charged assemblies. The most famous of these was the gathering of

student prodemocracy protestors in late spring of 1989. That movement and the government's violent suppression of it still define the square in most minds, Chinese as well as foreign. All physical traces of the crackdown disappeared after the square received a face-lift in 1999, just in time to celebrate the 50th anniversary of the founding of the People's Republic, but reminders remain in the stiff-backed soldiers and video cameras since put in place to ensure order is maintained.

There isn't much to do in the square, but early risers can line up in front of Tian'an Men at sunrise to watch the **flag-raising ceremony,** a unique suffocation-in-the-throng experience on National Day (Oct 1), when what seems like the entire Chinese population arrives to jostle for the best view.

Chairman Mao's Mausoleum (Mao Zhuxi Jinian Guan) A trip here is one of the eeriest experiences in Beijing. The decision to preserve Mao's body was made hours after his death in 1976. Panicked and inexperienced, his doctors reportedly pumped him so full of formaldehyde that his face and body swelled almost beyond recognition. They drained the corpse and managed to get it back into acceptable shape, but they also created a wax model of the Great Helmsman just in case. There's no telling which version is on display at any given time. The mausoleum itself was built in 1977, near the center of Tian'an Men Square. However much Mao may be mocked outside his tomb (earnest arguments about whether he was 70% right or 60% right are perhaps the biggest joke), he still commands a terrifying sort of respect inside it. This is not quite the kitsch experience some expect. The tour is free and fast, with no stopping or photos and no bags allowed inside.

South end of Tian'an Men Square. ✆ **010/6513-2277.** Free admission. Tues–Sun 8am–noon. Bag storage across the street, directly west, ¥14. Metro: Qian Men.

Qian Men The phrase Qian Men (Front Gate) is actually a reference to two separate towers on the south side of the square that together formed the main entrance to the Tartar (or Inner) City. The southernmost Arrow Tower (Jian Lou) is no longer open to the public. You can, however, still climb the interior of the rear building (Zhengyang Men), where a photo exhibition depicts life in Beijing's pre-1949 markets, temples, and *hutong*.

Tian'an Men Square. ✆ **010/6511-8101.** Admission ¥20. 8:30am–4pm. Metro: Qian Men.

National Centre for the Performing Arts (Guojia Da Juyuan) The controversial National Theatre, designed by Paul Andreu, is due to open west of the Great Hall of the People within the lifetime of this book. Andreu was awarded the project in 2000, and Beijingers have nicknamed it *jidanke'r* (the Eggshell). Although the project has been downsized, it still features a dazzling titanium-and-glass dome perched on a lake, and encasing three auditoriums. Patrons descend on escalators through the waters of the lake. Performances usually start at 6pm.

Xi Chang'an Jie (west of Tian'an Men Sq. and the Great Hall of the People). Metro: Tian'an Men West.

The Temple of Heaven (Tian Tan; 天坛)

At the same time Yongle built the Forbidden City, he also oversaw construction of this enormous park and altar to heaven to the south. Each winter solstice, the Ming and Qing emperors would lead a procession here to perform rites and make sacrifices designed to promote the next year's crops and curry favor from heaven for the general health of the empire. The park is square (symbolizing Earth) in the south and rounded (Heaven) in the north.

ESSENTIALS

Temple of Heaven Park (Tian Tan Gongyuan; ✆ **010/6702-8866**) is south of Tian'an Men Square, on the east side of Qian Men Dajie. It's open from 6am to 8pm (may close earlier in winter, depending on weather and staff decisions), but the ticket offices and major sights are only open from 8am to 5:30pm, last ticket sold at 4pm. All-inclusive tickets *(lian piao)* cost ¥35 (¥30 in winter); simple park admission costs ¥15. The east gate *(dong men)* is easily accessed by public transport; take the no. 39, 106, or 110 bus from just north of the Chongwen Men metro stop to Fahua Si. However, the best approach is from the south gate *(nan men)*, the natural starting point for a walk that culminates in the magnificent Hall of Prayer for Good Harvests.

HIGHLIGHTS

Circular Altar (Yuan Qiu) This three-tiered marble terrace is the first major structure you'll see if you're coming from the south. It was built in 1530 and enlarged in 1749, with all of its stones and balustrades organized in multiples of nine (considered a lucky number by northern Chinese).

Imperial Vault of Heaven (Huang Qiong Yu) Directly north of the Circular Altar, this smaller version of the Hall of Prayer was built to store ceremonial stone tablets. The vault is surrounded by the circular **Echo Wall (Huiyin Bi).** In years past, when crowds were smaller and before the railing was installed, it was possible for two people on opposite sides of the enclosure to send whispered messages to each other along the wall with remarkable clarity.

Hall of Prayer for Good Harvests (Qinian Dian) ★★ This circular wooden hall, with its triple-eaved cylindrical blue-tiled roof, is perhaps the most recognizable emblem of Chinese imperial architecture outside the Forbidden City. Completed in 1420, the original hall burned to the ground in 1889, but a near-perfect replica (this one) was built the following year. It stands 38m (125 ft.) high and is 29m (98 ft.) in diameter, and is constructed without a single nail. The 28 massive pillars inside, made of fir imported from Oregon, are arranged to symbolize divisions of time: The central 4 represent the seasons, the next 12 represent the months of the year, and the outer 12 represent traditional divisions of a single day. The hall's most striking feature is its ceiling, a kaleidoscope of intricate painted brackets and gilded panels.

The Summer Palace (Yihe Yuan; 颐和园)

This expanse of elaborate Qing-style pavilions, bridges, walkways, and gardens, scattered along the shores of immense Kunming Lake, is the grandest imperial playground in China; it was constructed from 1749 to 1764. Between 1860 and 1903, it was twice leveled by foreign armies and then rebuilt. The palace is most often associated with the Empress Dowager Cixi, who made it her full-time residence.

ESSENTIALS

The **Summer Palace** (✆ **010/6288-1144**) is located 12km (7 miles) northwest of the city center in Haidian. Take **bus no. 726** from just west of Wudaokou light rail station; or take a 30- to 40-minute **taxi** ride for about ¥60 from the center of town. A more pleasant option is to travel here by **boat** along the renovated canal system; slightly rusty "imperial yachts" leave from the Beizhan Houhu Matou (✆ **010/8836-3576**), behind the Beijing Exhibition Center just south of the Beijing Aquarium (10am–4pm hourly, or every 30 min. during student summer holidays; 50-min. trip;

¥40 one-way; ¥70 round-trip; ¥100 includes round-trip travel and the entrance ticket), docking at Nan Ruyi Men in the south of the park. The gates open at 6am; no tickets are sold after 5:30pm in summer and 5pm in winter. Admission is ¥30 for entry to the grounds or ¥60 for the all-inclusive *lian piao,* reduced to ¥20 and ¥50, respectively, in winter (Nov–Mar). The most convenient entrance is Dong Gong Men (East Gate). Go early and allow at least 4 hours for touring on your own. Overpriced **imperial-style food** in a pleasant setting is available at the Tingli Guan Restaurant, at the western end of the Long Corridor. Spots around the lake are perfect for picnics, and Kunming Lake is ideal for skating in the depths of winter.

EXPLORING THE SUMMER PALACE

This park covers roughly 290 hectares (716 acres), with **Kunming Lake** in the south and **Longevity Hill (Wanshou Shan)** in the north. The lake's northern shore has most of the buildings and other attractions and is the most popular area for strolls, although it is more pleasant to walk around the smaller lakes behind Longevity Hill. The hill itself has a number of temples as well as **Baoyun Ge (Precious Clouds Pavilion),** one of the few structures in the palace to escape destruction by foreign forces. Dozens of pavilions and a number of bridges are on all sides of the lake, enough to make a full day of exploration, if you so choose.

RENSHOU DIAN (HALL OF BENEVOLENCE AND LONGEVITY) Located directly across the courtyard from the east gate entrance, Renshou Dian is the palace's main hall. This is where the empress dowager received members of the court, first from behind a screen and later from the Dragon Throne itself. North of the hall is Cixi's private theater, now a museum that contains an old Mercedes-Benz—the first car imported into China.

LONG CORRIDOR (CHANG LANG) ★ Among the more memorable attractions in Beijing, this covered wooden promenade stretches 700m (nearly half a mile) along the northern shore of Kunming Lake. Each crossbeam, ceiling, and pillar is painted with a different scene taken from Chinese history, literature, myth, and geography (roughly 10,000 in all).

SEVENTEEN-ARCH BRIDGE (SHIQI KONG QIAO) ★ This 150m-long (490-ft.) marble bridge connects South Lake Island (Nan Hu Dao) to the east shore of Kunming Lake. There is a rather striking life-size bronze ox near the eastern foot of the bridge.

Other Sights in Beijing

TEMPLES, MOSQUES & CHURCHES

Dongyue Miao ★ This Daoist temple, built in 1322 and beautifully restored a few years ago, is most famous for a series of 76 stalls ("heavenly departments") that surround its main courtyard. Garishly painted divine judges in each stall can offer relief from practically every ill—for a price. The most popular stall, not surprisingly, is the Department of Bestowing Material Happiness. English signs explain each department's function.

Chaoyang Men Wai Dajie 141, Chaoyang Qu (10-min. walk east on the north side). ✆ **010/6551-0151.** Admission ¥10; free during festivals. Tues–Sun 8:30am–4:30pm. Metro: Chaoyang Men.

Fayuan Si (Source of Dharma Temple) 🎁 Despite guides droning on about a long and glorious history, most of Beijing's sights are relatively new, dating from within the last 600 years. This temple, constructed in 645 in what was then the southeast corner of town, retains both an air of antiquity and the feel of a genuine Buddhist monastery. Orange-robed monks, housed in the adjacent Buddhist College, go about their business in earnest. The ancient *hutong* immediately surrounding the temple are "protected" and well worth a wander.

Fayuan Si Qian Jie 7, Xuanwu Qu. Admission ¥5. Thurs–Tues 8:30–11am and 1:30–4pm. Metro: Xuanwu Men.

Guo Zi Jian and Kong Miao This classic temple-school compound, buried down a tree-shaded street east of the Lama Temple (see below), is still in use. The Kong Miao, China's second-largest Confucian Temple, is on the right, and the Guo Zi Jian (the Imperial College) is on the left, both originally built in 1306. The front courtyard of the temple contains several dozen stelae inscribed with the names of the last successful candidates in the *jinshi* (highest level) imperial examinations. The college, imperial China's highest educational institution, contains a striking glazed-tile gate with elaborately carved stone arches.

Kong Miao at Guo Zi Jian Jie 13 (walk south from station along west side of Lama Temple, turn right onto street marked with arch), Dong Cheng Qu. ✆ **010/8401-1977.** Admission ¥30 to both. Kong Miao 8:30am–5:30pm; Guo Zi Jian 8:30am–5:30pm. Metro: Yonghe Gong/Lama Temple.

Ox Street Mosque (Niu Jie Qingzhensi) This is Beijing's largest mosque and the spiritual center for the city's estimated 200,000 Muslims. Built in 996, the complex looks more Eastern than Middle Eastern, with sloping tile roofs similar to those found on Buddhist temples. Halls are noticeably free of idols, however. A small courtyard on the south side contains the tombs and original gravestones of two Arab imams who lived here in the late 13th century.

Niu Jie 88 (on east side of street), Xuanwu Qu. ✆ **010/6353-2564.** Admission ¥10 for non-Muslims. All day. Bus: 61 to Libaisi from Changchun Jie metro.

White Cloud Temple (Baiyun Guan) This sprawling complex, said to have been built in 739, is the most active of Beijing's Daoist temples. Chinese visitors seem intent on actual worship rather than on tourism, and the blue-frocked monks wear their hair in the rarely seen traditional manner—long and tied in a bun at the top of the head. One notable structure is the Laolu Tang, a large hall in the third courtyard built in 1228, now used for teaching and ceremonies.

On Baiyun Guan Lu, east of the intersection with Baiyun Lu (1st right north of Baiyun Qiao, directly across from Baiyun Guan bus stop), Haidian Qu. ✆ **010/6346-3531.** Admission ¥10. 8:30am–4:30pm. Bus: 727 from Muxidi metro to Baiyun Guan.

Yonghe Gong (Lama Temple) ★★ If you visit only one temple after the Temple of Heaven, this should be it. A complex of progressively larger buildings topped with ornate yellow-tiled roofs, Yonghe Gong was built in 1694 and originally belonged to the Qing prince who would become the Yongzheng emperor. As was the custom, the complex was converted to a temple after Yongzheng's move to the Forbidden City in 1744. The temple is home to several beautiful **incense burners,** including a particularly ornate one in the second courtyard that dates from 1746. The Falun Dian (Hall of the Wheel of Law), second to last of the major buildings, contains a 6m-tall (20-ft.) bronze statue of Tsongkapa (1357–1419), the first Dalai Lama and founder of the Yellow Hat sect of Tibetan Buddhism. The final of the five central halls, the Wanfu Ge (Tower of Ten Thousand Happinesses), houses the temple's prize possession—an ominous Tibetan-style **statue of Maitreya** (the future Buddha), 18m (60 ft.) tall, carved from a single piece of white sandalwood.

Yonghe Gong Dajie 12, south of the N. Second Ring Rd. (entrance on the south end of the complex). ✆ **010/6404-3769.** Admission ¥25; audio tours in English additional ¥25 plus ¥200 deposit. Summer 9am–4:30pm, winter until 4pm. Metro: Yonghe Gong/Lama Temple.

PARKS & GARDENS

Aolinpike Gongyuan (Olympic Park) ★ Everything in Beijing is big. Tian'an Men Square is roughly the size of 90 football fields, wandering through the Forbidden City feels like a mini-marathon, and of course the Great Wall is . . . very long. It is fitting then that hosting the Olympics in Beijing meant building awe-inspiring, people-dwarfing structures. And all at a sizeable price tag of $40 billion.

Beijing's **Olympic Green** is the main attraction. Wear comfortable shoes, because the green covers an area roughly six times the size of Athens' Olympic Green and three times the size of New York's Central Park. Electric trolleys with tours in Chinese only will take you around the green for ¥20, round trip. The biggest draw is the **Beijing National Stadium,** dubbed "the Bird's Nest" because its oblong shape and interlocking steel grids closely resemble the twigs and branches of, well, a bird's nest. The original design featured an innovative retractable roof, but that was scrapped due to cost and time pressures. But even without a fancy convertible-like ceiling, the Bird's Nest is an impressive architectural feat. It was designed by architecture darlings Jacques Herzog and Pierre de Meuron, cost roughly $400 million, and can hold 91,000 spectators. It hosted the opening and closing ceremonies, as well as athletics events and football. The ¥50 entrance fee (ticket booths are at the north end of the nest) gets you into the stadium, where you can walk right onto the field and have your picture taken with the Olympic torch for ¥15. An on-site post office sells commemorative stamps and a few other stores sell Olympic kitsch inside. A healthy stone's throw away from the Bird's Nest is the **National Aquatics Center,** also known as "the Water Cube" (it's actually a rectangle, but "Water Rectangle" didn't have the same ring), which was recently converted into the **Happy Magic Watercube Waterpark** (p. 108). North of the Water Cube is the **National Indoor Stadium,** which hosted gymnastics and handball events. Its design plays on the theme of a traditional Chinese folding fan. Unlike its neighbors, it doesn't have a cutesy nickname.

Behind the Olympic Green is the **Olympic Forest Park.** During the Olympics, the park hosted tennis, archery, and hockey events. This spacious bit of greenery includes **Main Mountain,** a man-made pile of 3.98 million cubic m (141 million cubic ft.) of earth, and **Main Lake,** a 110-hectare (272-acre, roughly 205 football fields) body of water shaped like the Olympic torch. While this is Beijing's largest city park at 640 hectares (1,581 acres), there's nothing terribly special here. It's over 1km (less than 1 mile) north of the Water Cube and Bird's Nest, so if your feet are already aching, you can skip this.

Beichen Dong Lu. ✆ **010/8437-3017.** Free admission to the Olympic Green. Open 24 hr. Admission to National Stadium ¥50, ¥25 for children under 1.2m/4 ft. and seniors. National Aquatics Center: ✆ 8437-0112. Admission ¥30, free for children under 1.5m/5 ft. and seniors 65–69. 9am–5:30pm. Opening times for both stadiums will vary in the case of sporting or entertainment events. Swimming at National Aquatics Center ¥50 for 2 hr. weekdays 1–9pm, weekends 9am–9pm. Free admission to Olympic Forest Park. Mar 15–Nov 15 6am–8pm; Nov 16–Mar 14 8am–6pm. Metro: Olympic Sports Centre.

Bei Hai Park (Bei Hai Gongyuan) ★★ This is Beijing's oldest imperial garden, roughly 800 years old, and the one city park you should not miss. Most of the park is actually a man-made lake, **Bei Hai (North Sea),** part of a series of lakes that run north along the eastern edge of the Forbidden City. The central feature is a 36m (118-ft.) Tibetan-style **White Dagoba (Bai Ta),** similar to the one at Bai Ta Si, built in 1651 to commemorate a visit by the Dalai Lama. The pagoda stands atop the artificial hill that dominates Qionghua Dao, also known as the **Jade Islet.** A hike around the island, and around the shore of Bei Hai, will take you past several beautiful pavilions and gardens. The **Round City (Tuan Cheng),** located just outside the south entrance of the park, stands on the site where Kublai Khan built his palace after establishing the Yuan dynasty (1279–1368). It contains a massive jade bowl that once belonged to him, and a 3m (10-ft.) Buddha carved out of white jade.

Wenjin Jie 1, Xi Cheng Qu (south entrance is just west of the north gate of the Forbidden City; east entrance is opposite the west entrance of Jing Shan Park). ✆ **010/6404-0610.** Admission summer ¥10; winter ¥5; ¥10 extra for Yong'an Si; ¥1 extra for Tuan Cheng. 6am–10pm. Bus: 812 from Dong Dan metro stop to Bei Hai.

Happy Magic Watercube Waterpark ★ ☺ Formerly the site of the swimming pool where Michael Phelps won his gold medals during the 2008 Olympics, the National Aquatics Center has been converted into a new waterpark, which swarms with ecstatic children careening down waterslides and playing in the wave pool. The various rides, some of which pile up to four guests in giant inner tubes, and are titled "Tornado" and "Bulletbowl," offers thrills for all ages. Adults can laze in the hot Jacuzzi pools. It's an ingenuous use of a former Olympics space.

Beichen Lu, Aolinpike Gongyuan, Chaoyang Qu. ✆ **010/84372030.** Free admission for children under 1.2m (3¾ ft.); ¥180 for children between 1.2–1.4m (3¾–4½ ft.; ¥200 for adults and children over 1.4m (4½ ft.). 10am–9:30pm.

Jing Shan Park (Jing Shan Gongyuan) If you want a clear aerial view of the Forbidden City, this is where you'll find it. The park's central hill—known both as Jing Shan (Prospect Hill) and Mei Shan (Coal Hill)—was created using earth left over from the digging of the imperial moat and was the highest point in the city during the Ming dynasty. A locust tree on the east side of the hill marks the spot where the last Ming dynasty Chongzhen emperor hanged himself in 1644, just before Manchu and rebel armies overran the city.

Jing Shan Qian Jie 1 (opposite Forbidden City north gate), Dong Cheng Qu. ✆ **010/6404-4071.** Admission ¥2. Jan–Mar and Nov–Dec 6:30am–8pm; Apr–May and Sept–Oct 6am–9pm; June–Aug 6am–10pm.

National Museum of China (Guojia Bowuguan) ★ After a decade-long effort that cost nearly $400 million, the newly opened version combines the Museum of the Chinese Revolution and the Museum of History. The result is a massive space intended to impress with its trove of more than 1 million cultural relics from China's lengthy history. Of particular note is the exhibit on Ancient China, which covers in exhaustive detail the prehistoric era through the Ming and Qing dynasties. Among the highlights is a Han Dynasty jade burial suit sewn with gold thread, an enormous Shang Dynasty bronze vessel, and delicate ceramics from the Song Dynasty. Also worth a look is the central gallery containing a collection of antique wood, bronze and porcelain Buddha sculptures from India, Pakistan and China. Less satisfying are the

WITH A new museum COMES NEW HISTORY

With a new National Museum that rivals the Louvre Museum in size, China set out to showcase the country's history and its modern rise to power. The new museum measures a staggering 192,000 sq. m (2,066,671 sq. ft.) and boasts priceless cultural relics. Yet for all its historical treasures, critics say the new museum has failed to measure up because it doesn't confront controversial aspects of China's tumultuous past. Instead, the exhibits paint a Communist Party-approved version of the country's more recent economic-powered triumphs, from recent space flights to its hosting of the 2008 Olympic Games. Pig-tailed female guides in gray Mao uniforms give perky and sanitized history lessons, sans death and destruction. The result is less an examination of China's past than a revisionist spin by a Communist government determined to mold its version of truth.

sections on contemporary Chinese history (see box). Still, it's easy to spend a half-day wandering through the galleries.

East side of Tian'an Men Square, Dong Chang'an Jie 16. ✆ **010/6511-6400.** www.chnmuseum.cn. Free admission for permanent exhibitions. However, you have to get a ticket from the West Gate office using valid ID. Last ticket issued at 4:30pm. ¥10 for special exhibits; ¥30 English audio guides. Tues–Sun 9am–5pm. Closed Mon. Metro: Tian'an Men East.

Old Summer Palace (Yuan Ming Yuan) ★ ☺ An amalgamation of three separate imperial gardens, these ruins create a ghostly and oddly enjoyable scene, beloved as a picnic spot. Established by the Kangxi emperor in 1707, Yuan Ming Yuan is a more recent construction than the New Summer Palace to the west, but it is misleadingly called the Old Summer Palace because it was never rebuilt after troops looted and razed it during the Second Opium War of 1860. Ironically, some of the buildings were filled with European furnishings and art. Two Jesuit priests, Italian painter Castiglione, and French scientist Benoist were commissioned by Qianlong to design the 30-hectare (75-acre) **Xiyang Lou (Western Mansions)** in the northeast section of the park. Inaccurate models suggest that the structures were entirely European in style, but they were curious hybrids, featuring imperial-style vermilion walls and yellow-tiled roofs. Recently, the park has been the center of environmental controversy: Park management decided to line the lakes (an integral part of Beijing's water ecology) with plastic sheeting to save on water bills and raise the water levels to allow for a duck-boat business.

Qinghua Xi Lu 28 (north of Peking University), Haidian Qu. ✆ **010/6262-8501.** Admission ¥10, ¥25 to enter Xiyang Lou. 7am–7pm (to 5:30pm in winter). Bus: 743 from east of Wudaokou metro stop to Yuan Ming Yuan.

MORE MUSEUMS & OTHER CURIOSITIES

Ancient Observatory (Gu Guanxiang Tai) ☺ Most of the large bronze astronomical instruments on display here—mystifying combinations of hoops, slides, and rulers stylishly embellished with dragons and clouds—were built by the Jesuits in the 17th and 18th centuries. You can play with reproductions in the courtyard below.

Jianguo Men Dong Biaobei 2 (southwest side of Jianguo Men intersection), Dong Cheng Qu. ✆ **010/6512-8923.** Admission ¥10. Tues–Sun 9am–4:30pm. Metro: Jianguo Men.

Factory 798 (Qijiuba Gongchang) ★★ Optimistically billed as Beijing's Soho district, this Soviet-designed former weapons factory is a center for local art and fashion, but its long-term survival is uncertain. Purchase a map for ¥2 on arrival. Establishments worth your time include **798 Space,** still covered with slogans offering praise to Mao; **798 Photo,** immediately opposite; and **Beijing Tokyo Art Projects** (www.tokyo-gallery.com), which has a formidable stable of local and international artists.

Jiuxian Qiao Lu 4, Chaoyang Qu (north of Dashanzi Huandao). www.798space.com. 10:30am–7:30pm, some galleries closed Mon. Bus: 813 east from Chaoyang Men metro to Wangye Fen.

Former Residence of Lao She (Lao She Jinianguan) Lao She (1899–1966) was one of China's greatest 20th-century writers, lauded by early Communists for his use of satire in novels like *Teahouse* and *Rickshaw Boy* (or *Camel Xiangzi*) and persecuted for the same books during the Cultural Revolution. He is said to have committed suicide but might instead have been murdered by Red Guards. The rooms here contain photos, copies of his books, and his own library (Hemingway, Dickens, Graham Greene). Most interesting is his study, supposedly preserved the way he left it, with a game of solitaire laid out on the bed and the calendar turned to August 24, 1966—the day he disappeared.

Fengfu Hutong 19, Dong Cheng Qu (from Wangfujing Dajie, turn left at the Crowne Plaza along Dengshikou Xi Jie to the 2nd *hutong* on your right). ✆ **010/6514-2612.** Free admission. 9am–4:30pm. Metro: Wangfujing.

Museum of Ancient Architecture (Gudai Jianzhu Bowuguan) ★★ This exhibition, a mixture of models of China's most famous architecture and fragments of buildings long disappeared, is housed in halls as dramatic as those on the central axis of the Forbidden City. These were once part of the **Xian Nong Tan,** or Altar of Agriculture, now as obscure as neighboring Tian Tan, the Temple (properly Altar) of Heaven, is famous. From about 1410, emperors came to this once-extensive site to perform rituals in which they started the agricultural cycle by playing farmer and plowing the first furrows. Models of significant buildings around Beijing can help you select what to see in the capital during the remainder of your trip. As of press time, this museum was under renovation.

Dong Jing Lu 21, Xuanwu Qu (from bus stop, take 1st right into Nan Wei Lu and walk for 5 min., look out for an archway down a street on the left). ✆ **010/6301-7620.** Admission ¥15. 9am–4pm. Bus: 803 from just south of Qian Men metro stops to Tian Qiao Shangchang.

Prince Gong's Mansion (Gong Wangfu Huayuan) ★ This imperial residence belonged to several people, including the sixth son of the Guangxu emperor (Prince Gong), and is thought to have been the inspiration behind the lushly described mansion in Cao Xueqin's canonical 18th-century work, *Dream of the Red Chamber.* Only the garden is open to visitors, but its labyrinthine combination of rockeries and pavilions offers plenty to see.

Liuyin Jie 17 (signposted in English at top of Qian Hai Xi Dajie running north off Ping'an Dadao opposite north gate of Bei Hai Park; turn left at sign and follow alley past large parking lot; entrance marked with huge red lanterns). ✆ **010/8328-1758.** Admission ¥40; ¥70 including guide and opera performance. 7:30am–4:30pm.

The Hutong

As distinct as Beijing's palaces, temples, and parks may be, it is the ***hutong*** that ultimately set the city apart. Prior to the 20th century, when cars and the Communist love of grandeur made them impractical, these narrow and often winding lanes were the city's dominant passageways. Old maps of Beijing show the city to be an immense and intricate maze composed almost entirely of *hutong,* most no wider than 10m (30 ft.) and some as narrow as 50cm (20 in.).

Beijing's other famous feature is the ***siheyuan*** (courtyard house)—traditional dwellings typically composed of four single-story rectangular buildings arranged around a central courtyard with a door at one corner (ideally facing south). Originally designed to house a single family, each one now houses up to five or six families. Until recently, as much as half of Beijing's population lived in some form of *siheyuan,* but large-scale bulldozing of the *hutong* has resulted in significant migration into modern apartment buildings. Foreign visitors charmed by the quaintness of the old houses often assume this migration is forced, and it often is. But many who move do so willingly, eager for central heating and indoor plumbing (both rare in the *hutong* neighborhoods).

The *hutong* are being leveled so rapidly that the term "fast-disappearing" is now a permanent part of their description. The best-preserved *hutong,* and the ones most likely to survive because of their popularity with tourists, are those found in the Back Lakes (Shicha Hai) and nearby Di'an Men.

The most dynamic of these hutong can be found around the alley of Nan Luogu Xiang, a gentrifying neighborhood filled with Chinese hipsters, grungy French and Americans, and old Beijingers. Nan Luogu Xiang is the name of the north-south alley filled with a growing number of cafes, bars, restaurants, and hotels listed throughout our pages. Bar highlights include Mao Livehouse (p. 120).

Pedicab tour companies offer to bike you around this area and take you inside a couple of courtyards, but they all charge absurd rates. It's much cheaper, and far more enjoyable, to walk around on your own (see "Walking Tour: The Back Lakes," below). If you must, the **Beijing Hutong Tourist Agency** (✆ **010/6615-9097**) offers tours in English.

WALKING TOUR: THE BACK LAKES

START: **Drum Tower (Gu Lou), north end of Di'an Men Wai Dajie.**

FINISH: **Prince Gong's Palace (Gong Wang Fu), west side of Qian Hai.**

TIME: **Approximately 3 hours.**

BEST TIMES: **Morning (9am) or just after lunch, no later than 1:30pm (or you risk getting locked out of Prince Gong's Palace).**

There is, quite simply, no finer place to walk in Beijing. The Back Lakes area (Shicha Hai) is composed of three idyllic lakes—Qian Hai (Front Lake), Hou Hai (Back Lake), and Xi Hai (West Lake)—and the tree-shaded neighborhoods that surround them. Combined with other man-made pools to the south, these lakes were once part of a system used to transport grain by barge from the Grand Canal to the Forbidden City. Prior to 1911, this was an exclusive area, and only people with connections to the imperial family were permitted to maintain houses here (a situation that seems destined to return). A profusion of bars and cafes has sprung up around the lakes in recent years (p. 91), providing ample opportunities to take breaks from your walk.

Beyond the lakes, stretching out to the east and west is the city's best-maintained network of *hutong.* Many families have lived in these lanes for generations, their insular communities a last link to Old Beijing.

Begin at Mei Mansion, at the northwest corner of Deshengmen Nei Dajie and Huguosi Jie:

1 Mei Mansion

This former museum and residence of Beijing's best-known Peking opera star was recently converted into a pricey Chinese restaurant called Mei Mansion (✆ **010/6612-6845**), but you can still peek in to get a sense of the grandness of the quarters. The pictures of the opera singer displayed inside demonstrate the wide-ranging number of expressions used in the art form.

Turn left out of Mei Lanfang Guju and cross Deshengmen Nei Dajie onto Dingfu Jie. Continue and on the left, you'll walk past:

2 Former Campus of Furen Daxue (Furen University)

The original campus of Furen University (1 Dingfu Jie), a Catholic institution set up by Chinese priests, was built in 1925. The university was shuttered after the Communists came to power and was moved to Taiwan. Note the ornate facade featuring an arched doorway and the traditional sloping Chinese roof.

Walk to the end of Dingfu Jie through the messy 5-way intersection, turn left onto Liuyin Jie and follow the road as it curves. On your left is:

3 Prince Gong's Mansion (Gong Wang Fu Huayuan)

This is the most lavish courtyard residence (Liuyin Jie 14; ✆ **010/**8328-8149**;** admission ¥40; 7am–4:30pm) in the Back Lakes. The 1777 mansion was occupied by Heshen, a corrupt official who was rumored to be the Qianlong emperor's lover. Later, it became the home of Prince Gong, who negotiated on behalf of China at the end of the Second Opium War. See p. 110 for a more detailed description of Prince Gong's Mansion.

Turn right when leaving the mansion, and follow Liuyin Jie to the end. Make a left at the T onto Yangfang Hutong. Take a right at the gray brick pedestrian path, walk through the park, and turn right on the path next to the lake:

4 Take a Break

At **Family Fu's Teahouse** (✆ **010/6616-0725**), you can relax lakeside on Ming Dynasty furniture while sipping longjing, a green tea from Hangzhou, one of China's famed tea-producing areas. The English-speaking owner is particularly friendly.

From the teahouse, turn left and follow the path along the lake to:

5 Wild Duck Island

Beijing is full of loopy attractions, including this man-made island built of steel in Hou Hai Lake for the ducks in the area. March is a particularly busy time on the island as it's mating season.

Continuing along the path, you'll pass Kong Yi Ji, one of Beijing's most famous restaurants on the left. Turn right at the footbridge and continue around the lake. On the left is:

6 Jiumen Xiao Chi (Nine Gate Snacks)

The sprawling restaurant (✆ **010/6402-6868;** 10am–10pm) is worth a peek even if you aren't hungry—the vendors crammed down one hall of the dining

Walking Tour: The Back Lakes

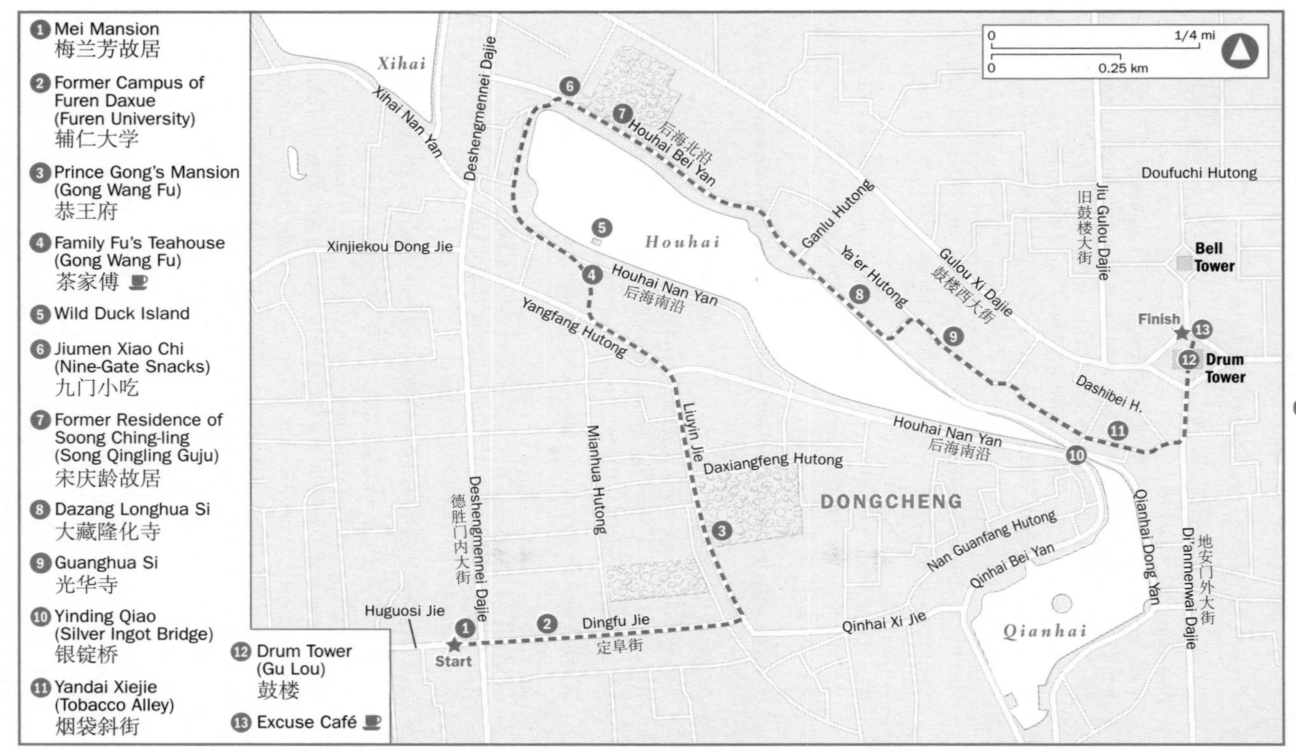

room offer snacks that are disappearing from Beijing's streets, including quick-fried tripe soup *(baodu)*, dumplings shaped to resemble large stubby door nails, and an array of sweet glutinous rice cakes. (See p. 92 for more background.)

Return to the path along the lake and continue to:

7 Former Residence of Soong Ching-ling (Song Qingling Guju)

This former imperial palace (© **010/6404-4205;** admission ¥20; 9am–6pm, winter 9am–4pm) once famously housed the wife of Sun Yat-sen, modern China's founder. This feminist hero later became a friend of Mao's and a Communist sympathizer. China's last emperor, Henry Puyi, is said to have been born on this site. On weekends, there's a risk of being trampled by soon-to-be-wed brides in their finery.

Turn left from the residence and continue along the lake. After passing the outdoor exercise equipment, continue for a few minutes until you see on your left:

8 Dazang Longhua Si

This temple dates back to 1719. Though it's now the grounds of a kindergarten, the facade—with intricate animal-shaped stone gargoyles—has been nicely preserved.

Continue along the lake and turn left at Lotus Place Hotel, then take a quick right on Ya'er Hutong to:

9 Guanghua Si

Though this temple is not officially open to the public, monks have snuck us in more than once. China's last known eunuch was a caretaker of this temple for two decades and died here in 1996.

Continue and turn right down a narrow alley, then left at the lake path and walk until you reach:

10 Yinding Qiao (Silver Ingot Bridge)

This bridge separates Hou Hai from Qianhai (Front Lake). It's usually a mess of tourists, aggressive rickshaws, and cars.

Turn left at the bridge onto Xiao Shi Bei Hutong, then right onto the pedestrian alley:

11 Yandai Xiejie (Tobacco Alley)

This touristy pedestrian street houses a few gems. No. 63 on the left, a folk art store, features stylish Chinese pillow covers, framed paper cuts, and cloth coasters. On the left, in between No. 37 and 51 is Guangfu Daoism Temple, built in 1459. No. 20 on the right sells cute totes and lipstick cases made with Chinese patterns. No. 12 is the Tibetan Jewelry & Tea Bar where you can stop for a drink in the airy back room and browse their collection of Tibetan bracelets, rings, and clothing.

The end of Yandai Xiejie brings you to Dianmen Wai Dajie. Turning left, you will see a number of kitchen supply shops on your left, and in front of you, the looming:

12 Drum Tower (Gu Lou)

Drumming performances are held daily every half hour (from 9–11:30am and 1:30–5pm), underneath the bright yellow tile roof of the looming Drum Tower (admission ¥20; 9am–4:40pm). Highly recommended. For an extra ¥10 you can get a ticket that also allows entry to the more understated Bell Tower (Zhong Lu) just behind the Drum Tower.

13 Winding Down

Just across the street from the Drum Tower, on the right, is **Excuse Café** (68 Zhonglou Wan Hutong; ✆ **010/6401-9867**; 7:30am–10pm) serving terrific coffee and sandwiches

SHOPPING

Stores and markets in Beijing sell everything from cashmere and silk to knockoff designer-label clothing to athletic wear, antiques, traditional art, cloisonné, lacquerware, Ming furniture, Mao memorabilia, and enough miscellaneous Chinesey doodads to stuff Christmas stockings from now until eternity. Prices are reasonable (certainly lower than in the Asian-goods boutiques back home), though increasingly less so.

Before you rush to the ATM, however, it is important to remember that not all that is green and gleams in Beijing is jade. Indeed, the majority of it is colored glass. The same principle holds for pearls (see below), famous-brand clothing, antiques, and just about everything else. Shoppers who plan to make big purchases should educate themselves about quality and price well beforehand.

You should also be leery of any English-speaking youngsters who claim to be **art students** and offer to take you to a special exhibit of their work. This is a scam. The art, which you will be compelled to buy, almost always consists of assembly-line reproductions of famous (or not-so-famous) paintings offered at prices several dozen times higher than their actual value.

Top Shopping Areas

The grandest shopping area in Beijing is on and around **Wangfujing Dajie,** east of the Forbidden City. The street was overhauled in 1999, the south section turned into a pedestrian-only commercial avenue lined with shops, fast-food restaurants, and the city's top two malls—the Sun (Xin) Dong An Plaza and the Oriental Plaza (Dongfang Guangchang). **Dong Dan Bei Dajie,** a long block east, is a strip of clothing boutiques and CD shops popular among fashionable Beijing youth. **Nanluoguxiang** is a popular renovated *hutong,* or alley, just east of the **Drum Tower** lined with boutiques and independent stores offering creative, original designs.

Other major Westernized shopping areas include the section of **Jianguo Men Wai Dajie** between the Friendship Store and the China World Trade Center, and the neighborhood outside the **Northeast Third Ring Road North,** southeast of Sanyuan Qiao around the new embassy district.

Beijing's liveliest shopping zone, the one most beloved of tourists for its atmosphere and Chinese-style goods, is the centuries-old commercial district southwest of Qian Men. **Liulichang** is an almost too-quaint collection of art, book, tea, and antiques shops lining a polished-for-tourists, Old Beijing–style *hutong* running east-west 2 blocks south of the Hepingmen metro station. The street is good for window-shopping strolls and small purchases—like the unavoidable **chop** (*tuzhang;* stone or jade stamp), carved with your name—but beware large purchases: Almost everything here is fake and overpriced. **Qianmen Dajie** is the new Disneyland-esque ancient

BUYING pearls

Most of the pearls on sale at Hongqiao Market are genuine, although of too low a quality to be sold in Western jewelry shops, but there are some fakes floating around. To test if the pearls you want to buy are real, try any one of the following:

- Nick the surface with a sharp blade (the color should be uniform within and without)
- Rub the pearl across your teeth (this should make a grating sound)
- Scrape the pearl on a piece of glass (real pearls leave a mark)
- Pass it through a flame (fake pearls turn black, real ones don't)

Strange as it may feel to do these tests, vendors are generally willing to let you carry them out and might even help, albeit in bemusement. If you'd rather not bother (and most don't), just assume the worst, shop for fun, and spend modestly.

street south of Qian Men (Front Gate). Most stores are Western (H&M, Zara, and so on). It's pedestrian only and has a trolley running down the middle of it.

MARKETS

Although malls and shopping centers are becoming more popular, the majority of Beijing residents still shop in markets. Whether indoors or out, these markets are inexpensive, chaotic and, for the visitor, tremendously interesting. Payment is in cash, bargaining is universal, and pickpockets are plentiful.

Hongqiao Market (Hongqiao Jimao Shichang) ★ An outlet for cheap jewelry better known as the **Pearl Market,** Hongqiao Market is just northeast of the Temple of Heaven at Tian Tan Lu 9. The first floor smells awful (there's a seafood market in the basement), but the upper floors have cheap Western clothing, luggage, old Chinese curios, and, of course, pearls (third floor). The prices here are good and the bargaining fierce. The market is open from 8:30am to 7pm.

Panjiayuan Antique (Panjiayuan Jiuhuo Shichang) ★★★ Eureka! Also known as the Dirt or Ghost Market, this is the Chinese shopping experience of dreams: row upon crowded row of calligraphy, jewelry, ceramics, teapots, ethnic clothing, Buddha statues, paper lanterns, Cultural Revolution memorabilia, PLA belts, little wooden boxes, Ming- and Qing-style furniture, old pipes, opium scales, and painted human skulls. There are some real antiques scattered among the junk, but you'd have to be an expert to pick them out. Locals arrive Saturday and Sunday mornings at dawn or shortly afterward (hence the "Ghost" label) to find the best stuff; vendors start to leave around 4pm. Initial prices given to foreigners are always absurdly high—Mao clocks, for instance, should cost less than ¥40 rather than the ¥400 you'll likely be asked to pay. The market is located on the south side of Panjiayuan Lu, just inside the southeast corner of the Third Ring Road.

Handily located just south of Panjiayuan on the west side of Huawei Qiao, **Curio City** (**Guwan Cheng;** ✆ **010/6774-7711**) has four floors of jewelry (including diamonds and jade), old clocks, cloisonné, furniture, and porcelain, as well as curios and the odd genuine antique. International shipping is provided. Curio City is open daily from 10am to 6:30pm.

Silk Market (Xiushui Fuzhuang Shichang) This is not a place to go for silk, but rather for knock-offs of your favorite brands and trendy items, like Ugg Boots,

Louis Vuitton handbags, and North Face jackets. Beijing's most famous market among foreign visitors is a crowded maze of stalls with a large selection of shoes and clothing. Vendors formerly enjoyed so much trade they could afford to be rude, but the knockoff boot is now firmly on the shopper's foot, as Silk Alley now sees only a fraction of the business of Yaxiu (see below). Most of the original vendors are gone, unwilling (or unable) to pay the new steep rental fees. Good riddance. Under no circumstances pay more than ¥200 for a North Face (North Fake, the expats call it) jacket, ¥100 for a business shirt, or ¥150 for a pair of jeans. Stores that sport a red flag are purported to "subscribe to higher ethics." Spot the ethical pirates. Open 9:30am to 9pm. 8 Dong Xiushui Jie. ✆ **010/5169-9003.** www.silkmarketbeijing.com.

Yashow Clothing Market (Yaxiu Fuzhuang Shichang) ★ Whatever you may think of their business practices, Beijing's clothing vendors are nimble: Here you'll find refugees from two outdoor markets, Yabao Lu and Sanlitun. The fourth floor is a fine hunting ground for souvenirs and gifts—there are kites from Weifang in Shandong, calligraphy materials, army surplus gear, tea sets, and farmer's paintings from Xi'an. The basement and the first two floors house a predictable but comprehensive collection of imitation and pilfered brand-name clothing, shoes, and luggage. The market has been "discovered" by fashion-conscious locals, and starting prices are ridiculous. The market is west of Sanlitun Jiuba Jie, at Gongti Bei Lu 58 (✆ **010/6415-1726**), and is open from 10am to 9pm.

MORE MARKETS

True bargain hunters who don't mind immersing themselves into the fray should head to the Zoo Market (Xizhimen, just east of the Beijing Zoo; no phone), for samples of Diane Von Furstenberg and other high-end labels. Ri Tan Shangwu Lou, at Guanghua Lu 15A (just east of the south gate of Ri Tan Park; ✆ **010/8561-9556**), is not as cheap as Yaxiu, but is far less nasty. From outside, it looks like an uninspiring office building; inside is shopping nirvana: more than 70 shops stocking high-quality women's clothing, footwear, and accessories. There is a smattering of shops for the chaps, too. Open 10am until 8pm. For value housewares, bric-a-brac, and anything wholesale, head to Tianyi Market (259 Fuchengmen Wai Dajie; no phone).

Department Stores

Landao Dasha Though it's state-owned (and therefore, pretty unhip), Landao boasts a good location near the CBD and, surprisingly, you can find just about anything you need here, from Columbia Sportswear to a decent suitcase (re: not a knockoff) to tote back everything you've bought while in Beijing. Open 9:30am to 9:30pm. 8 Chaoyangmen Wai Dajie. ✆ **010/8561-7838.** www.ldds.com.cn.

Xi Dan Baihuo Shangchang Crowded and chaotic, this is an old-school four-story department store selling everything from cosmetics to appliances, with good deals on denim and shoes. Open 9am to 8pm. East side of Xi Dan Bei Dajie (north of Xi Dan metro stop).

MALLS & SHOPPING PLAZAS

Oriental Plaza (Dongfang Guangchang) Asia's largest shopping/office/apartment/hotel complex covers 4 city blocks of prime real estate from Wangfujing Dajie to Dong Dan Bei Dajie. The two-story arcade has hip clothing stores such as π Art of Shirts and Kookai; the Wangfujing Paleolithic Museum; and another Ole supermarket. The Grand Hyatt (p. 68) stands above all the consumption. Summer hours are from 10am to 10:30pm; winter 9:30am to 10pm. Dong Chang'an Dajie. Metro: Wangfujing.

The Place (Shimao Tianjie) This new behemoth, marked by a huge outdoor screen playing clips of random fashion shows, sees plenty of fashionista traffic. Spanish retailer Zara chose to set up shop here; their arrival in Beijing was highly anticipated by locals and expats alike. Makeup gurus MAC also chose The Place for their flagship store. Other retailers like French Connection, Mango, and Adidas ensure this place is virtually bargain-hunter-free. Open 10am to 10pm. Guanghua Lu Jia 9. ✆ 010/8595-1755. Metro: Yong'anli. Guanghua Lu 9. ✆ **010/6587-1188.** Metro: Yong'anli.

Shin Kong Place (Xin Guang Tiandi) Shin Kong Place sets the gold standard in Beijing luxury shopping. This indoor mall has all the labels that break the bank: Coach, Gucci, Salvatore Ferragamo, and Marc Jacobs, as well as high-end but more-affordable retailers, such as Juicy Couture, Diesel, and Club Monaco. Open 10am to 10pm. Jianguo Lu 87, Chaoyang Qu. ✆ **010/6530-5888.** www.shinkong-place.com. Metro: Dawang Lu.

The Village at Sanlitun ★★ The Village is comprised of several freestanding, multi-story buildings connected by covered walkways and surrounding a central outdoor courtyard. A team of well-known and international names from the architect world is responsible for the modern shopping complex. Anchor stores include the first **Apple Experience Store** and the world's largest **Adidas** flagship. Aside from shopping, there are popular restaurants on the second and third floors, a movie theater in the basement, and cafes are on the main level. Sanlitun Bei Jie 19, Chaoyang Qu. ✆ **010/6417-6110.** www.sanlitunvillage.com. Metro: Tuanjiehu.

BEIJING AFTER DARK

It wasn't so long ago that the after-dark options available to foreigners in Beijing were limited to a short list of tourist-approved activities: Beijing opera, acrobatics, and wandering listlessly around the hotel in search of a drink to make sleep come faster. Now opera and acrobatics are still available, but in more interesting venues, and to them have been added a range of other worthwhile cultural events: teahouse theater, puppet shows, traditional music concerts, and even the occasional subtitled film. Beyond such edification, Beijing has China's most diverse stable of bars, clubs, discos, and cafes, cheaper and often more interesting than those of Hong Kong or Shanghai.

Performing Arts

BEIJING OPERA

A relatively young opera form dating from only 300 years to the early Qing dynasty, Beijing Opera (Jingju) dazzles as much as it grates. Performances are loud and long, with dialogue sung on a screeching five-note scale and accompanied by a cacophony of gongs, cymbals, drums, and strings. This leaves most first-timers exhausted, but the exquisite costumes, elaborate face paint, and martial arts–inspired movements ultimately make it worthwhile. Several theaters now offer shortened programs more amenable to the foreign attention span, sometimes with English subtitles and plot summaries.

Most tourists on tours are taken to the bland, cinema-style **Liyuan Theater (Liyuan Juchang)** inside the Qian Men Hotel, where nightly performances at

7:30pm cost ¥80 to ¥480. The venues below offer essentially the same performances in much better traditional settings.

Huguang Guild House (Huguang Huiguan) This combination museum-theater was originally built in 1807. The theater is a riot of color, with a beautifully adorned traditional stage and gallery seating. It is currently Beijing's best opera venue. Nightly performances take place at 7:30pm. Hufang Lu 3, at intersection with Luomashi Dajie. ✆ **010/6351-8284.** Tickets ¥180–¥280. Metro: Hepingmen; walk south 10 min.

Mei Lanfang Grand Theatre (Mei Lanfang Da Ju Yuan) This brand new, multi-story theater was built specifically for Peking Opera. The performance quality and times vary so be sure to check the schedule ahead of time. If you don't want to chance sitting through a bad Peking opera show, the ultra-modern glass theater and the giant bust of Mei Lanfang in the foyer are worth viewing on their own. Ping'anli Xi Dajie 32. ✆ **010/5833-1388.** Tickets ¥50–¥280.

Zhengyici Peking Opera Theatre (Zhengyici Xilou) Rumors that this 300-year-old theater had gone under are untrue, but funding problems and its position at the center of a massive urban reconstruction project have limited the number of performances. The theater is similar to the Huguang Guild House but less ostentatious, with a more local feel. Shows are held most nights at 7:30pm (call to check). This is the first choice of venue for Beijing Opera when it's open. Pray it survives. Qian Men Xi Heyan Jie 220 (walk south of the Hepingmen Quanjude, take 1st left). ✆ **010/6315-1650.** Tickets ¥150–¥280. Metro: Hepingmen.

ACROBATICS

China's acrobats are justifiably famous, and probably just a little bit insane. This was the only traditional Chinese art form to receive Mao's explicit approval (back flips, apparently, don't count as counterrevolution). Not culturally stimulating, it's highly recommended nonetheless.

The city's best acrobatics venue is the **Wansheng Juchang** on the north side of Bei Wei Lu, just off Qian Men Dajie (west side of the Temple of Heaven; ✆ **010/6303-7449**). The fairly famous Beijing Acrobatics Troupe performs nightly shows here at 7pm. Tickets cost ¥180 to ¥580. The acrobats of **Chaoyang Theatre** (**Chaoyang Juchang;** ✆ **010/6507-2421**) at Dong San Huan Bei Lu 36 are slightly clumsier. Nightly shows at 5:15 and 7:15pm cost ¥180 up to ¥880. Metro: Hujialou.

TEAHOUSE THEATER

Snippets of Beijing opera, cross-talk (stand-up) comedy, acrobatics, traditional music, singing, and dancing flow across the stage as you sip tea and nibble snacks. If you don't have time to see these kinds of performances individually, the teahouse is a perfect solution. Performances change nightly at **Lao She Teahouse** (**Lao She Chaguan;** Qianmen Xi Dajie 3, west of Qian Men on street's south side; ✆ **010/6303-6830;** tickets ¥180–¥380), a somewhat garishly decorated teahouse but always include opera and acrobatics. It pays to buy the more expensive tickets, as rear views are obscured. Nightly shows take place at 7:50pm.

PUPPETS

Puppet shows (*mu'ou xi*) have been performed in China since the Han dynasty (206 B.C.–A.D. 220). Most theatrical performances, including weekend matinees, are held at the **China Puppet Art Theater (Zhongguo Mu'ou Juyuan),** in Anhua Xili near the North Third Ring Road (✆ **010/6424-3698**). Tickets cost ¥90 to ¥380.

SMALL LIVE-MUSIC VENUES

CD Jazz Cafe (Sendi Jueshi) After much upheaval, this amalgamation of CD Cafe and the short-lived Treelounge is the best place to see local jazz and blues acts in Beijing. If it's a special act, get there early. Open 4pm until very late. Dong San Huan, south of the Agricultural Exhibition Center (Nongzhanguan) main gate (down small path behind trees that line sidewalk). ✆ **010/6506-8288.** Metro: Nongzhanguan.

MAO Livehouse This live music venue is backed by Japanese label Bad News, home of local punk band Brain Failure. Plenty of aspiring punk rockers are loyal fans of both the band and the bar. The exterior looks like a rusty, unfinished steel warehouse. Inside, the decor is an eclectic mix of chairs and tables sandwiched between black walls. Performances generally start at 8:30pm. 111 Guloudajie. ✆ **010/6402-5080.** www.maolive.com. Cover ¥40–¥60. Metro: Bei Xin Qiao.

The Star Live Cool musicians (Ziggy Marley, The Roots, Sonic Youth) are finally coming to Beijing, and they seem to enjoy playing at Star Live. This place is nothing like its thumping, downstairs neighbor Tango; it's small and intimate and has excellent acoustics. Ticket prices depend on the artist, but expect to pay between ¥50 and ¥300. 3/F, Tango, 70 Heping Xijie (50m/164 ft. north of subway station). ✆ **010/6426-4628.** www.thestarlive.com. Metro: Yonghegong.

Yugong Yishan This wonderful performance space is the best live music venue in Beijing, period. The sound isn't perfect, it can get plenty stuffy in summer, and its location in the middle of a parking lot–cum–bus depot lends it a certain seediness, but the owners have a knack for turning up the best local acts. Run by the owners of the now defunct Loup Chante, the diverse lineup—from punk to Mongolian mouth music—means you can visit night after night. It's open from 2pm to 2am. Zhangzizhong Lu, east of Lotus Lane. ✆ **010/8402-8477.** www.yugongyishan.com. Cover varies for performances. Metro: Zhangzizhong Lu.

OTHER PERFORMING-ARTS VENUES

Beijing hosts a growing number of international music and theater events every year, and its own increasingly respectable troupes—including the Beijing Symphony Orchestra—give frequent performances.

Among the most popular venues for this sort of thing is the **National Centre for Performing Arts** (also known as "the Egg"), the modern egg-shaped glass structure next to the Great Hall of the People (Xi Chang'an Jie 2; ✆ **010/6655-0000**), the **Forbidden City Concert Hall** inside Zhongshan Park (✆ **010/6559-8285**), and the **Beijing Concert Hall** (**Beijing Yinyue Ting;** ✆ **010/6605-5812**), at Bei Xinhua Jie in Liubukou (Xuanwu). The **Poly Theater** (**Baoli Dasha Guoji Juyuan;** ✆ **010/6506-5343**), in the Poly Plaza complex on the East Third Ring Road (northeast exit of Dong Si Shi Tiao metro station), also hosts many large-scale performances, including the occasional revolutionary ballet. For information on additional venues and the shows they're hosting, check one of the expatriate magazines or ticket sellers Piao (Dongzhimenwai Dajie 48, Dongfang Yingzhuo Building A 17/F; ✆ **010/6466-9968;** www.piao.com).

Bars & Clubs

Beijing's oldest and still most popular drinking district is **Sanlitun.** The name comes from Sanlitun Lu, a north-south strip of drinking establishments east of the Workers' Stadium between the East Second and Third ring roads that at one time contained practically all of the city's bars. Now known as North Bar Street (Sanlitun Jiuba Jie, though the official street sign reads Sanlitun Bei Lu), it has been joined by other bars in the Xingfu Cun area to the west, and scattered around the stadium area. Bars here are rowdy and raunchy, and are packed to overflowing on weekends.

Popular bars in this district include the **Saddle Cantina,** aka "The Saddle," 81 Sanlitun Bei Lu, inside Nali Patio (✆ **010/5208-6005**), which draws big crowds with its gigantic balcony and slushy-style margaritas; around the corner, a more classy choice frequented by foreigners is **Apothecary,** Sanlitun Beilu 81 Nali Patio 3/F (✆ **010/5280-6040**), known for its extensive collection of expert cocktails. Upstairs is **Migas,** a trendy rooftop bar that features Spanish tapas downstairs and music and cocktails upstairs. Other hotspots in the area include **The Tree,** 43 Bei Sanlitun Nan, 100m (109 yards) west of Sanlitun Bei Lu (✆ **010/6415-1954**), with the city's best selection of Belgian beer; and the classy **Q Bar,** 6/F Eastern Hotel (✆ **010/6595-9239;** www.qbarbeijing.com), which produces the city's finest martinis—don't be put off by the fact that you have to walk through a dumpy hotel to get here, this place is gorgeous and has a great balcony. Just north is **Glen,** 16 Sanlitun Nanlu, Taiyue Apartments Suite 203 (✆ **010/6591-1191**), modeled after a Japanese whisky bar. Just below Glen is **Beer Mania,** 16 Sanlitun Nan Lu, Taiyue Apartments Ground Floor (✆ **010/6500-059l**). The extensive beer menu, served in an unpretentious and laid-back environment, is a refreshing change from the standard light Chinese beer served at most places. **Mesh** and **Punk,** both inside the Opposite House hotel at 11 Sanlitun Bei Lu (✆ **010/6417-6688**) are hip new places serving pricey drinks in stylish environs—best to visit during happy hour (8–11pm Thurs at Mesh, Fri at Punk). Punk has a small dance floor that doesn't start grooving until around midnight.

Worker's Stadium has become a thriving area for dance clubs and bars in Beijing. Just inside the north entrance of Worker's Stadium. **Mix** (✆ **010/6506-9888**) and **Vic's** (✆ **010/5293-0333**) are two of Beijing's well-known establishments that play hip hop and electronic music respectively. If you're looking for something a less hyped and full of young clubbers, stop by **Fubar** (✆ **010/6546-8364**), a "speakeasy" bar at Gongti West gate, sneakily located just behind **Stadium Dog,** a hotdog stand opened by the same owner. Fubar has a very social atmosphere, not to mention their occasional martini happy hours.

Another bar district surrounds the west gate of **Chaoyang Park** (tell the cab driver *Chaoyang Gongyuan Xi Lu*) in the east, an area the government has tried to promote as the new drinking district because it has fewer residential buildings. Worth checking out is the seedy **Club Suzie Wong** (Suxi Huang Julebu; ✆ **010/6500-3377**), the see-and-be-seen venue for nouveau riche Chinese and new expatriates. If you're visiting during the summer, continue north from Suzie Wong's to the chic balcony at **The Beach,** in the Block 8 Complex at 8 Chaoyang Gongyuan Xi Lu (✆ **0/13521882889;** open during the summer only), which is known for a beautiful rooftop and its equally beautiful guests. Be prepared to wait in line.

The fastest-growing spot for late-night drinking is the **Back Lakes** (Shicha Hai or Hou Hai), a previously serene spot with a few discreetly fashionable bars that now threatens to explode into a riot of hip. Neon has become a common sight, and several dance clubs are in the works, but for now this remains the finest place in the city for a quiet drink. Good bars here include supercool **Bed Tapas and Bar** (Chuang Ba), where you can enjoy an excellent caipirinha or mojito while lounging on a traditional four-poster bed in a delightful courtyard setting, at Zhangwang Hutong 17, northwest of the Drum Tower (✆ **010/8400-1554**); and **Pass-by Bar** (Guoke Jiuba), which also serves passable Italian food, at Nan Luogu Xiang 108 (alley to the left/west of the Muslim restaurant on the north side of Ping'an Dadao; walk north 150m/492 ft.; ✆ **010/8403-8004**). If you're looking for an inventive cocktail or a pizza, stop by **Mao Mao Chong** (✆ **010/6405-5718;** www.maomaochingstore.com), located on Banchang Hutong 12. During the winter they have a delicious adult chai, or you can cool off in the summer with a Mao Mao Chong Iced Tea.

You can also go off the beaten path to get a microbrew in an open courtyard at **Great Leap Brewery** (✆ **010/5715-1399;** www.greatleapbrewing.com), at Dou-Jiao Hutong no. 6 (check the website for a map to get there). Have a seat in their traditional courtyard and sample their variety of home brews, something that is not commonly found in Beijing.

Finally, there is **Haidian,** the city's university district to the northwest. Bars and clubs are congregated around gates of several universities and cater to a crowd of film students, English-language majors, and aspiring writers.

GAY & LESBIAN BARS

Beijing is a quiet scene for lesbians, somewhat less so for gay men. The best gay club in Beijing is **Destination (Mudidi),** Gongti Xi Lu 7, south of the Worker's Stadium west gate (✆ **010/6551-5138**), where the crowd revels and the beats are right. For the gals, it's a slow-developing scene: Aside from Thursday nights at Destination, try the Feng Bar, just east of the south gate of the Worker's Stadium on Saturday nights.

SIDE TRIPS FROM BEIJING

The Great Wall 长城

Even after you dispense with the myths that it is a single continuous structure and that it can be seen from space, China's best-known attraction is still a mind-boggling achievement. Referred to in Mandarin as the Wanli Changcheng (10,000-Li Long Wall) or just Changcheng for short, the Great Wall begins at Shanhaiguan on the Bo Hai (sea; p. 135) and snakes west to a fort at Jiayu Guan in the Gobi Desert (p.285). Its origins date from the Warring States Period (453–221 B.C.), when rival kingdoms began building defensive walls to thwart each other's armies. The king of Qin, who eventually conquered the other states to become the first emperor of a unified China, conscripted around 300,000 laborers to combine the walls into a more or less uninterrupted rampart. During the Han dynasty (206 B.C.–A.D. 220), the Wall was extended farther west, with subsequent dynasties adding their own bits and branches, which makes it difficult to pin down the Wall's precise length. It is at least 10,000km (6,200 miles) long by common estimates, but some guesses go as high as 50,000km (31,000 miles).

Most sections of the Great Wall visible north of Beijing were reconstructed by the Ming dynasty (1368–1644) in an (ultimately vain) effort to defend against attack by Manchus and Mongols from the north. The four sections we recommend, which we present from easiest and more popular to less traversed and remote: **Mutianyu, Juyongguan, Simatai,** and **Jiankou.** Avoid Badaling, the most popular section, which has become a Disneyfied mess of tour groups and touts.

Note: For Chinese translations of major sites in this section, turn to chapter 16.

On the Wild Wall

Sections of the Great Wall listed below are easy to reach and suitably stunning, but they represent only a part of what the Wall has to offer. People with time and an inclination to explore beyond these sections are strongly encouraged to join one of the excellent, usually multiday "Wild Wall" trips to the crumbling **"unofficial" sections of the Wall** that snake through more remote areas north of Beijing. Most weekend trips cost ¥3,600 and are based at one of two **modernized farmhouses** (one better outfitted than the other). The fee includes guided hikes, 2 nights' accommodations, six meals, drinks and snacks, research and conservation contribution, and book. Details and booking information about weekend trips, day hikes, and "Extreme" treks can be found on the Wild Wall website at **www.wildwall.com**.

MUTIANYU 幕田峪 ★

Opt for this wall, restored in 1986, rather than the overcrowded Badaling. Mutianyu is a bit rougher than Badaling, but it does have its own traffic jams in summer. Cable-car transportation is available. Sadly, a fence prevents you from walking onto the tempting unrestored sections. The ticket office is open 7:30am to 6:30pm. Admission is ¥40 and the cable car costs ¥50 round-trip.

Mutianyu is 90km (56 miles) north of Beijing. Most hotels can arrange **guided group tours** for around ¥250. The **tourist (*you*) bus no. 6** combines the trip to Mutianyu with visits to a temple and a lake for ¥50; it leaves from the northeast side of the Xuanwu Men metro station every 30 minutes from 6:30 to 8am. A **taxi** will cost ¥500.

Tip: In a quiet river valley close to Mutianyu lies Beijing's most appealing Great Wall resort, **Red Capital Ranch** ★ (✆ **010/8401-8886;** ¥850–¥1,500 including breakfast, plus 15% service charge; Apr–Nov) with small studio villas and new Tibetan tent accommodations Fishing, bike riding, hiking on the Wall, and even a Tibetan essential oil massage are offered. A shuttle connects with the Red Capital Residence. Another option is the **Schoolhouse at Mutianyu** (Mutianyu Cun 12; ✆ **010/6162-6506;** www.theschoolhouseatmutianyu.com; ¥3,200), which offers cozy villa accommodations for hefty prices.

JUYONGGUAN 居庸关 ★

This is the most recently restored section of the Great Wall, and the closest to Beijing (55km/34 miles northwest, on the road to Badaling), definitely a plus for time-pressed travelers. The restoration is crisp and the sense of history rather distant. But there are fewer tour groups here, and a number of impressive Buddhist bas-relief carvings on the separate and genuinely old Yun Tai (Cloud Platform) built in 1342. The ticket office is open from 7:30am to 5pm. Admission is ¥45 in summer, and ¥25 for students.

The **tourist (*you*)** and **public buses** that go to Badaling also stop here. A round-trip **taxi** ride should cost around ¥400.

SIMATAI 司马台 ★★

Somewhat tamed after a series of deaths led to the closing of its most dangerous stretch, Simatai nevertheless remains one of the best options for those who want

A Great Hike on the Great Wall

Jinshanling ★★ (✆ **010/8402-4628;** ¥50), along with Jiankou, is one of the all-time Great Wall hikes. It's not as steep as Simatai and is more heavily restored, but with fewer visitors. The hike from here east to the Miyun Reservoir is roughly 10km (6 miles) and takes 3 to 4 hours. The middle part of the hike, as the people fall away and the Wall begins to crumble, can be truly sublime. A number of hostels provide transportation for this hike, including the Beijing Downtown Backpacker's Hostel, Nanluoguxiang 85 (✆ **010/8400-2429;** ¥280). You can take an air-conditioned bus from the Xi Zhi Men long-distance bus station to Miyun (every 30 min.; 6am–4pm; ¥15), then hire a minivan *(miandi)* to drop you off at Jinshanling and pick you up at Simatai for around ¥100—make sure you withhold payment until after you're picked up.

more of a challenge from the Great Wall. The most harrowing portion, steep and unrestored, is on the east side of the Miyun Reservoir. Several gravel-strewn spots here require all four limbs to navigate. The endpoint is Wangjing Ta, the 12th watchtower from the bottom. Beyond this is the appropriately named **Tian Qiao (Heavenly Bridge),** a thin, tilted ridge where the Wall narrows to only a few feet—this section is now off-limits. Despite the danger, this part of the Wall can get crowded on weekends, especially since the cable car was installed. Souvenir vendors can also be a nuisance. The round-trip hike to Tian Qiao takes roughly 3 hours at a moderate pace. The section of Simatai west of the reservoir is better restored (in the beginning at least) and connects to another section of the Great Wall, Jinshanling, in Hebei Province. The ticket office is in a small village 10 minutes' walk south of the reservoir; it's open from 8am to 5pm. Admission is ¥40. The cable car runs April to November from 8am to 4:30pm; a round-trip ride to the No. 8 Tower costs ¥50.

Simatai is 110km (68 miles) northeast of Beijing. The best no-hassle option is to go there with one of the **Youth Hostel** tours (✆ **010/6551-5362**); this leaves from the Beijing City Central Youth Hostel at Beijing railway station. The van leaves once a day and costs ¥220 from May to October and ¥180 from November to April. The **tourist *(you)* bus no. 12** travels to Simatai from northeast of the Xuanwu Men metro stop (Apr to mid-Oct Sat–Sun 6:30–8:30am, every 30 min; ¥70); you get about 3 hours at the site. A round-trip **taxi** ride should cost less than ¥500.

Responding to the popularity of the Jinshanling-to-Simatai hike (see above), the **Simatai YHA** (✆ **010/8188-9323;** dorm bed ¥70; standard room ¥320) opened in 2004. Courtyard-style rooms are basic, but the coffee is superb, and the view of the Wall from the patio is wonderful.

JIANKOU 箭口 ★★★

This is our favorite part of the Wall. Few tourist buses make the journey here, and there is no cable car shuttling out-of-shape tourists to the top. Even more amazing, there are no touts selling knickknacks. This section is for serious hikers only. Start at Xin Zhai Zi Cun where the road dead-ends into a parking lot, following the trail up to the Wall. Turn left once you reach the wall, and prepare yourself for an intense 5-hour hike. The tallest watchtower in the distance is Jiankou, and just before you reach it, there is a turn-off point that is marked by a flat, paved section of the Wall that leads you back down to the road. From the road, it's a 20-minute walk back to the parking lot. The ticket office is open 8am to 5pm. Admission is ¥20. Parking is ¥5.

Jiankou is 70km (44 miles) northeast of Beijing. There are no public transportation options here. A round-trip **taxi** will cost ¥500, including driver's waiting time.

Other Sights Outside Beijing

THE MING TOMBS (SHI SAN LING; 十三陵)

Of the 16 emperors who ruled China during the Ming dynasty (1368–1644), 13 are buried in this valley north of Beijing (hence the Chinese name Shi San Ling, the 13 Tombs). The Yongle emperor, who also oversaw construction of the Forbidden City, consulted geomancers before choosing this site, considered advantageous because it is bounded to the north by a range of protective mountains. The geography of the valley is mirrored in the tombs themselves, with each emperor buried beneath a tumulus protected from the rear by a mountain. Only three of the Ming Tombs—**Ding Ling, Chang Ling,** and **Zhao Ling**—have been restored, and only one (Ding Ling) has been fully excavated. Many of the buildings mirror Ming palaces found in the city. Because of this, the sight can be boring to people who've already had their fill of imperial architecture. However, several attractions, particularly the **Shen Dao (Spirit Way),** make the trip worthwhile for those who have the time.

The valley is 48km (30 miles) north of Beijing, on the same road that goes to Badaling. Many **tours** to Badaling also come here, but if you want time to explore some of the unrestored tombs (highly recommended), you'll have to make a separate trip. A **taxi** hired in Beijing should cost about ¥500. The most comfortable form of public transport is the air-conditioned **bus no. 345** from Jishuitan to Changping. Then cross the street and take bus no. 314 to the Da Gong Men stop.

Shen Dao (Spirit Way) ★ The main entrance to the valley is the **Da Hong Men (Great Red Gate),** remarkably similar to gates found in the Forbidden City, beyond which is a pavilion housing China's largest memorial stele, and beyond that the Spirit Way. The path, slightly curved to fool evil spirits, is lined on either side with willows and remarkable **carved stone animals** and human figures, considered among the best in China and far better than those found at the Qing Tombs. Not be missed.

Ticket office north of stele pavilion. Admission summer ¥30, winter ¥20. 8:30am–6pm. Simple bilingual maps available here for ¥3.

Chang Ling This tomb, home to the remains of the Yongle emperor, is the largest and best preserved of the 13. It is essentially a Forbidden City in miniature, and perhaps disappointing if you've seen the palace already. Most striking is the **Ling'en Dian,** an immense hall in which the interior columns and brackets have been left unpainted, creating an eye-catching contrast with the green ceiling panels.

4km (2½ miles) due north of the Shen Dao. Admission summer ¥45, winter ¥30. 8:30am–5:30pm. Bus: no. 314 to Chang Ling stop from lighted intersection just beyond north end of Spirit Way.

Ding Ling The 4,000-sq.-m (13,000-sq.-ft.) **Underground Palace** discovered here in 1956 was the burial place of the Wanli emperor, his wife, and his favorite concubine. The "palace" is a plain marble vault, buried 27m (88 ft.) underground and divided into five large chambers. It's all a bit disappointing. The corpses have been removed, their red coffins replaced with replicas, and burial objects moved to aboveground display rooms. The original marble thrones are still here, though, now covered in a small fortune of Renminbi notes tossed by Chinese visitors in hopes of bribing the emperor's ghost. Outside, behind the ticket office, is the respectable **Shisan Ling Bowuguan (Ming Tombs Museum)**.

Admission summer ¥60, winter ¥40. 8:30am–6pm. On west side of valley; walk south from Chang Ling, take 1st right, and walk west 20 min.

Eastern Qing Tombs (Qing Dong Ling; 清东陵) ★★

The Qing Dong Ling have been open for more than 20 years but they are still little visited, despite offering considerably more to visitors than those of the Ming. Altogether, 5 emperors, 15 empresses, 136 concubines, 3 princes, and 2 princesses are buried in 15 tombs here. The first to be buried was Shunzhi—the first Qing emperor to reign from Beijing—in 1663, and the last was an imperial concubine in 1935. The tomb chambers of four imperial tombs, the **Xiao Ling** (the Shunzhi emperor), **Jing Ling** (Kangxi), **Yu Ling** (Qianlong), and **Ding Ling** (Xianfeng), are open, as well as the twin **Ding Dong Ling** tombs (the Cixi dowager empress and the Ci'an empress). Also of interest is a group site for the Qianlong emperor's concubines.

The tombs are in Zunhua County, Hebei Province, 125km (78 miles) east of Beijing. They are open from 8am to 5:30pm in summer, 9am to 4:30pm in winter. The *tong piao,* which offers access to all the tombs, costs ¥120. A special Qing Dong Ling tourist bus leaves at 7:30am from northeast of the Xuanwu Men metro stop (departures 6:30–8am; ¥170, includes admission ticket) and allows you about 3 hours onsite before beginning the return journey. If you want to explore at your own pace, you'll have to hire a cab; a round-trip costs around ¥500.

The **Xiao Ling** was the first tomb on the site, and a model for others both here and at the Western Qing Tombs, although few others are so elaborate. Each tomb has an approach road or Spirit Way, which may have guardian figures. The entrance to the tomb itself is usually preceded by a large stele pavilion and marble bridges over a stream. To the right, the buildings used for preparation of sacrifices are now usually the residences of the staff, and hung with washing. Inside the gate, halls to the left and right were for enrobing and other preparations, and now house exhibitions, as usually does each **Hall of Eminent Favor,** at the rear, where ceremonies in honor of the deceased took place. Behind, if open, a doorway allows access past a stone altar to a steep ramp leading to the base of a **soul tower.** Through a passageway beneath, stairs to either side lead to a walkway encircling the mound, giving views across the countryside. If the tomb chamber is open, a ramp from beneath the soul tower leads down to a series of chambers.

The twin **Ding Dong Ling** tombs have nearly identical exteriors, but empress dowager Cixi had hers rebuilt in 1895, 14 years after empress Ci'an's death (in which she is suspected of having had a hand), using far more expensive materials. Everywhere are reminders of the Forbidden City, such as the terrace-corner spouts carved as water-loving dragons (*che*). The interior has motifs strikingly painted in gold on dark wood, recalling the buildings where the empress spent her last years. There are walls of carved and gilded brick, and columns writhing with superbly fearsome wooden dragons. After this, the other tombs seem gaudy.

The enclosure of the **Yu Fei Yuan Qin (Garden of Rest)** contains moss-covered tumuli for 35 of the Qianlong emperor's concubines. Another is buried in a proper tomb chamber, along with an empress whom Qianlong had grown to dislike.

The **Yu Ling** has the finest tomb chamber, a series of rooms separated by solid marble doors, with walls and arched ceilings engraved with Buddha figures and more than 30,000 words of Tibetan scripture. The 3-ton doors themselves have reliefs of bodhisattvas (beings on the road to enlightenment) and the four protective kings usually found at temple entrances. This tomb is worth the trip in its own right. The **Jing Ling** is the tomb of Qianlong's grandfather, the Kangxi emperor. It's surprisingly modest given that he was possibly the greatest emperor the Chinese ever had, but that's in keeping with what is known of his character. The Spirit Way leading to the tomb has an elegant five-arch bridge; the guardian figures are placed at an unusual curve in the way, quite close to the tomb itself, and are more decorated than those at earlier tombs.

Western Qing Tombs (Qing Xi Ling; 清西陵) ★★

The Yongzheng emperor broke with tradition and ordered his tomb to be constructed here, away from his father (the Kangxi emperor). His son, the Qianlong emperor, decided to be buried near his grandfather and that thereafter burials should alternate between the eastern (see above) and western sites, although this was not followed consistently. The first tomb, the **Tai Ling,** was completed in 1737, 2 years after the Yongzheng reign. The last imperial interment was in 1998, when the ashes of Aisin-Gioro Henry Puyi, the last emperor, were moved to a commercial cemetery here. He and two consorts were added to four emperors, four empresses, four princes, two princesses, and 57 concubines. The site is rural, with the tombs lapped by orchards and agriculture, and with chickens, goats, and the odd rabbit to be encountered.

Chang Ling (the Jiaqing emperor's tomb) and **Chong Ling** (Guangxu) are also open, as well as **Chang Xi Ling,** with the extraordinary sonic effects of its **Huiyin Bi**—an echo wall where, as the only visitors, you'll actually be able to try out the special effects available only in theory at the Temple of Heaven.

The **Qing Xi Ling** are located 140km (87 miles) southwest of Beijing, outside Yi Xian in Hebei Province. The ticket office is open from 8am to 5pm; a *tong piao* (good for access to all the tombs) costs ¥120 and is good for 2 days. There's no access by tourist bus, but that is part of the appeal for most visitors. The best way to get here is by taxi, which costs around ¥500 (round-trip, including driver's waiting time). It's possible to visit **Marco Polo Bridge (Lu Gou Qiao)** on the way.

Unless you make a very early start, you may want to spend the night at the modest, Manchu-themed **Ba Jiao Lou Manzu Zhuangyuan,** just east of Tai Ling (✆ **0312/826-0828;** ¥120 standard room). **Xing Gong Binguan,** near Yongfu Si on the eastern side of the tomb complex (✆ **0312/471-0038;** standard room ¥150 after discount), was where Manchu rulers stayed when they came to pay their respects, and the room constructed in 1748 to house the Qianlong emperor is now rented out as two suites (¥660 after discount).

The **Da Bei Lou,** a pavilion containing two vast stele, is on the curved route to the **Tai Ling.** The general plan of the major tombs follows that of the Eastern Tombs, above. In fact, the **Chang Ling,** slightly to the west, is almost identical, brick for brick, to the Tai Ling, although the rear section with soul tower and tomb mound is not open. The Jiaqing empress is buried just to the west in the **Chang Xi Ling,** on a far smaller scale, the tomb mound a brick drum. But the perfectly semicircular rear wall offers the whispering-gallery effects found at some domed European cathedrals; clapping while standing on marked stones at the center of the site produces multiple echoes, while speech is amazingly amplified. The empress can't get much peace.

Jiaqing's son, the Daoguang emperor, was meant to be buried at Qing Dong Ling, but his tomb there was flooded. The relocated **Mu Ling** appears much more modest than those of his predecessors. No stele pavilion or Spirit Way, largely unpainted, and the tomb mound is a modest brick-wall drum, but this is the most expensive tomb: Wood used to construct the exquisite main hall is fragrant *nanmu,* sourced from as far away as Myanmar. The Guangxu emperor was the last to complete his reign (although his aunt, Cixi, is again suspected of shortening it), and his **Chong Ling,** which uses more modern materials than other tombs, wasn't completed until 1915, well after the last emperor's abdication.

Several other tombs are open, and more are being restored. The recently opened **Tai Ling Fei Yuan Qin** is a rather battered group of concubine tumuli, individually labeled with the years in which each concubine entered the Yongzheng emperor's service, and their grades in the complex harem hierarchy.

The ashes of **Puyi** (properly known as the Xuantong emperor) lie buried on the eastern end of the site, up a slope behind a brand-new Qing-style memorial arch *(pailou),* and behind a shoddy modern carved balustrade. Neighboring plots are available for the right price.

Western Temples

Buried in the hills west of Beijing, **Tanzhe Si (Temple of the Pool and Wild Mulberry)** and **Jietai Si (Temple of the Ordination Platform)** are the tranquil kinds of Chinese temples people imagine before they actually come to China. Foreign travelers seldom visit them, but the effort to come out here is worth it, if only to escape the noise and dust of the city center.

Both are easily accessible by taking **bus no. 931** from the Pingguoyuan metro station at the far western end of Line 1. Take a right out of exit D and continue straight a few minutes to the bus station (be sure to take the plain red-and-beige, rather than the red-and-yellow *zhi,* version of the bus). Tanzhe Si is the last stop on this line; the trip takes 1 hour and costs ¥2.50. Basic but acceptable accommodations are available at both temples, for those who want (or need) to spend more time in quietude.

Tanzhe Si ★★ This peaceful complex dates from the Western Jin dynasty (265–316), well before Beijing was founded. In the main courtyard on the central axis is a pair of 30m (100-ft.) ginkgo trees, supposedly planted in the Tang dynasty (618–907), as well as several apricot trees, cypresses, peonies, and purple jade orchids. The **Guanyin Dian,** at the top of the western axis, was favored by Princess Miao Yan, a daughter of Kublai Khan; she is said to have prayed so fervently she left footprints in one of the floor stones (now stored in a box to the left).

48km (29 miles) west of Beijing. ✆ **010/6086-2244.** Admission ¥55. 8am–5pm. Bus: 931. Get off at last stop and hike up stone path at end of parking lot.

Jietai Si ★ The **ordination platform** here, China's largest, is a three-tiered circular structure with 113 statues of the God of Ordination placed in niches around the base. It is located in the Jietai Dian, in the far-right corner of the temple. Ceremonies conducted on this platform to commemorate the ascension of a devotee to full monkhood required permission from the emperor. Other courtyards have ancient, twisted pines, as venerable as the temple itself.

13km (8 miles) east of Tanzhe Si. ✆ **010/6080-3428.** Admission ¥45. 8am–5:30pm. Bus: 931 from Tanzhe Si. The stop is marked with a huge sign pointing the way to the temple.

CHENGDE 承德 ★★

Hebei Province, 233km (146 miles) NE of Beijing

If you can do only one overnight side trip from Beijing, make it Chengde—the summer camp of the Qing emperors. Here, in a walled enclosure containing numerous palaces, pavilions, and pagodas as well as a vast hunting park, the emperors escaped Beijing's blazing summer temperatures, entertained delegations from home and abroad, and practiced the mounted military skills that had originally gained them their empire. The design of the resort, built between 1703 and 1794, was shaped by its varied diplomatic functions. Some buildings are plain and undecorated to show visiting tribesmen that the emperors had not lost touch with their roots or been too softened by luxury; others were copies of some of China's most famous and elegant buildings; and some were giant edifices with hints of minority architecture, intended both to show the emperor's sympathy for the traditions of tributary and border-dwelling peoples, and to overawe their emissaries.

In 1794 Britain's Lord Macartney arrived on a mission from George III, and not finding the Qianlong emperor at home in Beijing, followed him up to Chengde. He was impressed by the resort's vast scale, and was shown around by people who anticipated modern guides' hyperbole by telling him that the gilded bronze roof tiles of the Potala Temple were of solid gold.

The Jiaqing emperor died here in 1820, as did the Xianfeng emperor in 1861, having signed the "unequal" treaties that marked the close of the Second Opium War. The place came to be viewed as unlucky, and was already decaying by the fall of the Qing in 1911. But the **Mountain Retreat for Escaping the Heat,** along with the remaining **Eight Outer Temples** around its perimeter, still form one of the greatest concentrations of ancient buildings in China. It's an 18th-century version of a "Splendid China" theme park (as seen in Florida and Shenzhen), but with oversize buildings rather than the miniatures offered there.

Ordinary Beijingers now follow imperial tradition by flocking here to escape the baking summer heat. You can hurry around the main sights by spending a night here, but you might want to spend 2.

Essentials

GETTING THERE Chengde has no airport, and although it's an easy side trip from Beijing, it's not well connected to anywhere else except the Northeast. A convenient morning all-seater **train** from Beijing Zhan, the K7711, departs at 6:30am, arriving in Chengde at 10:48am. It returns to Beijing as the K7712, leaving Chengde at 1:30pm, arriving in Beijing at 5:48pm. Soft seat costs ¥61, hard seat ¥41. The railway station is just south of the city center, and bus no. 5 from outside to your right runs to several hotels and to the Mountain Resort. The ticket office (up the stairs and to the right) is open from 5am to 10:30pm with brief breaks. There are also limited services to Shenyang and (nine high-speed D-series trains daily) Shijiazhuang (four trains daily, one D-series train at 5:14pm).

The soft-seat waiting room is through a door at the far left-hand end of the main hall as you enter, while luggage storage is on the right-hand side. On the train both to and from Beijing, enterprising staff sell tea for ¥3, instant coffee for ¥5, maps, and hotel reservations (do *not* book with them). About 1¼ hours after you leave Beijing, you'll see a crumbling stretch of the Great Wall.

At least until construction of a new road/rail interchange station at Dongzhi Men is complete, **bus** departures for Chengde from Beijing are more frequent from Liu Li Qiao Changtu Qiche Keyun Zhan (southwest of the Liu Li Qiao bridge; ✆ **010/8383-1717** or 010/8383-1720). The 233km (144-mile) trip costs ¥73 for an Iveco or similar, with departures about every 30 minutes from 5:40am to 6:40pm. The current journey takes about 5 hours. At the moment it's possible to alight and see the Great Wall at Jinshanling en route, and subsequently flag down a passing bus to finish the trip. Express buses from Beijing run to and from the forecourt of Chengde railway station. Escape the pestering of touts by dodging into a branch of the Sichuan restaurant Dongpo Fanzhuang, opposite and to the left (south) where you alight, and if you're ready for a quick lunch, have it here. The main long-distance bus station has been demolished to make way for an extension of the Sheng Hua Dajiudian, and most buses now depart from the **Qiche Dong Zhan** (✆ **0314/212-3588**), a ¥20 taxi ride south, or take bus no. 118, which passes Yingzi Dajie and the Mountain Resort. The ticket office is open from 5:30am to 5pm. There are two services to Shijiazhuang (7am, 9am, 11am, and 2pm; 10 hr.; ¥121), with seven buses connecting with Qinhuangdao (6:30am, 7:30am, 8:05am, 8:30am, 10am, 1pm, and 5pm; 4 hr.; ¥97). Buses to Beijing run every 20 minutes, but it's easier to flag an Iveco from outside the railway station.

GETTING AROUND **Taxi** meters are generally not used. The fare is ¥5 in town, or ¥10 to the outer temples. If the meter is started, ¥5 flagfall includes 1km; then ¥1.40 per kilometer, jumping 50% after 8km (5 miles). **Buses** usually charge ¥1.

VISITOR INFORMATION For tourist complaints, call ✆ **0314/202-4549.**

[Fast FACTS] CHENGDE

Banks, Foreign Exchange & ATMs The main foreign exchange branch of the Bank of China (9am–5pm) is at the junction of Dong Dajie and Lizheng Men Dajie. Another convenient branch is at Lizheng Men Dajie 19, just east of the Mountain Villa Hotel. Both have ATMs that accept foreign cards, as does a branch on the corner of Nan Yingzi Dajie and Xinhua Lu.

Internet Access Internet cafes are few and mostly far from the usual visitor areas. Follow Nan Yingzi Dajie south until you cross the railway line, turn right into Shanxi Ying to find a cluster of Internet bars (8am–midnight) on the first corner, which charge ¥1.50 per hour.

Post Office The post office is on Yingzi Dajie at its junction with Dong Dajie. It's open from 8am to 6pm (to 5pm in winter).

Visa Extensions Walking south along Nan Yingzi Dajie, turn right after the Xinhua Bookstore into Xiao Tong Gou Jie, then take the first left. Next to a branch of CITS you'll find a sign that reads aliens exit-entry department. Open Monday to Friday 8:30am to noon; 2:30 to 5:30pm in summer (1:30–5:30pm in winter).

Relaxing with the Emperors

Bishu Shanzhuang (Mountain Resort for Escaping the Heat) ★ While the "Winter Palace," as Beijing's Forbidden City was sometimes called, was the creation of the indigenous Ming dynasty, the summer palace at Chengde was entirely the creation of the Manchu Qing, and lay beyond the Great Wall in the direction of their homelands. Here the emperor and the Manchu nobility would play at the equestrian

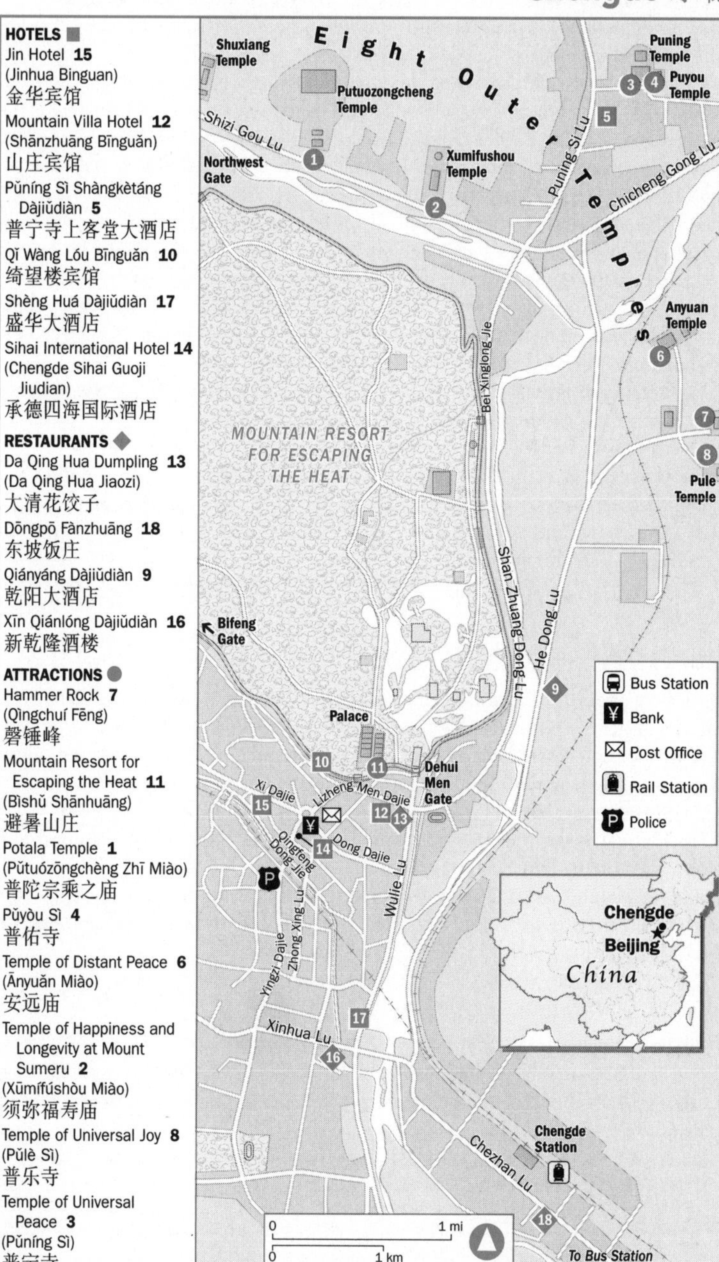
HOTELS
Jin Hotel 15
(Jinhua Binguan)
金华宾馆
Mountain Villa Hotel 12
(Shānzhuāng Bīnguǎn)
山庄宾馆
Pǔníng Sì Shàngkètáng Dàjiǔdiàn 5
普宁寺上客堂大酒店
Qǐ Wàng Lóu Bīnguǎn 10
绮望楼宾馆
Shèng Huá Dàjiǔdiàn 17
盛华大酒店
Sihai International Hotel 14
(Chengde Sihai Guoji Jiudian)
承德四海国际酒店
RESTAURANTS
Da Qing Hua Dumpling 13
(Da Qing Hua Jiaozi)
大清花饺子
Dōngpō Fànzhuāng 18
东坡饭庄
Qiányáng Dàjiǔdiàn 9
乾阳大酒店
Xīn Qiánlóng Dàjiǔdiàn 16
新乾隆酒楼
ATTRACTIONS
Hammer Rock 7
(Qìngchuí Fēng)
磬锤峰
Mountain Resort for Escaping the Heat 11
(Bìshǔ Shānhuāng)
避暑山庄
Potala Temple 1
(Pǔtuózōngchèng Zhī Miào)
普陀宗乘之庙
Pǔyòu Sì 4
普佑寺
Temple of Distant Peace 6
(Ānyuǎn Miào)
安远庙
Temple of Happiness and Longevity at Mount Sumeru 2
(Xūmífúshòu Miào)
须弥福寿庙
Temple of Universal Joy 8
(Pǔlè Sì)
普乐寺
Temple of Universal Peace 3
(Pǔníng Sì)
普宁寺
Eight Outer Temples
Shuxiang Temple
Putuozongcheng Temple
Xumifushou Temple
Puning Temple
Puyou Temple
Anyuan Temple
Pule Temple
Shizi Gou Lu
Northwest Gate
Puning Si Lu
Chicheng Gong Lu
Bei Xinglong Jie
MOUNTAIN RESORT FOR ESCAPING THE HEAT
Shan Zhuang Dong Lu
He Dong Lu
Bifeng Gate
Palace
Dehui Men Gate
Xi Dajie
Lizheng Men Dajie
Dong Dajie
Qingfeng Dong Jie
Zhong Xing Lu
Yingzi Dajie
Wulie Lu
Xinhua Lu
Chezhan Lu
Chengde Station
To Bus Station (10km)
Bus Station
Bank
Post Office
Rail Station
Police
Chengde
Beijing
China
0 1 mi
0 1 km

4 BEIJING & HEBEI | Chengde

and military talents that had won them China in the first place, both with formal contests in archery and with hunting in the well-stocked park. The lakes and their many pavilions, stuffed with treasures, provided the emperor and his consorts with more refined diversions.

There's a half-day of wandering here, although many of the buildings shown as lying within the park have long since vanished. The most important remaining is the **Zheng Gong (Main Palace).** The message here is one of simplicity and frugality (the beams and columns are very plain, although actually made of hardwoods brought long distances at great expense), with a pleasing elegance in great contrast to the usual Qing gaudiness. The palace now serves as a museum, displaying ancient military equipment in the front rooms and period furnishings and antiquities at the rear.

Straight north, up the west side of lakes dotted with pavilions and crossed by many bridges, lies the **Wenjin Ge (Pavilion of Literary Delight),** a ripple-roofed southern-style building reached through a rockery, which is a copy of a famous library building from Ningbo.

A little farther northeast, the handsome **Liu He Ta (Pagoda of the Six Harmonies)** is the most striking building in the park. Its nine brick stories have green- or yellow-tiled eaves hung with bells and topped by a golden knob.

The pagoda is near the east entrance of the park, close to which the retired and unemployed can be found enjoying a game of croquet. If you've already examined the gaudy pavilions around the lakes, it's possible to leave this way to walk or catch a bus to the Eight Outer Temples.

Main entrance (Zheng Men) in Lizheng Men Dajie. ✆ **0314/207-6089.** Admission ¥90, ¥60 in winter. 6am–6pm.

Wai Ba Miao (Eight Outer Temples; 外八庙) ★★

There were originally 12 temples, built between 1713 and 1780, and not all of those that remain are open to the public. Summer hours are May 1 to October 15; outside these times, some lesser temples may be shut. Several temples have features unique to Chengde. Most are extremely grand and suitably impressive (their purpose, after all), with successive halls on rising ground.

Tip: Puning Si and the other northern temples are on morning itineraries for tour groups, followed by Pule Si and the eastern temples in the afternoon. If you're traveling independently, work the other way around. You can also buy a *tao piao* for ¥80, which includes entry to Xumifushou Miao, the Potala Temple, Pule Si, and Anyuan Miao.

Bus no. 118, from Yingzi Dajie or the Mountain Resort main entrance, will take you to the northern group of temples.

Xumifushou Miao (Temple of Happiness and Longevity at Mount Sumeru) Partly inspired by Tashilhunpo in Tibet (p. 773), this temple was constructed to make the Panchen Lama, number two in the Tibetan religious hierarchy, feel at home during a visit in 1780.

Shizi Gou Lu. ✆ **0314/216-2972.** Admission summer ¥30, winter ¥20. 7:30am–6pm (8:30am–5pm in winter). Bus: 118 to Xumifushou Zhi Miao.

Putuozongcheng Zhi Miao (Potala Temple) Five minutes' walk west, the Potala Temple, its tapering windows and slab-sided walls obviously influenced by Tibet, is in no way "a copy of the Potala Temple in Lhasa" (p. 764), as local guides like to say. Many windows are blind, and several outbuildings are solid, just intended to add to the massy splendor of the whole. Items on display in the surrounding galleries include two nine-story sandalwood pagodas climbing through holes cut in the floors, young girls' skulls fused with silver and once used as drinking vessels, and anatomically detailed esoteric statuary of sexual acts.

Shizi Gou Lu. ✆ **0314/216-3072.** Admission summer ¥40, winter ¥30. 7:30am–6pm (winter 8:30am–5pm). Bus: 118 to Putuozongcheng Zhi Miao.

Puning Si (Temple of Universal Peace) The main Hall of Mahayana is impressive—story upon story of red walls and yellow roofs, topped with a gold knob surrounded by four mini-pagoda-like points. More impressive still is its contents, a giant copper-colored wooden Guanyin figure more than 22m (73 ft.) high, the largest of its kind in the world. It's possible to climb three levels of interior galleries to look the figure in the eye, as she sits in dusty gloom. While other sights in Chengde are managed by the sleepy local tourism bureau, this temple is run by an entrepreneurial group of monks: The temple now sports a hotel (see below) and a tacky but entertaining re-creation of a Qing market, and offers an evening show promising blessings and exorcisms by "real Tibetan lamas."

Off Puning Si Lu. ✆ **0314/205-8203.** Admission ¥50–¥100 to climb the Hall of Mahayana. 7:30am–6pm (winter 8:30am–5pm). Bus: 6 or 118 to Puning Si.

Puyou Si The point of entering is to see the remainder of a collection of statues of the 500 arhats (the first followers of the Sakyamuni Buddha). Many of these were destroyed in 1937 during the Japanese occupation, but the remainder have a lively jollity and are hung with scarves placed by respectful devotees.

✆ **0314/216-0935.** Admission ¥20. 8am–5:30pm (winter 8:30am–4:30pm).

Pule Si (Temple of Universal Joy) Tibetan advisors were employed in the design of this temple, built to receive annual tributary visits from defeated Mongol tribes. But the most striking element is the copy at the rear of the circular Hall of Prayer for Good Harvests from the Temple of Heaven. Shady benches around the quiet courtyards make perfect picnic stops.

Off Hedong Lu. ✆ **0314/205-7557.** Admission summer ¥30, winter ¥20. 8am–5:30pm (winter 8:30am–4:30pm). Bus: 10 from Wulie Lu to terminus. Taxi: a short ride from Puning Si.

Qingchui Feng (Hammer Rock) Bus no. 10's terminus is actually the cableway to Hammer Rock. The characters specifically mean a kind of hammer for striking a Buddhist musical instrument, but the shape of this clublike column will inevitably remind all who see it of something completely different. It reminds the Chinese of that, too—they're just being polite. Pleasant strolls across the hills and sweeping views of the valley await those who ascend.

✆ **0314/205-7135.** Admission ¥25. 24 hr. Cable car ¥27 one-way; ¥42 round-trip. Apr 1–Oct 30 7:30am–5:30pm.

Anyuan Miao (Temple of Distant Peace) Built in 1764, this is another example of architectural diplomacy, built in imitation of a temple (now long-vanished) in Yining on China's remote western borders (p. 332) to please Mongol tribes that were resettled around Chengde. You'll almost certainly be the only visitor.

✆ **0314/205-7809.** Admission ¥10. Summer only 8:30am–5pm. A 15-min. walk north of Pule Si.

Shopping

A lively **market** takes over the upper part of Yingzi Dajie at night, interesting for its color rather than for what's on sale. The street also has several department stores with ground-floor supermarkets. Toward the post office there's a couple of bakeries where you can pick up snacks for the onward journey.

Where to Stay

From the first week of May to the first week of October the town is busy, weekends particularly so, but only during the weeklong national holidays should it be difficult to find a room. Otherwise, the town has an excess of accommodations and, even in peak season, all hotels will have 20% discounts, rising to as much as 70% in the off season for the gently persuasive bargainer who just shows up. A 50% discount is taken for granted; you work down from there.

EXPENSIVE

Puning Si Shangketang Dajiudian ★★ Run by the market-savvy monks of Puning Si, this newly opened hotel offers cozy accommodations within the west wing of the temple. Rooms are tastefully decorated with dark wood furniture and handmade paper lamps and are set around eight tranquil courtyards, which have rock gardens and ponds. Buddhist touches are in evidence: There's a large (if overpriced) vegetarian selection in the main restaurant, the proscription against soft beds is enforced, and there's little chance of sleeping in—the temple bells peal at 7:30am.

Puning Si. ✆ **0314/205-8889** for reservations. 60 units. ¥488 standard room. 30% summer discounts offered. V. **Amenities:** 2 restaurants; exercise room; indoor pool. *In room:* A/C, TV, fridge.

Sheng Hua Dajiudian The four-star Sheng Hua is Chengde's best hotel when it comes to furnishings. Rooms are spacious; luxury twin (standard) rooms even come equipped with their own computer. Bathrooms are well outfitted and come with elaborate massage-jet showers. A new wing, located on the site of the old bus station, opened in 2006. It houses a pool and fitness center. Staff is helpful with inquiries, and speaks English and French.

Wulie Lu 22. ✆ **0314/227-1188.** Fax 0314/227-1112. 114 units. ¥700–¥780 standard room. 30%–40% summer discounts offered. AE, MC, V. **Amenities:** 2 restaurants; teahouse; forex. *In room:* A/C, TV, fridge, hair dryer, Internet.

Sihai International Hotel The hotel locals will point you in the direction of is Sihai International Hotel—but be warned. The hotel has an institutional feel, which is continued through the rooms, though they are quiet spacious. The only other redeeming feature is the marble bathtubs in each room. Like most nice Chinese hotels, there is a KTV in the complex and one Chinese restaurant.

Huo Shen Miao Re He Daxia Building B. www.shihotel.com. ✆ **0314/209-1666.** Fax 0314/209-6625. 186 units. ¥480–¥1,200. AE, MC, V. **Amenities:** Restaurant, KTV, ticket center. *In room:* A/C, cable TV, cable Internet.

MODERATE

Shanzhuang Binguan (Mountain Villa Hotel) Once the only hotel in town, this six-building monster directly opposite the Mountain Resort underwent a full renovation. Unfortunately, the hotel recently eliminated a variety of simpler, cheaper rooms with common bathrooms for budget travelers but the standard rooms are still a good deal. Usually these longer-standing hotels should be your last choice, but here a real effort has been made to stay in competition with the newer hotels.

Li Zhen Men Dajie 11 (opposite main entrance to Mountain Resort). mvhotel@cs-user.he.cninfo.net. ✆ **0314/209-1188.** ✆ 0314/202-2457 for reservations. Fax 0314/203-4143. 370 units. ¥580–¥780 standard room; ¥800–¥2,000 suite. 20% discount in summer. AE, DC, MC, V. Bus: 5 from railway station to Bishu Shanzhuang. **Amenities:** 2 restaurants; forex; fitness room. *In room:* A/C, TV, hair dryer, Internet (on request).

INEXPENSIVE

Jin Hua Binguan This might be the best of the inexpensive bunch, however mediocre this choice may be. Suited for the budget minded, the hotel offers private rooms and dorm beds—with the usual hard mattress and pillows. Private rooms are spacious and feature deep red Chinese carpets but could use an extra scrubbing. The hotel offers guided tours of the town for a bargain price of ¥50.

Xi Dajie and MaShi Jie West Corner. ✆ **0314/203-5055.** ¥180 single bed; ¥280 double bed; ¥380 triple bed. **Amenities:** A/C.

Where to Eat

The **nightmarket** on Yingzi Dajie runs through the heart of town. Stalls sell kabobs for ¥1 and other Chinese fast food, eaten at tables behind each stall.

As befits a former hunting ground, Chengde's specialty is game. The town is almost like a remote outpost of Guangdong, of whose residents other Chinese say, "They eat anything with legs except a table, and anything with wings except an airplane." Donkey, dog, and scorpion are on menus. But so are deer, *shan ji* ("mountain chicken"—pheasant), and wild boar—often as unfamiliar ingredients cooked in familiar styles. Stir-frying makes venison tough, but wild boar softens up nicely while retaining its gamey flavor.

The best restaurants are in larger hotels such as the **Qianyang Dajiudian.** Try *lurou chao zhenmo* (venison stir-fried with hazel mushrooms) and *quechao shanji pian* ("Sparrow's nest" pheasant slices). The **Xin Qianlong Dajiudian,** just south of the Sheng Hua Dajiudian on Xinhua Lu (✆ **0314/207-2222**), open from 10am to 8:40pm, has attentive service, good portions, and a picture menu. Plump dumplings stuffed with donkey meat and onions are called *lurou dacong shuijiao;* 200 grams or four *liang (si liang)* should be enough per person. *Cong shao yezhurou* (wild boar cooked with onions) and *zhenmo shanji ding* (nuggets of pheasant with local mushrooms) are both good. As long as you don't venture into scorpion or roe deer backbone marrow, a meal costs around ¥80 for two. There's an older branch at Zhong Xing Lu 2. **Da Qing Hua Dumplings** on Shan Zhuang Lu 19 across from De Hui Gate (✆ **0314/203-6111**), a Manchurian restaurant, boasts an interior and tables all made of out wood. Dumplings are featured, as well as roast duck, venison, and steamed meats. The menu isn't in English, but you can point to the photos. A meal for 2 runs ¥100 to ¥150.

SHANHAIGUAN 山海关 ★

Hebei Province, on the Bo Hai coast, 439km (274 miles) E of Beijing

Eventually the Great Wall gives up its mad zigzagging from high point to high point and plunges spectacularly down a mountainside to run across a small plain and into the sea. On its way it briefly doubles as the eastern city wall of the garrison town of Shanhaiguan (Pass between Mountains and Sea), built during the Ming dynasty to prevent the easy passage of mounted invaders from the Northeast.

The Wall was never an effective defense mechanism, and Shanhaiguan became irrelevant after 1644 when, following the overthrow of the Ming dynasty by peasant rebellions, the dismayed defenders here allowed Qing forces through. Once the enemy was within the gates, the Wall became pointless, lying as it did within Qing territory, and it was allowed to fall into ruin until the imperatives of tourism rebuilt parts of it.

Each year large quantities of material are still carted away for incorporation in domestic buildings, and local governments breach the Wall when it suits them. At Shanhaiguan a local vegetable wholesaler was made to rebuild a section of the Wall when he pulled it down to expand his warehouse. The local government then plowed a new expressway straight through it and permitted the display of advertising on its side, to ". . . rejuvenate the national industry that will face increased competition after China's entry into the World Trade Organization," according to *China Daily.*

Entrance prices to attractions in Shanhaiguan are in constant flux, and off season may be as low as half the high-season rates quoted here, although that fact isn't often posted. Whatever the season, always ask for a discount.

Note: Turn to chapter 16 for Chinese translation of key locations in this section.

Essentials

GETTING THERE Qinhuangdao **airport** is just outside town to the south, reached by taxi, with infrequent flights from Taiyuan, Harbin, Changchun, Dalian, and Shanghai. **Train** services from major cities in the Northeast pass through Shanhaiguan on their way to many southern destinations, but Qinhuangdao is better served from Beijing—take the T509 at 7:30am, arriving in Qinhuangdao at 10:28am. This is an all soft-seat train that marks the return of class designations to Chinese trains—imagine the embalmed Mao a-spin. Yi deng (first class) is ¥97. Outside the Qinhuangdao railway station, cross the road and turn left to find bus no. 33. It reaches Shanhaiguan in about 30 minutes, for a fare of ¥2. The bus drops you at the south gate of the old city walls (Nan Men). Trains directly to Shanhaiguan from Beijing tend to be slower or ill-timed, although the T11 departing at 10am and arriving at 7:06pm is a possibility. Shanhaiguan's new railway station, Shenyang North station (© **0335/794-2242**), is a few minutes' walk southeast of the south gate. The T12 leaves Shanhaiguan at 10:11am, arriving in Beijing at 1:22pm, and the speedier T94 departs at 7:04pm, arriving at 9:49pm. Tickets are set aside for both trains, but unless you're fortunate, you'll probably have to buy a seatless ticket and upgrade on the train. It's safer to return to Qinhuangdao, where the T510 at 1:37pm reaches Beijing Station at 4:42pm trains leave every couple of hours.

For **bus** services it's again better to return to Qinhuangdao, with twice-daily connections to Beijing's Xi Zhi Men bus station and others to Beijing Railway Station, for ¥60 Bus no. 33 to Qinhuangdao Railway Station runs every 2 to 5 minutes from 6:20am to 7pm.

GETTING AROUND **Buses** have conductors and cost ¥1. A **tourist shuttle service** runs from Nan Men (South Gate) to the Tianxia Diyi Guan and Jiao Shan at 8:30am, 11am, and 3:30pm, summer only. Most **taxis** have a flagfall of ¥8, which includes 2km (1¼ miles), then charge ¥1.20 per kilometer up to 8km (5 miles), then

¥1.80 per kilometer thereafter. Use one taxi to see all the sights. Insist that the "one-way" button is not pushed, and then this should be about 32km (20 miles), and cost less than ¥50, including waiting time. There's also an assortment of meterless rickety three-wheelers with extravagant ideas about the depth of foreigners' pockets. A better choice is to rent a **bicycle** from one of the cluster of stores on Nan Dajie.

[Fast FACTS] SHANHAIGUAN

Banks, Foreign Exchange & ATMs The main Bank of China (8:30am–5pm) is just inside the city wall's southeast corner at Diyi Guan Lu 60. There is no ATM.

Internet Access The Lingshi Wangba, between the post office and the Friendly Cooperate Hotel, charges ¥2 per hour.

Post Office The post office is on Nan Guan Dajie, right next to the Friendly Cooperate Hotel. Hours are from 8am to 6pm.

Inspecting China's Defenses

Tianxia Diyi Guan The "First Pass under Heaven" is the east gate of the city's walls and a gate through the Great Wall itself, originally defended by towers overlooking a large walled enclosure, most of which still stands. The only entrance was from the south, and would have required a sharp left turn to reach the main gate while coming under attack from all sides. To the north and south the Wall is heavily restored, the odd reconstructed tower holding either a small exhibition or a shop. It was once possible to walk north to Jiao Shan; the way is now barred by a metal door.

✆ **0335/505-1106.** Admission ¥40–¥100, ¥70 students. 7am–6pm (winter 7:30am–5:30pm). From the south gate, walk north up Nan Dajie and turn right at Dong Dajie, or walk west outside the walls and turn left up Diyi Guan Lu inside the east wall—also the route any taxi will take. Alternatively, enter the south gate and simply zigzag through the back streets—worthwhile in itself—because there's no way through the walls once you're inside; you can't get lost.

Jiao Shan ★ The rebuilt Wall plunges spectacularly down the mountainside, so your climb up it is consequently steep. There are handrails to assist you, and ladders up the sides of watchtowers, or the alternative of a chairlift for ¥15 one-way, ¥20 round-trip. The towers are certainly worth scaling for the views of the Wall wriggling down the hillside and running away to the sea. Higher up, the Wall becomes more attractively decayed but still safely passable, and those with the stamina (and a picnic) can travel some distance.

✆ **0335/505-2884.** Admission ¥15. Open 24 hr. 3km (2 miles) north of Shanhaiguan, and best reached by taxi.

Lao Long Tou A few years ago the "Old Dragon's Head" was just rubble, with the odd stone sticking out of the sea. The Great Wall's final kilometer was re-created in 1992, and it runs past a brand-new "old barracks area" (with shops) and a final tower before it expires in the sea. Stand at the Wall's end, look back, try to see beyond the tawdry desperation for the tourist dollar, and view the Wall as the beginning of a vast drama, ending thousands of kilometers away in Gansu Province (p. 288). It's the culmination of a Ming dynasty arms race, the "Star Wars" project of its time, which nearly sank the national economy and turned out to be pointless, since scruffy little men on ponies armed with bows and arrows, the "terrorists" of their day, regularly got through it.

Stairs to the right lead down to a beach where Chinese, most of whom live a very long way from the sea, paddle in search of pebbles and shells. Beyond lies a small temple to the Sea God, rebuilt in 1989, an excellent vantage point for photography of the "Old Dragon's Head" itself.

✆ **0335/515-2996.** Admission ¥50. 7:30am–6pm (winter until 5:30pm). Bus: 35 south down Nan Hai Xi Lu (everyone knows where you want to get off, at a point where the road forks) or 25 (which terminates here).

Mengjiangnu Miao This temple, a reminder of the Great Wall's human cost, is linked to a myth that crops up repeatedly around China, where compulsory labor on vast civil engineering projects led to the deaths of tens of thousands: Husband goes off to imperial construction project, and nothing more is heard. Eventually wife goes to look for husband, discovers that he has died during his labors, and the Wall crumbles under the weight of her tears to reveal his bones. She subsequently chooses suicide in preference to becoming an imperial concubine.

Such was the fate of the probably mythical Mengjiangnu. Her temple is on a look-out point up a steep flight of stairs, called "Looking for Husband Rock," and consists of some remarkably battered halls and oddly shaped rocks, labeled opportunistically as her bed, dressing table, and so on.

✆ **0335/505-3159.** Admission ¥25. 7am–7pm (winter until 6pm). 8km (5 miles) east of town.

Wang Jia Dayuan ★★ This small but fascinating folk museum provides a clue as to what the Cultural Relics Bureau could achieve if it were properly funded and had some marketing savvy. With investment from a Beijing entrepreneur, part of a courtyard mansion that once housed Shanhaiguan's wealthiest burgher has been sensitively renovated and is slated to expand farther south. Exhibits are crammed with curiosities: a mustache comb, a portable barber's chair, sepia pictures of the former residents, and an impressive collection of shadow puppets and ceramics. Four of the rooms are available for overnight stays for ¥298 to ¥398, with meals included.

Dong San Tiao 29. ✆ **0335/506-7700.** Admission ¥30. Includes English-speaking guide. Open daylight hours. From Nan Men, walk north up Nan Dajie, take the 5th turn on the right.

Where to Eat

Close to the Jiguan Zhaodaisuo on Nan Dajie is the friendly **Si Tiao Baoziguan,** which has an English-speaking staff member. Smock-clad ladies roll the dumplings in an open kitchen while locals queue out the door for dumpling heaven. Perfect for an early start, they're open 6am to 6:30pm. Shanhaiguan's locals wistfully recall a time when they dined on unfarmed fish, but despite the depletion in fish stocks, Shanhaiguan is still renowned for its seafood.

SHIJIAZHUANG 石家庄

Hebei Province, 269km (168 miles) SW of Beijing

Hebei's nondescript capital is one of the few places in China where the intention to rebuild everything from scratch in only 20 years is actually improving the city. Down-at-the-heel Shijiazhuang is an accident arising from the crossing of major north-south and east-west railway lines—here X really does mark the spot. It's grown from village to provincial capital in 100 years.

Even that status is a hand-me-down from Tianjin, after the metropolis gained the right to report directly to Beijing rather than through the provincial government. As a result there's little glamour here. But the city has a decent infrastructure for visitors and provides a base for exploring marvelous sights in the surrounding countryside, including **Zhengding ★★**, about 15km (10 miles) northeast. It was an important town for centuries before anyone had heard of Shijiazhuang. Today it is still home to **Longxing Si ★★**, one of the oldest, most atmospheric, and (luckily) least "restored" Chinese temples. Zhengding is also home to a number of pagodas so different from each other it's hard to believe they were produced by the same culture. **Zhao Xian,** 42km (26 miles) southeast, has an important example of religious revival in the large Zen (Chan) Buddhist temple, the **Bailin Si.** It also has the elegant **Zhaozhou Qiao ★**—the first bridge of its kind in the world. Roughly 80km (50 miles) southwest, **Cangyan Shan** has the bridge-top temple featured in the closing scenes of *Crouching Tiger, Hidden Dragon.* **Note:** Turn to chapter 16 for Chinese translation of key locations in this section.

Essentials

GETTING THERE The **airport** is 33km (20 miles) to the northeast. A shuttle bus for ¥20 meets flights and runs to the CAAC ticket office at Zhongshan Dong Lu 471, on the east side of town at the terminus of bus no. 5 to the center. **CAAC** (8am–8pm) has a 24-hour flight-booking line (✆ **0311/8505-4084**). Buy in town from agents such as the **Hebei Oversea Tour Aviation Ticket Center** (Hebei Haiwai Luyou Hangkong Piaowu Zhongxin), inside the Tiedao Dasha, Zhongshan Dong Lu 97 (✆ **0311/8607-7777;** 8am–9pm) on the corner of Ping'an Bei Dajie. They also have a branch inside the Hebei Century Hotel (9am–9pm). There are air connections to most provincial capitals, including daily flights to and from Beijing, Hohhot, Shanghai, and Xi'an.

Since Shijiazhuang's prosperity, such as it is, originates with its railway connections, it's right that the **railway station** is in the center of town. Getting there from **Beijing West** couldn't be easier, with six daily express trains taking 2 hours and 40 minutes; tickets (¥64) can be bought outside waiting room 3 or on the train itself. These are all-seat double-decker trains with snack service. Taking the T511 from Beijing at 7:35am and returning by the T514 at 5:58pm can make Shijiazhuang a possible day trip. Shijiazhuang is also a stop on the T97/98 run between Beijing West and Kowloon (¥705 soft sleeper; ¥458 hard sleeper), arriving at 3:18pm from Kowloon and leaving at 12:47pm headed south. You will need your passport to book this ticket. Most south- and southwest-bound trains from Beijing stop at Shijiazhuang, offering connections to Taiyuan, Xi'an, and points as far flung as Ürümqi. **Rail tickets** can be booked by telephone (✆ **0311/8699-5426;** 8am–6:30pm) for a ¥10 to ¥15 commission, depending on if you buy a sitting seat or bed. The railway station has been renovated, and has 17 windows from which tickets can be purchased. Window 1 is for soft-seat tickets only, windows 8 through 19 are normal ticket windows, and 20 through 24 are for 10-day advance purchases. There's even a screen displaying the availability of tickets.

Shijiazhuang is littered with **bus stations.** The most important of them, **Changtu Keyun Zhan,** is a 5-minute walk south of the railway station on Zhan Qian Lu. Destinations served include Ji'nan (241km/149 miles; ¥82); Tai'an (281km/174 miles; ¥60), Zhengzhou (437km/271 miles; ¥45), and Qinhuangdao (480km/298 miles; ¥130). There are frequent connections to several Beijing bus stations, including Lize Qiao (7am–5:30pm) and Lianhua Chi (6:30am–4pm; 3½ hr.). But the real competition with the rail link to Beijing is just to the right at the **Keyun Zong Zhan,** where the Alsa company runs luxury coaches to Beijing Liu Li Qiao (roughly every 25 min. 6am–7pm; returning 12:30–7:30pm; ¥70). In addition, twice-daily super luxury buses have large, airline-style tiltable seats, only three across the bus (¥90), departing at 8:10 and 9:25am, returning at 3:10pm and 4:40pm. For service from Beijing call ✆ **010/6386-1262;** from Shijiazhuang call ✆ **0311/8702-5775.** They also run two morning services to Ji'nan and Zhengzhou, with afternoon returns.

GETTING AROUND **Taxis** are mostly Jettas and Fukang, and cost ¥2 per kilometer. Hyundai cost ¥2 per kilometer. Add 50% after 6km (3¾ miles), and 20% from 11pm to 5am.

VISITOR INFORMATION **CITS,** at Donggang Lu 26, quotes imaginative prices for cars and guides. However, it does have some good English-speakers, so if you're desperate, call them at ✆ **0311/8581-5102.**

[Fast FACTS] SHIJIAZHUANG

Banks, Foreign Exchange & ATMs There's a handy branch of the Bank of China on the north side of the Dongfang Dasha, Zhongshan Xi Lu 97, close to the railway station. Hours are Monday through Friday from 8:30am to noon and 2:30 to 5pm. Forex is available at counters 4 to 7. Another useful branch lies near a KFC just west of the World Trade Plaza on Zhongshan Dong Lu (same hours). Both branches have ATMs that accept foreign cards.

Internet Access Dial-up is ✆ 163 or 169.

Post Office The post office near the railway station (corner of Gongli Jie and Zhongshan Xi Lu) is open from 8:30am to 6pm. There's a more centrally located post office in Jianshe Nan Dajie; its hours are 8:30am to 6:30pm.

Visa Extensions The city **PSB** is a block north of Zhongshan Xi Lu, and 2 blocks east of Zhonghua Bei Dajie, at Liming Jie 8. The visa office has a separate entrance on the east side of the building. Walk up Qingnian Jie on the west side of the Huabei Shangcheng (department store), across the next junction, and the office is on your left (✆ **0311/8686-2500**). Hours are Monday to Friday from 8:30am to noon and 1:30 to 5:30pm.

WALKING TOUR: THE PAGODAS OF ZHENGDING ★★

GETTING THERE: **Take minibus no. 201 from the enclosure between Zhan Qian Jie and the railway station; it drops you at Zhengding bus station for ¥3. Ignore *sanlunche* (three-wheeler) drivers and take minibus no. 1 from the same spot to its terminus outside Longxing Si (¥1). A *sanlunche* will cost you ¥5. A harder-to-find alternative is a tourist service that runs every 15 minutes from near the no. 50 bus stop farther south on the road running directly in front of the station, just north of the bus station, to outside Kaiyuan Si; the fare is ¥3. It is possible to stay at the (nominally) four-star Golden Star Holiday Hotel (✆ 0311/825-8888), just north of Longxing Si, at Xingrong Lu 68.**

START:	**Longxing Si.**
FINISH:	**Changle Men.**
TIME:	**At least half a day.**
BEST TIMES:	**Weekdays between 8am and 4pm.**

In once-important, long-irrelevant Zhengding, only a little exertion brings a lot of pleasure, including sights like some of the oldest surviving wooden buildings in China, a vast 27m (90-ft.) 10th-century bronze statue of Guanyin, four very different pagodas, and a fragment of city wall.

Bus no. 1 terminates at the main entrance. We recommend that you purchase an all-inclusive ticket *(tao piao)* for ¥60, which covers all the sights described here, except for the Linji Si, which is managed by the Religious Affairs Bureau. The ticket includes entrance to a Confucian Temple of minor interest, containing a rather gruesome exhibition on the Japanese occupation.

1 Longxing Si 龙兴寺

Open 8am to 5:30pm (¥40), the Longxing Si dates its foundation from the Sui dynasty (581–618), and has three particularly unusual and interesting halls. The **Moni Dian (Manichean Hall),** built around 1052, rebuilt in 1563, and restored with tact from 1977 to 1980, is almost square in plan, with gabled porches on all four sides. Inside, five gilded figures are approached across a dark uneven floor past vast columns, some of which have a slight lean; the walls carry faint traces of early frescoes, miraculously unretouched. Through a gate beyond, a small altar building houses a two-faced, four-armed and rather delicately executed figure from 1493, hung with scarves of honor. To the right the Pavilion of Kindness contains a 7.4m (24-ft.) Maitreya carved from a single piece of wood. To the left, the two-story **Zhuanlun Cang Dian (Turning Wheel Storage Hall)** of the Northern Song (960–1127) seems to have three stories due to an external gallery with "waist eaves." The ground floor is dominated by a 7m-high (23-ft.) octagonal revolving bookcase, as complex in its design as a miniature temple. The climax is the **Pavilion of Great Benevolence,** also Northern Song, a vast hall seven bays wide containing a massive 27m (90-ft.) bronze Guanyin with a "thousand arms" whose angularity gives her a rather crustacean look. The figure was cast upon the instructions of the first Northern Song emperor in about 971. You can climb several dusty floors to look her in the eye. The rearmost Ming-era hall was brought to the site from another temple in 1959, and contains a remarkable three-layered statue of 12 figures seated on lotus thrones. One side hall contains a bizarre exhibition (¥5) that includes what is claimed to be a 2,100-year-old Han dynasty jade burial suit, reconstructed from hundreds of small jade plates and held together with cloth-covered gold wire. If it's the genuine article, it's priceless, but the presence in the exhibition of a pickled turtle, a dilapidated butterfly collection, and other bric-a-brac suggests otherwise. Continue through to **Kunlu Dian (Hall of Vairocana),** an exquisitely carved effigy of four bodhisattvas, dating from the late Ming.

Leaving the temple, note the rough map near the ticket office to the right. Turn right (west) from the temple and walk for 10 minutes.

2 Tianning Si 天宁寺

If you are here in the spring, the *wutong* (Chinese parasol) trees you'll see will have spectacular cascades of pink blossoms. The **Lingxiao Ta** (pagoda), all that remains of the temple, is clearly visible to your right. Open 8am to 5:30pm (¥10), the Song dynasty nine-story octagonal brick structure, at 41m (134 ft.), is the tallest of the town's remaining pagodas. To climb it, enter from the far (north) side. If you are lucky the attendant will hand you a flashlight, but if not, the climb to the second, third, and fourth floors is through narrow passages within the brick walls, with short periods of pitch-darkness to start with. Keep your head *down*. The remainder of the climb to the ninth floor is by wooden staircases in the interior. A central set of trunks bound with hoops of iron, which radiate support beams, sit on fat brackets.

From the top, looking southwest, you can see the squat, square form of your next destination.

Return to the main road and turn right. After less than 5 minutes, Lishi Wenhua Jie "Historical and Cultural Street" is on the left at a bizarre statue-cum-roundabout. Turn left. There's a supermarket with snacks on the corner, and the street has a number of modest restaurants, which are less modest than anything else in the town. Kaiyuan Si is a short distance down to the right.

3 Kaiyuan Si 开元寺

Two minor buildings stand here, including a heavily renovated late-Tang bell tower, which can be climbed for a closer view of a 2.9m (9½-ft.) bronze bell. Open 8am to 5pm (¥15).

The nine-story **Xumi Ta** will seem familiar to those who've visited Xi'an—a tapering, brick, four-sided building, with a projecting ridge between each floor and a plainness that makes the Lingxiao Ta look fussy. There are local claims that it dates from 636, but as Xi'an's Great Goose (p. 259) is supposedly based on information brought back to China by the peripatetic monk Xuanzang, and its construction didn't start until 16 years later, one story is wrong (although Xuanzang is said to have been in the area—see Bailin Si, below). But the stately Xumi Ta certainly looks its age—quite a few of the bricks have fallen out, providing handy niches for nesting sparrows, and it's fenced off. Around the base are eight tubby martial figures, simply carved but full of life. If you do go in, note the carvings of dragons and flowers. The interior floors are missing, and the main floor is slippery with guano, but there's an impressive view up the resulting vertical tunnel.

One area of the temple's ruined remains has been labeled STONE INSCRIPTION GARDEN and contains forlorn rows of chipped statuary and chunks of stelae probably smashed in the Cultural Revolution, along with the cracked remains of the largest *bixi* you'll ever see, its claws 6 inches long. Often mistakenly described as turtles, *bixi* are in fact a primitive kind of dragon (not only with claws, but teeth). This one was accidentally discovered in June 2000 during construction work, as illustrated by photographs in the entrance hall as you leave.

Outside, turn right. You'll see a few street vendors selling birds, flowers, plants, and fish, and almost immediately on the left the entrance to the ancestral hall of the Liang family.

4 Liangshi Zongci 梁室宗祠

This hall is a single unit five bays wide in brown wood, containing a small exhibition (pictures, family tree) of the Liang family. Open 8am to 5pm (closed at lunchtime; ¥5).

Outside, turn left. Along the length of this street are antiques and memorabilia shops (with lower prices than most because they are aimed at domestic tourists) selling everything from Buddhist bits and pieces to Mao memorabilia. Still, expect most objects to be fake, and pay only a small fraction of initial asking prices. There are also places to buy ice cream, and assorted restaurants offering *jiaozi* and Beijing duck. Keep looking on the left for a large sign with a picture of a pagoda, and turn left there.

5 Linji Si 临济寺

Open 7:30am to 5pm (¥15), this temple claims to have been founded by the Eastern Wei dynasty (534–49). Its **Chengling Ta** was built to house the remains of the founder of a Zen Buddhist (Chan) sect still popular in Japan, who died late in the Tang dynasty in 867. The slender, octagonal brick pagoda is in a highly ornamental style; an elongated lower floor sits on a brick plinth carved with lotus petals. Eight further tiny stories, each with decorative brick brackets and eave figures, are topped by an umbrella spire. Roughly 30m (98 ft.) high, the pagoda was restored in 2001 and cannot be climbed. A handful of monks are in residence.

Turn right out of the temple and left at the main street. The Guanghui Si is a well-signposted left turn a few minutes farther along.

6 Guanghui Si 广化寺

This temple's bizarre **Hua Ta,** dating from around 1200, is obviously a direct descendant of Indian stupas, consisting of a central brick pavilion topped with a stone spire covered with intricate statuary of elephants, other animals, and figures—some headless, some faceless, and some intact—finished with a brick point on top. The central pavilion is supported by four smaller, rebuilt pavilions. A climb up two floors to a platform (again, watch your head) gives views of the earthen core of the old city wall, the fields still inside it, and a modern mosque. Open 8am to 5:30pm (¥10).

Again return to the main road and turn left. The south gate of the city wall is straight ahead; the entrance is to the right.

7 Changle Men长乐门

As is usual with city walls, the brick has been taken away to use in domestic construction—all except for those structurally necessary to maintain the gates, unless the wall is breached elsewhere (or removed, earthworks and all). Here the gate and its tower have been rebuilt. Open 8am to 5:30pm (¥10).

To return to Zhengding, flag down the yellow bus no. 2, which returns in the direction you have walked to the long-distance bus station.

Other Area Attractions

Bailin Si The Cultural Revolution was so thorough here that only the Jin dynasty (1115–1234) pagoda was left standing. The extensive complex has been reconstructed over the last few years entirely with donations from the faithful, and includes one of the largest "10,000 Buddha" halls in the world.

The temple saw the foundation of a sect of Zen (Chan) Buddhism, and its beginnings date from 220 during the Eastern Han dynasty. Xuanzang is said to have studied here before his trip to India in search of authoritative texts. The temple is entered through a small grove of cypresses (for which it is named), and has a calm bustle of activity from shaven-headed monks in orange and brown robes. One or two English-speakers tend to seek out foreign visitors and are happy to answer queries, show you around, and explain Zen principles and the *Shenghuo* (life) variant introduced by Venerable Master Jinghui, the driving force behind the temple's change from weeds and rubble into an impressive complex. Then-President Jiang Zemin visited in 2001. Perhaps the rumors are true and he is a closet Buddhist.

Free admission. 8am–4pm. In Shijiazhuang, take bus no. 26, 30, or 35 from the train station to Nan Jiao Keyun Zong Zhan and catch a bus to Zhao Xian (30–45 min.; ¥9) tell the driver that you wish to get off at Bailin Si, and he or she will drop you off at the gate. If you can't make yourself understood, jump off at a traffic island with a mini-pagoda in the middle. The road to the left, Shi Ta Lu, takes you to Bailin Si in 10 min. on foot. Alternatively, if you head straight on down Shi Qiao Dajie (Stone Bridge St.), you'll pass the earthen core and 1 or 2 watchtowers of the city wall, and get to a major junction, straight over which is Zhaozhou Qiao, about a 30-min. walk. Or take a *sanlunche* (¥3) or minivan (¥5).

Zhaozhou Qiao ★ Also known as Anji Qiao (Safe Crossing Bridge) and Da Shi Qiao (Big Stone Bridge), this is often labeled the oldest surviving bridge in China. There are probably older bridges, but this one was constructed between 595 and 605, and unlike China's wooden structures it is largely original in its current form. A mecca for architects and civil engineers as well as historians, it was the first bridge in the world to use a segment of an arc rather than a complete semicircle for its arch, giving a far more shallow curve to the road deck and thus making crossings for carts and horses much easier. This was a major design breakthrough, but it would be 800 years before a similar approach would be tried in Europe, and nearly 1,300 years before Europe tried the spandrel—piercing the buttresses at either end of the bridge so as to reduce pressure on the foundations and allow floodwaters to pass without sweeping the bridge away.

The parallel stone ribbons that form the main arch are surprisingly flexible and things of beauty in themselves. Until recently the bridge was still in use, but traffic is now diverted, and some of the damaged carvings on the superstructure, including scowling mythical beasts called *taotie,* have been replaced.

Sadly, the bridge's conversion to a tourist site has brought pedalos (pedal boats) that wallow in the murky, tadpole-filled waters beneath, as well as construction of a hideous parallel concrete pedestrian bridge, mainly to obscure views from the new road bridge and thus increase receipts. But don't let this stop you from viewing China's most significant contribution to architectural method.

See directions for Bailin Si, above. The ticket booth is to the right of the main entrance. Admission ¥35. 7:30am–6:30pm (winter until 7pm). ✆ **0311/8490-2618.** To find buses to Shijiazhuang, return to the traffic island by foot or taxi, and continue to the next T-junction. (If you turn left and walk for a few minutes, on your right you'll find another, smaller bridge constructed in the same style, with no entrance fee at all.)

Cangyan Shan This wooded mountain is part of the Taihang range, about 80km (50 miles) southwest of Shijiazhuang; its summit is at 1,044m (3,424 ft.). The main point of visiting is a staircase of more than 300 steps leading up a cleft and beneath two parallel bridges, each topped by a temple, originally Sui dynasty (518–618). The setting is as spectacular as it looks in the closing scene of the film *Crouching Tiger, Hidden Dragon* (although the final jump is reportedly from Huang Shan), and the location, especially from the stairs below and on a misty day, makes for some spectacular photography. The paths that lace the mountainside do not lead to any other equally spectacular sights, and some have crumbled away. Take a picnic. The 2-hour minibus trip begins rather early in the morning.

Admission ¥50. ✆ **0311/8232-4128.** Bus: to Cangyan Shan from the Xiwang Changtu Keyun Chezhan (take bus no. 9 from the rail station to the terminus) in Xinhua Lu. It departs at 7am and returns late afternoon. Return fare is ¥26.

Where to Stay

EXPENSIVE

Hebei Century Hotel (Hebei Shiji Dafandian) This Chinese five-star, 29-floor glass cylinder tower has a cavernous lobby and good-size rooms, if typically tiny bathrooms. The guest rooms have the standard neoclassical cabinetry of international five-stars, but someone involved in the design has been a bit more adventurous with color than is common to Chinese-run hotels, and service is a notch above average, too.

Zhongshan Xi Lu 145 (just west of the city PSB, corner of Zhonghua Bei Dajie). www.hebei-centuryhotel.com. ✆ **0311/8703-6699.** Fax 0311/8703-8866. 439 units. ¥480–¥780 standard room; ¥520–¥6,800 suite. 30%–50% discounts easily obtained. AE, DC, MC, V. Bus: 1 west along Zhongshan Xi Lu. **Amenities:** 4 restaurants; badminton court; billiards; children's play area; fitness room; nightclub; indoor pool; sauna. *In room:* A/C, satellite TV, computer (executive floors), hair dryer, Internet, minibar.

World Trade Plaza Hotel (Shimao Guangchang Jiudian) ★ This former Crowne Plaza was recently the victim of a buy-out by its Chinese partner. For the moment, this centrally located five-star hotel is the first choice for foreign visitors, but parts of the operation are already veering out of control, particularly the enthusiastic "massage" service, which occasionally solicits from door to door. North-facing rooms are quieter, and the larger "executive rooms" *(shangwu jian),* which are appealingly arranged with a glass divider between the resting and the work area, are excellent value. The second-floor restaurant offers the finest Western cuisine in town.

Zhongshan Dong Lu 303 (opposite Sheng Bowuguan/Provincial Museum). www.wtphotels.com. ✆ **0311/8667-8888**. Fax 0311/8667-1694.. 238 units. ¥788-¥941 standard room; from ¥991-¥1,231 suite. Best rates often 50% less. AE, DC, MC, V. **Amenities:** 3 restaurants; cafe; forex; fitness room w/access to off-site facilities

MODERATE

Huiwen Jiudian The 26-floor Huiwen is the best choice of a clutch of hotels conveniently opposite the railway station, and less than 10 minutes' walk north of the long-distance bus station. The hotel is clean and well run, but it needs at least one more elevator, and lighting in the bathrooms is poor. Still, this is a perfectly adequate choice and a good value for the traveler on a budget. Public transport to most out-of-town sites leaves from stops nearby.

Zhan Qian Jie 6 (opposite railway station exit—look for Xinhua Bookstore sign). ✆ **0311/8787-9988.** Fax 0311/8786-5500. 180 units. ¥268–¥438 standard room; ¥588 suite. Discounts around

20%. No credit cards. **Amenities:** 3 restaurants; teahouse; bowling; fitness room; nightclub; pool table. *In room:* A/C, TV, hair dryer, Internet.

Where to Eat

The usual fast-food culprits are here: KFC is opposite the Yanchun Garden Hotel, Zhongshan Dong Lu 195, and just west of the World Trade Plaza on Zhongshan Dong Lu, along with a McDonald's. Extensive Western menus are available at both hotels. You can also find a branch of the excellent Shanghai restaurant, **Soup Best Shen,** at the Yanchun Garden. There's budget eating opposite the station, including two branches of **California Beef Noodle King (Meiguo Jiazhou Niurou Mian Dawang),** and a branch of the **Malan** noodle chain next to Quanjude (see below). The vast Renren Le Supermarket is located underneath the Mao park, just east of the Yanchun Garden Hotel. Another supermarket for travel snacks, open from 9am to 7:30pm, is located at Zhongshan Xi Lu 83, just west of the station. Shijiazhuang is best at offering Beijing specialties in quieter environments and for lower prices.

Quanjude ★ BEIJING The national capital's best-known supplier of its signature roast duck dish provides a better atmosphere, better service, and lower prices at this provincial branch than it does at home. The grand two-story building with a sweeping central staircase bustles pleasantly. The ovens are visible at the rear and use the traditional fruitwood method for baking the duck, which is as moist and succulent as it should be. The downstairs area also offers Shandong dishes, which you select from illuminated shelves. Upstairs has full waitress service. If you are by yourself, a half duck *(ban zhi)* is only ¥49. There's another branch on the south side of Heping Xi Lu just west of Ping'an Jie.

Jianshe Nan Dajie 7, just south of the Yanchun Garden Hotel. ✆ **0311/8621-1566.** Duck sets (with pancakes, condiments, and soup) ¥100–¥200. No credit cards. 10am–2pm and 5:30–8:30pm.

THE NORTHEAST

by Lee Wing-sze

The frigid lands to the northeast, once known as Tartary or Manchuria and now referred to simply as Dongbei (the Northeast), represent one of the least visited and most challenging regions in China and its last great travel frontier.

Dongbei was the birthplace of China's final dynasty, the Manchu-ruled Qing (1636–1912). It was declared off-limits to Han Chinese from 1644, when the first Qing emperor took up residence in the Forbidden City, until the dynasty began to lose power in the late 19th century. The ban preserved Dongbei's image as a mysterious and menacing place separate from China proper. "The Chinese talk of Tartary as a country half as big as the rest of the world besides," Lord Macartney, George III's emissary to the court of the Qing Qianlong emperor, wrote in the early 18th century. "But their conceptions of its limits are very dark and confused. There is a wide difference between pretension and possession."

Japan and Russia waged a series of battles for control of Dongbei in the first half of the 20th century; the Chinese finally took genuine possession of the region at the end of World War II. Using Japanese- and Russian-built railroads, China's new Communist leaders made it the center of their efforts to bring the country into the industrial age.

The name "Dongbei," which conjured images of wild invaders on horseback or ruddy-faced factory workers, is on its way to being a modern area. Despite industrialization, Dongbei still claims China's largest natural forest, its most pristine grasslands, one of its most unspoiled mountains (Changbai Shan), and celebrated lakes (Tian Chi). The architectural remnants of the last 350 years—early Qing palaces and tombs, incongruous Russian cupolas, and eerie structures left over from Japan's wartime occupation—also make the region unique. It also houses one of the four biggest snow events (Harbin Ice and Snow Festival) in the world.

The region has been undergoing a tourism makeover in an attempt to replace income lost in the spate of state-owned factory closures. With a boost in hotels, modernization, and standard of English, it is not as difficult a place to visit as it once was. But at the same time, it still offers visitors the chance to travel in a place largely free of the exploitation and cultural hyperbole common to tourism in more accommodating parts of China.

The region is notoriously freezing cold in winter, from December to February. But this extreme weather also creates an incredible venue for the celebrated Harbin Snow Festival. From July to September, the flora blossoms on the grasslands and in the mountains, and the rice fields turn spring green. ***Note:*** Unless noted otherwise, hours listed in this chapter are the same daily.

SHENYANG 沈阳

Liaoning Province, 868km (538 miles) NE of Beijing, 544km (337 miles) SW of Harbin

Shenyang is the largest city in Dongbei and on its way to becoming a lovely gateway to the region. The city—formerly an industrial area sprawling with the chaos of dirt and noise—has gradually transformed into a cleaner modern city where historical buildings stand bathed in new consumerism. As one of the four hosting cities for the 2008 Olympics soccer matches, it has benefited from efforts to reduce pollution and boost citizens' English efficiency. It was the birthplace of the Qing dynasty in the 15th century and is now the capital of Liaoning, Dongbei's southernmost and wealthiest province. Many travelers spend only enough time here to switch trains, but it is worthwhile to linger in the city, which is home to several of Dongbei's most fascinating historical attractions.

Shenyang has existed under various names since the Tang dynasty (618–907) and has been the region's most strategically important city since 1625, when Jurchen founders of the Qing dynasty (1626–1912) made it their capital (Shenjing). The Qing's leaders stayed here for 19 years, perfecting a system of government modeled on the Chinese and plotting an attack on the weakened Ming from inside their palace, which still stands in the city center. With the decline of the Qing at the start of the 20th century, the city (renamed Fengtian) fell under the influence of legendary warlord Zhang Zuolin. Zhang ruled Manchuria from his downtown residence courtyard complex just south of the Qing palace, until his assassination by Japanese soldiers in 1928. The city drifted without obvious leadership until the fall of 1931, when Japan's Kwantung Army used the "discovery" of a small hole blasted in their railway line north of the city (known to them as Mukden) as a pretense to invade. The attack, referred to in China as the September 18th (or Mukden) Incident and immortalized in a museum in the north part of the city, eventually led to the establishment of Manchukuo (Mandarin: *Manzhou Guo*), the puppet state Japan used to mask its territorial ambitions during World War II.

The mayor who transformed Dalian (p. 164) into the shimmering pride of northern China, now the governor of Liaoning Province, has vowed to work his magic on the capital. Shenyang has never been pretty, but perhaps it doesn't need to be. "[Mukden] is ancient and dusty, with nothing especially attractive," one visiting Catholic missionary wrote in 1919. "I found it very interesting." The same holds true today.

The city is building its subway system to ease its busy traffic. One of the three lines started to run in late 2009, with stations at popular spots such as Shenyang Zhan, Nanjing Jie, and Zhong Jie. The entire network is target to be completed in 2015.

Essentials

GETTING THERE Flights connect Shenyang's **Taoxian International Airport (Taoxian Guoji Jichang)** with every major Chinese city, such as Beijing (10 to 12 flights daily), Shanghai (13 to 14 flights daily), Guangzhou (five to six flights daily), Shenzhen (seven flights daily), Harbin (four flights daily,) and Hong Kong (one flight

daily); there are also connections to New York, California, Munich, Frankfurt, Irkutsk, Novosibirsk, Seoul, Busan, Pyongyang, Tokyo, Osaka, and Nagoya. Flights can be booked at the **China Northern Airlines** ticket office (**Zhongguo Beifang Hangkong Shoupiao Chu; © 024/2383-4089**), located at Zhonghua Lu 117, north of Shiyi (11) Wei Lu. The office is open from 8am to 5pm. The airport is 30km (19 miles) south of downtown. One of the **airport shuttles** runs from Terminal One to Shenyang Bei Railway Station, while another airport bus route runs from Terminal Two to Maluwan (southeast of Zhonghua Lu). The 45-minute ride costs ¥15. Free buses to the airport depart from Chengshi Houji Lou at Qingnan Dajie 56 every hour from 6am to 6pm. **Taxis** charge ¥80. Cash and traveler's checks can be exchanged at a kiosk near the international arrivals area.

Shenyang 沈阳

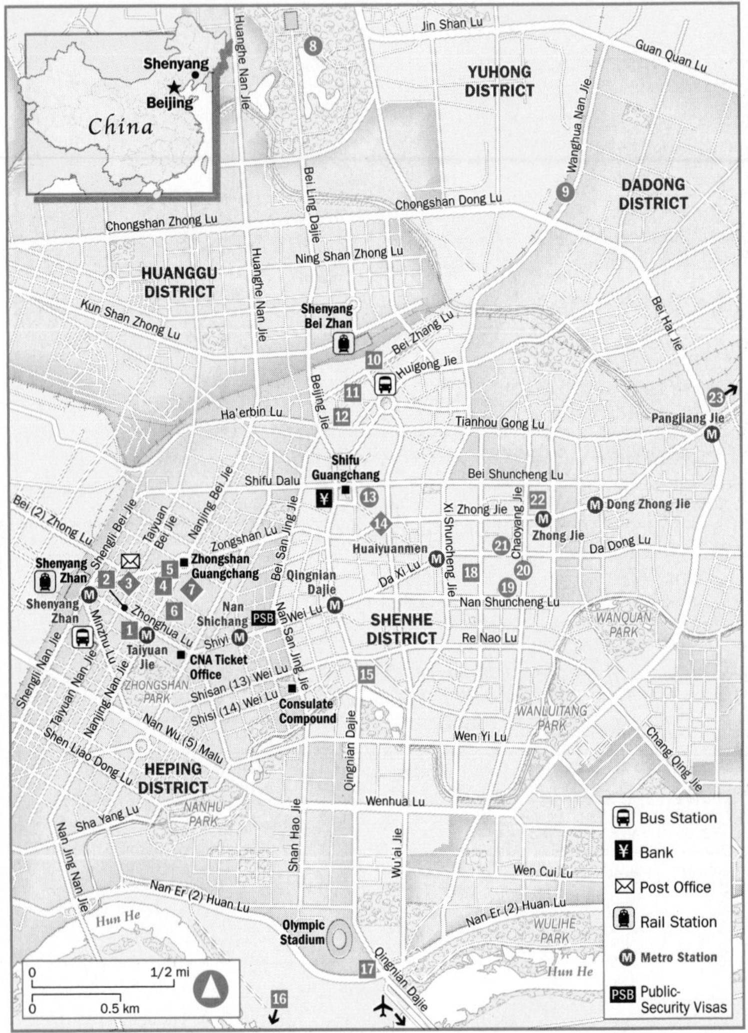

Shenyang has two main **railway stations:** the Russian-built **Shenyang Zhan (Shenyang Railway Station)** on the western edge of downtown, and the modern **Shenyang Bei Zhan (Shenyang North Station),** north of Shifu Guangchang. D-series trains leave from Shenyang Bei Zhan to Beijing (17 trains daily; 4–4½ hr.; ¥218 second class/¥261 first class), Tianjin (three trains daily; 4½ hr.; ¥213 second class/¥256 first class), Changchun (11 trains daily; 2 hr. 15 min.; ¥93 second class/¥111 first class), Jilin (three trains daily; 3 hr.; ¥127 second class/¥153 first class), Harbin (five trains daily; 4 hr.; ¥169 second class/¥203 first class). Express trains to Shanghai (four trains daily; 25–27 hr.; ¥409–¥430 hard sleeper/¥627–¥658

Shenyang Key

HOTELS ■

Crowne Plaza Shenyang Zhongshan **4**
沈阳中山皇冠假日酒店

Gloria Plaza Shenyang **11**
(Shenyang Kailai Dajiudian)
沈阳凯莱大酒店

Home Inn **18**
(Rujia)
如家酒店

Ibis (Yibisi) **6**
宜必思

Kempinski Hotel Shenyang **15**
(Shěnyáng Kǎibībsījī Fàndiàn)
沈阳凯宾斯基饭店

Lexington Shenyang Rich Gate Hotel **12**
(Shěnyáng Huáfǔtiāndì Láixīngdùn Jiǔdiàn)
沈阳华府天地莱星顿酒店

Liaoning Hotel **5**
(Liaoning Binguan)
辽宁宾馆

Maritim Hotel Shenyang **16**
沈阳碧桂园玛丽蒂姆酒店

New World Shenyang Hotel **1**
沈阳新世界酒店

Regar Hotel Shenyang **22**
沈阳天伦瑞格酒店

Sheraton Shengyang Lido Hotel **17**
(Shenyang Lidu Xilaideng Fandian)
丽都喜来登饭店

Times Plaza Hotel **10**
(Shídài Guǎngchǎng Jiǔdiàn)
时代广场酒店

Traders Hotel **2**
(Shangmao Fandian)
沈阳盛贸饭店

RESTAURANTS ◆

Ma Family Shaomai **3**
(Ma Jia Shaomai Guan)
马家烧麦馆

Mulligan's **7**
爱尔兰酒吧

Xinglongxuan Jiaozi Guan **14**
兴隆轩饺子馆

ATTRACTIONS ●

9.18 Museum **9**
(Jiuyiba Bowuguan)
九一八历史博物馆

Bei LIng **8**
北陵

Dong LIng **23**
东陵

Gu Gong (Imperial Palace) **21**
故宫

Liaoning Provincial Museum **13**
(Liaoning Sheng Bowguan)
辽宁省博物馆

Shenyang Financial Museum **20**
(Shenyang Jinrong Bowuguan)
沈阳市金融博物馆

Zhang Residence **19**
(Zhangshi Shuaifu)
张氏帅府

soft sleeper); Dalian (six trains daily; 3¾–4⅓ hr.; ¥55 hard seat/¥87 soft seat), Dandong (seven trains daily; 3½–5 hr.; ¥21–¥42 hard seat) stop at both railway stations.

Shenyang's main **long-distance bus station, Qiche Kuaisu Keyun Zhan** (ticket office open 6am–9pm; ✆ **024/6223-3333**), is on Huigong Jie 120. **Luxury coaches** go to Dandong (6am–7pm; 3 hr. 10 min.; ¥80), Dalian (6:30am–7pm; 4½ hr.; ¥129), Changchun (7:40am–5pm; 4 hr. 20 min.; ¥68), Jilin (7:30am, 11:30am, and 1:40pm; 4 hr. 50 min.; ¥105), Harbin (11am and 2:30pm; 6½ hr.; ¥98), and Beijing (eight trains daily; 8am–9pm; 7½ hr.; ¥129).

GETTING AROUND The two areas in Shenyang where it is feasible to walk are the old city center, a 5-sq.-km (2-sq.-mile) area surrounding the Imperial Palace (Gu Gong), and the shopping district Taiyuan Lu and Zhonghua Jie, east of Shenyang Zhan. Most sights, however, are scattered in the sprawl outside these areas. **Buses** charge ¥1 to ¥2 and congregate at the two railway stations. Bus no. 203 travels from Shenyang Zhan via Maluwan and Taiyuan Jie to Shenyang Bei Zhan; a circle-line *(huan)* bus goes from Shenyang Bei Zhan past Taiyuan Jie to Zhong Jie (see "Shopping," later in this chapter) and the Gu Gong. Maps can be bought at Shenyang Bei Zhan. The **Metro** Line One, running from 5:30am to 10pm, have stops in Shenyang Zhan, Taiyuan Jie and Zhong Jie. Tickets ¥2–¥4.

Taxis charge ¥8 for the first 3km (2 miles), then ¥1 per 0.6km (⅓ mile).

[Fast FACTS] SHENYANG

Banks, Foreign Exchange & ATMs The main branch of **Bank of China** is at Shifu Da Lu 253, west of the Shifu Guangchang (Mon–Fri 8:30am–5pm, public holidays 9am–4pm; ✆ **024/2281-0777**). Traveler's checks and cash can be exchanged at window 28 on the second floor; credit card transactions are handled on the third floor. International ATMs are on the first floor of the bank.

Consulates Most consulates are located in a single, heavily fortified compound at the intersection of Shisi (14) Wei Lu and Bei San Jing Jie. The **Consulate General of United States** (Mon–Fri 8:30am–noon and 1:30–5:30pm; ✆ **024/2322-1198**) is closest to the corner at Shisi Wei Lu 52. The **Japanese Consulate** (Mon–Fri 9am–noon; ✆ **024/2322-7490**) is next door, and the **Korea Consulate** (Mon–Fri 9am–noon and 1:30–5:30pm; ✆ **024/2385-3388**) is across the road. The **Democratic People's Republic of Korea Consulate** (Mon–Fri 9am–noon and 2–5pm; ✆ **024/2324-0009**) is situated at Sijing Jie 109. The **France Consulate** (✆ **024/2319-0000**) is at Nan Shisan (13) Wei Lu 34. The surly staff at the **Russian Consulate** (Mon–Fri 9:30am–12:30pm and 3–4pm; ✆ **024/2322-3527**), at Shisan (13) Wei Lu 31, don't speak English.

Exploring Shenyang

The one attraction within walking distance of the downtown hotels is **Zhongshan Guangchang (Sun Yat-sen Square),** 4 blocks northeast of Shenyang Zhan on Zhongshan Lu. It's notable for its striking **statue of Mao,** which stands proudly surrounded by a teeming mass of soldiers, peasants, and workers all bearing weapons of the revolution (guns, sledgehammers, Mao's *Little Red Book*) and staring grim-faced at the banks and hotels that now surround the square.

In winter, from December to February, **Shenyang International Ice and Snow Festival** is held at **Qipanshan (Qipan Mountain).** With spectacular giant ice sculptures, skiing facilities, and winter sports events, it is not as extensive as the

THE MINORITIES & THE manchu myth

Manchurians, one of China's more numerous ethnic minorities with a population of 11 million, did not actually exist until a dozen years before they conquered China. Originally a loose alliance of nomadic tribes, they became Manchus (the exact meaning is unknown but the name was probably taken from a Buddhist term meaning "great good fortune"), after Qing founder Huang Taiji invented the label to unify his people and distance them from their barbarian roots. But it was Nurhaci, Huang Taiji's father, who paved the way for the Manchu conquest of Ming China. Nurhaci was bent on instilling loyalty and demanded men who surrendered to him to imitate the Manchu tradition of shaving the front of the forehead and braiding hair in the back into a long "queue," a law that was also enforced during the reign of Huang Taiji. By 1645, any man who did not comply faced execution. The Chinese were humiliated by the order at the time, but the queue has recently been reclaimed as Chinese cultural history, and makes frequent appearances on dozens of widely popular Chinese period soap operas.

Manchu culture borrowed heavily from a number of ethnic groups, especially in architecture (see Gu Gong, below), but many of their customs disappeared after they established the Qing and adopted Chinese habits—a phenomenon Chinese historians still note with pride. Some aspects of Manchu culture have survived, however. Most notable among these are *kang,* heated brick beds still found in some Dongbei homes, and *qipao* (traditional fitted dresses), made famous in 1930s Shanghai.

Dongbei is technically home to more than a dozen other ethnic groups, including Mongolians, Russians, and Koreans. But the majority of them were, at one time or another, considered Manchurian. Victims of successive assimilation, most are now practically indistinguishable from Han Chinese. A few distinct minority cultures have managed to survive, if only barely, in the more remote corners of the Northeast. These include a few nomadic **Oroqen** hunters and reindeer-herding **Ewenkis** in the Greater Xing'an Mountains (on the border between Inner Mongolia and Heilongjiang Province), and the **Hezhe,** the majority of whom live in northeastern Heilongjiang Province. Numbering fewer than 5,000, Hezhe are famous for their fish-skin clothing, a typical suit of which costs between ¥5,000 and ¥6,000 and uses roughly 250 kilograms (550 lb.) of pike, carp, or salmon.

celebrated Harbin Snow Festival (p. 191) though. Bus no. 168 from Maluwan or Zhongjie.

Bei Ling ★★ This august tomb at the center of an Eastern Eden of ponds, pavilions, twisting paths, and 300-year-old pines contains the remains of Qing dynasty founder Huang (the Manchurian Tai Zong emperor, Abahai). The eighth son of Nurhaci, the Jurchen chieftain who unified Manchuria in the early 17th century, Huang Taiji rose to power shortly after his father's death, proclaimed the founding of the Qing dynasty in 1636, then conquered Korea.

Construction of the tomb (also known as Zhao Ling) began in 1643, the year Huang Taiji died, and took 8 years to complete. A central path leads visitors through the front gate, past a stone army of guardian animals and into Long'en Dian, a large hall housing the emperor's memorial tablet. Climbing up onto the encircling wall at the northern end will put you at eye level with the tomb itself, a simple dirt hill topped by a lonely tree. Huang Taiji's body lies somewhere beneath. The tomb lies at the northern end of Bei Ling Park, former imperial cemetery turned public space.

Taishan Lu 12, at northern end of Bei Ling Dajie. ✆ **024/8689-6294.** Admission ¥50 plus ¥6 for Bei Ling Park entrance. May–Oct 8am–5pm; Nov–Apr 8am–4:30pm. Bus: 148 from Shenyang Bei Zhan or 218 from Zhong Jie; get off at Bei Ling Gong Yuan Zhan. Taxi: about 20 min. from downtown (¥20).

Dong Ling ★★ Also known as Fu Ling, this is the tomb of Qing Dynasty founder Nurhachi and his wife, Empress Xiaocigao. Built in 1629, the year the first Qing Emperor died after a defeat in a battle with Ming general Yuan Chonghuan, Dong Ling is the first imperial mausoleum of the Qing Dynasty. The tomb is perched on Mount Tianzhu and encircled by thousands of 400-year-old pine trees.

With an architectural structure similar to Bei Ling, it features a unique design of a 108-step staircase. The 40-m-long (131-ft.) slope begins at the Sacred Way and leads to the Stand Stele Pavilion.

Dongling Lu 210, Dongling District. ✆ **024/8803-1748.** Admission ¥40, Apr 1–Oct 31; ¥30, Nov 1–Mar 31. May–Oct 8am–5pm; Nov–Apr 8am–4:30pm. At Zhong Jie Metro Station Exit A, walk east to Dong Shun Cheng Jie, take bus no. 218 to Dongling Gongyuan at Zhong Jie bus stop (south of Dong Shun Cheng Jie). Taxi: about 35 min. from downtown (¥30).

Gu Gong (Imperial Palace) ★ For those who have visited its predecessor in Beijing, the first and most obvious difference will be size. Shenyang's humble imperial abode covers roughly 60,000 sq. m (645,835 sq. ft.), less than a 10th the area of the Forbidden City. This means you don't have to run a tourist marathon to see all the offerings, nor do you need to devote an entire day to exploration.

The palace, built from 1625 to 1636, is largely modeled after Beijing's Gu Gong, but architecturally blends intricate Mongolian- and Tibetan-influenced carvings favored by the early Qing. Unfortunately, many of the exhibitions are poorly cared for, such as Zhong Zheng Dian, where the emperor once attended to political affairs. Viewed from afar, the carved oak throne and emperor-yellow cushion have faded under a thick layer of dust into dull wood and a sickly pale color.

On the northeastern side is the oldest and most impressive structure in the Gu Gong: **Da Zheng Hall (Da Zheng Dian)** and the surrounding **Pavilion of Ten Kings (Shi Wang Ting).** The original gate housed to the east of the main entrance is now closed to the public, so visitors will stumble upon this homage to the Manchurian army either from a small door on the west, or from the back. The two pavilions closest to the hall display the offices of the left and right wings, while the remaining eight pavilions display various Qing weaponry and replicas of the armor and the colorful banners (two each of yellow, red, blue, and white) of the eight divisions of the Manchu army. Da Zheng Hall is where Dorgon, Huang Taiji's younger brother and regent to his successor Shunzhi (the first Qing emperor to rule from Beijing), is said to have given the orders to invade China.

Shenyang Lu 171. ✆ **024/2484-2215.** Admission ¥60. May–Oct 8:30am–6pm; Nov–Apr 8:30am–4:30pm Bus: 213 from Bei Ling Park Zhan to Gu Gong stop; walk north to Shenyang Lu, then walk west along Shengyang Lu. Metro: Huayuan Men; walk 440m east along Shenyang Lu.

Liaoning Provincial Museum (Liaoning Sheng Bowuguan) ★ This museum, formerly the Liaoning Museum, which opened back in 1949 and was revamped in 2007, houses an impressive collection of pieces from cave age-era fossils to Qing dynasty precious artifacts. The large, circular layout gives the museum a comfortable, open feel, while the vaulted ceilings absorb the sounds of chattering tour groups. The entire third floor hosts the **Liao River Civilization** exhibition, with five different rooms and 1,400 items displaying the history and culture of the provinces. Other notable exhibits include the **Crafts of the Ming and Qing Dynasties** and **the Gem of Porcelains of The Ming and Qing Dynasties,** showcasing an imposing collection of imperial pieces such as jade, lacquer, enamels and bamboo, wood, ivory carvings and porcelains from two of the most flourishing periods in Chinese history, and the **Chinese Money exhibition,** which displays everything from rudimentary seashell beads to ancient gold ingots from which the auspicious Chinese delicacy *jiaozi* (steamed dumplings) get their shape.

Shifu Da Lu 363, east side of Shifu Guangchang. ✆ **024/2274-1193.** Free admission. Audio tours in English and Chinese (available at coat check) ¥10 plus ¥100 and ID deposit. 9am–5pm. Closed Mondays (except public holidays) and New Year's Eve. Bus no. 214, 215, 216, 221, 228, 230, 243, 248, 260, or 800.

9.18 Museum (Jiuyiba Bowuguan) This museum in northern Shenyang offers a decidedly biased view of the Mukden Incident (1931) in which Japan staged an attack on its own South Manchurian railway line at Liutiao Hu as a pretense to invade the Northeast. Four large characters displayed under a clock frozen at 10:20 read *"Wu wang guo chi"*—"Never forget the national disgrace." The museum strives to offer a variety of unorthodox presentations. One exhibition, documenting the Rise of the Anti-Japanese Army of Resistance (coincidentally supported by the CPC, and in direct disobedience of Kuomintang orders of nonresistance) replicates a guerrilla warfare conference using full-size wax figures meeting in a large fake forest. Nearby are miniature clay figurines behind glass casing, with stunted comical bodies and expressions, celebrating the army's successes. Oil paintings and blown-up photos adorn the walls. The mixing and matching of presentation styles makes for muddled exhibitions. Other displays touch on the Unit 731 biological weapons experiments (see "Harbin," p. 191) and the Nanjing Massacre (p. 398).

Wanghua Jie 46 (at Chongshan Lu, southeast of Bei Ling). ✆ **024/8832-0918.** Free admission. 9am–4:30pm. Bus: 253 from Da Xi Men (west of Gu Gong).

Shenyang Financial Museum (Shenyang Jinrong Bowuguan) Opened in 2006, this museum is now the biggest of its kind in China. The European-style structure, listed in the National Important Relics Protective Institutions, is the former site of the Frontier Bank, a private bank of warlord Zhang Zuolin and his son, established in the 1930s. The ground floor, decorated in the style of the original Frontier Bank lobby, is filled with over 80 vivid full-size wax figures demonstrating how the bank worked before computers dominated our lives. The museum has 23 rooms displaying the financial history of the Northeast, ancient Chinese currencies discovered in the area, and 1940s money featuring portraits of Dr. Sun and Mao, as well as different versions of Renminbi and other early foreign paper money. It also has an interactive corner to show how to identify counterfeit money. However, the descriptions are mostly in Chinese, with little and simple English.

Shao Shuai Fu Xiang 8, Chaoyang Jie. East of Zhang Residence (below). ✆ **024/2486-7711.** Admission ¥30 and combo ticket ¥60 include Zhang Residence. English audio guide ¥20 plus ¥200 and ID deposit. 8:30am–5pm.

Zhang Residence (Zhangshi Shuaifu) This resurrected courtyard house south of the Gu Gong, originally known as Shuai Fu (the Commander's Palace), was the home of warlord Zhang Zuolin and his celebrated son, Marshal Zhang Xueliang.

The residence provides a glimpse into the almost-imperial world inhabited by the powerful warlords who ruled parts of China after the Qing dynasty collapsed. A study in the Xiaoqing Lou, a small European-styled house next to the main courtyard complex, is where Zhang Zuolin died after Japanese assassins exploded a bomb under his private train in 1928.

Corner of Chaoyang Lu and Nan Shuncheng Lu. ✆ **024/2484-2454.** Admission ¥60 (includes Shenyang Financial Museum). Apr 15–Oct 15 8:30am–5pm; Oct 16–Apr 14 8:30am–4:30pm. Walk west from Gu Gong; take a left on Zhengyang Jie. Or from Huayuan Men Metro station Exit B, walk south to Daxi Men bus station and take bus no. 503 or 260 to the next station, Shi Huan Bao Ju.

OUTSIDE SHENYANG

Qian Shan ★ Once a quiet mountain retreat, Qian Shan, one of Dongbei's most accessible getaways, is slowly being taken over by tourists scrambling over the Song dynasty temples and zipping through the park on electric shuttle buses that charge ¥10 a ride. Getting off the main road, which twists through the national park, leads to a more serene and pleasant experience. Climbing is not highly favored by the teeming hordes of visitors, so it's quite easy to escape to a pleasant hike off the well-worn paths leading to sites and temples, though you have to climb quite a distance to get away from the karaoke bar speakers blasting on the northeastern slope.

The Bei Bu (Northern Ravine), with signs in English, can be seen in 1 day. Xianren Tai (Peak of the Immortals), site of the legendary Da'an Temple, requires an overnight trip. Several affordable hotels are in the area. Modest rooms are available in some of the Buddhist temples if you ask nicely.

17km (11 miles) south of An Shan. Admission at main gate ¥80, temples ¥5–¥20. Open 24 hr. Bus: Catch large air-conditioned bus to An Shan (every 15 min.; 2 hr., ¥27) near Wenhua Gong, 3 blocks southeast of Shenyang Zhan on Minzhu Lu; then take minibus from Jian Guo Nan Lu (40 min.; ¥2) to Qian Shan. Last bus back to Shenyang leaves An Shan at 7pm.

Where to Stay

High season in Shenyang runs from March to mid-October. Hotels become especially crowded with conventions in early September. More budget options are now available.

VERY EXPENSIVE

Kempinski Hotel Shenyang (Shenyang Kaibinsiji Fandian) ★ Overlooking the lofty TV tower and lake at Qingnian Park, the rooms here are restful with light caramel and sophisticated purple background and decorated with classy patterned mirrors and glass panels. The view from the rooms is imposing when the lights of the park and the tower are on at night. The bathroom has a stylish oval glass washbasin and shelves, separate shower, and bath tub. Its service is one of the best in the city. Free broadband Internet access is in all rooms.

Qingnian Lu 109, Shenhe District. www.kempinski.com. ✆ **024/2298-8988.** Fax 024/2298-8888. 332 units. ¥1,199 standard room. ¥1,449–¥2,489 suite. 15% service charge. AE, DC, MC, V. **Amenities:** 2 restaurants; deli; bar; concierge; executive-level rooms; fitness center; indoor pool; room service; spa; ticketing. *In room:* A/C, floor heating, satellite TV, hair dryer, free broadband Internet, minibar.

Sheraton Shenyang Lido Hotel (Shenyang Lidu Xilaideng Fandian) ★ This is the best five-star hotel in Shenyang. Decorated throughout with fine, original artwork, it offers the city's classiest rooms. Standard guest rooms have large bathrooms with separate bathtub and shower. The hotel features some unique perks, including a climbing wall on the fourth floor.

Qingnian Dajie 386 (south of Wulihe Stadium). www.sheraton.com/shenyang. ✆ **024/2318-8888.** Fax 024/2318-8000. 590 units. ¥1,095 standard room; ¥1,460 suite. 15% service charge. Rates include breakfast. AE, DC, MC, V. **Amenities:** 3 restaurants; deli; bar; concierge; executive-level rooms; forex; golf simulator; health club and spa; indoor pool; room service; smoke-free floors. *In room:* A/C, satellite TV, fridge, hair dryer, Internet, minibar.

EXPENSIVE

Crowne Plaza Shenyang Zhongshan (Shenyang Zhongshan Huangguan Jiari Jiudian) ★ Rebranded as Crowne Plaza in 2010, this hotel is the only five-star around the Zhongshan Guangchang area and still a good choice in the city center. Service here is top-notch. Rooms are comfy and clean, though the in-room facilities are a bit outdated. Food at its Italian restaurant is delectable and close to authentic.

Nanjing Bei Jie 208, Heping District. www.crowneplaza.com. ✆ **024/2334-1999.** Fax 024/2334-1688. 278 units. ¥1,088–¥1,588 standard room; ¥1,888–¥2,088 suite. 15% service charge. AE, DC, MC, V. **Amenities:** 5 restaurant; bar; concierge; executive-level rooms; forex; fitness center; indoor pool; smoke-free floors; ticketing. *In room:* A/C, LCD/satellite TV, hair dryer, Internet, minibar.

Lexington Shenyang Rich Gate Hotel (Shenyang Huafutiandi Laixingdun Jiudian) ★ This is the most luxurious lodge in the Shenyang Bei Zhan area and has the most capacious standard rooms in the city. It is situated on top of a new entertainment complex comprised of shopping malls, restaurants, and a movie theater. The rooms have LCD TV, pleasing and stylish geometric furniture, and impressionist paintings hanging on the wall. Beds are plush and comfy. Bathrooms are large, with separate tub and shower. Through the glass panel separating the bathroom and bedroom, you can watch TV while having a relaxing soak. Its top-floor restaurant enjoys a great view of the city

Ha'erbin Rd. 128, Shenhe District. www.lexingtonhotels.com. ✆ **024/2259-8888.** Fax 024/2259-8999. 573 units. ¥1,288 standard room; ¥2,088 executive-level room. Over 30% discount. 15% service charge. AE, DC, MC, V. **Amenities:** Restaurant; deli; babysitting; concierge; executive-level rooms; forex; ticketing. *In room:* A/C, LCD/satellite TV, floor heating, hair dryer, Internet, minibar.

Maritim Hotel Shenyang (Shenyang Biguiyuan Malidimu Jiudian) ★ Launched in mid-2011, Maritim is now the largest hotel in the city. Perched on the outskirts of Shenyang city, the resortlike property has a huge artificial lake surrounded by a lush garden and planked path. Exquisite ceiling paintings along the promenade of the high-ceiling lobby are imposing. The spacious rooms have a balcony overlooking the lake or the garden. The marble bathrooms are equipped with separate showers and bathtubs.

Datonghu Lu 168, Yuhong District. www.maritim.com. ✆ **024/2526-8888.** Fax 024/2259-8999. 631 units. ¥1,200 standard room; ¥2,000 suite. Over 30% discount. 15% service charge. AE, DC, MC, V. **Amenities:** 2 restaurants; bar; babysitting; bowling center; concierge; executive-level rooms; forex; fitness center; indoor pool; room service; sauna; smoke-free rooms; tennis court; Wi-Fi. *In room:* A/C, plasma/satellite TV, hair dryer, free broadband Internet, minibar.

Traders Hotel (Chengmao Fandian) ★ Its convenient location, in the midst of the Taiyuan Jie shopping district and within walking distance of Shenyang Zhan, is the number-one advantage of this Shangri-La-managed four-star hotel. The stellar service of this hotel, open for over 15 years, also makes it stand out from the competitors. Rooms are decently sized with a subtle Oriental touch. The bathrooms are virtually spotless. The hotel provides free broadband Internet connection in all rooms.

Zhonghua Lu 68 (at Taiyuan Jie). www.shangri-la.com. ✆ **024/2341-2288.** Fax 024/2341-1988. 407 units. ¥668 standard room. ¥1,788 suite. 15% service charge. Rates include breakfast for 1. AE, DC, MC, V. **Amenities:** 2 restaurants; deli; bar; concierge; executive-level rooms; small exercise room; forex; Jacuzzi; room service; sauna; smoke-free rooms. *In room:* A/C, satellite TV, fridge, hair dryer, free broadband Internet, minibar.

MODERATE

Gloria Plaza Shenyang (Shenyang Kailai Dajiudian) The Gloria Plaza was the first international hotel to open in the Shenyang Bei Zhan area and is still a reliable standby. Well-maintained guest rooms are unremarkably decorated but comfortable and have small but clean bathrooms.

Yingbin Jie 32 (at Bei Zhan Lu). www.gphshenyang.com. ✆ **024/2252-8855.** Fax 024/2252-8533. 283 units. ¥398–¥468 standard room. ¥588–¥888 suite. Rates include breakfast and service charge. AE, DC, MC, V. **Amenities:** 2 restaurants; bar; babysitting; concierge; health club and spa; KTV; room service. *In room:* A/C, satellite TV, fridge, Internet, minibar.

Liaoning Hotel (Liaoning Binguan) ★ Originally part of the illustrious Japanese-run Yamato chain, the Liaoning is one of a very few truly charming hotels in the Northeast. The building (constructed in 1927) underwent an admirable $3.75-million restoration, giving new life to the original marble staircase with its well-worn brass handrails and intimate green-and-white tile lobby. Guest rooms have high-ceilings, while bathrooms are small but pleasant. The Liaoning's central location on Zhongshan Guangchang adds to the charm.

Zhongshan Lu 97, south of Zhongshan Guangchang. ✆ **024/2383-9166.** Fax 024/2383-9103. 77 units. ¥358–¥398 standard room. AE, MC, V. **Amenities:** 2 restaurants; exercise room; sauna; outdoor tennis court. *In room:* A/C, TV, fridge, hair dryer, free broadband Internet.

New World Shenyang Hotel (Shenyang Xin Shijie Jiudian) The New World was Shenyang's first international joint-venture hotel and a luxury choice in the downtown area when it opened back in the '90s. Though it's not as swanky as it once was, it is now a good mid-priced option in the Taiyuan Jie commercial area. Rooms of the conveniently located hotel were renovated in recent years, and now have large flat-screen TVs and new furniture. Bathrooms are cramped but clean, and service is courteous.

Nanjing Nan Lu 2, Heping District. www.newworldhotels.com. ✆ **024/2386-9888.** Fax 024/2386-0018. 258 units. ¥388 standard room. AE, DC, MC, V. **Amenities:** Restaurant; cafe; concierge; forex; small exercise room; room service; ticketing. *In room:* A/C, satellite TV, fridge, hair dryer, free broadband Internet, minibar.

Shenyang Regar Hotel (Shenyang Tianlun Ruige Jiudian) Positioned right in the heart of the Zhong Jie shopping area, this four-star hotel has the advantage of being within walking distance to several attractions such as Gu Gong. Rooms are clean and pleasantly decorated, and staff are amiable.

Chaoyang Street 23, Shenhe District. www.regarhotel.com. ✆ **024/2487-6666.** Fax 024/2487-6999. 243 units. ¥468 standard room without breakfast. AE, DC, MC, V. **Amenities:** 2 restaurants; bar; concierge; exercise room. *In room:* A/C, cable TV, fridge, free broadband Internet, minibar.

Times Plaza Hotel (Shidai Guangchang Jiudian) Located just opposite Shenyang Bei Zhan, the well-situated Times Plaza is another good four-star selection in the area. Though guest rooms are fairly standard, the beds are comfy and the bathrooms are compact but clean, with shower and tub. The Hong Kong management, Rosedale, has given the hotel an entire revamp after taking over in 2007. Service is satisfactory, with a very nice staff. The fitness club has two squash courts.

Beizhan Lu 99, Shenhe (opposite to Beizhan Railway Station). www.rosedalehotels.com. ✆ **024/2253-2828.** Fax 024/2253-0588. 274 units. ¥388 standard room. AE, DC, MC, V. **Amenities:** 2 restaurants; deli; concierge; forex; exercise room; limited room service; squash courts. *In room:* A/C, satellite TV, fridge, minibar.

INEXPENSIVE

Mainland economy hotel brand **Home Inn (Rujia)** has opened 12 hotels in the city. One of them at Zhengyang Jie 196 (✆ **024/2486-1999;** www.homeinns.com; ¥199 standard room) is just a 10-minute walk from Gugong and offers clean and cozy rooms. Its proximity to a number of attractions and the Zhong Jie business area makes it a good budget pick. **Ibis (Yibisi,** Nanjing Bei Jie 161; www.ibishotel.com; ✆ **024/3131-5555;** ¥178), close to the Taiyuan Street commercial district, is another convenient choice. It has simple and comfy rooms, with LCD TV, Japanese-style partitions and small but clean bathrooms.

Where to Eat

Shenyang has a wide selection of cuisines from Dongbei, to Sichuan, Japanese, Korean, and Western. For Japanese food, the classiest is **Mikado,** in the Marvelot Shenyang Hotel (Qingnian Dajie 388, next to the Sheraton), with a specialization in *teppanyaki* and fine sushi served in private tatami-mat rooms. Cheaper and more convenient is the **Qianyi Lamian Dian,** Tianjin Bei Jie, north of the Dongbei Cinema (✆ **024/2341-9941**), open from 10am to 10pm. For groceries, go to **Walmart** on Zhonghua Jie, near Shenyang Zhan, or the **Carrefour** near Shenyang Bei Zhan.

Ma Family Shaomai (Ma Jia Shaomai Guan) ★ CHINESE Great-great-great-grandpa Ma is rumored to have first sold these award-winning *shaomai* (steamed open-top dumplings) from a street-side wheelbarrow in 1796. Prices on the menu are for a plate of 10 dumplings—eight dumplings for one hungry person are more than enough. The most delicious offering here is the *chuantong* (traditional) *shaomai,* with beef and ginger. *Yu cui* (jade green) *shaomai,* with egg and spring onion, is excellent vegetarian fare.

Taiyuan Bei Jie 12, Heping. ✆ **024/8383-1555.** Meal for 2 ¥70–¥80. No credit cards. 10am–10pm. Metro: Shenyang Zhan; from Exit A, walk along Shengli Bei Jie for about 10 minutes to Bei Si Ma Lu, turn right and walk 3 blocks.

Xinglongxuan Jiaozi Guan ★ CHINESE Unmistakable with its bright red facade, this restaurant is cheaper and livelier than the "tourist-approved" Laobian Jiaozi Guan, and its *jiaozi* are more delicious. Try the *bianxian sanxian* (egg, shrimp, and chives stir-fried before wrapping) or the standard *zhurou baicai* (pork and cabbage).

Xiaoxi Lu 75, Shenhe District. ✆ **024/2290-8858.** Meal for 2 ¥50–¥70. No credit cards. 9am–10pm. Walk south at the Liaoning Province Museum exit along Xiaoxi Lu to the intersection of Zhongshan Lu.

Shenyang After Dark

Dongbei entertainment, ***errenzhuan,*** a mix of opera, stand-up comedy and singing, is popular in Shenyang. **Liulaogen Dawutai (Liulaogen Theatre),** on Zhong Jie

(✆: **0431/2484-5532**), is one of the most prominent stages for the more than 300-year-old folk performance art, recognized as an intangible heritage in China. The classic lanterns, gigantic fans, red-colored Chinese surname characters, and flashy lights adorn the distinctive exterior of the Chinese-style theater. Show costs ¥200 to ¥460, starting at 7pm nightly and running for 2½ hours. Conducted in Dongbei dialect, some of the gags are hard to catch even for those who understand Mandarin. But audiences are kept entertained and amused by the animated actors, roaring with laughter all night. Shows are always full; buy tickets early at the ticket office, which opens at 10am and sells tickets on the same day only.

Like most cities in the Northeast region in China, Shenyang doesn't have a lively pub scene and goes to bed at around 10pm on most Fridays and Saturdays, but late nights can still be had. **Mulligan's,** an Irish pub inside the Holiday Inn Hotel, at Nanjing Bei Jie 206 (✆ **024/2334-1888**), with its wide selection of international beers and a tolerable level of kitsch, is not a bad choice. **Shamrock Irish Pub (Sanyecao Ai'erlan Jiuba),** located at Changjiang Jie 134-11 (✆ **024/8608-5856**), is well received by expats, being one of the few survivors on the bar street near Liaoning University. Chef and co-owner is a Chinese who lived in Ireland for over three decades and the pub serves refreshing Guinness beer imported from Ireland. **Q7,** inside Times Plaza Hotel, at Beizhan Lu 99 (✆ **024/2396-6666**), has one of the best club scenes. It is famous for its big video wall, impressive lighting and DJ stage, and selection of dance music.

DANDONG 丹东

280km (173 miles) S of Shenyang, 370km (229 miles) NE of Dalian

Visitors come to **Dandong** for one reason: to see North Korea. Situated on a bend in the Yalu Jiang (Green Duck River) and connected by rail bridge to the North Korean town of Sinuiju, the city has built a robust economy around the geographical voyeurs who rush to the border every summer. For all its wealth, Dandong remains a Chinese city, with crowded tenement buildings and a new riverside development area already stained by pollution, but it gleams in comparison with its neighbor.

Essentials

GETTING THERE **Flights** leave the airport (Dandong Jichang), 13km (8 miles) west of town, for Beijing (8 flights weekly), Shanghai (10 flights weekly), and Shenzhen (4 flights weekly). Purchase tickets at the **CAAC ticket office** (**Minhang Shoupiao Chu;** ✆ **0415/221-7999;** Mon–Sat 8–11:30am and 1–4:30pm) at Jinshan Dajie 50 (intersection with San Wei Lu). The **airport shuttle** (30 min.; ¥5) leaves from the CAAC office 2 hours before each flight. By **taxi,** it's a 20-minute ride for ¥40.

Dandong's **railway station** is on Shi (10) Wei Lu, on the western edge of town. Trains go to Beijing (6:31pm; 14 hr.; ¥263), Shenyang (12 daily; 4–5⅓ hr.; ¥24–¥42), Dalian (8:31am; 10 hr. 13 min.; ¥99 hard sleeper), and Changchun (6:47am and 3:26pm; 10 hr. and 8¾ hr., respectively; ¥89 hard sleeper). **International trains** go to Sinuiju three weekly (¥150); tickets are available in the **CITS** office (✆ **0415/217-6728;** Mon–Fri 8:30–11am and 1:30–5pm). The office is located in the double-spired

Dandong 丹东

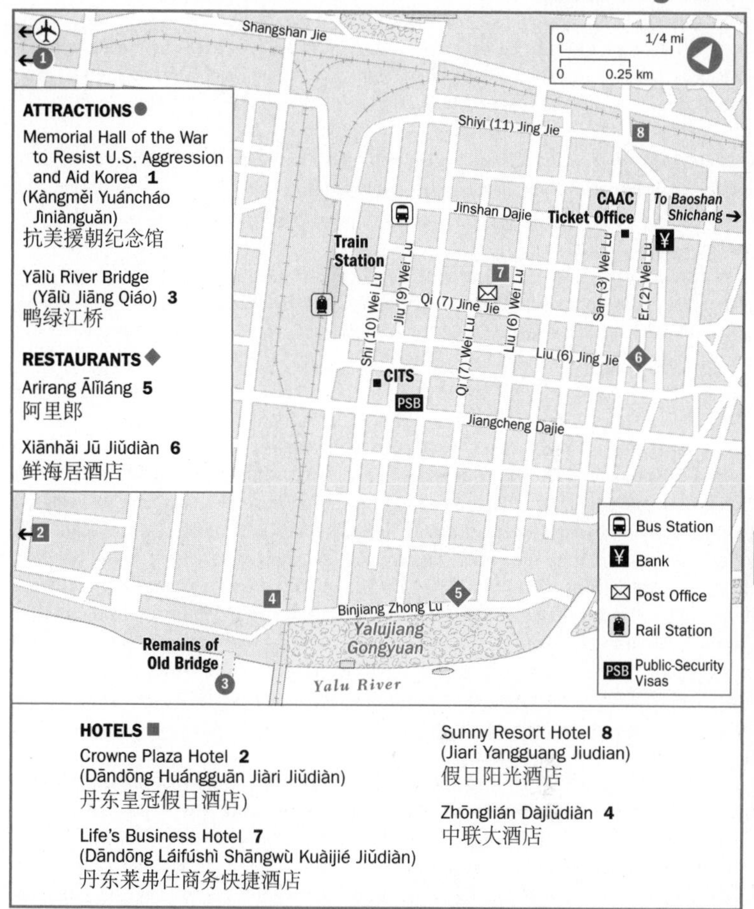

Shuangxing Dasha across from the station (see "Border Crossing: North Korea & Russia" p. 163).

The **long-distance bus station** (✆ **0415/213-4571**) is across the street from the railway station, at the corner of Shi Wei Lu and Gong'an Jie, with coaches to Shenyang (3 hr. 10 min.; ¥80) and Dalian (eight daily; 4 hr.; ¥99).

VISITOR INFORMATION For tourist complaints, call ✆ **0415/314-7937.**

GETTING AROUND Most of Dandong lies north of a V formed by the Yalu Jiang and the train tracks. Shi Wei Lu follows the tracks to the Yalu Jiang Gongyuan, facing North Korea. **Taxis** are ¥5 for the first 2km and ¥2/km thereafter; from 9pm to 5am, they charge ¥6 for the first 2km.

[Fast FACTS] DANDONG

Banks, Foreign Exchange & ATMs Cash and traveler's checks can be exchanged from 8am to 4pm inside the **Bank of China** branch at Jinshan Dajie 60 (at its intersection with Er Wei Lu; Mon–Fri 7:30am–5pm). A 24-hour international ATM is located at the bank's entrance.

Internet Access The 24-hour **Wuxian Wangyuan** is on Shiyi (11) Jing Jie, north of Liu (6) Wei Lu. It charges ¥3 per hour. Dial-up is ✆ **96163.**

Post Office The main post office, open from 8am to 5:30pm, is on the corner of Qi (7) Wei Lu and Qi Jing Jie.

Visa Extensions For visa extensions, go to room 112 of the main **PSB** office at Jiangcheng Dajie 15, behind Shuangxing Dasha (✆ **0415/210-3393;** Mon–Fri 8am–noon and 1:30–5:30pm). You'll have to show a hotel registration card and proof that you have $100 per day of the extension.

Exploring Dandong

There isn't much to see at the **North Korean border,** but the contrast between lively Dandong and depressed Sinuiju does provide a vivid illustration of the different paths to development taken by China and its Communist ally. There are two ways to see the border—by boat and by bridge. Most visitors do both. A 10-minute walk south of the railway station to the end of Shi Wei Lu and a few blocks west, along Jiangyan Jie, is the **Yalu Jiang Qiao ★** (✆ **0415/312-4767;** 7:30am–6pm; ¥20), a unique horizontal rotation bridge bombed by the United States in 1950. Korea dismantled its half shortly after the Korean War armistice, rendering the bridge useless. You can wander out to the still-mangled end of the Chinese section, where someone has installed a pair of bomb casings as a reminder. **Boats** leave from the pier adjacent the Yalu Jiang Qiao entrance (8am–5pm; ¥50 boats; ¥70 speedboats), allowing you to see the shore of North Korea more up-close.

You might guess what kind of perspective a museum clunkily named the **Memorial Hall of the War to Resist U.S. Aggression and Aid Korea** (**Kangmei Yuanchao Jinianguan;** 8am–4pm; free admission) might have. Nevertheless, it offers an interesting Communist revisionist's look at the Korean War with black-and-white photos, surprisingly clear English translations, and patriotic music piped in. The museum requires some effort to reach—not just because it's located on a hill on the north side of Shangshan Jie, in the northwest part of town, but because the stairs to the memorial are quite a climb. The museum is to the right of the memorial, and behind the museum are some rusty rail cars, tanks, and fighter planes used during the war. Take bus no. 21 from the railway station, get off at the Tiyuguan, and walk northwest.

Outside Dandong

Five Dragon Mountain (Wu Long Shan) The 30-minute drive from downtown Dandong puts you in an idyllic setting with plenty of hikes and a temple housing 20 monks. Ignore the tacky faux-Japanese "villas" at the front of the park, and concentrate on the nature within. It's particularly nice in the autumn when the leaves change colors.

Admission ¥35. 7:30am to 5pm. Bus runs from the left side of the train station plaza every hour ¥3. Round-trip taxi from center of town ¥80.

border crossing: NORTH KOREA & RUSSIA

Tour groups to North Korea stopped for a short while after the death of Kim Jung Il, but the communist country has now reopened to tourists. At press time, United States citizens are allowed to travel to North Korea by plane only. In Shenyang, there are planes to Pyongyang. CITS in Dandong can arrange tours for other nationalities who have applied for visas to North Korea. The paperwork takes at least a week to process. Independent Beijing-based operations like foreign-run Koryo Tours (www.koryogroup.com) also have trips that end in Dandong, charge roughly the same rates, and have more experience with foreigners.

Crossing the border from Dongbei into **Russia,** either on the Trans-Siberian train or at one of the border posts in Heilong Jiang and Inner Mongolia, is easier but also requires a visa. Tourist visas can usually only be arranged at the Russian Embassy in Beijing. Keep in mind you'll have to arrange for a Chinese **double-entry visa** if you plan to come back to China from either country.

Tiger Mountain Great Wall (Hushan Changcheng) ★ Tiger Mountain, a short, steep, and impeccably restored section of the Great Wall located 30km (19 miles) northeast of Dandong, forms part of China's border with North Korea. A brief hike along the Wall provides beautiful views of surrounding cornfields, and the return path takes you right up against the small stream that separates Chinese and North Korean territory. South Chinese sometimes wander onto stones set in the stream just behind the Wall to trade goods and information with North Korean soldiers and farmers. ***Warning:*** Cross over on the stones yourself and you risk arrest.

✆ **0415/557-8511.** Admission ¥60. Museum ¥10. 7am to 5pm. Bus no. 15. (40 min.; ¥11 round-trip) leaves from left side of long-distance bus station.

Where to Stay

A recent boom in hotels in Dandong means that travelers have a lot more choices and bargaining power. The new and only five-star hotel, **Crowne Plaza Dandong (Dandong Huangguan Jiari Jiudian) ★**, Binjiang Zhong Lu 158 (www.crowneplaza.com; ✆ **0415/318-9999;** fax 0415/318-9888; 356 units; ¥1,180–¥1,280, over 50% discount available; 15% service charge; AE, DC, MC, V), offers the best and most luxurious rooms in town. Situated in the west end of the river, it is comparatively a bit far from downtown. Its American-style rooms are cozy, filled with wooden furniture and equipped with a LCD TV and a computer. Bathrooms have comfy bathtub and shower cubicle. It also has an indoor pool, well-equipped fitness center, outdoor badminton and tennis courts.

Sunny Resort Hotel (Dandong Jiari Yangguang Jiudian) ★, Xian Qian Jie 1 (www.jryghotel.com; ✆ **0415/288-3333;** fax 0415/288-7999; 180 units; ¥368–¥508; 15% service charge; AE, DC, MC, V), has clean and modern rooms, with a soothing ambience. Another four-star hotel is the **Zhonglian Hotel (Zhonglian Jiudian) ★**, Binjiang Zhong Lu 62 (www.zlhotel.com.cn; ✆ **0415/233-3333;** fax 0415/2337-3888; 165 units; ¥388–¥518; AE, DC, MC, V), located opposite the Yalu Jiang Qiao. The hotel offers a nice Western food buffet, a bowling center, and surprisingly large rooms with generously sized beds and impeccable bathrooms. The hotel cafe looks onto North Korea; come with a pair of binoculars that you can use to gaze at North Korea from rooms overlooking the river. **Life's Business Hotel (Laifushi Shangwu Kuaijie Jiudian),** Liu Wei Lu 29 (www.lifeshotel.com; ✆ **0415/213-9555;** ¥198–¥298; cash only), has clean standard rooms with a minimal style and provides free broadband Internet access, though carpets are somewhat stained. It also has rooms decorated with special themes and is within walking distance to the Yalu Jiang Park and Bridge.

Where to Eat

Downtown Dandong is full of small, nondescript home-style restaurants and *jiaozi* houses, and the river promenade has a number of upscale Japanese and Korean eateries. Along the strip of Korean eateries that line the river, locals consider **Arirang** (**Alilang;** Binjiang Zhong Lu 46; ✆ **0415/212-2333;** 9am–9:30pm) a pretty good choice. The Korean setting with comfortable booths and private rooms is a nice place to relax after boating. Try the *shiguo Banfan* (stone pot rice), known as *bibimbop* in Korean, the *huoguo* (hot pot), or the *shengban niurou* (raw beef). If you're really feeling adventurous, you might consider the *xiangla gourou* (spicy dog). The best place to try the local seafood, which area residents rave about, is **XianhaiJu Jiudian,** located at the intersection of Liu (6) Jing Jie and Er (2) Wei Lu (✆ **0415/216-5763;** 9am–midnight). It offers a simple, clean interior and a back room of tanks of live seafood that you can wander through. A meal for two costs about ¥140–¥160.

DALIAN 大连 ★★ & LUSHUN 旅顺

397km (246 miles) S of Shenyang

Dalian is the supermodel of Chinese cities. Thoroughly modern, sartorially savvy, and unabashedly narcissistic, it is also the largest and busiest port in northern China. Dalian's straightforward beauty can be refreshing in a region where most towns are of the interesting-but-homely type, and indeed, there are few more enjoyable activities after a week in the Dongbei gloom than a sunlit stroll along the city's supremely walkable streets. The mere fact that the city has a definable downtown, unlike other cities in China, is to be lauded.

Like Shanghai and Hong Kong, the cities to which it is most often compared, Dalian isn't really Chinese. Located just north of the Lushun naval base at the tip of the Liaodong Peninsula, it was conceived by Russia's czarist government as an ice-free alternative to Vladivostok. Construction of the port, originally called Dalny, got off to a quick start after Russia secured a lease on the peninsula in 1898; however, it lost the city and Lushun to Japan in the Russo-Japanese War (1904–05). Dalian (in Japanese: *Dairen*) soon grew into the pleasantly sophisticated port Russia had imagined.

Communist-era industrial development swamped Dalian in thick clouds of factory smoke, but it was miraculously resurrected in the mid-1990s by Mayor Bo Xilai, who tried to model the new Dalian on cities he had seen in Europe. This led him to introduce several revolutionary measures—including a hefty fine for public spitting—that have become a model for urban renewal projects throughout China. Today, Dalian is considered a vision of China's future both by optimists, who laud its beauty and modernity, and by more cynical observers, who point wryly to the same silver skyscrapers and note how many are empty. Striking as the modern buildings are, it is the

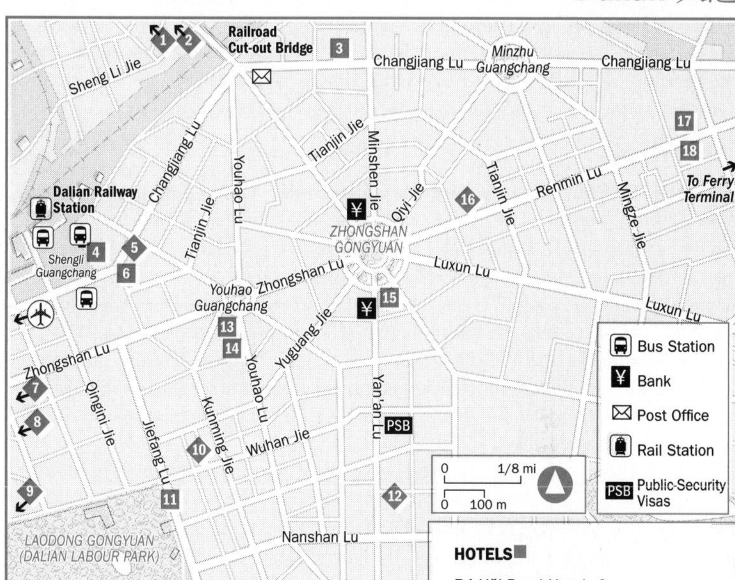

RESTAURANTS & NIGHTLIFE ◆

Blossom Jazz Music Club **10**
(Huāmǎndōu Juéshì Jūlèbù)
花满都爵士俱乐部

Chu-Shin-ya **12**
(Zhōngxīn Wū)
中心屋

Daliang Gu Tou Zong Dian **8**
(Dàliáng Gǔtou Zǒngdiàn)
大梁骨头总店

Dave's Bar **16**

I-55 Coffee Stop & Bakery **9**
(Àiwǔwǔ Měishì Kāfēizhàn I-55)
咖啡站

Lónghǎi Yúwān Měishí Guǎngchǎng **7**
龙海渔湾美食广场

Russian Street (Éluósī Fēngqíng Jiē) **2**
俄罗斯风情街

Taineng **5**
(Taineng Shaokao Dian)
太能烧烤店

Tapas (Dápàsī) **1**
达帕斯西班牙餐厅

HOTELS ■

Bó Hǎi Pearl Hotel **4**
(Bó Hǎi Míngzhū Dàjiǔdiàn)
渤海明珠大酒店

Dàlián Hotel (Dàlián Bīnguǎn) **15**
大连宾馆

Gloria Plaza Hotel **13**
(Dàlián Kǎilái Dàjiǔdiàn)
凯莱大酒店

Kempinski Hotel Dalian **11**
(Dàlián Kaibinsiji Fandian)
大连凯宾斯基饭店

Motel 168 **14**
(Mòtài Yīliùbā)
莫泰168

New World Hotel Dalian **18**
(Dàlián Xīnshìjiè Jiǔdiàn)
大连新世界酒店

Nikko Hotel Dalian **3**
(Dàlián Rihang Jiǔdiàn)
大连日航饭店

Ramada Plaza Dàlián **6**
(Jiuzhou Huameida Dàjiǔdiàn)
九州华美达大酒店

Shangri-La Dàlián **17**
(Dàlián Xiānggélǐlā Dàfàndiàn)
大连香格里拉大饭店

old colonial architecture, remnants of Japanese and Russian rule contrasting pleasantly with the newness around them, that is the city's most interesting attraction.

Fashion designers and consumers from China, Japan, Korea, and Hong Kong descend on Dalian in mid-September for the 2-week **Dalian International Fashion Festival (Dalian Guoji Fuzhuang Jie).** The festival isn't as important or glamorous as the city claims, but it's worth seeing if you're in the area.

Essentials

GETTING THERE Dalian's **airport (Zhoushuizi Guoji Jichang)** is roughly 11km (6 miles) northwest of downtown. Destinations include Beijing (12–15 flights daily), Shanghai (16–18 flights daily), Guangzhou (5 flights daily), Shenzhen (1 flight daily), Hong Kong (1 flight daily), and Seoul. Airport buses cost ¥10 and take you to Qingniwa Jie and the Railway Station in about 35 minutes. A taxi costs ¥30 and takes 25 minutes to city center. **Air China** has an office in the Guohang Dasha, at Zhongshan Lu 578 (✆ **0411/8480-1161;** 9am–6pm). **All Nippon Airways** has a ticket counter on the first floor of the Sen Mao building at Zhongshan Lu 147 (intersection of Zhongshan Lu and Wuhui Lu; ✆ **4008-82-8888;** Mon–Fri 9am–5pm). The counter sells tickets to Tokyo (daily) and Osaka (daily).

From city center to airport, take **bus** no. 710 outside Time Square on Renmin Lu (40 min.; ¥1).

Dalian's **railway station (Dalian Zhan)** is in the center of town, opposite Shengli Guangchang (Victory Sq.). Trains go to Beijing (3 daily; 10½ hr.; ¥390 soft sleeper; 11½ hr.; ¥257 hard sleeper), Shanghai (12:02noon; 24½ hr.; ¥446), Shenyang or Shenyang Bei (32 daily; 3¾–6½ hr.; ¥28–¥55), Harbin (7 daily; 9½–14¼ hr.; ¥136–¥231 hard sleeper), Dandong (9:38am; 9 hr. 40 min.; ¥99 hard sleeper), and Lushun (6:42am and 2:52pm; 1¾ hr. and 1 hr., respectively; ¥9 and ¥11 soft seat). Most **long-distance buses** congregate around Shengli Guangchang (✆ **0411/8362-8681**). Express air-conditioned coaches to Dandong (eight daily; 4 hr.; ¥99) and Lvshun (1 hr.; ¥14; 7am–6pm) leave from the square's west side; buses to Shenyang (23 daily; 4 hr. 50 min.; ¥127) leave from the east side.

Ferries leave from the Dalian Gang Keyun Zhan, on Gangwan Jie 1 (east end of Renmin Lu; ✆ **0411/8263-6061** or 0411/8262-5349), for Yantai (8:30am; 6 hr.; ¥380 second class), or from Dalian Xingang, for Yantai (8:30am, 10:30am, 2:30pm, 9pm, and 10:30pm; ¥380 second class). The ticket office is open from 4am to 10pm; Tickets are also sold at booths outside railway station.

VISITOR INFORMATION The **Tourism Bureau** has an information line (✆ **0411/96181**) and a complaint line (✆ **0411/8433-9970**).

GETTING AROUND Downtown Dalian is arranged around a series of traffic circles. The two most important are **Youhao Guangchang (Friendship Square),** dominated by a glass globe in the center, and **Zhongshan Guangchang,** the city's transportation center. Ten roads radiate from Zhongshan Guangchang, including Renmin Dajie, a major avenue that runs east to the wharf, and Zhongshan Lu, which runs west past the railway station to the city's far southwestern corner. **Taxis** charge ¥8 for the first 3km (2 miles), then ¥2 per kilometer; it's 30% extra from 10pm to 5am. Regular **buses** cost ¥1 without air-conditioning, air-conditioned buses cost ¥2; pay as you get on. Bus no. 801 runs the length of Zhongshan Lu and Renmin Dajie. A **tour bus** takes visitors around the city from the south side of Dalian Railway Station South Square to Zhongshan Guangchang (every 30 min.; 1½ hr.; ¥10). Real

Japanese-built **trolleys** go from Erqi Guangchang in the east to Xinghai Gongyuan in the southwest. The fare is ¥1. The city's underground railway is in the pipeline. Its first two lines are scheduled to run in late 2012.

[Fast FACTS] DALIAN

Banks, Foreign Exchange & ATMs The main **Bank of China** branch is in a large tower on the corner of Yan'an Lu and Baiyu Jie, behind the Dalian Hotel on Zhongshan Guangchang (Mon–Fri 8:30am–4:30pm). Traveler's checks and cash can be exchanged at window 32, and credit cards are handled at window 11 (both on the second floor). International **ATMs** are next to the old Bank of China on Zhongshan Guangchang and inside the Nikko's shopping arcade.

Internet Access **Bincheng Wangba (Coast City Internet),** open from 9am to midnight (¥3–¥5 per hour), is located underground of Shengli Guangchang. The entrance is next to the east bus station. **Shengli Gainian Wangcheng (Victory Concept Net City),** on the fifth floor of Huang Bin Lou, Shengli Guangchang, opens from 8am to midnight. Take the lift from the entrance of Hisound KTV. Both are the most central Internet bars. Dial-up is ✆ **165** or 169.

Post Office The central post office is located at Zhongshan Guangchang 10, northwest of the Guangchang (8am–5pm).

Visa Extensions Visa extensions can be obtained at the **PSB** Exit/Entry Office on Zhonghua Dong Lu (second floor; ✆ **0411/8676-6108;** Mon–Fri 8:30am–4:30pm). Extensions take 5 days to process.

Exploring Dalian

Dalian's most impressive buildings surround **Zhongshan Guangchang ★**. Highlights are the late Renaissance–style white-brick and green-domed Bank of China (built in 1909) on the north side of the square, and the Dalian Hotel (see "Where to Stay," below) directly opposite. Head to **Renmin Guangchang** (1km/½ mile east of the railway station on Zhongshan Lu; bus: 701), a large square surrounded on three sides by government buildings, to get an interesting taste of modern Chinese architecture. The city made an effort to recapture some of its Russian history with **Eluosi Fengqing Jie (Russian Street),** a collection of mostly new Russian-style structures north of the railway cutout, above Shanghai Lu. The large, dilapidated yellow-brick building at the end of the street was the municipal government office when Russia still controlled the city. But the street is only filled with shops selling kitsch and souvenirs.

The Beaches & Binhai Lu ☺ Dalian's seaside location is the major draw for Chinese tourists. Most of its beaches are pebbly and polluted, but the simple presence of the ocean and its attendant sea air provide respite from the rigors of travel. Binhai Lu meanders next to the coastline and gives breathtaking views of the sea. Start your journey by taking a taxi or bus no. 201 to Haizhiyun Gongyuan (¥10), formerly Donghai Gongyuan, located about 5km (3 miles) east of downtown. In a nearby plaza at the north gate of the park, locals enjoy watching the sun rise. Continue on, by taxi, to **Bangchui Dao.** It was once the exclusive playground of Communist Party higher-ups and is now a pristine, hedge-lined country club only accessible by car (15 min.; ¥20). The city's nicest beach is a 30-minute walk past the gate (¥20). Just west of Bangchui Dao is **Laohu Tan (Tiger Beach),** a popular beach that also features Dalian's aquatic theme park, **Laohu Tan Haiyang Gongyuan** (¥190). A few kilometers west is the relatively clean **Fu Jia Zhuang Beach** (¥5). This is where the city's serious swimmers gather for a brisk dip before work. Take bus no. 5 (25 min.) from Qingniwa Qiao (north of Shengli Guangchang). **Xinghai Gongyuan,** 5km (3 miles) southwest of downtown, was originally a Japanese resort and is now Dalian's most accessible but crowded beach. Now, luxurious mansions have been newly built along the coastal line. Nearby is **Xinghai Guangchang** where it houses a seaside carnival in summer from April to September and an international beer festival in the end of July. Take bus no. 531 or 23 from Qingniwa Qiao.

Discoveryland ☺ This theme park is the Chinese answer to Disneyland with seven zones: American Street, Legendary Castles, Magical Forrest, Metallic Factory, Mysterious Desert, Mad Village, and Wedding Hall. Opened in 2006 and situated at the Jinshi Tan resort area (see below for Jinshi Tan), it has stolen the focus of the city's tacky old theme park Tiger Ocean Park. Its resort hotel opened in 2011.

Jinshi Tan. ✆ **0411/8790-0000.** www.discoveryland.cn. Admission ¥170 adults, ¥125 students; ¥85 children. Free admission for children below 1.2m (3.6 ft.). Night admission ¥100 adults, ¥75 students, ¥50 children. Apr–Oct. 9:30am–6pm; 9:30am–9:30pm from late June to early Sept. Light-rail to Jinshi Tan (50 min. from Train Station), then take shuttle bus to the theme park.

Jinshi Tan (Golden Pebble Beach) ★ With a little effort you can enjoy a clean beach without loudspeakers, tour groups, or other tackiness that infects the city shores. Hop on the light rail *(qinggui)* at the Dalian Zhan railway station and take it to the last stop, Jinshi Tan; the ride takes about an hour and passes by suburbs and factories along the coast. Taxis are sparse, so once you arrive, take a private car (¥5) or a horse-drawn carriage (¥10) to the area's best strip of beach, **Huangjin Hai'an.** It's a good swimming spot and the fine-pebble beaches are nearly empty except during the high season (July–Sept). The 36-hole golf course in the resort area is well received by golfers for its full-fledged facilities and picturesque coastline view.

Jinshi Golf Club, Golden Pebble Beach National Holiday Resort. ✆ **0411/8791-2343.** Fax 0411/8791-2260. www.dalianjinshigolf.com.

Sun Asia Ocean World & Polar World (Shengya Haiyang Shijie & Jidi Shijie) ☺ The theme park has three aquariums, Ocean World, Polar World, and Coral World. The Ocean World exhibit is set as a submarine cruising undersea and features a dolphin show. It has a 118m-long (380-ft.) underwater aquarium tunnel. The Polar World, which houses such polar animals as polar bears, polar wolves, penguins, and sea lions, and the underwater performance by a beluga whale may make it a worthwhile stop. Call ahead for free English-speaking guides, who will explain which of the animals in the tanks are edible.

Just east of Xinghai Park. ✆ **0411/8458-1113.** www.sunasia.com. Admission (to Ocean World only) ¥110 adults; ¥80 adults (to Polar World only); ¥50 adults (Coral World only). Combo tickets to Ocean, Polar, and Coral World ¥190 adults; to Ocean and Polar World ¥160 adults. Free admission for children 1.3m (4.2 ft.) or below in height. Summer 8:30am–6:30pm; winter 9am–4:30pm. Bus: 16, 22, 23, 406, 531 or 901 from Dalian Railway Station to Medical University. Taxi: 10 min.; ¥19.

LUSHUN ★

Known to war historians as Port Arthur, Lushun has been the most important, and most sensitive, naval base in northern China for roughly 100 years. Little used during the Qing dynasty, it became a formidable installation under Russia, was captured and expanded by Japan after the Russo-Japanese War, and was finally returned to Chinese control after World War II. ***Warning:*** The military zone is officially off-limits to the public; do not cross the railroad tracks, which mark off the restricted area.

Most of the sights in Lushun touch on its military history. During the cherry picking season from May to June, the cherry gardens in the area are popular leisure spots for local tourists. Air-conditioned coaches to Lushun (1½ hr.; ¥14) leave from the west side of the Shengli Guangchang every hour from 7am to 6pm. It drops you at the Waimao Xuexiao (Foreign Trade Institute) in the new development zone. The latest return bus departs at 6pm.

Across from the Waimao Xuexiao is **Taishan Jingang Gongyuan** (Taishan Jingang Park). On a clear day, from Taishan Biaozhita (Taishan Tower), the views of the Lushun development zone, nearby outlying islands such as Niao Dao (Bird Island) and She Dao (Snake Island), and Yueliang Wan (Lunar Bay) are impressive.

The **Ri'e Jianyu Jiuzhi (Lushun Prison Relic Museum)** ★ (www.lsprison.com; ✆ **0411/8661-0675;** 7:30am–5:30pm in summer; 8am–4:30pm in winter), located north of Lushun Railway Station, at Xiangyang Jie 139, recorded a sadistic history of World War II. Also known as the Japan-Russia Prison Site, the prison was first built by Russia in 1902. After Japan took control of the peninsular, it was extended to a 26,000-sq.-m (279,862-sq.-ft.) prison, with three extensive wards, detaining and torturing patriots and revolutionists from China, North Korea and Russia. The museum displays the inhuman living condition of the prison and how the detainees were tormented. From 1942 to 1945, about 2,000 people were detained and over 700 detainees were killed in the prison. Take bus no. 3 to Yuanbaofang. Admission ¥25.

Lushun Bowuguan (**Lushun Museum;** Liening Jie 42; ✆ **0411/8638-3334;** 9am–4pm; closed Mon), west of the train station, houses over 60,000 items, such as bronze wares, ceramics, jade, lacquer, enamel and ancient paintings, dated back from the New Stone Age, to Han Dynasty, to Tang, Ming and Qing dynasties, discovered from different parts of China. Highlights of its collection are the oldest sutra written in Chinese and the six mummies unearthed in Xinjiang by a Japanese exploration team during the Second World War. Admission ¥20. Take bus no. 2, 3 or 5 to Youyi Lu from Lushun Railway Station.

The **Shuishi Ying** (✆ **0411/8623-3509;** ¥40; 7:30am–5pm), in the village of Shuishi, is where commanders of the Japanese and Russian armies met to discuss and sign Russia's surrender of Lushun in 1905. The historical sight, visited mainly by Japanese tour groups, might appeal primarily to military history buffs. The tiny house, chosen because it was the only major structure still standing after both sides bombed the town, contains the original table, which was an operating table before on which the agreement was signed. A small display room outside the house exhibits a handful of old Japanese posters and old photos of Lushun. Take bus no. 8 to the terminus on Shuishi Ying Lu, keep walking toward the end of the road, the ticket selling office is just across the street.

The **203-Meter Mountain (Erlingsan Gaodi)** ★ was Russia's rear defense base during the Russo-Japanese War and the site of one of the war's most pivotal battles. Between 10,000 and 17,000 Japanese soldiers, including the Japanese commander's son, died taking the mountain. A few of the trenches where they fought have been preserved, served by trails near the summit. An exhibition room halfway up the hill contains several Qing-era photos of the port and a few rusted swords and bullets used in the battle. Most striking is a large, bullet-shaped monument on the summit, erected by the Japanese and defaced by Russian tourists. You can look down into the port itself from here. From late April to mid-May, the Dalian Lushun International Cherry Blossom Festival is held at the site. Take bus no. 5 to Shibanqiao. It is open 24 hours; admission is ¥30; for information, call ✆ **0411/8639-8277.**

Shopping

Dalian is a petite female shopper's paradise, with a range of Japanese, Korean, and western fashions. **Qingniwa Jie,** south of Shengli Guangchang (9am–9pm), is a materialistic mecca of malls, hotels, fast-food outlets, boutiques, and elaborate window displays unlike anything in China outside Shanghai or Hong Kong. The prices are very reasonable. If the labyrinth of underground shops, called the **Dixia Shangchang,** is too overwhelming, try the Japanese department stores **Itokin (Yidujin). Time Square,** next to Hotel Furama, is the high-end shopping mall in the city.

Where to Stay

Dalian has the Northeast's largest selection of luxury hotels. Rooms are expensive during the September Fashion Festival, but discounts otherwise typically reach 50%.

VERY EXPENSIVE

Kempinski Hotel Dalian (Dalian Kaibinsiji Fandian) ★★ Operated by a German hotelier group and located just a street across from the commercial and shopping center, the Kempinski Dalian is one of the best choices in the city. The guest rooms, overlooking the picturesque Labor Park, are spacious, with stylish European furniture and a glass wall with an artistic Chinese ink bamboo pattern against the bed. A sliding wooden partition is used to separate the bathroom and bedroom in some rooms. Rooms in the Park View Tower, are with lower ceilings and simple furnishings. Bathrooms are nice and have a separate shower and tub. All rooms have a small flatscreen TV and free broadband. Its Paulaner Brauhaus & Restaurant is now one of the hottest nightspots in the city.

Jiefang Lu 92 (east of Labor Park). www.kempinski-dalian.com. ✆ **0411/8259-8888.** Fax 0411/8259-6666. 454 units. From ¥1,100 standard room. 15% service charge. Rates include breakfast. AE, DC, MC, V. **Amenities:** 6 restaurants; deli; bar; concierge; executive-level rooms; health center and spa; indoor pool, Wi-Fi. *In room:* A/C, flatscreen satellite TV, fridge, hair dryer, free broadband Internet, minibar.

New World Hotel Dalian (Dalian Xinshijie Jiudian) ★★ This is one of the newest luxury hotels in the city. Located in the city center and across from the well-established Shangri-La, the hotel provides another option for travelers looking for youthful and stylish digs. Rooms are large, comfy, and equipped with big flatscreen TVs, chic beige and wooden colored fittings and plush beds. Bathrooms are spacious with separate shower and a big and sleek bath tub. The bathrobe is remarkably soft and smooth. Its sizable indoor pool and poolside bar, with plenty of natural light, is decorated with a water fountain at the entrance and lined by comfortably and modish rattan chaise longues. Staff is friendly.

Renmin Rd. 41. www.dalian.newworldhotels.com. ✆ **0411/8807-8888.** Fax 0411/8807-8899. 429 units. ¥750–¥2,185 standard room; ¥2,000–¥3,220 suite. 15% service charge. AE, DC, MC, V. **Amenities:** 2 restaurants; 2 bars; concierge; executive-level rooms; forex; luxurious health club and recreation rooms; large indoor pool; room service; smoke-free rooms. *In room:* A/C, LCD satellite TV, fridge, hair dryer, Internet, minibar.

Nikko Hotel Dalian (Dalian Rihang Jiudian) ★ This hotel has been under Japanese management since 2005. Guest rooms are tasteful and decorated in solid colors. Bathrooms have a separate tub and shower. Units at the top of the tower have spectacular views of the city. It's close to Zhangshan Guangchang, so traffic noise can be problematic.

Changjiang Lu 123 (at Minsheng Jie). www.nikkodalian.com.cn. ✆ **0411/8252-9999.** Fax 0411/8252-9900. 372 units. ¥870–¥1,300 standard room; ¥1,480–¥2,950 suite. 15% service charge. AE, DC, MC, V. **Amenities:** 3 restaurants; deli; bar; concierge; executive-level rooms; forex; health club and spa; indoor pool; room service; smoke-free rooms, Wi-Fi. *In room:* A/C, satellite TV, fridge, hair dryer, free broadband Internet, minibar.

Shangri-La Dalian (Dalian Xianggelila Dafandian) ★★ With over 10 years in the city, Shangri-La's northeast flagship seems to be the most reliable option in town. Standard rooms are incredibly spacious, tasteful, and comfortable, with a sophisticated oriental touch. Bathrooms have separate shower stalls and tub. Service is impeccable. The lobby, most of the public area, and the Chinese restaurant got a facelift in 2011. The central courtyard garden is a pleasant place to rest your feet after a walk on Binhai Lu. Free broadband Internet and Wi-Fi access is available in all rooms. Rooms on executive floors provide French toiletries, l'Occitane, and have DVD players. Breakfast is delectable and has a wide selection.

Renmin Lu 66. www.shangri-la.com. ✆ **0411/8252-5000.** Fax 0411/8252-5050. 563 units. ¥1,000–¥1,500 standard room. ¥2,300–¥2,600 suite. 15% service charge. AE, DC, MC, V. **Amenities:** 3 restaurants; deli; bar; cigar room; concierge; executive-level rooms; forex; health club and spa; indoor pool; room service; smoke-free rooms; outdoor tennis courts; Wi-Fi. *In room:* A/C, satellite TV, DVD player (in executive rooms), fridge, hair dryer, broadband Internet and Wi-Fi, minibar.

EXPENSIVE

Bo Hai Pearl Hotel (Bo Hai Mingzhu Dajiudian) This Chinese-run four-star is typically tacky (note the frightening harpy statues at the door), but the hotel's location directly east of the railway station is as convenient as it gets in Dalian. Standard rooms are small with undersize bathrooms. Facilities and staff are slightly above par.

Shengli Guangchang 8. ✆ **0411/8882-8333.** Fax 0411/8881-8158. 366 units. ¥388–¥488 standard room. AE, DC, MC, V. **Amenities:** 2 restaurants; bar; concierge; forex; gym; small indoor pool; room service; sauna. *In room:* A/C, satellite TV, fridge, hair dryer, minibar.

Ramada Plaza Dalian (Jiuzhou Huameida Dajiudian) The hotel is well located near the railway station and popular among Japanese travelers. Rooms are spacious and plainly appointed, with large beds and flatscreen TVs. The bathrooms are clean, but somewhat incommodious.

Shengli Guangchang 18. www.ramada.com. ✆ **0411/8280-8888.** Fax 0411/8280-9704. 366 units. ¥550–¥800 standard room. AE, DC, MC, V. **Amenities:** 2 restaurants; bar; concierge; gym; indoor pool; room service; sauna; smoke-free rooms. *In room:* A/C, satellite TV, fridge, hair dryer, Internet, minibar.

MODERATE

Dalian Hotel (Dalian Binguan) ★ 🎁 The Dalian, built in 1909 on the south side of Zhongshan Guangchang, was described in a 1920s guidebook as "one of the finest hotels in the Far East." Originally a part of the Japanese-owned Yamato Hotel chain, it was restored to a semblance of its former appearance in 1997 but still lacks the charm of its counterparts in other northeastern cities. Guest rooms are large with small beds but clean, sizable bathrooms. Furnishings fail to match the grandeur of the building itself, but no other hotel in Dalian can claim as much history.

Zhongshan Guangchang 4. www.dl-hotel.com. ✆ **0411/8263-3111,** ext. 1101. Fax 0411/8263-4363. 86 units. ¥300–¥450 standard room. ¥350–¥680 suite. AE, MC, V. **Amenities:** 3 restaurants; forex. *In room:* A/C, satellite TV, fridge, hair dryer.

Dumplings & Dog Meat

Generally speaking, food is not one of Dongbei's finer attractions, but there is at least one aspect of Dongbei cuisine that will appeal to epicures: the delectable meat- and vegetable-filled ravioli-like dumplings known as ***jiaozi.*** Cheap and satisfying, *jiaozi* are popular all over China but are nowhere as divine as in the Northeast. Cooked in one of three ways—boiled *(shuijiao),* steamed *(zhengjiao),* or pan-fried *(jianjiao)*—they are most commonly filled with a mix of pork and cabbage *(zhurou baicai)* and served with a soy-and-vinegar dipping sauce, to which you add your own chopped garlic, chili oil, and mustard. Alternatives are endless. Absolutely not to be missed.

Probably better known but significantly less appetizing is **dog *(gourou),*** Dongbei's other signature food. A Korean import shunned by Manchurians but valued among Chinese for its warming properties, it is a winter item most commonly eaten in hot pot. Dog meat turns greenish when boiled; trying it, according to one traveling companion of mine, is "like eating a piece of beef, then licking a filing cabinet."

Gloria Plaza Hotel (Dalian Kailai Dajiudian) After an upgrade, the Gloria Plaza is now a more pleasant place to stay. Guest rooms and bathrooms are now bigger in size, everything is clean, and the staff is friendly. There is a new women-only floor decorated with a feminine touch, catering to women traveling alone. Cheaper units on lower floors receive little natural light.

Yide Jie 5 (at Youhao Guangchang). www.gphdalian.com. ✆ **0411/8280-8855.** Fax 0411/8280-8533. 211 units. ¥428–¥781 standard room. 10% service charge. AE, DC, MC, V. **Amenities:** 2 restaurants; executive rooms; forex; room service; women's floor. *In room:* A/C, satellite TV, fridge, Internet, minibar.

INEXPENSIVE

Motel 168 (Motai Yiliuba) This economical hotel is right next to Gloria Plaza Hotel. It offers small and simple but clean standard rooms. Bathrooms have shower only.

Yide Jie 11. www.motel168.com. ✆ **0411/8282-3333.** Fax 0411/8282-3218. 321 units. ¥258–¥368 standard. No credit cards. **Amenities:** Restaurant; smoke-free rooms; ticketing; vending machines. *In room:* A/C, satellite TV, Internet, hair dryer (upon request), Internet.

Where to Eat

Dalian's specialty is seafood and the city has a cosmopolitan range of international restaurants. For excellent **dim sum** head to the Shangri-La Hotel's Shang Palace, Renmin Lu 66 (✆ **0411/8252-5000**). A cluster of **Japanese restaurants** are around Yan'an Lu, south of Zhongshan Guangchang, as well as in the neighborhood of New World Hotel. A number of **fast-food outlets** such as McDonald's, KFC, Pizza Hut, and Starbucks can also be found at Shengli Guangchang and on Qingniwa Jie. Youhao Guangchang boasts a couple of **burger and pizza restaurants.**

Chu-Shin-ya (Zhongxin Wu) ★★ JAPANESE This small joint, with a wood-paneled facade, offers authentic and tasty Japanese food and is popular among the city's Japanese community. Cold tofu with shredded chicken, sprouts, carrot toppings, and special sauce is a nice appetizer to start. Rolled egg with grilled eel is mouthwatering, tender, and freshly cooked. Also, try the grilled ox tongue. The special meatballs served with barbecue sauce are the house specialty, but it isn't as tasty as it looks. The menu has photos and English translation. Ask staff for the daily special menu, which is only written in Japanese.

Liulin Jie 16-18 (across Xin Tiantian Yugang on Yan'an Lu). ✆ **0411/8282-1000.** Meal for 2 ¥180–¥300. AE, MC, V. 5pm–midnight.

Daliang Gu Tou Zong Dian ★ HOME-STYLE The popular local restaurant with three branches in the city is famous for its tender and melt-in-your-mouth *da gutou* (big ribs). Almost every table will order one plate of *da gutou,* stewed with special sauce. A small plate is enough for two people. A pair of plastic gloves is offered to you to savor the dish. Try the delicious *qing tang da gu bang* (big bone soup). The menu has photos but is in Chinese only.

Wusi Lu 151. ✆ **0411/8431-3771.** Meal for 2 ¥80–¥100. No credit cards. 10am–10pm.

I-55 Coffee Stop & Bakery (Aiwuwu Meishi Kafeizhan) ★ AMERICAN Owned by an American expatriate who made sure to include all the typical coffee-shop details—chalkboard menus and corner couches, world music soundtrack, a Scrabble set propped on a shelf—I-55 is a good place to satisfy a craving for American food. The cafe roasts its beans on-site and serves a good cup of coffee. The Philly cheesesteak is outstanding, with freshly baked bread, lots of flavorful beef, cheese, and mayo. It also offers good desserts and a weekend breakfast buffet. The staff speaks English but service is a bit lousy. Relax with a book on the peaceful outdoor patio during summer.

Gaoerji Lu 67 (at Jinian Jie, Renmin Guangchang). ✆ **0411/8369-5755.** Coffee drinks ¥32–¥48, weekend brunch ¥55; food ¥20–¥40. No credit cards. 9am–midnight. Bus: 502, 406, or 505.

Longhai Yuwan Meishi Guangchang ★ SEAFOOD This is a gaudy sight, with its faux-marble staircase, but the dishes here make up for it. Recommended by a local food writer, this recent addition to the Dalian restaurant scene is located near Xinghai Guangchang. Try the salt-dried yellow fish *(yancheng huanghuayu),* spinach with mussels *(buocai ban maoxian),* pig stomach cabbage soup *(nongtang zhudu wawacai),* and fish dumplings *(bayu shuijiao).* Be prepared for plenty of raw garlic. This place is best for groups, with each table set in a private room with a flatscreen television.

Tongtai Lu 21. ✆ **0411/8368-5555.** Meal for 2 ¥150–¥400. MC, V. 11am–10pm.

Taineng (Taineng Korean Restaurant) ★ KOREAN This always-packed joint offers authentic and good-value Korean dishes. The items off its grilled menu are popular, but its main dishes are impressive. Try the stone pot rice *(shiguo banfan):* It's tasty and not too spicy, with loads of different toppings. The restaurant also makes delicious Korean noodle soup, cold noodles, and grilled fish. It's so popular that it has added one more floor to house more customers. The menu has pictures and English translation.

Shengli Guangchang 18 (G/F of Ramada Hotel). ✆ **0411/8263-3676.** Meal for 2 ¥60–¥150. DC, MC, V. 11am–10pm.

Tapas (Dapasi) SPANISH On the edge of Russian Street, this two-level restaurant feels more like a hacienda in Galicia than a restaurant in Dalian. The wine list features wines from Spain, and the menu offers an exhaustive list of tapas good for a snack or a whole meal. Try the gratin mushroom tart, the pancetta with garlic, and the baked peppers on toast. Staff can speak English.

Tuanjie Jie 19 (near Russian St.). ✆ **0411/8254-0996.** Tapas ¥8–¥30; meal for 2 ¥70–¥100. AE, MC, V. 11:30am–10:30pm.

Dalian After Dark

Besides karaoke catering to naughty Japanese businessmen, there are few nice nightspots in the city. Resident foreigners favor the subterranean Makewei, known to English-speakers as **Dave's Bar,** south end of Qiyi Jie (✆ **0411/8282-2345;** from 1pm until late), a U.N. of watering holes just northeast of Zhongshan Guangchang. Americans, Russians, Europeans, Asians, and Africans mix and flirt at Dave's over bottles of Tsingtao beer. If you love live jazz and blues, go to **Blossom Jazz Music Club (Huamandou Jueshi Julebu),** Kunming Jie 50 (✆ **0411/82802216;** 5pm–1:30am), with a local band playing there from 8:30pm to midnight every night. **I-55** (see "Where to Eat," above) and its neighboring pubs are open until midnight.

CHANGCHUN 长春

Jilin Province, 302km (187 miles) NE of Shenyang, 250km (155 miles) SW of Harbin

Changchun is remote enough to feel authentic, is friendly and modern enough to be comfortable, and has just enough pop-history background to make it interesting. Between 1932 and 1945, it was the capital of Japanese-controlled Manchukuo (Manzhou Guo) and home to puppet ruler Henry Puyi, the bespectacled final Qing emperor best known to Westerners as the subject of Bernardo Bertolucci's lush biopic *The Last Emperor.* The city provided a base for Japan's brutal World War II colonization campaign and was slated to sit at the center of a postwar empire that never materialized.

Changchun, now the capital of Jilin Province, has gained fame in the modern era as the Detroit of China, producing first Red Flag cars for Communist Party cadres and later Volkswagens for China's new middle class. Recent economic hardships have sent the city in search of tourism dollars and prompted admirable restorations of several Manchukuo-era buildings. But the city's greatest attraction is still its people, as unpretentious, warm-hearted, and quick-witted as any in the country.

The rest of Jilin Province mirrors Changchun in many ways. Less convenient than Liaoning to the south and lacking the "extreme travel" cachet of Heilong Jiang and Inner Mongolia to the north and west, it quietly offers several of Dongbei's most enjoyable attractions. **Changbai Shan** (p. 187), a dramatic mountain straddling the China–North Korea border, is the most famous. Just as compelling is the seldom-visited **Yanbian Korean Autonomous Prefecture** (p. 184) to the north.

Essentials

GETTING THERE Changchun's **Longjia Airport** is 31km (19 miles) northeast of town. Flights connect it to major cities including Beijing, Shanghai, Guangzhou, Dalian, Hong Kong, Seoul, and Tokyo. **China Southern Airlines** (✆ **0431/8862-0522**) is on the first floor of Tonggang Guoji Dasha, at Yatai Dajie 3218. **Asiana Airlines** (✆ **400/650-8000**) is at Unit 1004 of Shangri-la Hotel. Airport buses from Menghan Binguang go to the airport every hour from 6am to 6pm; it takes 45 minutes and costs ¥20. By taxi, fares cost ¥60 to ¥70.

D-series express **trains** connect to Beijing (six daily; 6 hr. 30 min.; ¥239 second class; ¥299 first class), Harbin (six daily; 1 hr. 45 min.; ¥76 second class; ¥91 first class), Shenyang (11 daily; 2 hr. 15 min.; ¥93 second class; ¥111 first class), Jilin City (frequent trains 6:50am–9:55pm; 34–39 min.; ¥34 second class; ¥41 first class). Fast train to Shanghai (three daily; 29 hr.–35 hr. 40 min.; ¥458–¥499 hard sleeper), and Dalian (6:12am and 10:20pm; 7 hr. 30 min.–8 hr.; ¥175 hard sleeper). The railway station (Changchun Zhan) is north of downtown, at the top of Renmin Dajie.

Air-conditioned **buses** to Harbin (all day; 3 hr. 30 min.; ¥76) and Shenyang (all day; 3 hr. 30 min.; ¥82) leave from a white building at Renmin Dajie 6 (behind the Chunyi Binguan). Regular buses to Jilin City (2 hr.; ¥24) leave every few minutes from the north side of the building.

GETTING AROUND Jetta **taxis** charge ¥5 for the first 2.5km (1½ miles), then ¥1.30 per kilometer. **Buses** (¥1–¥2) are pay-as-you-board. Bus no. 6 runs from the railway station through the middle of town on Renmin Dajie; bus no. 62 and 362 both wind from the railway station to Renmin Guangchang and pass Xinmin Guangchang, with stop announcements in English. The **Light Rail** system now has two lines in service. Line no. 3 runs from Changchun Zhan (the station is outside the west wing of the Changchun Train Station) to Changchun Movie Wonderland. The newly opened Line no. 4 running from Changchun Zhan Bei Guangzhang (the North Plaza of Changchung Train Station), via Wei Huanggong, to Nan Si Huan (South Fourth Ring). The interchange station of these two lines is Weixing Lu Zhan. Ticket ¥2 to ¥4.

[Fast FACTS] CHANGHUN

Banks, Foreign Exchange & ATMs The most convenient **Bank of China** branch is on Tongzhi Jie, south of the Xi'an Dalu intersection (Mon–Fri 8:30am–4:30pm). Traveler's checks and credit card transactions are handled on the second floor (*not* available 11:30am–1pm), and an ATM is on the first floor. Another ATM across the street from the Shangri-La hotel dispenses up to ¥2,500.

Internet Access Several Internet bars can easily be found near the train station. Most open from 8am to midnight and charge ¥2 to ¥4 per hour. **Into Internet Bar,** which is located at the intersection of Tongzhi Jie and Guilin Lu, can hold up to 1,000 people. Dial-up is ✆ **169.**

Post Office The most convenient post office (Kuancheng Youdianju; May–Sept 8:30am–5pm; Oct–Apr 8:30am–4:30pm) is in an old green building south of the long-distance bus station on Renmin Dajie.

Visa Extensions Visa extensions are easy to obtain (passport, hotel registration, and proof of $100 available to you per day of extension) at the imposing **PSB** Exit/Entry office, Guangming Lu 688 (✆ **0431/8890-8465;** Mon–Fri 9am–noon and 1:30–5:30pm), behind PSB headquarters on the southwest side of Renmin Guangchang.

Exploring Changchun

Changchun's chief attraction is the ghost of Japanese occupation, which still lingers in the more than two dozen ministry buildings left scattered throughout the city. The **former Kwantung Army headquarters (Guandongjun Xianbing Silingbu)** is an impeccably preserved Japanese-style castle on Xinfa Lu (now occupied by the Communist Party). Guards might let you roam around the grounds if you promise not

Changchun 长春

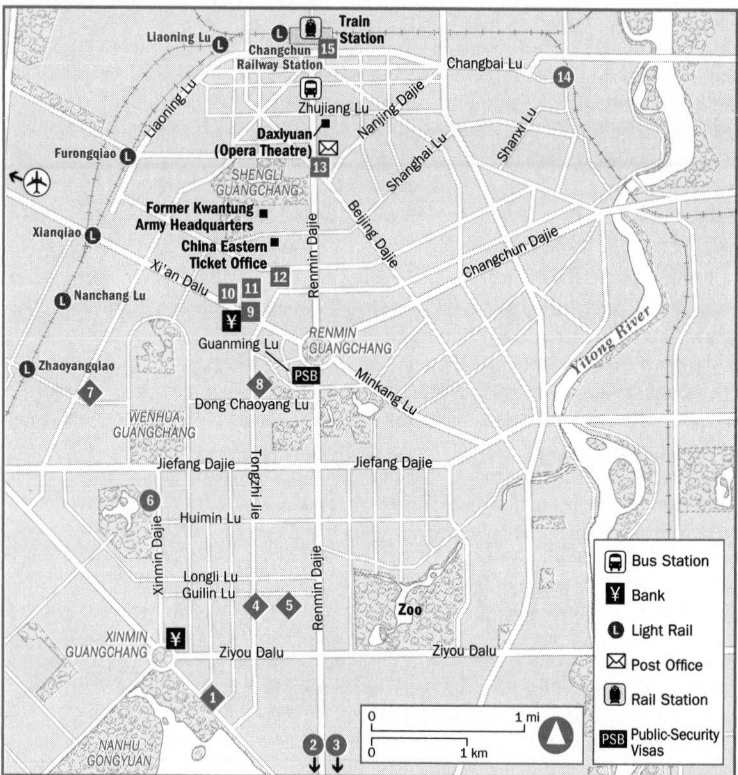

to take pictures. There are also a number of buildings lining Xinmin Lu south of the **Wenhua Guangchang (Culture Square),** site of a never-completed imperial Japanese palace and now home to the main building of Jilin University. The grim building southeast of the square, at Xinmin Dajie 2, fronted by a statue of infamous Canadian doctor Norman Bethune, is the former site of the **Wei Manzhouguo Guowuyuan (Manchukuo State Council).** A bizarre English-language tour here (8:30am–6pm; ¥20) includes a ride in a 70-year-old solid brass Otis elevator once used by Henry Puyi (see Wei Huanggong, below). Take bus no. 13, 240, 264 or 276 to Jida Yi Yuan. Bilingual maps are available (¥5) at the Wei Huanggong.

Changchun Movie Wonderland (Changying Shiji Cheng) ☺ The theme park is China's answer to Hollywood's Universal Studios. Investor Changchun Film Group, formerly known as Changchun Film Studio, was produced an abundance of movies during the 1950s, but ceased operations after World War II. Posters and photos of some popular Chinese actors and actresses in Changchun Film Studio productions are exhibited in the park to evoke visitors' nostalgic memories. The park features attractions such as 3D and 4D movies, water curtain film theatre, spherical screen theatre, behind-the-scene tour and adventurous rides. However, all movies are in Mandarin only without subtitles.

HOTELS ■	**RESTAURANTS ◆**
Chángchūn Maxcourt Hotel **10** (Chángchūn Jílóngpō Dàjiǔdiàn) 长春吉隆坡大酒店	Bar Street (Jiuba Jie) **5** 酒吧街
Changchun Zhuozhan Days Hotel **11** (Chángchūn Zhuózhǎn Tiāntiān Jiǔdiàn) 长春卓展天天酒店	French Bakery (Hóng Mòfáng) **4** 红磨坊
Chūnyí Bīnguǎn **15** 春谊宾馆	Lao Ma Shuo Gan Mian **1** 老妈手擀面
Paradise Hotel **13** (Yuèfǔ Dajiǔdiàn) 乐府大酒店	Renfengge **7** 仁凤阁
Shangri-La Chángchūn **9** (Chángchūn Xiānggélǐlā Dàfàndiàn) 长春香格里拉大饭店	Xiàngyáng Tún **8** 向阳屯
Star-moon Fashion Inn **12** (Xīyuè Shísàng Jiǔdiàn) 星月時尚酒店	

ATTRACTIONS ●

Changchun World Sculpture Park **3** (Changchun Shijie Diaosu Gongyuan) 长春世界雕塑公园

Manchukuo State Council **6** (Wěi Mǎnzhōu Guó Guówùyuàn) 伪满洲国博物馆

Movie Wonderland **2** 长影世纪城

Puppet Emperor's Palace **14** (Wěi Huánggōng) 伪皇宫

4.5km (3 miles) from Changshuang Highway, Jingyue Development Zone. ✆ **0431/8455-0888.** www.changying.com. Admission: ¥240 (Apr 1–Oct 31); ¥198 (Nov 1–Mar 31); free admission for children under 1.1m (3½ ft.). Half price for children from 1.1–1.4m (3½–4½ ft.). Apr–Oct 31: 9am–5:30pm; Nov 1–Mar 31: 9am–4:30pm. Take Light rail to the Changying Shiji Cheng terminus.

Changchun World Sculpture Park (Changchun Shijie Diaosu Gongyuan) ★ Over 390 sculptures by artists from 172 countries such as China, Russia, Africa, and Korea are exhibited inside this park, which is located in the south of the city. The vast 92-hectare (227-acre) park has artworks placed along two main roads as well as surrounding the lake in the center of the park. The art gallery at the right side of the entrance features different exhibitions from time to time. Though not every piece of the artwork is exceptional, some of them are pretty impressive. Outstanding pieces include Russian artist Pavel Shaposhnik's *Golden Dream,* a cast bronze sculpture featuring a man falling asleep on a bench, placed near the exit of the art gallery; and mainland artist Chen Tao's *Dressing Girl,* outside the art gallery.

Renmin Dajie 9518. ✆ **0431/8537-9001.** Admission (park and art gallery) ¥20. Park 7am–6pm; gallery 9am–4pm. Bus: 112, 240, or 270 to Weixing Guangchang.

Wei Huanggong ★★ "The Puppet Emperor's Palace" is where Aisin-Gioro "Henry" Puyi, China's last emperor, spent 13 years as an impotent sovereign under Japanese control. This complex of imperial-style buildings, formerly criticized by travelers as shabby and boring, recently underwent a multimillion-dollar makeover and is now among the Northeast's premier historical attractions.

Installed as emperor of China in Beijing in 1908, at the age of 3, Puyi was deposed by Republican forces in 1912 (at a time when he was still breastfeeding) and eventually fell into the hands of the Japanese. In 1932, eager to use Puyi's Manchurian face as a screen for its war efforts in the Northeast, Japan convinced him to move to Changchun and made him president (later emperor) of Manchukuo. He lived a futile life here, taking orders from the Japanese army and subsisting on Qing restoration fantasies, until he was captured by the Soviets in 1945. He spent 14 years in prison, was "rehabilitated," and worked as a gardener until his death in 1967.

The palace was damaged when Soviet troops occupied Changchun, so much of the furniture and trappings on display here are replicas. Otherwise, the restoration is meticulous. Most impressive is the Tongde Dian (originally the Jilin Salt Tax Collection Office, and therefore sometimes referred to as the Salt Palace because it was built using money from Japan's salt-mining operations), a building Puyi supposedly never used for fear the Japanese had bugged the rooms. The main hall is recognizable as the setting for a dance party scene in *The Last Emperor,* although it was never actually used for that purpose.

Guangfu Bei Lu 5. ✆ **0431/8286-6611.** Admission ¥80. May 1–Oct 10 8:30am–5:20pm; Oct 11–Apr 30 8:30am–4:50pm. English audio guide ¥20, deposit ¥100. Bus: 70, 80, or 264 (from the Wenhua Guangchang).

Shopping

Changchun is one of China's top producers of ginseng, available in any one of the city's ubiquitous pharmacies. For more conventional shopping, try the upscale **Chongqing Lu** or **Guilin Lu** (east of the Tongzhi Jie intersection), a hip and haphazard street lined with Korean clothing shops and stuffed-animal stores. The **underground market** in front of the railway station was once part of an underground bomb shelter connected by tunnels to the Manchukuo ministries.

Where to Stay

Rooms are scarce from July until late summer, when the city hosts a series of conferences and industry fairs, but discounts of up to 30% are common at other times of the year.

VERY EXPENSIVE

Shangri-La Changchun (Changchun Xianggelila Dafandian) ★★ The Shangri-La is Changchun's oldest five-star property and still the only hotel in town that provides luxury with class. After a facelift in 2011, the new lobby and lobby lounge highlight Jilin's local character with an extensive wall painting of Changbai Shan landscapes. Standard rooms are spacious, with large flatscreen TVs, large beds, and generously sized bathrooms, and the hotel's staff is head-and-shoulders above any other in the city. The Shangri-La is centrally located at the edge of the city's most upscale shopping district, a short walk from Renmin Guangchang. Free Internet access is in all rooms.

Xi'an Dalu 569. www.shangri-la.com. ✆ **0431/8898-1818.** Fax 0431/8898-1919. 458 units. ¥1,400 standard room. ¥2,288 suites. 15% service charge and ¥5 government development fund. AE, DC,

MC, V. **Amenities:** 2 restaurants; 2 bars; concierge; executive-level rooms; forex; health center and spa; small indoor pool; room service; smoke-free rooms. *In room:* A/C, satellite TV, fridge, hair dryer, free Internet, minibar.

EXPENSIVE

Zhuozhan Days Hotel (Zhuozhan Tiantian Jiudian) The four-star hotel is popular among business travelers and is frequently booked up. Rooms are standard with great beds. Bathrooms have separate shower and bath tub. A humidifier is placed in each room to help tackle the region's dry weather. The hotel is conveniently situated on top of the Zhuozhan shopping mall.

Chongqing Lu 1255. www.zhuozhandayshotel.com. ✆ **0431/8848-6888.** Fax 0431/8848-62481. 188 units. ¥750–¥770 standard room. 15% service charge. Rate includes breakfast. AE, DC, MC, V. **Amenities:** 3 restaurants; forex; health club; room service; ticketing. *In room:* A/C, satellite TV, fridge, hair dryer, humidifier; Internet, minibar.

MODERATE

Changchun Maxcourt Hotel (Changchun Jilongpo Dajiudian) This Malaysian-run four-star is the best deal in town. Bathrooms are small, but guest rooms are some of the most comfortable in the city—especially those on the newly renovated 19th and 20th floors—and service is decent.

Xi'an Dalu 823. www.maxcourt.com. ✆ **0431/8896-2688.** Fax 0431/8898-6288. 266 units. ¥498 standard room. ¥598 suite. 15% service charge. Rate includes breakfast. AE, DC, MC, V. **Amenities:** 2 restaurants; bar; forex; health club; KTV; room service. *In room:* A/C, satellite TV, fridge, hair dryer, free broadband Internet, minibar.

Chunyi Binguan The Chunyi, built in 1909, is the least impressive of the former Yamato Hotels, and is attractive now only for its convenient location just across the street from the railway station. The original gate is still here, but the exterior is crumbling and the interior retains only a whisper of history. The hotel was undergoing renovation at press time. Rooms, which used to be worn and small, are expected to be upgraded and have better facilities.

Renmin Dajie 80 (southeast of railway station). ✆ **0431/8209-6888.** Fax 0431/8896-0171. 280 units. ¥249–¥298 standard room. Rates include breakfast. AE, DC, MC, V. **Amenities:** Restaurant; bar; forex; room service; massage. *In room:* A/C, TV, Internet.

Paradise Hotel (Yuefu Dajiudian) An institution among travelers in Changchun, the Paradise is one of a handful of state-run three-stars in China that have a firm grasp on the concepts of service and maintenance. Newly renovated doubles, equipped with a queen-size bed, are cramped. Standard rooms are larger but older. Both are nicely appointed with lacquer furniture, large TVs, and small but very clean bathrooms. Some of the staff speak English. The place fills up in summer, so call ahead.

Renmin Dajie 1078 (south of the Agricultural Bank of China building). ✆ **0431/8209-0999.** Fax 0431/8271-5709. 202 units. ¥328–¥398 standard room. AE, DC, MC, V. **Amenities:** 4 restaurants; bar; gym. *In room:* A/C, satellite TV.

INEXPENSIVE

Star-moon Fashion Inn (Xiyue Shishang Jiudian) A number of cheap hotels have opened in Changchun over the last few years and Star-moon, with a dozen locations in the city, is a preferable brand. One is well-situated near the Chongqing Lu shopping area. Rooms are kept clean and have shower only. The one close to Nanhu Gongyuan (South Lake Park) has more stylish design and larger rooms.

Chongqing Lu Dian: Bei'an Lu 36 (north of Zhuozhan Shopping mall). www.starmooninn.com.cn. ✆ **0431/8898-4000.** ¥138–¥168 standard room. Nanhu Dian: Changqing Jie 2809 (outside the north gate of Nanhu Gongyuan). ✆ **0431/8556-4000.** ¥168–¥218. No credit cards. *In room:* A/C, TV, Internet.

Where to Eat

A number of restaurants in Changchun serve reasonable regional cuisine. Otherwise, the Sheng Cafe of Shangri-La has satisfying Western dishes.

French Bakery (Hong Mofang) WESTERN This dark and low-ceilinged cafe with French movie posters pasted to its fake brick walls has long been a haven for Changchun's foreign residents. A very clean kitchen produces simple sandwiches, omelets, pizza, pasta and near-authentic pastries. Coffee drinks are excellent, but it takes too long to get the pasta ready to serve. Ring the bell on the table to order and for service. Olive oil, Tabasco sauce, Heinz barbecue sauce, and ground coffee are for sale on a small shelf near the door.

Guilin Lu 745 (east of Tongzhi Jie intersection). ✆ **0431/8562-3994.** Meal for 2 ¥80–¥100; coffee ¥20–¥30. No credit cards. 8am–10:30pm.

Lao Ma Shuo Gan Mian ★ SICHUAN This successful chain has a handful of branches in Changchun. Its original shop at Changqing Road, with home-style decor, is the busiest one; it's hard to find a table during peak hours. The food is generally tasty. The Sichuan dishes—such as mouthwatering chicken *(kou shui ji),* served with a special hot-and-sour sauce, crushed peanuts, and green onion—leave me wanting more after finishing one dish. The noodles are also good, but most of them are served in red spicy broth.

Changqing Lu 46-2. ✆ **0431/8563-0696.** Meal for 2 ¥60–¥80. No credit cards. 9am–10pm.

Renfengge ★★ KOREAN What makes this joint attractive and exotic is not just its authentic Korean food, but also the well-trained waitresses who all sport traditional Korean dress and hail from mysterious North Korea. It is said that all the staff of the restaurant are either top students in universities or children of top government officers. A piano and a stage are placed right in the center of the first floor. It is where the North Korean performers play Korean folk songs and Chinese classics every night. The restaurant, decorated with wooden tables and Korean lanterns, is spacious, but somewhat raucous. Customers have to take off shoes to climb up a low platform to the seats. The Pyongyang cold noodles *(Pingrang leng mian),* served with beef, boiled egg, cucumber, radish, and sweet and sour broth, are one of the best delights in the city. Other dishes, such as stone pot rice (shiguo banfan) and grilled beef, also taste delicious. The menu is in Chinese and pinyin only, but has clear pictures. It has a long wait during dinner hours.

Xichaoyang Lu 221. ✆ **0431/8858-0668.** Meal for 2 ¥100–¥140. No credit cards. 11am–9:30pm.

Xiangyang Tun ★★ HOME-STYLE This delightful countryside eatery, with a statue of Mao out front and calligraphy-covered walls in the main dining room, is the favorite for home-style fare. Try the *jiaji dun zhenmo*—tender pieces of chicken stewed with mushrooms in a dark savory sauce—and the *da paigu* (big ribs), a melt-in-your-mouth house specialty with meat that literally falls off the bone.

Dong Chaoyang Lu 433 (east of Tongzhi Jie intersection). ✆ **0431/8898-2876.** Meal for 2 ¥80–¥100. No credit cards. 10:30am–11pm.

Changchun After Dark

Changchun is the birthplace of the first ***errenzhuan*** theater, **Heping Daxiyuan (Heping Theatre).** The popular Dongbei entertainment is a mix of stand-up comedy and opera that is thoroughly vulgar and, for those who can understand Dongbei dialect, very amusing. Real fans head to the raucous, smoke-filled **Heping Daxiyuan,** a block north of the post office on Renmin Dajie (✆ **0431/893-4304**), where tawdry performances get audiences roaring with laughter and keep them that way most of the night. Nightly shows at 7:40pm cost ¥30 to ¥180. The Longli Lu, near Guilin Lu and Renmin Jie, is the "Bar Area," with a number of local bars. One of the two popular disco clubs is **Mayflower (Wuyuehua Jiuba;** ✆ **0431/8564-8098;** www.mayflowerbar.com), at the intersection of Mudan Jie and Ziyou Dalu. The club is so well-received that it opened its second branch in the city inside Shangri-la Hotel (see above). **Letou Shishang Yinyue Ba** (✆ **0431/8893-9288**) on the south side of the Wenhua Huadong Zhongxin, at Renmin Dajie 92, is also popular with party goers.

JILIN CITY 吉林

Jilin Province, 128km (79 miles) E of Changchun

Jilin, one of the oldest settlements in the province and a legendary shipbuilding center during the Qing dynasty, is famous now for its delicate winter scenery. The city's original name was *Jilin Wula* (Manchurian for "along the river"), because it straddles a bend in the Songhua Jiang (Sungari River). It was hit hard in World War II and, despite one of the country's more impressive urban renewal plans, it will probably never recover its old prestige.

Essentials

GETTING THERE **Express D-series trains** connect **Jilin Railway Station (Jilin Zhan)** to Changchun (frequent trains 6:25am–9:05pm; 34–39 min.; ¥34 second class/¥41 first class), Shenyang (three daily; 2 hr. 50 min.; ¥127 second class/¥153 first class), and Harbin (one daily; 2 hr. 33 min.; ¥111 second class/¥133 first class). **Fast trains** depart from **Jilin West Railway Station (Jilin Xi Zhan)** to Songjianghe (one daily; 15 hr. 24 min.; ¥116 hard sleeper), Baihe (one daily; 17 hr. 19 min.; ¥125 hard sleeper), Yanji (one daily; 6 hr. 50 min.; ¥106 hard sleeper), and Beijing (two daily; 12–17 hr. 30 min.; ¥263–¥290 hard sleeper). The Jilin Zhan is north of the river, at the intersection of Zhongkang Lu and Chongqing Jie. Bus no. 34 connects Jilin Zhan to Jilin Xi Zhan in 40 minutes. The **long-distance bus station (Keyun Zhan)** was relocated from the west of the railway station to Wusong Lu in mid-2011; buses leave from here for Dandong (9:05am; 8 hr.; ¥146), Harbin (6 hr. 30 min.; ¥138), and Yanji (8am; 6 hr.; ¥84).

VISITOR INFORMATION For tourist complaints, call ✆ **0432/6245-7524.**

GETTING AROUND Jilin Dajie, the main thoroughfare, runs north-south through the middle of town. Most **buses** (¥1) stop at the railway station; bus no. 32 leaves from the railway station and travels along Jilin Dajie. **Taxis** charge ¥5 for the first 2km (1¼ miles) and ¥1.80 per kilometer after that.

[FastFACTS] JILIN CITY

Banks, Foreign Exchange & ATMs The main **Bank of China** branch is inconveniently located on Shenchun Jie, at the east end of the Linjiang Qiao (Linjiang Bridge). It's open from 8:30am to 4:30pm, Monday to Friday, and from 9am to 4pm on public holiday. Windows on the left handle traveler's checks and credit card transactions (*not* available 11:30am–1pm). An international ATM is just inside the door.

Internet Access Several **24-hour Internet bars** charge ¥2 to ¥4 per hour on Chaoyang Jie. Dial-up is ✆ **16300.**

Post Office The main post office is on Jilin Dajie 153 (8:30am–4:30pm), north of the Jilin Bridge.

Exploring Jilin City

Jilin is host to a scene of unearthly beauty in winter, when steam rises from the Songhua River and condenses on nearby trees. The phenomenon, dubbed ***wusong* (ice-rimmed trees)** ★ in Mandarin, is a byproduct of the nearby Fengman Hydroelectric Dam, which feeds warm water into the Songhua and keeps it from freezing despite air temperatures of –22°F (–30°C). To see this, get up early and walk along any section of the pleasant riverside promenade that follows Songhua Jiang Lu, or you can take the touring cart (¥2 single trip;¥4 round-trip) on Jiangbin Xi Lu, outside the Shijie Guangchang, to enjoy the beautiful river. Also beautiful is an old **Catholic Church (Tianzhu Jiaotang),** built in 1917 and restored in 1980, opposite the promenade on the west side of Jiangcheng Guangchang square; it isn't open to tourists, but you might convince someone in the attached hospice to let you in for a look.

Wen Miao This decrepit, charming Confucian temple is notable for its exhibition on the Qing dynasty imperial examination system, inside the first hall on the right. A mural at the entrance to the exhibit depicts a mountain of men stepping on each other in an effort to climb the Confucian hierarchy. Inside are reproductions of "cheat sheets"—pieces of clothing covered in thousands of near-microscopic characters found on Qing-era candidates in Beijing.

Nanchang Lu 2. Free admission. 8:30am–4pm (May 1–Oct 1 until 5pm); closed holidays. Bus: 130 to Jiangcheng Guangchang, then walk east 2 blocks on Ankang Hutong.

Yunshi Bowuguan (Meteorite Museum) ☺ On March 8, 1976, one of the largest meteorite showers in recorded history fell on a 500-sq.-km (195-sq.-mile) area around Jilin, pelting the city with 4,000 kilograms (4.4 tons) of rock and giving it a reason to open this museum. This simple facility is more like a display room for the world's largest stony meteorite (1,774kg/3,921 lb.), which hovers dressed in a blue velvet skirt in the middle of the hall. Records show that the meteorite's impact registered 1.7 on the Richter scale. It has few English captions.

Jilin Dajie 100. ✆ **0432/6466-1214.** Admission ¥80 adults, ¥40 children. 8:30am–4:30pm. Bus: 59 to Bowuguan, then walk south past a large statue of Mao.

Where to Stay

Jilin's hotels are busy year-round but only fill up during major Chinese holidays. Discounts range from 15% to 25% in summer.

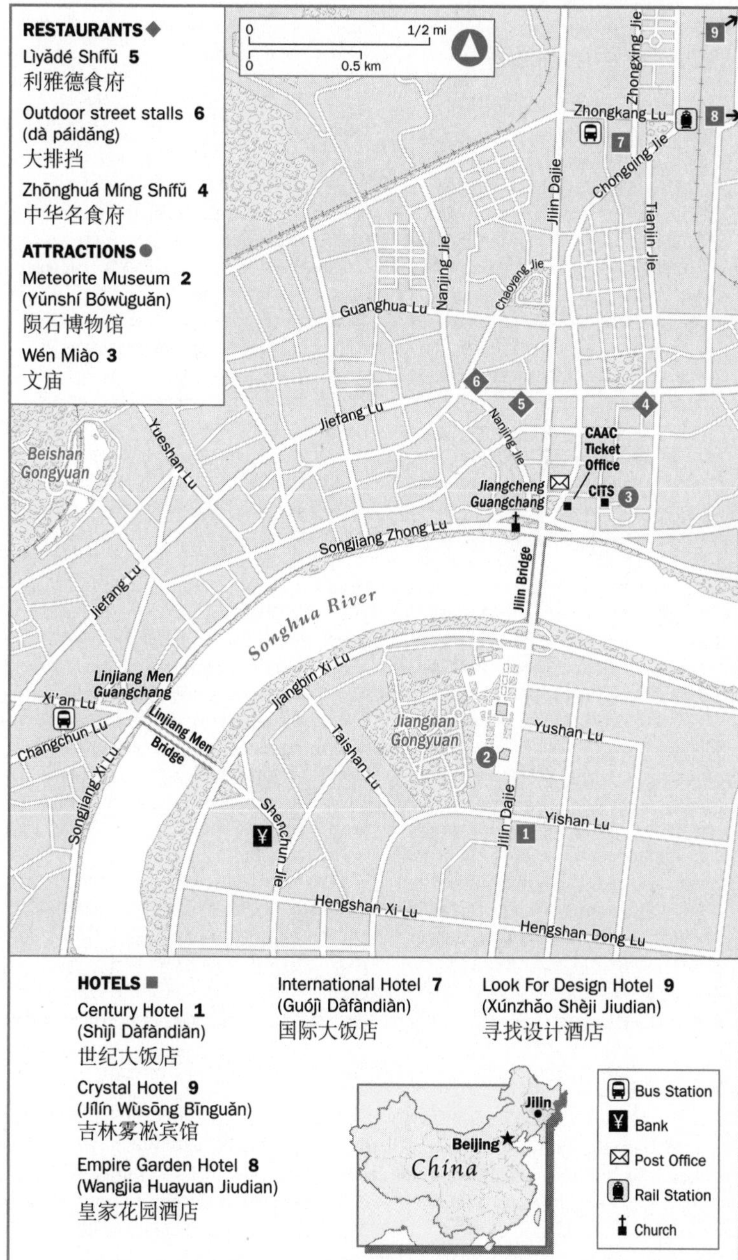

RESTAURANTS
Lìyǎdé Shífǔ 5
利雅德食府
Outdoor street stalls 6
(dà páidǎng)
大排挡
Zhōnghuá Míng Shífǔ 4
中华名食府
ATTRACTIONS
Meteorite Museum 2
(Yǔnshí Bówùguǎn)
陨石博物馆
Wén Miào 3
文庙
0 1/2 mi
0 0.5 km
Zhongxing Jie
Zhongkang Lu
Chongqing Jie
Jilin Dajie
Tianjin Jie
Nanjing Jie
Chaoyang Jie
Guanghua Lu
Jiefang Lu
Nanjing Jie
CAAC Ticket Office
CITS
Jiangcheng Guangchang
Beishan Gongyuan
Yueshan Lu
Songjiang Zhong Lu
Jilin Bridge
Jiefang Lu
Songhua River
Linjiang Men Guangchang
Xi'an Lu
Changchun Lu
Linjiang Men Bridge
Songjiang Xi Lu
Jiangbin Xi Lu
Taishan Lu
Jiangnan Gongyuan
Yushan Lu
Jilin Dajie
Yishan Lu
Shenchun Jie
Hengshan Xi Lu
Hengshan Dong Lu
HOTELS
Century Hotel 1
(Shìjì Dàfàndiàn)
世纪大饭店
Crystal Hotel 9
(Jílín Wùsōng Bīnguǎn)
吉林雾凇宾馆
Empire Garden Hotel 8
(Wangjia Huayuan Jiudian)
皇家花园酒店
International Hotel 7
(Guójì Dàfàndiàn)
国际大饭店
Look For Design Hotel 9
(Xúnzhǎo Shèji Jiudian)
寻找设计酒店
Jilin
Beijing
China
Bus Station
Bank
Post Office
Rail Station
Church

wild china: **YANBIAN** 延边

Koreans first fled across the border to Yanbian, a seldom-visited area of greener-than-green hills and fertile fields nestled in the northeastern corner of Jilin Province, after the first of several severe famines struck the Korean peninsula in 1869.

Subsequent diasporas in the 20th century, the result of continued food shortages and a pair of brutal Japanese occupations, turned the area into what many now call the Third Korea. Now officially called the Yanbian Chaoxian (Korean) Autonomous Prefecture, it is home to the largest population of ethnic Koreans outside the peninsula itself.

Many parts of Yanbian have only recently been opened to tourists, and even those areas that have been open for years see few Westerners. Facilities are minimal and English almost nonexistent. But people adventurous enough to travel here can enjoy one of Dongbei's most peacefully stunning landscapes—a sublime combination of Scotland and Japan—and interact with one of China's only truly bicultural societies.

The capital of Yanbian is **Yanji,** a rapidly developing city where all of the street signs, and most of the residents, are bilingual. Bland and somewhat rigid, its chief value is as a base for journeys to the surrounding countryside, Changbai Shan, and the North Korean border.

A late-afternoon bus ride through the **Yanbian countryside ★★**, as sunlight glitters on fields of rice and warms the upturned roofs of Korean huts, is one of the most exquisite experiences available in the Northeast during July. The best excuse to take such a ride is **Fangchuan,** a tiny town at the end of a needle-thin strip of Chinese territory between North Korea and Russia, and China's preeminent border-viewing spot. A view from the tower here (¥20) provides vistas of Russia, North Korea and, on a clear day, the northern edge of Japan. You can first take a bus from Yanji to Hunchun (1 hr. 30 min.; ¥25). In Hunchun, you have two choices: public transportation or taxi. A **taxi** will save you a lot of hassle; a round-trip ride from Hunchun to Fangchuan costs ¥100 to ¥120. You can have the driver wait for you while you sightsee. Have the driver wait outside the ticketing area or pay an additional ¥10 to take the car all the way to the tower. Otherwise, once you arrive in Hunchun, take a mini-bus (¥1) to Hunchun's Zhonghe Shichang, where you can take a minibus (¥10 one-way) to the border's edge. It will only drop you off about 3km (2 miles) from the viewing tower in Fangchuan. Be certain to ask about the availability of return buses to Hunchun, as schedules are virtually nonexistent and service is largely determined by whether or not there are enough passengers to fill a bus.

Warning: North Koreans continue to flow into Yanbian, but without official permission. Though identity checks aren't as strict as they used to be, it is

EXPENSIVE

Century Hotel (Shiji Dafandian) ★ An exaggerated statue of Cretheus on Argus at the entrance is the first of many ancient Greek and Roman flourishes installed throughout this odd hotel. Nominally managed by Swiss-Belhotel but dominated by its Chinese owner, the Century feels grossly out of place in Jilin. Still, it is the city's nicest hotel, and close to the sights. Rooms are spacious and opulent, with fluffy beds, pale walls, and dark wood furniture.

Jilin Dajie 77 (at Yishan Lu). www.centuryhotel.com.cn. ✆ **0432/6216-8888.** Fax 0432/6216-8777. 230 units. ¥800–¥880 standard room. ¥1,380 suite. Rates include breakfast. 10% service charge. AE, always a good idea to carry your passport with you at all times.

Getting There Trains connect Yanji to Beijing (12:24pm; 23 hr. 30 min.; ¥353 hard sleeper), Changchun (six daily; 8–9 hr. 30 min.; ¥78–¥131 hard sleeper), and Shenyang or Shengyang Bei (5 daily; 12 hr. 20 min.–17 hr.; ¥125–¥197). The **railway station (Yanji Zhan)** is to the south, at the end of Zhan Qian Jie. **Buses** to Changbai Shan (p. 187) and towns in the countryside leave from the Dongbeiya Keyun Zhan (on Chang Bai Lu, northeast of railway station); the ticket office is open from 5am to 4:30pm. Buses also leave from the railway station parking lot. **Flights** to Beijing (three to four daily; ¥1,130), Shanghai (two daily; ¥1,760), Changchun (one daily; ¥770), Shenyang (six weekly; ¥740), Dalian (one daily, except Wed; ¥1,100), Guangzhou (one daily; ¥2,560), and Seoul (one daily, except Tues; ¥2,510) depart from a small airport 6km (3¾ miles) west of the railway station; a taxi ride there costs ¥10. Taxis do not use meters; rides are either ¥5 or ¥10, depending on distance. Negotiate the price before you get in. Purchase flight tickets at the **CAAC ticket office** (✆ **0433/291-5555;** 8am–9pm) inside the Xiangyu Dajiudian above the Yanxin Bridge, north of the railway station.

Where to Stay & Eat Yanji's most convenient hotel is the **Dazhou Hotel,** Tiebei Lu 439 (✆ **0433/619-5555;** fax 0433/619-5999), across from the railway station. The four-star hotel opened in late 2005, has clean and spacious units (¥428) standard room), with competent service. The joint-venture **Yanbian International Hotel (Yanbian Dayu Fandian) ★**, Youyi Lu 118, Juzi Jie intersection (✆ **0433/250-9999;** fax 0433/250-6999), is Yanji's largest and most luxurious hotel, overlooking the Bu'er Hatong River. The small but tasteful rooms cost ¥660 and come with breakfast. **Home Inn (Rujia),** 2 blocks south of the train station, offers clean and minimally decorated budget rooms (Changbaishan Lu 2562; ✆ **0433/280-5599;** fax 0432/290-6899; ¥218). Yanji's food specialty is the authentic Korean cuisine. A favorite dish is *lengmian* (cold noodles), semi-translucent wheat noodles served in a cold broth with various toppings such as pickled cabbage, beef, pine nuts, and Korean chili paste garnished with an apple slice. Both **Jindalai Fandian,** Hailan Lu 42, at Xinhua Jie (✆ **0433/252-8590**), and **Mozhate Kuaicandian ★**, Hailan Lu 29 (✆ **0433/253-8198**), serve great and good-value Korean food and the best *lengmian* in town. The former offers less of a third-grade cafeteria ambience, while the latter has a more comfortable setting and serves tasty tofu hot soup *(doufutang)* and grilled fish. Both restaurants are open from 10am to 10pm. The Gouwu Guangchang shopping area has some Western outlets.

DC, MC, V. **Amenities:** 3 restaurants; bar; badminton courts; forex; health club and spa; small indoor pool; room service; sauna; tennis and squash court. *In room:* A/C, satellite TV, Internet, fridge, hair dryer, Internet, minibar.

Empire Garden Jilin (Jilin Wangjia Huayuan Haihang Jiudian) ★ Situated in the east of the railway station, the five-star hotel is far from the city's attractions, but provides good service and comfy rooms. The lobby has a large, pretty garden with loads of greenery and wooden furniture.

Liaoning Lu 10, Jiefang Dalu Bei Duan (east of railway station). ✆ **0432/6216-9999.** Fax 0432/6216-9000. 307 units. ¥400–¥460 standard room. ¥700–¥800 suite. AE, DC, MC, V. **Amenities:** 2

restaurants; bar; tea house; indoor badminton court; small indoor pool; room service; spa. *In room:* A/C, satellite TV, fridge, Internet, minibar.

Jilin Crystal Hotel (Wusong Binguan) ★ Once the only luxury hotel in Jilin, this four-star still offers the city's best combination of comfort and service. Perched several kilometers northeast of the railway station on the east bank of the Songhua Jiang, it is far from most sights in the city but provides good views of the ice-rimmed trees in winter. The corner rooms are larger and offer the best river views. Rooms in building A are equipped with more traditional and oriental decor, while the design of rooms in building B are younger and stylish. Spacious standard rooms on floors 1 through 3 of satellite building C are a good value at about 20% less than comparable rooms in the main building.

Longtan Dajie 29 (south of Longtan Bridge). www.crystal-hotel.com.cn. ✆ **0432/6391-9999.** Fax 0432/6398-6501. 228 units. ¥312 standard room in bldg. C; ¥380 standard room in building A, ¥460 standard room in building B. AE, DC, MC, V. 15% service charge. Rates include breakfast for 2. **Amenities:** 4 restaurants; 2 bars; bowling alley; small exercise room; indoor pool; room service; spa w/river view. *In room:* A/C, satellite TV, fridge, hair dryer (upon request), Internet.

MODERATE

Jilin International Hotel (Jilin Guoji Dajiudian) This three-star no longer gleams the way it used to, but it's the best-equipped hotel in the railway-station area. Well-maintained standard rooms are the most expensive; the cheapest rooms, on the seventh and eighth floors, are with hard beds.

Zhongxiling Jie 20 (southwest of railway station). ✆ **0432/6657-0300** or **0301.** 191 units. ¥180–¥280 standard room. ¥380 suite. AE, DC, MC, V. **Amenities:** 3 restaurants; bowling alley; exercise room; pool. *In room:* A/C, TV.

INEXPENSIVE

Look For Design Hotel (Xunzhao Sheji Jiudian) A small and cozy lodging, the hotel's owner and his designer friend have put a lot of heart and effort into every corner of the hotel. Each room has a distinct theme and ambience, from garden, to Mediterranean, to classic European style. Even the design and decor of the bathrooms match the specific themes of the rooms. Despite that some facilities and fittings have become a bit worn, the comfortably sized rooms are basically clean with shower only.

Yan'an Lu, Donghong Lu 18. ✆ **0432/258-5499.** 10 units. ¥118–¥168 standard room. No credit cards. **Amenities:** Small coffee shop. *In room:* TV, Internet.

Where to Eat

A **KFC** and a **McDonald's** are inside the Fu-Mart at the intersection of Jiefang Lu and Hunchun Lu; the Fu-Mart also has a **supermarket.** The Century Hotel's Western restaurant serves decent pizza and salads and offers occasional buffet promotions for about ¥60 per person. A popular **Korean cold-noodle** restaurant, **Chaoxianzu Dalengmian,** is situated at the intersection of Chongqing Jie and Dongshi Buxing Jie (see box, "Wild China: Yanbian," p. 184). For a more adventurous and truly local dining experience, try the block of **outdoor street stalls *(da paidang)*** at the night market on **Hunchun Jie ★**, just north of Jiefang Zhong Lu. You can choose from hot pot, seafood, or *guotie,* meat and vegetables you cook yourself at the table in an iron pan. It's open nightly May through October, from 5pm until late.

Liyade Shifu ★ MUSLIM By far the most upmarket Muslim restaurant in the city, Liyade lacks the gritty appeal of Jilin's other Hui minority eateries but still manages to serve some fine mutton dishes. Portions are small but well presented. Don't miss the *shousi yangrou,* tender bits of torn lamb served with soy-and-garlic dipping sauce.

Jiefang Zhong Lu 56 (west of Jilin Dajie). ✆ **0432/208-1010.** Meal for 2 ¥70–¥120. No credit cards. 10am–10pm.

CHANGBAI SHAN 长白山 ★

Jilin Province, 565km (350 miles) E of Jilin City

Changbai Shan (Long White Mountain) is the mythical source of Manchurian and Korean culture, the center of the 200,000-hectare (494,000-acre) **Changbai Shan Nature Preserve,** the tallest peak in Dongbei, and the region's most impressive attraction. The main reason to visit is **Tian Chi (Heavenly Lake) ★**, a pristine, 2-million-year-old fog-enshrouded lake set deep in the crater at the top of the mountain. Roughly 13km (8 miles) in circumference, it straddles the Chinese–North Korean border and is the source of the Songhua River. Below the lake, the mountain is home to a truly impressive range of flora—over 80 tree and 300 medicinal plant species, including ginseng, Korean pine, and the rare Chang Bai larch. The **Jinjiang Canyon ★**, a 70km-long (43-mile) valley, over 200m (656 ft.) wide and 160m (525 ft.) deep formed from molten lava situated in the dense forest, is another must-see sight of the mountain. The valley offers a magnificent landscape as the lava formed different fascinating shapes after years of wind erosion, rain invasion, freezing, and thawing.

The mountain was considered forbidden territory throughout most of the Qing dynasty, and Han Chinese who wandered into the area, usually in search of ginseng, were sometimes beaten to death with sticks. Extreme as it sounds, visitors today might find themselves wishing for a similar policy to protect the mountain from new hordes of Chinese and South Korean tourists. The mountain's UNESCO World Natural Reserve status has done little to this end and the staff of the mountain seems helpless to rectify the situation.

Snow makes routes impassable from early October to late May, but this turns the western slope into an extensive and pleasant skiing spot. In summer the weather is maddeningly unpredictable (bring a raincoat). To see the lake, the best time to visit is from July to September, when the weather clears somewhat and the lake is most likely to be visible. Unfortunately, August is the busiest time being flooded with tourists, and September is also when an army of South Koreans flood the area, taking up hotel rooms as far west as Jilin City and driving up prices.

Note: Turn to chapter 16, p. 824, for Chinese translations of key sights.

The Northern Approach

One of only two routes open to foreigners (the others enter or venture too close to North Korea), this is the most convenient and scenic way to tackle the mountain. It is possible to see Tian Chi and return to Erdao Baihe (see below) in a single day using this approach, but it's worthwhile to spend at least 2 days here.

ESSENTIALS

GETTING THERE The route begins at **Erdao Baihe** (Baihe for short), a small town 25km (16 miles) north of the mountain, named for a river that flows down from Tian Chi. From the south, the easiest approach is by **train** from Shenyang (one daily;

13 hr. 20 min.; ¥103 hard sleeper), or from Dandong (one daily; 17 hr. 50 min.; ¥139 hard sleeper). From the north, a train departs from Changchun (15 hr. 15 min.; ¥110 hard sleeper) to Baihe daily. The best way to reach Baihe from the north is through Yanji (see "Wild China: Yanbian," above); during peak season, which starts around mid-June, a **tourist express** leaves Yanji's long-distance bus station at 4:30am and goes directly to the mountain gate in 4 hours. It returns to Yanji at 3pm same-day and costs ¥110. Or you can catch one of several Baihe-bound buses (191km/118 miles; 4 hr.; ¥32) that leave from the Yanji railway station. The Baihe long-distance bus station is 150m (164 yards) southeast of the railway station.

From the west gate of the mountain, a taxi to Erdao Zhen costs ¥200; to the North gate ¥260.

Admission at the main gate costs ¥100 for adults and ¥50 for students and children. Tour bus (¥85) at *daozhankou* takes you around the park and to a parking lot in front of the hot springs just below Tian Chi. The gate opens at 6:30am.

TOURS Many travel agents in Jilin offer a 3-day Changbai Shan tour for ¥500 to ¥700. The tours are certainly reasonably priced but they don't leave much time to enjoy anything but the lake. In Yanji, **CITS,** located at Chongqing Lu 2222 and close to Wen Miao (✆ **0433/6245-3773**), offers a 2-day tour for ¥480, which includes lunch, one night of accommodation, and all fees for the mountain during weekends.

SEEING THE LAKE

To view the lake, you will have to climb an incredible number of paved stairs (¥25). More enjoyable is the 2-hour hike, which follows a smaller road up a narrow valley, crosses a bridge, then climbs past the 68m (223-ft.) **Changbai Shan waterfall** to the north shore *(bei po)* of the lake. Rock slides sometimes block the trail, in which case you may be able to seek out a freelance guide (¥100 per person) to show you an alternate route. Go early in the morning to avoid the crowds. Once you arrive, search out Mr. Song, an ex-reporter and photographer who lives by the lake and likes to tell tales of the mythical **Tian Chi monster *(guaiwu)*** over glasses of harsh Chinese moonshine.

OTHER SIGHTS

Changbai Shan is home to a number of volcanic **hot springs,** the largest of which seeps steaming out of the rock south of the waterfall. Water from the springs commonly reaches 180°F (80°C); vendors sell eggs boiled in the springs (¥10 for four). The **Wenquan Yu,** in a small white building that's a 10-minute walk below the waterfall (on the left side as you descend), charges ¥80 for a pleasant soak in its hot-spring baths. Also on the mountain, 4km (2½ miles) below the *daozhankou,* is the truly magical **Dixia Senlin (Underground Forest)** ★ (includes the **Heavenly Pool [Xiao Tian Chi]**), a lush forest that becomes progressively more alien as it descends, with the Erdao Baihe 60m (200 ft.) below the mountain stratum (bring bug spray). In Baihe itself, between the railway station and the rest of town, is **Meiren Song Senlin** (**Sylvan Pine Forest;** 6am–6pm; ¥8), with a stunning forestry of sylvan pines *(meiren song),* a rare species that grow only on the northern slope of Changbai Shan between 650m and 1,600m (2,100–5,200 ft.).

WHERE TO STAY & EAT

Rooms in most hotels are outfitted with ***kang***—heated brick platform beds, favored by Korean and manchus, either raised or sunk into the floor and covered with quilts.

A group of families have set up small guesthouses next to the railway station in Baihe, where it is possible to sleep on a *kang* and enjoy home cooking for as little as ¥50.

In Baihe, the largest and nicest hotel is **Jin Shui He International Hotel (Jinshuihe Guoji Jiudian;** www.cbs-jsh.com.; ✆ **0433/607-7777;** fax 0433/607-7700; 340 units), at Tongchang Lu 36, south of the railway station. Spacious and clean rooms with bathrooms cost ¥880–¥980.

If you plan to spend more than a day at Changbai Shan, it makes sense to pay the extra money and stay on the mountain. The **Landscape Hotel & Resorts (Lanjing Wenquan Dujia Jiudian)** ★★ offers the most luxurious and comfortable stay on the mountain. The hotel (✆ **0433/574-5678**; fax 0433/574-5555; 200 units; ¥880–¥1,080 standard room; ¥1,580 duplex; ¥2,380–¥3,380 suite) developed into a full-fledged resort, with a well-equipped hot springs and spa facilities. Located just right outside the park entrance, the attractive wooden hotel has clean and spacious standard rooms, with separate showers and tubs. All duplexes and suites overlook the sizable and nicely decorated outdoor hot springs, and enjoy plenty of natural light and relaxing sounds of the flowing stream. Free broadband Internet is available in rooms. The hot springs are introduced from Changbai Shan's Julong Quan.

The **Athlete's Village,** at the *daozhankou* (**Yundongyuan Cun;** ✆ **0433/574-6008;** fax 0433/574-6055; 56 units), offers basic but comfortable rooms with TVs and small, clean bathrooms in a ski-lodge setting for ¥560. A 15-minute walk up the road, in a large, traditional Korean-style building, is the **Changbai Shan International Hotel** (**Changbai Shan Guoji Binguan;** ✆ **0433/574-6004;** fax 0433/574-6002; 42 units; ¥700; AE, DC, MC, V), which offers relatively luxurious standard rooms with plush beds and clean marble bathrooms. Next door, the impeccable **Chang Bai Shan Daewoo (Chang Bai Shan Dayu Fandian)** ★ (✆ **0433/574-6011;** fax 0433/574-6012; 59 units) offers a choice of bed or water-heated *kang* (¥960; AE, DC, MC, V).

All of the hotels mentioned above serve overpriced but adequate food. Restaurants in town are mostly dives, but they are significantly cheaper and serve comparable fare. The best meal (also the most expensive) can be found at the Chang Bai Shan Daewoo.

If you prefer a mattress, Baihe's largest and nicest hotel is the **Xinda Binguan** (✆ **0433/572-0111;** fax 0433/572-0555; 116 units), on the east side of Baishan Dajie just south of the Meiren Song Senlin. Simple but spacious and clean rooms with slightly dirty bathrooms cost ¥380. The **Fubai Binguan** (✆ **0433/571-8372;** www.cbstianchi.com/fb-about.asp; 68 units), inside the Baihe Forestry Bureau complex south of the railway station, has clean guest rooms with small but tidy bathrooms for ¥200 to ¥220, as well as beds for ¥50.

The Western Approach

This route has been more developed over the last couple of years and has a more subtle beauty. The starting point is the dusty village of Songjiang He, 40km (25 miles) west of Changbai Shan, connected by a newly paved road to a saddle of rock overlooking Tian Chi on the border with North Korea. The chief attractions here are the **Jinjiang Grand Canyon,** the plant life, which changes gradually from ghostly forests of birch at the lower elevations to vivid fields of wildflowers and grassy tundra just below the lake, and the newly open ski park. The flowers at the **Alpine Garden** and **Iris Garden** are at their most vibrant in early June. This path also offers a wonderful panorama of the Changbai Shan mountain range.

ESSENTIALS

GETTING THERE Since the **Changbai Shan Airport,** 18km (11 miles) from the western slope entrance, started operating in 2008, the mountain has become increasingly more accessible. The 40-minute flights connecting to Changchun cost ¥580 one-way, four flights weekly; flights to Beijing take 1 hr. 40 min. and cost ¥1,130. There is also a daily flight from Yanji, ticket costs ¥400. Discount is available. Book tickets with **China Southern Airline** (✆ **8620/95539;** www.cs-air.com).

Another way to get to Songjiang He is by **train** from Dandong (16 hr.; ¥131 hard sleeper), Shenyang (11 hr. 15 min.; ¥92 hard sleeper) or Tonghua (6:30am; 4 hr. 30 min.; ¥12–¥14 hard seat). Taxi is the only way to go to the entrance of the mountain from the railway or long-distance bus station. It takes about 30 minutes and costs ¥50.

TOURS The **Songjiang He Forestry Company** (✆ **0439/631-8461**), with a travel office inside the Songjiang He Binguan (see "Where to Stay & Eat," below), is the only organization officially allowed to run tours of the western slope. The 2-day tour costs ¥440 and includes admission and lunch, but no English is spoken. If you can speak Mandarin, it's much cheaper to hire a private car; drivers will approach you at the railway station. A reasonable price range is ¥150 to ¥250.

EXPLORING THE MOUNTAIN

The **Xi Po Shan Men (West Slope Mountain Gate),** located 44km (27 miles) west of Tian Chi, is open from 7am to 4pm; admission is ¥100. Tour buses (¥85 per person) travel from the gate to all sights below Tian Chi. To go to **Jinjiang Canyon ★**, a 1km-deep (⅔-mile) valley formed from molten lava, change buses at the transportation service center. One of the best times to visit the mountain is late June to mid-July, when the birch forests and fields of wildflowers in **Alpine Garden ★** flourish. The tour bus drive ends at a steep set of 1,236 stairs that leads to **Tian Chi ★** and the **No. 5 border stone,** which marks the beginning of North Korea. Birds and Chinese tourists cross the border at will, but soldiers stationed by the stone keep foreigners from doing the same. There is a 3-hour round-trip hike from here to Baiyun Feng, the highest point (2,691m/8,826 ft.); it's the second peak to the left as you face the lake.

WHERE TO STAY & EAT

One of the best lodgings in the western slope area is the well-equipped resort hotel **Days Hotel Landscape Resort (Changbai Shan Lanjing Daisi Jiudian) ★**

Hiking West to North

Development of the western approach has made it possible to hike around Tian Chi and see both sides of the lake in 2 days, provided you have a tent, warm clothes, and plenty of food and water. The **hike from the west shore ★★** along the ridge past Baiyun Feng to the waterfall on the north shore takes roughly 6 hours. Once you reach the waterfall, you can hike down to the hot spring, camp, and catch a ride to Baihe the next morning. Buses back to Songjiang He (3 hr.; ¥21) leave from the long-distance bus station on Baishan Dajie at 2pm.

Warning: The path is rocky and the weather unpredictable—for experienced hikers only.

(✆ **0439/633-7999;** fax 0439/633-7888; 112 units; ¥850–¥1,100), adjacent the western slope gate. The environmentally friendly resort uses solar power to heat the water and provides decently sized and soothing standard rooms. It also has a handful of rooms with *kangs*. Bathrooms have shower only but are spotless. The hotel only has a Chinese restaurant and staff speaks limited English. Outside the resort, is an 800m (2,625-ft.) wooden trail into the forest where you can enjoy a pleasant walk after breakfast. **Horizon Resort & Spa Changbai Mountain (Changbaishan Tianye Dujia Jiudian)** ★ (www.horizoncbs.com; ✆ **0439/655-8888;** fax 0439/655-8999; 280 units; ¥1,500–¥2,100 standard room), located a 10-minute drive away from the west gate entrance, is the newest and swankiest hotel in the west of the mountain. Rooms are large and comfortable, with beige wallpaper and furniture that echo the natural environment.

HARBIN 哈尔滨

Heilong Jiang Province, 1,421km (881 miles) NE of Beijing, 553km (342 miles) NE of Shenyang

Harbin (Ha'erbin), originally a Russian-built railway outpost carved out of the wilderness on the banks of the Songhua Jiang (Sungari River), is the northernmost major city in China and capital of Heilong Jiang Province. Named for the Black Dragon River that separates Dongbei from Siberia, Heilong Jiang represents China's northern limits. It is the country's coldest province, with winter temperatures that hover, on average, around –15°F (–26°C). Like many border regions, it is an amalgamation of clashing extremes, home to one of China's roughest mountain ranges (the Greater Hinggan or Da Xing'an Ling), some of its most fertile soil, its largest oil and coal fields, its most pristine wilderness, and most of its few remaining nomad groups.

Harbin itself suffers from a similar internal antagonism, one that ultimately makes it the most compelling destination in Dongbei. The city was founded in 1897 as a camp for Russian engineers surveying construction of the eastern leg of the Trans-Siberian railroad (called the China Eastern Railroad, or CER). Demand for labor and the city's laissez-faire atmosphere quickly attracted a diverse population of outcasts from Latvia, the Ukraine, and Poland, as well as Manchuria. It was, at its height, one of the most bizarrely cosmopolitan cities in Asia—cold, dirty, rife with speculation and venereal disease, architecturally vibrant, and a model for ethnic and religious tolerance. The town fell under Japanese control during World War II and was finally recaptured in 1946.

Most original foreign residents fled at the end of World War II. The city has begun to recover some of its former face, however, as trainloads of Russian merchants and prostitutes flood back to take advantage of China's new economic momentum. Harbin attracts visitors year-round, especially in winter, when it hosts the famous **Ice and Snow Festival (Bingxue Jie)** ★★★. The summer's mild temperatures allow for leisurely strolls past the truly stunning clusters of Russian buildings, with their lonely cupolas and embellished pediments that still brighten older parts of town.

The Ice and Snow Festival has successfully turned the city's worst feature—villainous winter cold—into its greatest asset. The winter, despite the frostbite-inducing weather, is the best time to come as it's the town's most festive time of year. The festival now covers most of the city and features some truly outstanding ice and snow sculptures. Past highlights have included translucent reproductions of the Great Wall and Beijing's Gate of Heavenly Peace (Tian'an Men), life-size pagodas, structurally sound multilevel houses, and a massive statue of Elvis—all equipped with internal lights.

It's easy to underestimate the cold (temperatures often drop below –22°F/–30°C), so bring more warm clothing than you think you'll need. Wearing five layers of sweaters and a down coat might sound ridiculous until you get there. Admission can be expensive, but there are increasing numbers of free displays on Zhongyang Dajie and other major streets. Major venues include **Zhaolin Gongyuan** (admission ¥100 adult, ¥50 children and students 4–9:30pm; ¥50 adult, ¥25 children and students 10am–4pm) on Shangzhi Jie for giant ice lanterns; **Taiyang Dao Gongyuan** (**Sun Island Park;** admission ¥150 adult, ¥75 children and students), across the river for snow sculptures; and **The Grand World of Ice and Snow (Bingxue Dashijie),** a collection of buildings constructed entirely of ice and snow, takes place in the north of the Songhua Jiang and west of Sun Island Park. Admission is ¥280 for adult and ¥140 for children and students, from Monday to Thursday; ¥330 for adult, and ¥165 for children and students, from Friday to Sunday and on public holidays.

Essentials

GETTING THERE **Flights** connect Harbin with Beijing, Shanghai, Dalian, and Guangzhou; international routes include Hong Kong (Mon and Sat), Seoul (daily), Niigata (Mon, Wed, Fri, and Sun), and Taipei (Tue). The **Taiping International Airport (Taiping Guoji Jichang)** is 30km (19 miles) south of central Harbin. An ICBC booth next to the international departures area on the second floor exchanges traveler's checks and cash. The **CAAC ticket office** (**Minhang Shoupiao Chu; ✆ 0451/8265-1188;** fax 0451/8231-9343; domestic 6am–9pm, international 8am–4pm) is in a large white tiled building with a red roof, 4km (2½ miles) south of the railway station at Zhongshan Lu 99. An **airport shuttle** (50 min.; ¥20) leaves the CAAC office every 30 minutes from 6am to 6pm. **Taxis** to the airport from downtown (¥100), including ¥20 toll, take between 40 minutes and an hour, depending on traffic. Leave early either way.

Harbin's **main railway station (Ha'erbin Zhan)** is on Tielu Jie, between Nangang and Daoli districts. D-series trains depart from here for Beijing (three daily; 8–8 hr. 45 min.; ¥281 second class/¥351 first class), Tianjin (daily; 8 hr. 45 min.; ¥281 second class/¥351 first class), Shenyang Bei (five daily; 4–4 hr. 15 min.; ¥169 second class/¥203 first class), Changchun (six daily; 1 hr. 45 min.; ¥76 second class/¥91 first class), and Jilin (daily; 2 hr. 30 min.; ¥111 second class/¥133 first class). Fast trains depart from here for Dalian (9:04pm; 9 hr.; ¥231), Shenyang (six daily; 4 hr. 30 min.–6 hr.; ¥76 hard seat; ¥139 hard sleeper), Qiqihar (seven daily; 2 hr. 45 min.–3 hr. 30 min.; ¥44–¥55 hard seat), and Manzhouli (six daily; 12 hr. 20 min.–16 hr.; ¥130–¥222). The ticket sales office is on the right side of the station (**✆ 0451/8690-2828**); tickets can be bought 5 days in advance. For tickets to Khabarovsk and Vladivostok, visit the **Harbin Railway International Travel Service** (**Ha'erbin Tiedao Guoji Luxingshe; ✆ 0451/5361-6721;** www.ancn.net; Mon–Fri 8am–5pm) on the seventh floor of the Kunlun Hotel, west of the main station. **CITS** (Hongjun Jie 66; **✆ 0451/8886-6662;** 8:30am–5:30pm) and the **Heilong Jiang Overseas Tourist Company** (**Heilong Jiang Haiwai Luyou Gongsi; ✆ 0451/5363-4000;** fax 0451/5362-1088), on the 11th floor of Hushi Dasha, Haiguan Jie 182, on the west side of the railway station, both sell tickets for the **Trans-Siberian Railroad** (2 weeks to process).

Harbin 哈尔滨

ATTRACTIONS ●

Church of St. Sofia **15**
(Shèng Suǒfēiyà Jiàotáng)
圣露西亚教堂

Confucian Temple **23**
(Wén Miào)
文庙

Flood Control Monument **2**
(Fánghóng Shènglì Jìniàntǎ)
防洪胜利纪念塔

Gémìng Lǐngxiù Shìchá Jìniànguǎn **21**
革命领袖视察纪念馆

Heilongjiang Science and Technology Museum **4**
(Hēilóngjiāng Shěng Kēxué Jìshùguǎn)
黑龙江省科学技术馆

Jewish Synagogue
(Yóutài Xīn Huìtáng) **12**
犹太新会堂

Siberian Tiger Park **1**
(Dōngběi Hǔ Línyuán)
东北虎林园

Temple of Bliss (Jílè Sì) **22**
极乐寺

HOTELS ■

7 Days Inn **11**
(Qītiān Liánsuǒ Jiǔdiàn)
7天连锁酒店

Days Hotel Xin Kai Lai Harbin **3**
哈尔滨新凯莱戴斯大酒店

Holiday Inn City Center **13**
(Hā'ěrbīn Wàndá Jiàrì Fàndiàn)
哈尔滨万达假日饭店

Ibis **9**
(Yíbìsī Jiǔdiàn)
宜必思酒店

Jīngǔ Hotel (Jīngǔ Bīnguǎn) **7**
金谷宾馆

Lóngmén Guìbīn Lóu **20**
龙门贵宾楼

Modern Hotel **10**
(Mǎdiē'ěr Bīnguǎn)
马迭尔宾馆

Shangri-La Hotel Harbin **16**
(Hā'ěrbīn Xiānggélǐlā Dàfàndiàn)
哈尔滨香格里拉大饭店

Sofitel Wanda Harbin **18**
万达索菲特大酒店

RESTAURANTS ◆

Běiláishùn **5**
北来顺

Dà Fēngshōu **21**
大丰收

Dōngfāng Jiǎozi Wáng **14**
东方饺子王

Portman
(Bōtèmàn Xīcāntīng) **8**
波特曼西餐厅

Russia
(Lùxīyà Xīcāntīng) **6**
露西亚西餐厅

Xuēfǔ Yīpǐn Jiàng Gǔ **17**
薛府一品酱骨

The central **long-distance bus station (Changtu Keyun Zhan)** is across from the railway station, a building next to the Beibei Hotel on Chunshen Jie. Luxury air-conditioned buses go to Qiqihar (4 hr.; ¥71), Wu Da Lianchi (7:30am and 1:30pm; 5 hr. 30 min.; ¥95), and Changchun (3 hr. 30 min.; ¥76). Regular buses go to Yanji (3:30pm; 9 hr.; ¥112). The ticket sales office is open from 5:30am to 6pm (luxury tickets at windows 7–11).

GETTING AROUND Nearly everything of interest falls into one of two old districts—Daoli and Nangang—divided by the train tracks that run past the main station. The Songhua Jiang (Sungari River) forms the city's northern border and divides it from Taiyang Dao, a new island development area that seeks to imitate Pudong in Shanghai.

Taxis cost ¥8 for first 3km/2 miles, then ¥1.90 per kilometer. A number of useful **buses** (¥1–¥2) stop at the railway station; **bus no. 13** goes from the station through the heart of Daoli.

[FastFACTS] HARBIN

Banks, Foreign Exchange & ATMs The main **Bank of China** branch (Mon–Fri 8:30am–4:30pm) is at Hongjun Jie 19, near Hongbo Guangchang. Credit cards and traveler's checks are handled at window 2 on the second floor (*not* available 11:30am–1pm). An international ATM is on the premises. A second branch at Xi Shi (10) Daojie 29 (east of Zhongyang Dajie) exchanges traveler's checks and cash (Mon–Fri 8:30am–4:30pm).

Internet Access Go online at the 24-hour **Yidu Kongjian Wangba** (¥3 per hour) on the north side of Hongzhuan Jie, a block west of Zhongyang Dajie. Dial-up is ✆ **16900** or 165.

Post Office The main post office (**Nangang Youzhengju;** 8:30am–5pm) is on the corner of Dong Dazhi Jie and Jianshe Jie, several blocks east of Hongbo Guangchang.

Visa Extensions Visa extensions are available inside the **PSB** Exit/Entry Administration Office (✆ **156/4508-0750;** Mon–Fri 8:30–11:30am and 1:30–4:30pm) at Jingwei Tou Dao Jie 6. Passport, hotel registration and proof of available funds (US$100 per day) are required.

Exploring Harbin

ZHONGYANG DAJIE ★★

A cobbled, tree-lined street located in the heart of Daoli District, Zhongyang Dajie was once the buzzing heart of social and commercial life in Harbin, home to the city's most exclusive hotels and shops. "From 3am until nightfall, it was alive with throngs of people," a Japanese visitor wrote of the avenue, originally known as Kitaiskia (Chinese) Street, in 1926. "The Russian women with their gaudy early summer hats and clothing together with their white shoes formed a spectacle to be seen nowhere else in the Far East save Shanghai." The scene today is much the same. Particularly vibrant is the **pedestrian-only section** at the southern end, where Chinese women in absurd fur coats window-shop a new generation of boutiques set up in the old Russian buildings, beautifully restored with explanatory plaques in English. The old-world charm, however, has not stopped the commercial invasion of fast-food restaurants, Wal-Mart, and two movie theaters. The luxury department store Lane Crawford has opened a branch, selling pricey Dunhill, St. John, and Mont Blanc items.

At the top of the street, constructed along a large embankment erected after the Songhua River flooded and covered Harbin under several feet of water in 1932, is

Zion That Wasn't

Unlikely as it sounds, Jews fled to Harbin in such numbers in the early 1900s (the population reached 25,000 at its height) that Manchuria ranked just below Morocco and Palestine on early-20th-century lists of potential sites for a Jewish homeland. Fleeing official discrimination and a revival of pogroms in czarist Russia, they were instrumental in Harbin's development but fled en masse for the real Zion shortly after World War II. The only obvious Jewish structures still remaining in the city are the **Modern Hotel** (see "Where to Stay," p. 198); **Youtai Xin Huitang (Jewish Synagogue),** see p. 197; and a **music and Torah school** at Tongjiang Jie 86 (a block west of Zhongyang Dajie), a ragged structure built in 1919 with Star of David window frames that now houses the No. 2 Korean Middle School (Chaoxian Er Zhong).

Sidalin Gongyuan (Stalin Park), a stretch of trees and benches where locals gather to exercise and gossip. In the center of the park is the **Fanghong Shengli Jinianta (Flood Control Monument).** The monument commemorates the city's struggle against the floods of 1957, when the river rose 1.2m (4 ft.) above street level but was kept from spilling into town by an army of soldiers and volunteers. Water levels from other big floods are marked at the base of the monument.

Church of St. Sophia (Sheng Suofeiya Jiaotang) ★★ The brick spires and green dome of the Church of St. Sophia rising out of the chaos east of Zhongyang Dajie are the divine reminders of a more inspired age in architecture. Erected in 1907 and rebuilt several times, the church took its current form in 1932. The handiwork is still visible on the vaulted ceilings and painted chambers, despite near-destruction by the Red Guards in the 1960s and a restoration in 1996. The church is now home to the **Harbin Architecture Arts Center.** An exhibition inside contains photos of other churches, old newspaper clippings, and an interesting scale model of Nangang District in the 1920s. The rear cloister, once used for storage, now contains a small but interesting collection of religious objects. The church's incongruous beauty is enhanced by dozens of white pigeons (kept in place with the promise of free food from feeders in the surrounding square).

Toulong Jie 88, intersection of Toulong Jie and Zhaolin Jie. ✆ **0451/8468-6904.** Admission ¥15 adults, ¥10 students and children from 1.2–1.4m (3½–4½ ft.). 8:30am–5pm. Bus: 2, 8, 13, 74, 83, or 116 to Jianzhu Yishu Guangchang, then walk north on Zhaolin Jie.

Dongbei Hu Linyuan (Siberian Tiger Park) ✋ The Siberian Tiger Park is more like an impoverished prison for the tigers—with rusty fences and dilapidated watchtowers—but it may be worth a visit to see the rare felines. Your entrance fee gets you a seat on a typical Chinese minibus that rolls onto the fenced-in .4-sq.-km (.2 sq.-mile) premises on a dirt road. The bus gets close enough for you to snap good photos and ogle the tigers' paws that are as large as human heads. The park increased its tiger population from the original 8 to nearly 300, but the facility is more tourist attraction than breeding center. For your sadistic pleasure you may order a meal for the tigers, served via a caged jeep; on the feeding menu are a live bird (¥40), a live duck (¥100), and a live cow (¥1,500). Sadly, some of the tigers are confined to tiny cages, pacing about in their mini insane asylums; others seem to be in a semipermanent state of slumber.

Songbei Jie 88, 10km (6 miles) north of the city center. ✆ **0451/8808-0098.** www.dongbeihu.net.cn. Admission (including tour) ¥90 adults, ¥45 children. 9am–4pm. Last tour 30 min. before closing. Bus: 85 from south end of Gonglu Daqiao (40 min.).

Geming Lingxiu Shicha Jinianguan This elegant mansion, built in 1919 by a Polish merchant and opened as a museum after a 3-year restoration effort, was where China's top Communist leaders stayed during official inspections of Heilong Jiang. Sumptuously designed rooms on the first floor contain several mementos, including a bathrobe once used by Zhou Enlai. An impressive spiral staircase leads up to the room where Mao slept, still with the original bed.

Yiyuan Jie 1 (off Hongjun Jie). ✆ **0451/5364-2522.** Admission ¥6. 9am–5pm. Located behind Sinoway Hotel; it's the 2nd old mansion on the left.

Heilongjiang Science and Technology Museum ☺ It is pleasurable to spend a morning or few hours touring this educational museum, which has an armillary sphere sundial sitting outside the entrance. The three-story museum houses interactive models and simple experiments to explain science knowledge such as fundamental mechanical principles, different forms of power, and human senses. At the exhibits on the third floor, children can play and get wet. A range of shows are performed throughout the day.

Sun Island Scenic Spots. ✆ **0451/8800-2728.** www.hstm.cn. Admission ¥24. Tues–Sun 9am–4pm (ticket selling stops after 3:30pm). Bus no. 80, 85, 88, or 29.

Jile Si (Temple of Bliss) Jile Si is the largest active Buddhist temple in Heilong Jiang Province, a beautiful complex welcoming tourists but not made for them. Most impressive are the halls on either side of the main pavilion in the northeastern half, each filled with 500 individually carved arhats *(luohan)*, or Buddhist saints. The hall on the right is devoted to Manchu namesake Wenshu Pusa (Sanskrit: *Manjusri*), the tiger-riding Bodhisattva of Wisdom (see "Minorities & the Manchu Myth," p. 153). There's a smaller temple next door called Puzhao Si that is open on the 1st and 15th day of each Chinese lunar month.

Dong Dazhi Jie 9. Admission ¥10. May–Sept 8am–4:30pm; Oct–Apr 8am–4pm. Bus: 104/14 from Hongbo Guangchang to Youleyuan; walk northeast on Xuanpu Jie, then take a left on Dong Dazhi Jie.

Unit 731 Museum (Qinhua Rijun Diqisanyao Budui Jiuzhi) ★★ What happened here is little known in the Western world, which makes this museum a very worthwhile visit despite being located in Harbin's inconvenient suburbs. Between 1939 and 1945, members of Japan's Unit 731 killed roughly 3,000 Chinese, Russian, Mongolian, and North Korean prisoners of war in a series of nauseating experiments designed to perfect their biological weapons program. Japanese soldiers blew up most of the 6-sq.-km (2-sq.-mile) facility at the end of the war, and the unit's existence was kept covered up for decades with the help of the United States government, rumored to have purchased the research with a promise of immunity for participating doctors. A documentary about 731 released in the 1990s prompted Harbin to renovate the facility and add English signs. Ironically, the museum now stands in an area of town where many of China's pharmaceutical companies are located.

What's best about the museum is that it lets the images and details tell the story, rather than resorting to the heavy-handed propaganda that plagues other Chinese war memorials like the Nanjing Massacre Site. An exhibition in the main office building contains a series of grim but nicely presented displays on the experiments, in which victims (called *maruta,* Japanese for "log") were frozen, burned, injected with hemorrhagic fever virus, exposed to plague and cholera, and sometimes dissected alive. Most chilling is the medical instruments display (room 9), with its test tubes, needles, saws, and coat rack vivisection hooks (used to "hang human viscera," aka organs). The smokestacks of a large incinerator, where dead *maruta* were burned, still stand on the edge of a weed-strewn field in back.

Once you tour the museum, go to the museum's backyard to see where the original germ factory stood (now a pit with overgrown weeds), the remnants of a power-generating facility for the factory, and a series of sheds where the Japanese once bred disease-carrying rats for the experiments.

Xinjiang Dajie 25, Pingfang Qu. ✆ **0451/8680-1556.** Admission ¥20. 9am–3pm. Bus: 338 or 343 from Ha Zhan on Tielu Jie, west of railway station (20km/12 miles; 45 min.; ¥2.50) to Shuangyoug Lu; walk south and turn left at the intersection.

Wen Miao (Confucian Temple) If you're looking for a brief respite from grimy urban life and a more solemn place than Jile Si, visit this wooden temple, one of the largest Confucian temples in China. Built in 1926, Wen Miao, with its 20m-high (66-ft.) ceilings, is now part of Harbin Engineering College campus. At the time of writing, the buildings adjacent to the main palace that make up the temple's main courtyard were being converted into the Nationalities Museum of Heilong Jiang Province. Students painting still lifes in the courtyard and the temple's huge pine trees give it an air of tranquillity.

Wenmiao Jie 25. Admission ¥15. 8:30am–4pm. Walk from Jile Si across the street to the Harbin Engineering College, then walk inside about 5 min.

Youtai Xin Huitang (Jewish Synagogue) ★ Once the center of Harbin's vibrant Jewish community that numbered around 25,000 during the early 20th century, this three-story temple recently underwent an extensive renovation. Today, with few Jews remaining in the city, government officials turned the synagogue into a contemporary art museum featuring Jewish and Russian artists.

Jingwei Jie 162, Dao Li District. ✆ **0451/8468-6904.** Admission ¥25 adults, ¥15 students and children. 8:30am–4:30pm. Bus: 21, 116, or 105.

Where to Stay

If you want to visit Harbin during the Ice and Snow Festival—December to early March, when thousands flood the city—try to book a room at least 2 weeks to a month in advance. Some hotels offer minor discounts during the festival. Discounts at other times range from 30% to 50%.

VERY EXPENSIVE

Shangri-La Hotel Harbin (Ha'erbin Xianggelila Dafandian) ★★ The Shangri-La is the finest hotel in central Harbin, and the only five-star in Daoli District. Rooms are comfortable and tasteful. Bathrooms are spotless. Service is fantastic. Some rooms overlooking Songjiang River. The only drawback is that the hotel is not within walking distance of Harbin's fabled architecture, but its location on the river (across from the Ice and Snow Palace) becomes ideal in winter. An adorable little ice cafe is erected in the outdoor area of the hotel during the winter.

Youyi Lu 555 (east of Songhua Jiang Gonglu Bridge), Daoli District. www.shangri-la.com. ✆ **0451/8485-8888.** Fax 0451/8462-1777. 404 units. ¥1,450 standard room. 15% service charge. Rate includes breakfast for 1. AE, DC, MC, V. **Amenities:** 2 restaurants; bar; concierge; executive-level rooms; forex; health club and spa; indoor pool; room service; smoke-free rooms; outdoor tennis courts (only open in summer); Wi-Fi. *In room:* A/C, satellite TV, fridge, hair dryer, free broadband Internet, minibar.

Sofitel Wanda Harbin (Ha'erbin Wanda Suofeite Dajiudian) ★ Located in the Xiangfang district, the hotel is a bit far away from the city center. Rooms are stylish, with a taste of European charm. Some of the rooms have a view of the golf course across from the hotel. Suites are very large with an exercise pad and Hermès toiletries provided.

Ganshui Lu 68, Xiangfang Daoli District. ✆ **0451/8233-6888.** Fax 0451/8233-1818. 322 units. ¥1,400 standard room. 15% service charge. Rate includes breakfast for 1. AE, DC, MC, V. **Amenities:** 3 restaurants; 2 bars; concierge; executive-level rooms; forex; fitness center; indoor pool; room service; sauna; smoke-free rooms; spa; Wi-Fi. *In room:* A/C, satellite TV, fridge, hair dryer, minibar, free broadband Internet and Wi-Fi.

EXPENSIVE

Days Hotel Xin Kai Lai Harbin (Ha'erbin Xinkailai Dajiudian) This hotel, formerly the Songhua Jiang Gloria Plaza Hotel, has an unmatched location right next to the Flood Control Monument and at the north of Zhongyang Dajie. The hotel is inside a large European-style premise. Rooms in A Wing are appointed with European style furniture and fittings. Some rooms have a balcony facing the hotel's garden cafe. Rooms in B Wing are plain, and bathrooms have shower only. The suites on the top floor share a common private balcony overlooking the river.

Zhongyang Dajie 259, Daoli District. www.daysinn.cn. ✆ **0451/8677-0000.** Fax 0451/8677-0088. 259 units. ¥880–¥980 standard room; ¥1,880–¥2,880 suite. 15% service charge. 30%–50% discounts. AE, DC, MC, V. **Amenities:** 2 restaurants; bar; forex; room service; ticketing and tour arrangements. *In room:* A/C, TV, Internet.

Holiday Inn City Center (Ha'erbin Wanda Jiari Fandian) The Holiday Inn, which used to be one of the finest hotels in Harbin, now feels more like a mid-range Chinese hotel than a respectable joint-venture. But its convenient location at the bottom of Zhongyang Dajie, solid service, and one of the best Western restaurants in Harbin still make it an attractive option. Rooms are large, clean, and comfortable but somewhat worn and outdated.

Jing Wei Jie 90, Daoli District. www.holidayinn.com. ✆ **0451/8422-6666.** Fax 0452/8422-1661. 155 units. ¥700 standard room. 15% service charge. Rates include breakfast. AE, DC, MC, V. **Amenities:** 2 restaurants; bar; executive floors; forex; basic health club; room service; sauna; smoke-free rooms; Wi-Fi. *In room:* A/C, satellite TV, fridge, hair dryer, broadband Internet and Wi-Fi, minibar.

Jingu Hotel (Jingu Dasha) Located on Zhongyang Dajie, this hotel's location puts you in the heart of the pedestrian walk. The beds here are slightly hard, but the bathrooms are sparkling clean. Some English is spoken by the staff.

Zhongyang Dajie 185, Daoli District. www.jinguhotel.com.cn. ✆ **0451/8469-8700.** Fax 0451/8469-8458. 213 units. ¥700–¥778 standard room. 20% discounts. 10% service charge. AE, DC, MC, V. **Amenities:** 2 restaurants; bar; bank; bowling; forex; room service; sauna; ticketing center. *In room:* A/C, satellite TV, Internet, minibar.

Modern Hotel (Madie'er Binguan) ★ The most glamorous hotel in Harbin during the city's heyday, the three-story Art Nouveau hotel, built in 1906, fell on hard times in the early Communist era. While it's improved significantly since, say, the Cultural Revolution, the rooms don't measure up to the history of the place. Still, the location smack in the middle of Zhongyang Dajie and the fair prices make it a very good choice. Standard rooms are rather lackluster and devoid of character; bathrooms are small but very clean.

Zhongyang Dajie 89 (at Xiba Daojie, entrance in back), Daoli District. ✆ **0451/8488-4000.** Fax 0451/8461-4997. 141 units. ¥718–¥788 standard room. Rates include breakfast. AE, DC, MC, V. **Amenities:** 2 restaurants; bar; forex; indoor pool and health club (in neighboring building). *In room:* A/C, satellite TV, fridge, Internet, minibar.

MODERATE

Longmen Guibin Lou ★★ Built in 1901, this inexplicably ignored yellow-and-white Russian building behind the nondescript Longmen Hotel is the most beautifully restored of the old Yamato Hotels. Rooms are spacious and nicely appointed with period furniture. History buffs with money to spare can stay in the suite, outfitted with a beautiful bed from the 1930s, where Zhang Xueliang (see "Shenyang," p. 148) held court when in Harbin. Dining rooms on the first floor still display the original Russian woodwork and contain several turn-of-the-20th-century relics, including an old wooden icebox and a still-functioning phonograph.

Hongjun Jie 85 (at Jianzhu Jie, opposite the railway station), Nangang District. ✆ **0451/8311-7777.** Fax 0451/8363-9700. 30 units. ¥380 standard room, ¥600 suite. MC, V. **Amenities:** 2 restaurants; bar; billiards room; forex; room service. *In room:* A/C, TV, fridge, Internet, minibar.

INEXPENSIVE

More budget options are available since a range of economic hotel brands have established outlets in Harbin over the last few years. The most convenient and better quality are **Ibis (Yibisi)** and **7 Days Inn (Qitian Liansuo Jiudian),** which are well situated around the Zhongyang Dajie area. Both offer clean and cozy rooms, and satisfying service. Ibis at Zhaolin Jie 92 (www.ibishotel.com; ✆ **04518/750-9999;** fax 0451/8750-6575; 215 units) charges ¥189–¥219 for a standard room; at 7 Days, Tongjiang Jie 55 (www.7daysinn.cn.; ✆ **0451/5882-5888**), a room costs ¥195 to ¥239.

Where to Eat

The basement of the Zhongyang Shangcheng, at Zhongyang Dajie 100, has a **food court** with point-to-choose Chinese food and a well-stocked **supermarket.** Zhongyang Dajie is also home to several of the usual western chains. For quick and convenient local food from 9am to 9pm, try the *shaguo shizitou* (smoky tofu, carrots, and a large meatball in savory broth) and pancakes *(bing)* at **Lao Shanghai** (✆ **0451/8262-6335**), located above a bakery at the corner of Zhongyang Dajie and Da'an Jie.

Beilaishun MUSLIM This long-running Muslim restaurant, named after the legendary Donglaishun restaurant in Beijing, is often packed in winter, when believers and atheists alike quiet their shivers over the steam from brass hot pots *(huoguo)*. Thin-sliced mutton is the main hot pot ingredient, but it's big on the menu, too: Try the *pa yangrou tiao*—tender, baconlike strips of lamb braised in a simple soy-and-garlic sauce.

Youyi Lu 51 (next to Children's Hospital). ✆ **0451/8461-5531.** Meal for 2 ¥80–¥100. No credit cards. 11am–9pm.

Da Fengshou ★★ DONGBEI Everything about this immensely popular place is authentic Dongbei: Diners sit on benches and drink beer out of bowls, waitresses unceremoniously dump handfuls of sunflower seeds on the table as appetizers, and the dishes are immense. Avoid the pig-face set dinner and go instead for *jiachang* *tudouni,* a Chinese take on garlic mashed potatoes. The entrance is marked by a huge neon sign and a long, lantern-lit pathway.

Yimian Jie 283 (north of traffic circle next to railway bridge). ✆ **0451/5364-6824.** Meal for 2 ¥80–¥100. No credit cards. 9am–9pm.

Dongfang Jiaozi Wang ★ JIAOZI So popular it inspired a region-wide chain, this original branch is classier than other members of the "Eastern Dumpling King" family and serves some of the best *jiaozi* in China. Order a cold dish and a plate of *sanxian* (shrimp, pork, and Chinese chive) or *songren yumi* (corn and pine nut) *shuijiao,* then wander over to the glass-enclosed kitchen to marvel as the restaurant's army of chefs wrap and boil the dumplings with inconceivable speed.

Zhongyang Dajie 39. ✆ **0451/8465-3920.** Meal for 2 ¥40–¥60. No credit cards. 10:30am–9:30pm.

Russia (Luxiya Xicanting) ★ COFFEE/RUSSIAN This small cafe decorated with heirlooms left behind by a Russian family is a rare reminder of China's treaty port days, when expatriates would suffer the chaos of prewar China by day and retreat at night to the softly lit, lace-covered comfort of their homes to drink coffee and write fantastic letters to the people they'd left behind. The cafe, nestled inside the cracked-wall room of an old Russian building near the top of Zhongyang Dajie, serves a small selection of Western dishes. The hearty red vegetable soup is satisfying; however, their signature dish, "pot beef," a steaming stew of beef, carrot, and tomato, is not particularly outstanding. It's lovely to spend a day here, whiling away the hours with a few cups of coffee and a book.

Xitou Daojie 57. ✆ **0451/8456-3207.** English menu. Meal for 2 ¥60–¥100. No credit cards. 9am–midnight.

Xuefu Yipin Jiang Gu ★ DONGBEI This loud establishment is a favorite among locals. Though there are no English-speakers here, the simplicity of ordering is a huge bonus: Simply go to the display section in the back and point to what you want. The advertised specialty is the pork ribs *(jiang gu).* If you're adventurous, you can get the *gubang* (pork legs); locals enjoy sucking the marrow out of the bones. Every table setting comes with a pair of plastic gloves that diners don to pick up the giant drumsticks. Also try the tasty four-mushroom soup *(Yipin Juntang),* the pumpkin fries, and the fried crepes with vegetables and egg *(Danhuang Junangua).*

Tongda Jie 329, Daoli District. ✆ **0451/8762-1288.** Main courses ¥80–¥100. No credit cards. 10:30am–9pm.

Shopping

Aside from **Zhongyang Dajie,** the biggest commercial street is **Guogeli Jie,** where the government has recently organized several streets around themes. There is a street for children (clothing and toys) and one for women (clothing). The **Churin Department Store (Qiulin Baihuo),** located in an immense green baroque-style building on the north side of Dong Dazhi Jie (opposite the main post office), was once one of the largest department stores in East Asia. The first floor is where you'll find Harbin's best *dalieba*—heavy circular loaves of crusty bread—and Russian-style red sausage *(hongchang),* which you can take for a picnic in the nearby Children's Park. A few blocks west, at the intersection of Dong Dazhi Jie and Hongjun Jie, is the **Hongbo Shichang,** one of the largest underground markets in the Northeast. The market is set up inside an old air-raid shelter, located underneath the former site of the St. Nicholas Church (destroyed by Red Guards in the 1960s), and offers everything from fur hats to black-market video games.

Harbin After Dark

The Popov distillery left town long ago, but foreign residents still imbibe plenty of vodka at **Blue Kiss** (**Bulusi Jiuba; ✆ 0451/8461-3854**). The drinks-and-dance venue at Diduan Jie 100, near Toulong Jie, is open from 1pm to very late; go late on a weekend night for the must-see variety show, a mix of high-kick quasi-striptease numbers that leaves even regular visitors shaking their heads in slack-jawed wonder. **St. Petersburg (Shengbidebao),** on Guogeli Jie (Guangmang Jie 140; **✆ 0451/8261-7070**), offers an environment similar to an American chain restaurant. Wherever you end up, do try the refreshing and light Harbin Beer, known as *Hapi* by the locals, which is China's oldest brew.

WU DA LIANCHI 五大连池

Heilong Jiang Province, 340km (210 miles) NW of Harbin

Wu Da Lianchi (Five Linked Lakes) is an utterly strange health retreat wedged between the Greater and Lesser Hinggan (Xing'an) mountains, several hundred miles north of Harbin. The area is named for a series of connected lakes, formed 260 years ago by lava flows from the two youngest of 14 local volcanoes. Wu Da Lianchi is celebrated among Chinese for its pungent natural springs, water from which is rumored to cure everything from gastritis to chronic cardiocerebral angiopathy. The springs are disgusting, but the area's physical oddity is fascinating. Avoid the summer miracle-cure crowd if at all possible.

Essentials

Air-conditioned **coaches** (5 hr. 30 min.; ¥95 luxury bus) that leave the **Harbin long-distance bus station** (**✆ 0451/8283-0117**) at 7:30am and 1:30pm stop at the park entrance. Return buses leave from the same spot at 6:50am, 8:20am, and 3pm.

Exploring Wu Da Lianchi

Wu Da Lianchi's most impressive sight is not the lakes but the lava fields, collectively dubbed **Shi Hai (Sea of Stone),** which spread out for miles around the area's two largest volcanoes and look vaguely like charred marshmallow. At the center of this is **Laohei Shan ★** (also known as Heilong Shan, or Black Dragon Mountain), tallest of the Wu Da Lianchi volcanoes. An hour-long circumnavigation of the crater's edge, with its twisted birch trees and lichen-covered desolation, provides panoramic views. The **Bing Dong** (8am–4pm; ¥30), 7km (4⅓ miles) east of the Worker's Sanatorium, is a system of sub-freezing caves that contains an exhibition of colorful but underwhelming ice lanterns. Avoid going to **Nan Quan;** it charges ¥20 for drinking the "natural spring water," which has an unpleasant rusty taste.

Private **minivans** are the only way to see most sights in Wu Da Lianchi. Drivers gather near **a large bilingual map** of the area opposite the entrance to Nan Quan (South Spring), a 30-minute walk east of the Worker's Sanatorium. Negotiations for a full tour of the area (25km/16 miles) usually start at around ¥150 a car or ¥50 per person. **Entrance** costs ¥105, including access to the volcano and lava fields.

Where to Stay

Wu Da Lianchi swims with sanatoriums (Chinese for a spa and wellness center) and guesthouses, all offering the same basic accommodations. The most convenient and popular option is the **Wu Da Lianchi Worker's Sanatorium** (**Gongren Liaoyangyuan; ✆ 0456/722-1569;** fax 0456/722-1814; 490 units), a large complex just east of the central traffic circle. Rooms were recently upgraded. Standard rooms in the main building (¥400–¥580) are clean but small. Suites with European-style furniture (¥2,400) are in a separate building. It caters mainly to tour groups from Russia, and individual tourists must call for reservations beforehand.

MANZHOULI 满洲里

Inner Mongolia, 981km (608 miles) NW of Harbin

A frontier town of 260,000 lost in a sea of grass in the northeast corner of Inner Mongolia, Manzhouli is the East-meets-Wild-West frontier outpost the late David Carradine should have used as the backdrop to *Kung Fu.* Born almost overnight in the early 1900s, it was once the primary channel for trade between China and Russia. Russians can be seen everywhere in the streets. Most of the signs are written in Chinese, Russian, and Mongolian and many businessmen speak fluent Russian. A new wave of Russian traders has revitalized the city, affecting a return to the rough-and-tumble days of its founding. It is the most convenient base for trips into the gorgeous **Hulun Buir,** home to China's most pristine grasslands.

Essentials

GETTING THERE The **Manzhouli Airport** (Manzhouli Xijiao Jichang) is located 9km (6 miles) southwest of the town. Purchase tickets for flights to Beijing (one to three flights daily), Harbin (two flights daily), Hohhot (two to three flights daily) at the **CITS** at 35 Erdao Jie, the International Hotel ticket office (**✆ 0470/624-8288;** 8:30–11:30am and 2–5pm). There is no airport shuttle to Manzhouli airport, but a taxi ride takes 20 minutes and costs ¥50.

Trains connect Manzhouli to Beijing (3 daily; 29 hr. 30 min.–32 hr. 20 min., ¥316–¥428 hard sleeper), Harbin (6 daily; 12 hr. 15 min.–15 hr. 30 min.; ¥130–¥222 hard sleeper), Qiqihar (4 daily; 10–11 hr. 20 min.; ¥103–¥175 hard sleeper), and Hailar (11 daily; 2–3 hr. 30 min.; ¥14–¥29 hard seat). The Trans-Siberian train comes through twice a week, usually Friday and Sunday morning, with stops in Irkutsk and Moscow; book tickets through CITS. The **railway station** (**✆ 0470/225-2261**) is opposite downtown, south of the tracks; ticket office is open from 5am to 10pm. Purchase tickets for the Trans-Siberian at the business center inside the International Hotel. (***Note:*** You must have arranged a Russian tourist visa in Beijing if you want to board the train.)

The **long-distance bus station (Guoji Keyun Zhan)** is north of the tracks on Yi Daojie, a 5-minute walk west of the railway footbridge. Iveco buses depart from here for Hailar (3 hr.; ¥35) every 30 minutes from 7:30am to 5:30pm.

GETTING AROUND Most of Manzhouli is located north of the train tracks (behind the railway station) and is easily navigated on foot. **Taxis** charge ¥7 for the first 2km, and ¥1.8/km after. Several bus routes, from 7am to 7pm, costing ¥1, go around the town.

[FastFACTS] MANZHOULI

Banks, Foreign Exchange & ATMs The **Bank of China** (Mon–Fri 8am–5pm) is at San Daojie 28. Cash and traveler's checks are exchanged in the main hall on the right; credit card transactions (MC, V) take place inside a separate entrance on the left.

Internet Access A row of 24-hour basement-level **Internet bars** line Er Daojie, near the International Hotel; one of them is **Meng Gongchang** (✆ **1394/700-8393**); and charges ¥3 per hour of access. Dial-up is ✆ **16900** or 16901.

Post Office The post office (Mon–Fri 8:30am–5:30pm; Sat–Sun 9am–4pm) is located at the corner of San Daojie and Haiguan Lu.

In & Around Manzhouli

A few Russian wood houses still stand in the center of Manzhouli, and the free flow of cash and vodka lends a certain exhilaration to the place, but most points of interest lie elsewhere. The closest attraction, only 10km (6 miles) west of town, is the **Sino-Russian border crossing** (**Guo Men;** ✆ **0470/629-1562;** 8am–5pm; admission ¥20). The old Guo Men built in 1989 was replaced by this new and fifth generation doorway in 2008. If you want your taxi to drive onto the premises, they'll charge you an extra ¥5. Nothing much happens here anymore, as most Russians enter China through a new border crossing farther north, but you can still watch trains pass across the border between China and Russia. There is a small exhibition that tells the history of the area inside the building. Access is by taxi only (20 min.; ¥40 round-trip). A **trade market (Zhonge Hushi Maoyi Qu)** is located in a pink Russian-style building beside Guo Men; it opens in the morning, and all kinds of products, from food to furs (including fakes) can be bought there On the way to the Sino-Russian border crossing, you will see the new **Eluosi Taowa Guangchang (Russian Matryoshka Dolls Plaza)** on the right-hand side. Opened in 2006, the plaza has a giant Russian Matryoshka doll towering 30m (90 ft.) and over 200 colorful nesting dolls representing different countries. There are also several fairy-tale-like Russian-style structures built around the plaza to give the place an exotic ambience. A light and fountain show is staged at the plaza at 9pm every night. On **Nanerdao Jie ★**, alongside the train station, stand a number of classic Russian houses aged over 100 years. Some of these well-preserved log and stone houses are still residences, while some have transformed into restaurants and coffee shops. It's nice to have a walk along the street during late afternoon.

Dalai Hu ★ Also known as Hulun Hu (*Hulun Nur* in Mongolian), this immense lake emerges seamlessly out of the landscape 36km (22 miles) south of Manzhouli—a liquid equivalent to the grasslands that surround it. Dalai Hu is China's fifth-largest lake (2,399 sq. km./936 sq. miles) and a popular feeding ground for rare bird species. A small resort on the north shore offers boating, swimming, and fishing. In pleasant weather vendors sell barbecued fish and shrimp skewers fresh from the lake for ¥2 to ¥3. The lake is also open in the winter, but is much less interesting without boat access.

The only way to get to the lake from Manzhouli is by taxi (1 hr.; ¥100–¥150 round-trip). Admission at the main gate, just north of the resort, costs ¥20 for each person including the driver plus another ¥10 for taxi entrance. A boat ride on the lake costs ¥20 and a motorboat ride costs ¥10 for 10 minutes.

Hulunbuir Grasslands (Hulunbei'er Caoyuan) ★★★ No other grasslands in Inner Mongolia can match the Hulun Buir, an emerald expanse shot through with radiant patches of wildflowers that spreads over the hills outside Manzhouli. The grass here is twice as long as anything found outside Hohhot, and people are scarce. Nothing this beautiful lasts long, though: The season for seeing the grasslands at their most vibrant runs only from late June to mid-August.

CITS, inside the International Hotel, Erdao Jie 38 (✆ **0470/855-5155;** fax 0470/855-5155; 8:30am–5pm), and **Hulunbuir Express Travel Service** (**Hulunbei'er Yuntong Lvxingshe;** http://en.nmgtrip.com; ✆ **0400/660-6000**) offer different types of tours around the grasslands. Four- to 9-day tours (¥2,600–¥4,800 per person) include accommodations in a yurt, horse riding, a mutton banquet, and a visit to Dalai Hu (see above); 2- and 3-day tours are also available. Other attractions around Manzhouli, such as Golden Shore (Jin Hai'an) and the Birds' Kingdom (Wulan Pao), may be added to your tour. If you speak Mandarin and don't mind modest facilities, a better option is to negotiate a stay with one of the local families that approach visitors at the railway station. If you decide to do this, be clear about the details and withhold final payment until your stay is over.

The Hulunbuir is the backdrop to one of China's most authentic **Naadam** festivals (see also "Hohhot," p. 214), held every summer, usually between mid-July and mid-August. Call CITS for details about the date and location.

Zhalainuo'er (Jalainur) The turn-of-the-20th-century Russian-built open coal mine *(meikuang)* is a hideous scar on an otherwise pristine landscape, but few other places in Asia can offer what it does: the chance to see 22 steam trains from the 1920s and 1930s in still-chugging order. CITS (see "Hulunbuir Grasslands," above) offers multi-day tours that include a ride on one of the working engines; the price depends on which attractions you choose. It is possible, however, to visit on your own. The mine is 18km (11 miles) south of Manzhouli, and admission is free. The best time to visit is between October and March, when the steam from the trains is most dramatic. A bus to Zhalainuo'er (30 min.; ¥3) leaves from the intersection of Si Daojie and Xinhua Lu in Manzhouli and drops you in the center of town. From there, hire a taxi to tour the mine for ¥40 to ¥60. The easier but pricier option is to simply hire a taxi in Manzhouli for ¥70 to ¥100.

Where to Stay

All of Manzhouli's hotels are located north of the train tracks. Most offer discounts of 20% or more throughout the year.

Duolisi Yishu Jiudian Opened by a Manzhouli native who studied and lived in the Russian city Chita for 8 years, the three-star hotel stands out with its celebration of Russian arts and culture. Paintings by Russian artists are displayed in different corners inside the hotel. The hotel also organizes exhibitions by contemporary Russian painters from time to time. The hotel's on-site restaurant, run by a Russian chef, serves western cuisine with ingredients imported from the Eurasia country. Rooms are clean and simple.

Yi Daojie (west side of Tielu Lianjian Dalou). ✆ **0470/282-8888.** Fax 0470/622-0518. 133 units. ¥680 standard room. No credit cards. **Amenities:** Restaurant; gallery. *In room:* A/C, TV, Internet.

Home 1 Hotel (Jiayi Shishang Jiudian) This modern and small hotel is located in the city center. There are no extra amenities in the six-story hotel, but service is satisfying. The rooms are small but comfy and clean, with flatscreen TVs, stylish lamps, and minimal design. Bathrooms are cramped, with showers only. A big pane of glass is used to separate the bathroom and bedroom.

Xinghua Lu 8. ✆ **0470/623-1888.** Fax 0470/623-9222. 72 units. ¥488 standard room. No credit cards. *In room:* Satellite TV, Internet.

Friendship Hotel (Manzhouli Youyi Binguan) The formerly unremarkable Friendship Hotel now offers nice rooms, with good service and easy access to the railway station. Standard rooms are clean and bright, with large beds and compact but clean bathrooms. The hotel isn't as lively as some of its competitors, but this could change as word spreads.

Yi Daojie 26 (between Xinhua Lu and Haiguan Lu). ✆ **0470/624-8888.** Fax 0470/622-3828. 190 units. ¥480–¥700 standard room; ¥1,010–¥1,500 suite. Rates include breakfast. No credit cards. **Amenities:** 2 restaurants; bar; executive floor, forex; fitness centre; sauna;

Shangri-la Hotel (Manzhouli Xianggelila Dajiudian) ★★ Opened in 2011, Shangri-la is the city's first five-star hotel and the first international brand to come to town. The hotel stands in the neighborhood of the Xiaobei Lake and enjoys the best view in town. Rooms are sizable and restful, dignifiedly appointed with exquisite oriental touches. Some look over the lake. Marble bathrooms are large and sparkling clean. Service is remarkable. If you have the means to afford it, this is the best luxury option in Manzhouli.

Liudao Jie 99. www.shangri-la.com. ✆ **0470/396-8888.** Fax 0470/391-9777. 235 units. ¥1,138–¥1,338 standard room; ¥3,558 suite. Rates include breakfast. AE, DC, MC, V. **Amenities:** 3 restaurants; bar; concierge; executive floor; forex; fitness center; indoor pool; sauna; smoke-free floor. *In room:* A/C, satellite/cable TV, fridge, hair dryer, free broadband Internet, minibar.

Where to Eat

The local specialty is *shuan yangrou,* a form of mutton hot pot that uses plain boiling water instead of broth. You'll find it offered all over town, but the best version is found at **Mengxiangyuan Huoguo** (✆ **0470/622-0989;** 10am–5am; meal for two ¥30–¥50), an unassuming restaurant on Wu Daojie. They're famous for their fresh lamb, but you'll also find some vegetarian-friendly options (called *qingshui guodi*).

Russian restaurants abound here. The city's busiest Russian restaurants are **Xinmanyuan Xicanting,** San Daojie 38 (✆ **0470/622-2008;** 7am–1am; meal for two ¥30–¥50), and **Beijiaerhu Xicanting,** Zhongsu Jie 23 (✆ **0470/623-4689;** 7am until late; meal for two ¥40–¥70), a strange and raucous eatery-cum-nightclub located behind the International Hotel (look for the white-and-green awning). A visit isn't complete without sampling the bowls of hearty *suba tang* (beef, potato, and carrot in tomato broth).

6 ALONG THE YELLOW RIVER

by Simon Foster

The Yellow River is one of China's great waterways, and from its source high on the Tibetan Plateau, it snakes its way through the arid northwestern provinces of Ningxia, Inner Mongolia, Shanxi, and Shaanxi before spilling into the Sea of Japan in Shandong. Like the Yangzi (known in Chinese as Changjiang, meaning Long River), the Yellow River is a literal translation derived from the jaundiced hues of the loess sediment that it collects along its 5,471-km (3,400-mile) course. Long held as one of the cradles of Chinese civilization, the Yellow River valley is overloaded with history, and the six cities and one mountain village covered in this chapter present more historical sites than many a small country. From the incredible Buddhist grottoes at Datong, all the way through to "modern" sights such as the communist base of Yan'an, there is plenty to keep you occupied here for at least a fortnight, all the more so since the opening of excellent new museums at Hohhot, Yinchuan, and Taiyuan.

From Beijing, Datong has always been the traditional gateway to the region, but with the commencement of fast Beijing-Taiyuan trains, this is now a viable starting point. From Taiyuan one can visit Pingyao, one of China's best preserved walled cities, and the sacred Buddhist mountain retreat of Wutai Shan, before heading north to Datong. Proceeding west to Hohhot, some relief can be found from the barren dryness of this part of China by making a side-trip out to the grasslands before continuing on to Yinchuan, capital of Ningxia Hui Autonomous Region. If you have the time, and an interest in communist history, Yan'an makes a good last stop on the loess loop before returning to Beijing (or Xi'an).

Piercing winds and icy air currents from the north keep most travelers away from this region from late November to mid-March. Moving south, summer temperatures can be scorching, but evenings are generally comfortable.

Note: Unless noted otherwise, hours listed in this chapter are the same every day.

DATONG 大同

Shanxi Province, 379km (236 miles) W of Beijing, 284km (176 miles) SE of Hohhot, 350km (217 miles) N of Taiyuan

In 398, Datong (then Ping Cheng) became the capital of the Xianbei tribes' first Chinese-style state—as opposed to a tribal confederation—under the

Northern Wei dynasty. Modeled after the Han Chinese capital of Chang'an (Xi'an), Datong remained their political center for the next hundred years, and it was during this period that most of the Yungang Buddhist Caves were carved out. Four hundred years after the Wei moved their capital south to Luoyang in a step toward Sinicization, the Khitan (or Qidan) established their Liao dynasty (907–1125) capital in Datong. Two buildings from that era survive at Huayan Monastery, which with the Yungang Caves and the spectacular Hanging Temple give ample reasons to visit.

Modern Datong is an industrial center with an abundance of coal that is both a blessing and a curse. Without it, Datong's economy would collapse; with it, skies are rarely clear and lung disease is common. In 2001, the city began implementing pollution-control measures; while some industries have been closed and air quality has certainly improved, don't breathe too deeply in Datong. At the time of writing the city's roads were undergoing a major overhaul, resulting in chaotic traffic, particularly around the south part of the walled city. A new city, east of Datong's current center, is also planned, and when complete, many of the government buildings will relocate there.

It's possible to visit Datong as a long day trip from Beijing (see "Tours" on p. 209), but to see all the sights, 2 days are needed.

ATTRACTIONS ●

Drum Tower (Gǔ Lóu) **6**
鼓楼

East Gate **5**
(Dōngmén)
東門

Huáyán Sì **3**
华严寺

Nine Dragon Wall **4**
(Jiǔ Lóng Bì)
九龙壁

Shanhua Monastery **8**
(Shànhuà Sì)
善化寺

Bank ¥
Bus Station
Post Office ✉
Rail Station
Public Security PSB
Visas
Travel Agent TA

HOTELS ■
Dàtóng Bīnguǎn **10**
大同宾馆

Holiday Inn **9**
(Jiàrì Jiǔ Diàn)
假日酒店

Jiahe Express Hotel **12**
(Jiā Hé Kuài Jí Shāng
Wù Jiǔ Diàn)
嘉和快捷商务酒店

Jiahe Hotel **2**
(Jiā Hé Guó Jì Kuài
Jí Jiǔ Diàn)
嘉和国际快捷酒店

Huāyuán Dàfàndiàn **7**
(Dàtóng Garden Hotel)
花园大饭店

RESTAURANTS ◆
Kaige Feiniu Hotpot **13**
(Kaigē Feíniú Huǒguō)
凯鸽火锅

Tonghe Dafandian **1**
(Tónghē Dàfándiàn)
同和大饭店

Yonghe Food City **11**
(Yǒng Hé Měi Shí Chéng)
永和美食城

Essentials

GETTING THERE Datong's **airport** offers flights to Beijing (daily), Shanghai (Tues, Thurs, and Sat) and Guangzhou (daily). The airport is 15km (9 miles) east of the city and can be reached by taxi (¥40).

Plenty of **trains** run between Beijing Xi Zhan and Datong, which take around 6 hours. Trains from Taiyuan take a similar length of time and include the K7801 at 3:21pm. Heading west, the Beijing-Baotou line has plenty of services, connecting Datong with Hohhot in around 4 hours.

Large, deluxe **buses** travel between Datong and Beijing (5 hr.; ¥120) several times a day from the Datong's new **south bus station (Qiche Nanzhan; ✆ 0352/502-5222**); passengers are dropped off at the Liuliqiao Bus Station in the west part of Beijing. **Minivans** for Beijing also leave from outside the train station and charge ¥100; while they are slightly quicker and cheaper than the buses, they can be cramped, you'll have to wait for the van to fill up with passengers and drivers often give little thought to road safety. Air-conditioned buses connecting with Hohhot arrive and depart hourly from the south station (4 hr.; ¥70). Regular buses also connect to Taiyuan (3 hr. 30 min.; ¥97) and two daily services for Wutai Shan (4 hr.; ¥66). Share taxis for Yingxian and Wutai Shan (¥100–¥150 per person) wait outside the train station, although unless you're prepared to pay the cost of the whole car (¥400–¥600) you'll have to wait for other passengers before you depart.

GETTING AROUND Although the city is spread out, it can be toured on foot because the few tourist sights are in a fairly compact area south of Da Xi and Da Dong Jie. **Taxis** charge ¥6 for the first 3km (2 miles), then ¥1.40 per kilometer thereafter. Beyond 8km (5 miles), the fare is ¥2.10 per kilometer. Between 10pm and 7am, the first 3km (2 miles) is ¥6, then ¥1.80 per kilometer. Most trips within 3km (2 miles) in the city are ¥6 to ¥9. For longer trips, negotiate a price before you set off.

TOURS A helpful branch of **CITS** (**✆ 130/-0808-8454**) is in the courtyard of the Tai Jia Hotel, a 5-minute walk from the train station; turn right out of the station and follow the CITS signs. The office is managed by helpful William Gao and offers 1-day tours to the Yungang Buddhist Caves, the Hanging Temple, and the Ying Xian Wooden Pagoda. You can choose from either tour 1 (Yungang Caves and the Hanging Monastery) or tour 2 (the Hanging Temple and the Wooden Pagoda). Tours operate with a minimum of five passengers, start at 9am from the train station and cost ¥420 including entrance fees and lunch, or ¥100 without. Some visitors arrive overnight from Beijing, take this tour, and return overnight. CITS also has a helpful office outside the Datong Binguan (**✆ 0352/510-1021**).

[FastFACTS] DATONG

Banks, Foreign Exchange & ATMs You can't walk more than a few minutes in downtown Datong without stumbling across a Bank of China with an ATM. The main **Bank of China,** Yingbin Lu near Hongqi Nan Jie (Mon–Fri 8am–6pm) has full-service foreign exchange and an ATM that accepts international cards. An ATM is in the lobby of the Huayuan Dafandian (p. 213).

Internet Access Several Internet cafes are close to the train station, including the 24-hour **Hongxin Wangba** opposite the police station 5 minutes' walk southeast along Dongma Lu (look for the blue and white sign). Connection here costs ¥3 per hour. In the south of town a good option is at 11 Yingbin Dong Lu, just west of the intersection with Yuhe Nan Lu where connection costs ¥2 per hour and opening times are from 8am to midnight.

Post Office The main post office is in Hongqi Square (8am–6:30pm) and another branch is across from the train station.

Visa Extensions The **PSB** (**Gong'anju; ✆ 0352/232-1311;** Mon–Fri 9am–noon and 2–5pm) is on Xinjian Bei Lu. Visas can be extended while you wait.

Exploring Datong

If you have time after a visit to Huayan Si, Datong's **Jiulong Bi (Nine Dragon Wall;** Da Dong Jie), east of Da Nan Jie (¥10; May–Sept 7:30am–7:30pm, Oct–Apr 8am–6pm; bus: 4) is a fine example of a spirit screen to fend off ghosts and evil spirits that can only move in straight lines. The brightly colored glazed wall with nine writhing dragons was built in 1392 in front of a prince's mansion, long ago razed by fire. The much-restored **Shanhua Si** (¥20; 8am–6pm) west of Nan Men Jie, last rebuilt in 1445, is also a pleasant escape from Datong's dusty streets. Most impressive are the beautiful timber doors of the **Hall of Three Sages (San Sheng Dian).** The old **city wall** has also been recently restored, and visitors can now walk a section accessible from the East Gate (¥15); the remainder of the wall is also under restoration and in the future you should be able to make a complete circuit.

Huayan Si ★ This monastery has separate upper and lower temples that share a lane. The upper temple's massive main hall, the **Daxiong Bao Dian** of 1140, is one of China's few surviving 12th-century buildings. Inside are the lined-up Buddhas of the Five Directions (including the center), seated on elaborately decorated lotus thrones and set off by small standing attendants.

Most significant of all the halls in the two temples is the **Bojia Jiaozang Dian** of 1038, a very rare example of a Liao dynasty building. Inside, Buddhist sutras (scriptures) are stored in one of the finest and best-preserved examples of the miniature timber buildings favored by the period's architects for housing sutras. Named the **Celestial Palace Pavilion (Tiangong Louge),** the sutra cabinet is an exquisite dollhouse with elaborate bracketing, an arched bridge, curved eaves, and balconies. The 31 elegant stucco statues in the hall also date from the Liao dynasty. One of the most prized is the female bodhisattva on the right-hand side. Her palms are pressed together as if in prayer, and her lips are parted, revealing her teeth—a rarity in Chinese sculpture.

Both Upper and Lower temples are down a lane off the south side of Da Xi Jie. Admission ¥20 each temple. May–Sept 8am–6pm; Oct–Apr 8:30am–5:30pm. Bus: 4 from railway station.

Out of Town

Yungang Shiku (Yungang Caves) ★★★ Influenced by the Buddhist site of Bamiyan in Afghanistan and the caves of Kizil and Kuqa (in Xinjiang, p. 314), the stone carvings of Yungang are the earliest of their kind in China. Hewn in three stages between 460 and 524, they show the movement from a heavy reliance on Indian and central Asian artistic models to an emergence of Chinese traditions. The caves numbered 16 to 20 (the "Five Caves of Tan Yao") were carved between 460 and 465 under the supervision of a Buddhist monk. Caves 1, 2, and 5 to 13 were carved in the second stage, which began in 470 and ended when the Wei dynasty capital was moved from Datong (at that time Ping Cheng) to Luoyang in 494. The remaining caves, carved without imperial patronage, are less notable.

For sheer size, **Caves 16 through 20** are the most impressive. Made in part to honor the reigning emperor, Wen Cheng, and his four predecessors, each cave contains one central Buddha figure (representing an emperor) and his attendants. The best of them, **Cave 18,** contains the colossal image of Sakyamuni, the 10 *arhats* (enlightened disciples) associated with him, and two attendant Buddhas. The Buddha to the right of Sakyamuni has a webbed hand—one of the 32 marks of a superior being. His robe was originally red, his face white, and his hair black. Traces of his green mustache and beard can still be seen, and echo the art of Iran.

Largest of the Buddhas in the Tan Yao caves is the sitting figure in **Cave 20,** now exposed by the collapse of the top and sides of the cliff. Holes for beams indicate that a wooden structure was built to protect the Buddha, but that, too, is long gone. The squared figures and static style are typical of this early period of Northern Wei statuary; they also suggest that the artists may have worked from sketches or drawings brought back by pilgrims from Indian holy sites. Notice in the later carvings the fluidity of line in the postures and draped clothing.

Many caves in the second group depict stories from Buddhist scriptures. **Cave 1** is interesting for its Chinese-style architectural features in the bas-reliefs of buildings, though many of the images have eroded. **Cave 3** is the largest of the caves. The fuller bodies of the three Buddhist images it contains suggest it was carved as late as the Sui or the Tang dynasties. **Caves 5 and 6** were both carved before 494, but the four-story wooden facade dates from 1651. **Cave 5** houses the largest carving at Yungang—a stunning Sakyamuni in meditation. In **Cave 6** look for the two Buddhas, Sakyamuni and Prabhutaratna, facing each other. This customary pairing alludes to an episode from the Teaching of the Lotus Sutra. In this episode, a *stupa* (shrine) containing the relics of the Prabhutaratna Buddha appears in the sky. Surrounded by Buddhas and bodhisattvas, Sakyamuni rises to the stupa and unlocks it with his finger. Out comes the extinct Prabhutaratna, who praises and congratulates him. Other episodes from the life of Sakyamuni decorate the walls. On the entrance arch of **Cave 8** are contented images of Shiva and Vishnu (two of several Hindu deities who found their way into Buddhism). The discs they hold represent the sun and the moon. Some sources identify the small bird on Vishnu's chest, and the larger one on which his feet rest, as the mythical *garuda*—the vehicle (and disciple) of Vishnu; others, less convincingly, call them phoenixes, a Chinese motif. Traces of ancient Greece appear in the classical bow with inward curve at its center. (As in this relief, the bow is commonly held in the left "wisdom" hand. Presumably the missing right "method" hand held an arrow.) A seated Maitreya Buddha (Future Buddha) dominates **Cave 13.** Most delightful about this statue is the figurine of a four-armed attendant who stands on the Buddha's thigh while supporting its huge raised arm—the artists' solution to a crack in the stone. Allow yourself at least 2 hours to see the main caves.

16km (10 miles) west of Datong. Admission ¥150. 8:30am–5:30pm. Buses no. 4 to the terminus (¥1), then bus no. 3. (¥3). A taxi should charge ¥40 one-way, or ¥80 round-trip, including waiting time.

Xuankong Si (Hanging Temple) ★ This temple, clinging to the side of a cliff in an impressive gorge, is composed of some 40 connected halls that appear to be supported by toothpicks. Looking more like a wooden model than anything weight-bearing, it is actually supported by sturdy timbers that extend deep into the mountain. Founded in the Northern Wei dynasty (386–534), the temple contains Buddhist, Daoist, and Confucian chambers, along with a chamber, the Sanjiao Dian (Three Teachings Hall), which combines all three. Sakyamuni is in the center with Confucius to his right and Lao Zi to his left. The hour or so drive out from Datong passes through some incredibly barren mountain scenery and if you take a taxi you can also ask to stop at the cave dwelling of septuagenarian Zhang Dehua, which gives a fascinating insight into the way many people still live in this part of China. His home is on the left-hand side, 5 minutes into the first mountains you reach coming from Datong; ¥5 or ¥10 per person should be offered.

62km (39 miles) south of Datong. Admission ¥130. Summer 8am–7pm; winter 8am–6pm. Minibuses to Hunyuan (near the monastery) leave from the station opposite the railway station when they fill up. Price isn't fixed, so bargain; expect to pay ¥8–¥12 for the 90 minute journey. From Hunyuan, it's another 6km (4 miles) to the monastery by minibus (about ¥5) or taxi (about ¥9). To take a taxi the whole way from Datong expect to pay ¥300 return including waiting time.

Ying Xian Mu Ta (Ying Xian Wooden Pagoda) ★ Built in 1056 during the Liao dynasty, this impressive building is China's oldest surviving wooden pagoda. From the outside, it appears to have only five stories, though it actually has nine; and its complex system of supports includes 54 kinds of brackets. Frescoes on the ground floor and a gilded statue of Sakyamuni date from the Liao dynasty. During a 1974 renovation, engraved sutras and documents related to the construction of the pagoda were discovered inside one of the statues of Buddha. Unfortunately, visitors are now only allowed to climb to the second level of this delicate structure.

For those on their way from Datong to Wutai Shan, it's possible to visit the Hanging Temple and Wooden Pagoda in a day, then spend the night in Ying Xian and leave the next morning for Wutai Shan. East of the pagoda, the friendly, affordable **Lihua Chun Binguan,** Yinghun Lu (eastern extension of Xinjian Dong Lu; ✆ **0349/502-9593**), is the best hotel in Ying Xian, and its restaurant serves good Cantonese and local dishes. Standard rooms go for ¥88 to ¥108. The hotel can arrange for north- or south-bound hotel pickup. The minibus to Wutai Shan charges ¥55 for the 2-hour trip.

76km (47 miles) south of Datong. Admission ¥60. Winter 7:30am–7pm; summer 8am–6pm. Minibuses to Ying Xian leave from the new south bus station (¥20; 2 hr.) and drop passengers near the Wooden Pagoda. Minibuses also leave from Hunyuan (¥15 for the 90-min. drive). Taxis to both the Hanging Temple and the Wooden Pagoda charge around ¥400 for the round-trip including waiting time. To visit both and then head on to Wutai Shan by taxi, expect to pay ¥600 plus.

Jing Xia You (Coal Mine Tour) One of Datong's latest travel fads is a visit to a local coal mine. You get to suit up in a real coal miner's outfit complete with boots and light-equipped helmet and spend 2 hours underground, albeit at a distance more comfortable than the coal miners are used to. A miner's elevator will take you down into the mine, and then you'll board a small train to reach a point where miners are digging. You may also have lunch with the coal miners in their cafeteria. Tours can be arranged by CITS. To reserve a place call 1 day in advance; a minimum of 10 are required for the tour to run.

30 min. outside Datong. Call CITS for reservations ✆ **0352/510-1021.** Tour price ¥150.

Where to Stay

Accommodation choices have expanded dramatically in Datong in recent years and now include everything from international chains to inexpensive but well-managed and maintained budget business hotels. Year-round discounts at some of the more expensive options can offer very good value.

EXPENSIVE

Holiday Inn (Jiari Jiudian) ★ The latest addition to Datong's high-end line-up, the Holiday Inn has the best standard rooms in the city, very professional staff, and a host of amenities and facilities including a pool and a gym. Rooms are ultra-modern, and styled in subtle tones, with large armchairs, and large tubs with a separate shower cubicle in the attractive bathrooms. At the time of writing the hotel was offering very appealing promotional rates.

Yingbin Xi Lu 37. www.holidayinn.com ✆ **0352/211-8888.** Fax 0352/586-8200. 212 units. ¥1,288 standard room; ¥1,588 suite. Up to 55% discount. AE, DC, MC, V. Bus: 15 from train station. **Amenities:** 2 restaurants; bar; forex; gym; indoor pool; room service; ticketing. *In room:* A/C, TV, fridge, hair dryer, Internet.

MODERATE

Datong Binguan ★★ With its manicured gardens, park-size lawn with gazebo, and manor-house facade, this is one of the more pleasant of Datong's hotels. Service is excellent; rooms are well-appointed, clean, and comfortable; and the price is reasonable. Some of the Standard A rooms have small balconies, which are worth requesting. Rooms facing the street overlook the front lawn and fountain.

Yingbin Xi Lu 37. www.datonghotel.com. ✆ **0352/586-8666.** Fax 0352/586-8200. 188 units. ¥580 standard room A; ¥500 standard room B; suite ¥1,180. Up to 50% discount. Some rates include breakfast. 15% service charge. AE, DC, MC, V. Bus: 15 from train station. **Amenities:** 2 Restaurants; bar; forex; room service; ticketing. *In room:* A/C, TV, fridge, hair dryer, Internet.

Huayuan Dafandian (Datong Garden Hotel) The Datong Garden Hotel is clean, well priced, and the service is friendly. The guest rooms in this four-star hotel are well sized and furnished with Ming and Qing dynasty-style pear-wood furniture; it's worth spending extra for the larger superior rooms. The hotel is conveniently located in the center of Datong, near the Drum Tower, restaurants, and shopping centers.

Da Nan Jie 59. ✆ **0352/586-5825.** Fax 0352/586-5824. 108 units. ¥1,380 standard room; ¥1,580 superior standard; ¥2,880 suite. Rates include breakfast. Up to 65% discount available. 15% service charge. AE, MC, V. **Amenities:** 2 restaurants; bar; forex; room service, ticketing. *In room:* A/C, TV, fridge, hair dryer, Internet, minibar.

INEXPENSIVE

Jiahe Hotel (Jiahe Guoji Kuai Jiudian) Budget backpacker favorite Feitian Binguan has been remodeled as the Jiahe Hotel, and now offers significantly better rooms at very reasonable prices. Rooms are still small, but now feature modern black furnishings, flat screen TVs and decent showers. The location right next to the train station remains both a convenient blessing and a noisy curse, and at the time of writing there was also construction work at the rear of the property. Nonetheless for budget-minded travelers taking the train in or out of town, the Jiahe is a decent choice. The chain has another similarly priced property **(Jiahe Kuai Shangwu Jiudian)** close to a good selection of restaurants on Yingbin Dong Lu.

Zhangqian Jie (across from the train station). ✆ **0352/555-9555.** 150 units. ¥188 standard room. No credit cards. *In room:* A/C, TV, Internet.

Where to Eat

The residents of Datong enjoy a good meal out and the city has no shortage of restaurants catering to all tastes. The bulk of good Chinese eateries are to be found on Xiao Beimen, Nanmen Jie, and Da Bei Jie, but for something cheaper look out for the beef noodle joints around the train station. If you want some Western food then you'll find **KFCs** just south of the Huayuan Dafandian and another in the main square, Hongqi Guangchang, as well as a McDonald's on Jiaochang Jie. A **UBC Coffee** is on Da Bei

Jie. For a Western buffet meal, the **Huayuan Dafandian** is a good, but expensive option (¥228 per person).

Kaige Feiniu Huoguo ★★ HOTPOT For something really special it's worth heading south to this hugely popular upmarket hotpot restaurant. Kaige offers a one-of-a-kind hotpot experience where waiters on roller skates rush around serving a mouthwatering array of meat and vegetable plates for customers to cook in their own individual spicy or vegetable broth hotpots. Things are made easier for non-Chinese speakers by photographs of dishes but another easy tactic is to just look around and ask for what you see other people cooking.

South side of Yingbin Dong Lu, halfway btw. Nan Guan Nan Jie and Yuhe Nan Lu. ✆ **0352/209-5218.** Reservations recommended. Meal for 2 ¥60–¥80. No credit cards. 10am–1:30pm and 5:30–8:30pm.

Tonghe Dafandian CHINESE This Chinese banquet hall restaurant serves a wide range of inexpensive local and Chinese dishes including Shanxi Fried Noodles, sweet corn and mushrooms, and dumplings. For those with a sweet tooth, for dessert there's *basi pinguo* (caramelized apples). Staff should be able to track down their one basic English menu.

Next to the Hongqi Hotel in the railway station square. ✆ **0352/281-7222.** Meal for 2 ¥40–¥60. No credit cards. 10am–2pm and 5–10pm.

Yonghe Food City (Yonghe Meishicheng) ★ CHINESE Another opulent dining option on Yingbin Lu, three-story Yonghe Food City offers a host of regional favorites including green onion pancakes and carrot and mutton dumplings, along with a smattering of specialties from around the country. For the adventurous, you can try sea cucumber (¥118), escargot (¥28), and Bird's Nest Soup (¥128), or for spice lovers, Sichuan dishes include *yuxiang rousi* (fish-flavored pork) and *gongbao rouding* (diced pork with chili and peanuts).

South side of Yingbin Dong Lu, just east of Nan Guan Nan Jie. ✆ **0352/510-0333.** Reservations recommended. Meal for 2 from ¥80. No credit cards. 11:30am–2pm and 6–9pm.

HOHHOT 呼和浩特 ★

Inner Mongolia, 410km (255 miles) W of Beijing

By Chinese standards, Hohhot, the capital of Inner Mongolia Autonomous Region, has a short history. In 1557, when the Mongolian prince, Altan Khan, ordered the construction of a large Tibetan-Buddhist complex, he had his own agenda. (In a historical twist, his workforce was made up of captured Han Chinese artisans and Han peasants forced into labor.) Completion of such a complex would legitimize his rule over the southern Mongolian tribes and secure the recognition of the Ming Empire. By 1579, Da Zhao Temple, which still survives, was completed, and by 1590 the town of Hohhot (in Mandarin Huhehaote, or simply Hu Shi) had sprung up around it.

From the beginning, the city was both Mongolian and Han Chinese, and though the ratio has fluctuated wildly over 4 centuries, the population has always been culturally mixed. In the 19th century, the Hui (Chinese Muslims) became the third-largest ethnic group in the city. Population claims are rarely reliable when they're about China, but it's said that currently for every Mongolian in Hohhot, there are 9 Han Chinese. Inner Mongolia's economy is booming, even by Chinese standards, and as the capital of the province, Hohhot is at the heart of the action. This means better

HOTELS
Bāyántălā Fàndiàn 8
巴彦塔拉饭店
Holiday Inn Hotel 11
(Hūhéhàotè Jiàri Jiŭdiàn)
呼和浩特假日酒店
Inner Mongolia Hotel 6
(Nèiménggŭ Fàndiàn)
内蒙古饭店
Jinjiang Inn 4
(Jĭn Jiāng Zhī Xīng Lŭguǎn)
锦江之星旅馆
Shangri-La Hotel & Shang Palace Restaurant 9
(Xiāng Gē Lĭ Lă)
香格里拉
Xīnchéng Bīnguǎn 5
新城宾馆
RESTAURANTS
Bàn Mŭ Dì Yóumiàn Dàwáng 10
半亩地莜面大王
Bā Yán Dē Lē Haí 2
巴彦德乐海
Ménggŭ Dayin 1
赛马场蒙古大营
Shang Palace 9
香宫
Warm 6
暖
Yōng Bū Lākàng Zháng Cǎn Bā 7
雍卜拉康藏餐吧
ATTRACTIONS
Dà Zhāo Monastery 14
(Dà Zhāo Sì)
大昭寺
Great Mosque 12
(Qīngzhēn Dà Sì)
清真大寺
Inner Mongolia Museum 3
(Nèiměnggŭ Bówùguǎn)
内蒙古博物馆
Wŭtă Sì 15
五塔寺
Xílìtú Zhāo 13
席力图召
Horse Track
Hulun Beier Bei Lu
Rail Station
Bus Station
0 1/2 mi
0 0.5 km
Xilin Guole Bei Lu
Xinhua Dajie
Xincheng Nan Jie
Tongdao Bei Jie
Tongdao Nan Jie
Zhongshan Dong Lu
Hulun Beier Nan Lu
Wulan Chabu Xi Lu
Minzu Shangchang (Department Store)
Xilin Guole Nan Lu
Zhongshan Xi Lu
Daxue Dong Lu
Daxue Xi Lu
Gongyuan Nan Lu
Tongshun Dong Jie
Hohhot
INNER MONGOLIA
Beijing
China
Bank
Mosque
Museum
Post Office
Temple
Travel Agent

employment prospects, infrastructure, hotels and restaurants, which has given rise to a wave of new residents from elsewhere in China. Mongolians though, often feel left out of the changing picture, and as in other Han-controlled outposts around the country, tension is mounting. The situation was brought to a head when a Mongolian herder was hit and killed by a Han truck driver in the grasslands in May 2011. Following protests in the capital, the government employed the same control techniques as in Tibet and Xinjiang: The army moved in, students were locked down, and Internet was censored. The truck driver was sentenced to death, and peaceful co-existence has been re-established, but in the face of increasing Han migration, and the day-by-day dilution of Mongolian culture, the road ahead looks uncertain at best.

Essentials

GETTING THERE The **airport** is 16km (10 miles) east of town. A taxi into town costs about ¥30. Locals negotiate the price in advance and don't use the meter. The CAAC (Zhongguo Minhang) shuttle (¥5) meets flights and heads to **Inner Mongolia Airport's main ticket office** (✆ **0471/693-4005;** daily 8am–6pm) on Xilinguole Lu just south of Wulanqiate Xi Jie. **Air China** (✆ **0471/461-3319**) is next door. Direct daily flights to and from many major cities in China include Beijing, Shanghai, and Chengdu. Hohhot is also linked to Guangzhou by three weekly flights. **Aero Mongolia** (www.aeromongolia.mn) and Tianjin Airlines each operate three-times-weekly flights to Ulaan Baatar for ¥1,652. In order to purchase a ticket you'll need a Mongolian visa (p. 217), although U.S. citizens can enter Mongolia for 90 days without a visa.

The **old railway station** is in the north part of town and serves destinations to the west. Useful services include the K43 link with Lanzhou (17 hr.), which leaves at 10:41pm and also stops at Yinchuan (8 hr.). Trains for eastern destinations (including Datong and Beijing) leave from the brand new Hohhot East station, a ¥25 taxi ride from the city center. Of the many trains linking Hohhot with Beijing, the K264 (10 hr.) at 10:23pm is one of the most convenient. Datong (4 hr.) is also on this line and is served by numerous services including T284 at 12:14pm. Tickets can be bought in advance at all windows, but sleepers are often in short supply. Try agents in hotels for these.

The **Long-Distance Bus Station** (✆ **0471/696-5969**) is immediately west of the old railway station. Hourly buses go to Beijing (7 hr.; ¥150) and Datong (4 hr.; ¥70). Yinchuan is served by one bus daily at 9:30am (10 hr.; ¥155). To get to the grasslands, Xilamuren is served by hourly buses (2 hr.; ¥21) from 6:55am.

GETTING AROUND **Bus** fare is ¥1; **minibus** fare is ¥1.50. The **taxi** rate for the first 2km (1¼ miles) is ¥7; after that, it's ¥1.30 per kilometer.

TOURS The helpful **CITS** office on the third floor of Yishuting Nan Jie 95 (✆ **0471/620-1602;** Mon–Fri 8am–6pm) can arrange a variety of tours to different areas of the grasslands and desert dunes with an English-speaking guide (from ¥150). Most hotels have tour desks that can book grassland and desert trips; most are guided in Chinese only, but the Bayantala Hotel's desk offers trips in English.

FESTIVAL & SPECIAL EVENTS Da Zhao has more than a dozen temple festivals. Among the best are **Songjing Da Fahui** (8th–15th days of the first and sixth lunar months), 8 days of prayer and chanting sutras; **Songbalin** (14th day of the first and sixth lunar months), a morning spent exorcising demons—chanting, performing ritual dance, burning of demon effigy; **Liang Dafo** (15th day of the first and sixth lunar months), which begins with the Sunning of the Maitreya *thangka* (a giant image of the Future Buddha hung in the courtyard to air and be admired), and is followed by prayer, chanting, ceremonial dance and music, circumambulation, and alms-giving; and **Mani Hui** (14th–17th days of the eighth lunar month), Da Zhao's most solemn festival of the year, 3 days and nights of continuous prayer for good fortune (at the end, visitors who give alms are rewarded with a packet of "sacred medicine," said to cure all manner of illness and disease).

The traditional sports festival, **Naadam,** which features wrestling, horse and camel racing, and archery, occurs when and if the grasslands turn green. That's usually mid-August, but it can be as early as July. Last-minute cancellations aren't uncommon. Check with CITS for details. Note that the dates don't coincide with (the People's Republic of) Mongolia's Naadam festival, which is tied to their National Day and always occurs from July 11 to July 13.

[FastFACTS] HOHHOT

Banks, Foreign Exchange & ATMs Two branches of **Bank of China** that have full-service foreign-exchange counters and 24-hour ATM access are at Xincheng Nan Jie (a block south of the Xinhua Dajie intersection); and on the south side of Xinhua Dajie between Xilinguole Bei Lu and Yingbin Nan Lu. Hours are 8:30am to 5:30pm. An ATM is in the lobby of the Guohang Dasha hotel.

Consulates The **Mongolian Consulate (Menggu Lingshiguan; ✆ 0471/490-2325)** issues 30-day tourist visas at Dongying Nanjie 5. Visa service is available Monday, Tuesday, and Thursday from 8:30am to 12:30pm. Two photographs and a letter of invitation (available from travel agents) are required. The next-day fee is ¥495; regular processing takes 3 days and costs ¥270. For a surcharge this process can be arranged for you by CITS. U.S. citizens can enter Mongolia for up to 90 days without a visa.

Internet Access A huge 24-hour Internet room is on the second floor of the bus station. Access costs ¥4 per hour.

Post Office The main branch of the post office is east of the railway station (8am–5:30pm). Other branches are on Zhongshan Dong Lu and Xinhua Dajie.

Visa Extensions The **PSB (Gonganju; ✆ 0471/669-9053)** is on Dong Erhuan Tongfei Dadao. Opening hours are Monday to Friday 8am to noon and 2:30 to 5:30pm.

Exploring In & Around Hohhot

Da Zhao Si Once at the heart of old Hohhot, this temple is now surrounded by a modern imitation of itself, *sans* residents, and while this takes away from the flavor of the neighborhood, this vast temple is still worthy of a visit. It's said that at one time this 6th-century temple had over 400 lamas in residence. Later, the Qing government (1644–1911) decreed that no more than 80 could live in Hohhot's earliest Tibetan temple. Today Da Zhao houses 16 students from all over Inner Mongolia and only about 50 monks, but it is still an active center of Buddhist worship. Unlike Beijing's famed lamasery, Yonghe Gong, Da Zhao looks and feels much more like the monasteries of Tibet, but with Chinese characteristics. Instead of offerings of *tsampa* (roasted barley), devotees leave mounds of uncooked rice; and the pervading smell is of incense rather than rancid yak butter. But as in Lhasa, worshipers here drape their favorite Buddhas and bodhisattvas with shiny white ceremonial *khata* scarves. As you make your way through the complex, look for Da Zhao's three most prized holdings:

the 400-year-old Silver Buddha; in front of it, a pair of vivid golden dragons coiled around two floor-to-ceiling pillars; and exquisite Ming wall murals (in their original paint) depicting stories from Buddhist lore. Go all the way to the back of the complex to find a library full of antique sutras wrapped in orange and yellow cloth. Peek into the less-visited side chambers, too, where you're likely to find a lone lama chanting and playing Tibetan cymbals or a devotee kowtowing in the half-dark.

Tongshun Dong Jie, just off Da Nan Jie. Admission ¥30. 8:30am–6:30pm.

Neimenggu Bowuguan (Inner Mongolia Museum) ★★ ☺ Hohhot's huge museum presents an incredible variety of exhibits that range from space rockets and dinosaurs to traditional costume and archeological finds. One of the main draws, especially for kids, is the extensive display of dinosaur remains found within the region; the enormous wooly mammoth, adult protoceratops, and iguanodon skeletons are particularly impressive. Kids will also enjoy the collection of spacecraft on the ground floor; Inner Mongolia is China's Cape Canaveral, and it was from Dongfeng Space City that China's first satellite, Long March I, was launched in 1970, along with more recent projects including Shenzhou V, China's first manned space flight in 2003. The remaining exhibit halls are a little more conventional, but none the less worthwhile, and include fascinating displays of Mongolian folk customs, much of which revolve around their famous horsemanship. Not to be missed are the graceful gold Xianbei belt buckles, to which a 4th-century poet compared a maiden's "exquisite neck." Also of note are sets of pottery figures from a nearby Northern Wei tomb. Among them is a pair of troll-faced pottery tomb-guardians, and eight pottery figurines of a musical troupe and a dancer who look more like a mime troupe, their wooden instruments having long ago disintegrated. After seeing this collection, you may never think of ancient Mongols, Huns, or Tartars in terms of "hordes" again.

Xinhua Dong Dajie. Free admission. Tues–Sun 9am–5:30pm (last ticket 4pm). Bus: 3 or 29.

Qingzhen Da Si (Great Mosque) As beautiful as this 360-year-old mosque is, it has yet to become a standard tourist sight. Typically, a few seniors are chatting and passing time in the courtyard. The buildings include the prayer hall with a beautiful ceiling painted with pink flowers; the teaching hall; and a 15m-tall (49-ft.) wooden pavilion (a Chinese version of the minaret). (***Note:*** A sign in Chinese at the mosque's entrance requests no shorts, short skirts, smoking, or loud talking.) The back exit leads through a small street lined with food stalls.

Tongdao Jie (near Zhongshan Xi Lu intersection). Free admission. 10am–4pm. Bus: 3, 19, or 21 to Tongdao Jie and Zhongshan Xi Lu intersection.

Wuta Si This rare Indian-style five-pagoda Buddhist temple is one of only six *jingang baozuo* (diamond throne pagodas) in China. Built between 1727 and 1732, it was quite likely modeled after Beijing's Wuta Si, constructed 300 years earlier. Like that one, Hohhot's Wuta Si is the only remaining structure of a much larger temple complex that fell into disrepair. Notable features are the 1,561 stone-carved images of Buddha that cover the middle and top portions of the temple; the graceful bas-relief images of bodhisattvas, bodhi trees, and sacred creatures gracing the base of the temple; and the astronomical map on the back wall purported to be the only one of its vintage written in Mongolian script. Carved in stone, it depicts the 24 seasonal periods of the lunar year, 28 planets, some 270 constellations, over 1,550 stars, and the 12 astrological divisions. Climb to the top of the temple for a view of this rapidly changing neighborhood.

Wuta Si Hou Jie. Admission ¥30. 8am–6pm.

Xilitu Zhao Si Like Da Zhao, this Buddhist temple was constructed during the Wanli reign (1572–1620) of the Ming dynasty and remains active, with 16 monks in residence. Razed by fire in the 19th century, it was rebuilt only to be damaged during the Cultural Revolution (1966–76). Its latest humiliation is the transformation of its front buildings into souvenir shops. However, a short distance into the complex, it starts feeling more like a temple than a tourist spot. One highlight is the Buddhist ornaments crowning the central hall. In front is the Wheel of Dharma flanked by two deer, representing the Buddha's first turning of the dharma wheel in the Deer Park at Sarnath in India. Behind the wheel are two victory banners and a jeweled trident symbolizing the Three Buddhas (past, present, and future) and the Three Jewels (the Buddha, the doctrine, and the monastic community; or body, speech, and mind). Inside the main building is a typical Tibetan prayer hall with cylindrical banners that hang from the ceiling, a white elephant (identified with the Buddha), and sutras lining the walls. On the first day of each lunar month, from 9am to noon, the monks can be heard (and viewed) chanting sutras in the main hall.

Da Nan Jie, across from Da Zhao Si. Admission ¥35. 8am–6:30pm.

Three Ways to the Grasslands

BY BUS Hourly buses head for Xilamuren Da Caoyuan from the bus station. For a day trip, take the 6:55am bus and return on the last bus around 3pm (check on the exact time before leaving). The drive takes about 2 hours—much of it through the scrub, wild grass, and cultivated forests that carpet the Da Qing Mountain range. About 65km (40 miles) out of Hohhot, the bus makes a 10-minute stop in the small town of Wuchuan. Before leaving Wuchuan, let the driver know you wish to get off at **Luyou Dujiacun (Traveler's Holiday Village),** which is about 30km (19 miles) from Wuchuan. A set of tourist *ger* (the Mongolian word for the circular felt tents known in central Asia as yurts, or *menggu bao* in Chinese) are visible across the street about 300m (1,000 ft.) away. Mr. Bao, who operates these with his wife, has horses, and though he's not inclined to let you ride off on your own, he and his yellow dog are affable riding companions. (When the mood strikes, he breaks into song—anything from Mongolian folk to "The East Is Red.") With an hour, he can take you to a famous *oboo* (stone memorial) in the area. More time allows you to ride deeper into the grasslands and visit a herdsman's family living in a real *ger* rather than one for tourists. The going rate is ¥50 per hour. The Bao family can also prepare a delicious Mongolian lunch (even vegetarian, if requested), which will include Mongolian milk tea and the homemade snacks that go with it. You may get *shouba rou* (hand-held meat)—mutton on the bone, eaten with the hands. The return bus passes the spot by the roadside where you were dropped off in the morning.

BY TAXI If you balk at taking a crowded, smoke-filled rattletrap with no air-conditioning, opt for a private taxi. Drivers are at the ready at the bus and railway stations. Prices can vary drastically, so ask around and compare. (This will amount to you and the driver pushing a calculator back and forth at each other.) Round-trip fare should be around ¥300, but you'll want to be certain the driver is taking you to a set of *ger* where you'll be able to ride horses and get a Mongolian meal.

BY TOUR One-day tours are available from city hotels and travel agents. Most go to Xilamuren Da Caoyuan and tours start at ¥100 per person. Tours normally include a visit to a herding family, performance of Mongolian song and dance, and a wrestling demonstration. Unless you speak Mandarin, **CITS** on the third floor of Yishuting

Nan Jie 95 (✆ **0471/620-1602**) is the most reliable way to go, although not the cheapest, with tours starting at ¥180 per person. The travel office in the Bayantala Hotel can also arrange trips to Xilamuren guided in English. For something fractionally less touristy you could ask CITS about trips to Gegentala, which translates as "beautiful grasslands," and is only a little further than Xilamuren.

Shopping

The third floor of **Minzu Shangchang (Mongolian Minority Department Store)** on Zhongshan Xi Lu has a great selection of traditional Mongolian items including carpets, knives, and costumes (also available in kids sizes). More modern shopping options include the nearby **Wanda** and **Wangfujing** shopping centers. For travel snacks, **Spar** supermarket in the Victory Plaza shopping center has just about anything you could want. Be prepared to check your bag. It's located on the southwest corner of the intersection of Xinhua Dajie and Hinggan Nan Jie.

Where to Stay

Hohhot's hotel scene is developing quickly, and new options have opened in all categories. The Shangri-La is the most striking addition to Hohhot's hotels, but a league of new business hotels have also joined the fold and, at the other end of the scale, plenty of cheapies are still near the train station where you can get a passable room with en-suite for around ¥150.

VERY EXPENSIVE

Neimenggu Fandian (Inner Mongolia Hotel) ★ The Neimenggu was entirely rebuilt to five-star standards in 2001. Although it lacks the spacious grounds of the Xincheng around the corner, a public park is across the street and its rooms now far surpass those of its competitor. In addition to having all the trappings of an international hotel (including a sweeping lobby staircase), it has some of the best non-Chinese cuisine in the province, served in three of Hohhot's handsomest restaurants. Guest rooms and bathrooms are spacious and attractive and service is excellent. If you're on a budget and can put up without a window then the economy rooms, which are otherwise the same as the plush ¥960 rooms, are worth considering, and give access to all of the hotel's facilities.

Wulanchabu Xi Lu (east of Hulunbei'er Nan Lu). www.nmghotel.com. ✆ **0471/693-8888.** Fax 0471/695-2288. 343 units. ¥960 standard room; from ¥1,600 suite; economy room ¥360. AE, MC, V. Bus: 72 from the railway station to Wulan Chabu Xi Lu. **Amenities:** 4 restaurants; bar; forex; health club; Jacuzzi; large indoor pool; room service; sauna. *In room:* A/C, satellite TV w/pay movies, fridge, hair dryer, Internet, minibar.

Shangri-La ★★ Hohhot's only international five-star, the gleaming edifice of the Shangri-La, offers first class rooms, state-of-the-art facilities, and excellent service. What's more the hotel enjoys a prime location in the center of town and prices are very reasonable. Rooms are spacious, well-designed, super-comfortable and enjoy good views over the city, particularly those on higher floors. Rooms on the Horizon Club floors (19–23) are worth the extra investment and include use of the club lounge, afternoon cocktails, and late checkout. Some of the city's best dining is also to be found at the Shangri-La.

Xilinguole Nan Lu 5. www.shangri-la.com. ✆ **0471/336-6888.** Fax 0471/336-6666. 375 units. ¥848 deluxe room; from ¥1,488 suite. AE, MC, V. **Amenities:** 2 restaurants; bar; forex; health club; Jacuzzi; large indoor pool; room service; sauna. *In room:* A/C, DVD player, satellite TV, fridge, hair dryer, Internet, minibar.

EXPENSIVE

Huhehaote Jiari Jiudian (Holiday Inn Hohhot) ★ Rates at the city's first four-star hotel have dropped in light of new competition that makes the Holiday Inn a great deal. Rooms are spacious and comfortable, but the executive eighth and ninth floors are particularly good and include a free nightly snack buffet in the executive lounge. The hotel is within walking distance of Hohhot's shopping and commercial areas and the temples in the south of the city are also close at hand.

Zhongshan Xi Lu 185. www.holidayinn.com. ✆ **0471/635-1888.** Fax 0471/635-0888. 197 units. ¥580 standard room; from ¥1,270 suite. Rates do not include breakfast. AE, DC, MC, V. **Amenities:** 3 restaurants; ATM; health center w/sauna and whirlpool. *In room:* A/C, satellite TV, fridge, hair dryer, Internet.

Xincheng Binguan ★ ☺ The grounds of this hotel and garden complex in the heart of the city cover 119,000 sq. m (1,280,904 sq. ft.) and include a lake, a park, a large sports complex, and a set of *ger* tents. Originally built in 1958, the Xincheng underwent a 2001 renovation that produced Hohhot's first five-star hotel. The standard rooms in the Xingbin building now seem dated, but newer, more expensive rooms in the Yingbin and Xingjun buildings are spacious and well-appointed. But rooms are only a part of the package here, and the Xincheng remains a decent place to take a break from traveling. If you have kids, send them off to swim, bowl, or play video games while you treat yourself to a massage. If you opt for a deluxe standard, ask for a room with a front view (overlooking gardens, a fountain, and, in the distance, a bustling avenue) in the renovated building A.

Hulunbei'er Nan Lu 40. www.xincheng-hotel.com.cn. ✆ **0471/666-1888.** Fax 0471/693-1141. 370 units. From ¥680 standard room; from ¥1,280 suite. AE, DC, MC, V. Bus: 37 from railway station. **Amenities:** 12 restaurants; bar; bike rental; billiards; bowling alley; forex; health club; large indoor pool; room service; sauna; squash court; indoor tennis courts; video arcade. *In room:* A/C, TV, fridge, hair dryer, Internet, minibar.

MODERATE

Bayantala Fandian The VIP Building in this hotel near Xinhua Guangchang offers well-maintained rooms with twin beds and small bathrooms although those on the street side are a little noisy. The VIP Building has a satellite branch of Beijing's most famous Peking Duck restaurant, Quanjude, and there are a host of other eateries to choose from on the premises. Though the "Main Building" is less charming, it too is clean, and offers standard twins and a range of economy rooms which do not have bathrooms.

Xilinguole Bei Lu 46 (btw Xinhua Dajie and Zhongshan Xi Lu). ✆ **0471/666-3002.** Fax 0471/696-7390. 173 units with bathroom in VIP Building; 218 economy units (with common bathroom) in Main Building. ¥480 standard room in VIP Building; ¥800 suite. Rates in VIP Building include breakfast. ¥360 standard room in Main Building; ¥70–¥90 economy room in Main Building. Up to 55% discount available (except for economy rooms). No credit cards. Bus: 34 from the railway station. **Amenities:** 7 restaurants. *In room:* A/C, TV, Internet (in VIP Building).

INEXPENSIVE

Jinjiang Inn (Jinjiang Zhixing Luguan) Part of a new chain of budget business hotels sweeping the nation, the Jinjiang offers clean, modern rooms decked out with cheap, functional furniture. Bathrooms are the only slight let-down; although clean and perfectly functional they are entirely made of plastic and look as if they've been stolen from a port-a-loo. The hotel's location is close to Ba Yan De Le Hai (below) restaurant and on the way out to the Inner Mongolia Museum in the west of town.

61 Xinhua Da Jie. www.jinjianginns.com. ✆ **0471/666-8111.** 274 units. ¥218 standard twin. MC, V. **Amenities:** Restaurant. *In room:* A/C, TV, Internet.

Where to Eat

Hohhot's varied and satisfying Mongolian cuisine offers a big change from the mainstream Chinese diet and is definitely worth sampling at least once. In addition to the Mongolian restaurants listed below, you'll find plenty of good street eats; tables are set up along Xilinguole Bei Lu near the junction with Zhongshan Lu on a summer's evening and sell beer and tasty kabobs. If you're really in need of a Western splurge then the daily buffets at the Shangri-La's **Xin Café** (second floor; ¥148), or the Nei Menggu Fandian's **Warm** (¥148), should comfortably sate your needs, or for Italian try **Buon Appetito** in the Holiday Inn. Cheaper Western options include the usual array of **McDonald's** and **KFC**s, along Zhongshan Xi Lu, where you'll also find a **Pizza Hut.**

Ban Mu Di Youmian Dawang ★★ MONGOLIAN Eating in this lively restaurant specializing in pastas and pancakes made of husked wheat will put you in a good mood. The decor is a mix of Mongolian *ger* and prettified farmhouse. The walls are brightly decorated with floral and folk designs. The waitresses, dressed in equally bright colors and busy patterns, are friendly and efficient. Best of all, the food is inexpensive and exceptionally tasty. Try house specialties like *wowo,* husked wheat pasta shaped by curling the dough around the little finger then pressed together in a bamboo steamer, forming what looks like honeycomb made of pasta. *Dundun*—husked-wheat pancakes filled with carrots, potato, and cabbage—are rolled up and sliced like Mediterranean Levant sandwiches.

Xilinguole Lu (just north of the Shangri-La). ✆ **0471/691-0168.** Reservations recommended. Meal for 2 under ¥60. No credit cards. 11:30am–2pm and 6–9:30pm.

Ba Yan De Le Hai ★★ MONGOLIAN This is a great place to tuck into meaty Mongolian specialties surrounded by traditionally dressed wait-staff and decor. Most famous for its barbecued *(kao)* beef *(niurou)* and lamb *(yangrou),* you'll also find a host of other regional delicacies and snacks here including *suan nai* (yoghurt) and *nai cha* (bitter milk tea without the potent yak butter smell and taste associated with the Tibetan variety). If there's a group of you, ask about dining in one of the four yurts at the rear of the property.

Xinhua Da Jie 75. ✆ **0471/493-6600.** Reservations recommended. Meal for 2 ¥100. No credit cards. 9am–2pm and 5–9:30pm.

Shang Palace ★★ CANTONESE Hong Kong chef Lee Chiu Hung prepares a feast of Cantonese culinary masterpieces at this most opulent of Hohhot's dining establishments. House signature dishes include Double-boiled Aged Chicken Soup with Cordyceps (which tastes far better than it sounds) and foie gras with raspberry. There are also a host of other choices from across the country, including Sichuan dishes and a contemporary take on Mongolian cuisine, best of which is the Boiled Grass-fed Lamb in Broth with Mongolian Spices and Herbs. If you've got a hungry group of 20 or so friends you could even try and work your way through a whole roast lamb, Genghis Khan style, although it doesn't come cheap at ¥2,588.

1st Floor Shangri-La, Xilinguole Nan Lu. ✆ **0471/336-6888.** Meal for 2 from ¥200. AE, MC, V. 11am–2:30pm and 6–10:30pm.

Yong Bu Lakang Zhang Can Ba ★ TIBETAN Beautifully decked out in Tibetan style, this small, homey restaurant offers a real change from both Chinese and Mongolian fare. The owners are from Aba in Tibet and their dishes are as genuine as you'll get outside of the TAR. As you'd expect yak features heavily on the menu; cold yak, yak soup, and yak pie are all well accompanied by a (pricey) Tibetan beer. If you want something other than yak then try another Tibetan staple, *tsampa* (roasted wheat or barley flour) or head for another restaurant!

Just down the alleyway that runs along the north side of the Bayantala Hotel on Xilinguole Bei Lu. It's the 1st restaurant on your left. ✆ **0471/693-6388.** Meal for 2 ¥60–¥80. No credit cards. 11am–2pm and 5–10:30pm.

Hohhot After Dark

Menggu Dayin Nightly shows at this famous restaurant offer an easy way to see Mongolian folk music and dance whilst enjoying hearty local fare from noodles to barbecued goat. Performances start at 9pm and last a couple of hours.

Saima Chang (Hohhot's horse-racing track). ✆ **0471/651-5858.** No credit cards. Restaurant: 9am–2:30pm and 5–11pm. Performance: 9-11pm. Bus: 13 or 24 north along Hulunbei'er Lu to the racetrack.

YINCHUAN 银川 ★

Ningxia Province, 1,369km (845 miles) W of Beijing, 723km (450 miles) NW of Xi'an

Compared to the other major cities in this chapter—particularly the dirty duo of Datong and Taiyuan—Yinchuan is a breath of fresh air. Capital of the Ningxia Hui Autonomous Region, it has a population of around a million, and it has escaped the extreme poverty associated with this province by having the good fortune to be hydrated by the Yellow River and an irrigation system first built during the Han dynasty. Nearly a quarter of the region's population is Hui (Chinese Muslims), and a significant percentage live in the capital, adding a cultural diversity less apparent in other Chinese capitals. This is an easy town to settle down in for a few days. Hotel rates aren't exorbitant, the food is good, the weather is great and most of the sights are within walking distance or easy to get to by bus or taxi.

The best time to visit is between May and October. Though summer temperatures can soar, the dry climate makes even the hottest days bearable. ***Note:*** Yinchuan holds its annual Motorcycle Tourism Festival for a week in September (check with CITS for exact dates). The emphasis is on tourism, so unless you're prepared for throngs of unregenerate cap-wearing tourists and dancers in go-go boots performing the "songs and dances of the Western Xia," it may be a good time to stay away.

Essentials

GETTING THERE Direct **flights** from major cities include Beijing, Shanghai, Chengdu, Guangzhou, Taiyuan, and Xi'an. Discounts are usually available. The **CAAC** office (✆ **0951/691-3456**) is on Changcheng Dong Lu. Buses for **Hedong Airport** (30 min.; ¥15) leave from the intersection of Nanhuan Dong Lu and Bei Jie, south of Nan Men, 2 hours before flights. A taxi into town costs about ¥80.

The **railway station** is in the new part of town, but there's a booking and ticket office just south of the Drum Tower at Gongnong Xiang 15. Major connections are

THE (NEARLY) lost dynasty OF THE XI XIA

After Genghis Khan died in 1227 near the Xi Xia (Western Xia) capital of Zhongxing Fu (present-day Yinchuan), his corpse was carried in an ox-drawn chariot—the centerpiece of a grand procession that led back to the Mongolian steppe. En route, any person or beast in the procession's path was slaughtered—in offering to the Khan's spirit and to keep news of his death from spreading. As dour as it must have been, the escorting soldiers might have smiled to themselves in the knowledge they were returning home victorious—having once and for all defeated the Xi Xia (Western Xia) dynasty (1038–1227), which had lasted almost 200 years.

Today the Xi Xia is somewhat of a mystery. Until recently it wasn't recognized as a legitimate dynasty by the Chinese, so there is no official history of the empire or its people, the Tangut; and Xi Xia documents—written in a system fashioned after but different from Chinese—have been difficult to decipher. It's known that the ancient Tangut nomads came from what is now Sichuan, Qinghai, and Tibet. By the Tang dynasty (618–907), they had a leader and were one of the major players (along with the Khitan and Jurchen) in the ongoing struggle for territory. By the early 11th century they had defeated the Song imperial army, declared an independent empire, and extracted an annual tribute of tea, cloth, silk, and silver from the Song empire. Almost a century later, the Xia's alliance with the Jin (the Jurchen state) ignited the wrath of Genghis Khan, who personally led his troops south to destroy the "Great Xia," as they called themselves. At its height, the Xi Xia Empire controlled much of what is now Qinghai, Gansu, Ningxia, and Inner Mongolia. This obscure Buddhist state left behind imperial mausoleums, religious monuments, its own written language, and cultural relics that reveal a passion for Buddhist art, fine pottery, sculpture, and exquisite gold and silver artifacts. Much of what remains can be seen at the new Ningxia Museum.

with Beijing (T275; 13 hr.) and Xi'an (K1087; 14 hr.). Trains connecting Hohhot and Lanzhou stop in Yinchuan (2636; 9 hr.).

The new **Nanmen Zhan long-distance bus station** (**✆ 0951/789-9633**) is in the new city, reachable by bus numbers 1, 19, 23 and 101, or a 20-minute taxi ride from the old city. Xi'an (720km/447 miles; 9 hr.; ¥169) is served by express buses that leave hourly from 7:30am to 8:30pm. Lanzhou buses leave every 45 minutes (514km/320 miles; 6 hr.; ¥120). Two buses connect with Taiyuan (763km/474 miles; 10 hr.; ¥205) at 11:40am and 7:30pm; five express buses connect with Yan'an (449km/279 miles; 6 hr.; ¥143). Tickets can be bought up to 3 days in advance at the bus station.

GETTING AROUND Yinchuan has a new city (as of the 1960s) and an old city, and the distance between them is rapidly being filled with vast new developments, including the grand Ningxia Museum. The railway station is in the new city, but everything else the traveler would need or want is in the much more charming old city 10km (6 miles) to the east. **Taxis** wait in the parking lot at the railway station to transport passengers to the old city (around ¥20). **Bus** no. 1 goes from the railway station to Nanmen via Jiefang Jie, which runs east to west through the center of the old city; the fare is ¥3. Bus fare within the old city is ¥1. Taxi rates are ¥5 for the first

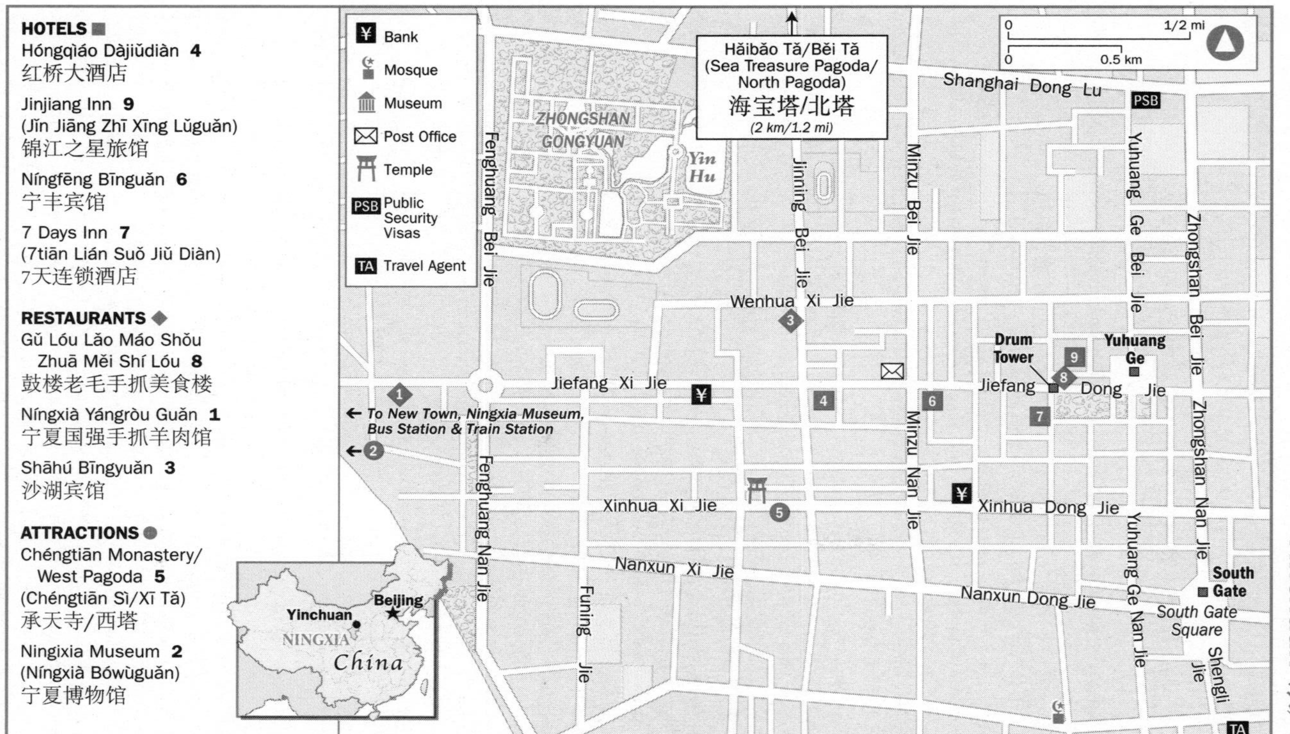
HOTELS ■
Hóngqìáo Dàjiǔdiàn 4
红桥大酒店
Jinjiang Inn 9
(Jǐn Jiāng Zhī Xīng Lǚguǎn)
锦江之星旅馆
Níngfēng Bīnguǎn 6
宁丰宾馆
7 Days Inn 7
(7tiān Lián Suǒ Jiǔ Diàn)
7天连锁酒店
RESTAURANTS ◆
Gǔ Lóu Lǎo Máo Shǒu Zhuā Měi Shí Lóu 8
鼓楼老毛手抓美食楼
Níngxià Yángròu Guǎn 1
宁夏国强手抓羊肉馆
Shāhú Bīngyuǎn 3
沙湖宾馆
ATTRACTIONS ●
Chéngtiān Monastery/West Pagoda 5
(Chéngtiān Sì/Xī Tǎ)
承天寺/西塔
Ningixia Museum 2
(Níngxià Bówùguǎn)
宁夏博物馆
Bank
Mosque
Museum
Post Office
Temple
PSB Public Security Visas
TA Travel Agent
Hǎibǎo Tǎ/Běi Tǎ
(Sea Treasure Pagoda/
North Pagoda)
海宝塔/北塔
(2 km/1.2 mi)
0 1/2 mi
0 0.5 km
ZHONGSHAN GONGYUAN
Yin Hu
Shanghai Dong Lu
Fenghuang Bei Jie
Fenghuang Nan Jie
Jinning Bei Jie
Minzu Bei Jie
Minzu Nan Jie
Yuhuang Ge Bei Jie
Yuhuang Ge Nan Jie
Zhongshan Bei Jie
Zhongshan Nan Jie
Wenhua Xi Jie
Jiefang Xi Jie
Jiefang Dong Jie
Xinhua Xi Jie
Xinhua Dong Jie
Nanxun Xi Jie
Nanxun Dong Jie
Funing Jie
Shengli Jie
Drum Tower
Yuhuang Ge
South Gate
South Gate Square
To New Town, Ningxia Museum, Bus Station & Train Station
Beijing
Yinchuan
NINGXIA
China

3km (2 miles), then between ¥1.20 and ¥1.40 per kilometer. Beyond 8km (5 miles), the rate is ¥1.50 per kilometer. Fares within the old town will rarely exceed ¥7.

TOURS Ningxia **CITS,** at Beijing Dong Lu 375 (© **0951/671-9792**), arranges pricey tours to nearby sites, Zhongwei, and Shapotou.

[FastFACTS] YINCHUAN

Banks, Foreign Exchange & ATMs The **Bank of China,** at Jiefang Xi Jie 80, has 24-hour ATMs. All windows can change traveler's checks and foreign currency. Other useful branches with ATMs are at Xinhua Xi Jie 69, and Xinhua Dong Jie 43. Bank hours are Monday through Friday from 8:30am to 5:30pm in winter, and until 6pm in summer.

Internet Access Several Internet cafes are on Yuhuang Ge Nan Jie, including **Hongma Wangba,** just south of the Nanxun Dong Jie intersection. The cafe is open from 8:30am to 8:30pm and charges ¥2 to ¥3 per hour.

Post Office The main post office (8am–8pm) is on the northwest corner of the Jiefang Xi Jie and Minzu Bei Jie intersection.

Visa Extensions The Exit-Entry Office of the **PSB** is at Yuhuang Ge Bei Jie 203. It's open Monday through Friday from 8:30am to noon and 2:30 to 6:30pm. The official processing time is 3 to 5 days, but it's usually done overnight.

Exploring In & Around Yinchuan

As well as the attractions listed below the recently re-opened **Xi Ta (Western Pagoda;** ¥3, or ¥18 to climb the tower; 9am–5pm) is worth a wander for its pretty gardens and the views over town gained from the top.

Haibao Ta/Bei Ta (Sea Treasure Pagoda/North Pagoda) In a province that has more than its share of stately pagodas, Haibao Ta is one of the loveliest. Originally built in the 5th century, it was toppled by the 1739 earthquake and rebuilt in the original style some 30 years later. Restored since then, it has retained its distinctive cross-shaped ground plan that adds depth and complexity to the four-sided tower. Its rare peach-shaped steeple of glazed green tiles is one of only two—the other crowns Chengtian Temple's West Pagoda. After a visit take a stroll through the recently completed Haibao Park, which has lakeside paths extending all the way to Shanghai Lu.

3km (1¾ miles) north of the old town center along Jinning Bei Jie. Admission ¥10. 8am–5pm. No public bus. Taxi from old city ¥5.

Najiahu Qingzhensi (Na Family Mosque) A good time to visit this 490-year-old wooden mosque is morning, as the town begins to stir. From the three-storied entrance gate, you can look east over the flat-topped brick houses and into small yards and alleys. The population of greater Yongning (which is a half-hour drive south of Yinchuan) is about 80% Hui, while this old village that immediately surrounds the mosque is 100% Hui—that being one of the requisites of residing in this well-preserved section of town. To this day a majority of residents are part of the Na family after which the mosque was named. According to the caretaker, the mosque escaped the destruction of the Cultural Revolution because the tightly knit community kept constant watch over it and refused entrance to the Red Guards. These days, visitors are invited into the pretty and peaceful courtyard. If you come alone or with only a few people, the caretaker may also let you into the prayer hall.

23km (14 miles) from Yinchuan in the town of Yongning, at Guo Dao 109. Admission ¥30. 6am–noon and 1:30–4pm. Bus: green no. 9 opposite Nan Men to Yongning; you'll be dropped at the Xinzhaizi Lukou (Xinzhaizi intersection). Walk west about 300m (1,000 ft.). You'll cross a small timber bridge. Look for the mosque on your left. Taxis charge around ¥80–¥100 for the round-trip, including waiting time.

Ningxia Museum ★ Yinchuan's state-of-the-art new museum highlights Ningxia's importance as a gateway between China and its peripheral territories and their communities, ranging from the so-called barbarians to the north to Silk Road traders like the Sogdians. Most importantly it sheds some light on the near mythical Xi Xia dynasty (p. 224) and the Hui people. The edifice itself follows the big, bold, and beige format of China's other recently constructed museums and Yinchuan's 30,000 or so years of history are told on three levels set around a grand central atrium. The story starts on the ground floor with an interesting display of prehistoric cave-art from the region. It then continues on the second floor with the seemingly obligatory Paleolithic caveman models, and follows through the various dynasties, with an all-Chinese section on Communist China. But the main attraction of the museum is the section on the Xi Xia. Xi Xia artifacts have been discovered all over the province and beyond, and the pieces on display on the second floor illustrate the highly cultured nature of their society. Some of the most impressive pieces in the Xi Xia collection were discovered in a subterranean cellar when the Xinhua Department Store was being extended in 1986; the cache of treasures included an exquisite gold-gilded copper Buddha astride an elephant. Other items to seek out include fine gold cap ornaments, the muted tones of the Xi Xia's distinctive pottery, and Buddhist sutras found in caves in the Helan Mountains, some of which include translations from the Xia language into Han Chinese.

The Hui display begins on the second floor and includes a model of the Na Family Mosque (see below) as well as some fine Qing dynasty enamel and filigree work. While the mock-up Hui street on the third floor isn't a promising introduction to this level, and actual artifacts are scant here, the difference in the style of the porcelain and copperware is immediately obvious. The floor design echoes this difference, using Islamic alcoves and geometric patterns. The explanations about Hui culture and Islam are interesting if simplistic. Allow a couple of hours for a visit.

Renmin Guangchang Dongjie; 3 miles west of the old city. Free Admission. Tues–Sun 9am–5pm. Taxi from old city ¥10.

Qingtong Xia Yibailingba Ta (108 Dagobas) Little is known about the 108 dagobas that stand like bowling pins on the side of the Qingtong Gorge, near the Yellow River. In the Ming dynasty they were referred to as the "ancient pagodas" *(gu ta)* and their origin was already a mystery. Today scholars associate them with the Western Xia dynasty because other relics and remains from the Xia culture have been unearthed in the vicinity. Their shape—like a Buddhist alms bowl—is similar to that of the classic Tibetan stupa, supporting the accepted belief that Tibetan Buddhism thrived in this area during the Western Xia and Yuan dynasties. Extensive repairs were made to them in 1987, but the dagobas are unusual and worth the visit. On the way, consider stopping at the Najiahu Qingzhensi (see above).

82km (51 miles) south of Yinchuan, near Qingtong Xia Zhen. Admission ¥60. 7:30am–7pm. Bus: 153 to Qingtong Xia Zhen (not to be confused with Qingtong Xia Shi, where the bus may stop on the way). Minibuses wait at the drop-off point. The asking price will be higher if the minibus isn't full. Hard bargaining might get it down to ¥20. If the minibus is full, it should be considerably less. To walk from the drop-off junction, take the road to the right. Turn left at the hydroelectric plant; then continue toward the right until you reach the dam. (Signs in English point the way.) Cross the Yellow River by ferry (¥15), then hike up and over. Follow the trail to the dagobas. A taxi from Yinchuan and back, including road toll and parking, should be around ¥250 and take 90 min. one-way.

Xi Xia Wang Ling (Western Xia Tombs) As the tourism bureau develops this spot, it is fast acquiring a theme-park aura. But if you can forgive the modern "Spirit Way" (fashioned after the path to the Ming tombs), skip the cheesy reenactment scenes of Xia life in the "Art Hall," and ignore promoters' claims that these are "China's Pyramids," you'll be able to appreciate this intriguing site. The tombs of nine Xia kings are spread across a 5×11km (3×7-mile) area at the foot of the Helan Mountains. In the fashion of Tang imperial tombs, each of these was originally surrounded by a 1-hectare (2½-acre) mausoleum composed of eight different types of traditional buildings. While only ruins survive, all but one of the nine imperial tombs remain intact. Dotting the landscape, the eerie, mud-encased pyramids resemble giant termite mounds. A two-story museum contains most of the relics, such as compelling stone plinths carved to look like potbellied gnomes on their knees, eyes and foreheads bulging as if from the weight they bear.

38km (24 miles) west of Yinchuan on eastern slopes of Helan Mountains. Admission ¥60. 8am–7pm. Public buses leave from Nan Men. Taxi round-trip: negotiate for ¥100–¥150.

Shopping

The largest supermarket in town is the **Beijing Hualian Chaoshi** (9am–10pm) under Nan Men Square opposite the bus station. Another good basement supermarket can be found on the north side of Xinhua Dong Jie, just east of the Gulou Nan Jie intersection.

Where to Stay

Yinchuan has an evergrowing selection of hotels, notably the newly opened five-star Holiday Inn on Jiefang Xi Jie. Choices at the bottom end are more limited: Cheapies are by the train station in the new city although cleanliness is not a strong point, and it's only really worth staying here if you have an early train to catch. Aside from the Jinjiang Inn (see below), the best budget option in the old city is the **7 Days Inn** (✆ **0951/561-2888**), directional signs point off pedestrianized Gulou Nan Jie, where the cheapest doubles go for ¥137.

Hongqiao Dajiudian The Hongqiao remains a fair mid-range option, although room sizes vary, so ask to have a look at another if the first one you're shown looks small. Rooms are well maintained and carpets are clean (if a little worn) while mid-size bathrooms have combo tub/showers. The hotel isn't in the heart of the tourist area, but it's only a few blocks west of Gulou (the Drum Tower), which is the center of town. It's popular, and is especially busy on weekends.

Jiefang Xi Jie. ✆ **0951/691-8579.** Fax 0951/691-8788. 231 units. ¥478 standard room. Up to 45% discount. AE, DC, MC, V. Bus: 1 or 11 from railway station. **Amenities:** 2 restaurants; bar; forex; room service; ticketing. *In room:* A/C, TV, fridge, Internet, minibar.

Jinjiang Inn (Jinjiang Zhixing Luguan) ★ Part of the ever-growing Jinjiang chain, this brand-new branch offers modern, attractively decorated and furnished business-style rooms at great prices. The hotel is a stone's throw from many of the old city's attractions and has friendly, English-speaking staff. It's certainly worth spending the extra ¥10 for a standard B room, which gives you a larger room with sofa and bigger window.

Gulou Bei Jie 15. www.jinjianginns.com. ✆ **0951/602-9966.** Fax 0951/602-8252. 173 units. ¥189–¥199 standard room. MC, V. **Amenities:** Restaurant. *In room:* A/C, TV, Internet.

Ningfeng Binguan ★ This large, business-oriented hotel offers some of the best rooms in Yinchuan and enjoys a good location in the center of town within walking distance of many of the city's tourist sites. The recently renovated rooms are tastefully styled in muted tones and feature large flatscreen TVs, crisp white linen, modern bathrooms with separate toilet and shower cubicles, and bathrobes. Service is friendly.

Jiefang Dong Jie 6. www.ningfenghotel.com. ✆ **0951/609-0222.** Fax 0951/609-0202. 163 units. ¥688 standard room; from ¥988 suite. Up to 30% discount. AE, MC, V. Bus: 1 from railway station. **Amenities:** 3 restaurants; ticketing. *In room:* A/C, TV, fridge, Internet, minibar.

Where to Eat

You'll find opportunities to sample Hui food on almost every street corner, but for a really special local meal it's worth heading out to Ningxia Yangrou Guan on Jiefang Xi Jie. Closer to the center **Gulou Lao Mao Shouzhua Meishi Lou** on the northeast corner of the Drum Tower circle has similar fare, and delicious and filling stretched beef noodles *(niurou lamian)* can be found in the southeast corner of Nan Men Square. If you're in need of a Western fix, Dicos hamburger joints abound. All can be found on Xinhua Dong Jie by the intersection with Gulou Jie. For a change from the usual fast-food options, just south from here, **Domis Pizza,** in the basement of Dicos, has an all you can eat (in 90 min.) buffet for ¥50 that includes pizza, salad, drinks, desserts, and coffee.

Ningxia Yangrou Guan ★ HUI This large local restaurant at the west end of town is out-of-the-way but worth the trip. Over 100 well-trained staff ensure that the restaurant is spotless, service is swift, and most importantly, that the food is delicious. Try the *shouba rou* (hand-held mutton; ¥58 per jin), *liangfen* (cold noodles in vinegar sauce) or take your pick from the picture menu. If it's full, then Minzu Fanzhuang, next door, has a similar choice of Hui fare.

Jiefang Xi Jie 410. ✆ **0951/503-6220.** Meal for 2 ¥30–¥50. No credit cards. 9:30–11:30am and 4:30–9pm.

Shahu Binguan ★ CHINESE FAST FOOD By 7am customers are lined up at this restaurant's outdoor stand to buy *baozi* (stuffed steamed buns) for takeout. Generous portions of good, inexpensive food have turned this restaurant into the most popular breakfast spot in Yinchuan. According to one taxi driver, a ¥3 *baozi* at Shahu is one and a half times the size of a ¥3-*baozi* anywhere else. For very little money you can sample lots of local specialties; choose from among noodle dishes, savory pancakes, eight-treasure soups *(babao zhou)*—of which there are many kinds—and every sort of *baozi, jiaozi,* and *hezi* (steamed buns, Chinese ravioli, fried meat or vegetable pies). And there are many more choices for meat eaters and vegetarians alike. Customers pay food servers with coupons purchased in advance from the cashier. Unspent coupons can also be redeemed there.

Wenhua Xi Jie 22 (on the ground floor of the Shahu Hotel). ✆ **0951/501-2128.** Meal for 2 under ¥20. No credit cards. 6am–2pm and 5–9pm. Bus: 105.

YAN'AN 延安

Shaanxi Province, 371km (230 miles) N of Xi'an

For 10 years between 1937 and 1947, the dusty, desolate town of Yan'an in Shaanxi Province (spelled with two *a*'s to distinguish it from its neighbor, Shanxi) was the site from which the Chinese Communist Party consolidated power and spread revolution. It was here that Mao seized leadership of the party and formulated the theories that came to be known as "Mao Zedong Thought." As the Japanese took control of the eastern part of the country, intellectuals from all over China moved to impoverished Yan'an, eager to make their contribution and share in the collective experiment. Among them were the writer Ding Ling (who was chastised by Mao for her essay on International Women's Day—"Thoughts on March 8"—that pointed out gender inequities in Yan'an) and the Shanghai starlet Jiang Qing, who became Mao's third wife and, later, a key player in the Cultural Revolution.

Like Mao's birthplace of Shao Shan, Yan'an was a place of pilgrimage during the 1960s, and today is a major point for Chinese making Red Tours, or visiting revolutionary sites, but quite what The Great Helmsman would make of the town's recent headlong jump into capitalism is an interesting question. Nevertheless, the appeal of this part of Shaanxi is its very austerity—the cave dwellings, the dry terraced hills, and the yellow loess that covers it all. The "revolutionary sites" that have become such a part of the founding myth of the PRC will also draw anyone with an interest in modern Chinese history, and, Yan'an feels refreshingly undiscovered by foreign travelers. ***Note:*** Turn to chapter 16 for Chinese translations of key locations.

Essentials

GETTING THERE **Yan'an Airport** is 10km (6 miles) northeast of town. A shuttle bus to the town center costs ¥5 or taxis are ¥40. Yan'an is connected to Beijing by one daily flight, and Xi'an is served twice daily.

The Yan'an **railway station** is at the south end of town. Fast trains to Xi'an (Z53; 5:06am) take as little as 3 hours, while the Z54 that leaves at 10:34pm takes 10 hours to reach Beijing. You can buy tickets at the station, but it's easiest to proceed through the train ticket booking office in town, next to the Yan'an Tourist Hotel (Yan'an Luyou Dasha) on Zhongxin Jie.

Most buses arrive and depart from the **South Bus Station** (**✆ 0911/249-2777**) opposite the railway station, although some services leave from the **Dongguan Jie Station** (**✆ 0911/211-2531**). From Pingyao or Taiyuan, it's easiest to go to Xi'an first, then transfer to bus or train for Yan'an. From the South Bus Station services connect Xi'an and Yan'an throughout the day for the 4-hour journey and cost ¥91. One daily bus at 1:40pm connects Yan'an to Luoyang (16 hr.; ¥222) from the South Bus Station. For the 5-hour journey to Yinchuan (¥143), four services per day leave from the Dongguan Jie station.

GETTING AROUND Shaped like a Y, the city of Yan'an traces the Yan River as it forks to the east and west. The town is small by Chinese standards and easy to navigate on foot, since its commercial district is concentrated in a few blocks around Zhongxin Jie (Central St.) and Da Qiao Jie (Big Bridge St.). City **bus** rides cost ¥1. Rates for **taxis** are ¥6 for the first 3km (2 miles), then ¥1.40 per additional kilometer. Between 10pm and 7am, the first 3km (2 miles) are ¥7. Most destinations within the city are under ¥10.

TOURS CITS (© **0911/228-6488**) is at Da Jie 10. Hours are Monday through Friday from 8:30am to noon and 2 to 5:30pm.

[FastFACTS] YAN'AN

Banks, Foreign Exchange & ATMs The **Bank of China,** at Zhongxin Jie and Bei Guan Jie, changes cash and has an international ATM. Another convenient branch offers the same services next to the Yinhai Guoji Dajiudian. Both branches are open Monday through Friday from 8:30am to 5:30pm, and 9am to 4pm on weekends.

Internet Access A handy 24-hour Internet cafe is above the post office (the stairway is in between the post office itself and the China Postal Savings next door). **QQ Internet** is another central *wangba* and its second floor location in a building halfway along a market lane can be found by following the English "QQ" sign from Er Dao Jie. Both places charge ¥3 per hour. **King Coffee** (p. 233) has free Wi-Fi for customers.

Post Office The post office is on Zhongxin Jie, south of Yan'an Binguan. It's open 8am to 6pm.

Exploring In & Around Yan'an

Between 1936 and 1947 the Communists had four different bases in Yan'an, each of which comprised cave homes common to the area. Each site is actually very similar, featuring homes cut out of the side of the loess hills, and with a spartan air about them. The rooms are simple, with only basic comforts, such as a desk, chair, and *kang,* the coal-heated brick platform beds. Shops at each of the sites sell a variety of revolutionary kitsch. Admission fees for many of the sites have recently been reduced or even withdrawn. You can take public buses as listed to visit most of these sites, or a taxi can be hired to visit all five for about ¥100.

Bao Ta (Bao Pagoda) ★ Built in the Song dynasty and renovated in the 1950s, the 44m (144-ft.) Bao Pagoda, which can be seen from almost anywhere in the city, is a national symbol of China. Located on a hill on the southeast side of the Yan River and offering excellent views of the city and nearby countryside, the pagoda is attractively lit up at night giving a great backdrop to evening strolls along the river.

Bao Pagoda, seen from anywhere in the city, can be reached on foot from the downtown area within just a few minutes. Admission ¥65. 8am–6pm (to 5:30pm in winter).

Geming Jinianguan (Revolutionary Memorial Hall/Museum) While Mao lies under glass in Beijing, the trusty white steed that transported him through northern Shanxi in 1947 stands stuffed behind glass at this museum. According to the sign on the window, the horse, who was then living in the Beijing Zoo, one day turned in the direction of Zhong Nan Hai (where Mao was living at the time), neighed loudly, and went on to join Marx. Unfortunately, there is no English signage, so without a familiarity with the players, the photographs on display have little meaning. The museum houses an interesting collection of old weapons, many of them handmade and crude, personal effects, and military gear. Unless you have a deep knowledge of Communist Party history, the museum—established in 1950 as "a classroom for advancing patriotism, revolutionary tradition, and the Yan'an spirit"—shouldn't take more than a half-hour of your time.

Northwest of the city center along Zaoyuan Lu. Admission ¥5. 8am–6pm (to 5:30pm in winter). Bus: 1 or 3.

Wangjiaping Geming Jiuzhi (Former Revolutionary Headquarters at Wangjiaping) ★ A 5-minute walk south of Geming Jinianguan is the site of the general office of the Eighth Route Army and headquarters of the CCP Central Military Commission from 1937 to 1947. Mao, Zhu De, Zhou Enlai, and other top brass also lived here at various times. In March 1947, as the Kuomintang (KMT) army moved into northern Shanxi, the CCP abandoned Yan'an, and during the following 13 months of Nationalist government occupation, the Wangjiaping buildings were destroyed. Some years later, after the end of the civil war, they were restored according to the original layout and design. The simple mud dwellings and halls, with their low-pitched rooflines and arched doorways and windows that mimic the surrounding hills, are worthy of Frank Lloyd Wright in the way they blend with the natural environment.

Zaoyuan Lu. Admission ¥5. 8am–6pm (to 5:30pm in winter). Bus: 1 or 3.

Yangjialing Jiuzhi (Yangjialing Revolutionary Headquarters) The Communist pantheon of Mao, Zhu De, Zhou Enlai, and Liu Shaoqi all lived here at one time or another, but this was also the site of the famous Yan'an Forum on Literature and Art in May 1942. The forum, in which Mao argued that art and literature should serve the people, was to have a profound impact on the arts in China in the following decades. Visitors to Mao's room toss cigarettes onto the former leader's bed as a sign of respect.

Northwest of the Revolutionary Memorial Hall. Free admission. 8am–6pm (to 5:30pm in winter). Bus: 1 or 3.

Where to Stay

Yan'an has a reasonable choice of hotels, an expanding number of which are open to foreigners. If you're after something cheaper than those listed below, a few options are near the train and bus stations, and plenty of choices are along Er Dao Jie, including **Jinrong Binguan** (✆ **0911/288-5001**), which has passable twins for ¥180; and **Tianzi Shangwu Jiudian** (✆ **0911/211-0800**) with clean and modern, but cramped rooms for ¥190, or ¥220 with a computer in the room.

Yan'an Binguan Dignitaries such as Ho Chi Minh, Lee Kuan Yew, Zhou Enlai, and Jiang Zemin have stayed at this Soviet-style hotel, but until an upgrade in 2000, it had only three stars. While the rooms are now looking a little worn, and there's no hot water from the sink faucets in the spacious bathrooms, service has definitely moved up a gear. Gone are the days of old, when guests were subjected to suspicious glances from front-desk staff; instead reception is friendly and helpful, and the hotel even managed to win a provincial tourism award in 2005.

Zhongxin Jie 56. ✆ **0911/288-6688.** Fax 0911/211-4297. 193 units. ¥380 standard room; ¥880 suite. Most rates include breakfast. 10% service charge. No credit cards. Bus: 3, or 12 from railway station. **Amenities:** 2 restaurants; room service; ticketing. *In room:* A/C, TV, fridge, Internet.

Yasheng Dajiudian A welcoming, efficient staff and bustling lobby make this three-star hotel instantly seem inviting. However, hallways are dim and rather cavernous, and the smallish guest rooms are past their best, particularly given the price tag. The hotel's location in the center of town and close to restaurants and food stalls is about its only plus point—stay here only if the other listings are all full.

Er Dao Jie, Zhong Duan. ✆ **0911/2666-000.** Fax 0911/2666-2222. 189 units. ¥328 standard room. 15% discount available. No credit cards. **Amenities:** 2 restaurants; room service; ticketing. *In room:* A/C, TV.

Yinhai Guoji Dajiudian (Silver Seas International Hotel) ★ The city's best hotel is holding its own, and good discounts and service make it as popular as ever. Bathrooms are a little cramped for the price, but rooms are comfortable and hotel facilities are good. Ask for one of the newly renovated rooms on the seventh floor, which cost the same as the older rooms.

Da Qiao Jie. ✆ **0911/213-9999.** Fax 0911/213-9666. 228 units. ¥688–¥738 superior and deluxe rooms. Up to 55% discounts. No credit cards. **Amenities:** 2 restaurants; health club; indoor pool; room service; ticketing. *In room:* A/C, TV, fridge, Internet.

Where to Eat

One of the best areas to find good, inexpensive dishes is at the junction of Er Dao Jie and Zhongxin Jie, where streetstalls set up every evening selling everything from hotpots to dumplings, *yangrouchuan, yangrou pao mo* (mutton soup), and pasta, including *daoxiao mian*—knife-pared noodles—made by paring slices off a block of pasta dough into a large pot of boiling water. Supposedly, in earlier days, the chef placed a clump of dough atop his cotton skullcap and, with a knife in each hand, whittled away above his head—pasta strips flying—until all the dough was in the pot.

Western fast food has also recently exploded onto Yan'an's eating scene and KFC, Subway, and Dairy Queen can all be found on Da Qiao Jie. For a decent cup of coffee looking out over the muddy Yan River, **King Coffee** is on the 3rd floor above Subway, and also has free Wi-Fi and a selection of Chinese meals.

Wuqi Dajiudian ★★ SHANXI Despite its simple, somewhat dingy (but clean) appearance, this is probably the best restaurant in the city. Locals crowd the place every evening, chatting noisily as they toast each other between mouthfuls of tasty Shanxi specialties. The drink of choice is *mijiu,* an alcoholic beverage made from millet; this local version, served heated from a small kettle, is a bit cloudy and sweet, and it goes well with the local cuisine. Among the tasty offerings are *huangmomo* (sweet steamed millet cake), *youmomo* (fried doughnut made of millet), *kucai tudou* (mashed potatoes with wild vegetables), *qiaomian hele* (pressed buckwheat noodles with a vinaigrette dressing), and *yougao* (a pan-fried sticky rice cake).

Beiguan Jie, opposite Yan'an Middle School. ✆ **0911/213-9720.** Meal for 2 ¥25–¥40. No credit cards. 7:30am–11pm.

PINGYAO 平遥 ★

Shanxi Province, 616km (383 miles) SW of Beijing, 100km (62 miles) S of Taiyuan, 540km (335 miles) NE of Xi'an

The great majority of Chinese cities have histories extending back hundreds and often thousands of years, but few have anything outside of a museum to show for it. The central Shanxi city of Pingyao is an exception. This 2,700-year-old city had its heyday during the late Ming and Qing dynasties, and the walled city that survives today was largely built then, though a few Yuan dynasty structures also survive. Chinese and overseas travelers come to this area to see some of the best-preserved traditional architecture in China: gray-brick courtyard homes *(siheyuan),* extravagant family mansions (one of which was the set for Zhang Yimou's *Raise the Red Lantern*), a Ming city wall, Daoist and Buddhist temples, and China's earliest commercial banks. Visitors also get to stay in restored courtyards, sleep on a *kang* (heated brick bed), and eat wonderful Shanxi cuisine, which for some reason has yet to catch on in the West.

But Pingyao isn't all quaintness and old-world charm. Like any place in China dependent on tourism, it has an overabundance of vehicles of every kind, fake antiques, touts, and, well, tourists. Visitors on foot will have to avoid the speedy electric buggies that cart Chinese tourists around and as more residents of the old city are moved to modern apartments with modern plumbing, this World Heritage city faces the threat of becoming an over-precious imitation of itself. However, for now, Pingyao still has the vitality of a thriving town behind the veneer of an ancient one. ***Note:*** Turn to chapter 16 for Chinese translations of key locations.

Essentials

GETTING THERE Overnight **trains** from Beijing or Xi'an save you a night's hotel stay and arrive in Pingyao in the morning. The 1163 (12 hr.) that leaves Beijing at 7:03pm is the most convenient train. Several trains during the day come from Xi'an (8–9 hr.), or the 2672, which leaves at 10:48pm and arrives in Pingyao early the following morning; this train then continues on to Datong (8 hr.). Moving on to Beijing, the K604 leaves at 6:47pm and arrives at Beijing West at 6:28am the following morning. To Xi'an, the 2669 departs at 9:38pm and arrives the following morning at 6:55am. Pingyao has a tiny sleeper allocation, so if you want a berth you'll have to pay the price of a ticket from Taiyuan and will be given a photocopy of the ticket that you can exchange onboard. Most hotels can arrange this service for ¥30 to ¥40.

Luxury **buses** from Beijing's Lize Qiao Long-Distance Bus Station leave every 45 minutes for Taiyuan (7 hr.; ¥149), where you'll need to change bus stations to transfer to a Pingyao service (2 hr.; ¥26).

GETTING AROUND Trains and buses arrive at the Pingyao **railway station** in the "modern" city that is west of the ancient wall. Taxis aren't allowed into the narrow streets of old Pingyao, so walk a short stretch or take a motorcycle rickshaw (¥10), or cycle rickshaw (¥2–¥10 depending on your negotiating skills). Many of the better courtyard hotels will arrange free pickup for guests. Most of the courtyard hotels are in the vicinity of the Shi Lou (Market Building)—the tallest building in sight—at the center of the ancient town, on Nan Dajie (also called Ming Qing Jie).

The old town has only four main streets and a number of small lanes, so most places are within walking or biking distance. A ride on a motorcycle or bicycle rickshaw to places within the wall costs only a few yuan. A bicycle rickshaw that can accommodate two people can be hired for around ¥50 for a whole day. Several of the courtyard hotels rent bicycles for ¥10 per day. A **bike rental** store is at Xi Dajie 73, where they also have tandems for ¥20 a day. If you want to join the hordes you can also take a seat on one of the numerous electric buggies that circuit the main sites for ¥10.

TOURS Most of the courtyard hotels can arrange cars and buy bus and train tickets for a small fee.

[Fast FACTS] PINGYAO

Banks, Foreign Exchange & ATMs None available, but many of the hotels will exchange major foreign currencies, including U.S. dollars, euros, and yen.

Internet Access Internet cafes can be found in the lobby areas of many courtyard hotels and access is often free if you eat there. Some of the better ones (including both listed) also now provide free Wi-Fi. For a good old-fashioned Chinese Internet cafe where you'll be surrounded by teenage online gamers, head to Bei Dajie 74 (8am–midnight).

Post Office The old town's post office is at Xi Dajie 1 and is open from 8am to 6pm.

Exploring Pingyao

The ancient town within the 6km-long (4-mile) city wall is ideal for walking. Take your map, head in any direction, and you're bound to find traditional architectural and cultural gems. Indeed, the town's charm is most alive away from the tourist crowds at the main sights—heading east along Dong Dajie from Ming Qing Jie and then into the narrow lanes of the southeastern quadrant is a good start. On the way, you'll get to see how some of the 20,000 current residents of Pingyao's old city live. While in the past tickets had to be purchased separately for each site, visitors must now buy a **3-day pass** for ¥150 that allows entrance to the town's 19 most popular sites. These sites are open from 8am to 7:30pm in the summer, and 8am to 6pm in winter. Passes are available from all 19 site ticket offices. A few sites in town, including Shi Lou, still require a separate ticket. **English audio guides** for the main sites included on the pass are available at all of these locations. They cost ¥40 (plus ¥200 or passport as deposit) and are valid for 2 days. The audio guides are satellite-linked and are prompted into action to give a short introduction to each site as you arrive.

A good first stop is the three-story **Shi Lou** (**Market Building;** not included in 2-day pass; ¥5; 8am–7pm) that marks the city center and affords the best view of the old town. The well-preserved Ming dynasty **ancient city wall** ***(gu chengqiang),*** made of rammed earth and bricks, also affords views of the old city and outlying areas. It takes about an hour to walk the circumference of the wall. Near the center of town, **Ri Sheng Chang** and **Bai Chuan Tong**—headquarters of two of 19th-century China's leading money exchanges—are reminders that this remote town was once the financial center of the Qing government. Both compounds have been transformed into museums that look much more like elegant courtyard residences than banks. Restored and rebuilt, Ri Sheng Chang (Xi Dajie 38) is an engaging museum of three courtyards and almost two dozen halls and rooms. Bai Chuan Tong (Nan Dajie 109) is now a furniture museum consisting of bedrooms, parlors, a kitchen, and a room for taking snuff (and probably opium)—all furnished and decorated in Ming and Qing styles.

A few blocks southeast of the Market Building on Chenghuang Miao Jie are three Daoist temples in one, the **Chenghuang Miao, Caishen Miao,** and **Zaojun Miao,** honoring the City God, the God of Wealth, and the Kitchen God. The separate but connected buildings are meant to imitate the arrangement of the government seat and its offices. Start at the Temple of the City God. At the back, where scriptures would normally be, the walls have *trompe l'oeil* murals of bookshelves filled with books and scrolls. Turn right (east) to get to the Kitchen God Temple. To get to the less obvious Temple of the God of Wealth, go to the back of the first temple and take the door to the left (west). This Ming dynasty complex burned down twice and was last rebuilt in 1864. Follow Chenghuang Miao Jie west (where it becomes Zhengfu Jie) to visit the **Xianya Shu** (or Yamen). This was the administrative office that meted out justice, such as it was, during the Ming and Qing dynasties. On the east side sat a summoning drum *(dengwen gu)*. When someone had a complaint, they beat the drum to call for the Yamen chief, who would then hear the case and make his judgment. You may catch performers in rehearsal for operas and reenactments of trials that are performed here at select times throughout the week. A fine example of a wealthy urban residence, the former home of pioneering banker Lei Lutai, **Lei Lutai Guju,** Shuyuan Jie, is also worth a visit for its four rows of connecting courtyards, each in a different style. In the front courtyard, a "certified fortuneteller" reads hands, faces, and astrological charts—alas, only in Chinese.

Out of Town

A Buddhist temple (8am–6pm; ¥20) within biking or driving distance of Pingyao is **Zhenguo Si,** 12km (7½ miles) northeast of the old town. Its **Wanfo Dian (Palace of Ten Thousand Buddhas),** from the Tang dynasty, is another of China's oldest timber-frame buildings. Inside, its impressive statuary dates to the Five Dynasties (907–960). One of the pleasures of this less-visited temple is its tranquil atmosphere, due in part to an absence of touts and souvenir stalls.

Qiao Jia Dayuan ★★ This is the best-known of Shanxi's merchant-family mansions (*dayuan,* or "grand courtyards"), and where Zhang Yimou's *Raise the Red Lantern* was filmed. Almost midway between Taiyuan and Pingyao, it is easily reached from either city, but this also makes it popular with large Chinese tour groups. Containing six large courtyards and 313 houses, the compound was constructed in 1755 by Qiao Guifa, the first member of the family to strike it rich selling tea and bean curd in Baotou, beyond the Great Wall. Returning to his hometown, he built his dream home, to which successive generations added until it reached its present size. Give yourself at least 2 hours.

Admission ¥40. 8am–7pm (6pm in winter). Avoid weekends. Buses between Pingyao and Taiyuan will drop you off. Follow signs to Qiao Family Courtyard (10-min. walk). Round-trip taxi from Pingyao (or Taiyuan), is ¥200–¥250, or ¥300 if you want to continue on to Taiyuan.

Shuanglin Si ★ This Buddhist temple is 6km (4 miles) southwest of Pingyao and easily reached by bicycle, motor-rickshaw (¥40 round-trip), or taxi (¥60–¥80 round-trip). Built in the 6th century, the complex underwent large-scale renovations during the Ming dynasty. It is most famous for the 2,000-plus painted statues distributed among 10 halls in three connected courtyards. Highlights include the arhats in **Tianwang Dian.** Princely and dignified, they are a refreshing change from the usual gilded, grotesque variety. Statues of worshipers depict commoners in everyday dress looking humble and devout and nothing like the serene, finely clad bodhisattvas nearby. In the **Pusa Dian (Bodhisattva Palace),** which contains a thousand-armed Guanyin, look up at the ceiling where the green, three-clawed, round-bellied figure of a guard keeps watch.

Qiaotou Cun. Admission ¥25. 8am–6pm (8:30am–5pm winter). ¥40 round-trip taxi.

Wang Family Courtyard (Wang Jia Dayuan) ★★ Sixty kilometers (37 miles) south of Pingyao, this *dayuan* dwarfs the Qiao family's mansion. First constructed in the mid–17th century, its expansion continued for over a century. Walking through the 123 courtyards and 1,118 houses takes around 3 hours, but the time is well spent. The decorative lattice screens and windows, shaped openings between rooms and courtyards, and undulating partition walls are exquisite examples of Ming and Qing vernacular architecture. Rarely are so many classic styles found all in one place. Also of note and well worth looking for are the cave dwellings at the compound's periphery.

Admission ¥66. 8am–6:30pm (to 6pm in winter). Buses connect Taiyuan and Pingyao to the town nearest Wang Jia Dayuan, Lingshi Cheng. Buses between Lingshi Cheng and Wang Jia Dayuan leave every 10 min. and cost ¥1. Round-trip taxi from Pingyao is ¥200–¥250.

Zhangbi Ancient Castle (Zhangbi Gubao) ★★ Nearly 50km (31 miles) south of Pingyao, this ancient underground fortress is an architectural marvel. Built in the 7th century, the castle village's walled exterior, cobbled lanes, and collection of temples are worthy of a visit in their own right, but what makes this place so special is the three-layer tunnel system that runs beneath it. An inconspicuous entrance (aside from the sign) inside a house leads down to more than 10km (6 miles) of tunnels running at depths of 1m (3 ft.) to 18m (59 ft.) below the castle. Many tunnels were damaged by earthquakes and floods, but visitors can still walk safe sections, although a (Chinese-speaking) guide is recommended to make sure you don't get lost.

10km south of Jiexu. Admission ¥60; guide fee ¥20. 8am–6:30pm. Round-trip taxi from Pingyao is ¥150, or ¥250 if you combine it with Shuanglin Si and Wang Jia Dayuan.

Where to Stay

The old town has many courtyard hotels, and more are opening every day. Prices vary and bargaining is expected. Standard and deluxe rooms are decorated in Qing style and have large *kang* heated brick beds and small modern bathrooms. Budget rooms have conventional beds and less traditional ornamentation. Some of the better guesthouses now accept foreign credit cards as well as exchange major foreign currencies. Most, including the two guesthouses recommended here, have bike rentals for ¥10 per day.

Deju Yuan ★ A gracious host, excellent cooking, attention to decor, and reasonable prices make this one of the better courtyard guesthouses in town, but this also makes it popular with tour groups—reserve in advance. Attractive standard rooms come with large *kang* beds. A three-room suite has two bedrooms connected by a central hall and is ideal for families. The most peaceful rooms (022, 023, and 024) are in a secluded courtyard garden at the rear of the property.

Xi Dajie 43. www.pydjy.net. ✆ **0354/568-5266.** Fax 0354/568-5366. 26 units. ¥280–¥480 small to large standard rooms; ¥1,480 suite. 20% discount Nov–Mar. V. **Amenities:** Restaurant; ticketing; free transport from railway station. *In room:* A/C, TV, Wi-Fi.

Kylin Grand Hotel A sign of things to come, the Kylin Grand is Pingyao's most upmarket hotel, and whilst the grounds are pleasant and the rooms are undoubtedly the most luxurious and comfortable in the walled town, it all feels a bit bland compared with the more moderately priced historic courtyard guesthouses. Nonetheless the proprietors have made an effort, and the hotel is attractively designed with traditional style. Rooms are plush and comfortable and feature good bathrooms, although it's worth spending a little extra for one of the larger deluxe rooms.

Chenghuang Miao Jie. 76. ✆ **0354/568-9988.** Fax 0354/568-9918. 65 units. ¥718 standard twin, ¥960 deluxe twin; ¥1,550 suite. MC, V. **Amenities:** Restaurant; ticketing; free transport from railway station. *In room:* A/C, TV, Internet.

Tian Yuan Kui ★★ ☺ This is the pick of the courtyard guesthouses and it is often full with a mix of Chinese, European, and North American guests. Aware of growing competition, its savvy proprietors have continually renovated, and added rooms, services, and facilities to keep ahead of the pack. Rooms are set around a series of tranquil courtyards with the odd well-placed Buddha statue, cauldron or plant completing the picture. Rooms come in a variety of shapes and sizes, and prices vary accordingly, so check out a few before you choose (8017 is my favorite). Staff is young and friendly and enjoys helping with foreign kids. The hotel also has a good restaurant and in summer Shanxi opera performances (*Jin ju*) can be arranged for ¥500.

Nan Dajie (Ming Qing Jie) 73. www.pytyk.com. ✆ **0354/568-0069.** Fax 0354/568-3052. 35 units. ¥280–¥580 small to large standard room. ¥898 suite. 30% discount Nov–Mar. AE, DC, MC, V. **Amenities:** Restaurant; ticketing; free transport from railway station. *In room:* A/C, TV, Wi-Fi.

Where to Eat

Most Pingyao restaurants specialize in Shanxi and local cuisine, which emphasize wheat pastas, meat pies, Pingyao beef (similar to corned beef in color and taste), and fried cakes and breads. All are well-accompanied by a bottle of the local Xinghuacun beer. Two of the best restaurants in town are in the recommended **Deju Yuan** and **Tian Yuan Kui** guesthouses. Dinner for two costs ¥30 to ¥50. Nearly every restaurant in town serves a version of *laolao youmian* (sometimes called *wowo*). These small rings of husked-oat pasta are served pressed together in a bamboo steamer. The sauce that accompanies the dish varies from place to place, but Deju Yuan serves one of the best. The pasta is so substantial that it almost tastes like cornmeal, while the tomato-based sauce—flavorful and slightly hot—is reminiscent of a light tamale sauce. *Xiangsu ji* (crispy aromatic chicken) is also highly recommended, as is the lightly sweet *youzha gao* (crispy puff with date and red bean paste). Try corned beef with potatoes (*tudou shao niurou*) at Tian Yuan Kui; or try any of their numerous noodle dishes, made from husked oat, yellow bean, or sorghum flour. Most famous is the pasta shaped like little cats' ears (*mao erduo*). Both restaurants also serve good Western breakfasts, including delicious omelets and fruit crepes. For a drink, dessert or snack, try the **Sakura Café** (8am–midnight), located on the corner of Dong Dajie and Nan Dajie, which serves an all-encompassing range of Western and local dishes. Another outlet, Sakura Café 2, is on Nan Dajie, and other branches are throughout China, and even in Laos and Thailand. The apple pie and ice cream is recommended. For a quiet drink, the cozy **Jincheng Bar** at 81 Xi Dajie is worth seeking out.

TAIYUAN 太原

Shanxi Province, 500km (310 miles) SW of Beijing, 651km (405 miles) NE of Xi'an

During the 77 years of disunion that followed the collapse of the Tang dynasty, northern China was up for grabs by the various kingdoms that came to be known as the Five Dynasties (907–960). Each laid claim to Taiyuan (then called Jinyang) until the first emperor of the Song dynasty (960–1279) stepped in and annihilated the city, going so far as to divert the Fen River so that it would wash away any evidence that Jinyang ever existed. Modern Taiyuan—the capital of Shanxi Province—is located on the site of the rebuilt city.

Today things are more tranquil, but not necessarily better for your health. A 1999 report found this sooty industrial city to be the most polluted in the country and city officials, shamed into action, began to take strides toward cleanup. The main thoroughfare, Yingze Dajie, was widened in 2007, and while Taiyuan is still unlikely to win any awards for its living conditions, the new Shanxi Museum makes the city definitely worth a day or two of your time en route to Wutai Shan or Pingyao.

HOTELS ■
Bīngzhōu Fàndiàn **5**
并州饭店

Jinjiang Inn **12**
(Jǐn Jiāng Zhī Xīng Lǚguǎn)
锦江之星旅馆

Shānxī Grand Hotel **11**
(Shānxī Dàjiǔdiàn)
山西大酒店

Shānxī World Trade Hotel **2**
(Shānxī Guómào Dàfàndiàn)
山西国贸大饭店

Yíngzé Bīnguǎn **7**
迎泽宾馆

RESTAURANTS ◆
Hongbin Lou Kaoya **8**
(Hóng Bīn Lóu)
鸿宾楼烤鸭店

Tàiyuán Miànshídiàn **9**
太原面食店

UBC Coffee **1**
(Shàngdǎo Kāfēitīng)
上岛咖啡厅

ATTRACTIONS ●
Chóngshàn Monastery
(Chóngshàn Sì) **3**
崇善寺

Chúnyáng Gōng **6**
纯阳宫

Confucian Temple
(Wén Miào) **4**
文庙

Jin Temple **13**
(Jìn Cí)
晋祠

Shānxī Museum **10**
(Shānxī Bówùguǎn)
山西博物院

Essentials

GETTING THERE   Wusu Airport is 15km (9 miles) southeast of town. Useful connections include flights from Hong Kong (two flights weekly), and several daily services to and from Beijing, Shanghai, Xi'an, and Shenzhen. Tickets can be booked at **China Eastern Airlines** at Yingze Dajie 158 (✆ **0351/417-8605**). To get to the airport a shuttle bus (¥15) runs from Shanxi Guomao Dafandian, or bus no. 201 leaves from the train station. Taxis cost around ¥50 from town to the airport.

The main **railway station** is on the east side of town at the start of Yingze Dajie. **Fast intercity CRH trains** to Beijing take a mere 3 hours, with 9 links per day. The fastest train to Datong is the K7808, which leaves at 1:30pm and takes a little over 5 hours. Pingyao is served by several daily trains on the Taiyuan-Yuncheng route (90 min). Of the services to Xi'an, the 1095 is convenient, leaving at 7:14pm and arriving at 7:22am.

Most long-distance buses connect with Taiyuan's **Main Bus Station** (© **0351/404-2346**) west of the railway station, but Wutai Shan (4 hr.; ¥66), is served from the shiny new easterly **Dong Kezhan,** while Pingyao (2 hr.; ¥26) buses leave from the **Jian Nan** station. Luxury buses link Taiyuan's Main Bus Station with Beijing's Lize Qiao Bus Station (7 hr.; ¥149) every 45 minutes and Datong (4 hr.; ¥120) every 20 minutes.

GETTING AROUND City **bus** fare is ¥1; with air-conditioning, the fare is ¥2. **Taxis** are abundant and the fare for the first 3km (2½ miles) is ¥8 (plus ¥1 fuel surcharge at the time of writing); after that it's ¥1.10 per kilometer. Beyond 10km (6¼ miles), it's ¥1.60 per kilometer.

TOURS A helpful branch of **CTS** is at Pingyang Lu 8 (© **0351/724-2162;** Mon–Fri 9am–noon and 2–6pm).

[Fast FACTS] TAIYUAN

Banks, Foreign Exchange & ATMs The **Bank of China** (Mon–Fri 8am–5:30pm) at Yingze Dajie 288 has an ATM and full foreign-exchange facilities.

Internet Access A *wangba* is near Chongshan Si at Shangma Jie 20. It is open from 8am to midnight and charges ¥2 per hour.

Post Office The main post office (Mon–Fri 8am–7pm) is opposite the railway station.

Visa Extensions The **PSB** is at Houjia Xiang 19 (© **0351/202-3011;** Mon–Fri 8–11:30am and 2:30–5:30pm).

Exploring Taiyuan

The new provincial museum (see below) has superseded the collections to be found at the Daoist temple Chunyang Gong and the former Confucian temple Wen Miao; nevertheless, both are still worth visiting for the tranquil escape from the mean streets of Taiyuan. **Chunyang Gong,** Qifeng Jie 1 (around the block from KFC) is dedicated to Lu Dongbin, the Tang dynasty poet, calligrapher, and wine connoisseur who, by the time of the Song dynasty, was worshipped as one of the Eight Immortals of Daoism. He's usually depicted as an impassive scholar with two long wisps of mustache and a thin pointed beard, holding a double-edged sword given to him by a dragon. The main hall, **Lu Zu Dian,** is dedicated to him. The temple is open from 9am to 5:30pm; admission is ¥10. The grounds of the **Confucian Temple (Wen Miao)** on Shangguan Xiang have gardens and covered walkways, making this a pleasant place to amble, and the handicrafts collection (from the Ming and Qing dynasties) includes paper cuttings, traditional dress, jewelry, and jade work. Hours are from 9am to 5pm Tuesday to Sunday and admission is ¥5.

Shanxi Museum (Shanxi Bowuguan) ★★ The imposing new Shanxi Museum proudly reinforces the province's status as the cradle of Chinese civilization. The first floor has some interesting photographs of the various excavated sites around the province, while the second floor details Shanxi's history from earliest times through to the Jin dynasty. Along with the seemingly obligatory ridiculous caveman models, sections on Neolithic and Paleolithic history have some genuine finds such as arrowheads, flints, and teeth. Excavations at Taosi walled town have helped further convince historians that the town was the legendary capital of Yao, and jade and lacquer items from the site are on display. The best displays on this floor, though, are the articles discovered in Minister Zhao's tomb, which include enormous bronze cauldrons, bells, stone chimes, and a life-size chariot. The wealth of treasures found in this tomb and the 10,000 articles retrieved from the Marquis of Jin's tombs are indicative of the rising power of the Jin at that time.

The third floor is another winner and offers an exquisite collection of Buddhist statuary and stelae from around the province. The statues are tastefully set into alcoves in the mock-adobe walls, and the lighting is subtle yet clearly defines the fine craftsmanship of the stone carving. The fourth floor holds a series of collections including the standard coins and currency, and calligraphy and painting, along with some beautiful Buddhist frescoes and fine jade pieces. A display of Shanxi architectural splendor includes some beautifully detailed roof ornaments and models of some of the province's most famous buildings. However, it seems that the powers that be ran out of time, energy, or translators by the time they reached the fourth floor; while floors two and three have detailed English captions, the fourth floor has only the most cursory of introductions in English. English-speaking guides can be arranged for ¥100. English audio guides are available for ¥10. Allow a couple of hours for a visit.

Binhe Xi Lu. ✆ **0351/878-9555.** Free admission. Tues–Sun 9am–5pm. Bus no. 6 or taxi ¥10–¥12).

Out of Town

Jin Ci (Jin Temple) ★★ The site of Jin Ci is a large park with gardens and a lake, as well as pavilions, halls, and temples from various dynasties, beginning with the Song (960–1279). It isn't known when the original temple was built, but the earliest written reference to Jin Ci is from the 6th century. As you stroll the grounds, the one building that must not be overlooked is **Shengmu Dian (Hall of the Holy Mother).** Located at the back of the park, it is recognizable by its double-eaved roof and its extraordinary writhing dragons, each carved out of wood and coiled around one of the building's eight front columns. First completed in 1032, the hall was restored several times—most recently in the Ming dynasty—but without ever altering the original architectural style and design. Today, along with a handful of other Shanxi buildings, it is one of the earliest surviving wooden halls in China.

The contents of the hall are equally impressive. Inside is a statue of the honored matriarch—the mother of the founder of Jin—surrounded by a retinue of life-size handmaidens, actresses, and eunuchs. Dating from the Song, these gorgeous painted clay figures reveal much about court customs and dress. Sitting in lotus position, the Holy Mother is the picture of composure. Standing third in attendance on her right is a eunuch with one ear bigger than the other and one eye crossed—from listening intently to his mistress while never daring to look at her directly. Some of the actresses are dressed as male characters, evident from their stances—toes pointed outwards—and flat-topped headdresses.

Directly opposite the Hall of the Holy Mother, across the **Flying Bridge Over the Fish Pond (Yuzhao Feiliang),** is the **Xian Dian (Hall of Offerings),** where offerings were made to the Holy Mother, believed to have magic powers. Built in 1168 and rebuilt 400 years later, the hall was last restored in 1955.

Admission ¥70. Summer 8am–6pm; winter 8:30am–5:30pm. Bus: 804 or 856 from railway station or on Xinjian Nan Lu, just south of Yingze intersection in front of the Industrial and Commercial Bank. On arrival, motorcycle-taxi drivers may try to convince you that the distance to the temple is too far to walk; in fact, it's a short (10-min.) walk through the park.

Where to Stay

Most of Taiyuan's accommodation options lie along or near Yingze Dajie. While there are plenty of upscale and midrange options, good budget choices are more limited although a newly opened Jinjiang Inn has improved the situation a little. Other relatively inexpensive options include the scrappy East Wing rooms at the Yingze (see below), or the past-it but functional budget rooms in the West Wing of the **Bingzhou Fandian** (✆ **0351/882-1188**). The hotel is on the southwest corner of Wuyi Square; rooms can be bargained down to ¥190.

Jinjiang Inn (Jinjiang Zhixing Luguan) Once again here to save the day for budget travelers is the Jinjiang Inn, a chain with locations all over China. The hotel has comfortable, functional rooms. Service is very good, and it has a convenient location that's right in the center of Taiyuan.

Jiefang Nan Lu 5. www.jinjianginns.com. ✆ **0351/525-0998.** 128 units. ¥219–¥239 standard room. MC, V. **Amenities:** Restaurant. *In room:* A/C, TV, Internet.

Shanxi Dajiudian (Shanxi Grand Hotel) Plush sofas, high-ceilinged guest rooms, quality bathrooms, and business suites featuring computers with Internet access make this four-star hotel a good choice. The hotel is popular with tour groups, which maybe explains why staff always seem hurried.

Xinjian Nan Lu 5. www.sxgh.com. ✆ **0351/882-9999.** Fax 0351/404-3525. 167 units. ¥670 standard room; ¥920 business room; from ¥1,988 suite. Most rates include breakfast. Up to 20% discount available. 15% service charge. AE, DC, MC, V. Bus: 1 from railway station. **Amenities:** 2 restaurants; bar; ATM; forex; health club; indoor pool; room service; ticketing. *In room:* A/C, satellite TV, fridge, hair dryer, Internet, minibar.

Shanxi Guomao Dafandian (Shanxi World Trade Hotel) This is Taiyuan's first five-star hotel, and while the lobby is grand, and the rooms quite spacious and comfortable, the service is still a bit rough around the edges for an expensive hotel. That said, this is the most comfortable and modern hotel in the city, with most facilities and amenities to be expected in a five-star international hotel. Superior rooms are a little on the small side for the money, making it worth opting for a larger deluxe room, which is better laid out and has a good desk, comfy armchairs, and a bigger bathroom.

Fuxi Jie. www.sxwtc.com. ✆ **0351/868-8888.** Fax 0351/868-9888. 398 units. ¥1,258 superior room; ¥1,398 deluxe room; ¥2,478 suite. Up to 35% discount available. AE, DC, MC, V. **Amenities:** 4 restaurants; bar; fitness center; forex; indoor pool; room service; sauna; ticketing. *In room:* A/C, satellite TV, fridge, hair dryer, Internet, minibar.

Yingze Binguan ★ This pleasant hotel has a recently renovated five-star (west) and an older two-star (east) wing, and is conveniently located less than 3km (2 miles) west of the railway station. Some English is spoken and management and staff go out of their way to meet guests' needs, and the business center's post office is convenient and reliable. Guest rooms in the east wing are the standard issue (two beds, two chairs, and coffee table) but are very shabby. The west wing offers decidedly more luxury and features spacious, thick carpeted rooms, some of which have computers.

Yingze Dajie 189. www.shanxiyingzehotel.com. ✆ **0351/882-8888.** Fax 0351/882-6688. 378 units. West wing ¥1,180 standard room; from ¥2,200 suite. East wing ¥190 standard room. Up to 35% discount available in west wing. AE, DC, MC, V. Bus: 1 or 6 from railway station. **Amenities:** 3 restaurants; bar; fitness center; forex; room service; sauna; ticketing. *In room:* A/C, satellite TV, fridge (West Wing), hair dryer (West Wing), Internet (West Wing), minibar (West Wing).

Where to Eat

Shanxi cuisine is famous for its buckwheat, sorghum, bean, and potato-flour pastas—all currently enjoying increased popularity in China—as well as for its vinegar *(cu)*. A favorite dish that employs potato-flour noodles, vinegar, soy sauce, and spring onion is *liangfen.* Served cold, the dish is particularly refreshing on muggy summer evenings. Like Italian pastas, *cuojianer* (twisted points), *mao erduo* (cats' ears), and a variety of others are named for their shapes. Two winter specialties are Shanxi beef or lamb hot pot *(huoguo)* and—for breakfast—mutton soup *(tounao)*. Made with fatty mutton, yam, lotus, and herbs (to mask the gamey taste), it goes well with the flatbread called *xiaobing* and fortifies you against the winter cold.

The best place to get these local specialties is at the Shipin Jie **night market,** parallel and east of Jiefang Lu, which is lined with some small stands and a number of restaurants serving local specialties and various other Chinese cuisines.

For fast food, a 24-hour **McDonald's** is on the southeast corner of Wuyi Square. For a decent cup of coffee and passable pizza, sandwiches, steak, and spaghetti, a branch of **UBC Coffee (Shangdao Kafeiting)** is just west of Shanxi Guomao Dafandian on Fuxi Jie. For snacks and supplies, the **Meet All supermarket** on the northeast corner of Wuyi Square has a good range of products.

Hongbin Lou Kaoya BEIJING DUCK With the capital now just 3 hours away by fast train, this traditional roast duck restaurant makes more sense than ever. The duck skin is nice and crispy on the outside, and the meat succulent and juicy on the inside; in other words it's pretty authentic and delicious.

Jiefang Lu. ✆ **0351/202-7118.** Whole roast duck ¥108. No credit cards. 11am–2:30pm and 6–9:30pm.

Taiyuan Mianshidian ★ SHANXI This excellent restaurant serves typical Shanxi dishes. Try *guoyou rou* (pork "passed through oil"), *mao erduo, liangfen,* and other local dishes. The bright and clean restaurant is spread over the second and third floors and is popular with businesspeople and families.

Jiefang Lu 5. ✆ **0351/202-2230.** Meal for 2 ¥20–¥40. No credit cards. 11am–3pm and 5:30–9:30pm.

WUTAI SHAN 五台山 ★

Shanxi Province, 327km (203 miles) SW of Beijing, 210km (130 miles) S of Datong, 238km (148 miles) N of Taiyuan

The mountain known as Wutai or "Five Platforms" is actually a cluster of mountains, which long ago collectively became the northernmost sacred peak of Buddhism. Situated roughly halfway between Datong and Taiyuan, Wutai Shan is, in Buddhist lore, the earthly residence of the great bodhisattva Manjusri. Often depicted astride a lion, he is said to embody the perfection of wisdom. To this day, though tourists far outnumber them, pilgrims come entreating Manjusri to reveal himself again. The peaks of Wutai Shan have an average height of 2,000m (6,561 ft.) above sea level, and from northeast to southwest they stretch 120km (75 miles). Cradled at their center is the small town of Taihuai Zhen, with an elevation of 1,680m (5,500 ft.). Part tourist slum, part sacred site, the town is a combination of souvenir shops, hotels, restaurants, temples, and shrines. Summer is the best time to visit—when Wutai Shan offers an escape from the heat and humidity of lower climes. In July and August, the average temperature is only about 50°F (10°C), with warm days and cool nights. Even at this most temperate time of year, the mountain itself is rarely overcrowded during the week. Weekends are another story, and national holidays should be avoided at all costs. Winters are severely cold, with temperatures dipping as low as –40°F (–40°C). Even in June, snow is not unheard of.

One of the liveliest of Wutai's temple festivals is held on the 14th and 15th days of the sixth lunar month, when demons are exorcised and the Diamond Sutra is honored in a ritual dance. All who join the parade from Pusa Ding to Luohan Temple are promised blessings. ***Note:*** Turn to chapter 16 for Chinese translations of key locations.

Essentials

GETTING THERE Most visitors arrive by bus from Taiyuan to the south or Datong to the north. Wutai Shan has no airport. The Wutai Shan **railway station** is in Shahe, 48km (30 miles) and an hour-plus drive from Taihuai. Daily fast trains run to and from Beijing (7 hr.) and Taiyuan (4 hr.). **Buses** between Shahe Railway Station and Taihuai Zhongxin Tingche Station leave regularly throughout the day for ¥20. A **taxi** between Shahe and Taihuai is around ¥150. Allow 2 hours if you're catching a train in Shahe. Plentiful buses connect Taihuai with Taiyuan (4 hr.; ¥74) and two daily buses connect with both Datong (4 hr.; ¥66) and Beijing (6 hr.; ¥131), and one daily bus is for Hohhot (7 hr.; ¥85) at 7am. Arriving, buses drive into Taihuai and will drop you at your hotel if you know where you're staying; otherwise, you'll be ushered out of the bus at the Chaoyang Binguan. The bus station is in the south of town. Coming from Datong there are also share taxis (¥100 per person or ¥400 for the whole car) from the train station.

Admission to the Wutai Shan area is ¥168. All vehicles are stopped at the gate and passengers have to disembark to buy tickets, grumbling about government corruption all the way. The ticket price includes use of the tourist bus, which shuttles visitors between the main temples. Many temples are included in the ticket price, but some also charge a small additional entry fee (¥4–¥10). Temples are open from 7am to 6pm or later.

GETTING AROUND The town of Taihuai runs along the valley nestled between the peaks of Wutai Shan and is small enough to cover on foot in under an hour. The main street (Taihuai Jie/Yingfang Jie) runs north-south along the Qingshui River. Minivans trawl the stretch from town to the area in the south where the best hotels are, picking up passengers for a few yuan. The mountains rise to the immediate east, while two small streets running west off the main street lead to Taihuai's temple area. Although the streets have names, nobody uses them; even maps dispense with them.

Directions to anyplace begin with the name of the nearest temple, many of which can be reached on foot. East of the village a chairlift goes up to **Dailou Peak** (6am–6pm; ¥35 up; ¥30 down; ¥60 round-trip), which offers good views over the valley. Alternatively you can walk there in under an hour, or ride a horse for ¥35; ¥60 round-trip.

TOURS Minibuses and taxis go to the mountain temples from Yingfang Street and should cost ¥70 per person to visit two of the five mountain areas. **CITS** has a number of generally unhelpful branch offices in Taihuai. The main office is at Ming Qing Jie 18 (© **0350/654-3138;** 7:30am–8pm). They don't have their own vehicles, but they will arrange a car and driver for ¥360 per day, and English-speaking guides for ¥180 per day.

[Fast FACTS] WUTAI SHAN

Banks, Foreign Exchange & ATMs The **Bank of China,** Yingfang Jie (8am–noon and 2:30–6:30pm; winter 8:30am–6pm), only exchanges U.S. dollars; no traveler's checks. There's an **Agricultural Bank of China** ATM just south of the Yiyuan Hotel that accepts MasterCard, Maestro, and Cirrus. Restaurants will sometimes change foreign currency, but it's best to arrive with enough yuan for the duration of your stay.

Internet Access A 24-hour Internet cafe is in the far right hand corner of the Jinjie Binguan courtyard. Access costs ¥3 per hour.

Post Office The post office (8am–7pm; winter 8am–6pm) is just north of the Xinhai Hotel on Yingfang Jie.

Around the Mountains

One of the delights of Taihuai Village is the variety of people it attracts. Nuns, monks, and lamas from different orders and from all over China, Japan, Nepal, and Thailand come to Wutai Shan in the summer—some to climb the five terraces, others to simply take part in the many temple activities. The mountain also has a special religious significance for Tibetan Buddhists and so attracts Tibetan monks, nuns, and laypeople from all over China. Ask around and you will usually learn of some mass gathering in one or another of the temples. Alms meals *(dazhai)* for the nuns and monks (paid for by wealthy patrons to amass good karma) take place frequently all summer. Observers are welcome as long as you're quiet and very discreet with cameras.

TEMPLES IN TAIHUAI (台坏)

The small town of Taihuai Zhen has close to a dozen temples. West of town, next to the bell tower, **Xiantong Si** is the largest and one of the oldest of the temples at Wutai Shan. It was first built in A.D. 68; the surviving halls date from the Ming and Qing dynasties. Climb the belfry for a commanding view of the town and mountains. Also be sure to visit the **Tong Dian (Bronze Hall),** lined with thousands of miniature statues said to symbolize the myriad bodhisattvas to whom Manjusri read the Buddhist scriptures while he lived on Wutai Shan. The bronze roof and outside structures are remarkable for their flawless imitation of timber construction and wood design.

A 5-minute walk south of Xiantong Si is **Tayuan Si,** easily recognized by its tall white pagoda that dominates Taihuai's skyline and has become the symbol of Wutai Shan. A smaller pagoda is said to contain strands of Manjusri's hair. Equally famed is the two-story **Sutra Library** in Tayuan Si. At its center is a revolving wooden bookcase that dates from the Ming dynasty. Now empty and unable to turn, it once held more than 20,000 volumes of Buddhist scriptures, written in Chinese, Mongolian, and Tibetan.

MOUNTAIN TEMPLES

The temples on the mountains are generally of less note than those in town, but two of the most famous are **Nan Shan Si** and **Longquan Si.** The former is 2km (1¼ miles) south of Taihuai Zhen. Longquan Temple is another 2km (1¼ miles) in the same direction, so they are easily visited together and, within a few hours, can be done on foot. Like several of Wutai's temples, they claim 108 stairs leading to the entrance gate. Though none of them seem to have exactly that number, the point is that the steps represent the 108 worries (or delusions) of mankind. With each step a worry is cast off, so that by the time visitors reach the gate, you are cleansed with sweat and worry-free. A variation on the theme equates the silent and earnest counting of each stone stair with the meditative chanting of the Buddhist rosary (of 108 beads). With every step, the pilgrim has a chance to reach a pure land, free of temptations and defilements.

Founded in the Later Liang dynasty (907–23) and rebuilt in 1937 on seven terraced levels, Nan Shan Si is one of Wutai Shan's largest temples. Visitors come to see its 18 superb clay arhats (enlightened disciples) in the **Hall of the Great Buddha (Dafo Dian)**—the sleeping arhat is considered the best for its lifelike posture and craftsmanship. In the same hall, to the right of the large gilded Sakyamuni, look for the white marble statue of Avalokitesvara (Guanyin) holding a plump baby boy on her knee. Worshippers bring offerings to her in hopes of male offspring.

Located at the foot of Wutai Shan's central peak, Longquan Si or Dragon Spring Temple has three courtyards connected to one another by moon-shaped gates. The main halls can be found in the east courtyard. At the front, the **Hall of Celestial Kings (Tian Wang Dian)** houses, among others, the Buddha with a Cloth Sack (Budai Fo). This rotund Buddha with an exposed potbelly was a Tang dynasty monk who—with his walking stick and sack of worldly belongings—roamed carefree and begging. He had in his favor the gift of predicting the future and forecasting the weather, and was believed to be an incarnation of Maitreya, the Future Buddha. A purely Chinese creation, he only appears in temples built after the Ming dynasty (1368–1644). The stupa in the central courtyard contains the remains of Puji, the abbot of Nan Shan Temple who died in 1917 believing he, too, was an incarnation of Maitreya. The four images on the sides of the stupa are of Puji/Maitreya at different ages.

TEMPLES BELOW

Two of only three Tang dynasty (618–907) wooden buildings still standing in China—**Nanchan Si** and **Foguang Si**—are located between Wutai Shan and Taiyuan. With 120km (75 miles) separating them, visiting both in 1 day is best done en route from one town to the other rather than as a day trip from either point. A taxi between Taiyuan and Taihuai Village that stops at both temples costs ¥600 to ¥800. A day trip from Taihuai Village to both temples and back costs ¥400. Allow 6 to 7 hours for the round-trip. Buses to Taiyuan pass the turnoffs to these temples, and those with light luggage can hop off and negotiate with waiting taxis for each side trip.

Nanchan Si (Temple of Southern Meditation) ★ About 177km (110 miles) south of Wutai Shan, turning west off the main road to Taiyuan, a dusty road leads to this tranquil ancient temple (¥15). It's said that this temple escaped the great Tang persecution of Buddhism in 845 because it was so far from the temples on Wutai Shan. Today, its small, perfectly proportioned main hall, **Dafo Dian (Hall of the Great Buddha),** is reason enough to make the trip. Built in 782, the wooden-frame building has been much restored, but—unlike the other halls in this complex, which are distinctly of Ming and Qing design—it has its original proportions and graceful Tang design. Note its gently sloping roof, markedly different from the steep gabled roofs of the previous Northern Wei and Sui dynasties. Along the main roof ridge, the pre-Ming ornaments that curl toward each other are called *chiwei,* meaning "owl tails." The word refers to a mythical sea monster—one of the sons of the dragon—believed to protect against fire. Inside the hall are 17 Tang dynasty painted clay statues around the large figure of Sakyamuni. The large statue in the far left corner is Manjusri riding a lion.

Foguang Si (Temple of Buddha's Light) ★ The temple (¥15) is 35km (22 miles) south of Taihuai Village. First built during the Northern Wei dynasty when Buddhism was the official religion, it had greatly expanded by the time it fell victim to the Tang anti-Buddhist campaign of 845. After its total destruction, it was rebuilt 12 years later with the help of a female benefactor named Ning Gongyu. The one hall associated with her, **Dong Dadian (Eastern Great Hall),** survives today. Like the Nanchan's Hall of the Great Buddha, it is the only Tang-style building amid a cluster of mostly Ming and Qing dynasty halls.

To get to the Eastern Great Hall, follow the cobblestone path through the first courtyard. This leads through a deep archway similar to a city-wall gate, followed by a steep stone staircase. The statues, calligraphy, and wall paintings within are from the Tang (618–907) and Song (960–1279) dynasties, while the 296 arhats (enlightened disciples) on either side—remainder of the original 500—date to the Ming. Note the more elaborate bracketing, double roofs, and ridge ornaments of this hall compared with the simple elegance of Nanchan Si.

Shopping

All manner of Buddhist art, clothing, and accouterments are sold on and off the main street. Paintings on fabric *(tiaofu)* and religious scrolls are around ¥25, Buddhist pilgrim bags are ¥15, and the biggest prayer beads you'll see cost a mere ¥20.

Where to Stay

Wutai Shan's best accommodation lies east of the river along Ming Qing Jie and farther south (see listings below). High season is May through October, but even then hefty discounts are possible Monday through Thursday.

Numerous small, very inexpensive hotels are further north in the center of Taihuai Zhen, but cleanliness and heating is a problem, so they're only for people traveling on a very tight budget. You'll be approached by hotel touts if you get off the long-distance bus in this part of town. If you do want to stay in the center, the **Jinjie Shanzhuang** (**✆ 0350/654-5568**), at the base of the Dailou chairlift in the north of town, offers acceptable accommodations for ¥200. If you arrive after dark, chances are the bus will pull up outside the **Chaoyang Binguan,** just below Xiantong Si, where the surly staff will offer you rooms for ¥100 to ¥150 depending upon your bargaining prowess. While the shabby rooms at this place can hardly be recommended, if you're tired and just need a bed for the night, it does at least have hot water and heating.

Xinjinlun Guoji Jiudian (Xinjinlun International Hotel) Located on the contrived but attractive old-world Ming Qing Street, this is a decent mid-range option. Rooms are spread over two buildings on opposite sides of the street; those in the east building are set around a courtyard and are larger, plusher and consequently more expensive than those in the west building. The west building rooms are still clean and pleasant and worth considering if you don't want to spend too much. Staff is friendly and helpful.

Northern end of Ming Qing Jie. ✆ **0350/654-2396.** Fax 0350/654-2332. 40 units. ¥420 standard room East Building; ¥320 standard room West Building; ¥580 suite. Discounts of up to 40%. No credit cards. **Amenities:** Restaurant. *In room:* AC, TV, Wi-Fi (East Building).

Yinhai Shanzhuang Built in the Qing style, this three-story complex, with its gray buildings, red trim, and bright green and gold roofs with upturned eaves, looks almost like another mountain temple. Its clean, carpeted rooms are some of the best to be found in Wutai Shan and it is popular with tour groups. For the best view, request a room facing Nan Shan Si, which is just a 20-minute walk away.

Xiao Nanpo Cun, on the main street, 3km (2 miles) south of town, opposite Nan Shan Si. ✆ **0350/654-2676.** Fax 0350/654-2949. 96 units. ¥788 standard room; ¥1,388 suite. 30% discount sometimes available. MC, V. **Amenities:** 2 restaurants; bar; room service; ticketing. *In room:* A/C, TV, fridge, hair dryer, Internet.

Where to Eat

Wutai Shan's main strip is lined by identical restaurants that mostly offer the same variety of overpriced, bland Chinese staple dishes, so it's worth trying one of the decent vegetarian or specialty restaurants in town. If you want to eat cheaply though, the tiny **Hui Yuan** canteen, just south of the Jiabin Hotel on the same side of the road, has an English menu featuring all of the usual dishes including sweet and sour pork, *yuxiang rousi,* and dumplings.

Jingxin Zhai ★★ VEGETARIAN Hunting out the drab grey exterior of this traditional Buddhist restaurant is quite a challenge, but once inside it's all decked out in temple yellow and excellent vegetarian food is on offer. Try some of the following dishes as you listen to soft Buddhist chants being played over and over again: *iqi yaangyaang* (spicy mock chicken cubes fried with dried red peppers), *luohan zhai* (traditional mixed vegetables fried with bean-starch noodles), and *supaai* (deep-fried "meat" smothered with succulent brown sauce).

North end of Ming Qing Jie, inside the courtyard of Jinwei Binguan. ✆ **0350/654-2791.** Meal for 2 from ¥80. No credit cards. 7–9am, 11am–2:30pm, and 5–9:30pm.

Jinjie Si Fu SHANXI This banquet hall restaurant serves a good range of local specialties, albeit at a price. Everything from dog to pigeon is on offer, but tamer specialties such as mountain mushrooms are also available. The comprehensive English picture menu can help you choose; indeed it's almost worth dining here for the menu translations alone ("the hand rips the donkey meat" and "cool self-torture" are both better than they sound). Service is quick and friendly.

East of the river in the north part of town next to the Dailou chairlift. ✆ **0350/654-5878.** Meal for 2 ¥100. No credit cards. 6am–10pm.

Yizhan Mingdeng Quaansu Zhai ★★ VEGETARIAN Maitreya and a small army of grey-clad staff greet you as you enter this quality Buddhist restaurant. A good variety of delicious vegetarian dishes make it popular with local and visiting monks, nuns, and laypeople. Some of the excellent dishes here include *baaiguo naangua bao* (stewed gingko nut with pumpkin), *lancai roumo sijidou* (olive leaf fried with string beans), *jinshang tianhua* ("shredded pork" with yuxiang flavor), and *tieban heijiao niupaai* (grilled "steak" with black-pepper sauce).

Signed off Yingfang Jie just south of Shuxiang Temple. ✆ **0350/654-5674.** Meal for 2 ¥80–¥100. No credit cards. 10:30am–9pm.

THE SILK ROUTES

7

by Simon Foster

China was first known in the West as Seres, the land of silk or serica. The Romans were entranced by this strong but delicate thread, and believed it was combed from trees. But it was also viewed as a decadent luxury—for the appetite of Rome's better classes for silk was rarely sated, and without a luxury (other than glass) to export in return, silk imports emptied Rome's coffers. As a result, in A.D. 14 the Roman Senate forbade the wearing of silk by men, and Caligula, who was fond of diaphanous silk garments, was disparagingly referred to as Sericatus.

In Tang China, silk was the most important form of legal tender; taxes, fines, and officials' wages were all measured in bales of silk. Silk was used to buy off raiding armies of Uighurs and Tibetans and (it was hoped) make them a bit less barbaric.

The term "Silk Road," coined in the 19th century by German geographer Ferdinand von Richthofen, is both an evocative and misleading appellation. The trade routes that connected China and the West from the 1st century B.C. until the 10th century A.D. carried a whole inventory of luxuries and necessities beyond silk, from gold and jade to wool and rhubarb. Nor was the road traveled from end to end. Chinese merchants rarely went beyond the edges of the **Taklamakan Desert** before turning the goods over to Sogdian or Parthian caravans, who were left to face the forbidding mountain passes of the Pamirs. Only devoted missionaries went farther, like the legendary monk Xuanzang, who spent 15 years traveling across India and central Asia in search of Buddhist sutras.

Silk was just one of many goods transported over these vast distances. Apricots, peaches, and pears reached the West, while China gained the fig tree and the grapevine. China imported spices, woolen fabrics, horses for military campaigns, and foreign novelties such as musical instruments, coral, colored glass, and jewels, which fascinated the courts.

Traders also brought foreign ideas, and were soon followed by missionaries of many faiths. Nestorian Christianity, Zoroastrianism, Manichaeism, and, most significantly, Buddhism, were welcomed by a confident and cosmopolitan civilization. Doctrines and art spread eastward, leaving spectacular monuments in the cave temples of **Dunhuang, Maiji Shan,** and **Kizil.**

The Silk Routes

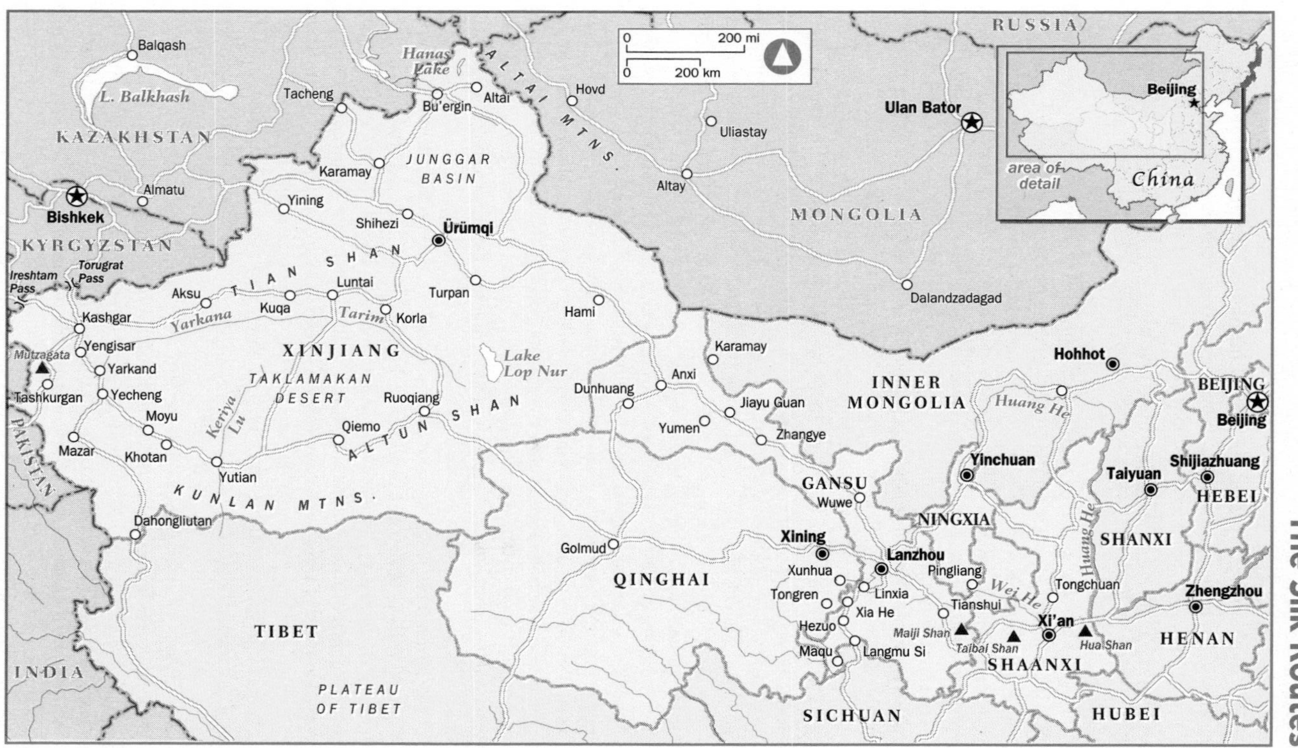

The Silk Road wasn't one road at all, but a series of routes emanating from the capital of Chang'an. From Chang'an camel trains would follow the Wei River west before branching into several different routes.

The southern route passed through **Dunhuang, Miran,** and **Khotan,** in the shadow of the mighty **Kunlun Shan,** whose meltwater streams fed thriving Buddhist communities. Intrepid travelers today, tolerant of bare-bones transportation and accommodations, can still traverse the route, which will lead to bustling towns such as Khotan with ancient markets and traditions little disturbed by either tourism or modernization.

The middle route was initially (1st c. B.C.–4th c. A.D.) popular, allowing merchants to float on barges down the Tarim River from the garrison town of Loulan to Korla and **Kuqa.** But when the river changed course, and Lop Nor Lake "wandered off," this route was abandoned. Thanks to more recent nuclear testing, which finally ended in 1996, this route will likely remain closed for the half-life of plutonium.

The northern routes, skirting the northern and southern foothills of **Tian Shan (the Heavenly Mountains),** were menaced by Kazakh and Kyrgyz bandits. The bandits are less of a problem these days, and most travelers follow the northern route along the He Xi corridor to the mighty fort of **Jiayu Guan,** the peerless Buddhist caves of Dunhuang, and the grape trellises of **Turpan.** Beyond, the road leads to fascinating oasis towns such as Kuqa, and the great market town of **Kashgar,** skirting the northern edge of the Taklamakan Desert. (Taklamakan is commonly translated as "go in and you don't come out," but in ancient Uighur it means "vineyard," evoking a time when the region was more fertile.) The desert dunes have been marching south for many years, threatening the oasis towns of the ancient southern route.

The present character of the Silk Road is Islamic rather than Buddhist. An exodus of the Turkic Uighur peoples from western Mongolia displaced the Indo-European inhabitants, the Tang dynasty fell, and Islam gradually spread east through the Tarim Basin. With the rise of sea trade, land routes fell into disuse. Settlements and temples (which also functioned as banks) were abandoned to the desert. They remained undisturbed until the turn of the 20th century, when archaeologists from Britain, France, Germany, Russia, Japan, and (later) America came searching for lost Buddhist kingdoms.

The adventurers saw the Han Chinese as fellow colonizers, keeping the Turkic Uighurs in their place. British diplomat Eric Teichman believed "the Turkis are a patient, contented and submissive people, made to be ruled by others." Xinjiang means "new territories," rather a giveaway in itself, but many Han guides will try to persuade you that this region has always belonged to China. Turkic Uighurs make up the majority of the population in Xinjiang, but they are gradually being displaced by a wave of migrants from the east. After an absence of over a millennium, Han Chinese are reasserting control over the Silk Routes with a ruthlessness that the Wudi emperor (reigned 141–87 B.C.)—the first ruler to control the Silk Routes—would have envied. Most Uighurs would prefer to rule themselves though, a fact that is becoming ever clearer in the increasing tensions in Xinjiang. Fatal attacks on police in Kashgar and Kuqa in 2008 were followed by full-scale riots in Ürümqi in 2009 that left many Han Chinese dead and injured. The army was sent in to quell the protests and Internet connection was cut throughout the province, technology that was subsequently used in Egypt during the last days of Hosni Mubarak's presidency. Fears that the "Jasmine Revolution" could spread to China's Islamic heartland have once again heightened tensions. Check travel advisories for the latest before you plan a trip to Xinjiang.

Travel along the Silk Routes has always been arduous, temperatures are extreme, the distances involved are considerable, and it's *very* dusty. Peak season is early May and mid-July to mid-October. Outside of Xi'an, Lanzhou, Dunhuang, Ürümqi and Kashgar, expect little in the way of luxurious lodgings. The more adventurous should seek out the Uighur trading centers of Khotan, and Kuqa, or the Tibetan monastic settlements of **Xia He** and **Langmu Si.** ***Note:*** Unless otherwise noted, hours listed for attractions and restaurants are daily.

XI'AN 西安

Shanxi Province, 1,200km (744 miles) SW of Beijing

Surrounded by rich loess farmland, Xi'an (Western Peace), the present capital of Shanxi Province, was home to the ruling houses of the Qin, Han, Sui, and Tang dynasties, when it was known as Chang'an (Eternal Peace). The city reached a peak during the Tang dynasty (618–907), when it was the military and trading base for China's shaky control of the Silk Routes. During the Xuanzong reign of the Tang (712–55), Chang'an swelled with two million taxable inhabitants and was the largest, most cosmopolitan settlement in the world.

The scale of the metropolis is readily imagined—what are now referred to as the city walls were rebuilt during the Ming dynasty (1644–1911) on the remains of Tang palace walls. The Tang city walls extended 8km (5 miles) north-south and almost 10km (6 miles) east-west, and the south gate opened onto a tree-lined avenue 150m (500-ft.) wide, down which foreign emissaries would once approach the metropolis. The Tang era was a high point for advocates of "foreign religions" as Manicheans, Nestorians, and Buddhists flocked to the capital. Buddhism in particular enjoyed royal patronage.

Surviving monuments open a window onto the imperial power and cosmopolitan style of the old capital. The short-lived totalitarian state of Qin Shi Huangdi is reflected in the awe-inspiring massed terra-cotta armies of the **Qin Bingmayong Bowuguan.** The more peaceful and settled times during the reign of Emperor Jingdi are evidenced by the miniature, but no less impressive collection of statuettes guarding his tomb north of the city. The influence of Buddhism is clear from the majestic spire of the **Da Yan Ta (Great Goose Pagoda),** constructed under the supervision of Xuanzang (d. 664), who returned to China in 645 after 15 years of travel across India and central Asia. Evidence of the flourishing trade along the Silk Routes may be found in the **Shanxi History Museum** and **Famen Si.**

Today, in spite of ever expanding city limits, pollution, searing summer heat, and freezing winters, Xi'an is a joy to visit. Central Xi'an is pleasantly compact and its grid layout within the city walls makes it easy to navigate. There is enough to see in and around Xi'an to keep even the most energetic visitor busy for a week. It's the most-visited town on the Silk Routes, which brings the usual annoyances. Nevertheless, locals are easygoing and disparaging of their ancient capital, shaking their heads in regret that their ancestors "fell behind" their richer cousins in Beijing. However, the armies of Chinese tourists and foreign visitors, along with the legion of upscale new malls full of well-dressed shoppers let you know Xi'an's not that far behind.

Xi'an 西安

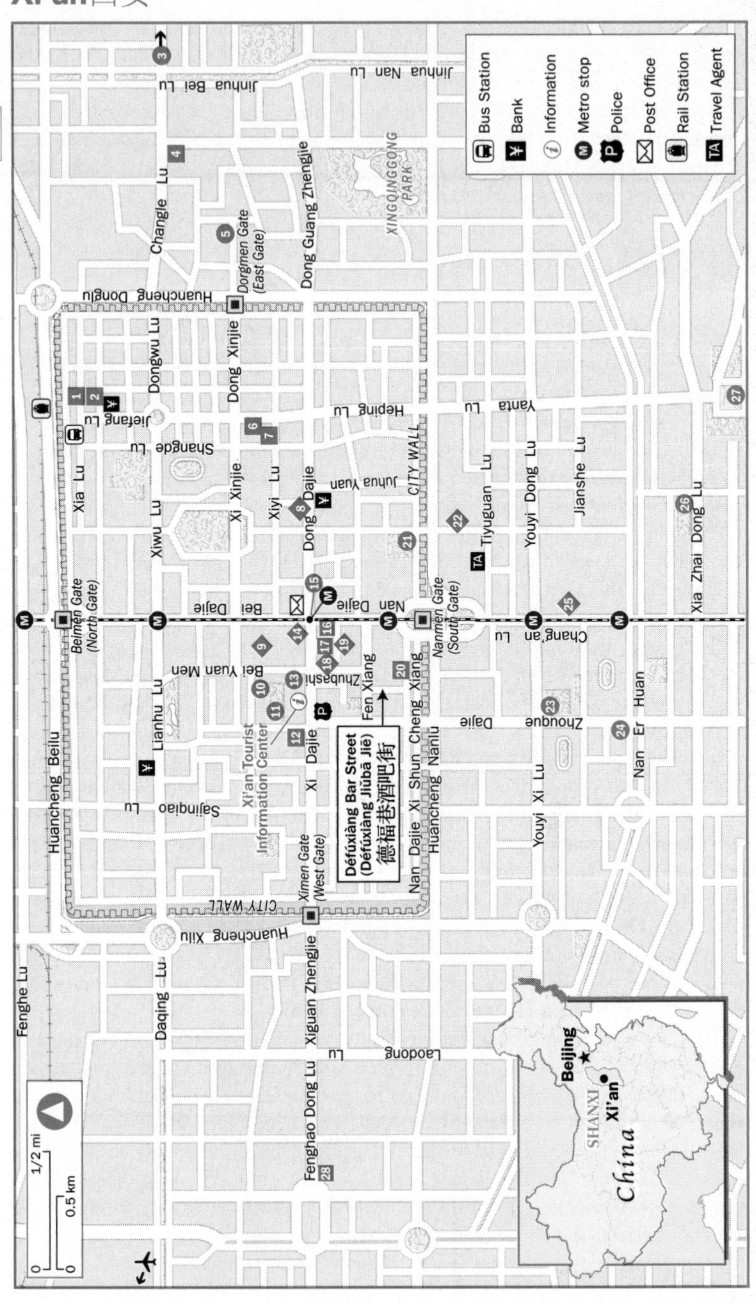
Bus Station
Bank
Information
Metro stop
Police
Post Office
Rail Station
Travel Agent
Défúxiàng Bar Street
(Défúxiàng Jiǔbā Jiē)
德福巷酒吧街
Xi'an Tourist Information Center
Beimen Gate (North Gate)
Nanmen Gate (South Gate)
Ximen Gate (West Gate)
Dongmen Gate (East Gate)
CITY WALL
XINGQINGGONG PARK
Huancheng Beilu
Huancheng Donglu
Huancheng Xilu
Huancheng Nanlu
Jinhua Bei Lu
Jinhua Nan Lu
Changle Lu
Dong Guang Zhengjie
Dongwu Lu
Dong Xinjie
Jiefang Lu
Shangde Lu
Heping Lu
Xia Lu
Xiwu Lu
Xi Xinjie
Xiyi Lu
Dong Dajie
Juhua Yuan
Bei Dajie
Nan Dajie
Bei Yuan Men
Zhubashi
Fen Xiang
Lianhu Lu
Xi Dajie
Sajinqiao Lu
Nan Dajie Xi Shun Cheng Xiang
Tiyuguan Lu
Yanta Lu
Youyi Dong Lu
Youyi Xi Lu
Jianshe Lu
Chang'an Lu
Zhouque Dajie
Nan Er Huan
Xia Zhai Dong Lu
Fenghe Lu
Daqing Lu
Xiguan Zhengjie
Fenghao Dong Lu
Laodong Lu
0.5 km
1/2 mi
Beijing
SHANXI
Xi'an
China

Xi'an Key

HOTELS ■

Bell Tower Hotel **16**
(Zhōnglóu Fàndiàn)
钟楼饭店

Bestay Express **7**
(Bǎi Shí Kuài Jié Jiǔ Diàn)
百时快捷酒店

Grand Soluxe Hotel **2**
(Xī'ān Yanguāng Guójì Dàjiǔdiàn)
西安阳光国际大酒店

Jiěfàng Fàndiàn **1**
解放饭店

Jinjiang Inn **6**
(Jǐn Jiāng Zhī Xīng Lǚguǎn)
锦江之星旅馆

Meihua Golden Tang **12**
(Meǐhuá Jīn Táng Guójì Jiǔdiàn)
美华金唐国际酒店

Melody Hotel **17**
(Měilún Jiǔdiàn)
美伦酒店

Shangri-La Golden Flower **4**
(Jīnhuā Fàndiàn)
金花大酒店

Sheraton Xian **28**
(Xīláidēng Dàjiǔdiàn)
喜来登大酒店

Xī'ān Shūyuàn Qīngnián Lǚshè **20**
西安书院青年旅社

ATTRACTIONS ●

Banpo Neolithic Village **3**
(Bànpō Bówùguǎn)
半坡博物馆

Bell Tower **15**
(Zhōng Lóu)
钟楼

Drum Tower **13**
(Gu Lóu)
鼓楼

Forest of Stelae **21**
(Bēilín Bówùguǎn)
碑林博物馆

Gaojia Dayuan **10**
(Gāojiā Dàyuàn)
大清真寺/化觉巷清真大寺

Great Goose Pagoda **27**
(Dà Yàn Tǎ)
大雁塔

Great Mosque **11**
(Dà Qīngzhēnsì)
大清真寺

Shǎnxī History Museum **26**
(Shǎnxī Lìshǐ Bówùguǎn)
陕西历史博物馆

Small Goose Pagoda **23**
(Xiǎo Yàn Tǎ)
小雁塔

Temple of the Eight Immortals **5**
(Bā Xiān Ān)
八仙庵

Xī'ān Gǔwán Chéng **24**
西安古玩城

RESTAURANTS & NIGHTLIFE ◆

Dé Fā Chāng **14**
德发长

Fánjì Làzhī Ròudiàn **19**
樊记腊汁肉店

Jiasan Guàntang Baozi **9**
贾三灌汤包子

Lǎ Sūn Jiā **8**
老孙家

Shanxi Grand Opera House **22**
(Shǎnxī Gēwǔ Dà Xìyuàn)
陕西歌舞大戏院

Star Ferry **18**
(Tiān Xīng Mǎtoú)
天星码头

Tang Dynasty **25**
(Táng Yuè Gōng)
唐乐宫

Essentials

GETTING THERE Daily **flights** connect Xianyang Airport with all major cities in China, including Beijing, Shanghai, Chongqing, Chengdu, Kunming, Shenzhen, Ürümqi, Lhasa, and Hong Kong. You can book flights through the ticketing agency on the ground floor of the Melody Hotel on Xi Dajie (✆ **029/8728-3333**). **Airport shuttle buses** (¥26) depart from outside of the Melody Hotel on the hour from 6am to 7pm; aim to leave 3 hours before your flight. A **taxi** from the airport into town costs about ¥150 to ¥180 dependent on the time of day.

The **railway station** is located outside the northeast side of the city wall, 20 minutes by double-decker bus no. 603 from the main hotel area. The station square has recently been redeveloped and now has a KFC, a McDonald's, and a 24-hour Internet cafe. The station itself is open 24 hours, and window 3 or 4 should have an English-speaker. Ticket refunds can be obtained from window 2. The fastest trains to Beijing are the Z20 (11 hr.) at 7:30pm and the T44 (13 hr.) at 7pm, although a new high-speed line is due to open by 2012 and will cut the journey time to an unbelievable 4 hours! The line will have its own designated terminus near the airport. Other useful trains are the Z94 to Shanghai (14 hr.) at 5pm; the K84 to Guangzhou (26 hr.) at 8:35am; the T164 to Lanzhou (7 hr.) at 10:11am; the K165 at 10:18pm, which passes through Chengdu (16 hr.) and terminates in Kunming (36 hr.); the T52 to Ürümqi (27 hr.) at 12:36pm; and the T224 to Chongqing (11 hr.) at 10:28pm.

The **bus station (Xi'an Qiche Zhan; ✆ 029/8742-7420)** is directly opposite the railway station. Regular buses connect with Zhengzhou (573km/355 miles; 7 hr.; ¥133), Luoyang (425km/264 miles; 4 hr.; ¥108), Taiyuan (685km/425 miles; 8 hr.; ¥190), Tianshui (380km/236 miles; 4 hr.; ¥120), and Tongchuan (100km/62 miles; 2 hr.; ¥29). Afternoon sleeper buses connect with Yinchuan (720km/446 miles; 9 hr.; ¥200). For Hua Shan (2 hr.; ¥22) buses leave from east of the station square. For Yan'an (402km/249 miles; 4 hr.; ¥98), you'll need to head to the east station **(Dong Keyun Zhan).**

CITY LAYOUT The center of town is generally denoted by the massive Ming **Bell Tower (Zhong Lou),** which marks the crossroads between the main north-south and east-west roads—which connect with the four main city gates. The main arteries are **Bei, Nan, Dong,** and **Xi Dajie** (North, South, East, and West aves.). Most of the main hotels, and many of the main sights and restaurants, are along these roads.

GETTING AROUND Regular **buses** cost ¥1, while K buses, which are air-conditioned, charge ¥2. Most **taxis** are green Santana sedans that charge ¥7 for the first 2km (1¼ miles), then ¥1.50 per additional kilometer; add ¥1 if you're traveling between the hours of 10pm and 5am. The first **subway** line, running north-south through the city, is due to open by 2012 and an east-west line will follow by 2014.

Xi'an is flat and thus seems suitable for **biking,** but the streets are congested, and traffic rules are often ignored by motorists. Aside from a ride along the top of the city walls, cycling in Xi'an is only recommended for the experienced urban cyclist.

TOURS While you can arrange tours of the sites within Xi'an, it's easy enough, more fun, and cheaper to see the town by yourself. For trips outside of the city it is worthwhile to book a tour and many travel agencies and hotels offer 1-day tours. The most popular tour follows the **Eastern Route (Dong Xian),** which usually includes the **Terra-Cotta Warriors (Qin Bingmayong Bowuguan), Huaqing Chi (Huaqing Pools), Banpo Bowuguan,** and sometimes **Da Yan Ta.** The more expensive and less-traveled **Western Route (Xi Xian)** should include Famen Si,

Qian Ling (Tang dynasty tombs), and perhaps Mao Ling (Han dynasty tombs), and Xianyang Bowuguan (Xianyang Museum); in this book, we'll focus on the Eastern Route.

CITS, at Chang'an Bei Lu 48 (✆ **029/8526-2066;** www.citsxa.com; 8am–8pm), charges ¥350 for the Eastern Route, which includes all transport, an English-speaking guide, entrance fees, and lunch. They have plenty of branches around the city including one on the second floor of the Bell Tower Hotel (✆ **137/0921-7156**). Most hotels offer their own tours, and hostels offer cheaper versions of the same. **Shuyuan Hostel** (✆ **029/8728-7721**) offers Terracotta Warrior tours for ¥220, and day trips out to Hua Shan for ¥390. Another useful resource is the **Xi'an Tourist Information Centre,** just west of the Drum Tower (✆ **029/8763-0166;** 8:30am–9pm), where English-speaking staff can provide detailed information on local attractions, and also assist with tour booking.

[FastFACTS] XI'AN

Banks, Foreign Exchange & ATMs Plenty of banks around town offer cash and travelers check exchange, credit card advances, and ATMs. The city branch of the **Bank of China** is at Jiefang Lu 157 (✆ **029/8762-0755;** Mon–Fri 9am–6pm, Sat and Sun 9am–4pm). It's about 400m (¼ mile) south of the railway station, on the west side of Jiefang Lu, next to the Silk Road Hotel. The provincial branch is located in the center of town, on the corner of Juhua Yuan at Dong Dajie 306 (same hours). Several ATMs are accessible 24 hours and accept foreign credit cards. There's also a branch, with an ATM, just 180m (590 ft.) south of the Bell Tower at Nan Dajie 29 (✆ **029/8728-1287;** same hours).

Internet Access The most convenient and comfortable net cafe in the downtown area is 24-hr. **T8,** on the second floorin between De Fa Chang and the Wenyuan Hotel on the Bell Tower Square. Charges range from ¥2.50 to ¥4 per hour and there's a small cafe on site. Opposite the railway station on the second floor of the McDonald's there's a good 24-hour net cafe that charges ¥4 per hour.

Post Office The **main branch** is at the northeast corner of the Bell Tower at Bei Dajie 1, open 9am to 7pm.

Visa Extensions Extensions can be obtained from the **PSB** at Xi Dajie 58 (✆ **029/8727-5934**). They are open Monday to Friday 8:30am to noon and 3 to 6pm and they take 3 days to process extensions.

Exploring Xi'an

Xi'an has a bewildering array of sights that can confound the visitor with little time to spare. The Terra-Cotta Warriors are a must, likewise Emperor Jingdi's Mausoleum and the Shanxi History Museum, but make sure you also leave time for a walk or bike ride along the city walls, a dumpling banquet, and a wander through the Muslim quarter prior to an alfresco meal of kabobs.

Ba Xian An (Temple of the Eight Immortals) ★ Tucked away in a narrow alley the tour buses can't reach is the most charming temple in Xi'an. As with the Great Mosque, the walk into it is half the adventure, with a flea market out front in some of the temple's old buildings. This becomes a huge antiques market on Sunday mornings (see "Shopping," below). Inside the temple, monks, their hair tied up in traditional Daoist fashion, play chess and are always keen for a chat. The folk legend of the **Eight Immortals (Ba Xian)** is said to have originated here during the late

Tang dynasty. The temple was expanded during the Qing dynasty and was a favorite haunt of the Cixi dowager empress during the time she spent in Xi'an after her escape from Beijing following the Boxer Rebellion. As you look at the temple murals, note the influence of Confucianism on its supposed alter-ego, Daoism: The Eight Immortals have a strict hierarchy, with Lu Dongbin in front on his tiger, the rotund Tieguai Li waddling along with his crook to his side, and the one woman, He Xiangu, near the back, carrying a lotus flower.

Wu Dao Shizi Dongjie (from An Ren Fang, continue east 135m/450 ft. before heading south down the 1st alley on your right; turn right when the road meets a T-junction. Immediately take a left and continue south to the back of the temple, following the incense vendors). Admission ¥3. 8:30am–6pm. Bus: 13 or 42 from the station, or 4 or 11 from the Bell Tower to An Ren Fang.

Beilin Bowuguan (Forest of Stelae) ★ Formerly the Shanxi Provincial Museum, the Forest of Stelae is situated in a former Confucian temple (ca. 1087) that the literature describes as "unsophisticated and elegant." Originally forming the basis of a Tang university, many of the stelae have traveled a long way to get here; they were floated downriver on rafts to Luoyang during the Song dynasty before returning here in 1087. Stelae are often borne on *bixi,* legendary turtlelike creatures descended from the Dragon King *(longwang)* that were renowned for their incredible strength and endurance. As there is little English signage, the stelae can be a little hard to appreciate for non-Chinese-speakers, but the serene atmosphere of the courtyards and their contorted time-old trees require no translation.

In the main courtyard, the first major stele was composed by the Xuanzong emperor in 745; the exposition on filial piety predated the influential "three character classic" *(san zi jing).* Room 1 houses the Confucian classics, including The Analects, The Spring, and Autumn Annals. Candidates for official examinations would pore over rubbings taken from these stelae and would be expected to know the classics by heart—an educational style that unfortunately still holds sway in China. Immediately to your left in room 2 is the Nestorian Stele. Nestorian Christians were drummed out of the Church for maintaining that Jesus was both human and divine and that Mary was the mother of "the man Jesus," and not the mother of God. The stele records the visit of a Nestorian priest to Chang'an and the founding of a Nestorian chapel, providing evidence of a Nestorian presence in China as early as A.D. 635. The influence of other faiths is clear—the Maltese cross is set amid Daoist clouds, supported by a Buddhist lotus flower. Rooms 2 and 3 also house the work of master calligraphers, such as Wang Xizhi, whose writings are still used as models by calligraphy students. Room 4 has pictorial stelae, including a famous image of Confucius. Here you will encounter a demonstration of "rubbing," whereby moistened paper is hammered onto the inked stones, color is tapped on using a wooden disk wrapped in a cloth, and the impression is dried before being gobbled up by Japanese tour groups. It isn't a gentle process, and it's easy to see why many stelae are almost unreadable. Double back to your left to enter rooms 5 to 7, as well as a gallery of stone sculpture containing an exquisite statue of a bodhisattva that shows Indian and Grecian influences.

Wenyi Bei Lu 18. ✆ **029/8725-8448.** Admission ¥75. Summer 8:30am–6pm; winter 8:30am–5:30pm. Bus: 14, 402, or 239.

Da Qingzhensi (Great Mosque) ★ Founded during the height of the Tang dynasty in 742, this is one of the most tranquil places in town and the center of a sizable Muslim community, residents in Xi'an for over 1,200 years. As with Baxian An, half the adventure is getting there, as you veer left just north of the Drum Tower. The covered alleyway, Huajue Xiang, has good-humored vendors selling all manner of weird merchandise (see "Shopping," below) and it may take you a few attempts to find the mosque. The courtyards are spacious and have a gardenlike feel, with a wonderful fusion of Arabian and Chinese architectural styles. To the right of the entrance is a hall filled with exquisite Ming furniture. The central courtyard has a triple-eaved octagonal "minaret" from which worshipers were traditionally called to prayer, although it is far more akin to a Chinese pagoda. The prayer hall is normally closed to non-Muslims. As this is an active mosque, be circumspect in taking photographs. Avoid visiting on Friday, when access to the mosque is restricted. Be sure to bring mosquito spray in the summer. Combine your visit with a wander through the lanes of the Muslim quarter (below).

Huajue Xiang 30. ✆ **029/8727-2541.** Admission ¥25. Apr–Oct 8am–7pm; Nov–Mar 8am–6pm. Bus: 221, 29, 6, or 618.

Da Yan Ta (Great Goose Pagoda) & Da Ci'en Si (Temple of Great Goodwill) ★ This is the best-known temple in Xi'an, and worth a visit if, like many in the U.K. and Australia, you were entranced by the TV version of "Monkey" as a child. The scripture-collecting journey of Xuanzang (596–664) to India, on which the show was based, lasted 15 years, and was immortalized and lampooned in Wu Cheng'en's novel *Journey to the West (Xi You Ji).* But the journey was not the end of Xuanzang's travails. Upon his return, he requested the construction of a pagoda to house the scriptures; his request was accommodated inside a temple built from 647 to 652 by Prince Li Zhi in honor of his mother, Empress Wen De. Construction of the pagoda commenced in 652, in a style similar to those seen by Xuanzang in India—hence the simple, tapering structure. Xuanzang is credited with translating 75 texts into over 1,000 volumes, an amazing feat since the originals contained a host of specialized terms with no Chinese equivalents.

Halls at the back of the temple contain murals depicting Xuanzang's journey—in many pictures, he is shown holding a fly whisk, intended to send evil spirits into flight. To the left and right of the pagoda's south entrance are prefaces to the texts written by Taizong and Gaozong. Above the east and west doors are barely visible Tang carvings of the Buddha. The temple's perimeter has recently undergone redevelopment and the result is as good as Chinese urban planning gets. To the north of the pagoda is the north plaza *(bei guangcang),* which boasts a large pool of fountains, benches, and retail shops lining the mall. A water fountain and light show kicks off nightly at 8pm.

Admission ¥50, plus an additional ¥20 to climb the tower. 8:30am–5pm. Bus: 610 (from the station).

Muslim Quarter ★★ A wander through the timeless lanes of the Muslim quarter is one of the highlights of a visit to Xi'an, and provides an alluring taste of what lies farther west for travelers setting out along the Silk Road. The Hui have been living here for centuries and in the lanes white-capped men and headscarved women tend small noodle and kabob houses, whilst carts laden with fruit and nuts bustle by. North of the Drum Tower, Bei Yuan Men is the natural entrance to the quarter, and is a great place for a kabob meal and some souvenir browsing along Huajue Xiang, but to really experience the feel of the quarter you need to head out into the sidestreets. Approach the quarter from Xi Dajie, head through the red arch onto Da Xue Xi Xiang, and then work your way east toward the Great Mosque and Bei Yuan Men.

Shanxi Lishi Bowuguan (Shanxi History Museum) ★★★ With the completion of recent renovations, one of China's best museums just got better and displays its unrivalled collection of treasures even more alluringly. Items are displayed chronologically, starting with the Shang dynasty (ca. 17th c.–11th c. B.C.) and the Zhou dynasty (ca. 11th c.–221 B.C.) on the ground floor, including items that speak to eating, drinking, and merriment in the Western Zhou (ca. 11th c.–771 B.C.).

Things take a martial turn as you enter the Qin dynasty (221–206 B.C.): Aside from the bronze swords and rusting iron weapons (which gave the Qin a decisive military edge), a striking exhibit is a **tiger-shaped tally** covered in characters *(duhu fu)* that gave its owner, one General Du, imperial authorization to mobilize over 50 soldiers at will. As you move on to the Tang dynasty (618–907), the influence of Buddhist art from the Silk Routes becomes apparent—carvings are more sophisticated, and bright colors are introduced. Perhaps the most startling exhibits are the frescoes *(bihua)* relocated from the Tang tumuli around Xi'an. A depiction of **ladies-in-waiting *(gongnu tu)* ★★** shows nine women carrying the tools of their trade—candelabras, fans, cloth bundles, powder boxes, even fly swatters. Two of them are dressed in male clothing. Another fresco *(ma qiu tu)* shows noblemen enjoying the newly imported game of polo. **Ceramic tomb guardians** point to a lively trade with the outside world—there's a trader from Africa and a fanciful depiction of a man on horseback battling a leopard. You can easily spend 3 or 4 hours here.

Xiao Zhai Dong Lu 91. ✆ **029/8525-4727.** Free Admission. Visitor numbers are restricted to 2,500 in the morning and 1,500 in the afternoon, so get there early and take your passport. Tues-Sun 8:30am–5pm (last admission 4pm). Bus: 5 (from the station) or 610 (from just north of the Bell Tower to Lishi Bowuguan).

Xi'an Chengqiang (City Wall) ★ The largest and best-preserved city wall in China is definitely worth a visit. The pieces of the wall have recently been reconnected so that you can do the 14km (8¾-mile) loop around it by foot, bicycle, or a golf cart. The walls were built during the early Ming dynasty, on the remains of Tang palace walls. The original city walls were much farther out, well past Da Yan Ta. The surrounding moat has recently undergone an extensive clean-up and is fringed by a narrow strip of parkland popular with tai chi practitioners, dog-walkers, and young couples. The South Gate (Nan Men) is the best place to start your exploration. Individual (¥20) and tandem bicycles (¥30) may be rented (per 100 min.) from here, or just east of Heping Men. A ride on a golf cart around the wall costs (¥50). To do the entire loop takes 3 to 4 hours by foot, less than 2 hours by bicycle, or 1 hour by cart. The wall provides little protection from sun or wind, so dress accordingly.

Admission ¥40. Apr–Oct 8am–9:30pm; Nov–Mar 8am–6pm.

Around Xi'an

Bingmayong (Terra-Cotta Warriors) ★★★ This is the reason most visitors come to Xi'an, and unlike some big sights in China, it does not disappoint. Amazingly, the warriors are just one piece of Qin Shi Huang's attempt to reconstruct his empire for the afterlife. The tomb to the west is supposedly booby-trapped and is still to be fully excavated, but it is said to include a full reconstruction of the ancient capital, complete with rivers and lakes of mercury. According to historian Sima Qian, over 700,000 workers were drafted for the project, and those involved in the construction of the tomb were rewarded with graves beside their emperor. Tourism officials pray that the warriors are "just the tip of the iceberg," but it is just as likely that the tomb was plundered during the Tang or Song dynasties. ***Tip:*** To fully appreciate the majesty of the warriors, try to get to the site as early as possible and race to Pit 1; if you get here ahead of the crowds, you should manage a few minutes of solitude with one of the world's greatest historical finds.

It's hard not to get a shiver down your spine as you survey the unromantically named **Pit 1 ★★★**, with four columns of warriors in each of the 11 passageways; there are over 1,000 infantry in battle formation, stretching back 182m (600 ft.). Originally painted in bright colors, they were constructed from interchangeable parts sealed together by clay. Because the heads were hand-molded, no two appear the same. Qin Shi Huang's army was drawn from all over his vast empire, and this ethnic diversity is reflected in the variety of hairstyles, headdresses, and facial expressions. Even on the mass-produced bodies, the level of detail is striking, down to the layering of armor and the studs on archers' shoes that prevented them from slipping. The average height of the warriors is 1.8m (5 ft. 11 in.); senior officers are taller. Most of the 1,400 soldiers in **Pit 2** are less intact than those in Pit 1, although the statues show greater diversity of posture. The highlights here are encased in glass cabinets around the edge of the pit; look for the 2m (6½-ft.) general. **Pit 3** is much smaller and houses the headquarters, with 68 senior officers.

A **small hall** just to the right of Pit 1 contains a display of two magnificent bronze chariots, reconstructed from nearly 3,500 pieces excavated from a pit to the west of the tomb.

The tour bus will drop you off in a parking lot; you can either walk the 1km (⅔ mile) to the museum's entrance or take a trolley for ¥15 round-trip ticket. An English-speaking guide (¥100), or an audio guide (¥40) can be arranged on the spot at the main entrance.

✆ **029/8391-1961.** Admission: Main exhibits Mar–Nov ¥110; Dec–Feb ¥65. 8:30am–5:30pm. Bus: 306 (¥8) leaves from the front of the railway station, on the east side. Round-trip taxi from the city costs ¥200–¥300.

Banpo Bowuguan (Banpo Neolithic Village) If you're interested in archaeology, this is an essential visit. Otherwise, you can give it a miss. Given the amount of material unearthed here since its discovery in 1953 (tools, pottery, burial jars, and so on), it's amazing that only one-fifth of the site has been excavated (mostly due to the cost of preserving what has been discovered). The village, traced from the Yangshao culture, was occupied from about 5000 to 4000 B.C.

Banpo Bowuguan (from the Banpo Bowuguan bus stop, walk back toward town and turn left at the 1st cross street). Admission ¥35. 8:30am–5:30pm. Bus: 11 (from just north of the Bell Tower) or 105 (from the station). Continuing on to Huaqing Pools and Bingmayong is tricky, but possible. Take bus no. 105 back toward town as far as Wanshou Lu. Catch bus no. 512 north far as Wang Jia Fen (3 stops) and then catch bus no. 306 east.

Emperor Jingdi's Mausoleum (Han Yanling) ★★ Discovered by a works crew building the new airport road in 1990, Han Yanling, the mausoleum of Emperor Jingdi (157-141 B.C.), deserves far more attention than it has been getting. This is a good thing, and while everyone scrambles for a glimpse of the terra-cotta warriors at Lintong, far fewer make it to Han Yanling. Those that do are rewarded by an intimate journey through time in an incredible underground museum that allows visitors to get up close to tens of thousands of ancient clay figurines displayed in their originally discovered state.

Of course comparisons with the "original" warriors are unavoidable, and also offer insight into the changes in China during this 4-century period. Qin Shi Huang's terra-cotta army was built during a turbulent time, when the great tyrant emperor was trying to unify the country for the first time, and the focus is thus military and grand. Three centuries later, Emperor Jingdi ruled over a far more stable and agrarian empire, and this is reflected by the fact that along with soldiers, nobles, government officials and servants, there are herds of pigs, sheep and cows. While the terra-cotta warriors at Lintong were Qin Shi Huang's last great gesture, economic measures and looking to the future prevailed during the reign of Jingdi, meaning that the figurines were built to a third-size (albeit in their thousands).

As at Lintong, the figures are laid out in a series of pits surrounding the unexcavated mausoleum itself. In some of the pits the figures are toppled like skittles, in others they remain caked in loess, with only columns of protruding heads to indicate what lies beneath. There are also examples of the molds used to cast the figures, which help to illustrate their production, said to have taken some 17,000 workers nearly three decades. The figures were cast without arms, which were fashioned from wood and added later. More important figurines were also clothed in miniature silk garments, but these have long since perished. Some of the figures are clearly identifiable as eunuchs, and as such this is also the earliest evidence of this practice in the Chinese court.

The whole experience is assisted by state-of the-art display techniques, including the glass walkway that allows visitors to gain a bird's-eye view of the pits, excellent low-lighting, audio guides in English, French, German and Japanese, and an unbelievable holographic video that is worth seeing for the technology more than the content. The site is close to the airport and is well-combined with your arrival or departure. Allow 90 minutes.

Han Yanling (10 min. drive from the airport). Admission ¥40. 8:30am–6:30pm. No Public Transport. ¥250–¥300 taxi return from Xi'an.

Shopping

Along with good clothes and sports shops on Dong Dajie, and a decent supermarket in the **Century Ginwa** (below Bell Tower Square), Xi'an has plenty of decent markets.

Ba Xian An The outdoor antiques market on Sunday mornings is the most atmospheric in town. Despite a sign warning that antiques must be declared with Customs before you leave China, there's no guarantee that what you buy is a genuine antique. But there is a buzz to the place, and you can find some wonderful Cultural Revolution kitsch, ceramics, bronze Buddhas, and Qing coins. See the Ba Xian An review in "Exploring Xi'an," above, for directions.

Huajue Xiang An enjoyable place to shop for souvenirs is the covered alleyway that leads to **Da Qingzhensi.** Shopping here is a blood sport, and you are the game, but the vendors are friendly. Interesting finds include feng shui compasses, Mao lighters, Tibetan prayer wheels, copies of *Little Red Book* in French, and gnarled walking sticks.

Shuyuan Xiang This fun street for browsing is east of Nan Men, on the way to Beilin Bowuguan. Shops sell huge paint brushes, rubbings, paintings, and musical instruments, and you can watch artists at work in this faithfully restored street.

Xi'an Guwan Cheng With peasants finding that their fields are full of valuable antiques stored in the graves of their prosperous ancestors, digging is going on at a furious pace in the countryside surrounding Xi'an. Factories producing excellent copies are also very busy. If you're after a genuine antique, you have some chance of finding one here. There are fakes aplenty, but this market is geared to locals, so asking prices are not as absurd as elsewhere. There are bronzes of all kinds, heroic comic books from the Cultural Revolution, and weird *Kama Sutra*–inspired woodcarvings. Be wary when purchasing bronzes, which tended to be melted down and reused over the ages (unless they were buried). Your best bets are ceramics and pottery. Open April through October from 9:30am to 6pm, and November through March from 10am to 6pm.

Zhu Que Dajie Zhong Duan 2. Bus no. 610 from south of Bell Tower to Xi'an Guwan Cheng.

Where to Stay

Xi'an has an ever-increasing array of accommodation options to choose from. Hostels are popping up all over the city and, at the other end of the scale, many international five-stars are staking their claim in this increasingly competitive market, including a newly opened Shangri-La in the Gao Xin hi-tech zone, plus another Sheraton and a Westin, both of which are set to receive guests in 2012. Most of Xi'an's luxurious hotels are to be found outside of the city walls, though the Hyatt is a notable and longstanding exception. North of here the Accor group has opened a development containing a Sofitel, Mercure, and Grand Mercure, but its location is a little too far from the sights, and the hodgepodge of styles and poor service have thus far proven to be stumbling blocks. Mid-range options abound and many enjoy prime locations within minutes of the Bell and Drum Towers and the Muslim quarter. Most hotels listed below will offer some discount, and reductions of as much as 50% off the rack rates can be achieved with bargaining out of peak season.

Unless you have an early train, staying by the station has little merit, but if you must, try the **Jiefang Fandian,** Jiefang Lu 181 (✆ **029/8769-8888;** ¥328 standard room, ¥638 suite; 20% discount available), directly across from the railway station, or the **Grand Soluxe (Xi'an Yangguang Guoji Dajiudian;** ✆ **029/8735-8888;** ¥880 standard room, ¥1,380 suite; up to 40% discount available), directly behind the Jiefang.

VERY EXPENSIVE

Shangri-La Golden Flower (Jinhua Fandian) ★★ Xi'an's first international five-star venture, the Golden Flower continues to impress with its switched on service, spacious well-appointed rooms, huge beds, and nice bathroom and lighting fixtures. Located outside the city wall, the hotel is inconvenient for walking around, but a 15-minute taxi ride will get you to the center of town. Stay here if you're in town just to see the Terra-Cotta Warriors, as it is closer to the expressway leading to the treasures than other luxury hotels.

Changle Xi Lu 8 (3km/2 miles east of city wall). www.shangri-la.com. ✆ **029/8323-2981.** Fax 029/8323-5477. 416 units. ¥888 standard room; from ¥2,788 suite. 15% service charge. AE, DC, MC, V. Bus: 105 (from the station) or 11 (from east of Bell Tower). **Amenities:** 2 restaurants; bar; cafe; concierge; executive-level rooms; forex; health club and spa; large indoor pool; room service. *In room:* A/C, satellite TV, DVD player, fridge, Internet, minibar.

Sheraton Xi'an (Xilaideng Dajiudian) ★★ Located over 1.6km (1 mile) west of the city walls, the Sheraton has improved remarkably in recent years, and service is excellent. Rooms are bright, modern and well-appointed, with sturdy beds and plush carpets. After a day braving the grimy air of Xi'an, seek refuge in the immaculate bathrooms. The Gate West Restaurant offers tasty Western fare.

Fenghao Dong Lu 262. www.sheraton.com/xian. ✆ **029/8426-1888.** Fax 029/426-2188. 338 units. ¥830 standard room; from ¥2,400 suite. 15% service charge. AE, DC, MC, V. Bus: 611 from the station and west of the Bell Tower to Fenghao Dong Lu. **Amenities:** 3 restaurants; cafe; bar; airport shuttle; concierge; executive-level rooms; forex; health club; game room; large indoor pool; room service; spa. *In room:* A/C, satellite TV, fridge, hair dryer, Internet (¥50 per day), minibar.

EXPENSIVE

Bell Tower Hotel (Zhonglou Fandian) ★ This is a solid choice with a fantastic location and one notch down in price from the international hotels. Rooms are spacious and bathrooms are modern and clean. English-speaking staff is surprisingly competent for a state-run hotel. A helpful branch of CITS is on the second floor.

Nan Dajie 110 (southwest corner of Bell Tower). ✆ **029/8760-0000.** Fax 029/8721-8767. 300 units. ¥798 standard room; from ¥1,280 suite. Up to 20% discount. AE, DC, MC, V. Bus: 603 from the station. **Amenities:** 3 restaurants; cafe; concierge; forex. *In room:* A/C, TV, fridge, hair dryer, Internet, minibar.

Meihua Golden Tang ★ This stylish new hotel has a great location, tucked away on a lane west of the Drum Tower. Rooms are trendily decorated in subtle tones, and bathrooms are tastefully designed; deluxe rooms are larger and have a sofa rather than a recliner. Ask for a room with an external window rather than those that look over the atrium. Service is competent, courteous, and English-speaking.

Xi Dajie 126 (1 block west of the Drum Tower). www.mandarin-cn.com. ✆ **029/8761-6666.** 265 units. ¥1,300 standard room; from ¥2,200 suite. Up to 60% discount. AE, DC, MC, V. **Amenities:** 2 restaurants; forex; gym. *In room:* A/C, TV, DVD library, fridge, hair dryer, Internet, minibar.

MODERATE

Melody Hotel (Meilun Jiudian) The Melody's location and price make it a good midrange choice. Although service is lackluster and rooms are on the small side and showing signs of wear, they are, at least, clean and bright. If you don't mind a bit of street noise, then the pricier rooms with Drum Tower view are also worth considering.

Xi Dajie 86 (opposite the Drum Tower). ✆ **029/8728-8888.** Fax 029/8727-3601. 138 units (shower only). ¥398–¥498 standard room; ¥888 suite. 40% discount AE, DC, MC, V. **Amenities:** Restaurant; concierge. *In room:* A/C, TV, fridge, Internet, minibar.

INEXPENSIVE

Jinjiang Inn (Jinjiang Zhixing Luguan) The Jinjiang comes through with the usual clean, comfortable and functional rooms, with good beds and showers. Service is friendly and the location, within 10 minutes' walking distance of the train station, isn't too bad given the price. If you want to go cheaper still, try the Bestay Express (Baishi Kuaijie Jiudian) just around the corner on Xiyi Lu, a zero frills chain also owned by the Jinjiang group.

Jiefang Lu 110. www.jinjianginns.com. ✆ **029/8743-9695.** 171 units (shower only). ¥229 standard room. No credit cards. **Amenities:** Restaurant. *In room:* A/C, TV, Internet.

Shuyuan Qingnian Lushe (Xi'an Shuyuan Youth Hostel) ★★ 🎁 Of the various hostels in Xi'an, this is the best choice. A restored courtyard residence, it formerly housed the Xianyang County government. The hostel has been extensively renovated and has clean, basic dorm beds, as well as simple twins with good modern bathrooms. You also get English-speaking staff, an excellent location, impartial and useful information, free Internet access, a decent bar and restaurant, and that rare commodity in China—ambience.

Nan Dajie Xi Shun Cheng Xiang 2A (27m/90 ft. west of the South Gate, just inside the city wall). www.hostelxian.com. ✆ **029/8728-7721.** 45 units (shower only). ¥200 standard room; from ¥40–¥60 dorm bed. No credit cards. Bus: 603 from the railway station to Nan Men. **Amenities:** Cafe; bar; bike rental; concierge; railway station courtesy car; Internet; kitchen. *In room:* A/C, TV, no phone.

Where to Eat

Xi'an has a good variety of eateries, with some fine dumpling houses and atmospheric restaurants with outdoor seating along Bei Yuan in the **Muslim quarter.** If you feel the need for some Western intake, there's an overload of chains around the Bell Tower central intersection. For something vaguely healthier, there's also a **Subway** just west of Watsons on Xi Dajie.

De Fa Chang ★★ ☺ DUMPLINGS Dumplings are raised to a high art form at this huge and lively restaurant located next to the Bell Tower Square. The canteen downstairs is always bustling and serves a variety of dumplings and side dishes wheeled around on carts. Upstairs De Fa Chang is a little more refined, and serves an unbelievable 18-course dumpling meal (¥118). Tasty *xiaochi,* or little eats, resembling flying saucers, mouse heads, and walnuts will also come in a steady stream to your table.

Zhonglou Guangchang. ✆ **029/8721-4060.** Meal for 2 ¥40–¥200. No credit cards. 8:30am–9:30pm.

Fanji Lazhi Roudian SHANXI This is the most famous vendor of Shanxi's most widely consumed snack—*rou jia mo,* finely chopped pork pressed between two halves of a solid steamed bun. Xi'an's answer to the hamburger makes a perfect snack on the run, but you can almost feel your arteries clogging up as you wolf it down. Ask for the good-quality *(youzhi)* bun (¥8).

Zhubashi Jie 53 (from Gu Lou, the shop is opposite, 45m/150 ft. south of Xi Dajie on the road's east side). ✆ **029/8727-3917.** Meal for 2 less than ¥20. No credit cards. 8:30am–8:30pm. Bus: 611 from the station to Gu Lou.

Jiasan Guantang Baozi ★ MUSLIM Still the most famous of the Jia Brothers' restaurants, you'll know you're there when you see the monstrous eaves over the entrance and a wall festooned with photographs of Xi'an notables—TV hosts, writers, and musicians. The specialty dish is *guantang baozi,* with a choice of beef, lamb, or "three flavors"—lamb, mushroom, and prawn. The dumplings have piping-hot soup inside, so let them cool before testing your chopstick skills. This dish is best washed down with *ba bao tian xifan,* a sweet rice porridge filled with peanuts, sultanas, hawthorn, and medlar berries.

Bei Yuan Men 93 (135m/450 ft. north of Drum Tower, on the east side). ✆ **029/8725-7507.** Meal for 2 less than ¥40. No credit cards. 8:30am–11pm.

Lao Sun Jia ★ SHANXI Lao Sun Jia first opened its doors in 1898, and it remains the best place to sample Xi'an's most celebrated dish, *yangrou paomo.* There are now three branches, two of them on Dong Dajie. The most convenient branch is the first one you'll reach on Dong Dajie (coming from the Bell Tower). Both the clientele and the minimalist, modern decor is a little more upscale than in days of old, but the food remains the central attraction. As well as the *yangrou paomo,* recommended dishes include the lamb dumplings *(suan tang shuijiao)* and a local favorite,

Catching Chinese Shadows

Piying was the staple entertainment of rural Shanxi before karaoke. Puppets are carved from leather and dyed dazzling colors—many date from the Qing dynasty (1644–1911). There are over 600 different plays, ranging from legends to love stories to kung-fu epics. Unlike opera, this is loud, irreverent entertainment for the masses. Piying is a dying art form; it takes 10 years to learn the craft, and for most, driving a taxi is a more appealing option, but tourism may just save the day and short performances (¥15) can now be seen on request at Gaojia Dayuan (8:30am–11pm; entrance ¥15) on the western side of Bei Yuan Men in the Muslim quarter. This traditional courtyard residence, once home to Qing official Gao Yuesong, has been well restored and also contains an art gallery and a teahouse.

fenzheng yangrou, two steamed buns perched delicately to the side of a pile of mince and flour. You will face an empty bowl and two steamed buns, as well as plates of chili, coriander, and cloves of garlic that have been marinated in vinegar and sugar for several months. Tear the buns into tiny pieces and pop them into the empty bowl. When you've finished, your bowl will be taken away and refilled with broth and noodles. Stir in the coriander and chili, and when your palate gets greasy, nibble a clove of garlic and encourage your friends to do likewise. If the star dish doesn't fill you up, the stewed oxtail *(hongshao niuwei)* and bok choy with mushrooms *(bilu za shanggu)* are recommended.

Dong Dajie, just west of Nan Xinjie (look for the 1898 sign and take the lift to the 5th floor). ✆ **029/8742-1858.** Reservations recommended. Meal for 2 ¥150. No credit cards. 9am–9pm.

Star Ferry CANTONESE Right next to the Melody Hotel, this lively, bright, and modern canteen serves excellent Cantonese favorites like shrimp wonton and noodles (¥20). They also serve a few Hakka *(kejia)* dishes including braised pork and have a good range of tea on offer.

Xi Dajie 86. ✆ **029/8725-6611.** Meal for 2 ¥50. No credit cards. 8am–1am.

Xi'an After Dark

As well as the cultural entertainment options listed below, Xi'an also has a fairly lively nightlife scene; the best place to sample this is **Defuxiang Bar Street (Defuxiang Jiuba Jie),** northwest of Nan Men, where there are plenty of different bars to choose from.

THE PERFORMING ARTS

Two companies perform Tang-style banquets and musicals to entertain visitors. The competition for the group-tour dollar is fierce.

Shanxi Grand Opera House (Shanxi Gewu Da Xiyuan) While it can't compete with Tang Yue Gong (see below) as a spectacle, this opera company has a more authentic feel, with revolutionary credentials tracing its origins to the Northwest Culture Work Group in Yan'an. If you opt for the dinner, you'll gorge on dumplings with 20 different fillings. Be sure to book in advance. Voice-overs are in Chinese and English. Dinner starts at 7pm, and the show starts at 8pm.

Wen Yi Lu 161. ✆ **029/8785-6012.** Reservations required. Dinner and show ¥298; show only ¥238. AE, DC, MC, V. Bus: 14 from the station, or no. 208 from south of the Bell Tower to Diao Jia Cun.

Tang Dynasty (Tang Yue Gong) Run by a Hong Kong entrepreneur, this show delivers all your fantasies of Asia at once: lavish costumes modeled on the Mogao cave paintings, a six-course banquet (watch out for the rice wine), hammy acting, and some amazing music and dance. Gao Ming's performance of the Spring Oriole's Song on a vertical bamboo flute, the *pai xiao,* is almost worth the money in itself. If you can get past the slickness and the feeling that it's just for foreigners (the voice-overs are all in English), the show makes a spectacular night out. Dinner starts at 7pm; the show begins at 8:30pm.

Chang'an Lu 75. ✆ **029/8782-2222.** Fax 029/8526-1619. www.xiantangdynasty.com. Reservations required. Dinner and show ¥500; show only ¥220. AE, DC, MC, V. Bus: 603 from station or north of Bell Tower to Cao Chang Po.

A Side Trip from Xi'an: The Potters of Chen Lu (陈炉镇) ★★

This tiny group of villages in undulating terrain north of Xi'an has been turning out exquisite pottery since the Tang dynasty, and is free of the hype that surrounds Jingde Zhen (p. 521). Locals joke that Chen Lu "eats pottery," and while this may be fiction, walls are made of ceramic urns rather than bricks. Elegant cups that would fetch tidy sums in Xi'an lie by the side of the road. Numerous small factories turn out different styles of pottery, ranging from the sleek black *heiyou* to the rusty shades of *tiexiu hua* and the blues and whites of *qing hua.* It's an old-fashioned town: People call each other "comrade" *(tongzhi)* without the overtone of homosexuality that it now usually bears in urban China, wear Lei Feng hats with thick tops and earflaps without irony, and offer cigarettes on reflex when they meet a stranger.

If you visit on a day trip, it's doubtful you'll have time to explore all the factories and shops. The best bargains are found in the factory showrooms, where the starting prices will have you offering more money, but you're more likely to come across original works in the houses of individual artisans. Exquisite bowls in *qing hua* style cost as little as ¥20, while original works are considerably more expensive. Individual artisans are proud to display their wares and may hail you in the street. The main factory, **Chen Lu Taoci Chang** (✆ **0919/748-3343**), has an exhibition of antique ceramics, including Tang dynasty moxibustion cups, hat canisters from the Yuan dynasty, and ceramic pillows—still used by some villagers today. Visit the exhibition before going on a spending spree, as staff can advise you on which factories make which kinds of pottery. Other factories worth visiting include **Zhong Guo Yao Zhou Ci** (✆ **0919/748-3623**) and the workshop of renowned local artisan **Xu Kuai Le** (✆ **0919/748-2235**).

Chen Lu is a 1½-hour drive from Xi'an, but most tour agencies will give you a blank look when you mention it. A taxi should cost no more than ¥500 for the round-trip. Air-conditioned buses depart for Tongchuan (100km/62 miles; 1½ hr.; ¥29) from the main bus station every 15 minutes from 6:30am to 9pm. In Tongchuan, continue north to the first roundabout for 630m (2,066 ft.), or catch bus no. 8 to the roundabout at Yigu Liangzhan. From south of the roundabout, white minivans leave when full for Chen Lu (18km/11 miles; 40 min.; ¥3).

HUA SHAN 华山

Shanxi Province, 120km (74 miles) E of Xi'an

The first king of Shang made a sacrifice on Hua Shan in 1766 B.C., and Han Wudi (reigned 141–87 B.C.) declared it the Sacred Mountain of the West. The mountain's present popularity with Chinese tourists was aided by Jin Yong's martial-arts novel *Hua Shan Lun Jian,* which is filled with heroic swordsmen, mythical beasts, and beautiful maidens. Add a popular soap opera set against the granite bluffs, precariously perched pine trees, and Daoist temples dangling from precipitous peaks, and Hua Shan's popularity with the locals was guaranteed. Hua Shan sees comparatively few foreign visitors, but the scenery is spectacular, the Daoist monks are friendly, and the air is clear enough to make the sunrise worth seeing. The best times to visit are mid-autumn, when the trees are a magical, colorful jumble, or spring, when the wildflowers bloom. Winter is picturesque but bitterly cold.

Essentials

GETTING THERE Hua Shan can be visited as a 1- or 2-day trip from Xi'an. Regular **buses** leave from the main bus station from 7am (2 hr.; ¥22), or there are private buses for ¥33. All buses should drop you in the village from where you can walk to the ticket office. To take the cable car you'll need to take another bus (¥20 return), which departs from the ticket office and takes 20 minutes to reach the terminus. Entry to Hua Shan is ¥120. The last bus returns to Xi'an from the cable car stop at 4pm, and minibuses run until 7pm.

You can also connect by **rail** via Hua Shan railway station. Express G trains to and from Xi'an take just 35 minutes and depart every hour or so. From the station there is a minibus every half-hour to Hua Shan Kou (20 min.; ¥3), or you can hail a taxi for ¥20.

Exploring Hua Shan

Consider the cable car, particularly if you only have 1 day in your schedule. The mountain is a tough 2,000m (6,600-ft.) climb, especially if you don't have a head for heights. If you have 2 or more days, walk up and stay at one of the simple guesthouses on the mountain. You will enjoy a feeling of smugness when you meet the masses piling out of the cable cars at **North Peak** (**Bei Feng;** 1,613m/5,295 ft.). By staying on the mountain, you can see the sunrise and the sunset, and enjoy the mountains when the light is soft.

Some Chinese guidebooks recommend climbing up at night with a flashlight to see the sunrise (presumably skipping the entrance fee). The locals say, "You don't fear what you can't see" *("Bu jian bu pa")*. This is not sensible. The main 8km (5 miles) path starts from the village of Hua Shan and takes around 4 hours to reach the summit. The last mile to North Peak is steep, narrow, and slippery, particularly through **Heaven's Well (Tian Jing).** If your time is limited the cable car (¥150 round-trip; ¥80 one-way) is a far quicker option and reaches Bei Feng in 10 minutes. Climbing up, exploring the peaks, and then taking the cable car down will save your knees and leave you more time on the mountain.

Chinese tour groups, bedecked in yellow hats and white gloves, will gape at you, and souvenirs, bottles of water, and cucumbers will be waved in your face, but there is an enjoyable spirit of camaraderie among the hikers. And at least one of the souvenirs is worth purchasing. As at many of China's holy mountains, Chinese visitors have their name engraved on a brass padlock wishing good health for the family (or a long and happy relationship for young couples) and attach it to one of the many chain railings.

Where to Stay & Eat

Outside of early May and mid-October, there is a surplus of accommodations on Hua Shan, so discounts of 30% to 50% are easily obtained. Dining on the mountain is basic and overpriced; take as much food as you can carry.

If you arrive at Hua Shan late at night, there are a couple of passable hotels in **Hua Shan Kou,** and unlike the lodgings on Hua Shan itself, they have en-suite showers. The best places to stay in the village are the **Hua Shan Kezhan** (✆ **0913/465-8111;** ¥580 twin; discount of up to 45%), and the new **Bijiayi Kuaijie Jiudian** (✆ **0913/465-8000;** ¥238 standard twin).

On the mountain, facilities are basic, there are no private bathrooms or showers, and pit toilets are common. The **Bei Feng Fandian,** Hua Shan Fengjing Qu Bei Feng (¥240 twin without bathroom), is a 5-minute walk from the cable car—perfect for the lazy and the late. Both the sunset and the sunrise can be enjoyed from the North Peak. The hotel offers a competent staff, clean rooms, a restaurant, and magnificent views, and as a result it is often fully booked. Other decent mountaintop options include the **Dongfeng Binguan** (¥320 double), which is great for easy sunrise viewing.

TIANSHUI 天水

Gansu Province, 385km (239 miles) W of Xi'an, 294km (182 miles) SE of Lanzhou

Tianshui is divided into two parts—the main town of **Qin Cheng,** and the smaller township of **Beidao Qu,** 15km (9 miles) down the Wei river valley to the west, but the main reason to visit is a clamber around the stunning Buddhist caves of Maiji Shan, a 1-hour bus ride from Beidao Qu. Whilst both townships are unexceptional, Qin Cheng is a more attractive base, and has a few other sights to explore. ***Note:*** Turn to chapter 16 for Chinese translations of key locations.

Essentials

GETTING THERE The **railway station** is in the north of Beidao Qu, with many trains from Lanzhou (4 hr.) and farther west, and from Xi'an (4 hr.) and farther east. Tianshui's allocation of tickets is limited, so you may need to proceed through CITS in Qin Cheng. Heading west for Lanzhou there are plenty of options; the K591 (4 hr.; 2:43pm) is convenient. To Xining, the speediest choice is the T151 (7 hr.; 6:52am). To Chongqing, the only direct train is the K544 (17 hr.; 8:14pm). Pray for an upgrade. To Xi'an (4 hr.), take the T152 (6:47pm) or the T54 (5:55pm) that continues to Shanghai (20 hr.). Beijing trains include the T152 (17 hr.; 6:47pm).

The **main bus station** in Qin Cheng (✆ **0938/821-4028**) is at Shandong Lu 31, but many services also stop in Beidao Qu. Buses depart from Qin Cheng for Xi'an (380km/236 miles; 6 hr.; ¥69) every 40 minutes; Lanzhou (381km/236 miles; 4 hr.; ¥67) every 20 minutes; one daily service also runs to Linxia (4 hr.; ¥80) at 6:30am, and there are two buses a day for Yinchuan (610km/378 miles; 10 hr.; ¥125–¥143) at 4:30pm and 6:30pm.

GETTING AROUND Bus nos. 1 and 6 from the railway station connects Qin Cheng with Beidao Qu (15km/9¼ miles; 30 min.; ¥3). The first bus is at 6:20am; the last bus departs at 11:30pm. Share taxis in between the two cost ¥10, or you can hire the whole cab for ¥30 to ¥40. Regular flagfall is ¥6 for the first 2km (1¼ miles).

TOURS & GUIDES **CITS** at Minzhu Lu 8 (✆ **0938/273-3710**) is useful if you are looking for a guided tour or an English-speaking guide (¥200 per day). They are open from 8:30am to 6pm.

[FastFACTS] TIANSHUI

Banks, Foreign Exchange & ATMs The main **Bank of China** is located at Jianshe Lu 8 in Qin Cheng, 800m (2,624 ft.) east of the northeast corner of the main square on the north side of the road. The building has massive bronze lions out front. It's open from 8:30am to noon and 2:30 to 6pm on weekdays. There are other branches with ATMs on Minzhu Lu and Jiefang Lu.

Internet Access Mayi Wangba next to the Hualian Hotel on Gong Lu, just off Zhongxin Guangchang, has Internet access for ¥2 per hour.

Post Office The main post office (8am–8pm) is located on the northwest corner of the main square (Zhongxin Guangchang) in Qin Cheng.

Exploring Tianshui

The principal reason to visit Tianshui is to visit the remarkable Buddhist caves at Maiji Shan, but Qin Cheng also holds a couple of worthwhile temples. **Yuquan Guan** (8am–6pm; ¥20) rises above Renmin Xi Lu and offers some respite from the city, whilst **Fuxi Miao** (8am–6pm; ¥30) displays some wonderfully ornate woodcarving. The latter is dedicated to the semi-mythical figure Fuxi, one of the forefathers of Chinese civilization, believed to be responsible for the creation of the eight trigrams *(bagua)*. The temple dates to the Ming dynasty, and in its tranquil courtyards ancient cypresses are positioned in accordance with the corresponding 64 hexagrams. The surrounding area has been redeveloped in traditional style, and is now a wide pedestrianized boulevard lined with antique and wood-carving shops.

MAIJI SHAN SHIKU 麦积山石窟 ★★

These are some of the most remarkable Buddhist caves in China, demonstrating a fine range of statuary styles amid spectacular scenery. Located 30km (19 miles) southeast of Tianshui, the haystack-shaped mountain that gives the caves their name, is home to 194 extant caves, most on the western side of the mountain. The first caves were carved out during the Later Qin (384–417), a non-Han dynasty established during the Sixteen Kingdoms Period. Unlike other Buddhist caves, these saw little construction during the Tang dynasty, due to a series of earthquakes. The most serious occurred in 734, when the middle part of the grottoes collapsed. In 2008 some of the statues were damaged during the Sichuan earthquake. In spite of all of this seismic activity, significant statuary remains from the Northern Wei, Northern Zhou, and Sui dynasties.

Unlike other sites, the statuary here was not carved from the crumbling red rock, but added to it. **Grotto 18** explains the method of construction: A wooden superstructure is hauled up the mountain, bored into the soft cliffs, and coated with clay. Striking grottoes include **no. 191,** which houses a menacing winged figure with bulging eyes as its centerpiece; **no. 13,** with a huge Buddha and two attendant bodhisattvas dating from the Sui dynasty; and **no. 5,** with a sensuous bodhisattva dating from the Tang dynasty. As you scramble up the ladders that connect the caves, the charming scenery complements the statuary.

Many of the most interesting caves are off-limits without payment of ¥500 per group. If you have either the money or many like-minded friends, cave **no. 133,** from the Northern Wei, is recognized as Maiji Shan's best. It contains 18 carved granite stones that depict the life of the Buddha. A sublime statue stands to the right, depicting one of Buddha's disciples, Bhiksu, smiling enigmatically as he listens to the master. When (now ex-) Prime Minister Zhu Rongji visited in 2001, he was depressed by the poverty he saw on his tour of Gansu. After staring at this statue, his good humor returned.

Buses for Maiji Shan (1–1 hr. 30 min.; ¥10) leave Beidao Qu railway station from 7am, with the last bus leaving the mountain at 6pm. The bus will stop at a ticket office, where you pay ¥70 to enter the "scenic area." Collect a map of the area, which is included in the price but is not offered without prompting. From the ticket office a 2km (1¼ miles) walk, or ¥10 buggy ride will bring you to the caves, where, as ever, you'll have to brave the gauntlet of souvenir stalls. There are no English-speaking guides on-site, so unless you are fluent in Mandarin, there is no need to pay for a guide unless you arrange one in advance through CITS. Take a picnic, and leave time to explore the surrounding mountains and the botanical gardens.

✆ **0938/223-1031.** Admission: Scenic area and caves ¥70; entrance to "special caves" ¥500. 8am–6pm. Minibus from railway station ¥5; taxi return including waiting time should be ¥100.

Where to Stay

While Beidao Qu is more convenient for onwards transport, if you're not in a hurry to move on, better hotels and atmosphere are to be found in Qin Cheng, or to maximize your time at the caves you could choose to stay at Maiji Shan. The best hotel in Qin Cheng is the **Mingyuan Dajiudian** on Taishan Lu (✆ **0938/823-8888;** ¥298–¥398 standard room), opened in 2010, which offers comfortable, carpeted and well-appointed rooms, although it's worth spending the extra on a deluxe as the standard doubles are on the small size. Whilst the location isn't as good as those in the main city square, it is just a short walk from the bus station. Cheaper options include the **Hualian Fandian** on Dazhong Bei Lu (✆ **0938/821-5501;** ¥180 standard room), which has small rooms but a great position just off Zhongxin Guangchang; or the clean, bright and modern rooms at the **Tianshui Fandian** (✆ **0938/821-4056;** ¥160 standard room), which are handy for the bus station across the road, but can be noisy. For those on a very tight budget, the shabby and noisy rooms at the **Tianshui Dajiudian** (✆ **0938/828-9999;** ¥110–¥130) are right next to the KFC on Zhongxin Guangchang.

If you want to spent the night at Maiji Shan, **Zhiwuyuan Zhaodaisuo** (✆ **0938/223-1025;** ¥100 twin in old wing, ¥360 cabin) is a real find. The setting is the botanical gardens behind the mountain, amid imposing oak and birch forests, and the cabins are good value—you can pay by the bed. By car, take a road to the left 720m (2,362 ft.) past the scenic area ticket office and continue uphill for 3km (2 miles), or walk 15 minutes past the Maiji Shan caves. Finally, if you have an early train to catch, the three-star Dong'an Fandian (✆ **0938/261-3333;** ¥168 standard twin) next to the railway station in Beidao Qu is a decent choice

Where to Eat

In Qin Cheng there are plenty of small canteens serving *mianpi,* the local specialty noodle dish, or in the evening you could head to **Xiaochi Jie (Snack Alley),** which is packed with food stalls. For another cheap eat, just off the main square, **Pei Feng Beef Noodles (Pei Feng Niurou Dian)** serves up warming bowls of beef noodles for ¥4.50. Nearby on Dazhong Bei Lu, just off Zhongxin Guangchang, **Shengan Coffee (Shengan Kafei)** has window tables looking out over the street where you can sip expensive coffee and choose from a range of Western and Chinese dishes. If you visit Fuxi Miao then it's worth stopping by for lunch at **La Fu Chuan Xiang Guan** (© **187/9416-5400**), opposite the entrance gate on the main road. Choose from the enticing array of fresh produce displayed at the back of this friendly family-run hotpot restaurant and then get ready for a seriously spicy hotpot.

Beidao Qu may not be a culinary paradise, but it sports honest eateries serving generous portions for around ¥10 per person. Elbow past the locals to find a seat in **Niu Dawan,** a halal restaurant north of the bus station on Er Ma Lu. There's one dish to order—*niurou mian* (beef noodles), and two choices to make—thick *(kuan)* or thin *(xi)* noodles, and whether to add more beef *(jia rou).*

A friendly establishment just west of the Gonghui Dasha, the **Tian Xi Xiaochidian** is run by three retired sisters and serves filling *chao mian* (stir-fried noodles) or a stone bowl of bubbling *shaguo jikuai* (chicken clay pot), both of which are perfect after a hike in the mountains. For picnic supplies there's a supermarket 200m (656 ft.) west of the Tianshui Dajiudian in Qin Cheng.

LANZHOU 兰州

Gansu Province, 665km (412 miles) W of Xi'an, 514km (319 miles) SW of Yinchuan

This was once the point where the Silk Routes crossed the Yellow River; however, whatever charms the old town possessed were buried long ago. In 1998, **Lanzhou** won the title of the planet's most polluted city by a considerable margin (Chinese towns filled 7 of the top 10 places). This dubious distinction led to numerous and humorous attempts to rectify the problem—one entrepreneur got backing for a scheme to knock a hole in the surrounding mountains to "open the window" on Lanzhou's smog. Spring dust storms can worsen the situation to the point that the mountains surrounding the city can disappear for days at time.

Air quality aside, today Lanzhou is a wealthy, bustling modern city and aesthetic improvements are continually being made; the riverside area has been converted into a large park that makes a pleasant place for a stroll. However, Lanzhou still offers few reasons to linger. The museum is worth a look, and the town is a comfortable base for trips south to Bingling Si, Xia He, and Langmu Si. But your first action should be to book a ticket out of town.

Essentials

GETTING THERE The airport is 75km (47 miles) to the north. Lanzhou is served by daily flights to and from Shenzhen, Guangzhou, Xi'an, Beijing, Shanghai and Urumqi. **China Eastern Airlines** (© **0931/882-1964;** 8:30am–7:30pm) has its main office opposite the JJ Sun Hotel. Next door the **Lanzhou Ticket Center** (© **0931/888-9666;** 8:30am–7pm) can also book flights. Regular airport buses

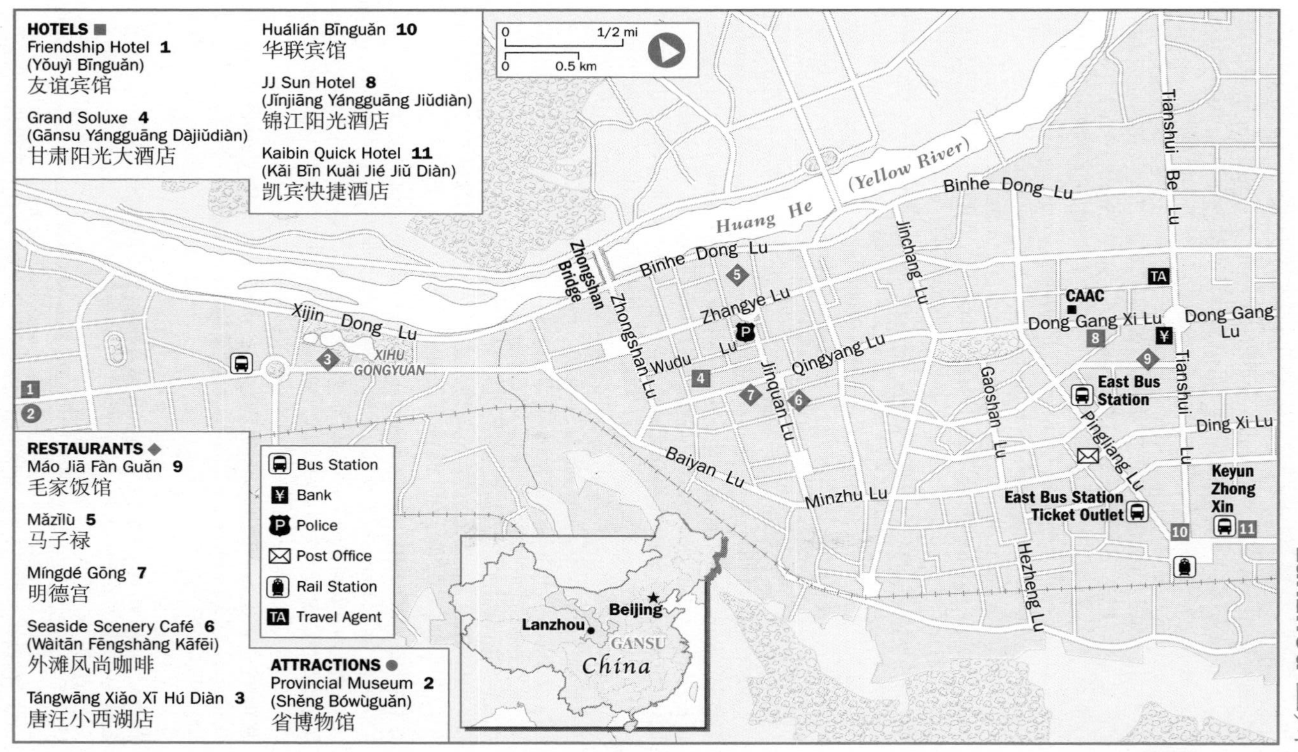
HOTELS ■
Friendship Hotel 1
(Yǒuyì Bīnguǎn)
友谊宾馆
Grand Soluxe 4
(Gānsu Yángguāng Dàjiǔdiàn)
甘肃阳光大酒店
Huálián Bīnguǎn 10
华联宾馆
JJ Sun Hotel 8
(Jǐnjiāng Yángguāng Jiǔdiàn)
锦江阳光酒店
Kaibin Quick Hotel 11
(Kǎi Bīn Kuài Jié Jiǔ Diàn)
凯宾快捷酒店
0 1/2 mi
0 0.5 km
(Yellow River)
Huang He
Binhe Dong Lu
Tianshui Be Lu
Zhongshan Bridge
Xijin Dong Lu
XIHU GONGYUAN
Zhongshan Lu
Zhangye Lu
Wudu Lu
Jinquan Lu
Qingyang Lu
Jinchang Lu
Gaoshan Lu
CAAC
Dong Gang Xi Lu
Dong Gang Lu
Tianshui Lu
East Bus Station
Ding Xi Lu
Pingliang Lu
Baiyan Lu
Minzhu Lu
East Bus Station Ticket Outlet
Keyun Zhong Xin
Hezheng Lu
RESTAURANTS ◆
Máo Jiā Fàn Guǎn 9
毛家饭馆
Mǎzǐlù 5
马子禄
Míngdé Gōng 7
明德宫
Seaside Scenery Café 6
(Wàitān Fēngshàng Kāfēi)
外滩风尚咖啡
Tángwāng Xiǎo Xī Hú Diàn 3
唐汪小西湖店
Bus Station
Bank
Police
Post Office
Rail Station
Travel Agent
ATTRACTIONS ●
Provincial Museum 2
(Shěng Bówùguǎn)
省博物馆
Lanzhou
Beijing
GANSU
China

(1 hr.; ¥30) leave from outside China Eastern. Alternatively a taxi costs around ¥150 on the meter.

Queues at the new **railway station** (✆ **0931/492-2222**) in the south of town generally aren't too bad and given the number of trains that pass through Lanzhou you've got a good chance of securing a berth this way. Alternatively, sleeper tickets may also be purchased through your hotel, or an agent, for a commission.

Trains from Lanzhou connect with Beijing (T28: 3:29pm, 17 hr.), Shanghai (T118: 12:41am, 24 hr.), Ürümqi (T192: 1:57pm, 20 hr.), Xi'an (T166: 1:16pm, 10 hr.), Guangzhou (T266: 1:40pm, 29 hr.), Chengdu (T24: 2:25pm, 17 hr.), Pingliang (K9664: 7:14pm, 12 hr.), Jiayuguan (K9661: 8:50pm, 11 hr.), Xining (T209: 12:40pm, 3 hr.), Golmud (T27: 1:19pm, 13 hr.), and Lhasa (numerous, including T27). The speediest connection with Yinchuan is the K916 at 10:40pm (9 hr.).

Lanzhou has a confusing number of bus stations, the most useful of which is the **East Station (Qiche Dong Zhan)** on Pingliang Lu (✆ **0931/456-2222**). The station is a 20 minute walk northwest of the railway station, or alternatively you can buy your ticket at the outlet opposite the Hualian Binguan, and will then get a complimentary transfer. Heading west, the East Station has buses that connect with Xining (3 hr.; ¥56) every 30 minutes between 7:30am and 7:30pm; Dunhuang (12 hr.; ¥283) is served by one bus daily at 6am. For eastwards travel there are buses to Tianshui (3–4 hr.; ¥73) every half-hour, and there are two daily sleeper buses to Xi'an (10 hr.; ¥178) at 11:30am and 6:30pm. A new bus station, **Keyun Zhong Xin** (✆ **0931/880-7114**), just to the east of the train station, also serves Xining and Tianshui (same times and prices), and is convenient if you arrive by train and want to head straight out of town. Heading for Xia He you'll need to make your way to the hectic **South Bus Station (Nan Zhan)** in the far southwest of town (✆ **0931/291-4066**), a ¥15 taxi ride from the center. There are buses for Xia He (256km/159 miles; 4–5 hr.; ¥71) at 6:30, 7:30, 8:30am, and 2:30pm. Be prepared for some aggressive touts and if you arrive with a long wait for a direct service, head to Linxia (or Hezuo) and change there—don't believe a word the touts tell you about the availability of onward buses. Buses connect with Hezuo (258km/160 miles; 4 hr.; ¥46) every half-hour from 7am to 4pm; with Linxia (149km/92 miles; 3 hr.; ¥28) every 20 minutes from 7am to 6pm. The **West Bus Station** at Xijin Dong Lu 486 (✆ **0931/291-9537**) has direct buses to Liujia Xia (2 hr.; ¥18) that run regularly between 7am and 6pm.

GETTING AROUND Green Santanas charge ¥7 for the first 3km (2 miles), then ¥1.40 per kilometer; add a night surcharge of ¥1.60 from 10pm to 5am. Buses start at ¥1, which is paid on boarding at the front of the bus. Bus no. 1 is useful; it starts at the railway station and passes the Bank of China, the JJ Sun Hotel, the Grand Soluxe, and the Friendship Hotel (opposite the Lanzhou Museum).

TOURS Most **hotels** have tour desks that offer tours to Bingling Si. There are numerous **CITS** offices, including a helpful branch located at Pingliang Lu 498 (✆ **0931/887-7111**).

[Fast FACTS] LANZHOU

Banks, Foreign Exchange & ATMs The **Bank of China** (Mon–Fri 8:30am–5:30pm) at Tianshui Lu 525 accepts traveler's checks and credit cards. To the left of the building, ATMs accept foreign cards. Another useful branch is on Qingyang Lu, just west of the Grand Soluxe Hotel.

Internet Access Next to Hualian Binguan, second-floor **Hongchen Wangba** provides reliable 24-hour connection for ¥2.50 per hour. There are also plenty of places around Lanzhou University including **E Hang Wang Lou** on Tianshui Nan Lu (¥2 per hour).

Post Office The post office (Minzhu Dong Lu 104; Mon–Fri 8am–7pm) is located on the corner of Minzhu Dong Lu and Pingliang Lu near the East Bus Station. There's another branch on Qingyang Lu, a little west of the Grand Soluxe Hotel, on the south side of the road.

Visa Extensions Visa extensions are processed promptly up to 2 weeks before the expiration date at a helpful **PSB,** just west of the city government building at Wudu Lu 310 (✆ **0931/871-8606;** Mon–Fri 8:30–11:30am and 2:30–5:30pm).

Exploring Lanzhou

Sheng Bowuguan (Provincial Museum) The renovated Provincial Museum displays its healthy collection in state-of-the-art form. The late Neolithic pottery is particularly impressive, most of it from the region around Tianshui, displaying the rapid progress in both pottery and painting during this period (ca. 3000 B.C.–1900 B.C.). The museum's most famous exhibit is the **Flying Horse (Tong Ben Ma) ★**, taken in 1969 from the tomb of an Eastern Han (25–220) general near Wuwei. Staff admit that the bronze horse on display is a replica; the real article is in the vaults of the museum, and another copy is in Beijing. However, the original was damaged in the copying process, and the mold was either lost or destroyed, so this copy is priceless. Other items from the tomb include bamboo strips containing meticulous instructions on the etiquette of drinking, marriage, and death. Call in advance or contact CITS to arrange an English-speaking guide, and allow a couple of hours for a leisurely visit.

Directly opposite the Friendship Hotel (Youyi Binguan). ✆ **0931/234-6306.** Free admission; English-speaking guide ¥100. Tues–Sun 9am–5pm. Bus: 1 to Youyi Binguan.

A NEARBY GROTTO: BINGLING SI 炳灵寺

Once a long day trip from Lanzhou, **Bingling Si** is now far more accessible. The town nearest Bingling Si is Liujia Xia, which was recently connected with Lanzhou by an expressway. The trip takes about 90 minutes. Unless you have a passion for cave temples, this one's probably not worth the long haul from Lanzhou, but if you have your own vehicle it can make an agreeable stop en-route to Xia He.

You can get to the caves by bus from the West Bus Station at Xijin Dong Lu 486, or more simply arrange a private car through CITS (¥400). However you get here, on arrival at Liujia Xia, you'll be bundled off to the boat ticket office. The public ferry runs in summer and costs ¥30, though it's a long 6- to 7-hour return trip, and you're better off negotiating a place on a shared boat for ¥60 to ¥80. Alternatively you could hire a private speedboat (¥200–¥400), which will allow you to explore the caves at your leisure rather than rushing around in 90 minutes, which is the standard waiting time for shared boats. Those continuing to Linxia (25km/16 miles; 40 min.; ¥10; last minibus 6pm) and then Xia He (107km/66 miles; 2 hr. 30 min.; ¥9) should ask to be dropped at Lianhua Tai on the way back. (If you've got your private boat, you can ask that they take you here.) The last bus back to Lanzhou (¥16) leaves at 6:30pm. If you stay in Liujia Xia, the best lodgings are the Huang He Binguan and the cheaper Liu Dian Binguan.

Two-thirds of the caves were carved in the Tang dynasty, but examples range from the Northern Wei (368–534) to the Ming dynasties. Pay ¥80 at the ticket office and turn right; follow a narrow pathway around. A 27m (90-ft.) Maitreya (Buddha of the Future) with prominent nipples—a decidedly non-Han Chinese touch—dominates the valley. Higher up the cliff face is **Cave 169** ★ (¥300 extra!), one of the most ancient in China, showing Indian influences. Unlike most cave temples, the upper caves are natural. Unfortunately, 200 lower caves were flooded when the San Xia Dam (formerly the largest in China) was completed.

Shopping

For those who don't have the time to head up to Xia He, there are plenty of shops stocking Tibetan jewelry around the train station. There are also numerous small supermarkets here to stock up for journeys, but for a wider selection try **Vanguard** on the south side of Gannan Lu, just west of the Bank of China on Tianshui Lu.

Where to Stay

Lanzhou has plenty of new hotels with comfortable beds where 30% to 50% discounts are often negotiable.

VERY EXPENSIVE

Grand Soluxe Hotel Gansu (Yangguang Dajiudian) ★★ Easily the best hotel in town, the flagship Grand Soluxe property has great service and comfortable rooms. The standard rooms have plush beds and thick carpets but it's worth spending extra for the more spacious deluxe rooms, which have raised sitting areas and bathtubs. Facilities for travelers with disabilities are available.

Qingyang Lu 428. www.grandsoluxehotel.com. ✆ **0931/460-8888.** Fax 0931/460-8889. 225 units. ¥1,060–¥1,160 standard room; ¥1,260 deluxe room; from ¥1,580 suite. Discounts of 30%. Rates include breakfast. 15% service charge. AE, DC, MC, V. **Amenities:** 2 restaurants; concierge; forex (no traveler's checks); game room; room service. *In room:* A/C, satellite TV, fridge, hair dryer, Internet, minibar.

EXPENSIVE

Jinjiang Yangguang Jiudian (JJ Sun Hotel) A quick taxi ride from the railway station, this Shanghai-managed hotel is a good option. Renovated rooms on floors 13 to 17 are light and bright, have comfortable bedding, decent bathrooms and good views. The only downside to a stay here is that you may end up spending a fair proportion of your time in Lanzhou waiting for the hotel's glacial elevator.

Donggang Xi Lu 589. www.jjsunhotel.com. ✆ **0931/880-5511.** Fax 0931/841-2856. 236 units. ¥800 standard room; from ¥1,500 suite. Discounts of up to 40%. Rates include full breakfast. AE, DC, MC, V. **Amenities:** 2 restaurants; cafe; concierge; forex. *In room:* A/C, TV, fridge, hair dryer, Internet (¥30 per day), minibar.

MODERATE

Youyi Binguan (Friendship Hotel) While it won't win any awards, the long-established Friendship has good facilities and pleasant enough rooms, and its location directly opposite Lanzhou's only real "sight"—the museum—makes it a convenient option. There are several wings to this monster of a hotel; the west wing has light, bright, and quiet rooms, although carpets and furnishings are worn. The hotel is popular with tour groups.

Xijin Xi Lu 16. ✆ **0931/268-9169.** Fax 0931/233-0304. 575 units. ¥290 standard room; from ¥490 suite. Discounts of 20–30%. AE, DC, MC, V. **Amenities:** Several restaurants; forex; health center; tennis court. *In room:* A/C, TV, Internet (¥30 per day).

INEXPENSIVE

Hualian Binguan Directly opposite the train station, this budget favorite has recently renovated many of its rooms and is very convenient if you want to minimize your time in Lanzhou. Standard twins and doubles on the 6th to 9th floors have computers and Internet access, but if you don't need this facility, the rooms on the 21st floor are similar, but cheaper and quieter.

Tianshui Nan Lu. ✆ **0931/499-2101.** 400 units. ¥279–¥479 standard room. Discounts of up to 50%. No credit cards. **Amenities:** 2 restaurants. *In room:* A/C, TV, Internet (6th–9th floors only).

Kaibin Quick Hotel (Kaibin Kuaijie Jiudian) Less than 5 minutes' walk from Lanzhou train station, Kaibin Quick Hotel has once again opened its doors to foreigners, and while they may fumble over your passport details, staff is friendly and rooms are great value. While starting to show signs of wear, rooms are nonetheless clean and comfortable, and perfect for a short stay. There are several categories of room, with more money buying you a bigger room, plus carpet rather than tile.

Above Keyun Zhong Xin Bus Station. ✆ **0931/880-7777.** 200 units. ¥178–¥208 standard room. No credit cards. **Amenities:** Restaurant. *In room:* A/C, TV, Internet.

Where to Eat

Those craving junk food will find plenty of **KFCs** including one at the train station and another on the northeast corner of the junction of Qingyang Lu and Jiuquan Lu. **Seaside Scenery Cafe (Waitan Fengshang Kafei)** at Nanguan Shizi Shiyou Dasha 1 Lou (✆ **0931/844-8396**), serves eminently drinkable coffee (from ¥30)—but be sure to specify hot *(re)*, iced *(bing)*, or by the pot *(hu)*. The menu offers a host of Western dishes including steaks and spaghetti.

Maojia Fanguan ★ HUNAN Look for the red plastic statues beckoning you into the restaurant, and then head upstairs and settle into a booth overlooking the street for a fiery Hunanese dining experience. Maojia translates as Mao's home, Hunan, and at the top of the stairs diners are greeted by a statue of the man himself, while historic photographs of the Great Helmsman adorn the walls. Most importantly, the spicy Hunan dishes are as tasty as they are authentic—the chicken and potato stewpot will serve three to four people and is well accompanied by the spicy eggplant with green beans. A picture menu will help you make your choices, but don't trust the English captions!

Gannan Lu. ✆ **0931/841-5566.** Meal for 2 ¥100. No credit cards. 11:30am–2pm and 5–9pm.

Mazilu ★★ GANSU Be prepared to have one of the best noodle experiences of your life. The drafty, warehouse-style restaurant, open for breakfast and lunch, doesn't have much atmosphere, but no one's here for the decor—it's all about the beef noodles, which is the only thing you can get here. Lanzhou *niurou lamian* has migrated to all parts of the country by way of little street-side noodle shops, but this is the real deal, and known by locals as the best place to sample the dish. Pay your ¥5 to the cashier, who will give you a ticket to collect your bowl at the back of the restaurant. The tender, thin noodles are boiled in a huge vat of beef broth, then chili and sesame sauce and bits of beef are tossed in at the last minute.

Dazhong Xiang. ✆ **0931/845-0505.** Meal for 2 ¥10. No credit cards. 6:30am–2pm.

Mingde Gong ★ GANSU The Mingde Gong, a four-story palace that gets progressively more luxurious as you ascend, is the flag-bearer for Gansu cuisine—*"long* *cai."* While the boss is a Hui entrepreneur, the chefs hail from Beijing and Guangzhou. Signature dishes include the huge and spicy *kao yangtui* (roast leg of lamb with walnuts), a deep-fried lamb and green-pepper pancake (bobing *yangrou*), and the sweet vegetarian dish, *xishi jinju baihe.*

Qingyang Lu. ✆ **0931/843-3599.** Meal for 2 ¥90–¥170. No credit cards. 10am–9:30pm.

Tangwang Xiao Xi Hu Dian GANSU Regional specialties are scarce, but locals are proud of *shouzhua rou* (grabbed meat): hunks of beef dunked in salt and pepper and chased by a clove of raw garlic (optional!). Ask for a lean portion *(shou fen)*, unless you want to guzzle huge lumps of lard. Lanzhou's liveliest nightmarket, Xiao Xihu Yeshi, is directly across the road.

✆ **0931/260-2398.** Meal for 2 less than ¥40. No credit cards. 9:30am–10:30pm. Bus: 1 to Xiao Xi Hu.

LINXIA 临夏

Gansu Province, 149km (92 miles) SW of Lanzhou, 107km (66 miles) NE of Xia He

"All writers agree on the commercial ability and energy of the T'ung-kan [Hui], as well as on their surliness, ill manners and hostile suspicion of strangers. . . ." This judgment by American journalist Owen Lattimore seems harsh until you visit Linxia, a predominantly Hui town (with a smattering of Bao'an and the Altaic Dongxiang minorities). Those wishing to stay in a traditional, non-Uighur Islamic town should visit Xunhua in eastern Qinghai. However, if you arrive late en-route to Xia He, an overnight stay in Linxia may be unavoidable.

GETTING AWAY The **West Bus Station** (**Xi Zhan;** ✆ **0930/621-2177**) has buses every half-hour for Lanzhou (149km/92 miles; 3 hr.; ¥30) from 7am to 3pm; Hezuo (106km/66 miles; 2 hr.; ¥20) every half-hour from 6:30am; Xining (269km/167 miles; 6 hr.; ¥56) at 6am; Xunhua (115km/71 miles; 2 hr. 30 min.; ¥19), and Tongren (183km/113 miles; 5 hr.; ¥34) at 6:30am. Heading to Xia He (107km/66 miles; 2 hr. 30 min.; ¥19), you'll need to transfer to the **South Bus Station** (**Nan Zhan;** ✆ **0930/621-2767**); a bus runs every half-hour from 7am to 4:30pm.

Where to Stay

As long as you get here by midafternoon, there's really no need to stay in Linxia, but if you find yourself stuck here, the **Linxia Fandian** at Hongyuan Lu 9 (✆ **0930/623-0080;** fax 0930/621-4412) is a reasonable option with twin rooms in the old wing for ¥180, and better rooms in the new wing for ¥258. Head east from Xi Zhan along Minzhu Xi Lu, then turn down the first street on your right (south).

HEZUO 合作

Gansu Province, 258km (160 miles) SW of Lanzhou, 72km (45 miles) SE of Xia He

Aside from a substantial Tibetan population and the impressive Milarepa Tower, the capital of Gan Nan (Southern Gansu) Prefecture is much like any other Han town of recent construction. However, as a transit point, it is infinitely preferable to Linxia.

Essentials

GETTING THERE Hezuo has two bus stations. Most buses from Lanzhou arrive at the Central Bus Station, which is far more convenient than the new South Bus Station, in the far south of town. The Central Bus Station, Hezuo Qichezhan

(© 0941/821-2422) has buses for Linxia (106km/66 miles; 2 hr.; ¥20) every 20 minutes from 6am to 5:40pm and Xia He (72km/45 miles; 1 hr. 30 min.; ¥14) every 30 minutes between 6:30am and 5:50pm. Regular buses depart for Lanzhou (258km/160 miles; 5 hr.; ¥60) and there is one daily service for Xining at 6:30am (331km/205 miles; 5 hr.; ¥64). For Langmu Si (173km/107 miles; 3 hr.; ¥33) there's one daily bus at 9am, plus another three services (7am, 10:20am, and 12:20pm) from the South Bus Station (Qiche Nan Zhan; © 0941/821-3039). The south station also has one bus daily for Ruo'ergai (4 hr.; ¥65) in northern Sichuan at 7:30am; and this service then continues on to Aba (583km/361 miles) the following day.

[FastFACTS] HEZUO

Visa Extensions The Hezuo **PSB** office is on Sanqu Lu (© **0941/821-0862**).

Exploring Hezuo

Milarepa Tower ★ Part of the Hezuo Monastery, this nine-story tower was built in 1678, but was burned down during the Cultural Revolution. In the late 1980s, government officials allowed the tower's rebuilding, which was completed in 1994. It's worth a rickety climb up the nine floors not only for the artifacts but also for the decent view of the city from the top. A nice monk named Chinpa who oversees the grounds may invite you in his office for tsampa and tea if you speak a bit of Chinese or Tibetan.

At the north end of Renmin Lu. Admission ¥20; if you look Chinese, they'll let you in half price. Open daylight hours.

Where to Stay

Although it's a better transit option than Linxia, given the proximity to Xia he, there's little need to stay in Hezuo. Nevertheless, if you find yourself here for the night, **Jiaotong Binguan** (Traffic Hotel; © **0941/822-1300;** ¥90 standard room) is hardly the Hilton, but it's cheap, central, and only a couple of minutes' walk from the bus station (turn right at the station and the hotel is on your right). Better rooms can be found at **Xiangbala Dajiudian** (Renmin Jie 53; © **0941/821-3222;** ¥196 standard room), which also has a Tibetan-style bar that features a nightly dancing and singing performance.

Where to Eat

Not far from the bus station on the corner of Renmin Lu and Dong Er Lu the market has an interesting mix of street stalls and small restaurants selling dumplings, Muslim food, and noodles. Once you've sated your hunger, you can stroll around the market, which features everything from live birds to athletic shoes.

XIA HE (LABRANG; 夏河) ★★★

The delightful monastery town of Xia He is nestled north of the banks of the **Da Xia He (Sang Qu)** at an elevation of 2,900m (9,500 ft.). Not surprisingly, it gets very cold in winter, dipping to –4°F (–20°C); even in August, the average temperature is a cool 59°F (15°C). The town is divided into two sections. Primarily Han and Hui at its ever-expanding eastern end, it changes abruptly to Tibetan as you approach the monastery in the west. Monks in Xia He staged demonstrations in March 2008 in solidarity with their T.A.R. brethren, and an unconfirmed number of people were killed in the ensuing conflict. As a result the town was closed to foreigners until mid-2009, and even when it re-opened private transport and guaranteed hotel bookings were required. At press time, things were back to normal and travelers could easily visit the town, however tensions lie not too far beneath the surface. Recently Xia He has become increasingly popular with Chinese tourists. A new upscale hotel and an airport will make the town more accessible to a wider range of visitors, but for the meanwhile pilgrims still outnumber tourists 10 to 1. ***Note:*** Turn to chapter 16 for Chinese translations of key locations.

Essentials

GETTING THERE Xia He's airport is due to open in 2013, but for the meanwhile road offers the only access. Check with Overseas Tibetan hotel for the latest. **Buses** (**© 0941/712-1462**) connect with Hezuo (72km/45 miles; 1 hr. 30 min.; ¥14) every 30 minutes from 6:10am to 5:40pm; Linxia (107km/66 miles; 2 hr.; ¥30) every 30 minutes from 6am to 5:30pm; Lanzhou (256km/159 miles; 4 hr. 30 min.; ¥70) at 6:30am, 7:30am, 8:30am, 2:30pm and 2:55pm; Tongren (107km/66 miles; 3 hr.; ¥25) at 7:30am; and Amchog (72km/45 miles, 2 hr.; ¥19) at 10am and 11am. There's one daily bus for Xining at 6:10am (¥77), and one for Langmu Si at 7:40am (4 hr.; ¥44).

If there's a group of you, **minivans** to Langmu Si (5 hr.; ¥700) can be arranged through the Overseas Tibetan Hotel, Tara Guesthouse or at the bus station. ***Warning:*** If you're taking the rough but scenic route southeast via Amchog, hire a Tibetan driver and bring cigarettes; banditry, in the form of determined children with large rocks, or nomads on horseback, is common.

GETTING AROUND **Bicycles** can be rented from most guesthouses for ¥20 per day. **Shared taxis** or **motorcycle carts** should take you anywhere in town for ¥1, but they'll try for more.

TOURS & GUIDES Losang at the Overseas Tibetan Hotel is the best source of information and trip organizer in town. Tsewong of Tsewong's Cafe is also a good resource for local travel information.

[FastFACTS] XIA HE

Banks Forex services are unavailable in Xia He, and the ICBC ATM in the east of town only accepts Union Pay cards.

Internet Access Internet access can be found at many of the guesthouses and cafes including the Overseas Tibetan Hotel. The charge is ¥5 to ¥6 per hour.

Post Office The post office (8am–6pm) is a few hundred meters west of the bus station on the south side of the road.

Visa Extensions You used to be able to previously get them done here, but now it's only possible in at the Hezuo PSB office (p. 279).

Exploring Xia He

A 3km (2-mile) clockwise perambulation *(kora)* of the monastery is an excellent way to begin the day. You may find yourself befriended by delightful elderly pilgrims or by young monks keen to practice their English. If your schedule allows, time your visit to coincide with the **Monlam Festival,** held on the 4th to 16th days of the first lunar month (Feb–Mar). The monastery is open to all during the festival, and on the 13th day you can watch the "sunning of the Buddha." An enormous *thangka* (silk painting) is spread across a **Thangka Wall** on the south bank of the Sangchu. When sanctified, it effectively becomes the Buddha in the minds of believers. The following days feature religious dancing and the offering of *torma* (butter sculptures).

A hike up into the hills gives you a magnificent view of the monastery. Just west of it is a small, friendly nunnery.

Labuleng Si (Labrang Monastery) ★★ As any monk you come across will tell you, Labrang Monastery, founded in 1709, is one of the six largest monasteries of the Geluk order, and the largest monastery in Amdo. Unlike most large religious institutions, it escaped desecration during the Cultural Revolution, although the number of monks and nuns was reduced from over 4,000 to the present number of just over 1,000. Despite the fact that he is only 10 years old and still studying, the resident Gunthang Lama ranks behind only the Dalai Lama and the Panchen Lama. There are colleges for esoteric and exoteric Buddhism, astronomy, mathematics, geography, and medicine. Amdo monks see themselves as the true holders of the faith—looking down on the Khampas and central Tibetans as soldiers and politicians respectively—and the monks take pride in the appearance of their monastery. Stunning *thangkas* adorn the walls, and many beams and finials are inscribed with sacred and protective script.

The most striking building is the **Assembly Hall ★**, with its golden roof. This is a recent addition, as the original burned down in 1985. The **museum** and a display of frozen **butter sculptures** are also worth seeking out. Just to the right of the main entrance is the School of Buddhist Studies, where monks are often keen to practice their English. There is no charge for wandering at will through the various buildings, but to get a better understanding of the monastery, taking one of the two daily English-speaking tours is advised (10:15am and 3:15pm). There's an entry fee of ¥10 to visit the golden **Gongtang Pagoda,** reached from the south *kora,* which is thoroughly worthwhile as from the top you'll get fine views over the monastery.

Free admission; ¥40 for twice-daily English tour from the front gate. No guided tours Nov–Feb.

Around Xia He

About 13km (8 miles) up the Da Xia He are the grasslands of **Sangke,** an ideal place for horse riding (¥40 per hour). The grasslands are most spectacular in July and August, when the canola is flowering. Minivans wait outside the Tara Guesthouse and should charge about ¥30 round-trip; or you can ride out by bike in an hour or so. Some of the recently developed tourist holiday villages in the grasslands are so appalling they are attractions in their own right. More authentic and spectacular grasslands can be reached by hiring a car and driver for the day (¥200–¥350) to take you out to **Ganjia,** an hour's drive over the beautiful Naren-Ka mountain pass. Once here expansive vistas of green rolling hills abound, dotted with sheep, horses, yaks and nomads. There are also a couple of monasteries worth seeking out. **Drockar Gompa** (¥30), nestled below dramatic vertical cliffs, belongs to the yellow-hat sect and is home to some 90 monks; **Tseway Gompa** is a Bon Monastery (remember to complete the *kora* anti-clockwise here) in another incredible location—climb up to the prayer flags for commanding views over the monastery and back to Drockar. In between the two you can stop at Ba Jia (Eight Corners; ¥15) Village, a simple settlement contained by

2,000-year-old walls and inhabited by friendly Tibetans. You can arrange camping trips out to these grasslands through Tsewong's Cafe and the Overseas Tibetan Hotel.

Shopping

The western end of Xia He is chock-a-block with small shops selling all manner of Tibetan goods for pilgrims (and tourists). *Thangkas,* prayer wheels, belts inlaid with coins, door-hangings, boots and bulky Tibetan coats are all for sale. Asking prices are generally fair, with the exception of jewelry, for which you'll have to haggle hard. For guaranteed quality yak textiles, don't miss out on **Norlha,** which is reached by turning right at Nomad Restaurant. Products on offer include super-soft shawls, bags, and cuddly yak toys.

Where to Stay

Xia He's hotel scene is on the move upscale with the recent completion of the Labuleng Civil Aviation Hotel, but the budget cheapies remain, although note that most of these places only have hot water for a limited number of hours in the morning or evening.

Labuleng Minhang Dajiudian (Labuleng Civil Aviation Hotel) ★ In the eastern part of town, but just a 15-minute walk from the monastery, the mammoth Labuleng is set to change the face of accommodation in little old Xia He. The author visited 2 days before the official opening, and the corridors were warm, the hot water worked and staff was keen to please. Rooms feature dark wood furnishings, flat-screen TVs and some have carpets and computers. Only the suites offer any Tibetan style though.

Opposite the post office. ✆ **0941/712-888.** 154 units. ¥668 standard room; ¥988 suite. Up to 20% discount. No credit cards. **Amenities:** Restaurant. *In room:* TV, hairdryer, Internet.

Overseas Tibetan Hotel (Huaqiao Fandian) ★ The manager, Losang, is a Nepalese Tibetan who earned an MBA in the U.S. and does his best to instill a service ethic into his erratic staff. Once a dreary concrete monolith, this hotel has been greatly improved by successive additions to the second and third floors. The midsize rooms with twin beds on the third floor are in need of renovations, but are some of the best value in town, with tasteful Tibetan decorations. On the second floor cheaper *kang* rooms are also decent, but the first-floor dormitory rooms suffer from dampness. All day hot showers were apparently on the way at the time of writing.

Renmin Xi Jie 77, 747100. ✆ **0941/712-2642.** Fax 0941/712-1872. info@overseastibetanhotel.com. 35 units. ¥160–¥200 standard room; ¥20 dorm bed. No credit cards. **Amenities:** Restaurant; bike rental (¥20 per day); Internet. *In room:* TV, no phone.

Tara Guesthouse (Zhuoma Lushe) A mecca for backpackers, the rooms at Tara have improved in recent years, and if you can put up without an en suite bathroom this place is a good deal, especially given the location right across from the monastery. The pine rooms with raised sleeping area are tastefully done, and a TV and heater can be added for ¥30 each. The dorms are the cheapest in town and the cafe downstairs has Wi-Fi.

Yage Tang 268, 747100. ✆ **0941/412-1274.** 19 units (shared bathroom). ¥10 dorm bed; ¥100 standard room. No credit cards. **Amenities:** Restaurant; bike rental.

Where to Eat

Everest Cafe WESTERN/CHINESE Attached to the Overseas Tibetan Guesthouse, the restaurant is conveniently located for you to grab a tasty breakfast in the mornings before you start your pilgrimage around the monastery. Along with toast, eggs, real juice and coffee, the ¥20 set breakfast also includes local yogurt and honey. They also offer a range of sandwiches, milkshakes, *lassis,* and, of course, momos.

Renmin Xi Jie 77. ✆ **0941/712-2642.** Meal for 2 ¥30–¥50. No credit cards. 6:30am–11pm.

Nomad Restaurant ★★ TIBETAN Good Tibetan food, friendly service, views over the monastery and the company of monks make Nomad Xia He's best dining experience. The fried yak momos quite literally burst with flavor and if you're feeling brave, you can wash them down with a glass of Labrang barley beer. There are also a few Chinese items on the menu including caramelized bananas, which make a tasty dessert.

3F, next to the monastery. ✆ **138/9390-9709.** Meal for 2 ¥30–¥50. No credit cards. 8am–11pm.

Tsewong's Cafe ★ WESTERN/CHINESE Opened by a former employee of the Overseas Tibetan Guesthouse, this cafe serves better than average Western food in a clean environment. The "real pizza by oven" is recommended—the crust is nice and cheesy and the sauce consists of fresh tomatoes. The burritos come a close second, and the Chinese dumplings are also popular. Internet access is available for ¥6 per hour and Tsewong is also a helpful resource for information about day trips around Xia He.

Renmin Xi Jie, located on the same side of street as the Overseas Tibetan Hotel, about 100m (328 ft.) in the opposite direction of the monastery on the 2nd floor. ✆ **138/9397-9763.** www.tsewongs-cafe-xiahe.de. Meal for 2 ¥30–¥80. No credit cards. 8am–8pm.

LANGMU SI (TAKTSANG LHAMO; 郎木寺) ★★

Gansu Province, 431km (267m) S of Lanzhou, 91km (56m) NW of Ruo'ergai

Perched on the border of Sichuan and Gansu, this Tibetan monastic center is slowly becoming known to Chinese tourists, but still lacks the commercial feel of Xia He. The tranquil mountain village is reminiscent of Lijiang before it was "discovered." It is hoped Langmu Si can escape UNESCO listing and the inevitable crowds for a few more years.

Essentials

GETTING THERE Daily **buses** connect with Hezuo (173km/107 miles; 3 hr.; ¥33) at 6.30, 7:30am and noon. There is one direct bus for Xia He each day at 2pm (¥47). To the south, a bus connects with Ruo'ergai (91km/56 miles; 2 hr.; ¥22) at 7am. Plans for a daily Songpan bus have yet to materialize, but a minivan to Songpan can be arranged through the Langmu Si Binguan or Langmu Si Tibetan Horse Trekking for ¥700.

Exploring Langmu Si

The town is home to two major Geluk monasteries, **Sertri Gompa** (¥20) and **Kirti Gompa** (¥15), situated in Gansu and Sichuan respectively. Both were razed during the Cultural Revolution and rebuilt during the early 1980s. Together, they house about 1,000 monks. True to the factional traditions of Tibetan Buddhism, they refer to each other as "that place in the other province." While the buildings are of recent construction, both are lively centers of worship, and the sound of monks chanting the scriptures may be heard throughout the day. A magnificent view of the surrounding countryside may be had from Sertri Gompa.

There are some delightful rambles around Langmu Si. If you head southwest beyond Kirti Gompa, a succession of narrow ravines and moraine valleys crowded with wildflowers, birds, and bubbling springs show the way to an abrupt pass. Continuing over the pass, you eventually connect with the Langmu Si–Maqu road, but this is a strenuous tramp through wild nomad country and should only be attempted by well-equipped parties. Another stiff hike is to the top of the distinctively shaped **Hua Gai Shan (Flower Cap Mountain) ★★**; this is best done as part of a horse trek (¥180 per day for a minimum of two guests), camping overnight on the peak. Traditionally, only men are allowed to sleep on the mountain, but this taboo is relaxed for foreigners. On a clear morning, you can see the holy mountain of Amnye Machen in Qinghai. On the 15th day of the 6th month of the lunar calendar, a magnificent **"sunning of the Buddha" festival** takes place on a broad plateau just below the peak, the consecration of the *thangka* heralded by lamas trumpeting from the summit. A nearby hot spring is also a popular destination for horse treks. **Langmu Si Tibetan Horse Trekking** (✆ **138/9399-1541**), opposite the Langmu Si Binguan, can arrange horse treks and hiking trips.

Langmu Si is a popular spot to attend a **sky burial** or *chadur* (¥20 admission to Sertri Gompa). To reach the spot, head past the gate of Sertri Gompa and veer toward the left, walking about 1km (⅔ mile). In this arid, treeless land, an alternative to cremation or burial had to be found for the people of the Tibetan plateau. The remains of the deceased (whose soul is thought to have already left the body) are dismembered and offered to huge vultures. Nothing is wasted; even the bones are ground up by attendants. If attending the funeral of a stranger doesn't put you off, be aware that this is not a tourist show and you should keep a respectful distance. A large breakfast beforehand is not advised.

Where to Stay

Langmu Si has a reasonable collection of hotels, although rooms with bathrooms are few and far between, and wherever you stay hot water will only be available for a limited period in the evening.

Langmu Si Binguan Clean and simple rooms with bathrooms and friendly English-speaking staff make this a popular backpacker choice. The owner Kelsang is also a bounty of information on the local area and can assist with everything from trekking advice to guides and arranging homestays.

Langmu Si. ✆ **0941/667-1086.** 55 units. ¥160–¥180 standard room. No credit cards.

Langmu Si Dajiudian ★ This grand new edifice looks a little out of place in ramshackle Langmu Si, but it's by far the most comfortable offering in town. The rooms are clean, modern, and tasteful and are decked out with pine furniture. The suites are plushly carpeted, and the rooms at the front of the hotel enjoy good views over Kirti Gompa. Rooms are a little overpriced at high-season rack rate, but outside of the May and October holidays, you should be able to negotiate a good deal. Not to be confused with the Langmu Si Binguan, opposite the bus stop, which is a far cheaper (but still perfectly acceptable) option.

Langmu Si (opposite the Kirti Gompa ticket office and the mosque). ✆ **0941/667-1555.** 55 units. ¥380 standard room; ¥800 suite. No credit cards. *In room:* TV.

Nomad's Youth Hostel (Lupeng Qingnian Luguan) ★ Opened by an avid Chinese backpacker from Henan province, this second-floor guesthouse has great service, wood floors, and a row of airy communal rooms with dorm beds. Try to snag the one private room here by calling in advance. When the hostel is full, Tibetan dance performances are held in the grounds behind the hostel, which inevitably turn into a late-night drinking fest. The owner, Mr. Zhang, is an encyclopedia of travel information and can help arrange treks around the area. There is usually an English-speaking staff member around.

Langmu Si (halfway to Sertri Gompa from the bus stop). ✆ **0941/667-0004.** lphy717@163.com. 20 dorm beds, 1 standard room. ¥20 dorm bed; ¥50 standard room. No credit cards. *In room:* No phone.

Sana Hotel (Sana Binguan) The plentiful standard rooms don't come with private bathrooms but offer a nice view of the temple from their windows and the sound of a stream will lull you to sleep. The Muslim owner Yang Jincai is a jolly fellow who will encourage you to soak in the hot springs.

Langmu Si (a little beyond Nomad's toward Sertri Gompa). ✆ **0941/667-1062.** 30 units. ¥30 dorm bed; ¥60 standard room. No credit cards. *In room:* No phone.

Where to Eat

Black Tent Café, operated by Langmu Si Tibetan Horse Trekking, has comfy seating and tasty cakes and coffee, and is also a good place to source local information. Just before the turn to Sertri Gompa, **Ali's Café ★★** (✆ **0941/667-1090**), predictably owned by (the very affable) Ali, offers a homey ambience and cheap prices making it a great place to relax after a hike. Hearty backpacker fare is offered by **Leisha's Café** (✆ **0941/667-1179**), near the bus stop. Fans of "competitive eating" should inquire about the Yak Burger Challenge. Another cafe worthy of note is **Shanghai Times (Shanghai Shiguang),** which offers freshly ground coffee with one refill for ¥10 and a decent spaghetti Bolognese. Shanghai Times is on the second floor of the building opposite the bus stop.

JIAYU GUAN 嘉峪关

765km (474m) NW of Lanzhou, 383km (237m) E of Dunhuang

At the northwest end of the narrow **He Xi corridor** lies a fort that marks the western extremity of the Ming Great Wall. During the Ming dynasty, **Jiayu Guan** was regarded as the end of the Chinese world, beyond which lay the strange lands and peoples of the western lands. Just as transportation to Australia struck fear into Britons, exile ranked just behind decapitation and death by strangulation in the Qing penal code. Many common criminals passed through the gates of Jiayu Guan, but so did victims of court intrigues, such as commissioner Lin Zexu (1785–1850), who tried to suppress the opium trade in Guangzhou (Canton) but found himself banished to Yining. The only people regarded as less fortunate were those who built the Ming Wall. Its construction was estimated to have claimed eight million lives—one life for every yard. Jiayu Guan today is a modern and quietly prosperous steel town. It's worthwhile to spend a day here to visit the fort and outlying sections of wall.

Essentials

GETTING THERE The **airport** is 15km (9 miles) northeast of downtown. A taxi there costs ¥40 to ¥50. Jiayu Guan has daily connections with Beijing, Shanghai, Xian and Lanzhou.

The **railway station** is 4km (2½ miles) southeast of the center of town. A taxi from the station should cost less than ¥10. Heading west, your chances of obtaining a sleeper ticket are slim, but for the 4-hour ride to Dunhuang a hard seat train is bearable. Heading farther west proceed through a travel agent (around ¥50 commission), or buy a hard-seat ticket and try to upgrade. Heading east, things are a little easier, and the T9204 is a good option to Lanzhou (7:16am; 7 hr.).

The **bus station** (✆ **0937/622-5242**) is on the southeast corner of Shengli Zhong Lu and Xin Xi Lu. Daily buses connect with Dunhuang at 9am, 10:30am, 11:30am, and 2:30pm (383km/237 miles; 5 hr.; ¥70). A sleeper bus leaves for Lanzhou (765km/474 miles; 12 hr.; ¥150) at 6:30pm.

GETTING AROUND **Taxis** cost ¥6 for the first 3km (2 miles), ¥1.20 per kilometer thereafter, with a night surcharge of ¥1.40 from 10pm to 5am. For trips to outlying sights charter a taxi for half-a-day for ¥100 to ¥150, depending upon where you plan to visit. **Bus** nos. 1 and 2 run from the railway station; both cost ¥1.

TOURS **Junhe International Travel Service** has offices on the fourth floor of the Jiugang Hotel at Xiongguan Xi Lu 2 (✆ **0937/626-2696;** www.jhitsonline.com). Hours are Monday to Friday from 8:30am to 6:30pm. They charge ¥50 commission on train ticket bookings and can arrange private tours with a driver and an English, French, or German speaking guide. Guides cost ¥200 per day regardless of group size and vehicles range from ¥350 per day for a three-passenger car to ¥500 for an eight-person van. As well as the sites listed below, Junhe can also arrange trips to a local winery where you can enjoy a tasting session for ¥50.

[FastFACTS] JIAYU GUAN

Banks, Foreign Exchange & ATMs You can change traveler's checks at the **Bank of China** (Mon–Fri 9am–5pm, Sat–Sun 10am–4pm) at Xinhua Zhong Lu 42, and there's an ATM that accepts foreign cards.

Internet Access There's a large 24-hour Internet cafe just east of the China Telecom and Post Office on Xiongguan Dong Lu. Access costs ¥1.50 to ¥2 per hour.

Post Office The main post office is on the main square in the south of town, but a more convenient branch is inside the China Telecom building on the southeast corner of the main roundabout at Xinhua Zhong Lu 1. Both branches are open from 8:30am to 6:30pm.

Visa Extensions The **PSB** is in the east side of Xiongguan Guangchangon (✆ **0937/630-2618**). The office is open Monday through Friday 8:30am to noon and 2:30 to 6pm. Processing takes 2 or 3 days.

Exploring Jiayu Guan

The three "wall sights" around Jiayu Guan are all covered by a joint ticket *(tongpiao)* costing ¥120, which is cheaper if you plan to visit the fort plus either (or both) the

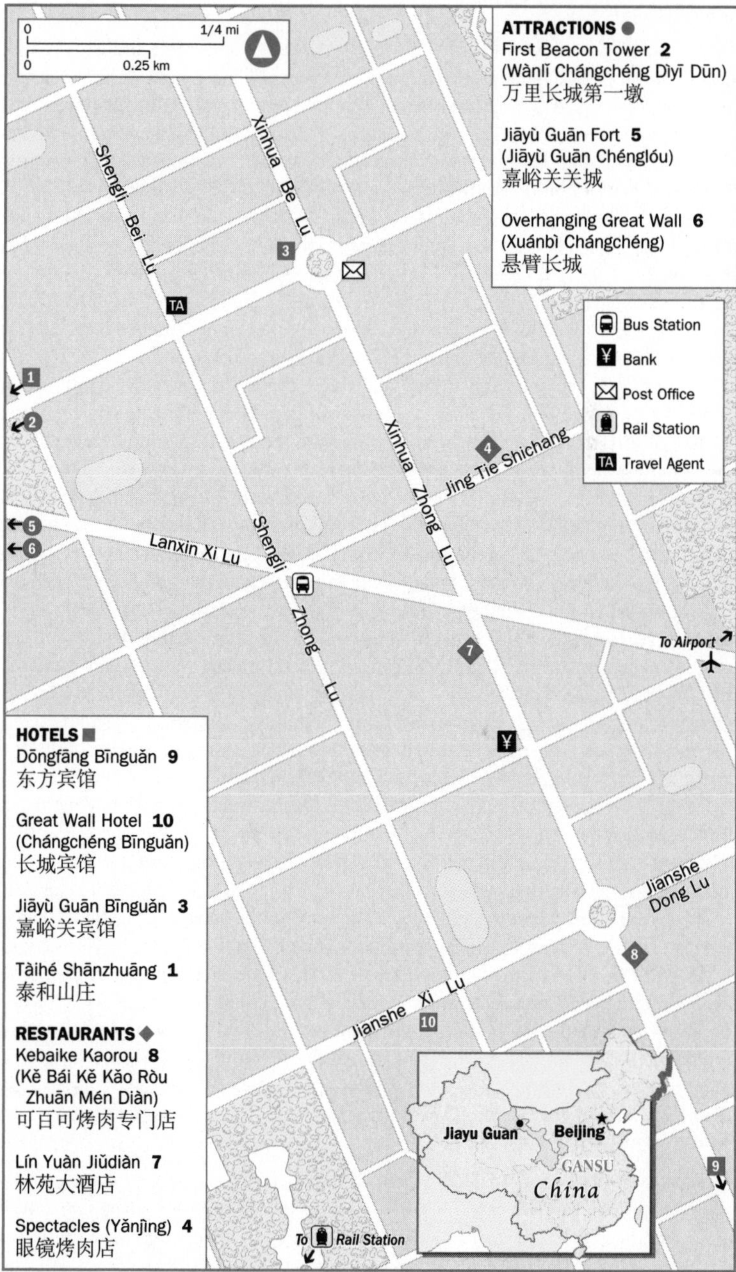
0
1/4 mi
0
0.25 km
ATTRACTIONS ●
First Beacon Tower 2
(Wànlǐ Chángchéng Dìyī Dūn)
万里长城第一墩
Jiāyù Guān Fort 5
(Jiāyù Guān Chénglóu)
嘉峪关关城
Overhanging Great Wall 6
(Xuánbì Chángchéng)
悬臂长城
Bus Station
Bank
Post Office
Rail Station
Travel Agent
HOTELS ■
Dōngfāng Bīnguǎn 9
东方宾馆
Great Wall Hotel 10
(Chángchéng Bīnguǎn)
长城宾馆
Jiāyù Guān Bīnguǎn 3
嘉峪关宾馆
Tàihé Shānzhuāng 1
泰和山庄
RESTAURANTS ◆
Kebaike Kaorou 8
(Kě Bái Kě Kǎo Ròu
Zhuān Mén Diàn)
可百可烤肉专门店
Lín Yuàn Jiǔdiàn 7
林苑大酒店
Spectacles (Yǎnjìng) 4
眼镜烤肉店
Xinhua Be Lu
Shengli Bei Lu
Xinhua Zhong Lu
Jing Tie Shichang
Lanxin Xi Lu
Shengli Zhong Lu
To Airport
Jianshe Dong Lu
Jianshe Xi Lu
To Rail Station
Jiayu Guan
Beijing
GANSU
China

Overhanging Great Wall and the First Beacon. These sights are also linked by a tourist bus (¥10), which is a cheap way of seeing all three, but leaves less flexibility than hiring a taxi.

Jiayu Guan Chenglou (Jiayu Guan Fort) ★★ The Ming dynasty's rebuilt section of the Great Wall is still most people's image of China, and this final outpost, surrounded by desert and backed by snowcapped mountains, is the best-preserved and most spectacular of the lot. First built in 1372, then expanded and reinforced in 1539, it was the final project of the Ming rebuilding. Entering from the east, you first come to the **Wenchang Pavilion,** restored in the late Qing dynasty, where intellectuals were said to compose poems, lamenting their rotten luck in being sent to live with the barbarians beyond the Wall. Before leaving, they could enjoy performances at the open-air theater opposite. After passing through **Guanghua Men,** the first of the three main 17m (56-ft.) towers, they would hurl a stone against the Wall to find out whether they would ever return to civilization. If the stone bounced back, all was well, but if it slithered quietly down the Wall, hope was lost.

Another legend associated with the Wall shows that obsession with quantification started long before 1949. The project's supervisor demanded an exact estimate of the number of bricks to be used in the construction of the fort; if the number was off by one brick, the death penalty awaited one Engineer Yi. When the fort was completed, Yi found that there was one brick left over. Faced with evidence of his failure, Yi declared it "the brick to balance the fort" *(ding cheng zhuan)* and walked away unscathed. The brick sits on the side of **Hui Ji Men,** and locals joke about tripping on it. Inside the main courtyard is the **Youji Yamen,** where the unfortunate generals were stationed with their families. The second main tower, **Rou Yuan Men,** represents the Ming policy of peaceful coexistence with the ethnic minorities beyond the Wall, a policy that ended in the Qing dynasty, when Xinjiang was dragged back into the Chinese empire. Continuing west, you face the massive outer Wall, over 10m (33 ft.) high, and pass through **Jiayu Guan Gate.** Chinese tour groups joke about forgetting their passport, ride camels, and dress up in funny minority costumes, but in the past it was no joke. Locals called it the Gate of Sighs, and the walls were scrawled with hastily composed poems by unfortunate exiles. A wander into the desert north of here gives some sense of both the isolation, and strategic significance of the fort, and if you're feeling brave you can also take short ultra-light flights (¥260 for 5 min.), which give an exhilarating perspective.

The **Great Wall Museum** (admission included in the price of the ticket; located near the fort's exit; July–Oct 8am–8pm, Nov–June 8:30am–6:30pm) is worth a visit for its well-curated exhibition and models of various spots along the Great Wall. The section on traditional weaponry and methods of protecting the wall are also interesting: As well as raked sand to trace would be deserters, dried cow-dung dust was used to blind attackers.

Joint ticket (¥120); regular admission ¥100, both including entry to the Changcheng Bowuguan (Great Wall Museum). Summer 8am–8pm; Winter 9am–5:30pm; Spring and Autumn 8:30am–6pm. Take a ¥10 taxi ride from town.

Wanli Changcheng Diyi Dun (First Beacon Tower) Seven kilometers (4⅓ miles) away from the Fort lies this fairly untouched crumbling bit of the Great Wall and watchtower. The Taolai River that runs through a steep gorge near the tower makes for a dramatic sunset photo op. On the way you'll notice that, true to form, history hasn't stood in the way of "progress" and an expressway runs directly under the wall, while the rail line runs through it! If the glass-floored platform over the gorge at the "visitor center" isn't scary enough you can strap on a body harness and be pitched out over the gorge via a cable (¥31), but remember that in the event of an accident, you're unlikely to sue and win in China. From the visitors center it's also worth visiting the mock-up Chinese military encampment 1km (½ mile) back toward the ticket office. There are stone yurts, catapults, cannons, and the opportunity to try your hand at some archery (¥1 per arrow). But best of all is a rickety suspension bridge across the gorge that gives stunning views in both directions. Make sure your taxi waits for you, as it's difficult to arrange a car back to town.

Joint Ticket (¥120); regular admission ¥21. 8am–8pm. Take a taxi, round-trip for ¥30–¥40.

Xincheng Wei Jin Mu (Wei-Jin Tombs) Twenty kilometers (12 miles) northeast of Jiayu Guan, this is sometimes misleadingly called the Dixia Hualang (Underground Art Gallery). The thousands of tombs in this area date from the Wei (220–65 B.C.) and Jin (A.D. 265–420), but only one is open to the public. You will see the tomb of a sixth-rank official, the lowest rank in the imperial pecking order. The valuables were plundered soon after the tomb was sealed, probably by the builder, judging from the accuracy of the thief's tunnel. Compared with Buddhist art, the murals in the tomb are crude cartoons. Detailed instructions on slaughtering pigs, goats, and cows leave no doubt as to what the owner was hoping for in the next world. There is evidence that sericulture had already spread to this part of the empire, that barbecues were enjoyed before Australia was colonized, and that officials were plumper than their servants. Murals detail the official's trip to the capital in Luoyang, doubtless the highlight of his career. The remaining contents of the tomb are on display in an **exhibition center,** and include black stone pigs found in the hands and the mouth of the official's corpse. He liked his pork.

Admission ¥45. 8:30am–7pm.

Xuanbi Changcheng (Overhanging Great Wall) This dramatic desert section of the Great Wall snakes its way up into the desolate **Hei Shan (Black Mountains).** Originally built in 1539, it was restored in 1988 and is supposedly as far northwest as the Wall goes, but there are actually sites farther west near Dunhuang. Two sections of Wall are here, both of which are worthwhile, although the second one is included in the *tongpiao* (joint ticket) and offers better views over the desert. The Wall here rises at a 45-degree angle for half a kilometer (1,640 ft.), which makes for a sweaty 20-minute climb, but the effort is rewarded with astounding views over the seemingly endless flat desert. You can take a different path back down from the last watchtower. At the top, past visitors have arranged stones into the equivalent of "John loves Mary." This section is 8km (5 miles) north of the fort, and can be reached by taxi or bike. Take plenty of water.

1st Section ¥25 admission; 2nd Section Joint Ticket (¥120), regular admission ¥21. Apr–Oct 8:30am–dusk; Nov–Mar 8:30am–6pm.

Shopping

For a supermarket try the Xinhua Chaoshi, on Xinhua Nan Lu, 250m (820 ft.) south of the junction with Jianshe Lu.

Where to Stay

Jiayu Guan suffers from a glut of mediocre three-star options. Outside the busy season in early May and mid-July to October, occupancy rates run as low as 20%, so discounts of at least 40% can be obtained. During the busy season, a 20% discount should be given.

EXPENSIVE

Changcheng Binguan (Great Wall Hotel) A favorite with tour groups since 1987, this sprawling, comfortable three-star hotel, whose exterior is a tacky replica of the Jiayuguan Fort outlined in white Christmas lights at night, is set in pleasant grounds. Service in the hotel is friendly, but they won't offer much of a discount in the high season. The deluxe rooms have been renovated more recently and feel plusher than standard rooms, but are no bigger and have the same amenities.

Jianshe Xi Lu 6. ✆ **0937/622-5288.** Fax 0937/622-6016. 153 units. ¥560–¥760 standard room; from ¥980 suite. Discounts of up to 50%. AE, DC, MC, V. Bus: 2. **Amenities:** Restaurant; concierge; exercise room; pool. *In room:* A/C, TV, fridge, hairdryer, Internet (¥20 per day).

Jiayu Guan Binguan ★ Right in the center of town, this well-run four-star hotel has been giving birth to new wings since 1983. Rooms in Building 1 are modern, comfortable and well-equipped, whilst those in Building 2 are older and smaller, but well-maintained and still perfectly comfortable. This is where government officials stay when they come to Jiayu Guan.

Xinhua Bei Lu 1. ✆ **0937/620-1588.** Fax 0937/622-7174. 177 units. ¥768 standard room in Building 1; ¥680 standard room in Building 2; from ¥1,880–¥2,680 suite. Discounts of 40%–50%. AE, DC, MC, V. Bus: 1 to Youdian Dalou. **Amenities:** 2 restaurants; concierge; 24-hr. forex; game room. *In room:* A/C, TV, fridge, hair dryer, Internet.

MODERATE/INEXPENSIVE

Dongfang Binguan This budget hotel out toward the train station offers decent but small rooms at a good price. Bathrooms don't quite live up to the quality of the rooms. Service is friendly and attentive, though little English is spoken. The downstairs canteen and second floor restaurant are both deservedly popular, and there's a supermarket right next door.

Yingbin Xi Lu. ✆ **0937/630-1866.** Fax 0937/630-1027. 78 units (shower only). ¥320 standard room; ¥480–¥680 suite. Discounts of 45%. No credit cards. **Amenities:** 2 restaurants. *In room:* A/C, TV, hair dryer, Internet (¥10 per day).

Taihe Shanzhuang ★ Located within the grounds of the Jiayu Guan Fort, this replica of a Qing dynasty courtyard house allows you to spend more time at Jiayu Guan's main attraction and to view the fort at sunrise and sunset, when the earthen ramparts are highly photogenic. The standard rooms are small and shabby, so it's worth the extra outlay to take a suite. Beds are hard and bathrooms are slightly grimy but the atmosphere is unbeatable. The restaurant fare is decent.

Jiayu Guan Chenglou (150m/492 ft. past the back entrance to the fort). ✆ **0937/639-6622.** 16 units (shower only). ¥120 standard room; ¥180 suite. No credit cards. **Amenities:** Restaurant. *In room:* TV (in suite).

Where to Eat

Jiayu Guan is a prosperous steel town, so the restaurants—unlike the hotels—do well year-round. The main outdoor food markets are Fuqiang Shichang and Jingtie Shichang. The nightmarket on the north side of Jingtie Shichang is the liveliest in town. Sheep carcasses dangle, beer flows, and vendors make fun of their regular customers. The nightmarket's greatest showman, simply called **Yanjing (Spectacles)** serves tasty Uighur lamb skewers (*yangrou chuan;* ¥1 each) and mini–lamb chops (*yangpai;* ¥10 for 8).

Lin Yuan Jiudian ★★ CANTONESE/HOTPOT This lively restaurant is one of the best in town and offers fiery hotpot on the ground floor and Cantonese and Sichuanese cuisine on the second. If you don't like spicy food, this hotpot restaurant also serves *yuanyang huoguo,* where you choose between a spicy or a vegetable broth in which to cook your meat and vegetables. Upstairs, the *fugui niurou* is akin to roast beef on sesame toast, while *xiqinbaihe chao xian you* (fresh squid on a bed of celery, field mushrooms, and lotus) is a Cantonese favorite.

Xinhua Zhong Lu 34 (2nd floor of the Lin Yuan Hotel). Hotpot ✆ **0937/620-3666;** Cantonese ✆ **0937/620-3777.** Meal for 2 ¥60–¥120. No credit cards. 9am–2pm and 5–9pm. Bus: 1.

Kebaike Kaorou ★ BARBECUE A popular choice with families and young couples, Kebaike is a modern restaurant where you get to barbecue your own food. Choose from a host of options including spicy beef, aubergines with cumin or needle mushrooms wrapped in bacon, and order a cucumber salad to refresh your palate. A picture menu and accommodating staff makes ordering simple. There's also a bakery on the premises.

Xinhua Nan Lu—look for the English Xililai sign. ✆ **0937/628-7922.** Meal for 2 ¥80. No credit cards. 10am–midnight. Bus: 1.

DUNHUANG 敦煌

Gansu Province, 383km (237 miles) W of Jiayu Guan, 524km (325 miles) NE of Golmud

Dunhuang's name (blazing beacon) derives from its function as a Han Chinese garrison town, but the Tang name of Sha Zhou (sand district) describes it better, hemmed in by sand dunes and bleak, pebbly desert. The middle and southern Silk Routes set off from Dunhuang, passing through the remote garrison town of **Loulan** (abandoned when Lop Nor Lake "wandered off" in the 4th c.) and through the **Lop Desert.**

A large number of the early residents of Dunhuang were not Han, and the town came under the sway of the Tibetans, the Uighurs, and the Xi Xia, only really becoming a Han town after the colonization of the western regions was initiated during the Qing dynasty. The town is dependent on tourism, and despite efforts to develop other sites, it is the peerless **Mogao cave-temple complex** that makes Dunhuang the essential stop on the Silk Routes.

Essentials

GETTING THERE The **airport** is 13km (8 miles) east of Dunhuang, just past the turnoff to the Mogao caves. Public buses (¥10) connect with flights, or you can try your luck bargaining with taxi drivers without meters, who should charge no more than ¥50 to the center of town. The most useful flight booking office (8am–9pm) is by the Dunhuang Binguan at 246 Yangguan Dong Lu (✆ **0937/882-9000**). In summer daily flights connect with Lanzhou, Ürümqi, Xi'an and Beijing. There are fewer flights in winter.

Dunhuang's tiny new **railway station** is 6 miles out of town (¥15–¥20 by taxi or ¥3 by local bus), and has year-round services to Lanzhou, Jiayuguan, and Xi'an, and sometimes there are summer services to Turpan and Ürümqi. Coming to or from Beijing or Shanghai you'll still have to come via the old railhead 130km (81 miles; 2 hr.) away at Liuyuan. From Liuyuan station, you will have no trouble finding taxi or minibus drivers, who ask ¥30 per person to Dunhuang, or ¥120 for the whole taxi. If you are the last tourist around after a train pulls away, you can bargain hard as the station suffers from a glut of drivers. Buses for Liuyuan railway station leave hourly from Dunhuang's long-distance bus station (¥20). You can buy train tickets at either rail station, from the Booking Office for Train Tickets (8am–4pm) opposite the Dunhuang International Hotel at 31 Ming Shan Lu, or through an agent.

The new **bus station** is in the east of town on Sanwei Lu (✆ **0937/882-2129**). Construction was ongoing at the time of writing, but bus services were not affected. Daily buses connect with Jiayu Guan (383km/237 miles; 5 hr.; ¥62–¥86) from 8am to 7pm; with Lanzhou at 11am and 3pm (1,148km/713 miles; 20 hr.; sleeper bus; ¥226); with Golmud at 9am and 7:30pm (524km/325 miles; 9 hr.; ¥100); and with Xining at 12:30pm (1,067km/662 miles; 18 hr.; ¥208).

GETTING AROUND **Taxis** fill Dunhuang's narrow streets. Meters aren't commonly used and the rate should be ¥5 for a short ride or ¥10 for a longer one. Get around on foot, or hire a **bike** for ¥3 to ¥5 per hour. There are also a few **bus** routes, of which no. 3 ¥1) running to the Singing Sand Mountains, the unnumbered airport (¥10), and train station (¥3) routes are the most useful. A new bus service (again unnumbered) runs every 30 minutes from the Dunhuang Fandian near Charley Johng's cafe to the Mogao Caves for ¥8.

TOURS **CITS** is inside the compound of the Dunhuang Guoji Dajiudian at Ming Shan Lu 32 (✆ **0937/882-2474;** www.dhcits.com; Mon–Sat 8am–noon and 3–6pm), on the right as you enter. For camel rides into the desert contact Charley Johng at his cafe, hostel, or dune guesthouse (p. 298).

[Fast FACTS] DUNHUANG

Banks, Foreign Exchange & ATMs You can change cash and traveler's checks at the **Bank of China** (8:30am–6pm) at Yangguan Zhong Lu 13. There's also a 24-hour ATM here. There's another branch with ATM opposite the tourist nightmarket on Yangguan Dong Lu.

Internet Access Most of the backpacker cafes on Ming Shan Lu offer Internet access for ¥6 per hour, often giving 30 minutes free use if you eat there. There's a genuine 24-hour Internet cafe on the east side of Ming Shan Lu, just north of the Dunhuang International Hotel.

Post Office The main post office (8am–6:30am summer; 8:30am–6pm winter) is on the north side of Yangguan Zhong Lu, just west of the junction with Sha Zhou Lu.

Exploring Dunhuang

As well as the sites listed below there's also the opportunity to take a **camel ride ★★** out into the desert away from the crowds. Trips last anything from a couple of hours to a month and can be arranged through any of the Western cafes on Ming Shan Lu. They cost ¥160 for a 3-hour sunset trip, or ¥300 to ¥400 per day for longer trips, but prices are scheduled to increase. Longer trips include guide, food and water, tent, sleeping bag, and a warm coat in the colder months. Even a short trip works out cheaper than the cost of an entry ticket and a touristy camel ride at Mingsha Shan, and the experience feels far more authentic.

Mingsha Shan & Yueya Quan (Singing Sand Mountains & Crescent Moon Spring) ★ When Aurel Stein settled down by the spring to churn out his

Dunhuang 敦煌

HOTELS
Charley Johng's Hostel 7
(Mèng Tuó Líng Qīng Nián Lǎshè)
梦驼铃青年旅社
Dunhuang International Hotel 13
(Dūnhuáng Guóji Dàjiǔdiàn)
敦煌国际大酒店
Dunhuang Legend Hotel 4
(Dūnhuang Fēitiān Dàjiǔdian)
敦煌飞天大酒店
Fēitiān Bīnguǎn 12
飞天宾馆
Grand Soluxe 2
(Dūn Huáng Yáng Guān Shā Zhōu Dà Jiǔ Diàn)
敦煌阳光沙洲大酒店
Jīnyè Bīnguǎn 14
金叶宾馆
Silk Road Dunhuang Hotel 15
(Dūnhuáng Shānzhuāng)
敦煌山庄
RESTAURANTS
Charley Johng's Café 8
Dá Jì Lūròu Huángmiàn Guǎn 3
达记胪肉黄面馆
John's Information Café 11
(Yuēhàn Cāntīng)
约翰餐厅
Night Market (Yèshì) 5
夜市
Shirley's Café 10
Siji Xiang Meishicheng 9
(Sì Jì Xiāng Měishíchéng)
四季香美食城
ATTRACTIONS
Mogao Caves 6
(Mògāo Shíkū)
莫高石窟
Singing Sand Dunes 16
(Míngshā Shān)
鸣沙山
Western Thousand Buddha Caves 1
(Xī Qiān Fó Dòng)
西千佛洞
Airport
Bank
Bus Station
Police
Post Office
Travel Agent
Dang River
Dunhuang
Beijing
GANSU
China
Yanguan Zhong Lu
Yanguan Dong Lu
Shazhou Bei Lu
Shazhou Nan Lu
Henshui Lu
Jinshan Lu
Shichang Xiang
Mingshan Lu
Xinjian Lu
Huancheng Nan Lu
Dunyue Lu
To Airport (13 km) & Bus Station
0 1/8 mi
0 100 m
TA

memoirs, he opined, "It lay hidden away amidst high sands beyond the southern edge of the oasis and about 3 miles from the town. For the desert wanderer there could be no more appropriate place of rest, I thought, than this delightful little pilgrimage place enclosed all around by sand-ridges rising to over 75m in height. There was a limpid little lake, of crescent shape and about a quarter of a mile long, which has given the locality its name and its sanctity."

Stein's peaceful temple was razed during the Cultural Revolution and is now a souvenir shop. The limpid "lake" is a fenced-off dank pond reduced to half the original size, a result of the ongoing exploitation of underground water. The pilgrimage is marked by a gauntlet of stalls selling stuffed toy camels, batik, and glow-in-the-dark cups, culminating in a ticket office charging ¥120 to see a naturally formed attraction. Inside the entrance are carts (¥10) to take you to the lake, and toboggans (¥20) to take you down the sand dunes, which make for a fun, if sandy experience. To get deeper into the dunes you can hire a camel (¥80 for an hour including the ridiculous bright orange gaiters you'll see most domestic tourists sporting), a jeep (¥260 for up to four people for an hour), or an ATV (¥120 for two people). If you've never seen desert dunes, it's worth the effort, especially just before sunrise or sunset, when the delicate contours and colors of the dunes are beguiling. The best way to avoid the crowds is to hike up the first ridge you see as you enter, get as high as you can (it's hard work) and then roam at leisure.

Admission ¥80. Summer 6am–9pm; winter 8am–7pm. Taxi ¥10 or minibus no. 3.

Mogao Shiku (Mogao Caves) ★★★ Here is the biggest, best-preserved, and most significant site of Buddhist statuary and frescoes in all of China—and the best-curated site, too. A guide is compulsory, as is leaving your camera (no charge) at the gate. Generally the guides, who all have bachelor's degrees, are excellent, sometimes going well beyond the script. Tours, which depart every few minutes and are limited to about 20 people, usually take 2 hours and cover 10 of the 40 caves that are open to the public; Caves 16, 17, 96, and 148 are included on all tours. Tours in the afternoon are less crowded, and you may get a guide to yourself. Or come right as the caves open in the morning, before the tour groups arrive. Although guides have powerful flashlights, it's worth bringing your own to see the murals in some of the darker caves.

Before you reach the grottoes you'll see the **Dunhuang Exhibition Centre ★**, which includes copies of several of the grottoes, including **cave 285,** which tells the tale of 500 rebels who fought against the corrupt King Prasenajit and had their eyes gouged out and were banished to the wilderness before the gods took pity on them and allowed them to be tonsured as monks, their sight restored by the Buddha. Upstairs is a stunning exhibition of Tibetan bronze statues, both complete and beheaded, that were rescued from Red Guards by the canny curator.

All together, there are 492 caves, of which you will see a mere 10 on the 2-hour tour. Your first stop on the tour will likely be **Caves 16 and 17** (the Library Cave). The cave was sealed off sometime after 998 (the year of the last dated manuscript), perhaps out of fear of the spread of Islam—the Buddhist kingdom of Khotan was captured and sacked in 1006. In 1900, the cave was rediscovered by Wang Daoshi (Abbot Wang), the self-appointed guardian of the caves. First among the villains was archaeologist Aurel Stein, a Hungarian who obtained British citizenship (and later a knighthood), and who arrived during the winter of 1907. The Chinese commentary is only slightly more damning than the English translation, accusing Stein of "purchasing by deceit" over 7,000 complete manuscripts and silk paintings from the "ignorant" Abbott Wang for a paltry £130. Next came young French Sinologist Paul Pelliot, whose mastery of Chinese gave him a selectivity his predecessor lacked—Stein returned to London with over 1,000 copies of the Lotus Sutra. Pelliot obtained thousands of documents for even less—only £90! The Chinese save their greatest condemnation for Langdon Warner, who removed 12 murals **(Cave 323)** and a statue **(Cave 328).** Warner justified his theft as a way of avoiding the "renovations" funded by Abbot Wang. A map in the small museum opposite the Library Cave illustrates how the contents are spread around the world.

Curators, fearing that increased tourist activity is damaging the coloration of the frescoes, are closing some caves to the public. Some caves, considered of particular interest and import (such as Caves 275 and 285, detailed above), can be visited for an additional fee of ¥200 per cave per person. The caves depicting acts of love-making, much touted in other guidebooks, are generally off-limits. Remarkable early caves (usually open) include **Cave 259,** commissioned during the Northern Wei (A.D. 386–535); and **Cave 428,** where an early incarnation of the historical Buddha sacrifices himself to feed a tigress and her cubs. It's also worth asking to see **Cave 249,** which dates from the Western Wei; the cave's small size allows in enough daylight to see the exquisite lapis lazuli artwork on the ceiling. Later caves, such as **Cave 96,** which houses a 36m (116-ft.) Buddha, and **Cave 148,** which contains a serene 17m (56-ft.) Sleeping Buddha, indicate that artisans from the Tang court found their way to Mogao. Some lower caves were affected by floodwaters from the Daquan River, and sunlight has caused lead-based pigments to turn black, but the overall state of preservation is incredible. Caves are grouped roughly by period, and it is intriguing to view the steady transformation of facial features from Greco-Indian to plumper, more feminine Chinese features.

Admission May-Oct ¥180, Nov-Apr ¥100, includes English-speaking guide. Summer 8am–5:30pm, Winter 9am–5pm (ticket booth hours; the caves close at 6pm). To make the 30-min. journey to the caves, green minibuses leave every 30 min. (from 8am, last bus returns at 6pm; ¥8 each way) from just north of Charley Johng's Cafe. Taxis cost ¥100 for the round-trip.

Xi Qian Fo Dong (Western Thousand Buddha Caves) The missionary Mildred Cable described the scene: "At the edge of the cliff was a rough opening, and from it a very precipitous path led down to a narrow ledge from which the new caves opened . . . they were comparable to the better known Thousand Buddha Grottoes . . . the figures were free and stately, with flowing lines and elegant draperies, and the frescoes showed the same clear warm tints."

Located 35km (22 miles) southwest of town, the valley is easily accessed as a half-day trip, but it's still a scramble down to the caves. They were largely built by locals from the nearby village of Nan Hu, and have several *Jataka* stories not covered by the Mogao caves. Most of the statuary (with the exception of Caves 5 and 16) was repainted to poor effect during the Qing dynasty. The most spectacular murals are located in **Cave 15 ★**, which is not open to the casual visitor without payment of an additional fee. The stunning blues and muscular bodhisattvas of the Northern Wei **(Cave 5)** and Northern Zhou **(Cave 6)** are in real contrast to the plump, feminine bodhisattvas of the Middle Tang **(Cave 15).** To reach the site, a taxi may be hired for ¥60; or take any bus heading west from Dunhuang for ¥5. From the road, it's a 15-minute walk south to the cliff face, with a set of stairs to the left leading down to the ticket office.

Admission ¥30. 8am–6pm. No English tour guide. Taxis make the trip from Dunhuang for ¥80 round-trip.

A Side Trip to Han Dynasty Ruins ★

If you're a history buff who is tired of seeing fake renditions of the Great Wall, this 92km (57-mile) journey into the desert to visit these desolate Han dynasty ruins is a worthwhile day trip. The ruins comprise three separate locations: **Yumen Guan (Jade Gate),** an ancient watchtower made of mud, straw, and stone, and the lesser-known **He Cangcheng** and **Han Changcheng.** On the way to these ruins you'll pass another historic site called Yang Guan (Sun Gate). Yumen Guan and Yang Guan were the traditional border crossings that marked the beginning of the territory ruled by the Han dynasty. Today, however, Yang Guan (¥50) is a tacky site geared toward Chinese tour groups; it features an unspectacular watchtower surrounded by a fake village, and a terribly curated museum. Skip this and continue to the Yumen Guan ticket counter, which appears in the middle of the desert, along a long stretch of road. Pay here (¥40) and drive for another 30km (19 miles) to reach Yumen Guan. The highlight of the three is **Han Changcheng ★★**, which is 13km (21 miles) east of Yumen Guan on a dirt road and is a rather crumbling building that was used as a storage unit. Five kilometers (8 miles) to the east of Yumen Guan is Han Changcheng, which features one watchtower and a remnant of the Great Wall that's several hundred yards long. Another 80km (50 miles) farther west will bring you to the **Yardang Geological Park** (¥50), a collection of peculiarly shaped rocks formed by the action of wind, setting for the final scenes of Zhang Yimou's epic movie *Hero,* starring Jet Li. Plan for a day trip that takes roughly 8-10 hours. A round-trip taxi ride costs around ¥400.

Where to Stay

Dunhuang has a surplus of accommodations. During the peak season, hotels offer 20% discounts; during the low season, discounts of up to 60% are readily negotiated. In spite of what you may be told, most of the budget accommodations (including the Feitian Binguan) only have hot water for a limited number of hours in the evening; if you're told the hotel has 24-hour hot water, ask for a demonstration.

VERY EXPENSIVE

Dunhuang Shanzhuang (The Silk Road Dunhuang Hotel) ★★ This four-star Hong Kong venture is the finest hotel on the Silk Routes, and one of the most unique hotels in the country. It lies 4km (2½ miles) south of town, just before the Ming Shan Dunes, which loom in the background. Designed by a Chinese-American architect, the gigantic, airy lobby gives you a sense of calm that rarely exists in China. The main building mimics the look of the Mogao Caves, and the high-ceilinged rooms feature finely crafted wooden furnishings, cool stone floors and Xinjiang rugs that mesh perfectly with the desert surroundings. Bathrooms, which feature enormous showerheads and are lined with black stone, are fantastic. During a visit, Bill Gates was duly impressed with the villas, which feature a mixture of Tang and Han architectural styles. For those on a budget the "professional quarters" offers simpler rooms set around an empty courtyard, but some have great dune views, and all benefit from full use of the hotel's facilities. Next-door an aptly named "student building" with beds for ¥80 (sometimes discounted to ¥30) also houses the staff. Service is top-notch. The **rooftop patio ★★** is a must for sunset and beautiful views of the dunes—guests can take breakfast there, and it's open to the public in the evenings. Dinner at the restaurant adjoining the hotel is decent, featuring spicy Chinese dishes. Barbecues in the desert outside of the hotel can be arranged in summer for ¥268 per person. In season (May–Oct), if there are big groups staying (more than 30 people total), dance performances can sometimes be enjoyed and begin at 9pm (¥69). The hotel features a very professional massage center, as opposed to the dodgy kind on offer at many Chinese hotels.

Dunyue Lu. www.dunhuangresort.com. ✆ **0937/888-2088.** Fax 0937/888-2086. 269 units including villas. ¥800–¥1,200 standard room; from ¥2,000 suite; from ¥2,000 villa room; professional room ¥350. Discounts of 25–45%. AE, DC, MC, V. **Amenities:** 2 restaurants; cafe; bar; bike rental; concierge; 24-hr. forex; room service; sauna; evening shuttle bus to town. *In room:* A/C, TV, fridge, hair dryer, Internet (¥50 per day).

Grand Soluxe Hotel (Dunhuang Yangguang Shazhou Dajiudian) While it certainly doesn't have the style, character, or great location of Dunhuang Shanzhuang, in terms of luxury and amenities, the Soluxe wins hands down. The huge glass monolith looks somewhat out of place in sleepy Dunhuang, but inside the rooms it's all muted tones accented with the group's signature burgundy. Spend a little extra on a deluxe room with tub and ask for a high floor overlooking the river.

Yangguan Zhong Lu 31. www.grandsoluxehotel.com. ✆ **0937/886-2888.** Fax 0937/886-2889. 250 units. ¥860 standard room; ¥1,360 deluxe room; from ¥1,600 suite. Discounts of 15–20%. AE, DC, MC, V. **Amenities:** 3 restaurants; concierge; 24-hr. forex; room service; swimming pool. *In room:* A/C, TV, fridge, hair dryer, Internet.

EXPENSIVE

Dunhuang Feitian Dajiudian (Dunhuang Legend Hotel) ★ Not to be confused with the cheaper Feitian Binguan down the road (see below), this new hotel in the center of town provides clean, comfortable, spacious, and quiet rooms, some of which have computers with Internet access. Rooms are well furnished, with good bathrooms. Discounted prices are competitive and staff is keen to please.

Ming Shan Lu 2. www.dhlegendhotel.com. ✆ **0937/885-3999.** 134 units. ¥698 standard room; ¥1,588 suite. Up to 40% discount. V. **Amenities:** Restaurant. *In room:* A/C, TV, hair dryer, Internet (¥30 per day).

Jinye Binguan (Golden Leaf Hotel) Located 1.6km (1 mile) south of the center of town, this recently renovated hotel is a sound three-star choice. An orchard provides grapes, apricots, and peaches for the hotel restaurant. Rooms are tastefully styled and feature photos of local scenes, but it's worth asking for a room overlooking the orchard, as rooms facing the main road are noisy. "Golden leaf" is a reference to tobacco: The hotel is owned by the Gansu Tobacco Company.

Ming Shan Lu 37. ✆ **0937/885-1246.** Fax 0937/885-1248. 91 units. ¥880 standard room; ¥1,680 suite. Rates include full breakfast. Discounts of up to 40%. No credit cards. **Amenities:** Restaurant; bar; concierge; large exercise room; game room. *In room:* A/C, TV, fridge, Internet (¥20 per day).

MODERATE

Dunhuang Guoji Dajiudian (Dunhuang International Hotel) While its bathroom-tile exterior may give you pause, the rooms here are some of the best in town for the price. The rooms are decorated in simple tones and feature modern headboards and comfy beds, but service is hit-or-miss. You can save ¥100 by choosing a standard room over a deluxe room, the only difference being that the deluxe rooms have tubs and are slightly bigger.

Ming Shan Lu 28. www.dhih.cn. ✆ **0937/885-3348.** Fax 0937/882-1821. 150 units. ¥588 standard room; ¥998–¥1,288 suite. Up to 50% discount. AE, DC, MC, V. Rates include full breakfast. **Amenities:** 2 restaurants; cafe; bar; concierge; forex; karaoke; room service. *In room:* A/C, TV, fridge, Internet (¥40 per day), minibar.

INEXPENSIVE

Charley Johng's Hostel (Mengtuo Ling Qingnian Lushe) This newly opened hostel presents bright, clean, simple and airy doubles and twins in a good location near the tourist nightmarket. There are also spacious dorms with bathrooms, plus free Wi-Fi and computer terminals with Internet access. The outdoor bar is a good place to meet fellow travelers and Charley is a great source of local information. If you want to experience a meal in a traditional-style courtyard house, Charley can take you out to his simple dune guesthouse, set amid apricot orchards just yards from the sand.

Behind the Mosque. ✆ **0937/885-7298.** 22 units. ¥120 standard room; ¥35 dorm bed. No credit cards. **Amenities:** Restaurant; Wi-Fi. *In room:* TV.

Feitian Binguan (Feitian Hotel) ★ This old backpacker favorite has an old wing with dated twins, which at full discount still offer one of the best budget deals in the city. There's also a newer wing with better rooms, which is popular with domestic tour groups. As the bus station has now moved to the east of the city, the hotel's location is no longer as convenient for onwards travel, nevertheless, it is still at the heart of the Western cafe ghetto on Ming Shan Lu, and the friendly staff are used to dealing with foreigners.

Ming Shan Lu 22. ✆ **0937/882-2337.** 81 units. ¥320 standard room in old wing; ¥558 standard room in new wing. Discounts of 40–60%. No credit cards. **Amenities:** Restaurant. *In room:* A/C, TV, Internet (¥30 per day.

Where to Eat

Clustered around the Feitian Hotel are small restaurants with English menus, offering "Western" food and overpriced Chinese fare. My favorite is the newly expanded **Shirley's,** but **Charley Johng's Café** and **John's Information Café** are also worth a try. A favorite local drink served at many restaurants, including John's and Shirley's, is the delicious *xingpishui* (dried apricot juice), which is generally home-brewed by soaking the apricots in water, then adding sugar for a tart and sweet combination. For a decent cup of coffee (¥18–¥50) in a comfy setting, head to **Memory Box Café (Shiguan Hezi Kafeiguan),** just off the main nightmarket drag near the mosque.

Da Ji Lurou Huangmian Guan GANSU Surprisingly, the specialty dish of Dunhuang is *lurou huangmian* (donkey meat yellow noodles). More surprisingly, it's delicious. It is claimed that the method of making the noodles is revealed in Cave 265, but the cave isn't open to the public and the owners of this noodle shop aren't talking. The noodles are cooked with tofu, mushrooms, and plenty of garlic—a small plate *(xiaopan)* is more than sufficient. To accompany the main dish, order some donkey meat *(lurou)*. Half a *jin* (*ban jin;* ¥25), which is half a kilo, is enough for two. The meat is lean and tastes a little like roast beef. You'll be served a bowl of finely chopped garlic, to which you should add chili sauce and vinegar to taste, before dipping the meat in it. If you want to meet some locals, this market street is a better choice than the tacky main nightmarket *(yeshi)*. An after-dinner stroll through the charming narrow lanes provides a rewarding glimpse of the old town.

Jinshan Lu (just south of the gate that marks the entrance of the market from Yangguan Zhong Lu). ✆ **0937/383-7228.** ¥8 small bowl of *huangmian.* No credit cards. 10:30am–10:30pm.

Siji Xiang Meishicheng CHINESE This clean restaurant presents a wide range of Chinese favorites in its English menu, along with (expensive) specialties such as Camel's Paw and donkey noodles. Service is good and the *gongbao jiding* (diced chicken with peanuts), *yuxiang rousi* (fish-flavored pork), and *tudou si* (finely sliced potatoes) are all delicious.

Ming Shan Lu. ✆ **0937/882-4430.** Meal for 2 ¥50–¥70. No credit cards. Noon–2pm and 6–9pm.

TURPAN (TULUFAN; 吐鲁番) ★★

Xinjiang Province, 187km (116 miles) SE of Ürümqi

Early European visitors were preoccupied with the overwhelming heat of this delightful oasis town. Set in the **Turpan Depression,** 154m (505 ft.) below sea level at its lowest point at **Lake Ayd Inkol (Aiding Hu),** the town experiences noon temperatures hovering above 113°F (45°C) during the summer months. The American journalist Lattimore found some relief: "Over the central streets, which are at once passageways and market-places, are trellises, covered with mats, gourd-vines, and the branches of willows and poplars. In the checkered shade the people step softly, loose-robed and barefooted or slipper-shod; as they chatter in Turki, guttural but soft, the eyes of women flash under stenciled eyebrows and the teeth of men flash from black beards. . . ."

The green fields that surround Turpan are sustained by the *karez* irrigation system, thought to have been introduced in Persia 2 millennia ago. A web of 1,610km (1,000 miles) of covered water channels brings water from the mountains to the north and west of Turpan. Keeping the *karez* clear requires considerable effort, and locals are proud of this ongoing engineering achievement. Turpan is surrounded by significant ancient sites and some magnificent desert scenery, all readily accessed by car or minibus. Often an independent kingdom, it has maintained a strong sense of local identity, and observes a relaxed and tolerant version of Islam.

The annual grape festival, which runs in late August for about a week, brings fruit vendors, winemakers, and loads of tourists from around China. It's a fun time to visit—as the city becomes a lively, teeming mass of humanity, you can sample unlimited grapes on the trellis-lined streets of Turpan and witness a fantastic fireworks display on the night before the festival officially kicks off.

Warning: In contrast to its torpid, laid-back feel, Turpan has an unfortunate but deserved reputation as a town in which you should be wary of your belongings; petty theft and pickpocketing (usually while you are being distracted) are rife. Leave your valuables in the hotel safe and be very aware of your personal space.

Essentials

GETTING THERE As yet, talk of an airport at Turpan remains just that, and the nearest **airport** is at Ürümqi.

The **railway station** is located 54km (33 miles) north of Turpan in the drab town of Daheyan. Minibuses connect with **Turpan's long-distance bus station** for ¥7.50. The **bus station** in Daheyan is reached by heading up the hill in front of the station, turning right, and continuing along the road for about 180m (600 ft.). The bus station is on your left. Some buses wait at the station, along with individual taxis that charge ¥100 to Turpan, or ¥25 per person, as long as they are able to fill a car with four passengers. Getting to Daheyan from Turpan the same options are available; either flag a taxi on the street or head to the long distance bus station to take the bus or a share taxi.

To connect with Kashgar, the best choice is the N9787 at 12:02pm; the trip takes 23 hours. Except in peak season, sleeper tickets are readily purchased in Daheyan.

Those heading to Ürümqi are better served by bus. Heading east, sleeper tickets are tighter; your chances are best on the T194 to Hankou at 8:53pm or the T198 to Zhengzhou at 9:12pm, both of which make stops at Jiayuguan (11 hr.), Lanzhou (18 hr.), Tianshui (23 hr.), Xi'an (27 hr.), and Luoyang (32 hr.). It's easiest to proceed through a travel agent; CITS charges a commission of ¥40 or John's Information Café, which charges ¥30 to ¥50.

The **bus station** is at Lao Cheng Lu 27 (✆ **0995/852-2325**), about 90m (300 ft.) west of the central intersection. Buses for Ürümqi (187km/116 miles; 2 hr. 30 min.; ¥40) leave every 20 minutes from 7:30am to 8pm. Share taxis also work this route for ¥65 per person or ¥260 for the whole vehicle. There's a daily sleeper bus at 3pm for Kuqa (638km/396 miles; 14 hr.; ¥118 lower berth, ¥108 upper berth).

GETTING AROUND Turpan is a small town, and nearly everything is within walking distance of the center, marked by the intersection of Lao Cheng Lu and Gaochang Lu. Taxis within the city cost ¥5. Most sights are outside town and require a **taxi, minibus,** or **bike,** the latter of which can be hired from John's Information Café for ¥5 an hour. Your presence is noted by local drivers when you arrive. They will politely but insistently offer tours of the eight sights *(bage difang)*. Decline.

TOURS **CITS** (✆ **0995/818-2318;** turpancitsoasis@hotmail.com; 9am–1pm and 4:30–8:30pm) is located in the Tulufan Dafandian at 422 Gaochang Zhong Lu.

[Fast FACTS] TURPAN

Banks & Foreign Exchange You can change traveler's checks and draw money on your credit card from counters 3 to 5 at the **Bank of China,** at Lao Cheng Lu 18, just west of the intersection with Gaochang Lu. It also has an ATM and is open April to September from 9:30am to 12:30pm and 4:30 to 7pm; October to March 10am to 1pm and 3:30 to 6:30pm.

Internet Access **Zhixin wangba** is up the decrepit looking stairwell at Gaochang Lu 441 next to the China Construction Bank, just north of Wenhua Lu. It's open from 10am to 2am and Internet access costs ¥2 per hour. Another nameless ¥2 per hour *wangba* can be found on the west side of Bezeklik Lu, just south of the junction with Wenhua Lu. You can also use the Internet for ¥5 per hour at John's Information Café in the Turpan Hotel on Qingnian Lu.

Post Office The main post office (May–Oct 9:30am–8pm, Nov–Apr 10am–7pm) is next to the Hongyuan Hotel on Gaochang Lu, just north of the junction with Lao Cheng Lu. There's another branch with the same hours just west of the bus station.

Visa Extensions The **PSB office** (Mon–Fri 9:30am–1pm and 4:30–8pm) on Gaochang Lu (✆ **0995/856-5316**) can process visa extensions.

Exploring Turpan

Tulufan Bowuguan Housed in a bold, beige edifice festooned with frescoes, Turpan's brand new museum opened its doors in September 2009, and houses a wide-ranging and worthwhile collection of artifacts including everything from dinosaurs to Tang dynasty pottery. The museum's key exhibits trace the regions' history from the Neolithic all the way through to the Qing dynasty, with a focus on the Gaochang Prefecture era (A.D. 327–640)—the intricately carved horn sculpture is a highlight from this period. Many of the most interesting finds come from Astana, and include dumplings, cakes, and sultanas, all at least 13 centuries past their best. The

HOTELS ■

Dōngfāng Jiǔdiàn **3**
东方酒店

Jiaotong Binguan **5**
(Iāo Tōng Bīn Guǎn)
交通宾馆

Jīnxīn Bīnguǎn **1**
金新宾馆

New Fortune Hotel **2**

Tulufan Huozhou Hotel **11**
(Tǔlǔfán Huǒzhōu Dàjiǔdiàn)
吐鲁番火洲大酒店

RESTAURANTS ◆

Ātàchì Cāntīng **7**
阿太赤餐厅

Hanzha Da Haohua Canting **6**
(Hán Zhādá Háo Huá Cān Tīng)
韩扎达豪华餐厅

John's Information Cafe **8**
(Yuēhàn Cāntīng)
约翰餐厅

Orda (Oū Ěr Dá) **12**
欧尔达

ATTRACTIONS ●

Sugong Minaret **9**
(Sūgōng Tǎ)
苏公塔

Turpan Bazaar **4**
(Tǔlǔfān Bāzhā)
吐鲁番巴扎

Turpan Museum **10**
(Tǔlǔfān Bówùguǎn)
吐鲁番博物馆

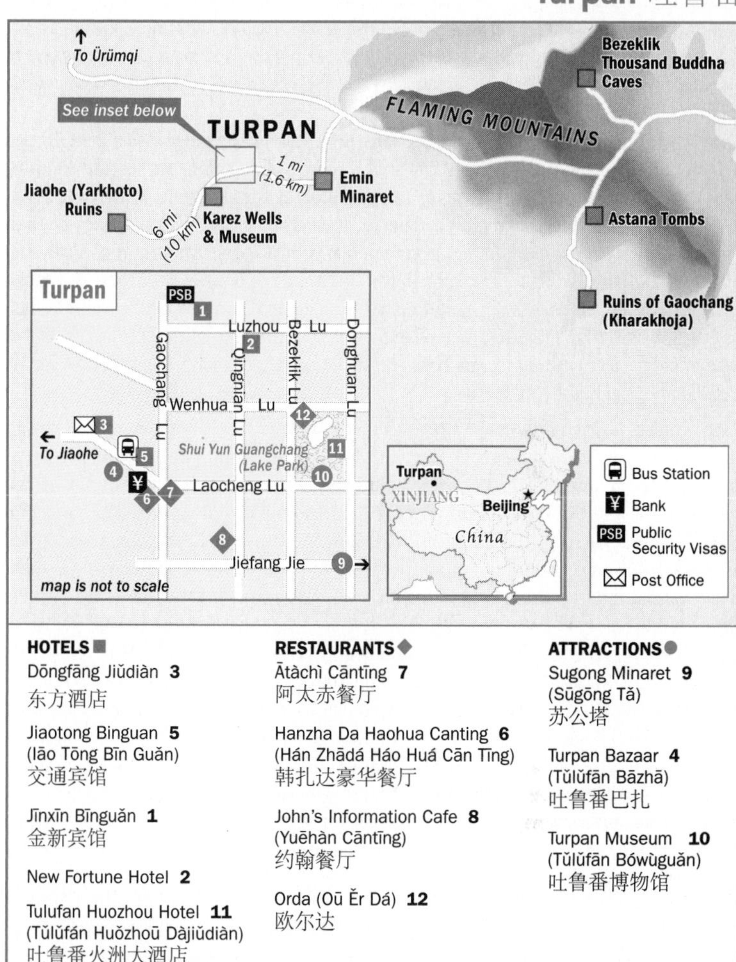

famed Astana mummies are housed at the museum, but were not on display at the time of writing. Other exhibits to look out for include a beautiful Han dynasty golden earring, and make sure you don't miss the fossil rooms, which contain an impressive array of dinosaur skeletons (that kids will love), notably a giant rhinoceros.

Muna'er Lu. Admission Free (with passport). Tues–Sun 10:30am–6:30pm.

AROUND TURPAN

The "eight sights" around Turpan can easily be visited in 1 day. These are the ancient city of **Gaochang**, the **Astana tombs**, the **Bezeklik Caves**, the **Flaming Mountains** (made famous by Ang Lee's *Crouching Tiger, Hidden Dragon*), **Putao Gou** (Grape Valley), **Sugong Minaret (Sugong Ta)**, the *karez* irrigation channels, and the ancient city of **Jiaohe.** Private minibus drivers charge around ¥50 to ¥60 per person for the tour. During July and August an air-conditioned CITS minibus leaves at 9am for five of the eight sights (Jiaohe, the *karez* irrigation channels, Grape Valley, Bezeklik and the Flaming Mountains) for ¥80 per person. Hiring a taxi allows you to be selective, and prices can be as low as ¥200 for a Santana in the off season, rising to a CITS high of ¥300.

Several of the eight sights are not worthwhile. The ticket seller at Astana tells you to "save your money for the museum." The road to Gaochang passes the Flaming Mountains, and Bezeklik is in them, so don't stop at the designated site unless you want to spend ¥40 to accompany hordes of tour groups having camel rides or their photo taken next to a giant tacky thermometer. Whilst extensive and historically significant, the *karez* wells tourist spot (¥40) isn't that impressive, and there are grape vines in Turpan, so there's no need to pay ¥60 for a look around Grape Valley. Organize a half-day tour including Gaochang, Bezeklik, Sugong Minaret, and Jiaohe, or take a 1-day tour with a visit to Tuyoq in the morning. Sugong Minaret and Jiaohe can also be reached by bike.

Bozikelike Qian Fo Dong (Bezeklik Thousand Buddha Caves) The setting of Bezeklik Caves, in a ravine deep in the Flaming Mountains, is more spectacular than the contents of the caves. Bezeklik was stripped by several German expeditions—led by Albert Grunwedel and his nominal understudy, Albert von Le Coq—and relocated to the Museum fur Indische Kunst in Berlin. Grunwedel was reluctant to remove Buddhist antiquities, but Le Coq deemed it essential for their preservation, sparing them from Muslim iconoclasts and practical-minded farmers who would scrape off paintings for use as fertilizer. Nearly all the large wall paintings were destroyed during Allied bombing raids on Berlin in 1943 and 1945. What little is left in the few caves that are open, particularly in no. 39, hints at a distinctly Indo-Persian style. The new *Journey to the West* statue outside is rather special. About 1.6km (1 mile) back down the road, is another collection of new statues, including a Laughing Buddha, which aren't worth paying the ¥20 to look around, but the picturesque vineyard set at the verdant valley bottom (included in the same ticket) is worth a wander down to, even if you don't enter the site.

Admission ¥20. 8:30am–9pm summer; 9:30am–7:30pm winter.

Gaochang (Karakhoja) Located 45km (28 miles) southeast of Turpan, Gaochang was founded during the Han dynasty as a garrison town to supply troops engaged in the conquest of the "Western Regions." Gaochang rose to prominence, becoming the capital of the region and maintaining its influence even when it passed from Chinese hands. Xuanzang visited in A.D. 630, and the king of Gaochang was so impressed by his preaching that he took the young monk captive. Xuanzang went on a hunger strike and was released with a promise to return. He wriggled out of his pledge, returning to China by the southern Silk Route. In any event, the king was dead before he returned, as Turpan returned to Chinese control.

During the Tang dynasty, Gaochang was a thriving artistic and spiritual center for Buddhism and Manichaeism, and most relics recovered by Albert von Le Coq, Stein, and Chinese archaeologists date from this period. There is a **Manichean shrine** northeast of the city walls, but the contents of its library were thrown into a river 5 years before Le Coq arrived. The man feared "the unholy nature of the writings and . . . that the Chinese might use the discovery as a pretext for fresh extortions."

Gaochang is a significant site, but aside from the city walls and the restored **Buddhist temple,** the weathered mud-brick buildings are hard to discern, although on a clear sky day, the backdrop of Flaming Mountains adds drama to the scene.

Admission ¥40. 9am–8pm.

Jiaohe (Yarkhoto) ★ Ten kilometers (6¼ miles) west of Turpan, these ruins are less historically significant, but better preserved, easier to access, and enjoys a more spectacular location than Gaochang; if you have time for only one set of ruins, come here. Originally a Han garrison town, it has no city walls, as the site (which means "meeting of the rivers") is bounded by steep ravines. A clear central avenue runs east-west through the town, with residential, religious, and governmental areas delineated. The reason for the demise of the settlement during the Yuan dynasty is unclear, but the depth of the numerous wells suggests the water supply may have run out. Sunset is the best time to go; not only for photos, but to avoid most of the tour groups. Walk in a clockwise direction to further avoid the remaining tour groups (which always seem to make their pilgrimages in a counterclockwise circle, sometimes only getting as far as the viewing platform before turning around). Jiaohe can be reached by taxi for ¥40 round-trip; make sure your driver waits for you as there aren't many spare drivers in the parking lot.

Admission ¥40. 9am–9:30pm summer; 10am–8pm winter.

Sugong Ta or Emin Ta (Sugong Minaret) The mosque was built in 1778 by Prince Suleiman in honor of his father, Prince Emin, one of the few rulers of Turpan to have made the pilgrimage to Mecca. One of the first Western visitors was Francis Younghusband, who was less than overawed: "Some 3 miles from Turfan we passed a mosque with a curious tower, which looked as much like a very fat factory chimney as anything else. It was about 80 feet high, circular, and built of mud bricks, and it was ornamented by placing the bricks at different angles, forming patterns." However, on a deep blue-sky day, the mosque's graceful combination of adobe curves and angles are beautifully softened by the surrounding grapevines and it's hard not to be drawn to the "chimney," which is actually 40m (132 ft.) tall. The style is neither Han nor Hui, but similar to those found farther west on the Silk Routes. The mosque is not the oldest in Turpan, but it's the best preserved. It's open for worship on Friday lunchtime, when entry for non-Muslims is restricted.

Admission ¥30. 9:30am–7:30pm summer; 10am–7pm winter. Bus: 6 to the terminus; continue east for 10 min.

An Uighur Stronghold: Tuyoq 吐峪沟 ★

Less than 20km (12 miles) beyond Gaochang, the idyllic Uighur village of Tuyoq is a fine day trip, and can be included in a tour. A leisurely day trip to Tuyoq, stopping at Gaochang (or Bezeklik) on the way back, can be arranged with individual taxis for ¥250. Buses to **Lukeqin** (1 hr.; ¥12) pass Tuyoq, and leave every half-hour from 10:30am; the last bus back to Turpan leaves Lukeqin at around 5pm, passing Tuyoq about 20 minutes later. If you catch the Lukeqin bus, you will be dropped at the south end of the sprawling settlement, leaving a hot but fascinating 5km (3-mile) walk north to the village proper. Three-wheelers also make the trip for ¥3.

Tourist officials hoped that the recent opening of some Buddhist caves here would boost revenues; in spite of the fact that the caves are currently closed to visitors, the village still charges a ¥30 fee to walk around. If the caves have re-opened by the time you get here, you'll see all that's left are small patches of cave paintings with the faces of Buddhas scratched out. Bring a flashlight for a closer look. The village itself is nice to wander through, and several courtyard homes will open their doors for you at lunchtime. The cost of a meal should be ¥20—make sure you agree on the price before you settle in. Something else to be wary of is young children approaching you and asking to have their photograph taken and then aggressively demanding money; best to avoid the situation and only photograph people with whom you've had some prior interaction.

Where to Stay

Although a few new hotels have opened in Turpan over the past few years, the choices are still limited given the number of tourists that pass through. At the time of writing the Turpan Oasis Hotel, owned by the same Hong Kong group as the excellent Silk Road Hotel in Dunhuang, had been closed for renovations for more than 2 years—when it re-opens, this is one to watch out for. During the peak season, discounts of 20% are standard. During the off season, discounts of 40% to 60% are possible.

Huozhou Dajiudian (Tulufan Huozhou Hotel) ★ Turpan's top hotel has a central location next to an attractive lake park in the heart of town. Rooms are tastefully styled in muted tones and have decent sized beds and modern dark-wood furnishings. Bathrooms are also good and have small tubs. Ask for a lakeview room in Building A. Service is friendly but not exceptional.

Donghuan Lu and south side of Shui Yun Guangchang. www.tlfhuozhou-hotel.com. ✆ **0995/866-6888.** 109 units. ¥680 standard room; ¥2,180 suite. Up to 40% discount on standard rooms; up to 60% discount on suites. MC, V. **Amenities:** Restaurant. *In room:* A/C, TV, fridge, hair dryer, Internet.

Jiaotong Binguan (Traffic Hotel) Having undergone a complete makeover and now housed in an Uighur-style building, the Traffic Hotel offers compact, clean, modern and comfortable standard rooms with flat-screen TVs. Proximity to the bus station and bazaar are advantages, but also means that rooms can be a little noisy. Photos of local landscapes and life line the corridors and service is friendly.

Lao Cheng Xi Lu. ✆ **0995/625-8688.** 104 units. ¥380 standard room. Up to 50% discount. No credit cards. *In room:* A/C, TV, hair dryer, Internet.

Jinxin Binguan (Jinxin Hotel) One of the taller buildings around, the Jinxin offers well-furnished, but worn rooms with comfy beds and passable bathrooms. Some rooms (¥380) have computers with Internet access. The hotel is well managed, and they're used to dealing with foreigners. A recent benefit is the demise of the noisy karaoke parlor on the 9th floor.

Luzhou Zhong Lu 390. ✆ **0995/856-0222.** Fax 0995/856-0403. 54 units. ¥360 standard room; ¥888 suite. Up to 40% discount. No credit cards. **Amenities:** Restaurant; conference room. *In room:* A/C, TV, Internet.

New Fortune Hotel After staying 3 nights at the New Fortune not long ago, the author was then ordered to leave, as the hotel didn't have a license to accept foreigners. The hotel now has the license, and, although the staff aren't used to dealing with foreigners, rooms are clean, modern, and tastefully decorated, and some look down onto the grapevine trellises of Qingnian Lu. The hotel's good value is evidenced by its popularity with domestic businessmen and tourists.

Luzhou Zhong Lu 289. ✆ **0995/852-8900.** Fax 0995/852-3888. 40 units. ¥220 standard room. No credit cards. **Amenities:** Restaurant; conference room. *In room:* A/C, TV, hairdryer, Internet.

Where to Eat

Western breakfasts can be found at **John's Information Café** (7am–10pm) at the back of the Turpan Hotel on Qingnian Lu 41; John's is also a good place for a drink under the shade of grapevine trellises in the heat of the day. Other Western options are limited to branches of Best Food Burger, one of which can be found on Lao Cheng Xi Lu, just west of the junction with Gaochang Lu. Hotels offer safe but boring Muslim and Chinese fare and evening performances of singing and dancing. For real food, during the day head for the bazaar just west of the Bank of China, where you can enjoy pastries stuffed with minced lamb *(samsa)*, kabobs, and homemade ice cream scraped from gigantic sweet orange mounds. Around 8pm, when the heat of the day has passed, nightmarkets selling fantastic kabobs, Uighur dumplings, and noodles set up all around the city. The **market outside of Hongyuan Binguan** on Gaochang Lu (next to the post office) is one of the best. Just point to what you want. To stock up on snacks for long journeys head for the **Tianmajiayuan Supermarket** on the northeast corner of the junction of Wenhua Lu and Bezeklik Lu; there's also a nightmarket here.

Ataichi Canting UIGHUR This is Turpan's original dinner and dance restaurant for the locals. Although its underground location keeps it cool, it has a dungeonlike feel, and the print of a whole roast sheep sitting contentedly with a knife through its back on a tablecloth in a meadow may be enough to convert you to veganism. Busiest on Friday and Saturday, the banquets are an excellent way to try a variety of foods without wearing out your phrasebook.

Basement 1015 Lao Cheng Lu (on the southeast side of the intersection with Gaochang Lu). ✆ **0995/852-9775.** Banquets ¥39–¥89 per person. No credit cards. 10am–10pm (performance starts 8pm).

Hanzha Da Haohua Canting ★★ UIGHUR Another great local option, this opulent dining hall is frequently packed full of locals in their best clothes, sharing vast mounds of *pilaf* and bowls of *naren*. As well as these dishes and the obligatory *yangrou chuan* there are few Chinese dishes on the menu. Little English (or Chinese) is spoken, but service staff are accommodating.

2nd floor (up the outside steps) on the southeast corner of the junction of Gaochang Lu and Lao Cheng Lu. ✆ **0995/857-7777.** Meal for 2 ¥50. No credit cards. 9am–11pm.

Orda (Ou Ai Da) ★★ UIGHUR Pleasantly located on the edge of the lake park, Orda is a great local choice, and serves all the regular Uighur dishes cooked to perfection. In summer carpeted eating platforms with low tables are set up outside of the restaurant, right next to the lake, and make an ideal place to watch the world go by with a local beer and some fine dining. There's a Chinese-only picture menu, but if you stick to the *laghman, naren, pilao,* and kabobs you won't go far wrong.

Shui Yun Guangchang. ✆ **0995/761-8003.** Meal for 2 ¥50. No credit cards. Noon–midnight.

ÜRÜMQI (WULUMUQI; 乌鲁木齐)

Xinjiang, 1,470km (911 miles) NE of Kashgar, 692km (429 miles) E of Yining

Early visitors to Ürümqi came back with mixed reviews. Missionary Mildred Cable (1878–1952) thought the town "has no beauty, no style, no dignity and no architectural interest. The climate is violent, exaggerated and at no season pleasant. . . ."

However, acerbic American author Owen Lattimore loved Ürümqi "in the spring, when along the liquescent streets the Chinese began to appear in gay colors and flowered silks and satins, and the Turkis, abandoning the reds and purples of their long winter gowns, to put on the white cotton robes of warm weather; and in the beginning of summer, when the early leafage of trees was not yet dulled with dust, and to walk on the city walls at sunset was the crowning glory of the day."

Opinions on the city are still divided, but everyone agrees that Ürümqi is best avoided in winter. Ringed by factories and relying on coal heating, the city sees its first snow coated by a film of soot within hours. But, in spite of its modern Chinese appearance, for those who fly in from the east, Ürümqi provides a tantalizing first taste of a different culture, and there are fascinating markets to explore, all to the backdrop of snow-clad mountains that appear and vanish as the weather (and pollution) allows.

In July 2009, the city became the focus of international news when Uighur anti-Han colonization riots broke out, leaving over 150 Han Chinese dead. The city was locked down, curfews were imposed, and the army rolled in. For the meanwhile things have returned to normal, but these tensions aren't going to just disappear. Following events in North Africa in 2011 heavily armed riot police patrols are a conspicuous addition to the streets of Ürümqi.

GETTING THERE **Ürümqi airport,** to the north of town, has an enormous wave-roofed terminal (terminal 3) that opened in 2010, which serves both domestic and international flights, and leaves terminals 1 and 2 somewhat redundant. Taxis into town should cost around ¥40, although some unscrupulous drivers will ask for as much as ¥80—check to be sure the driver will use the meter as soon as you get in, or be prepared to bargain hard. Alternatively there's a free shuttle bus for China Southern passengers to and from their office on Youhao Nan Lu; other passengers must pay ¥10 for this service. **China Southern** handles most flights within Xinjiang and its main office (✆ **95539;** 9am–9:30pm) is next to the CSA (China Southern Airlines; formerly the Kempinski) Hotel on Youhao Nan Lu. A ticket office is also at the airport. Several daily flights connect with Beijing, Shanghai, Guangzhou, Chengdu, Xi'an, Lanzhou, Kashgar, Khotan, and Kuqa. There are thrice weekly domestic connections with Dunhuang. The airport has also expanded its international connections and destinations now include Islamabad, Istanbul, Mashhad, Taskent, Tehran, and Tblisi.

Ürümqi's **railway station** is located in the southwest corner of town. Nearly all trains from the east and west terminate here. Tickets may be purchased at the station, at the **railway ticket office** (7:30am–9pm) next to the courtyard of the Laiyuan Binguan at Jianshe Lu 3 (where you pay a ¥5 commission), or through an agent (around ¥30 commission). There are direct express trains to Beijing (T70; 33 hr.) at 10:13am, and to Shanghai (T54; 44 hr.) at 5:14pm, passing through Lanzhou (20 hr.) and Xi'an (29 hr.). There are also speedy connections with Lanzhou (T298; 20 hr.) at 3pm, and with Dunhuang (T70; 9 hr.) at 10:17am. Sluggish trains head for Chongqing (K544; 47 hr.) at 2:06pm, and for Chengdu (K454; 49 hr.) at 1:34pm. Heading west, the fastest train is the K9786, which leaves at 10am and passes through Kuqa (15 hr.) on its way to Kashgar (25 hr.). For Yining train K9789 leaves at 10:54pm and takes 11 hours.

Tickets for Almaty in Kazakhstan may be purchased in a ticket office in the foyer of the **Ya Ou Jiudian** (✆ **0991/777-0898**), next to the train station. The office (no

Ürümqi 乌鲁木齐

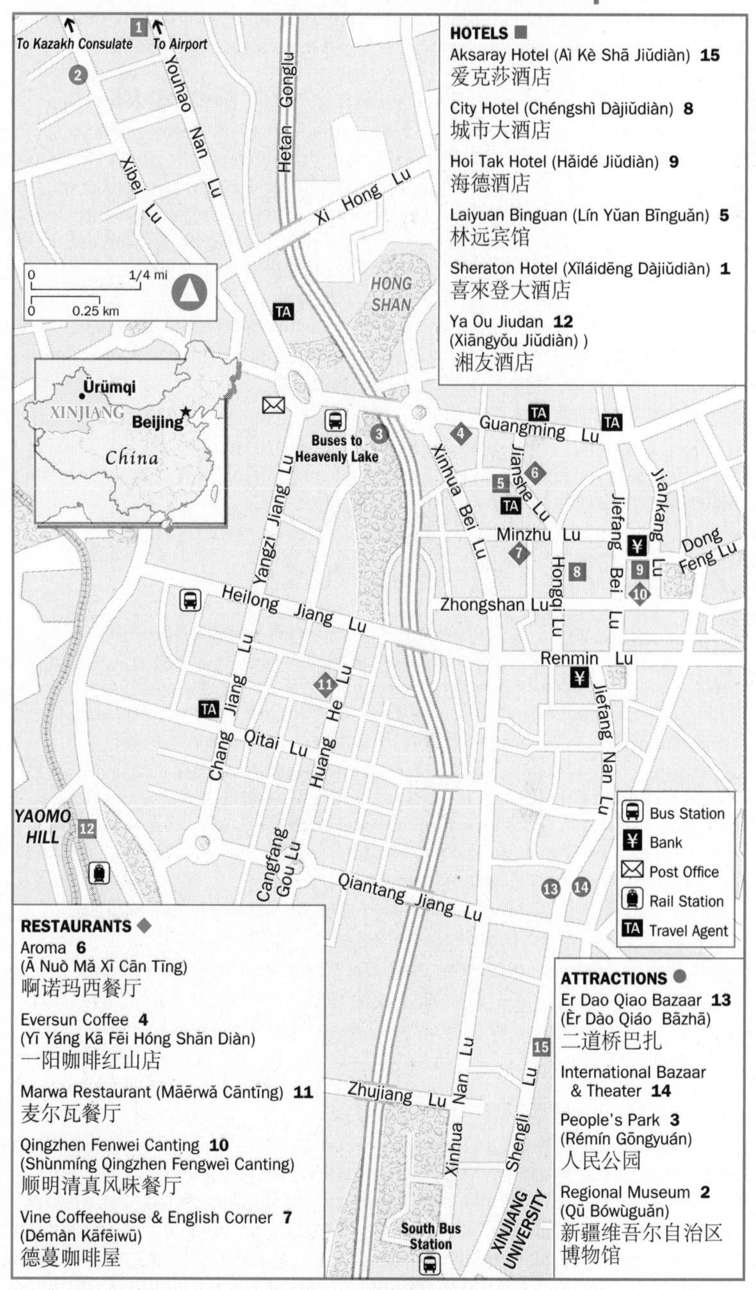
To Kazakh Consulate
To Airport
1
2
Youhao Nan Lu
Xibei Lu
Hetan Gonglu
Xi Hong Lu
0 1/4 mi
0 0.25 km
HONG SHAN
TA
Ürümqi
XINJIANG
Beijing
China
Buses to Heavenly Lake
3
4
Guangming Lu
Xinhua Bei Lu
Jianshe Lu
5
6
Jiefang Bei Lu
Jiankang Lu
Dong Feng Lu
Minzhu Lu
7
Hongqi Lu
8
9
10
Zhongshan Lu
Yangzi Jiang Lu
Heilong Jiang Lu
Renmin Lu
11
Huang He Lu
Chang Jiang Lu
Qitai Lu
Jiefang Nan Lu
YAOMO HILL
12
Cangfang Gou Lu
Qiantang Jiang Lu
13
14
Bus Station
Bank
Post Office
Rail Station
Travel Agent
15
Zhujiang Lu
Xinhua Nan Lu
Shengli Lu
South Bus Station
XINJIANG UNIVERSITY
HOTELS
Aksaray Hotel (Aì Kè Shā Jiǔdiàn) 15
爱克莎酒店
City Hotel (Chéngshì Dàjiǔdiàn) 8
城市大酒店
Hoi Tak Hotel (Hǎidé Jiǔdiàn) 9
海德酒店
Laiyuan Binguan (Lín Yǔan Bīnguǎn) 5
林远宾馆
Sheraton Hotel (Xǐláidēng Dàjiǔdiàn) 1
喜來登大酒店
Ya Ou Jiudan 12
(Xiāngyǒu Jiǔdiàn))
湘友酒店
RESTAURANTS
Aroma 6
(Ā Nuò Mǎ Xī Cān Tīng)
啊诺玛西餐厅
Eversun Coffee 4
(Yī Yáng Kā Fēi Hóng Shān Diàn)
一阳咖啡红山店
Marwa Restaurant (Māērwǎ Cāntīng) 11
麦尔瓦餐厅
Qingzhen Fenwei Canting 10
(Shùnmíng Qingzhen Fengweì Canting)
顺明清真风味餐厅
Vine Coffeehouse & English Corner 7
(Démàn Kāfēiwū)
德蔓咖啡屋
ATTRACTIONS
Er Dao Qiao Bazaar 13
(Èr Dào Qiáo Bāzhā)
二道桥巴扎
International Bazaar & Theater 14
People's Park 3
(Rémín Gōngyuán)
人民公园
Regional Museum 2
(Qū Bówùguǎn)
新疆维吾尔自治区博物馆

phone) is open on Mondays, Wednesdays, Thursdays, and Saturdays between 10am and 1pm and 3:30 and 6pm. Trains leave on Mondays and Thursdays and sleeper class tickets start at ¥826. Both trains take around 31 hours to complete the journey, but the Kazakh train is more comfortable. You'll need a **Kazakh visa** (see below) in advance to buy a ticket.

The **main bus station** at Heilongjiang Lu 51 (**© 0991/5878-898**) can be reached by local bus no. 3. From here there are seven daily buses to Yining (692km/429 miles; 10–12 hr.; ¥176 lower berth, ¥160 upper berth); and to the border town of Tacheng (633km/392 miles; 12 hr.; ¥150) at 10am, 11am and noon. The **Southern Bus Station** (**© 0991/286-6635**) has regular connections with Turpan from 9am to 8pm (187km/116 miles; 2 hr. 30 min.; ¥41); Kuqa (745km/462 miles; 14 hr.; ¥185 lower berth, ¥175 upper berth) every hour from 3:30pm to 7:30pm; and Kashgar (1,470km/911 miles; 24 hr.; ¥235 lower berth, ¥220 upper berth) every half-hour from 10:40am to 8pm. Express buses across the Taklamakan Desert to Khotan (1,777km/1,101 miles; 20–24 hr.; ¥260–¥360) leave hourly between 2 and 8pm. Bus nos. 1, 7, and 101 all connect with this bus station.

GETTING AROUND A legion of Santana **taxis** charge ¥6 for 3km (2 miles), then ¥1.30 per kilometer; ¥2.10 midnight to 7am. For the useful **bus** nos. 1, 2, and 7, pay ¥1 into a box as you enter, or ¥1 to ¥2 to a conductor. Riding a **bike** through the smog and traffic snarls is not recommended.

[Fast FACTS] ÜRÜMQI

Banks, Foreign Exchange & ATMs The main **Bank of China** (Mon–Fri 10am–6:30pm, and Sat–Sun 11am–4pm) is opposite the Hoi Tak Hotel at Dongfeng Lu 1. Cash and traveler's checks can be exchanged at counters 7 and 8 and there's the added convenience of black-market dealers operating outside the bank! ATMs (left of the entrance) accept foreign cards. Another ATM is located at the intersection of Jianshe Lu and Wenyi Lu.

Consulates Kazakh visas are available from the **Kazakh Consulate** at Kunming Lu 31 (**© 0991/383-2324**) for ¥261. They are issued in 3 to 5 working days. The consulate is open Monday through Friday from 10am to noon for drop-offs and between noon and 1pm for collections. One passport photo and a photocopy of your passport are required. The consulate is not easily located, so take a taxi.

Internet Access A 24-hour Internet cafe is above the **Chengshi Dajiudian** and charges ¥3.80 to ¥5.80 per hour dependent on where you decide to sit.

Post Office The main post office on Yangzi Jiang Lu is open from 10am to 8pm.

Visa Extensions The busy, but friendly **PSB** at Kelamayi Dong Lu 27 (**© 0991/491-8435**) offers 1-month visa extensions up to 20 days in advance. Processing takes 3 to 5 working days.

Exploring Ürümqi

Qu Bowuguan (Regional Museum) This museum recently had a full renovation, and its exhibits are now well presented in the shiny interior of this massive building. Don't miss the remarkably well-preserved **mummies ★★**, many with Indo-European features: high cheekbones, long noses, brightly colored woolen kilts. The mummies, some of which date from 2000 B.C., were unearthed from tombs scattered around the Taklamakan in **Loulan, Astana, Hami,** and **Charchan (Qiemo)**—see map on p. 251. They do little to further Han claims over Xinjiang. Add the cost of preservation and you might believe, as some suggest, that additional finds are being deliberately left in the ground. Han Chinese chauvinists point out that Uighurs, a Turkic people who migrated from western Mongolia, have nothing in common with the indigenous Indo-European Tocharians, who spoke a language that resembles a Celtic tongue. But there are enough blue- or green-eyed folk on the streets of Turpan and Kuqa (former Tocharian strongholds) to suggest that interbreeding was common. As my Uighur companion remarked, "So we killed all of them?"

Han Chinese guides make much of the relatively young mummy of General Zhang (d. A.D. 633), commander of the armies in Gaochang, whose wife rests in the Turpan Museum. Other interesting items on exhibit are lead and bronze eyeshades used in sandstorms, and a hunting boomerang unearthed in Hami. For those journeying farther along the Silk Road, the sections on each of the province's ethnic minorities is also worthwhile.

Xi Bei Lu 132. Free admission. Tues–Sun 10:30am–5pm; last entry 4:30pm). Bus: 7 to Bowuguan.

Shopping

You'll find a wide range of Uighur handicrafts on sale at **Er Dao Qiao Bazaar** and across the road at the **International Bazaar,** but the environment has been turned into a tacky tourist trap. On what used to be an airy outdoor market now stands a Hong Kong developer's interpretation of Uighur architecture, massive beige-brick buildings, complete with a Carrefour and KFC. For more of a local flavor, head to **Ribiya Dasha,** a building erected by the Uighur businesswoman Rebiya Kadeer who became famous in the Western press after being jailed in China as a political prisoner. Outside, around the perimeters of the building and in the nearby lanes, bright fabrics, televisions, jewelry, and appliances are sold. Also nearby is **Baihetiya'er Huangjin Shoushidian** at Jiefang Nan Lu 288, which sells affordable gold, silver, and platinum jewelry. The necklaces are particularly elegant. Watch the Uighur women bargain, and see if you can get a similar price.

For carpets, you should avoid Er Dao Qiao Bazaar and its scary assortment of pushy salespeople who don't know the first thing about carpets; instead head behind the market to **Tianhaai Lu** where several stores have genuine antiques, but prices are high. Opposite the Ramada on Changjiang Lu, **Western Folk Fengwu** is an easy place to pick up tasteful products from around the region, ranging from pashminas to locally grown lavender. To stock up on snacks before a long bus or train journey, there are plenty of supermarkets around the town center; the one in the basement of the **Parkson shopping center** at the southern end of Youhao Nan Lu is particularly good, as is the vast and always busy **Carrefour** at Er Dao Qiao Bazaar.

Where to Stay

Ürümqi has an increasing array of places to stay in all categories. The best hotels are in the central downtown area and to the north, however if you want to sample Uighur life in Ürümqi then you might want to consider the **Aksaray Hotel (Ai Ke Sha Jiudian)** at 160 Shengli Lu (✆ **0991/620-0555**) in the south of town. Popular with traders (some of whom set up discount suit stores in their rooms), the Aksaray has clean, spacious twins with windows that can be negotiated to ¥150, or rooms with internal windows for ¥130.

VERY EXPENSIVE/EXPENSIVE

Haide Jiudian (Hoi Tak Hotel) ★ The Hoi Tak benefits from aggressive Hong Kong management, rigorous staff training, and plenty of capital from its parent company. Regular rooms are spacious and comfortable, if a little dated, while recent renovations have brought modern furnishings and DVD players to the deluxe rooms on floors 24 and 27. Bathrooms in all rooms are well-equipped. On clear days, rooms on higher floors enjoy a magnificent view of the Tian Shan range.

Dongfeng Lu 1. www.hoitak.com. ✆ **0991/232-2828.** Fax 0991/232-1818. 318 units. ¥1,400 standard twin room; ¥1,600 deluxe twin room; from ¥2,080 suite. 50% discounts are standard. 15% service charge. AE, DC, MC, V. **Amenities:** 4 restaurants; bar; cafe; billiards and table tennis rooms; 8-lane bowling alley; concierge; forex; health club; nightclub; large indoor pool; room service. *In room:* A/C, TV, DVD player (in deluxe rooms), fridge, hair dryer, Internet, minibar.

Sheraton (Xilaideng Dajiudian) ★★ Set up in the quickly developing northwest of town, Ürümqi's newest five-star might not have a great location for travelers, but the facilities, rooms and service certainly live up to the brand standards. The plush rooms are decorated in neutral tones and have glassed off bathrooms with separate bath and shower cubicles. King-bed rooms feature comfy loungers while the twin versions have armchairs and a coffee table. It's worth paying the extra for an executive room on floors 26 to 32, which gives not only good views, but also access to the executive club lounge and all this entails; express check-in and check-out, complimentary breakfast and happy hour drinks, and guaranteed late check-out until 4pm.

Youao Bei Lu 669. www.sheraton.com/urumqi. ✆ **0991/669-9999.** 398 units. ¥1,300 superior room; ¥1,820 executive deluxe room; from ¥4,488 suite. AE, DC, MC, V. **Amenities:** 3 restaurants; bar; cafe; concierge; courtesy car; forex; health club; nightclub; large indoor pool; room service. *In room:* A/C, satellite TV, fridge, hair dryer, Internet, minibar.

MODERATE/INEXPENSIVE

City Hotel (Chengshi Dajiudian) ★ Right in the center of town, located on a crowded street, the facilities and service at this three-star hotel are better than you would anticipate for the outlay. The beds are firm and the bathrooms are spotless, if a little cramped. It's worth spending a little extra for the rooms with windows that open. Service has improved to meet the expectations of the primarily foreign clientele. Taking the elevator here feels a bit like stepping into the United Nations—you'll be sharing your space with Russians, Africans, and Americans.

Hongqi Lu 119. ✆ **0991/220-7336.** Fax 0991/230-5321. 226 units. ¥483 standard room; from ¥1,952 suite. Discounts of up to 60%. Discounted rates exclude breakfast (¥20). AE, DC, MC, V. **Amenities:** 2 restaurants; concierge; 24-hr. forex; nightclub; teahouse. *In room:* A/C, TV, fridge (some rooms), Internet, minibar.

Linyuan Binguan ★ A central location, newly renovated rooms, helpful staff and decent discounts make this place worth considering. Rooms are fitted with dark wood furnishings and flat-screen TVs, and those on higher floors and facing the rear are quieter. The hotel is popular for weddings and conferences so it's worth reserving a room in advance.

Jianshe Lu 3. ✆ **0991/293-3888.** 111 un/its. ¥528 standard room; from ¥1,280 suite. Standard discount of 50%. AE, MC, V. **Amenities:** Restaurant. *In room:* A/C, TV, fridge (some rooms), hair dryer, Internet (¥100 deposit for cable).

Where to Eat

As well as the restaurant options listed below there are also plenty of good street eats to be enjoyed in Ürümqi. The streets around Er Dao Qiao are full of Uighur stalls and restaurants serving tasty dumplings stuffed with lamb and pumpkin, lamb skewers, and *laghman,* or noodles. In the evenings barbecue stalls set up at the intersection of Jianshe Lu and Wenyi Lu, or if you've had your fill of Uighur food, there's also a **Best Food Burger** and a **Dicos** to be found here.

Aroma (A'nuoma Xi Canting) ★ ITALIAN A short climb up an unpromising looking stairwell brings you into the large, but somehow cozy, interior of Aroma. The owner is Maltese, the clientele mostly local, and the cuisine is Italian, including tasty stone-baked pizzas, delicious carbonara and vegetable risotto. Desserts are also a highlight, and range from crème brûlée to tiramisu, which go down well with an Italian coffee. Imported wines feature on the wine list (¥128–¥498).

Jianshe Lu 193, 2F. ✆ **0991/283-5881.** Main courses ¥30–¥55. AE, MC, V. 11am–11:30pm

Eversun Coffee (Yiyang Kafei Hongshan Dian) WESTERN This is a trendy and popular cafe-bar with cozy booths, some of which have window views of the city and make a particularly nice place to escape the hustle and bustle. You can try your luck with the entrees, which range from steaks to pizza and Sichuan dishes, but it's the rich coffee that stands out. The drinks list also includes local and imported wines (¥88–¥1,080).

Xinhua Bei Lu 108. ✆ **0991/230-5559.** Meal for 2 ¥100. AE, DC, MC, V. 11am–2:30am.

Marwa (Maerwa Canting) ★ 🎁 UIGHUR To plunge straight into Uighur cuisine, this refined restaurant is a fine first choice. Smartly uniformed staff present a range of traditional dishes including *pilao* (served with delicious dates and raisins), chunky kabobs, and for dessert lovers, *suan nai* (yogurt) with sugar is a real treat. The clean dining hall features carved wooden chairs and a vaulted ceiling and is always busy. There's no English menu but the open kitchen at the front of the restaurant means you can just point at what you want. To find the restaurant, look for the oval white sign reading Marwa in green writing.

Huang He Lu 103. ✆ **0991/581-8188.** Meal for 2 from ¥50. No credit cards. 9:30am–11pm.

Qingzhen Fenwei Canting UIGHUR This big, bustling canteen provides easy, no-frills, around-the-clock access to Uighur cuisine. Kabobs are ¥4, rice pilaf can be ordered hot or cold and there's a range of stretch noodles to choose from. There's no English menu, so just point to what you want.

Next to the Hoi Tak Hotel on Jiankang Lu. ✆ **0991/281-5182.** Meal for 2 ¥30–¥40. No credit cards. 24 hr.

Vine Coffeehouse & English Corner (Deman Kafeiwu) CARIBBEAN A friendly Caribbean cafe is not something you expect to find in downtown Ürümqi, but travel is all about challenging expectations. The halal menu was established by the head chef of the Plaza Hotel, Curaçao. Try his signature dish, the Jacques Steak, pan-fried with green peppers, tomatoes, and onions, and served with a chunky side salad and fries. Other hits are the Island Cheese Chicken, which comes with fried rice and banana fritters or for a quick snack, try the cookies and cakes under the front counter with a *batida* (fruit shake). "English Corner" is currently held on Sunday afternoons at 4:30pm; it's a nice way to meet locals, and possibly find a guide who isn't out to rip you off. The restaurant is down a small alley (Xinsheng Xiang) off Minzhu Lu.

Xin Sheng Xiang 28, off Minzhu Lu. ✆ **0991/230-4831.** Main courses ¥38–¥60. AE, MC, V. Tues–Sun 1:30–10:30pm.

Ürümqi After Dark

Most Han Chinese believe that Uighurs, like all Chinese ethnic minorities, love to sing and dance *(neng ge shan wu)*. As one Chinese guidebook notes, "although very few Uighurs speak Chinese well, they will often spontaneously break into song and dance to show their friendship." If you're not already exhausted by all the singing and dancing, the easiest way to enjoy a performance is to attend one of the nightly shows at the theater (✆ **0991/855-5485**) in the International Bazaar. Mainly attended by Chinese tour groups, these shows are performed by the acclaimed **Bazaar Ensemble of Song and Dance,** and often feature huge casts and dramatic stage sets. The exact program changes monthly, but performances start at 8pm and last for 90 minutes. Tickets cost from ¥168 to ¥298 depending upon the show, seating and whether you want snacks during the performance.

Around Ürümqi

While Ürümqi has improved, an explosion in domestic tourism means that **Tian Chi** (**Heavenly Lake;** admission ¥100) is on the way to becoming the world's largest public convenience. If you do go, stay the night, as the lake is more tranquil after buses return to Ürümqi around 5pm. In summer a place in a yurt can be negotiated for around ¥50 including meals. Avoid Rashid's Yurt, which is listed in every guidebook—fame is not good for everyone. Hikes and horse treks are other good ways to escape the crowds, and maybe even find a spot of pristine solitude. Buses depart for the lake from the entrance to Ürümqi's **Renmin Gongyuan** at 9:30am (120km/74 miles; 1 hr. 30 min.; ¥40 round-trip) and return at 5:30pm. A similar day trip is to **Baiyang Gou (White Poplar Gully;** ¥15), where you can ride horses, stay in yurts, and enjoy lush countryside. Buses depart at 9:50am (76km/47 miles; 1 hr. 30 min.; ¥40) and return midafternoon.

KUQA (KUCHE; 库车) ★

Xinjiang Province, 748km (464 miles) SW of Ürümqi, 723km (448 miles) E of Kashgar, 591km (366 miles) SE of Yining

A maverick Silk Route kingdom, Kuqa was the center of the ancient kingdom of **Qiuci.** The inhabitants were Indo-European Tocharians, who migrated down from Anatolia (Turkey) and the Caucasus. Drawing on inspiration from Gandhara and Persia, Kuqan musicians and artists were very much the fashion in the cosmopolitan capital of Chang'an. Monks adhered to Hinayana Buddhism, in contrast to other Tarim basin towns and China proper, which adhered to the more complex Mahayana tradition.

Kuqa's most famous son was **Kumarajiva** (A.D. 343–413), uniquely qualified to be a translator, with a Brahmin father and a Kuqan mother. His father wanted him to be ordained as a Buddhist monk, but his mother sent him to Kashmir and Kashgar to be instructed in Indian literature, astronomy, and Buddhism. He arrived in Chang'an in 401 as a prisoner of Chinese raiders, and soon caught the eye of the fervently Buddhist Tibetan ruling house. Kumarajiva oversaw the largest "translation team" in history. Although the Kuqan scholar was skeptical that the scriptures could ever be rendered faithfully from the Sanskrit, the team of around 1,000 scholars translated the *Diamond Sutra,* which became one of the most influential texts in Chinese Buddhism.

Present-day Kuqa is a friendly, ramshackle Uighur town with a great Friday market. The fertile soil and relatively temperate climate yield delicious apricots, grapes, peaches, and plums. ***Note:*** Turn to chapter 16 for Chinese translations of key locations.

Essentials

GETTING THERE There is one flight a day from Ürümqi. For times, check with **China Southern** on Wenhua Lu (✆ **0997/712-9390**).

The **railway station** is on the southwest side of town. Taxis (¥10) and bus no. 6 (¥1.50) take you into town. Heading west the times aren't great, but the train is preferable to the bus; the K9787 for Kashgar (9 hr.) leaves at 1:58am. Heading east, the K9788 for Ürümqi (16 hr.) leaves at 10pm. The railway ticket office, open from 9am to noon, 1 to 8pm, and 9pm to midnight, sells tickets up to 10 days in advance. Sleeper tickets are only available for express trains; soft sleeper tickets are hard to come by, but hard sleepers are often available.

The **bus station** at Tian Shan Lu 125 (✆ **0997/712-2379**) has no direct buses to Kashgar, and no guarantee of a berth on sleeper buses from Korla. However, hourly buses run to Aksu (275km/171 miles; 4 hr.; ¥42, where you'll need to take a taxi (¥5) to Zhongxin Keyun Zhan in order to board a Kashgar-bound bus (8 hr.; ¥60). Heading east, regular buses connect with Luntai (111km/69 miles; 2 hr.; ¥20); with Korla (285km/173 miles; 5 hr.; ¥49); and with Ürümqi (748km/464 miles; 12 hr.; ¥185 lower berth, ¥175 upper berth).

GETTING AROUND **Taxis** have no meters; most trips within town cost ¥5. There are **three-wheelers** and **pedicabs,** as well as six **bus** routes. Bus fare is ¥.50. Donkey-drawn **carts** for ¥1 connect the bus station with the old part of town.

[FastFACTS] KUQA

Banks The **Bank of China** (Mon–Fri 9:30am–8pm), Tian Shan Lu 25, has an ATM, can change cash and draw money on credit cards, but it doesn't change traveler's checks. There's another branch with an ATM on the southeast corner of the intersection of Wenhua Zhong Lu and Youyi Lu.

Internet Access There are plenty of Internet cafes on Tianshan Lu near the junction of Wuyi Lu, which charge ¥2 per hour.

Post Office The post office is at Wenhua Lu 8, open from 10am to 7:30pm.

Exploring Kuqa

Kuqa's market day has recently changed to Sunday, which makes seeing this bazaar and the famous Kashgar Sunday Bazaar impossible without spending a week in between. Humanity pours in from the surrounding countryside for the **Kuqa**

Bazaar ★★, filling the old town with unforgettable sights and smells. Eric Teichman, making the first motorized journey across Xinjiang, found himself greatly inconvenienced: "The streets were so packed with Turki peasants that it was difficult to force a passage with the trucks. . . . We lost our way in the maze of narrow streets round the bazaar of Kuchar and it was after 4pm by the time we cleared the town."

There has been no attempt to "modernize" this bazaar, which spills out in front of the mosque, just across the **Kuqa River.** Get there early when the light is ideal for photography. If you're not bazaared out, it's also worth making a late afternoon trip to the new city market on Wuqian Lu, which stretches south off Tian Shan Lu.

On any day of the week, the old town is worth exploring. Make for the **Kuqa Grand Mosque (Kuche Da Si),** the only mosque in Xinjiang that retains a religious court (ca. 17th c.). Bus no. 1 connects the old town with the bus station, or you can hail a donkey-drawn cart.

Kizil Thousand Buddha Caves (Kezi'er Qian Fo Dong) Those without a special passion for cave temples should save themselves for Dunhuang, but for those seeking a complete picture of the transmission of Buddhist art and ideas, this site might offer some more insights. Seventy-eight kilometers (48 miles) from Kuqa, the site can be reached by arranging a tour or hiring a taxi (¥200–¥250 round-trip).

Currently, only the Western Section (Xi Qu) is open to the public, and none of the caves actually have much in them except for **Cave 17,** which has several walls worth of Buddhist cave drawings intact. Even so, the blue tones in some of the caves, produced by lapis lazuli from Afghanistan (which was worth twice its weight in gold during the Middle Ages), are stunning. To visit other caves, you'll have to fax a letter in advance to ask for permission.

The site predates Dunhuang, and painting continued until the Ming dynasty, when Islam fully displaced Buddhism. It lies in a spectacular and remote valley beside the Muzart River, where the lack of Han influence is striking. Persian, Gandharan, Indian, and Grecian motifs dominate. Black suns, Garuda (a bird god borrowed from Indian mythology), and Apollo riding in a chariot are common decorations on the axis of the roofs. Most caves have a central pillar for perambulation, with a sleeping Buddha at the rear, presided over by mourning disciples. Buddhas and bodhisattvas are lean and muscular, with Indian features.

Unfortunately, little statuary remains, and many of the wall paintings have been removed to Europe and Japan. The eyes and mouths of most remaining images have been defaced by Muslim iconoclasts. There are also some inappropriate recent additions, particularly a ridiculous man-made lake less than 180m (600 ft.) from the caves, which depend on aridity for their preservation. **The Exhibit of Kizil Artifacts ★**, just inside the entrance, is also worthwhile and features reproduction drawings from many caves that you won't be allowed to enter, and other artifacts.

✆ **0997/893-2235.** Fax 0997/893-2247 (fax request if you're seeking permission to visit closed caves). Admission ¥55. The price of a tour guide can be shared among several tourists, but few individual travelers visit the site. Summer 9:30am–8pm; winter 10am–6pm.

Subashi Gucheng Originally called Jarakol (Headwater) Temple when it was established in the 4th century, this ruined town 24km (15 miles) northeast of Kuqa is evidence of Buddhist parishioners' penchant for spectacular sites. Kumarajiva and Xuanzang both preached here, the latter recording, "The images of the Buddha in these monasteries were beautiful almost beyond human skill: And the Brethren were punctilious in discipline and devoted enthusiasts." A large fire devastated the town in the 9th century, and it was gradually abandoned from the 11th century as the populace converted to Islam. There were still Buddhist relics (brought by Prince Asoka) housed in the main pagoda when the enigmatic Count Otani visited during the early 19th century.

Admission ¥25. Open daylight hours. Taxi round-trip ¥80.

Tianshan Gorge (Tianshan Da Xia Gu) For a break from markets and ruins, a 90-minute drive north of Kuqa, this spectacular gorge slices its way nearly 6km (3¾ miles) through the deep red rock that gives Keziliya Mountain its name. Starting as a chasm beckoning travelers away from the desert sun, the gorge gradually narrows to just a few feet, leaving only a sliver of sky above. The narrow trail is sometimes blocked by storm debris—flashfloods are a real danger, so you should check weather conditions before heading out. Take plenty of water. If you want to stay overnight, there's a tourist hotel (✆ **0997/678-0366;** ¥240 standard room, ¥50/¥60 per bed in 4-/6-bed room) at the main entrance, which also serves meals.

63km north of Kuqa. Admission ¥40. 9am–7:30pm. Taxi round-trip ¥150–¥200.

Where to Stay

Kuche Binguan ★ While options are limited, this is certainly the best place to stay in Kuqa. The hotel offers a central location, helpful staff, and a good range of rooms. Rooms in the recently renovated Yibin Building have thick carpets, decent furnishings, and clean bathrooms with showers. Cheaper rooms in the South Building (on the left as you approach the hotel) are smaller and don't have Internet connection, but they come with bathtubs.

Jiefang Bei Lu 17. www.kcbg.com. ✆ **0997/712-2901.** 200 units. ¥280 standard room in Yibin Building; ¥180 standard room in South Building; from ¥688 suite in Yibin Building. No credit cards. **Amenities:** Restaurant. *In room:* A/C, TV, Internet.

Kuche Fandian Tour groups often find themselves staying here and while the rooms are clean and spacious and the large complex is peaceful and pleasant, its location 3km (2 miles) from the railway station is a little isolated. Of the standard rooms offered, those in building 9 have better bathrooms. The best rooms are those in the villas, but at the time of writing these could only be booked by the villa (that is, all 12 rooms).

Tian Shan Dong Lu 8. ✆ **0997/723-3156.** Fax 0997/713-1160. 384 units. ¥388–¥488 standard room; ¥688–¥888 suite. Up to 50% discount. No credit cards. Bus: 6 from the railway or bus station. **Amenities:** Restaurant; gift shop; sauna. *In room:* A/C, TV, Internet.

Where to Eat

For some cheap alfresco dining, the pedestrianized street running east from the southern end of Tuanjie Lu (near the junction with Tian Shan Lu) has a number of atmospheric Uighur restaurants serving kabobs. In the evenings barbecue stalls set up outside. **Best Food Burger** is, as the name suggests, Kuqa's top Western choice. It's located on the north side of Wenhua Lu, just west of the junction with Tuanjie Lu.

Wumai'erhong Meishi Cheng ★★ UIGHUR Elsewhere, you can polish off 20 kabobs and still not be sated, but three kabobs are sufficient at this famous eatery.

Chinese businessmen stroll in before noon and groups of Uighurs soon follow. The *pilao,* or rice pilaf, is excellent, as is the *laghman* (spicy cold noodles). Other items worth trying include *laohu cai,* a spicy salad of cucumber, carrot, and red peppers; and the fruit salad *(shuiguo shala)*.

20 Tuanjie Lu. ✆ **0/133-990-50505.** Meal for 2 ¥40–¥100. No credit cards. 8am–11pm.

Wuqia Guoyuan Canting (Uqa Bhag Restaurant) ★ UIGHUR At this garden restaurant, a favorite among Kuqans for special occasions, you risk becoming the guest of honor, especially if you're game to sing, dance (be prepared to make a fool of yourself attempting Uighur-style dancing), and imbibe. The *dapan ji* is excellent value, though you'll need a party of four to polish off this tasty meal of whole chicken, peppers, potato, and tomatoes covered in thick noodles. Other dishes include spicy beef strips *(ganzha niu rou tiao)* and a cold platter of sweet cucumber *(tangban huanggua)*.

Wuqia Lu. ✆ **0997/713-3665.** Meal for 2 ¥60–¥150. No credit cards. 6:30pm–12:30am. Donkey cart or motorbike ride (¥1 south from the intersection of Tian Shan Lu and Youyi Lu.

KASHGAR (KASHI; 喀什)

Xinjiang Province, 1,470km (911 miles) SW of Ürümqi, 520km (322 miles) NW of Khotan

The northern and southern Silk Routes joined at ancient **Kashgar** and bifurcated again, leading south through the **Pamirs** to Gilgit, and west through **the Ferghana Valley** to Samarkand. At the height of the Han and Tang dynasties, Kashgar was in Chinese hands. The Chinese were routed by the Arabs in 751 in the Battle of Talas River (northeast of Tashkent). This allowed Islam to spread east into the Tarim Basin, displacing Buddhism and Manichaeism. Kashgar subsequently became a center of Islamic scholarship and, but for a brief return during the Mongol Yuan dynasty, it lay outside the sphere of Chinese influence. During the Qing dynasty the Chinese reasserted control, and Kashgar became a key site for players of the **Great Game**—it had both a Russian and a British consulate.

Trade is the lifeblood of Kashgar, and with the opening of border crossings at **Khunjerab, Torugart,** and the **Irkeshtam route to Osh,** it is now once again an international trading center. Kashgar's strategic position has unfortunately made it a priority in efforts to "Sinicize" border areas, and since the opening of the railway line in 2000, Han settlers have arrived by the trainload.

At press time, plans to redevelop the old city were well underway, and large portions of the historic quarter had already been demolished. The tourist version of the old city looks safe for now, but south of Ordaisnki Lu resembles a construction site, with hundreds of residents being re-located. Some residents are being given the choice to have their houses reconstructed on the same spot, and re-developed areas are supposed to accord with Islamic style, although there is little evidence of this in the bland high-rises that are springing up around the city. This will likely only add to the tension that boiled over in the July 2009 riots in Ürümqi. The government cites the risk of earthquakes as the reason for the re-development, and undoubtedly much of the old town is dilapidated. However, critics argue that as much of the old town has survived for hundreds of years, that this is just an excuse to further impose Han culture on the Uighur population.

HOTELS ■
Chini Bagh Hotel 7
(Qīníwǎkè Bīnguǎn)
其尼瓦克宾馆
Eden Hotel 6
(Hái ěr Bā Gé Dà Fàn Diàn)
海尔巴格大饭店
Seman Hotel (Sèmǎn Bīnguǎn) 1
色满宾馆
Taxinan Barony Hotel 3
(Tǎxīnán Bāngchén Jiǔdiàn)
塔西南邦臣酒店
Tianyuan International Hotel 13
(Guoji Dajiǔdiàn)
天缘国际酒店
ATTRACTIONS ●
Abakh Hoja Mausoleum 16
(Xiāngfēi Mù)
香妃墓
Central Asia International Grand Bazaar 15
(Xīngqītiān Dàshìchǎng)
星期天大市场
Id Kah Mosque 11
(Àitígǎ'ěr Qīngzhēn Sì)
艾提尕尔清真寺
Ordaisnki Mosque 12
(Aodàyìxìkè Qingzhensì)
奥大伊西克清真寺
RESTAURANTS ◆
Altun Orda 2
(Yín tí Zá ěr Jīn Ō Er Dá Yǐnshì)
银提扎尔快餐厅
Eden Café 6
(Diàn Kā Fēi)
一甸咖啡
John's Information Café 1
(Yuēhàn Cāntīng)
约翰餐厅
Karakoram Café 9
Orda (Ōurìdá) 14
欧日大
Pakistan Café 8
(Bājīsītǎn Kāfēi)
巴基斯坦咖啡店
Pigeon Restaurants 10
(Gēzi Diàn)
鸽子店
Rixta 5
Samawer 4
(Cháyuán Dàjiǔdiàn)
茶园大酒店
0 1/2 mi
0 0.5 km
Kashgar
XINJIANG
Beijing
China
To Airport
International Bus Station
Jichang Lu
Xia Malebag Lu
Seman Lu
Aodayixike Lu (Ordaisnki Rd.)
Aizilaiti Lu
Jiefang Bei Lu
OLD TOWN
Mao Statue
Ferris Wheel
Tawuguzi Lu
To Railway Station
Renmin Xi Lu
Renmin Dong Lu
Youmulake Xiehai'er Lu
Regional Bus Station
East Lake
PEOPLE'S PARK
Tiannan Lu
Jiefang Nan Lu
Tiyu Lu
Wenhua Lu
Kezi Duwei Lu
Saglam Lu
To Ivan Bazaar
Airport
Bus Station
Bank
Police
Post Office
Rail Station

Whatever your opinion, the redevelopment marks the end of an era, and will undoubtedly change the face of old Kashgar forever. Fortunately the depth of tradition here is such that a change of exterior appearance will by no means result in a change of culture, and Uighurs will continue to thrive and trade as they have done for the last thousand years. The markets are still a riot of color and exotic scents, donkeys pull rickety carts laden with watermelons and cotton bales in and out of town, gray-bearded mullahs call the faithful to prayer on every street corner, and serene old men enjoy long chats over tea. The city also remains a great place from which to explore the stunning landscapes and as yet untouched market towns within a few hours' drive.

Essentials

GETTING THERE The **airport** is 12km (7½ miles) north of downtown. Take a taxi from the airport for ¥20 to ¥30, or you can take bus no. 2, which terminates to the west of the Peoples' Square. Most hotels have travel agents and flight booking offices, or you can book through the **Airline Ticket Office** (✆ **0998/284-1186;** 10am–8pm) on Jiefang Nan Lu, where the staff can also arrange ticket delivery. Several daily flights connect with Ürümqi, and onward **flights** can also be booked.

The **railway station** is southeast of town. Take a 15-minute taxi ride for ¥10, or take bus no. 28 to immediately east of the Peoples' Square. The station sells tickets up to 10 days in advance, and is open from 8:30am to 6pm, but if you want sleeper tickets in the high season it's easiest to proceed through a travel agency, or line up at the Kasha Huochezhan Shoupiao Chu (ticket office) at counter 5 of the Regional Bus Station on Tiannan Lu. The ticket office is open from 9:30am to 1:30pm and 3 to 7:30pm. The K9788 for Ürümqi (24 hr.) leaves at 1:16pm, and the 7558 (31 hr.) departs at 8:18am.

Most **buses** connect to the grandly named **International Bus Station (Guoji Qichezhan)** in the north of town at Jichang Lu 29 (✆ **0998/296-3630**). Fast, comfortable sleeper buses link with Ürümqi every 50 minutes between 9:50am and 9:30pm (24 hr.; ¥248 lower berth, ¥229 upper berth). There are also regular buses to Aksu (468km/290 miles; 7–8 hr.; ¥80), and four daily services (2, 4, 6, and 8pm) to Kuqa (723km/448 miles; 12–13 hr.; ¥150 lower berth, ¥140 upper berth) and Korla (1,003km/622 miles; 17–18 hr.; ¥182 lower berth, ¥168 upper berth). There are three departures daily (11am, 3pm, and 6pm) for the long trip to Yining (1,644km/1,019 miles; 37–38 hr.; ¥334 lower berth, ¥310 upper berth). Summer buses to Sost operate on demand (minimum of 10) and cost ¥270 for the 2 day journey.

Twice a week a direct bus heads to Bishkek for the scenic ride over the Torugart Pass (¥570), but at press time, foreigners were not allowed on it. Until the pass is upgraded to a "first level" border crossing, travelers will need to charter a vehicle through a travel agency in Kashgar.

It is now possible to take a bus to Osh in southern Kyrgyzstan via Irkeshtam for ¥570. No permit is required, only a valid Kyrgyz visa. At present, the bus departs at 9am on Mondays and Thursdays. In winter, you may need to proceed through travel agencies.

The **Diqu Keyun Zhan** (**Regional Bus Station;** ✆ **0998/282-9673**) on Tiannan Lu has buses to Khotan every 90 minutes from 10am (520km/322 miles; 8 hr.; ¥90), as well as a sleeper bus that leaves at 8:30pm (¥95 lower berth, ¥87 upper berth). There are also two daily local buses to Karakul (¥45) and Tashkurgan at

The Back Door to Lhasa

A 4-hour bus ride south of Kashgar, **Yecheng** is the main point for hitching an illegal ride to **Ali (Shiquan He),** the main town in western Tibet. In the past numerous travelers managed to sneak through, but since the troubles in both Xinjiang and Tibet, things have tightened up. Truck drivers ask in the vicinity of ¥1,000 for the 1,100km (680-mile) trip that takes at least 4 days. It is likely to take several days to arrange a lift. Aside from tales of Frenchmen freezing to death in the backs of trucks, be aware that if you manage to negotiate a ride you will be putting your driver at risk. Even if you make it to Ali without incident, at the very best you should expect to be fined by the PSB (¥400–¥500) and issued with an Aliens Travel Permit to continue on to Lhasa, but far more likely you'll be turned around and sent back where you came from. It is now possible to undertake the journey legally, but for a price. **Uighur Tours** and **Kashgar Mountaineering Adventures** (see below for contact details) organize 2- or 3-week trips, the longer of which also take in Mount Kailash. Expect to pay at least US$2,500 per person. Permits, 4WD, drivers, accommodation, and entrance fees are generally included in the price, but not food.

11:30am and 12:30pm (294km/182 miles; 6 hr.; ¥65). There are regular buses to Yecheng 4 hr.; ¥35), for those considering the illegal journey to Tibet (see below).

Departure times and tickets are quoted in Beijing time (2 hr. ahead of local time), but be sure to double-check when you buy your ticket.

TOURS & GUIDES Kashgar has an overload of travel agents, touts, and tour guides, many of whom are just out for a fast buck, but there are also some decent and professional agencies and individuals. **Uighur Tours** (✆ **0998/298-1073;** www.uighurtour.com) in the lobby of the Chini Bagh is managed by a friendly local, Ali Tash, who can assist with everything from general advice on what to see in the city through to booking bus, plane, and train tickets, permit assistance, day trips to local markets and full-blown tours. Ali has appeared on National Geographic, and genuinely takes pleasure in sharing the nuances of Uighur culture and a trip with him is highly recommended. Other places to try include Abdul Wahab Tours (✆ **0998/220-4012**) and John's Information Café (✆ **0998/258-1186;** www.johncafe.net), both at the Seman Hotel, or Imam Husan (✆ **0998/295-1029;** www.kashgarguide.com), in the lobby of the Eden Hotel. Those interested in adventure travel such as the popular trek out to **Mustagh Ata;** an assault on the world's second-highest mountain, **K2;** or following in the footsteps of Swedish explorer Sven Hedin into the mountains south of Khotan, should connect with **Kashgar Mountaineering Adventures** at 41301 Yudu Mansions, 43 Jiefang Nan Lu (✆ **0998/282-1832;** www.ksalpine.com).

[FastFACTS] KASHGAR

Banks, Foreign Exchange & ATMs Both traveler's checks and credit cards are accepted at the main **Bank of China** (Mon–Fri 9:30am–1:30pm and 4–7pm) on the eastern side of Renmin Square, and there are also several ATMs here. There are other branches with ATMs on the south side of Renmin Xi Lu, and on Seman Lu, a few minutes' walk east of the Seman Hotel.

Internet Access The **Karakoram Café** offers 30-minutes free Internet for customers and also has free Wi-Fi, and there are various Internet cafes around the city. Try the 24-hour second-floor *wangba* next to the Karakoram Café, or the basement *wangba* on the east side of Jiefang Nan Lu, just south of the junction with Renmin Lu, both of which charge ¥2 per hour.

Post Office The main post office (10am–7:30pm) is at Renmin Xi Lu 7.

Visa Extensions The **PSB** (✆ **0998/282-2030**) is located next to the Home Inn on Youmulake Xihai'er Lu. They are open Monday to Friday 9:30am to 1:30pm and 4 to 8pm and can process visa extensions in a day, but will generally only extend them if you have less than a week left on your current visa.

Exploring Kashgar

The wide, main streets brought in by the Han have long threatened Kashgar's atmosphere, but now the redevelopment of substantial sectors of the old city will forever change the feel of this ancient trading post. A small part of the old city (with a ¥30 2-day pass; daily 10am–7:30pm) should remain architecturally intact, but the rest of the city looks like it's either becoming a sea of bland high-rises, or at best a themed imitation of itself. It's a sad sight to watch the adobe houses of old Kashgar come down one by one, whilst cranes blight the skyline above; however, the indomitable spirit of the people and their culture endures and one senses it will continue to prevail in spite of the physical changes afoot.

The tourist area of the **old city** remains home to some 2,000 families, and is certainly still worth a visit, either independently, or with one of the free guides assigned by the ticket office. Guides can facilitate interactions with the locals, and will take you to a few open houses (read shops), but if you like getting lost, exploring independently is also a fun option—note that hexagonal paving indicates a main road, whilst regular brick paving means you're heading to a dead end. Reconstruction will take some years, and it remains unclear whether the bulk of displaced communities will be re-housed in new houses on the same spot, or in the anodyne tower blocks that are rapidly dominating the city. For the meanwhile there are still pockets of intact and genuine old city, notably at **Koziqiyabixi,** just across the river from the Central Asian Market, and nearby up the hill **west of Azilaiti Lu,** and also **around the Abakh Hoja Mosque.**

Ordaisnki Lu also seems to be surviving the changes well, and remains a narrow, busy commercial street where coppersmiths beat out pots, while street vendors sell boiled lamb's heads, fresh yellow figs, Hami melon, and rotisserie chicken. Proceeding west toward Jiefang Bei Lu, old men sitting on rows of old iron benches watch Uighur music videos while drinking a yogurt-and-ice concoction. Just before you reach Jiefang Bei Lu, there will be an alley, Areya Lu, to your left. Proceed south and you'll see hat vendors touting a range of eclectic styles, ranging from fluffy sheepskin caps with earflaps to tall, narrow white-and-black felt ones worn by Kyrgyzs to cowboy hats popular with Chinese tourists. Following this road down, you'll continue through a weave of streets that will eventually spit you out on **Remin Dong Lu.** Walking west on Remin Dong Lu, you'll pass Renmin Square and the notorious, giant Mao statue that is also one of the largest in China.

Abakh Hoja Mausoleum (Xiangfei Mu) ★ The tomb of one of Kashgar's most renowned kings and spiritual leader of the **Bai Shan sect** is several miles northeast of the town center. Five generations of his family are housed in a domed mausoleum decorated with green, blue, orange, and white tiles. The cool interior houses 58 tombs draped with silks. The admission ticket means that the tomb is not a center of worship, but the adjacent mosque is active. The **Gaodi Mosque** to the left of the entrance has swastika motifs decorating its columns, trays for washing corpses, and wooden stretchers for transporting them to the graveyard. The cemetery is now cut off from the mausoleum by a high wall, hopefully not impeding the smooth passage of believers to the afterlife.

The tomb is known to the Chinese as **Xiangfei Mu,** or **Tomb of the Fragrant Concubine,** a member of the Hoja clan known for her "exceptional body aroma," probably due to the sprig of oleaster she was fond of wearing. A favorite of the Qianlong emperor (1711–99), she constantly refused his advances, but all tales have him devastated by her death. She was either murdered by Qianlong's mother, committed suicide rather than sleep with the emperor, or died naturally, depending on which account you believe. The sedan just inside the tomb is labeled as the one that brought her back to her beloved Kashgar, although her remains are almost certainly buried in the Eastern Qing Tombs in Hebei.

Admission to the tomb ¥30. 10am–7:30pm. Bus: 20 from Peoples' Sq. to the terminus. Taxi ¥10.

Id Kah Mosque (Aitiga'er Qingzhen Si) Xinjiang's largest mosque dates from the 15th century and can house up to 20,000 worshippers. Impressive statistics aside, the mosque looks at its best from the square outside, but its prayer hall and leafy courtyard do offer some relief from the bustling markets.

Admission ¥20. Sat–Thurs 7:40am–2pm and 4–8:30pm; Fri 7:40am–11am and 4:30–8:30pm.

Kashgar Sunday Bazaar (Kashi Xingqitian Da Shichang) You might expect the world's most famous open-air market to be safe from the meddlings of bureaucracy, if only in the name of financial gain. But you would be wrong. Several years ago the Bazaar became *two* bazaars, making the original site a covered bazaar marked as CENTRAL ASIA INTERNATIONAL GRAND BAZAAR ★, while the livestock market was moved out of town. In 2010 the livestock market, known as **Ulagh Bazaar ★★** was moved again to a location by the motorway east of town, but remains the dusty, noisy spectacle you'd hope for. Efforts to herd all the traders into an enclosure are cheerfully ignored by small traders, who haggle on the road outside, blocking traffic. Ignore demands for payment on entry, unless you have donkeys to trade. Bearded Uighur men in traditional blue-and-white garb sharpen their knives and trim their sheep; small boys wearing Inter Milan stripes gorge themselves on Hami melons; Kyrgyz in dark fur hats pick up and drop dozens of lambs to test their weight and meatiness before settling deals with vigorous and protracted handshakes. No fewer than 10 people act as witnesses.

Arrive early before the (tourist) herds, and while the market is still setting up, when the light is perfect for some unforgettable photography. Shelter under colorful awnings during the midday heat, enjoying tea, buns stuffed with minced lamb (*samsas*), and bagels. Taxis (¥10–¥15), and noisy three-wheelers (¥1 per person) connect the Central Asia Bazaar with the Ulagh Bazaar. Bus no. 28 also heads to Ulagh Bazaar.

If the Ulagh Bazaar is all about livestock and the men who come to buy and sell them, then the Sunday Bazaar, as the Central Asia Bazaar is known, is the place to see the ladies of Kashgar eagerly snapping up glistening garments. The market operates every day and is a good place to haggle over hats, pashminas, or musical instruments, but if you want to see it at its liveliest, then Sunday is the day. While the bazaar can initially seem a little touristy, the deeper you delve into its passages, the more local it feels. Bus nos. 7 and 20 serve the bazaar.

Ordaisnki Mosque (Aodayixike Qingzhensi) Islamic visitors looking for a less scrutinized place to worship can visit the oldest mosque in Kashgar (c. 1119), about 270m (900 ft.) east of Id Kah Square on Ordaisnki Road. Follow your nose—the city government has so much respect for religion it has placed huge rubbish bins outside, and the mosque is now scheduled for demolition.

Shopping

The lanes surrounding the **Id Kah Mosque** are ideal for browsing for gifts. Just north of the mosque is a line of carpet shops with nice antique rugs from Khotan, Afghanistan, and Turkmenistan. Prices start around ¥1,000. Another great place for browsing is the **Central Asia International Grand Bazaar** (see above). Wares include embroidered fabrics, dried fruit, knives, spices, hats, musical instruments, and wooden handicrafts.

There are plenty of small supermarkets around town, but for more choice try the huge **Yi Jia Hui Hao Supermarket** on Renmin Xi Lu; look for the red and white sign in English in the pedestrianized area on the south side of the road 5 minutes' walk west of the Jiefang Lu intersection.

Where to Stay

Kashgar's hotel scene is developing apace, and several five-star ventures should be complete within the next few years. Two of the most popular hotels, the Chini Bagh and the Seman, are located on the grounds of the former British and Russian consulates, respectively. The former enjoys a great location; the latter offers the rare opportunity to escape the bland uniformity of mainstream hotel rooms in China. More upscale offerings can be found in the center of the new city, so for the meanwhile, the decision to be made is whether you want luxury or proximity to the "real Kashgar" because with the current options, it's one or the other.

EXPENSIVE

Guoji Dajiudian (Tianyuan International Hotel) ★ In the center of the new city, this new hotel offers Kashgar's best rooms and service. While its location just across the road from the Mao statue and People's Park is a world away from the Kashgar most travelers come to see, if it's a hint of luxury away from the dust you want, stay here. Rooms are furnished with solid dark wood pieces, carpets are only mildly worn and higher floor rooms facing the front have great views over (what's left of) the old city, and, on clear days, to the mountains beyond. The square outside is lively in the evenings and the old city is only a 10-minute walk away.

Renmin Dong Lu 8. ✆ **0998/280-1111.** 168 units. ¥980 standard room; ¥1,180 deluxe standard room; ¥2,880 suite. Up to 50% discount. MC, V. **Amenities:** Restaurant. *In room:* A/C, TV, fridge, hair dryer, Internet.

Taxinan Bangchen Jiudian (Tarim Barony Hotel) Located opposite the old city wall on a stretch of road between the Seman and the Chini Bagh Hotels, this newer hotel is one of the few in town that meets four-star standards. While service isn't quite international, rooms are well appointed, particularly the deluxe and executive rooms on the 5th and 6th floors, which all come with computers. The garden cafe is also a pleasant place for a drink.

Seman Lu 242. www.baronyhotels.com. ✆ **0998/258-6888.** Fax 0998/258-5888. 108 units. ¥880 standard room; ¥1,680 suite. 20%–45% discounts. AE, MC, V. **Amenities:** Restaurant; billiards; concierge; conference center; gift shop; gym. *In room:* A/C, TV, fridge, hair dryer, Internet, minibar.

MODERATE/INEXPENSIVE

Chini Bagh Hotel (Qiniwake Binguan) Nothing about the two main white-tiled buildings of this aging hotel lends any hint of its history as the former British Consulate. Neither does the enormous five-star tower, which was under construction at the time of writing and due to open in 2012. However, its location just across the road from a lively Uighur street that quickly brings you to Id Kah Mosque, makes it a good choice. There are also several decent cafes and restaurants within a 2-minute walk. Furthermore service is generally friendly and a host of room choices are available. Previously the cheapest rooms and dorms were on the upper floors of the Jingyuan Building, located toward the back of the complex, but this was closed at the time of writing. The best value rooms are within the North Building (Beilou), but until construction of the five-star tower has finished, these are best avoided. This leaves only the rooms in the circular Friendship Building (Youyilou), which (just) meet three-star standards, though plumbing is sketchy and bathrooms are a bit dank.

Seman Lu 144. ✆ **0998/298-2103.** Fax 0998/298-2299. 258 units. ¥180–¥280 standard room; ¥680 suite; ¥30–¥50 dorm bed. Discounts of 30%. V. **Amenities:** 2 restaurants; concierge; forex. *In room:* A/C, TV, Internet.

Eden Hotel (Hai'erbage Dafandian) A recent addition with a great location, unfortunately Eden doesn't quite live up to the expectation set by the wonderfully themed restaurant downstairs. Nevertheless, rooms have touches of Uighur flavor, such as rug-style carpets and gold flourishes, and mod-cons including flat-screen TVs, making them a good deal. Bathrooms are tiny though. Rooms at the front are a little noisy, so pick a room at the back (even numbers), providing the construction has finished at the Chini Bagh.

Seman Lu 148. ✆ **0998/266-4444.** 86 units. ¥188 standard room; ¥318 suite. No credit cards. **Amenities:** Restaurant. *In room:* A/C, TV, hair dryer, Internet.

Seman Binguan (Seman Hotel) Although its location is farther from the old town than the Chini Bagh and service can be erratic, the Seman has managed to retain some of its original character. The best rooms are to be found in **building 3 ★** and have a gaudy central Asian feel, intricately carved walls, beaded lampshades, and nice carpets. Bathrooms are decent, but still a bit worn for a three-star hotel. Building 1 also has some rooms like this along with a motley collection of cheap and grubby twins, triples and dorms, some with bathrooms, others without; none of them is worth staying in unless you're on a very tight budget. The hotel is "ground-zero" for foreign tourists who frequent the travel agencies and restaurants nearby (including a branch of John's Information Café within the complex), but its location is not as good as the Chini Bagh's for those who want to spend time in the old quarter of town.

Seman Lu 337. www.semanhotel.com. ✆ **0998/258-2129.** 206 units, 133 of which are Uighur-style rooms. ¥280 Uighur standard room in buildings 1 and 3; ¥160 standard room in building 1; ¥20–¥30 dorm bed in 3- to 6-bed rooms. No credit cards. **Amenities:** 4 restaurants; concierge. *In room:* A/C, TV.

Where to Eat

Kashgar has plenty of culinary opportunities, from Western-style cafes serving tasty sandwiches to opulent Uighur dining halls, street food, and beyond. The **nightmarket** across from Id Kah Mosque in the streets east of Jiefang Bei Lu is lively and other good bets include the whole pigeon soup (*gezi tang;* ¥20) to be found at a collection of 11 small canteens across the street and about 300m (981 ft.) left out of the Chini Bagh Hotel. As well as the Western options listed below there's a **Best Food Burger** and a **Dicos** on Renmin Xi Lu and a branch of the ubiquitous **John's Information Café** in the Seman Hotel (8am–midnight).

Altun Orda (Jinao Erda Tese Cai) ★★ UIGHUR Altun Orda is an opulent affair that serves a delicious selection of local dishes, cooked to perfection. The clientele comprises mostly wealthy locals enjoying foot-long lamb skewers, sumptuous pilaf rice, and *laghman,* all washed down with fresh pomegranate juice and plenty of local tea. Decor is fresh from Arabian Nights and service staff is smartly turned out in Uighur attire. A table on the second floor overlooking the atrium allows you to fully soak up the scene. The English picture menu also features some Chinese dishes (the shredded potato and peppers with vinegar is good). After dinner you can retreat down to the basement for a local coffee and even a strawberry *shisha.*

Renmin Xi Lu 320. ✆ **0998/258-3555.** Meal for 2 ¥60–¥100. No credit cards. 10:30am–midnight.

Eden Café (Dian Kafei) ★ INTERNATIONAL Very popular with wealthy locals, this huge new Uighur style cafe-restaurant is divided into sections featuring cozy booths, with low-lighting, exposed brickwork, adobe, and rugs completing the scene. The menu is broad-ranging, but the Turkish dishes, especially the kebabs and kofta, are recommended. The fresh juices are also excellent.

Seman Lu 148, on the ground floor of Eden Hotel. ✆ **0998/266-5555.** Main courses ¥35–¥48. No credit cards. 9am–late.

Karakoram Café ★★ WESTERN The Karakoram Café is an oasis of cleanliness, calm, and cappuccino in the dusty desert that is Xinjiang. Owned by the same Singaporean group that established Tashkurgan's Crown Inn, the cafe's smart and courteous Uighur staff present first-rate breakfasts, sandwiches, shakes, and coffees. The cafe is minimally but attractively decorated and has Wi-Fi and the cleanest toilets in Xinjiang. The on-site travel service can arrange trips to the mountains and desert.

Seman Lu. ✆ **0998/282-2669.** Main courses and sandwiches ¥10–¥68. No credit cards. Noon–midnight.

Orda (Ourida) ★ UIGHUR This is Uighur dining, made easy; with its kitchen in the center of the restaurant you can just point to what you want. Try the *pilao* (rice pilaf) set meal, which comes with yogurt that you can dole onto your rice to give it a creamy texture. The whole roast chicken (¥68) is also delicious. The atmosphere is pleasant, with walls decorated in colorful tiles and Uighur musicians that play traditional instruments. If you order the fruit plate, remember to eat the watermelon first, before the grapes and the Hami melon—it's an Uighur taboo to do it in reverse. No photography is allowed inside.

Renmin Dong Lu (Diqu Sifa Duimian). ✆ **0998/265-2777.** Meal for 2 ¥60–¥100. No credit cards. 10am–11:30pm. Bus: 10.

Pakistan Cafe (Bajisitan Kafei) ★★ PAKISTANI Despite its slightly grubby appearance and garish posters, this tiny cafe is a gem, offering a taste of what lies just over the border in Pakistan. The menu is simple but the staff is friendly and the food is sumptuous and authentic. Try the chicken curry or *aloo gobi* served with fresh-from-the-oven *chapati* and round the meal off with a cup of sweet *chai.*

Seman Lu. No phone. Meal for 2 ¥30–¥40. No credit cards. 9am–11pm.

Rixta ★ UIGHUR This place is famous for one dish, *dapanji* (Xinjiang Big Chicken), and the huge mound of perfectly–cooked chicken, spicy sauce and miles of noodles will easily fill four people for just ¥60. Decor is basic, customers are locals, and service staff are efficient and friendly.

Seman Lu (look for the Rixta sign in English). ✆ **139/9964-8803.** Dapanji ¥60. No credit cards. Noon–midnight.

Around Kashgar

Shipton's Arch (Tushuk Tagh) The world's largest natural arch stands, largely unheralded, about 50km (31 miles) northwest of Kashgar. Known locally as "Gate of the Sky", and located at an elevation of 3,168m (10,394 ft.), the arch towers 366m (1,200 ft.) above the canyon floor. It is composed of crumbling conglomerate and is exceedingly difficult to reach. Eric Shipton, Britain's final representative in Kashgar and an accomplished mountaineer, failed several times from the southern route via Muk and Mingyol, finally gaining access from the north via Artux and Karakum. His wife described the scene: "We found ourselves looking straight across at the immense curve of the arch. Its upper half soared above us, but the walls continued down into an unfathomable gorge below. It was as if we stood on a platform some few feet away from a giant window. . . ."

Uighur Tours runs day trips to the arch and charge ¥700 to ¥800 for a jeep that can hold up to four people and a driver.

Tomb of Mohammed Kashgari The tomb of this eminent 11th-century translator (¥30; 10am–8pm) lies 30km (19 miles) southwest of Kashgar, west of the charming Uighur town of **Opal (Wupa'er).** The scholar spent most of his years in Baghdad and is credited with compiling the first Turkic dictionary in Arabic. The site itself is surprisingly expansive, spreading over a hillside, and as well as the tomb itself there's a small museum, cave and good views to the dusty desert below. Hire a taxi (¥200 return) or take bus no. 4 (¥2.50) from Kashgar's Opal bus station (a block south of the Seman Hotel) as far as Shufu, then share a taxi to Opal for ¥5. Motorbike carts, charging ¥4, leave for the tomb from under a red-and-yellow arch in the center of Opal. If you haven't sated your appetite for markets after a Sunday in Kashgar, Opal's Monday market offers a smaller scale version, replete with all the usual trimmings—cattle, donkey carts, and enigmatic faces all vie for your attention.

TASHKURGAN (TASHIKUERGAN; 塔什库尔干) & KARAKUL 喀拉湖

Xinjiang Province, 295km (183 miles) SW of Kashgar

Nestled in a basin 3,100m (10,171 ft.) up in the Pamirs, Tashkurgan marked the end of the Silk Routes for Chinese traders arriving from Kashgar or Yarkand. Their goods would be transferred to Bactrian, Persian, or Sogdian caravans, which continued on to Gilgit and thence either south to the Indian Ocean along the Indus River, or west through Kabul, Herat, and Mashhad, ultimately reaching the Mediterranean Sea at Antioch or Tyrus. Described by British consul Eric Teichman as the "storm centre of Asian politics," the town has a strong military presence, but it is still a traditional Tajik town and you'll see plenty of elaborately dressed local women sporting distinctive cylindrical headgear. ***Note:*** Turn to chapter 16 for Chinese translations of key locations.

Essentials

GETTING THERE After recent repairs, the stunning drive from Kashgar to Tashkurgan along the fabled Karakoram Highway is now a smooth 6-hour journey (bar the odd landslide). Roughly two-thirds of the way to Tashkurgan is **Karakul (Black Lake),** over which towers the magnificent **Mustagh Ata** (7,546m/24,757 ft.). Buses leave for Karakul and Tashkurgan at 9:30 and 10:30am from Kashgar's Diqu Bus Station. The cost is ¥45 to Karakul and ¥65 to Tashkurgan. Return buses leave from Tashkurgan's neglected bus station at 8am and then again at 3pm; the station is beyond the Jiaotong Binguan on Tashkurgan Lu. Provided you have a Pakistani visa you can also continue on to **Sost** on the 10am bus for ¥230; the 8-hour trip arrives in town in late afternoon after many inspections. Returning to Kashgar from Karakul may be a little trickier; buses are supposed to stop on their way back from Tashkurgan, but they'll often plow ahead without stopping. The bus down to Kashgar should pass by around 10:30 or 11am, while the buses up to Tashkurgan should arrive at around 12:30 or 1pm, but check this with the locals. Far easier, and better for sightseeing is to rent a taxi and driver for up to four people to take you there and back; overnight trips to Karakul cost ¥700 to ¥800, while overnight trips to Tashkurgan are ¥1,000 to ¥1,200 for 2 days. **Uighur Tours** and most agencies in Kashgar can arrange drivers, or you could negotiate with a local taxi driver; **Mohammad Tursun** (**© 0/1389-913-3306**) is a friendly and reliable driver who speaks a little English and is often to be found outside the Chini Bagh Hotel in Kashgar.

Nearly 4,000m (13,123 ft.) up in the Pamirs, icy Karakul Lake now has an entry fee (¥50), and staying in Kyrgyz yurts is no longer assured, but it is still definitely worth making the spectacular drive here. Previously Kyrgyz families owning yurts could take in visitors between May and the end of October. However, the building of a new hotel at the lake has led to "licensing issues" for the yurts. At the time of writing the hotel had yet to open, but yurts were not allowed to take in guests, meaning there's nowhere to stay at the lake itself. When the hotel opens this will obviously be an option, albeit more expensive and less authentic than staying at the yurts, otherwise travelers will need to continue on to Tashkurgan (2 hr.), or head back down the road 15 minutes to Bulung Kol, where a local family should be able to take you in. If the situation at Karakul changes, the first yurts you'll encounter belong to Nazerbik and his Kyrgyz family and are recommended. A place in a yurt should cost ¥40 to ¥50 per person and simple meals of bread and noodles are available, or for more choice head to the hotel (when it opens). It is not recommended to camp at the lake alone. Locals can arrange horse (¥50–¥60) or motorbike (¥100) rides around the lake. A few kilometers along the road beyond Karakul lies Subash, and then a little farther brings you to Point 204, the trailhead for Mustagh Ata ascents.

Exploring Tashkurgan

National Culture and Arts Center While it's hardly a national treasure, Tashkurgan's small museum has some interesting local finds and detailed English explanations of traditional Tajik customs. Two rooms in the basement display funerary items discovered in the region, the most fascinating (and grisly) of which are the 2,500-year-old mummies of an adolescent female and a 3-month-old baby, which were discovered during the construction of a hydro-electric power project in 2004. Other finds include a finely crafted miniature sheep from the Tang era. Upstairs focuses on the Tajik people and their customs and is made all the more enjoyable by the local tunes and hawk dance video in the background. There are displays of traditional clothing, jewelry, and instruments and good English labeling. Boards detail Tajik architecture, cuisine, greetings, marriage, festivals, music, and games, the latter of which includes "goat tossing" from the back of a yak!

Honqilapu Lu, on the roundabout with the Hawk Statue. Admission ¥20. 10am–2pm and 4–7pm.

Tashkurgan Fort Dating from the 14th century, this crumbling fort is accessed by a small lane just east of the Pamir Hotel. You can enjoy an impressive view of the surrounding fields, mountains, and military complexes from the old walls, but the best view of the fort is from the pastures below in the early morning light.

Admission ¥8. 8am–8pm.

Where to Stay

Tashkurgan isn't a major tourist destination and most of its hotels reflect this, in terms of both price and quality; nevertheless things have picked up recently with the opening of the Crown Inn. Note that many hotels (including the Crown and Pamir) are closed between November and April.

Crown Inn (Taxian Huangguan Dajiudian) ★ Undoubtedly Tashkurgan's top choice, the Singaporean-owned Crown Inn offers superclean, simple but stylish and modern rooms. The queen-bedded rooms have full-size tubs that are definitely welcome at this altitude. The hotel's location, a little out of the center, affords fine mountain views especially from the roof terrace. Service is friendly and the hotel can also arrange local treks, horse rides and visits to nearby Kayrgyz and Tajik villages. The restaurant here is also the best in town, and a small shop selling Kyrgyz handicrafts made by local villagers should open in 2012.

Pamir Lu. www.crowninntashkorgan.com. ✆ **0998/342-2888.** 30 units. ¥980 standard room. Discounts of 30%. No credit cards. **Amenities:** Restaurant; Wi-Fi in the lobby and restaurant. *In room:* A/C, TV.

Jiaotong Binguan (Traffic Hotel) Dorms without bathrooms are spartan, better furnished standard twins are chilly, and hot water is talked about but seldom seen. Nevertheless the Jiatong Binguan is at least cheap and open year-round.

Tashikuergan Lu 50. ✆ **0998/342-1192.** 33 units. ¥120 standard twin; ¥15 dorm bed. No credit cards. **Amenities:** Restaurant. *In room:* TV.

Pami'er Binguan (Pamir Hotel) This two-star right by the fort on the far side of town offers more comfortable rooms than the Traffic Hotel. Rooms in the new wing are worth the minimal extra outlay, although all rooms suffer from temperamental showers.

Tashikuergan Lu 207. ✆/fax **0998/342-2660.** 54 units. ¥286 standard room. Discounts of 50%. No credit cards. **Amenities:** Restaurant. *In room:* TV.

Stone City Hotel (Tashikuergan Shitou Cheng Binguan) A compact hotel just a few minutes' walk from the center of town or the museum, Stone City has dated but adequate twins with TV and underfloor heating, plus there's hot water in the mornings and evenings. Rooms on the second floor are brighter.

Pamir Lu. ✆ **0998/342-2600.** 28 units. ¥180 standard room. No credit cards. **Amenities:** Restaurant. *In room:* TV.

Where to Eat

Tashkurgan is hardly a culinary center, but you'll find a number of basic options along Tashikuergan Lu near the junction with Hongqilapu Lu, including **Wushi Lao Huimin Canting** (✆ **0998/342-17167;** 10am–1am), which offers beef stretch noodles (¥15) and hand-held yak (¥80 good for four). The restaurant is signed "Wushi Huimin Old Dining Restaurant" and has a red signboard with a picture of a gold mosque. For something a little spicier, a few meters farther toward the junction **Chongqing Quan Jia Fu** (10am–midnight) turns out Sichuan favorites including *gongbao jiding, yuxiang rousi* (both ¥24), and *huoguo* (¥30).

The only upscale option is the **Karakoram Restaurant** ★ at the Crown Inn (9–10:30am, 1–3pm, and 6–10pm), which offers a wide range of well-presented local, Chinese, and Western dishes. Specialties not to be missed include "High Altitude Fish seasoned with Xinjiang Spices and cooked on Tashkurgan Stones" (¥168), "Spiced Horse Salami with Sesame Seeds" (¥38), and the huge grilled yak ribs (¥188). Western dishes include pizzas and pastas (¥45–¥98), and there are tasty desserts such as apple strudel (¥18). To stock up on snacks, try **Arman Supermarket** on the junction of Tashikuergan Lu and Hongqilapu Lu.

KHOTAN (HETIAN; 和田) ★★

Xinjiang, 520km (322 miles) SE of Kashgar, 1,509km (936 miles) SW of Ürümqi

Khotan was once a more important trading and religious center than Kashgar. From ancient times, jade was "fished" from the 24 rivers in the Khotan area, and "jade routes" to Mesopotamia and China flourished from the 3rd millennium B.C. onward. Passing through on his way to India in the 5th century, the Chinese Buddhist monk Faxian found a purely Buddhist population in the order of "several myriads." Returning to China after his adventures in India, Xuanzang found a thriving center: "the country produced rugs, fine felt, and silk of artistic texture, it also yielded black and white jade. The climate was genial, but there were whirlwinds and flying dust. The people were of gentle disposition, and had settled occupations. The nation esteemed music and the people were fond of dance and song; a few clothed themselves in woolens and furs, the majority wearing silk and calico. . . . The system of writing had been taken from that of India."

From 1901, Aurel Stein visited several sites around Khotan, concluding that the ancient capital was at **Yoktan (Yaotegan),** 9.7km (6 miles) to the west. He found Roman coins, and some delightful paintings and sculptures (ca. 2nd c.) showing Grecian influence. Protected from inundation by Han settlers until the arrival of the passenger rail line in 2011, Khotan remains a bustling commercial city, home to one of the liveliest **bazaars** in Xinjiang, and is a must for experiencing traditional Uighur culture and markets. *Note:* Turn to chapter 16 for Chinese translations of key locations.

Essentials

GETTING THERE Khotan's **airport** (✆ **0903/293-3200**), 10km (6¼ miles) west of downtown has four daily flights to Ürümqi. A taxi into the center of town should cost ¥20 to ¥30. The **Hotan Airport Booking Office** at Wulumuqi Nan Lu 14 (✆ **0903/251-8999**) is open from 9:30am to 2pm and 3.30 to 7.30pm.

The main **bus station** (✆ **0903/202-2688**) is on Taibei Xi Lu. Sleeper buses cross the Taklamakan Desert Highway to Ürümqi every couple of hours; afternoon services are more comfortable and cost more (1,509km/936 miles; 20–24 hr.; ¥256–¥348). There are also several daily buses to Korla (15 hr.; ¥78). A new road also cuts through the desert between Khotan and Aksu. Buses leave every 90 minutes and cost ¥125 to ¥157 for the 8-hour journey; some of these buses continue on to Kuqa (13 hr.; ¥159–¥177). Alternatively, you could buy a ticket to Luntai (874km/542 miles; 10 hr.; ¥160–¥178) from where there are buses for Kuqa (110km/68 miles; 2 hr.; ¥10) that leave when full. For Kashgar (520km/322 miles; 9 hr.) there are buses every couple of hours, both regular (¥67) and evening sleeper services (¥93). For destinations east, buses depart from the **east station** (**Dongjiao Keyun Zhan;** ✆ **0903/202-5487**) on Taibei Dong Lu. These buses stop at the oasis towns of Keriya (Yutian; 177km/110 miles; 3 hr.; ¥25), Niya (Minfeng; 294km/182 miles; 5 hr.; ¥55), and Charchan (Qiemo; 603km/374 miles; 8–10 hr.; ¥105–¥147).

GETTING AROUND **Taxis** are plentiful, but seldom use their meters; ¥5 is sufficient for most journeys within town. **Bus** fare is usually ¥1, paid to the conductor.

TOURS & GUIDES **Hetian CITS** is on the first floor of Tamubage Lu 23 (✆ **0903/251-6090**). It's open from 10am to 1:30pm and 3:30 to 7:30pm and can arrange guides (¥200–¥300 per day) and transport. A cheaper alternative is to make arrangements through friendly local Kurban Siraji (✆ **137/7929-1939;** treklab@gmail.com), who also works with CITS, but can be booked as a guide independently from ¥150 per day.

[FastFACTS] KHOTAN

Banks, Foreign Exchange & ATMs If you are continuing east along the southern Silk Route, change your money in Khotan, as there are no facilities before Golmud or Dunhuang. There are several branches of the **Bank of China** around Khotan, the most convenient of which is at Beijing Xi Lu 38. This branch accepts traveler's checks and credit cards and has an ATM. It's open weekdays in summer from 9:30am to 1:30pm and 4 to 8pm; weekdays in winter from 10am to 2pm and 3:30 to 7:30pm.

Internet Access Several Internet cafes are on Nawake Lu, including **Crazy Boy,** a little east of Gaoyang Kaorou restaurant. It's open 24 hours and charges ¥2 per hour.

Post Office On Beijing Xi Lu 1 (✆ **0903/202-1885**), a little west of the intersection with Wenhua Lu, the post office's narrow frontage belies its size. It's open in summer from 9:30am to 8pm and in winter from 10am to 7:30pm.

Visa Extensions The **PSB** at Beijing Xi Lu 92 (✆ **0903/202-3614**) offers one of the speediest visa extensions available. It's open weekdays from 9:30am to 1:30pm and 4 to 7:30pm and processing takes a day.

Exploring Khotan

Khotan Museum ★ Given the wealth of discoveries unearthed and taken from the Southern Silk Road by the likes of Hedin, Stein and von Le Coq, it's surprising that Khotan's Museum has much to offer, but the centerpiece of two Five Dynasties mummies, complete with hair and teeth, are worth a visit in their own right. Other notable exhibits include Buddhist frescoes from Keriya and Niya, reinforcing the regions' pre-Islamic religious history. Tiny camel figurines from the Han dynasty show the importance of these beasts of burden since the beginnings of the Silk Road, and of course, this being Khotan there's also plenty of jadework on display. Most exhibits are labeled in English. Allow 45 minutes.

Beijing Xi Lu. Free. No photos. Thurs–Tues 10am–1:30pm and 3:30–7pm.

Sunday Market, Xingqitian Dashichang ★★★ This is everything the Kashgar Market once was. You'll need an early start and an empty memory card to make the most of Khotan's lively bazaar, set in the heart of the Uighur part of town. The intersection between Gujiang Bei Lu and Jiamai Lu marks the center of the action, and you're unlikely to see a Han face as the streets fill with livestock and people throughout the day. Jewelers pore over gemstones, blacksmiths busy themselves shoeing horses and repairing farm tools, blanket makers beat cotton balls, rat-poison sellers proudly demonstrate the efficacy of their products—the sights and smells are overwhelming. Don't miss the **horse riding enclosure** toward the north side of the melee, where buyers test the roadworthiness of both beast and attached cart, with frequent spectacular tumbles. Head southeast from the bus station or simply follow the crowds.

Shopping

Khotan is famous for jade, silk, and carpets and you can visit workshops and factories to all three in and around town.

Jade Factory (Gongyi Meishu Youxian Gongsi) Khotan has long been China's source of jade (nephrite). The jade was first noticed by Zhang Qian, sent to Khotan on a reconnaissance expedition by Han Wudi, prior to the first successful Chinese invasion of the Western Regions. He believed women were adept in finding the gem, and they would dive for jade in the rivers around Khotan. Diving in the muddy and much diminished Khotan River now is not recommended, regardless of your gender. Those contemplating jade purchases should do their homework with a reputable jeweler before leaving home. While this place is reliable (if expensive), fake jade is one commodity Khotan never runs short of. The smallest pieces here start from a few hundred yuan, whilst there are exquisitely carved larger pieces costing tens of thousands. Visit the dusty workshop beside the shop, where artisans turn, carve, and polish the jade. The Jade Factory is open every day from 9:30am to 2pm and then 3:30 to 7:30pm, but note that you'll only see the artisans at work if you come during the week. Gujiang Bei Lu 1, 2F. ✆ **0903/203-5281.**

Khotan Old and New Carpet Store Directly below the Jade Factory, this tiny store in the Uighur part of town has a decent selection of carpets from the surrounding areas. While the shop carries just a few hard-to-find antique carpets, this is probably the best selection you're going to get for old carpets in Khotan, as most stores only sell new ones, in fairly tacky designs, to locals. If you're serious about making a purchase, call the owner, Abdujilil, and he'll come and pick you up. The shop is usually open 9am to 9pm. Gujiang Bei Lu 1-1. ✆ **0903/687-0430.**

Carpet Factory (Ditan Chang) In the 1980s, factory inspections were an unavoidable part of any trip to China. Fortunately, you can examine the workings of this factory without listening to a cadre reciting statistics. Workers sit outside the main carpet-making hall, their hands, feet, and hair stained red by henna dye. The gentle rattle of the looms and swoosh of the combs is almost drowned out by the banter of Uighur women. At the back is the inevitable shop, but much of the art of carpet weaving was lost during the Cultural Revolution, so you won't find anything to match the splendor of carpets in your average Uighur home. The factory is open Monday through Saturday from 9:30am to 1:30pm and 3:30 to 7:30pm. Nawake Jie 6. ✆ **0903/205-4553.** Take a cab (about ¥20) or bus no. 2 east along Beijing Lu to the terminus, then bus no. 5 heading south, again to the end of the line.

Silk and Mulberry Research Center (Si Sang Yanjiusuo) ★ Khotan is said to have broken the closely guarded Chinese silk monopoly in the 5th century. According to legend, a Chinese princess was instructed by the king to smuggle silk-moth eggs in her hairpiece, as frontier guards, however zealous, would never touch a lady's hair.

The front building houses offices, and possibly someone willing to show you around, but the surest way to see the center is to arrange a tour through CITS, who will also show you "their" traditional silk makers. You can view the entire mysterious process, from sorting and boiling the cocoons, to reeling off the thread—typically 900m (2,950 ft.) long—through to the final weaving into the wavelike ikat patterns characteristic of Khotan silk. While the primitive (and deafening) technology makes for a good tour, business is not good. A sign near the gate opens with a statement of the company's bold production targets, and ends with the modest objective, DON'T LOSE MONEY *(bu kui)*. You'll find few tasteful products in the shop; buy your silk in a large city. This difference in tastes is nothing new. Chinese silk patterns were never in vogue among the Romans, who usually imported silk thread—Plinius recorded that Chinese cloth would be unraveled and rewoven. Hemo Lu 107. Bus: 1 from north of the main roundabout on Hetian Lu to the terminus, then walk back about 225m (750 ft.).

Where to Stay

Khotan, surprisingly enough, has a decent selection of midrange options.

Hetian Binguan (Hotan Hotel) If you want a retreat from the bustle of central Khotan, this spacious hotel, set amid rose gardens and grapevine-trellised walkways

A REMOTE manchu outpost: YINING (GULJA; 伊宁)

Yining, 692km (429 miles) west of Ürümqi, has always been a tenuous possession of the Chinese empire, surrounded by the richest farmland in central Asia, and closer to Moscow than Beijing. Just how tenuous was illustrated in 1997, when peaceful anti-colonization protests were met with an armed military response leaving countless dead and injured. Today, surrounded by high peaks and blessed with a mild climate and hearty cuisine, Yining feels like a sleepy agricultural settlement, but talk behind closed doors soon brings to light the true feelings of the Kazaks, Uighurs and Uzbeks who still live in this now predominantly Han Chinese city.

The colonization of Xinjiang began with the fierce ancestors of the current residents of **Qapqal Xibo Autonomous County (Chab u Cha'er Xian). Qapqal,** 25km (16 miles) west of Yining. In 1764, 1,000 Xibo soldiers (followed "secretly" by 4,000 family members) were dispatched from Manchuria by the Qianlong emperor, with the promise that they would be allowed to return after 50 years. After putting the natives to the sword and hunting the region's animals to near extinction, the Xibo accepted there was no prospect of a return home, settled down, and took to farming.

While the **Manchu language** died out in northeast China, this outpost maintained their written and spoken language, and traditions such as the **hanging family tree *(jiapu).*** Most houses have one, with coins to represent the family coming into money, clubs and arrows the birth of a boy, and ribbons and boots the birth of a girl. Take a round trip taxi for ¥100 (including waiting time), or catch a bus from outside the Yining bus station to Cha Xian (30 min.; ¥5) and take a three-wheeler (¥5) onward to **Jingyuan Si** (admission ¥30; daily 10am–7:30pm). The Lamaist complex itself is nothing out of the ordinary, but the small museum near the entrance affords the opportunity to see Manchu calligraphy scrolls, and the exhibition of **Xibo** culture, which features clothing, farm tools and weaponry, is fascinating. After a visit, wander among the fields of sunflowers and wheat, dotted with earthen courtyard houses with pastel-blue doors.

In Yining itself it's worth stopping at the daily **Uighur Bazaar** on Xinhua Dong Lu (just south of Renmin Square), then wandering through the grand Islamic arches into the old part of town to check out the **Hui** and **Uzbek mosques,** and the **beautiful Uzbek houses** west of here. Predominantly one-story, these old residences feature carved wooden lintels, with doors and window frames painted in a pleasing turquoise.

Getting There The **airport** is connected to town by taxi (¥20–¥30) and shuttle bus (¥3). **CAAC** (✆ **0999/809-5777;** daily 10am–7:30pm) is in the foyer of the **Yilite Dajiudian,** Shengli Jie 98. Yining has daily flights connecting with Ürümqi. The **train station** in the northwest of town has daily services to Ürümqi, of which the K9790 (11 hr.) is

is a good option. While the rooms are blandly functional, bathrooms are a little shabby, and service is unremarkable, outside in the grounds, the Islamic architecture lends the hotel a decidedly central Asian feel. Avoid the ground floor rooms with windows that look out onto a brick wall.

the best option. The **bus terminal** on Jiefang Lu in the northwest of town (✆ **0999/813-9263**) has hourly connections with Ürümqi (12 hr.; ¥150–¥160). Buses for the daily 8am bus for Almaty (10 hr.; ¥150) leave from the Taoyuan Dajiudian in the south of town. There are abundant **taxis,** which charge ¥5 for 2km (1¼ miles), then ¥1.30 per kilometer thereafter; add ¥.20 from midnight to 5am. **Buses** charge ¥1, dropped in a box when you board.

Where to Stay & Eat Yili Binguan, Yingbin Lu 8 (✆ **0999/802-3799;** fax 0999/802-4964), is Yining's oldest hotel, set in the extensive (30,000-sq.-m/322,917-sq.-ft.) grounds of the former **Soviet consulate,** which are particularly charming in autumn. There's a huge array of rooms on offer, from basic, but overpriced twins (¥388) in buildings 1 to 3, through to plusher accommodations on the four-star floors of buildings 3 and 4, but service is frosty throughout. Yining's swankiest new hotel, the four-star **Yili Xinjiang Dajiudian** (✆ **0999/802-6666;** fax 0999/802-5678; ¥680, discountable to ¥288), is unmissable, dominating the corner of Jiefang and Stalin Lu, but inside rooms are already starting to show their age. For a friendlier experience and a better location, try rooms on the renovated 7th and 8th floors of the **Yilite Dajiudian,** Shengli Jie 98 (✆ **0999/782-9666;** fax 0999/782-9888). The hotel is situated on the northeast corner of the Peoples' Square, the scene of the 1997 anti-government riots. Cheaper rooms are available on other floors (¥118–¥168).

For dining, in the evenings, food night-markets set up around town—the one next to Renmin Square is easy to find. Nearby, **Youli Gongshi Shan** (✆ **0999/803-0005**) has a great location in a Chinese–style building with a balcony looking out over the square, and serves the usual range of Uighur dishes, plus dumplings (¥1 each), along with a vast selection of teas. For something Western, **Eversun Café** has a second-floor branch on Jiefang Lu, near the junction with Feijichang Lu. The vast menu has everything from sashimi to steaks (both ¥58), the latter of which are surprisingly good. Out of town, **Uyhur Taamuri** (✆ **0999/832-3580**) is an atmospheric spot, set in the middle of apple orchards and just a few minutes' walk down to the river. Wusu beer (¥4) is served to wash down the pilaf (¥20–¥30), kabobs (¥2) and huge plates of *naren* (¥50). This is a popular spot for wedding parties, so if you're lucky you might see some traditional Uighur or Kazak dancing in the raised rotunda. To get here turn left down the final road before the Yili Bridge south of town and continue for 455m/1,500 ft. The entrance is signed off the road on the right and then it's a couple of hundred meters through the orchard to the restaurant. Back down at the old river bridge, there are a host of small open-air canteens, some of which have river views. You can stock up on snacks at the **supermarket** across from the Yili Xinjiang Binguan.

Wulumuqi Lu 10. ✆ **0903/251-3563.** Fax 0903/251-3570. 70 units. ¥360 standard room; from ¥688 suite. 50% standard discount. No credit cards. **Amenities:** Restaurant. *In room:* A/C, TV, Internet (¥10 per day).

Wenzhou Dajiudian (Wenzhou Hotel) ★ Recent renovations and an extension have once again made this one of the best places to stay in town. The prime location on Beijing Xi Lu is close to lively Tuanjie Square and plenty of restaurants and the old town are also within walking distance. Rooms are clean and bright with a beige and gaudy white and gold color scheme, and rooms on higher floors enjoy views out over the city. Bathrooms are modern and in good order.

Beijing Xi Lu 49. ✆ **0903/202-6666.** 156 units. ¥228 standard room; ¥418 suite. No credit cards. **Amenities:** Restaurant; concierge. *In room:* A/C, TV, Internet, water cooler.

Zhejiang Dajiudian (Zhejiang Hotel) ★ Brought to you by coastal Chinese investors this hotel, right next to Tuanjie Square, has sleek, modern and well-appointed rooms. Reception is friendly, and the hotel remains popular, making booking ahead advisable. My only criticism would be that while the bathrooms are sparkling clean, the plumbing is starting to show its age and showers are weaker than you might hope.

Beijing Xi Lu 75. ✆ **0903/202-9999.** Fax 0903/203-6688. 74 units. ¥418 standard room; ¥458 suite. Up to 50% discount. No credit cards. **Amenities:** Restaurant; concierge; conference rooms. *In room:* A/C, TV, fridge, Internet (¥10 per day), minibar.

Where to Eat

Khotan has plenty of Uighur options, but if you feel in need of some Western fare, there's a bakery next to the Zhejiang Hotel on Beijing Xi Lu or unique fast-food dining at **Weilimai Burger** (**Weilimai Hanbao;** 10am–midnight) on the northeast corner of Tuanjie Square. From the outside this fast-food joint looks like any other, but Weilimai offers the opportunity to enjoy a decidedly mediocre burger and better fries with a beer in its unexpectedly expansive upstairs dining room surrounded by booths full of young couples, while families take in the views over the square to the Mao statue. Just across Beijing Xi Lu from the Zhejiang Hotel, **Meile Pizza** (11am–10:30pm), has friendly staff and passable pizzas (¥39–¥46) and tasty soups (¥15).

Gaoyang Kaorou Kuaicandian ★ UIGHUR The prize for Xinjiang's best *samsa*—a package of lamb and spices baked in pastry—easily goes to this delightful restaurant, distinguished by its twin chimneys and metal blue awning. You can join the ever-present line outside for takeout, or head into the atmospheric smoky, gold-wallpapered interior. The kabobs and nan are also excellent and are well followed by the slightly sweet medicinal tea that is common to many restaurants—the tea leaves *(jiankang cha)* can be purchased from the **Uighur Hospital,** Jiamai Lu 2.

Nawake Lu 317. ✆ **138/0998-0965.** Meal for 2 less than ¥50. No credit cards. 8am–2am.

Marco Dream Café (Make Yizhang) MALAYSIAN Run by a friendly Malaysian couple, this eclectic little cafe is Khotan's only backpacker cafe per se, although most of the year the clientele is local. Dishes range from beef rendang to tropical chicken, and there's a smattering of Western dishes including shepherd's pie and moussaka (both ¥30), although these need to be ordered at least 2 hours in advance. It's also worth asking about the daily specials, and maybe taking a cupcake with you for later.

Minjie Jie, Youyi Lu 57. ✆ **0903/202-7515.** Mains from ¥15. No credit cards. Tues–Sun 1:30–10:30pm.

Marwa (Maerwa Canting) ★ UIGHUR The best of Khotan's numerous upscale Uighur restaurants, Marwa offers a taste of local food in a vaulted wooden dining hall, often heaving with locals. The *naren* is filling and tasty, as is the *laghman*, and the delicious *yangrou chuan* deserves a special mention. Wash it all down with plenty of local tea and fresh juice.

Urumqi Nan Lu, near the Hotan Airport Booking Office. ✆ **0903/686-0778.** Meal for 2 ¥50–¥100. No credit cards. Daily 9:30am–midnight.

EASTERN CENTRAL CHINA

by Candice Lee & Tini Tran

8

If Shanxi Province is the cradle of Chinese civilization, then the stretch of eastern central China between the Yellow River (Huang He) and the Yangzi River (Chang Jiang)—an area covering the provinces of Henan, Shandong, Jiangsu, and Anhui—can be seen as the cradle in which Chinese culture subsequently developed and flourished. Bounded by the Yellow Sea and the East China Sea on the east, and buffered from ethnic minority influences from the north, west, and south, this swath of China is a region that, except for some Western influence late in China's history, has remained unapologetically and overwhelmingly Han Chinese in character.

Early Chinese civilization may have developed around the Yellow River in Henan Province with the Shang dynasty (1700–1100 B.C.), but Chinese culture as it is widely perceived today really started to take shape only some 600 years later with the birth of the most influential figure in Chinese history, Confucius, in Qufu in Shandong Province. By the time of the "golden age" of the Han dynasty (206 B.C.–A.D. 220), Confucianism, that quintessentially Chinese philosophical tradition, had become the official state philosophy, and would be put to the test in the subsequent 2,000 years of dynastic changes. Arguably, no region or place in China has seen the rise and fall of more dynasties than this eastern central section of the country, with the ancient capitals of Luoyang (capital of nine dynasties), Kaifeng (six dynasties), and Nanjing (eight dynasties) serving as China's seat of power 23 times. Today, though none of these former capitals has retained much of their previous glory, all contain vestiges of a Chinese imperial past, and are worth visiting. Chinese history buffs may be interested as well in some lesser-known but intriguing finds such as the miniature terra-cotta army in Xuzhou, and the horse and chariot funeral pits in Zibo.

The influence of that other indigenous Chinese religious-philosophical tradition, Daoism, is also very strong in this region, which is home to two of Daoism's sacred mountains: **Tai Shan,** the most climbed mountain in China, and **Song Shan,** the central Daoist mountain. Though not indigenous to China, Buddhism's influence on Chinese

Eastern Central China

culture has also been profound. Some of China's finest Buddhist art and sculpture can be seen at the magnificent **Longmen Grottoes (Longmen Shiku)** in Luoyang.

Historically, this region has also been the cultural bridge between the political center of gravity mostly in the north and the economic center in the south, especially around the fertile lower deltas of the Yangzi River. The physical link was the great Chinese engineering feat of the **Grand Canal,** built between the Sui dynasty (581–618) and the Yuan dynasty (1206–1368) to link the Yangzi and Yellow rivers. Although much of the canal is no longer navigable, it gave rise in its heyday to many flourishing river towns, including Suzhou, Zhou Zhuang, and the underrated but delightful **Yangzhou,** the economic and cultural capital of southern China during the Sui and Tang dynasties. The gardens that were built here by merchants and retired officials, with rocks hauled up from nearby **Tai Hu (Lake Tai),** have created in many a mind's eye the quintessential Chinese garden. But it is at nearby **Huang**

Shan (Yellow Mountain) that you find the ultimate Chinese landscape, as wispy clouds hover over a lone pine tree on a distant mountaintop.

Today, this eastern central region of China continues to function as a modern microcosm. Traveling in this area, you will encounter two of China's richest provinces (Shandong and Jiangsu) bordering one of its poorest (Anhui). You will see some of China's oldest temples standing next to some of its newest skyscrapers. The region sees hot, humid summers, while winters can be bone-chillingly cold; spring and fall are the best times to visit. ***Note:*** Unless otherwise noted, hours listed for attractions and restaurants are daily.

ZHENGZHOU 郑州

Henan Province, 689km (413 miles) SW of Beijing, 998km (599 miles) NW of Shanghai

Zhengzhou, a sprawling industrial city of six million and a major railway stop on the Beijing-Guangzhou rail lines, was once a Shang dynasty (1700–1100 B.C.) capital, though few traces of its 3,000-year history remain. Many travelers simply overnight here en route to Kaifeng and Luoyang, but a few lesser known but intriguing sights are in the surrounding area. Zhengzhou's proximity to the Yellow River (30km/18 miles to the north) also makes it a convenient base from which to explore the river.

Essentials

GETTING THERE Zhengzhou is connected by **air** to many major Chinese cities, including Beijing (1 hr. 30 min.), Guangzhou (2 hr. 10 min.), Hong Kong (2 hr. 30 min.), and Shanghai (1 hr. 20 min.). Tickets can be purchased at the **CAAC office** at Airport Hotel (Minhang Dajiudian) Jinshui Lu 3 (© **0371/6599-1111**). The airport is about 35km (21 miles) southeast of the city. Sofitel and Crowne Plaza have booths at the airport and can arrange transportation into the city if you contact them ahead of time. **Taxis** make the run for around ¥100. **CAAC airport shuttles** (40 min.; ¥16; 6am–8pm) depart every hour for the airport from the Airport Hotel (Minhang Dajiudian; © **0371/6578-1111,** ext. 2350) and also meet incoming flights.

Trains run from Zhengzhou's **railway station** (© **0371/6835-6666**) to Luoyang (2 hr.), Kaifeng (1 hr.), Xi'an (10 hr.), Beijing (12 hr., or 5 hr. on the D-series **express trains** five times daily), Shanghai (14 hr., or 7 hr. on twice-daily D-series trains), Guangzhou (36 hr.), and a host of other cities in between.

From the **long-distance bus station** (© **0371/6696-3818** or 0371/6696-6107) opposite the railway station, Iveco buses depart for Luoyang (every 30 min. 7:30am–7pm, public buses depart every 25–45 min. 6:50am–6:30pm; 2–2 hr. 30 min.; ¥40), Dengfeng (every 30 min. 6am–7:40pm; 30 min.; ¥26), and Gongyi (every 30 min. 6:40am–6:30pm; 1 hr. 30 min.; ¥24). Buses to Kaifeng (every 20 min. 7:30am–7pm; 1 hr.; ¥7) leave from the **East Bus Station (Keyun Dong Zhan)** on Jichang Lu; it will cut down your travel time significantly. If you're traveling in the summer, make sure to ask if your bus has air-conditioning (*you mei you kongtiao?*). For guaranteed air-conditioning, a private bus service, **Henan Yu An Kuaiyun** (© **0371/6638-3055**), runs air-conditioned buses to Luoyang (every 30 min. 7am–7pm; 2 hr. 30 min.; ¥40), Beijing (9:30pm; 9 hr.; ¥180).

Zhengzhou 郑州

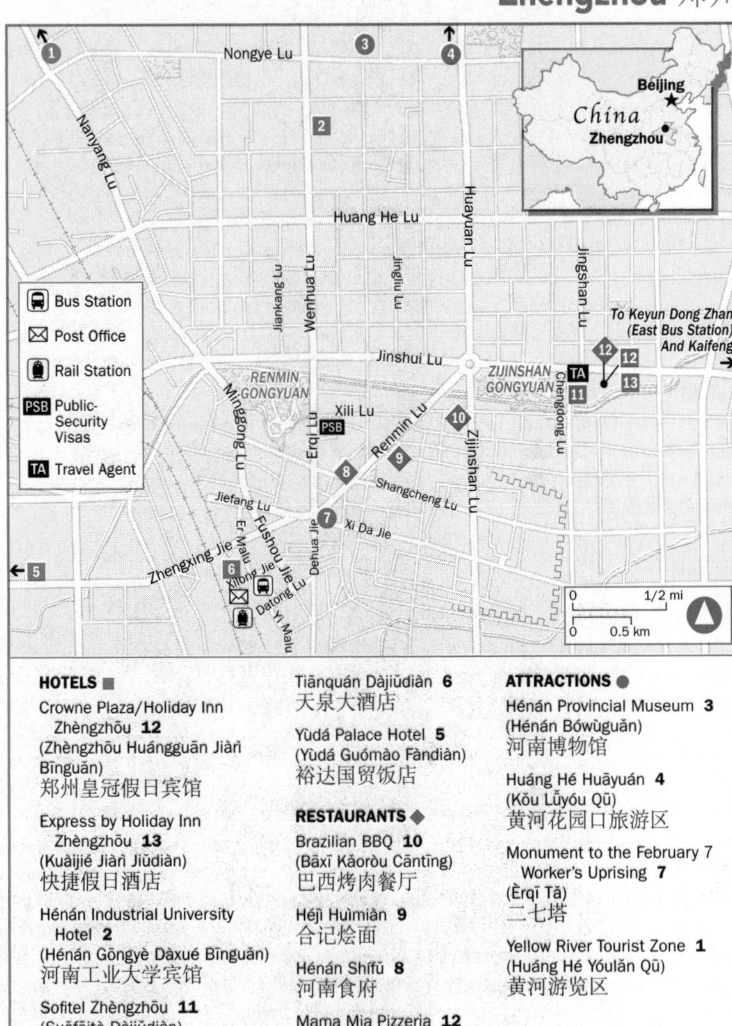

GETTING AROUND **Taxis** charge ¥6 for 2km (1¼ miles), then ¥1.50 per additional kilometer until 12km (7½ miles), after which the price rises to ¥2.25 per kilometer. From 11pm to 5am, prices rise to ¥8 per 2km (1¼ miles). City **buses** cost ¥1 flat fare. Bus no. 26 runs from the railway station to Jinshui Lu via Renmin Lu, while bus no. 16 runs from Erma Lu to the Yellow River.

[Fast FACTS] ZHENGZHOU

Banks, Foreign Exchange & ATMs A convenient **Bank of China** branch (✆ **0371/6597-7640;** Mon–Fri 9am–noon and 1–5pm) is at Jinshui Lu 266. Counters 3 and 4 are for foreign exchange. This location also has an ATM.

Internet Access If you have your own computer, most hotels have in-room high-speed Internet access. Free Wi-Fi is available in the public areas of the Sofitel and the Crowne Plaza. For those without computers, Crowne Plaza's business center charges ¥1 per minute (6am–11pm).

Post Office The post office (8am–6:30pm) is just south of the railway station.

Visa Extensions The **Gonganju (PSB)** is located at Erqi Lu 70 (✆ **0371**/6962-0359; Mon–Fri 8:30am–noon and 3–6:30pm). Allow 5 business days, though emergency 3-day visas can also be processed.

Exploring Zhengzhou

The 11-story twin-tower pagoda in the heart of town is the **Erqi Ta (Monument to the February 7 Workers' Uprising),** which commemorates the February 7, 1923 strike on the Beijing-Hankou rail line against the warlord authorities. The workers were fighting for their rights, but the uprising was bloodily suppressed.

Henan Bowuguan (Henan Provincial Museum) ★★ Located in the northern part of town, this marvelous museum—the fourth largest in China, it claims—is well worth a couple of hours of your time. Housed in a pyramid-shaped structure, it has a strong collection of prehistoric and early Chinese artifacts such as oracle bones, tools, and pottery from the Yangshao culture, the Longshan culture, and the early Xia, Shang, and Zhou dynasties, as well as bronzes, jades, and Han dynasty funeral objects. Exhibits are well documented in English, and the English-language audio tour—¥30 with a deposit of either ¥400 or your passport—is quite helpful. English-speaking museum guides are available for ¥100.

Nongye Lu 8. ✆ **0371/6351-1237.** Free admission. Tues–Sun 9am–4:30pm. Bus: no. 30, K39, or 61.

Huang He (Yellow River) ★ Prone to flooding because of silt deposits in its upper reaches, the mighty Yellow River (Huang He) has long been known as "China's Sorrow," having wreaked untold damage and taken countless lives through the ages. Here the river can be visited from two different locales. The first is at **Huang He Youlan Qu (Yellow River Tourist Zone),** a large park on the river's southern bank. You can take the hydrofoil on a 40-minute round-trip tour for ¥80 per person, which includes a stop at a sandy islet in the middle of the river.

About 15km (9 miles) east of the Yellow River Tourist Zone, the **Huang He Huayuan Kou Luyou Qu** was where Chiang Kai-shek ordered his army to blow up the dikes in order to halt the advance of the Japanese troops in 1938. The tactic worked temporarily, but in the process it flooded 44 counties, killed almost a million people, and left another 12 million homeless and destitute. Today, stone tablets in this tourist park commemorate the event, as does a four-character inscription, ZHI LI HUANG HE, on the embankment by Mao Zedong, meaning "Control the Yellow River."

Yellow River Tourist Zone. ✆ **0371/6379-9500.** Admission ¥60. 8am–8pm. Bus: no. 16 (¥5) from corner of Erma Lu and Zhengxing Jie to its terminus. Huayuan Kou Tourist Region of the Yellow River: ✆ **0371/6563-2119.** Admission ¥20. 8am–6:30pm. Bus: no. 520 (¥1.50) from railway station; get off at Jin Shui Cun, then take a motorcycle taxi.

Where to Stay

EXPENSIVE

Crowne Plaza/Holiday Inn Zhengzhou (Zhengzhou Huangguan Jiari Binguan) ★ Situated in the northeastern part of town, this hotel chain is in the rather unusual position of having the five-star **Crowne Plaza** and the four-star **Holiday Inn** right next to each other and sharing many of the same facilities and management. The three-star **Express by Holiday Inn Zhengzhou** (see listing below), converted from the former International Hotel, joined the party in 2005 (but does not share in the amenities). The Crowne Plaza's copious use of marble and gold trim makes it feel like you're walking through a cheesy Roman movie set. But the rooms are a good size, beds are comfortable, and bathrooms are stocked with good amenities. Service is warm and helpful, and the breakfast buffet is tops. Rooms at the Holiday Inn, geared more toward the business traveler looking for a less flashy, quieter environment, are smaller but were recently renovated and are very comfortable with clean and modern bathrooms. It shares the amenities of the Crowne Plaza, but you have to walk across a parking lot to get to them.

Jinshui Lu 115. www.ichotelsgroup.com. ✆ **0371/6595-0055.** Fax 0371/6599-0770. Crowne Plaza 222 units; Holiday Inn 230 units. Crowne Plaza: ¥1,188 standard room; ¥4,030 suite. Holiday Inn: ¥698 standard room; ¥2,750 suite. 35%–40% discounts possible. 15% surcharge included, 5% council tax. AE, DC, MC, V. **Amenities:** 5 restaurants; bar; lounge; concierge; driving range; executive rooms; forex; small health club; small indoor pool; room service; sauna; smoke-free rooms; spa. *In room:* A/C, TV, hair dryer, Internet, minibar.

Sofitel Zhengzhou (Suofeite Dajiudian) ★★ This hotel just underwent a massive face lift and is hands down the most luxurious, contemporary place to stay in Zhengzhou. The public spaces have all been redone with new modern decor such as carpets with geometric patterns, plush chairs in purple and dark turquoise, and a funky tiered bar in the lounge area. The old desks and chipped marble counters in the bathrooms have been replaced and new rooms are now sleeker and more stylish than those at their neighbor's, the Crowne Plaza. Service is professional and impeccable; I mentioned that I had a cold and a pot of hot Coke and ginger—a cold remedy the Chinese swear by—was sent to my room. Business travelers will like the e-business rooms, which come with a fax machine, a plasma TV hooked up to a computer and wireless keyboard, and a desk stocked with tape, a stapler, and other stationery items.

Chengdong Lu 289. www.sofitel.com. ✆ **0371/6595-0088.** Fax 0371/6595-0080. 240 units. ¥2,700 standard room; from ¥4, 298 suite. 30%–60% discounts possible. 15% surcharge, 5% council tax. AE, DC, MC, V. **Amenities:** 2 restaurants; 2 bars; lounge; concierge; executive rooms; forex; small health club and spa; small indoor pool; room service; sauna; smoke-free rooms. *In room:* A/C, TV, hair dryer, Internet, minibar, scale.

Yuda Guomao Fandian (Yuda Palace Hotel) ★★ This handsome, modern, 45-story building is Zhengzhou's grandest and most opulent hotel, but its location in the western part of town makes it inconvenient for independent travelers. Rooms are enormous—the largest in the city—comfortable, and gorgeously furnished with classic Italian furniture and a high-tech Bose surround-sound audio system. The spacious all-marble bathrooms come with separate tub and shower, except for corner rooms.

Zhongyuan Zhong Lu 220. www.yudapalacehotel.com.cn. ✆ **0371/6743-8888.** Fax 0371/6742-2539. 365 units. ¥1,826 standard room; ¥2,401 suite. 30%–40% discounts possible. 15% surcharge. AE, DC, MC, V. **Amenities:** 5 restaurants; bar; lounge; concierge; disco; executive rooms; forex;

health club; indoor pool; room service; sauna; smoke-free rooms. *In room:* A/C, TV, hair dryer, Internet, minibar, scale.

MODERATE

Express by Holiday Inn Zhengzhou (Kuaijie Jiari Jiudian) ★ If you'd like to stay at an internationally managed hotel but balk at the prices, this new property is a good option. While it has a slightly institutional feel (note the staff uniforms, for example—employees look like fitness coaches), this hotel will suit any international traveler fine, if you don't require too many frills. The bathrooms are a bit small and without bathtub, but rooms are bright, stylish for the price, and of a good size to boot.

Jinshui Lu 114. www.ichotelsgroup.com. ✆ **0371/6595-6600.** Fax 0371/6595-1526. 269 units. ¥988 standard room; ¥1,288 suite. 40% discounts possible. AE, DC, MC, V. **Amenities:** Restaurant. *In room:* A/C, TV, hair dryer, Internet.

Tianquan Dajiudian Conveniently located next to the railway station, this three-star hotel offers relatively clean accommodations at reasonable prices. Guest rooms are a little dark, with forgettable furnishings, but are otherwise comfortable. Bathrooms are a bit old, but clean. Be sure to ask for a room in the back, as the honking taxis in the front of the square can be a rude surprise at 3am. The staff tries to be helpful.

Xi Datong Lu 1. ✆ **0371/6698-6888.** Fax 0371/6699-1814. 214 units. ¥388–¥588 standard room; from ¥1,198 suite. Rates include Chinese breakfast. 20%–40% discounts possible. MC, V. **Amenities:** Restaurant; bar; exercise room; nightclub; room service. *In room:* A/C, TV.

INEXPENSIVE

Henan Gongye Daxue Binguan (Henan Industrial University Hotel) Located just opposite the university's campus gates in the northeastern part of town, not far from the Henan Provincial Museum, this basic guesthouse is one of the best budget choices in town. Rooms are a little musty but well kept and the bathrooms are clean and outfitted with new fixtures. Little English is spoken at the front desk, but the receptionist says a staff member is usually on duty to help with translations.

Wenhua Lu 48. ✆ **0371/6388-7704.** 86 units. ¥248 standard room. No credit cards. *In room:* A/C, TV.

Where to Eat

EXPENSIVE

Mama Mia Pizzeria (Mama Miya Bisa) ★ CONTINENTAL/WESTERN This low-key restaurant offers many of the comfort foods of home. The ambience is casual and unpretentious, with low lighting and checkered tablecloths. Pizzas and pastas are popular here; the spaghetti carbonara is pretty good. Other favorites include the U.S. Angus T-bone steak and the grilled salmon. Service is attentive.

In the Crowne Plaza Hotel, Jinshui Lu 115. ✆ **0371/6595-0055.** Main courses ¥100–¥200. AE, DC, MC, V. 11:30am–2pm and 5:30–10pm.

MODERATE

Baxi Kaorou Canting (Brazilian BBQ) BRAZILIAN There's nothing really Brazilian about this buffet restaurant, but the atmosphere makes for a fun night. Servers wearing cowboy hats walk around tables carrying metal rods laden with roasted meat that is then doled out onto your plate. The roast duck is excellent, and the roasted lamb pieces pretty much taste like the ones at the local Xinjiang restaurant. The buffet selection is all Chinese food, but mostly safe stuff like ginger pork, sautéed broccoli, fried rice, and a rather strange, ketchuplike pasta. It's a decent place to come for something in between hotel dining and hole-in-the-wall Chinese restaurant.

Zijing Shan Lu 6. ✆ **0371/6623-9728.** Buffet ¥38–¥48 per person. No credit cards. 11:30am–2:30pm and 6:30–9:30pm.

Henan Shifu ★★ HENAN Located in a recessed courtyard off Renmin Lu in the center of town, this is one of Zhengzhou's more popular and long-standing restaurants. The decor here is traditional Chinese and there's a festive atmosphere during peak dining hours. The food is uniformly excellent and intriguing, especially the *xiangma shaobing jia niurou* (also known as Zhengzhou's "hamburger"); it consists of marinated cold beef sandwiched in fried sesame bread—a subtle but sublime mix of cold and hot, savory and sweet. Other noteworthy dishes include *ba sushijin,* a vegetarian dish of mushrooms, seasonal greens, and bamboo shoots; and *guotie doufu,* a tofu casserole. Service is efficient and friendly but the staff doesn't speak English, nor is there an English-language menu.

Renmin Lu 25. ✆ **0371/6622-2108.** Meal for 2 ¥60–¥200. 10am–2pm and 5–9pm.

INEXPENSIVE

Heji Huimian NOODLES The specialty at this always crowded halal restaurant in the center of town is the *teyouhuimian* (house specialty noodles), which consists of fresh coarse noodles served with a variety of mushrooms and small chunks of lamb in broth. Chilies, cilantro, and vinegar can be added at the table to taste. The first floor offers no-frills fast-food dining: Order your noodles at the counter by simply asking for a small bowl *(xiao wan)* for ¥7.50 or a large bowl *(da wan)* for ¥8; then grab a table and hand your ticket to the waitress. You'll be served within minutes. The second and third floors offer a la carte dining in a more pleasant, well-lit environment, but menus are in Chinese only.

Renmin Lu 3. ✆ **0371/6622-8026.** Meal for 2 ¥25–¥60. No credit cards. 1st floor: 9am–10pm; 2nd and 3rd floors: 10:30am–10pm.

Zhengzhou After Dark

Target Pub (Mubiao Jiuba), at the south end of Jing Liu Lu (✆ **0138/038-57056**), is a cool place for those in the know. You can actually have a conversation here or simply sit at the bar and let Lao Wang regale you with tales of off-roading in Lhasa, Mongolia, and the Gobi Desert.

DENGFENG 登封 & SONG SHAN 嵩山

Henan Province, 63km (40 miles) SW of Zhengzhou, 87km (53 miles) SE of Luoyang

Located south of the Yellow River in northwest Henan Province, Song Shan is the central mountain of the five holy Daoist mountains. Today, it's better known as the home of the Shaolin Temple (Shaolin Si), birthplace of the eponymous brand of kung-fu martial art (Shaolin *gongfu*) that has long been popular in Asia but has only in recent years become increasingly known to the Western world. The main town serving Song Shan is Dengfeng (meaning "Ascending to Bestow Honor"), named by the Tang dynasty empress Wu Zetian who preferred Song Shan to Tai Shan (Mount Tai) in Shandong Province, traditionally the favorite mountain of most emperors.

Song Shan can be visited in conjunction with Luoyang, or as a day trip from Zhengzhou. ***Note:*** For Chinese translations of selected establishments in this section, turn to chapter 16.

Essentials

GETTING THERE The nearest **airport and rail connections** are in Zhengzhou, but air tickets can be bought from an English-speaking agent at **CITS** at the Guolu Dalou on Beihuan Lu Xiduan (✆ **0371/6288-3442**). *Luyou che* (tour buses) connect Zhengzhou directly to Shaolin Si (Shaolin Temple). Unfortunately, you waste a lot of time waiting around because buses don't leave until they're full, there's a 30-minute stop at an uninteresting temple in Dengfeng, and another stop at a random Chinese restaurant right before the mountain (everyone on my bus put up a protest and we were able to boycott the restaurant stop). What should have been a 1½-hour trip can quickly turn into 2 or 2½ hours. You're better off taking the 30-minute bus from Zhengzhou for ¥21 to Dengfeng and grabbing a 20-minute, ¥3 **minibus** ride to Shaolin Si (Shaolin Temple). Minibuses also connect Dengfeng to Luoyang (every hour 8am–noon and 2–6pm; 1 hr. 30 min.; ¥20) and Gongyi (7am–6pm; 1 hr.). In Dengfeng, all minibuses depart from the ramshackle **West Bus Station** (**Xi Kechezhan;** ✆ **0371/6287-2049**) on Zhongyue Dajie just west of Songyang Zhong Jie. Buy your tickets on the bus. A **taxi** from Zhengzhou to Dengfeng will cost about ¥400, subject to negotiation.

GETTING AROUND The town of Dengfeng is small enough to **walk** or traverse by **bus** (¥1). Bus no. 2 runs from the Songyang Academy (Songyang Shuyuan) through town to the Zhongyue Miao (temple). Bus no. 1 connects the Tianzhong Hotel with the West Bus Station.

[FastFACTS] DENGFENG

Banks, Foreign Exchange & ATMs The **Bank of China** (✆ **0371/6287-5633**; Mon–Fri 9am–noon and 2–5pm) is at Shaolin Dadao 186. An ATM is on the premises.

Post Office The main post office (✆ **0371/6287-2969;** 8am–6pm) is at Song Shan Lu 358 (corner of Aimin Lu).

Exploring the Central Mountain

Song Shan is made up of two mountain ranges, each with 36 peaks and dotted throughout with temples and pagodas. The larger range to the east is known as **Taishi Shan,** and the lesser range to the west is **Shaoshi Shan.**

TREKKING Ascending the **eastern** or greater range **(Taishi Shan)** of Song Shan is more challenging as there are no cable cars to bail out the weary. The trail typically starts behind the Songyang Academy (Songyang Shuyuan). Stone steps lead all the way up to the 1,470m-high (4,900-ft.) **Junji Feng** where, unlike at China's other sacred mountains, there is no temple or building at the summit, just patches of grass and all of Song Shan below you. Allow 4 hours to reach the top. A ¥100 entrance fee gets you into the Taishi Shan Scenic Area and is required to go up the road to the **Songyue Temple Pagoda.** You can use the same ticket to get into Shaolin Monastery.

Climbing the **western** or lesser range **(Shaoshi Shan)** is made easier by three cable cars. Just west of Tai Lin (Forest of Stupas) is the **Shaolin Suodao** (¥30), which runs up the northern side of the mountain and has back views of the monastery and the forest. A better option, the **Songyang Suodao,** is up the road another 150m (492 ft.). This pleasant ¥30, 20-minute ride on a chairlift runs less than halfway up the mountain. The ride (or hike) back down affords some marvelous views of the Shaolin Monastery and the Forest of Stupas nestled in the foothills. The **Song Shan Shaolin Suodao** is another 300m (984 ft.) from the lower terminus of the first gondola, and is a ¥50 one-way (¥60 round-trip), 40-minute cable-car ride that goes past Ladder (Tizi) Gully to just below the summit. From here, trails lead to the **Song Shan Diaoqiao,** a suspension bridge stretched over a deep ravine of tall bald rocks. You can climb back down either the northern side of Shaoshi Shan underneath the cable cars, or the sheer southern face lined with steep narrow trails. At the parking lot below Sanhuang Xinggong (Sanhuang Palace), you can hire a taxi back to Dengfeng. For the relatively fit, climbing Shaoshi Shan takes 5 to 6 hours round-trip.

SHAOSHI SHAN 少室山

Shaolin Si (Shaolin Monastery) ★ Most visitors these days come to Song Shan not for the mountain climbing but for this famous monastery, better known for its martial arts than for its religious affiliations. Today's Shaolin, more loud marketplace than quiet monastery, is overrun with vendors, tourists (up to 10,000 a day in the summer), and martial-arts students.

Located 15km (9 miles) west of Dengfeng at the northern base of Shaoshi Shan, the monastery was built in A.D. 495 during the Northern Wei dynasty. Legend has it that the Indian monk Bodhidharma (Damo in Chinese), founder of the Chan (Zen) school of Mahayana Buddhism, retreated here in 527 after failing to convince the emperor of Liang in Nanjing of the "nothingness" of everything. With the Chan emphasis on meditation, Damo is said to have sat praying in a cave for 9 years. As an aid to, or perhaps relief from, meditation, Damo's disciples apparently developed a set of exercises based on the movements of certain animals like the praying mantis, monkey, and eagle, which eventually developed into a form of physical and spiritual combat known as Shaolin kung-fu (*gongfu*). In the Tang dynasty, Prince Li Shimin (later to be the Tang Taizong emperor) was rescued from a battle by 13 Shaolin monks. Thereafter the emperor decreed that the monastery always keep a troop of fighting monks, a practice that reached its apogee during the Ming dynasty (1368–1644), when 3,000 Shaolin monks were engaged in fighting Japanese pirates off the coast of China. The Shaolin monks' exploits, depicted in countless Hong Kong and Chinese films, have in recent years caught on with Western audiences. It's not unusual to see Western faces leaping and stomping at the more than 60 martial-arts schools around the monastery.

Pugilism aside, the temple itself has a number of religious relics and frescoes worth viewing. In the **Wenshu Dian (Wenshu Hall),** visitors can squint through the protective glass casing at a piece of rock supposedly imprinted with Damo's shadow from all those months of meditation. On the base before you get to the final three halls, stop to take a look at the bas-reliefs. Instead of the same old dragon carvings seen at other temples, there are peaceful-looking monks in kung-fu and meditation poses. In the last hall, **Qian Fo Dian (Thousand Buddha Hall),** is a gorgeous Ming dynasty fresco of 500 *arhats* (Buddhist disciples) worshiping Pilu, a celestial Buddha embodying wisdom and purity. About 400m (1,312 ft.) west of the temple is the impressive **Ta Lin (Forest of Stupas) ★**, the monastery's graveyard where 243 brick stupas built between the Tang (618–907) and Qing (1644–1911) dynasties contain the remains of notable monks. The oldest stupa, honoring Tang dynasty monk Fawan Chanshi, was built in 791 and features a simple stupa on a two-tiered brick pedestal. High on the mountain behind the forest is the **cave (Damo Dong)** where Damo was said to have meditated for 9 years.

Finish your visit with a free kung-fu show that takes place near the entrance at the **Shaolin Wushu Guan (Martial Arts Training Center).** Shows take place every half-hour between 9:30am and noon and 2 and 6pm. Come at least 20 minutes in advance if you want a seat.

Shaolin Si. © **0371/6274-8276.** ¥100 includes admission to the Forest of Stupas. 6:30am–6pm. To reach Shaolin Temple, see "Getting There," above, for directions.

MARTIAL ARTS TRAINING The **Shaolin Wushu Guan** (**Martial Arts Training Center;** © **0371/6274-9016**), inside the main entrance near the Shaolin Monastery offers classes only.

The **Shaolin Si Tagou Wushu Xuexiao** (**Shaolin Monastery Wushu Institute at Tagou;** © **0371/6274-9627;** www.shaolintagou.com), just outside the monastery's main entrance, is one of the largest and oldest schools, with 20,000 students. The fee for foreigners is ¥150 per day, ¥5,000 per month, including lodgings.

It is also possible to study at one of the many private schools in the area. A very unfriendly **CITS,** Beihuan Lu Xiduan, Guolu Dasha 203 Dalou (© **0371/6288-3442** or 0371/62872137; fax 0371/6287-3137), can arrange such study trips with students staying from a week to 6 months and longer. The office is open Monday through Friday from 7:30am to noon and 3 to 6:30pm.

TAISHI SHAN 太室山

Songyue Ta (Songyue Pagoda) ★ Five kilometers (3 miles) northwest of town, nestled at the foot of the Taishi Shan Scenic Area (Fengjingqu) is the oldest surviving (A.D. 520) brick pagoda in China, originally part of the Songyue Temple built in 509 as an imperial palace for the Xuan Wu emperor of the Northern Wei. The Tang Gaozong emperor and empress Wu Zetian stayed at this temple every time they visited Song Shan. One of the few relics from the temple still stands today: The gracefully curving, 15-story hollow pagoda is 40m (131 ft.) tall. It features arched doorways and windows at its thick base, and increasingly narrow upper stories separated by layers of stepped brickwork. Today, the pagoda is still beautiful but not well kept, and it seems to attract more bats than humans. Motorcycle taxis run here from the nearby Songyang Academy for around ¥10 each way.

Taishi Shan Scenic Area (Fengjing Qu). © **0371/6287-2138.** Admission Taishi Shan Scenic Area ¥80; Songyue Pagoda ¥20. 8am–6:30pm.

Zhongyue Miao About 5km (3 miles) east of Dengfeng on the road to Zhengzhou, this is the largest Daoist temple in Henan Province, and one of the oldest dating from before 110 B.C. Today's complex dates from the Qing dynasty (1644–1911). In the courtyard after the Chongsheng gate (Chongsheng Men) are four 3m-high (9¾-ft.) Song dynasty iron guards originally cast in 1064 with weapons in their hands, but these were supposedly sawed off during the Cultural Revolution. Just before the central gate (Lingji Men) is a rather unusual 1604 **stele with carvings** of the five sacred Daoist mountains: Song Shan stands in the middle, Tai Shan in the east, Heng Shan Bei in the north, Heng Shan Nan in the south, and Hua Shan in the west. The temple's central hall, the impressive golden-roofed, double-eaved **Zhongyue Dadian,** resembles the Forbidden City's Taihe Gong and has a statue of the god of Song Shan.

Zhongyue Dajie. Admission ¥80. 8am–6:30pm. Bus: no. 2.

Where to Stay

Fengyuan Dajiudian This three-star hotel is just west of the Tianzhong and has several wings with two grades of standard rooms. Opt for the more expensive rooms (¥518), which at least are larger, newer, and brighter. The staff tries to be helpful.

Zhongyue Dajie 52. ✆ **0371/6286-5080.** Fax 0371/6286-7090. 132 units. ¥328–¥518 standard room; ¥1,080–¥1,288 suite. 40%–60% discounts possible. No credit cards. **Amenities:** Restaurant; bar; lounge; concierge; forex; room service; sauna. *In room:* A/C, TV.

Shaolin Guoji Dajiudian (Shaolin International Hotel) The first hotel in this area to cater to Western tourists, this three-star property is still popular with independent travelers, but the facilities and service do not match those at the Fengyuan hotel. The hotel's saving grace is its location, which puts you close to the temple. Rooms are comfortable enough, even though they're unremarkably decorated with standard-issue brown furniture and old carpets. The bathrooms could use a scrubbing.

Shaolin Dadao 20. ✆ **0371/6286-6188.** Fax 0371/6285-6608. 60 units. ¥780 standard room; ¥1,118 suite. 20%–30% discounts possible. MC, **Amenities:** Restaurant; bar; lounge; concierge; room service; sauna. *In room:* A/C, TV.

Zen International Hotel ★ This new hotel is located inside the Shaolin Martial Arts Training Center. Here, you can search for your inner Zen in sophisticated, modern surroundings. The decor is minimalist, with rectangular furniture and monochrome shades of black, white, and gray in rooms and public spaces. Bedrooms are spacious, beds are comfortable, and the bathrooms are sparklingly clean. It's a popular destination for Russian and European tour groups. The location is ideal for having a leisurely stroll around the mountain (rather than the usual 1-day marathon to hit all the sights), and you get to see the monastery and temples at night, when they are all lit up.

500m (1,640 ft.) east to Shaolin Si, inside the Shaolin Wushu Guan (Martial Arts Training Center). www.shaolinsi.gov.cn/hotel.asp. ✆ **0371/6274-5666.** Fax 0371/6274-5669. 69 units. ¥680 standard room; ¥1,280 suite. 40% discounts possible. No credit cards. **Amenities:** Restaurant; vegetarian hall; bar; tearoom; lounge; executive rooms; room service; smoke-free rooms. *In room:* A/C, TV, hair dryer, Internet, minibar.

Where to Eat

For the adventurous, a **nightmarket** sets up at the corner of Zhongyue Dajie and Caishi Jie, a block east of Song Shan Zhong Lu, where you can eat your fill of spicy kabobs, stir-fries, and the local noodles, *daoxiao mian*. The **Jinguan Mianbao Xidian Fang** on the western side of Song Shan Zhong Lu, just north of Shaolin Dadao, has a wide selection of breads and pastries and is open from 6:30am to 9:30pm. Just up the street from the bakery is the small **Xiangji Wang,** selling fried chicken. A favorite restaurant frequented by foreigners who live at Shaolin is **Fuyuan Nong Jia Le** (✆ **01390/381-1423;** 500m/1,625 ft. to the right after you leave the temple; 7am–10pm). The proprietor, Mr. Chiu (aka "Uncle Tom," as he's been dubbed by foreigners), makes delicious fresh-cut fries, sweet-and-sour chicken and fish, kung pao chicken, and potatoes and chicken. If you can't find the place, give him a call and he'll pick you up in his trishaw.

LUOYANG 洛阳

Henan Province, 322km (200 miles) E of Xi'an, 150km (93 miles) W of Zhengzhou

Situated in western Henan Province at the junction of the Grand Canal and the ancient Silk Road, Luoyang (literally "north of the river Luo") was the capital of nine dynasties from the Eastern Zhou (770–221 B.C.) to the Late Tang (923–36). Today, this industrial town with a population of 1.3 million is better known as home to the magnificent UNESCO World Heritage Site **Longmen Grottoes (Longmen Shiku) ★★★**, a must-see for anyone interested in Buddhist art and sculpture. A visit in April will allow you to take in Luoyang's famous **Peony Festival** as well. ***Note:*** For Chinese translations of selected establishments listed in this section, turn to chapter 16.

Essentials

GETTING THERE Luoyang's small airport is located about 11km (7 miles) north of the city center. Daily **flights** go from Luoyang to Beijing (1 hr. 30 min.) and Shanghai (1 hr. 30 min.). Tickets can be purchased at the **CAAC office** (**Minghang Shoupiao Chu; ✆ 0379/6231-0121**) on Minghang Dasha, Shachang Lu crossing Daobei Lu Guo Hua Lu just north of the railway station. **CITS** can arrange tickets and is at Jiudu Xi Lu 4, Luyou Dasha (**✆ 0379/6432-5061**).

From the **railway station** (**✆ 0379/6256-1222**) just north of the city center on Daonan Xilu, trains run to Beijing (express train 8 hr.) starting around 7pm until 3am, Shanghai (14 hr.), Xi'an (5 hr.), Zhengzhou (1 hr. 30 min.), and Kaifeng (2 hr. 30 min.).

From the **long-distance bus station** (**✆ 0379/6323-9453**), opposite the railway station on Jinguyuan Lu, buses run to Zhengzhou (every 30 min.; 6:30am–7:30pm; 2–2 hr. 30 min.; ¥40), Kaifeng (hourly; 7:14am–4:40pm; 3 hr.; ¥50), and Dengfeng (hourly; 1 hr. 30 min.; 5:30am–6pm; ¥20). High-end hotels can arrange comfortable **private cars** from Zhengzhou to Luoyang for around ¥1,500. A better deal can be found by hiring a **city taxi** for ¥400 to ¥500, subject to negotiation.

GETTING AROUND Most **taxis** charge ¥5 for 3km (2 miles), then ¥1.50 per kilometer until 10km (6 miles), after which the price rises to ¥2.25 per kilometer. From 10pm to 5am, prices rise to ¥5.80 for 2km (1¼ miles), then ¥1.75 per kilometer thereafter. The bus costs ¥1. From the railway station, bus no. 81 runs to the Longmen Grottoes, bus no. 83 runs to the airport, and bus no. 11 runs to the western part of town via the Friendship Hotel.

[Fast FACTS] LUOYANG

Banks, Foreign Exchange & ATMs The **Bank of China** (**✆ 0379/6332-0031;** Mon–Fri 9am–noon and 1–5pm) is located at Zhongzhou Zhong Lu 439. Foreign exchange is available at counters 3 to 5. An ATM is located here.

Post Office The main post office at Zhongzhou Zhong Lu 216 (**✆ 0379/6391-1123;** 8am–5pm) has a Western Union in addition to the usual services.

Visa Extensions Located at Tiyuchang Lu 1, the **Gonganju (PSB; ✆ 0379/6393-8397** or 0379/6313-3239; Mon–Fri 8am–noon and 3–6:30pm in summer, 8am–noon and 2–5:30pm in winter) can process visa extensions in 5 business days.

Longmen Shiku (Dragon Gate Grottoes; 龙门石窟) ★★★

Located 13km (8 miles) south of the city center, on the banks of the Yi River (Yi He) which divides Xiang Shan to the east from Longmen Shan to the west, these caves are considered one of the three great sculptural treasure-troves in China. (The other two are the Mogao caves in Dunhuang, and the Yungang Grottoes in Datong, the precursor to Longmen.) In general, the limestone is harder at Longmen than at Yungang, and the caves closer to the river, making it easier to discern the details but more difficult to see the caves as a whole.

The first caves were carved in the Northern Wei dynasty in A.D. 493, when the Xiao Wen emperor moved his capital from Pingcheng (today's Datong) to Luoyang. Over the next 400 years, cave art and sculpture flourished, reaching their zenith during the Tang dynasty (618–907) and even continuing into the Northern Song. Benefactors of the Longmen Caves included imperial families, high-ranking officers, Buddhist leaders, and merchants as well as common folk, many of whom could only afford the smaller honeycomb niches. Today, there are 2,300 caves and niches with more than 2,800 inscriptions and over 100,000 Buddhist statues on both East Hill and West Hill. About 30% of the caves are from the Northern Wei dynasty (386–584); their statues are more elongated, static, and lacking in complexity and detail than the later Tang dynasty sculptures which account for about 60% of the caves, with their fuller figures, gentle features, and characteristic liveliness. The section of Longmen Shiku currently open to visitors is concentrated in a 1km-long (⅔ mile) stretch on the West Hill side of the Yi River. Morning is the best time to visit the Longmen Grottoes, which mainly face east and catch the light from the rising sun. Try to arrive before 8am to avoid the tour groups which usually descend on the caves around 9am. April, one of the peak tourist months, sees at least 300,000 visitors every year.

Following are the best caves of the lot, starting at the entrance and running south. Displays have rudimentary English captions, but even for the most independent traveler, this is one of those times when a guided tour is highly recommended. English-speaking guides are available for hire just inside the main entrance for ¥100.

Golf carts run the 500m journey between the parking lot and the main gate. A round-trip costs ¥10 and is well worth it during hot summer months. Once you've toured the first side of the mountain, you can either walk across a long bridge to get to the other side, or take a boat for ¥20 per person.

Binyang San Dong (Three Binyang Caves) Work here began in the Northern Wei dynasty from 500 to 523 A.D., but the carver died in 523 after completing only the middle cave. The other two were finished later. All three were commissioned by the Xuan Wu emperor, who dedicated the middle cave to his father, the Xiao Wen emperor, the southern cave to his mother, and the northern cave to himself. The figures in the middle cave are comparatively longer and thinner than their fleshier, curvier Sui and Tang dynasty counterparts in the other two caves. Missing reliefs are now in the Metropolitan Museum of Art in New York and the Nelson-Atkins Museum of Art in Kansas City.

Wan Fo Dong (Ten Thousand Buddha Cave) ★ Finished in A.D. 680, this exquisite cave actually contains carvings of 15,000 Buddhas, mostly in small niches in the north and south walls, with the smallest Buddha measuring only 4cm (1½ in.) high. Even more remarkable is the fact that this cave was commissioned by two women, an indication perhaps of the comparatively elevated status of females during empress Wu Zetian's reign. The centerpiece is the Amitabha Buddha, whose delicate rounded features are said to be modeled on those of one of the cave's patrons.

Lianhua Dong (Lotus Flower Cave) Carved during the Northern Wei dynasty around A.D. 527, this cave's highlight is a lotus flower, measuring 3m (10 ft.) in diameter, carved in high relief on the ceiling. Representing serenity and purity, lotus flowers are common motifs in Buddhist art. Surrounding the lotus are some faded but still fine apsaras (Buddhist flying nymphs).

Fengxian Si (Ancestor Worshiping Temple) ★★★ Carved in the Tang dynasty between 672 and 675 A.D., this majestic cave is the largest and most beautiful at Longmen. Originally started by the Tang Gaozong emperor, it was expedited by empress Wu Zetian, an ardent Buddhist, who poured money (from her cosmetics budget, it is said) into its completion, no doubt because the central Buddha's face is thought to be modeled on hers. This main Buddha, Vairocana, seated on a lotus flower, is a stunning 17m (56 ft.) tall, with a 4m-high (13-ft.) head, 1.9m-long (6-ft.) earlobes, a wide forehead, a full nose, and serene eyes, which were painted black at one time.

Flanking the Buddha are the disciple Kasyapa (the elder) to the left, and Sakyamuni's cousin, the clever disciple Ananda (the younger), to the right. Beside the disciples are two attending bodhisattvas (Buddhas who delay entry into nirvana in order to help others), Manjusri and Samantabhadra, who are decorated with exquisitely fine beads and ornamental drapes. It is said that this tableau of statues is a distilled replica of the Tang imperial court, with the dignified main Buddha representing the emperor (or empress), the obedient disciples representing the ministers, the heavenly kings standing in for the warriors and soldiers, the richly dressed bodhisattvas evoking the imperial concubines, and the flying devas (spirits) recalling palace maids.

Yaofang Dong (Medical Prescription Cave) This small cave was first carved in the Northern Wei dynasty but appended in subsequent dynasties. The main Buddha here is a Northern Qi (550–77) creation, its fuller figure emblematic of the transition from the thin Wei figures to the fuller Tang sculptures. At the entrance are stelae carved with Chinese medicine prescriptions for 120 diseases, including diabetes and madness.

Guyang Dong First carved during the Northern Wei sometime between 488 and 528, this is the oldest cave at Longmen, though additions were being made well into the Tang dynasty by different benefactors. Nineteen of the famous "Longmen Twenty" (20 pieces of calligraphy deemed especially fine and representative of their time) are found here. The central Buddha's head was restored during the Qing dynasty, and is said to resemble Daoist master Lao Zi.

Shiku Dong (Stone Room Cave) This last of the major caves was carved in the Northern Wei between 516 and 528 and has the best worshiping scenes in Longmen. On both sides of the wall are niches with low-relief carvings of officials in high hats, court ladies in flowing robes carrying single lotus flowers, and servants carrying sheltering canopies, all in a procession to honor Buddha.

Luolong Lu. Admission ¥120. Mar 1–Oct 7 7am–6:30pm; Oct 8–Nov 10 7am–5:30pm; Nov 11–Jan 31 8am–5pm; Feb 7:30am–5:30pm. Bus: no. 53, 60 (from the western part of town opposite the Friendship Hotel), or 81 (from the railway station) runs to the caves (35–45 min.; ¥1.50). Taxi about ¥30.

Other Attractions

Baima Si (White Horse Temple) It is more than likely that earlier Buddhist temples were built along the Silk Routes in what is today's Xinjiang (the path by which Buddhism entered China), but this is widely held to be the first officially sanctioned Buddhist temple built in China proper. Located 13km (7 miles) to the east of Luoyang, this temple was built by the Eastern Han Ming Di emperor (reigned A.D. 58–76) to honor and house two Indian monks who, the story goes, came from India bearing Buddhist scriptures on two white horses. Two stone horses (likely from the Song dynasty) stand guard outside the gate to today's temple, mostly a Ming construction. Just inside the main entrance in the southeastern and southwestern corners of the complex are the tombs of the two Indian monks. In the impressive Yuan dynasty Daxiong Dian (Great Hall), there are 18 arhats (disciples) of ramie cloth.

Baima Si Lu. ✆ **0379/6378-9053.** Admission ¥50. 7am–6pm. Bus: no. 56 (from Xigua stop on Zhongzhou Zhong Lu).

Gumu Bowuguan (Ancient Han Tombs) ★ This fascinating museum features 25 reconstructed underground ancient tombs dating from the Western Han dynasty (206 B.C.–A.D. 9) to the Northern Song dynasty (960–1127). By the Eastern Han dynasty (25–220), the use of hollow bricks with painted designs gave way to larger stone vault tombs made of solid carved brick. Eleven of the tombs also have elaborate wall murals, the most famous of which is the Western Han "Expelling the Ghost Mural Tomb," which features a faded but still gorgeous fresco of celebrants holding a feast before the exorcism. The tombs are about 10km (6 miles) north of town on the road to the airport.

Jichang Lu. ✆ **0379/6226-5737.** Admission ¥20. 8:30am–5pm. Bus: no. 83 (Gumu Bowuguan stop).

Luoyang Bowuguan (Luoyang Museum) Standouts in this museum of local relics include a section dedicated to the Xia (2200–1700 B.C.) and Shang dynasties (1700–1100 B.C.), with an emphasis on items excavated at Erlitou (an important Shang site 30km/18 miles east of Luoyang), including jade, bronzes, and pottery artifacts; Han dynasty exhibits of painted pottery and tomb frescoes; and some fine Tang dynasty glazed pottery.

Zhongzhou Zhong Lu 298. Admission ¥20. 8am–5pm. Bus: no. 4, 11, or 50.

Wangcheng Gongyuan Every April during the Luoyang Peony Festival (Apr 15–25), this park, built on the former site of a Zhou dynasty city, Wangcheng, is awash in a riot of colors: red, white, black, yellow, purple, pink, blue, green, and every shade in between. Luoyang produces the best peonies China has to offer, so don't miss paying a visit if you're in town then. For an extra ¥5, you can visit the zoo. The zoo and gardens, which open at the crack of dawn, are perfect for early risers.

Zhongzhou Zhong Lu. ✆ **0379/6393-8545.** Free admission to park, zoo entrance ¥15, 6am–6pm. Park is open 24 hr. Bus: no. 2, 4, 101, 102, or 103.

Where to Stay

Luoyang has several low-quality four-star-rated hotels with reasonable prices. Most hotels regularly give 20% to 30% discounts unless otherwise noted. There is usually a 5% city tax but no additional service charge. If you're going to be in town for the Peony Festival, book a room in advance.

EXPENSIVE

Huayang Guangchang Guoji Dajiudian (Huayang Plaza Hotel) ★ This white behemoth looks more like a casino than a hotel. Thankfully, the tackiness of the exterior does not continue indoors; guest rooms are classy with tasteful headboards, plush and comfy beds, and subtle lighting fixtures. They're the finest you'll find in town. Bathrooms can be a bit cramped but they're sparkling clean and modern. Some guests to the new hotel complain that service is a bit shaky.

Kaixuan Xi Lu 88. ✆ **0379/6558-8123.** Fax 0379/6488-4777. 530 units. ¥980–¥1,280 standard room; ¥1,680–¥2,400 suite. 20%–35% discounts possible. AE, DC, MC, V. **Amenities:** 2 restaurants; bar; lounge; concierge; forex; health club; indoor pool; sauna. *In room:* A/C, TV, hair dryer, minibar.

MODERATE

Mudan Cheng Binguan (Peony Plaza) ★ This four-star hotel offers some of the flashiest and most modern accommodations in town. A wall of smoked blue glass on the outside, the 28-story tower has a revolving rooftop restaurant and a wide range of facilities. Guest rooms are cozy enough but the furniture is showing wear. Bathrooms are a good size and come with scales. Service is not quite up to four-star international standards but is adequate. A Western buffet breakfast is served.

Nanchang Lu 2. ✆ **0379/6468-1111.** Fax 0379/6493-0303. 190 units. ¥800 standard room; ¥1,500 suite. 40%–50% discounts possible. AE, DC, MC, V. **Amenities:** 3 restaurants; bar; lounge; concierge; forex; health club; indoor pool; room service; sauna. *In room:* A/C, TV, minibar.

Xin Youyi Binguan (New Friendship Hotel) Located in the western part of town, this three-star annex to the old Friendship Hotel has pleasant, modern rooms. Units come with the usual nondescript brown furniture but beds are comfortable. Bathrooms are small but clean. The hotel also has a Western restaurant, part of its entertainment center that includes a pool table, coffee bar, and shuffleboard.

Xiyuan Lu B6. ✆ **0379/6468-6666.** Fax 0379/6491-2328. 120 units. ¥574–¥1,200 standard room; ¥1,200 suite. 30% discounts possible. AE, DC, MC, V. **Amenities:** 2 restaurants; bar; lounge; concierge; forex; room service; sauna. *In room:* A/C, TV, fridge.

INEXPENSIVE

Mingyuan Dajiudian (Mingyuan Hotel) Not far from the railway station, this hotel, which is affiliated with Hostelling International, gets a fair share of greasy-haired foreign backpackers. The rooms, which are characterless but totally adequate, are a better bargain than the dorm beds, which come with an attached bathroom. Bathrooms, though somewhat worn, are acceptably clean. The karaoke on the lower floors of the building may give the place a slightly dodgy feel.

Jiefang Lu 20. ✆ **0379/6319-0378.** Fax 0379/6319-1269. 80 units. ¥50 dorm bed; ¥150 standard room. No credit cards. **Amenities:** Restaurant; karaoke; sauna. *In room:* A/C, TV.

Where to Eat

For Western food, hotel dining offers the most reliable fare. The **Luoyang Peony Hotel** (Luoyang Mudan Dajiudian) at Zhongzhou Xi Lu 15 (✆ **0379/6468-0000**) has a Western dining room that serves fish and chips, pizzas, and lamb chops for dinner at ¥30 to ¥90 per entree.

MODERATE

Lao Luoyang Mianguan (Old Luoyang Noodle House) ★ HENAN Bright, unpretentious, and packed with locals, this a fantastic place for a casual meal. Order the *zhajiangmian* (noodles with bean sauce) and the *tangcu liji* (sweet-and-sour fish). The place is tastefully decorated with simple Ming-dynasty-style chairs.

On Changchun Xi Lu, near the corner of Jinghua Lu (no number). ✆ **0379/6861-1658.** Meal for 2 ¥60. No credit cards. 11:20am–2:30pm and 6–9pm.

Zhen Bu Tong ★ LUOYANG The specialty at this popular restaurant housed in a huge five-story Chinese-style building is the famous *Luoyang Shuixi* (Water Banquet), consisting of 8 cold and 16 hot dishes variously cooked in broth, soup, or juice (examples include *zhenyancai,* a soup made of ham, radish, mushrooms, and eggs; and *mizhi tudou,* sweet-potato fries in syrup). The full complement of dishes, designed for a table of 10 people, costs ¥500 and up, but happily, the first-floor dining hall offers more reasonably sized four- or five-dish minibanquets. The staff is a little surly, but this is a unique local dining experience that shouldn't be missed.

Zhongzhou Dong Lu 369. ✆ **0379/6395-2609.** Reservations recommended. Meal for 2 ¥40–¥80. AE, DC, MC, V. 10am–9pm.

KAIFENG 开封 ★

Henan Province, 70km (43 miles) E of Zhengzhou

Located in central Henan Province, just 9km (6 miles) south of the Yellow River (Huang He), Kaifeng has a history lasting more than 2,700 years as the capital of seven dynasties. Its heyday was during the Northern Song, when it was known as East Capital (Dongjing), the most prosperous city in the world, with a population of 1.5 million. Kaifeng is also believed to be the first place the Jews settled when they arrived in China. Having survived fire, earthquake, and flooding from the Yellow River, Kaifeng today is a sleepy but charming town not yet overtaken by massive development, though the government's efforts to capitalize on tourism are kicking into high gear.

Essentials

GETTING THERE The nearest major **airport** (✆ **0371/6851-9000**) is at Zhengzhou. Frequent **trains** serve Kaifeng from Zhengzhou (40 min.; D-series train, 3 daily; 30 min.), Xi'an (5 daily; 6 hr.), and Shanghai (6 daily; 11 hr.; D-series train, 2 daily; 6 hr. 30 min.). Kaifeng's railway station is in the south part of town.

Buses run to Zhengzhou (every 20 min. 6am–7pm; 1 hr. 20 min.; ¥17) from the **Keyun Xi Zhan (West Bus Station)** on Yingbin Lu; but as this bus station seems to have some unscrupulous and dodgy drivers, go to the **long-distance bus station (Qiche Zhongxin Zhan)** across from the railway station. Private **taxi** rental between Zhengzhou and Kaifeng costs around ¥300 round-trip.

GETTING AROUND **Taxis** cost ¥5 for 3km (2 miles), then ¥1 per kilometer. Between 11pm and 6am, the rate increases to ¥5.60 for 3km (2 miles), then ¥1.20 per kilometer. All **buses** cost ¥1 per ride. **Tricycle taxis** cost ¥2 for most places within the city walls.

Bus no. 1 runs from the railway station through the center of town to the Dragon Pavilion and Iron Pagoda. Bus no. 15 connects Po Pagoda in the southeast to the Dragon Pavilion in the northwest. Kaifeng is also an easy city to get around by **bike;** ask your hotel for information on rentals.

VISITOR INFORMATION Kaifeng no longer has a tourism bureau, but answers can be found by calling Mr. Shilei at the Zhengzhou Tourism Bureau ✆ **0371/6585-2319.**

[Fast FACTS] KAIFENG

Banks, Foreign Exchange & ATMs A **Bank of China** (9am–5pm), equipped with ATMs, is at Zhongshan Lu 32.

Post Office The main post office (8am–6:30pm) is at Ziyou Lu 33.

Visa Extensions The **PSB** is at Zhongshan Lu Zhongduan 86 (✆ **0378/595-8899;** Mon–Thurs 8:30am–noon and 3–7pm, Fri 8:30am–noon).

Exploring Kaifeng

Da Xiangguo Si Originally built in A.D. 555, this temple, one of China's more famous Buddhist shrines, had its heyday during the Song dynasty (960–1279), when there were 64 Sutra Halls on the premises. Destroyed in the flood of 1642 and rebuilt in 1766, the temple's main attraction is the magnificent four-sided statue of Avalokitesvara (the male Indian bodhisattva who became transfigured over the years into the female Guanyin), with 1,000 hands and 1,000 eyes (all-seeing and compassionate), who stands surrounded by 500 arhats. Weighing 2,000 kilograms (2¼ tons), the 7m-high (23-ft.) statue was said to have been carved from the trunk of a 1,000-year-old ginkgo tree and required 58 years to complete.

Ziyou Lu 54. ✆ **0378/566-5090.** Admission ¥30. 8am–6pm. Bus: no. 5, 9, or 15.

Kaifeng Bowuguan (Kaifeng Museum) Located just south of Lord Bao Lake (Bao Gong Hu), this rather dilapidated and neglected museum is ordinarily not worth visiting, but the fourth floor houses three stone tablets that record early Jewish history in Kaifeng. In order to see the stelae, you should contact CITS (Yingbin Lu 98; ✆ **0378/393-9032**) a day or two in advance to get permission (¥50 per person).

Yingbin Lu 26. ✆ **0378/393-3624.** Free admission. Tues–Sun 8:30–11:30am and 3–6pm. Bus: no. 1, 7, 9, 12, or 16.

Long Ting Gongyuan (Dragon Pavilion Park) This park sits on the site of the former imperial palaces of six dynasties from the time of the Later Liang dynasty (907–23) through part of the Jin dynasty (1115–1234). The park's entrance is at the northern end of **Songdu Yujie (Imperial Street of the Song Dynasty),** once exclusively reserved for use by the emperor, imperial family, and aristocrats. Inside the park's main entrance, the imperial way continues past two lakes, Panjia Hu to the east and Yangjia Hu to the west, and ends at the foot of Long Ting (Dragon Pavilion), reconstructed in 1692 for worship of the emperor. Seventy-two steep steps to the top reward you with views of Kaifeng.

Zhongshan Lu Beiduan. ✆ **0378/566-0142.** Admission ¥35. 8am–6pm. Bus: no. 1, 15, or 20.

Po Ta (Po Pagoda) ★ Tucked away in a maze of alleys in the southeastern corner of town, this hexagonal pagoda, the oldest standing building in Kaifeng, was originally

Kaifeng 开封

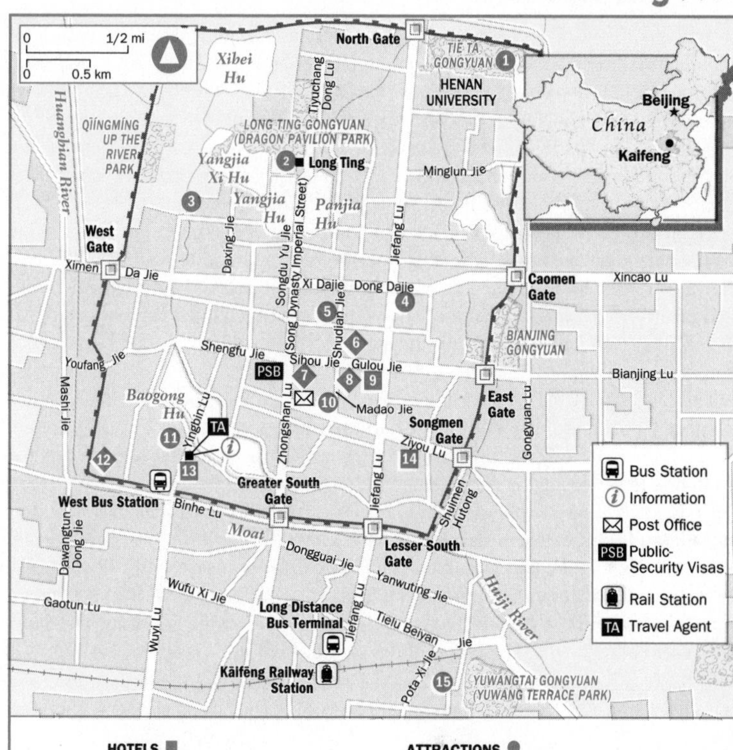

HOTELS ■

Dàjīntái Bīnguǎn (Dàjīntái Hotel) **9**
大金台宾馆

Dōngjīng Dàfàndiàn **13**
东京大饭店

Kāifēng Bīnguǎn (Kāifēng Hotel) **14**
开封宾馆

RESTAURANTS ◆

Huáng Jiā Lǎo Diàn **12**
黄家老店

Night market (Yèshì) **8**
夜市

Number One Dumpling Restaurant **7**
(Dìyīlóu Bāozi Guān)
第一楼包子馆

Xīnshēng Měishíyuán **6**
新生美食园

ATTRACTIONS ●

Dà Xiàngguó Sì **10**
大相国寺

Dragon Pavilion Park (Lóng Tíng) **2**
龙亭

Former Kāifēng Synagogue **4**
(Kāifēng Yōutaī Jiàotáng)
开封犹太教堂遗址

Iron Pagoda (Tiě Tǎ) **1**
铁塔

Kāifēng Museum (Kāifēng Bówùguǎn) **11**
开封博物馆

Pō Pagoda (Pō Tǎ) **15**
繁塔

Qīngmíng Shànghé Yuán **3**
清明上河园

Shānshǎngān Huìguǎn **5**
山陕甘会馆

built in 974 with nine floors. The 37m-tall (121-ft.), three-story Ming dynasty pagoda is covered both inside and out with gray brick tiles, each meticulously carved with a Buddha image. There are 108 such images, including those of Sakyamuni, Amitabha, and various bodhisattvas and apsaras. Hiring a taxi is the easiest way to reach the pagoda.

Po Ta Xi Jie 30. Admission ¥10. 8am–5:30pm. Bus: no. 15 (ask to be dropped off at Po Ta Xi Jie, then follow the red arrows on the walls).

Qingming Shanghe Yuan ★ ☺ Just west of the Long Ting Gongyuan, this manufactured theme park is modeled after painter and poet Zhang Zeduan's famous 12th-century scroll painting *Qingming Shanghe Yuan* (Festival of Pure Brightness on the River)—now hanging in the Forbidden City in Beijing—that depicts Kaifeng at its height. The park contains reconstructed traditional restaurants, shops, and bridges, and hosts performances by dancers and musicians who reenact Song dynasty rituals. An exciting show for the little ones is an action-filled reenactment of a battle between two old wooden ships held at the north end of the park. The kids can also try their hand at operating traditional flour mills or take a ride on horse- or camel-drawn carriages. Young women demonstrating traditional embroidery emulate skilled artisans in the imperial workshops who embroidered the emperor's robes using silk threads that were one-fifth the thickness of today's threads, and pulled by needles as thin as human hairs.

The highlight of the park for interested Western visitors is the **Jewish Cultural Exhibit Center (Youtai Wenhua Zhanlanguan),** located in the western part of the park behind the Wang Yuanwai Jia building. The history of Jews in the city (see "Kaifeng's Jews," below) is documented in four rooms, with exhibits on early Jewish life in the city, as well as photographs of Jewish graves and synagogues that once stood in Kaifeng. If you're here when the center is closed, check with the Tourist Service Center just before the park's main entrance. The eager-to-please staff will often open up the Jewish Center for inquiring Western guests. For ¥10/hour with a ¥300 deposit plus one piece of ID, the Tourist Service Center also provides an occasionally clumsy but nevertheless helpful audio tour of the park in English.

Long Ting Xi Lu 5. ✆ **0378/566-3633.** Admission ¥80; 9am–10pm. Dec–Feb ¥40; 8:30am–5:30pm (last ticket sold at 6pm). Jewish Cultural Center 9:30–11:30am and 3–5:30pm. Bus: no. 1, 15, or 20.

Shanshangan Huiguan ★ This magnificent guild hall was built during the reign of the Qianlong emperor (1736–96) by businessmen from the three provinces of Shanxi, Shaanxi and, later, Gansu, who were living in Kaifeng. All the buildings, from the stage, bell tower, and drum tower, to the double-eaved, three-gate archway and the Main Hall, have overwhelmingly vivid and exquisite wood, brick, and stone carvings.

Xufu Jie 85. Admission ¥20. 8am–6:30pm. Bus: no. 1 or 14.

Tie Ta (Iron Pagoda) ★ Kaifeng's most famous landmark is located in the northeast corner of town. This beautiful 11th-century pagoda is actually a brick structure whose facade of glazed brown tiles gives the impression of cast iron. Originally built in 1049, the building has survived earthquakes, fires, and the great flood of 1642, which buried the base under several meters of silt. The 13-story, 55m-tall (180-ft.) octagonal structure has brick panels featuring exquisite designs of apsaras, *qilin* (Chinese unicorns), dragons, and flowers. For another ¥10, you can climb the 168 steps to the top, though the experience can be a bit claustrophobic.

Jiefang Lu 175. ✆ **0378/282-6629.** Admission ¥40. 7am–7pm. Bus: no. 1 or 3.

Shopping

Songdu Yujie (Imperial Street of the Song Dynasty) is lined with shops that sell souvenirs, embroidery, silk screen paintings, calligraphy, paintings, seals, and ink

KAIFENG'S jews

The origins of Kaifeng's Jewish community are a mystery. Three stone tablets (dated 1489, 1663, and 1679) from Kaifeng's old synagogue record different dates of arrival. Although inscriptions on the 1663 stele record the arrival of Jews during the Zhou dynasty (1100–221 B.C.), it is now more widely accepted that the early Jews likely came from Persia via the Silk Routes sometime in the late 10th century during the Song dynasty. According to the 1489 stele, the first arrivals were traders who were invited to stay on in Kaifeng by the Song emperor, who also bestowed his surname and those of his six ministers on the Jews who were said to have arrived with 73 surnames, and who subsequently took on the Chinese surnames of Zhao, Li, Ai, Zhang, Gao, Jin, and Shi. A synagogue was established in 1163 but was often rebuilt, usually after natural disasters like the Great Flood of 1642, which damaged much of the town.

By most accounts, the Jews in Kaifeng did not retain any contacts with other Jews outside of China. The first Western report of their existence came from Jesuit priest Matteo Ricci in 1605 when he met Ai Tian, a Kaifeng Jew who had come to Beijing seeking office. Ricci later sent one of his Chinese converts to Kaifeng, who confirmed Ai Tian's story that the town had many Israelite families and a magnificent synagogue containing the five books of Moses.

The Jewish community continued to worship in Kaifeng until the flood of 1852 again destroyed their synagogue, which was never rebuilt after that. Evidence indicates that the remaining Jews became completely assimilated. Today, with renewed interest in the Jews of Kaifeng, there are a few self-identified Chinese Jews making themselves known again, the most notable being Zhang Xingwang, who has been working with the Kaifeng Museum to preserve the history of Kaifeng's Jews. He can be contacted through CITS or the Kaifeng Tourism Bureau (Luyouju; ✆ **0378/398-8488**). In the United States, information about Kaifeng's Jewish heritage, sometimes including special-interest tours, is available through the Sino-Judaic Institute, 232 Lexington Dr., Menlo Park, CA 94205 (www.sino-judaic.org).

stones. There's also a touristy shopping district called Gudai Wenhua Qu (Gudai Culture Area); expect plenty of kitsch and bargain hard. For specialty snacks from Henan, visit the **Kaifeng Tutechan Shichang** (8:30am–9pm), on Long Ting Xi Lu, near Songdu Yujie. Goodies include *huasheng gao* (peanut cake) and *xingren cha* (almond tea), which is more like a gelatin than a tea.

Where to Stay

Dajintai Binguan (Dajintai Hotel) This guesthouse's location and price make it a standout. Located next to the nightmarket, the rooms are nothing special, just standard two-star fare, but you'll be saving a few bucks by opting to stay here over competitors. Bathrooms are very clean, and the tile floors in the rooms sparkle. Rooms facing the street may be noisy, especially at night when the market kicks into full gear.

Gu Lou Jie 23. ✆ **0378/255-2888.** Fax 0378/595-9932. 113 units. ¥160–¥200 standard room. 25% discounts. No credit cards. **Amenities:** Restaurant. *In room:* A/C, TV.

Dongjing Dafandian Located across from the West Bus Station, this sprawling hotel's lily pond and pavilions are charming, but the guest rooms are rather characterless and bathrooms could be a bit cleaner. The staff doesn't speak much English but tries to be helpful. Rooms in the VIP building (presumably for such folk as former president Jiang Zemin, who is said to have stayed here) are gaudily decorated and overpriced—you're better off staying in the recently renovated building 4.

Yingbin Lu 99. ✆ **0378/398-9388.** Fax 0378/393-8861. 221 units. ¥120–¥800 standard room. 30%–50% discounts possible. MC, V. **Amenities:** 2 restaurants; bar; lounge; concierge; forex; health club; indoor pool; room service; sauna. *In room:* A/C, TV, fridge.

Kaifeng Binguan (Kaifeng Hotel) ★ This is hands-down the best choice in town. Situated in a courtyard with a variety of rooms to fit different budgets, this hotel offers a charming environment and friendly service. The building in the center of the courtyard was a Buddhist nunnery in the early 20th century and is now a protected landmark; the rooms in this building are nice, though a bit gaudy in style. The hotel's best rooms are in the slightly less historic building 5, each room recently remodeled and outfitted with sleek white armchairs and modern beds. The bathrooms are sparkling clean and feature massaging shower heads. There are no nonsmoking rooms, so some units have a very strong cigarette smell; you may want to see/smell your room beforehand. The hotel was undergoing a renovation at press time, but it should be done by the time you read this.

Ziyou Lu 66. ✆ **0378/595-5589.** Fax 0378/595-3086. 187 plus units. ¥280–¥438 standard room; ¥800–¥1,800 suite. 30%–50% discounts possible. AE, DC, MC, V. **Amenities:** Restaurant; bike rental; concierge. *In room:* A/C, TV, Internet.

Where to Eat

Hotels catering to foreigners all have Chinese restaurants that offer decent if forgettable fare, with a meal for two averaging ¥40 to ¥80. Locals agree that the city's best *xiaolong bao,* small dumplings filled with pork and a hint of broth, is at the humble **Huang Jia Lao Dian,** Binhe Lu 1 (✆ **0378/397-2768**). For the meat-adverse, try the *su baozi,* stuffed with vermicelli noodles, egg, carrots, mushrooms, and spring onions. A lot of tourists get sent to **Diyilou Baozi Guan (Number One Dumpling Restaurant),** Sihou Jie 8 (✆ **0378/599-8655;** 10:30am–8pm), another local institution specializing in dumplings and buns. A bit farther to the east at Gu Lou Jie 66 is the informal diner **Xinsheng Meishiyuan** (✆ **0378/597-9191;** 10am–2:30pm and 5–9:30pm), which offers a wide variety of noodles, kabobs, stir-fries, pastries, and snacks. There is no English menu, but purchase your meal tickets for ¥10 and up, then go around to the different stalls and order. The Dongjing Hotel has a **fast-food eatery** out front that offers convenient and inexpensive dining for ¥4 to ¥8 per person. Just point to choose from the many buffet dishes.

For the more adventurous, the **nightmarket** ★ which starts around 7pm on Sihou Jie and closes early in the morning, offers delicious local snacks such as *wuxiang shaobing* (five-spice roasted bread) and *zhima duowei tang* (sesame soup). The shish kabobs, especially the *yangrou chuan* (spicy lamb kabob), are especially tasty. The market is located on a street filled with charming old architecture in a variety of styles, which makes for a pleasant stroll even if you're not hungry.

JI'NAN 济南

Shandong Province, 497km (308 miles) S of Beijing

With few tourist attractions, the capital of Shandong Province is a major rail and air junction that's best used as a base for exploring more worthwhile attractions in nearby towns such as Tai'an, Qufu, and Zibo. ***Note:*** For Chinese translations of selected establishments listed in this section, turn to chapter 16.

Essentials

GETTING THERE Ji'nan is connected by **air** to many Chinese cities, including Beijing (1 hr.), Shanghai (1 hr. 30 min.), Xi'an (1 hr. 30 min.), Guangzhou (2 hr. 30 min.), Chongqing (2 hr.), Zhengzhou (1 hr.), and Hong Kong (2 hr. 30 min.). CAAC buses (1 hr.; ¥20) depart for the Yao Qiang Airport 40km (25 miles) to the east from Yu Quan Sen Xu Xin Hotel at Luoyuan Dajie 68 every hour from 6:10am to 6:10pm. Buses also meet incoming flights (last bus at 10pm) and end their run at the same hotel. Plane tickets can be purchased at the **CAAC office** (✆ **0531/8602-2338**) from 9am to 5:30pm. **China Eastern Airlines** is at Jingshi Lu 23806 (✆ **0531/8796-4445;** 8:30am–5pm).

From Ji'nan's main **railway station** (✆ **0531/8601-2520**) in the west of town, trains run to Beijing (16 trains daily, 4 hr. 30 min.–7 hr.; 5 D-series trains daily, 3½ hr.), Shanghai (6 trains daily, 9–14 hr.; 1 D-series train daily, 7 hr. 20 min.), Tai'an (1 hr.), Yanzhou (2 hr.), Qufu (3 hr.), Zibo (1 hr.), Weifang (2 hr. 30 min.), Qingdao (5 hr., 2 hr. 30 min. on D-series trains), and Xi'an (19 hr.). Train tickets can be bought 5 days in advance at the railway station.

From the **long-distance bus station** (✆ **0531/96369**) in the northern part of town, buses depart for Tai'an (every 30 min. 6:30am–6:10pm; 1–1 hr. 30 min.; ¥20–¥24, different types of buses), Qufu (every 40 min. 6:50am–6:30pm; 1 hr. 30 min.–2 hr.; ¥39–¥43), Qingdao (various times; 6:50am–8:30pm; 5 hr.; ¥70–¥99), Zibo (every 30 min. 6am–7pm; 1 hr. 40 min.; ¥28–¥35), and Weifang (every 40 min. 7am–6pm; 3 hr.; ¥55–¥65).

GETTING AROUND Most **taxis** charge ¥7.50 for 3km (2 miles), then ¥1.50 per kilometer until 5.5km (3½ miles), after which the price rises to ¥2 per kilometer. From 10pm to 5am, the rates increase very marginally.

TOURS The **China Shandong Travel Service (Zhongguo Shandong Luxingshe)** at Lishan Lu 185 (✆ **0531/8260-8108**) can arrange customized tours of other Shandong destinations like Tai Shan, Qufu, Weifang, and Zibo.

[Fast FACTS] JI'NAN

Banks, Foreign Exchange & ATMs The **Bank of China** at Luoyuan Dajie 22 (Mon–Fri 9am–5pm) is open for foreign exchange.

Post Office The main post office (8:30am–6pm) is in the old part of town at Jing Er Lu 162 (corner of Weier Lu).

Visa Extensions The local **PSB** is in the old part of town at Jing San Lu 145 just east of Wei Wu Lu (✆ **0531/8508-1088;** Mon–Fri 8:30–11:30am and 1:30–4:30pm). The surly staff at counter 8 can process visa extensions; allow 5 business days.

Exploring Ji'nan

Ji'nan is known for its 72 famous **springs** around town, which are really only worth visiting during the rainy season (July–Aug) when water levels are actually high enough to produce any activity. The most famous and also the first of the 72 springs is **Baotu Quan (Baotu Spring),** located in the center of town at Baotu Quan Nan Lu 1; admission is ¥15 in the evening and ¥20 during the daytime. The Qing Qianlong emperor drank from the spring waters and declared it the "First Spring Under Heaven" *(Tianxia Diyi Quan)*. The park is open from 7am to 10pm. The best time to visit is in the evening, under a starlit sky. You can enjoy tea in the pavilion by the spring.

More interesting is a walk around the western part of town near the railway station. This area was the **old German Concession,** which came into being when Ji'nan was opened to foreign trade in 1906. There are still a number of German-style buildings around, but you'll have to look for them under webs of telephone poles and wires and years of grime and soot.

Da Ming Hu Gong Yuan (Da Ming Hu Park) Located in the heart of town, this lake park, popular with locals, is situated by a set of hot springs. The park is most famous for its lotus flowers, which are best viewed during the Lotus Festival (July–Aug). There's a memorial for the female poet Li Qingzhao, who romanticized the park's flowers 800 years ago in her poems. A sightseeing cable car whisks you to the top of the hill in 13 minutes and costs ¥10.

Minghu Lu, Li Xia District. Admission ¥30 or ¥45 (includes visit to skippable stone museum). 6am–6:30pm. Bus: no. 41 or 66.

Where to Stay

Nearly all rooms in Ji'nan come with free Internet, either in room or in the hotel's business center. Inquire at check-in.

EXPENSIVE

Crowne Plaza Guihe Ji'nan (Guihe Huangguan Jiudian) ★★ This handsome structure with thick Western-style columns and arches sits atop six floors of the Guihe Shopping Center and offices. Arranged around a square atrium coffee shop, rooms are large and beautifully appointed, with full amenities. Marble bathrooms are brightly lit and spacious, and come with separate tub and shower. The only flaw seems to be that some of the bathrooms are already showing cracks. Service is efficient.

Tianditan Lu 3. www.ichotelsgroup.com. ✆ **0531/8602-9999.** Fax 0531/8602-3333. 306 units. ¥1,495 standard room; from ¥2,300 and way up suite. 40%–60% discounts online or by phone. AE, DC, MC, V. **Amenities:** 4 restaurants; bar; lounge; airport shuttle service; babysitting; concierge; executive rooms; forex; health club; indoor pool; room service; sauna; smoke-free rooms; rooms for those w/limited mobility. *In room:* A/C, TV, hair dryer, Internet, minibar.

Longdu International Hotel (Longdu Guoji Fandian) This is a five-star hotel, Chinese-style. That means the public areas are very chintzy (think wall murals of Renaissance scenes) and over-the-top. The rooms, however, are pretty tasteful. Cream-colored carpets cover the floors, and beds have cozy white duvets and maroon bed skirts. Walls are done in two-tone, pale yellow stripes and it's all fairly warm and inviting, which is not the impression you get when you walk into the glitzy hotel lobby. Bathrooms are a reasonable size, with bathtubs and standard amenities. Staff is helpful, but service in English is a challenge. The rack rates at this hotel are sky high, but discounts are very common (my room was 65% off), and it's very likely you'll get it for much cheaper than either of the other five-star hotels listed here.

Beiyuan Dajie 421. ✆ **0531/8591-8888.** Fax 0531/8591-6868. 142 units. ¥988 standard room; ¥1,688–¥1,988 suite. Discounts up to 40%–65%. **Amenities:** 2 restaurants; bar; karaoke bar; concierge; forex; health club; indoor pool; sauna; smoke-free rooms. *In room:* A/C, TV, Internet.

Sofitel Silver Plaza Ji'nan (Suofeite Yinzuo Dafandian) ★★ Until the arrival of the Crowne Plaza, this was *the* hotel at which to stay, and it continues to attract a large percentage of the foreign market with its good service and luxurious facilities. In the center of town, this modern 49-story edifice incorporates classical European elements in its decor, from chandeliers and thick columns in the lobby to traditional furniture in the rooms. Guest rooms are spacious and offer impeccable luxury and comfort, high above Ji'nan. The marble bathrooms, which come with separate tub and shower, are on the small side. The hotel is a tightly run operation with friendly and obliging staff.

Luoyuan Dajie 66. www.sofitel.com. ✆ **0531/8606-8888.** Fax 0531/8606-6666. 326 units. ¥1,725 standard room; ¥2,564 suite. Discounts up to 40%–60%. AE, DC, MC, V. **Amenities:** 6 restaurants; bar; lounge; airport shuttle service; concierge; executive rooms; forex; health club; nightclub; indoor pool; room service; sauna; smoke-free rooms. *In room:* A/C, TV, hair dryer, Internet, minibar.

MODERATE

C.SOHOH Business Hotel (Shanhe Shangwu JiuDian) Located in a convenient and central part of town, this hotel is a less expensive option to the Sofitel across the street. The rooms are sparsely decorated with cozy, wood paneled floor. Each room is equipped with its own computer, printer, and fax machine. The bathrooms are cleaned and tiled, surrounded by glass (don't worry; there is a curtain to partition off from the rest of the room). In the evenings, the breakfast restaurant morphs into a Brazilian barbecue joint with servers in Hawaiian shirts.

Luoyan Dajie 53. ✆ **0531/8613-8888.** Fax 0531/8615-1388. ¥398 standard room, ¥880 suite. MC, MC, V. **Amenities:** 2 restaurant; concierge; train ticket booth; wireless in lobby. *In room:* A/C, TV, fax machine, computer, cable Internet.

Silver Plaza Quan Cheng Hotel (Yinzuo Quancheng Dajiudian) ★ This four-star hotel in the heart of town offers modest accommodations at reasonable prices. Rooms in the south tower are elegant and have modern furniture and comfortable beds with pristine white comforters. The marble bathrooms are on the small side, but are bright and clean. North tower rooms are larger though the furniture and carpets are worn. Service is adequate and some staff members speak a little English.

Nanmen Dajie 2. ✆ **0531/8692-1911.** Fax 0531/8692-3187. Quancheng488@sohu.com. 310 units. ¥580–¥680 standard room; ¥780–¥880 suite. 20%–30% discounts. 10% service charge. AE, DC, MC, V. **Amenities:** 2 restaurants; bar; lounge; airport shuttle service; concierge; exercise room; forex; nightclub; room service; sauna. *In room:* A/C, TV, hair dryer, Internet, minibar.

INEXPENSIVE

Gui Du Dajiudian Conveniently located about 1km (⅔ mile) from the railway station, this hotel sits on a quiet street near city government offices. The rooms in the auxiliary building, which lacks an elevator, are cheaper and smaller. Rooms in the main building are a little dark and old but have decent-size bathrooms.

Sheng Ping Jie 1. ✆ **0531/8690-0888.** Fax 0531/8690-0999. 236 units. ¥688–¥888 auxiliary building; ¥1,090–¥1,290 main building. 20%–30% discounts available. AE, DC, MC, V. **Amenities:** Restaurant; airport shuttle service; concierge. *In room:* A/C, TV, Internet (main building).

Where to Eat

The top hotels offer reliable, if expensive, Western food. There is a **bakery,** Dasanyuan, at Chaoshan Jie Beishou; it's open from 8am to 9pm.

Set back from Quancheng Lu's main shopping drag is **Furong Jie,** a small street redone to look like a traditional Chinese alley. It's atmospheric and not too touristy. The entrance is marked by a traditional Chinese archway at Quancheng Lu 197. Head in and take your first right. You'll find several restaurants serving standard, tasty Chinese fare and traditional Ji'nan snacks like *youxuan,* a small, flat bun with spring onions twisted and baked in the street-vendor equivalent of a coal-fired Dutch oven.

Jingya, Daminghu Lu 100 (✆ **0531/8272-0268**), is known to many foodies in Shandong and Beijing as the premier restaurant for Lu cuisine. The humble restaurant serves food that packs a punch. Try the spicy mountain chicken *(lazi shanji),* shrimp with cabbage *(daxia baicai),* or three-flavor pan-fried dumpling *(sanxian guotie).*

Restaurants serving traditional Shandong cuisine are on Chaoshan Jie near the heart of the town. Try the *ma popo men shuangsun* (steamed bamboo and asparagus). The various kinds of *zhou* (rice porridge) at **Lao Hangzhou Jiu Wan Ban,** Chaoshan Jie 18 (✆ **0531/8612-7228**), where a meal for two costs ¥30 to ¥50. The restaurant provides special slender chopsticks unique to the coastal town of Hangzhou. If you have a hankering for something other than Chinese food, **Jenny's Café/Umart,** Wenhua Xi Lu 2-2 (✆ **0531/8260-8477**), is a Western-style cafe with a variety of treats such as tacos or burgers. Though the dishes might be a bit pricey (¥50–¥300), it will satisfy your Western food craving. Another option is Modern Thai Cuisine (Foshan Jie 25, ✆ **0531/8691-8806**) for decent curries and papaya salads.

TAI SHAN 泰山 & TAI'AN 泰安

Shandong Province, 66km (40 miles) S of Ji'nan; 68km (42 miles) N of Qufu

Inscribed on the UNESCO World Heritage List in 1987, Tai Shan (Great Mountain) is the most famous of the five Daoist sacred mountains in China, located midway between Beijing and Shanghai. Its base, in the town of Tai'an, is 150m (492 ft.) above sea level, and its summit is at 1,545m (5,068 ft.). With annual visitors numbering over four million, Tai Shan is and has always been the most climbed mountain in China. The first emperor of China scaled it. From the summit, Confucius declared that "the world is small," while Mao Zedong proclaimed that the "East is Red." Today, tourists and pilgrims, young and old, continue to make the journey, accompanied practically each step of the way by vendors peddling everything from snacks to souvenirs. Neither the highest nor the most impressive mountain in China, Tai Shan attracts visitors because of its cultural and historical significance, much of which, along with the colorful legends surrounding the different sights along the way, is lost on Westerners. However, the mountain still offers scenic vistas, plenty of chances to chat with fellow hikers, and a good workout. During the annual International Tai Shan Climbing Festival in early September, hundreds of runners race up the mountain. Check with CITS or Tai'an Tourism (see below) for the exact dates.

Essentials

GETTING THERE The nearest major **airport** to Tai Shan is at Ji'nan, 66km (40 miles) south. From the **Tai'an railway station** (✆ **0538/218-1040**) located just

Tai Shan 泰山

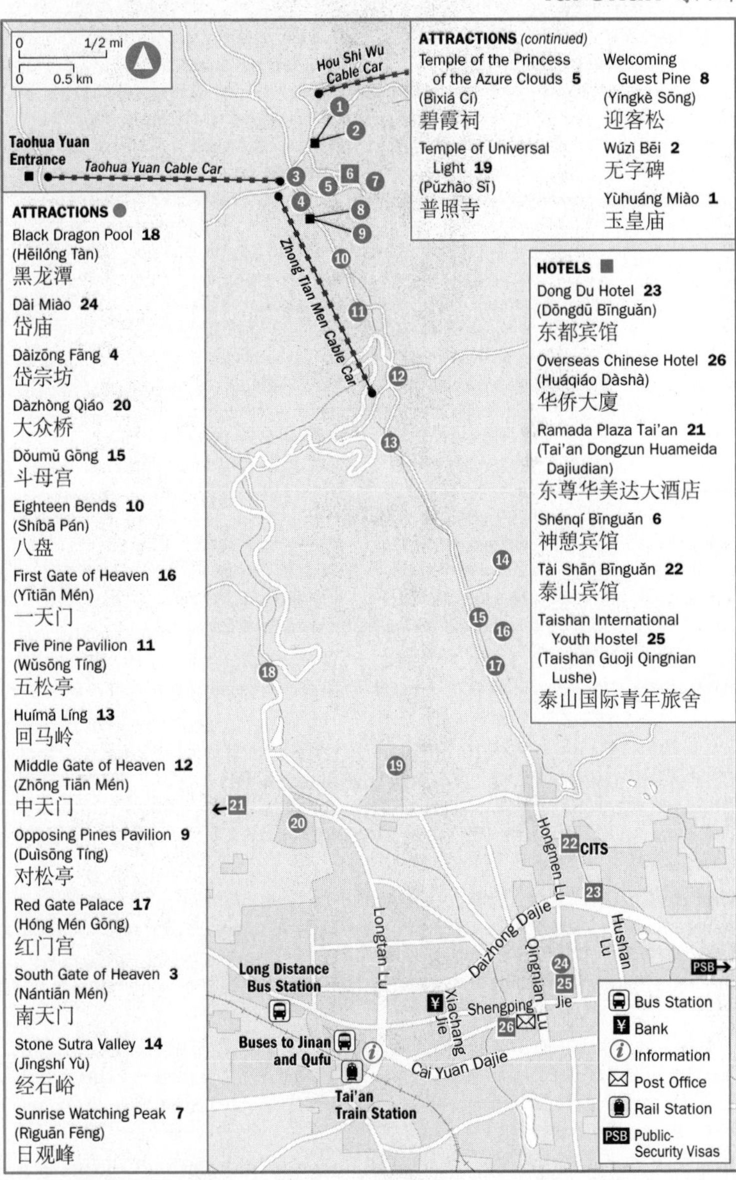

west of the center of town, trains run to Beijing (7 hr.; one D train daily, 4½ hr.), Ji'nan (1 hr.), Shanghai (11 hr.; two D train daily, 6 hr. 30 min.), and Qingdao (6 hr.). Frequent **buses** to Ji'nan (every 30 min. 6am–5:30pm; 1 hr. 10 min.; ¥17–¥18) and Qufu

THE GREAT mountain

The significance of Tai Shan to the Chinese can be traced to their creation myth in which Pan Gu, after creating the sky and earth, died from exhaustion, his head and limbs falling to earth as five sacred mountains. Tai Shan, formed from the head and situated in the east (an auspicious direction signifying birth), became the most revered of the sacred mountains. The other four mountains are Song Shan in Henan (center), Heng Shan Bei in Shanxi (north), Heng Shan Nan in Hunan (south), and Hua Shan in Shaanxi (west). Although Tai Shan is not particularly high, the ancient Chinese came to regard it as the symbol of heaven. Historically, the Chinese emperor was considered to be the son of heaven, and many emperors, starting from China's first, the Qin Shi Huangdi emperor, climbed the mountain to perform sacrificial ceremonies to express their gratitude for being chosen to lead all below them, and to report to heaven on their progress. This also served to legitimize the emperors' power, as only those able to scale the mountain successfully were considered legitimate rulers. Today, hundreds, if not thousands of historical relics, carved inscriptions, temples, and sacrificial altars provide a fascinating record of the imperial presence on the mountain. Countless ordinary Chinese have also made the pilgrimage to this holiest of holy mountains. They believed that the god of Tai Shan ruled the heavens and the earth and governed life and death. Although he has continued to be greatly revered through the years, his daughter Bixia (Princess of the Azure Clouds) has for many years now surpassed him in popularity. Today's pilgrims, many of them elderly, female, and working class, scramble up the mountain paths, stopping at every altar to light incense and pray to the goddess for blessings and protection.

(every 30 min. 6am–6:30pm; 1 hr. 10 min.; ¥20) depart from the square in front of the railway station. From the **Tai'an long-distance bus station** (✆ **0538/833-2656**) in the western part of town on Dongyue Dajie Xishou, buses run to Beijing (11:20am and 2:50pm; ¥130; 5 hr.), Shanghai (5:30am; ¥246; 12 hr.), and Ji'nan (every 30 min. 6:40am–5:30pm; ¥23; 1 hr.).

GETTING AROUND **Taxis** are plentiful in town and charge ¥5 for 2km (1¼ miles), then ¥1.50 per kilometer. From 10pm to 5am, the price rises to ¥5.80 for 2km (1¼ miles), then ¥1.70 per kilometer. **Bus** no. 3 (¥1) runs from the railway station to Dazhong Qiao and also into town and up Hongmen Lu to the main entrance of Tai Shan.

TOURS & GUIDES **CITS,** at Hu Shan Lu 158 (✆ **0538/826-2456**), can arrange private guided tours of Tai Shan for around ¥700, including transportation, English-speaking guide, entrance fees, and lunch. They can also arrange accommodations and book tickets.

VISITOR INFORMATION The **Tai'an Tourism Information Centre,** located just outside the railway station to the right as you exit (✆ **0538/688-7358;** www.travelshandong.us), can answer questions and direct travelers to hotels, sights, and travel agencies.

[Fast FACTS] TAI'AN

Banks, Foreign Exchange & ATMs The **Bank of China** is located at Dongyue Dajie 48. Foreign exchange is available Monday through Friday from 8am to noon and 1:30 to 5pm. There is an ATM here.

Internet Access There are Internet cafes along Hongmen Lu north of Daizong Dajie. Most are open 24 hours and charge ¥2 to ¥3 per hour.

Post Office The main post office (8am–5pm) is at Dongyue Dajie 3.

Visa Extensions The **Gonganju (PSB)** is in the eastern part of town at Dongyue Dajie Dongshou (✆ **0538/827-5264;** Mon–Fri 8:30am–noon and 1–5pm). Allow 5 business days. Take a taxi or catch bus no. 3 or 4.

Exploring Tai Shan

Dai Miao ★ Chinese emperors would come to this awesome temple at the southern foot of Tai Shan to offer sacrifices and pay homage to the god of Mount Tai before tackling the mountain. The present structures date mostly from the Song dynasty (A.D. 960–1127). Built in 1009, the nine-bay **Tianhuang Dian (Hall of Heavenly Gifts),** decorated with yellow glazed tiles, red pillars, and colorful brackets, houses a statue of the god of Tai Shan and a gorgeous, if faded, 62m-long (203-ft.) **Song wall mural ★** depicting, from right to left, the Zhenzong emperor (998–1023) as the god of Tai Shan embarking on an inspection tour. In the courtyard in front of the Hall of Heavenly Gifts, blindfolded visitors to the **Cypress of Loyalty** literally run circles around a nearby rock (three times clockwise, three times counterclockwise), after which they try to touch the fissure on the south side of the tree. It is said that those who succeed (and very few do) will have luck.

In the back of the complex is a lovely 1615 bronze pavilion, **Tong Ting,** which was formerly housed in the Bixia Temple on the mountaintop. West of the pavilion is an octagonal iron pagoda, **Tie Ta,** originally built in 1533 with 13 stories, each one cast separately, but only three survive today. The northern gate of the temple marks the beginning of Hongmen Lu and the imperial way up the mountain.

Sheng Ping Jie. Admission ¥30. 7:30am–6pm. Bus: no. 1 or 4.

CLIMBING THE MOUNTAIN

Tai Shan is a challenging but manageable climb. Two trails lead up to the midway point, Zhong Tian Men (Middle Gate of Heaven): a shorter but less-often hiked **western route** (7.8km/4.75 miles) which starts at Dai Miao but detours west before Hong Men; and the much more popular **eastern route** (11km/6.5 miles), which runs from Dai Miao up to the main entrance on Hongmen Lu. As the former imperial way, the eastern route features more cultural and religious sights. The relatively fit should allow a total of about 4 to 5 hours to reach the summit: It's 2 hours to the halfway point, where there are some hotels and a cable car, and another 2 hours minimum to reach Nan Tian Men (South Gate of Heaven) near the summit. Water and snacks become increasingly expensive the higher you climb, so pack enough beforehand. A walking stick, which can be purchased in stores in town or at the mountain's entrance, can come in handy. Temperatures at the summit can differ considerably from Tai'an's, so dress in layers. Climbing Tai Shan would not be complete without viewing sunrise from the summit. Some Chinese climb at night, making it to the top just in time to catch the first rays, but this is not advisable for the average foreigner. If you plan to overnight at the top, be sure to pack warm clothing and a flashlight.

BY BUS & CABLE CAR Those not inclined to climb day *or* night can now take one of three cable cars up to Nan Tian Men, though you'll still have to walk another 1.5km (1 mile) to the summit. The first and most popular option involves taking bus no. 3 (or a taxi) from the railway station to Dazhong Qiao (Tian Wai Cun also), where you transfer to a minibus (¥30) to Zhong Tian Men. You will have to purchase a ticket for entrance to Tai Shan, which costs ¥125, here. (There are also direct buses to Zhong Tian Men from the railway station, but these only run in the morning.) From Zhong Tian Men, the 10-minute ride to Nan Tian Men on a six-person cable car costs ¥80 one-way, ¥140 round-trip. The second cableway runs between the Tianjie Suodao Zhan and Taohua Yuan (Peach Blossom Ravine) on the western flanks of the mountain and costs ¥80 one-way. The third option connects the summit to the more rural Hou Shi Wu (Rear Rock Basin) and Tianzhu Feng (Tianzhu Peak) on the northeast side of the mountain; the cost is ¥20 one-way.

ENTRANCE FEE Prices used to vary by entry point, but in early 2007 a standard ¥125 (plus the mandatory ¥2 insurance) admission was decreed, regardless of whether you enter at Hongmen Lu, Wan Xian Lou, Taohua Yuan, or Dazhong Qiao. The price drops with seasonal temperatures to ¥100 (Dec–Jan).

EASTERN ROUTE Heading north from Dai Miao, visitors soon pass through the Ming dynasty **Daizong Fang,** a three-portal gate that leads to **Yi Tian Men (First Gate of Heaven),** which marks the beginning of the imperial ascent. Just inside is another arch commemorating the site where Confucius is said to have rested when he visited the mountain. North of the arch is **Hong Men Gong (Red Gate Palace),** which is also the main entrance to the mountain. Purchase your ticket about 200m (656 ft.) north of here. One kilometer (⅔ mile) farther is **Doumu Gong,** a Daoist nunnery whose origins are obscure, though the temple was completely renovated in 1542; it houses a statue of the goddess Doumu with 24 heads and 48 hands and eyes in the hollows of her palms. Behind Doumu Gong, a 1km (⅔-mile) detour to the east leads to **Jingshi Yu (Stone Sutra Valley),** an enormous flat piece of rock carved with the text of the Buddhist *Diamond Sutra.* Another 1.8km (1 mile) farther along the main path, an arch, **Huima Ling,** commemorates the spot where the Tang Xuanzong emperor had to dismount and continue by sedan chair when his horses could no longer navigate the steep twists and turns.

Less than a kilometer away, **Zhong Tian Men (Middle Gate of Heaven)** marks the halfway point up the mountain (elev. 850m/2,788 ft.), as well as the intersection of the eastern and western routes. There are restaurants, snack shops, and very crude hostels, as well as a cable car that runs to Nan Tian Men. A little farther on, those continuing on foot approach **Wu Song Ting (Five Pine Pavilion),** where the Qin emperor Shi Huangdi sought shelter from the rain in 219 B.C. He later conferred on the sheltering pine the title of fifth-grade official, hence the name of this spot. Just to the north, **Yingke Song (Welcoming Guest Pine),** immortalized in countless paintings, extends a drooping branch in welcome. Recharge at **Dui Song Ting (Opposing Pines Pavilion)** before the final assault on the daunting **Shiba Pan (Eighteen Bends),** the steepest and most perilous 1,633 steps of the mountain. Allegedly built in the Tang dynasty (618–907), the steps lie at a gradient of 80 degrees and rise over 400m (1,312 ft.) in height. Emperors used to be carried up this final stretch in sedan chairs. Today's climbers can only cling to the side railings as you straggle up the steps.

At the top, **Nan Tian Men** (**South Gate of Heaven;** elev. 1,460m/4,788 ft.) is probably the most welcome and most photographed sight of Tai Shan. Originally built in 1264, this two-story red arched gate tower was completely renovated in 1984. A little farther on, the shop-lined **Tian Jie (Heavenly Lane)** brings you to a small Ming dynasty **Wen Miao (Temple to Confucius)** rebuilt in 1995, and above that the hotel Shenqi Binguan. Below, on the southern slope of the summit, is **Bixia Ci (Temple of the Princess of the Azure Clouds),** built in 1009 and renovated and expanded during the Ming and Qing dynasties. Admission is ¥5; hours are from 8am to 6pm. The roof of the main hall is covered with copper tiles, while those on the side chambers are cast with iron to protect the buildings from the fierce elements on the summit. Elderly and female pilgrims flock here to burn incense and pray to Bixia and her different incarnations, Yanguang Nainai (Goddess of Eyesight), and Songsheng Niangniang (Goddess of Fertility).

Northeast of the temple, **Daguan Feng** is a gigantic sheer cliff face carved with inscriptions by different emperors, including the Tang Xuanzong emperor and the later Qing Kangxi and Qianlong emperors. A little farther north of here is the highest point of Tai Shan, **Yuhuang Ding** (elev. 1,545m/5,067 ft.). A temple, **Yuhuang Miao,** houses a Ming dynasty bronze statue of the Jade Emperor, considered by many Daoists to be the supreme god of heaven. Outside the temple is the 6m-high (19-ft.) **Wuzi Bei (Stele Without Words).** One version has it that the first Qin emperor had this tablet erected in A.D. 219, but years of exposure to the elements have weathered away the text. Another story tells of the stele being erected by the sixth emperor of the Han dynasty, who modestly left it blank to suggest that the virtue of the emperor was beyond words. About 200m (656 ft.) to the southeast is **Riguan Feng (Sunrise Watching Peak),** where hundreds of bleary-eyed visitors wrapped in thick jackets congregate every morning around jutting **Tanhai Rock** to watch the sunrise. On this peak emperors such as the Tang Gaozong and Xuanzong emperors and the Song Zhenzong emperor conducted the Feng and Shan ceremonies. In 1747, two boxes of jade inscriptions by the third emperor of the Song dynasty, once thought to be lost during the Ming dynasty, were unearthed here.

If you choose this route, you should take a minibus to **Zhong Tian Men (Middle Gate of Heaven)** for ¥30 and then climb to **Nan Tian Men (South Gate of Heaven)** yourself. You can then ride the cable car (¥80) back down to **Zhong Tian Men,** as it is rather steep to climb down.

WESTERN ROUTE This route has fewer cultural attractions than the eastern route and emphasizes more natural sights such as pools and forests. The trail (not always clearly marked) converges at times with the main road running to Zhong Tian Men. A little over 3km (2 miles) down from Zhong Tian Men is **Shanzi Ya,** strangely shaped rock formations named for various animals they resemble. About 2km (1¼ miles) farther down past Changshou Qiao (Longevity Bridge) is the main attraction, **Heilong Tan (Black Dragon Pool),** a pleasant enough waterfall in the summer and early fall. Another kilometer (½ mile) brings you to **Dazhong Qiao** and the terminus for the Zhong Tian Men buses. The path continues to **Puzhao Si (Temple of Universal Light),** a Buddhist temple built during the Northern and Southern dynasties (A.D. 420–589) and rebuilt in the Ming. Between 1932 and 1935, Feng Yuxiang (1882–1948), the "Christian General," stayed in the hall in the back of the temple complex. Born in Anhui Province, Feng was a warlord of the north who supported Sun Yat-sen but who later mounted a challenge to Chiang Kai-shek in 1929. He used to baptize his troops with a fire hose, and is buried on the southern slope of Tai Shan. From the temple, it's another 2km (1¼ miles) to the Dai Temple.

Where to Stay

Dongdu Hotel (Dongdu Binguan) This three-star hotel is conveniently located about 2 blocks east of the Dai Temple, and higher floors have good views of Tai Shan. Rooms are basic, with dorm-room-style gray carpets and somewhat shabby sheets. The walls, painted sea-foam green, add a bright splash of color to the otherwise bland decor. Bathrooms are small, with no separate shower. Ask to see a room first, as some have a strong musty smell.

Daizong Dajie 279. ✆ **0538/822-7948.** Fax 0538/822-5223. 146 units. ¥380–¥580 standard room; ¥880–¥4,888 suite. 30%–50% discounts possible. AE, MC, V. **Amenities:** Restaurant; lounge; concierge; dance hall; outdoor pool; room service; sauna. *In room:* A/C, TV, Internet.

Huaqiao Dasha (Overseas Chinese Hotel) This 14-story hotel is supposed to be the most luxurious in town, but it is a rather colorless place even though its rooms and facilities meet the minimum standards for a four-star hotel. Guest rooms are fitted with large twin beds and standard nondescript brown furniture, and are comfortable enough for a night or two. The decent-size bathrooms are a little dark but clean.

Dongyue Dajie Zhongduan. ✆ **0538/822-8112.** Fax 0538/822-8171. 207 units. ¥600–¥800 standard room; ¥600–¥1,580 suite. 30%–60% discounts possible online. 10% service charge. AE, DC, MC, V. **Amenities:** Restaurant; bar; lounge; bowling alley; concierge; forex; health club; Internet; indoor pool; room service; sauna. *In room:* A/C, TV (in-house movies), computers (14th floor only), minibar.

Ramada Plaza Tai'an (Humeida Dajiudian) Ramada has carved itself a beautiful space in the base of Taishan mountain. The tall windows shine a lot of light on the lavish interior composed of white marble and gold trimmings. One drawback: this hotel is no stranger to large business conventions, so be prepared for the hoards. The rooms are big with a contemporary feel and are fit for people who want to spoil themselves for a weekend.

Yingsheng Lu 16. www.ramada.com. ✆ **538/836-8888.** Fax 538/836-8666. Units 330. ¥996 deluxe room; ¥1,400–¥1,440 deluxe king; ¥1,460 suite. Breakfast included. AE, DC, MC, V. **Amenities:** 2 restaurants; bar; business desk; Internet; 11 meeting rooms; spa. *In room:* TV, fridge; hair dryer; Internet.

Tai Shan Binguan A trusty old standby, this popular, well-located hotel between the main gate of Tai Shan and the Dai Temple is comfortable and reasonably priced. Guest rooms come with high ceilings and basic but functional furniture. Bathrooms are clean. The whole place has a friendly feel to it and the staff seems to know what they're doing. CITS is conveniently located right next door.

Hongmen Lu 26. ✆ **0538/822-4678.** Fax 0538/822-1432. 110 units. ¥480–¥600 standard room; ¥1,280 suite. 30% discounts possible online. V. **Amenities:** Restaurant; bar; lounge; concierge; exercise room; forex; room service; sauna. *In room:* A/C, TV, fridge, hair dryer.

Taishan International Youth Hostel This friendly hostel is located in a traditional Chinese-style outside mall. There is a night market and small shops within the mall that are great for snacking and shopping for gifts. The hostel is very clean and welcoming with a staff that speaks English and is very helpful and friendly. The standard rooms are simple and spacious with a large bathroom. A taxi to Taishan only takes about 10 minutes, and a great night market with lots of outdoor eating space is within walking distance.

Fuquan Jie 8. Tai'an City. www.yhats.cn. ✆ **0538/628-5196.** ¥45 dorm room; ¥188 standard room. MC, V. **Amenities:** Restaurant; bike rental; Internet. *In room:* A/C.

ON THE MOUNTAIN

Shenqi Binguan This overpriced, overrated three-star perched atop some steep steps is nevertheless the best place to stay at the summit. It's only 30m (98 ft.) from Yuhuang Ding and 100m (328 ft.) from Riguan Feng. Rooms are somewhat dark but are clean enough and come with small twin beds and a small, clean bathroom; TVs are in place, but they receive no stations. The hotel only has hot water between 8 and 11pm. Thick jackets are provided for the sunrise viewing, and the staff will make sure you're awake in time. A buffet lunch starts at ¥60.

1km (½ mile) from Nan Tian Men along Tianjie. ✆ **0538/822-3866.** Fax 0538/833-7025. 66 units. ¥1,480 standard room. Discounts possible up to 30% except on Sat nights Apr–Oct. AE, DC, MC, V. **Amenities:** Restaurant; bar; sauna. *In room:* A/C, TV.

Where to Eat

In Tai'an, the **Baihua Canting** restaurant in the Tai Shan Binguan (✆ **0538/826-9977;** 7–9pm) offers decent Chinese food in a clean environment. Simply point to choose. A meal for two costs ¥70 to ¥100. **Huanqiu Xishi Mianbao Fang,** Hongmen Lu 7, sells pastries and snacks for the long hike.

On the **mountain,** food is comparatively more expensive along the trail and on the summit than in town. Trailside vendors offer ice cream, bottled drinks, instant noodles, and boiled eggs. At the summit, **Shenqi Binguan** has a restaurant that serves basic Chinese fare *(jiachang cai)* as well as delicacies made from local ingredients such as pheasants, wild vegetables, and local medicinal herbs. A meal for two is ¥80 to ¥120.

QUFU 曲阜 ★

Shandong Province, 150km (90 miles) S of Ji'nan, 68km (42 miles) S of Tai'an

Qufu, the home of Confucius, is a small town of 630,000 people, 125,000 of whom are surnamed Kong (though few are direct descendants). The town is dominated by the magnificent Temple of Confucius, the Confucian Mansion, and the Confucian Forest, all UNESCO World Heritage Sites. Qufu is often visited as a somewhat hurried day trip from Ji'nan. If you would like a more leisurely appreciation of the sights or merely wish to soak up the rarefied air, consider staying overnight and combining this with a visit to nearby Tai Shan. If you like celebrations, the ideal time to visit is on the occasion of Confucius's birthday, September 28. During this time, parades and musical and dance performances take place throughout Qufu. Book well in advance. ***Note:*** For Chinese translations of selected establishments in this section, turn to chapter 16.

Essentials

GETTING THERE The nearest major **airport** is in Ji'nan, 150km (90 miles) away. The **train** situation is a little confusing, as there are two railway stations: **Qufu Zhan,**

confucius SAYS . . .

Confucius's tremendous impact on Chinese society was not felt during his lifetime. Born Kong Qiu (also Kong Zhongni) to a minor noble family, Confucius (551–479 B.C.) spent most of his life wandering the country as a teacher after the various feudal lords with whom he sought positions all rejected him. Confucius himself never wrote his teachings down. It was only later, over the course of several generations, when his disciples like Zengzi and Mengzi collected and compiled his teachings in *The Analects (Lun Yu)*, that Confucianism began to take a firm hold.

A philosophical tradition that has come to underpin much of Chinese society, Confucianism is a series of moral and ethical precepts about the role and conduct of an individual in society. Essentially conservative, Confucius was concerned about the breakdown in human, social, and political affairs he observed in the world around him during the Spring and Autumn Period of the Eastern Zhou dynasty (770–221 B.C.). Expounding on the traditional rites and rituals set forth during the previous Western Zhou dynasty (1100–771 B.C.), Confucius formulated a code of conduct governing what he saw as the five basic hierarchical relationships in society: between father and son, husband and wife, older and younger brothers, ruler and subject, and friend and friend. At its crux was the supreme virtue of benevolence *(ren)*, and the ideal relationship was one in which the dominant figure (always the male) would rule benevolently over the subordinate, who would in turn practice obedience and piety *(xiao)* toward the authority figure. This concept of *xiao*, which so permeates Chinese familial relations (from parents to in-laws to siblings), is the glue that holds much of Chinese society together.

After an inauspicious beginning when the Qin dynasty Shi Huangdi emperor (China's first) rejected all things Confucian and implemented a book-burning campaign in 213 B.C., Confucianism became the official state philosophy from the Han dynasty (206 B.C.–A.D. 220) until the fall of the Qing in 1911, with different rulers seizing on different aspects of Confucius's teachings to justify their rules and methods. Over the years, Confucianism underwent many changes, but Confucian temples *(wen miao)* continued to proliferate and the stature of the Kong family continued to rise; by the Qing dynasty, the Kong family had attained a status equal to that of the imperial family. To be sure, there were many detractors throughout the years, too, none more so than during the Cultural Revolution (1966–76) when, encouraged to reject tradition and authority, children openly criticized and humiliated their parents and teachers. The bonds of *xiao* were broken.

Today, Confucianism struggles to remain relevant. Some younger people scoff at it for being rigid and outdated, while a smaller group lays at its feet the onus of over 2,000 years of Chinese patriarchy. Indeed, where once the concept of *zhongnan qingnu* (the value of males over females), an extension of Confucius's emphasis on the importance of male heirs to continue the family lineage, was held absolute and paramount, today that practice is being very slowly, if not surely, challenged. Yet those fearing the imminent demise of Confucianism need only take a closer look at the family flying a kite in the park, at the crowds who show up to sweep the graves of their ancestors, at the teeming masses who burden the Chinese transportation system in the days leading up to the Spring Festival (Chun Jie) so they can all rush home to celebrate the Chinese New Year with their family, at the peasant woman who is allowed to have a second child if her first one is a girl. For good or ill, tradition is alive and well, and the family is still the strongest and most important social unit in Chinese society.

about 5km (3 miles) southeast of the city center, where several trains a day stop between Beijing and Rizhao and between Ji'nan and Rizhao. The K51 from Beijing (9 hr.) arrives in Qufu at 7am, while the return K52 departs Qufu at 9:27pm. Bus no. 5 runs from the railway station into town, though service is infrequent. **Yanzhou Zhan** (✆ **0537/341-5239**), 15km (9 miles) west of Qufu, sits on the Beijing-Shanghai rail line and sees much more traffic. From Yanzhou are daily connections to Tai'an (1 hr.), Ji'nan (2 hr.), Beijing (5 hr.), and Shanghai (10 hr.). There are a limited number of assigned berths on trains serving both stations, so be sure to book your ongoing ticket as soon as you reach town. To avoid the hassle of running back and forth between Yanzhou and Qufu, use a ticketing agency like the **Qufu Shoupiao Chu** in the north Da Cheng Lu (Huadeng Jie; ✆ **0537/335-2276**). They have the only computer booking system in Qufu. The staff here is friendly and helpful.

From the **Qufu Qiche Zhan** (✆ **0537/441-1241**), located 1 long block south of the Temple of Confucius at the corner of Shendao Lu and Jingxuan Dong Lu, **buses** run to Ji'nan (every 30 min. 6:45am–6pm; 2 hr. 30 min.–3 hr.; ¥43), Tai'an (every 30 min. 6:30am–6:30pm; 1 hr. 10 min.; ¥19), Weifang (8:20am, 9:30am and 1:30pm; 4 hr.; ¥75), and Qingdao (8:30am, 1:30pm and 4:30pm; 7 hr.; ¥125). The several daily sleeper buses to Beijing daily are often booked (8am, 11:20am, and 3pm, ¥130). **Minibuses** run to the railway station at Yanzhou (every 10 min. 6am–7pm; 25 min.; ¥5). The taxi to **Yanzhou Zhan** from town costs ¥30 and takes 20 minutes.

GETTING AROUND It is possible to tour temple, mansion, and cemetery on foot, though hiring a pedicab or horse-drawn taxi to the cemetery is an inexpensive option. Unmetered *miandi* (minivan) **taxis** cost ¥5 per 2km (1¼ miles). Around town, **horse-drawn carriages** cost ¥2 to ¥4 per person, while a **tricycle taxi** costs ¥1 to ¥3 per person. You can hire a tricycle taxi for 1 day for ¥20 to ¥30, but make sure you agree on the price and what attractions you want to see before starting the ride. The infrequent **bus** no. 1 runs from the southwest of town past the bus station all the way up Gu Lou Jie to the Confucian Forest. Bus no. 2 travels an east-west route along Jingxuan Jie.

VISITOR INFORMATION The **Qufu Tourist Information Center** at Gu Lou Bei Jie 4 (✆ **0537/441-4789;** Mon–Fri 8:30am–noon and 2–6pm) can provide information and direct travelers to sights and accommodations.

[FastFACTS] QUFU

Banks, Foreign Exchange & ATMs The **Bank of China** is at Dongmen Dajie 96 just east of Gu Lou Bei Jie. Foreign-exchange hours are Monday to Friday from 8am to noon and 2 to 6pm.

Internet Access If you have your own laptop, free Internet access is available at most hotels around town. Otherwise, access is pretty limited. Just east of Gou Lou Nan Jie is **Xingji Wangba,** a large Internet bar with decent connections for ¥5 per hour. To get there, head east along the nightmarket street Wumaci Jie and take your first right down the small alley. The Internet bar is about 150m (492 ft.) in on your right.

Post Office Located north of the Drum Tower at Gu Lou Bei Jie 8–1, the post office is open from 8am to 6pm.

Visa Extensions The **PSB (Shi Gonganju)** is at Wuyuntan Lu 1 (✆ **0537/296-0153;** Mon–Fri 9–11:30am and 2–4pm). Take a taxi or bus no. 3 from the Kongfu Fandian (Kongfu Hotel) at the corner of Datong Lu and Jingxuan Lu, and ask to be let off at Wuyuntan.

Exploring Qufu

Kong Miao (Confucius Temple) ★★★ One of the great classical Chinese architectural complexes (along with Beijing's Forbidden City and Chengde's Imperial Summer Resort), the magnificent Confucius Temple was first built in 478 B.C. by the king of Zhou, Lu Aigong, who converted three rooms from Confucius's residence into a temple to offer sacrifices to the Sage. The temple grew from the Western Han dynasty (206 B.C.–A.D. 24) onward due to the increasing number of titles conferred on Confucius. Many of today's structures, done in typical imperial fashion with red pillars and yellow-glazed tiles, and oriented on a north-south axis, date to the Ming and Qing dynasties.

Over a kilometer long (½ mile), the temple is first approached from the main south gate in Qufu's city wall. Then, a series of gates and courtyards lead eventually to **Dazhong Men,** a gate and former temple entrance (during the Song). In the next courtyard is the marvelous three-story, triple-eaved **Kuiwen Ge (Worship of Literature Pavilion),** first built in 1018 and rebuilt in 1191. This wooden building with stone pillars survived a major earthquake during the reign of the Qing dynasty Kangxi emperor (1654–1722) that destroyed much of the rest of Qufu. In the next courtyard are **13 stelae pavilions** all constructed during different periods, from the Jin (A.D. 265–420) to the Republican period (1914–19), and housing stelae recording the visits of different emperors.

The central gate, **Dacheng Men,** leads into the heart of the temple complex and the magnificent **Dacheng Dian (Hall of Great Achievements) ★★★**, originally built on this site in 1021 and rebuilt in 1724. Constructed on a two-tiered sculptured marble terrace, the building is supported by 28 carved stone pillars and majestically capped by a double-eaved, yellow-tiled roof. Individually carved from whole blocks of stone, the 10 columns in front each depict two dragons playing with pearls amid a sea of clouds. The remaining 18 octagonal pillars each bear 72 smaller dragons. Inside the temple is a statue of Confucius flanked by four of his students. These statues, destroyed during the Cultural Revolution, were replaced in 1983. Also on display is a set of bronze vessels and musical instruments that were used in ceremonial rites to honor the Great Sage, still occasionally performed here. In front is **Xing Tan (Apricot Altar),** where it is said Confucius delivered lectures to his 72 disciples. Behind the Great Hall is the **Hall of Bedroom** used to honor Confucius's wife, Lady Yuangong, who married him at the age of 19 and died 7 years before her husband.

The original Confucius's temple stands in the eastern section, only three shanties by legend. Also noteworthy is a 3m-deep (10-ft.) **well** in the eastern section of the complex from which Confucius is said to have drunk. East of the well, a screen wall, **Lu Bi,** commemorates the successful attempt by the ninth generation of Confucius's descendant Kong Fu to hide all the Confucian classics such as *The Analects* and *The Book of Rites* in the walls of Confucius's residence during Qin Shi Huangdi's book-burning campaign in 213 B.C. The books were later discovered during the Han dynasty (206 B.C.–A.D. 220), when the residence was torn down in order to enlarge the temple.

✆ **0537/441-4002.** Combined admission ¥150 to Kong Miao, Kong Fu, and Kong Lin saves you ¥40. Admission to Kong Miao only ¥90. 8:10am–5:30pm.

Kong Fu (Confucian Mansion) ★★★ Until 1949 the mansion on the north-east side of the Confucius Temple had been home to 77 generations of Confucius's direct descendants, although the mansion's present location dates only from the end of the 14th century and the complex really grew to its current size (with a total of 463 halls) only in the Ming and Qing dynasties. If you've mostly been visiting temples around China, one of the most striking things about this place is the color and architecture. Temples and palaces are usually towering, majestic buildings that make you feel small and insignificant among all that red and imperial yellow. The Confucian Mansion, a residential dwelling, is a beautiful mix of gray stone walls, black columns, and black, red, and white trim throughout. The colors may remind you of 1950s Art Deco, but with a flourish of antique Chinese style. It's also smaller in scale, so you don't feel dwarfed by the surrounding architecture, and there are plenty of small passageways and paths that make this a very fun place to explore.

Here lived the Yansheng ("Continuing the Line of the Sage") duke, a title first conferred upon the 46th-generation descendant of Confucius by the Song Renzong emperor in 1055, and subsequently passed down. During the Ming dynasty, the duke's stature grew, and by the time of the Qing, he and the Kong family had attained a status equivalent to that of the imperial family. He was exempted from taxes, given power over his own court of law and subjects, and was the only one besides the emperor who could ride his horse within the Forbidden City. The Qing Qianlong emperor (reigned 1736–96) even married his daughter to a Yansheng duke in 1772, because only marriage to someone from a family equal in stature could dispel the misfortune that had been predicted for her by fortunetellers because of the mole on her face. To circumvent the law that prohibited Manchus from marrying the Chinese, Qianlong first gave her to a Chinese official, Yu Minzhong, for adoption, and her name was changed from Aixin Jueluo to Lady Yu.

The mansion is divided into three sections. The front part is reserved for formal and public business, the second serves as private family quarters, and the third is a garden. Inside the main gate is a large courtyard with the free-standing **Chongguang Men,** a gate built on eight stone drums that was only opened when emperors or imperial edicts arrived. In the three halls to the north, starting with the main hall, **Da Tang,** the Yansheng duke proclaimed imperial edicts, received visitors, and tended to business. In the second hall, where the duke received high-ranking officials, are seven tablets inscribed by various emperors, including one with the character *shou* (longevity) inscribed by the empress dowager Cixi. Northeast of the third hall is a small alley leading to a four-story **Binan Lou (Tower of Refuge),** which was meant to shelter the duke in case of attack. It was never used.

Behind the third hall, the **Neizhai Men (Gate to the Inner Apartments)** marks the beginning of the private quarters restricted to family members and a handful of trusted, mostly female servants. Even the water carrier had to pour his well water through a tiny trough in the wall just west of the gate. Behind the Front Reception Hall used for family banquets, weddings, and funeral ceremonies, the two-story **Qiantang Lou** was where the 76th duke, Kong Lingyi, lived with his wife, Madame Tao, his two concubines, and his two daughters from Concubine Wang. After the 76th duke's death, one concubine gave birth to the 77th duke, Kong Decheng. It is widely held that Madame Tao, who produced no surviving heirs herself, poisoned his mother 17 days after she gave birth. The boy was to grow up with his sisters in relative isolation under the tyrannical Madame Tao, Qufu's equivalent of the powerful and manipulative empress dowager Cixi. As depicted in *The House of Confucius* by Decheng's sister Kong Demao and Ke Lan, life in the Confucian Mansion in those days was full of intrigue and betrayal for the adults and loneliness and sadness for the children. Decheng married and lived here until 1940, when he fled the Japanese invasion and then the Communists, ending up in Taiwan; he was the last of Confucius's descendants to occupy the mansion.

A large garden in the rear occupies the rest of the mansion grounds. A complete tour of the mansion will take 2 hours. Budget another 1 to 2 hours if you want to tour Kong Miao. It's best to do both in the morning hours, as there are fewer tourists.

Entrance opposite the back gate of Kong Miao. Admission ¥60 or by combination ticket; see Kong Miao, above. 8am–5:30pm.

Kong Lin (Confucian Forest & Cemetery) ★★★ Slightly over a kilometer (½ mile) north of the Confucian Mansion and Temple, Kong Lin is the burial ground for Confucius and his family, and is the largest and oldest cemetery park in China. Covering 2 sq. km (1¼ sq. miles), the forest has thousands of graves and over 20,000 trees, including cypresses, maples, and willows, many collected and planted by Confucius's disciples over the years. It's interesting to note that women, monks, criminals, and aborted fetuses cannot be buried here. Some 4,000 remaining gravestones span the dynasties, and the different styles make the cemetery worth visiting. It is a place both large and atmospheric enough to lose yourself in for a few hours. It can be delightfully eerie in the morning before the fog lifts. Bikes can be rented at the entrance for ¥10.

Tip: After or between visiting the main attractions noted below, get off the main road and walk along the dirt paths to explore the myriad of gravestones and statues. You'll get away from the tour groups, flittering butterflies will keep you company, and the cicadas and warbling birds will drown out the sounds of the outside world.

The walkway leading to the forest from the south is lined with 73 trees on the right representing Confucius's age when he died, and 72 trees on the left signaling the number of his disciples. Passing through another two gates, visitors arrive at the forest proper, which is surrounded by a 3m-high (10-ft.) and 5m-thick (16-ft.) wall. To get to Confucius's grave, turn left inside the second entrance, walk along the **Imperial Carriageway** for about 200m (654 ft.), cross the Ming **Zhushui Bridge,** and continue along the "Spirit Way" *(shen sao),* which is flanked by four pairs of Song dynasty stone sculptures. At the end of the Spirit Way is **Confucius's tomb,** a mound of packed earth in front of which are two stelae. The front Ming dynasty tablet is inscribed with the characters DACHENG ZHI SHENGWEN XUAN WANG MU or "Tomb of the Ultimate Sage of Great Achievements." Local lore has it that the last two characters, *"wang mu"* (king's tomb), are partially hidden from view by the stone altar in front to reassure visiting emperors who came to pay their respects that no matter how respected and exalted the Sage was, there was only one emperor. To the right (east) of Confucius's grave is that of his son Kong Li, who died before his father. To the south lies the tomb of Confucius's grandson, Zisi, who was Mencius's (Mengzi's) teacher and the author of *The Doctrine of the Mean.*

Following the main road to the left of Confucius's grave brings you to a group of Ming Tombs. Continuing to the north eventually leads you to an archway and **tomb for Lady Yu,** the Qianlong emperor's daughter. (While Confucian wives were allowed to be buried in the forest, Confucius's female descendants were restricted to burial outside the forest.) Not far to the east is the **Tomb of Kong Shangren** (1648–1718), a 64th-generation descendant and author of the famous classical play *Taohua Shan (The Peach Blossom Fan).* East of Kong Shangren's tomb is the Tomb of the 76th Yansheng duke, Kong Lingyi, and his wretched wife Madame Tao. Concubine Wang was also reburied here, despite laws prohibiting concubines from being buried within the forest. Following the road south brings you back to the main entrance.

Lindao Lu. Admission ¥40 or by combination ticket; see Kong Miao, above. Mar–Nov 8am–6pm; Dec–Feb 8am–5pm. Bus: no. 1.

OTHER ATTRACTIONS

Kongzi Yanjiuyuan (Confucius Academy) ★ Designed by the famous Chinese architect Wu Liangyong, this academy is a combination museum, research center, and exhibition space. Six rooms are dedicated to Confucius's life and theory, with drawings of the Sage and also some antiques from Kong Fu (Confucian Mansion) on display. Unfortunately, the place lacks English signage and English-speaking guides, but it's still worthwhile for the fantastic architecture.

Da Cheng Lu 9. Admission ¥40, includes guide (no English-speaking guides available, though). 7:30am–5:30pm.

Shao Hao Ling (Tomb of the Emperor Shao Hao) ★ Located 4km (2½ miles) east of town, this unusually shaped tomb was built in 1111 by the Song Huizong emperor to honor Shao Hao, one of the legendary five emperors who succeeded the even more legendary first Chinese emperor, Huang Di (the Yellow Emperor). This flat-topped pyramid-shaped structure capped by a small brick altar with a yellow-tiled roof was supposedly built from 10,000 pieces of stone. Also here are two 17m-tall (56-ft.) stelae, **Wanrenchou Jubei (Sorrow of Ten Thousand Stelae),** meant to honor the Yellow Emperor, but the Song dynasty was driven from power before the stelae could be erected. Lying facedown since then, the tablets were hacked at by zealous Red Guards during the Cultural Revolution but were restored and set upright in 1992.

4km (2½ miles) northeast of Qufu in Jiuxian Village. Admission ¥10. 8am–5pm. Shao Hao Ling is best reached by taxi (about ¥10–¥15) Bus: no. 2 from outside the bus station heading east on Jingxuan Dong Lu. Ask to be dropped of at Shao Hao Ling, then head north for another 400m (1,308 ft.).

Shopping

Popular souvenirs include the "Four Treasures of the Study": seals, ink stones, calligraphy brushes, and rice paper, all of which are available at **Chunqiu Ge** at Gu Lou Bei Jie 5 (8am–7:30pm). The store also sells ceramics, jewelry, cloisonné, and jade, and accepts international credit cards.

Where to Stay

Queli Binshe (Queli Hotel) ★ The best place to stay in town, this three-star hotel just east of the Confucius Temple has traditional Chinese buildings in a courtyard setting. Legend has it that Confucius lived nearby. Rooms, while not luxurious, are spacious, comfortable, and decorated in a style that combines traditional Chinese motifs with modern flourishes. Bathrooms have black marble walls and are small and a bit old but acceptably clean. Most rooms have views of the hotel's traditional Chinese rooftops and the central courtyards below. Service can be spotty.

Queli Jie 1. www.quelihotel.com. ✆ **0537/486-6818.** Fax 0537/441-2022. 160 units. ¥568–¥598 standard room; ¥2,288 suite. 10%–20% discounts possible. MC, V. **Amenities:** Restaurant; bar; bowling alley; concierge; room service; sauna. *In room:* A/C, TV w/free Internet, fridge.

7 Days Inn A very popular hotel chain with many locations around China, the 7 Days' rooms are nothing special, but are clean and suited for the budget-minded. Though this hotel sits outside of the city wall, it's a quick walk over to the temples and forest. There is also a handy train ticket vendor just next to the entrance of the hotel.

Dacheng Lu 1. www.7daysinn.cn. ✆ **0537/460-8777.** Fax 0537/460-1777. ¥151 1 bed; ¥173 2 beds. 20%–30% discounts available at counter. No credit cards. **Amenities:** Wi-Fi. In Room: A/C, TV.

Yu Long Dafandian (Yu Long Hotel) Located in the north part of the old town, the quiet hotel has a good view of the city wall. It provides huge and acceptably clean rooms, though the furniture is worn. The staff are friendly, and they can book train tickets for you.

Gu Lou Bei Jie 15. ✆ **0537/441-3469.** Fax 0537/441-3209. ¥300 standard room; ¥800–¥1,180 suite. 20%–30% discounts possible. No credit cards. **Amenities:** Restaurant. *In room:* A/C, TV, Internet.

Where to Eat

The **Confucius Restaurant and Western Dining Room** in the Queli Hotel offers the best dining in a relatively clean environment, but watch out for shenanigans with prices. Just to the east of the Queli, the clean and well-lit **Kong Fu Dajiujia** (**✆ 0537/441-1048**) has an English menu and serves local Confucian specialties like *yangguan sandie* (chicken, vegetables, and egg folded together like a fan), *daizi shangchao* (stewed pork, chicken, chestnuts, and ginseng), and *shili yinxing* (sweet ginkgo). A meal for two averages ¥40 to ¥160. Farther east along Wumaci Jie, a lively **nightmarket** proffers a variety of snacks, including delicious grilled kabobs, roasted nuts, and bean curd. Set among several food stalls and restaurants just outside the south city wall is a hidden gem, **Sanbao Congee Shop** (Sanbao Zhoupu; Shendao Lu, outside of Confucian Temple South gate; no phone). This very clean, homey restaurant is a nice change from the smaller and dirtier restaurants within the city walls. The menu features about 60 different types of rice porridges ranging from salty to sweet, and stir-fry dishes. The fried eggplant and the pork and thousand-year-old egg porridge are highly recommended. A meal for two averages ¥30 to ¥80.

Qufu After Dark

The Queli Hotel (see above) has **Confucian musical performances.** Tickets are ¥80 per person for 10 reservations or more (smaller audiences can expect to pay higher ticket prices) and are sold in the hotel lobby. From April to October are nightly "Confucius Dream" musical performances at 8:30pm at **Xing Tan Juchang (Apricot Altar Theater; ✆ 0537/441-3565**) where some of the rites mentioned in the *Analects (Lun Yu)* are performed. The theater is on Da Cheng Lu, about 800m (2,624 ft.) south of Kong Miao (Confucius Temple).

QINGDAO 青岛 ★★

Shandong Province, 318km (197 miles) E of Ji'nan, 890km (551 miles) SE of Beijing

Qingdao's strategic location at the mouth of a natural inlet on the south coast of the Shandong Peninsula has long made it attractive to foreign powers. When two German missionaries were killed in the Boxer Rebellion at the end of the 19th century, that was all the excuse Kaiser Wilhelm II needed to wrest Qingdao, then a small fishing town, from the weak Qing government, which ceded the port to the Germans on November 14, 1897, for 99 years. The Germans moved in, set up the Tsingtao Brewery, established churches and missions, built a railway to Ji'nan, and stationed 2,000 men in the garrison. But they were forced out at the beginning of World War I in 1914, and the Japanese took over, staying on after the 1919 Treaty of Versailles granted them authority over all ex-German territories in China. The Japanese ceded Qingdao back to the Kuomintang (Nationalist Government) in 1922 but occupied the town again from 1938 to 1945 during World War II.

Today, Qingdao, which has retained much of its Teutonic architecture, remains one of China's more charming and relaxing cities. With its year-round mild climate, Qingdao also hosts many fairs and festivals throughout the year, the most famous of which is the annual Qingdao International Beer Festival, held the last 2 weeks of August and attracting upwards of a million visitors. Summers see the town packed with Chinese visitors, making spring and fall better times to visit if you hope to avoid the crowds. In recent years, thanks to its vaulted position as host city to the watersports events of the 2008 Olympics, Qingdao has also seen many new hotels, restaurants, and faster connections to major cities. The **Olympic Sailing Center** is on the far eastern bay, with views of the central business district's sleek and glossy buildings, the international image of Qingdao broadcast worldwide during the XXIX Olympiad.

Essentials

GETTING THERE Qingdao is well connected by **air** to many Chinese cities, including Beijing (1 hr. 15 min.), Guangzhou (2 hr. 45 min.), and Shanghai (70 min.). Tickets can be purchased at the **CAAC office (Minhang Dasha)** at Xianggang Zhong Lu 30 (✆ **0532/8577-5555;** 24 hr.). International destinations served include Hong Kong, Seoul, Fukuoka, Tokyo, Pusan, and Bangkok. **Dragonair** (✆ **0532/8577-6159**) has an office at the Hotel Equatorial, Xianggang Zhong Lu 28, as does **Japan Airlines,** Xianggang Zhong Lu 76 (✆ **0532/8571-0088**). Qingdao's **Liu Ting Airport** (✆ **0532/8471-5777**) is located 30km (19 miles) north of the city; the 40-minute taxi ride costs ¥80 to ¥100. Airport shuttles charging ¥20 depart from the Haitian Fandian (Haitian Hotel), and make a stop at the Equatorial Hotel on the hour between 6am and 9pm. The bus also meets incoming flights.

The brand-new D-series **express trains** from Beijing take 5 to 5½ hours (6:57am D60, 8am D58, 10:51am D62, 2:58pm D52, 5:19pm D56, 6:05pm D54, and 7:53am D58, 5 hr.; 5:30pm D56, 5½ hr.). The old overnight express **train** from Beijing (T26) takes 10 hours. A slow overnight train from Shanghai (K29) takes 19½ hours, while the 10:30am D75 train takes 10 hours. Several trains a day connect to Weifang (2 hr.), Zibo (3–4 hr.), Ji'nan (4–5 hr. 30 min.), Tai Shan (6 hr.), and Qufu/Yanzhou (7 hr.). Tickets can be bought at the railway station (✆ **0532/8297-5207**) at Hai'an Lu 1, 5 days in advance.

The long-distance bus station is in the northern part of town, but the **bus station** (✆ **0532/4006-916916**) just outside the railway station should serve most travelers' needs. Intra-province buses depart from the lot south of the railway station for Weifang (every 40 min. 6:30am–5:20pm; 2 hr. 40 min.; ¥49) and Ji'nan (every 1 hr. 6:50am–7pm; 5 hr.; ¥84–¥113). Purchase your tickets at the little green kiosks. Long-distance sleeper buses depart from the front of the railway station for destinations farther afield such as Shanghai (noon, 5pm, 6pm, 7pm, 8pm; 11 hr.; ¥200) and Hangzhou (6am, 3:50pm and 6:30pm; 14 hr.; ¥310).

Qingdao 青岛

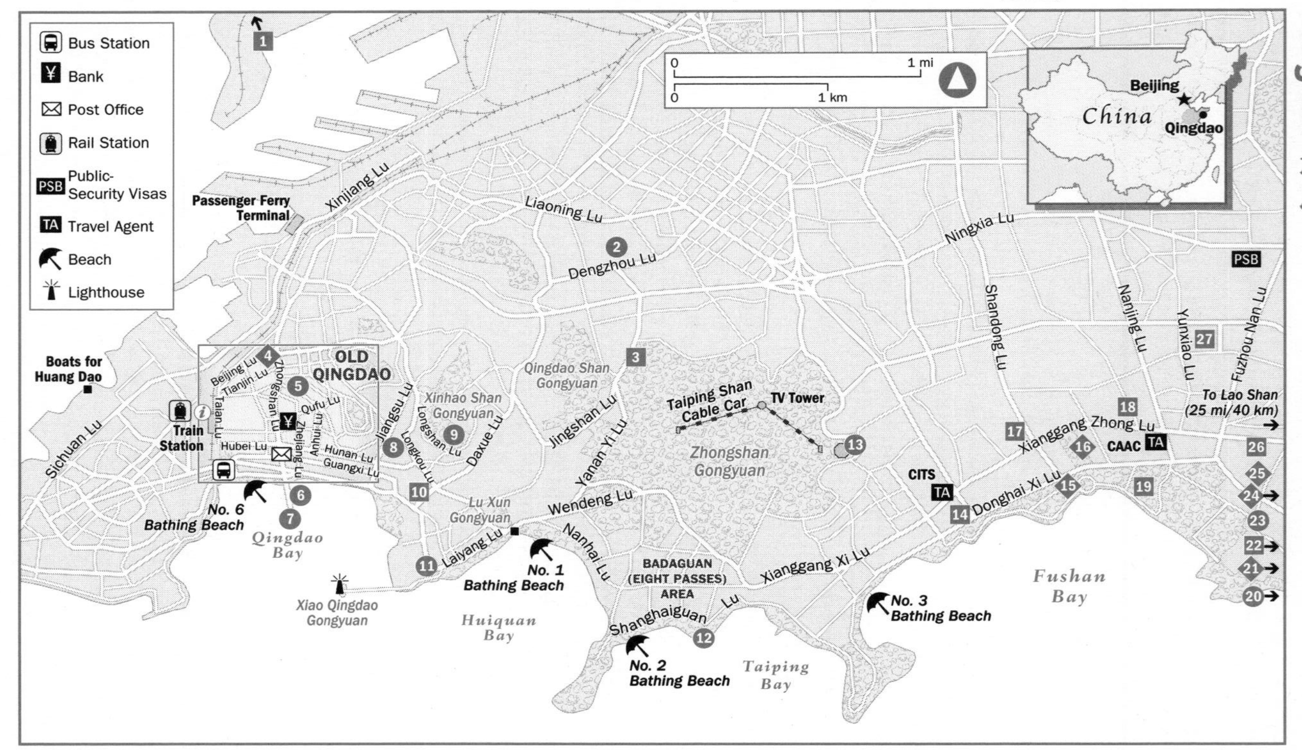
Bus Station
Bank
Post Office
Rail Station
PSB Public-Security Visas
TA Travel Agent
Beach
Lighthouse
0
1 mi
0
1 km
Beijing
China
Qingdao
Passenger Ferry Terminal
Xinjiang Lu
Liaoning Lu
Dengzhou Lu
Ningxia Lu
PSB
Shandong Lu
Nanjing Lu
Yunxiao Lu
Fuzhou Nan Lu
To Lao Shan (25 mi/40 km)
Boats for Huang Dao
OLD QINGDAO
Beijing Lu
Tianjin Lu
Zhongshan Lu
Qufu Lu
Taian Lu
Anhui Lu
Zhejiang Lu
Hubei Lu
Hunan Lu
Guangxi Lu
Train Station
Sichuan Lu
Jiangsu Lu
Longshan Lu
Longkou Lu
Xinhao Shan Gongyuan
Daxue Lu
Qingdao Shan Gongyuan
Jingshan Lu
Yanan Yi Lu
Taiping Shan Cable Car
TV Tower
Zhongshan Gongyuan
Xianggang Zhong Lu
CAAC
CITS
Donghai Xi Lu
No. 6 Bathing Beach
Qingdao Bay
Lu Xun Gongyuan
Wendeng Lu
Laiyang Lu
Nanhai Lu
No. 1 Bathing Beach
Xiao Qingdao Gongyuan
Huiquan Bay
BADAGUAN (EIGHT PASSES) AREA
Xianggang Xi Lu
Shanghaiguan Lu
No. 2 Bathing Beach
Taiping Bay
No. 3 Bathing Beach
Fushan Bay

Qingdao Key

HOTELS ■

China Community **27**
(China Gōngshè)
公社文化艺术酒店

Copthorne Hotel **18**
(Guodun Da Jiudian)
青岛国敦大酒店

Crowne Plaza Qīngdǎo **26**
(Qīngdǎo Yízhōng Huángguān Jiàrì Jiǔdiàn)
青岛颐中皇冠假日酒店

Dōngfāng Fàndiàn **10**
东方饭店

Doubletree Hotel **1**
(Qīngdǎo Xīn Jiāng Xīèrdùn Yìlín Jiǔdiàn)
青岛市鑫江希尔顿逸林酒店

Gloria Garden Resort Qingdao **14**
(Kǎilái Guójì Jiǔdià)
凯莱花园酒店

Intercontinental Qingdao **19**
(Qīngdǎo Hai'er Zhōuijì Jiǔdiàn)
青岛海尔洲际酒店

Qingdao Kilin Crown Hotel **22**
(Qīngdǎo Lù Lín Huángguān Dà Jiǔdiàn)
青岛麒麟皇冠大酒店

Shangri-La Hotel Qīngdǎo **17**
(Qīngdǎo Xiānggélǐlā Fàndiàn)
青岛香格里拉饭店

Super 8 Motel **3**
(Su Bā Jǐu Diàn)
速8酒店

ATTRACTIONS ●

Catholic Church **5**
(Tiānzhǔ Jiàotáng)
天主教圣弥厄尔大教堂

China Navy Museum **11**
(Hǎijūn Bówùguǎn)
海军博物馆

Huāshí Lóu **12**
花石楼

Huílán Gé **7**
迴澜阁

Protestant Church **8**
(Jīdū Jiàotáng)
基督教堂

Qīngdǎo Beer Park **23**
(Qīngdǎo Píjiǔ Chéng)
青岛啤酒城
only open during the Tsingtao Beer Festival

Qingdao Olympic Sailing Center **20**
(Qīngdǎo Àolínpīkè Fānchuán Zhōngxīn)
青岛奥林匹克帆船中心

Qīngdǎo Welcome Guesthouse **9**
(Qīngdǎo Yíng Bīnguǎn)
青岛迎宾馆

World of Tsingtao Beer **2**
(Qīngdǎo Píjiǔ Chǎng)
青岛啤酒厂

Zhàn Qiáo **6**
栈桥

Zhàn Shān Sì **13**
湛山寺

RESTAURANTS ◆

Beida Huang Ren **21**
(Běi Dà Huāng Rén)
北大荒人

Bellagio **15**
(Xiānggǎng Xiǎo Zhèn)
鹿港小镇

Chūnhé Lóu **4**
春和楼

Steven Gao's Restaurant **24**
(Liè Nóng Cānbā)
列侬餐吧

SPR Coffee **16**
(Yēshì Kāfēi)
耶士咖啡

Yijing Lou Hongkong 97 **25**
(Yíjǐng Lóu Xiānggǎng 97)
怡景楼香港97

Ferries to Incheon, South Korea (17 hr.) run three times a week (Mon, Wed, Fri). Tickets can be bought at the **Qingdao Port Passenger Terminal (Qingdao Gang Keyun Zhan)** at Xinjiang Lu 6 (✆ **0532/8282-5001**).

GETTING AROUND Downtown and the German Quarter can be toured on foot, but taxis and buses are more convenient ways to get to some of the beaches and attractions farther afield. **Taxis** charge either ¥10 for 3km (2 miles), then ¥1.70 per kilometer until 6km (5 miles), when the price rises to ¥2.55 per kilometer; or ¥7 for 3km (2 miles), then ¥1.20 per kilometer until 6km (5 miles), when the price rises to ¥1.80 per kilometer. Kilometer rates for either type of taxi increase by 50% after 10pm. **Bus** nos. 26 and 301 run from the railway station along the southern edge of the peninsula toward the commercial district on Xianggang Zhong Lu; the fare is ¥1.

VISITOR INFORMATION A **Tourism and Information Service Center** (✆ **0532/8591-2029;** 8:30am–6pm) is located 200m (656 ft.) to the left when you exit the railway station. They can provide information and direct travelers to sights and accommodations.

TOURS & GUIDES If you haven't become frustrated enough by other **CITS** offices around the country, you can give this one a shot. It's located at Xianggang Xi Lu 73 (✆ **0532/8389-3001;** fax 0532/8389-3013). For the latest information on the city and the rest of the province, look for the monthly English-language *Red Star* magazine, available at most international hotels or on the Internet at www.myredstar.com.

[Fast FACTS] QINGDAO

Banks, Foreign Exchange & ATMs The **Bank of China** at Zhongshan Lu 66 (✆ **0532/8286-1234**) has an ATM and is open for foreign exchange Monday through Friday from 8:30am to 5pm, Saturday and Sunday from 9:30am to 4pm. An **HSBC** ATM is also conveniently located inside the Crowne Plaza Hotel (Yizhong Huangguan Jiari Jiudian).

Internet Access If you're traveling with your own laptop, most hotels offer free in-room high-speed Internet connections. There is a small **Internet cafe** across from the post office on Anhui Lu. It's open from 9am to midnight.

Post Office Located at Anhui Lu 5 (8am–6pm) and another in the commercial district at Xianggang Zhong Lu 56 (8:30am–5:30pm).

Visa Extensions The **PSB** office for visa extensions (✆ **0532/6657-3259;** Mon–Fri 8:30–11:30am and 1:30–5:30pm) is inconveniently located in the eastern part of town at Ningxia Lu 272. Bus no. 301 runs there from the railway station.

Exploring Qingdao

GERMAN QINGDAO

Many houses and shops in the former German Concession still retain their original European architecture. In addition to the sights that follow, other noteworthy buildings include the **Railway Station** at Tai'an Lu 2, a classical European structure built in 1901 with a 35m-high (115-ft.) bell tower; the former **Public Security Bureau** at Hubei Lu 29, built in 1904 and 1905 in the style of a medieval village church; and the **Princess House** at Juyongguan Lu 10, a villa built in 1903 by the Danish consulate general for a Danish princess.

East of the old town near the Number Two Bathing Beach, the **Ba Da Guan (Eight Passes)** area, named for the eight famous passes of the Great Wall, was and still is the toniest address in town. Unfortunately for the visitor, most of the well-preserved European mansions and villas here are hidden behind high walls and fences. Still, it's a lovely area to stroll, as the streets are wide and sheltered by a canopy of trees, with each street (or "pass") planted with a different bloom, including crab apples, peaches, pines, magnolias, and ginkgoes.

Haijun Bowuguan (China Navy Museum) ★ ☺ Briefly wander through the drab indoor exhibition showing old photos and navy uniforms. Now on to the fun part: the outdoor exhibition of a torpedo boat, a surface-to-air missile, and plenty of old planes and helicopters. Kids can playfully scramble over small replicas nearby (though they're pretty much allowed to run at will through the exhibition as well). You can also walk through a docked destroyer and a jet, and for some family bonding time, take a crawl through a real submarine. It's claustrophobically tiny, so you get up close and personal with the bunkers, gauges, and inner workings of the deep-sea vessel.

Southernmost tip of Laiyang Lu. ✆ **0532/8286-6784.** Admission ¥60, extra ¥20 to tour ship and submarine.8:30am–5:30pm.

Huashi Lou (Hua Shi Villa) ★ This Bavarian medieval castle built in 1903, with a tall round turret, chimneys, balconies, and Greek-style columns, was originally a Russian aristocrat's villa but was later taken over by the German governor general as a fishing retreat. In 1946, Chiang Kai-shek secretly retreated here to plan the Kuomintang's next moves. These days, the villa, a big hit with wedding parties, can't exactly be called quiet or relaxing. Climbing to the top affords the visitor a grand view of the surrounding Ba Da Guan area.

Huanghai Lu 18. ✆ **0532/8387-2168.** Admission ¥9. Apr–Oct 8am–6pm; Nov–Mar 8am–5pm. Bus: no. 26 or 31.

Jidu Jiaotang (Protestant Church) ★★ One of Qingdao's more attractive sights, this simple but beautiful church was designed by German Curt Rothkegel in the style of a Western medieval castle and completed in 1908. A red tile roof and a pretty green bell tower with a three-sided clock face cap the squat yellow structure. Visitors can climb the tower to see the original bells that still toll here. More popularly known to locals as Zhongbiao Lou (Clock Tower), the building was spared destruction during the Cultural Revolution, as few knew it was a church.

Jiangsu Lu 15. Admission ¥7 to acess bell tower. Mon–Sat 8am–5pm; Sun noon–5pm. Bus: no. 1 to Jiangsu Lu.

Qingdao Yingbinguan (Qingdao Welcome Guest House) ★★★ Built between 1905 and 1908 in the style of an old fortress with Tudor motifs, this magnificent building, the former residence of the German governor general, looks like it leaped from a Grimm Brothers' fairy tale. In 1934, the house became a hotel and is now a museum. Visitors can see the office where Mao Zedong slept during his month-long summer vacation in July 1957. Much of the stained glass, dark woods, and plush furnishings have survived, including an exquisite green marble fireplace with ornamental tiles in the study and an original 1876 German grand piano. There's an audio guide for ¥30 available at the information center to the left when you enter the house. The information given is pretty general, and includes facts like the height and length of the windows in the atrium.

Longshan Lu 26. ✆ **0532/8288-9888.** Admission ¥15 in summer; ¥10 in winter. Apr–Oct 8:30am–5:30pm; Nov–Mar 8:30am–5pm. Bus: no. 25, 26, or 214 to Daxue Lu.

Tianzhu Jiaotang (Catholic Church) ★ The former St. Michael's Cathedral was designed by German architect Pepieruch in a Gothic and Roman style and built between 1932 and 1934 with 60m-high (197-ft.) twin bell towers housing four bronze bells. Much of the church's interior was destroyed during the Cultural Revolution. Today, the inside has been given a bit of a tacky paint job and all the stained glass is new except for the small triangular panels in the round window in the eastern wall of the church. The Sunday morning 8am service is open to the public. It's become a popular spot for wedding couples, who can be found posed in front of its gates at all hours. Note: At time of writing the church was closed for renovations and staff could not confirm when it will re-open to the public. Be sure to check with your hotel beforehand for the latest news on opening dates and admission prices.

Zhejiang Lu 15. ✆ **0532/8286-5960.** Admission ¥5. Mon–Sat 8am–5pm; Sun noon–5pm. Bus: no. 26.

World of Tsingtao Beer ★ The Tsingtao beer factory was closed to the public until recently; now, it's become a must-see attraction for most visitors to Qingdao. The well-curated museum offers a history of the beer, which debuted in China in 1903 as a British-German venture. Displays of print and film advertisements from the 1930s are worth checking out as is the actual bottling assembly line. The tour ends at the Tsingtao Bar, where you'll be treated to a pitcher (half a pitcher if there's only two of you) of beer. English signage in the museum is adequate for explaining most of the exhibits, but you can call ahead to arrange for an English-speaking guide.

Dengzhou Lu 56. ✆ **0532/8383-3437.** Admission ¥50. 8:30am–4:30pm. Bus: no. 205, 217, 221, or 604.

BEACHES

Qingdao's beaches are a top attraction for many Chinese, attractive if you're coming from any one of China's many dull, gray, overcrowded cities. Just don't expect a white-sand tropical paradise. From June to September, the beaches are packed. All the main public beaches, seven in the urban area, have changing booths where you can shower for ¥3, as well as medical stations and lifeguards on duty. Watersports range from water-skiing to parasailing.

Starting from the western tip of the peninsula, the beach nearest the railway station is the **Number Six Bathing Beach (Diliu Haishui Yuchang);** its rocky terrain makes it the least desirable for sunbathing. The big attraction here, however, is Qingdao's former pier, **Zhan Qiao** (¥2; 7am–8:30pm), originally built in 1892 for the Qing army. It now juts 440m (1,300 ft.) into the bay and is considered the city's symbol. At the end of the pier is the octagonal **Huilan Ge** (¥4), a pavilion that currently houses a small tacky aquarium with a coral exhibit.

Continuing east around the headland into the next bay past the aquarium, the 800m-long (2,624-ft.) **Number One Bathing Beach (Diyi Haishui Yuchang)** is one of Qingdao's longest, but the sand here is somewhat coarse and pebbly. Between April and June, this is where you'll find couples posing for wedding photos, with photographers and lighting equipment balanced precariously on the rocks and the stony piers that jut into the water. Around the next headland is the **Number Two Bathing Beach (Di'er Haishui Yuchang) ★**, much nicer and more secluded than either numbers One or Six. Little wonder that this beach used to be popular with political figures like Mao Zedong and other government officials. You must pay a ¥2 entrance fee from 9am to 6pm, but at other times, it's free. In the next bay is the 400m-long (1,312-ft.) **Number Three Bathing Beach (Disan Haishui Yuchang) ★**, also nice, quiet, and a bit out-of-the-way. **Shi Lao Ren (Old Man Rock) ★** is a quiet beach farther to the east. It's named for a rock that sits several hundred yards out from the bay and has the curved, stooped shape of an elderly man. Shi Lao Ren is far away from the business district, so things are less hectic here. It's also Qingdao's longest beach.

Far out to the west, half an hour by boat and then another half-hour by bus, is the beach of **Huang Dao ★**, cleaner and quieter than Qingdao's beaches, and until recently known only to locals—a real find. Take the Qingdao Huang Dao Lundu (ferry; hourly 6:30am–9pm; 30 min.; ¥10) from the local ferry terminal (Lundu Zhan) on Sichuan Lu west of the railway station, then bus no. 1 to its terminus.

PARKS

Qingdao has a multitude of parks, some of them worth exploring. **Zhongshan Gongyuan,** Xianggang Xi Lu (free admission; 8:30am–5pm) offers some pleasant strolls and is especially pretty during April and May when the cherry trees are in bloom. Northeast of the park is the **Taiping Shan Gongyuan,** where visitors can take a cable car up to a TV tower at the summit. The cable-car fare is ¥40 one-way, ¥50 round-trip. At the summit you can see lovely views of the city. From there, you can hike down the way you came, take the cable car, or hike down the back of the mountain to **Zhan Shan Si** (Ziquan Lu 4), the largest Buddhist temple in Qingdao. Admission to the temple is ¥10; hours are from 8:30am to 4:30pm. Note that the cable-car terminus is still a 15-minute walk to Zhan Shan Si; the fare to Zhan Shan Si is ¥20 one-way, ¥30 round-trip.

Xinhao Shan Gongyuan (Signal Hill Park), at Longshan Lu, just west of the Qingdao Welcome Guest House, was the location of a German navigating signal tower in 1898. Today the tower has been replaced by someone's bad idea of postmodernist architecture—three carbuncular mushroom-domed pink buildings meant to simulate signaling torches. Kitsch aside, the revolving viewing platform inside the main "mushroom" does afford some lovely views of Qingdao. Admission is ¥2 for the park only, ¥15 including tower entrance. Hours are from 7am to 7pm (to 6pm in winter). **Qingdao Shan Gongyuan,** northwest of Zhongshan Gongyuan, has the remains of an old German fort (or rather, the underground command post). Admission is ¥15; hours are from 8:30am to 4:30pm.

OTHER ATTRACTIONS

About 15km (9 miles) east of town, **Qingdao Pijiu Cheng** (Xianggang Dong Lu and Hai'er Lu) is a European-themed amusement park only open during the 2-week International Beer Festival in September. In this Bavarian bacchanal, there's something for everyone, from amusement park rides for kids, to drinking contests for adults, to go-karting for the kid in the adult. The beer festival also takes place closer to town at the Huiquan Guangchang, which offers a slightly more sanitized, calmer experience next to the ocean. Both are worth checking out, though you can expect a lot of kitsch at the first location. Check with CITS for exact dates.

Where to Stay

Qingdao has a glut of upmarket hotels, many of which offer 20% to 30% discounts. All rooms are subject to a 15% surcharge unless otherwise noted.

EXPENSIVE

Crowne Plaza Qingdao (Qingdao Yizhong Huangguan Jiari Jiudian) ★

Located in the heart of the commercial and shopping district, this hotel is popular with Western independent and business travelers. Rooms have a slightly claustrophobic, dark feel as windows are small, but they are well furnished and the beds are comfortable. Views of the sea are especially fine, though somewhat obstructed due to recent construction. Service is friendly here, but not as polished as at the pricier Shangri-La. With six restaurants on the premises, the hotel also has some of the most diversified dining choices; the Italian restaurant offers some of the best Western food in town.

Xianggang Zhong Lu 76. www.crowneplaza.com ✆ **0532/8571-8888.** Fax 0532/8571-6666. 388 units. ¥1,176 standard room; ¥1,376 suite. AE, DC, MC, V. **Amenities:** 6 restaurants; bakery; bar; lounge; free airport shuttle service; babysitting; bowling alley; concierge; executive rooms; forex; health club and spa; newsstand; indoor pool; room service; sauna; smoke-free rooms. *In room:* A/C, TV, hair dryer, Internet, minibar.

DoubleTree Qingdao (Qingdao Xinjiang Xi'erdun Yilin Jiudian) ★ Choose this Hilton-family hotel if you need to stay close to the airport. It opened in mid-2009, so the rooms and facilities are brand spanking new. Spacious rooms have plush carpets and tasteful modern decor, using warm amber and chocolate brown colors throughout. This really is like staying at a Hilton, with stylish appointments and great amenities like the sleek bathroom stocked with Crabtree & Evelyn products. The drawback is the location. This seems to be a hotel set up for company events, where guests fly in for a meeting and fly out the next day. It's 10 minutes from the airport, but over a half-hour from downtown and close to an hour away from the sites in the old German Concession.

220, 308 National Rd. www.doubeltree.com. ✆ **0532/8098-8888.** Fax 0532/8092-8666. 200 units. ¥700 standard; ¥895 executive room; ¥1,436 suite. 20% discounts available. AE, DC, MC, V. **Amenities:** 3 restaurants; lounge; babysitting; concierge; executive rooms; golf driving range; health club; 25m/82-ft. heated indoor pool; room service; smoke-free rooms; squash court; tennis court; Wi-Fi. *In room:* A/C, TV, hair dryer, minibar.

InterContinental Qingdao (Qingdao Haier Zhouji Jiudian) ★★ Occupying prime territory at the waterfront marina, this hotel served as the athletes' village during the 2008 Olympic games, when Qingdao hosted the sailing events. The hotel is huge and plush, spread among four interconnected towers. Decor is crisp and contemporary, with rooms equipped with plasma TVs by Haier, the Chinese appliance giant that owns the hotel. Spacious and luxe, rooms feature dark wood paneling, inset lighting, and silk brocade coverlets. Curtains silently open with the flick of a switch, showcasing a ceiling-to-floor panorama of the ocean and marina, if you requested a room with a view. Bathrooms are huge, with separate tub and shower facilities. Service is top-notch and professional; the busy concierge desk is particularly helpful. The breakfast buffet is immense and sumptuous, with a dining room that offers a glimpse of the water.

Ao Men Lu 98. www.intercontinental.com. ✆ **0532/6656-6666.** Fax 0532/6656-6888. 438 units. Standard rooms ¥1,800; suites ¥2,200. AE, DC, MC, V. **Amenities:** 4 restaurants; 2 bars; babysitting; concierge; executive-level rooms; 24-hr. health club; indoor pool; room service; Wi-Fi. *In room:* A/C, TV/DVD, CD player, fridge, hair dryer, Wi-Fi.

Qingdao Kilin Crown Hotel (Qingdao QiLin Huangguan Da Jiudian) This five-star hotel is a franchise of the Best Western group. It attracts many Korean vacationers who are looking for a beach vacation away from the city center; the hotel is less than a 5-minute walk from Shi Lao Ren Beach (Old Man Rock Beach). Rooms are more functional than luxe on the lower floors, with blond furniture, forgettable carpets, and cramped bathrooms. Rooms on the 36th floor and up are much nicer, with dark wood floor entryways and pretty silk bed throws. Ask to see rooms before you commit, as they vary by floor, and some seaside views are blocked by the exposed elevator that runs the length of the hotel's front side. There's a revolving restaurant on the top floor that has top-notch views of nearby Old Man Rock Beach.

Xianggang Dong Lu 197. www.bestwestern.com ✆ **0532/8889-1888.** Fax 0532/8889-1777. 405 units. ¥943–¥1,012 standard; ¥1,300 suite. Discounts possible up to 30%. AE, MC, V. **Amenities:** 2 restaurants; bar; concierge; forex; exercise room; small indoor pool; room service; sauna. *In room:* A/C, TV, hair dryer, Internet, minibar.

Shangri-La Hotel Qingdao (Qingdao Xianggelila Fandian) ★★ This is your top choice in Qingdao. The hotel added a new building in recent years and the rooms are outstanding. Bathrooms are spacious and luxurious, with L'Occitane bath amenities, his-and-her sinks and freestanding tubs separated from rooms by sliding doors. Rooms here are slightly larger than at the nearby InterContinental (see above). The hotel is also cozier and more stylish than the aging Crowne Plaza (see above), but often more expensive. The hotel has been revamping their rooms in the hotel's old wing for several years, with half now redone (along with building a new wing with 100 more rooms), and the other half of the old wing beginning renovation in fall 2012. Offering the full range of facilities and fine dining, the signature Shangri-La service and luxury is very much in evidence here.

Xianggang Zhong Lu 9. www.shangril-la.com. ✆ **0532/8388-3838.** Fax 0532/8388-6868. 696 units. Old building: ¥1,300 standard room; from ¥2,800 suite. New building: ¥1,950 standard room; ¥3,450 suite. AE, DC, MC, V. **Amenities:** 2 restaurants; bakery; bar; lounge; airport shuttle service; babysitting; concierge; executive rooms; forex; health club and spa; Jacuzzi; newsstand; indoor pool; room service; sauna; smoke-free rooms; outdoor tennis court. *In room:* A/C, TV, DVD player (in executive rooms and suites), hair dryer, Internet, minibar.

MODERATE

China Community (Zhongguo Gongshe) ★★ For those who love boutique hotels, look no further than this cool property. The owners, a husband-and-wife team from Sichuan and Shandong, already own a group of successful restaurants in Qingdao and Ji'nan. They've taken their love of traditional Chinese elements and added a healthy dollop of contemporary flair for this property. Each room has a different theme, but you can expect modern, design-heavy decor such as sliding doors with latticework carved to look like Chinese paper cuts, or traditional Chinese chairs painted metallic silver and paired with red and black silk cushions. Most rooms are open concept, with sinks on wooden countertops near the bed and in some rooms, toilets behind glass panels. The hotel features a striking architectural signature—a cylindrical Hakka-style building known as a *tulou,* which houses a popular three-story restaurant that also showcases cultural performances.

Min Jiang San Lu 8. www.chinagongshe.com. ✆ **0532/8576-8776.** Fax: 0532/8077-6776. 126 units. ¥408–¥588 standard room; ¥858–¥998 suite; ¥1,298 villa room. AE, DC, MC, V. **Amenities:** Restaurant; room service. *In room:* A/C, TV; hair dryer; Internet.

Copthorne Hotel (Guodun Da Jiudian) Formerly the Equatorial Hotel, this four-star hotel has all the modern amenities in the central business district. The marble lobby shares space with a well-lit buffet restaurant and a smart-looking bar with comfortable lounging areas. Rooms are perfectly comfortable though not lavish.

Décor is blonde wood and golden furnishings. Bathrooms are clean. Decent city views can be had from some rooms. The hotel's Chinese restaurant is a popular choice for local wedding receptions.

Xianggang Zhong Lu 28. www.milleniumhotels.com ✆ **0532/8668-1668.** Fax 0532/8668-1699. 455 units. ¥860 standard; from ¥1,698 suite. AE, DC, MC, V. Amenities: 2 restaurants; bakery; bar; lounge; concierge; executive rooms; fitness center and sauna; indoor pool; room services. *In room:* A/C, TV, hair dryer, Internet, minibar.

Dongfang Fandian ★ For those who don't require a beach location, this four-star hotel, about a 10-minute walk from the Protestant church, is probably the best deal around. Many Western travelers give it good marks for its comfortable, clean rooms at reasonable prices. It's not luxurious, but there's a full range of facilities and the service is quite good overall. The helpful staff speaks some English.

Daxue Lu 4. ✆ **0532/8286-5888.** Fax 0532/8286-2741. 146 units. ¥1,088 standard room; from ¥1,588 suite. 50% discounts possible. AE, DC, MC, V. **Amenities:** 3 restaurants; bar; lounge; concierge; forex; health club; room service; sauna; tennis court. *In room:* A/C, TV, hair dryer, minibar.

Gloria Garden Resort Qingdao This Hong Kong–managed three-star hotel catering mostly to Japanese, Korean, and domestic guests is the place to stay if you want to be closer to the sea and don't require luxurious amenities. An ugly white-tiled structure on the outside, the hotel has rooms that are comfortable enough on the inside. Bathrooms are bright and clean. The rooms facing the sea are bigger and a bit pricier. Views from seaside rooms are somewhat restricted by apartment blocks, but are pleasant. Service is decent, though getting an extra towel is harder than it should be.

Zhengyangguan Lu 19. ✆ **0532/8387-8855**. Fax 0532/8386-4640. 238 units. ¥880–¥1,580 standard room; ¥2,180 suite. 50%–60% discounts possible. AE, DC, MC, V. **Amenities:** 2 restaurants; bar; lounge; airport shuttle service; babysitting; concierge; executive rooms; forex; health club; indoor pool; room service; sauna; smoke-free rooms. *In room:* A/C, TV, minibar.

INEXPENSIVE

Super 8 Hotel (Su Ba Jiu Dian) This minihotel is the same chain as Super 8 in the U.S. and Canada. The Chinese version attracts the midrange, fairly well-to-do Chinese travelers and business folk. It's super-clean and service is excellent, international-quality. Rooms are decorated like a photo from an IKEA catalog. There are plush orange or white sofas, sleek lamps, and blond wood furniture. Beds are clean and white with cozy duvets.

Yan'an Yi Lu 86. ✆ **0532/8288-1888.** Fax 0532/8271-1888. 85 units. ¥388–¥458 standard; ¥528 superior room. AE, DC, MC, V. **Amenities:** Restaurant; room service; smoke-free rooms. *In room:* A/C, TV, Internet.

Where to Eat

Qingdao's seafood and its variations of local Shandong cuisine *(lu cai)* are all worth trying. Two long blocks east of the Shangri-La Hotel along Xianggang Zhong Lu is **Yunxiao Lu,** a lively street of bars and restaurants serving all types of Chinese cuisine into the wee hours. Just outside the Tsingtao Beer Museum is also a busy strip of streetside restaurants that offer up seafood and, of course, the local brew.

Coffee aficionados can get a fix at **Starbucks** on Xianggang Zhong Lu in the Sunshine Plaza (Yangguang Baihuo) or at **SPR Coffee** in the May 4th Square (north of the monument) on 35 Donghai Xi Lu. If you have your own computer, the SPR location also has Wi-Fi.

Bei Da Huang Ren ★★ DONGBEI Chinese measure the quality of a restaurant by the number of people inside and level of noise. So this place is of very serious quality! Bei Da Huang Ren is packed at dinnertime and the surrounding diners chattering away and clanking plates and chopsticks provide an atmospheric din to a tasty meal. Try the signature dish, *Bei Da Huang Kong Fu* (white fish served in a spicy broth with Sichuan peppercorns). The staff is super-friendly and efficient.

Liao Yang Xi Lu 48. ✆ **0532/8565-9999** or 0532/8565-6999. Meal for 2 ¥80–¥200. No credit cards. 11am–9:30pm.

Bellagio (Xianggang Xiao Zhen) ★ TAIWANESE This popular chain has made its way to Qingdao city. As with their Shanghai and Beijing locations, the decor is stylish and hip. The signature icy desserts are melt-in-your-mouth divine; I highly recommend the *huasheng bingsha* (peanut ice smoothie).

Aomen San Lu 19. ✆ **0532/8387-0877.** Meal for 2 ¥100–¥250. AE, MC, V. 11am–11pm.

Chunhe Lou ★ SHANDONG This long-standing institution for Shandong cuisine is located in an old two-story corner building in the German Concession. The first floor serves casual fast food while the second floor has large tables and private rooms. Despite the modest ambience, the food has its devotees. House specialties include *youbao hailuo* (fried sea snails), *songshu guiyu* (deep-fried sweet-and-sour fish), and *xiang su ji* (fragrant chicken). With less than a dozen tables and booths, not including the private rooms that require an extra fee, this popular spot quickly fills up.

Zhongshan Lu 146. ✆ **0532/8282-4346.** Meal for 2 ¥80–¥150. No credit cards. 1st floor 10am–2:30pm and 5–8:30pm; 2nd floor 11am–9pm.

Hongkong 97 (Xianggang 97) ★★ SEAFOOD Seafood doesn't get more delicious or fresh than at this popular chain, especially when you're asked to point and choose it from the tank yourself. Ordering is super easy here: There's no menu—just a range of aquariums and sample dishes on display. A waiter will follow you around to write down what you want. The highlight of our meal was the fresh *hualong,* a lobster-like creature without claws, prepared three ways: served raw (brought to our table with the head still moving), deep-fried with salt and pepper, or made into a rice porridge. Other highlights included *youba gufa zheng qiezi* (steamed eggplant), *gongzhu yu* (princess fish cooked in oil and steamed), and *tieban heli kao dan* (iron plate clams with scrambled eggs). Service is good, though comically formal—they presented our Sprite the way a sommelier would show a bottle of wine before opening it.

Xiang Gang Zhong Lu 90. ✆ **0532/8588-3388.** Meal for 2 ¥300–¥500. No credit cards. 10am–2pm and 4:30–9pm.

Steven Gao's Restaurant SHANDONG Okay, it's a strange setting for authentic Lu cuisine: The two-story pub with a pool table, booths, and a stage is owned by a local named Steven Gao, who has a love affair with British culture. John Lennon's image decorates the menu cover, and Beatles posters hang from the walls. The food, though, is pure home-style Shandong cuisine. Try the sautéed mini clams with chili pepper *(lachao xiao geli)* and the savory stir-fried noodles with beef tendon *(niujin chaomian).* Finish it off with one of our favorite Chinese desserts, candied, lightly battered and fried apple chunks *(basi pingguo).*

Zhuhai Lu 20. ✆ **0532/8589-3899.** ¥30–¥60. No credit cards. 9am–3am.

Lao Shan 崂山 ★★

Located 40km (24 miles) east of Qingdao, Lao Shan is a mountain range that is part Daoist sanctuary, part natural wonder; with waterfalls, streams, and walking trails

WILD CHINA: THE funeral pits OF ZIBO 淄博

Once the capital of the Qi State—during the Spring and Autumn (722–481 B.C.) and Warring States periods (475–221 B.C.)—Zibo today is a dusty industrial town better known for its glass and ceramic production.

The town is located 116km (70 miles) east of Ji'nan in Shandong Province, but most of its worthwhile sights are actually in Linzi District about 35km (21 miles) east of Zibo. The **Linzi Zhongguo Guche Bowuguan (Li Museum of Chinese Ancient Chariots)** ★★ (Qilin Zhen, Houli Guanzhuang), is about 6km (3½ miles) from the Linzi bus station. Admission is ¥25 and hours are from 8am to 6pm. Here you'll see two fascinating ancient horse-and-chariot funeral pits which predate Xi'an's terra-cotta army by more than 280 years. The horses' remains, dating from the Spring and Autumn Period, have been left as they were found. The first pit contains the remains of 10 chariots and 32 horses, all facing west. From the positions of the horses, with bronze bits still intact, archaeologists concluded that the animals were either anesthetized or otherwise rendered unconscious before burial. The second pit features the bones of four horses plus six chariots, which remain buried underneath the horses. Visitors can get a close look, which is a fascinating, if eerie, experience.

Ten minutes to the northwest, **Xun Ma Keng (Ancient Horse Relics Museum)** ★, Heyatou Cun (¥10; 8am–5pm) is a series of over 20 tombs believed to have belonged to Qi Jing, the 25th monarch of the Qi State. The tombs contain the fossils of 600 horses. Only **tomb 5** (106 horses) in the southwestern section is open, however. Unearthed in 1982, the horses are arranged in two rows with their heads facing outward. No other funerary objects were found, as the tombs were long ago robbed.

Ceramic production developed around Zibo as early as the period of the Houli culture 8,000 years ago. Four exhibit halls at the town's ceramics museum, **Zibo Zhongguo Taoci Guan** ★, Xincun Xi Lu (✆ **0533/217-2300;** ¥40; May–Oct 9–11:30am and 3–6pm; Nov–Apr 9–11:30am and 2–5pm), trace the evolution of Zibo's ceramics from the Neolithic Longshan and Houli cultures to its zenith in the Tang and Song dynasties with the development of celadon ware and black glaze porcelain. Notable items on display

snaking through wooded hills; and jagged cliff faces rising dramatically from the blue sea. Daoism spread to the mountain during the Western Han dynasty (206 B.C.–A.D. 9), and emperors throughout the ages have dispatched envoys to scale the mountain in search of the elixir of life. While the water that originates from here didn't perform any miracles, today it is famous and is used in brewing Tsingtao beer.

Admission to Lao Shan is ¥70, but thanks to greedy tourist officials you must now purchase additional tickets, ranging from ¥4 to ¥30, to gain entry to specific attractions on the mountain. The most popular sightseeing route is the **southern route,** which takes in Daoist temples, caves, and ponds, with stupendous sea views along the way. The main Daoist temple here is **Taiqing Gong,** first built in 140 B.C., now with over 140 rooms and an equally mind-boggling number of gods from the Daoist pantheon. Admission is ¥15; hours are from 6am to 6pm. East of the temple, a trail leads up to **Yakou temple,** where you can either take a cable car or continue on foot up to Yao Lake and Mingxia Cave, where admission is ¥4. The trail down leads past **Shangqing Gong** (¥4), another Daoist temple; and the impressive waterfall, **Longtan Pu.**

include the dainty eggshell earthenware of the Longshan culture and the rare "Blue and Yellow Celestial Dragon" patterned porcelain reserved strictly for use by the emperor. The store here (8–11:30am and 2:30–6pm, to 5pm in winter) sells surprisingly inexpensive locally produced vases, cups, and individual sculptures. Only cash is accepted.

Getting There From Zibo's **railway station** (✆ **0533/258-2522**) in the southern part of town, daily trains run to Ji'nan (2 hr.), Weifang (1 hr.), Qingdao (1 hr. 40 min.–3 hr.), and beyond. From Zibo's **bus station** (✆ **0533/9671-7533**), just west of the railway station, buses run to Ji'nan (every 20–30 min. 6am–7pm; 1 hr. 30 min., ¥27–¥36), Qingdao (every 1 hr. 7:30am–4pm; 3 hr. 30 min., ¥75), Weifang (every 30 min. 6:30am–6pm; 1 hr. 30 min., ¥25–¥30), and Tai'an (every 40 min., 6:30am–5:30pm; 1 hr. 30 min., ¥40).

Getting Around Take bus no. 6 or minibus no. 20 for ¥3 from Dongyi Lu just east of the railway station to its terminus at Linzi Bus Station; then take tourist bus no. 5, which stops at all the main sights listed here (¥4 for the entire loop). Alternatively, a **taxi** from Zibo will cost ¥60 to ¥80 one-way. In town, taxis charge ¥5 per 3km (2 miles), then ¥1.20 per kilometer thereafter.

Where to Stay & Eat Located in its own garden compound in the center of town, the four-story, four-star **Zibo Binguan,** Zhongxin Lu 189 (✆ **0533/228-8688;** fax 0533/218-4990) offers rooms that lack charm but are comfortable, with clean bathrooms. Rooms go for ¥680, and can be discounted 60%. The 31-story **Zibo Fandian ★**, Zhongxin Dadao 177 (✆ **0533/218-0888;** fax 0533/218-4800) was the town's first four-star hotel (opened in 1999). What it lacks in charm is made up for with a host of modern conveniences. The rack rates are absurd here, but you can bargain them down considerably. Standard rooms, with discount, cost ¥360 and have large, comfortable beds and standard four-star furnishings, though the carpets are old. The spacious marble bathrooms are dark but clean. Suites can be had for ¥480 to ¥680. The hotel's revolving restaurant on the 31st floor offers Shandong cuisine (also known as "Lu") in one of the city's more elegant settings. The Demeanor Bar serves real cappuccino and Colombian coffee, plus cocktails and imported wine.

To get to Lao Shan, tourist buses depart from the eastern end of Qingdao's railway station square every half-hour from 6:30am to 6pm. The 1-hour trip costs ¥20. Public bus no. 304 runs from the Ferry Terminal (Lundu) on Sichuan Lu all the way to Yakou. The Taiqing Gong cable car costs ¥50 round-trip (¥40 in low season).

NANJING 南京 ★★

Jiangsu Province, 306km (189 miles) NW of Shanghai

First the nation's capital in the early years of the Ming dynasty (A.D. 1368–1644), then the capital of the Republic of China from 1911 to 1937, and now capital of Jiangsu Province, this bustling city of six million is left off many China itineraries, lacking many visible reminders of what has in fact been a highly tumultuous and storied past. Except for Zhongshan Lin, the tomb of Sun Yat-sen, the scope of Nanjing's attractions do not accurately reflect the magnitude and importance of its place in China's history, which is a shame, because the city deserves at least a day or two

Nanjing 南京

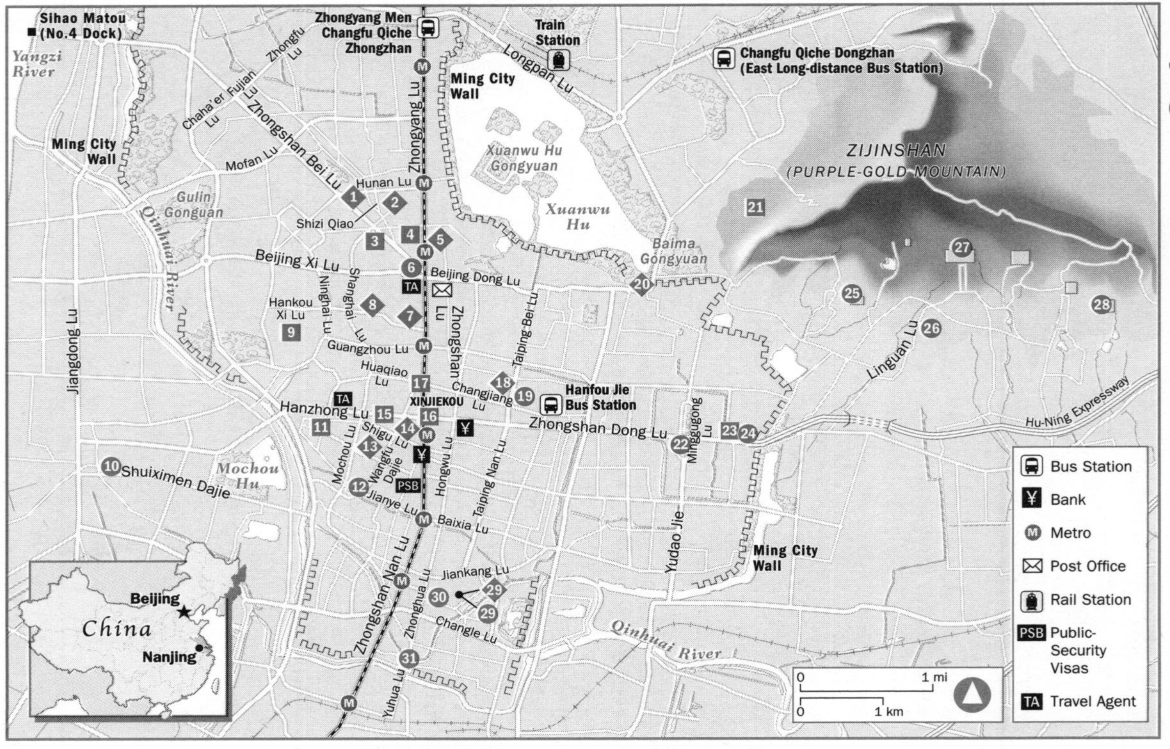
Sihao Matou (No.4 Dock)
Yangzi River
Zhongyang Men Changfu Qiche Zhongzhan
Train Station
Changfu Qiche Dongzhan (East Long-distance Bus Station)
Ming City Wall
Longpan Lu
Zhongfu Lu
Chaha'er Lu
Fujian Lu
Zhongshan Bei Lu
Zhongyang Lu
Xuanwu Hu Gongyuan
Xuanwu Hu
ZIJINSHAN
(PURPLE-GOLD MOUNTAIN)
Mofan Lu
Hunan Lu
Gulin Gonguan
Qinhuai River
Shizi Qiao
Baima Gongyuan
Beijing Xi Lu
Beijing Dong Lu
Shanghai Lu
Ninghai Lu
Hankou Xi Lu
Zhongshan Lu
Taiping Bei Lu
Jiangdong Lu
Guangzhou Lu
Huaqiao Lu
Changjiang Lu
Hanfou Jie Bus Station
Linguan Lu
XINJIEKOU
Hanzhong Lu
Shigu Lu
Zhongshan Dong Lu
Minggugong Lu
Hu-Ning Expressway
Mochou Lu
Wangfu Dajie
Hongwu Lu
Taiping Nan Lu
Shuiximen Dajie
Mochou Hu
Jianye Lu
Baixia Lu
Yudao Jie
Jiankang Lu
Zhongshan Nan Lu
Zhonghua Lu
Changle Lu
Yuhua Lu
China
Beijing
Nanjing
0 1 mi
0 1 km
Bus Station
Bank
Metro
Post Office
Rail Station
PSB Public-Security Visas
TA Travel Agent

Nanjing Key

HOTELS ■

Celebrity City Hotel **4**
(Míngrén Chéngshì Jiǔdiàn)
名人城市酒店

Central Hotel (Zhōngxīn Dàjiǔdiàn) **17**
中心大酒店

Crowne Plaza Nanjing Hotels and Suites **15**
(Qiáo Hóng Huángguān Jiǔdiàn)
南京侨鸿皇冠假日酒店

Grand Metropark Hotel Nanjing **23**
(Nánjīng Wéi Jǐng Guójì Dàjiǔdiàn)
南京维景国际大酒店

Hotel Sheraton Nánjīng Kingsley Hotel and Towers **11**
(Nánjīng Jīnsīlì Xǐláidēng Jiǔdiàn)
南京金丝利喜来登酒店

Jīnlíng Fàndiàn **16**
金陵饭店

Nánshān Bīnguǎn **9**
南山宾馆

Sofitel Galaxy Nanjing **3**
(Nánjīng Suǒfēitè Yínhé Dàjiǔdiàn)
南京索菲特银河大酒店

Sofitel Zhongshan Golf Resort **21**
(Suǒfēitè Gāo'ěrfū Jiǔdiàn)
南京索菲特钟山高尔夫酒店

RESTAURANTS ◆

Bǎnián Lǎo Fèng Xiǎochī **29**
百年老风小吃

Bellagio (Xiānggǎng Xiǎo Zhèn) **18**
鹿港小镇

Ciao Italia (Nǐhǎo! Yìdàlì Cāntīng) **13**
你好！意大利餐厅

Da Pai Dang **1**
大牌档

Golden Harvest Thai Opera Café **2**
(Jīnhé Tài Cāntōng)
金禾泰餐厅

Jīnyīng Dàjiǔlóu **14**
金鹰大酒楼

Le 5 Sens (Lè Shàng Fǎguó Cāntīng) **8**
乐尚法国餐厅

New Magazine Café (Xīn Zázhì Kāfēi) **7**
新杂志咖啡

Prime Restaurant **5**
云端西餐厅

Skyways Bakery and Deli **20**
(Yún Zhōng Cānpǐndiàn)
云中食品店

South Beauty **18**
(Qiào Jiāng Nán)
俏江南

ATTRACTIONS ●

Cháotiān Gōng **12**
朝天宫

Confucian Temple (Fūzǐ Miào) **29**
夫子庙

Dàzhōng Tíng **6**
大钟亭

Gǔ Lóu **6**
鼓楼

Jiāngnán Gòngyuàn Lìshǐ Chénlièguǎn **29**
江南贡院历史陈列馆

Línggǔ Sì **26**
灵谷寺

Memorial to the Victims of the Nánjīng Massacre **10**
(Nánjīng Dàtúshā Jìniànguǎn)
南京大屠杀纪念馆

Ming Filial Tomb (Míng Xiào Líng) **25**
明孝陵

Míng Gù Gōng **22**
明故宫

Nánjīng Museum (Nánjīng Bówùguǎn) **24**
南京博物院

Presidential Palace (Zǒngtǒng Fǔ) **19**
总统府

Sòng Měilíng's Villa (Sòng Měilíng Gōngguǎ) **28**
宋美龄别墅

Tàipíng Heavenly Kingdom Historical Museum **30**
(Tàipíng Tiānguó Lìshǐ Bówùguǎn)
太平天国历史博物馆

Zhōnghuá Mén Chéngbǎo **31**
中华门城堡

Zhōngshān Líng **27**
中山陵

of your time. In addition to some Ming dynasty attractions are reminders that Nanjing was also the seat of the Taiping Rebellion and the site of one of history's most brutal massacres. Spring and fall are the best times to visit, as Nanjing in the summer is well known as one of China's three furnaces.

Essentials

GETTING THERE From Nanjing's **airport**, just under 50km (31 miles) southwest of the city, daily flights connect to Beijing, Guangzhou, Wuhan, Chengdu, Kunming, Guilin, and Hong Kong. There are also twice-weekly flights to Macau and Bangkok. Tickets can be purchased at hotel tour desks and at the **CAAC** at Ruijin Lu 50 (✆ **025/8449-9378**). **China Eastern** has an office at Zhongshan Dong Lu 402 (✆ **025/8445-4325;** 8:30am–6pm), while **Dragonair** offices are at Hanzhong Lu 2, nos. 751–753 (✆ **025/8471-0181;** 7am–11pm). CAAC airport shuttles depart from the CAAC office every 30 minutes from 6am to 7pm, and also meet arriving flights. The trip takes 50 minutes and costs ¥25. ***Note:*** The bus leaves once full; those left behind must take taxis. A metered **taxi** into the Xinjiekou area should run about ¥140, including toll.

Nanjing's **railway station,** Longpan Lu 264 (✆ **025/8582-2222**) is conveniently linked to Nanjing's metro. A 5-minute ride to a central station (such as Xinjiekou) will cost ¥2. The city is an important rail junction along the Beijing-Shanghai railway line. Trains heading east to Shanghai (2 hr.; D-series trains 1 hr ½ hr.) connect to Wuxi (1½–2 hr.), Suzhou (2–2 hr. 30 min.), and Hangzhou (5 hr.; 1 D-series train daily 4 hr.). Heading west, there are trains to Huang Shan (6–10 hr.) You can buy tickets on the second floor of the three-story annex west of the station's exit. A special window selling only Shanghai tickets is marked in green; its hours are from 7 to 11am and from 11:30am to 6:30pm. You can also buy tickets at the Gu Lou ticket-booking office at Zhongshan Lu 293.

Nanjing has seven **long-distance bus stations,** but the main one, Nanjing Zhongyang Men Changtu Qiche Zongzhan, at Jianning Lu 1 (✆ **025/8553-1288**), just west of the Nanjing Railway Station, should serve most travelers' needs. From here, large, air-conditioned buses run to Suzhou (every 30 min.; 6:50am–7:30pm; 2 hr. 40 min.; ¥70), Shanghai (every 90 min.; 7:30am–4:40pm; 3 hr. 30 min.; ¥68), and Hangzhou (hourly; 6:20am–8pm; 5 hr.; ¥118). The East Long-Distance Bus Station (Changtu Qiche Dong Zhan) at Huayuan Lu 17 services Yangzhou (every 30 min.; 6:30am–6:40pm; 1 hr.; ¥33) and Yixing (every 20 min. 6am–6:40pm; 2 hr. 30 min.; ¥50). There are also express "business" buses for ¥88 that leave for Shanghai at 8, 9, and 10am and 2, 3:30, and 4:30pm from the back entrance of the Jinling Hotel.

GETTING AROUND Nanjing is a sprawling city not particularly conducive to walking, with sights scattered in different directions. The rate for **taxis** is ¥8 for 3km (2 miles), then ¥2.40 per kilometer. From 11pm to 6am, the price rises to ¥2.70 per kilometer after 3km. All taxi rides come with a ¥1 fuel surcharge. The **metro** is a fast and convenient way to get around town. Tickets are ¥2 to ¥4 depending on distance. Single-journey "tokens" that look remarkably similar to poker chips are available at vending machines in the station or at ticket windows. Swipe tokens when entering the subway, and deposit the plastic coin in the slot on the way out. Nanjing Public Utility IC Cards (or *Yika Tongpiao*) can be used for metro and bus rides, offering 5% discounts on the metro and 20% discounts for buses. Buy them for a ¥30 refundable deposit at ticket counters in the metro station. **Buses** are a cheap way to get around Nanjing, although they are almost always full. Pay ¥2 for air-conditioned buses and ¥1 for all others, or use an IC card (see above). No change is given. Some of the main bus routes include: no. 1: Nanjing Railway Station–Xinjiekou–Fuzi Miao; no. Y1: Nanjing Railway Station–Xinjiekou–Zhongshan Ling; no. Y2: Yuhua Tai–Zongtong Fu–Zhongshan Ling.

TOURS **Jiangsu Zhongshan International Travel Service,** Zhongshan Bei Lu 178 (✆ **025/8629-2086**) works with the major hotels to offer a standard 1-day tour of Nanjing, including visits to Zhongshan Ling (Dr. Sun Yat-sen's Mausoleum), Zongtong Fu (the Presidential Palace), and Chaotian Gong (Worshipping Heaven Palace), among other places. The cost of ¥230 includes entry fees and the use of a guide and bus driver.

VISITOR INFORMATION *MAP,* the free local English-language monthly magazine featuring the latest on dining and entertainment in Nanjing, is available in any of the top hotels or in Western restaurants. Try the government-run **Nanjing Tourist Information Center** (**Nanjing Luyou Zixun Fuwu Zhongxin;** ✆ **025/5226-9008;** 9am–5pm) in Confucius Temple for advice on sightseeing, restaurants, and hotels. The office is staffed by two very helpful employees.

[FastFACTS] NANJING

Banks, Foreign Exchange & ATMs The main branch of the **Bank of China** is located at Zhongshan Nan Lu 148. Hours for foreign exchange are Monday through Friday from 8:30am to noon and 2 to 5pm. ATMs accept international cards. Another branch is at Hongwu Lu 29 with the same hours.

Internet Access Free wireless laptop access is available at the **Coffee Beanery** (in the 1912 restaurant/pub complex at the corner of Changjiang Hou Jie and Taiping Bei Lu) and at all locations of **New Magazine Cafe** (p. 403).

Post Office The main post office (8:30am–5:30pm) is at **Gu Lou,** Zhongshan Lu 366.

Visa Extensions The **PSB** is located at Honggong Ci 1 (✆ **025/8442-0004;** Mon–Sat 8:30–11:30am and 2–5pm). Same-day visas are possible. From Xinjiekou, walk 5 minutes south on Zhongshan Nan Lu, then head west onto Sanyuan Xiang for about 300m (980 ft.).

Exploring Nanjing

HISTORIC SIGHTS

Sadly, Nanjing's Ming legacy can be found in only a few buildings and ruins today. In the center of town, the drum tower **Gu Lou** was built in 1382 and contained a series of drums used to mark the night watches, welcome guests, and occasionally warn of approaching enemies (admission to grounds free, ¥5 to enter the second floor of tower and teahouse, metro: Gu Lou). Close by is a pavilion, **Dazhong Ting,** which houses a 23,000-kilogram (25-ton) bronze bell from 1388. Toward the eastern part of town are the ruins of the first Ming dynasty imperial palace, **Ming Gu Gong.** All that remains of the once massive palace, destroyed in the Taiping Rebellion, are the Wu Men (Meridian Gate) that once marked the front gate of the palace wall, five small marble bridges, and 12 large plinths that were once the foundation of another large gate. Sections of the Ming **city wall** are still visible.

THE TAIPING heavenly kingdom

During the mid–19th century, natural disasters, catastrophic floods and famines, Western excesses, and Qing government neglect and corruption had all coalesced to create widespread unrest in China. It was in such a setting that the largest uprising in modern Chinese history occurred. Known as the **Taiping Rebellion,** its impact continues to be felt even today.

The Taiping Rebellion started in the mind of Hong Xiuquan (born Hong Huoxiu, 1814–64), a teacher and a farmer's son from Guangdong Province. After Hong failed his civil-service exams for the third time, he had a feverish dream of a bearded man and a younger man, whom he later decided were God the Father and Jesus. Hong also kept seeing part of his own name, "Huo" in the Christian tract, which he interpreted as another divine calling. Convinced that he was God's son and Jesus' younger brother, and his mission from God was to "slash the demons"—the twin demons of the Manchu government and the traditional Chinese folk religion—Hong formulated his own ideology, a mix of Christian ideals and Confucian utopianism. He soon amassed a large anti-Manchu, anti-establishment following in the south and in 1851 led a group of 20,000 followers to establish the **Taiping Heavenly Kingdom,** with Hong himself as king. Using their army and any number of ragtag peasant militias they could muster along the way, the Taipings swept up through south and central China and established themselves in Nanjing in 1853, renaming the city Tianjing (Heavenly Capital).

The Taipings preached a new order based on the equal distribution of land, equality between the sexes, monotheism, and the existence of small communities ruled by religious leadership, an order that, save for the religious bit, was to prefigure some of the tenets of the Chinese Communist movement. Feudalism, slavery, concubinage, arranged marriages, opium smoking, foot binding, prostitution, idolatry, and alcohol were all to be abolished (at least in theory). While women under the Taiping were allowed a greater degree of freedom (there was even a Taiping army made up entirely of female troops), Taiping morals continued to stress obedience and chastity in women. Hong Xiuquan and other Taiping leaders also continued to keep harems, in that way no different from any of China's emperors or even Mao Zedong, who was known to maintain his own.

In the end, however, the Taipings were doomed by a combination of internecine struggles, corruption, defections, flawed policies, and external forces made up of a reconstituted Qing army aided by Western powers who had apparently decided they would rather deal with the devil they knew (the Qing government) than contend with the uncertainties of a strong Taiping force, even though they were closer to them in ideals. The counterattack was brutal and merciless, and by the time the Chinese army succeeded in crushing the revolt 14 years after it began, a reported 30 million lives had been lost. Hong Xiuquan himself died of illness in 1864 but his successor, his 14-year old son, was killed by Qing troops.

It is uncanny how so many facets of the Taiping Rebellion would be echoed in later Chinese events. The ability of one man to command such a large fanatical uprising and sustain it for so long would later be paralleled in Mao's Cultural Revolution (1966–76). The effects of such large mass uprisings also help explain the current Chinese leadership's fear of them.

Zhonghua Men Chengbao ★ Located in the southern part of town, this is the biggest and best-preserved of the city wall's original 13 gates. Built by the Hongwu emperor between 1366 and 1386, the wall, at 33km (20 miles), was the longest city wall in the world, made of uniform bricks cemented with a mortar of lime, sorghum, and glutinous rice. Zhonghua Gate, first built in 1386, actually consists of four rows of gates, the first one 53m (173 ft.) long. Each gate entrance had a vertically sliding stone door lifted with a mechanical winch. Twenty-seven arched vaults inside the first gate could house up to 3,000 soldiers, who were set to ambush the enemy should the latter be so unfortunate as to be trapped within the gates. Climb to the top for some good views of the city, and to gaze at the kitschy fake guards. Along the way, watch for bricks that still bear the carvings of their maker and supervisor. In front of the walls, locals fly kites bought from vendors for ¥8.

Zhonghua Men. Admission ¥35. 8am–9:30pm. Metro: Zhonghuamen.

Zongtong Fu (Presidential Palace) ★★ The last time we visited this fascinating site, it was worn around the edges and attracted very few visitors, but it had an authentic air of historical significance to it. Now, likely capitalizing on its location next to the big tourist attraction of 1912 (see "Where to Eat" later in this chapter), the palace has undergone a massive renovation. Columns have been repainted bright red and there are new window frames with frosted glass in place. There are also more areas on display, like the rock gardens on the west and the Taiping Lake on the east. The palace was the seat of government of the Liangjiang viceroy's office (1671–1911), the Taiping Heavenly Kingdom (1853–64), Sun Yat-sen's provisional government (1912), and the Nationalist government (1927–37 and 1946–49). It has borne witness to all the important events and personalities in Nanjing's history. Though this presidential palace dates from the Ming dynasty, today's buildings were all built after 1870. Just inside the main entrance, the Great Hall marked by the words TIAN XIA WEI GONG (the world belongs to all) used to be the first in a series of nine magnificent halls during the Taiping Heavenly Kingdom. On January 1, 1912, provisional president of the new Chinese republic Sun Yat-sen held his inauguration here.

After the second hall, the next series of rooms were used by Chiang Kai-shek, the leader of the Nationalist Party, to receive foreign guests, among them U.S. Gen. George Marshall, who was attempting to broker a truce between Chiang and Mao Zedong. In the back, Chiang Kai-shek's former office has an interesting old-fashioned hand-operated Otis elevator, which has now been restored. In Xuyuan, the garden on the western side of the compound, a stone boat is the only remaining original artifact from the days of the Taiping Heavenly Kingdom.

Changjiang Lu 292. Admission ¥40. English-speaking guides an exorbitant ¥150. 7:30am–5pm. Bus: no. 1, 2, 29, 44, 65, 95, or 304. Metro: Xinjiekou.

Fuzi Miao (Confucian Temple) Kitschy it may be, but this is where you'll get a good idea of the modern interests of Nanjing's youth. Once a place of intense study and quiet contemplation, Fuzi Miao is now the site for everything from tattoo parlors to pirated music stores selling the latest Mandarin hits. To the right (east) was once the Jiangnan Gongyuan, an academy first built in 1169, which later became the largest imperial civil examination halls during the Ming and Qing dynasties, with over 20,000 cells for examinees. Today, a handful of rooms have been restored into a museum, the **Jiangnan Gongyuan Lishi Chenlieguan.** Tourists can reenact part of the examination process by donning period robes and Ming dynasty hats and sequestering themselves in the cells, which have white walls, bare concrete floors, and two boards stretched across the cells as a seat and a table.

Jiankang Lu. Confucian Temple ¥25. 9am–10pm (last ticket sold at 9:30pm, Fri–Sat 10:30pm). Bus: no. 1 from Nanjing Railway Station or Xinjiekou to Fuzi Miao. Metro: Sanshan Jie.

Chaotian Gong One of the earliest documented sites in Nanjing, this former foundry and soldier training ground during the Spring and Autumn Period (722–481 B.C.) was a temple used by the Hongwu emperor (1382–98) as a ceremonial place of worship, hence Chaotian or "heaven-worshiping." The place was rebuilt in the Qing dynasty as a Confucian temple and academy. Today, the main hall, Dacheng Dian, houses a fascinating **Six Dynasties museum.** Exhibits include a locally unearthed Roman glass, a compass vehicle, and immortality pills, which obviously didn't work. The English explanations are quite good. Outside of the temple, an antiques market sells jade knickknacks and Mao posters.

Chaotian Gong 4. Admission ¥30. 8am–5pm (last ticket sold at 4:30pm). Bus: no. 4 from Fuzi Miao to Chaotian Gong. Metro: Zhangfuyuan.

MEMORIALS & MUSEUMS

For ¥140 you can buy a combination ticket that will give you access to Zhongshan Ling, Ming Xiao Ling, and Linggu Si; a shuttle (¥3) runs between these sights from morning until evening.

Zijin Shan (Purple Gold Mountain), on the eastern edge of town, got its name from the mountain's purple shales, said to have lent the place a mysterious purple aura at dawn and dusk. Covered with dense forests and dotted with the occasional lake, the mountain has always been a pleasant retreat for locals seeking relief from Nanjing's heat. It's also home to some important historical sites. Spend the day if you can, but if you have limited time, then the highlight is surely Zhongshan Ling.

Zhongshan Ling ★★ This magnificent mausoleum for Dr. Sun Yat-sen (Sun Zhongshan), widely revered as the founder of modern China, has become a mecca for Chinese tourists seeking to pay their respects. Sun Yat-sen died in Beijing in 1925 but wasn't interred here until 1929, when construction of the mausoleum was complete. (In 1912, while hunting with friends in Zijin Shan, Sun had expressed his wish to be buried here.) The tomb itself is at the end of a long, steep set of stairs beginning with a Memorial Archway made of white Fujian marble and capped by blue glazed tiles. Symbolizing the white sun on the blue background of the Kuomintang flag, the colors also marked a departure from the yellow tiles used to honor all of China's previous emperors. At the top of the 392-step grand tomb passage, a white marble statue of Dr. Sun sits under the pretty mosaic roof of the Memorial Hall. The Republican government's constitution is inscribed on the side walls. Dr. Sun's marble coffin lies in the hushed domed chamber in the back. On the way down, you'll be treated to a nice view of downtown Nanjing and its surroundings. Make sure to get here early or late in the afternoon, as the place fills up like a zoo.

Located at the center of Zijin Shan park, on the eastern edge of the city. ✆ **025/8444-8978.** Admission ¥80, or by ¥140 combination ticket (see above). 6:30am–6:30pm. Bus: no. Y1 (from the Nanjing Railway Station) or 9 (from Xinjiekou).

Ming Xiao Ling (Ming Filial Tomb) ★ More peaceful than Sun Yat-sen's mausoleum is the tomb of the founder of the Ming dynasty, Zhu Yuanzhang (1328–98), also known as the Hongwu emperor. The tomb served as a model for subsequent Ming and Qing emperors' tombs in Beijing. The site has recently been polished up with funds from UNESCO after being deemed a World Heritage Site, but the explanations of the tombs are in Chinese only with strange diagrams. Zhu Yuanzhang was the only Ming emperor to be buried in Nanjing. The Sacrificial Palace, one of the tomb's main buildings built in 1383, houses memorial tablets. The Ming Tower, a rectangular citadel, served as the command point of the tomb. Nearby, **Shixiang Lu** is a pleasant walkway half a kilometer long lined with stone carvings of 12 pairs of animals. The second half of the passageway, flanked by pairs of soldiers and mandarins, leads to Four Square Pavilion, which consists of a tall stone tablet enclosed by four walls. Built in 1413, the pavilion's tablet contains 2,000 characters inscribed with the life story of Emperor Zhu Yuangzhang, written by his son Zhu Di.

Admission ¥70, or by ¥140 combination ticket (see above). 6:30am–6:30pm. Bus: no. Y2 or Y3.

Linggu Si Hidden amid the tall conifers east of Zhongshan Ling, the fascinating Wuliang Dian (Beamless Hall), the only surviving edifice of this original Ming dynasty temple, is notable for having been built entirely from bricks without a single wood beam. From the outside, the building is beautiful, but unfortunately, the inside has been turned into a wax museum of key historical leaders from the early 20th century. China's Republican government erected a cemetery on the grounds of the temple in 1933 to commemorate soldiers.

Admission ¥35; also included in the ¥80 entrance fee for Zhongshan Ling, or with the ¥140 combination ticket (see above). 6:30am–6:30pm.

Song Meiling's Villa A beautiful, high-ceilinged villa with a traditional Chinese roof, this is where Chiang Kai-shek and his wife, better known as Madame Chiang Kai-shek, often spent weekends when China's capital was located in Nanjing. The second floor consists of a massive bedroom, parlors, and a dining room decorated with large national government maps.

Admission ¥10. 7:30am–6pm.

OTHER ATTRACTIONS

Nanjing Bowuguan (Nanjing Museum) ★ Situated in an impressive and sleek building near the entrance to Zijin Shan, the Nanjing Museum is worth at least an hour or two of your time. Standouts include the **Lacquerware Hall** with an exquisitely carved Qing dynasty throne; the **Jadeware Hall** featuring an Eastern Han dynasty jade burial suit sewn together with silver from A.D. 200; and the **Fabric Embroidery Hall,** where visitors can view a demonstration of cloud-pattern brocade weaving on an old-fashioned loom. The basement level houses a nice folk-art section and earthenware from the Tang dynasty. The museum shop sells a wide selection of art and crafts.

Zhongshan Dong Lu 321. ✆ **025/8480-2119.** Free admission. 9am–5pm (last ticket sold at 4:30pm). Bus: no. Y1, Y2, or 9 to Zhonghua Men.

Nanjing Datusha Jinianguan (Memorial to the Victims of the Nanjing Massacre) ★ While worth a visit, this memorial museum, detailing the atrocities suffered by the Chinese during the Japanese invasion of Nanjing in 1937, certainly does a heavy-handed job of explaining history, from the funerary-style orchestral music piped on the grounds to the giant statues of human limbs that greet visitors at the museum's entrance. Located at Jiang Dong Men, itself an execution and mass burial site during the invasion, the museum consists of an outdoor exhibit, a coffin-shaped viewing hall containing some excavated victims' bones, and pictures and

THE NANJING massacre

On December 13, 1937, Japanese troops invaded Nanjing. What followed were the darkest 6 weeks of Nanjing's history, as over 300,000 Chinese were bayoneted, shot, burned, drowned, beheaded, and buried alive. The city was looted and torched, and corpses were thrown into the Yangzi River. Women suffered the most: During the first month of occupation, 20,000 cases of rape were reported in the city. Many of those who survived were tortured.

During this time, a small number of Western businessmen and American missionaries, who stayed behind when their compatriots fled after the departing Chinese government, used their privileged status as foreign nationals to create a 3.9-sq.-km (1½-sq.-mile) safety zone covering today's Hanzhong Lu in the south, Zhongshan Lu in the east, Shanxi Lu in the north, and Xikang Lu in the west. Around 250,000 Chinese found safe haven in 25 refugee camps inside it. The head of the safety zone was German businessman John Rabe, chosen in part because he was a Nazi. Often described as the Oskar Schindler of China, Rabe's initial determination to save his Siemens Chinese employees eventually took on a larger purpose as he even sheltered hundreds of Chinese women in his own backyard. There were countless individual moments of courage, too, as Chinese clawed their way out of mass graves, crawled to hospitals with bullet wounds, or sheltered their brethren at great risk to themselves.

artifacts documenting the Japanese onslaught, the massacre, and the aftermath. Photographs of tortures and executions, many taken by Japanese army photographers, are quite gruesome, as are reproductions of the blood-soaked clothing of the victims. The final room documents the reconciliation, however tenuous, between the Chinese and Japanese.

Shuiximen Dajie 418. ✆ **025/8661-2230.** www.nj1937.org/english. Free admission. 8am–5pm. Bus: no. Y4 or 7.

Taiping Tianguo Lishi Bowuguan (Taiping Heavenly Kingdom Historical Museum) The largest uprising in modern Chinese history, the Taiping Rebellion is documented here in pictures and artifacts including Taiping maps, coins, and weapons. Unfortunately, the descriptions don't explain the rebellion particularly well. The museum itself is located in **Zhan Yuan,** a garden that was the residence of the Taiping "Eastern Prince," Yang Xiuqing, and the young "Western Prince," Xiao Youhe. Visitors can relax in the garden and ponder China's 5,000 years of history while watching goldfish in a pond.

Zhan Yuan Lu 128. ✆ **025/8662-3024.** Admission ¥10. Museum 8:30am–5pm; park 8am–11pm. Bus: no. Y2 or 14 to Changle Lu.

Shopping

Nanjing's biggest **art gallery,** Jinying Yishu Zhongxin Hualang (Golden Eagle Art Center), located at Hanzhong Lu 89, 11th floor, has a large collection of traditional Chinese ink paintings, calligraphy, and modern oil paintings. Nanjing Yunjun Yanjiusuo (Brocade Research Institute) at Chating Dong Lu 240 (8:30am–4:30pm) sells **cloud dragon brocade** once reserved exclusively for use by emperors. Prices are high, but this is the real deal. The Nanjing Gongyi Meishu Dalou Gouwu Zhongxin at Beijing Dong Lu 31; 9am–5:40pm) has two floors of fairly expensive **handicrafts** from all over China, including jade, silk embroidery, fans, lacquerware, pottery, and jewelry. At the other end of the price and taste spectrum, shops at Fuzi Miao sell all kinds of local products, including rain flower pebbles, rain flower tea, hanging ornaments, and Nanjing salted duck.

The trendy **nightmarket** on Hunan Lu between Zhongshan Bei Lu and Zhongyang Lu has pretty much turned into a clean and orderly shopping arcade. There's still a small nightmarket at Yunnan Lu hosting vendors who sell ethnic batik arts, embroidered bags, jewelry, underwear, and household items.

Where to Stay

The glut of upmarket hotels in Nanjing has resulted in generous discounts, averaging between 30% and 50% in low season (plus a 15% service charge).

EXPENSIVE

Crowne Plaza Nanjing Hotels and Suites (Qiao Hong Huangguan Jiudian) ★★ Incredibly spacious suites, complete with living area and separate dressing area, are the big draw at this centrally located hotel in the heart of the city's Xinjiekou shopping thoroughfare. With prices only a little higher than for a standard room, the suites are especially popular with business travelers who make up a large bulk of the hotel's repeat customers. Attached to a major shopping mall and office buildings, the hotel's lobby is located on the 7th floor while guest rooms and suites occupy the 37th to 58th floors. Decorated in glass chandeliers and gilt-edged furniture, the lobby area displays a more formal design. Guests are all given club floor treatment, including seated, personalized check-ins. Once the city's tallest building, the hotel has given up its claim to the highest perch to the newly built InterContinental Hotel but still offers decent views from its rooms. Bathrooms are especially roomy with double sinks and separate shower and tub facilities.

Hanzhong Lu 89. www.ichotelsgroup.com. ✆ **025/8471-8888.** Fax 025/8471-9999. 300 units. ¥1,000 standard room; ¥1,200 and up suite. AE, DC, MC, V. **Amenities:** 4 restaurants; bar; lounge; airport shuttle; babysitting; concierge; executive rooms; forex; health club; nightclub; indoor pool; room service; sauna. *In room:* A/C, TV, hair dryer, Internet, minibar.

Hotel Sheraton Nanjing Kingsley Hotel and Towers (Nanjing Jinsili Xilaideng Jiudian) ★★ Located about 1km (⅔ mile) west of Xinjiekou, this sleek and modern glass tower with a state-of-the-art elevator control system (makes a maximum of three stops per run) is a popular choice with foreign business travelers. The Sheraton also has the largest hotel swimming pool and health club in town. Rooms are tastefully decorated and comfortable, and afford good views of the city; those on executive floors come with personal butler service. Bathrooms are large and contain separate shower and tub.

Hanzhong Lu 169. www.starwoodhotels.com/sheraton. ✆ **025/8666-8888.** Fax 025/8666-9999. 350 units. ¥1,780 standard room; ¥1,980–¥3,280 suite. Discounts possible up to 60%. AE, DC, MC, V. Metro: Xinjiekou. **Amenities:** 4 restaurants; bar; lounge; concierge; disco; health club and spa; indoor pool; room service; sauna; tennis court. *In room:* A/C, TV, hair dryer, Internet, minibar.

Jinling Fandian ★ Don't let the fact that this is a state-owned hotel turn you off. The 37-story Jinling has been a local institution since it opened in 1983 and has worked to keep its reputation. Its exalted status has made it arrogant on occasion but its wide range of facilities and shops, not to mention its ideal location right at the city center, make it the place to be for many business travelers and tourists. Standard rooms run small but are functional, and come with large plasma-screen TVs. Rooms are decorated in a smart, minimalist style and bathrooms are sparkling clean.

Hanzhong Lu 2. www.jinlinghotel.com ✆ **025/8472-2888.** Fax 025/8471-1666. 600 units. ¥698 standard room; ¥1,698 suite. Discounts possible. AE, DC, MC, V. Metro: Xinjiekou. **Amenities:** 7 restaurants; bar; lounge; bowling alley; cigar bar; concierge; disco; executive rooms; forex; simulated golf driving range; health club and spa; karaoke; indoor pool; room service. *In room:* A/C, TV, hair dryer, Internet, minibar.

Sofitel Galaxy Nanjing (Nanjing Suofeite Yinhe Dajiudian) ★★★ Sleek and stylish, this hotel is one of the most luxurious in town. The decor is muted with browns and gold. Standard rooms are spacious with floor-to-ceiling glass windows offering great views from the 48-story tower. Framed black-and-white photos of Nanjing on the walls give a contemporary flair. Marble bathrooms are huge with separate tub and shower facilities. Beds are wonderfully soft. The heated indoor swimming pool, part of the fitness center, is a marvel, with an enormous domed ceiling of glass.

Shanxi Lu 9. www.sofitel.com/asia. ✆ **025/8371-8888.** Fax 025/8371-0505. 278 units. ¥1,180 standard; from ¥1,600 executive/suite. AE, DC, MC, V. Metro: Gulou. **Amenities:** 3 restaurants; bar; lounge; concierge; executive rooms; forex; health club; nightclub; indoor pool; room service; sauna; shuttle service to town; spa; tennis court. *In room:* A/C, TV, hair dryer, Internet, minibar, scale.

Sofitel Zhongshan Golf Resort (Nanjing Suofeite Gao'erfu Jiudian) ★★ Located way the heck out of town on the eastern side of Purple Mountain, this creamy white hotel with towering columns looks like an old French colonial mansion. Coincidence? We think not—this is after all a Sofitel resort. Rooms come with balconies and are as lovely and luxe as you can expect from this brand. Standard rooms are done in light blond wood (sleek dark wood for executive suites), and silk accent pillows and bed throws patterned with Chinese characters adorn the beds. Unlike its sister location, which is a popular business hotel, rates at this resort tend to be much higher on weekends when all the business folk head for the hills and the golf range.

Huanling Lu. www.sofitel.com/asia. ✆ **025/8540-8888.** Fax 025/8430-8001. 140 units. ¥1,500 standard; from ¥3,088 suite. Discounts possible up to 50%. AE, DC, MC, V. **Amenities:** 3 restaurants; bar; concierge; forex; health club; mahjong rooms; indoor pool; room service; smoke-free rooms. *In room:* A/C, TV, hair dryer, Internet, minibar.

MODERATE

Celebrity City Hotel (Mingren Chengshi Jiudian) This hotel was meant to be a Marriott, but after negotiations fell through, it opened as a Chinese-owned four-star establishment instead. Rooms are tastefully decorated, and deluxe rooms come with desktop computers. One big draw is that the hotel offers free high-speed Internet access in its rooms. Bathrooms have a slight funky smell to them, but on the plus side, they come with a self-cleaning Japanese-style toilet and a massaging shower head.

Zhongshan Lu 30. www.yilaicch.com ✆ **025/8312-3333.** Fax 025/8212-3888. 368 units. ¥1,480 standard room; ¥1,880–¥2,180 deluxe room. 50% discounts possible. AE, DC, MC, V. Metro: Gulou. **Amenities:** 2 restaurants; bar; conference center; fitness center; karaoke; indoor pool; room service; sauna; smoke-free rooms; rooms for those w/limited mobility. *In room:* A/C TV, desktop computer (deluxe rooms and suites), Internet.

Central Hotel (Zhongxin Dajiudian) ★ Looking somewhat weathered on the outside, this popular four-star hotel still draws visitors with its spacious, recently renovated rooms, competitive prices, and great location a block north of Xinjiekou.

Amenities, however, do not seem particularly standardized in the rooms, so be sure to request rooms containing whatever specific item you may need. Bathrooms are clean.

Zhongshan Lu 75. ✆ **025/8473-3888.** Fax 0258/473-3999. 320 units. ¥650–¥800 standard room; ¥1,600 suite. 20% discounts possible. AE, DC, MC, V. Metro: Xinjiekou. **Amenities:** 5 restaurants; bar; lounge; bowling alley; concierge; forex; health club; nightclub; outdoor pool; room service; sauna. *In room:* A/C, TV, hair dryer, Internet (in some), minibar.

INEXPENSIVE

Nanshan Binguan Located in the southwestern corner of the Nanjing Normal University campus about a 15-minute taxi ride northwest of Xinjiekou, this hotel is a no-frills clean and comfortable budget choice. The hotel also houses foreign students studying at the university. Rooms are spartan but the small bathrooms are clean.

Ninghai Lu 122. ✆ **025/8371-6440.** Fax 025/8373-8174. 200 units. ¥198–¥268 standard room; ¥268–¥380 suite. No credit cards. **Amenities:** Cafeteria; Internet bar. *In room:* A/C, TV.

Where to Eat

There are several upmarket, modern restaurants in **1912,** a restaurant and bar district on the corner of Changjiang Lu and Taiping Bei Lu. 1912 has been constructed to create an "Old China" feel: gray stone, traditional roofs, and pedestrian walkways. Everything feels a bit geared for the tourists and most restaurants are expensive or overpriced. Western standbys like KFC and Starbucks are here. For finer dining, head to the hip Taiwan chain **Bellagio** (beside Starbucks), or the popular Sichuanese chain **South Beauty** (see reviews below). Other lively places to grab a late-night bite include **Shizi Qiao,** a popular pedestrian restaurant street off Hunan Lu, and the **Confucius Temple** area, which attracts swarms of people when it is all lit up at night.

EXPENSIVE

Jinhe Tai Canting (Golden Harvest Thai Opera Cafe) THAI Located in the Hunan Lu dining area known as Shizi Qiao, this restaurant serves decent Thai food and is popular with Nanjing's expats. A golden Buddha statue outside greets arriving guests, while the decor inside is tasteful and subdued. Besides the typical solid curries and pad thai, Golden Harvest features several specialties, including a good fried crab with Thai curry sauce and a casserole of baked king prawns with vermicelli noodles.

Hunan Lu Shizi Qiao 2. ✆ **025/8324-2525.** Reservations recommended. English menus with pictures. Meal for 2 ¥150–¥250. AE, DC, MC, V. 10:30am–2:30pm and 5–10pm. Metro: Gulou.

Jinying Dajiulou ★ HUAIYANG Established in 1998 with only eight tables, this restaurant has since grown into a top restaurant with two locations. The house specialty is *Tianmuhu yutou,* a delicious white fish–head soup made with fish from nearby Tianmu Lake. Other tasty dishes here include *shuijing xiaren* (tender sautéed shrimp) and *pansi yu* (deep-fried fish-tail filets in sweet-and-sour sauce).

Wangfu Dajie 9. ✆ **025/8452-0088.** Reservations recommended. Meal for 2 ¥120–¥250. No credit cards. 11am–2pm and 6–9pm. Metro: Xinjiekou.

Le 5 Sens (Le Shang Faguo Canting) ★ FRENCH You found it—the most charming, affordable French restaurant in town. Tucked away on a small street beside Nanjing University, this intimate place serves savory, home-style French dishes. Part-owner Michael Martin originally came to Nanjing as a student and was compelled to extend his stay. He tried working at the five-star hotels, but opening his own restaurant proved to be the better path. The Quiche Lorraine is rich and flavorful, and we highly recommend the chocolate profiteroles. The vanilla ice cream sandwiched between puff pastries is just a way to get to the star of the dish: the warm chocolate sauce made from imported Belgian chocolate (Martin: "I can not work wit' zomething else!"). They've also got free Wi-Fi.

Hankou Lu 52-1. ✆ **025/8359-5859.** Dinner for 2 from ¥230. MC, V. 11:30am–10:30pm.

Prime ★ CONTINENTAL Perched on the 78th floor of the InterContinental Hotel, the restaurant has the best view in town overlooking the busy streets of Nanjing, with nearby Lake Xuanwu and Zijin Shan in the distance. The menu is high-end Western, with perfectly grilled steaks and seafood, along with imaginative appetizers like deconstructed ceviche and creamy soups. The service is attentive without being overbearing; the decor is smart and sleek. Attached to the restaurant is a martini bar and wine and cigar lounge hosting regular music acts.

InterContinental Hotel (Zifeng Tower), Zhong Yang Lu 1, ✆ **025/8353-8888.** Reservations recommended. Meal for 2 ¥800–¥1,200. AE, DC, MC, V. 5:30–10:30pm. Bar: 5:30pm–1am.

MODERATE

Bellagio (Lu Gang Xiaozhen) ★ TAIWANESE Bellagio is one of our favorite chains in China. True to form, this Nanjing outlet serves up tasty "rebel island" staples like savory Taiwanese stewed fatty pork and refreshing shaved ice desserts either served as a tall mound of ice shavings (*bingshan,* or ice mountain) or blended like a smoothie (*bingsha,* or ice sand). I highly recommend the *mangguo bingshan* (mango ice mountain), which consists of fresh mango cubes served over ice shavings drizzled with sweetened condensed milk. The restaurant interior is chic and comfortable, with fluffy blue overstuffed seats and beaded curtains throughout.

1912, Building A1, Changjiang Lu 288 ✆ **025/8452-2281.** Meal for 2 ¥80–¥110. MC, V. 11am–3am.

Ciao Italia (Ni hao! Yidali Canting) ITALIAN The fine homemade pasta and wood-fired pizzas at this classic-style Italian trattoria should satisfy anyone's craving. Naples-born chef Giuseppi Parisi recently left Bella Napoli Restaurant due to, er, artistic differences. He took his signature fresh and homemade style of cooking and opened this new outlet, which has quickly become a hit with local expats. Try the signature dish (Giuseppi's own creation), the Mezza-Luna, a half-moon pizza that's part calzone.

Shigu Lu 193-2. ✆ **025/8660-8807.** Main courses ¥25–¥140. AE, DC, MC, V. 11am–11pm.

Da Pai Dang ★ HUAIYANG An institution showcasing Nanjing specialties, this restaurant brings in the crowds with its loud and lively atmosphere. Diners are crowded together on stools at wooden tables in a huge dining hall, built in the style of a traditional teahouse. The dishes includes *yaxie fensi tang,* duck-blood soup with glass noodles, *shizi tou,* delicate pork meatballs, and roast duck steamed buns. Guests can order off the menu or peruse the side stalls where dishes are being made. By flashing a placard with their table number, diners can point to what they want and food will be delivered to their table. Entertainment comes in the form of traditional singers on a small stage. Located in the middle of the pedestrian eating area of Shizi Qiao (Stone Lion Bridge), the popular eatery has other branches in the city.

Hunan Lu Shizi Qiao 2. ✆ **025/8330-5777.** www.njdapaidang.com. Meal for 2 ¥80–¥150. AE, DC, MC, V. 10:30am–2:30pm and 5–10pm.

South Beauty (Qiao Jiang Nan) ★ SICHUANESE This reliable chain serves up fiery Sichuanese fare. The kung pao chicken is fantastic here; it is loaded with *mala* (spicy Sichuan peppercorns) and the chicken cubes are cooked to tender perfection. Regulars love the spicy *shui zhu yu*—a white fish fried in hot oil infused with giant red peppers, garlic, and Sichuan peppercorns. The decor is stylish, but not exactly comfortable. The entire restaurant is decked out in minimalist fusion furniture—think traditional Chinese tables and chairs done in white lacquer—which makes for a rather stiff dining environment.

1912, Building 17, Taiping Bei Lu 52. ✆ **025/8451-1777.** Meal for 2 ¥100–¥155. MC, V. 10am–10pm.

INEXPENSIVE

Bainian Lao Feng Xiaochi ★ NANJING STREET FOOD For a fun and authentic experience, head to this cafeteria located in Confucius Temple. It's a lively joint where diners go to the cashier to trade money for paper tickets, before heading to individual stalls where the tickets can be redeemed for an array of snacks, including steamed dumplings and glutinous rice wrapped in bamboo leaves. The best part is just being able to point to what you want. The wonton soup (¥3) and the steamed buns are the most popular dishes.

122 Gongyuan Jie (on the main street near the Confucius Temple, 300m/984 ft. east of McDonald's). No phone. ¥4–¥10 per person. No credit cards. 10:30am–8:30pm.

New Magazine Cafe (Xin Zazhi Kafei) ECLECTIC You might come here for the free Wi-Fi but you should stay for the food, which ranges from Western-style pastas to chicken teriyaki to Sichuanese spicy noodles. Teas, in flavors from hazelnut to almond, are brought to the table in porcelain pots resting on a small fire. The cafe also features a rack of Chinese magazines for sale and a range of pastries.

3 locations: Hankou Lu 42, ✆ **025/8324-8932;** Changbai Jie 488, ✆ **025/8451-2013;** and Hunan Lu 18, ✆ **025/5791-3508.** Main courses ¥25–¥40. AE, DC, MC, V. 10am–1:30am.

Skyways Bakery and Deli EUROPEAN This place serves excellent, generously sized pastries and proper homemade breads. Skyways is also a good place to meet other Nanjing expats (the Nanjing Running Club indulge themselves here after Sun runs around the nearby lake). Deli sandwiches are a steal and done the way you like 'em. The Taipingmen Jie location is more popular, but Hankou Lu 3-6 is more centrally located.

2 locations: Taipingmen Jie 10, ✆ **025/8481-2002;** Hankou Lu 3-6, ✆ **025/8663-4834.** Pastries ¥5–¥15 or ¥42 for an entire pie; sandwiches ¥20. No credit cards. 9:30am–8:30pm.

Nanjing After Dark

To find out what's happening in the arts, pick up a copy of the free English-language monthly *MAP.*

Chinese *kun ju* opera is usually performed at the **Jiangnan Theater,** Yanling Xiang 5 (✆ **025/8450-7397**), while traditional Beijing Opera is performed at the **People's Theater,** Yanggongjing 25 (✆ **025/8664-1100**). Performances usually begin at 9pm.

Around the corner from the Presidential Palace, **1912** is a district of bars, cafes, clubs, and restaurants. With its Euro-dance music and funky interior **7 Club,** about 500m (1,640 ft.) down the way from KFC, is the current hip place to grab a drink. **Danny's Irish Pub (Danni'er Ai'erlan Jiuba),** located on the fourth floor of the Sheraton Hotel, Hanzhong Lu 169 (6:30pm–2am) is the most popular bar with Nanjing's expatriates. For dancing, **Time Tunnel (Shiguang Suidao),** at Taiping Nan

Lu 354, has the largest dance floor in Nanjing and a nightly laser show to boot. The wild **Scarlet (Luanshi Jiaren),** at Gu Lou Chezhan Dongxiang 29, has been known to give foreigners a discount on entry fees in order to entice the locals.

YANGZHOU 扬州 ★★

Jiangsu Province, 240km (149 miles) NW of Shanghai, 100km (62 miles) NE of Nanjing

Located at the junction of the Yangzi River and the Grand Canal, Yangzhou was known during the Sui and Tang dynasties as the economic and cultural center of southern China, home to scholars, painters, poets, literati, and merchants. It was also the playground of the rich and famous, starting with the 6th-century Sui Yangdi emperor, who visited courtesans here. The Qing Qianlong emperor visited six times. Today Yangzhou is a charming town with broad, tree-lined boulevards, and a network of canals and lakes. Known for its handicrafts, cuisine, and landmarks, Yangzhou certainly has enough to keep you occupied for a couple of days, but it can also be a day trip from Nanjing.

Essentials

GETTING THERE The nearest **airport** is in Nanjing and the closest **railway** station is in Zhenjiang. **Buses** serve Zhenjiang (every 15 min. 6:30am–6:30pm; 1 hr.; ¥15) and Nanjing (every 20 min. 6:30am–6:30pm; 1 hr. 30 min.; ¥33) from the **West Bus Station** (**Yangzhou Xi Zhan; ✆ 0514/8796-3658**) in the southwest of the city. Buses to Shanghai (seven daily 6:40am–6:25pm; 3–3 hr. 30 min.; ¥98) and Suzhou (seven daily 6:50am–6:30pm; 2 hr.; ¥73) depart from the **long-distance bus station** in southeast Yangzhou on Dujiang Nan Lu 27 (**✆ 0514/8510-5207**).

GETTING AROUND Most of Yangzhou's sights are in the north of town. **Taxis** charge ¥6 for 3km (2 miles), then ¥1 per kilometer until 10km (6 miles), after which the price rises to ¥1.50 per kilometer. **Bus** no. 5 (¥1) runs from the long-distance bus station in the southwest of town up Huaihai Lu to Daming Si.

TOURS & GUIDES **China Travel Service (CTS)** at Wenchang Zhong Lu 200 (**✆ 0514/8734-0524;** Mon–Fri 8–11:30am and 2–6pm) can arrange accommodations, plane tickets, and city tours. English-speaking guides will cost around ¥200 a day, transportation not included.

[Fast FACTS] YANGZHOU

Banks, Foreign Exchange & ATMs The **Bank of China** at Wenchang Zhong Lu 279 conducts foreign exchange Monday to Friday from 8:30am to 5:30pm. An ATM is located here.

Internet Access There's a **24-hour Internet cafe** at Liuhu Lu 34. It charges ¥2 per hour.

Post Office Located at Wenchang Zhong Lu, it is open from 8am to 6:30pm.

Visa Extensions The **PSB** is at Run Yang Zhong Lu 98, visa extensions are done on the first floor (**✆ 0514/8703-1651;** Mon–Fri 8–11:30am and 2:30–6pm, 2–5:30pm in winter).

Exploring Yangzhou

GARDENS

Shou Xi Hu (Slender West Lake) ★★ Located in the northwest part of town, Yangzhou's premier attraction got its name during the Qing dynasty, when Hangzhou

HOTELS ■

Grand Metropark Hotel **12**
(Yángzhōu Jīnghuá Dàjiǔdiàn)
扬州京华大酒店

Ramada Casa Hotel Yangzhou **9**
(Hua Mei Da Jiudian)
华美达凯莎酒店

Xīyuán Dàjiǔdiàn **5**
西园大酒店

Yángzhōu Guesthouse **3**
(Yángzhōu Yíngbīnguǎn)
扬州迎宾馆

RESTAURANTS ◆

Fùchūn Cháshè **11**
富春茶社

ATTRACTIONS ●

Dàmíng Sì **1**
大明寺

Gè Yuán **7**
个园

Hàn Dynasty Tomb
Museum **4**
(Hàn Mù Bówùguǎn)
汉墓博物馆

Hé Yuán **13**
何园

Mountain Flattening Hall **1**
(Píng Shān Táng)
平山堂

Pǔhādīng Yuán **10**
普哈丁园

Slender West Lake **2**
(Shòu Xī Hú)
瘦西湖

Wàng Shì Xiǎ Yuàn **8**
汪氏小苑

Yángzhōu City Museum **6**
(Yángzhōu Shì Bówùguǎn)
扬州博物馆

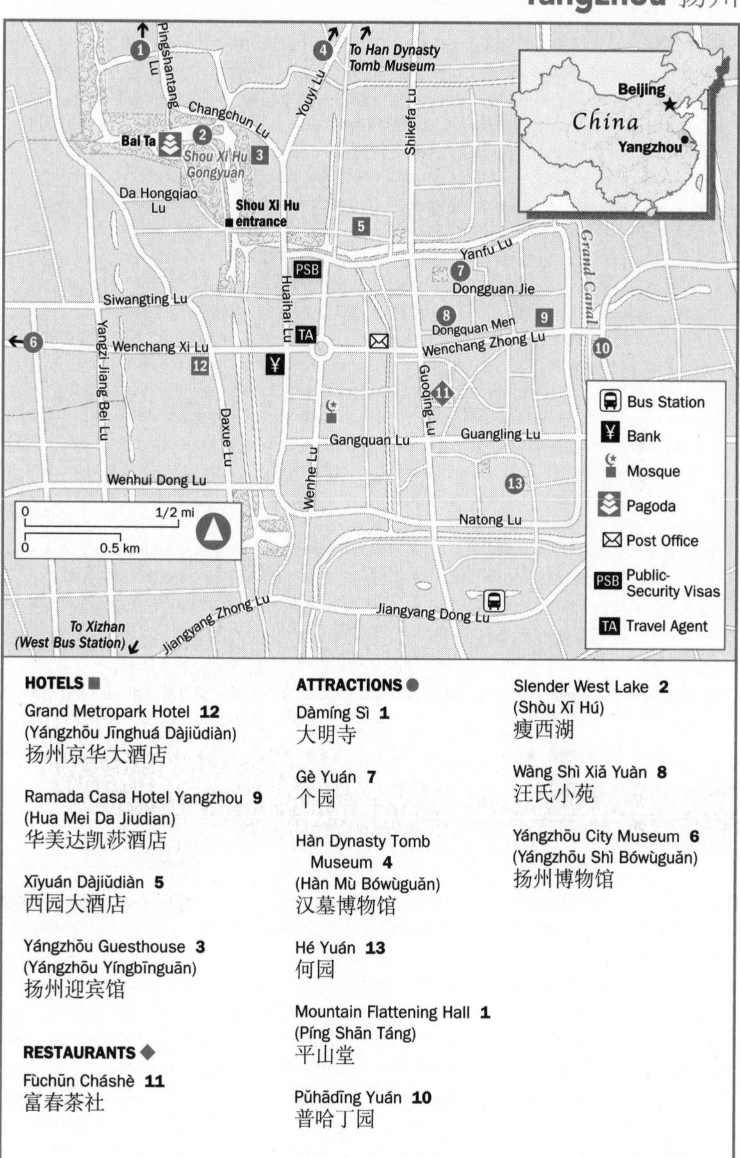

poet Wang Kang, on passing through the area, noted that it resembled a slender version of Hangzhou's West Lake (Xi Hu). The most popular photo spot is the impressive **Wu Ting Qiao (Five Pavilion Bridge),** built in 1757 by a salt merchant who, in anticipation of the Qianlong emperor's arrival, modeled the bridge after one in the

THE grand CANAL

At 1,800km (1,116 miles), the Grand Canal (Da Yunhe) is the longest canal in the world. Together with the Great Wall of China, this waterway, which runs from Beijing to Hangzhou, is one of China's great engineering feats. The first 85km (52 miles) were constructed as early as 495 B.C., but the Herculean task of linking the Yellow River and Yangzi River began in earnest in the early 7th century, when the second Sui dynasty Yang Di emperor had the waterway dug from his capital at Luoyang to Beijing in the north and to the Yangzi River basin. Due to the differences in terrain and water levels, locks and dams were built along the way.

The original purpose of the canal was to transport the plentiful grains of the affluent south to the poorer north, but over the course of the years, the canal became a major trade conduit as commodities such as tea, silk, porcelain, lacquerware, and salt were all shipped up north. By the time of the Yuan dynasty (1206–1368), the final stretch of the canal was completed, linking Beijing all the way to Hangzhou. Many of the bricks and stones used to build Beijing's temples and palaces arrived via the canal. By the time of the Southern Song dynasty (1127–1279), political power had shifted south to Jiangsu and Zhejiang provinces, as the Song emperors moved their capital to Hangzhou and the Ming emperors established themselves in Nanjing.

The canal only fell into disuse in the early 20th century, due to constant flooding from the Yellow River, silting, and the development of rail lines. Today, the navigable sections are primarily south of the Yangzi River in the region known as Jiangnan, which includes the cities of Wuxi, Yangzhou, Suzhou, and Hangzhou. Even here, some sections are so shallow and narrow that they are accessible only to small, flat-bottomed boats. North of the Yangzi, much is silted up and impassable.

imperial resort (Bishu Shanzhuang) in Chengde, Hebei. Many Qing dynasty salt merchants competed with each other to build gardens in order to impress the emperor.

Bai Ta (White Dagoba), a white Tibetan-style stupa also in the park, was built by another ingratiating salt merchant more than 200 years ago. The story goes that during one of his six visits to the lake, the Qianlong emperor remarked on the area's resemblance to Bei Hai Park in Beijing and inquired if there was a similar dagoba here. Eager to please, the salt merchant said yes, then spent the whole night panicking when the emperor insisted on seeing the dagoba. Finally, the merchant hit upon the idea to have a dagoba made out of salt, a tactic that apparently worked the next day when Qianlong saw the white structure from afar. Thereafter, the merchant commissioned a real dagoba to be built. The **Diaoyu Tai (Angler's Terrace)** on **Xiao Jin Shan (Small Golden Hill)** is where Qianlong came to fish, although he was such a terrible angler that the merchants took to putting fish on his hooks in order to avoid imperial wrath.

Da Hongqiao Lu 28. ✆ **0514/8735-7803.** Admission ¥90; ¥140 combo ticket includes admission to Ge and He Gardens, along with Daming Si, and a boat cruise. 6:30am–6pm.

Ge Yuan ★ This garden was built over 160 years ago as part of a salt merchant's residence. It features a ponderous rockery section quite cleverly designed according to the four seasons. "Summer," for example, features Tai Hu rocks designed to resemble clouds in the sky after a storm; magnolia trees provide welcome shade. There's also a variety of exotic bamboo here, including purple, turtle, and yellow bamboo.

Yanfu Dong Lu 10. Admission ¥40. 8am–6pm.

He Yuan ★★ Smaller than Ge Yuan, this garden offers some peace and quiet. Located in the southeast part of town, it is more residence than garden but still has its share of rockeries, pavilions, and ponds. Trees, plants, and an elevated walkway are used rather ingeniously to make the garden appear much larger than it really is, a tactic employed in many classical southern Chinese gardens.

Xuningmen Jie 77. Admission ¥40. 7:30am–6pm.

Wang Shi Xiao Yuan ★ Located in the center of town on Dong Quan Men, the street of preserved historic homes (including that of former Chinese president Jiang Zemin), this impressive late Qing dynasty residence of a local salt merchant is simple and understated from the outside but has almost 100 rooms inside, with the main rooms situated on a central axis. The furnishings are fine and reflect the wealth and status of the owner. The main Chun Hui Shi (Spring Hall), for example, contains a German chandelier, expensive marble wall panels whose patterns resemble Chinese landscapes, and a poem by Tang dynasty poet Bai Juyi.

Dongquan Men Lishi Jiequ 14. Admission ¥10. 8am–6pm.

OTHER ATTRACTIONS

Daming Si ★ Built more than 1,600 years ago, this major Buddhist temple is today best known for its **Jian Zhen Memorial Hall,** dedicated to a Tang dynasty abbot of the temple, Jian Zhen (688–763), who in 742 was invited to teach in Japan. After five unsuccessful attempts to cross the ocean in a wooden boat, Jian Zhen finally made it to Japan in 753, old and blind. He spent the next 10 years introducing Chinese Buddhism, medicine, language, and architecture to the Japanese. The Jian Zhen Memorial Hall, built in 1974, is modeled after the main hall of the Toshodai Temple in Nara, Japan, which Jian Zhen built. A cedar statue of the teacher stands in the hall and there are still religious and cultural exchanges between Nara and Yangzhou.

South of the temple is **Ping Shan Tang (Mountain Flattening Hall),** where famous Song dynasty writer Ouyang Xiu (1007–72) came to drink wine and write poetry when he was governor of Yangzhou. From here, his perspective was on the same level as the nearby hills, hence the hall's name.

Ping Shan Tang 1. Admission ¥45. Apr–Nov 8am–5:30pm; Dec–Mar 8am–4pm. Bus: no. 5.

Han Mu Bowuguan (Han Dynasty Tomb Museum) ★★★ This fascinating Western Han tomb of the king of Guangling Kingdom, Liu Xu, the fifth son of the Han Wu Di emperor (140–86 B.C.), is worth visiting. Sixty years in the making, Liu Xu's tomb is five levels deep. The second airtight layer is made up of 840 *nanmu* (cedar) bricks linked to each other lengthwise by tiny hooks on the inside surfaces. These bricks could only be disassembled, and the wall breached, by locating the first brick. On the third level was the warehouse, while the living quarters occupied the fourth level; the fifth and bottom level contained a coffin on wheels. In the northwest part of the tomb, there is even a bathroom, making this the first Han tomb to contain one. Despite the seemingly impenetrable defenses, the tomb was actually robbed about 100 years later. The thieves were able to dig right down to the residential level with relative ease, suggesting that the tomb was robbed by descendants of the very people who built it. East of Liu Xu's tomb is that of his wife, who died 10 years after him. Three levels deep, the queen's tomb, also made from *nanmu,* is approached from the bottom level.

Youyi Lu 16 (3km/2 miles north of town). Admission ¥30. 8:30am–4:30pm. Bus: no. 5.

Puhading Yuan ★ The central tomb at this Song dynasty Muslim graveyard belongs to Puhading, 16th descendant of the prophet Muhammad, who visited Yangzhou to help spread Islam. He built the Crane Mosque (Xian E Si) in town, and was buried in this graveyard in 1275 in a simple, stepped stone grave enclosed in a rectangular structure with a vaulted roof. Also here are the tombs of Muslim traders and other Arabs from the Yuan to the Qing dynasties.

Jiefang Nan Lu 17. Admission ¥12. 8am–5pm.

Yangzhou Shi Bowuguan (Yangzhou City Museum) Just east of the Yangzhou Hotel, this museum is housed in a temple complex dedicated to a local hero, the late Ming dynasty official Shi Kefa, who led Yangzhou's citizenry against the advancing Qing army. Shi was killed when he refused to surrender, his body cut up into five pieces and strewn to the wind. In the 10 days after his death, which came to be known as "Ten Days in Yangzhou," Qing troops killed 80,000 Yangzhou residents. Shi's jade belt, clothes, and cap are buried in the tumulus behind the hall. The museum itself features some Han coffins, a Tang canoe, and a jade funeral suit with copper threads.

Fengle Shang Jie 2. ✆ **0514/8759-7208** or 0514/8732-6156. Admission ¥10. 8:15–11:30am and 2:30–5:30pm.

Shopping

Yangzhou is famous for its **lacquerware,** which has a tradition stretching from 475 B.C. Red lacquered vases, mother-of-pearl inlaid screens, ink slabs, fans, jewelry, teapots, and lacquered furniture can all be purchased at the **Yangzhou Qiqi Youxian Gongsi** at Yanhe Jie 50 (7:45am–6pm). Prices range from the reasonable for small handicrafts to the thousands of dollars (yes, dollars) for the larger pieces of furniture. International credit cards are accepted.

Where to Stay

EXPENSIVE

Ramada Casa Hotel (Hua Mei Da Dajiudian) ★ Located in downtown, this recently opened Ramada hotel offers all the standard amenities of the American chain. Rooms are well-appointed and comfortable with decent views of the famed Grand Canal. However, bathrooms are on the small side, with full-length glass doors. The hotel gym, with its heated pool, is well-equipped and spacious.

Wenchang Zhong Lu 318. www.ramada.com ✆ **0514/8780-0000.** Fax 0514/8790-5888. 142 units. ¥560 standard room; ¥760 superior room; ¥1,200 suite. AE, DC, MC, V. **Amenities:** 2 restaurants; bar; forex; health center; pool; beauty salo room service; sauna. *In room:* A/C, TV, hair dryer, minibar.

Xiyuan Dajiudian ★ This four-star hotel has an ideal location that will allow you to walk to many sights, including Shou Xi Hu, or simply stroll along the nearby canals. With an interesting history—it was supposedly constructed on the site of Qianlong's imperial villa—this is the most popular choice with Western tour groups and independent travelers. Units are furnished with comfortable beds, clean bathrooms, and the

HUAIYANG cuisine

As one of the four major schools in Chinese cooking, **Huaiyang cuisine** (referring to the region between the Yangzi River and the Huai River in northern Jiangsu) has its origins in Yangzhou, even though it has been as much influenced these days by the different regional cooking styles of Jiangsu and Zhejiang provinces. The Ming dynasty Hongwu emperor employed a chef from Yangzhou, as did the famous 20th-century Chinese opera singer Mei Lanfang. Unlike Sichuan cooking with its reliance on peppers, Huaiyang cuisine aims to preserve the basic flavor of ingredients in order to achieve balance and freshness. River fish, farm animals, birds, and vegetables feature prominently. Some of the more famous dishes include *xiefen shizitou* (lightly braised meatballs with crabmeat, also known as Lion's Head Meatballs), *chaihui lianyutou* (stewed fish head with tofu, greens, and radish), and *bashao zheng zhutou* (stewed pig's head in a red glaze).

usual amenities, though some rooms show signs of age. Service is acceptable, but nothing more. ***Note:*** At time of research, the hotel was closed for renovations until 2012.

Fengle Shang Jie 1. ✆ **0514/8780-7888.** Fax 0514/8723-3870. 253 units. ¥680–¥780 standard room; ¥1,800–¥2,600 suite. 30%–50% discounts possible. AE, DC, MC, V. **Amenities:** 2 restaurants; bar; lounge; concierge; executive rooms; forex; indoor pool; room service, tennis court. *In room:* A/C, TV, hair dryer, minibar.

Yangzhou State Guesthouse (Yangzhou Yingbinguan) ★★ Major renovations in the last several years have transformed what was already the city's nicest hotel into a polished five-star property. Meticulously maintained gardens, with wooden pavilions and small footbridges, blend seamlessly with the Slender West Lake next door. Once reserved for senior government dignitaries, the hotel now caters to business and corporate travelers, though government-sponsored events and guests are still common. Rooms are spacious and elegant, with fine linens and chocolate brown furnishings. Spread between several low-rise buildings, the hotel has several restaurants, including one specializing in imperial cuisine. Private banquet spaces include a recreation of the literary Red Mansion. A hotel-owned dragonboat can be hired to ferry guests around the nearby lake. Former president Jiang Zemin, originally from Yangzhou, makes an annual visit here.

Youyi Lu 48. ✆ **0514/8780-9889.** Fax 0514/8780-0009. 306 units. ¥1,280 standard room; ¥4,800 and up suite. 60% discounts possible. AE, DC, MC, V. **Amenities:** 2 restaurants; teahouse; bar; lounge; concierge; forex; indoor pool; room service; tennis courts. *In room:* A/C, TV.

Where to Eat

The Xiyuan and Grand Metropark hotels both have restaurants serving decent Western food. The Yangzhou State Guesthouse (p. 409) does impressive Huaiyang style cuisine in elegant private rooms or its larger restaurant.

Fuchun Chashe ★ TEAHOUSE/DUMPLINGS Indulge in one of Yangzhou's favorite pastimes, drinking morning tea, at one of Yangzhou's oldest teahouses. The ritual starts with a pot of tea and a round of nine different snacks, including Yangzhou's famous *baozi* (steamed buns), which come with chicken, bamboo shoots, shrimp, crabmeat, tofu, or a variety of bean pastes. These steamed buns are also available at dinner, as are a variety of *jiaozi* (dumplings). This restaurant is so popular that it has branches in other Chinese cities and even Tokyo.

Desheng Qiao 35 (off Guoqing Lu). ✆ **0514/8793-0558.** Meal for 2 ¥20–¥50. AE, MC, V. 6:15am–1:30pm and 3:45–7:30pm.

WUXI (无锡), TAI HU (太湖) & YIXING (宜兴)

Jiangsu Province, 128km (79 miles) NW of Shanghai

Located in the southern part of Jiangsu Province, Wuxi, literally "without tin," was once "you xi" ("has tin"). The town changed its name during the Han dynasty when nearby deposits of tin were mined out. A Grand Canal port, Wuxi itself is not an exciting city but it's the best base for a visit to Tai Hu (Lake Tai), one of China's four largest freshwater lakes and its most fabled body of water. On the west shore of Tai Hu is Yixing, famous for its purple clay pottery. ***Note:*** For Chinese translations of selected establishments listed in this section, turn to chapter 16.

Essentials

GETTING THERE Wuxi has a small airport which is seldom used. Shanghai offers the nearest major **airline** connections. Wuxi is connected by daily **trains** to Shanghai (1–1 hr. 30 min.), Suzhou (25–35 min.), Hangzhou (4 hr. 30 min.via Shanghai), and Nanjing (2 hr.). The **railway station** (✆ **0510/8383-1234**) is in the northern part of town (counters 7–9 sell same-day tickets for Shanghai, Suzhou, and Hangzhou).

From the **Wuxi Qichezhan** (**Wuxi Bus Station;** ✆ **0510/8258-8188**) just north of the railway station, buses head to Shanghai (every 30 min. 7:10am–7:30pm; 2 hr.; ¥41–¥47), Suzhou (every 15 min. 6:30am–7:20pm; 1–2 hr.; ¥16–¥21), Hangzhou (every 30 min. 6:40am–6:30pm; 3 hr.; ¥82), Yixing (every 20 min. 6:30am–7:30pm; 1–2 hr.; ¥19–¥23), Nanjing (every 30 min. 6:30am–7pm; 2 hr. 10 min.; ¥57–¥63), and Yangzhou (every 40 min. 6:50am–5:30pm; 2 hr. 30 min.; ¥62).

GETTING AROUND **Taxis** cost ¥8 for 3km (2 miles), then ¥2.30 per kilometer, then ¥2.80 per kilometer after 8km (5 miles). Public **bus** no. 1 (¥1) and tourist bus no. G1 (same fare) run from the railway station to Yuantouzhu. Bus no. 2 from the railway station stops at Xihui Gongyuan.

TOURS & GUIDES **China Travel Service (CTS),** located directly across from the railway station at Chezhan Lu 88 (✆ **0570/8230-3366;** fax 0510/230-4143; 8am–6pm), can arrange customized tours around the city and to the pottery shops and caves in Yixing County.

[FastFACTS] WUXI

Banks, Foreign Exchange & ATMs The **Bank of China** at Zhongshan Lu 258 conducts foreign exchange Monday through Friday from 8:30am to 4:30pm. An ATM is inside the bank.

Internet Access Broadband Internet access is available for ¥.50 per hour at the library, south of Tai Hu Guang Chang (✆ **0510/8575-7830,** ext 8401; www.wxlib.cn; 9am–5pm). Dial-up is available at ✆ **163.**

Post Office There's a post office (7:30am–6:30pm) on Renmin Zhong Lu, west of Zhongshan Lu.

Visa Extensions The **Gonganju (PSB)** is located on the second floor at Chongning Lu 54 (✆ **0510/8270-6842**) and is open Monday through Friday from 8 to 11:30am and 1:30 to 5:30pm (2:30–5:30pm July–Sept). Allow 5 business days.

Exploring Wuxi

Tai Hu (Lake Tai) With its northern banks grazing the southwest edge of Wuxi, China's most fabled body of fresh water is the main attraction in town. Covering over 2,400 sq. km (950 sq. miles) with an average depth of only 2m (7 ft.), the lake is dotted with islands, fishing trawlers, low cargo boats, and small sampans. Often shrouded in mist, Tai Hu is also the source of many fantastically shaped limestone rocks that were submerged for years to achieve the desired effect, and that now decorate many a classical Chinese garden. It is said that the Huizong emperor of the Song dynasty nearly bankrupted the country's treasury in pursuit of increasingly bizarre Tai Hu rocks. For all its fabled status and storied history, however, today's lake, at least the parts accessible to tourists from Wuxi, is a bit of a disappointment, unashamedly geared as it is to the mass tourist trade.

The lake's most popular scenic spot is the peninsula **Yuantouzhu (Turtle Head Isle).** From the park's entrance, most tourists head straight for the ferry docks at the western edge of the peninsula. You can walk, take the tourist train (¥10 per trip), or ride the elevated tram (¥10 one-way, ¥16 round-trip) to the docks. The area south of the docks has some pleasant trails and is worth exploring if you have the time. A lighthouse marks the westernmost tip of the peninsula.

From the docks, ferries shuttle visitors to **San Shan Dao,** a hilly island connected by causeways to two flanking islets. The 15-minute boat ride, the highlight of a visit to Tai Hu, is usually refreshing, though you're likely to find yourself on a boat with chattering schoolchildren and loud tourists. The island itself is a tacky, commercialized affair complete with pushy vendors and wretched performing monkeys. All the structures here date from the mid-1980s, when the island was first opened to tourists.

Yuantouzhu. Admission ¥105 (includes ferry ride). 6am–6pm. Bus: no. 1 or 212.

Xihui Gongyuan This park in the northwestern part of town is dominated by two hills that have become symbols of Wuxi: **Xi Shan** after which the city was named, and **Hui Shan** to the west. It's a bit of a climb up to the seven-story octagonal brick-and-wood **Longguang Ta (Dragon Light Pagoda)** atop Xi Shan, but there are some good views of the Grand Canal snaking through the city. From 8:30am to 5pm you can also ride a chairlift (¥15 one-way, ¥28 round-trip) from the bottom of Xi Shan to the peak on Hui Shan. The ride offers even more commanding views of the surrounding area.

At the foot of Hui Shan is the famous Ming dynasty garden, **Jichang Yuan,** laid out in classical southern style with walkways, rockeries, ponds, and pavilions. The garden is said to have so captivated the Qianlong emperor on one of his visits south that he commissioned a copy of it to be built in the Yihe Yuan (Summer Palace) in Beijing. Just southwest of the garden is the **Second Spring Under Heaven (Tianxia Di'er Quan),** three wells containing the putative second-best water source in China for brewing tea, according to Lu Yu's Tang dynasty *Cha Jing (Tea Classic).* From May to October, nightly traditional music performances are held in the garden.

Huihe Lu. Admission to park ¥25. 8:30am–5pm. Bus: no. 2.

Shopping

Wuxi's famous folk-art **Hui Shan clay figurines,** which some consider rather ugly, are available at the **Hui Shan Clay Figurine Factory** store at Xihui Lu 26 (8:30am–5pm). Credit cards are accepted.

Where to Stay

Most hotels regularly offer 20% to 30% discounts, and add a 15% service charge.

EXPENSIVE

Grand Park Hotel Wuxi (Wuxi Junle Jiudian) ★★ Formerly a Sheraton, this hotel remains a comfortable place to stay in the city without the hefty five-star prices. Rooms are spacious, comfortable, and equipped with a full range of amenities, including robe and slippers. Marble bathrooms are bright and clean. The four restaurants offer reliable fine dining. Staff is friendly and very helpful.

Zhongshan Lu 403. www.parkhotelgroup.com ✆ **0510/8272-1888.** Fax 0510/8275-2781. 396 units. ¥600 standard room; from ¥1,000 suite. 20%–30% discounts possible. AE, DC, MC, V. **Amenities:** 4 restaurants; bar; lounge; concierge; cigar bar; executive rooms; forex; health club and spa; Jacuzzi; indoor pool; room service; sauna. *In room:* A/C, TV, hair dryer, Internet (in some), minibar.

Hubin Fandian ★★ Set on beautiful grounds along the shores of Lake Tai, this hotel is a good place to escape the bustle of the city. A five-star hotel, this 10-story European-style luxury hotel has whitewashed walls, elegant marble floors, and wrought-iron balustrades and balconies. Rooms are not outstanding but they do have thick carpets, redwood furniture, and some gorgeous views of the lake. Beds are big but firm. Bathrooms are small and slightly worn.

Huanhu Lu, Li Yuan. ✆ **0510/8510-1888.** Fax 0510/8510-2637. 281 units. ¥1,280–¥1,500 standard room; ¥2,800) suite. New building ¥1,600–¥1,800 standard room; ¥4,000 suite. 40%-60% discounts possible. AE, DC, MC, V. **Amenities:** 3 restaurants; bar; lounge; bowling alley; concierge; executive rooms; forex; health club; outdoor pool; room service; sauna; spa; tennis court. *In room:* A/C, TV, hair dryer, minibar.

MODERATE

New World Courtyard Wuxi (Wuxi Xinshijie Wanyi Jiudian) ★★ This hotel, operated by the Marriott Courtyard chain, caters mostly to business travelers and a few tour groups. Located in the heart of town near shops and restaurants, the hotel prides itself on having the largest standard guest rooms around. Rooms are tastefully decorated and fitted with a full range of amenities. Bathrooms are spacious and clean, and service is friendly and efficient.

Zhongshan Lu 335. ✆ **0510/8276-2888.** Fax 0510/8551-7784. www.courtyard.com. 266 units. ¥465 standard room; ¥788 suite. AE, DC, MC, V. **Amenities:** 3 restaurants; bar; lounge; concierge; executive rooms; forex; health club and spa; room service; sauna. *In room:* A/C, TV, hair dryer, Internet, minibar.

Where to Eat

The top hotels all offer reliable dining. Western fast food is readily available in the center of town. Babaiban (Yaohan Department Store) at Zhongshan Lu 168 has a **food court** on the sixth floor.

MODERATE

San Feng Jiujia ★ WUXI While Wuxi isn't exactly known for its cuisine, this restaurant does a superb job making the best of the regional fare. Order the *paigu,* delicious Chinese-style baby back ribs cooked in sugar and soy sauce, or the local specialty *mianjin,* which are fried balls of flour that are shredded and stir-fried with meat and vegetables. The restaurant also has fresh seafood and fresh squeezed juices.

Zhongshan Lu 240. ✆ **0510/8272-5132.** Meal for 2 ¥80–¥160. AE, DC, MC, V. 11am–1:30pm and 5–8:15pm.

Wuxi Kaoya Guan (Wuxi Roast Duck Restaurant) ★★ WUXI This popular four-story restaurant serves its excellent signature Wuxi roast duck in two ways: with steamed bread, chives, cucumbers, and sweet sauce; and as a soup. Other specialties include *Taihu yinyu* (deep-fried Lake Tai fish) and the mouthwatering *Wuxi xiaolong* (Wuxi dumplings). Service is friendly.

Zhongshan Lu 218. ✆ **0510/8272-9623.** Reservations recommended. English menu. Meal for 2 ¥90–¥200. AE, DC, MC, V. 11:30am–2pm and 5–9pm.

INEXPENSIVE

Wangxing Ji DUMPLINGS One of Wuxi's most famous and popular places for casual dining, this assembly-line cafeteria has pretty good crabmeat dumplings *(xiefen xiaolong)* and pork wontons *(xianrou huntun).* A variety of noodles are also available. Don't expect much from the apathetic service, and try your best to grin and bear the beggars who stumble in here asking for money—or a dumpling.

Zhongshan Nan Lu 221. ✆ **0510/8275-1777.** Meal for 2 ¥20–¥40. No credit cards. 6:30am–8pm.

A Side Trip to Yixing (宜兴)

Located 60km (37 miles) southwest of Wuxi on the western shores of Tai Hu, Yixing is famous for its "Yixing ware" pottery, specifically small teapots and decorative objects made from a distinctive dark red clay (often referred to as "purple sand" due to a high level of iron in the soil). You can see a collection of Yixing pots, flasks, and urns from over 6,000 years ago, as well as the latest vases and teapots from contemporary masters, at the ceramics museum **Yixing Taoci Bowuguan,** Dingshan Bei Lu 150 (¥20; 8am–5pm) in Dingshu Town, 15km (9 miles) southwest of Yixing. Recently renovated, the museum offers coherent explanations in English and is pretty well put together for a small-town museum. It's worthwhile for visitors who are really into pottery. You can purchase a certified Yixing teapot set (teapot with six cups) for ¥200 to ¥300 at the museum store. Outside are workshops where visitors can watch ceramics artisans at work. Across the highway is a dusty market, where amazing deals can be struck for a wide range of pottery from ¥25 to ¥200.

Yixing also has some karst caves near Dingshu Town. **Shanjuan Dong** (¥120; 7:30am–5pm) located 25km (15 miles) southwest of Yixing, has three main chambers of oddly shaped rocks. Visitors may climb to the upper cave or take the more interesting short ride on a flat-bottomed boat in the lower cave along a 120m-long (393-ft.) underground stream that leads out to a tacky temple complex commemorating China's Romeo and Juliet, Liang Shanbo and Zhu Yingtai. Twenty-two kilometers (13 miles) southwest of town, a Daoist temple fronts the large **Zhanggong Dong** (¥305; 7:30am–5:30pm), which contains a labyrinthine 72 halls. The Hall of the Dragon King has wide steps that run all the way to the top of the hill, where there's a view of the dusty countryside.

From the **Yixing Bus Station** (**Sheng Qichezhan;** ✆ **0510/8794-5031**), buses depart regularly for Wuxi (90 min.; ¥23) and Nanjing (2 hr. 30 min.; ¥57). Once in Yixing, tourist bus no. Y1 (¥5) will take you from the bus station to the ceramics museum and Zhanggong Dong (Zhanggong Cave), while tourist bus no. Y2 heads to Shanjuan Dong (Shanjuan Cave).

Yixing is usually a day trip from Wuxi or Nanjing, but for those who wish to stay over, the renovated three-star **Yixing Guoji Fandian (Yixing International Hotel) ★**, Tongzhengguan Lu 52 (✆ **0510/8791-6888;** fax 0510/8790-0767), has clean and comfortable rooms for ¥498 to ¥798, with 20% to 30% discount possible. The rooms are fitted with all new furniture, fridge, and satellite TV. The hotel has three restaurants serving decent fare.

HEFEI 合肥

Anhui Province, 615km (381 miles) NW of Shanghai, 321km (199 miles) NW of Huang Shan

As the provincial capital of Anhui, this industrial city of 1.3 million has few attractions for the tourist but sees a constant flow of business travelers. Hefei is also home to the University of Science and Technology, where Chinese dissident Fang Lizhi was vice-president until he sought asylum in the West after the 1989 Tian'an Men Square massacre. ***Note:*** For Chinese translations of selected establishments listed in this section, turn to chapter 16.

Essentials

GETTING THERE Hefei has daily **flights** to Beijing (1 hr. 10 min.), Guangzhou (1 hr. 45 min.), Shanghai (1 hr.), and Qingdao (1 hr. 30 min.), and several flights a week to Xi'an (Mon, Thurs–Sun; 2 hr. 10 min.), Hangzhou (Thurs and Sun; 50 min.), Guilin (Tues and Thurs; 90 min.), Huangshan (Mon, Wed, Fri, Sun; 50 min.), Hong Kong (Mon and Fri; 2 hr.), Ji'nan (1 hr.), and Zhengzhou (1 hr.). Tickets may be purchased at the 24-hour **CAAC Booking Center (Minghang Shoupiao Zhongxin)** at Meiling Dadao 368 (✆ **0551/467-9999**). **Taxis** (20 min.; ¥20) are your best option for getting to Hefei's airport, which is about 10km (6 miles) south of town. There are no airport buses, but public **bus** no. 11 runs there from the railway station.

From Hefei's railway station (✆ **0551/424-3311**) in the northeast part of town, daily **trains** run to Beijing (10 hr.), Zhengzhou (8 hr.), Shanghai (8 hr. 30 min.; seven D-series trains daily; 3 hr. 30 min.), Huang Shan (6 hr. 30 min.), Xi'an (16 hr.), and Hangzhou (7 hr.). Tickets can be purchased at the railway station or, more conveniently, at ticket outlets at Changjiang Zhong Lu 376 (✆ **0551/264-0000**).

Hefei has several bus stations, but the **long-distance bus station** (✆ **0551/429-9111** or 0551/429-9161) at the corner of Shengli Lu and Mingguang Lu should serve most travelers' needs. Buses run to Shanghai (every 1 hr. 6:40am–5pm; 6 hr.; ¥150), Zhengzhou (10am, noon, and 4pm; 8 hr.; ¥165), Huang Shan (8:30am; 4 hr.; ¥114), and Nanjing (every 25 min. 6am–7:20pm; 2 hr. 30 min.; ¥45).

GETTING AROUND **Taxis** charge ¥6 for 2.5km (1.55 miles), then ¥1.20 per kilometer. From 11pm to 5am, prices rise ¥6 for 2.5km (1.55 miles), then ¥1.20 per kilometer.

Most public **buses** (¥1 flat fee) require exact change. Bus no. 1 runs from the railway station down Shengli Lu onto Changjiang Zhong Lu before heading south on Jinzhai Lu. Bus no. 11 runs from the railway station to the airport along Changjiang Zhong Lu.

[FastFACTS] HEFEI

Banks, Foreign Exchange & ATMs The **Bank of China** is at Chang Jiang Dong Lu 789. Foreign exchange is available at all counters Monday through Friday from 8:30am to 5pm. An ATM is located here.

Internet Access Dial-up is ✆ **163.**

Post Office The post office (8am–6pm) is at Changjiang Zhong Lu 110.

Visa Extensions The **Hefei Municipal Administration Service Center (Shi Xingzheng Fuwu Zhongxin)** is at Jiu Shiqiao Jie 45. Open year-round Monday through Friday from 8am to noon; May to October, 3 to 6pm and November to April 2:30 to 5:30pm. Allow 5 business days for processing.

Exploring Hefei

Hefei's nicest park, **Bao He Gongyuan** in the center of town, has an arched bridge over a placid lake, whispering willows on the shores, and schools of fish in lily ponds, all making for some pleasant strolls. Entrance is free and the park is open 24 hours. The park is also home to **Bao Gong Muyuan (Lord Bao's Tomb)** at Wu Hu Lu 58. It commemorates one of China's most respected iconic figures, local son Bao Zheng (999–1062), a conscientious and impartial Northern Song dynasty judge who fought for the common folk. Admission to the tomb is ¥50, open daily 8am to 6pm.

For an eclectic range of activities, head to **Xiaoyaojin Gongyuan.** It features a peaceful lake where the elderly practice tai chi, but also offers a range of tacky roller-coaster-type rides for kids, a petting zoo, a circus, paintball, and best of all, crocodile wrestling. Admission is free and the cost of individual activities ranges from ¥3 to ¥30; the park is open from 8am to 5:30pm.

North of the Xiaoyaojin Gongyuan along the pedestrian street **Shangye Buxing Jie** is **Li Hongzhang Guju,** Huaihe Lu 208 (✆ **0551/261-6772;** ¥20; 8:30am–6pm), the former residence of Li Hongzhang (1823–1901), a highly successful Qing dynasty military commander who is perhaps best known as one of the chief architects of the destruction of the Taipings (p. 394). His residence has been well preserved, complete with beautiful lattice windows and Qing dynasty furniture.

The **Anhui Sheng Bowuguan (Anhui Provincial Museum),** at Anqing Lu 268 (¥10; Tues–Sun 8:30–11:30am and 2:30–5pm), is a rather forlorn place. It has a modest bronze collection, some Han tomb engravings, and a fairly comprehensive display on the Huizhou-style architecture of southern Anhui. The museum closes early if there are no visitors, which is often. There's a decent flower and bird market outside of the museum.

Where to Stay

EXPENSIVE

Holiday Inn Hefei (Hefei Gujing Jiari Jiudian) ★★ Just east of the commercial heart of town, this luxurious five-star, 29-story hotel has rooms that are large, well-appointed, and decorated with classical furniture. The marble bathrooms are a bit small but very clean. Rooms on the higher floors provide panoramas of the city. Service is professional and efficient.

Changjiang Dong Lu 1104. www.holidayinn.com ✆ **0551/220-6666.** Fax 0551/220-1166. 338 units. ¥630 standard room; from ¥750 suite. AE, DC, MC, V. **Amenities:** 4 restaurants (including

Noodle in Chopsticks, see below); bar; lounge; cigar bar; concierge; disco; executive rooms; forex; health club; indoor pool; room service. *In room:* A/C, TV, hair dryer, Internet, minibar.

Novotel Hefei (Weishang Qiyun Shanzhuang) ★★ Renovated in recent years, the trendy four-star Novotel has standard rooms that are a little small but perfectly comfortable. They are fitted with modern light-wood furniture and all the expected amenities. Bathrooms are sparkling clean. Consider upgrading to a superior room, which is spacious and refreshingly decorated with hip blue and orange futon sofas. Service is excellent, and the staff is professional and exceedingly friendly.

Wu Hu Lu 199. www.accorhotels.com/asia ✆ **0551/228-6688.** Fax 0551/228-6677. 245 units. ¥475 standard room; ¥760 superior. Discounts possible up to 50%. AE, DC, MC, V. **Amenities:** 3 restaurants; pastry shop; bar; lounge; airport shuttle; concierge; executive rooms; forex; health club; room service. *In room:* A/C, TV, hair dryer, Internet, minibar.

Sofitel Grand Park Hefei (Hefei Suofeite Mingzhu Guoji Dajiudian) ★★ This long, colonial white building looks like it belongs somewhere in Bavaria. But here it is, right in the middle of Hefei's technological zone. The hotel is a bit far from the city center, but it's close to the exhibition center, making it a comfy choice for business travelers. Expect luxuriously soft beds, excellent service, and a sleek decor.

Hefei Economic and Technological Development Zone, Fanhua Rd. www.sofitel.com ✆ **0551/221-6688.** Fax 0551/221-6699. 261 units. ¥550 standard; from ¥785 suite. AE, DC, MC, V. **Amenities:** 3 restaurants; 3 bars; concierge; executive rooms; forex; health club; indoor pool; room service; tennis court; table tennis. *In room:* A/C, TV, hair dryer, Internet, minibar.

Where to Eat

All the top hotels catering to foreigners serve very credible Western and Chinese food.

Jin Man Lou Huayuan Jiudu ★ CHAOZHOU/CANTONESE This popular, clean restaurant offers reliable and tasty fare at very reasonable prices, though service is uneven. Start with a cold dish of spicy mushrooms with broad beans or the house specialty, *taiji sucai geng,* a puréed vegetable soup. Graduate to the *huishi xiaochao,* a light stir-fry mix of pork, leeks, and bean curd strips. Also try *suan zheng shanbei,* garlic steamed scallops with glass noodles.

Tongcheng Lu 96. ✆ **0551/287-7777.** Meal for 2 ¥40–¥120. AE, DC, MC, V. 11am–2pm and 5–9pm.

Lao Xie Longxia ★★ SEAFOOD Located on a street that's been dubbed "*longxia yi tiao lu*" or "a street filled with lobsters," this restaurant packs them in every night of the week. *Longxia* really means Chinese-style crayfish here, which is steamed in spices and served with beer. In the warmer months, locals cram themselves on outdoor tables and enjoy grilled corn on the cob, fish, and meat-and-vegetable skewers along with the crayfish. The mustachioed Mr. Xie has been at it for more than a decade, and while there are other restaurants on the street that serve the same thing, he keeps drawing the crowds that come until the wee hours of the morning.

Wu Hu Lu 265. ✆ **0551/288-4799.** Meal for 2 ¥20–¥50. No credit cards. 9:30am–4am.

Noodles in Chopsticks (24 Xiaoshi Mian) ★ NOODLES Located in the Holiday Inn, this noodle house will satisfy your hunger pangs 24 hours a day. There's a noodle for practically every taste, from the simple Sichuan-style *dandan mian* (spicy noodles with meat sauce) to Japanese udon; egg and spinach noodles may substitute regular noodles in any of the dishes.

Holiday Inn, 2nd floor. ✆ **0551/220-6228.** Meal for 2 ¥20–¥60. AE, DC, MC, V. Open 24 hr.

HUANG SHAN 黄山 ★★★

Anhui Province, 501km (315 miles) SW of Shanghai, 65km (40 miles) NW of Tunxi

If you climb one mountain in China, let it be Huang Shan (Yellow Mountain). In southern Anhui Province, and inscribed on the UNESCO World Heritage List in 1990, Huang Shan, with its 72 peaks, is China's most famous mountain for scenic beauty. Having no religious significance, the mountain is known instead for its sea of clouds, strangely shaped rocks, unusual pine trees, and bubbling hot springs—four features that have mesmerized and inspired countless painters and poets for over 1,500 years.

Huang Shan is enshrouded in mist and fog 256 days a year, while snow covers the mountain peaks 158 days a year. Trails are usually packed with hikers from May to October, so April is often cited as the best time to visit. Local tourism authorities, however, like to boast that each season highlights a uniquely different aspect of Huang Shan, and have taken to pushing Huang Shan winter tours, when hotel, restaurant, and ticket prices are at least lower. Whenever you visit, allow at least 2 days for the mountain, and another day or two for the attractions around **Tunxi.**

Essentials

GETTING THERE The nearest **airports** and **railway stations** are at Tunxi, 65km (40 miles) and a 1½-hour bus ride away. The Tunxi Airport is more commonly called Huang Shan Airport. In Tangkou, the nearest town serving the mountain, buses leave for Tunxi from the **long-distance bus station** (✆ **0559/256-6666**) just before the main gate to Huang Shan and from the main bridge area in town. Slow long-distance buses also run to Hefei (every 35 min., 7:30am–4:20pm; 6 hr.; ¥108), Shanghai (every hour 7:10am–6pm; 8 hr.; ¥132), and Hangzhou (every hour 6:50am–5:50pm; 6 hr.; ¥85).

GETTING AROUND *Miandi* (van) taxis charge ¥3 to ¥5 for trips in town. The start of the Eastern Mountain Trail (Eastern Steps) or the cable car at Yungu is another hour away by minibus (¥5) or taxi (approximately ¥30 per trip or ¥10 per person depending on the number of people). The Peach Blossom Hot Springs area and the start of the Western Mountain Trail (Western Steps) will require a 30-minute walk or a taxi ride from the Tangkou bus station (¥10–¥15). If you want to take the cable car up the western slopes, take a minibus for ¥5 to ¥10 or a taxi for around ¥40, subject to bargaining, from Tangkou to the Mercy Light Temple (Ciguang Ge).

Exploring Huang Shan

ORIENTATION & INFORMATION

Buses from Tunxi usually drop off passengers in Tangkou by the bridge or at the bus station in upper Tangkou near the Huang Shan Front Gate.

Two main trails lead up the mountain. The 7.5km-long (4.5-mile) **Eastern Steps** (3–4 hr. hike) are compact and steep and are generally considered less strenuous than the 15km-long (9.25-mile) **Western Steps** (4–6 hr. hike), which are longer and steeper but which have some of Huang Shan's most spectacular vistas. For the fit, it's entirely possible to climb the mountain in the morning and descend in the afternoon in about 10 hours. But an overnight stay at the summit would allow a more leisurely appreciation of the sights and views along the way.

Sedan chairs can be hired on both routes and can cost up to ¥500 for a one-way trip, though there is plenty of room for bargaining. Just be very clear beforehand on all the terms of the deal, including exact starting and ending points, and the price per passenger. If you hire a porter to tote your bags, be clear as to whether you're being charged by the piece or by weight. If the latter, insist, if you can, that the items be weighed *before* you embark so you have an idea of the total cost, and not when you're at the end, for the load at the end has an uncanny way of weighing three times more than you'd imagined.

For those preferring the path of least resistance, three **cable cars** go up the mountain: the Eastern Trail's **Yungu Si (Cloud Valley) cable car** (Mar 15–Nov 15 6:30am–4:30pm; otherwise 8am–4pm) has a waiting line for the 6-minute ascent that can take up to 1 to 2 hours. The Western Trail's **Yuping (Jade Screen) cable car** (Mar–Nov 6am–5pm; Dec-Feb 7am–4pm) runs from Ciguang Ge (Mercy Light Temple) to Yuping Lou, which is just over halfway up the western slope; the third, with a length of 3,709m (12,166 ft.) and less frequently used because it spits you west of the summit, is **Taiping cable car** (same times as above). The trip back to Tangkou takes 30 minutes to 1 hour by taxi or infrequent minibus. The one-way cost of each cable car is ¥80. When climbing the mountain, always carry layers of clothing: sweaters and raincoats as well as T-shirts. Hats and umbrellas are useful, too, as temperatures, even in summer, are subject to sudden changes due to the altitude and winds. You might also consider packing your own food and drink, as these become considerably more expensive the higher you climb.

From March 10 to November 15, the park entrance fee is ¥230; from November 16 to March 9 it's ¥150.

EASTERN STEPS At 7.5km (4.5 miles) long, these paved, cut-stone stairways are considerably easier to negotiate than the Western Steps, though this is definitely not a walk in the park. Shortly after the start of the trail, considered the Yungu Si cable car terminus, see if you can spot Eyebrow Peak (Meimao Feng) to the south, said to resemble what else but a pair of eyebrows. When you're not huffing and puffing, the climb, which takes you past bubbling streams and pretty pine and bamboo forests, is quite pleasant.

WESTERN STEPS Most hikers begin their assault on the 15km (9-mile) Western Steps at **Ciguang Ge,** where you can burn incense and offer prayers for safe trails, not a bad idea considering that the serpentine Western Steps, hewn out of the sheer rock face, can be precipitously steep and narrow. Rest stops are along the way at the **Yueya Ting (Crescent Moon Pavilion)** and the **Banshan Si (Mid-Level Temple,** a misnomer—it should be the Quarter-Way Temple, for that's about where you are).

The real midpoint of the trail is **Yuping Feng (Jade Screen Peak),** with the Yuping Lou Binguan (Jade Screen Hotel) nestled like a jewel among the pointed vertical peaks. About 20 minutes by foot to the west is the upper terminus for the Yuping *suodao* (cable car). Before you reach Jade Screen Peak, however, a narrow path hewn between two large rocks named **Yi Xian Tian** (literally "A Thread of Sky" because only a sliver of sky is visible through this passage) leads to the distinctive **Yingke Song (Welcoming Guests Pine),** which extends a long tree branch as if in greeting.

South of Jade Screen Peak, an incredibly steep and exposed stairway (often called the Aoyu Bei—Carp's Backbone) snakes its way to the magnificent **Tiandu Feng ★★★**, the third-highest peak at 1,810m (5,937 ft.). Young lovers often bring

Huang Shan 黄山

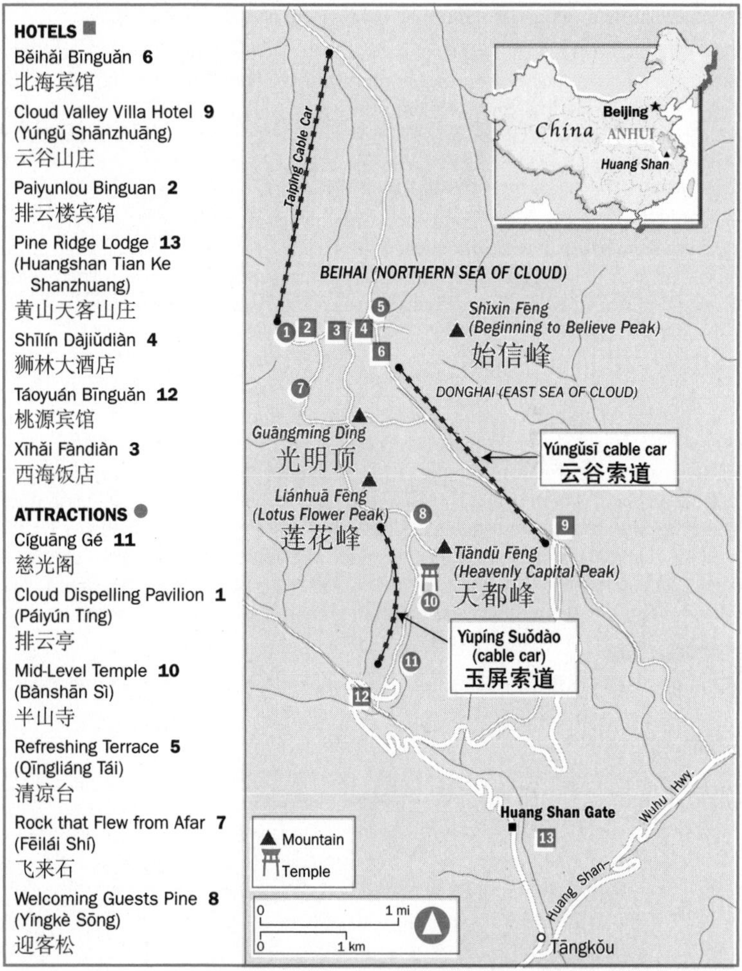

HOTELS
Běihǎi Bīnguǎn 6
北海宾馆
Cloud Valley Villa Hotel 9
(Yúngǔ Shānzhuāng)
云谷山庄
Paiyunlou Binguan 2
排云楼宾馆
Pine Ridge Lodge 13
(Huangshan Tian Ke Shanzhuang)
黄山天客山庄
Shīlín Dàjiǔdiàn 4
狮林大酒店
Táoyuán Bīnguǎn 12
桃源宾馆
Xīhǎi Fàndiàn 3
西海饭店
ATTRACTIONS
Cíguāng Gé 11
慈光阁
Cloud Dispelling Pavilion 1
(Páiyún Tíng)
排云亭
Mid-Level Temple 10
(Bànshān Sì)
半山寺
Refreshing Terrace 5
(Qīngliáng Tái)
清凉台
Rock that Flew from Afar 7
(Fēilái Shí)
飞来石
Welcoming Guests Pine 8
(Yíngkè Sōng)
迎客松
Beijing
China
ANHUI
Huang Shan
Taiping Cable Car
BEIHAI (NORTHERN SEA OF CLOUD)
Shǐxin Fēng
(Beginning to Believe Peak)
始信峰
DONGHAI (EAST SEA OF CLOUD)
Guāngmíng Dǐng
光明顶
Yúngǔsī cable car
云谷索道
Liánhuā Fēng
(Lotus Flower Peak)
莲花峰
Tiāndū Fēng
(Heavenly Capital Peak)
天都峰
Yùpíng Suǒdào
(cable car)
玉屏索道
Huang Shan Gate
Wuhu Hwy.
Huang Shan
Mountain
Temple
0
1 mi
0
1 km
Tāngkǒu

padlocks inscribed with their names to affix to the railings at the peak in proof and hope of being "locked" together in eternal love. The views from this "heavenly capital" are simply extraordinary. If you suffer from vertigo or acrophobia, give this peak a pass. ***Note:*** The stairway to Tiandu Feng is a steep, 85-degree angle slope; CITS recommends skipping this peak on rainy days.

Past the Jade Screen Hotel is a steep hike to Huang Shan's highest summit, **Lianhua Feng** (**Lotus Flower Peak;** elev. 1,873m/6,143 ft.), so named because it resembles a lotus shoot among fronds. From here it's another 20 to 30 minutes or so to the second-highest peak, **Guangming Ding** (Brightness Peak; elev. 1,860m/6,100 ft.), where there's a weather station and a hotel. Farther along is the famous **Feilai Shi (Rock That Flew from Afar),** a large vertical rock standing on a tapered end. Another half-hour brings you to the Beihai Binguan (North Sea Hotel).

ON THE SUMMIT The highlight at the summit is the **Beihai Sunrise ★★**, the only reason for overnighting on the summit. Weather permitting, the moment when the first golden ray hits and spills onto the sea of clouds is truly breathtaking. Be forewarned, however, that you'll be sharing this special moment with hundreds of other chattering tourists bundled up in the thick jackets provided by the summit hotels. The **Qingliang Tai (Refreshing Terrace),** less than 10 minutes from the Beihai Binguan, is the best place to view the sunrise. Alternatively, the **Paiyun Ting (Cloud Dispelling Pavilion)** between the Feilai Shi and the Xihai Fandian is the place to catch the equally pretty sunsets. Another popular photo op is the **Shixin Feng (Beginning to Believe Peak)** between the Beihai Binguan and the Yungu cable car terminus.

Where to Stay & Eat

Tangkou's hotels are not quite up to international standards but are adequate in a pinch. Hotels at the hot springs are generally overpriced, and staying there only makes sense if you plan to indulge in the waters or if you plan an early-morning assault on the Western Trail. The Yungu Si area is more remote, and hotels there generally cater to large tour groups. Although prices are significantly higher on the summit, spending a night at the top in order to catch the famed Beihai sunrise is highly recommended. Phone ahead for reservations, particularly if you plan to visit May through October when rooms are difficult to come by.

TANGKOU

A **bakery,** Weitejia Mianbaofang, is on Yin Shi Jie, the main street under the bridge. Next door is a tiny **supermarket** where you can stock up on snacks, groceries, and drinks for the climb.

Pine Ridge Lodge (Huangshan Tian Ke Shanzhuang) Set just outside the south entrance to Huangshan, this new hotel, opened in 2009, is the closest accommodation to the national park. With simple but tasteful furnishings, spotless bathrooms, and comfortable beds, the 33-room lodge set on a small hill amid a grove of pine trees is a quiet gem with friendly staff that can help arrange onward travel. The U.S.-born and educated owner is especially helpful to guests in offering advice on hiking Huangshan and exploring local villages nearby. A small restaurant on the premises specializes in tasty local cuisine.

Huang Shan Nan Men ✆ **0559/556-3388.** 33 units. ¥175–¥235 standard room; ¥265–¥320 deluxe room. Only Chinese credit cards. **Amenities:** Restaurant; airport pickup; concierge; shuttle service. *In room:* A/C, TV, Wi-Fi.

YUNGU SI (CLOUD VALLEY TEMPLE) CABLE CAR STATION

Yungu Shanzhuang (Cloud Valley Villa Hotel) Down the road from the Yungu Si cable car, this remote three-star hotel popular with Taiwanese tour groups is nicely designed in the traditional Huizhou architectural style, with stark white walls and gray tiled roofs. Rooms are a little dark and damp, but are otherwise furnished with the basic amenities.

Yungu Si. ✆ **0559/558-6444.** Fax 0559/558-6018. 100 units. ¥580 standard room; ¥4,880 suite. 20% discounts possible. AE, DC, MC, V. **Amenities:** Restaurant; bar; lounge; concierge; forex (US$ only); room service; sauna. *In room:* A/C, TV.

SUMMIT AREA

Beihai Binguan Originally established in 1958 as a guesthouse for Chinese leaders, which in more recent years has included Deng Xiaoping and Jiang Zemin, this four-star outfit has staked out the best position for sunrise-viewing and charges accordingly. Recent renovations, including a new wing built in 2009, have given the hotel a needed-makeover. Rooms are well-appointed with firm beds, and some have good views of the surrounding peaks. Closets are stocked with down jackets for the often-chilly dawn viewing of the famed sunrise over the sea of clouds. Service is uneven.

Beihai Fengjingqu. ✆ **0559/558-2555.** Fax 0559/558-1996. 370 units. ¥1,680 standard room; ¥5,800 suites. 10-30% discounts possible. AE, DC, MC, V. **Amenities:** Restaurant; bar; lounge; concierge; room service. *In room:* TV, heater.

Paiyunlou Binguan ★ A large and slick marble lobby gives this renovated four-star hotel an upscale feel. Its location near Tianhai Lake and nice views make it a decent spot for the night. Rooms are clean and comfortable, with newer Chinese furnishings. This hotel, like most on the mountain, also offers dorm rooms, with bunk beds for 6-8 people, for a sharp discount if you don't mind sharing with others.

Tianhai Fengjing ✆ **0559/558-1558.** Fax 0559/558-3999. 137 units. ¥800 standard room; ¥1,680 suite. 30% discount possible. AE, DC, MC, V. **Amenities:** 2 restaurants; bar; concierge; forex (US$ and yuan only); room service. *In room:* TV, heater, minibar.

Shilin Dajiudian ★ This four-star hotel close to Beihai Binguan has rooms that are small but cozy and furnished with the usual amenities. Bathrooms are small but clean and come with glassed-in cylindrical showers. The hotel's restaurant can serve Western breakfasts upon request. Service is adequate if not particularly memorable.

Beihai Fengjingqu. www.shilin.com ✆ **0559/558-4040.** Fax 0559/558-1888. 142 units. ¥780 standard room; ¥1,480 suite. 30% discount available. AE, DC, MC, V. **Amenities:** 2 restaurants; bar; lounge; concierge; forex; room service; smoke-free rooms. *In room:* A/C, TV, minibar.

Xihai Fandian ★ This Swiss-designed hotel remains quite popular with tour groups. Its rooms, decorated like ship cabins, are a bit worn around the edges but comfortable enough. The hotel's banquet dining hall is considered one of the better restaurants spots on the mountain At the time of a recent visit, the main section of the hotel was undergoing major renovations to become a five-star spot, slated for completion in 2012. Guests were being housed in the older north building.

Xihai Fengjingqu. ✆ **0559/558-8888.** Fax 0559/558-8988. 125 units. ¥900–¥1,000 standard room; 30% discount possible. AE, DC, MC, V. **Amenities:** 2 restaurants; bar; concierge; forex (US$ and yuan only); room service. *In room:* TV, heater, minibar.

TUNXI

Anhui Province, 67km (41 miles) SE of Huang Shan, 27km (17 miles) W of She Xian

After arriving in Tunxi, the gateway to Huang Shan, it used to be that visitors would bypass this small town and head directly for the mountain. Nowadays, however, the beautiful countryside around Tunxi, with its paddy fields and gorgeous traditional architecture, provides a draw in its own right, and a visit here is well worth combining with your trip to Huang Shan. ***Note:*** For Chinese translations of selected establishments listed in this section, see chapter 16.

Essentials

GETTING THERE Located about 8km (5 miles) northwest of town, **Tunxi airport** has daily flights to Shanghai (1 hr.), Beijing (2 hr.), and Guangzhou (1 hr. 30 min.), and less frequent flights to Hong Kong (2 hr.) and Hefei (40 min.). Tickets can be bought at the **Airport Booking Office (Minghang Huang Shan Shoupiao Zhongxin)** at Huashan Lu 23 (✆ **0559/293-4111;** daily 8am–6pm). Taxis to the airport cost ¥20.

Two **trains** a day connect Tunxi to Shanghai (N204, 12 hr.; ¥252 soft sleeper, ¥175 hard sleeper). Tickets can be bought at the **railway station** (✆ **0559/211-6222**), at CITS, or at hotel tour desks.

Tangkou-bound **buses** (1 hr. 30 min.; ¥13) regularly leave from Tunxi's bus station and the square in front of the railway station. They start as early as 6:30am to catch arriving train passengers and run until around 6pm. Buses become less frequent in the afternoon and only depart when full.

GETTING AROUND **Taxis** charge ¥5 for 3km (2 miles), then ¥1.50 per kilometer thereafter until 10km (6 miles), then ¥2.70 per kilometer. Smaller *miandi* (van) taxis charge ¥3 per 2km (1¼ miles) or ¥5 for destinations in town. Private taxi rental out to Yi Xian will run around ¥300, subject to negotiation.

TOURS & GUIDES **CITS** at Binjiang Xi Lu 1 (✆ **0559/251-5303;** fax 0559/ 251-5255) can arrange private day trips to surrounding areas like Yi Xian and She Xian. Car rental for a day (guide not included) will run ¥600 depending on your itinerary; an English-speaking guide will cost another ¥300.

[FastFACTS] TUNXI

Banks, Foreign Exchange & ATMs The **Bank of China** at Xin'an Bei Lu 9 (✆ **0559/251-4983**) is open for foreign exchange Monday through Friday from 8am to 5:30pm. An ATM is outside the bank.

Internet Access A **24-hour Internet cafe** is at the southern end of Xianrendong Lu; it charges ¥2 per hour. If you have your own computer, the **UBC Coffee Shop** next to the Bank of China has free Wi-Fi access.

Post Office The post office (✆ **0559/232-2361;** July–Oct 8am–noon and 3–6pm; Nov–June 8am–noon and 2:30–5:30pm) is in the southern part of town at Qianyuan Nan Lu 39.

Visa Extensions The **PSB** is at Changgan Lu 108 (✆ **0559/255-5011;** July–Sept 8am–noon and 3–6pm; Oct–June 8am–noon and 2:30–5:30pm).

Where to Stay

EXPENSIVE

Huang Shan Guoji Dajiudian (Huang Shan International Hotel) ★ This four-star hotel in the northwestern part of town is the top choice for visiting Chinese dignitaries also popular with Western visitors, although it's starting to show signs of age. Rooms are spacious, comfortable, and equipped with extra amenities like robes, bathroom scale, and in-house movies. Bathrooms are bright and clean, and the service is quite friendly and efficient. The hotel's restaurant, featuring Anhui cuisine, is known by locals as one of the better establishments in town.

Huashan Lu 31. ✆ **0559/256-5678.** Fax 0559/251-2087. 215 units. ¥880 standard room; from ¥1,800 suite. 40% discounts possible. AE, DC, MC, V. **Amenities:** 2 restaurants; bar; lounge; concierge; forex; health club; room service; outdoor tennis court. *In room:* A/C, TV, hair dryer (4th floor and up), minibar.

Jianguo Shangwu Jiudian (Jianguo Garden Hotel) ★ Located near the International Hotel on the road to the airport, this four-star hotel catering mostly to Asian tour groups is a modern but charmless white-tiled affair on the outside. Happily, rooms are more tastefully decorated with comfortable beds and inoffensive furnishings. The clean bathrooms have bathroom scales and the basic amenities. The friendly staff speaks a little English.

Jichang Dadao 6. ✆ **0559/256-6688.** Fax 0559/235-4580. 130 units. ¥680–¥780 standard room; ¥1,380–¥4,800 suite. 20% discounts possible. AE, DC, MC, V. **Amenities:** 2 restaurants; bar; lounge; concierge; forex; health club; outdoor pool; room service; outdoor tennis court. *In room:* A/C, TV, hair dryer.

Xiang Ming Hotel ★ A five-star hotel finally arrives in (okay, *near*) Huang Shan. This new hotel is the brainchild of, oddly, a tea company. As such, it should come as no surprise that while this is a luxurious hotel relative to other digs in the vicinity, you should not expect the service or amenity standards of an international five-star chain. That said, staff here are extremely friendly and speak English well enough, the environs are new and squeaky clean, and the morning Western (or Chinese, if you prefer) breakfast is filling. Rooms are spacious, with off-white carpets and comfortable beds. The decor is low-key, with silk bed throws and a few matching pillows. Modern bathrooms come with Kohler bath fixtures, including a fabulous rain shower. The long walkway to the rear building is done in traditional Chinese style, with sloping, covered pavilions and a long archway overhead—a very nice touch.

Yingbing Lu 2. ✆ **0559/257-9999.** Fax 0559/257-8888. 500 units. ¥1,080 standard room; ¥1,500 suite. Discounts possible. AE, DC, MC, V. **Amenities:** Restaurant; bar; basic gym; Internet; indoor pool; room service; free walking sticks. *In room:* A/C, TV, fridge, hair dryer, minibar.

Where to Eat

Lao Jie Diyi Lou ★ HUIZHOU Housed in a traditional three-story Huizhou-style building at the eastern end of Old Street, this is an excellent place to try Huizhou cuisine, which is typically strong and pungent, emphasizing spicy and salty flavors. Specialties include *Huang Shan suweiyuan* (stir-fried mountain vegetables, tofu, pumpkin, bamboo shoots, mushrooms, and medicinal herbs), *wucai shansi* (eel stir-fried with peppers, mushrooms, and bamboo shoots), and *chou doufu* (smelly tofu). The food is tasty but service is a bit uneven.

Lao Jie 247. ✆ **0559/253-9797.** Meal for 2 ¥50–¥100. English menu available. AE, DC, MC, V. 10:30am–1:30pm and 4:30–9pm.

Shopping

In the southwestern part of town 1 block north of the river is **Lao Jie (Old Street),** a 1.3km (¾-mile) street lined with restored Song dynasty wooden houses and shops. The usual souvenirs are here, from ethnic batik and Mao buttons to Chinese paintings

HUIZHOU architecture

The main courtyard in Huizhou is flanked on three sides by buildings with downward-sloping roofs, meant to aid the collection of rainwater, which symbolized wealth. This open-air courtyard provides the only illumination as there are few, if any, outside windows. Buildings typically have two or three overhanging stories; these upper floors were the havens (or prisons) of the women of the house, who had to rely on peepholes and small windows in the closed-off verandas to survey the goings-on in the courtyard below.

The average family home had a single courtyard, but those of higher status were allowed two or even three courtyards. Because building courtyards beyond one's rank was a punishable offense, many owners attempted to enhance their prestige by building more side rooms and by improving the ornamental and decorative fixtures in the house. As a result, many of Huizhou's houses have some of the best stone, brick, and wood carvings in China.

Huizhou houses are also separated from each other by high, crenellated walls called **horse-head walls *(matou bi)*,** so named because the wall is said to look like a horse's head with its convex-shaped, black-tiled gable roof over stark white or gray stones. These walls were used both to prevent fires and to deter burglars and bandits, especially when the merchants were away on business.

Stone **memorial archways *(paifang)*** built to honor ancestors typically have calligraphic inscriptions detailing the reason for the arch, have two or four supporting posts, and have anywhere from two to five tiered roofs.

and dried foodstuffs. Shops are open from 8am to 10pm. This is a fun place to stroll even if you're not in the buying mood.

Around Tunxi

Formerly known as Huizhou (from which Anhui derived part of its name), this region was home to many wealthy salt merchants who in the Ming and Qing dynasties built many memorial arches and residences in such a unique style as to create a distinct regional *Huizhou* style of architecture. The district of Huizhou and the counties of She Xian and Yi Xian are famous for their well-preserved memorial arches *(paifang)*, memorial halls *(citang)*, and traditional villages of narrow streets and flowing streams.

Yi Xian is approximately 50km (30 miles) northwest of Tunxi, while the **Huizhou District** and **She Xian** are to the north and northeast. All three can easily be visited as separate day trips, but a combination of the three will be trickier. It is possible to visit both She Xian and Yi Xian in a long day, but you'll most likely only be able to visit one or two sights in each place and you won't have time to linger. You'll also have to rent a private taxi or car for the day (see "Tours & Guides" on p. 422), since public transportation to and between sights is slow and infrequent. If you have some command of Chinese or would simply like to brave it on your own, you can hire a taxi in Tunxi for the day to **Xidi, Hong Cun,** and **Nanping** in Yi Xian for ¥250 to ¥300, and to **She Xian, Qiankou,** and **Chengkan** for around ¥280. Minibuses also leave for She Xian (30 min.; ¥4) and Yi Xian (1 hr.; ¥8) from the bus station and the roundabout in front of the railway station.

Yi Xian 黟县

The first village you encounter on the way to Yi Xian (7km/4 miles away) is **Xidi ★** (¥104; 8am–5:30pm), a UNESCO World Heritage Site famous for its over 300 well-preserved ancient residences. The houses, with their amazingly ornate stone, brick, and wood carvings, are really the highlight here at this boat-shaped village, which dates from the Northern Song dynasty (960–1127) but which developed into its present size during the Ming and Qing dynasties. The memorial archway (built in 1578) that greets visitors is the sole remaining archway in the village and is said to have survived the Cultural Revolution because it was covered with Mao slogans.

Another UNESCO World Heritage Site, **Hong Cun ★★** (¥104; 8am–5:30pm), located 11km (7 miles) northeast of Yi Xian town, is probably the most picturesque of the towns, with two spots in the village vying for top honors: the exterior view with an arched bridge across a large lily pond; and the crescent-shaped pond Yuezhao Tang, whose reflection of the surrounding traditional houses on a clear day is truly magnificent. If these vistas appear familiar, it is probably because the two locations were used in the movie *Crouching Tiger, Hidden Dragon.* Water is the main feature at this village, with the two large ponds connected to a series of flowing streams and canals that pass by every house, providing water for washing, cooking, and bathing, and that taken altogether are said to outline the shape of a bull.

Just over 5km (3 miles) west of Yi Xian, **Nanping ★** (¥43; 8am–5:30pm) is a late Tang, early Song dynasty town that served as the location for Zhang Yimou's 1990 film, *Ju Dou.* In fact, so many films have been made in this picturesque village that it is also unimaginatively called Movie Village of China. All the houses in the village have concave corners that bow inward, the absence of rigid sharp edges symbolizing the avoidance of quarrels in the community. With 72 lanes that seem to double back on each other like an Escher maze, the village is best visited with a local guide (included in the price of admission), even though he or she speaks practically no English. The guide also has the keys to open various halls, including the 500-year-old, 1,500-sq.-m (16,146-sq.-ft.) Ye's Ancestral Hall, where the teahouse fight scene from *Crouching Tiger, Hidden Dragon* was filmed.

Where to Stay

Pig's Inn Xidi (Zhu Lan Jiu Ba Xidi) ★ Set in the UNESCO-honored village of Xidi, this small farmer's home was lovingly restored by a Shanghainese couple who came looking for a quieter way of life. Rustic and charming, this is a great place to stay if you want to experience the idyllic pace of rural life. Views from the open-air third-floor lounge overlooking the picturesque gray-tiled rooftops and lush mountains in the distance are spectacular. Meals in the dining room, the former site of the pig sty that gives this hotel its unique name, are made to order with village-grown ingredients. The homemade breakfasts are ample, with tasty soup dumplings, congee, and fried eggs. You may also opt to stay at their sister property 15 minutes away, **Pig's Inn Bishuan,** a gorgeously upscale renovation of a wealthy merchant's home.

Xidi Cun. http://blog.sina.com.cn/zhulanjiuba. ✆ **0559/515-4555.** 5 units. ¥360 standard room; ¥880 suite AE, DC, MC, V. **Amenities:** Restaurant. *In room:* A/C, hair dryer, Internet.

She Xian 歙县

Although She Xian has 94 memorial arches scattered throughout the county, **Tangyue Paifang Qun (Tangyue Memorial Arches) ★**, with its collection of seven four-pillared arches, is the best place to view these impressive structures. Located about 6km (3¾ miles) west of She Xian, the arches may be viewed from 6:30am to 6:30pm for a fee of ¥80. The arches were built by a salt merchant family named Bao over 400 years in the Ming and Qing dynasties. If you're coming by minibus (¥4) from Tunxi, ask to be dropped off at the archways. From there, it's another 1.5km (1 mile) to the arches. Walk or take a tricycle taxi for ¥5 to ¥10.

She Xian claims the only eight-pillared memorial archway in China, the **Xuguo Shifang (Xuguo Stone Archway) ★★**. Built in 1584 to honor a local scholar named Xu Guo, this magnificent structure has eight pillars decorated with carved lions, phoenixes, and *qilin* (Chinese unicorns). Up the hill from the archway and down a left side street is **Doushan Jie,** a narrow alley lined with traditional houses and shops.

Huizhou Qu (Huizhou District; 徽州区)

The highlight at **Chengkan village ★★** (¥60; 7am–5:30pm; Nov 16–Mar 15 8am–4:30pm), 34km (20 miles) north of Tunxi, is **Baolun Ge (Baolun Hall) ★★**. The impressive building alone is worth the trip. Located in the back of the **Luo Dongshu Ci (Luo Dongshu Ancestral Hall),** the bottom half of the structure, with stone square pillars supporting exquisitely painted (though now faded) wooden beams and brackets, was built in the Ming dynasty to honor the Luo family ancestors. The top half, with wooden windows and tiled roof, was built 70 years later to honor the emperor. At Zhongying Jie 12 is a Qing dynasty house with intricate wooden doors and panels.

Qiankou village has a Museum of Ancient Residences (¥40; 7:30am–6pm), a collection of 12 Ming dynasty Huizhou-style residences formerly scattered throughout She Xian county but relocated here and restored. This museum provides a comprehensive overview of local architecture if you can't see each individual town.

SHANGHAI

While Beijing may be the capital of China, Shanghai is China's economic, financial, and commercial center, its largest city, and the key to China's future. As the Middle Kingdom re-emerges as a major global power in the 21st century, Shanghai—the "city above the sea"—is the economic engine that is leading the way. No other super city in China, or anywhere else in the world for that matter, is more vibrant or fascinating.

9

As Chinese cities go, Shanghai is comparatively young, gaining its identity only after the First Opium War in 1842, which opened up this heretofore small fishing village at the mouth of the Yangzi River to foreign powers. The British, French, Americans, Germans, and Russians moved in, erecting their distinct Western-style banks, trading houses, and mansions, leaving an indelible architectural legacy to this day.

During its heyday in the 1920s and 1930s, Shanghai, dubbed the "Paris of the East" (and more ignominiously, the "Whore of Asia"), was a cosmopolitan and thriving commercial and financial center. It attracted legions to its shores: explorers and exploiters, gangsters and businessmen alike. After the Communist victory in 1949, however, Shanghai went into a commercial slumber for the next 40 years. In 1990, then dour Shanghai was picked to spearhead China's economic reform. The city embarked on an unprecedented building boom, and has not looked back or paused for breath since.

Today, neighborhoods of foreign architecture have been preserved and restored and are wonderful for a stroll. Shanghai's great river of commerce, the Huangpu, a tributary of the Yangzi River, is lined with a gallery of colonial architecture, known as the Bund, grander than any other in the East, beckoning to the curious visitor and locals alike. The mansions, garden estates, country clubs, and cathedrals of the Westerners who made their fortunes here a century ago are scattered throughout the city, and the city even has a synagogue, dating from the days of an unparalleled Jewish immigration to China.

At the same time, the creations of a strictly Chinese culture have not been entirely erased. A walk through the chaotic old Chinese city turns up traditional treasures: a teahouse that epitomizes Old China; a quintessential southern-Chinese classical garden; active temples, and ancient pagodas.

But the city is not only a museum of East meeting West on Chinese soil. Overnight Shanghai has become one of the world's great modern capitals, the one city that best shows where China is headed at the dawn of the 21st century. Across the Huangpu River, Pudong, serving as the face of new Shanghai, now has the tallest hotel in the world, Asia's largest shopping mall, China's largest stock exchange, and the highest observation deck in the world, in the Shanghai World Financial Center.

Shanghai is also once again a leading trendsetter in fashion, design, culture, and the arts, and it is arguably the best city in China for dining and shopping.

Bearing the burden of all these superlatives, the Shanghainese—frank, efficient, chauvinistic, and progressive—are using their previous international exposure to create China's most outward-looking, modern, and brash metropolis. The city set the stage for becoming one of the world's leading cities when it hosted the World Expo in 2010 and broke the record for most visitors, with 73 million attendees.

Visitors dizzy from the frenzy can find, within an easy day trip, two slightly more pastoral spots that are worth visiting. To the northwest, Suzhou, with its classical gardens and canals, is known as the "Venice of China." To the southwest is Hangzhou, renowned for beautiful West Lake and the surrounding tea plantations.

Winter in Shanghai is windy and chilly; summer is oppressively hot and humid, making late March or late October/early November ideal for a visit.

Note: Unless otherwise noted, hours listed for attractions and restaurants are daily.

ORIENTATION: SHANGHAI 上海

Arriving

BY PLANE

Shanghai has an older airport to the west, **Hongqiao International Airport,** and a newer airport to the east, **Pudong International Airport,** which began operations late in 1999. Virtually all of the international carriers use the Pudong airport, which serves all major international destinations from Amsterdam to Vancouver. Every major city in China is also served with multiple daily flights, mostly to and from Hongqiao, but the most important, such as Beijing, also have services to Pudong.

The **Pudong International Airport** (**✆ 021/96990;** www.shairport.com), your likely point of arrival, is located about 45km (28 miles) east of downtown Shanghai. Transfers into the city take 45 minutes to 1 hour. The airport has two terminals serving both international and domestic flights that are connected by indoor corridors and free shuttle buses. Hotel counters, money exchange, and ATMs are in both terminals. ***Note:*** It is important that you verify with your airline which terminal you will be arriving at and departing from.

The older **Hongqiao Airport** (**✆ 021/6268-8899**), now largely reserved for flights within China, is located 19km (12 miles) west of the city center. New **Shanghai-Beijing express shuttle flights** depart practically every half-hour from Hongqiao Airport that promise a maximum 3-hour turnaround from check-in to baggage claim. There are some hotel counters here, and ATMs, but no money exchange. These shuttle flights are run by a number of airlines including Shanghai Airlines (www.shanghai-air.com), China Eastern Airlines (www.ce-air.com), Air China (www.airchina.com.cn), and Hainan Airways (http://global.hnair.com).

Getting into Town from the Airport

HOTEL SHUTTLES Many of Shanghai's hotels maintain service counters along the walls in the main arrivals halls in both airports, though in most cases, the hotel's airport staff is primarily there to help you find a taxi or arrange for an expensive private car to take you to the hotel in the city.

AIRPORT TAXIS The legitimate taxis are lined up just outside the arrivals halls of both airports. Taxis into town from Hongqiao Airport take anywhere from 20 to 40 minutes depending on traffic and should cost between ¥40 and ¥90. Taxi transfers on the highway to hotels in Pudong and downtown Shanghai run between 45 minutes and 1½ hours for ¥160 and up. Insist on seeing the meter started.

METRO The world's first commercially operating maglev (magnetic levitation) line uses German technology to whisk you the 30km (19 miles) between Pudong Airport and the Longyang Lu metro station in Pudong in 8 minutes (¥50 one-way; ¥80 round-trip within 7 days). Maglev trains run every 20 minutes between 6:45am and 9:40pm daily. For information, call ✆ **021/6255-6987.** From the Longyang Lu station, travelers can connect to the rest of Shanghai using metro line 2.

AIRPORT BUSES There are several buses making transfers from **Pudong** airport into town: Airport Bus Line no. 1 goes to Hongqiao Airport; airport Bus Line no. 2 (Jichang Er Xian) goes from Pudong to the City Air-Terminal Building (Chengshi Hangzhan Lou) at Nanjing Xi Lu 1600 every 15 to 20 minutes, from 7:20am to 11pm, with taxis providing the final link to hotels. Bus no. 5 goes to the Shanghai Railway Station, and bus no. 7 to the Shanghai South Railway Station. Fares range from ¥18 to ¥30. Shuttle buses no longer run between Pudong Airport and select hotels.

From **Hongqiao,** several buses also make the run into town. A CAAC shuttle, Minhang Zhuanxian (Airport Special Line), goes to the Chengshi Hangzhan Lou (City Air-Terminal Building) at Nanjing Xi Lu 1600, every 20 minutes from 6am to 8pm. Tickets cost ¥4. Airport Bus Line no. 1 (Jichang Yi Xian) goes to Pudong Airport (buses depart every 20 min. from 6am–9pm). Public bus no. 941 goes to the railway station and bus no. 925 runs to People's Square (Renmin Guangchang).

BY TRAIN

Shanghai Railway Station (**Shanghai Huochezhan;** ✆ **021/6354-3193** or 021/6317-9090) is massive. You will have to walk a block to the metro station (follow the signs for lines 1, 3, and 4) or hail a taxi on the lower level of the terminal. Express T trains run to destinations such as Dalian, Ürümqi, Nanjing, Yangzhou, Hangzhou, Xi'an, Lanzhou, and Ji'nan. It's also the terminus of the main train line to Beijing (though bullet trains now depart from Hongqing; see below). The T99 runs on alternate days to Hong Kong. The station also is the stop for K trains to Changsha, Guangzhou, Kunming, Wuhan, Yinchuan, Xining, Fuzhou, Xiamen, Chongqing, Shenyang, Qingdao, Taiyuan, Harbin, and Jilin. Trains arriving from Hangzhou and select destinations south now arrive at the **Shanghai South Railway Station** (**Shanghai Nan Zhan;** ✆ **021/6317-9090**) in the southwestern part of town. This station is reachable by metro lines 1 and 3.

The new, ultra-modern **Hongqiao Railway Station (Shanghai Hongqiao Zhan)** opened in 2010, and is now the largest train station in Asia. Spread over 4 levels, it serves several high-speed bullet trains, including trains to Nanjing, Hangzhou, and the Beijing-Shanghai high-speed railway. Located west of the city center, the station connects to Hongqiao International Airport (see above) and lies on lines 2 and 10 of the Shanghai metro.

BY SHIP

International arrivals from Japan are at the **International Passenger Terminal (Guoji Keyun Matou)** at Yangshupu Lu 100, not far north of the Bund. Ships of the **Japan-China International Ferry Company (Chinajif)** line sail between Shanghai and alternately Osaka and Kobe every week. The **Shanghai Ferry Co. Ltd.** has a weekly sailing from Osaka on Friday, and to Osaka on Tuesday; see **www.shanghai-ferry.co.jp** (in English). Tickets are available at the terminal or at travel agencies such as CITS. Domestic ships arriving from the Yangzi River and Putuo Shan now arrive at the **Wusong Passenger Terminal (Shanghai Gang Wusong Keyun Zhongxin),** Songbao Lu 251 (✆ **021/5657-5500**), at the intersection of the Huangpu and Yangzi rivers. If you arrive here as an independent traveler, you will have to hail a taxi at the passenger terminal to reach your hotel, which is likely another 30 to 45 minutes away.

Visitor Information

The best source of visitor information is the 24-hour **Shanghai Call Center** (✆ **021/962-288**) with very helpful English and Chinese-speaking university graduates providing information on almost all Shanghai-travel-related topics. There are about a dozen **Travel Information Service Centers (TIC)** in the city, and they appear to only sell tours and book hotels but, depending on who's behind the desk, you may get some guidance. The main office is at Zhongshan Xi Lu 2525, room 410 (✆ **021/6439-9806**), with smaller branch offices scattered throughout the city.

The best sources of **current information** about Shanghai events, shopping, restaurants, and nightlife are the mostly free English-language newspapers and magazines distributed to hotels, shops, and cafes around town, such as *that's Shanghai,* and *City Weekend* (www.cityweekend.com.cn). The newspaper *Shanghai Daily* (www.shanghaidaily.com) provides the sanitized official view.

City Layout

Shanghai, with one of the largest urban populations on Earth (more than 18 million residents), is divided by the Huangpu River into Pudong (east of the river) and Puxi (west of the river).

For the traveler, the majority of Shanghai's sights are still concentrated **downtown** in Puxi, whose layout bears a distinct Western imprint. After the First Opium War in 1842 opened Shanghai up to foreign powers, the British, French, Germans, Americans, and others moved in, carving for themselves their own "concessions" where they were subject not to the laws of the Chinese government but to those established by their own governing councils. Colonial Shanghai is especially visible downtown, along the western shore of the Huangpu River up and down the **Bund (Waitan),** which has always been and still is the symbolic center of the city; from here, **downtown Shanghai** opens to the west like a fan. Today's practical and logistical center, however, is **People's Square (Renmin Guangchang),** about 1.6km (1 mile) west of the Bund. This is the meeting point of three of Shanghai's main subway lines, as well as the location of the Shanghai Museum, Shanghai Art Museum, and Shanghai Grand Theatre. The Bund and People's Square are linked by several streets, none more famous than **Nanjing Lu,** historically China's number-one shopping street.

Southwest of the Bund is the historic **Nanshi District,** Shanghai's Old Chinese city. As its name suggests, located here are some typically Chinese sights, such as the quintessential Southern-Chinese Garden, Yu Yuan, the famous Huxin Ting teahouse, and several temples.

About 1.6km (1 mile) west of the Bund and south of Nanjing Lu, Shanghai's former **French Concession** is still one of Shanghai's trendiest neighborhoods, chock-full of colonial architecture and attractions. It is also home to some of the city's most glamorous shops and restaurants, as seen in the mega-development **Xin Tiandi.** Farther west still is the **Hongqiao Development Zone,** where modern commercial and industrial development was concentrated beginning in the 1980s.

North Shanghai has a scattering of interesting sights, including the Jade Buddha Temple, the Lu Xun Museum, and the Ohel Moshe Synagogue. **South Shanghai** has the Longhua Pagoda, the Shanghai Botanical Garden, and the cafes and shops of Hengshan Lu.

East of the Huangpu River, the district of **Pudong** is all about Shanghai's future, as epitomized by its ultramodern skyscrapers such as the Oriental Pearl TV Tower, the 88-story Jin Mao Building, and the 100-story Shanghai World Financial Center, which houses the highest hotel in the world.

Neighborhoods in Brief

The Shànghǎi municipality consists of 14 districts, four counties, and the Pǔdōng New Area, and covers an area of 6,341 sq. km (2,448 sq. miles), with its urban area measuring 2,643 sq. km (1,020 sq. miles). The seven main urban districts, running from east to west, are identified here.

Pǔdōng Located across the Huángpǔ River from the Bund, Pǔdōng (literally "east of the Huángpǔ") was formerly backwater farmland before 1990 when it was targeted by then-Chinese President Dèng Xiǎopíng to lead Shànghǎi and the rest of China into a new age of economic growth. Today, it is home to the Lùjiāzuǐ Financial with its many modern economic monuments (Jīn Mào Tower, Shànghǎi World Financial Center), the Shànghǎi stock exchange, Asia's second-largest department store, a riverside promenade, the Pǔdōng International Airport, and the 2010 World Expo grounds.

Huángpǔ (Downtown Shànghǎi) The city center of old Shànghǎi lies in a compact sector west of the Huángpǔ River and south of Sūzhōu Creek. It extends west to Chéngdū Běi Lù (the North-South Elevated Hwy.), and encompasses the Bund, People's Square (Rénmín Guǎngchǎng), and the Shànghǎi Museum. The district now also stretches to the south to encompass **Nánshì,** the old Chinese city, with the Old Town Bazaar, Yù Yuán (Yù Garden), Shànghǎi's old city wall, and the Confucian Temple.

Hóngkǒu (Northeast Shànghǎi) Immediately north of downtown Shànghǎi, across Sūzhōu Creek, this residential sector along the upper Huángpǔ River was originally the American Concession before it became part of the International Settlement in colonial days. Today, it's a developing neighborhood with a few sights: the Ohel Moshe Synagogue, the Lǔ Xùn Museum, and the Duōlún Lù Commercial Street.

Lúwān (French Concession) Beginning at Xīzàng Lù at the eastern end of People's Square and continuing west to Shǎnxī Nán Lù, this historic district was the domain of the French colonial community up until 1949. The French left their mark on the residential architecture, which boasts such tourist sights as Fùxīng Park, the historic Jǐn Jiāng Hotel, the shops along Huáihǎi Zhōng Lù, the Xīntiāndì development, and the former residences of Sun Yat-sen and Zhōu Ēnlái.

Jìng Ān (Northwest Shànghǎi) North of the French Concession and part of the former International Settlement, this district has its share of colonial architecture, as well as the modern Shànghǎi Centre. Two of the city's top Buddhist shrines, Jìng Ān Sì and Yùfó Sì (Jade Buddha Temple), are located here, as are a number of Shànghǎi's top hotels and restaurants.

Xúhuì (Southwest Shànghǎi) West of the French Concession and south along Héngshān Lù, this area is one of Shànghǎi's top addresses for cafes, bars, and shops. Sights include the Xújiāhuì Cathedral, Lónghuá Pagoda, the Shànghǎi Botanical Garden, and the former residence of Soong Ching-ling.

Chángníng (Hóngqiáo Development Zone) Starting at Huáihǎi Xī Lù, directly west of the Xúhuì and Jìng Ān districts, this corridor of new international economic ventures extends far west of downtown, past Gǔběi New Town and the Shànghǎi Zoo, to the Hóngqiáo Airport.

GETTING AROUND

By Metro

The Shanghai metro *(ditie)* is the fastest and cheapest way to cover longer distances: Rides cost ¥3 to ¥7 depending on the number of stops. Operating from 5:30am to 11pm, the metro has nine main lines, with plans to expand to 11 lines in 2010, and 13 lines in 2012. At press time, the most useful lines for visitors are metro lines 1 and 2. **Metro line 1,** the red line, winds in a roughly north-south direction connecting the Shanghai Railway Station in the north, through the French Concession to the Shanghai South Railway Station and points southwest. Its central downtown stop is People's Square (Renmin Guangchang) near Nanjing Xi Lu, which is where it connects with **metro line 2,** the green line, which runs east-west from Pudong across downtown Shanghai. **Metro line 3,** actually more of an aboveground light rail, encircles the western outskirts of the city and also links Shanghai's two train stations, though it is seldom useful for sightseeing except for its stop near Lu Xun Park. **Metro line 4,** the purple line, forms a ring around the city and connects Pudong to the Shanghai Railway Station. **Metro line 5 and 6** runs in the far southwest reaches of the city and in the eastern part of Pudong respectively, and is not useful for most tourists. **Metro line 8** runs from Pudong through downtown (up Xizang Lu) to Hongkou, and will be useful for seeing the World Expo sites, and **metro line 9** in the southwest takes visitors out to Qibao and Sheshan. See the map on the inside back cover for all stops.

NAVIGATING THE METRO Subway platform signs in Chinese and English indicate the station name and the name of the next station in each direction, and maps of the metro system are posted in each station and inside the subway cars. English announcements of upcoming stops are also made on trains. To determine your fare, consult the fare map posted near the ticket counters and on ticket vending kiosks. Fares range from ¥3 for the first few stops to ¥7 for the most distant ones. ***Note:*** Hang onto your electronic ticket, which you have to insert into the exit barrier when you leave.

By Taxi

With over 45,000 taxis in the streets, this is the visitor's most common means of getting around Shanghai. Taxis congregate at leading hotels, but are better hailed from street corners. Your best bets for service and comfort are the turquoise-blue taxis of **Da Zhong Taxi** (✆ **021/6258-1688**), the yellow taxis of **Qiang Sheng Taxi** (✆ **021/6258-0000**), and the blue taxis of **Jinjiang Taxi** (✆ **021/6275-8800**). Regardless of the company, the fare is ¥11 for the first 3km (1¾ miles), and ¥2.10 for each additional kilometer. There's a 30% surcharge for trips after 11pm, and for bridge and tunnel tolls. Expect to pay about ¥20 to ¥35 for most excursions in the city and up to ¥60 for longer crosstown jaunts.

By Bus

Public buses *(gonggong qiche)* mostly charge ¥2, but they are more difficult to use and less comfortable than taxis or the metro. Tickets are sold on board by a roving conductor, though some buses have no conductors and require exact change. Be prepared to stand and be cramped during your expedition, and take care with backpacks and purses, as these are inviting targets for thieves.

By Bridge, Boat & Tunnel

To shift the thousands of daily visitors between east and west Shanghai, there are a multitude of routes. Three are by bridge, each handling around 45,000 vehicles a day: the 3.7km-long (2⅓-mile), harp-string-shaped **Nanpu Daqiao,** and the **Lupu Daqiao,** both in the southern part of town; and the 7.6km-long (4¾-mile) **Yangpu Daqiao** northeast of the Bund. A fourth route (and the cheapest) is by water, via the **passenger ferry** that ordinary workers favor. There are numerous ferry crossings but one of the main ones for visitors is the ferry terminal located at the southern end of the Bund on the west shore (ticket price: ¥2), and at the southern end of Riverside Avenue at Dongchang Lu on the east shore. Other routes across the river make use of tunnels. Motor vehicles make use of the Yan'an Dong Lu Tunnel (though taxis are barred 8–9:30am and 5–6:30pm), the Fuxing Lu Tunnel, the Dalian Lu Tunnel in the north, and the Dapu Lu tunnel, with at least three more tunnels under construction. Metro lines 2, 4, and 8 also make the crossing, and the **Bund Sight-Seeing Tunnel (Waitan Guanguang Suidao)** is equipped with glassy tram cars that glide through a tacky subterranean 3-minute light show with music and narrative (8am–10pm; ¥40 one-way, ¥50 round-trip).

[FastFACTS] SHANGHAI

If you don't find what you're looking for in these listings, try the **Shanghai Call Center** (✆ **021/962-288**) or inquire at your hotel desk.

Banks, Currency Exchange & ATMs

The most convenient place to exchange currency is your hotel, where the rates are the same as at the Bank of China and exchange desks are often open 24 hours. Convenient **Bank of China** locations for currency exchange and credit card cash withdrawals are located on the Bund at the Bank of China building, Zhongshan Dong Yi Lu 23 (✆ **021/6329-1979**); at Nanjing Xi Lu 1221 (✆ **021/6247-1700**); at Yan'an Xi Lu 2168 (✆ **021/6278-5060**); and at Huaihai Zhong Lu 1207 (✆ **021/6437-8753**). Bank hours are Monday to

Friday from 9am to noon and 1:30 to 4:30pm, and Saturday from 9am to noon.

There are also branches of **Hongkong and Shanghai Bank (HSBC)** at the Shanghai Centre (Nanjing Xi Lu 1376) and at G/F, HSBC Tower, Lujiazui Huan Lu, Pudong, that can change U.S. traveler's checks and cash. All have 24-hour **ATMs.** Although there are now many ATMs around town with international logos for Plus or Cirrus, not all of them take international cards. It's best to stick to Bank of China, HSBC, and Citibank ATMs.

Doctors & Dentists Shanghai has the most advanced medical treatment and facilities in China. The higher-end hotels usually have in-house or on-call doctors, but almost all hotels can refer foreign guests to dentists and doctors versed in Western medicine. The following medical clinics and hospitals specialize in treating foreigners and provide international-standard services: **Parkway Health Medical Center** (formerly World Link Medical Center), Nanjing Xi Lu 1376, Shanghai Centre, Suite 203 (24-hr. hot line ✆ **021/6445-5999;** www.parkwayhealth.cn), has several clinics around town, 24-hour emergency services, offers Western dental care, and OB-GYN services; walk-in hours at the Nanjing Lu branch are from 9am to 7pm Monday through Friday, from 9am to 5pm on weekends. Call for times at other clinics. **Hua Shan Hospital,** Wulumuqi Zhong Lu 12, Jing'an District (✆ **021/6248-9999,** ext. 2500), has a special Foreigner's Clinic on the 8th floor of building 1, and a 24-hour hotline (✆ **021/6248-3986**). A representative office of **International SOS,** Hongqiao Lu 3, 2 Grand Gateway, Unit 2907-2910 (✆ **021/5298-9538**), provides medical evacuation and repatriation throughout China on a 24-hour basis.

Dental care to foreign visitors and expatriates is provided by Parkway Health Dental Centers Monday to Saturday (see above); and by **DDS Dental Care,** Huaihai Zhong Lu 1325, Evergo Tower, B1-05 (✆ **021/5465-2678;** www.ddsdentalcare.com). DDS Dental Care has multilingual Western-trained dentists, and their own lab.

Embassies & Consulates The consulates of many countries are located in the French Concession and Jing'an districts several miles west of the city center. The consulates are open Monday through Friday only, and often close for lunch from noon to 1pm. The Consulate General of **Australia** is in CITIC Square at Nanjing Xi Lu 1168, 22nd floor (✆ **021/2215-5200;** fax 021/2215-5252; www.shanghai.china.embassy.gov.au). The **British** Consulate General is in the Shanghai Centre, Nanjing Xi Lu 1376, Suite 301 (✆ **021/3279-8400;** fax 021/6279-7651; www.uk.cn). The **Canadian** Consulate General is in the Shanghai Centre at Nanjing Xi Lu 1376, West Tower, Suites 604 and 668 (✆ **021/3279-2800;** fax 021/3279-2801; www.shanghai.gc.ca). The **New Zealand** Consulate General is at Changle Lu 989, The Centre, room 1605-1607A (✆ **021/5407-5858;** fax 021/5407-5068; www.nzembassy.com). The Consulate General of the **United States** is at Huaihai Zhong Lu 1469 (✆ **021/6433-6880;** fax 021/6433-4122; http://shanghai.usembassy-china.org.cn), although U.S. citizen services are available at Nanjing Xi Lu 1038, 8th floor (✆ **021/3217-4650**).

Hospitals See "Doctors & Dentists," above.

Internet Access Business centers at most three-star and up Shanghai hotels provide online access and e-mail services. Broadband Internet access is now commonplace in many of Shanghai's hotels, a large number of which also offer Wi-Fi in their lobbies, executive lounges, and rooms. A number of Shanghai restaurants and cafes also offer free Wi-Fi access to their patrons. The most reliable and the cheapest Internet access can be found at the **Shanghai Library (Shanghai Tushuguan),** Huaihai Zhong Lu 1557 (✆ **021/6445-5555** ext. 2001), in a small office on the ground floor underneath the main entrance staircase. It's open from 8:30am to 8:30pm (¥4 per hour).

Maps & Books The biggest and best selection of English-language books in Shanghai, as well as the bilingual *Shanghai Tourist Map*, can be found at the **Shanghai Foreign Language Bookstore (Shanghai Waiwen Shudian),** Fuzhou Lu 390 (✆ **021/6322-3200;** 9am–6pm). **Chaterhouse Book Trader,** Shanghai Times Sq., Huaihai Zhong Lu 93, Shop B1-E (✆ **021/6391-8237**), and **Garden Books,** Changle Lu 325 (✆ **021/5404-8728**), also have an extensive English-language book selection. The **Shanghai Museum,** Renmin Da Dao 201 (✆ **021/6372-3500**), has selections of books on Shanghai and Chinese art and culture, as do the gift shops and kiosks in major hotels. Most hotel concierges should also be able to provide bilingual maps of the city.

Pharmacies The best outlet for Westerners is **Watson's Drug Store,** which has branches throughout town, including at Huaihai Zhong Lu 787–789 (✆ **021/6474-4775;** 9:30am–10pm). Prescriptions can be filled at the **Parkway Health Medical Center,** Nanjing Xi Lu 1376, Shanghai Centre, Suite 203 (✆ **021/6279-7688**).

Post Office Most hotels sell postage stamps and will mail your letters and parcels, the latter for a hefty fee. The main post office (*youzhengju;* 7am–10pm) is located at Bei Suzhou Lu 276 (✆ **021/6325-2070**), at Sichuan Bei Lu, in downtown Shanghai just north of Suzhou Creek; international parcels are sent from a desk in the same building, but its entrance is actually around the corner at Tiantong Lu 395. Another post office where employees can speak some English is at Shanghai Centre, Nanjing Xi Lu 1376, East Suite 355 (✆ **021/6279-8044**).

Taxes Most four- and five-star hotels levy a 10% to 15% tax on rooms (including a city tax), while a few restaurants and bars have taken to placing a similar service charge on bills. There is no sales tax. Airport departure taxes are now included in the price of your airline ticket.

Taxis See "Getting Around," above.

Visa Extensions The **PSB** office for visa extensions is at Minsheng Lu 1500 (✆ **021/2895-1900,** ext. 2; metro: Shanghai Kejiguan/Science and Technology Museum, Exit 3) in Pudong. Hours are Monday to Saturday 9am to 5pm.

Weather The *China Daily* newspaper, CCTV 9 (China Central Television's English language channel), and some hotel bulletin boards furnish the next day's forecast. You can also dial Shanghai's weather number, ✆ **121.**

WHERE TO STAY

With so many international chains and new luxury hotels, Shanghai offers excellent accommodations, but few bargains. The room rates listed are rack rates, but you'll be able to negotiate much better rates in person. The top hotels all levy a service charge of 10% to 15%, though this is usually waived or included in the final negotiated price at smaller hotels. All rooms have TVs with foreign channels unless otherwise noted.

Huángpŭ (Downtown)

VERY EXPENSIVE

Fairmont Peace Hotel (Hépíng Fàndiàn) After more than a 2-year renovation, Shànghǎi's best-known historic hotel is back in business. Originally built in 1929, the Peace—known in its heyday as the Cathay Hotel—is where Noël Coward

Shanghai Hotels & Restaurants

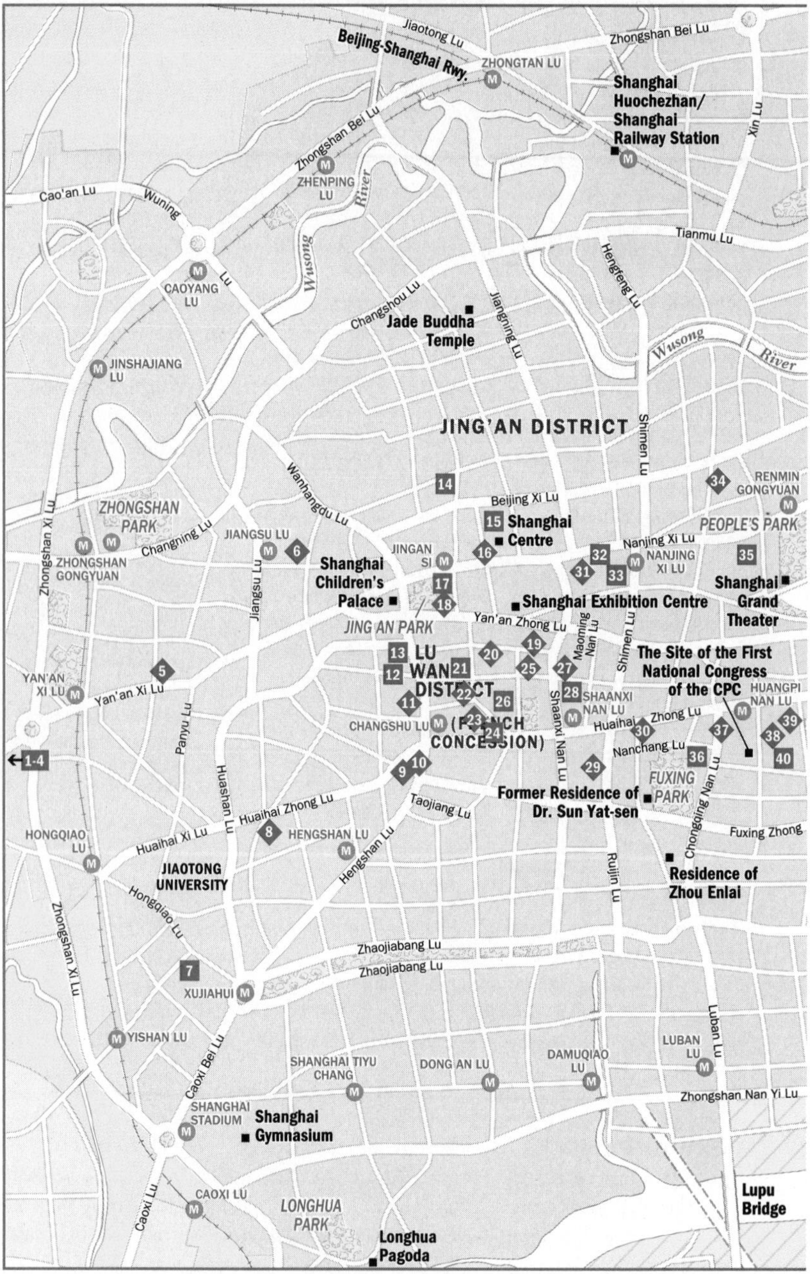

Jiaotong Lu
Zhongshan Bei Lu
Beijing-Shanghai Rwy.
ZHONGTAN LU
Shanghai Huochezhan/ Shanghai Railway Station
Xin Lu
Zhongshan Bei Lu
ZHENPING LU
Wusong River
Cao'an Lu
Wuning Lu
Tianmu Lu
CAOYANG LU
Hengfeng Lu
Changshou Lu
Jade Buddha Temple
Jiangning Lu
Wusong River
JINSHAJIANG LU
JING'AN DISTRICT
Shimen Lu
Wanhangdu Lu
14
34
RENMIN GONGYUAN
Beijing Xi Lu
ZHONGSHAN PARK
15 Shanghai Centre
PEOPLE'S PARK
Zhongshan Xi Lu
Changning Lu
JIANGSU LU
6
JINGAN SI
16
Nanjing Xi Lu
32
NANJING XI LU
35
ZHONGSHAN GONGYUAN
Shanghai Children's Palace
31
33
Shanghai Grand Theater
Jiangsu Lu
17
18
Shanghai Exhibition Centre
JING AN PARK
Yan'an Zhong Lu
Maoming Nan Lu
19
Shimen Lu
13 LU WAN DISTRICT (FRENCH CONCESSION)
20
The Site of the First National Congress of the CPC
5
12
21
25
27
YAN'AN XI LU
Yan'an Xi Lu
11
22
26
28
SHAANXI NAN LU
HUANGPI NAN LU
CHANGSHU LU
23
24
Huaihai Zhong Lu
30
37
38
39
Panyu Lu
Shaanxi Nan Lu
Nanchang Lu
36
40
1-4
9
10
29
FUXING PARK
Huashan Lu
Former Residence of Dr. Sun Yat-sen
Huaihai Zhong Lu
Taojiang Lu
Chongqing Nan Lu
HONGQIAO LU
Huaihai Xi Lu
8
HENGSHAN LU
Fuxing Zhong
Hengshan Lu
JIAOTONG UNIVERSITY
Residence of Zhou Enlai
Ruijin Lu
Hongqiao Lu
Zhongshan Xi Lu
Zhaojiabang Lu
Zhaojiabang Lu
7
XUJIAHUI
Luban Lu
YISHAN LU
Caoxi Bei Lu
LUBAN LU
SHANGHAI TIYU CHANG
DONG AN LU
DAMUQIAO LU
Zhongshan Nan Yi Lu
SHANGHAI STADIUM
Shanghai Gymnasium
Caoxi Lu
CAOXI LU
LONGHUA PARK
Lupu Bridge
Longhua Pagoda

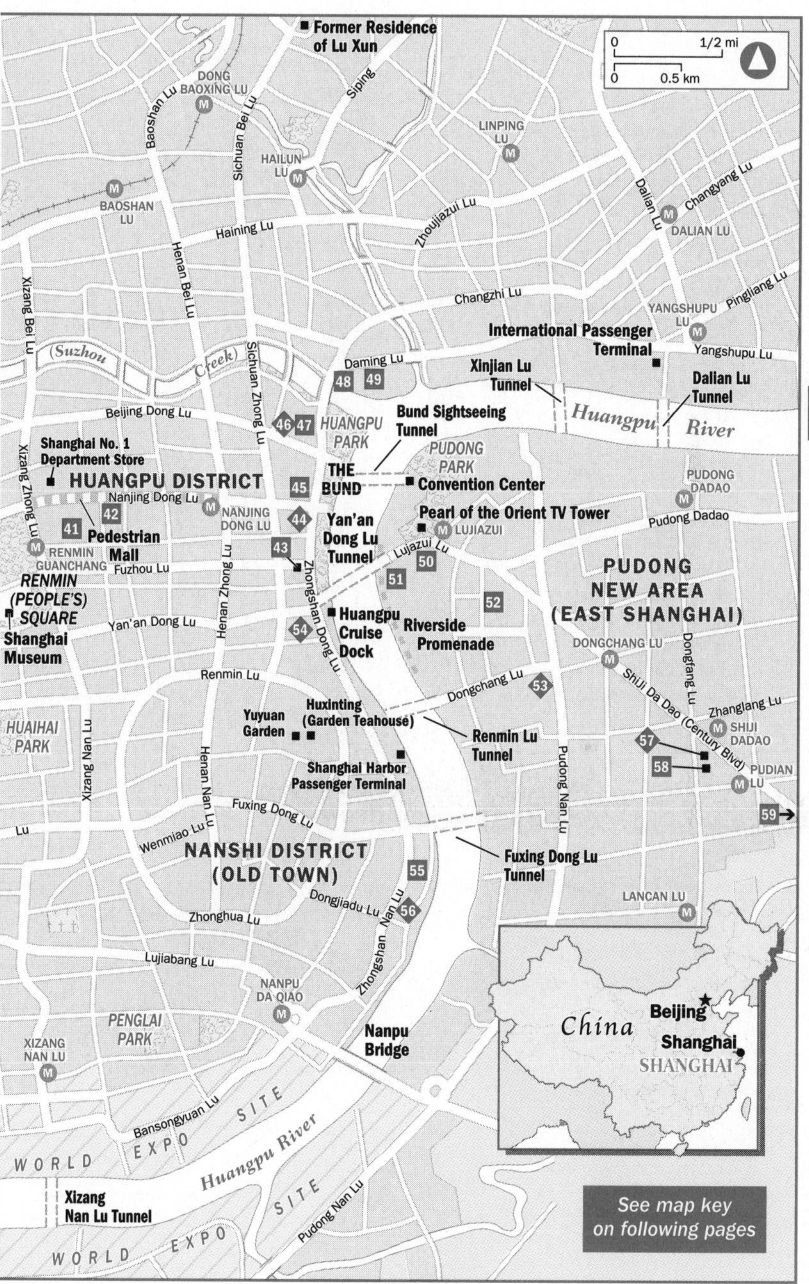

9
SHANGHAI | Where to Stay

Shanghai Hotels & Restaurants Key

HOTELS ■

88 Xīntiāndì Hotel **40**
88 新天地酒店

Argyle International Airport Hotel Hóngqiáo **1**
(Shànghǎi Huá Gǎng Yǎ Gé Jiǔ Diàn)
上海华港雅阁酒店

Astor House Hotel **48**
(Pǔjiāng Fàndiàn)
浦江饭店

Captain Hostel **43**
(Chuánzhǎng Qīngnián Jiǔdiàn)
船长青年酒店

Courtyard Shanghai Xujiahui **7**
(Shànghǎi Xīzàng Dàshà Wànyí Jiǔdiàn)
上海西藏大厦万怡酒店

East Asia Hotel **42**
(Dōngyà Fàndiàn)
东亚饭店

Fairmont Peace Hotel **45**
(Hépíng Fàndiàn)
和平饭店

Four Seasons Hotel Shànghǎi **33**
(Shànghǎi Sìjì Jiǔdiàn)
上海四季酒店

Hyatt On The Bund **49**
(Shànghǎi Wàitān Màoyuè Dàjiǔdiàn)
上海外滩茂悦大酒店

JIA Shanghai **32**
家上海

JW Marriott **35**
(Wànháo Jiǔdiàn)
万豪酒店

The Langham, Yangtze Boutique, Shanghai **41**
(Shànghǎi Lángyán Yángzǐ Jīngpǐ Jiǔdiàn)
上海朗延扬子精品酒店

Magnolia Bed & Breakfast **21**

Mansion Hotel **26**
(Shǒuxí Gōngguǎn Jiǔdiàn)
首席公馆酒店

Marriott Hotel Hongqiao **2**
(Wànháo Hóng Qiáo Dàjiǔdiàn)
上海万豪虹桥大酒店

Motel 168 Pudong Aiport **59**
(Mótài Shànghǎ Pǔdōng Jīchǎng Kōnggǎng Bīnguǎn)
莫泰上海浦东机场空港宾馆

Okura Garden Hotel Shànghǎi **28**
(Huāyuán Fàndiàn)
花园饭店

Old House Inn **13**
(Lǎo Shí Guāng Jiǔdiàn)
老时光酒店

Park Hyatt Shànghǎi **52**
(Shànghǎi Bǎiyuè Jiǔdiàn)
上海柏悦酒店

The Peninsula Hotel, Shanghai **47**
(Shànghǎi Bàndǎo Jiǔdiàn)
上海半岛酒店

Portman Ritz-Carlton Hotel **15**
(Shànghǎi Bōtèmàn Lìjiā Dàjiǔdiàn)
上海波特曼丽嘉大酒店

Pudi Boutique Hotel **36**
(Pǔdǐ Jīngpǐn Jiǔdiàn)
璞邸精品酒店

Pǔdōng Shangri-La Hotel **51**
(Pǔdōng Xiānggélǐlā Fàndiàn)
浦东香格里拉饭店

The Puli Hotel and Spa **17**
(Pǔlí Jiǔdiàn)
璞麗酒店

Quintet **12**

Ramada Pǔdōng Airport Shànghǎi Hotel **59**
(Shànghǎi Jīchǎng Huáměidá Dàjiǔdiàn)
上海机场华美达大酒店

Ritz-Carlton Pǔdōng **50**
(Shànghǎi Pǔdōng Lìsī Kǎěrdūn Jiǔdiàn Fàndiàn)
上海浦东丽思卡尔顿酒店

St. Regis Shànghǎi **58**
(Shànghǎi Ruìjí Hóngtǎ Dàjiǔdiàn)
上海瑞吉红塔大酒店

Tàiyuán Villa **24**
(Tàiyuán Biéshù)
太原别墅

URBN Hotel **14**
(Yǎyuè Jiǔdiàn)
雅悦酒店

The Waterhouse at South Bund **55**
(Shuǐshè Jiǔdiàn)
水舍酒店

RESTAURANTS ◆

1221 **5**

Art Salon **30**
(Wù Li Xiāng)
屋里香

Băoluó **25**
保罗

Blue Frog **3**
(Lán Wā)
蓝蛙

Dī Shuĭ Dòng **27**
滴水洞

Element Fresh **16**
(Yuán Sù)
元素

el Willy **22**

Fu 1088 **6**
(Fú 1088)
福一零八八

The Grape **19**
(Pútao Yuán Jiŭjiā)
葡萄园酒家

Haiku by Hatsune **9**

Hot Pot King **11**
(Lái Fú Lóu)
来福楼

Jiā Jiā Tāng Bāo **34**
佳家汤包

Jing'an Restaurant **18**

Jishi (Jesse Restaurant) **8**
吉士

Kebabs on the Grille **56**

Lost Heaven on the Bund Yunnan Folk Cuisine **54**
(Wàitān Huāmă Tiāntáng Yúnnán Cāntīng)
外滩花马天堂云南餐厅

Mr and Mrs Bund **44**

Méilóngzhèn **31**
梅陇镇

Nepali Kitchen **20**
(Níbō'ěr Cāntīng)
尼泊尔餐厅

O'Malley's **10**
(Ōu Mă Lì Cāntīng)
欧玛莉餐厅

Shànghăi Xīnjiāng Fēngwèi Fàndiàn **4**
上海新疆风味饭店

South Beauty **19**
(Qiào Jiāng Nán)
俏江南

Sū Zhè Huì **57**
(Jade Garden)
苏浙汇

Wagas (Wògēsī) **53**
沃歌斯

Xīndàlù China Kitchen **???**
新大陆

Xīntiāndì **37**
新天地

Xīn Wàng **29**
新旺

Yi Long Court **46**
(Yì Lóng Gé)
逸龙阁

Zăo Zĭ Shù **39**
枣子树

wrote *Private Lives* in 1930, and Steven Spielberg filmed scenes for *Empire of the Sun.* Although the hotel had just reopened and was unavailable for review at press time, expect that many of the original highlights of the hotel, including the masterpiece Art Deco lobby, the magnificent rooftop views, the world-famous Jazz Bar, and the "Nine Nations" deluxe suite (each decorated in the style of a particular country, for example, Chinese, British, American, French, Indian, and others) should all be well preserved, with guest rooms elegantly appointed and fitted with the latest state-of-the-art amenities. The Fairmont Hotels chain now manages the hotel with the local Jiǎnjiāng group, which means that service should be a considerable improvement from before.

Nánjīng Dōng Lù 20 (on the Bund); see map p. 436. www.fairmont.com/peacehotel. ✆ **021/6321-6888.** Fax 021/6329-0300. 270 units. ¥2,900 standard; ¥3,500 executive level; from ¥7,000 suite. AE, DC, MC, V. Metro: Nanjing Rd. (E). **Amenities:** 3 restaurants, deli, lounge, bar; babysitting; concierge; executive-level rooms; health club w/Jacuzzi and sauna; indoor pool; 24-hr. room service; spa. *In room:* A/C, TV/DVD, movie library, CD player, fridge, hair dryer, minibar, MP3 docking station, Wi-Fi.

JW Marriott (Wànháo Jiǔdiàn) ★★ Conveniently located a short walk from the main People's Square subway station and attractions such as the Shànghǎi Museum, Grand Theatre, Nánjīng Lù Pedestrian Mall, and Xīntiāndì, this is a handsome five-star hotel lodged primarily on the 38th to 60th floors of Tomorrow Square, a fascinating futuristic tower. Boasting a penthouse library billed as the tallest in the world by *Guinness World Records,* and China's first Mandara Spa, the hotel has luxurious rooms furnished with three telephones, CD radio, laptop safe, thick bathrobes, and brilliant city views. Marble bathrooms have separate showers with power massage jets and antifog mirrors. Service is top-notch.

Nánjīng Xī Lù 399 (at Huángpí Běi Lù, west side of People's Square); see map p. 436. www.marriott.com. ✆ **800/228-9290** or 021/5359-4969. Fax 021/6375-5988. 342 units. ¥2,500 standard; ¥3,150 executive level; from ¥3,900 suite (regular 30% discounts, up to 60% pending occupancy). AE, DC, MC, V. Metro: People's Square. **Amenities:** 3 restaurants, deli, 2 lounges; babysitting; concierge; executive-level rooms; health club w/Jacuzzi and sauna; indoor/outdoor pool; 24-hr. room service; spa. *In room:* A/C, TV, movie library, CD player, fridge, hair dryer, minibar, Wi-Fi (¥120 per day).

The Langham, Yangtze Boutique, Shànghǎi (Shànghǎi Lángyán Yángzǐ Jīngpǐn Jiǔdiàn) ★ Located a block south of the Nánjīng Lù pedestrian mall and a block east of People's Square, this striking, 1934 Art Deco hotel has undergone a complete overhaul from a three-star outfit into a handsome, ultraluxurious boutique hotel. The luxe interiors combine the best of colonial Shànghǎi ambience with the most modern amenities, including plush beds, a 42-inch LCD TV in the bedroom, and a 19-inch LCD set in the large marble bathroom. Ask for a room with a balcony, which, though small, provides a delightful perch to take in the hubbub of the city. The staff was very friendly and helpful, and housekeeping very prompt in replacing amenities missing from the room during my stay. The hotel also boasts a fine Cantonese restaurant, **T'ang Court.**

Hànkǒu Lù 740 (east of Xīzàng Zhōng Lù, 1 block south of Nánjīng Dōng Lù); see map p. 436. www.langhamhotels.com. ✆ **021/6080-0800.** Fax 021/6080-0801. 96 units. ¥3,300–¥3,600 standard; ¥4,000 suite (30%–50% discounts). AE, DC, MC, V. Metro: People's Square. **Amenities:** 3 restaurants, lounge, bar; airport transfers; babysitting; concierge; health club and spa; room service. *In room:* A/C, TV/DVD, hair dryer, minibar, MP3 docking station, Wi-Fi (¥5 per min., ¥120 per day).

The Peninsula Hotel, Shànghǎi (Shànghǎi Bàndǎo Jiǔdiàn) 上海半岛酒店 ★★★ The luxurious Peninsula Hotel sets a new standard for luxury hotels in Shànghǎi. Located at the top of Shànghǎi's most famous street next to the former British Consulate, the 14-story Peninsula is the only property allowed to be built on the Bund in the last 60 years. Tops at the hotel are the guest rooms, large, elegant, and fully appointed with walk-in closets, a nail dryer, a Nespresso coffee machine, a three-in-one printer, fax, and copier, a 46-inch plasma TV, a multimedia reader, free Wi-Fi, and a VOIP system that allows guests to call home anywhere in the world for free. What is especially impressive is the hotel getting right all the smallest details to ensure maximum guest comfort: Afraid you might wake up in the dark confused as to where you are? Wave your hand and the bedside lighting panel will slowly illuminate. Deluxe rooms with Bund and river views are well worth splurging on. Fully expect the refined and attentive service for which the Peninsula is well known. Those not staying here can still drop in for Peninsula's famous high tea (2–6pm), with a traditional 1930s tea dance held the first Saturday of every month.

Zhōngshān Dōng Yī Lù 32 (No. 32, The Bund, at Běijīng Dōng Lù); see map p. 436. www.peninsula.com. ✆ **021/2327-2888.** Fax 021/2327-2000. 235 units. ¥3,200–¥4,800 standard; from ¥6,400 suite (30%–40% discounts). AE, DC, MC, V. Metro: Nanjing Rd. (E). **Amenities:** 3 restaurants, lounge, bar; airport transfer; babysitting; children's programs; concierge; health club w/Jacuzzi and sauna; indoor pool; 24-hr. room service; spa. *In room:* A/C, TV/DVD, movie library, CD player, fax, fridge, hair dryer, minibar, MP3 docking station, free Wi-Fi.

EXPENSIVE

The Waterhouse at South Bund (Shuǐshè Jiǔdiàn) If post-industrial chic is your preferred style, consider staying at this newly opened boutique hotel lodged inside a 1930s warehouse near the Shíliùpǔ Wharf. With exposed brick, broken plaster walls, and splotchy concrete stairwells, it's hard not to feel like you're staying in a bomb shelter at times, albeit one that's a member of Design Hotels. But this bunker also has shiny wooden floors, glass windows, and lots of modern furniture and amenities to make up for any dystopian tendencies. No two rooms are alike here (some are noisier than others, some have showers only, so be sure to request a room with a bath if that matters to you), but all rates include breakfast, unlimited local phone calls, and complimentary nonalcoholic beverages from the minibar. The hotel is also home to the restaurant **Table No. 1,** opened and run by several former chefs at London's Maze restaurants. A rooftop cocktail bar has stunning views of the Huángpǔ River and Pǔdōng.

Máojiāyuán Lù 1 (north of Cool Docks, Zhōngshān Nán Lù 479); see map p. 436. www.waterhouseshanghai.com. ✆ **021/6080-2988.** Fax 021/6080-2999. 19 units. ¥1,600–¥1,900 standard; from ¥2,900 suite (30%–40% discounts). AE, DC, MC, V. No Metro. **Amenities:** Restaurant, lounge, bar; concierge; health club; room service. *In room:* A/C, satellite TV/DVD, CD player, fridge, hair dryer, minibar, MP3 docking station, free Wi-Fi.

INEXPENSIVE

Captain Hostel (Chuánzhǎng Qīngnián Jiǔdiàn) This maritime-themed hostel, lodged in a 1920s Art Deco–style building, is one of the most popular budget options in town. Among its recommendations, a superb location just off the Bund, clean "sailor bunk" dorms, comfortable if no-frills standards with in-suite bathrooms, and a rooftop bar offering views of the Huángpǔ River and Pǔdōng to rival those at the considerably more expensive bars and restaurants on the Bund, but with cold beer at half the price. All the usual hostel facilities, including a small Internet cafe, are also available.

Fúzhōu Lù 37 (just west of the Bund); see map p. 436. www.captainhostel.com.cn. ✆ **021/6323-5053.** Fax 021/6321-9331. 21 units. ¥500–¥600 standard (30% discounts); ¥90 dorm beds. AE, DC, MC, V. Metro: Nanjing Rd. (E). **Amenities:** Restaurant, bar; concierge; Internet. *In room:* A/C, TV (in some).

East Asia Hotel (Dōngyà Fàndiàn) If you don't mind the lack of frills and services, staying right in the thick of the Nánjīng Lù Pedestrian Mall doesn't come any cheaper than this. Located in the neoclassical former Shànghǎi Sincere Department Store, this hotel features rooms and furnishings that are a bit drab and subject to the usual wear and tear, but are still adequate for a few nights' stay for those on a budget. Guests are mostly Chinese, but bilingual signage and the staff's tenuous grasp of some English terms make this a manageable option for the foreigner. The deluxe rooms facing Nánjīng Lù are worth spending an extra ¥40.

Nánjīng Dōng Lù 680 (just west of Zhèjiāng Zhōng Lù); see map p. 436. ✆ **021/6322-3223.** Fax 021/6322-4598. 164 units. ¥400–¥520 standard; from ¥660 suite (30% discounts). AE, DC, MC, V. Metro: People's Square. **Amenities:** Restaurant, bar/lounge; concierge; room service. *In room:* A/C, TV, hair dryer.

Hóngkǒu (Northeast Shànghǎi)

VERY EXPENSIVE

Hyatt on the Bund (Shànghǎi Wàitān Màoyuè Dàjiǔdiàn) ★★ The second Grand Hyatt to open in Shànghǎi, this handsome contemporary hotel boasts a northern Bund address, but is actually situated on the western bank of the Huángpǔ River in Hóngkǒu, and is about a 10-minute walk from the Bund. All luxuriously appointed rooms have flatscreen LCD TVs, DVD players, and iPod docking stations. Floor-to-ceiling windows allow breathtaking views of either the Bund or Pǔdōng, while suites give you the best of both worlds. Staff is exceedingly friendly and helpful and the hotel's restaurants consistently provide quality dining. As Hóngkǒu district and the western shore of the Huángpǔ River continue to develop, look for this hotel to be much in demand from its river location.

Huángpǔ Lù 199 (north of the Bund, on the northeast side of Sūzhōu Creek); see map p. 436. www.shanghai.bund.hyatt.com. ✆ **021/6393-1234.** Fax 021/6393-1313. 631 units. ¥3,000–¥3,200 standard; ¥3,500 executive level; from ¥5,000 suite (up to 50% discount pending occupancy). AE, DC, MC, V. Metro: Nanjing Rd. (E) (about 1 mile away). **Amenities:** 4 restaurants, bar; babysitting; concierge; executive-level rooms; health club w/Jacuzzi and sauna; indoor pool; 24-hr. room service; spa. *In room:* A/C, TV/DVD, CD player, fridge, hair dryer, minibar, MP3 docking station, Wi-Fi (¥120 per day).

MODERATE

Astor House Hotel (Pǔjiāng Fàndiàn) Built in 1860 and reconstructed in late Renaissance style on its present site in 1910, this hotel north of the Bund is China's oldest, and the first place to use telephones and electric lights in the country. More recently, this cheap backpackers' favorite in the last decade has upgraded into a somewhat pricey, three-star outfit with executive-level rooms. Refurbished standard rooms have firm and comfortable beds, and bathrooms are large and clean. Visitors can also choose from four restored "celebrity rooms," once occupied by famous visitors such as U.S. President Ulysses S. Grant in 1879 (no. 410), Scott Joplin in 1931 and 1936 (no. 404), Bertrand Russell in 1920 (no. 310), and Albert Einstein in 1922 (no. 304). Service is adequate at best.

Huángpǔ Lù 15 (northeast side of Sūzhōu Creek, north of the Bund); see map p. 436. www.pujianghotel.com. ✆ **021/6324-6388.** Fax 021/6324-3179. 116 units. ¥1,280 standard; ¥1,680 celebrity room and executive level (20%–40% discounts). AE, DC, MC, V. Metro: Nanjing Rd. (E) (about 1 mile away). **Amenities:** 2 restaurants, bar; concierge; executive-level rooms; 24-hr. room service. *In room:* A/C, TV, hair dryer, Internet (¥60 per day), minibar (in some).

Lúwān (French Concession)

VERY EXPENSIVE

88 Xīntiāndì Hotel ★ Part of the trendy Xīntiāndì dining and entertainment complex in the heart of the French Concession, this small, luxury boutique hotel in the toniest of surroundings screams urban chic. All rooms here are plush residences, tastefully decorated with a combination of modern amenities, Chinese furnishings, and large, comfortable beds. Other welcome perks include a fax machine, free broadband connection, and kitchen facilities. Lake views are pleasant and worth the extra ¥200, and service is fine, though not particularly memorable.

Huángpí Nán Lù 380 (south block of Xīntiāndì); see map p. 436. www.88xintiandi.com. ✆ **021/5383-8833.** Fax 021/5383-8877. 53 units. ¥3,300–¥3,500 standard; from ¥3,800 suite (30%–40% discounts). AE, DC, MC, V. Metro: Huangpi Rd. (S). **Amenities:** Restaurant; concierge; health club w/Jacuzzi and sauna; indoor swimming pool; room service. *In room:* A/C, TV, fridge, hair dryer, minibar, free Wi-Fi.

EXPENSIVE

Pudi Boutique Hotel (Pǔdǐ Jīngpǐn Jiǔdiàn) ★ One of the earlier arrivals (2007) on the boutique hotel scene, the Pudi, well situated in the heart of the French Concession, goes all out to spoil its guests silly. Upon arrival in the dark lobby with its colorful fish tanks, you're whisked up to your very large room for a private check-in, after which you have your choice of pillows (goose down, perhaps?) and five different brands of amenities. Each room also has a fax, copier, and scanner, along with its own specially commissioned art, which guests can purchase. The Pudi tries to distinguish itself with funky twists like a plasma TV that swivels between the bedroom and the living area, and a bedside clock that projects the time onto the ceiling, though some guests might find the latter a little disturbing. The hotel tries hard with its butler service and its ratio of two staff for every guest. Some guests have complained of excessive noise, but the hotel's very reasonable prices are a bargain for the luxuries on offer.

Yàn dāng Lù 99 (south of Nánchāng Lù); see map p. 436. www.boutiquehotel.cc. ✆ **021/5158-5888.** Fax 021/5157-0188. 52 units. ¥1,677 standard; ¥2,277 suite (20%–30% discounts). AE, DC, MC, V. Metro: Huangpi Rd. (S). **Amenities:** Restaurant, rooftop bar, cigar lounge; babysitting; concierge; fitness room; rooftop Jacuzzi; 24-hr. room service. *In room:* A/C, TV/DVD, fridge, hair dryer, Internet (free), minibar.

Xúhuì (Southwest Shànghǎi)

EXPENSIVE

Mansion Hotel (Shǒuxí Gōngguǎn Jiǔdiàn) ★ Located in a French Concession villa built in 1932 for one of the partners of Shànghǎi's most infamous gang boss Du Yue Sheng, this exclusive boutique hotel is as luxurious and old school as they come. The lobby, cluttered with overstuffed armchairs, traditional Chinese furnishings, old gramophones, and colonial-era bric-a-brac, immediately transports guests back to old Shànghǎi. Rooms are individually decorated in a combination of Eastern and Western motifs, but all feature comfy king-size beds, armchairs with ottomans, Bose iPod sound docks, and 42-inch flatscreen TVs, while the marble bathrooms boast separate Jacuzzi tubs and high-pressure full body showers. Rooftop dining with superb views rounds out the whole dandy experience. For all its opulence, service is inconsistent and guest reactions have ranged from ecstatic to underwhelmed.

Xīnlè Lù 82 (west of Xiāngyáng Běi Lù); see map p. 436. www.chinamansionhotel.com. ✆ **021/5403-9888.** Fax 021/5403-7077. 32 units. ¥2,050 standard; ¥4,000 suite (30%–40% discounts). AE, DC, MC, V. Metro: Shaanxi Rd. (S). **Amenities:** 2 restaurants, lounge; babysitting; concierge; 24-hr. room service. *In room:* A/C, TV, CD player, fax, fridge, hair dryer, minibar, MP3 docking station, free Wi-Fi.

Tàiyuán Villa (Tàiyuán Biéshù) ★ This villa is a peaceful option. Also known as the Marshall House for American general George Marshall who stayed here between 1945 and 1949 when he was mediating between Máo Zédōng and Chiang Kai-shek, this magnificent mansion, originally built in 1920, was one of many homes of Jiāng Qīng (also known as Mme. Máo) between 1949 and 1976. Today this storied villa has dark wood paneling, a grand circular stairwell, and large, comfortable rooms (now carpeted and adorned with classical furniture and comfortable beds). Villa guests can use the pool and business center in the new, modern annex that usually caters only to long-term guests. The grounds are some of the quietest you'll find in central Shànghǎi.

Tàiyuán Lù 160 (south of Yǒngjiā Lù, east of Yuèyáng Lù); see map p. 436. ✆ **021/6471-6688.** Fax 021/6471-2618. www.ruijinhotelsh.com. 13 units. ¥2,000 standard; ¥5,000 master suite (30%–50% discounts). AE, DC, MC, V. Metro: Hengshan Rd. **Amenities:** Restaurant; concierge; fitness center; indoor pool; room service. *In room:* A/C, TV, fridge, hair dryer.

MODERATE

Courtyard Shànghǎi Xújiāhuì (Shànghǎi Xīzàng Dàshà Wànyí Jiǔdiàn) Housed in a tall tower capped by a Tibetan-style temple, the Courtyard is a thoroughly modern, four-star hotel that offers a comfortable stay at very reasonable prices. Rooms are spacious and furnished with modern furniture, LCD televisions, and all the standard amenities. Though the hotel caters mostly to business travelers, its convenient location next to the Xújiāhuì shopping area and subway station makes it an appealing option for tourists as well.

Hóngqiáo Lù 100 (west of Cáo Xī Běi Lù); see map p. 436. ✆ **021/6129-2888.** Fax 021/6129-2999. 364 units. ¥1,000 standard; ¥1,550 executive-level; from ¥2,000 suite (30%–40% discounts). AE, DC, MC, V. Metro: Xujiahui. **Amenities:** Restaurant, deli; babysitting; concierge; executive-level rooms; health club w/Jacuzzi and sauna; indoor pool; 24-hr. room service. *In room:* A/C, TV, fridge, hair dryer, minibar, Wi-Fi (¥60 per hour, ¥120 per day).

INEXPENSIVE

Magnolia Bed & Breakfast Conveniently located near the lively cafes and restaurants around Dōnghú Lù, this bed-and-breakfast in a quaint three-story French Concession house is a great choice for those looking for a more local stay. The rooms (two per floor) run a little small, but are clean with wooden floors, comfortable beds, high-pressure showers, and original art work by local artists. The Ink and Water suite on the top floor is more spacious, and also has a bathtub and small balcony. You are near the street so you will see and hear the sights and sounds of daily life. Those who are sensitive to noise may want to pack earplugs. The community room on the ground floor (where breakfast is served) has a Nespresso coffee machine, a computer, and books and information on local sights. Co-owner Miranda Yao and her staff are very friendly and helpful, and do their best to ensure a most pleasant stay.

Yánqìng Lù 36 (south of Dōnghú Lù); see map p. 436. www.magnoliabnbshanghai.com. ✆ **1381-794-0848.** 5 units. ¥650–¥1,200 standard. DC, MC, V. Metro: Changshu Rd. **Amenities:** Concierge. *In room:* A/C, TV, fridge, hair dryer, free Wi-Fi.

Jìng Ān (Northwest Shànghǎi)

VERY EXPENSIVE

Four Seasons Hotel Shànghǎi (Shànghǎi Sìjì Jiǔdiàn) ★★★ Well located in the thick of Pǔxī (Nánjīng Lù is a 5-min. walk and the Shànghǎi Museum a 10-min. stroll), the modern 37-story Four Seasons offers top-quality pampering. Each guest room is lavishly furnished with classical furniture, three telephones, thick robes, and DVD/CD players. The patented Four Seasons bed alone is worth the stay. Marble bathrooms have a separate shower and tub. Best of all, this hotel delivers impeccable service, from its 24-hour butler service for each guest to the highly efficient, friendly but discreet, multilingual staff throughout the hotel.

Wēihǎi Lù 500 (at Shímén Yī Lù, btw. Nánjīng Xī Lù and Yán'ān Zhōng Lù); see map p. 436. www.fourseasons.com. ✆ **800/819-5053** or 021/6256-8888. Fax 021/6256-5678. 422 units. ¥3,600–¥4,100 standard; from ¥5,400 suite; ¥500–¥700 extra for executive lounge benefits (up to 40% discount pending occupancy). AE, DC, MC, V. Metro: Nanjing Rd. (W). **Amenities:** 4 restaurants, lounge; free airport transfers; babysitting; children's programs; concierge; executive-level rooms; state-of-the-art health club and spa w/Jacuzzi and sauna; indoor pool; 24-hr. room service. *In room:* A/C, TV/DVD, movie library, CD player, fridge, hair dryer, minibar, MP3 docking station, Wi-Fi (¥120 per day).

Portman Ritz-Carlton Hotel (Shànghǎi Bōtèmàn Lìjiā Dàjiǔdiàn) ★★★ Despite some heavy competition, the 50-story Portman, having undergone a $40-million renovation, is still tenaciously guarding its position as Shànghǎi's top choice hotel for many business travelers and world leaders. Offering all the luxury and service associated with the Ritz-Carlton brand, the Portman exudes every elegance, from the two-story lobby, with its fiber-optic lighting, laminated stacked-glass sculptures, and marble and limestone walls, to rooms that are plush and well fitted with LCD televisions with DVD players, thick duvets, three phones, and all the amenities you could want. Service is as you'd expect—professional and excellent. The adjacent Shànghǎi Centre provides one-stop shopping with airline offices, a medical clinic, a supermarket, automatic teller machines, a performing arts theater, upscale boutiques, and a little-known cafe called Starbucks.

Nánjīng Xī Lù 1376 (Shànghǎi Centre); see map p. 436. www.ritzcarlton.com. ✆ **800/241-3333** or 021/6279-8888. Fax 021/6279-8800. 610 units. ¥4,200 standard; ¥4,800 executive level; from ¥5,200 suite (up to 50% discount pending occupancy). AE, DC, MC, V. Metro: Jing An Si. **Amenities:** 4 restaurants, 2 lounges; babysitting; concierge; executive-level rooms; health club and spa w/ Jacuzzi and sauna; indoor pool; 24-hr. room service; indoor tennis court; spa. *In room:* A/C, TV, CD player, fridge, hair dryer, minibar, Wi-Fi (¥120 per day).

The Puli Hotel and Spa (Pŭlí Jiŭdiàn) ★★★ Described as an "urban resort," the Puli Hotel and Spa is all that and more. Though it's located right in the center of town next to the Yán'ān Lù Elevated Highway, you won't find a more comfortable quiet oasis in the middle of Shànghǎi's concrete jungle. Blessedly set off from the road by a grove of bamboo, the hotel also adjoins the back of Jīng'ān Park. Decor throughout is classy and understated: Sleek modern furniture is complemented by Chinese flourishes like dragon screens, *shíkùmén* brick, and imperial black inkstone surfaces. The luxuriously appointed rooms are also fitted with low heat-emission glass windows and automated sunshades to help conserve energy, even as you avail yourself of the plush chaise longue, swiveling flatscreen TV, and free beverages from the minibar. The hotel serves an excellent breakfast, which you can have in the restaurant, in the Long Bar, in your room, or on-the-go. To top it off, service is first-rate: The staff does a very thorough job following up on guest requests. With the pampering Anantara Spa and the innovative **Jing'an Restaurant** (p. 457) on the premises, you may not want to leave this oasis.

Chángdé Lù 1 (at Yán'ān Lù); see map p. 436. www.thepuli.com. ✆ **021/2216-6973.** Fax 021/3251-8977. 229 units. ¥3,380–¥3,580 standard; from ¥3,980 club level; from ¥7,080 suite (30%–40% discounts). AE, DC, MC, V. Metro: Jing An Temple. **Amenities:** 2 restaurants, lounge, bar; babysitting; concierge; health club and spa w/Jacuzzi and sauna; indoor pool; 24-hr. room service; spa. *In room:* A/C, TV/DVD, movie library, CD player, fridge, hair dryer, minibar, MP3 docking station, free Wi-Fi.

EXPENSIVE

JIA Shànghǎi ★★ Lodged in a refurbished 1926 neoclassical building on Nánjīng Lù, the chic boutique hotel JIA (Mandarin for "home") wants to be your home away from home. Brought to you by the owner of the Philippe Starck–designed JIA Hong Kong, JIA Shànghǎi has maintained the building's original facade and structure, but has gussied up the interiors with some highly eclectic, modern design. While the interiors and bespoke furniture may not be to everyone's taste, the large, comfortable rooms, with fully equipped kitchenettes, microwaves, board games, and iPod docking stations that pipe your tunes to the room's stereo speakers, should make most people feel quite at home. Additional perks include free breakfasts and free local calls. Though the hotel attracts a trendy set, the vibe here is refreshingly informal.

Nánjīng Xī Lù 931 (at Tàixìng Lù); see map p. 436. www.jiashanghai.com. ✆ **021/6217-9000.** Fax 021/6287-9001. 55 units. ¥2,000–¥2,600 standard; from ¥4,000 suite (30%–40% discounts). AE, DC, MC, V. Metro: Nanjing Rd. (W). **Amenities:** Restaurant, lounge, bar; babysitting; concierge; 24-hr. room service. *In room:* A/C, TV/DVD, CD player, fridge, hair dryer, minibar, MP3 docking station, free Wi-Fi.

URBN Hotel (Yǎyuè Jiŭdiàn) This factory warehouse–turned–boutique hotel with a Zen garden–style courtyard prides itself on being the first carbon-neutral hotel in Shànghǎi: The hotel's furnishings and materials are locally sourced or recycled, and the hotel will pay for carbon offsets, which may explain the more expensive rates charged here. Rooms are decorated in a simple, contemporary style, but have all the necessary amenities, including DVD players and iPod docking stations. The living spaces are designed to be multifunctional, so you may find your bed on a platform facing a sunken wraparound lounge area, which can be innovative or impractical, depending on your needs. Not all guests may be willing to accept some of the hotel's design and functional quirks (such as the use of fluorescent lightbulbs) and occasionally spotty service, but this "green" property has its heart in the right place. Guests may also use the nearby boutique One Wellness gym, billed as the first carbon-neutral gym in Shànghǎi. The hotel's **Downstairs** restaurant offers wonderful alfresco dining in the warm summer months.

Jiāozhōu Lù 183 (south of Xīnzhá Lù); see map p. 436. www.urbnhotels.com. ✆ **021/5153-4600.** Fax 021/5153-4610. 26 units. ¥2,000–¥2,600 standard; ¥5,000 courtyard room; ¥8,000 penthouse (30%–50% discounts). AE, DC, MC, V. Metro: Jing An Si. **Amenities:** Restaurant, lounge; free airport transfers; concierge; access to nearby gym; 24-hr. room service. *In room:* A/C, TV/DVD, CD player, fridge, hair dryer, minibar, MP3 docking station, free Wi-Fi.

MODERATE

Old House Inn (Lǎo Shí Guāng Jiǔdiàn) One of the earliest outfits of its kind on the hotel scene, this boutique hotel in a 1930s French Concession lane house remains one of the more reasonably priced. Those nostalgic for old Shànghǎi Chinese style will surely love the rooms, some a little small, but all tastefully and elegantly refurbished with classic Chinese furniture, four-poster beds with wispy mosquito netting, and gorgeous hardwood floors. Bathrooms, however, are thoroughly modern. Breakfast is included. The inn's central location puts you in the heart of the French Concession within minutes. There have, however, been complaints of insufficient heating during the winter months.

Huáshān Lù Lane 351, no. 16 (in a lane just west of Chángshú Lù); see map p. 436. www.oldhouse.cn. ✆ **021/6248-6118.** Fax 021/6249-6869. 12 units. ¥640–¥1,250 standard. AE, DC, MC, V. Metro: Jing An Temple. **Amenities:** Restaurant, bar. *In room:* A/C, TV, hair dryer, minibar, free Wi-Fi.

Quintet ★ Independent travelers seeking a change from the usual hotel chains should definitely seek out this charming bed-and-breakfast inside a 1933 French Concession house that has been in the owner's family for three generations. The five rooms vary in size, and some have stairs leading to the ensuite baths. Rooms are intimate and boast a wonderful combination of old (original wood floors) and new (full amenities, including DVD players and free Wi-Fi). Breakfast (from the all-day restaurant in the building, the excellent **Closed Door Café**) is included, and can even be served in bed if so desired. The B&B's location on Chánglè Lù smack in the heart of the French Concession is ideal for those who want to explore on their own. Owner Fay and her excellent staff can also help with everything from airport transportation and tour planning to arranging Chinese cooking classes and in-room massages.

Chánglè Lù 808 (west of Chángshú Lù); see map p. 436. www.quintet-shanghai.com. ✆ **021/6249-9088.** Fax 021/6249-2198. 5 units. ¥800–¥1,100 standard. No credit cards. Metro: Changshu Rd. **Amenities:** Restaurant; concierge. *In room:* A/C, TV/DVD, CD player, fridge, hair dryer, minibar, MP3 docking station, free Wi-Fi.

Pŭdōng (East of River)

VERY EXPENSIVE

Park Hyatt Shànghăi (Shànghăi Băiyuè Jiŭdiàn) ★★ The Park Hyatt Shànghăi is scaling new heights of luxury. Occupying the 79th to 93rd floors of the 101-story, 492m (1,614-ft.) Shànghăi World Financial Center, this exclusive Hyatt brand now lays claim to the world's tallest hotel. Designed to be a cool refuge (in temperature and style) from the hustle and bustle of Shànghăi, the hotel has a direct elevator that whisks guests up to the 87th-floor lobby. Happily, a damper has been installed on the 90th floor, which should greatly reduce if not eliminate entirely the occasional swaying that guests staying at the neighboring and similarly high-flying Grand Hyatt would sometimes feel on a windy day. Guest rooms, reached via dimly lit vaultlike hallways, are the largest in the city (55 sq. m/592 sq. ft. and up), and some of the most comfortable with high ceilings, daybeds, DVD players, iPod docking stations, and flatscreen plasma TVs. Bathrooms are in a courtyard style with large rain showers and separate powder rooms, but the toilet lid that lifts automatically is perhaps trying a little too hard. Service is fine if not particularly memorable, but the views are brilliant when you're not socked in by clouds or smog.

Shìjì Dà Dào 100, World Financial Center (southeast of the Oriental Pearl TV Tower); see map p. 436. www.shanghai.park.hyatt.com. ✆ **021/6888-1234.** Fax 021/6888-3400. 174 units. ¥5,000–¥5,700 standard; from ¥11,500 suite (40%–50% discounts). AE, DC, MC, V. Metro: Lujiazui or Dongchang Lu. **Amenities:** 2 restaurants, lounge, 3 bars; babysitting; concierge; health club and spa w/Jacuzzi and sauna; indoor pool; 24-hr. room service. *In room:* A/C, TV/DVD, CD player, fridge, hair dryer, minibar, MP3 docking station, free Wi-Fi.

Pŭdōng Shangri-La Hotel (Pŭdōng Xiānggélĭlā Fàndiàn) ★★★ With the addition of a sleek new tower annex boasting a slew of trendy designer restaurants, the Himalayan-themed Chi spa, and a second health club and pool, not only is the Shangri-La currently the biggest and boldest hotel in town, but it has the best location in Pŭdōng, with unbeatable views of the Bund across the river. All guest rooms in the 36-story Grand Tower are spacious and superbly appointed with more amenities than you know what to do with, including DVD players, fax machines, 32-inch LCD TVs, and safes equipped to recharge your laptop computer. Original River Wing rooms were recently renovated with more classical furnishings. Staff is delightfully friendly and the service is of a high international caliber.

Fùchéng Lù 33 (southwest of the Oriental Pearl TV Tower/Dōngfāng Míngzhū, adjacent to Riverside Ave./Bīnjiāng Dà Dào); see map p. 436. www.shangri-la.com. ✆ **800/942-5050** or 021/6882-8888. Fax 021/6882-6688. 950 units. ¥1,850–¥3,000 standard; ¥2,250–¥3,750 executive level; from ¥4,050 suite (40% discounts). AE, DC, MC, V. Metro: Lujiazui. **Amenities:** 6 restaurants, deli, 2 lounges, 2 bars; babysitting; concierge; executive-level rooms; 2 health clubs w/Jacuzzi and sauna; 2 indoor pools; 24-hr. room service; spa; tennis court. *In room:* A/C, TV/DVD (Grand Tower rooms only), CD player (in some), fax (in some), fridge, hair dryer, minibar, free Wi-Fi.

Ritz-Carlton Pŭdōng (Shànghăi Pŭdōng Lìsī Kăĕrdūn Jiŭdiàn Fàndiàn) The second Ritz-Carlton to open in Shànghăi has all the luxury and high-caliber service that is associated with the brand. Lodged in the upper 18 levels of the 58-story South Tower of the Shànghăi International Finance Center (IFC), the hotel is like an Art Deco jewelry box (beige and gold dominate in the main areas) with Chinese flourishes. Rooms should please even the most exacting visitor: Amenities

airport HOTELS

The closest five-star hotel to the Hóngqiáo Airport is the **Marriott Hotel Hóngqiáo** (Hóngqiáo Lù 2270; www.marriott.com; ✆ **800/228-9290**), which is still about 6.4km (4 miles) to the east. The Australian-managed 205-unit **Argyle International Airport Hotel Hóngqiáo (Huá Găng Yă Gé Jiŭ Diàn,** Kōng Găng Yī Lù 458; ✆ **021/6268-7788;** fax 021/6268-5671) is the nearest major hotel within a 5-minute ride from the airport. Modern efficient standard rooms start at around ¥600.

There are several hotels serving Pŭdōng Airport. The best of the lot, **Ramada Pŭdōng Airport Shànghăi Hotel** (Shànghăi Jīchăng Huámĕidá Dàjiŭdiàn, Qĭháng Lù 1100; www.ramadaairportpd.com; ✆ **021/3849-4949;** fax 021/6885-2889), is a 2- to 3-minute free shuttle ride or a 10-minute walk from the airport. The hotel has 370 units. Rooms (¥880–¥1,080 standard) are clean and comfortable with the usual amenities, including safes and in-room movies. Both Western and Chinese dining are available. If you want to be really close to the terminal and don't mind basic accommodations, the gigantic **Motel 168** (Mótè 168 Shànghăi Pŭdōng Jīchăng Kōnggăng Bīnguăn, Yínbīn Dàdào 6001; www.motel168.com; ✆ **021/3879-9999;** fax 021/6885-2526) is located right on top of the Maglev station, just a few minutes' walk from both airport Terminals 1 and 2. The hotel has clean rooms with all the basic amenities, including free Internet, all for price levels starting around ¥398.

include 400-thread-count bed linens, a 42-inch LCD TV with Blu-ray disc player, and a Bose Wave Music System with iPod dock, among other indulgences. Expect the views from the hotel to be stellar on a good day: panoramic, but not so high up as to miss all the details. The hotel is well situated in Lùjiāzuĭ with easy access to sights like the Jīn Mào Building, the Shànghăi World Financial Center, the Riverside Promenade, and the slew of luxury shops at Shànghăi IFC. The subway station is nearby as well.

Shìjì Dàdào 8, Shànghăi IFC; see map p. 436. www.ritzcarlton.com. ✆ **021/2020-1888.** Fax 021/2020-1889. 285 units. ¥5,300 standard; ¥5,500 executive level; from ¥10,000 suite (40% discounts). AE, DC, MC, V. Metro: Lujiazui. **Amenities:** 4 restaurants, lounge, bar; babysitting; concierge; executive-level rooms; health club w/Jacuzzi and sauna; indoor pool; 24-hr. room service; spa. *In room:* A/C, TV/DVD, CD player, fridge, hair dryer, minibar, MP3 docking station, Wi-Fi (¥120 per day in standard rooms, free in other rooms).

St. Regis Shànghăi (Shànghăi Ruìjí Hóngtă Dàjiŭdiàn) ★★ The handsome St. Regis might well be *the* luxury hotel at which to stay in town were it not for its less-convenient location in Pudong. Standard rooms are large (48 sq. m/157 sq. ft.), and gorgeously furnished with comfortable sofas, ergonomic Herman Miller "Aeron" chairs, Bose CD radios, and "rainforest" showers in the spacious marble bathrooms. But what sets the St. Regis apart from its competitors is its signature 24-hour butler service, which the hotel initially pioneered and which other hotels have tried to copy. As part of their "Lifestyle Butler Service," St. Regis butlers can press clothing, make dinner reservations, and even act as tour guides about town, escorting guests interested in the Chinese art scene to galleries or the private studios of local Chinese artists. A ladies-only floor features women butlers and a host of special in-room amenities including toiletries by Bulgari. Service is top-notch throughout.

Dōngfāng Lù 889 (south central Pǔdōng); see map p. 436. www.stregis.com. ✆ **800/325-3589** or 021/5050-4567. Fax 021/6875-6789. 328 units. ¥3,390 standard; ¥3,970 executive level; from ¥4,270 suite (up to 60% discounts). AE, DC, MC, V. Metro: Pudian Rd. or Century Ave. **Amenities:** 3 restaurants, lounge; babysitting; concierge; executive-level rooms; health club w/aerobics classes; indoor pool; 24-hr. room service; spa. *In room:* A/C, TV/DVD, movie library, CD player, fax, fridge, hair dryer, minibar, Wi-Fi (¥120 per day).

WHERE TO EAT

Dozens of promising, mostly upscale, international restaurants and cafes open every month, too many to keep up with. The emphasis is on Shanghai's own renowned cuisine, commonly referred to as *benbang cai*. The most celebrated Shanghai dish is hairy crab, a freshwater delicacy that reaches its prime every fall. Also popular are any number of "drunken" dishes (crab, chicken) marinated in local Shaoxing wine, and braised meat dishes such as lion's head meatballs and braised pork knuckle. Shanghai dim sum and snacks include a variety of dumplings, headlined by the local favorite *xiaolong bao,* as well as onion pancakes and leek pies, all of which deserve to be tried.

The boom in Shanghai restaurants has brought with it a dramatic increase in Japanese, Thai, European, and American restaurants, too, with the international fast-food chains seemingly on every corner. For restaurant locations, see the map on p. 436.

Huángpǔ (Downtown)

VERY EXPENSIVE

Mr & Mrs Bund ★★★ FRENCH French brasserie cuisine never had it so good, creative, or playful. At international chef sensation Paul Pairet's excellent new modern French eatery—lodged on the sixth floor of the lavishly restored Chartered Bank of India, Australia, and China building on the Bund—the atmosphere is festive, and the more than 100 dishes on the menu are meant to be shared, family-style. Signature and more popular dishes are featured in the Rookie menu. Do try the foie gras light crumble, meunière bread (think butter and truffles), jumbo shrimp in citrus jar, steamed "Black Cod in the Bag," "Long Short Rib Teriyaki," and the to-die-for lemon tart. If none of that appeals, you can simply select your fish or viand to be cooked in a style (and sauce) of your own choosing. An Enomatic machine in the center of the restaurant dispenses 32 wines by the glass. Service is first-rate, and though the decor in classic black and red suggests formality, the place is surprisingly unpretentious. Request a table by the window for nighttime views of Pǔdōng.

Zhongshan Dong Yi Lu 18 Bund 18; see map p. 436. ✆ **021/6323-9898.** www.mmbund.com. Reservations required. Meal for 2 ¥700–¥1,200. AE, DC, MC, V. Mon–Fri business lunch (set menu) 11:30am–2pm; daily 6:30–10:30pm (4am Tues–Sat). Metro: Nanjing Rd. (E).

Yi Long Court (Yì Lóng Gé) ★★★ CANTONESE/SEAFOOD Under the guidance of Michelin star chef Tang Chi Keung, fresh from the Peninsula Tokyo, this restaurant in the Peninsula Shànghǎi serves up some of the finest haute Cantonese cuisine in town. Classic Hong Kong–style Cantonese cuisine means the emphasis is on seafood, and you can't go wrong with most of the meticulously prepared seafood dishes. Do try the delicious scallops stuffed with minced shrimp, beef with oyster sauce, the light and flaky barbecued pork puffs, and for dessert, the chilled sesame pudding, all complemented by a wide range of quality teas. The Western-style dining room with Art Deco flourishes provides a handsome setting, and table service is impeccable.

Zhōngshān Dōng Yī Lù 32 (Peninsula Hotel, by Běijīng Dōng Lù); see map p. 436. ✆ **021/2327-6742.** Reservations required. Meal for 2 ¥600–¥1,200. AE, DC, MC, V. 11:30am–2:30pm and 6–10:30pm. Metro: Nanjing Rd. (E).

EXPENSIVE

Kebabs on the Grille ★ INDIAN Spicy North Indian cuisine comes to the Cool Docks in the South Bund, but what sets this freshly scrubbed restaurant apart is its kebabs, finished off at individual grill sets at your table. The tandoori chicken is melt-in-your-mouth good, and the various curries spicy and flavorful. The mutton skewers and "Magic Mushrooms" should also be tried. Staff is friendly and helpful. Dinners can add up, but the restaurant has very reasonably priced business lunches for ¥70 and an all-you-can-eat Sunday brunch for ¥140 per person.

Zhōngshān Nán Lù 479, No. 8 (inside the Cool Docks, south of Fùxīng Dōng Lù); see map p. 436. ✆ **021/6152-6567.** www.kebabsonthegrille.com. Reservations recommended. Meal for 2 ¥200–¥300. AE, DC, MC, V. 11am–10:30pm. Metro: Nánpu Bridge.

Lost Heaven on the Bund Yunnan Folk Cuisine (Wàitān Huāmǎ Tiāntáng Yúnnán Cāntīng) ★★ YÚNNÁN If you fancy some different flavors from the typical Shanghainese cuisine, get thee to Lost Heaven. Steps from the Bund, this restaurant, popular with expats and locals, serves cuisine from the Tea Horse Trail (primarily that of the Dǎi, Bái, Nàxi, and Miáo minorities of Yúnnán Province in southwest China) with lots of Tibetan, Thai, and Burmese influences. Wooden floors and chairs, dark lighting, modern mood music, and photographs of Yúnnán's minorities and snow-capped mountains create just the right ambience. There's a separate menu (with pictures) of house favorites, as well as good English explanations of the various mushrooms and mountains of Yúnnán. Try the Yúnnán wild vegetable cake, Jicong mushrooms with assorted vegetables salad, Yi tribe stir-fry spicy beef, and spicy cod steamed in banana leaf. The tasty "Simmered Vegetables in Tamarind Juice," a typical West Yúnnán dish, actually comes with pork. Lost Heaven's original, smaller, outlet is in the French Concession.

Yán'ān Dōng Lù 17 延安东路17号 (east of Sìchuān Nán Lù); see map p. 436. ✆ **021/6330-0967.** www.lostheaven.com.cn. Metro: Nanjing Rd. (E). Xúhuì branch: Gāoyóu Lù 38 (by Fùxīng Xī Lù). ✆ **021/6433-5126.** Reservations recommended. Meal for 2 ¥200–¥300. AE, DC, MC, V. Daily noon–2pm and 5:30–10:30pm. Metro: Shanghai Library.

INEXPENSIVE

Jiā Jiā Tāng Bāo DUMPLINGS For many locals, this no-frills eatery just north of People's Square on one of Shànghǎi's "food streets" is one of the most famous and popular joints in town for Shànghǎi's favorite dumpling *xiǎolóng bāo,* with long lines inevitably forming during meal times. The restaurant serves several different kinds of dumplings (made only after you've ordered them) and not much else (though they do have the old-fashioned glass-bottled Coca-Cola). Order and pay at the front counter (there's no English menu, but you can point to the Chinese translations at the back of this book). The most basic is the pork-filled *chúnxiānròu tāngbāo* (with 12 in a steamer) or you can go all out with the pork and crab-roe version *xièfěn xiānròu tāngbāo*. For nonpork eaters, there's also a chicken dumpling *jīdīng xiānròu tāngbāo*. This is definitely a local experience you should try, but get here early as half the menu is usually sold out after lunch.

Huánghé Lù 90 (north of Nánjīng Lù); see map p. 436. ✆ **021/6327-6878.** Meal for 2 ¥20–¥50. No credit cards. 6:30am–7pm. Metro: People's Square.

Hóngkǒu District (Northeast Shànghǎi)

EXPENSIVE

Xīndàlù China Kitchen ★★ BÊIJĪNG/SHÀNGHǍI Xīndàlù is worth the trip to Hóngkǒu as it's easily the best place in town for succulent and tasty Peking duck done just right. Roasted in special wood ovens sent over from Běijīng, the duck here rivals some of the best in the capital itself. The restaurant, whose name means "New China," also features a dumpling and noodle section, along with traditional cuisine from Shànghǎi, Suzhou, and Hangzhou, but done in a modern, sophisticated style devoid of the usual oil and grease. In addition to the duck, try the smoked fish, the braised pork chop, or the delicious "Beggar's Chicken" (which has to be ordered in advance). Food presentation and service are sophisticated and the open kitchen allows you to watch the chefs at work—it's a grand time all around.

Huángpǔ Lù 199 (1st floor, Hyatt on the Bund, near Wǔchāng Lù); see map p. 436. ✆ **021/6393-1234,** ext. 6318. Reservations required. Meal for 2 ¥300–¥400. AE, DC, MC, V. 11:30am–2:30pm and 5:30–10:30pm. No Metro.

Lúwān District (French Concession)

EXPENSIVE

Xīntiāndì Restaurant Mall INTERNATIONAL A Starbucks stands at its entrance, the First National Congress of the Communist Party at its flanks, and in its midst, brilliant restorations of Shànghǎi's colonial Shíkù Mén ("stone gate") architecture. The place is **Xīntiāndì** (literally "New Heaven and Earth"), an upscale cultural mall where the moneyed East meets the moneyed West. Here you'll find the city's hottest dining spots. Located downtown a block south of the Huángpí Nán Lù Metro station, Xīntiāndì is a 2-block pedestrian mall with enough good eating to require weeks to experience it all. The best and the priciest are listed below. (See map p. 436.)

T8 ★★★ (North Block, House 8; ✆ **021/6355-8999;** www.t8shanghai.com; lunch 11:30am–2:30pm, tea 2:30–5:30pm, dinner 6:30–11:30pm) is the restaurant whose service and chefs easily rival, if not eclipse, those at M on the Bund, only with less attitude. Service and management are superb and unobtrusive, the decor is super chic, and the food is irresistible. Although there have been several chefs in the last decade, T8 has consistently been voted one of the top restaurants in town, and is highly recommended. The seasonal menu emphasizes Western dishes with Asian influences, and the latest recommendations include the pigeon popcorn, the sesame-crusted tuna, and the Wagyu beef. Do not miss the to-die-for chocolate addiction plate.

Crystal Jade Restaurant ★★★ (South Block/Nánlǐ 6–7, second floor–12A & B; ✆ **021/6385-8752;** www.crystaljade.com; Mon–Fri 11:30am–3pm and 5–10:30pm; Sat–Sun 10:30am–3pm and 5–10:30pm) serves up arguably the best *xiǎolóng bāo* (steamed dumplings with broth) and *lāmiàn* (hand-pulled noodles) south of the Yángzǐ. Must-tries include Shànghǎi steamed pork dumplings (the aforementioned *xiǎolóng bāo*), *lāmiàn* in Sìchuān style (noodles in a spicy peanut broth), roast pork buns, and the *hóngyóu cháoshǒu* (wontons with chili sauce). Reserve in advance or risk a long wait. There are two other branches at Huáihǎi Zhōng Lù 300, Hong Kong New World Building, B10, ✆ **021/6335-4188;** and Nánjīng Xī Lù 1038, #719, ✆ **021/5228-1133.**

Va Bene (Huá Wàn Yì) ★★ (North Block, House 7; ✆ **021/6311-2211;** Sun–Thurs 11:30am–2:30pm and 6–10:30pm; Fri–Sat 11:30am–3pm and 6–11pm) is an upscale Italian diner (from the owners of Hong Kong's Gaia) with warm Tuscan decor, patio dining, and a wide range of antipasti, pasta, and gourmet pizzas, all made from the freshest ingredients.

Paulaner Bräuhaus (Bǎoláinà) ★ (North Block, House 19–20; ✆ **021/6320-3935;** 11am–2am) is the Shànghǎi standby praised for its excellent German food, with authentic brews to match.

KABB (Kǎibó Xīcāntīng) ★ (North Block, House 5, Unit 1; ✆ **021/3307-0798;** Mon–Fri 7am–midnight, Sat–Sun 7am–2am) is a spiffy American bar and comfort-food cafe.

Dǐng Tài Fēng ★ (South Block, House 6, second floor, Unit 11A; ✆ **021/6385-8378;** 11am–2:30pm and 5–11pm), an upscale Taiwanese restaurant, serves *xiǎolóng bāo* dumplings (that come in a very close second to Crystal Jade's dumplings), as well as a whole host of Taiwanese dishes and snacks.

Xīn Jí Shì ★★ (Tàicāng Lù 181, No. 2, North Block; ✆ **021/6336-4746;** 11am–1:30pm and 5–9:30pm), a very popular but homey Shànghǎi eatery, features delicious local favorites such as braised home-cooked pork *(hóng shāo ròu)* and glutinous rice with red dates.

Yè Shànghǎi ★ (South Block, House 6; ✆ **021/6311-2323;** 11:30am–2:30pm and 5:30–11pm) is an elegant touch of old Shànghǎi, which Hong Kong visitors claim is better than the original Yè Shànghǎi restaurant back home.

Zen (Xiānggǎng Cǎidié Xuān) ★ (South Block, House 2; ✆ **021/6385-6395;** 11:30am–11:30pm), a modern Cantonese restaurant by way of Hong Kong, serves excellent dim sum for lunch.

MODERATE

Art Salon (Wū Lǐ Xiāng) ★ SHÀNGHǍI It's Matisse meets Shànghǎi when you dine in this cozy, somewhat ramshackle art salon lodged in a French Concession storefront. Paintings and art works by contemporary Chinese artists adorn the colorful walls, while mismatched traditional Chinese chairs and tables cram every available nook and cranny, but no matter, the overall effect is one of idiosyncratic charm.

The fairly extensive Chinese-only menu bulges with some excellent homemade local specialties. Happily, the brothers who own the place speak excellent English and can translate or make the appropriate recommendations. You can't go wrong with many of the dishes, but worth mentioning are the *pídàn dòufu* (preserved eggs with tofu), the fresh cucumbers with garlic appetizer, *hóngshāo huángyú* (braised yellow croaker), and their very own Shàoxìng-influenced *méigān cài shāo ròu* (braised pork with preserved mustard greens). Service is best described as deliberate, as the owners seem to place a premium on a leisurely appreciation of both the food and the art. Patrons are, of course, free to purchase anything that catches their eye, from the chopsticks in their hands and the chairs beneath them to the art on the walls.

Nánchāng Lù 164 (btw. Yándāng Lù and Sīnán Lù); see map p. 436. ✆ **021/5306-5462.** Reservations recommended for dinner. Meal for 2 ¥100–¥200. No credit cards. Daily noon–2pm and 5–10pm. Metro: Shanxi Rd. (S).

Dī Shuǐ Dòng ★★ HÚNÁN Rivaling Sìchuān cuisine in spiciness (though relying more on straight chilies and less on the mind-numbing, tongue-lashing peppercorn), the lesser-known cooking of Húnán Province can be tried at this delightful restaurant atop a flight of rickety wooden stairs inside a small French concession storefront. Highly recommended are *zīrán páigǔ* (cumin ribs), *gān guō jī* (chicken in chili pot), *suān dòujiǎo ròuní* (mashed pork with sour beans), *dòujiāo yútóu* (fish head steamed with red chili), and the spiced bullfrog leg. Or order just about anything in sight and plenty of cold beer to douse the fiery flames in your mouth. Service by the batik-clad waitstaff is no-nonsense, even occasionally impatient, but the food is superb and shouldn't be missed.

Màomíng Nán Lù 56 (north of Chánglè Lù); see map p. 436. ✆ **021/6253-2689.** Meal for 2 ¥80–¥140. No credit cards. 10am–1am. Metro: Shanxi Rd. (S).

Zǎo Zī Shù ★ VEGETARIAN This restaurant's name literally means "jujube tree," but the three characters that greet visitors upon arrival also cleverly play on the pun *zǎo chī sù,* advocating the early adoption of a vegetarian diet. Pleasant and contemporary, the restaurant takes its mission seriously: Fruit is served as an appetizer; organic tea is the norm; alcohol, dairy, and MSG are shunned; and smoking is definitively prohibited. The bean curd skin roll is a delicious appetizer, while the sweet-and-sour vegetarian pork and the pot with vegetable and curry are popular can't-go-wrong choices. Avoid the vegetarian steak with pepper sauce, though. Spinach dumplings and soup noodles with vegetables are also hearty alternatives for those less inclined to edible fungi. Waitstaff is friendly and helpful.

Sōngshān Lù 77, 1st floor (inside the Shànghǎi Huánggōng complex, south of Huáihǎi Lù, 1 block east of Huángpí Nán Lù); see map p. 436. ✆ **021/6384-8000.** Reservations recommended. Meal for 2 ¥80–¥140. AE, DC, MC, V. 11am–9pm. Metro: Huangpi Rd. (S).

INEXPENSIVE

Xīn Wàng HONG KONG Informal, inexpensive, yet tasty dining at its best, this small chain dishes up a hodgepodge of Chinese comfort foods guaranteed to please all comers. Rice, noodles, and congee form the base of most dishes, after which it's strictly variations on a theme. *Yángzhōu chǎofàn* (fried rice), *xiānxiā yúntūn miàn* (shrimp wonton noodles in soup), *mìzhī chāshāo fàn* (barbecue pork rice)—they're all here, along with casseroles, simple sandwiches, fruit juices, and milk teas. The scene is typically chaotic, the waitstaff is usually harried, but the food is delivered quickly. There is another popular branch at Hànkŏu Lù 309 (✆ **021/6360-5008**).

Chánglè Lù 175 (btw. Màomíng Nán Lù and Ruìjīn Yī Lù); see map p. 436. ✆ **021/6415-5056.** Meal for 2 ¥40–¥70. No credit cards. 7am–5am. Metro: Shanxi Rd. (S).

Xúhuì District (Southwest Shànghăi)

VERY EXPENSIVE

el Willy ★ SPANISH This contemporary Spanish restaurant is a favorite with expats, and frequently garners a host of awards from the local English-language lifestyle and dining magazines. This might lead some to expect the restaurant to be the greatest thing since the invention of paella, which it is not, but there are enough tasty dishes here for a perfectly fun and enjoyable evening, especially when you throw in the cozy French Concession mansion (the Diage house) with glass windows, one of the best *el fresco* garden settings in town, and the irrepressible charms of chef Guillermo "Willy" Trullas Moreno. Recommended tapas dishes (with the de rigueur modern twist) include the seared foie gras, scallop ceviche, seared red tuna loin, and lamb skewers with smoked eggplant, while the paellas are trusty standbys. There is a wide selection of wines and sherries, which just might make up for the average service.

Dōnghú Lù 20, 1st floor (north of Huáihăi Zhōng Lù); see map p. 436. ✆ **021/5404-5757.** www.elwilly.com.cn. Reservations required. Meal for 2 ¥400–¥800. AE, DC, MC, V. Mon–Sat 5:30–10:30pm. Metro: Changshu Rd.

Franck ★★ FRENCH Squirreled away in the French Concession in charming Ferguson Lane—a trendy little warren of shops, offices, and restaurants—is this cozy French restaurant serving the most authentic bistro fare in town. The red walls are adorned with French movie posters and maps. The menu, which changes daily, is carted around on a blackboard by the attentive and friendly staff, while owner Franck, originally from Aix-en-Provence, attends to every table. Menu choices are all solid here, judging from the many French-speaking repeat diners. You can't go wrong with the cold cuts or the *terrine de campagne* for starters, and classic *poulet rôti* (using free-range chicken from Mongolia, no less) and *tartare de boeuf* for main courses. When the delectable *confit de canard* makes an appearance, be sure to pounce on it. The extensive wine list has some pleasant French finds that complement the dishes well, and a small *boulangerie* sells meats and cheeses if you want to pack for a picnic the next day.

Wŭkāng Lù 376, Ferguson Lane (south of Húnán Lù). ✆ **021/6437-6465.** Reservations recommended. Meal for 2 ¥400–¥600. AE, DC, MC, V. 6–10:30pm. No Metro.

EXPENSIVE

Haiku by Hatsune ★ JAPANESE Sushi and sashimi purists might want to stay away, as it's all about the California-style rolls at this chic, highly popular Japanese haunt. Decor is minimalist, with low-slung banquettes and garden views. Favorites include the Moto-roll-ah, and 119 rolls (your standard spicy tuna roll), while the more adventurous can try the Alex Foie roll (seared foie gras with unagi, tempura, and shrimp). There's also a whole range of standard Japanese dishes like tempura, shabu shabu, and a variety of *izakaya*-style small dishes perfect for sharing. *Itadakimasu!*

Táojiāng Lù 28B (btw. Héngshān Lù and Wūlǔmùqí Lù); see map p. 436. ✆ **021/6445-0021.** Reservations recommended. Meal for 2 ¥200–¥300. AE, DC, MC, V. 11:30am–2pm and 5:30–10:30pm. Metro: Hengshan Rd. or Changshu Rd.

MODERATE

Hot Pot King (Lái Fú Lóu) ★ HOT POT Unlike most hot pot restaurants, which are packed, chaotic, and decor-free, Lái Fú Lóu provides some of the most elegant hot pot dining in town. Decor is sleek, with soft gray chairs and dark brown wooden tables spaced far apart, affording diners some welcome privacy. Your biggest decision will be to pick your soup base: There's a wide variety here from which to choose, including a special chicken soup stock, fish, or pig bone soup. Many folks opt for the *yuānyáng* version, which contains both a potent spicy stock and a more benign, pork-based broth. Besides all the usual meat and vegetable ingredients, the restaurant also specializes in handmade *yúwán* (fish balls) and *dànjiǎo* (egg-wrapped dumplings).

Huáihǎi Zhōng Lù 1416, 2nd floor (at intersection of Fùxīng Xī Lù); see map p. 436. ✆ **021/6473-6380.** Reservations recommended. Meal for 2 ¥80–¥120. AE, DC, MC, V. 11am–4am. Metro: Changshu Rd.

Jíshì (Jesse Restaurant) ★★ SHÀNGHǍI The progenitor of the Xīn Jíshì restaurants around town, this down-home restaurant in a tiny French concession cottage is one of my favorites for unrepentantly old-fashioned and delicious Shanghainese comfort food. The must-try's here include the wine-marinated crab, jujubes stuffed with glutinous rice, soy sauce stewed pork, and when in season, the *hóngshāo jiāo bái* (soy-braised wild rice stems). Service is brusque as the harried waitstaff is often eager to clear your table to accommodate the lines out the door. Don't expect to get in here without a reservation.

Tiānpíng Lù 41 (south of Huǎihǎi Lù); see map p. 436. ✆ **021/6282-9260.** Reservations required. Meal for 2 ¥120–¥200. AE, DC, MC, V. 11am–midnight. Metro: Xújiāhuì.

O'Malley's (Ōu Mǎ Lì Cāntīng) ☺ IRISH Best known as one of Shànghǎi's top bars and music spots, O'Malley's also sports a menu of Irish, English, and American favorites that range from bangers and mash to hearty helpings of mashed potatoes and flavorful steaks and burgers. Service is friendly and efficient. The old two-story mansion has been decorated like a down-and-out Irish pub, with plenty of cozy booths and tables on its main floor and balcony. In summertime, the large front lawn has courtyard dining and a children's playground, a handy feature during popular weekend brunches. The beers, of course, are quite good.

Táojiāng Lù 42 (1 block west of Héngshān Lù); see map p. 436. ✆ **021/6437-0667** or 021/6474-4533. Meal for 2 ¥80–¥150. AE, MC, V. Mon–Sat 11am–2am; Sun 10am–1am. Metro: Hengshan Rd. or Changshu Rd.

Shànghǎi Xīnjiāng Fēngwèi Fàndiàn UIGHUR Got lamb? Credible northwest Chinese cuisine can be found at this Uighur restaurant. Amid fake foliage and a miniature model of Xīnjiāng Province's Tiān Shān (Heavenly Lake), patrons are treated to a fun, raucous, and hearty dining experience complete with whooping and dancing waiters. The Uighurs are Muslim, so lamb dominates the Chinese-only menu. Definitely try the juicy *kǎo quányáng* (roast lamb), though if you plan to dine after 7pm, call ahead and reserve a portion, as this popular dish often runs out early. Other favorites include *kǎo yángròu* (barbecue lamb skewers), *dà pán jī* (chicken with cardamoms, peppers, tomatoes, onions, and potatoes), and *lǎohǔ cài,* a refreshing Xīnjiāng salad of cucumbers, tomatoes, and red onions. Noodles *(miàntiáo)* or baked bread *(bǐng)* make good accompaniments, as does Xīnjiāng black beer *(Xīnjiāng píjiǔ)*.

Yíshān Lù 280 (south of Nándān Lù); see map p. 436. ✆ **021/6468-9198.** Reservations recommended. Meal for 2 ¥120–¥240. No credit cards. 10am–2am (nightly dancing at 7:30pm). Metro: Xújiāhuì (20 min. away).

INEXPENSIVE

The Grape (Pútao Yuán Jiǔjiā) SHÀNGHǍI Located in part of a stunning, domed former Russian Orthodox church (though little of it is obvious in today's restaurant), the Grape was one of the first Shànghǎi eateries to attract foreign residents. Today, this friendly, down-to-earth (except for the clusters of plastic grapes that hang overhead) cafe keeps a core group of expats and locals happy with its reasonably priced homemade Shànghǎi cuisine and friendly service. The phoenix-tail shrimps with garlic, steamed clams with eggs, spicy chicken, and braised fresh bamboo shoots are all worth trying.

Xīnlè Lù 55 (2 blocks west of Shǎnxī Nán Lù, btw. Huáihǎi and Yán'ān Lù); see map p. 436. ✆ **021/5404-0486.** Meal for 2 ¥70–¥140. No credit cards. 11am–midnight. Metro: Shanxi Rd. (S).

Jìng Ān District (Northwest Shànghǎi)

VERY EXPENSIVE

Jing'an Restaurant ★★ CONTINENTAL Overlooking Jing'an Park, this classy restaurant on the second floor of the PuLi Hotel and Spa serves some delightfully tasty, chef-billed "hybrid nonesuch cuisine," which means the menu covers everything from artisan breakfasts to bistro lunches to more experimental, innovative dinner choices. Eschewing trendiness, Kiwi chef Dane Clouston is more about playing with the subtle and sophisticated flavors and textures of seasonal ingredients. Lunch is prix fixe and the only occasion to have the delightful Jing'an Burger, sandwiching a thin slab of foie gras, and sized just right (no Big Mac's here). Dinner recommendations include wonderful appetizers: pastrami of salmon and foie gras with smoked chocolate. The slow-roasted Wagyu beef and the maple-roasted duck breast main courses also fare well. Or you may just want to start with dessert first, with the lemon curd pie, strawberry trifle, and the five-spice *panna cotta* (cooked cream), all worth the extra calories. Service is attentive without being intrusive.

Chángdé Lù 1, 2nd floor, PuLi Hotel and Spa 常德路1号 (by Yán'ān Zhōng Lù); see map p. 436. ✆ **021/2216-6988.** www.jinganrestaurant.com. Reservations recommended. Meal for 2 ¥600–¥1,000. AE, DC, MC, V. 6:30–10am (11am Sun), noon–2:30pm, and 7–10:30pm. Metro: Jing'an Temple.

EXPENSIVE

Nepali Kitchen (Níbō'ěr Cāntīng) NEPALESE Fancy a trip to the Himalayas, if only through your taste buds? A favorite with many Shànghǎi expats, this charming three-story restaurant with colorful walls, pictures of snowy mountain ranges, and cushion seating in the back serves fairly authentic Nepali and Tibetan dishes. The cheese balls appetizer and the stir-fried tenderloin beef Nepali-style are always popular starters. For main courses, the Nepali-style grilled fish, the curries, and barbecues are also quite good. Service falls off a bit when it gets busy, which happens almost every night during prime dining hours; an early start will at least get you a little more attention.

Jùlù Lù 819, No. 4 (west of Fùmín Lù); see map p. 436. ✆ **021/5404-6281.** Meal for 2 ¥200–¥300. AE, MC, V. Mon–Sat 11am–2am; Sun 10am–1am. Metro: Changshu Rd.

South Beauty (Qiào Jiāng Nán) ★ SÌCHUĀN There are five South Beauty locations around town, but this one in an old financier's mansion off the old Avenue Edward VII (today's Yán'ān Lù) gets raves for its glamorous ambience. Given a contemporary makeover complete with Chinese motifs, lattice paneling, and wooden floors, the restaurant is huge, with a lounge, bar, cigar room, and different dining areas, including a patio that can be quite romantic at night. The food is not excessively spicy here, perhaps to accommodate local and expatriate tastes, but you can always request them to *jiā là* (pile on the spicy). Start with the Four Seasons Cold Dish Platter where you can select four appetizers from a wide range of choices; graduate to the "Australian Beef Tender in Hot Oil with Stones" (tender and succulent as the name suggests), and the delicious "Lan Style Spare Ribs with Chili and Spices." Save room for the *dan-dan* noodles in spicy peanut sauce. I found the staff to be attentive and efficient, but there have been occasional complaints of poor service.

Yán'ān Zhōng Lù 881 (just east of Tóngrén Lù); see map p. 436. ✆ **021/6247-5878.** Reservations recommended. Meal for 2 ¥200–¥400. AE, DC, MC, V. 11am–11:30pm. Metro: Nanjing Rd. (W).

MODERATE

Bǎoluó ★ SHÀNGHǍI One of the few constants in this ever-changing town is the long line that invariably forms outside Bǎoluó every evening. A seemingly tiny diner occupying a mere unit in a row of tightly packed Chinese houses until you step inside, the restaurant actually stretches four houses deep, every square inch buzzing with barely controlled chaos. The story goes that Bǎoluó's owner—a bicycle repairman who lived in this very lane—started the restaurant in his own home, but gradually bought up his neighbors' houses as business boomed. The extensive menu features many local favorites given a slight twist, including *huíguō ròu jiābǐng* (twice-cooked lamb wrapped in pancakes), *sōngshǔ lúyú* (sweet-and-sour fried fish), *xièfěn huì zhēnjūn* (braised mushroom with crabmeat), and the sinfully fatty, but absolutely delicious *hóng shāoròu* (braised pork belly).

Fùmín Lù 271 (north of Chánglè Lù, 1 block east of Chángshú Lù); see map p. 436. ✆ **021/6279-2827.** Reservations recommended. Meal for 2 ¥80–¥150. No credit cards. 11am–6am. Metro: Changshu Rd.

Méilóngzhèn ★★ SHÀNGHǍI Established in 1938, Méilóngzhèn is a Shànghǎi institution that still draws the crowds after all these years. Its cuisine has evolved over time from strictly regional fare to one incorporating the spices, vinegars, and chilies of Sìchuān cooking. Seafood is featured prominently, and popular favorites include deep-fried eel, lobster in pepper sauce, Mandarin fish with noodles in chili sauce, Sìchuān duck, and Méilóngzhèn special chicken, served in small ceramic pots. Renovations have turned the once-stodgy surroundings into a sparkling modern restaurant. Staff alternates between attentive and harried. There is another branch in the Westgate mall at Nánjīng Xī Lù 1038 (✆ **021/6255-6688**).

Nánjīng Xī Lù 1081, Building 22 (east of Shànghǎi Centre at Jiāngníng Lù); see map p. 436. ✆ **021/6253-5353.** Reservations recommended. Meal for 2 ¥120–¥240. AE, DC, MC, V. 11am–2pm and 5–10pm. Metro: Nanjing Rd. (W).

INEXPENSIVE

Element Fresh (Yuán Sù) ★ AMERICAN Even for a city as international and modern as Shànghǎi, finding a reasonably priced, delicious fresh salad on a consistent basis is not as easy as you might imagine. Thankfully, Element Fresh fills the niche for healthy dining by serving up a range of soups, salads, and sandwiches that are fresh, light, healthy, and an instant cure for any homesickness. This eatery has proved so popular that this original in Shànghǎi Centre has now spawned seven other branches. Also on the menu is a slew of smoothies, fresh fruit and vegetable juices, pastas, and a handful of Asian set meals, as well as some very popular breakfast sets. The place is jam-packed at lunchtime, as is the patio during warmer months. Another centrally located branch is on the fifth floor of the KWah Centre at Huáihǎi Zhōng Lù 1028 by Xiāngyáng Nán Lù (✆ **021/5403-8865**).

Nánjīng Xī Lù 1376 南京西路１３７６号, no. 112 (ground floor, Shànghǎi Centre); see map p. 436. ✆ **021/6279-8682.** www.elementfresh.com. Reservations recommended. Meal for 2 ¥35–¥140. AE, DC, MC, V. 7am–11pm (midnight Fri–Sat). Metro: Jing'an Temple.

Chángníng District/Hóngqiáo Development Zone (West Shànghǎi)

VERY EXPENSIVE

Fu 1088 (Fú 1088) ★★★ SHÀNGHǍI Tucked away behind an iron gate on a busy one-way street, this gem of a restaurant in a three-story mansion offers some of the best Shanghainese cuisine in town, and a much more fulfilling dining experience than its sister restaurant, Fu 1039. Guests here are in for a treat—dining is all in individual private rooms (there are 17 of them, seating 2–12 people), each furnished with early-20th-century furniture, cherry wood chairs, and chandeliers. Start with the chilled drunken chicken with rice-wine shaved ice, and the most delicious *xūn yú* (smoked fish) you'll ever taste, especially because it's served warm. For main dishes, dig into the glorious braised pork with soy and rock sugar, the deep-fried prawn with wasabi mayonnaise, and the steamed egg with crabmeat. Two local dishes you're unlikely to find back home that are also worth trying include *huáiyáng dàzhǔ gānsī* (bean curd sheet with garden greens and shrimp in thick soup), and the sautéed water bamboo in soy sauce. Service is very courteous and highly efficient. There is a ¥300 minimum charge per person, but for spot-on Shanghainese cuisine that is neither too sweet nor too oily, Fu 1088 is well worth the splurge.

Zhènníng Lù 375 (north of Yùyuán Lù); see map p. 436. ✆ **021/5239-7878.** Reservations required. Meal for 2 ¥600–¥900. AE, DC, MC, V. 11am–2pm and 5:30pm–midnight. Metro: Jiangsu Rd.

EXPENSIVE

Blue Frog (Lán Wā) ☺ AMERICAN This longstanding popular chain has outlets all over town, but this one in the Gubei area is extremely family-friendly with a large menu of familiar Western comfort foods (from nachos and chicken wings to juicy burgers and steaks) and a separate play area for kids. Portions are generous, the service is efficient, and best of all, the restaurant offers all kinds of specials, including discounted happy hour drinks every day and two-for-one burgers every Monday evening. Other branches are in the French Concession at Màomíng Nán Lù 207, #6 (✆ **021/6445-6634**), and in Pǔdōng at the Super Brand Mall, ground floor, no. 27, Lùjiāzuǐ Lù 168 (✆ **021/5047-3488**).

Hóngméi Lù 3338, #30 Hóngméi Leisure Pedestrian Street (south of Yán'ān Zhōng Lù); see map p. 436. ✆ **021/5422-5119.** www.bluefrog.com.cn. Reservations recommended. Meal for 2 ¥150–¥300. AE, DC, MC, V. 10am–late. Metro: Hóngqiáo Rd.

MODERATE

1221 ★★ SHÀNGHǍI Located at the end of an alley between the center of town and the Hóngqiáo district, the classy "One-Two-Two-One (Yī Èr Èr Yī)" has been quietly serving consistently fine food at reasonable prices for more than a decade. Offering Shànghǎi cuisine (with a touch of East/West fusion cooking) that's neither too greasy nor too sweet, this chic, tastefully decorated restaurant has a large and endearingly loyal following in the expatriate and business community. Most things on the menu will delight, but some standouts include drunken chicken, Shànghǎi smoked fish, lion-head meatballs, and braised pork with preserved vegetables. Also worth trying are the spicy Sìchuān beef with sesame bread, and the crispy duck. Wash it all down with eight-treasure tea *(bābǎochá),* steeped with streams of hot water skillfully poured from long-sprouted teapots. The efficient, no-nonsense service could be friendlier, but that seems a small quibble in an otherwise excellent dining experience.

Yán'ān Xī Lù 1221 (btw. Pānyú Lù and Dīngxī Lù); see map p. 436. ✆ **021/6213-6585.** Reservations recommended. Meal for 2 ¥120–¥250. AE, DC, MC, V. 11am–2pm and 5–11pm. No Metro.

Pǔdōng New Area

VERY EXPENSIVE

Guì Huā Lóu ★★ SHÀNGHǍI Restaurants serving regional cuisine are a dime a dozen, so it's nice to find one that does things just a little bit differently, and with a little more care. This award-winning restaurant in the Pǔdōng Shangri-La is such an outlet, serving up some excellent, very refined regional cuisine along with Cantonese and Sìchuān dishes, in an equally refined setting. You can't go wrong with most of the restaurant's signature dishes that have their own menu. The fried river shrimp, deep-fried duo of Mandarin fish (with both lemon and sweet and sour flavors), braised bean curd with ham and vegetable, braised pork belly, and "Lion's Head" meatballs with crabmeat roe are all excellent. Osmanthus tea *(guìhuā chá)* serves as a refreshing complement. Table service is stylish and impeccable.

Fùchéng Lù 33 (1st floor, River Wing, Pǔdōng Shangri-La Hotel). ✆ **021/6882-8888,** ext. 220. Reservations recommended. Meal for 2 ¥400–¥700. AE, DC, MC, V. Mon–Fri 11:30am–3pm; Sat–Sun 11am–3pm; daily 5:30–10:30pm. Metro: Lujiazui.

MODERATE

Sū Zhè Huì (Jade Garden) ★★ SHÀNGHǍI This branch of one of the more highly regarded and popular Shànghǎi chain restaurants offers diners its signature local dishes as well as Hong Kong–style dim sum in a classy and refined setting. Unadorned glass panels, marble floors, cream-colored chairs, and muted lighting all take a back seat to the food here. You can't go wrong with much of the menu: Tea-smoked duck, wine-preserved green crab, and *mìzhī huǒfǎng* (pork and taro in candied sauce) are all house specialties that live up to their renown; the noodles with scallions and small shrimp are some of the most delicious in town; and *qícài dōngsǔn* (fresh winter shoots with local greens) is something you're unlikely to get back home. Service is highly efficient.

Dōngfāng Lù 877 (just north of the St. Regis hotel); see map p. 436. ✆ **021/5058-6088.** Meal for 2 ¥120–¥200. AE, DC, MC, V. 11am–10:30pm. Metro: Century Ave.

Wagas INTERNATIONAL With many outlets around town, this highly popular cafe is best known for its simple but tasty sandwiches, salads, wraps, burgers, pastas, and smoothies, all served up sans preservatives, additives, or MSG. There is Wi-Fi for those who simply cannot be offline. Another branch in Pǔdōng is at Thumb Plaza, Fangdian Lu 199 (✆ **021/5033-6277**).

Pǔdōng Nán Lù 999, G104 (west of Shāngchéng Lù, near Bà Bǎi Bàn); see map p. 436 . ✆ **021/5134-1075.** Meal for 2 ¥120–¥200. AE, DC, MC, V. 7am–10pm. Metro: Century Ave.

EXPLORING SHANGHAI

The Bund (Waitan) ★★★

The Bund (Embankment) refers to Shanghai's famous waterfront running along the west shore of the Huangpu River, forming the eastern boundary of old downtown Shanghai. Once a muddy towpath for boats along the river, the Bund was where the foreign powers that entered Shanghai after the Opium War of 1842 erected their distinct Western-style banks and trading houses. Today, a wide avenue (Zhongshan Dong Yi Lu) fronts the old buildings, which date mostly from the prosperous 1920s and 1930s. On the east side of the road, a raised pedestrian promenade affords visitors pleasant strolls along the river and marvelous views of both the Bund and Pudong—its modern skyscrapers constituting Shanghai's "21st Century Bund"—across the river.

The highlights of the Bund are undoubtedly the colonial-era buildings lining the west side of Zhōngshān Dōng Yī Lù, standouts of which include the **former British Consulate, Customs House, former Hong Kong and Shànghǎi Bank, former Shànghǎi Club** (now the Waldorf Astoria Hotel), and the **Peace Hotel.**

Besides its landmark colonial architecture, however, the Bund has a few other small attractions. On its north end, the rehabilitated Sūzhōu Creek enters the Huángpǔ River beneath the 18m-wide (59-ft.) iron **Wàibáidù Bridge,** built in 1906 to replace the original wooden toll bridge constructed in 1856 by an English businessman. The bridge was most recently restored in 2009. On the river shore stands a granite obelisk, **Monument to the People's Heroes,** erected in 1993, and dedicated to Chinese patriots (as defined by the Communist Party) beginning in the 1840s. The **Bund History Museum** (9am–4:15pm; free admission), which contains

Shanghai Attractions

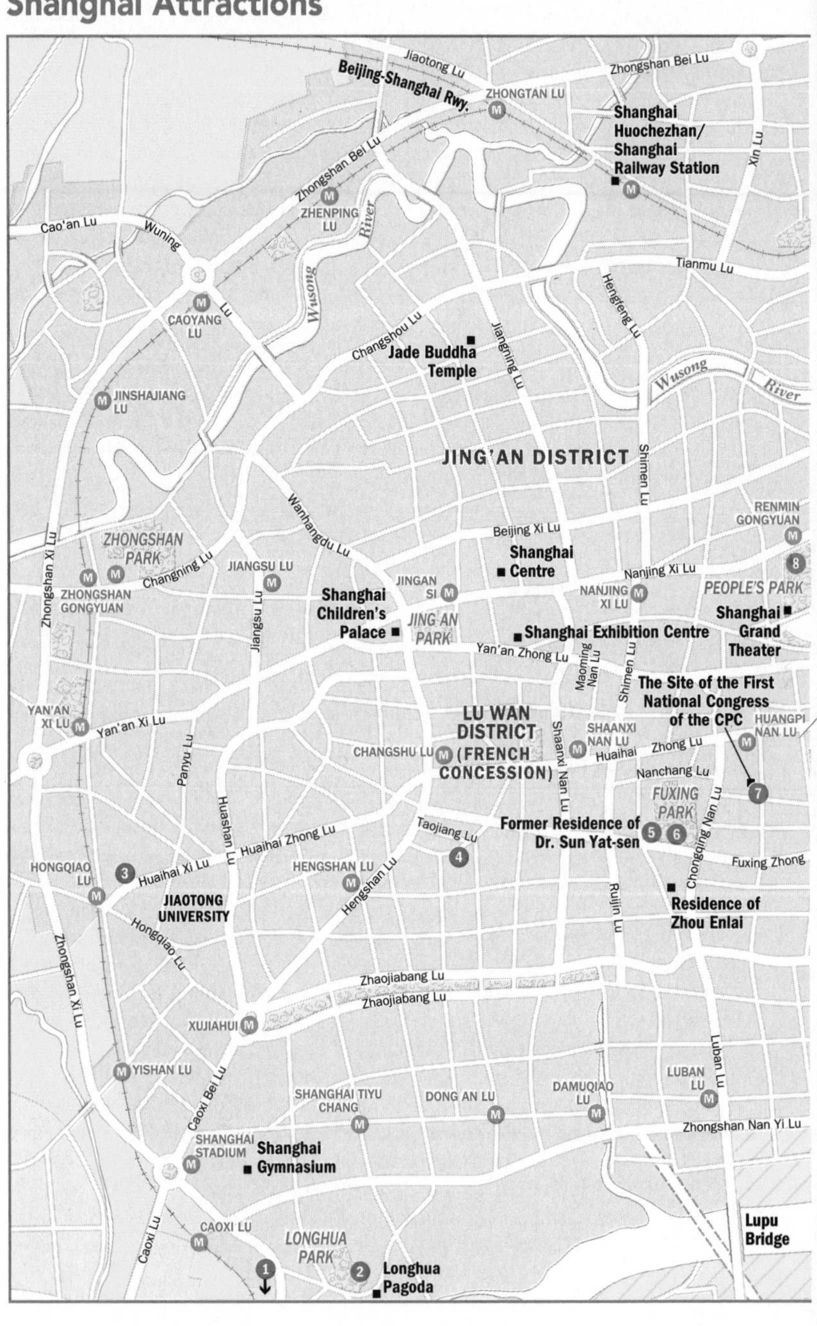

Jiaotong Lu
Beijing-Shanghai Rwy.
Zhongshan Bei Lu
ZHONGTAN LU
Shanghai Huochezhan/ Shanghai Railway Station
Xin Lu
Zhongshan Bei Lu
ZHENPING LU
Wusong River
Cao'an Lu
Wuning Lu
CAOYANG LU
Tianmu Lu
Hengfeng Lu
Changshou Lu
Jade Buddha Temple
Jiangning Lu
Wusong River
JINSHAJIANG LU
JING'AN DISTRICT
Shimen Lu
RENMIN GONGYUAN
Wanhangdu Lu
Beijing Xi Lu
ZHONGSHAN PARK
Shanghai Centre
Changning Lu
JIANGSU LU
JINGAN SI
Nanjing Xi Lu
NANJING XI LU
PEOPLE'S PARK
Zhongshan Xi Lu
ZHONGSHAN GONGYUAN
Jiangsu Lu
Shanghai Children's Palace
JING AN PARK
Shanghai Exhibition Centre
Shanghai Grand Theater
Yan'an Zhong Lu
Maoming Nan Lu
Shimen Lu
The Site of the First National Congress of the CPC
YAN'AN XI LU
Yan'an Xi Lu
LU WAN DISTRICT (FRENCH CONCESSION)
Shaanxi Nan Lu
SHAANXI NAN LU
HUANGPI NAN LU
Panyu Lu
CHANGSHU LU
Huaihai Zhong Lu
Nanchang Lu
Huashan Lu
FUXING PARK
Taojiang Lu
Former Residence of Dr. Sun Yat-sen
Chongqing Nan Lu
Huaihai Zhong Lu
HONGQIAO LU
Huaihai Xi Lu
HENGSHAN LU
Hengshan Lu
Fuxing Zhong
JIAOTONG UNIVERSITY
Ruijin Lu
Residence of Zhou Enlai
Hongqiao Lu
Zhongshan Xi Lu
Zhaojiabang Lu
Zhaojiabang Lu
XUJIAHUI
Luban Lu
YISHAN LU
Caoxi Bei Lu
LUBAN LU
SHANGHAI TIYU CHANG
DONG AN LU
DAMUQIAO LU
Zhongshan Nan Yi Lu
SHANGHAI STADIUM
Shanghai Gymnasium
Lupu Bridge
Caoxi Lu
CAOXI LU
LONGHUA PARK
Longhua Pagoda

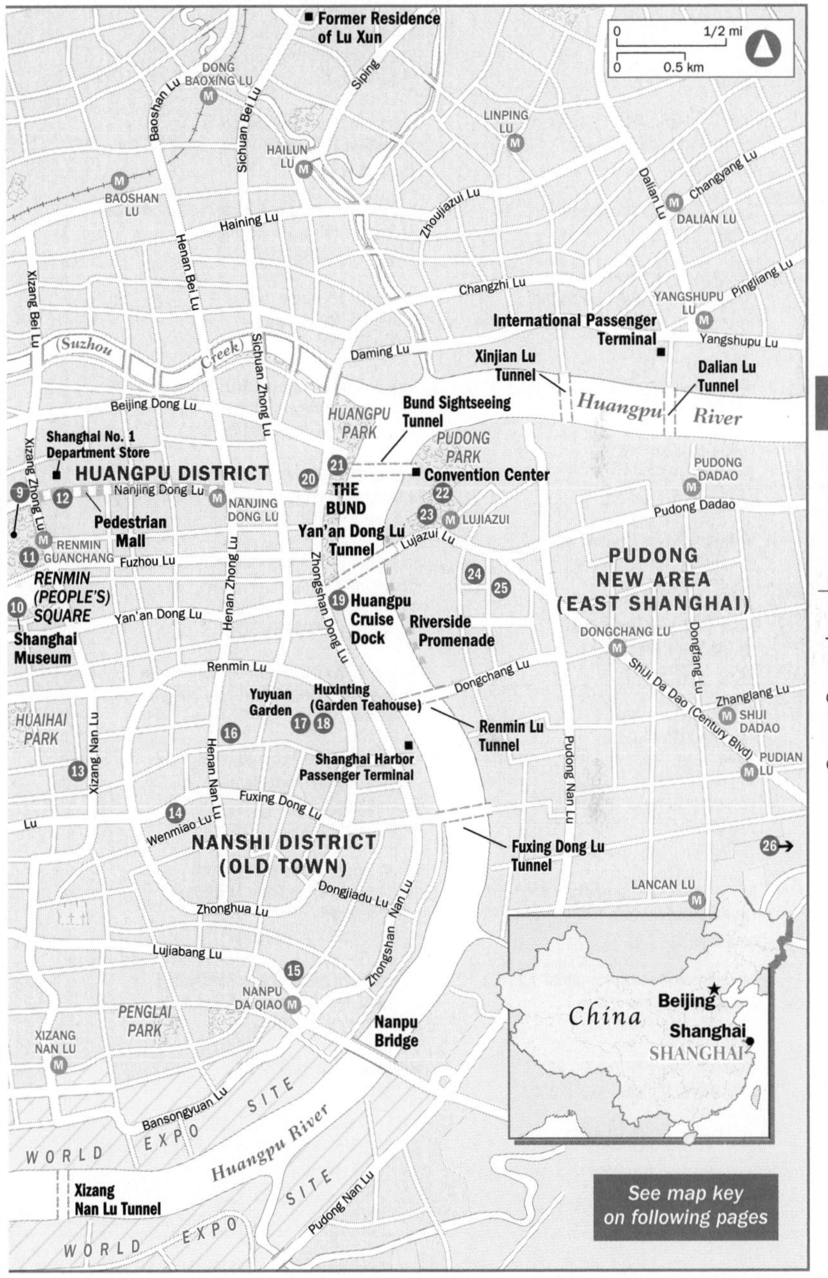
Former Residence of Lu Xun
0 1/2 mi
0 0.5 km
DONG BAOXING LU
Baoshan Lu
Sichuan Bei Lu
Siping
LINPING LU
HAILUN LU
BAOSHAN LU
Haining Lu
Zhoujiazui Lu
Dalian Lu
Changyang Lu
DALIAN LU
Henan Bei Lu
Xizang Bei Lu
Changzhi Lu
YANGSHUPU LU
Pingliang Lu
International Passenger Terminal
Yangshupu Lu
(Suzhou Creek)
Sichuan Zhong Lu
Daming Lu
Xinjian Lu Tunnel
Dalian Lu Tunnel
Huangpu River
Beijing Dong Lu
HUANGPU PARK
Bund Sightseeing Tunnel
PUDONG PARK
Shanghai No. 1 Department Store
HUANGPU DISTRICT
Convention Center
PUDONG DADAO
Nanjing Dong Lu
NANJING DONG LU
THE BUND
Pudong Dadao
Xizang Zhong Lu
Pedestrian Mall
LUJIAZUI
Yan'an Dong Lu Tunnel
Lujiazui Lu
RENMIN GUANCHANG
Fuzhou Lu
Henan Zhong Lu
Zhongshan Dong Lu
PUDONG NEW AREA (EAST SHANGHAI)
RENMIN (PEOPLE'S) SQUARE
Yan'an Dong Lu
Huangpu Cruise Dock
Riverside Promenade
Shanghai Museum
DONGCHANG LU
Dongfang Lu
Shiji Da Dao (Century Blvd)
Renmin Lu
Dongchang Lu
Yuyuan Garden
Huxinting (Garden Teahouse)
Zhanglang Lu
SHIJI DADAO
HUAIHAI PARK
Xizang Nan Lu
Renmin Lu Tunnel
Henan Nan Lu
Shanghai Harbor Passenger Terminal
Pudong Nan Lu
PUDIAN LU
Fuxing Dong Lu
Wenmiao Lu
NANSHI DISTRICT (OLD TOWN)
Fuxing Dong Lu Tunnel
Dongjiadu Lu
Zhongshan Nan Lu
LANCAN LU
Zhonghua Lu
Lujiabang Lu
NANPU DA QIAO
PENGLAI PARK
Nanpu Bridge
China
Beijing
Shanghai
SHANGHAI
XIZANG NAN LU
Bansongyuan Lu
WORLD EXPO SITE
Huangpu River
Xizang Nan Lu Tunnel
Pudong Nan Lu
See map key on following pages

Shanghai Attractions Key

The Bund **21**
(Wài Tān)
外滩

Century Park **26**
(Shìjì Gōngyuán)
世纪公园

Confucius Temple (Wén Miào) **14**
文庙

Dongtai Lu Antiques Market **13**
(Dōngtái Lù Gǔwán Shìchǎng)
东台路古玩市场

Fùxīng Park **6**
(Fùxīng Gōngyuán)
复兴公园

Fuyou Market **16**
(Fúyòu Shìchǎng)
福佑市场

Huangpu River Cruise **19**
(Huángpǔ Jiāng Yóulǎn)
黄浦江游览

Huxinting Teahouse **18**
(Húxīntíng Cháshè)
湖心亭茶社

Jin Mao Tower **24**
(Jīn Mào Dàshà)
金茂大厦

Longhua Temple **2**
(Lónghuá Sì)
龙华寺

Museum of Contemporary Art/MOCA **9**
(Shànghǎi Dāngdài Yìshù Guǎn)
上海当代艺术馆

Nanjing Lu Pedestrian Mall **12**
(Nánjīng Lù Bùxíngjiē)
南京路步行街

Oriental Pearl TV Tower **22**
(Dōngfāng Míngzhū Guǎngbō Diànshì Tǎ)
东方明珠广播电视塔

Peace Hotel **20**
(Hépíng Fàndiàn)
和平饭店

Shanghai Art Museum **8**
(Shànghǎi Měishùguǎn)
上海美术馆

Shanghai Botanical Gardens **1**
(Shànghǎi Zhíwùyuán)
上海植物园

Shanghai Municipal History Museum **23**
(Shànghǎi Shì Lìshǐ Bówùguǎn)
上海市历史博物馆

Shanghai Museum **10**
(Shànghǎi Bówùguǎn)
上海博物馆

Shanghai Museum of Arts and Crafts **4**
(Shànghǎi Gōngyì Měishù Bówùguǎn)
上海工艺美术博物馆

Shànghǎi Sculpture Space **3**
(Shànghǎi Chéngshì Diāosù Yìshù Zhōngxīn)
上海城市雕塑艺术中心

Shanghai Urban Planning Museum **11**
(Shànghǎi Chéngshì Guīhuà Zhǎnshìguǎn)
上海城市规划展示馆

Shanghai World Financial Center **25**
(Shànghǎi Huánqiú Jīnróng Zhōngxīn)
上海环球金融中心

Site of the First National Congress of the Communist Party **7**
(Zhōnggòng Yīdà Huìzhǐ)
中共一大会址

South Bund Fabric Market **15**
(Nán Wàitān Qīng Fáng Miánliào Shìchǎng)
南外滩轻纺面料市场

Sun Yat-sen's Former Residence **5**
(Sūn Zhōngshān Gùjū Jìniànguǎn)
孙中山故居纪念馆

Yu Garden (Yù Yuán) **17**
豫园

a few artifacts and some interesting photographs of the Bund, stands at its base; however, at press time, the museum was closed for renovation. Just south of the monument used to be the park **Huángpǔ Gōngyuán,** originally the British Public Gardens built in 1868. In the early days, only Chinese servants accompanying their foreign masters were allowed to enter the park. Dogs were also prohibited, leading in later years to the apocryphal NO CHINESE OR DOGS ALLOWED sign being attributed to the park. The park was eventually opened to Chinese in 1926, but today, has simply become part of the Bund promenade with the recent renovations. South of here, across from the Peace Hotel, is the entrance to the pedestrian **Bund Sightseeing Tunnel (Wàitān Guànguāng Suìdào;** daily 8am–10:30pm [until 11pm Fri–Sun]; admission ¥55 round-trip, ¥45 one-way) located under the Huángpǔ. Complete with tram cars and a light show, the tunnel connects downtown Shànghǎi to the Pǔdōng New Area and the Oriental Pearl TV Tower. Also here is a **statue of Chén Yì,** Shànghǎi's first mayor after 1949 and a dead ringer for Máo Zédōng, at least in bronze.

Farther south down the Bund Promenade are scores of vendors, a few restaurants, and excellent overlooks facing the river. At the intersection with Yán'ān Dōng Lù, you'll also notice a picturesque **Signal Tower,** a slender, round brick tower that served as a control tower for river traffic during colonial days. First built in 1884, the tower was rebuilt in 1907, and also relayed weather reports. In 1993 during the widening of Zhōngshān Lù, it was moved 20m (66 ft.) to its current site. About a 20-minute walk farther down the promenade are the docks for the Huángpǔ River cruises (p. 466).

Yu Garden (Yu Yuan)

Yu Yuan is a pleasant enough, well-contained classical Chinese garden, if not quite the loveliest of its kind, as local boosters would have you believe. Bearing the burden of being the most complete classical garden in urban Shanghai and therefore a must-see for every tourist, this overexposed garden overflows daily with hordes of visitors, and is no longer the pastoral haven it once was. Built between 1559 and 1577 by local official Pan Yunduan as the private estate for his father, Yu Yuan (meaning Garden of Peace and Comfort) is a maze of Ming dynasty pavilions, elaborate rockeries, arched bridges, and goldfish ponds, all encircled by an undulating dragon wall. Covering just 2 hectares (5 acres), it nevertheless appears expansive, with room for 30 pavilions.

Located in the heart of the old Chinese city, a few blocks southwest of the Bund in downtown Shanghai (nearest metro: Nanjing Dong Lu, which is still 1.6km/1 mile away), Yu Yuan has a ticket window on the north shore of the Huxin Ting Teahouse pond. The garden is open from 8:30am to 5pm; admission is ¥45.

The layout of Yu Yuan, which contains several gardens-within-gardens, can make strolling here a bit confusing, but if you stick to a general clockwise path from the main entrance, you should get around most of the estate and arrive eventually at the Inner Garden (Nei Yuan) and final exit.

Halls and pavilions of note (in clockwise order from the north entrance) include the **Hall for Viewing the Grand Rockery (Yang Shan Tang),** a graceful two-story tower serving as the entrance to the marvelous rock garden behind, which consists of 2,000 tons of rare yellow stones pasted together with rice glue and designed by a famous garden artist of the Ming dynasty, Zhang Nanyang; the **Hall of Heralding**

Spring (Dian Chun Tang), the most famous historical building in the garden, where in 1853 the secret Small Sword Society (Xiaodao Hui) plotted to join the peasant-led Taiping Rebellion and help overthrow the Qing dynasty; and the **Hall of Jade Magnificence (Yu Hua Tang),** opening to the most celebrated stone sculpture in the garden, the **Exquisite Jade (Yu Ling Long),** which was originally procured by the Huizong emperor of the Northern Song (reigned 1100–26) from the waters of Tai Hu (Lake Tai) where many of the bizarre rocks and rockeries found in classical Chinese gardens were submerged to be naturally carved by the currents. Such rocks represent mountain peaks in classical Chinese garden design. Just before the **Inner Garden (Nei Yuan),** where local artists and calligraphers often display and sell their works, is the garden's exit.

Shanghai Bowuguan ★★★

Frequently cited as the best museum in China, the Shanghai Museum has 11 state-of-the-art galleries and three special exhibition halls arranged on four floors, all encircling a spacious cylindrical atrium. The exhibits are tastefully displayed and well lit, and explanatory signs are in English as well as Chinese. For size, the museum's 120,000 historic artifacts cannot match the world-renowned Chinese collections in Beijing, Taipei, and Xi'an, but are more than enough to fill the galleries on any given day with outstanding treasures.

Located downtown on the south side of People's Square (Renmin Guangchang) at Renmin Da Dao 201 (✆ **021/6372-3500**), the museum has its main entrance on the north side of the building, facing the three monumental structures that now occupy the north half of the square (Grand Theatre to the west, City Hall in the middle, Shanghai Urban Planning Exhibition Center to the east). Metro lines 1, 2, and 8 all have stations on the northeast corner of People's Square. The museum is open 9am to 5pm (no tickets distributed after 4pm). Admission is free, though there is a limit of 5,000 visitors a day, so if you visit on the weekend, be sure to arrive early. Audio phones providing narratives of the major exhibits in English, French, Japanese, Spanish, German, and Italian are available for rent (¥40 plus a deposit of ¥400, or your passport) to your left as you enter the lobby.

Huangpu River Cruise

The Huangpu River (Huangpu Jiang) is the city's shipping artery both to the East China Sea and to the mouth of the Yangzi River, which the Huangpu joins 29km (18 miles) north of downtown Shanghai. It has also become a demarcating line between two Shanghais, east and west, past and future. On its western shore, the colonial landmarks of the Bund serve as a reminder of Shanghai's 19th-century struggle to reclaim a waterfront from the bogs of this river (which originates in nearby Dianshan Hu or Lake Dianshan); on the eastern shore, the steel-and-glass skyscrapers of the Pudong New Area point to a burgeoning financial empire of the future.

Many boat companies offer cruises; one of the main ones is the **Shànghǎi Huángpǔ River Cruise Company** (**Shànghǎi Pǔjiāng Yóulǎn Yoǔxiàn Gōngsī;** ✆ **021/6318-8888** or 021/6374-0091; www.pjrivercruise.com). They typically have a daily, full 3-hour afternoon cruise (2–5pm) to Wúsōng Kǒu and back. Cost is ¥150. As well, there are hour-long cruises (¥100) every day departing at 30-minute to 1-hour intervals between 9:30am and 4:30pm from the Bund to the Yángpǔ Bridge.

This company also offers a nightly cruise (45–60 min.; ¥100) every half-hour between 7 and 8:30pm. Cruise schedules vary depending on the season, and on Saturday and Sunday, additional cruises are sometimes added, so check ahead. Boats all depart from the Shíliùpǔ Wharf (Shíliùpǔ Lüyóu Jíshàn Zhōngxīn) at Wài Mǎ Lù 19, 1 block east of Zhōngshān Nán Lù 171, and just north of Fùxīng Dōng Lù. Tickets can be purchased through your hotel desk or at the Shíliùpǔ Wharf ticket office at Wài Mǎ Lù 80.

Temples

Lónghuá Sì (Lónghuá Temple) ★★ Shànghǎi's largest and most active temple is one of its most fascinating, featuring the city's premier pagoda, the delicate Lónghuá Tǎ. Local lore has it that the pagoda was originally built around A.D. 247 by Sūn Quán, the king of the Wú Kingdom during the Three Kingdoms period, but today's seven-story, eight-sided, wood-and-brick pagoda, like the temple, dates to the Sòng Dynasty (A.D. 960–1279). For a long time the tallest structure in Shànghǎi, today it can only be admired from a distance. The extensive temple grounds are often crowded with incense-bearing supplicants. There are four main halls (only a century old), the most impressive being the third, Dàxióng Bǎo Diàn (Grand Hall) where a gilded statue of Sakyamuni sits under a beautifully carved dome, flanked on each side by 18 *arhats* (disciples). Behind, Guānyīn, the Goddess of Mercy, presides over a fascinating tableau representing the process of reincarnation: A boat in the bottom right corner indicates birth, while death awaits at the bottom left corner. Behind the third and fourth halls is a basic, but popular vegetarian restaurant (11am–2pm). Lónghuá is also famous for its midnight bell-ringing every New Year's Eve (Dec 31–Jan 1). The Bell Tower's 3,000-kilogram (3.3-ton) bronze bell, cast in 1894, is struck 108 times to dispel all the worries said to be afflicting mankind. For a small fee, you, too, can strike the bell, but three times only.

Lónghuá Lù 2853, Xúhuì; see map p. 462. ✆ **021/6456-6085.** Admission ¥10. 7am–5pm. Metro: Lóngcáo Rd.

Wén Miào (Confucius Temple) Built in 1855 on the site of an earlier temple, and restored in 1999 to celebrate the 2,550th birthday of Confucius, this temple honoring China's great sage offers quiet refuge from the crowded streets of the old Chinese city. As at all Chinese Confucian temples, there's a *língxīn mén* (gate) leading to the main hall, Dàchéng Diàn. Inside are statues of Confucius flanked by his two disciples, Mèngzǐ (Mencius) and Yànhuī, and his two favorite musical instruments, a drum and set of bells. To the northeast, the Zūnjīng Gé, formerly the library, now houses a display of unusually shaped rocks. Back near the entrance, Kuíxīng Gé is a three-story 20m-high (66-ft.) pagoda dedicated to the god of liberal arts, and the only original structure left on these tranquil grounds. A lively book market is held here on Sunday mornings.

Wénmiào Lù 215, Huángpǔ (north side of Wénmiào Lù, 1 block east of Zhōnghuá Lù); see map p. 462. ✆ **021/6377-1815.** Admission ¥10. 9am–4:30pm. Metro: Laoximen.

Parks & Gardens

Fùxīng Gōngyuán (Fùxīng Park) ★ ☺ Formerly a private estate in the French Concession, Fùxīng Park was purchased by foreign residents and opened to the French public on July 14, 1909. It was popularly known as French Park, styled after your typical Parisian city park with wide, tree-lined walks and flower beds. Today, this is one of the city's most popular parks, home to a number of restaurants and nightclubs, as well as to pleasant fountains, a children's playground with a carousel and bumper cars, a rose garden to the east, 120 species of trees, and, near the north entrance, a statue of Karl Marx and Friedrich Engels in front of which Chinese couples often practice ballroom dancing.

Gāolán Lù 2, Lúwān (west entrance Gāolán Lù, north entrance Yándāng Lù, southeast entrance Chóngqìng Nán Lù off Fùxīng Zhōng Lù); see map p. 462. ✆ **021/6372-6083.** Free admission. 6am–6pm. Metro: Huangpi Rd. (S).

Shànghǎi Zhíwùyuán (Shànghǎi Botanical Gardens) ★ ☺ Somewhat inconveniently located in the southwest part of town, the city's premier and largest garden provides a pleasant reprieve from the urban hustle, but is not worth a special trip unless you really like your plants. The extensive grounds, covering 81 hectares (200 acres), are divided into different sections featuring peonies, roses, bamboo, azaleas, maples, osmanthus, magnolias, and orchids (considered the best in China). There are also a garden of medicinal plants and a greenhouse dedicated to tropical plants, but the hallmark section is the Pénjǐng Yuán (Bonsai Garden), which requires a separate admission (¥7), with hundreds of bonsai displayed in a large complex of corridors, courtyards, pools, and rockeries. There are restaurants, exhibition halls, vendors' stalls, and several children's playgrounds dotted throughout the park. The park is extremely crowded on weekends.

Lóngwú Lù 1111, Xúhuì; see map p. 462. ✆ **021/5436-3369.** www.shbg.org. Admission ¥15 garden only; ¥40 includes conservatory and Bonsai Garden. 7am–5pm. Metro: Shílóng Rd.

Shìjì Gōngyuán (Century Park) ★ ☺ Built to herald the new millennium, this sprawling 140-hectare (346-acre) park lies at the southern terminus of Century Boulevard (Shìjì Dà Dào), which runs from the Oriental Pearl TV Tower. Designed by a British firm, the park is divided into seven scenic areas, including a minigolf course, a beach area complete with man-made cobblestone beach, a bird-protection area, and an international garden area. The center of the park contains a lake where fishing poles and paddleboats can be rented. There's plenty here to distract the kids, but it's an even better place to watch local families enjoy themselves.

Jǐnxiù Lù 1001, Pǔdōng (south entrance at Huāmù Lù, next to Metro station); see map p. 462. ✆ **021/3876-0588.** Admission ¥10. 7am–6pm (to 5pm Nov 16–Mar 15). Metro: Century Park.

Museums & Mansions

Museum of Contemporary Art/MOCA (Shànghǎi Dāngdài Yìshù Guǎn) This beautiful, three-story glass structure houses Shànghǎi's first contemporary art museum, and has become a good pacesetter in China's contemporary art scene today. While not in the same league as better-known MOCAs around the world, the museum's two floors of exhibition space connected by a curving ramp are enough to showcase plenty of goofy, interesting, ridiculous, sublime, "this-is-art?" paintings, photographs, and installations by Chinese and international artists. For those immune to the charms of modern art, the building itself is quite interesting and can be appreciated gratis from the outside or at the door if you simply tell them you're going to the Art Lab restaurant on the third floor, where you can sip cocktails on the rooftop terrace.

Nánjīng Xī Lù 231, Gate 7, People's Park, Huángpǔ (inside People's Park/Rénmín Gōngyuán); see map p. 462. ✆ **021/6327-9900.** www.mocashanghai.org. Admission ¥20. 10am–9:30pm. Metro: People's Square.

Shànghǎi Art Museum (Shànghǎi Měishùguǎn) ★ Relocated in 2000 to the historic clock tower building on the northwest end of People's Square, the museum is more to be seen for its 1930s monumental interior architecture than for its art. The artwork in the 12 exhibit halls is certainly noteworthy, ranging from modern traditional oils to recent pop canvases, but it's overwhelmed by the fastidiously restored, wood and marble interiors of this 1933 five-story, neoclassical landmark. People's Square, today's Rénmín Guǎngchǎng, was a racecourse in colonial times, and today's clock tower, erected in 1933, marks the location of the original grandstand of 1863. After 1949, the building was used as the Shànghǎi Museum and the Shànghǎi Library. Today, in addition to the artwork, there is a classy American restaurant, Kathleen's 5, on the fifth floor.

Nánjīng Xī Lù 325, Huángpǔ (northwest edge of People's Park at Huángpí Lù); see map p. 462. ✆ **021/6327-2829.** www.sh-artmuseum.org.cn. Admission ¥20. 9am–5pm (last tickets sold 4pm). Metro: People's Square.

Shànghǎi Municipal History Museum (Shànghǎi Shì Lìshǐ Chénlièguǎn) ★★ This excellent museum in the basement of the Oriental Pearl TV Tower in Pǔdōng tells the history of Shànghǎi with an emphasis on the colonial period between 1860 and 1949. Fascinating exhibits include dioramas of the Huángpǔ River, the Bund, Nánjīng Lù, and foreign concessions, evoking the colorful street life and lost trades of the 19th and early 20th centuries; dozens of models of Shànghǎi's classic avenues and famous buildings; and a vehicle collection with trolley cars (the city line opened in 1908), 1920s sedans, and a U.S. jeep (popular after World War II), among others. Other intriguing bits include a gorgeously ornate wedding palanquin, boulders marking the concessions' boundaries, and visiting chits used in brothels. The museum takes about an hour to tour. Tickets are purchased at the Oriental Pearl TV Tower gate. Audio headsets (¥30) can enhance your visit, but are not crucial, as displays are well annotated in English and Chinese.

Lùjiāzuǐ Lù 2, Oriental Pearl TV Tower basement, Pǔdōng; see map p. 462. ✆ **021/5879-3003.** Admission ¥35. 9am–9pm. Metro: Lujiazui.

Shànghǎi Museum of Arts and Crafts (Shànghǎi Gōngyì Měishù Bówùguǎn) ★ This gorgeous, three-story late French Renaissance mansion was built in 1905 for the French Concession's Chamber of Industry director. The expansive lawns, sweeping marble staircases, stained-glass windows, dark wooden paneling, and ceiling beams of the mansion obviously appealed to many others as well, as it became the residence of Chén Yì, Shànghǎi's first mayor after 1949. For aficionados of Cultural Revolution (1966–76) history, it also served for a time as the residence of Lín Lìguǒ's (Lín Biāo's son's) mother-in-law, who tore down the glasshouse that used to be in the eastern section of the residence. After 1960, this became the Shànghǎi Arts and Crafts Research Center. Its many rooms were converted into studios where visitors could watch artisans work at traditional handicrafts. Today, some of the artists' studios remain, but it has been largely rearranged as a formal museum of the crafts produced in Shànghǎi over the past 100 years. On display are fine carvings in jade, wood, ivory, and bamboo, as well as gorgeously stitched costumes and tapestries, intricately painted vases and snuff bottles, and a variety of folk crafts from paper lanterns to dough figurines. A salesroom is attached, of course. Expect high prices, but also high quality.

Fēnyáng Lù 79, Xúhuì (at intersection with Tàiyuán Lù); see map p. 462. ✆ **021/6431-1431.** Admission ¥8. 9am–4:30pm. Metro: Changshu Rd.

Shànghǎi Urban Planning Museum (Shànghǎi Chéngshì Guīhuà Zhǎnshìguǎn) ★★ Filmmakers and science-fiction writers have imagined it, but if you want to see what a city of the future is really going to look like, take yourself over to this museum on the eastern end of People's Square. Housed in a striking, modern, five-story building made of Microlite glass, this is one of the world's largest showcases of urban development and is much more interesting than its dry name suggests. The highlight is on the third floor: an awesome, vast, scale model of urban Shànghǎi as it will look in 2020, a master plan full of endless skyscrapers punctuated occasionally by patches of green. The clear plastic models indicate structures yet to be built, and there are many of them. Beleaguered Shànghǎi residents wondering if their current cramped downtown houses will survive the bulldozer (chances are not good) need only look here for the answer. The fourth floor also has displays on proposed forms of future transportation, including magnetic levitation (maglev), subway, and light-rail trains that are going to change even the face of the Bund. The museum is well worth an hour of your time.

Rénmín Dà Dào 100, Huángpǔ (northeast of the Shànghǎi Museum; entrance on east side); see map p. 462. ✆ **021/6372-2077.** Admission ¥30. Tues–Thurs 9am–5pm (last ticket sold 4pm); Fri–Sun 9am–6pm (last ticket 5pm). Metro: People's Square.

Site of the First National Congress of the Communist Party (Zhōnggòng Yīdà Huìzhǐ) This historic building of brick and marble—a quintessential example of the traditional Shànghǎi style of *shíkùmén* (stone-framed) houses built in the 1920s and 1930s—contains the room where, on July 23, 1921, Máo Zédōng and 12 other Chinese revolutionaries founded the Chinese Communist Party. Also present were two Russian advisors. The delegates had to conclude their meeting on Nánhú Lake in Zhèjiāng Province when police broke up the party. The original teacups and ashtrays remain on the organizing table. As the anchor of the urban renewal project that spawned the open-air mall Xīntiāndì, this museum has been expanded to include several new galleries. There is the expected hagiographic treatment given the history of the Communist Party, but also more interesting displays of a Qīng Dynasty bronze cannon, swords and daggers used by rebels during the Tàipíng and Small Swords rebellions in 19th-century Shànghǎi, and a boundary stone used to demarcate the entrance to the British Concession, dated May 8, 1899.

Xīngyè Lù 76, Lúwān (south end of Xīntiāndì); see map p. 462. ✆ **021/5383-2171.** Free admission. 9am–5pm (last entry at 4pm). Metro: Huangpi Rd. (S).

Sun Yat-sen's Former Residence (Sūn Zhōngshān Gùjū Jìniànguǎn) ★ Sun Yat-sen (1866–1925), beloved founder of the Chinese Republic (1911), lived here with his wife, Soong Ching-ling, from June 1918 to November 1924, when the address would have been 29 Rue de Moliere. Here, Sun's wife later met with such literary stars as Lǔ Xùn and George Bernard Shaw (at the same dinner party), as well as political leaders including Vietnam's Ho Chi Minh (in 1933). Led by an English-speaking guide, visitors enter through the kitchen on the way to the dining room.

Sun's study is upstairs, complete with ink stone, brushes, maps drawn by Sun, and a "library" of 2,700 volumes (look closer and you'll see they're merely photocopies of book spines). The bedroom and the drawing room contain more original furnishings, including an original "Zhōngshān" suit, similar to the later Máo suit. The backyard has a charming garden.

Xiāngshān Lù 7, Lúwān (west of Fùxīng Park at Sīnán Lù); see map p. 462. ✆ **021/6437-2954** or 021/6385-0217. Admission ¥20. 9am–4pm. Metro: Shaanxi Rd. (S).

Special Attractions

Húxīntíng Teahouse (Húxīntíng Cháshè) ★ Shànghǎi's quintessential teahouse has floated atop the lake at the heart of Old Town, in front of Yù Yuán, since 1784. It was built by area cotton-cloth merchants as a brokerage hall. Tea drinking was forbidden inside until the late 1800s, when it became what it is today. Believed to be the original model for Blue Willow tableware, the five-sided, two-story pavilion with red walls and uplifted black-tiled eaves has served everyone from visiting heads of state to local laborers. This is the place in Shànghǎi to idle over a cup of tea, seated in front of the open windows. Húxīntíng (meaning "midlake pavilion") is reached via the traditional Bridge of Nine Turnings, so designed to deflect evil spirits who are said to travel only in straight lines.

Yùyuán Lù 257, Huángpǔ (at pond in the center of the Old Town Bazaar); see map p. 462. ✆ **021/6373-6950.** Free admission. 8:30am–9pm. Metro: Yu Garden.

Jīn Mào Tower (Jīn Mào Dàshà) ★★★ Built in 1998 as a Sino-American joint venture, this 421m-high (1,381-ft.) second-tallest building in China (to its neighbor the Shànghǎi World Financial Center) is simply sublime. Blending traditional Chinese and modern Western tower designs, the building, which boasts 88 floors (eight being an auspicious Chinese number), consists of 13 distinct tapering segments, with high-tech steel bands binding the glass like an exoskeleton. Offices occupy the first 50 floors, the Grand Hyatt hotel the 51st to the 88th floors, while a public observation deck on the 88th floor ("the Skywalk") offers views to rival those of the nearby Oriental Pearl TV Tower (its admission charge is also lower). High-speed elevators (9m/30 ft. per sec.) whisk visitors from Level B1 to the top in less than 45 seconds. The view from there is almost too high, but exquisite on a clear day. You can also look down at the 152m-high (499-ft.) atrium of the Grand Hyatt. Access the building through entrance no. 4.

Shìjì Dà Dào 2, Pǔdōng (3 blocks southeast of Oriental Pearl TV Tower); see map p. 462. ✆ **021/5047-5101.** Admission ¥88. 8:30am–10:30pm (last ticket sold 10pm). Metro: Lujiazui.

Oriental Pearl TV Tower (Dōngfāng Míngzhū Guǎngbō Diànshì Tǎ) The earliest symbol of the new China, this hideous gray tower with three tapering levels of pink spheres (meant to resemble pearls) still holds a special place in many a local heart and is still one of the first stops in town for Chinese visitors. Built in 1994 at a height of 468m (1,535 ft.), it is hailed as the tallest TV tower in Asia and the third-tallest in the world. Visit for the stunning panoramas of Shànghǎi (when the clouds and smog decide to cooperate) and the stellar Shànghǎi Municipal History Museum (p. 469) located in the basement. Various combination tickets are available for the tower and museum, but for most folks, the observation deck in the middle sphere (263m/863 ft. elevation), reached by high-speed elevators staffed by statistics-reciting attendants, is just the right height to take in Shànghǎi old and new, east and west. Those partial to vertiginous views can ascend to the "space capsule" in the top sphere (350m/1,148 ft. elevation).

Lùjiāzuǐ Lù 2, Pǔdōng; see map p. 462. ✆ **021/5879-1888.** Admission ¥100–¥150, depending on sections visited. 8am–9:30pm. Metro: Lujiazui (Exit 1).

Peace Hotel (Hépíng Fàndiàn) ★★★ Having reopened after a 2-year renovation, this Art Deco palace is the ultimate symbol of romantic colonial Shànghǎi. Built in 1929 by Victor Sassoon, a British descendant of Baghdad Jews who'd made their fortune in opium and real estate, the building was originally part office/residential complex known as the Sassoon House, and part hotel, the Cathay Hotel, one of the world's finest international hotels in the 1930s. Sassoon himself had his bachelor's quarters on the top floor where he threw lavish parties for the city's top denizens, and where you can again if you rent out the new Sassoon Presidential Suite. Or simply stroll through the wings of the finely restored lobby, and if possible (the hotel was not open for review at press time), head to the roof for a superb view of the Bund, Nánjīng Lù, the hotel's famous green pyramid roof, and Pǔdōng across the Huángpǔ River. Famous guests in the past have ranged from Charlie Chaplin and Noël Coward to Douglas Fairbanks and Mary Pickford.

Nánjīng Dōng Lù 20, Huángpǔ (on the Bund); see map p. 462. ✆ **021/6321-6888.** Free admission. 24 hr. Metro: Nanjing Rd. (E).

Shànghǎi Sculpture Space (Shànghǎi Chéngshì Diāosù Yìshù Zhōngxīn) In the vein of the recent Shànghǎi trend of converting abandoned industrial buildings into art centers, the space formerly occupied by the No. 10 Steel Plant of Shànghǎi (covering a total area of 50,000 sq. m/538,195 sq. ft.) on the edges of the French Concession has now been partially converted into a sprawling urban sculpture art center complete with galleries, artists' studios, restaurants, offices, and outdoor exhibition space. The original red-brick warehouses have been wonderfully preserved and are just as interesting architecturally as what they now house, from sculptures and installations to artwork by Chinese and international artists. If you like your art in 3D, this place, still being developed, is worth a visit.

Huáihǎi Xī Lù 570-588, Chángníng (east of Kǎixuán Lù); see map p. 462. ✆ **021/6280-7844.** www.sss570.com. Free admission to the grounds. Entrance fees for special exhibitions vary. Tues–Sun 10am–4pm. Metro: Hóngqiáo Rd.

Shànghǎi World Financial Center (Shànghǎi Huánqiú Jīnróng Zhōngxīn ★★ Opened in the middle of 2008, this tapering, 101-story, 492m-high (1,614-ft.) glass tower, resembling a giant, old-fashioned bottle opener, is the tallest building in China, and the tallest in the world, vis-à-vis the height to which visitors can ascend—which, in this case, is the stunning, all-glass 100th-floor observatory at a height of 474m (1,555 ft.). (The building, designed by American architect William Pedersen and developed by Minoru Mori and the Mori Group, which built the Roppongi Hills complex in Tokyo, is technically the third tallest in the world.) The rarefied air and views from up top are unparalleled, but can be stomach-churning for those prone to vertigo. The 94th-floor exhibition space, and the 97th-floor skybridge are nothing special, but the tony Park Hyatt Hotel on the 79th to 93rd floors is certainly good for a meal or drink after your visit, as are the restaurants in the basement.

Shìjì Dàdào 100, Pǔdōng; see map p. 462. ✆ **021/5878-0101.** www.swfc-observatory.com. 94th floor only ¥100; 94th–97th floors ¥110; 94th–100th floors ¥150. 8am–11pm (10pm last entry). Metro: Lujiazui.

Tours

Most Shànghǎi hotels have tour desks that can arrange a variety of day tours for guests. These tour desks are often extensions of **China International Travel Service (CITS),** now rebranded locally as **Jǐn Jiāng Tours.** CITS has its head offices near the Shànghǎi Centre at Běijīng Xī Lù 1277, Guólú Dàshà (✆ **021/6289-4510** or 021/6289-8899, ext. 263; www.citsusa.com). There's another branch at the Bund at Jīnlíng Dōng Lù 2 (✆ **021/6323-8770**) where you can purchase airline and train tickets.

Jǐnjiāng Tours operates many of the English-language group tours in Shànghǎi, even those booked in hotels. If you have little time, **group tours** are convenient, efficiently organized, and considerably less expensive than private tours. The **Jǐn Jiāng Tours Center,** which has its head office near the Jǐn Jiāng and Okura Garden hotels at Chánglè Lù 191 (✆ **021/5466-7936** or 021/6466-2828, ext. 0), offers several City Explorer group tours, including a half-day Shànghǎi tour and a 1-day tour of Shànghǎi by bus, with English-speaking guide and lunch, for ¥400; sites include Yù Yuán, the Bund, Jade Buddha Temple, Xīntiāndì, People's Square, the Shànghǎi Museum, and a quick drive-by of Pǔdōng. Another option is **Gray Line Shànghǎi,** located at Běijīng Xī Lù 1399, A/5F (✆ **021/6289-5221;** www.grayline.com), part of the international chain, which offers half-day (around ¥306) and full-day tours (around ¥496) of Shànghǎi.

As an alternative, **Big Bus Tours,** Hànkǒu Lù 515, Huì Jīn Tower, Room 1205, Huángpǔ (✆ **021/6351-5988;** www.bigbustours.com), has recently inaugurated two tour routes covering all the major landmarks in Pǔxī and Pǔdōng on its open-top double-decker buses. Your ticket (¥300) allows you to hop on/off at your leisure at any of the designated stops within a 24-hour period, and also includes audio commentary on the buses, free tickets to the Jade Buddha Temple, the Bund Sightseeing Tunnel, and a free River Cruise. Tickets can be purchased through your hotel, from the company's website, or on the bus (one of the main stops is at the northeast corner of People's Square opposite Madame Tussauds by Metro Exit 7).

Some other more specialized tour operators include **Bodhi Bikes,** Zhōngshān Běi Lù 2918, Building 2, third floor, Ste. 2308 (✆ **021/5266-9013;** www.bodhi.com.cn), which offers bicycle tours of Shànghǎi by night, as well as day trips to Chóngmíng Island and other nearby mountains; **China Cycle Tours** (✆ **0/1376-111-5050;** www.chinacycletours.com) has daily half-day and 1-day tours of Shànghǎi by bicycle, as well as a Chinese massage bike tour (includes a 1-hr. massage in your meanderings), and a nightly city tour. **Shanghai Sideways** (✆ **0/1381-761-6975;** www.shanghaisideways.com) arranges motorbike and sidecar tours of the city on a vintage 750cc Changjiang motorcycle, with a 4-hour tour costing ¥1,100 for the first passenger, and ¥750 for the second. There are also 1- and 2-hour tours.

SHOPPING

Shanghai's top street to shop has always been **Nanjing Lu,** enhanced recently by the creation of the **Nanjing Lu Pedestrian Mall** downtown, where the most modern and the most traditional modes of retailing commingle. More popular with locals, however, is **Huaihai Zhong Lu,** the wide avenue south of Nanjing Road and parallel to it. The modern shopping malls here have better prices than you'll find on Nanjing Road.

Some of the most interesting clothes and shoes shopping in the French Concession is concentrated in the **Maoming Lu/Changle Lu** area, and around **Taikang Lu,** while the **Old Town Bazaar** in Yu Yuan is the best place to shop for local arts and crafts, and antiques.

To preview what's available and for last-minute purchases, try the **Friendship Store (Youyi Shangdian)** at Changshou Lu 1188 (✆ **021/6252-5252**). It's open from 9:30am to 9:30pm. Another store is at Zunyi Nan Lu 6 (✆ **021/6270-0000**).

Shànghǎi is no Hong Kong, but it has some of the best **antiques** shopping in mainland China. A red wax seal must be attached to any item created between 1795 and 1949 that is taken out of China; older items cannot be exported. Many hotel shops and modern department stores will ship purchases to your home, and the Friendship Store has an efficient shipping department. **Furniture,** old or new, in traditional Chinese styles can be purchased or custom-ordered at several antiques stores. Prices are high, but still lower than you'd pay at home; shipping, however, can add considerably to the bill.

Shànghǎi is also known for its selection and low prices in **silk** (both off the bolt and in finished garments). The Shanghainese people are connoisseurs of fashion and style, so shops selling **fashionable clothing** in cotton, wool, silk, and just about any imaginable material are a dime a dozen, and prices are low. **Traditional clothing** such as *qípáo* (mandarin collar dresses) and *mián ǎo* (padded jackets sometimes referred to as Máo jackets or Zhōngshān jackets) are once again fashionable purchases.

Jewelry can be a bargain, particularly **jade, gold, silver,** and **freshwater pearls,** but bargaining and a critical eye are required. **Electronics, cameras,** and other high-tech goods are not particularly good buys, but if you need anything replaced, you'll find a wide selection from which to choose.

Among **arts and crafts,** there are also especially good buys in **ceramics,** hand-stitched **embroideries, teapots, painted fans,** and **chopsticks.** These are often sold in markets and on the sidewalks by itinerant vendors. Collectibles include **Máo buttons, posters of Old Shànghǎi** (covering everything from cigarette advertisements to talcum powder), old Chinese **coins, wood carvings,** and **screens**—all priced lowest at markets and stands. Other popular crafts made in Shànghǎi are **handbags, carpets, lacquerware, painted snuff bottles,** and **peasant paintings.** Prices vary considerably. The best rule is to find something you truly like, then consider how much it is worth to you.

Markets & Bazaars

DŌNGTÁI LÙ ANTIQUES MARKET (DŌNGTÁI LÙ GǓWÁN SHÌCHǍNG) ★

This largest of Shànghǎi's antiques markets has hundreds of stalls and many permanent shops along a short lane, located on Dōngtái Lù and Liúhé Lù, 1 block west of Xīzàng Nán Lù, Lúwān (about 3 blocks south of Huáihǎi Lù). Dealers specialize in antiques, curios, porcelain, furniture, jewelry, baskets, bamboo and wood carvings, birds, flowers, goldfish, and nostalgic bric-a-brac from colonial and revolutionary days (especially Máo memorabilia). When it rains, most stalls aren't open, but the stores are. The market is open 9am to 5pm.

FÚYÒU MARKET If you like rummaging through lots of junk for the chance to find the rare real nugget, this is still the best place to do it in Shànghǎi. This favorite for weekend antique and curio hunting, located in the Cángbǎo Lóu (building) at Fāngbāng Zhōng Lù 457 and Hénán Nán Lù (the western entrance to Shànghǎi Old St. in the Old Town Bazaar, Nánshì) is also called a "ghost market" because the traders set out their wares before sunrise (when only ghosts can see what's for sale). Come as early as possible on Saturday or Sunday morning, preferably the latter, when vendors come in from the surrounding countryside. The goods are various and few are polished up; many of the items are from the attic or the farm, though increasingly also from some factory backroom that churns out modern pieces that are then scuffed up with mud to look old. Porcelains, old jade pendants, used furniture, Qīng Dynasty coins, Chairman Máo buttons, old Russian cameras, Buddhist statues, snuff bottles, and carved wooden screens are just a few of the treasures here, none with price tags. Three floors of the market building are open daily from 9am to 5pm; the weekend market (on the third and fourth floors) runs from 5am to 6pm, but tapers off by noon.

SOUTH BUND FABRIC MARKET (NÁN WÀITĀN QĪNG FÁNG MIÁNLIÀO SHÌCHǍNG) ★ This popular fabric market, originally known as the Dǒngjiādù Fabric Market, moved from its original Dǒngjiādù location in 2006, hence the name change, though some taxi drivers and hotel concierges may still refer to it by its old name. Now relocated to nearby Lùjiābāng Lù 399 (intersection with Náncāng Jiē; ✆ **021/6377-5858**) in the southeastern corner of the old Chinese city, this former outdoor market, a favorite with expatriates, has moved indoors. Hundreds of stalls still sell bales of fabric at ridiculously low prices (though prices have increased slightly since the move), from traditional Chinese silk and Thai silk to cotton, linen, wool, and cashmere, though the heavier fabrics are only carried during the colder months. Many shops have their own in-house tailors who can stitch you a suit, or anything else you want, at rates that are less than half what you'd pay at retail outlets like Silk King. Come with a pattern. Turnaround is usually a week or more, but can be expedited for an extra fee. The market is open 8:30am to 6pm.

SHANGHAI AFTER DARK

Well into the 1990s, visitors retired to their hotels after dark, unless they were part of a group tour that had arranged an evening's outing to see the Shanghai acrobats. In the last few years, however, the possibilities for an evening on the town have multiplied exponentially, and Shanghai, once dubbed the "Whore of Asia" for its debauchery, is fast becoming again a city that never sleeps.

The Performing Arts

Shanghai acrobatics are world renowned, and a performance by one of the local troupes makes for a diverting evening. These days the juggling, contortionism, unicycling, chair-stacking, and plate-spinning have entered the age of modern staging; performances are beginning to resemble the high-tech shows of a Las Vegas–style variety act. That's exactly what you'll see at the **Shanghai Circus World (Shanghai Maxicheng),** Gonghe Xin Lu 2266 (✆ **021/5665-6622,** ext. 2027), a circus of many acts, headlined by acrobats. The Shanghai Acrobatic Troupe, one of the world's best, tours the world, but can often be found performing at the **Shanghai Centre Theatre (Shanghai Shangcheng Juyuan),** at Nanjing Xi Lu 1376 (✆ **021/6279-8663**), in a 90-minute variety show with a mix of standard and inventive acts. Check with the box office as performance schedules vary seasonally.

Shanghai has its own **Chinese opera** troupe that performs Beijing opera (*Jing Ju*) regularly at the Yifu Theatre at Fuzhou Lu 701, Huangpu (© **021/6351-4668**). Most opera performances these days consist of abridgements lasting 2 hours or less (as opposed to 5 hr. or more in the old days), and with their martial arts choreography, spirited acrobatics, and brilliant costumes, these performances can be a delight even to the unaccustomed, untrained eye. Regional operas, including the Kun Ju form, are also performed in Shanghai. Check with your hotel desk for schedules.

Jazz Bars

Shanghai was China's jazz city in the prerevolutionary days (before 1949), and it is once again becoming the home of some of the most creative and exciting jazz heard on the mainland. Most of the top-end hotel lounges and bars offer jazz performances, albeit of the easy-listening variety, by international artists. The famous **Peace Hotel Old Jazz Bar Band** (www.peacehotel.com.cn) is now back at its place of origin at 20 Nanjing Rd. on The Bund, after the hotel finished extensive renovation. For more modern and improvisational sounds, check out the following spots: the long-running **Cotton Club,** Fuxing Xi Lu 8 (© **021/6437-7110**); the intimate **House of Blues and Jazz,** Fuzhou Lu 60 (© **021/6323-2779**); and the jamming and jampacked **Club JZ,** Fuxing Xi Lu 46 (© **021/6431-0269;** www.jzclub.cn).

Dance Clubs, Discos & Bars

Some of the top spots to dance the night away are the long-running if somewhat pretentious **Babyface,** Huaihai Zhong Lu 138, Shanghai Square, Unit 101 (www.babyface.com.cn); the hip, hoppin' **Bling,** Danshui Lu 66; completely refurbished **Guandii,** Gaolan Lu 2 (inside Fuxing Gongyuan, Luwan), attracting a Taiwan, Hong Kong, and hip local crowd in a garden setting; **Muse,** Yuyao Lu 28 (the New Factories; www.museshanghai.cn), with its soundproof glass screens and weekend crowds; its new sibling **Muse at Park 97,** Gāolán Lù 2, which took over one of the original longstanding clubs in Shànghǎi in the lovely Fùxīng Park; and the popular, alternative-indie-music club in a former bomb shelter, **The Shelter,** Yongfu Lu 5.

Among the best bars are the Bund-situated **Bar Rouge,** Zhongshan Dong Yi Lu 18, 7th floor, *the* bar of choice for Shanghai's beautiful jet set, its gorgeous views and creative drinks; another Bund institution, the romantic **Glamour Bar,** in M on the Bund (Guangdong Lu 20, seventh floor), with great views; the Moroccan-themed **Barbarossa** in the middle of People's Park (Nanjing Xi Lu 231); **Constellation Bar,** Xinle Lu 86 (near Xiangyang Bei Lu) with its impeccably mixed cocktails; **Cotton's,** Anting Lu 132, located in a romantic French Concession mansion with a delightful garden bar for the warmer months; the classy **Manifesto,** Julu Lu 748; and **O'Malley's,** Taojiang Lu 42 (off Hengshan Lu), China's best Irish-style pub. In Pudong, **Jade on 36,** Fucheng Lu 33, on the 36th floor of the Shangri-La Hotel, offers the best views of the Bund and Puxi at night; **The Roof @ Waterhouse,** Máojiāyuán Lù 1-3, adjacent to the Cool Docks and the Shíliùpǔ Wharf, is a lovely terrace bar on the roof of the Waterhouse boutique with gorgeous rooftop views.

Gay-friendly nightspots (subject to change, as the scene shifts but never disappears) include the mainstay **Eddy's Bar,** Huáihǎi Zhōng Lù 1877, by Tiānpíng Lù; **Kevin's,** Chánglè Lù 946, no. 4, at Wūlǔmùqí Běi Lù; **Frangipani,** Dàgǔ Lù 399, by Shímén Yī; and the part bar, part art studio **Shànghǎi Studio,** Huáihǎi Zhōng Lù 1950, no. 4, by Xìngguó Lù.

SUZHOU 苏州

81km (50 miles) NW of Shanghai

Suzhou's interlocking canals, which have led it to be called the "Venice of the East," its classic gardens, and its embroidery and silk factories are the chief surviving elements of a cultural center that dominated China's artistic scene for long periods during the Ming and Qing dynasties. Rapid modernization in the last decade has robbed the city of much of its mystique, but enough beauty remains to merit at least a day of your time. ***Note:*** For Chinese translations of establishments listed in this section, turn to chapter 16.

Getting There

Sūzhōu can easily be visited on your own. There are frequent **trains** (approx. 40 min.; ¥26–¥31 from the Shànghǎi Railway Station), with the most popular trains for day-trippers being the D196, which leaves Shànghǎi at 7:56am and arrives at 8:32am; and the D232, which departs at 8:26am and arrives at 9:02am. There are many return trains to Shànghǎi in the afternoon, including no. D5435 (departs 5:54pm, arrives 6:38pm). There is also an express direct train from Sūzhōu to Běijīng, D386, departing at 9:38pm and arriving at 7:09am. At press time, there were plans for new China Railway High Speed (CRH) trains to depart from Shànghǎi's Hóngqiáo Railway Station (Hóngqiáo Huǒchē Zhàn) that will reduce travel time to Sūzhōu to less than 30 minutes. For the most up-to-date information on Sūzhōu train schedules in English, check the website travelchinaguide.com (www.travelchinaguide.com). The **Sūzhōu Railway Station** (**Sūzhōu Zhàn; ✆ 0512/6753-2831**) is in the northern part of town on Chēzhàn Lù just west of the Rénmín Lù intersection.

Sūzhōu is also well connected by **bus** to Shànghǎi. From Sūzhōu's **North Bus Station** (**Qìchē Běi Zhàn; ✆ 0512/6577-6577**), just to the east of the railway station, buses depart for Shànghǎi (90 min.; ¥33) every 20 minutes from 6:30am to 7:40pm. There is also a direct **airport bus** (at least one every hour between 10:40am and 7:40pm; ¥82) from Shànghǎi's Pǔdōng Airport (PVG) to Sūzhōu, but no direct return bus to PVG. You'll have to first take a bus from Sūzhōu's China Eastern Airlines office at Gānjiāng Xī Lù 115 to Shànghǎi's Hóngqiáo Airport (SHA; 11 buses between 6:20am and 2:50pm; ¥50) and then take Airport Bus 1 to Pǔdōng Airport. Buses depart hourly between 10am and 4pm and at 5:30pm and 7pm from Hóngqiáo Airport to Sūzhōu.

If you'd prefer a group bus tour to Sūzhōu, check with your hotel desk. The **Jǐn Jiāng Optional Tours Center,** Chánglè Lù 191 (**✆ 021/5466-7936**), offers a convenient 1-day group bus tour to Sūzhōu and the village of Zhōuzhuāng with an English-speaking guide and lunch, departing daily between 8am and 9am and returning in the late afternoon. At press time, the price was ¥650 for adults, ¥300 for children ages 2 to 7, and free for children up to age 2. The same tour operator can also arrange a private tour with a guide, air-conditioned car, lunch, and door-to-door service (¥2,000 for one person, ¥1,200 each for two people, ¥1,000 each for three or four people). **China International Travel Service (CITS),** at Dàjǐng Xiāng 18, off Guànqián Jiē (**✆ 0512/6511-7505**), can provide an English-speaking guide and vehicle for the day at around ¥500 (lunch and entrance tickets not included), but it's just as easy, and a whole lot cheaper, to see the town on your own.

Exploring Suzhou

Central Suzhou, surrounded by remnants of a moat and canals linked to the Grand Canal, has become a protected historical district, 3×5km (2×3 miles) across, in which little tampering and no skyscrapers are allowed. More than 170 bridges arch over the 32km (20 miles) of slim waterways within the moated city. The poetic private gardens number about 70, with a dozen of the finest open to public view. No other Chinese city contains such a concentration of canals and gardens.

CLASSIC GARDENS

Suzhou's magnificent formerly private gardens are small, exquisite jewels of landscaping art, often choked with visitors, making a slow, meditative tour difficult. Designed on principles different from those of the West, these gardens aimed to create the illusion of the universe in a limited setting by borrowing from nature and integrating such elements as water, plants, rocks, and buildings. Poetry and calligraphy were added as the final touches. Listed below are some classic gardens worth visiting.

FOREST OF LIONS GARDEN (SHĪZI LÍN YUÁN) ★★ Built in 1342 by a Buddhist monk to honor his teacher and reportedly last owned (privately) by relatives of renowned American architect I. M. Pei, this large garden consists of four small lakes, a multitude of buildings, and big chunks of tortured rockeries that are supposed to resemble lions. Many of these oddly shaped rocks come from nearby Tài Hú (Lake Tài), where they've been submerged for a very long time to achieve the desired shapes and effects. During the Sòng Dynasty (A.D. 960–1126), rock appreciation reached such extremes that the expense in hauling stones from Tài Hú to the capital is said to have bankrupted the empire. Containing the largest rocks and most elaborate rockeries of any garden in Sūzhōu, Shīzi Lín can be a bit ponderous, but then again, you won't see anything like this anywhere else. The garden is located at Yuánlín Lù 23 (**© 0512/6727-2428**). It's open daily from 7:30am to 5:30pm; admission is ¥30.

HUMBLE ADMINISTRATOR'S GARDEN (ZHUŌ ZHÈNG) ★★ Usually translated as "Humble Administrator's Garden," but also translatable tongue-in-cheek as "Garden of the Stupid Officials," this largest of Sūzhōu's gardens, which dates from 1513, makes complex use of the element of water. Linked by zigzag bridges, the maze of connected pools and islands seems endless. The creation of multiple vistas and the dividing of spaces into distinct segments are the garden artist's means of expanding the compressed spaces of the estate. As visitors stroll through the garden, new spaces and vistas open up at every turn. The garden is located at Dōng Běi Jiē 178 (**© 0512/6751-0286**). It's open daily from 7:30am to 5pm; admission is ¥70 from May to September, ¥50 from October to April.

LINGERING GARDEN (LIÚ YUÁN) ★★ This garden in the northwest part of town is the setting for the finest Tài Hú rock in China, a 6m-high (20-ft.), 5-ton contorted castle of stone called Crown of Clouds Peak (Jùyún Fēng). Composed of four sections connected by a 700m-long (2,297-ft.) corridor, Liú Yuán is also notable for its viewing pavilions, particularly its **Mandarin Duck Hall,** which is divided into two sides: an ornate southern chamber for men, and a plain northern chamber for women. Lingering Garden is located at Liúyuán Lù 80 (© **0512/6533-7940**). It's open daily from 7:30am to 5:30pm; admission is ¥40.

MASTER OF THE NETS GARDEN (WǍNG SHĪ YUÁN) ★★★ Considered to be the most perfect, and also smallest, of Sūzhōu's gardens, the Master of the Nets Garden is a masterpiece of landscape compression. Hidden at the end of a blind alley, its tiny grounds have been cleverly expanded by the placement of walls, screens, and pavilion halls, producing a maze that seems endless. The eastern sector of the garden consists of the residence of the former owner and his family. At the center of the garden is a small pond encircled by verandas, pavilions, and covered corridors, and traversed by two arched stone bridges. Strategically placed windows afford different views of bamboo, rockeries, water, and inner courtyards, all helping to create an illusion of the universe in a garden. In the northwest of the garden, don't miss the lavish **Diànchūn Yí (Hall for Keeping the Spring),** the former owner's study furnished with lanterns and hanging scrolls. This was the model for Míng Xuān, the Astor Chinese Garden Court and Ming Furniture Room in the Metropolitan Museum of Art in New York City. Master of the Nets Garden is located at Kuotao Xiāng 11, off Shíquán Jiē (© **0512/6529-3190**). It's open daily from 7:30am to 5:30pm; admission is ¥30. In the summer, daily performances of traditional music and dance are staged in the garden (7:30pm; ¥100).

TIGER HILL (HǓ QIŪ SHĀN) ★ This multipurpose theme park can be garishly tacky in parts, but it's also home to some local historic sights, chief among them the remarkable leaning **Yúnyán Tǎ (Cloud Rock Pagoda)** at the top of the hill. Now safely shored up by modern engineering (although it still leans), this seven-story octagonal pagoda dating from A.D. 961 is thought to be sitting on top of the legendary grave of Hé Lǚ, king of Wú during the Spring and Autumn period (770–464 B.C.), and also Sūzhōu's founder. Hé Lǚ was reportedly buried with his arsenal of 3,000 swords, his tomb guarded by a white tiger, which was said to have appeared 3 days after the king's death (hence the name of the hill).

Partway up Tiger Hill is a natural ledge of rocks, the **Ten Thousand People Rock (Wànrén Shí),** where according to legend a rebel delivered an oratory so fiery that the rocks lined up to listen. Another version claims they represent Hé Lǚ's followers who were buried along with him, as was the custom at that time. A deep stone cleavage, the **Pool of Swords (Jiàn Chí),** runs along one side of it, reputedly the remnants of a pit dug by order of the First Emperor (Qín Shǐ Huáng) 2,000 years ago in a search for the 3,000 swords. Tiger Hill is located 3km (2 miles) northwest of the city at Hǔqiū Shān 8 (© **0512/6532-3488**). It's open daily from 7:30am to 6pm; admission is ¥60.

WATER GATES & CANALS

Your best chance of catching what remains of Sūzhōu's once-famous canal life is in the southern part of town in the scenic area just south of the Pan Pacific Sūzhōu Hotel known as **Gūsū Yuán (Gūsū Garden).** Here, you'll find in the southwestern corner **Pán Mén (Pán Gate),** built in A.D. 1351, and the only major piece of the Sūzhōu city wall to survive. **Pán Mén** once operated as a water gate and fortress when the Grand Canal was the most important route linking Sūzhōu to the rest of China. To the south is a large arched bridge, **Wúmén Qiáo,** a fine place to view the ever-changing canal traffic. Near the main garden entrance in the east is **Ruìguāng Tǎ,** a seven-story, 37m-high (121-ft.) pagoda built in A.D. 1119, which affords some excellent views of the old city from its top floors. The rest of the grounds are not very interesting. Gūsū Yuán is located at Dōng Dà Jiē 1. It's open daily from 8am to 5pm; admission is ¥25.

In the northwest part of town near Liú Yuán, **Shāntáng Jiē (Shāntáng St.),** chock-full of Sūzhōu's old houses, narrow alleyways, arched bridges, and canals, is being slowly developed for tourists and pedestrians, with entrance to seven mansions and community halls of note being included in the ¥45 entrance fee (8am–9pm; ✆ **0512/6723-6980**). You can also take the de rigueur canal boat ride here (¥25 per person).

MUSEUMS

Sūzhōu is synonymous not only with gardens and canals, but also with silk. Its silk fabrics have been among the most prized in China for centuries, and the art of silk embroidery is still practiced at the highest levels. The **Sūzhōu Silk Museum (Sūzhōu Sīchóu Bówùguǎn),** Rénmín Lù 2001 (✆ **0512/6753-6538**), just south of the railway station, takes visitors through the history of silk in China, with an interesting section on sericulture complete with silkworms, cocoons, and mulberry leaves. Weavers demonstrate on traditional looms. The museum is open daily from 9am to 5pm; admission is ¥15.

Opened in 2006, the I. M. Pei–designed **Sūzhōu Museum (Sūzhōu Bówùguǎn)** just west of the Humble Administrator's Garden at Dōngběi Jiē 204 (✆ **0512/6757-5666;** www.szmuseum.com), and reportedly the last design of his career, combines characteristics of a typical Sūzhōu garden with modern geometric designs, and is worth a visit both for the building and its well-laid-out collection of locally discovered cultural relics, including an exquisite Pearl Pillar of the Buddhist Shrine from the Northern Sòng Dynasty. The museum is open Tuesday to Sunday, 9am to 5pm (last admission 4pm); free admission.

Where to Stay & Eat

If you plan to spend the night in Sūzhōu, a traditional favorite for its quintessential Chinese garden setting is the former Sheraton Hotel and Towers, now the **Pan Pacific Sūzhōu (Sūzhōu Wúgōng Zhī Tàipíngyáng Jiǔdiàn),** Xīn Shì Lù 259, near Pán Mén in southwest Sūzhōu (✆ **800/325-3535** or 0512/6510-3388; fax 0512/6510-0888; www.panpacific.com/suzhou). With 481 rooms and prices starting as low as around ¥800 to ¥1,000 in the low season for a standard room, this five-star hotel receives rave reviews for its Chinese-style buildings, which blend seamlessly into the environment. Another excellent choice is the luxury **Shangri-La Hotel Sūzhōu (Sūzhōu Xiānggélǐlā Fàndiàn),** Tǎyuán Lù 168 (✆ **0512/6808-0168;** fax 0512/6808-1168; www.shangri-la.com), but located less conveniently in the Sūzhōu Hi-Tech Industrial Development Zone about 20 minutes west of the old town. Delightfully luxurious rooms (¥1,880, 30% discount) offer high ceilings and panoramic views of the city. Between the Sūzhōu Industrial Park and the old city is the new **Sūzhōu Marriott Hotel (Sūzhōu Wànháo Jiǔdiàn)** at Gānjiāng Xī Lù 1296 (✆ **0512/8225-8888;** fax 0512/8225-8899; www.marriott.com), a modern high-rise with all the familiar luxury rooms and amenities. Standard rooms start at around ¥1,000.

WILD CHINA: THE water village OF TONGLI (同里)

Now that Suzhou, once the "Venice of the East," has grown into a modern city, visitors searching for a more traditional Yangzi River delta water town should visit the Song dynasty town of **Tongli,** 20km (12 miles) southeast of Suzhou and 80km (49 miles) west of Shanghai. The entrance fee for all sights is ¥50; hours are from 8am to 5pm. The main attraction in Tongli is **Tuisi Yuan (Retreat and Reflection Garden) ★**, in the center of the old town. Built in 1886 by a dismissed court official, the garden contains the family's residences in the west, meeting and entertaining rooms in the center, and a small but cleverly designed landscaped garden in the east. The use of winding walkways with different-shaped windows, jutting pavilions, and a reflecting pond make the garden appear larger than it is.

West of the garden are two of the town's better-preserved traditional residences. **Jiayin Tang,** built in the 1910s as the residence of a famous local scholar, Liu Yazi, has high white walls and doorways fronted by upturned eaves. The highlight at **Chongben Tang,** also with four courtyards and three doorways, is the refined brick, stone, and wood carvings of propitious symbols such as cranes and vases. Connecting the two residences are three bridges: **Taiping Qiao (Peace Bridge), Jili (Luck) Qiao,** and **Changqing (Glory) Qiao.** It was the custom in the old days to carry a bride in her sedan chair over all three. Today, tourists can don proper wedding finery and also be carried across the bridges in an old-fashioned sedan chair.

Getting There From the bus station in the new part of town on Songbei Gong lu, **buses** run to Suzhou (hourly 7am–5pm; 35 min.; ¥8). In Shanghai, the Jinjiang Optional Tours Center at Changle Lu 191 (✆ **021/6466-2828**) can organize a private tour with an English-speaking guide, air-conditioned car, and lunch for about ¥2,200 for one person and ¥1,200 each for two. Alternatively, a Tongli tourist bus (2 hr.; ¥110 round-trip) leaves from the Shanghai Stadium at 9am (returns at 4pm) and 10am (returns at 4:30pm). Check out the government-run www.tongli.net for more information.

Where to Eat Several small restaurants along **Mingqing Jie** serve basic *jiachang cai* (Chinese home-style cooking) at reasonable prices; a meal for two averages about ¥30 to ¥50. **Nanyuan Chashe,** located in a restored Qing dynasty building, serves tea and local snacks. Local specialties include *zhuangyuan ti* (the Tongli version of braised pigs' trotters), *xiao xunyu* (small smoked fish), and *min bing* (a sweet glutinous rice pastry).

If you want to be in the heart of the old town, the best location belongs to the **Sofitel Sūzhōu (Sūzhōu Xúanmiào Suǒfēitè Dàjiǔdiàn),** Gānjiāng Dōng Lù 818 (✆ **0512/6801-9888;** fax 0512/6801-1218; www.sofitel.com/asia), with plush standards (with free Internet access) starting at ¥1,488 (up to 50% discount), but its proximity to the nearby shopping and pedestrian streets can be a bit noisy for some guests. For those on a budget, the lovely 37-unit **Scholars Inn (Shūxiāng Méndì Shāngwù Jiǔdiàn)** in the center of town at Jǐngdé Lù 277 (✆ **0512/6521-7388;** fax 0512/6521-7326; www.soocor.com) offers simple but clean standard rooms with air-conditioning, phone, TV, showers, and broadband Internet for ¥520, with discounts up to 50%.

Although hotel restaurants serve the most reliable fare and accept credit cards, Sūzhōu has a number of good restaurants that deserve to be tried, many of which are located on Tàijiān Nòng (Tàijiān Lane), also known as Gourmet Street, around the Guànqián Jiē area. One of the most famous local restaurants on this street is the more than 200-year-old **Sōng Hè Lóu (Pine and Crane Restaurant)** at Tàijiān Nòng 72 (**© 0512/6727-2285;** 8am–9pm), which serves Sūzhōu specialties such as *Sōngshǔ Guìyú* (squirrel-shaped Mandarin fish), *Gūsū Lǔyā* (Gūsū marinated duck), *Huángmèn Hémàn* (braised river eel) and the exquisitely shredded *Luóbòsī Sū Bíng* (pan-fried turnip cake). Dinner for two ranges from ¥140 to ¥250. The **Bookworm (Lǎo Shū Chóng)** at Shíquán Jiē, Gǔnxiūfáng 77 (**© 0512/6526-4720;** www.suzhoubookworm.com), is a lovely bookstore-restaurant-cafe offering coffees, smoothies, salads, sandwiches, pastas, and desserts guaranteed to cure any homesickness.

HANGZHOU 杭州

185km (115 miles) SW of Shanghai

Seven centuries ago, Marco Polo pronounced Hangzhou "the finest, most splendid city in the world . . . where so many pleasures may be found that one fancies oneself to be in Paradise." Hangzhou's claim to paradise has always been centered on its famous **West Lake (Xi Hu),** surrounded on three sides by verdant hills. The islets and temples, pavilions and gardens, causeways, and arched bridges of this small lake (about 5km/3 miles across and 14km/9 miles around) have constituted the supreme example of lakeside beauty in China ever since the Tang dynasty when Hangzhou came into its own with the completion of the Grand Canal (Da Yunhe) in 609. Hangzhou reached its zenith during the Southern Song dynasty (A.D. 1127–1279), when it served as China's capital. In 2003, much to the horror of purists, Xi Hu was enlarged in the western section with an additional causeway along its new western shoreline. New sights, shops, and restaurants were added to the eastern and southern shores. ***Note:*** For Chinese translations of establishments listed in this section, turn to chapter 16.

Getting There

Hángzhōu-bound trains leave throughout the day from the **Shànghǎi South Railway Station** (**Shànghǎi Nán Zhàn; © 021/6317-9090**) in the southern part of town (reachable by Metro Lines 1 and 3). There are a few Hángzhōu-bound trains that leave from Shànghǎi Railway Station, but the times are less convenient and the journey takes longer than from South Station. The D5685, D3105, D5551, and D5689 bullet trains all depart the South Station between 7am and 8am and arrive in Hángzhōu around 90 minutes later. If you plan to stay overnight, the D5557 leaves Shànghǎi at 6:35pm and arrives at 8:04pm while the D5681 departs at 7:03pm and arrives at 8:21pm. Return train D5680 leaves Hángzhōu at 6:24pm and arrives at South Station at 7:42pm, and the D5672 leaves at 8:50pm and arrives at 10:12pm. Soft-seat train tickets range from ¥54 to ¥75, plus a typical ¥20 service charge if purchased from hotel tour desks. A daily express direct train D310 also leaves Hángzhōu at 8:15pm and arrives in Běijīng at 7:44am.

For the most up-to-date information on Hángzhōu train schedules, check the website **travelchinaguide.com** (www.travelchinaguide.com). The **Hángzhōu Railway Station** (**Hángzhōu Huǒchē Zhàn; ✆ 0571/5672-0222** or 0571/8782-9983) is in the eastern part of town. The no. 7 or no. K7 bus connects the station to downtown and the Shangri-La Hotel for ¥2, while a taxi should cost around ¥12 to West Lake.

There are also **buses** traveling between Shànghǎi and Hángzhōu, but they are a lot less convenient than trains. A direct bus (¥100) to Hángzhōu leaves from Shànghǎi Pǔdōng International Airport (**✆ 021/6834-5743** or 021/6834-6467) and runs between 9:30am and 7pm.

Hángzhōu also has an **airport** (**✆ 0571/8666-1234** or 0571/8666-2999; www.hzairport.com; airport code HGH) with a newly built international terminal (Terminal A) about a 30-minute drive from downtown, with international connections and connections to Běijīng and other major Chinese cities, but not Shànghǎi. A taxi into town costs around ¥130 while an air-conditioned airport bus (**✆ 0571/8666-2539;** ¥20) runs to the railway station, the Merchant Marco Hotel (nearest stop to the Shangri-La Hotel), and the Wǔlínmén CAAC ticket office.

If you want to see Hángzhōu on a group tour, the **Jǐn Jiāng Optional Tours Center,** Chánglè Lù 191 (**✆ 021/5466-7936**), in Shànghǎi offers a convenient, if expensive, 1-day group bus tour with an English-speaking guide and lunch, departing Shànghǎi around 8am every Tuesday, Thursday, and Saturday, and returning in the late afternoon. The price is ¥850 for adults. The same tour operator can also arrange a private 1- or 2-day tour (on any day) with a guide, air-conditioned car, lunch, and door-to-door service for significantly more. The top Hángzhōu hotels can also organize half- or full-day city tours.

Getting Around

The city surrounds the shores of West Lake, with modern Hángzhōu spread to the north and east. The lake is best explored on foot and by boat, while sights farther afield will require a taxi or bus. **Taxis** cost ¥10 for 3km (1¾ miles), then ¥2 per kilometer until 10km (6¼ miles) and ¥3 per kilometer after that. There is a ¥1 gas surcharge on all trips. Air-conditioned **buses** cost ¥2, while tour buses with a Y prefix *(yóukè)* cost ¥3 to ¥5. Bus no. K7 runs from the railway station to Língyǐn Sì via the northern shore of the lake (Bēishān Lù) and the Shangri-La Hotel, while bus no. 27 runs along Bēishān Lù to Lóngjǐng Cūn (Dragon Well Village), and bus no. Y1 makes a loop of the lake starting from Língyǐn Sì. **Bicycles** are available for rental at public leasing points around the city, but it's a bit of a hassle as you have to first purchase a stored value card at Lóngxiāng Qiáo 20 (**✆ 0571/8533-1122**), with proof of ID and a ¥300 deposit. **Water taxis** (**✆ 0571/8802-4368;** ¥3) also ply a small section of the Grand Canal in the northern part of town from Wǔlíng Mén (Wǔlíng Gate/Westlake Cultural Square) north to Gǒngchén Qiáo and Canal Cultural Square around Xiǎohé Lù, stopping at Xìnyìfáng along the way. Hángzhōu has a tourist information hot line (**✆ 0571/96123**).

Exploring Hangzhou

XI HU (WEST LAKE; 西湖)

Strolling the shores and causeways of West Lake and visiting the tiny islands by tour boat should not be missed. A **Lakeshore Promenade ★**—a combination walkway and roadway—encircles the lake, with the busiest parts along the eastern edge of the lake. The once-busy thoroughfare Hubin Lu has now become a pedestrian walkway home to such outlets as Starbucks and Häagen-Dazs, while the area immediately to the south around Nanshan Lu and Xihu Da Dao is now known as Xi Hu Tiandi (West Lake Heaven and Earth), a miniature version of Shanghai's Xin Tiandi, right down to the *shiku men* (stone-frame) style housing and with some of the exact same restaurants. Following are the top attractions around the lake:

SOLITARY ISLAND (GŪSHĀN DǍO) ★ Situated just off the lake's northwest shore, this big island is accessible via the Xīlíng Bridge in the west and the Bái Causeway (Bái Dī) in the northeast. A roadway sweeps across the island, which is home to a number of minor sights, including the park **Zhōngshān Gōnyuán** (daily sunrise–sunset; free admission), which was once part of the old Southern Song imperial palace built in 1252, though nothing remains of it. A climb to the top of the hill affords views of the lake to the south. Also here is Hángzhōu's famous restaurant, Lóu Wài Lóu, and the large **Zhèjiāng Provincial Museum** (**Zhèjiāng Shěng Bówùguǎn; ✆ 0571/8798-0281**), which contains the oldest grains of cultivated rice in the world (developed 7,000 years ago in a nearby Hémǔdù village). The museum is open Monday from noon to 4pm and Tuesday through Sunday from 9am to 4pm; free admission.

BÁI CAUSEWAY (BÁI DĪ) ★★ Solitary Island is connected in the east to downtown Hángzhōu by **Bái Dī,** a man-made causeway providing some of the finest strolls around West Lake. Named after famous Táng Dynasty poet Bái Jūyì, who served as prefectural governor here in A.D. 822 to 824, the causeway runs east for half a mile, rejoining the north shore road (Běishān Lù) at **Duàn Qiáo (Broken Bridge),** so named because when winter snows first melt, the bridge appears from a distance to be broken.

CRUISING WEST LAKE ★★ All along the lakeshore, but particularly on Húbīn Lù and near Gūshān Dǎo (northwest corner of the lake), there are boats for hire, from 3m (9¾-ft.), heavy wooden rowboats (where you take the oars) to small junks propelled by the owner's single oar to full-fledged ferries—flat-bottomed launches seating 20 under an awning. To tour the lake in a small junk costs ¥80 for an hour. Larger passenger ferries sell tickets for ¥35 (80-min. cruise with no stops), and ¥45, which includes entrance to the Island of Small Seas (below). Ticket booths are across the street from the Shangri-La Hotel and along the east side of the lake.

ISLAND OF SMALL SEAS (XIǍO YÍNG ZHŌU) ★★ Make sure your boat docks on this island at the center of West Lake. The **Island of Small Seas** was formed during a silt-dredging operation in 1607. As a Chinese saying goes, this is "an island within a lake, a lake within an island." Its form is that of a wheel with four spokes, its bridges and dikes creating four enclosed lotus-laden ponds. The main route into the hub of this wheel is the **Bridge of Nine Turnings,** built in 1727. Occupying the center is the magnificent **Flower and Bird Pavilion,** an exceedingly graceful structure that is notable for its intricate wooden railings, lattices, and moon gates, though it only dates from 1959. It's open daily from 8am to 5pm; admission is ¥20 (included if you take a large passenger ferry to the island).

THREE POOLS MIRRORING THE MOON (SĀN TÁN YÌN YUÈ) ★★ Located just off the southern shore of the Island of Small Seas are three little water pagodas, each about 2m (6½ ft.) tall, that have "floated" like buoys on the surface of West Lake since 1621. Each pagoda has five openings. On evenings when the full moon shines on the lake, candles are placed inside. The effect is of four moons shimmering on the waters. Even by daylight, the three floating pagodas are quite striking.

SŪ CAUSEWAY (SŪ DĪ) ★ The best view from land of the Three Pools Mirroring the Moon is from the Sū Causeway (Sū Dī), the original great dike that connects the north and south shores along the western side of the lake. (A third causeway added in 2003, the Yánggōng Dī running parallel to Sū Dī in the west, is primarily for vehicles and is not as scenic.) Running nearly 3km (1¾ miles), Sū Dī, named for Hángzhōu's poet-governor Sū Dōngpō (A.D. 1036–1101), is lined with weeping willows, peach trees, and shady nooks, and crosses six arched tone bridges.

Sū Dī begins in the north across from the **Tomb and Temple of Yuè Fēi** (Yuè Miào; ✆ **0571/8797-9133;** 7:30am–6:30pm; admission ¥25), a 12th-century general famous in Chinese history for his unwavering patriotism. He was nevertheless accused of treason and executed, though his reputation was later restored. Near the southern tip of Sū Dī is **Huāgǎng Yuán** (**Flower Harbor Park;** 8am–6pm; free admission), where there's a peony garden and ponds full of fat carp and goldfish.

LÉIFĒNG PAGODA (LÉIFĒNG TǍ) ★ On the south bank of West Lake, this modern steel-and-copper pagoda affords some of the best panoramic views of the lake. Beneath the modern construction are the brick foundations of the original Buddhist Léifēng Pagoda built in A.D. 977 by Qiān Chū, the king of the Wǔyuè Kingdom. The bricks you see were part of an underground vault used to store precious Buddhist relics, including a rare woodcut sutra, which was found among the ruins. The pagoda and surrounding gardens (✆ **0571/8798-2111,** ext. 123) are open daily from 7:30am to 9pm (to 5:30pm Dec–Mar); admission is ¥40.

OTHER ATTRACTIONS

LÍNGYǏN TEMPLE (LÍNGYǏN SÌ) ★ Located in the lush hills just west of West Lake, Língyǐn Sì (Temple of the Soul's Retreat) has been rebuilt a dozen times since its creation in A.D. 326. Don't expect to find much peace here, though, as the surrounding area seems to have been turned into one large amusement park. Entrance to the whole complex (7am–5:30pm) costs ¥35, while entrance to the temple itself is a separate ¥30.

The main attraction on the way to the temple is a limestone cliff, called **Fēilái Fēng (Peak That Flew from Afar),** so named because it resembles a holy mountain in India seemingly transported to China. The peak, nearly 150m high (492 ft.), contains four caves and about 380 Buddhist rock carvings. The most famous carving is of a Laughing Buddha from the year A.D. 1000. Scholars have deemed these stone carvings the most important of their kind in southern China.

The present temple buildings go back decades rather than centuries. The main Dàxióng Bǎodiàn (Great Hall) contains a gigantic statue of Buddha carved in 1956 from 24 sections of camphor and gilded with nearly 3,000 grams (106 oz.) of gold—the largest sitting Buddha in China, and not a bad modern re-creation.

If you want to get away from the crowds, farther west along the pathway past Língyǐn Sì is a quieter pretty temple, **Yǒngfú Sì (Temple of Goodness),** set amidst groves of bamboo and willow. A climb to the Dàxióng Bǎodiàn (Grand Hall) at the top allows wonderful views of the surrounding hills and even glimpses of West Lake on a clear day. More exalted views are available at two other temples even higher up, **Tāoguāng Guānhǎi Sì,** and the 1,600-year-old **Língshùn Sì,** often known as Cáishén Miào (Temple of Wealth), which sits atop **Běigāo Fēng (North Peak Mountain).** It's a fairly strenuous climb to the top, or you can take the cable car from behind Língyǐn Sì, the preferred transportation of the crowds who ascend the mountain to pray for wealth and good fortune.

DRAGON WELL TEA VILLAGE (LÓNGJǏNG WĒNCHÁ) West of West Lake is the village of **Lóngjǐng (Dragon Well),** the source of Hángzhōu's famous **Lóngjǐng tea,** grown only on these hillsides and revered throughout China as a supreme vintage for its fine fragrance and smoothness. The best tea here is still picked and processed by hand. A popular stop near the village is the **Zhōngguó Cháyè Bówùguǎn** (**Chinese Tea Museum; ✆ 0571/8796-4221**), open daily from 8:30am to 4:30pm. Here, you can comb through the extensive displays of Chinese teas, pots, cups, and ceremonial tea implements. Admission is free.

Dragon Well Village itself, a few miles beyond the museum, is where much of the tea is grown and processed. Independent travelers are sometimes accosted by local farmers who will invite them into their homes, ply them with tea, and sell them a few pounds at inflated prices. This can actually be a good opportunity to buy this relatively expensive vintage at the source if you know how to bargain. The highest grade Xī Hú Lóngjǐng tea retails in Hángzhōu's stores for around ¥68 to ¥88 per 50 grams (2 oz.), so aim for a price well below that. It also helps if you are or are with a tea connoisseur, as vendors may sometimes try to pass off last year's vintage as the most recent. Caveat emptor!

CHINESE MEDICINE MUSEUM (QĪNG HÉFÁNG/HÚQÌNGYÚTÁNG ZHŌNGYÀO BÓWÙGUǍN) Located east of West Lake in downtown Hángzhōu, **Qīng Héfáng Lìshǐ Jiē (Qīng Héfáng Historical Street)** has been the commercial center of Hángzhōu since the late 6th century. Restored in 2001 with Míng and Qīng dynasty–style buildings, this pedestrian mall has your usual quota of teahouses, restaurants, specialty stores, and also a few small museums. The most interesting of the lot is the **Húqìngyútáng Chinese Medicine Museum** on Dàjǐng Xiāng (**✆ 0571/8701-5379**). Established in 1874 by a rich merchant, Hú Xuěyán, the original apothecary, housed in a traditional courtyard mansion, has a striking dispensary hall with Chinese lanterns, and finely carved wooden pillars and brackets. Cubicle drawers along the walls contain an assortment of herbs, leaves, barks, seeds, and roots. There are English explanations throughout. The museum is open daily from 9am to 5pm; admission is ¥10.

Where to Stay & Eat

If you're spending the night, and don't mind splurging, a number of luxury resorts have opened in Hángzhōu in the last few years. The loveliest is **Amanfayun**

(Ānmànfǎyún), Fǎyún Nòng 22, Xīhújiēdào, in the redeveloped Táng dynasty village Fǎyún Cūn in the hills just west of Língyǐn Temple (✆ **0571/8732-9999;** fax 0571/8732-9900; www.amanresorts.com). Aspiring to the simplicity of village life (Fǎyún Cūn's villagers used to tend the neighboring tea fields), the hotel has 42 rooms, suites, and villas scattered among the original, but now refurbished (and unmarked) village houses. There's under-floor heating, free Wi-Fi, daybeds, but no bathtubs (except in the Aman spa), and TVs are available only on request. Lighting is on the dim side, but service is discreet and first-rate, making for a private pampering retreat. Rooms start from ¥3,944. To the west, nestled within the XīXī National Wetland Park is the **Banyan Tree Hángzhōu (Hángzhōu Xīxī Yuèróngzhuāng),** Zǐjīngǎng Lù 21 (✆ **0571/8586-0000;** fax 0571/8586-2222; www.banyantree.com). Highlights here include the resort's tranquil, traditional Chinese-garden setting with arched bridges and flowing streams, its 72 rooms and villas (all newly built), fully furnished with all the expected luxury amenities (including bathtubs), and the award-winning Banyan Tree Spa. Rooms start from around ¥2,500 to ¥2,700.

Closer to West Lake, the most atmospheric hotel is still the five-star, 382-unit **Shangri-La Hotel Hángzhōu (Hángzhōu Xiānggélǐlā Fàndiàn),** Běishān Lù 78, on the north shore of West Lake (✆ **800/942-5050** or 0571/8797-7951; fax 0571/8799-6637; www.shangri-la.com). Standard rooms, spacious and comfortable, cost ¥1,650 to ¥2,250, depending on whether they have garden or lake views. Expect around 35% discounts off the rack rate. Another top choice is the classy **Hyatt Regency Hángzhōu (Kǎiyuè Dàjiǔdiàn),** Hěbīn Lù 28, on the northeastern shore of West Lake (✆ **0571/8779-1234;** fax 0571/8779-1818; www.hangzhou.regency.hyatt.com). Rooms are plush and modern, with standard doubles ranging from ¥1,600 to ¥2,050 (30%–50% discount). Request a nonsmoking room if so desired.

For a cheaper alternative, the 60-unit **Jiéxīn Century Hotel (Jiéxīn Shìjì Jiǔdiàn),** also known as the Yìyuàn Bīnguǎn, Nánshān Lù 220 (✆ **0571/8707-0100;** fax 0571/8708-7010), on the eastern edges of the lake, is affiliated with the China Academy of Fine Arts and offers clean doubles from ¥680 (discounted to around ¥300 in low season).

For dining, the Hángzhōu institution **Lóu Wài Lóu,** Gūshān Lù 30 (✆ **0571/8796-9023**), on Solitary Hill Island, between the Xīlíng Seal Engraving Society and the Zhèjiāng Library, is a tourist favorite. Hours are daily from 11:30am to 2pm and from 5 to 8pm; local specialties, such as Beggar's Chicken *(jiàohuà jī),* the excellent local *dōngpō* pork, and Lóngjǐng shrimp can all be tried here. Or avoid the whole tourist trap (and prices) and head to where locals go for their Hángzhōu food fix: the perennially crowded **Wài Pó Jiā (Grandma's Kitchen),** with branches all over the city, including at Húbīn Lù 3, second floor (✆ **0571/8510-1939;** www.waipojia.com; 10:30am–2pm and 4:40–9pm). There's a picture menu with delicious local dishes; dinner for two ranges from ¥100 to ¥200. The international restaurants at **Xī Hú Tiāndì (West Lake Heaven and Earth),** on the southeastern shore of the lake, offer plenty of comfort food.

Hangzhou After Dark

If you're staying overnight in Hangzhou, the **Impressions West Lake** night show, 82 Beishan Rd. (opposite Yuefei Temple and Shangri-la Hotel; ✆ **0571/8796-2222;** www.hzyxxh.com/en) is a must-see. Performed on the West Lake (at the Yu

Lake portion), it was choreographed by Zhang Yimou, the famed movie director who directed the opening ceremony for the Beijing Olympics. The show incorporates the natural landscape with stunning use of light and music, employing hundreds of local actors. The show keeps the natural surroundings intact with eco-friendly initiatives, including the audience seats perched above the lake, which retract into the water during the day. The hour-long show is performed every night at 7:45pm, and on Saturday there's also a second show at 9:15pm. The steep price ($38 a ticket) is worth it; ask your hotel to book you a ticket.

THE SOUTHEAST

by Christopher D. Winnan

A quick glance at the topography of this area speaks volumes. Apart from a few scattered river deltas, this is harsh and unforgiving mountain country, with just a narrow ribbon of land next to the sea, into which most of China's modern coastal cities are all tightly squeezed.

Although the indigenous peoples of this area were assimilated by Han colonists long ago, the isolated terrain has fostered a strong feeling of independence in the coastal dwellers, forever aware that "the mountains are high and the emperor far away." In fact, it was probably their relative isolation and the establishment of small cell network economies that led to their early successes.

Few people realize that this was the part of the world that Columbus sought when he first set sail for the East Indies. While Europe had been blindly staggering through the Dark Ages, some of the foremost trading ports of their time had developed in this region. From then on, it was only a matter of time before the industrialization that swept across 18th-century Europe was to have similar disastrous effects in China. China's xenophobia, which appears currently to be aimed at Japan, was earlier focused on England, and China laid the blame for the subsequent "Opium Wars" firmly on the British, rather than on the emerging global economy and its corporate mercenaries, like the East India Company. Endless statues, museums, and memorials illustrate the "humiliations" of the Opium Wars to maximum effect for propaganda purposes, and yet nobody would dream of starting a cigarette war in retaliation for the 10,000 Chinese who now die from smoking-related illnesses every week. Still, beyond the misguided nationalism, this region is a treasure-trove of history for those willing to dig just a little bit further than the official media mouthpieces.

You'll experience the relentless pace of the modern economy in business cities like Guangzhou and Shenzhen. Tourists are relatively few compared to the unending stream of businessmen. Traveling in the region provides an opportunity to see the process of industrialization in action.

Summers are hot and extremely humid around the coast; the mild months of October through March are the best times to visit, although some offshore islands are appreciated year-round for their breezes. Inland Jiangxi suffers from drier but furnacelike summers and chilly dank winters, making spring and autumn the best times to travel. ***Note:*** Unless otherwise noted, hours listed for attractions and restaurants are daily.

THE BAMBOO TRIANGLE: MOGANSHAN (莫干山), ANJI (安吉) & LIN'AN (临安)

Moganshan 莫干山

Moganshan (719m/2,360 ft. high) was first used as a vacation destination in 1890 for Western missionaries and their families to escape the Shanghai summer furnace. By its peak in 1930, some 160 Western-style stone retreats dotted the cool glades, including 32 occupied by wealthy Chinese, and even Generalissimo Chiang Kai-shek brought his new bride Soong Mei-ling to Moganshan for their honeymoon in 1927. The Nationalists, never far behind, established their own resort called Wuling on the northeast side of the mountain.

The area's architecture is of an impressive variety, from the over-the-top Western opulence of the Chiangs' villa and the sprawling Chinese-style compound of Du Yuesheng ("Pock-marked Du," the notorious Green Gang boss from Shanghai who helped Chiang massacre the Shanghai workers' movement in 1927), to the simpler elegance of the Western vacationers' stone mansions. There were two churches, a swimming pool fed by icy water, seven tennis courts, and an amateur dramatics society. Many of the original houses, built by Western architects using the local gray dressed stone, still survive.

Mao Zedong was a frequent visitor to the area, and used a group of old stone foreign villas throughout the 1960s. By then Moganshan was a secret retreat for "the leadership" in case of war, with air-raid shelters for the Big Potatoes. Some of the houses even have secret tunnels that go right down to the valley.

ESSENTIALS

Zhejiang Province, 60km (36 miles) N of Hangzhou, 200km (124 miles) E of Shanghai

GETTING THERE Air-conditioned **buses** to Moganshan's nearest town, Deqing (also known as Wukang) leave every morning at 6:30, 11:50am, and 12:40pm from **Shanghai's Old North Station** at 80 Gong Xin Lu near Qiu Jiang Lu. This is in walking distance of metro line 3 and 4 Baoshan Lu Station, costing ¥55 and taking 4 hours. Alternatively, take the bus or train to Hangzhou (approximately an hour and a half) and then catch a bus to Wukang. An alternative is to jump on one of the semiofficial buses from Shanghai **South Railway Station** to Hangzhou; touts are all over the place. It costs about ¥50. Then make your way by bus or taxi from Hangzhou.

Regular buses leave from **Hangzhou North Bus Station,** on Moganshan Lu, at least every hour, and take about 40 minutes to Wukang bus station ¥15 (40 min.). In

The Southeast

Wukang you take a ¥50 mini bus or a ¥60 taxi to Moganshan, which takes another 45 minutes. A taxi from Hangzhou will run to about ¥250 and takes 1½ hours.

From Deqing, negotiate with a taxi or minivan outside the bus station to take you up to Moganshan. Taxis are normally ¥60, while a minivan can be had for ¥50. Insist that you go to the top of the mountain, not the village at the foot of the mountain or the ticket gate. There is now a new road through to Anji that cuts the trip from Moganshan down to about 45 minutes and costs about ¥80.

VISITOR INFORMATION Talk to Mark or Joanna at Moganshan Lodge for historical details, suggested walking routes, and even a couple of cross-country paths over to Anji. Tori, who lives close by to Prodigy, is also a valuable mine of information. The official Moganshan Travel Service number is ✆ **0572/803-3402.** The only local map available can be picked up at the bus station, but the map is in Chinese only, focuses more on Huzhou to the north, and only has a tiny insert map for Moganshan.

[Fast FACTS] MOGANSHAN

Post Office The post office (8am–4:30pm) is on Yinshanjie.

Visa Extensions The officers at the PSB (✆ **0572/803-3303**) are friendly but as with Anji, extensions are probably better handled back at Hangzhou (p. 482), where there are plenty of excellent English-speakers.

EXPLORING MOGANSHAN

Moganshan is crisscrossed with a maze of stone pathways and steps, and away from the small tourism industry there is plenty of wonderfully isolated mountain wandering to be had. Stone steps laid with expert precision over a century ago wind through the mountains. Flower gardens laid by generations of foreigners have gone wild, resulting in a mad cacophony of brilliant colors between the bamboo. And of course there are the imposing villas themselves: One of my own favorites is the impressive entrance to the China International Tea Culture Institute Communication Center, where huge blocks of stone lock together to create walls, stairs, and floors, all set into the mountain itself like a geological mosaic.

QINGLIANG TING As you climb the steep, windy road, near the Du Yue Sheng Villa, there is a great lookout point from which to view the surrounding sea of bamboo. Views down to the plain and across the hillside are spectacular on clear days.

SWORD FORGING POOL (JIAN CHI) Legend (or local tourism PR, at least) has it that Mo Xie and Gan Jiang, a pair of married sword smiths who lived in the 5th century B.C. and after whom the mountain is named, devoted their lives to making two incomparably beautiful swords for the emperor. According to lore, they would sit by this pool fed by three waterfalls and polish the swords they had just forged. The local administration bureau has done a remarkably good job of building walkways, wooden pagodas, and viewing points. Unfortunately, they are now charging an entrance fee of ¥60.

Steep steps lead down from the main Yinshanjie area but more interesting is the small **pagoda** about 100m (328 ft.) up and away to the left of the falls. What at first looks like a simple ornamental pagoda sits atop a cave that appears to be an early interrogation chamber complete with bars in the ceiling.

WHERE TO STAY

Hotels abound in Moganshan, and prices vary by day of the week and by season, with the peak in July and August and medium rates from April to June and from September to October. Be sure to ask about the Korean built earth-bag development to the west of Prodigy when you arrive. At the time of writing they were just beginning construction but it looks to be one of China's first true eco-tourism projects.

Moganshan Castle (Moganshan Zhuang) Originally called Mount Clare by foreigners, this spur of the mountain was the site of some of the earliest houses, in the very late 1800s. Its popularity is explained by the fact that there is a gully on the north side that sucks up a constant draft, which in the days before air-conditioning was the choicest spot on the mountain (Moganshan can be as much as 7° cooler than Shanghai in summer). These days the hotel is still impressive from the outside but retains a country-village feel to some of the rooms, which may be a little rural for some visitors, especially considering the high prices.

Wuling Cun, bldg. no 7. ✆ **0572/803-3421.** Fax 0572/803-3209. 30 units. ¥480 standard room; ¥900–¥2,600 suite. Rates include breakfast. Chinese credit cards only. **Amenities:** Restaurant; coffee shop; meeting room. *In room:* A/C, TV.

Moganshan Shangri-La Mountain Villa (Moganshan Xiangelila Shan Zhuang) Despite the fancy name, for those on a lower budget this is a reasonable option. It is a simple Chinese guest house with a friendly owner and good country-style food. This is where many mountain bikers stay when they come up for the weekend from Shanghai and Hangzhou. Try to get a room in the new building on the upper floor. While the rooms themselves are pretty basic, especially compared to the luxury hotels farther up the mountain, the place does have a nice shaded outdoor seating area, where you can chill with a few beers after a strenuous day on the slopes.

Fatouxiang, Shanshuiling no 2. ✆ **1395/726-5599.** 35 units. ¥100 standard room. No credit cards. *In room:* A/C, TV.

Prodigy Outdoor Club (Hu Wai Yun Dong Ji Di) ★★ Prodigy is nestled in the forest at the back of the mountain rather than in the resort area, so there is no need to pay an entrance fee. It is aimed at mountain bikers, hikers, and adventure sports fans, for whom there are plenty of great opportunities. The base can organize fishing, boating, climbing, swimming, and even canyoning and there is an extensive website to inspire the adventurous. The food is great, especially anything that comes out of their wood-fired pizza oven. Animal lovers will also feel at home here as the dogs and cats are all very friendly (one of the dogs, Happy, gave birth to 12 pups the night that I was there).

Fatouxiang, Houwucun. www.prodigyoutdoor.com. ✆ **0572/804-1168.** Mobile 18969260037 25 units ¥130 Dorms; ¥360–¥420 standard room. Rates include breakfast. **Amenities:** Restaurant; mountain bike and equipment hire; outdoor and rooftop terraces.

WHERE TO EAT

In Yinshanjie you can find several restaurants, hotels, and a Western-run coffee shop/restaurant. The local restaurants are in the village center. Here you'll be served tasty home-style food; be sure to try the local delicacies, including wild partridge, celery, mushrooms, and tea—all hunted down in the area's bamboo forests.

Moganshan Lodge (Song Liang Shan Zhuang) ★ WESTERN/CHINESE Mark Kitto, the founder of China's most popular English-language magazine, is enjoying his retirement immensely up in Moganshan, after the Shanghai government forcibly nationalized his publishing company (the phrase "to be kittoed" has quickly entered the expat vernacular, meaning to be screwed by the Chinese authorities, as his book *China Cuckoo* fully details). Now he and his family welcome escapees from Shanghai. The mouthwatering Full Fry Up includes all the usuals along with mushrooms, kidneys, and home-cured bacon, and lunch and dinner options include a three-course pork stroganoff a la Moganshan.

Yinshanjie. ✆ **0572/803-3011.** www.moganshanlodge.com. Meal for 2 ¥200. No credit cards. 11am–11pm.

Anji 安吉

Thanks to the enormous urban growth of cities like Shanghai, Hangzhou, and Suzhou, tourism has exploded in the bamboo forests inland, and this combined with the fact that a handful of scenes from the movie *Crouching Tiger, Hidden Dragon* were filmed here in 1999 makes Anji a very popular destination for city dwellers.

The vast swaths of bamboo have actually only appeared in the last few decades and before the mass deforestation of the Great Leap Forward, this area was mainly mountainous stretches of majestic pine forest. It is clear that the influence of foreign missionaries on Moganshan had a significant impact, as many of the mountain smallholders still hold Christian beliefs, and this might even stretch back as far as the Taiping Rebellion, when heavenly troops used these inaccessible areas as a stronghold against the imperial forces. More recently, the tortuous mountain passes provided safe havens for refugees fleeing the Japanese occupation of Shanghai and other large cities. Anji alone has over 90,000 hectares of bamboo plantations and is said to produce 12 million commercial bamboo poles annually ***Note:*** For Chinese translations of selected establishments listed in this section, turn to chapter 16.

Essentials

Zhejiang Province, 63km (34 miles) SE of Hangzhou, 220km (136 miles) SE of Shanghai

GETTING THERE Thanks to the expressway, Anji has rapid access to Hangzhou and Shanghai. The nearest airport is Xiaoshan airport on the other side of Hangzhou. **Anji Bus Station** (✆ **0572/522-9571**) is well served with comfortable modern coaches to and from Hangzhou North Station on Moganshan Lu 758 (✆ **0571/8809-7761;** 63km/34 miles; ¥26) almost every half-hour from 5:30am to 6:20pm. On this route, notice how the environment changes slowly from dirty concrete to an ocean of green as you leave Hangzhou and approach Anji's vast swathes of bamboo. Buses also run to Shanghai (220km/136 miles) Nanjing (240km/149 miles), and Suzhou (170km/106 miles). There is a left luggage office that is open from 5:20am to 5:30pm.

GETTING AROUND The downtown area of Anji is well served by ***sanlunche*** (cycle rickshaws) that will happily ferry you short distances for ¥5. For getting out of town, metered taxis are a better option, with flagfalls starting at ¥5; after that, it's ¥2.20 per kilometer. City bus lines run across the downtown with the no. 1 and no. 3 lines being the most useful for tourists. All have a flat fee of ¥1.

VISITOR INFORMATION Just down the road from Anji Bus Station is the Zhuyuan Travel Agency (586-588 Pu Yuan Da Dao; ✆ **0572/588-1766**), which has lots of brochures about the area. Ask for Ben, who is helpful and speaks reasonable English.

[FastFACTS] ANJI

Banks, Foreign Exchange & ATMs The main **Bank of China** (8am–5pm) is on Sheng Li Xi Lu and offers currency exchange. They also have an ATM for international credit cards.

Internet Access There is a cluster of net bars on Ying Bin Da Dao just across from the Xing He Holiday Hotel.

Map Only one city map is available at the moment and that is Chinese only. It costs ¥5 and is available from the shops around the bus station.

Post Office The post office (7:30am–9:30pm) is at Sheng Li Dong Lu (✆ **0572/502-3957**).

EXPLORING ANJI

The city itself is little more than furniture factories and construction, with most of the real sights a short bus ride outside of the town. Apart from the bamboo areas there has been an explosion in tacky theme parks recently. Unless you want to see tigers on scooters, or shoot your friends with paintballs, it is probably best to avoid the Zhongnan Baicao Garden, the Counterstrike Theme Park, and the bizarrely named Peasant's Paradise (Nong Fu Le Yuan). Be on your best behavior with the locals, as a surprisingly large number of them seem to have *chu tou* (bamboo-cutting billhooks) hanging on the back of their belts.

Bamboo Museum and Gardens (Zhu Bo Yuan) ★ A taxi from the bus station will cost around ¥20, but the budget conscious can hop on to any of the minibuses that head south for ¥3. The museum is directly behind the Sunny Holiday Resort.

The museum has half a dozen different display halls, all of which are fascinating in their own way. One deals with all the hundreds of different species of bamboo, another reveals some of the many products that have been made from bamboo in the last 6,000 years, while a third focuses solely on musical instruments fashioned from bamboo. Even so, aficionados may be disappointed at the limited scope of some of the displays.

Bamboo Museum and Gardens, Ling Feng Scenic Zone. ✆ **0572/533-8988.** www.cnbamboo.cn. Admission ¥60. 8am–5pm.

Big Bamboo Sea (Da Zhu Hai) From the bus station, take a mini bus out to the village of Gangkou. From there, jump in a three-wheeler for ¥5 to get to the park itself. The road is currently under construction, and on weekends is full of huge tour buses. A ¥45 ticket gains you access to several places, including a teahouse and a five-story lookout tower, but that all pales in comparison to the magnificent culms of the giant bamboo that grows in the area. While the Big Bamboo Sea tourist attraction is probably only worth an hour of your time, it is a good starting point for exploring the rest of this green ocean. In summer, the groves are cool and shaded. In winter, the mountain breezes summon a mysterious chanting as the huge plants move rhythmically back and forth. More serious hikers can get their bearings from the lookout tower and strike out to find a path that leads southwest, to Tian Huang Ping.

Gangkou County. ✆ **0572/521-0000.** www.dzhcn.com. Admission ¥50. 10am–5pm.

Tian Huang Ping Hydro Electric Facility (Tian Huang Ping Dian Zhan) Built in 1884, this mountaintop reservoir is the largest in Asia and second largest in the world, with perhaps the world's largest dirty bathtub ring on the upper tank where the water rises and falls on a regular basis. There is a small visitors' center, but it is the views out onto the surrounding bamboo forests that are the real draw up here. Down below is the actual power plant, where six enormous reversible pumps churn out a whopping 2,000 MVA that help bring the throbbing cities of Shanghai and Hangzhou and Suzhou to life.

Tian Huang Ping. ¥10 from Anji Bus Station ✆ **0572/504-1888.** Admission ¥50 for both sites. 8am–8pm.

Hidden Dragon Falls (Chan Long Pu Bu) ★ Of the more than 60,000 hectares (148,000 acres) of bamboo forest around Anji, this is one of the less industrial spots. There are around 60 individual waterfalls here, many with rope and bamboo bridges stretching across deep white water chasms. This area was the scene of some of the bloodiest fighting during the Taiping Rebellion (1853–1864) that aimed to topple the already corrupt and incompetent Qing Dynasty (1644–1912). If you are staying up in one of the farmer's guest houses, you can enter Hidden Dragon Falls from the very top late in the afternoon and save the ¥80 entrance fee. This is probably a good idea as it is a very steep climb up from the main gate, especially on some of the more precarious scaffolding walkways, where the sides of the gullies are simply too steep for rock-hewn steps. Back up at the top is a superb lookout point that provides amazing views over the entire valley. It is also a great spot to spend the early evening if you are lucky enough to be staying up here.

Hidden Dragon Falls, south of Tian Huang Ping. ✆ **0572/511-2357.** Admission ¥80. 10am–5pm.

SHOPPING

What appears at first glance to be a wholesale bamboo market at Tian Huang Ping Lu (10am–4pm) is actually a shopping stop for package tour day-trippers, although there are a few shops worth looking at. A favorite is the **Tianzhuzhuang Bamboo Fiber Company** (**✆ 0572/502-9911**), which has an extensive clothing stock, all made from 100% bamboo fiber, everything from socks and tennis sneakers to bath towels and winter long johns. I also like the outlet of the **Bamboo Charcoal Factory** (**Zhu Ye Cun; ✆ 0572/520-9588**), which sells bamboo shampoo, soap, and other toiletries, though prices have jumped up recently.

WHERE TO STAY

Up in the mountains surrounding Anji are literally hundreds of small guest houses to choose from, all offering basic accommodations at reasonable prices. A good example is the **Mountain Clan House (Gao San Ren Jia Ke Zhan),** Daxi Village, Chan Long Mountain (**✆ 0572/511-2505** or 1356/727-6184; twin ¥120, including breakfast), easily distinguishable by its two red lanterns. The owner, Miss Zhang, is a local bamboo farmer and will happily take guests out into the forest to instruct them in the art of cutting new shoots and picking white tea. She also provides meals of healthy local fare for between ¥20 and ¥30, including local specialties such as spicy cuckoo *(la wei bu gu niao)* and meat and potato stew *(rou shao tu dou li)*. She can also arrange a taxi from the bus station for you at just ¥100, a big discount on the ¥160 that local drivers will ask for.

Xing He Holiday Hotel (Xing He Jia Er Jiu Dian) Thanks to a very recent refurb, this is now one of the best value options in Anji, and certainly the best choice of all the other budget hotels on this road.

Yin Bing Da Dao Lu 505. www.ajxhjr.com. ✆ **0572/513-1001.** Fax 0572/513-1068. 52 units. ¥180 single; ¥220 standard room; ¥600 suite. No credit cards. **Amenities:** Restaurant; karaoke. *In room:* A/C, TV, fridge.

Sunny Holiday Resort (Xiang Yi Du Jia Cun) ★ About 10 minutes south of the city, beside the Bamboo Museum and Gardens is the beautiful Sunny Holiday Resort. Officially it's a four-star resort but it usually has standard rooms available at under ¥400 at many times of the year. The grounds are perfectly manicured and there is a pontoon bridge over the small dam, leading to the miniature Mount Lingfeng, complete with twisting staircases up to the summit. Furnishings are typically unimaginative, but this is made up for the large windows that give the rooms a light and airy feel as well as excellent views out over the grounds. The staff are very friendly and helpful. If you are with a group and looking for a special local treat try the Bamboo Shoot Banquet priced at ¥2,880 and ¥1,080, which might sound a lot, but both include at least 16 different dishes.

Anji Mount Lingfeng Scenic Spot. www.zjsunny.com. ✆ **0572/533-8888.** Fax 0572/533-8777. 149 units ¥380 standard room; ¥648 suite. AE, DC, MC, V. **Amenities:** 2 restaurants; bar; exercise room; pool. *In room:* A/C, TV, fridge, hair dryer.

WHERE TO EAT

Both of the larger hotels mentioned above have a selection of reasonable restaurants to choose from. A string of Western-style coffee shops have sprung up downtown, opposite the post office. These serve both local dishes and rough approximations of Western food.

Just down the road from the bus station is **Feimipin,** 763-769 Pu Yuan Da Dao (✆ **0572/566-6660**), a nice little cafe and bakery that is great for stocking up lunch and drinks before you head out exploring for the day. The exotic ice teas include kumquat, basil seed, and aloe. You should only buy drinks downstairs—a ¥12 fruit juice from the bakery costs a whopping ¥45 if purchased upstairs.

Niu Pai Ke Steak Restaurant, 180-184 Chang Shuo Dong Lu (✆ **0572/587-7677**), cannot seem to decide whether it is a fast food joint or an upmarket salon. Whatever the case, the food is good and staff are very welcoming. There are plenty of set meals including a T-bone, a sirloin, and an American Plum Set (steak with locally made plum sauce), all of which are very palatable.

Although difficult to find these days, look out for the local bamboo beer (Anji Bamboo Science Beer), which tastes great, especially when it is served in shallow pottery bowls. Other local specialties to look out for are *sha bing,* savory unleavened bread cooked in the same way that Indians fire chapattis, and delicious at only ¥.50 each. The area is famous for its hickory nuts *(shan he tao)* and its walnuts *(he tao)* with both deserving their well-earned reputations. You should also try the dried sweet potatoes *(hong shu gan)* that are wonderfully tender and the dried sliced kiwis *(qi yi guo)* that taste sweeter than most candy.

Lin'an 临安

Lin'an is yet another small Zhejiang town that has exploded in recent years, thanks to small manufacturing and an enormous overseas market. Unlike other towns that focus on just one item, such as buttons, bra clips, or coat hangers, Lin'an has concentrated on one raw material, bamboo. While touted as a green product, it has still devastated the area's natural forests and local authorities are now trying to diversify into multi-cropping strategies including hickory and ginkgo nuts. The city's other big market has been tourism. Back in 2004, the town hit the domestic radar by opening a naked swimming beach. Unfortunately, it only lasted 15 days before outraged authorities closed it down.

ESSENTIALS

Zhejiang Province, 45km (28 miles) SE of Hangzhou, 200km (136 miles) SE of Shanghai

GETTING THERE Lin'an is only half an hour away from **Hangzhou's West Bus Station,** which is down near Xixi Wetland Park. Big unmissable blue buses with the word LINAN emblazoned down the side run every 40 minutes at a cost of ¥15 arriving at the "chang tu ke yun zhong xin" old Station, 1 Ling Tian Lu (✆ **0571/6372-2070**). Hangzhou West Bus Station is one of the best in the country with a very helpful information desk and connecting buses to all parts of the city. Buses coming from Anji cost ¥26, take about 90 minutes and arrive at the Lin'an New West Station (pronounced "qi qe dong zhan"; Qian Wang Jie; ✆ **0571/6371-9562**). Although Lin'an does not have a train station, there is a train ticket office at Jin Cheng Jie (✆ **0571 8517-0900**), which is very useful if you want to get your tickets in advance.

GETTING AROUND Metered taxis are available, with flagfalls starting at ¥5; after that, it's ¥2.20 per kilometer. City bus lines are useful for tourists. All have a flat fee of ¥1.

[Fast FACTS] LIN'AN

Banks, Foreign Exchange & ATMs The main **Bank of China** (8am–5pm) BOC dual locations either side of Peoples Park (Wan Ma Lu) offers currency exchange. They also have an ATM for international credit cards.

Internet Access There are a number of net bars on Jin Cheng Jie, up from the Qian Wang Hotel.

Map Only one city map is available at the moment and that is Chinese only. It costs ¥5 and is available from the Xinhua Bookstore on Chen Zhong Jie.

Post Office The post office (8:30am–5:30pm) is at Qian Wang Jie.

EXPLORING LIN'AN

Prince Qian's Tomb (Qian Wang Ling) This is green oasis of peace and quiet among all the new skyscraper residential developments. The gardens are worth a stroll, even if the building is less than exciting. Most of the complex was built in 1997 when 3,000 year-old statues were excavated by what is now Yijing Road. One was a foundation stone, one an ancient mandarin and the third, a "Xiezhai," a mythical Chinese ram that can see through any lie and punishes evil doers with a mighty horn.

Yi Jing Jie. ✆ **0571/503-4887.** Admission ¥30. 10am–5pm.

Zhejiang Forestry University (Zheijiang Ling Xue Yuan) The East Lake campus is one of the most attractive university grounds in China and worth a visit if you want to get away from the downtown area.

South Gate—Nan Da Men Yi Jing Jie (take a K7 bus). ✆ **0571/6374-0038.** Admission free.

Tianmushan Ancient Forest Park ★ While Lin'an is famous for its bamboo, just a few hours outside of town are China's oldest and largest trees. The cryoptmeria conifers are a close relation to the sequoia and the redwood that completely covered the East China coastline many hundreds of thousands of years ago. Unfortunately, these are now the only remaining stands and tourist exploitation means that they are disappearing fast. From the ticket office it's a 6-hour climb up quite steep stairs to the ancient forest. Unless you're a serious hiker, we recommend that you take the mini bus from the main entrance around the back route for an extra ¥50. Once up at the Longfengjian area, check out the champion tree, the tallest in China at over 46m (151 ft.), and have your picture taken hugging the girths of some of the other monsters that still remain. But do so fast, as these fine specimens are experiencing a rapid die off. Hardcore hikers will find another ancient path behind the Lion Sect Temple that climbs an additional 500m (1,640 ft.) to the mountain peak, which is actually a flat plateau with a rather uninspiring meteorological center.

Tianmushan, take a bus from Lin'an old bus station (chang tu ke yun zhong xin, near the Qianwang Hotel) to the small town of Yuqian, which is about 1 hr. and ¥7 away. From there change buses (1 runs every 40 min.) to get to the West Tianmushan ticket office and resort. ✆ **0571/6375-1978.** Admission ¥150. 10am–5pm.

SHOPPING

Tianmushan Bamboo shoots are absolutely delicious (especially if you enjoy things like pickled onions) and are widely available in small packs of five for ¥4 upwards. The area is also famous for is green tea and hickory nuts, both of which are considerably more expensive.

WHERE TO STAY

Most businessman stay at the central, Qianwang Da Jiu Dian (518, Chen Zhong Jie; ✆ **0571/6371-8888**), a very standard four-star business hotel, but there are better options around the city.

Home Inn (Ru Jia Kuai Jie Jiu Dian) This familiar brand name is a much better option than the Cartier Hotel (Ka Di Ya Jia Er Jiu Dian) across the road and the Lin'an Square Hotel (Lin'an Guang Chang Da Jiu Dian). This one was recently gutted and refitted by the Home Inns chain and although the rooms are not huge, they are quite comfortable.

159 Ling Xi Rd. www.homeinns.com. ✆ **0571/6375-9997.** Fax 0571/6375-2668. 50 units. ¥169 standard room; ¥580 suite. International credit cards accepted. **Amenities:** Breakfast bar. *In room:* A/C, TV, Internet.

Wonderland Hotel (Zhong Dou Qing Shan Hu Pan Da Jia Dian) ★★ Well out of town near the K5 bus terminus, this huge five-star has luxurious rooms that look out onto Qingshan Lake. When Chinese basketball star Yao Ming got married, this is where he came to take those all important wedding photos. As well as all the usual five-star facilities, there are extensive gardens and even bikes for hire if you want to explore the rest of the lakeside, although they are asking a whopping ¥40 per hour for the privilege.

88 Shengyuan Rd., Jincheng Ave. ✆ **0572/803-3336.** Fax 0572/803-3274. 320 units. ¥380–¥480 standard room; ¥880 suite. International credit cards accepted. **Amenities:** Chinese restaurant; Western restaurant; coffee shop; lobby bar; airport pickup service, barbecue; chess/poker room; currency exchange; fitness facilities; flower shop; gift shop; karaoke; meeting facilities; Ping-Pong room; pool/billiards room; indoor and outdoor swimming pools; handicapped friendly rooms; room service; sauna, tennis; ticket office; free Wi-Fi in public areas. *In room:* A/C, mini fridge, hair dryer.

WHERE TO EAT

Sun-dried bamboo shoots (suan gan) are sometimes described as a kind of bamboo sausage that is woked with oil, garlic, peppers, meat and vegetables. *Chang hua dao qie mian* are long, flat, noodles served with soup and vegetables. Toppings include beef, pork, chicken, tofu, pork lungs, pork kidneys, and of course, bamboo sausage. Blackened dry tofu *(dou gan)*, commonly eaten individually as a snack, can also be stir-fried with vegetables and goes well with Chinese potato pancakes *(tu dou bing)*. In the Laio Bakery (Chen Zhong Jie, near the Qian Wang Hotel), staff with belt loop speakers and mikes offer deafening service as well as some interesting toastie concoctions and tasty meatball hotdogs.

Camphor Tree Cafe (Xiangzhang Shu Fan Dian) CHINESE/WESTERN Located inside the ZFU campus on the first floor of the student union building, this cafe is very popular with international students and teachers. Chinese and western dishes are served in a quiet, comfortable atmosphere.

Zhejiang Forestry University (Zheijiang Ling Xue Yuan). ✆ **0571/6374-0045.** Meal for 2 ¥80. No credit cards. 11am–11pm.

WUYISHAN 武夷山

Fujian Province, 369km (231 miles) NW of Fuzhou, 364km (228 miles) SE of Nanchang

I freely admit to having a love/hate relationship with Wuyishan. Choose the right time of year, get away from the domestic tourists, and you'll find one of the best places in China for hiking, climbing, and exploring. Unfortunately, the resort area has a well-deserved reputation for rip-offs, but there are still ways to avoid the scams and enjoy one of the most spectacular parts of China.

The resort and the main town are split into two separate areas by the airport and the railway station. While the surrounding scenery is gorgeous, the resort itself is an unsightly sprawl. Most of the hotels are on the east bank of the Chongyang Xi, with a little spillover onto the west bank, where the Fengjingqu (scenic area) can be found. This is prime Chinese tourist territory. Avoid summers, the week-long public holidays at the beginning of May and October, and weekends between those two holidays. But in November, daytime temperatures are a pleasant 59°F (15°C), just right for walking, and the fall colors are just as impressive as anywhere in Vermont. Wuyishan resort in winter and spring is usually a couple of degrees colder than the park area on the other side of the river, because the white plastered hotels and concrete reflect the heat. The mountains, however, are a thick black color and therefore absorb the heat. An important Song dynasty Confucian scholar, Zhu Xi, founded an academy on the mountain in 1183, during the Song dynasty. He taught there for 10 years and his teachings would influence Confucian thought in China up to the 20th century.

The subtropical forests carpet the mountain and in 1837 a French explorer discovered many new species of birds and animals. Since then more than 600 new species of animals have been found and the mountains are especially rich with snakes and insects. As early as the Qing dynasty, under Emperor Qianlong, the mountain was a protected nature reserve where fishing and logging was forbidden. In 1999 it became a UNESCO World Heritage Site.

Note: For Chinese translations of selected establishments listed in this section, turn to chapter 16.

Essentials

GETTING THERE The **airport** is served by flights from Beijing, Guangzhou, Shanghai, and Xiamen. The first three are generally limited to one per day but there are at least eight flights per day to Xiamen with plans to make it at least one per hour in the future. There are occasional flights from other cities. Bus no. 6 passes the airport entrance and runs the 8km (5 miles) to the resort for ¥3. The **railway station** is a little farther from the resort, also passed by bus no. 6, and three-wheelers run a shuttle the few hundred meters to the main road. There are useful train services from Hangzhou (509km/318 miles), Shanghai (710km/444 miles), Xiamen (590km/369 miles), Quanzhou (593km/371 miles), and other cities. Ticket offices are open from 3:30 to 5:30am, 8:30am to noon, 1:30 to 5:30pm, and 8:30 to 11:30pm. The station's left-luggage facility is open only from 6:30am to noon and 2:30 to 11pm. Agents in Wuyi Shan want a ¥40 commission for rail tickets. Fortunately, an official ticket office is located just next to the Xiamen Airlines Office in the Bank of China building that does not charge any commission. The train from Xiamen is now especially busy with tickets being booked up 3 weeks ahead last time I visited. I ended up taking an express bus to Fuzhou and then an overnight train from there.

GETTING AROUND Within the resort, everything is walkable. **Bus** no. 6 is the most useful of all; coming from Wuyi Shan town, it passes both the railway station and the airport, runs through the middle of the resort down Chongyang Dao, turns west along Wangfeng Dao, crosses the Chongyang Xi (river), and continues to Xing Cun. Minibuses in fairly good condition with air-conditioning cost a little more, but rides are typically ¥1. *Miandi* (minivans) to most destinations are ¥2 if you use them like buses, with others hopping on and off; you can use them to get to Xingcun for the *zhufa* (bamboo rafts), to get to the airport, or to get to the railway station. Bus no. 5 runs to the railway station when trains are scheduled, but not frequently. *Sanlunche* three-wheelers that charge ¥2 are everywhere. If you try to take one any distance, they will be straight onto one of their taxi friends to take over. It is generally assumed that you want to get wherever you are going as quickly as possible, when really the three-wheelers offer the chance to see and hear nature up close, something that most domestic tourists miss as they zip from sight to sight in their air-conditioned coaches. The resort has hundreds of shuttle buses for ticket holders as well as some newly imported German theme park type trains that give the whole place that little extra Noddy in Toyland feel.

[Fast FACTS] WUYISHAN

Banks, Foreign Exchange & ATMs The **Bank of China** (8am–5:30pm), with an ATM outside, is on San Gu Jie.

Internet Access While the usual Internet bars abound, there are a number of free access machines at the otherwise unhelpful tourist information office. This is located on the opposite side of the main intersection from Bank of China next to the large KTV complex.

Post Office The post office (summer 7:50am–9pm; winter 8am–5:30pm) is on Wang Feng Lu.

Wuyi Shan Fengjing Qu 風景區

The Danxia landforms of the Wuyishan are most commonly viewed from a bamboo raft (*zhufa* or *zhupai*) on **Jiu Qu Xi (Nine Bend Stream).** This area experienced tumultuous volcanic activity in the past and is now characterized by a maze of precipitous cliffs, huge vertical columns, and intricate gorges. On the western side of the stream, the rocks are volcanic, while to the east the geology is mainly sandstone with steep cliffs and flat tops.

This provides a spectacular contrast when viewed from the river itself, a very calm 9.5km (6 miles) that takes about an hour and 40 minutes. The river is only a meter deep in some parts and is clear enough to let you see the bottom. It's at its highest in July, and if it rises to a 2m (5½-ft.) height, trips are suspended.

Tickets can be purchased through your hotel or at the ticket office in Xincun, which is just behind the new Best Western Hotel. Take one of the many mini buses up to **Xing Cun** from Chongyang Dao or Wangfeng Lu for ¥3. Alight at the main traffic circle next to the vendors that sell a local type of pita bread so fiery that it ought to come with a government health warning. Walk up the hill to the post office and turn right heading down into the village proper, through wooden houses where weavers work bamboo the same way they have done for hundreds of years. Take the first major right turn down toward the river. The ticket office is down on the right, about 5 minutes' walk altogether. The *zhufa* depart in groups between 7:30am and 4pm, each with six life-jacketed passengers. In the peak season, tickets are so popular that they have to be booked at least 1 day in advance; they cost up to ¥180, but the official price is ¥100. Take a spare pair of shoes in a plastic bag if possible.

The river ride of about 9.5km (6 miles) takes an hour and 40 minutes, a lot of it right next to the main highway. The river is only a meter deep in some parts and is clear enough to let you see the bottom. It's at its highest in July, and if it rises to a 2m (5½-ft.) height, trips are suspended.

These days there is an almost continuous stream of rafts, scaring away what little is left of the wildlife. A much better way to appreciate the scenery is on foot in the park. Tickets are currently priced at ¥75 for a half day, ¥140 for 1 day, ¥150 for 2 days and ¥160 for 3 days.

Climbing **Da Wang Feng** officially takes 1½ hours, but it can be scaled by the moderately fit in an hour. At the top, the views are principally over the confluence of the rivers and the not particularly attractive sprawl of the resort. As you climb, you have several choices of route, which all lead eventually to the top; the routes include two horizontal galleries cut into the rock, the higher of which involves slightly less bending. It can be slippery when wet. The lower stairways wind wonderfully, but in some cases they are only wide enough for one—awkward when you encounter tour groups. At some points, the only thing that will catch you if you fall is a stand of bamboo. Nearly all the tour groups climb **Tianyou Shan** first thing in the morning so leave it until the afternoon. The paths are more solid, are broader, and have more hand holds than the paths of Wuyi Shan. Views are pretty, and you look down to the loop of the river's fifth and sixth bends, around which might drift some rafts. Halfway up, a pretty waterfall, multi-threaded and glued to the cliff face, seemingly moves in slow motion. Near the top are a house built for Chiang Kai-shek's wife, Soong Meiling, and a flat open space with teahouses. As you jostle your way to the top, the fantastic views will make you consider extending your stay. The turnoff is about halfway to Xing Cun, and the entrance to the mountain about 5km (3 miles) from the resort. A *miandi* will bring you here for ¥10, dropping you a 10- to 15-minute walk from the gate. If you're fit, the climb will not take more than about 30 minutes.

YU NU FENG 玉女峰

Hop off one of the many Xing Cun bound buses about halfway to the **Tian You Feng** at the signs for Yu Nu Feng, and you will see a small path leading down to the river and one of our favorite spots in the area known as **Shui Guang Du.** Few domestic tourists stop here as they are ferried between sights and so the grassy banks are ideal for a picnic lunch or a lazy afternoon. A small bridge leads away to the left, which is a great spot to take a picture beneath the iconic **Jade Beauty Peak (Yu Nu Feng).** (This is the one that is featured on the covers of all the maps and other promotional literature.) Just behind the bridge is a charming little set of stepping stones that leads under the main road and off to another set of steps just begging to be explored.

BEYOND WUYISHAN: SANDU & XIAOJIANG ★★

Heading north on the train from Wuyishan, the first few valleys are extremely impressive and provide enjoyable hikes. Take the no. 6 bus up to the Wuyishan town bus station, and jump on any of the buses headed north toward Da'an. For a warm hike, you might want to jump off at Sandu and follow the path that goes up behind the village to a little known temple. The wooden split-level shrine at the rear was especially impressive with its octagonal skylight bathing the tree deities in bright golden rays. From there the path goes up into orchards and pine forests, curving around to come down an hour or so later at the northern end of the village. Intrepid types can bushwhack their way up through the bracken and undergrowth following the loggers trails right up the top ridge, but beware of steep slippery slopes.

Off to the left of the main drag, the road through the sleepy village of Xiaojiang heads up to a large reservoir, where you can cross the bridge just in front of the flood gates. The earthen walls and tile roofs of Dong Tou Village should quickly come into view and from here you want to head up into the hills curving to the left so that you will descend back toward the main road. Low clouds roll majestically across the slopes of firs, bamboo, and abandoned terraces. The tracks range from steep overhangs that would stress out your average alpaca, to broad stone staircases that have obviously been used by tea farmers and pack animals alike for many centuries. As long as you keep the river valley to your right, it really does not matter where you descend, as all of the routes are fascinating in their own way. One route emerges just above Luo Dui, a stone village that has barely changed in the last hundred years and still boasts an impressive *miao* (ancestral hall) and numerous shrines. Another zigzags down through the ancient terraces, which for me with the lack of cafes and guest houses were far more impressive than Longsheng. Rushes have all but taken over many of the levels and this means you might surprise the odd grazing cow or water buffalo.

Another interesting hike heads under the railway bridge and past the small saw mills behind Da'an. Follow the track beside the stream up past the Aohu village orchards until you reach an abandoned apartment building. After this, there are many small apiaries and some fantastic swimming spots where the flow of the river has carved out natural bowls in the granite. Keep your eyes open for footprints, especially those of the elusive clouded leopard.

Try to get back to Wuyishan before 4pm, since buses stop running early. Locals pay ¥5 for a seat in a taxi or on the back of a motorbike back to Wuyishan, but foreigners are usually asked to pay ¥50.

Shopping

Various gift shops around town sell mountain produce such as dried roots, berries, and mushrooms, and specialist shops sell medicinal products (yes, including snake oil), but everything is ridiculously priced. Wuiyshan is also home to Lapsang Souchong, a delectable smoked black tea. A wholesale tea shop (Xiang Fa Yun; Cha Chang Yi Qu, Wu Yi Da Dao; ✆ **0599/530-2348**) is just around the corner from Dico's. Apart from lots of decorative wooden presentation boxes and other packaging, they also have other products such as tea oil and tea sets, which make nice gifts.

Nightlife

"Impression Dahongpao" is the fifth large-scale musical to which the acclaimed director Zhang Yi Mou has added his name. This one is about 70 minutes long, features a cast of hundreds, and has seats that revolve 360 degrees for added effect. Tickets range from ¥160 to ¥600 but if you have seen his shows in Yangshuo or Hangzhou, this might seem to be more of the same. For tickets, talk to your hotel or go to the San Yan Dao Fu Travel Agency (Guo Jia Lu Yo Du Jia Qu; ✆ **0599/515-3777**).

Where to Stay

Hotels are legion (with hundreds in the resort area, referred to as **Wuyi Gong,** alone), most of them the elevator-free, four-story model. Those that date from a building boom in 1995 are run down and worth avoiding, but some others just 2 or 3 years old are not much better. Generally speaking the resort is overpriced, almost two or three times the price of somewhere like Ligyun or Mile. The resort is very busy at Spring Festival (Chinese New Year) and during the first weeks of May and October. But on weekdays for the remainder of the May-to-October period, supply still outstrips demand, and you can pay half price. Outside those times you need not pay more than a third of the first asking price. Almost all the hotels have two or three stars; in addition to the choices below, glance into a few others. Avoid those with "beauty parlors" and those that offer karaoke. Although temperatures are well above freezing even in December, make sure that your hotel has the heat turned on and has hot water 24 hours during low season.

Wuyi Shanzhuang (**Wuyi Mountain Villa;** ✆ **0599/525-1888;** www.wysvilla.com) is the resort's most prestigious hotel, but staff tend to ignore the foreign customer in hopes he will go away. Budget options are out there but require some seeking out.

Fa Ting Jie Dai Chu Located in the greenest part of the resort, this is half guesthouse, half courthouse. Next door is the Yue Yi Hotel, which is not actually a hotel but a restaurant. Rooms are nothing to write home about but apart from the stream of overhead flights, rooms are quiet. And when you pull back the curtains in the morning, do not be alarmed to see that the parking lot is full of police cars.

Next to Yue Yi Hotel, Wuyi Gong. ✆ **1351/508-2933.** 30 units. ¥120 standard room. No credit cards. *In room:* A/C, TV.

Migrant's Home (Hou Niao Jia) Aimed squarely at younger travelers, this is more of a guesthouse than a regular hotel. The doubles with balconies at the front

Cheap Eats on the Street

The cheapest and probably the best food can be found at a handful of you zha stalls outside the Baodao Hotel. These nocturnal street eateries, frequented mainly by local foot-massage girls, offer a wide range of pan-fried meat and vegetables on kabob sticks. The small pumpkin cakes are delicious, and fried banana with ketchup seems to be a popular if strange local specialty.

are the best rooms, although there are also singles at the back and dorms downstairs. The front patio has a swing, barbecue, and very chatty mynah bird. This is also a good place to eat with fair prices.

42 Lantang Cun. (Cross the bridge out of the resort area and turn right, walking until you see the main traffic gate to the park area. Turn left just before this and head up the hill past the old grain house on the left. Bear right past the wooden bridge and the Migrants Home is off to the left.) www.houniaojia.cn. © **0599/525-2103.** Fax 0599/525-5555. 15 units. ¥30 dormitory; ¥110–¥200 standard room. Chinese credit cards only. *In room:* TV (in double and triples only).

Wuyishan Holiday Hotel (Jia Ri Hua Yuan Jiu Dian) ★ This place is characterized by its big airy rooms with lots of windows and very friendly and helpful *laobanyang* with three adopted strays who quickly befriend guests that bring them small meaty snacks. Chinese breakfast at just ¥15 is served on the nice patio and the corner rooms get great views of the mountains.

Lu Yo Du Jia Qu (San Gu). www.05995232088.com. © **0599/523-2088.** Fax 0599/523-2090. 50 units. ¥150 standard room. No credit cards. *In room:* A/C, TV.

Where to Eat

All the restaurants here have exotic displays of mushrooms, snakes, and bee larvae, as well as standard meat and vegetables. Unfortunately, proprietors are especially keen to take advantage of rich but scarce foreigners.

The handful of restaurants opposite the Holiday Hotel are as good (or as bad) as any other. Try asking for the following local specialties that are very tasty: wild celery fried with baby tree ears *(ye qing cai chao xiao mu er),* Indian pennywort omelet *(lei gong cai chao dan),* baked yellow horn fish *(men huang jiao yu),* and yam consommé *(san yao gen).* There are no English menus. The most comfortable dining is inside hotels, overpriced and of modest, if acceptable, quality. (Most three-star hotels charge under ¥100 for a meal for two.) Look out for local specialties including bears paws, Jian'ou salted preserved duck, and a plethora of snake dishes, including stir fried snake bones, stir fried snake eggs, and even stewed snake eyeballs.

QUANZHOU 泉州

Fujian Province, 593km (371 miles) SE of Wuyi Shan, 109km (68 miles) N of Xiamen

According to Marco Polo, Quanzhou, then known as Zaytun, was "one of the two greatest havens in the world for commerce." Franciscan friar Odoric da Pordenone, who was in China from 1323 to 1327, effused that it was "Twice as great as Bologna." The great Moroccan explorer Ibn Battuta, who visited the area in 1345 to 1346, lavished it with praise, "The harbor of Citong is one of the greatest in the world—I am wrong; it is *the* greatest. I have seen there about a hundred first-class junks together; as for small craft, they were past counting." The Franciscan bishop of Zaytun wrote of Genoese merchants in 1326, and the city had other foreigners, including many Arabs.

After the Ming expulsion of the Mongol Yuan dynasty in 1368, China gradually closed up, and by the time of Europe's next contact, via the Portuguese in the 16th century, Zaytun had withered. In the 19th and 20th centuries, while almost all its neighbors became treaty ports with resident foreigners and trading, Quanzhou was somehow overlooked. Today, Quanzhou's center has been overtaken by a different kind of commerce, mainly cheap sneakers and plastic sandals. The suburbs are filled with factories and white-tiled blocks of apartments. The downtown area is even more depressing, with Wenling Nan Lu, the main drag, consisting primarily of karaoke clubs interspersed with sleazy hotels. Still, Quanzhou's interesting history does manage to surface in places, and the city has a clutch of fairly new museums and a host of sites to explore outside of town. ***Note:*** For Chinese translations of establishments not on the map in this section, turn to chapter 16.

Essentials

GETTING THERE After 13 years of experimental opening and closing, **Quanzhou Jinjiang Airport** (✆ **1379/950-3010**) is now fully open with domestic flights to Beijing, Guangzhou, Shenzhen, Wenzhou, Nanjing, Shanghai, Zhoushan, Changsha, Hangzhou, Nanchang, and Wuhan as well as international flights to Manila. The number 16 bus takes passengers the 45-minute ride from downtown for just ¥4.50. The railway line down to Quanzhou is new, and the **railway station** is in the northeast suburbs. Bus nos. 19 and 23 run from the railway station to the center of town. Train tickets are on sale from 6:30 to 11:30am, 1:30 to 5pm, and 6:30 to 8:30pm. Trains to Zhejiang and elsewhere in coastal Fujian have to perform long loops. There are no longer any sleeper trains for Wuyi Shan. For that you have to travel to Xiamen, but the early riser can enjoy the winding mountain line by taking the K955 at 6:32am and arriving at 4:53pm (K9856 and K955; 594km/368 miles). There is a downtown train ticket office on Wenling Nan Lu (✆ **0595/2228-3192**).

The main bus station, the **Keyun Xin Zhan,** is full of yelling louts and has buses to Wuyi Shan (but the train is far better); to Xiamen (20 departures 6:35am–5:40pm; luxury bus ¥38). Some express buses to Xiamen drop off passengers at the airport entrance. Quanzhou does have its own Jinjiang airport but for short trips it is best just to bus it in from Xiamen.

GETTING AROUND While most youngsters seem to have bicycles with strange plastic spokes, older motorcyclists will ceaselessly beep at you and wave spare helmets, offering you a ride. Jetta **taxis** are ¥6 for 2km (1¼ miles), then ¥1.60 per kilometer up to 4km (2½ miles), then ¥1.80 per kilometer up to 30km (19 miles), then ¥2 per kilometer up to 50km (31 miles), and after that, ¥2.20 per kilometer. At night, from 11pm to 5am, rates begin at ¥1.80 per kilometer. To get to the suburbs, **buses** charge a flat fare of ¥1 on entry; buses without air-conditioning but with conductors charge ¥2.

VISITOR INFORMATION The **Quanzhou International Club** (**Quanzhou Guo Ji Ju Le Bu;** ✆ **1379/950-3010**) is organized by David Zeng (david@jinshow.com) of the Puppet Museum, who is a great source of local information. **CITS** is on the 1666, Wen Ling Nan Lu (✆ **0595/228-3192**). CITS's sales manager **Jackie Cai**

Quanzhou 泉州

(Cai Jian Jing) has also been reported as being very helpful. His office is in the Overseas Chinese Hotel, Baiyuan Road 362000 (✆ **0595/598-5940;** fax 228-2366).

[FastFACTS] QUANZHOU

Banks, Foreign Exchange & ATMs The main branch of the **Bank of China** (8–11am and 2:30–6pm) is in Fengze Jie just west of the Xiamen Airlines Hotel. Counter 14 handles checks and credit card withdrawals; it also handles cash exchanges during the same hours. ATMs at branches around town all accept foreign cards.

Internet Access The **Dadi Wangba** (8am–3am; ¥2–¥3 per hour) is just east of the PSB on Dong Hu Lu. The **Huanqiu Wangba** is at Zhuangyuan Jie 127, and another *wangba* is opposite it at no. 138. Both are full of chain-smoking youngsters playing shoot-'em-ups and hurling obscenities at each other. A quieter alternative, with two dozen or so PCs, is the public library at Donghu Lu 752 (8–11:30am and 2:30–10pm; ¥2 per hour).

Post Office The main post office (8am–8pm) is at Wenling Bei Lu 209, at the junction of Jiuyi Lu.

Visa Extensions Extensions are harder to obtain here than in most places. The PSB on Dong Hu Lu (✆ **0591/2218-0323;** Mon–Fri 8–11am and 3–6pm) requires evidence of the possession of $100 per day, for a single extension of up to 30 days.

Exploring Quanzhou

Maritime Museum (Haiwai Jiaotong Shi Bowuguan) ★ The Maritime Museum used to be one of the most interesting museums in China, especially for anybody who already has an interest in the sea. We recommend that you bypass the first floor with its xenophobic displays. The real gems are on the second floor: a priceless collection of hundreds of intricate scale models representing the whole of China's seafaring history. Each ship was handmade by master craftsman Chen Yanhong, and the level of detail is extraordinary. Highlights include imperial warships, caterpillar-like articulated vessels, and battleships that conceal secret launches. The English labels are better than you might expect, although, as so often seems to be the case, the authors claim the Chinese invented anything worth inventing long before the West. In this particular field, this includes anchors, rudders, watertight compartments, paddle-wheels, and even catamarans. Despite this pomposity, the construction of the models is of excellent quality and nobody leaves unimpressed. Unfortunately, much of the money for repairs, cleaning, and maintenance has been siphoned away to support other local museums, and many of the now-dusty exhibits are damaged, masts snapped by overenthusiastic visitors and sails ripped by grabbing youngsters.

Back on the first floor directly below the seafaring exhibit, visitors will find a collection of carved stonework, dating from the peak of Quanzhou's heyday. The displays are a lot less accessible for the casual visitor than the model ships but their significance is attested to by the fact that UNESCO funds are being used to help save these historical artifacts. Some of the inscriptions are carved in Syriac script, the written form of Aramaic, the language alleged to be spoken by Jesus. Five hundred years ago, this place was already a magnet for travelers of the world. Even though he ended up on the other side of the world, Columbus risked everything to find this already mythical city that had been made famous long before in the seven voyages of Sinbad, the tales of Marco Polo, and maybe even the mystical Christendom of Prester John.

Donghu Lu. ✆ **0595/2210-0561.** Admission ¥10. Tues–Sun 8:30am–5:30pm.

Quanzhou Museum (Quanzhou Bowuguan) The brand-new Minnan-style Quanzhou Museum is so new that you may be the only visitor in the place. The museum provides the usual political propaganda, but this is made up for by a very interesting *National Geographic*–style documentary, describing the *Taixing* wreck and how treasure hunters salvaged more than 350,000 pieces of porcelain from the ocean floor.

At press time, not all exhibits were open and the shops were just in the process of stocking their shelves, but one item caught my eye, the *Guide to Quanzhou Tourism.*

Although the descriptions are very brief and overly official, at just ¥15 it is a useful book to have if you plan to explore this area further.

North section of Xihu Lu. ✆ **0595/2228-3914.** Admission ¥10. 9am–5:30pm.

Quanzhou Taiwan Friendship Museum (Quanzhou Ming Tai Bowuguan) Both inside and outside, the design of this museum is impressive. The exterior seems to spread to fill as much area as possible while inside are three galleries of exquisite Minnan mosaic designs. In the main foyer is an 18m-high (59-ft.) gunpowder painting by a local artist that was created for the opening ceremony in May 2007, with the legend "Same wood, same seed, same root." The text of the displays, however, is filled with racist and venomous comments. My advice? Ignore the propaganda and enjoy the art.

North section of Bei Qing Lu. ✆ **0595/2275-1800.** Free admission with ID. 9am–4pm.

Cai Family Residence (Minnan Jian Zhu Da Guan Yuan) About 30 minutes out of the main town, this well-preserved complex of 16 Southern Fujian Qing dynasty residences is an interesting contrast to the conditions at nearby Chongwu (p. 510). Complexity abounds with fantastic relief carvings decorating almost every nook and cranny, as well as large wide boulevards that give a feeling of spaciousness. Look out for lots of building surprises such as drainpipes in the style of shubunkin and the large hollow Indian coral tree at the rear that has been adopted as home by a local stray. From Quanzhou bus station, take a no. 9 bus to Guan Qiao and then change onto a bus that heads out to Nan'an and get off outside the Yilida Hotel. Turn right off the main road and continue walking for about 10 minutes.

Nan'an City, Guan Qiao Town, Zhang Li Village. ✆ **0595/8689-2290.** Admission ¥15. 10am–6pm.

Statue of Zheng Chenggong At 38m (125 ft.) high, 42m (138 ft.) long, and weighing in at 500 tons, this huge monument is visible from just about any part of the city. Atop a mountain beyond the northern suburbs, this enormous statue portrays Zheng Chenggong, a Ming pirate who routed the Dutch from Taiwan and who, unlike most other pirates from around the world, has been a national hero ever since. The best way to get to this massive monolith is as a side trip on the way back from Chongwu. Once the general, who is seated astride an equally gigantic stallion, comes into view, jump off the bus and hail a moto-taxi to take you the rest of the way for ¥5 to ¥10. Up close, the monster statue of the great patriot on horseback is a bit disappointing, being of a hollow metal-plate construction rather than local stone. Still, the views of Quanzhou are excellent.

Puppet Museum (Muou Bowuguan) ★ While the idea of a puppet museum may sound a little dull, Quanzhou is full of surprises. Have you ever seen a puppet disrobe, smoke, or pour itself a drink? The marionettes in this small private museum have up to 30 strings and can be manipulated in the most fascinating ways. Ask the proprietor David Zeng to show you around as he can explain all the fascinating carving and outfit embroidery techniques. The range of puppets available for sale is equally impressive at very reasonable prices. There is also a second shop with lots more of interesting souvenir opportunities at Jin Xiu Zhuang, Li Cheng Qu, Da Xi Jie 124 (✆ **0595/2228-6924**).

Hou Cheng Wen Hua Jie 6, behind the Ashab Mosque. ✆ **0595/2216-3286.** www.jinshow.com. Free admission. 9am–9pm.

A Walk Around the Walls of Chongwu 崇武 ★★

A little over 50km (30 miles) from Quanzhou, Chongwu has one of the best-preserved city walls in China. Measuring 2.5km (1½ miles) long and dating from 1387, it is not yet the victim of much official recognition, and consequently is more natural than walls at Pingyao (p. 233).

The bus ride there departs from the main bus station every 30 minutes from 7am, with the last one heading back at 6pm; the fare is ¥9.50. The often crowded minibus takes an indirect 90-minute route through towns and villages almost entirely devoted to stone masonry. Stone is the traditional building material in this area. Houses are blocky, plain, and flat-roofed, with the occasional external stairway giving them a decidedly Middle Eastern look, reinforced by the tendency of local women to wear head scarves.

Before you even arrive at the old town, get off the bus and walk the last part of the way to see the amazing output of all the local **stone factories.** Alight at the circle with the three laughing Buddhas (known in Chinese as *Mi Le Fo*) and the huge triangular billboard. From there on in, not only do statues of every description line the road, but the front lots of the factories have thousands more. Apart from a complete pantheon of Asian deities, there are local celebrities of every age, right up to modern times with Mickey Mouse, Pokemon, and Hello Kitty. The biggest factories are clustered together, and a visit to these is especially recommended. Start out at **Haoxiang Stone,** Shan Xia Industrial Zone (✆ **0595/8761-9999;** www.haoxiang.cc); **Shi Xing Stone,** which is almost next door (✆ **0595/8760-9999;** www.cn-shixing.com); and then maybe ask for Miss Ye, who speaks a little bit of English at the **Hua Feng Sheng Stone Carving Company** (Shan Xia Chi Hu Gong Ye Qu), Shan Xia Industrial Zone (✆ **0595/8760-6210;** www.hfs-stone.come). The stockyards of these places are amazing, with everything from aliens and snowboarders to sumo wrestlers.

Modern Chongwu, reached after 1½ hours, is typically hideous, but walk straight from the bus terminus, and where the road swings right, go straight on up the narrower street of small shops. Continue uphill until you arrive in less than 10 minutes at the modest east gate of the old walls, its enceinte still intact. Through that gate, turn immediately right into an alley called Cui Shi Xiang, which is barely wider than your shoulders, and find steps up. Turn right and walk clockwise.

The wall is very solid, with varied construction styles much less regular than walls elsewhere. It is overgrown at times, but accessible. At each gate in the wall the enceinte is entered from one side with a turn forcing you to pass through the wall itself. You can look down on the passage of beeping motorbikes, and on meat sold from open trestles in the shade. Elsewhere, geese, ducks, and hens in backyards look up startled at your passage.

This makes an interesting contrast to other old towns such as Lijiang and Dali, where the whole layout has been expanded to make it more accessible for tourists. Inside Chongwu, conditions are cramped and claustrophobic. The stench of open sewers pervades the narrow alleys and yet motorbikes scream though the dark confines. Here is an authentic view of what really happens when an ancient Chinese town meets the 21st century head on.

After the north gate the wall has been cleared a little and rises to views of the sea across the roofscape. There's a modern statue of a heroic defender looking out to sea, and a little temple on the wall topped with marvelous dragons with green bodies and red tails and faces. Firecracker residue and incense ash indicate the temple's popularity. Another temple below is worth descending to see, its walls papered with lists of contributors to its restoration, and its hall again topped with rampant polychromic dragons.

Below the east gate, a group of bad modern statuary looks out over broad sand beaches, and there's a modern lighthouse at the southeast corner. It still is worth a visit (for ¥25) if you have not been to any of the statue factories, as it contains a truly bizarre sight, the 24 virtues of filial piety. Taken from a collection of popular Chinese folk tales available in every bookstore, the statues are great examples of weirdness.

On the south side there's more beach and neat topiary-lined pathways. At the south gate, the **Nan Men Guandi Miao** is a new but remarkably elaborate temple, its stone pillars carved fantastically into dragons. The ceiling inside is finely carved and gilded, and interior pillars are fabulously carved with birds and figures giving great liveliness to dead stone.

A ticket office at the base of the gate is unmanned but would attempt to charge ¥2 to visitors entering from the beach side if anyone could be bothered. The exterior of the wall here is bearded with creeper, and beyond it are cold-drink and ice-cream sellers, sly seafood restaurants, horse rides, lookout points labeled as suitable for photography, and more bad statuary. The final section is more overgrown but there's a clear path.

Where to Stay

Hotels in Quanzhou are unexceptional, and many at the three- and four-star levels are overpriced considering their dowdiness. Much renovation and new construction are going on, and there may be more choices by the time you arrive.

GP Hotel (Hao Di Fan Shang Wu Jiu Dian) While the corridors up on the guest floors still resemble the labyrinthine antechambers of a darkened karaoke club, the rooms, especially those at the front, are surprisingly comfortable. The bathrooms feature open-space planning. Best of all is the great location, literally at the rear of the Puppet Museum. By the way, GP stands for Good Place.

Bai Yuan Lu 1, Zhong Nan Shang Xia. ✆ **0595/2806-0000.** Fax 0595/2805-9928. www.goodplacehotel.com. 124 units. ¥160 standard room; ¥280 business room. AE, DC, MC, V. **Amenities:** Karaoke. *In room:* A/C, cable TV, Internet.

Quanzhou Hangkong Jiudian (Xiamen Airlines Quanzhou Hotel) An upper-end three-star hotel, with a free shuttle bus to Xiamen Airport, this fresh, modern, 16-story tower with well-maintained rooms has above-average service, except in the first-floor coffee shop, with its awful coffee, which is understandably always empty. This is a typical businessman's hotel where conformity to general standards is more important than imaginative design. Still, the bathrooms are slightly larger than would otherwise be expected, though on the downside the beds seemed much harder than the general standard. Larger and with more facilities than the Jian Fu, it has higher prices to match.

Fengze Jie 339. ✆ **0595/2216-4888.** Fax 0595/2216-4777. 177 units. ¥560 standard room; ¥998 suite. Rates include breakfast. 10% service fee not charged. 40%–50% discounts available. AE, DC, MC, V. **Amenities:** 2 restaurants; fitness room. *In room:* A/C, TV, video on demand, fridge, hair dryer, Internet, minibar.

Where to Eat

The liveliest eating is in the **Meican Shi Jie (the Delicacy Street)** running north from the arch on Jinhuai Jie, 1 block east and parallel to Wenling Bei Lu. Here rows of food stalls with tables and chairs in the open air or in air-conditioned interiors compete for your business until the small hours. There is seafood in buckets, *niupai* (beefsteak—a local favorite), dumplings, kabobs, hot pot, Sichuan food, and even Lanzhou "pulled" noodles. Especially interesting are the army-themed restaurants with pictures of aircraft carriers and stealth bombers on the walls. For more budget options such as rice boxes and barbecue, have a stroll up and down Yin Jin Jie opposite the Xinhua Bookstore. The excellent local wheat beer, Huiquan, will please anyone fond of Hoegaarden.

Those craving Western food will find several options around the city center, as well as a lot of smaller places trying to fake it until they make it. These include a CKF and even an imitation of the Filipino Jollibee brand, here called Jallie Bee.

Qing Qi Shen, near the GP Hotel, behind the Guandi Miao in Tumen Jie, is a very pleasant teahouse in a traditional multi-courtyard setting, where people sit playing board games beneath caged songbirds or watch the performance of a storyteller (in local Minnan dialect), and order snacks and tea from a bamboo slat menu: Oolong (Wulong) is ¥70 per pot; ordinary tea from ¥8.

Three Virtues Vegetarian Restaurant (San De Su Shi Guan) ★★, 124 Nan Jun Lu, 2nd floor, just opposite the Carp Hotel (✆ **0595/2291-0599**), opened by a locally based Hong Konger, is my favorite vegetarian place in all of China. The highly imaginative menu includes vegetarian "sushi" *(ri shi su ci shen),* deep-fried crab claws with minced vegetarian "squid" *(bai hua zha rang su xie qian),* vegetarian "spareribs" with sweet osmanthus sauce *(gui hua su wu pai),* and the huge durian pastries *(gan si liu lian su).*

XIAMEN 厦门 ★★

Fujian Province, 109km (68 miles) S of Quanzhou, 770km (481 miles) E of Guangzhou

The island of Xiamen, then better known to foreigners by its Fujian name of Amoy, became a foreign concession in 1903, with most of the foreigners living on the tiny islet of Gulang Yu just off Xiamen itself. By the 1930s there were about 500 resident foreigners and nine consulates, several of which still stand, as do the vast, European-style mansions of Chinese who returned wealthy from overseas.

Much of the island has unattractive white-tiled buildings, but even so, the odd turret and spire reflect the city's pride in its stock of original European-style architecture. The rest of the island is a refreshing change and full of character—narrow alleys connecting sinuous streets are laced together with power and telephone cables and house DVD shops, noodle restaurants, and hair salons. Vehicle-free Gulang Yu, a few minutes away by ferry, was until recently all pleasant strolls and quiet back streets full of mansions overgrown with brilliant bougainvillea. Be warned that this is now one of the busiest tourist locations in China. As the tourism boom continues, for rooms below ¥400, demand far outstrips supply, and will probably continue to be the case in the near future.

Essentials

GETTING THERE Xiamen's **Gaoqi International Airport** (✆ **0592/602-8940**) is on the north side of the island only 20 minutes from the downtown area. Airport

Xiamen 厦门

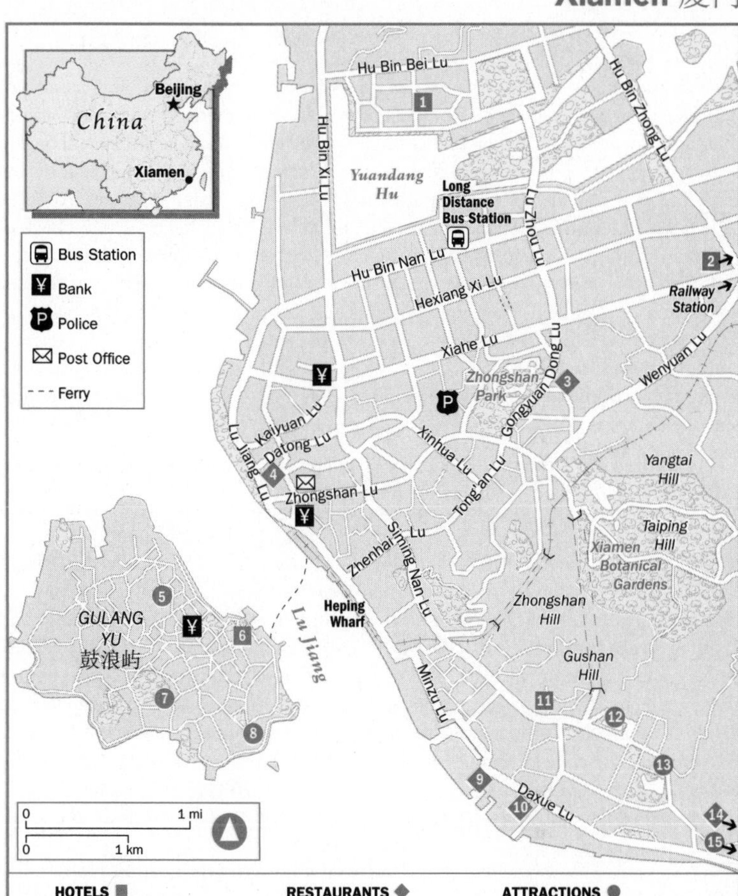

HOTELS ■

Hilford Hotel and Health Water Spa **11**
(Xī Ěr Fú Jiǔ Diàn)
希尔福酒店

Home Inn **2**
(Rú Jiā Jiǔdiàn)
如家酒店

Marco Polo Xiàmén **1**
马可波罗酒店

Miryam Boutique Hotel **6**
(Laŏ Bié Shù)
老别墅

RESTAURANTS ◆

The House **3**

Huāshēng Tāng Dián **4**
花生糖点

Miào Xiāng Biǎn Shí **9**
妙香扁食

Relax Cafe **10**
(Meiīi Shíguāng)
美丽时光

Temple Cafe **14**

ATTRACTIONS ●

City Museum **5**
(Xiàmén Shì Bówùguǎn)
厦门市博物馆

Húlǐ Shān Pàotái **15**
胡里山炮台

Jīnquán Qiánbì Bówùguǎn **8**
金泉钱币博物馆

Nán Pǔtuó Sì **12**
南普陀寺

Sunlight Rock (Rìguāng Yán) **7**
日光岩

Xiamen University **13**
(Xiàmé Dàxué)
厦门大学

taxis cost around ¥40 to downtown, and there's a shuttle to the railway station from the right of the terminal as you leave that charges ¥6. Marco Polo and the other big hotels have free shuttles for guests. There are some 20 international connections including Bangkok, Hong Kong, Kuala Lumpur, Manila, Osaka, Singapore, and Tokyo, with an assortment of domestic and foreign airlines including JAL, Philippine, ANA, and Dragonair; and regular flights to 60 major Chinese cities. While most airlines maintain offices in the Crowne Plaza or Marco Polo hotels, or in the Yinhang Zhongxin at the corner of Hubin Xi Lu and Xiahe Lu, you are better off purchasing your tickets from independent agencies, preferably away from your hotel. **Xiamen Airlines** (✆ **0592/222-6666;** www.xiamenair.com.cn) has a 24-hour ticketing and check-in desk for its own passengers and those of China Southern in the Jinyan Jiudian. It also sells tickets for other airlines with reasonable discounts. Its shuttle service is free for guests and for Xiamen/China Southern passengers. Reserve a seat on the shuttle in advance at ✆ **0592/221-8888,** ext. 34 or 6110.

At the airport, an **ATM** that accepts foreign cards is upstairs at international departures, as is a **Bank of China** forex counter open from 8:30am to 4:30pm. Just outside the airport is a bus station, and no. 27 goes all the way to Gulang Yu Ferry for ¥2, which is a good alternative to a ¥60 taxi.

On routes to neighboring coastal cities and to Hong Kong, luxury long-distance bus services are quickest, but there are useful **train** connections from Wuyi Shan (590km/369 miles), Shanghai (1,395km/872 miles), and Guangzhou (746km/389 miles). There is also a useful sleeper service to Wuyi Shan. The mostly single-track route through mountainous Fujian Province is pretty and winding, passing sugar-cane and banana plantations. There are also direct services from Beijing, Nanjing, and Xi'an. For **train inquiries,** call ✆ **0592/581-4340;** for **bookings** call ✆ **0592/398-8662** up to 12 days in advance. The railway station is a 10-minute cab ride east of the ferry dock, which can also be reached on bus no. 1. Ticket windows are open from 8am to 8:30pm, with tickets available up to 5 days in advance including day of travel. As you face the railway station, booking and left luggage are to the right of the entrance (6am–10:20pm). There is now also a North Railway that serves the new bullet train service between Xiamen and Fuzhou, cutting the trip down to around 1½ hours.

You can board most bus lines at the **Songbai Changtu Qichezhan,** Lian Yue Lu (✆ **0592/508-9328**). Services include Wenzhou, Wuyi Shan, Guangzhou, Shenzhen, and Quanzhou. From Songbai there is a free shuttle bus service (no. 816) to the other **long-distance bus station** (✆ **0592/221-5238**), officially described as the Xiamen Travel Distribution Centre, on Hubin Nan Lu 59, just north of downtown. It sells tickets from 5:30 to 10pm. Sample bus routes: Guangzhou (770km/481 miles), Shenzhen (680km/425 miles). There's even a direct bus route to Hong Kong (830km/519 miles).

Although Xiamen has recently opened an enormous new passenger cruise terminal (Dong Du Gang Guo Jie Ma Tou; ✆ **0592/202-2517**) for international cruise ships, all the coastal **ferry** routes are now long gone. It is no longer possible to go to Hong Kong or Shanghai by overnight ship as it was just a few years ago. The real irony is despite the vast new terminal, few cruise ships are coming and the city even had to offer a $100,000 incentive to get cruise ships to visit. The only ferry available is to

Jinmen Island (¥180; 1 hr., 10 per day 8am–6pm) where you can jump on a plane to Taipei, Taizhong, or Tainan in Taiwan.

GETTING AROUND While the old town and Gulang Yu can be explored **on foot,** the rest of Xiamen has quickly become a pedestrian's nightmare. Huge five-line highways carve up the entire downtown area and badly parked SUV's block up most of the pavements. Flagfall for taxis is ¥8 including 3km (2 miles), then ¥2 per kilometer up to 8km (5 miles), then ¥3 per kilometer. Add 20% from 11pm to 5am. **Buses** are frequent and reliable, with fare boxes into which you deposit ¥2 for air-conditioned service, ¥1 without. There are several **ferry** routes between the **Ferry Dock (Lundu Matou)** and Gulang Yu. The 5-minute main route is free outbound, but ¥8 to return. There's an optional ¥1 charge to sit on the top deck in either direction. Ferries run roughly every 10 to 15 minutes from 5:45am, every 20 to 30 minutes after 9pm; the last sailing is at 12:30am. To the right of the ferry boarding point are windows for a **daytime cruise** around Gulang Yu and to see Taiwanese Jinmen Dao. The 35-minute cruise departs roughly every 30 minutes from 7:40am to 5pm; call ✆ **0592/202-3493.** The next windows offer a **night cruise** (✆ **0592/210-4896;** 1 hr., 50 min.; ¥168 including snacks). There are also night trips to see the Haicang Da Qiao, a large, illuminated suspension bridge just to the north; the 40-minute trip is offered May through October from 8 to 8:45pm for ¥10 to ¥20. At the end farthest to the right is a second ferry service to Gulang Yu, running to San Qiu Tian, a little east of Gulang Yu's main dock, beneath the former U.S. consulate. Ferries depart every 30 minutes from 7:15am to 9:40pm; throughout the night, they depart roughly every hour.

A **tourist bus** now stops at the major tourist sites and charges ¥58 a day and includes lunch (✆ **0592/335-2833** or 0592/333-2702). The commentary is in Chinese, so take a good guidebook or carry an illustrated map with photos so you will know what you are seeing.

Lobbyists from King Long Bus and the Chinese auto industry scuttled plans for a metro in Xiamen, and the city has had to make do with a low budget, elevated Bus Rapid Transit instead. Fortunately, it is cheap and fast, costing as little as ¥.50 for five stops in places. The system currently has 3 operational lines: BRT 1 is the most useful, departing from No.1 Port to New Xiamen Railway Station, while BRT 2 takes passengers from Xiamen Gaoqi International Airport to Xike.

Hog fans may notice a large number of Chinese 750 military-style motorcycles with sidecars, very similar to the prewar BMW R71. As yet, there is nowhere to rent one of these monsters, but background details can be seen at the manufacturer's website, **www.chang-jiang.com/lsc**.

VISITOR INFORMATION For travel complaints, call ✆ **0592/505-6777.** A local agent that seems to have good information on a variety of locations is **Apple Travel,** 18-20 Guanren Rd. (behind the Marco Polo Hotel; ✆ **0592/505-3122;** susan@appletravel.cn). For more details about new developments in the area, check the *What's on Xiamen* website at **www.whatsonxiamen.com**. **Xiamen Travel Service** stated it had 10 English-speaking guides. It's at Lianhua Nan Lu 5 (✆ **0592/512-8855;** xm_travel@xiamenair.com.cn); ask for Chen Yu Cheng, Vice G. Manager, Foreign Liaison Center.

[Fast FACTS] XIAMEN

Banks, Foreign Exchange & ATMs All **Bank of China** ATMs take foreign cards, from the airport, via Gulang Yu (at Haitan Lu 2), to the convenient 10 Zhongshan Lu branch (8:30am–noon and 2:30–5:30pm) close to the Gulang Yu ferry dock in the center of town, which also has forex at counters 2 to 6. There's another Bank of China with forex and ATM in the Yinhang Zhongxin on the corner of Hubin Xi Lu and Xiahe Lu. Just next door is a branch of the **Hongkong and Shanghai Bank (HSBC),** whose ATMs take almost any card invented.

Internet Access Internet cafes are located all over the old town and around the university. Unfortunately, despite the city's vocal hype about the importance of education, the library facilities on Gong Yuan Nan Lu have been cut back extensively. Two floors have been closed completely and the Internet area has now been replaced with a souvenir shop.

Post Office The main post office (7:30am–7:30pm) is on Zhongshan Lu opposite the Bank of China. There's also a useful branch on Longtou Lu at Gulang Yu.

Visa Extensions The **PSB (Gong'anju;** Mon–Sat 8–11:45am and 2:30–5:45pm) is on 64 Zhenhai Lu (✆ **0592/226-2203**). Despite the glitzy appearance the second floor counter is still overly bureaucratic, demanding proof of funds of US$100 per day for a 30-day extension. Fees are currently ¥160 for most nationalities but a whopping ¥940 for Americans.

Consulates Consulates for the **Philippines, Singapore,** and **Thailand** are in Xiamen.

Exploring Xiamen

The narrow streets of the **old quarter** (bounded to the north by Xiahe Lu and to the south by Zhongshan Lu, which leads to the ferry docks) used to be a well-preserved area of treaty port–era shop-houses in a labyrinth of curling streets and narrow lanes, but has now been taken over by pedestrian shopping streets of the same domestic clothing brands that you see all over the rest of the country.

GULANG YU 鼓浪屿

Amoy, as Xiamen was then known, was one of the first five treaty ports to be opened to foreign residence and trade after the First Opium War, and a British consulate was opened in 1843. The first foreign settlements were on Amoy proper, but the town was then famously noisome, its alleys, some too narrow to allow the opening of an umbrella, funneling an extravagant palette of aromas from sewers inadequately concealed beneath the pavements. Xiamen was then reputed to be the filthiest city in China. (Now, it is touted as being one of the least polluted cities, and in the spring there are even a few days when the sky is almost blue. Even so, there's a high concentration of electronics factories in this area, along with a new benzene plant.)

The foreign community therefore moved to the 1.7-sq.-km (¾-sq.-mile) Gulang Yu but grew slowly (37 residents in 1836), although in 1852 the site became the first of the "concessions"—areas of land formally set aside for foreign residence, then parceled out to British citizens. By 1880, the now multinational foreign population was around 300 and sustained a daily English newspaper, an ice factory, a gentlemen's club, and tiger shooting (25 were bagged at the beginning of the 1890s alone). Amoy's main export was workers, the British having forced the Qing to permit Chinese emigration, and between 1883 and 1897 an estimated 167,000 left for labor overseas, founding Chinatowns around Asia and North America.

More recently, the population of this island has dropped to about 15,000 from 25,000 as the government returns houses to original owners. Its houses are being transformed into multi-storied resorts and apartments.

In treaty port days all transport was on foot, and no wheeled vehicles were allowed—a rule still enforced with the exception of some quiet electric carts used sometimes to take tourists on a circuit round the island (¥50).

First impressions of the island are not very favorable. The **ferry disembarkation area** consists of huge sliding steel gates that would be more at home on Alcatraz rather than a tourist hot spot. As you alight from the ferry, an office straight ahead as you dock offers a ¥80 ticket giving entrance to a variety of tawdry modern entertainments such as a fun fair and a laser show, so turn left instead to where the electric cars are parked. Proceed uphill straight to the area of finest mansions, on serpentine **Fujian Lu** and **Lujiao Lu.** The best examples are signposted, yet marked with unhelpful plaques giving construction dates and little more information; the former Japanese consulate is marked, however. Look out for the Catholic church of 1917 at Lujiao Lu 34. Some sources claim that 30% of the island's 20,000 residents are still practicing Christians. It's also a tradition that there are more pianos here than anywhere else in China, and tourism promoters claim that Gulang Yu is known as "Piano Island." Directly opposite Sunlight Rock is Asia's largest Piano Museum, testimony to the island's long love affair with the piano. There are over 70 historic pianos including the world's first square piano. A selection of them is used at the two major piano competitions held on the island, Gulang Yu Piano Festival and the National Competition for Young Pianists. Bach and Clementi can often be heard being hammered out rhythmically if unimaginatively, but that is only because the local high school uses concerto snippets instead of the usual school bells.

Fujian Lu 32 is particularly impressive—a vast porticoed mansion built in 1928 by a Vietnamese-Chinese real estate tycoon; the mansion later served as a hospital during the Japanese occupation of World War II, and today is the Art Vocation University of Xiamen. Dozens of families now occupy a range of such mansions and have bricked up entrances, walled in balconies to add floor space, and left gardens to turn wild. Pretty winding paths between mansions are now overgrown with hawthorn, but despite the sometimes dismaying crush on the ferry, the island has generous amounts of peace and quiet.

Farther on, clockwise around the island, is the **Jinquan Qianbi Bowuguan,** a museum of ancient coins housed in the handsome British consulate, originally built in 1843 and the earliest foreign building on the island. Recently opened, its hours and entrance fee seem not yet set, but beyond the building is one of the best lookout points back to Xiamen.

Follow signs down to the beach below. Chinese now paddle where foreigners once held bathing parties where they ate ginger cookies and drank cherry brandy. Just past the beach are shady benches beneath the trees, beyond which a short tunnel takes you through to the next beach. Immediately after that on the left, steps lead up the hillside through gardens to **Riguang Yan (Sunlight Rock),** a lookout point perhaps used by pirate and Ming loyalist Zheng Chenggong (1624–62), also known as Kongxia, a Dutch corruption of a title awarded him by the expiring Ming. He's an official state hero for being the first Han to invade Taiwan, which he did mainly for its silk and sugar, but is idolized for having kicked the Dutch off Taiwan in 1624. A dull museum to his memory is laced with the usual propaganda. It's a stiff climb (although there's a cable car alternative), the entrance fee is a hefty ¥60, and the view is overrated.

Past the beach, a right turn before a farther tunnel leads you into a maze of old mansions, but signs will direct you to the **Xiamen Shi Bowuguan (City Museum)** at Guxin Lu 43 (8:30am–5pm; ¥10). The museum is located in possibly the grandest of all the mansions, the swaggering, three-story, cupola-topped Bagua Lou or Eight Trigrams Building of 1907, designed by an American for a Taiwanese businessman. The ground floor has early examples of the Min Nan region (Quanzhou/Zhengzhou/Xiamen) specialty ware, *blanc de chine,* mostly Qing. There's other material on the Opium War and the Japanese occupation, as well as on the Communist forces' drive to Xiamen, which forced the Nationalists to Taiwan. The museum is dusty and rarely visited, but there are good views from upper balconies (hung with the attendants' washing) for a fraction of the cost of views from Sunlight Rock. A new building to one side has well-presented displays on fishing, local customs, and tea.

Tip: On Gulang Yu, look out for a delicious local specialty known as *ye shi ma ci.* These are deliciously sweet pockets of pounded sticky rice with a coating of black sesame powder.

AROUND XIAMEN

Southeast of the center, a series of sites make a pleasant excursion when seen together. Start by taking a taxi or bus no. 2 or 22 from Siming Lu to the **Huli Shan Paotai,** a platform (8:30am–5pm; ¥25) with a vast Krupp 280mm cannon overlooking the island-dotted ocean and offering a different kind of seashell. The huge gun, one of two originally sited here in 1893, sits on a vast rotating chain-driven mechanism and is credited with sinking a Japanese warship in 1937. When it was first fired, several nearby houses collapsed, too. The other gun emplacement now houses a tacky souvenir shop. The surrounding sunken barracks area has been turned over to the exhibition of peculiar stones and ancient weaponry that includes a rusty pistol said to have belonged to Opium warrior Lin Zexu. A boat at the pier below offers 1-hour trips to see Jinmen and Little Jinmen islands for ¥96; call ✆ **0592/208-3759** for information.

The ocean ring road (Huang Dao Lu) begins at Bai Cheng Beach outside the gates to Xiamen University and incorporates a substantial lane purely for cyclists, runners, and strollers. Bicycles can be rented from ¥10 per hour.

The vast Xiamen Botanical Gardens (Yuan Lin Zhi Wu Yuan—get off at Yi Zhong Zhan bus stop; ✆ **0592/2212-8577;** ¥40) that stretch almost all the way across the island are a good place to escape both the heat and the crowds. The palm collection is especially good.

For something a bit different, head to the **eco-park at Guangkou** (Kengnei Village; ✆ **0592/609-7977;** ¥50; 8am–5pm). Built by the same company that funded the Jimei Bridge, this is a definite work in progress and yet already there are plenty of exciting activities to fill the day. You might want to start with a go at grass skiing or tobogganing, perhaps followed by a bit of archery or even some horse riding. By the time that this guide is published, a large ATV track should be finished and the organic farm should be well up and running. Best of all, you only have to pay for the activities in which you partake rather than a hefty entrance fee that covers everything. The BRT extension of line 1 to Guangkou should be open soon, and from there it is a quick ¥10 on a motorbike or in a taxi up to the park at Kengnei Village.

Where to Stay

Xiamen has a surplus of luxury five-stars. Upmarket hotels add a 10% to 15% service charge and there is now an additional 4% local government tax.

Xiamen holds its annual marathon on the last Saturday of March when almost 20,000 athletes compete for a first prize of $25,000, so don't expect any hotel discounts that particular weekend. Xiamen tourism is busy March through May, after which Chinese tourism drops to almost nothing, and only the odd foreigner is seen midsummer; it picks up again September through early October for a trade fair. Typically, 40% discounts are available in non-peak periods, more in lower-level accommodations.

EXPENSIVE

Marco Polo Xiamen ★ Voted best business hotel in Xiamen many years running. Most of the rooms are arranged on eight floors around a central atrium with sandstone carvings of Marco Polo's travels, but a wing off to one side is a better choice for peace and quiet. Set on the lakeside, it's a short walk from coffee shops, restaurants, parks, and gardens. It has a complimentary shuttle from the airport 14 times a day. On Saturdays and Sundays, it has a shuttle to the main tourist attractions four times a day. The concierge desk is particularly well staffed with good English-speakers, both eager to help and capable of doing so. The center of town is only a few minutes away by taxi.

Jianye Lu 8 (off Hubin Bei Lu on the north shore of Yuandang Lake). www.marcopolohotels.com. ✆ **0592/509-1888.** Fax 0592/509-2888. 318 units. ¥1,280–¥2,000 standard room; ¥1,600–¥7,840 suite. 15% service charge. AE, DC, MC, V. **Amenities:** 4 restaurants; lobby lounge; poolside bar w/ views across the lake to the city skyline; free airport shuttle; babysitting; concierge; executive-level rooms; fitness room; forex; outdoor pool; room service; sauna, yoga center. *In room:* A/C, satellite TV, fridge, hair dryer, minibar.

Miryam Boutique Hotel (Lao Bie Shu) ★ Away from the tourist throngs, this Victorian building has just 15 designer rooms, each one with a feeling of opulence and grandeur. Features such as restored fireplaces and four-poster beds add to the effect, as do the balconies in the larger rooms with garden and sea views.

70, Huangyan Road Gulangyu. www.miryamhotel.com. ✆ **0592/206-2505.** Fax 0592/252-1600. 15 units. ¥688 deluxe room; ¥1,688 suite. 15% service charge. AE, DC, MC, V. **Amenities:** Restaurant; pool. *In room:* A/C, TV, fridge, hair dryer, Internet.

MODERATE

Hilford Hotel and Health Water Spa (Xi Er Fu Jiu Dian) ★★ Rooms here are opulent but still can be had for reasonable rates. Here ancient Chinese designs meet modern luxuries. The huge wooden doors are a breath of fresh air after so much flimsy plywood in cheap business hotels. Surprise extras include a balcony, a kitchen, and even a coffeemaker. Guests also have free access to the spa and water park next door.

Siming Nan Lu 495. www.hilford.com.cn. ✆ **0592/208-2222.** Fax 0592/209-2222. 165 units. ¥380 standard room; ¥738 suite. Rates include Chinese breakfast. MC, V. **Amenities:** 2 restaurants; airport shuttle; concierge. *In room:* A/C, TV, fridge, hair dryer, Internet access, kitchen.

Home Inn (Ru Jia Jiu Dian) This place is recommended for its reasonable cost and its location within easy walking distance of the train station. With a standard rate of ¥220 (plus an extra ¥20 at weekends) it is one of the city's best value accommodations. Like other hotels in this chain, the rooms have a garish color scheme including salmon duvets and bright yellow bathroom floors—you may feel like you're off to see the wizard while taking a shower. There are lots of small eateries close by as well as a large wet market and a Bank of China just next door.

99 Jingbang Lu. www.homeinns.com.cn ✆ **0592/589-9111.** Fax 0592/589-9188. 55 units. ¥220 standard room. No credit cards. **Amenities:** Restaurant; lounge. *In room:* TV, Internet.

7 Days Inn (Qi Tian Lian Suo Jiu Dian) This is my choice if you want to get away from the overcrowded downtown area. It's located in Tong'an, just 40 minutes by BRT. This simple business hotel is just 2 minutes' walk south of the third hospital BRT stop (san di yu yuan) but is ¥100 cheaper than the main town area.

920 Tongji Bei Lu, Tong'an District. www.7daysinn.cn. ✆ **0592/721-5777.** Fax 0592/721-5577. 55 units. ¥159 standard room. No credit cards. **Amenities:** Restaurant; lounge. *In room:* TV, Internet.

Where to Eat

Unsurprisingly for a port city, Xiamen is known for its fresh fish, and seafood can be found in the back streets of the old quarter or at small, hole-in-the-wall restaurants just up from the dock on Gulang Yu. Lunch will still be swimming or crawling in plastic tubs set out in the street, and is priced by weight. A waterfront **Pizza Hut** on the 24th floor of a tower in Lujiang Dao, visible for miles, has correspondingly excellent views once you get up there.

Relax Cafe (Mei Li Shi Guan), Daxue Lu 213 (opposite Xiamen University Medical School; ✆ **0592/219-1687**) with its spacious two-floor interior is popular with local and expat students alike who come here with their laptops to take advantage of the free wireless. There is an extensive Western menu and while items such as the Waldorf and duck breast salad look tempting, my advice is to choose something simpler to avoid any disappointment. The power-sets of three choices of juice and three choices of spaghetti at just ¥29 are especially good values. A pot of sour prune tea at ¥40 may be just what the doctor ordered.

Huang ze he, or peanut soup, from the **Huasheng Tang Dian** (peanut snack bar) on Zhongshan Lu, is the local dish that most tourists seek out, but you will have to battle through crowds. Fortunately you can avoid this by looking out for citywide brand **Miao Xian Bian Shi,** which turns out equally delicious peanut-based dishes. Try the local-style wonton soup *(bian shi)* and the tasty noodles *(ban mian).*

The Marco Polo is surrounded by upmarket fine dining options, but unless you are staying at this luxury five-star, places like The House and Le Cafe De Paris they may well be out of your budget. Instead you might want to head out to the village of Zeng Cuo An where a Taiwanese investor has restored a charming old temple and turned it into the very unusual **Temple Cafe,** 61 Zeng Cuo An (✆ **0592/209-6780**). Seating is inside an open courtyard that is completely dominated by a enormous red and gold ancestral shrine. It is slightly difficult to find, but if you get off at the Zeng Cuo An bus stop and walk straight north into the village you should not have too many problems. It's an interesting option for lunch during a day out at the beach, and certainly better than sand in your sandwiches.

JINGDE ZHEN 景德镇

Jiangxi Province, 280km (174 miles) NE of Nanchang, 430km (267 miles) E of Wuhan

Did you know that the English word "china" probably derives from Jingde Zhen's former name, Changnan? The place got its big break in the first year in Jingde Reign of Song dynasty (1004–07), when the potters of the town picked up a juicy commission from the Zhen Zong emperor. The royal court decreed that local artisans stamp their bowls and vases with the wording "Made during the Jingde Reign" printed on the bottom of every piece. Hence the city assumed the name of its imperial patron "Jingde Zhen."

By the Ming dynasty, Jingde Zhen had become a major export center. Several hundred kilns turned out hundreds of thousands of pieces each year and, conveniently located not far from the original Ming capital at Nanjing, it continued to keep the emperor and his concubines in teacups. When the capital moved north to Beijing, Jingde Zhen maintained its connection to the court via the waterways of Poyang Lake, the Yangzi, and the Grand Canal. Porcelain now runs deep in Jingde Zhen's history. The layer of discarded porcelain shards and kiln debris under its streets is said to be 9m (30 ft.) thick in places.

Although 17th-century Manchu riots destroyed much of the town, the Yangzi to the north, and river systems leading south to Guangzhou, enabled Jingde Zhen to get its wares around China for sale, and later, via the treaty ports, to an increasingly enthusiastic European market. Imperial support also helped—some kilns were employed solely for the making of wares for the emperors and their officials. The first kiln site to produce white china and to use certain underglaze painting techniques, Jingde Zhen reached its peak of technical brilliance during the mid–17th to late 18th century with the gaudy full-colored enamel overglaze illustrations of *famille vert* and *famille rose* china.

The secret, as Jingde Zhen potters had known for more than 1,000 years, lay in using the right combination of clays and feldspars. The most famous of these was kaolin, or china clay, which got its name from the high ridge, or Gao Ling, just north of Jingde Zhen combined with the timber from the surrounding hills as coal caused yellowing in the glaze. Industrialization of the area, which employed around half the town's workforce, soon stripped the hills bare and enough coal was fired to turn the skies black. Just 10 years ago, mass-production kilns began to be converted from coal to gas. The air is much better now and even the porcelain quality has improved thanks to this change in technology.

Essentials

GETTING THERE The **airport** is only 8km (5 miles) out of town, but it has a very limited number of flights only to Shanghai, Beijing, Xiamen, Chongqing, and Shenzhen. A **shuttle bus** runs to the Jichang Shoupiao Zhongxin (✆ **0798/822-3907;** ticket office 8am–5:30pm), in the center of town at Zhu Shan Lu 127. The shuttle fare is ¥10 and it leaves for the airport 1½ hours before each flight. A taxi ride costs about ¥30. For more choices, head to Nanchang's Changbei Airport, 4 hours north of Jingde Zhen.

Rail services are less limited than you might expect for its remote central location: Guangzhou, Kunming, three trains daily from Beijing Xi (West), one from Beijing, two from Shanghai and two from Xiamen. However, none start at Jingde Zhen, so ticket availability is limited. Nanchang and Jiujiang, both best reached by express bus from Jingde Zhen, have far more trains. Ticket windows at the station are open from 7:45am to 8pm, with brief breaks in between.

The **Main Bus Station** (**Keyun Zhongxin;** ✆ **0798/858-8787**) is on the northwest side of town and is open from 6am to 7pm. Express buses using the highway to Jiujiang and beyond, arrive and depart from here. Destinations include Jiujiang (134km/84 miles) and Nanchang (280km/175 miles), Shanghai, Hangzhou, and Nanjing. Left luggage doubles as a small store outside the ticket office, charges ¥3 per piece, and closes at 6pm. Another bus station (✆ **0798/820-8156**) opposite the railway station, open from 6:20am to 5:30pm, also serves Jiujiang and Nanchang.

GETTING AROUND **Taxis** have a flagfall of ¥5 that includes 2km (1¼ miles), after which the fare is ¥1 per kilometer up to 6km (3¾ miles), then ¥1.50 per kilometer thereafter. From 11pm to 5am the fare is ¥1.80. **Buses** charge a ¥1 flat fare deposited in the slot. Bus no. K35 starts at the Keyun Zhongxin and goes south past the Jinye Dajiudian and then east along Zhu Shan Zhong Lu. On Zhongshan Nan Lu there are a few cycle shops such as the one owned by Mr. Deng at no. 92 (✆ **0798/851-0687**), who will rent out bikes by the day. There is a Xinhua Bookstore on the corner of Lianshe Beilu facing People's Square that sells a map of the city.

[Fast FACTS] JINGDE ZHEN

Banks, Foreign Exchange & ATMs A useful **Bank of China** (8am–6pm, winter to 5:30pm) is just outside Kaimenzi Hotel on Xing Feng Lu.

Internet Access *Wangba*, such as the one on the south side of Zhu Shan Lu near the junction of Cidu Da Dao, usually charge ¥2 per hour.

Post Office The main post office (summer 8am–7pm, winter to 6:30pm) is on Zhu Shan Lu nearby the Jinjiang Inn.

Visa Extensions The PSB (Mon–Fri 8:30–11:30am and 2:50–5:30pm) is on the west side of Cidu Da Dao well south of the Zhu Shan Lu junction, in a tall white building with pink steps but the staff are neither friendly, nor helpful.

Exploring Around Town

Local authorities are starting to recognize the importance of tourism and, in 2004, first celebrated the area's 1,000th anniversary as an imperial kiln-production center. There is now a ceramics festival every October and a locally maintained website at www.jingdezhen.gov.cn.

Porcelain Culture Exhibition (Taoci Wenhua Bolanqu) ★ Although run down and desperately in need of a new coat of paint, this is still the best of several exhibitions devoted to ceramics, and includes several old kilns, areas demonstrating the production process, and ancient houses and temples. The site is down a winding country lane called Guyao Lu off an urban main street, providing an abrupt transition from town to countryside. The entrance to the left of the ticket office leads to rebuilt ancient kiln types in reddish brick, and a fine old mansion in local style, with black pillars, white walls, and richly carved and gilded interior beams. Glass cases in its three courtyards hold modest displays of ceramics. English signs guide you around the site, and visitors can even have a try at the ceramics process themselves.

A second entrance to the right of the ticket office leads to an area where, in theory, you can watch the production process in a series of sheds, which begins with pools of clay and continues with racks of pieces in various stages of preparation. But the kiln is no longer fired, weeds are growing from the clay pits, and this is all for show and shopping. I was especially interested to see that in a location famed for its technical expertise, potters still used hand-driven wheels to throw their clay.

Behind this area, what looks at first like a dry-stone wall is a large pile of firewood built into the shape of a cottage. Pine wood was carefully cut and stacked this way to guard against rain and spontaneous combustion, and to save the cost of building storage sheds, but the result is a work of art. The duck's-egg-shaped kiln to the right, one of Jingde Zhen's oldest, occupies only about a quarter of the area of a large barnlike building. The ground floor is a small forest of curved pillars that seem to be largely unfashioned tree trunks, between which are stacked piles of saggers, the rough ceramic outer cases into which pieces were placed for firing. A series of wall-mounted illustrations shows the process.

At the end of the low-ceilinged hall there's a ramp up through a narrow entrance into the arched brickwork of the kiln space itself, where the firewood would have been stacked in patterns depending on the effect required, and saggers (where a pot is placed before it is fired) containing porcelain requiring different temperatures would have been placed in different positions.

Guyao Lu, Exhibition area (just off Cidu Da Dao). Admission ¥50. 8am–5pm. Bus: 19 to the end of the route.

Water-powered Hammers (San Bao Shuidui) ★ A short way into the countryside, some fascinating primitive technology can be seen. Take bus no. K35 (¥1) to the east (look out for all the porcelain lamp posts and even porcelain traffic lights) and get off at the Hutian stop on Hangkong Lu, shortly before the terminus where the bus swings right outside the large red Ri Xin General Merchandise Store; walk on for 2.5km (1½ miles), or take a taxi. The route leads past a development of abandoned half-finished villas and smokeless chimneys peeping from among the green hills. The *shuidui* can be heard before they are seen, an irregular solid clunking from beneath a thatched hut to the left. In the middle of the town, look for the peoples' center with the Chinese opera stage inside; follow a path that crosses a stream and then swings around to the left of the hut. Inside, four giant wooden mallets with long heads and pointed noses, ingeniously driven by a small water wheel and among the last of their kind, pound soggy masses of clay.

Bus: K35 to Hutian; follow directions above.

Jingdezhen Imperial Kiln (Yu Yao Guo Jia Yi Zhi Gong Yuan) The kiln itself is little more than a pile of rubble, but the accompanying museum is well worth a look. The pottery here is displayed chronologically and by dynasty, so that you can quickly learn the differences between Yuan, Ming and Qing vases and impress your friends back home. A nice touch is a display recording the top prices ever paid for Jingdezhen porcelain at auction (though with the market still increasing, it's already quite a bit out of date).

169 Lianshi Bei Lu. ✆ **0798/820-1238.** Free admission. 9am–5pm.

Shopping ★★

Jingde Zhen is known for the thousands of porcelain shops that fill the city. The North Bus Station is surrounded by wholesale shops, but head further to the artisan

FRIENDS IN high places

The convenient location of **Wuyuan County,** on the boundary of three provinces in Jiangxi's North Eastern corner, just 80km (50 miles) from Jingdezhen and 114km (70 miles) from Huangshan, has helped it become a fast growing tourist destination, but it is the connection with China's former president, Jiang Zemin, that has really put it on the map. Jiang was born in Jiangwan, first built in the late Sui Dynasty (581–618) and early Tang Dynasty (618–907), but all the villages in the area are very photogenic and make an interesting side trip.

Wuyuan County comprises some of the most beautiful countryside in China with at least 50 old villages, all with stunning vernacular architecture with white walls and black tiles. The area's rivers with ancient trees are what many of us would consider a typical Chinese countryside scene. The hundreds of ancient houses date from the Ming (1368–1644) and Qing dynasties. In ancient times, Wuyuan was governed by Anhui and the merchant class dominated the Chinese economy back in Qing Dynasty.

There are regular buses from the Licun Bus Station (Lǐcūn zhàn) on Shuguang Lu in Jingdezhen to Wuyuan Town North Bus Station (Běizhàn; ✆ **0793/734-8585;** Wengong Beilu), the trip taking less than 2 hours with the first bus leaving at 6:30am (¥30). Wuyuan's North Station is far away from the main center of Wuyuan Town, but a taxi will take you into the town center for ¥5 and there is also a public bus for just ¥1.

From the old bus station in town you can hop aboard mini buses that go to all the major sites. Most of the villages (except Big Likeng) are now operated as tourist attractions complete with ticket offices, entry cards, and even fingerprint recognition in places. ¥60 will grant only one entrance, ¥180 grants all the scenic spots for 5 days except Big Likeng. Students can have a half-price entry with ID.

When you arrive at the North station there will be plenty of touts offering to take you up to **Big Likeng** (home to a number of prominent historical ministers, with courtyard houses boasting masses of intricate carving), but there are plenty

studios just to the south of **Renmin Square (Jing Chang Li Chi Mao Da Sha, Zhu Shan Zhong Lu),** where the large five-floor **ceramics market** showcases some very creative artists among the mass-produced stuff. Check out the deities and mythical figures in **Shang Ping Studio** (✆ **0798/822-2081**) on the third floor, as well as some of the porcelain paintings in **Tan Qing Xuan Zhi** (✆ **0798/823-5677**) on the fourth floor. Just along Lianshi Nan Lu are a cluster of 20 or 30 shops that sell local factory surplus at very good prices. There are some great bargains here, from cultural revolution tea mugs to ceramic knives at knock-down prices. Continue straight into the main wholesale area and on Mondays you will find a very bizarre street market where locals try to sell fragments and shards of plates and vases.

Gallery One (**Yi Hao Zhan Ting;** ✆ **0798/823-1116**) is one of many private galleries up on 116 Lianshe Beu Lu, but this one stands out for its interesting abstract work.

More finds can be had when exploring the back streets behind Zhejiang Lu. From the train station, head left for the Wen Yuan Business Hotel (Wen Yuan Shang Wu Da Jiu Dian, Tong Zhan Lu 36) with the golden Thai-style temple roof. On the opposite side of the road, venture into one of the small alleys next to the bus station to find of other villages to choose from. **Jiangling** boasts the most vivid rapeseed fields in spring and is a favorite with photographers. **Xiaoqi,** dating from the Song, has a number of shrines and mansions, all well preserved. **Sixi** is a strange claustrophobic village with tall gray walls and narrow mazelike streets that have been home to the Yu clan for generations. The most impressive house in the village is the **Jingxu Hall,** the grand abode of a wealthy family whose fourth generation still resides there. The buildings are under government protection, which means that the occupants are permitted to live there, but, to the disappointment of many collectors, they cannot sell any of the old relics. There are large wall maps of the area in both English and Chinese in almost every hotel, so there is no excuse for not getting out there and exploring.

The two best choices for local accommodation in Wuyuan Town are the **Meng Li Lao Jia Bing Guan** on Jing Guang Qiao Tou Lu (✆ **0793/720-1188**) on the banks of the river right next to China's largest wind-and-rain bridge, and the slightly cheaper **Fu Hao Da Jiu Dian** on Dong Sheng Lu (✆ **0793/721-1818**), just around the corner from the old bus station. The latter is adjacent to the best eating choice in town, the **Wuyuan Taste Restaurant** (Zi Yuan Wei Fu; ✆ **0793/721-1819**). Staff are helpful and there is a large picture menu although unfortunately without any English. We recommend sampling the delicate flavors of the large steamed frog as well as the potato fritters and pumpkin pancakes.

Local specialties are divided into four colors—red, green, black and white. Red is the local fish dish of Hebao Hongyu or Hebao Red Carp. Green is represented by local Wulu Tea a beverage that was celebrated as one of China's "six wonders" back in the Song Dynasty, and was given as tribute to the imperial court in the Ming and Qing dynasties. Locals claim that the best brands are Dazhangshan and Tianyou. Black is the Longweiyan or Dragon-Tail Inkstone and the white is a local fruit known as Jiangwanxueli or Jiangwan Snow Pear.

yourself in a rabbit warren of side streets and small wholesalers. Here you will find the more outlandish Cultural Revolution reproductions, and you can expect to see everything here from faux antique phones to porcelain weighing scales. Poison bottles make especially good gifts and look out for the Red Leaf Brand, which the government uses as gifts for visiting foreign heads of state.

Where to Stay

The largest and most expensive hotel in town is the four-star **Kaimenzi Dajiudian** (✆ **0798/857-7777;** www.kmz.cn/en/intro.html; it's the same company that supplies all the gas in Jingde Zhen), located in the old Telecom Building on Xing Feng Lu, but it would not be my first choice. Newer and more centrally located is the **Largos Hotel (Lang Yi Jiudian),** Zhu Shan Xi Lu 5 (✆ **0798/838-8888;** fax 0798/852-6666), which looks like a Bauhaus box hospital from the outside but has nicely appointed rooms inside. Standard rooms are ¥366, and suites ¥788 to ¥1,588. The usual credit cards are accepted, but there's no foreign exchange.

Of the many budget options along the main street, Zhu Shan Xi Lu, the three-star **Jinjiang Inn (Jinjiang Zhi Xing Lu Guan** at no. 1; ✆ **0798/857-1111;** fax

0798/857-1234) is the best choice. It was refurbished recently, but standard rooms still go for ¥120. This hotel has a nice riverside location. At the other end of town, the newly completed **Chang Xing Guoji Da Jiu Dian** (Zhejiang Lu; ✆ **0798/839-6666**) is slightly more upmarket if you are looking for a little extra luxury.

Sanbao Ceramic Art Institute (San Bao Tao Yi Yan Xiu Yuan) ★ This is an artists' retreat more than a hotel, but the rural location is fantastic and the owner, Jackson Li, is an expert in porcelain, ready to answer any and all questions. The institute stretches across a restored porcelain workshop complete with ancient kilns, water hammers, and a duck pond. At one end, Jackson has his own impressive office and studio. In the center are various workshops and studios for visiting artists, and at the other end are simple but authentic accommodations with shared facilities. Book early, as this place is very popular due to its reasonable prices (¥150 per night per person, full board) and is often filled with creative types from all over the world.

Sanbao Taoyi Cun, near Hutian (¥5 from the bus station by moto taxi). www.chinasanbao.org. ✆ **0798/849-7505.** Full room and board ¥150. MC, V. **Amenities:** Internet. *In room:* No phone.

Where to Eat

Yilong Dajiudian, Cidu Da Dao 908 (✆ **0798/833-3333;** 6:30–9:30am, 5–9pm, and 9:30pm–2am), next to the Customs Office, looks more like a hotel than a restaurant but offers a wide selection of *Gan cai* (Jiangxi dishes) and Chinese standards. The hot dishes (Jiangxi food is spicy) are labeled *huo la*—fiery hot. Try *sangna niurou,* "sauna" beef—tender slices in a garlicky, peppery oil, served in a clay pot and cooked by putting small heated stones in the liquid. The first floor has plenty of other dishes on display to make choosing easier, but bear in mind that this is not a cheap place and a bill of ¥200 for two should be expected. For local snacks, try Qianjie Pedestrian Street, which is also home to an interesting afternoon and evening market, just off Zhushan Road to the west of the river.

GUANGZHOU 广州

Guangdong Province, 163km (102 miles) NW of Hong Kong, 165km (103 miles) NE of Macau

While most of the city's history has been erased, Guangzhou still holds an endless fascination for anybody wishing to see the inner workings of the modern economy. If you enjoyed *Manufactured Landscapes,* then the commercial frenzy of the city will keep you enthralled for days, if not weeks. Few visitors manage to see beyond the superficial veneer of five-star hotels, shopping malls, and propaganda sightseeing, but those who do are rewarded with rare insights to equal those of Dickens. Guangzhou is the ideal starting point for those who wish to glimpse the dragon's underbelly, the result of combining Western capitalism and Eastern exploitation. Until recently, there were vast wholesale markets for every product imaginable, although shopping opportunities have declined with the onset of the global financial crisis.

Essentials

GETTING THERE Guangzhou's **Baiyun International Airport** (CAN) is 28km (17 miles) away from the center of Guangzhou City. It has already become the second busiest airport in all of China and is now planning a third runway. Guangzhou is now connected to well over 100 domestic cities and more than 60 international cities. There are several **information desks** (✆ **020/8613-7273**), both on the first and

Save Your ¥ When Flying to Hong Kong

For those heading to Hong Kong from elsewhere in China, it's often considerably cheaper to fly here or (even better) to Shenzhen instead, and then take a bus, train, or boat.

the third floor of the terminal building. Don't be surprised if your taxi driver asks for the ridiculous sum of ¥150 just to get out of town. If you are arriving later than 10pm, taxis are particularly bad about not wanting to run on the meter and charging exorbitant amounts.

Fortunately, plenty of regular **airport buses** run to dozens of locations within the city. Seven main bus routes traverse Guangzhou but nos. 1 and 2 will probably satisfy the short-term visitor. No. 1 goes to the old station and no. 2 goes through Tian He and past the big hotels on Huanshi Lu. Fares range from ¥10 to ¥30 by distance. Direct buses head for Zhuhai at ¥80 per person, running approximately every 2½ hours. The last bus leaves at about 8:30pm. For more information, contact the **Baiyun Port Bus Service** (✆ **020/3129-8077;** http://newsgd.com/specials/airportguide/airportqna/200407300080.htm). Line 3 was extended in 2010, and now reaches all the way up to Guangzhou Baiyun Airport from downtown.

Since 2007, passengers who pass directly through the territory of China on an international service or stay in Guangzhou less than 24 hours do not need a visa. They must however have a connecting flight and a booked seat.

As elsewhere, tickets are best bought from agents rather than directly from airlines. **CITS** (✆ **020/8669-0179** air tickets, or 020/8666-4661 train tickets; Mon–Fri 8:30am–6:30pm, Sat–Sun 9am–5pm) to the right of the main railway station as you face it, is unusually helpful, with some English spoken. Air ticket prices can be bargained down. For general airport inquiries in Mandarin, Cantonese, and English, call ✆ **020/360-66999.**

Most **trains** arrive at the main railway station **Guangzhou Huochezhan** (known locally as Lao Zhan, the old station 159, Huanshi Xi Lu; ✆ **020/613-57222**), which has services from Beijing Xi, Chengdu, Xi'an, Kunming, Xiamen, Guiyang, Wenzhou, and many more cities. There are a few services to Shenzhen. For information, call ✆ **020/6135-7412** or 020/6135-8952. An information counter is toward the right-hand end of the railway station as you face it, open from 5am to midnight. The 24-hour ticket windows are at the far right-hand end. Buy up to 12 days in advance. The 24-hour left-luggage windows are in the middle.

Direct trains from **Hong Kong** arrive at **Guangzhou Dong Zhan (East Station)** Linhe Zhong Lu, Tianhe District (✆ **020/6134-6222**), which is conveniently at the end of the first metro line (exit D). This station is on the express line from Beijing Xi through Jiujiang with direct trains that continue to Hong Kong on alternate days. There are also direct services to Changchun, Tianjin, Qingdao, Nanchang, and other cities. There are multiple train departures a day for **Hong Kong** between 8:30am and 9:20pm; the trip takes 1½ to 2 hours and costs from HK$190. For more information, see www.cantonfair.biz/hktrain.htm. There's also a very high-speed train service to **Shenzhen,** with departures every few minutes, some of which cover the 139km (87 miles) in under an hour and drop you right next to the border crossing to Hong Kong

Guangzhou 广州

Guangzhou Metro

Jiangxia
Xing Shi
Guangzhou Tiyuchang
Yuanjing
Sanyuanli
Guangzhou Huochezhan
Guangzhou Station
Yuexiu Gongyuan
Zhongshan Jiniantang
Gongyuanqian
Xi Men Kou
Chen Jia Ci
Changshou Lu
Huangsha
Fangcun
Huadiwan
Kengkou
Xi Lang
Haizhu Guangchang
Shi Er Gong
Jiang Nan Xi
Xiaogang
Zhong Da
Lujiang
Kecun
Chigang
Modiesha
Xingang Dong Lu
Pa Zhou
Nongjiangsuo
Lieshi Lingyuan
Dong Shan Kou
Yangji
Tiyu Xi Lu
Zhujiang Xin Cheng
Chigang Ta
Da Tang
Lijiao
Guangzhou East Station
Guangzhou Dong Zhan
Linhe Xi
Tiyu Zhongxin
Shipai Qiao
Gangding
South China Normal Univ.
Wu Shan
Tianhe Keyunzhan

Line 1
Line 2
Line 3
HUANGSHA Transfer Station

Guangzhou-Foshan Expressway
Jichang Lu
SANYUANLI
Guangzhou Train Station
1
GUANGZHOU HUOCHEZHAN
Zhan Xi Lu
Guangyuan Xilu
Huanshi Xi Lu
Zhan Qian Lu
2
YUEXIU GONGYUAN
Lia Hua Lu
Museum of the Nan Yue King
Lia Hua Hu Park
3
Dong Feng Xi Lu
ZHONGSHAN JINIANTANG
Xi Hua Lu
Temple of the Six Banyan Trees
Chen Clan Academy
Jiefang Bei Lu
Baisha River
DATANSHA
Donghai River
Nan An Lu
Zhongshan 8-Lu
Zhongshan 7-Lu
Zhongshan 6-Lu
CHEN JIA CI
XI MEN KOU
GONGYUANQIAN
Jiefang Zhong Lu
Li Wan Hu Park
CHANGSHOU LU
Huifu Xi Lu
15
Dade Lu
14
Jiefang Nan Lu
13
Shang Jiu Lu
Renmin Nan Lu
Di Shi Fu Lu
Xia Jiu Lu
Yide Lu
Huangsha Dadao
Fangcun Dadao Xi
Guangzhou South Train Station
HUANGSHA
Qingping Market
Yan Jiang Xi Lu
Bin Jiang Xi Lu
Pearl River
Liu'ersan Lu
16
SHAMIAN ISLAND
Tongfu Zhong Lu
Tongfu Xi Lu
NANTANG
Fangcun Dadao Zhong
FANGCUN
Kui Peng Lu
17
Hua lei Lu

Bus Station
Bank
Police
Post Office
Inner Ring Expressway

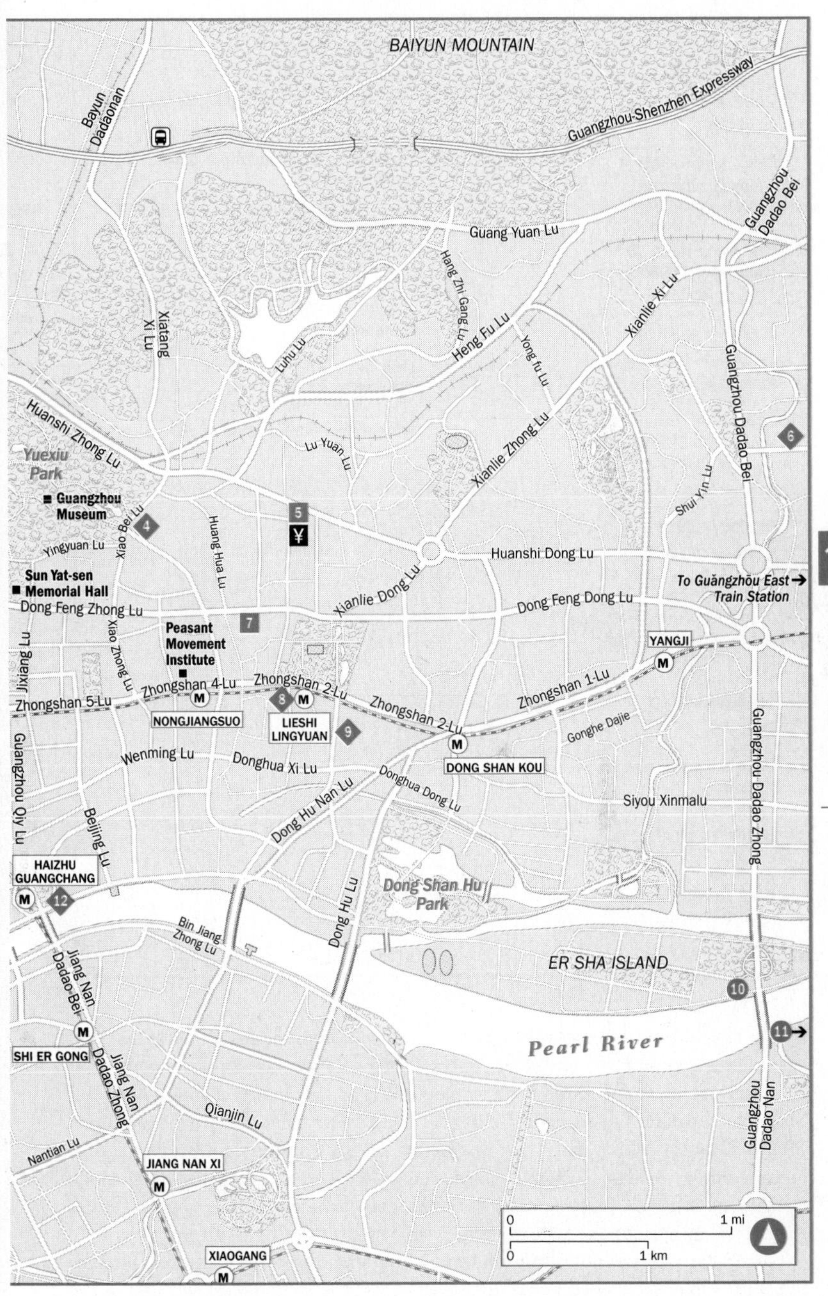

BAIYUN MOUNTAIN
Guangzhou-Shenzhen Expressway
Bayun Dadaonan
Guang Yuan Lu
Guangzhou Dadao Bei
Hang Zhi Gang Lu
Xiatang Xi Lu
Luhu Lu
Heng Fu Lu
Yong fu Lu
Xianlie Xi Lu
Huanshi Zhong Lu
Yuexiu Park
Lu Yuan Lu
Xianlie Zhong Lu
Guangzhou Museum
Xiao Bei Lu
Huang Hua Lu
Shui Yin Lu
Yingyuan Lu
Huanshi Dong Lu
Sun Yat-sen Memorial Hall
Xianlie Dong Lu
To Guǎngzhōu East Train Station
Dong Feng Zhong Lu
Dong Feng Dong Lu
Xiao Zhong Lu
Peasant Movement Institute
Jixiang Lu
YANGJI
Zhongshan 4-Lu
Zhongshan 2-Lu
Zhongshan 1-Lu
Zhongshan 5-Lu
NONGJIANGSUO
LIESHI LINGYUAN
Gonghe Dajie
Guangzhou Dadao Zhong
Wenming Lu
Donghua Xi Lu
DONG SHAN KOU
Donghua Dong Lu
Dong Hu Nan Lu
Siyou Xinmalu
Guangzhou Qiy Lu
Beijing Lu
HAIZHU GUANGCHANG
Dong Hu Lu
Dong Shan Hu Park
Bin Jiang Zhong Lu
ER SHA ISLAND
Jiang Nan Dadao Bei
Pearl River
SHI ER GONG
Jiang Nan Dadao Zhong
Qianjin Lu
Guangzhou Dadao Nan
Nantian Lu
JIANG NAN XI
XIAOGANG
0
1 mi
1 km

Guangzhou Key

HOTELS ■

Bauhinia Hotel **13**
(Baŏxuān Jiŭdiàn)
宝轩酒店

The Garden Hotel **5**
(Huāyuán Jiŭdiàn)
花园酒店

Guo Xiang Hotel **2**
(Guó Xiáng Dà Shà)
国祥大厦

New East Hotel **7**
(Xīndōngfāng Jiŭdiàn)
新东方酒店

White Swan Hotel **16**
(Bái Tiān'é Bīnguăn)
白天鹅宾馆

RESTAURANTS ◆

Bĕi Yuán Jiŭjiā **4**
北园酒家

Cháng Fĕn Fast Food Shop **9**
(Yín Ji Cháng Fĕn Diàn)
银记肠粉店

Dōng Bĕi Rén **3**
东北人

Dōng Jiāng Haĭ Xiān Dà Jiŭ Loú 3 **12**
东江海鲜大酒楼

Japan Fusion **6**
中森名菜日本料理

Kung Fu Fast Food **8**
(Zheng Gongfu)
正功夫

ATTRACTIONS ●

Canton Tower **11**
(Guăng Zhoū Xīn Diàn Shì Tă)
广州新电视塔

Guangdong Museum of Art **10**
广东美术馆

Guăngzhōu Old Railway Station **1**
广州老站

Guangzhou Wholesale Glasses Market **14**

Huādìwān **17**
花地湾

Wholesale Buddhist Market **15**

at Luo Hu/Lo Wu. (A few slower services run to and from the main railway station.) The railway station has a customer service center (5:30am–11:40pm), a number of air ticket agents (some surprisingly competitive), and a counter selling tickets for Shanghai, Taiyuan, Jiujiang, and Beijing Xi (West). The main ticket windows, open from 5:50am to 9:40pm with short breaks, are set back on the right, while the left-luggage office (8:30am–6:30pm) has moved to the central concourse. The Hong Kong ticket office (7:30am–6pm) is at the far end of the concourse, upstairs on the right. The entrance to Hong Kong trains, via Customs, is just beyond that.

Guangzhou has multiple **long-distance bus stations.** The **Liuhua Chezhan** (5am–10:30pm) is reached by an underpass across the station forecourt and to the right. It has buses to Shenzhen (75 departures 6am–10:30pm; ¥55, and a few more expensive services); and to Zhuhai (60 departures 5:45am–10pm; ¥65). From the far right-hand corner of the station forecourt as you leave it, turn right along Huanshi Xi Lu, and the 24-hour **Sheng Qiche Keyun Zhan (Guangdong Provincial Long-distance Bus Station)** is a couple of minutes farther on the right. Buses here are generally bound for Hunan, Jiangxi, Fujian, and Guangxi and cities in Guangdong Province. It has services to Shenzhen (¥60) every 12 minutes from 6:15am to 11pm; to Zhuhai Gong Bei for Macau (¥55) every 20 minutes from 6:30am to 8:30pm; and to Kaiping (¥45) every 40 minutes from 6:30am to 7pm. There are also services to Guilin, Nanning, and Beihai. The **Shi Qiche Keyun Zhan** opposite, over the foot-bridge, has more departures to the same destinations.

Unfortunately, nearly all of the **ferry services** to and from Hong Kong have been discontinued. Boats no longer depart from Guangzhou, only from some of the satellite towns such as Nansha, Panyu, and Shunde. The Garden Hotel has shuttles to Lian Hua Gang (Panyu) where there is still a boat to Hong Kong that takes about 2½ hours arriving at Zhong Gang Cheng, Kowloon. Shuttle buses leave the Garden Hotel at 8:30am, 10am, 4pm, and 6pm; the cost of the service is ¥145. Call the Garden Hotel for more information (✆ **020/8333-8989**).

GETTING AROUND **Taxi** fares are among China's most expensive with a flagfall of ¥9 including 2.3km (1¼ miles), then ¥2.60 per kilometer up to 15km (9 miles), then 50% more. There are no extra nighttime charges, but beware the 5-to-7pm rush hour, which will add significantly to your costs.

The **metro** is the most convenient way to get through Guangzhou's heavy traffic although with 144 stations and 236 km (147 miles) of track, it can be a little daunting to beginners. The useful line no. 1 (yellow on maps) runs from Xilang in the Fangcun district in southwest Guangzhou, passes Shamian Island (Huangsha Station) and two or three other major sights, and ends up at Guangzhou East railway station. Line no. 2 (blue), runs from Guangzhou South Railway Station to Wanshengwei and will eventually reach the current airport. It passes the main railway station and one or two useful hotels. Line 3 (orange) runs from the East Railway Station to Panyu Square; with a branch that runs from Tianhe Bus Station to West Tiyu Road via Gangding. Tickets cost ¥2 to ¥8 according to the distance to be traveled, as shown on a color-coded sign above ticket machines. Stored-value Yang Cheng Tong cards allowing multiple journeys are strangely unavailable from the metro station ticket desks, but can be found at the 7/11 nearby. The system runs from around 6am to 11pm. Ordinary **buses** charge a flat fare of ¥1; newer air-conditioned versions charge a flat fare of ¥2.

VISITOR INFORMATION Guangzhou supports several free magazines that tend to be more advertorial than useful, obtainable from hotel lobbies and expat hangouts. They contain reviews of new restaurants, clubs, and bars (usually paid for), and intermittently accurate listings. *That's PRD* (Pearl River Delta) is marginally better than *South China City Talk,* but not much since the English owner was pushed out in a very hostile takeover by the Chinese authorities.

A locally run agency used to dealing with the needs of foreigners is **Xpat Travel Planners,** Flat E, 20/F, Regent House, Taojin Lu 50 (✆ **020/8358-6961;** xpats@public.guangzhou.gd.cn).

American Express (✆ **020/8331-1311;** fax 020/8331-1616) has a branch in the office building of the Guangdong International Hotel. It's open Monday through Friday from 9am to 5pm. For official tourist information, call ✆ **020/8668-7051.**

[Fast FACTS] GUANGZHOU

Banks, Foreign Exchange & ATMs Most of the many branches of the **Bank of China** (9am–noon and 2–5pm) have forex services and ATMs accepting foreign cards, including the branch inside the Garden Hotel and the nearby Friendship Store. But be prepared to wait. Nearly all banks now have a ticket system like you find at a cheese counter. Just take a number and wait your turn. A newly opened branch of the **Hongkong and Shanghai Bank (HSBC)** is at the front of the Garden Hotel.

Consulates The consulate of **Australia** is on the 12/F Zhujiang New City Development Center, 3, Linjiang Lu (✆ **020/3814-0111;** fax 020/3814-0112). The consulate of **Canada** is in Suite 801, Wing C in the China Hotel (✆ **020/8666-0569,** ext. 0; fax 020/8667-2421). The **U.K.** consulate is on the second floor of the Guangdong International Hotel, Huan Shi Dong Lu 339 (✆ **020/8335-1354;** www.uk.cn/gz). The **U.S. Consulate** has moved to 5/F Phase 2, Tian Yu Gardens, 136-142 Lin He Zhong Lu 1 (✆ **020/8620-8121**). Onward visas for **Vietnam** are available on the second floor of B Building North at the Landmark Hotel, Qiaoguang Lu 8 (✆ **020/8330-5910**); hours are Monday through Friday from 9am to noon and 2 to 5pm. Cambodia, Denmark, France, Italy, Japan, Korea, Malaysia, the Philippines, Poland, Thailand, and the Netherlands also have consulates in Guangzhou.

Internet Access Internet cafes are everywhere, but most of them are dark, dingy places. A far cleaner alternative is on the second floor of the Guangzhou library, just outside the Lieshi Lingyuan subway stop. No smoking is allowed and the keyboards are legible—all for just ¥2 per hour. Deposit is (¥20); have your passport with you in case its requested. It's open Thursday to Tuesday (9am–5pm) and gets very busy on the second Monday of the month when access is free between 9am and noon; on Wednesdays, you can head to the nearby Zhongshan library (Zhongshan 4 Lu) instead.

Post Office A useful post office (Mon–Sat 9am–5pm) is in San Jie on Shamian if you happen to be staying in that part of town, but for sending anything bulky, try the branch outside the old railway station, where both of the packing guys are extremely helpful and speak excellent English.

Visa Extensions The PSB is at Jiefang Nan Lu 155 (✆ **020/8311-5808;** Mon–Fri 8:50–11:30am and 2:30–5pm) at the corner of Dade Lu. Check documents and pick up an application form upstairs in the zoo on the fourth floor (8–11:15am and 2:20–4:45pm) before being given access to the equally crowded and chaotic fifth floor. Extensions take 5 working days to obtain.

Exploring & Shopping Guangzhou

History buffs and culture vultures may well be disappointed in Guangzhou as this city moves to a very different beat, the vibrant pulse of international trade. The **Guangdong Museum of Art,** Yanyu Lu 38 (✆ **020/8735-1468;** www.gdmoa.org; ¥15; Tues–Sun 9am–5pm), is one of the best in the country and is definitely worth a visit, but apart from that the real highlights are the markets, the vast bazaars, and the huge numbers of people crammed into this small river delta. Those making a brief trip to Guangzhou from Hong Kong should concentrate on the commerce rather than the culture. The Provincial Museum, the Sun Yat-sen Memorial Hall, the Peasant Movement Institute, and other revolutionary sites are all dull and avoidable. Seek out instead what the Cantonese currently have passions for: business and food.

SHAMIAN ISLAND

Forced to relinquish a permanent trading base to the hated Westerners at the end of the First Opium War in 1841, the Guangzhou authorities probably snickered as they palmed off a sandbar to the British and French. Perhaps they snickered less when it was promptly bunded (made secure with artificial embankments); was provided with proper streets, drainage, and imposing buildings; and became home to a prosperous foreign enclave with everything from tennis courts to a yacht club. The rest of Guangzhou lacked even properly surfaced roads well into the 20th century. Resentment from the local authorities manifested itself in dictatorial regulations, restricting traders solely to the island (barely half the size it is today and resulting in the word "cantonment") and forbidding wives or families. There was a death penalty for anybody attempting to learn Chinese, and the only time that the foreigners were allowed to leave the island was by rowboat to visit the notorious flower boats upriver, lucrative sidelines for the same Cantonese merchants who monopolized the vast opium networks that quickly brought China to its knees.

Shamian (Metro: Huangsha on line no. 1) still retains some of its former grandeur in the mansions that served as foreign residences, business premises, banks, and consulates. The mansions were taken over by dozens of families after 1949, but they were recently restored, in many cases to their former splendor, with each major building labeled as to its former purpose. Now partly pedestrianized, its broader boulevards are like long thin gardens with a lot of topiary. A line of bars and cafes on the southwest side with views over the Pearl River serves modern expats. Avoid the dozens of small businesses close to the modern White Swan Hotel, which cater to people on organized tours.

Canton Tower (Guangzhou Xing Dian Shi Ta) At 610m (2,000 ft.) and 37 stories high, this was the tallest building in the world for about 5 minutes back in 2010 (since then, it's already dropped to ninth position and continues to fall as the building bubble surges on relentlessly). Opened to coincide with the city's hosting of the 16th Asian Games, it stands out with its thin hourglass design, which faces Zhujiang New Town. The world's highest Ferris wheel opened here in September 2011, with transparent pods that circle the roof, providing expansive views of the sprawling city. The ride lasts between 20 to 40 minutes and costs ¥130.

Zhujiang New Town Subway Station. ✆ **020/8933-8222.** www.cantontower.com. Admission ranges from ¥50–¥240. 9am–10pm.

Guangzhou Old Railway Station Here is a rare chance to see what China is undoubtedly most famous for: its enormous population. This old station and the adjacent large public square perpetually teems with humanity. It's certainly one of the best opportunities to visualize what a population of 1.6 billion really looks like. At Chinese New Year, this square is awash with more than 100,000 people a day, and ticket lines are as long as you would expect. Even at the non-peak times, being in this area is like being outside the stadium doors as a rock concert finishes and the audience pours out and is a great place to see what a human super-organism might look like. The area has a bad reputation for crime but this is rather undeserved, especially compared to the new East Station and the central business district of Tian He.

To cope with the enormous crowds, the station has at least 18 kinds of uniformed security as well as patrol cars ranging from converted golf carts to oversize SUVs. Business people from all over the province and much of the rest of the country converge here at the vast wholesale clothing markets nearby. Just opposite is the **Bai Ma (White Horse) wholesale clothing market** (Baima Fuzhuang Pifa Shichang; Mon–Sat 10am–5pm) probably one of the largest such markets in the world; and close by around the corner from the Provincial Bus Station is the shady fake-watch market. Simply find a vantage point and look on in awe, as immense flows of human traffic surge endlessly by.

Guangzhou Wholesale Buddhist Market While many visitors head to the Jade market, the best finds are on the upper floors. Here you can find everything you need to kit out your own personal monastery. There is everything here from Daoist ceremonial robes to full size ancestral shrines that probably need planning permission back home. Some parts of the outfits (especially the hats) make unusual gifts and there are more kinds of incense and ornate burners than you can shake a stick at. Also keep an eye out for beautiful Chinese lanterns, known as *gong deng*. If you explore even further, you will likely find one of the fake antique wholesale markets that supply all the trinket and curio shops that you see on your travels with old coins and Qing dynasty carvings. Both places are fascinating and well worth a morning of discovery.

Off Changshou Rd., behind the Hualin International.

Guangzhou Wholesale Glasses Market ★★ Of all the wholesale markets in Guangzhou, this is the one where most visitors find the best bargains. Start out at the main wholesale building where there are at least five floors of dealers. Sunglasses and novelty specs abound on the ground floor; fully operational opticians are up on the fifth floor. Stroll around and pick out some frames. Then head next door to Wider Lenses (ask for "Sweetie," who speaks surprisingly good English), get a quick eye test, and head off for some lunch. Finished frames and lenses are usually ready in less than 2 hours, and if you choose a reasonably priced frame the whole experience should not come to more than ¥200. Try finding that kind of bargain in the West.

Wider Lenses, 2nd floor, 260 Renmin Zhong Lu. ✆ **020/8188-9563.** www.founderoptical.com.

Huadiwan ★★ This market is great for an afternoon's wander. Start out in the furniture section where huge showrooms are devoted to replica Chinese furniture that make the Forbidden City look spartan in comparison. This is where locals come to furnish their most opulent teahouses and residential buyers can find everything from Qing-style four posters to floor-to-ceiling apothecary drawer cabinets. New additions to tempt your credit card might include the beautifully ornate jewelry boxes and the octagonal temple abaci. Passing through the life-size mythic figures of the woodcarving section, visitors move into the aquarium area where enormous arowana vie with king-size koi in gigantic tanks. An avenue of aquatic plants leads into the pet area proper where customers can purchase anything from scorpions to Saint Bernards. Be warned that animal lovers may be distressed at the mercenary puppy farming and the sight of cats and dogs in tiny cages. Aside from the yelps and whines, this huge expanse becomes a Chinese garden center with a clear emphasis on *sanshui* (mountain and water) features, viewing stones (oddly shaped rocks to the uninitiated), and forests of bonsai. Finally, the bird market showcases just about every kind of avian from plain homing pigeons to imported parakeets and full display peacocks. Huadiwan is a spectacular array of sounds and colors, but at the same time locals have little respect for concepts such as conservation and the protection of endangered species. Profit comes first, and so you will see stores piled high with coral and exotic animals of all shapes and sizes. My advice is to keep your hands firmly in your pocket and make a large donation to the World Wildlife Federation when you get home.

Huadiwan Subway Station on line no. 1. Look for exit C and head straight into the market complex directly ahead.

Yide Road Wholesale Markets ★★ The long stretch of road that runs from Haizhu Square down through Renmin Road and beyond is one of the most colorful and extensive wholesale markets in the world. Apart from the usual toys, furnishings, and electronics, this is a great place to find many of those souvenirs found in tourist shops around the rest of the country, with vast areas specializing in stationery, toys, and even dried foods. It is a shame that most people stop off in Guangzhou at the beginning of their trip into China, as this is the ultimate shopping stop and would be much more suitable on the return journey.

Metro: Haizhu Sq. on line no. 1.

Where to Stay

In the build-up to the Olympics and the Asian games of 2010, the Pearl River Delta has seen an explosion of glitzy five-star hotels (more than 30 in Guangdong province in the last 3 years alone, with another 20 still under construction) aimed at the mega-rich business elite and local nouveau riche. For the rest of us this means that all the other hotels in the everyday price range have had any staff with an iota of experience lured away or poached by the likes of the newly opened Westins and Ritz-Carltons. If you stay below four-star level, it's most likely that the staff won't speak English.

Guangzhou can be quite expensive. Don't visit in April or October when the main trade fairs are on, as you may have to pay even above rack rates. Sweltering July and August are popular with tour groups. However, from November to March, rates drop, with a further dip in December and after Chinese New Year.

This is one of the last cities where cavernous hotels with innumerable rooms and endless facilities have survived in any number. These are designed to serve the vast numbers of business people attending the main trade fairs in the last 2 weeks of October and April. These have an effect on room rates as far away as Hong Kong, and the major hotels, despite their cavernous size, are likely to be full in that period and offering no discounts. Otherwise, expect to cut 20% to 50% from the prices quoted, although major hotels also add a 10% service charge and a 5% city tax. Lesser hotels conform to normal Chinese standards by not adding service and including city tax in the quoted price.

MODERATE/INEXPENSIVE

Bauhinia Hotel (Bao Xun Jiu Dian) ★★ This hotel has an excellent location right in the heart of Guangzhou's busiest wholesale market area and only a few minutes away from the Haizhu Square subway station. The hotel is almost brand new and that means that the non-smoking rooms are fresh. Staff are attentive and speak good English.

151 Jiefang Nan Lu. www.bauhinia.com.cn. ✆ **020/6265-6888.** Fax 020/8186-2017. 406 units. ¥480 standard room; ¥580–¥880 suite. AE, DC, MC, V. **Amenities:** Chinese restaurant; coffee shop. *In room:* A/C, cable TV, Internet, minibar.

Guoxiang Hotel (Guoxing Da Sha) Even though the rooms have been halved in size and prices have doubled, this is still one of the favorite mid-range options in Canton. Rooms have recently been fully refurbed and are surprisingly opulent. The hotel is close by to the old station and is very popular with Arab and African traders. The staff speak reasonable English, although the smiles are rather forced.

66 Zhan Qian Lu. ✆ **020/8668-8188.** Fax 020/8667-762. gzguoxiang168@yahoo.cn. From Guangzhou Station take exit D1, which emerges outside the bus station. Turn right and look for the Number One Tunnel, which you can follow all the way to the end and the Guoxiang is about another 100m (328 ft.). 406 units. ¥380 standard room; ¥580–¥680 suite. AE, DC, MC, V. **Amenities:** A/C; cable TV; Internet; minibar.

Where to Eat

According to a national survey, the average Cantonese spends ¥4,413 on dining out annually, which is three times as much as the average Shanghainese, and a whopping seven times more than the national average. While it is Cantonese cuisine that captures the headlines, the local passion for eating has ensured that an eclectic mix of international flavors has established a presence here. Not only does Guangzhou provide the chance to sample many provincial cuisines, an abundance of Asian, Middle Eastern, and even European creativity can now be tasted here. Guangzhou's expat community has changed rapidly in the last few years and this can be seen in the number of international cuisines available. The city has a wide variety of flavors on offer, from Nigerian to Scandinavian.

Bei Yuan Jiujia CANTONESE The Bei Yuan dates from the 1920s, although the current two-story building with courtyards is newer, built around a garden and pond. There's dim sum here all day (about ¥5–¥10 per steamer) and a generous menu of Cantonese classics, with some English translations. Try *huadiao zhu ji* (chicken cooked in yellow wine—although some might argue this is really a Zhejiang dish), *tang cu su rou* (sweet-and-sour pork), and *jiuhuang rou si* (sliced pork with yellow chives). The typically garish carpets, screens, and chandeliers are in odd contrast to a central green space. There are twin entrances—the left is for the traditional Cantonese dishes; the right is for a Chaozhou (Chiu Chow) restaurant, with the roast goose dishes typical of that area of northeast Guangdong.

Xiao Bei Lu 202. ✆ **020/8356-3365.** Meal for 2 about ¥150. No credit cards. 6:50am–4:30pm and 5:30pm–12:10am.

Dong Bei Ren MANCHURIAN One of the most successful chains in the region, Dong Bei Ren offers the opportunity to try northern cuisine in a southern city. I highly recommend that you sample as many different kinds of *jiaozi* (resembling miniature ravioli) as possible. So many carts will come wheeling past your table that you may not even need to consult a menu; rest assured that you will not be disappointed by the selection. Accompany it with great-value fresh fruit juices or even a sweet red wine that might surprise with its potency. The bright flowery uniforms and decor should make branches easy to spot, but watch out for the copycats that are springing up. Additional branches at Tian He Nan Er Lu 36 (© **020/8750-1711**), Taojin Bei Lu 2/F (© **020/8357-1576**), and Lanbaoshi building of Renmin Bei Lu (© **020/8135-1711**).

He Qun Yi Ma Lu 65-7. © **020/8760 0688.** Main courses ¥30–¥100. No credit cards. 10:30am–10:30pm.

Dong Jiang Haixian Da Jiulou ★★ CANTONESE SEAFOOD While Cantonese food can now be found all over the world, the enormous, multistory, football field–size restaurants remain something that can only be seen in Guangzhou. Many places compete to be the largest (the title is currently held by Fishermans' City, more the size of a theme park than a restaurant, in the suburb of Panyu) but most branches of the Dong Jiang chain are vast enough to impress. This particular location stretches over five floors and even spills out on to the sidewalk later in the evening. There is no menu but huge tanks of seafood fill the first floor, with many obscure, strange-looking varieties available at higher prices. Beginners may want to start with a plate full of medium sized steamed shrimp and another of steamed jumbo scallops, before continuing with local exotica such as water beetles and horseshoe crabs. Restaurant rush hour is early Sunday evening, when it seems like every family in the city is heading out to eat. If you can even find a seat, the noise will be deafening, but it will be an experience that you will be unable to replicate elsewhere on the planet. Also at Huanshi Zhong Lu 276, opposite the children's activity center (© **020/8322-9188**).

Yanjiang Lu 2, beside Haizhu Sq. © **020/8318-4901.** Meal for 2 about ¥80–¥200. AE, DC, MC, V. 7am–4am.

Japan Fusion ★★ JAPANESE/CANTONESE Reputedly the largest Japanese restaurant in Asia, but the equally huge menu reveals a strong inclination toward Cantonese flavors. At lunchtime, the vast expanse of tables, teppanyaki plates, and sashimi bars is flooded to capacity, hardly a surprise considering the choice of excellent-value set lunches available. It's great for lunch on the way to or from the station, but watch out in the evening when prices rise sharply.

2/F Metro Plaza, Tian He Bei Lu 358–378. © **020/83884-5109.** Set lunches ¥20–¥100; specialty dishes can be much, much higher. AE, DC, MC, V. 11am–11pm.

Kung Fu Fast Food (Zheng Gongfu) CANTONESE With Chinese authorities growing increasingly nationalistic and the rest of the population following suit, locally branded fast-food chains are making an impromptu resurgence. Rather surprisingly, given what a huge hit Western chains were when they first opened in China, the passion for McDonald's is beginning to wane and some KFCs are even closing down. But fast-food fans need not fear, as the Kung Fu chain is quickly taking up the slack. Kung Fu, which opened its first branch in 1994, now operates 90 restaurants in Guangdong, 300 across the mainland, and hopes to become the top Chinese fast-food chain in the country within 5 years. Relying heavily on the Bruce Lee brand, the menu consists of steamed dishes with fresh ingredients and simple seasoning, such as pork ribs with soybean sauce, chicken with mushroom, beef with pickled vegetable, Taiwan-style minced pork, and eel, all priced between ¥22 and ¥29. The restaurant chain believes that a Cantonese-style steamed meal is a healthier alternative for customers—they're probably right. All dishes are accompanied by a choice of herbal soup such as chicken with ginseng soup (¥13), dried bok choy steamed with pig bones soup (¥11), or mushroom steamed with duck soup (¥12).

7/F, China Plaza. ✆ **020/8386-8999.** Meal for 2 about ¥80. No credit cards. 6:50am–4:30pm and 5:30pm–12:10am.

Yin Ji Chang Fan Dian ★★ CANTONESE Just 5 minutes' walk from China Plaza, Yin Ji is perhaps the best place on the planet to sample the most delicious *chang fen,* a steamed rice-flour pancake served in soy sauce. Although it is massively popular with locals and busy at all times of the day and night, the only other foreigner that you will ever see here is the author. Ask for *xian xia ji dan chang* and you will get a tasty shrimp and egg dish that is the epitome of Guangzhou food. Ask for some *jok* and *you tiao* and you will get some congee (thick rice broth with shredded pork skin) and tasty fried bread sticks for dipping. It's fantastic fare at ultra-low prices and a secret that few other tourists will ever find.

Dong Chuan Lu 94, on the left just past the Provincial Cardiovascular Hospital opposite the Songsha air-conditioner store. ✆ **020/8386-1967.** Meal for 2 about ¥20–¥50. No credit cards. 6:15am–1:15am.

SHENZHEN 深圳

Guangdong Province on the border with Hong Kong, 163km (102 miles) SE of Guangzhou

In the 1980s, Shenzhen grew seemingly overnight from nothing to a metropolis. The growth spurt came at the instigation of then-supreme leader Deng Xiaoping, and remains the primary symbol of the reform and opening policy he initiated. It's equally a symbol of everything that's wrong with what China has become—a jostle of shanty-towers with a rootless, money-grubbing, gone-in-a-day atmosphere. Hardly anyone here is a native, and many Chinese are here illegally. Shenzhen is trying to remake itself, attempting to disassociate itself from the fake handbag shops that line the border and focusing instead on a spanking new Central Business District in Futian.

If you're in Hong Kong and are considering Shenzhen as a side trip, then be aware that shopping is the main activity. Otherwise, the main point of visiting here is to use its airport to get somewhere else. ***Warning:*** Although Hong Kong has "returned to the motherland," this is a full-scale **international border crossing,** open from 6:30am to midnight, and is prohibited even to Chinese who don't have the right documentation. Lines can be long, especially during holiday periods. In either direction, allow *at least* an hour, and whether you're coming or going, be sure to collect immigration cards and fill them in while waiting in line. There are lines for Hong Kong residents, mainland Chinese, and foreigners—you'll be sent to the back again if you join the wrong one. Full Chinese tourist **visas** cannot be obtained here. A 5-day permit allowing access *only* to Shenzhen can be purchased at the border by citizens of most developed nations for ¥100, but the list of favored nations changes as high-level diplomatic spats eventually filter down to the ordinary traveler. ***Note:*** For Chinese translations of selected establishments listed in this section, turn to chapter 16.

Essentials

GETTING THERE It is usually much cheaper to **fly** into Shenzhen from other mainland cities than it is to fly directly to Hong Kong, and there are around 60 Chinese cities to choose from, including Beijing, Chengdu, Guilin, Hangzhou, Kunming, Shanghai, Xiamen, and Xi'an.

Shenzhen Bao'an International Airport (SZX), is the fifth-largest airport in China, and located 32km (20 miles) from downtown. It serves a dozen domestic airlines with regular flights to all the major tourist cities and beyond. Long distance international flights usually land at nearby Guangzhou, although Shenzhen is served by half a dozen Asian carriers. Convenient shuttle buses between Hong Kong International Airport and Shenzhen Airport run every 20 minutes costing HK$180 per adult and HK$100 per child, as well as buses going farther afield to locations such as Dongguan. Helicopter service between Macao and Shenzhen flies 10 times per day. Call ✆ **0852/2108-9898** for more details.

Airport bus no. 330 (✆ **0755/99788**) runs from the airport to the Hualian Dasha (a hotel and department store), just west of the center on Shen Nan Zhong Lu. The ride takes 40 minutes and costs ¥120; the buses run every 15 minutes from 6:20am to 9pm. When work on an extension to the KCR East Rail line is complete, buses will run to the railway station. For now it's a ¥20 taxi ride farther. (Coming from Hong Kong, ignore touts at Luo Hu, and make for the signposted taxi rank.)

The **railway station** (✆ **0755/8326-5043**) is 2 minutes' walk north of the Luo Hu/Lo Wu border and connected by elevated walkway. Tickets for Guangzhou are on sale at this level, and for elsewhere on the floor below, from 7am to 8pm. The express trains directly from Kowloon to Beijing and Shanghai pass through but do not stop here. Shenzhen has its own services from Beijing Xi (2,373km/1,483 miles). Tickets for this and many other **trains** from Shenzhen can be bought at CTS in Hong Kong, but there's a much greater choice of services and destinations from Guangzhou. Departures by express trains to Guangzhou Dong (East) leave 45 times a day from 7:18am to 8:45pm. They occasionally continue to the main station.

About 30 long-distance bus stations operate out of Shenzhen, but it is the **Luo Hu Qichezhan** (✆ **0755/8232-1670**) that visitors will find most useful as buses here depart to most cities of Guangdong Province. Buses for Guangzhou leave every 5 minutes and cost ¥60.

From **Hong Kong,** the easiest train route is via the KCR East Rail line from Hung Hom or Kowloon Tong to Lo Wu. The first train from Hung Hom is at 5:30am and the last at 11:07pm. *Only stay on for Lo Wu if you plan to cross the border, or you may be fined.* The long-distance bus station, **Luo Hu Qichezhan,** is beneath Luo Hu Commercial City, to your right as you leave Customs. There are rapid bus connections with Guangzhou, Zhuhai Gong Bei (the Macau border crossing, every 15 min. 7am–8:30pm), Kaiping, and most other corners of Guangdong Province. A cross-border coach service runs to the Shangri-La hotel directly from Hong Kong Airport's arrivals hall counter 4B; 16 services make the 2-hour trip from 10:30am to 8:30pm for HK$100. In the other direction, 10 services operate from 7:30am to 5:50pm. ***Warning:*** Access to Shenzhen is subject to extra controls. Have your passport ready if you're arriving or leaving by bus.

GETTING AROUND Few people get farther than Luo Hu, with its border station, railway station, bus station, shopping, restaurants, and hotels, all close together. **Red taxi** fares are among China's most expensive with a flagfall of ¥10 including 2.3km (1¼ miles), then ¥2.40 per kilometer up to 15km (9 miles), then 50% more. **Green taxis,** on the other hand, are a much more reasonable ¥7 including 2.3km (1¼ miles), then ¥1.60 per kilometer. *Never* deal with touts who approach you at the border. The taxi stand is signposted beyond Luo Hu Commercial City to your right. At the north end of the plaza, with the border on the south side and the station on the west, stands the Shangri-La hotel. The street leading north on the left side is Jianshe Lu, and the street on the right side is Renmin Nan Lu; between the two of them, they lead to everything you might want.

There are four Sightseeing Bus Lines. Number 1 runs from Nantou Checkpoint to Overseas Chinese Town East priced at ¥9, passing through Window of the World and Splendid China. Bus Line 2 runs from the Futian Agriculture Products Wholesale Market to Buji Union Inspection Station (¥3) and stops at some famous shopping centers, such as Women's World, Mao Ye Department Store and Buji Free Market. Da Yun Line (Sightseeing Line 3), runs from the Jin Long Hotel to the Futian Transportation Hub (¥10) and the Seashore Line (Line 4 ¥7) runs between Shenzhen Sea World and the Buji Union Inspection Station.

The new **metro** has four lines but is expanding fast thanks to the June 2011 Summer Universiade, when line five was completed. Line no. 1 (green on maps) runs 15 stations from Luo Hu to Airport East. Tickets cost ¥2 to ¥8 according to the distance to be traveled.

[Fast FACTS] SHENZHEN

Banks, Foreign Exchange & ATMs A branch of the **Hongkong and Shanghai Bank (HSBC)** is on the Renmin Nan Lu side of the Century Plaza Hotel—you can't change money here but you can use its ATM outside. A branch of the **Bank of China** (Mon–Fri 8:30am–5:30pm; Sat–Sun and holidays 9am–4pm), which has foreign-exchange service and an outside ATM, is nearby to the right and beyond the Shangri-La hotel.

Internet Access The 24-hour **PC-War E-Cafe** even has a nonsmoking area. It's on the fourth floor of the Cybermart at Renmin Nan Lu 3005 and charges ¥2 per hour. Use the side entrance from 7pm to 9am.

Post Office A useful post office (9am–noon and 12:30–5pm) is on the ground-floor level of the north end of Luo Hu Commercial City.

Visa Extensions Cross into Hong Kong and purchase a brand-new 3-month visa within 24 hours if you need one (see chapter 11).

Exploring Shenzhen

Newly minted Shenzhen is the face of modern China. Avoid the city's tawdry and occasionally offensive theme parks. Most attractions can be seen as a day trip from Hong Kong.

Dafen Painting Town ★★ Back in 1988, Hong Kong Businessman Huang Jiang set up the very first reproduction art studio among the paddy fields. These days Dafen houses more that 5,000 artists of all kinds, and it is estimated that they turn out at least five million Klimts, Bouguereaus, and Fragonards every year, an estimated 60% of all the world's oil paintings. This small enclave is surprisingly visitor-friendly, with lots of cafes and relaxed streets to stroll around, there is even an art museum (do not miss the amazing "Along the River During Qing Ming Festival" sculpture outside) and a 300 year old Hakka tea house. Artists will happily take commissions to copy photos or pictures so that you can immortalize that landscape of your childhood, or even have yourself and your family members painted into your favorite Botticelli. Expect to pay just a few hundred yuan but always insist on "A" quality. Of course, there is a great deal of controversy about this place, and some pundits claim that the output of Dafen is about as close to art as Wonderbread is to an artisan French loaf. Others remind us that in the times of the Old Masters, all training was done by copying, and that you can often learn a whole lot from carefully reproducing a Van Gogh. Visit and decide for yourself.

About 20 min. from Luohu in a taxi, which is maybe 50–60 RMB, or 40 min. on the number 300 bus for 5 RMB from Luohu station.

Shopping

It's an increasingly popular view among residents of Hong Kong that Shenzhen is a cheap place to shop. Compared to Hong Kong, it *is* cheap, of course, at least for domestic items, but many proclaiming this view have never been anywhere else in China (and many Hong Kong people have never been to the mainland at all). Those who do go to shop often get no farther than the overrated **Luo Hu Shangye Cheng (Luo Hu Commercial City),** five stories of shopping (8:30am–11pm) above the bus station to the right as you leave the border, where you find luggage, shoes, bags, CDs, clothes, toys, Chinese medicine, tea, tailoring services, portrait photography, bed linens, quilts, electrical goods, leather goods, pearls, jewelry, wigs, massages, pedicures, and even a Cantonese opera house. As elsewhere in the mainland, nearly everything is a fake.

Where to Stay

Business-oriented Shenzhen tends to be expensive. If you must spend a night, the best place to stay is the **Holiday Inn Express** (Luo Hu Kwai Jie Jia Er Jiu Dian) on 6 Guiyuan North Rd. (✆ **0755/2559-6999;** fax 0755/2559-6222), a luxury hotel at budget prices. All the basics are done extremely well as would be expected from such a big name, comfortable beds, excellent buffet breakfast, and full coverage Internet. It is well worth booking this hotel over the Internet where rates are usually in the region of ¥320 to ¥360 for a standard room. The OCT **Loft** (take the metro to the Qiao Cheng Dong stop) is currently one of the most fashionable areas away from the CBD. There is a youth hostel and also a branch of the **City Inn** chain, E-2 Building, Shantou Street (✆ 0755/2693-2828), which provides good value. At the other end of the scale is **the Mahayana OCT,** East OCT, Dameisha Yantian District (✆ **400/630-9996**), a Buddhist themed hotel with 22 Zen-inspired guest rooms, all decorated with religious frescoes. Among the extras are a vegetarian restaurant, meditation and chanting rooms, and Buddhist sermons held by the Huaxing Temple abbot for some soul-searching. There are even chanting robes and slippers in each of the rooms.

Where to Eat

Shenzhen has plenty of delicious culinary options to choose from. If you are just nipping over to Shenzhen for a shopping trip and do not plan to go much farther than

Expert Shopping

Nobody should spend any time in Shenzhen without consulting Ellen McNally's excellent insider's guide, *Shop in Shenzhen.* Widely available in Hong Kong yet strangely absent on the mainland, this handy little guide goes much further than detailed floor plans for Lo Wu, right out to Humen garment wholesale city. Check the Web at **www.shopinshenzhen.com**.

the Lo Wu complex, the top floor branch of the **Laurel Restaurant** (Dan Gui Xuan; ✆ **0755/**8232-3668; 7am–11:30pm) is a very popular choice. A dim sum favorite with Hong Kong day trippers, head there first and grab a reservation ticket and then head off and do your shopping. Depending on the day of the week, the wait might be as long as 3 hours before you are seated, so you'll have time to bargain hunt.

If you are staying longer, then you might like to try something a little less standard. For a change of pace from the rather predictable five-star hotels, try the **Da Shi Wu Jia Slow Food Restaurant,** 3rd floor of office building 88 in CBD in Futian district (✆ **0755/8828-4034**). Everything about the place, from the bamboo mats to the well thought out menu, is designed to calm and relax its guests, essential in one of China's most manic border towns. Prices reflect the fact that it is located in the middle of the new CBD and you should expect to pay around ¥400 for two people. For something even more bizarre, the **Modern Toilet Restaurant,** 2nd floor, Jiefang Lu 1004 Dongmen Buxing, Laojie Metro Station, would be something to write home about. All seats are toilets and dishes are served in miniature toilet bowls.

HONG KONG

11

by Beth Reiber

Hong Kong. The name alone conjures visions of the exotic, a destination molded by a colonial past but defined by its Chinese heritage. Viewed from Victoria Peak, it rates as one of the most stunning cities in Asia, if not the world, with skyscrapers ringing Victoria Harbour and its bustling traffic of historic Star Ferries, cruise liners, cargo ships, and wooden fishing vessels, all set against a dramatic backdrop of gently rounded mountains.

Hong Kong is also known for its streets ablaze with neon and surging with humanity, noisy Cantonese restaurants packed with extended families, and markets offering everything from live seafood to knock-off handbags. But Hong Kong is also one of Asia's most sophisticated cities and is synonymous with luxury hotels, trendy restaurants offering a staggering variety of international cuisines, and exclusive designer boutiques.

The juxtaposition of the past and present, the extreme differences between street life and the high life, has fueled my love affair with Hong Kong for more than 20 years. Ancient temples stand alongside some of the world's tallest skyscrapers; quaint villages slumber on the fringes of densely packed satellite towns; colorful traditional festivals share the stage with highbrow entertainment. You can eat dim sum for breakfast; cross the harbor on the historic Star Ferry; browse name-brand shops for designer wear; hike a solitary path through lush, tropical landscape; scout for cheap souvenirs at a street market; get a massage at a state-of-the-art spa; and then zip over to Macau for a Macanese meal—all in 1 day. Hong Kong's talent at constantly reinventing itself never ceases to amaze me; the promise of boundless possibilities draws me back again and again.

Hong Kong's blend of the exotic and the familiar was forged during its 156 years as a British colony—from 1842, when Britain acquired Hong Kong Island as a spoil of the first Opium War, to its 1997 handover to the Chinese. As a Special Administrative Region (SAR), with the Hong Kong dollar serving as legal tender and English an official language, Hong Kong may be pricier than most other Asian destinations but is a welcome respite for many travelers, with all the creature comforts of home.

Because of its subtropical location, Hong Kong's weather is generally mild in winter and uncomfortably hot and humid in summer, with an average annual rainfall of 2.3m (89 in.). ***Note:*** Unless otherwise noted, hours listed in this chapter are the same every day.

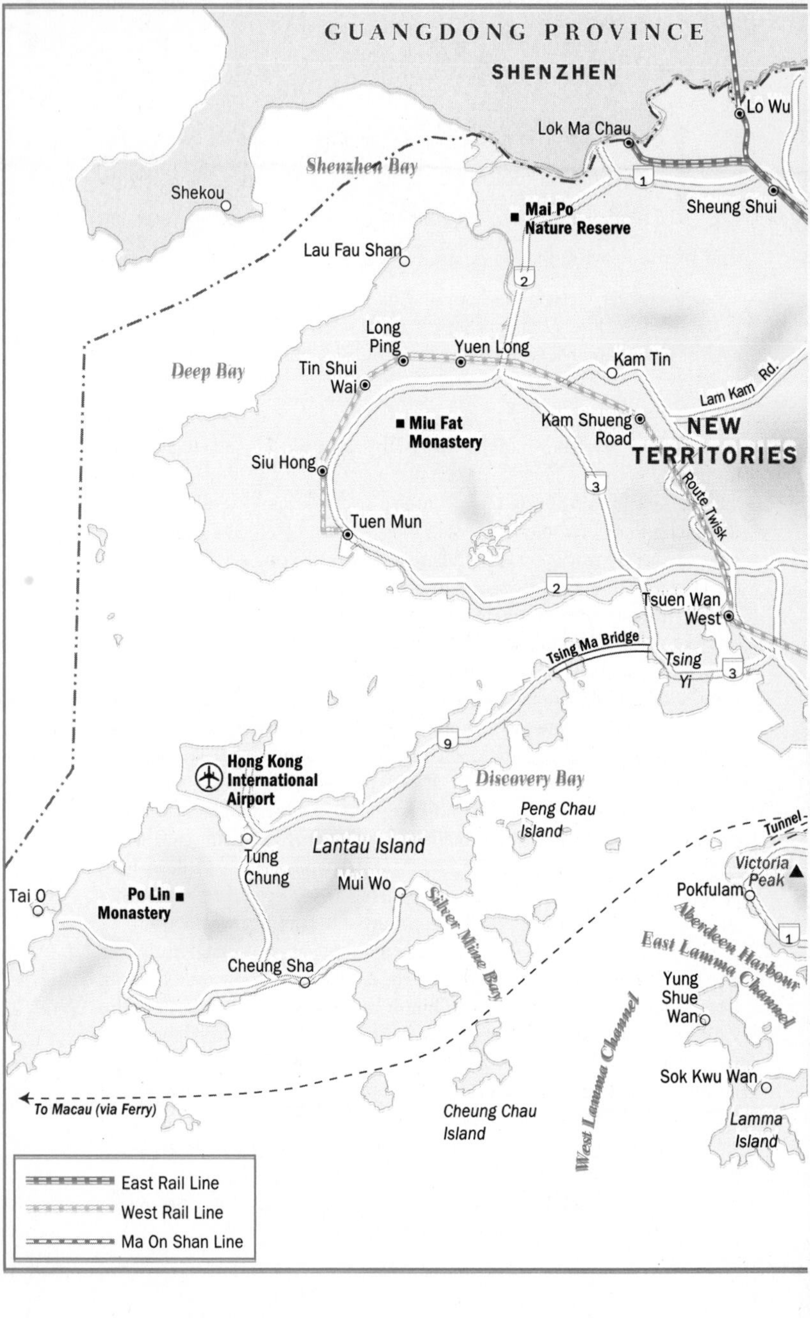

GUANGDONG PROVINCE
SHENZHEN
Lo Wu
Lok Ma Chau
Shenzhen Bay
Shekou
Mai Po Nature Reserve
Sheung Shui
Lau Fau Shan
Long Ping
Yuen Long
Kam Tin
Deep Bay
Tin Shui Wai
Lam Kam Rd.
Miu Fat Monastery
Kam Shueng Road
NEW TERRITORIES
Siu Hong
Route Twisk
Tuen Mun
Tsuen Wan West
Tsing Ma Bridge
Tsing Yi
Hong Kong International Airport
Discovery Bay
Peng Chau Island
Tunnel
Lantau Island
Tung Chung
Victoria Peak
Tai O
Po Lin Monastery
Mui Wo
Pokfulam
Silver Mine Bay
Aberdeen Harbour
East Lamma Channel
Cheung Sha
Yung Shue Wan
West Lamma Channel
Sok Kwu Wan
To Macau (via Ferry)
Cheung Chau Island
Lamma Island

East Rail Line
West Rail Line
Ma On Shan Line

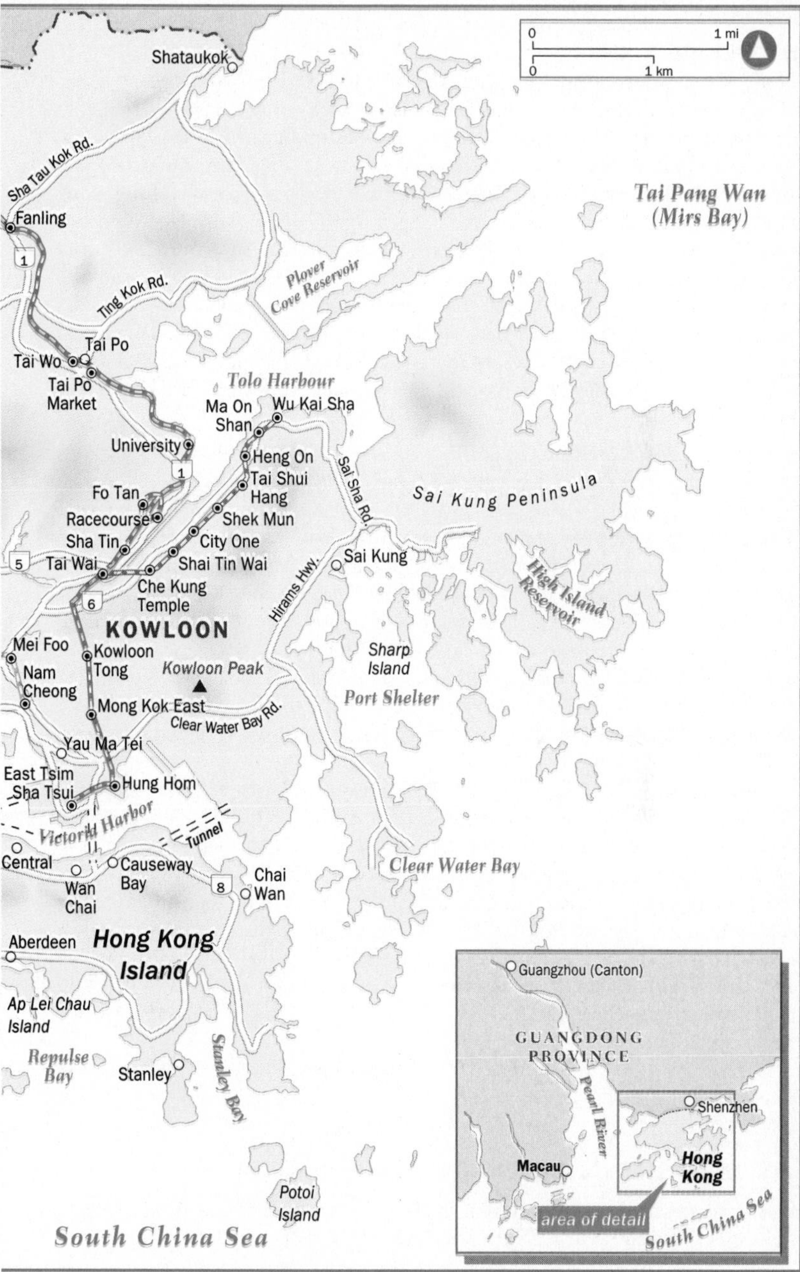
0 1 mi
0 1 km
Shataukok
Sha Tau Kok Rd.
Fanling
Ting Kok Rd.
Plover Cove Reservoir
Tai Pang Wan
(Mirs Bay)
Tai Po
Tai Wo
Tai Po Market
Tolo Harbour
Ma On Shan
Wu Kai Sha
University
Heng On
Tai Shui Hang
Fo Tan
Racecourse
Shek Mun
Sha Tin
City One
Tai Wai
Shai Tin Wai
Che Kung Temple
Sai Sha Rd.
Sai Kung Peninsula
Sai Kung
Hirams Hwy.
High Island Reservoir
KOWLOON
Mei Foo
Kowloon Tong
Kowloon Peak
Nam Cheong
Mong Kok East
Clear Water Bay Rd.
Sharp Island
Port Shelter
Yau Ma Tei
East Tsim Sha Tsui
Hung Hom
Victoria Harbor
Tunnel
Central
Wan Chai
Causeway Bay
Chai Wan
Clear Water Bay
Aberdeen
Hong Kong Island
Ap Lei Chau Island
Repulse Bay
Stanley
Stanley Bay
Potoi Island
South China Sea
Guangzhou (Canton)
GUANGDONG PROVINCE
Pearl River
Shenzhen
Macau
Hong Kong
area of detail
South China Sea

ORIENTATION

Getting There

BY PLANE

Hong Kong International Airport (✆ **852/2181 8888;** www.hongkongairport.com) is located about 32km (20 miles) from Hong Kong's central business district. In the arrivals hall, just past Customs, visitors can pick up English-language maps and sightseeing brochures and get directions to their hotel at the **Hong Kong Tourism Board (HKTB),** open 7am to 11pm. Also in the arrivals hall are the **Hong Kong Hotel Association** (www.hkha.com.hk), open from 7am to midnight, with a free booking service to some 90 member hotels; and the **Macau Government Tourist Office,** open from 9am to 1pm, 1:45 to 6pm, and 6:45 to 10pm. You can also exchange money in the arrivals hall, although because of the unfavorable rates, it's best to change only what's needed to get into town—about US$50 should more than do it. Otherwise, it's much cheaper to use the **Hongkong and Shanghai Bank (HSBC)** ATM at the departures level, which takes almost any card—ask HKTB staff for directions.

GETTING INTO TOWN The quickest way to get to downtown Hong Kong is via the sleek **Airport Express Line** (✆ **852/2881 8888;** www.mtr.com.hk), located straight ahead past the arrivals hall. Trains, which depart every 12 minutes between 5:50am and 1:15am, take 20 minutes to reach Kowloon Station and 24 minutes to reach Hong Kong Station (in Central on Hong Kong Island). Fares are HK$90 to Kowloon and HK$100 to Central. From both the Kowloon and Hong Kong stations, free shuttle buses (every 12–24 min. 6:12am–11:12pm) deposit passengers at major hotels. If you're returning to the airport via the Airport Express Line, consider purchasing the **Airport Express Travel Pass,** a stored-value pass that allows unlimited travel for 3 days. The HK$300 Travel Pass includes the trip from and to the airport, while the HK$220 pass covers only one trip on the Airport Express (for other options, see "Getting Around" on p. 551).

Airport Hotelink (✆ **852/3193 9333;** www.trans-island.com.hk) provides door-to-door airport bus service to major hotels for HK$130 to HK$150; the shuttle departs every 30 to 60 minutes and takes 30 to 40 minutes to reach Tsim Sha Tsui. Slower, with more stops, are **Cityflyer Airbuses** (✆ **852/2873 0818;** www.nwstbus.com.hk), serving major downtown areas. Most important for tourists are **Airbus A21,** which travels through Mongkok, Yau Ma Tei, and Jordan, and down Nathan Road through Tsim Sha Tsui on its way to the KCR East Rail Hung Hom Station; and **Airbus A11,** which travels to Hong Kong Island. Buses depart every 10 to 30 minutes, with fares costing HK$33 to Kowloon and HK$40 to Central and Causeway Bay.

On average, a **taxi** to Tsim Sha Tsui will cost approximately HK$300; a taxi to Central will cost about HK$365. Expect to pay an extra luggage charge of HK$5 per piece.

Traveling to & from the Mainland

If you plan to spend most of your time in Hong Kong and are considering just a brief trip to the mainland, avoid the massively overpriced tours peddled by Hong Kong agents—trips to Guangzhou and Shenzhen are easy to arrange for yourself. Neither of these cities should be picked as your sole experience of the mainland, however; nor, for longer stays, should they be your first choice as a point of entry. Instead, consider taking a ferry service to rural Kaiping, or a proper oceangoing vessel around the coast to Xiamen (perhaps providing the softest landing of all), and making easy connections up the coast.

A visit to mainland China requires advance purchase of a **visa,** but these are more easily obtainable in Hong Kong than anywhere else (both single- and double-entry visas are available in Hong Kong; multiple-entry visas must be obtained in your home country). Numerous agents are eager to act for you, but shop around—many agents within the tourist districts are also eager to charge you 50% to 100% more than you need to pay. The Hong Kong operation of **CTS (China Travel Service)** has approximately 40 branches, the best known of which is at 27–33 Nathan Rd., Tsim Sha Tsui (one floor up in Alpha House, entrance around the corner on Peking Rd.; **© 852/2315 7188;** fax 852/2315 7292; www.ctshk.com), open 365 days a year. Come here for commission-free ferry, train, and bus tickets to the mainland, as well as advance-purchase tickets for a limited selection of trains to Beijing, Shanghai, Hangzhou, Guangzhou, Xi'an, Guilin, and Shenzhen.

To fill out an application for your visa, you will need your passport (with an expiration date of not less than 6 months away) and one passport photograph. Prices for a visa, unfortunately, vary depending on nationality and are subject to change. It's cheapest, however, to turn in your visa application at least 4 business days prior to departure. At the time this book was going to press, Americans applying for a visa 4 days in advance at CTS, which is cheaper than most places (especially hotel tour desks), were required to pay HK$1,180 for either a single- or double-entry visa valid for 6 months. However, Americans in a hurry can obtain a visa more quickly by paying more: HK$1,530 for visa applications made 3 days in advance and HK$2,470 for same-day service (applications made before 9:30am will be available by 6:30pm the same day).

U.K. residents fare better: HK$600 for a single-entry visa (valid for 30 days) applied for 4 days in advance, HK$900 for 3 days in advance, HK$1,350 for next-day service, and HK$1,950 for same-day visa pickup. Otherwise, the regular price of a single-entry visa for many other nationalities, including Canadians, Australians, and New Zealanders, is HK$210 for applications made 3 days in advance; HK$480 for same-day pickup. In any case, visa requirements and prices can change overnight; call your embassy for updated information.

For air tickets, shop around the many budget-travel agents in the area, such as **Shoestring Travel,** also in the Alpha House, fourth floor (**© 852/2723 2306;** fax 852/2721 2085; www.shoestringtravel.com.hk). Entry visas are cheaper here, too, but agents farther away from the main shopping streets are even cheaper still.

BY PLANE

Various Chinese airlines connect Hong Kong with Beijing, Changsha, Chengdu, Chongqing, Dalian, Fuzhou, Guangzhou, Haikou, Hangzhou, Ji'nan, Kunming, Nanjing, Ningbo, Qingdao, Shanghai, Shantou, Shenyang, Tianjin, Wenzhou, Wuhan, Wuxi, Xiamen, and other minor destinations. Hong Kong's more expensive **Dragonair** flies to Beijing, Chengdu, Chongqing, Dalian, Fuzhou, Guangzhou,

Guilin, Hangzhou, Kunming, Nanjing, Ningbo, Qingdao, Shanghai, Tianjin, Wuhan, and Xiamen. Shop around with travel agencies and bargain for discount fares. Do *not* book with Hong Kong agents in advance online—prices are outrageous.

With the exception of rare special offers, it is almost always cheaper to fly from **Shenzhen** or **Guangzhou** to domestic destinations. Be sure to factor in transportation costs to Hong Kong International Airport and to Shenzhen or Guangzhou when making comparisons. **Shenzhen Bao'an Airport** has service to some 50 Chinese cities. Unfortunately, jetfoil service between Hong Kong International Airport and Shenzhen Bao'an Airport is only once daily (departing at 7:10pm from HKIA and at 6pm from Bao'an); there are, however, three bus companies at Hong Kong International Airport that provide service to mainland China, including Shenzhen Bao'an Airport. The **CTS Express Coach** (✆ **852/3604 0118;** http://ctsbus.hkcts.com), for example, offers hourly service to Shenzhen Bao'an Airport for HK$180.

BY TRAIN

The T98 leaves Hung Hom for Beijing at 3:15pm on alternate days, stopping at Dongguan (Changping), Guangzhou East, Shaoguan, Changsha, Wuchang, Hankou, Zhengzhou, and Shijiazhuang before arriving in Beijing West at 2:51pm the next day. The T97 departs Beijing at 1:08pm on alternate days and arrives in Hung Hom at 12:56pm the next day. The T100 departs Hung Hom for Shanghai at 3:15pm on alternate days, calling at Dongguan (Changping), Guangzhou East, Shaoguan, and Hangzhou East before arriving in Shanghai at 10am the next day. The T99 departs Shanghai at 6:20pm and arrives in Hung Hom at 12:56pm the next day.

Tickets for Beijing and Shanghai can be bought up to 60 days in advance and for Gunaghzhou 30 days in advance at Hung Hom or any MTR East Rail station, or through travel agents (with no commission payable). Tickets for Guangzhou can also be purchased with a prepaid Octopus at more than 40 MTR station. Online agents overcharge by as much as 70%. To find out whether your train is departing on odd or even days of the month, go to www.mtro.com.hk or call the **Intercity Passenger Services Hotline** at ✆ **852/2947 7888,** which also has details on Guangzhou services.

From Beijing, fares are HK$1,191 for *gaoji ruanwo*—a bed in a two-bed cabin—HK$934 for a soft sleeper, and HK$574 to HK$601 for a hard sleeper. From Shanghai, fares are HK$508 to HK$1,039.

There are 12 daily services to and from **Guangzhou Dong Zhan (East Station)** for HK$190 to HK$230; the trip takes a little less than 2 hours.

From Beijing and Shanghai, passengers are required to alight with all baggage and go through Customs and Immigration procedures about an hour out from Kowloon's Hung Hom Station, at Changping (Dongguan). Leaving Hong Kong, don't bother to stow heavy baggage until after you reboard the train. To and from Guangzhou, formalities are conducted at Guangzhou Dong station and on the train. Hong Kong Customs and Immigration procedures (including yet another X-ray of baggage) take place at Hung Hom station. Expect to spend about HK$35 for a taxi to a hotel in Tsim Sha Tsui or Tsim Sha Tsui East.

There are also services every few minutes to and from Lo Wu, Hong Kong's border crossing to Shenzhen, the last stop on the MTR East Rail. See "Getting Around" on p. 551, and "Shenzhen" (p. 538) for details. You should proceed as far as Lo Wu only if you intend to cross the border, which is open from 6:30am to midnight. Lines can be long—allow an hour.

BY FERRY

Up-to-date schedules of TurboJET jetfoil sailings from Hong Kong can be found at www.turbojet.com.hk or by calling ✆ **852/2859 3333** in Hong Kong, or ✆ **853/8790 7039** in Macau. There is round-the-clock service to Macau from the Macau Ferry Terminal on Hong Kong Island and nine daily sailings from the China (HK) Ferry Terminal in Tsim Sha Tsui in Kowloon (see "Macau," later in this chapter). There are also direct sailings from Hong Kong International Airport to Macau. Fares for a weekday sailing from Hong Kong Island to Macau are HK$134 for economy class and HK$236 for super class; fares are higher on weekends and holidays and for night service. Travelers who wish to journey in style can opt for the Premier Jetfoil, with up to 10 sailings daily offering such upgraded services as reclining leather chairs and complimentary food and beverage service. Prices for these run HK$212 to HK$312, depending on the class of seating, for day trips. Tickets are sold at ferry terminals and at the Shun Tak Centre 3/F (200 Connaught Rd. Central, Hong Kong), Hong Kong and Macau airports, and China Travel Service branches. Telephone reservations via credit card can be made up to 28 days in advance at ✆ **852/2921 6688** or online.

If your destination in Macau is Cotai, Taipa, or Colôane, you can travel from the Macau Ferry Terminal directly to Taipa every 15 to 30 minutes via **Cotai Waterjets** (✆ **852/2359 9990** in Hong Kong, **853/2885 0595** in Macau; www.cotaijet.com.mo); there are also a few morning departures from Tsim Sha Tsui's China Ferry Terminal. One-way fares are the same as the regular fares given above.

The **Chu Kong Passenger Transport Co.** operates a catamaran service to various ports in **Guangzhou,** as well as to the Taipa Ferry Terminal in **Macau,** from the China HK Ferry Terminal. See www.cksp.com.hk or call ✆ **852/2858 3876** for details.

BY BUS

Three coach operators, including **CTS Express Coach** (✆ **852/2365 0118;** http://ctsbus.hkcts.com), provide bus service directly from Hong Kong International Airport to more than 70 mainland destinations, including Shenzhen, Guangzhou, and Macau. In town, CTS sells tickets for a variety of cross-border bus services to destinations around Guangdong Province and beyond. Service from Causeway Bay (Metro Park Hotel) and from CTS offices in Wan Chai and Prince Edward to Guangzhou costs HK$100.

Visitor Information

In addition to its tourist counter in the arrivals hall of Hong Kong International Airport and at Lo Wu Arrival Hall (8am–4pm), the **Hong Kong Tourism Board (HKTB)** maintains two offices in town, on both sides of the harbor. On the Kowloon side, there's a convenient office in Tsim Sha Tsui right in the Star Ferry concourse, open 8am to 8pm. On the Hong Kong Island side, a HKTB kiosk is located on Victoria Peak, in a vintage tram car, open from 9am to 9pm. Otherwise, if you have a question about Hong Kong, you can call the **HKTB Visitor Hotline** (✆ **852/2508 1234**) from 9am to 6pm or visit HKTB's website at www.discoverhongkong.com.

The HKTB publishes a wealth of excellent free literature, maps, and the weekly *What's On—Hong Kong. Where Hong Kong, City Life,* and *bc* are other free monthly giveaways with event listings.

City Layout

The Hong Kong Special Administrative Region (SAR) is located at the southeastern tip of the People's Republic of China, some 2,000km (1,240 miles) south of Beijing. Hong Kong can be divided into four distinct parts: **Hong Kong Island;** the **Kowloon Peninsula;** the **New Territories,** which stretch north from Kowloon all the way to the mainland border; and 260 **outlying islands,** most of which are barren and uninhabited.

Neighborhoods in Brief

HONG KONG ISLAND

Central District Central serves as Hong Kong's nerve center for banking, business, and administration. It also has some of Hong Kong's most innovative architecture, some of the city's poshest hotels, high-end shopping centers, and restaurants and bars catering to Hong Kong's white-collar workers.

Lan Kwai Fong Named after an L-shaped street in Central, this is Hong Kong's premier nightlife and entertainment district, occupying not only Lan Kwai Fong but overflowing into neighboring streets like D'Aguilar and Wyndham.

Mid-Levels Located above Central on the slope of Victoria Peak, the Mid-Levels is a popular residential area with swank apartment buildings, grand sweeping views, lush vegetation, and slightly cooler temperatures. Serving white-collar workers who commute to Central is the Central–Mid-Levels Escalator, the world's longest people mover.

SoHo This up-and-coming dining and nightlife district, flanking the Central–Mid-Levels Escalator, is named for being "**So**uth of **Ho**llywood Road." It has blossomed into an ever-growing neighborhood of cafe-bars and intimate restaurants specializing in ethnic and innovative cuisine, centered mostly on Elgin, Shelley, and Staunton streets.

Western District The Western District, located west of Central, is a fascinating neighborhood of shops selling medicinal herbs, ginseng, medicines, dried seafood, and other Chinese products. It's also famous for Hollywood Road (long popular for its many antiques and curio shops) and for Man Mo Temple, one of Hong Kong's oldest, in a part of the Western District known as Sheung Wan. Unfortunately, modernization is slowly encroaching and replacing the older neighborhoods.

Wan Chai Once notorious for its sleazy bars and easy women, Wan Chai has become a little more respectable with mostly business-style hotels, the huge Hong Kong Convention and Exhibition Centre, and a small but revitalized nightlife scene.

Causeway Bay Just east of Wan Chai, Causeway Bay is popular as a shopping destination, with the Times Square shopping complex and department stores; clothing, shoe, and accessory boutiques; and restaurants. On its eastern perimeter is Victoria Park.

Aberdeen Aberdeen, on the south side of Hong Kong Island, was once a fishing village but is now studded with high-rises and housing projects. It remains famous for its hundreds of sampans and junks, and for a huge floating restaurant.

Stanley Located on the quiet south side of Hong Kong Island, this former fishing village is home to Hong Kong's most famous market, selling everything from silk suits to name-brand shoes, casual wear, and souvenirs.

KOWLOON PENINSULA

Kowloon North of Hong Kong Island, across Victoria Harbour, is Kowloon, 12 sq. km (4⅔ sq. miles) that were ceded to Britain in 1860. Kowloon includes the districts of Tsim Sha Tsui, Tsim Sha Tsui East, Yau Ma Tei, Hung Hom, and Mongkok. Boundary Street in the north separates it from the New Territories.

Tsim Sha Tsui Tsim Sha Tsui has an excellent art museum, a cultural center for the performing arts, Kowloon Park, one of the world's largest shopping malls, a broad selection of international restaurants, a jumping nightlife, Hong Kong's largest concentration of hotels, and Nathan Road, nicknamed the "Golden Mile of Shopping."

Tsim Sha Tsui East This area was built entirely on reclaimed land and is home to several hotels, shopping and restaurant complexes, museums, and East Tsim Sha Tsui Station, with train service to Hung Hom Station and onward to mainland China and connected to Tsim Sha Tsui MTR station via underground pedestrian passageway.

Yau Ma Tei Just north of Tsim Sha Tsui, Yau Ma Tei has an interesting produce market, a jade market, and the fascinating Temple Street Night Market. It also has several moderately priced hotels.

Mongkok This district north of Yau Ma Tei is a residential and industrial area, home of the Bird Market and the Ladies' Market on Tung Choi Street.

GETTING AROUND

Hong Kong is compact and easy to navigate, with street, bus, and subway signs clearly marked in English. Each mode of transportation—bus, ferry, tram, and train/subway—has its own fare system and requires a new ticket each time you transfer from one to another. However, if you're going to be in Hong Kong for a few days, consider purchasing the **Octopus** smart card, which allows users to hop on and off trains, trams, subways, buses, and ferries without worrying about purchasing tickets each time. It can also be used at convenience stores like 7-Eleven. Sold at MTR stations and some ferry piers, it costs a minimum of HK$150, including a HK$50 refundable deposit, and can be reloaded as necessary. For information, call the Octopus Hotline at ✆ **852/2266 2222** or check its website at www.octopus.com.hk. Other options include the Airport Express Travel Pass described above and the Tourist Day Pass for HK$55, which provides 24 hours of unlimited travel on the entire MTR network for visitors staying in Hong Kong fewer than 14 days.

Otherwise, transportation on buses and trams requires exact fare, making it imperative to carry lots of loose change wherever you go.

BY TRAIN & SUBWAY Hong Kong's **Mass Transit Railway (MTR)** is modern, easy to use, and very fast, consisting of nine color-coded subway and train lines, the Airport Express Line, and light rail service in the New Territories. The former Kowloon-Canton Railway (KCR), serving the New Territories, is now part of the MTR. Single-ticket, one-way fares start at HK$4 for most lines and increase according to the distance traveled. The train trip on the East Rail from Hung Hom to Sheung Shui, for example, the last stop before China's border, costs HK$8.50 for ordinary (second) class and HK$17 for first class for the 38-minute trip. Credit card–size plastic tickets are inserted into slots at entry turnstiles, retrieved, and inserted again at exits. The MTR operates from 6am to about midnight or 1am, and there are no public restrooms at any of the stations or on the trains. For general inquiries, call the **MTR Hotline** at ✆ **852/2881 8888** or check www.mtr.com.hk.

BY BUS Hong Kong buses are a delight—especially the British-style double-deckers. They're good for traveling to places other forms of transportation don't go, such as the southern part of Hong Kong Island like Stanley, the New Territories, or Lantau. HKTB has leaflets showing bus routes. Depending on the route, buses run from about 6am to midnight, with fares ranging from HK$1.20 to HK$45—exact fares required (or use an Octopus card). Few drivers speak English, so you may want to have someone at your hotel write your destination in Chinese. In rural areas, you must flag down a bus to make it stop. Otherwise, the best bet for tourists are open-top double-decker **Big Bus Tours** (✆ **852/2723 2108;** www.bigbustours.com/eng/hongkong), which offers hop-on/hop-off service to key attractions on Hong Kong Island and Kowloon. Operating from about 10am to 6pm at 30-minute intervals, the service costs HK$320 for 24 hours and HK$420 for 48 hours (children pay HK$200 and HK$300, respectively) and includes the Star Ferry, Peak Tram, and trips to Stanley. Rickshaw Sightseeing Bus (✆ **852/2136 8888;** www.rickshawbus.com) offers a similar service to major spots on north Hong Kong Island, with a day ticket costing HK$50.

BY TRAM Tram lines, found only along the north side of Hong Kong Island, are a nostalgic way to travel through the Western District, Central, Wan Chai, and Causeway Bay. Established in 1904, these old, narrow, double-decker affairs clank their way from Kennedy Town in the west to Shau Kei Wan in the east, with one branch detouring to Happy Valley. Regardless of how far you go, you pay the exact fare of HK$2 or use an Octopus card as you exit. Trams run from 6am to midnight. More information is available at ✆ **852/2548 7102** or www.hktramways.com.

BY FERRY A 5-minute trip across Victoria Harbour on one of the white-and-green ferries of the **Star Ferry Company** (✆ **852/2367 7065;** www.starferry.com.hk), in operation since 1898, is one of Hong Kong's top attractions. It costs only HK$2 for ordinary (second) class or HK$2.50 in first class on the upper deck Monday to Friday, with weekend and holiday fares HK$2.40 and HK$3 respectively. Ferries ply the waters between Central and Tsim Sha Tsui from 6:30am to 11:30pm, with departures every 6 to 10 minutes. Besides the Central-to-Tsim Sha Tsui route, Star Ferries also run between Central and Hung Hom and between Tsim Sha Tsui and Wan Chai.

A large fleet also serves the many outlying islands and the northern part of the mainland, with most ferries departing from the Central Ferry Piers (home also of the Star Ferry). The HKTB has ferry schedules, or you can also obtain information on schedules to Cheung Chau and Lantau at ✆ **852/2131 8181** and www.nwff.com.hk; for Lamma, call ✆ **852/2815 6063** or visit www.hkkf.com.hk.

BY TAXI Taxi drivers in Hong Kong are strictly controlled and as a rule are fairly honest. Fares start at HK$18 for the first 2km (1¼ miles), then HK$1.50 for each 200m (656 ft.). Luggage costs an extra HK$5 per piece, and taxis ordered by phone ✆ **852/2574 7311**) add a HK$5 surcharge. Extra charges are also permitted for trips through harbor tunnels and Aberdeen Tunnel. At major taxi stands, there are separate lines for Kowloon and Island-side taxis. A 24-hour hot line handles complaints about taxis (✆ **852/2889 9999**).

BY MINIBUS These small, 16-passenger buses are the poor person's taxis. There are two types of vehicles: The green-and-yellow public "light buses," which follow fixed routes, charge fixed rates ranging from HK$2 to HK$22.50 depending on the distance, and require the exact fare as you enter (many also accept Octopus cards); the red-and-yellow **minibuses** will stop wherever you hail them and do not follow fixed routes. Fares for these range from HK$2 to HK$23, and you pay as you exit. Just yell when you want to get off.

[Fast FACTS] HONG KONG

Banks, Foreign Exchange & ATMs Although opening hours may vary among banks, banking hours are generally Monday through Friday from 9am to 4:30pm and Saturday from 9am to 12:30pm. Some banks stop their transactions an hour before closing time. ATMs are everywhere, and almost all accept foreign cards.

Doctors & Dentists Most first-class hotels have medical clinics with registered nurses, as well as doctors on duty at specified hours or on call 24 hours. Otherwise, your concierge or the U.S. consulate can refer you to a doctor or dentist. In an emergency, dial ✆ **999** or call one of the recommendations under "Hospitals," below.

Embassies & Consulates The consulate of the **United States** is at 26 Garden Rd., Central District (✆ **852/2523 9011;** 852/2841 2211 for the American Citizens Service; http://hongkong.usconsulate.gov). The consulate of **Canada** is on the 12th to 14th floors of Tower One, Exchange Square, 8 Connaught Place, Central District (✆ **852/3719 4700;** www.canadainternational.gc.ca/hong_kong). The consulate of the **U.K.** is at 1 Supreme Court Rd., Central District (✆ **852/2901 3000;** http://ukinhongkong.fco.gov.uk/en). The consulate of **Australia** is on the 23rd floor of Harbour Centre, 25 Harbour Rd., Wan Chai (✆ **852/2827 8881;** www.hongkong.china.embassy.gov.au). The consulate of **New Zealand** is on the 65th floor of Central Plaza, 18 Harbour Rd., Wan Chai (✆ **852/2525 5044;** www.nzembassy.com/hong-kong). Most other nations, including all of China's neighbors—even hermit kingdoms like Bhutan—also have representation in Hong Kong. Collect onward visas here.

Hospitals Try **Queen Mary Hospital,** 102 Pokfulam Rd., Hong Kong Island (✆ **852/2855 3838;** www3.ha.org.hk/qmh/index.htm); and **Queen Elizabeth Hospital,** 30 Gascoigne Rd., Kowloon (✆ **852/2958 8888;** www3.ha.org.hk/qeh/index.htm).

Internet Access **Hong Kong Central Library,** 66 Causeway Rd., Causeway Bay, offers free Internet access for a maximum of 2 hours from 10am to 9pm. To avoid a wait, make a reservation at ✆ **852/2921 0348.** More convenient, perhaps, is **Cyber Pro Internet Cafe,** located in the Star House across from the Tsim Sha Tsui ferry terminal, next to McDonald's (no phone). Open daily from 10am to 2am, it requires a HK$40 deposit, plus a minimum charge of HK$20 for 1 hour. Four hours cost HK$60.

Newspapers The *South China Morning Post* and the *Standard* are the two local English-language daily newspapers. The *Asian Wall Street Journal, Financial Times, International Herald Tribune,* and *USA Today International* are also available.

Pharmacies There are no 24-hour drugstores in Hong Kong. One of the best-known pharmacies in Hong Kong is **Watson's,** with more than 100 branches, most of them open from 9am to 10pm.

Police You can reach the police for an emergency by dialing ✆ **999,** the same number as for a fire or an ambulance. There's also a 24-hour crime hotline at **852/2527 7177.**

Post Offices Airmail letters up to 20 grams (.7 oz.) and postcards cost HK$3 to the United States, Europe, or Australia. Most hotels have stamps and can mail your letters for you. Otherwise, most post offices are open Monday through Friday from 9:30am to 5pm and Saturday from 9:30am to 1pm. The main post office is at 2 Connaught Place, Central District, Hong Kong Island (✆ **852/2921 2222**). You can have your mail sent here "Poste Restante," where it will be held for 2 months; be sure to bring along your passport for identification. It's open Monday through Saturday from 8am to 6pm and Sunday and holidays from 9am to 5pm. On the Kowloon side, the Tsim Sha Sui main post office is at 10 Middle Rd., which is 1 block north of Salisbury Road (✆ **852/2366 4111**). It's open Monday to Saturday from 9am to 6pm and Sunday from 9am to 2pm. For more information, go to www.hongkongpost.com.

Smoking Smokers have a rougher time in Hong Kong now that it has gone mostly smoke free in public places, including restaurants and bars.

Weather To check the day's temperature and humidity level or the 2-day forecast, dial ✆ **187 8200** or go to www.hko.gov.hk.

WHERE TO STAY

Hotel rates listed below are the hotels' official or "rack" rates, which you might end up paying if you come during peak season (Chinese New Year, Mar–May, Oct–Nov, major trade fairs). Otherwise, you should be able to get a room for much less by calling the hotel directly to ask whether any promotional rates are available, or, even better, by checking the hotel's website.

Hong Kong's top hotels are among the best in the world, many with sweeping views of Victoria Harbour (for which you'll pay dearly) and superb service and amenities. Although the greatest concentration of hotels is on the Kowloon side, Hong Kong is so compact and easily traversed by public transportation that location is not the issue it is in larger, more sprawling metropolises. Moderate hotels comprise the majority of hotels in Hong Kong, with smaller rooms catering largely to the burgeoning growth of tourists from mainland China. Inexpensive hotels offer just the basics. A 10% service charge will be added to prices quoted below. All hotels below offer smoke-free rooms.

Kowloon

EXPENSIVE

Hotel InterContinental Hong Kong ★★★ The stylish InterContinental, located on the water's edge, has the best views of Victoria Harbour from Tsim Sha Tsui, with about 70% of its rooms commanding sweeping views of the harbor with floor-to-ceiling and wall-to-wall windows. Other notable features here are the highly rated restaurants; lobby lounge for tea or cocktails; upscale shopping arcade; state-of-the-art spa renowned for its healing treatments; free tai chi and yoga classes; contemporary rooms with air purification systems and huge walk-in closets adjoining the bathrooms (so you can shower and get dressed without disturbing another guest in the room); and Wi-Fi that enables guests to access the Internet even from poolside.

18 Salisbury Rd., Tsim Sha Tsui, Kowloon, Hong Kong. www.hongkong-ic.intercontinental.com. ✆ **800/327-0200** in the U.S. and Canada, or 852/2721 1211. Fax 852/2739 4546. 495 units. HK$4,700–HK$6,300 single or double; HK$900 extra per room per night for Club lounge privileges; from HK$6,800 suite. Children under 12 stay free in parent's room. AE, DC, MC, V. MTR: Tsim Sha Tsui. **Amenities:** 5 restaurants, including SPOON by Alain Ducasse (p. 562); lounge; bar; babysitting; concierge; executive-level rooms; exercise room and spa; Jacuzzis overlooking Victoria Harbour; outdoor pool w/underwater music; room service. *In room:* A/C, TV/DVD/CD, hair dryer, minibar, MP3 docking station, Wi-Fi (for a fee).

The Peninsula Hong Kong ★★★ This is Hong Kong's most famous hotel and *the* place to stay. Built in 1928, it exudes elegance, from its white-gloved doormen to one of the largest limousine fleets of Rolls-Royces in the world. Its lobby, with high gilded ceilings, pillars, and palms, has long been Hong Kong's foremost spot for

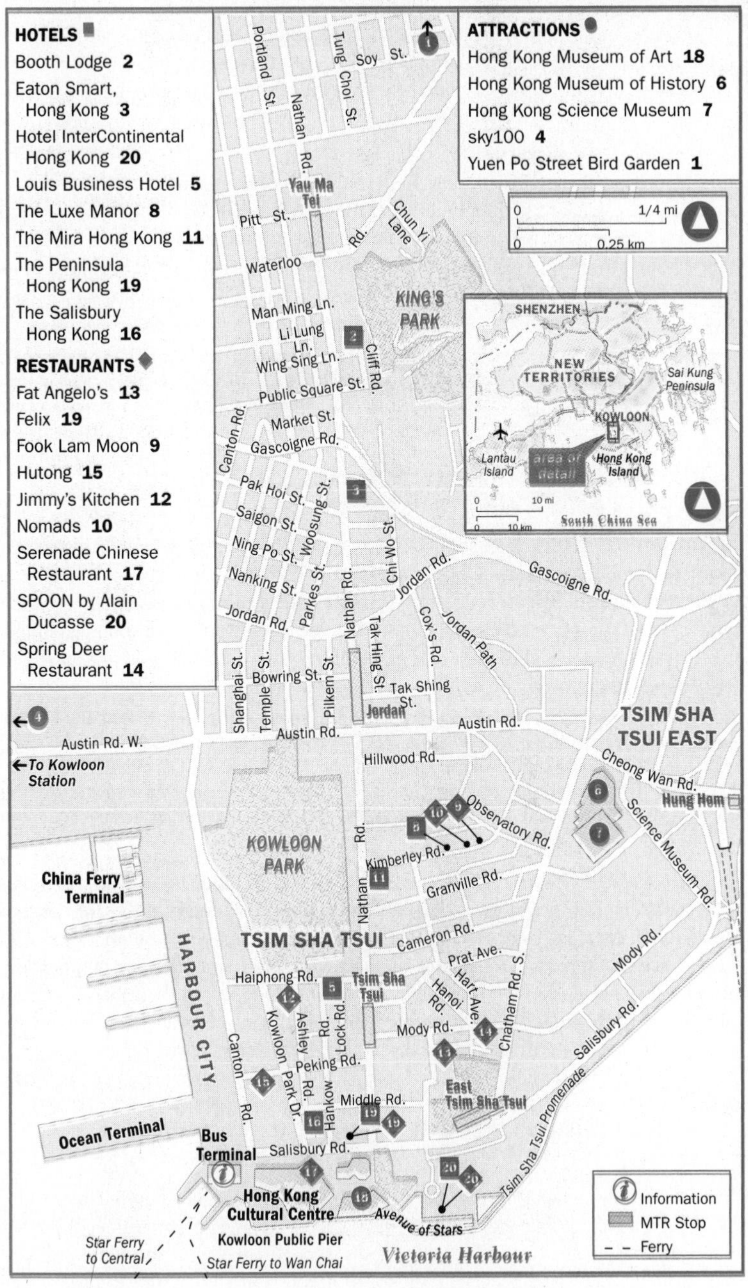
HOTELS
Booth Lodge 2
Eaton Smart, Hong Kong 3
Hotel InterContinental Hong Kong 20
Louis Business Hotel 5
The Luxe Manor 8
The Mira Hong Kong 11
The Peninsula Hong Kong 19
The Salisbury Hong Kong 16
RESTAURANTS
Fat Angelo's 13
Felix 19
Fook Lam Moon 9
Hutong 15
Jimmy's Kitchen 12
Nomads 10
Serenade Chinese Restaurant 17
SPOON by Alain Ducasse 20
Spring Deer Restaurant 14
ATTRACTIONS
Hong Kong Museum of Art 18
Hong Kong Museum of History 6
Hong Kong Science Museum 7
sky100 4
Yuen Po Street Bird Garden 1
0
1/4 mi
0
0.25 km
SHENZHEN
NEW TERRITORIES
Sai Kung Peninsula
KOWLOON
Lantau Island
area of detail
Hong Kong Island
0
10 mi
0
10 km
South China Sea
Portland St.
Tung Choi St.
Soy St.
Nathan Rd.
Yau Ma Tei
Pitt St.
Rd.
Chun Yi Lane
Waterloo
KING'S PARK
Man Ming Ln.
Li Lung Ln.
Wing Sing Ln.
Cliff Rd.
Public Square St.
Canton Rd.
Market St.
Gascoigne Rd.
Pak Hoi St.
Saigon St.
Woosung St.
Ning Po St.
Nanking St.
Parkes St.
Chi Wo St.
Jordan Rd.
Gascoigne Rd.
Jordan Rd.
Tak Hing St.
Cox's Rd.
Jordan Path
Shanghai St.
Temple St.
Bowring St.
Pilkem St.
Tak Shing St.
Jordan
Austin Rd.
TSIM SHA TSUI EAST
Austin Rd. W.
Austin Rd.
To Kowloon Station
Hillwood Rd.
Cheong Wan Rd.
Hung Hom
Observatory Rd.
Science Museum Rd.
KOWLOON PARK
Kimberley Rd.
China Ferry Terminal
Granville Rd.
TSIM SHA TSUI
Cameron Rd.
HARBOUR CITY
Prat Ave.
Mody Rd.
Haiphong Rd.
Tsim Sha Tsui
Hart Ave.
Hanoi Rd.
Chatham Rd. S.
Kowloon Park Dr.
Ashley Rd.
Lock Rd.
Mody Rd.
Salisbury Rd.
Canton Rd.
Peking Rd.
East Tsim Sha Tsui
Hankow Rd.
Middle Rd.
Tsim Sha Tsui Promenade
Ocean Terminal
Bus Terminal
Salisbury Rd.
Hong Kong Cultural Centre
Avenue of Stars
Information
MTR Stop
Ferry
Star Ferry to Central
Kowloon Public Pier
Star Ferry to Wan Chai
Victoria Harbour

Taxes Waived in Hong Kong & Macau

For several years, both Hong Kong and Macau have waived some taxes to encourage tourism. In Hong Kong, there is no accommodations tax, while Macau has waived government tax on the consumption of food and beverages.

afternoon tea and people-watching. Its restaurants are among the city's best, classes are offered on everything from tai chi and feng shui to cooking, its spa offers harbor views even from its sauna, and helicopter rides are offered from the roof. A magnificent 32-story tower added in 1993 provides fantastic views from guest rooms and its top-floor restaurant, **Felix,** designed by Philippe Starck. Spacious rooms are so wonderfully equipped that even jaded travelers are likely to be impressed.

Salisbury Rd., Tsim Sha Tsui, Kowloon, Hong Kong. www.peninsula.com. ✆ **866/382-8388** in the U.S., or 852/2920 2888. Fax 852/2722 4170. 300 units. HK$4,200–HK$5,800 single or double; from HK$6,800 suite. AE, DC, MC, V. MTR: Tsim Sha Tsui. **Amenities:** 6 restaurants, including Felix (p. 562) bar; 2 lounges; babysitting; concierge; health club and spa; indoor pool; practice music room w/grand piano; room service. *In room:* A/C, TV/DVD/CD w/free in-house DVD library, fax (silent, w/personal fax number), hair dryer, minibar, Wi-Fi.

MODERATE

Eaton Smart, Hong Kong ★★ This property near the Temple Street Night Market has more class and facilities than most in its price range. The lobby lounge is bright and cheerful, with a four-story glass-enclosed atrium that overlooks a garden terrace. Other pluses are the small but nicely done rooftop pool with sunning terrace, free daily guided tours of the jade and night market, free tai chi classes, and small but welcoming guest rooms with all the basic creature comforts.

380 Nathan Rd., Kowloon, Hong Kong. http://hongkong.eatonhotels.com. ✆ **800/588-9141** in the U.S. and Canada, or 852/2782 1818. Fax 852/2782 5563. 465 units. HK$2,100–HK$2,250 single or double; HK$2,500–HK$2,800 executive room; from HK$3,000 suite. AE, DC, MC, V. MTR: Jordan. **Amenities:** 3 restaurants; bar; lounge; babysitting; concierge; executive-level rooms; exercise room; small outdoor heated pool; room service. *In room:* A/C, TV, hair dryer, Internet (for a fee), minibar, MP3 docking station.

The Luxe Manor ★★ This whimsically designed boutique hotel looks like something Salvador Dalí might have dreamed up if asked to design the set for *Alice in Wonderland.* In other words, things are not as they seem, with wall-mounted TVs framed like gilded mirrors above faux fireplaces, picture frames framing nothing, and fun furniture like desks with four totally different leg shapes. In short, hoteliers from all over the world guilty of selling boring rooms should take lessons here, but visitors will have to decide for themselves if this is the Hong Kong they've come to see.

39 Kimberley Rd., Tsim Sha Tsui, Kowloon, Hong Kong. www.theluxemanor.com. ✆ **852/3763 8888.** Fax 852/3763 8899. 159 units (bathrooms have shower only). HK$2,400–HK$3,000 single or double; from HK$10,000 suite. AE, DC, MC, V. MTR: Tsim Sha Tsui. **Amenities:** Restaurant; bar; exercise room; room service. *In room:* A/C, TV, hair dryer, minibar, Wi-Fi.

The Mira Hong Kong ★★★ The Mira beats them all when it comes to in-room, high-tech convenience, not to mention cool decor and design, making this a hot choice for style-conscious IT junkies. Rooms, though small, rise above the ordinary, with vibrant color schemes of red, green, or purple and silver, Arne Jacobsen "Egg

Chairs," mood lighting, a seemingly endless choice of pillows, 40-inch LCD TVs that double as computers, Bose sound systems, and—an amazing perk—personal mobile phones you can take with you anywhere in Hong Kong. But what's most impressive about this hotel is its enthusiastic and personable young staff.

118–130 Nathan Rd., Tsim Sha Tsui, Kowloon, www.themirahotel.com. Hong Kong. ✆ **852/2368 1111.** Fax 852/2369 1788. 492 units. HK$1,700–HK$2,000 single or double; HK$2,300–HK$2,600 Mira Club rooms; from HK$3,400 suite. AE, DC, MC, V. MTR: Tsim Sha Tsui. **Amenities:** 3 restaurants; bar; lounge; executive-level rooms; health club and spa; indoor pool; room service. *In room:* A/C, TV/DVD/computer, hair dryer, minibar, MP3 docking station, Wi-Fi.

INEXPENSIVE

Booth Lodge ★ Close to the Jade Market, Temple Street Night Market, Ladies' Market, and MTR station, Booth Lodge is located just off Nathan Road on the seventh floor of the Salvation Army building. It has a comfortable lobby and an adjacent coffee shop offering reasonably priced lunch and dinner buffets. Rooms, all smoke-free twins or doubles and either standard or larger deluxe, are spotlessly clean. Some face the madness of Nathan Road; those facing the hillside are quieter.

11 Wing Sing Lane, Yau Ma Tei, Kowloon, Hong Kong. http://boothlodge.salvation.org.hk. ✆ **852/2771 9266.** Fax 852/2385 1140. 53 units. HK$620–HK$1,500 single or double. Rates include buffet breakfast. AE, MC, V. MTR: Yau Ma Tei. **Amenities:** Coffee shop. *In room:* A/C, TV, fridge, hair dryer, Wi-Fi (for a fee).

Louie Business Hotel With a good location across from Kowloon Park, the nonsmoking hotel—actually, it seems more like a barebones guesthouse—offers a variety of clean, basic rooms, from windowless (the cheapest) rooms to those on higher floors overlooking the park. You have to walk up the stairs to second floor reception, but an elevator delivers you to higher floors from there. If you don't expect much beyond a place to sleep at night and park your gear, you'll find this an adequate and conveniently located choice.

49–50 Haiphong Rd., Tsim Sha Tsui, Hong Kong. louiebusinesshotel@hotmail.com. ✆ **852/2311 1366.** Fax 852/2311 2166. 41 units (bathrooms have showers only). HK$400–HK$450 single; HK$500–HK$700 double; HK$750–HK$850 triple. MC, V. MTR: Tsim Sha Tsui *In room:* A/C, TV, fridge, hair dryer, Internet.

The Salisbury YMCA ★★★ ☺ For decades the number-one choice among low-cost accommodations, this YMCA right next to The Peninsula near the waterfront and Star Ferry offers 17 single rooms (none with harbor view) and more than 250 standards and singles (the most expensive provide great harbor views), as well as suites with and without harbor views that are perfect for families. Although simple in decor, these rooms are on a par with those at more expensively priced hotels in terms of in-room amenities. For budget travelers, there are also dormitory-style rooms, available only to visitors who have been in Hong Kong fewer than 7 days. Great for families is its sports facility, boasting two indoor swimming pools (one a lap pool, the other a children's pool, free to hotel guests), a gym, squash courts, and indoor climbing wall (fees charged). Because this is Tsim Sha Tsui's cheapest hotel with harbor views, make reservations far in advance, especially in peak times.

Salisbury Rd., Tsim Sha Tsui, Kowloon, Hong Kong. www.ymcahk.org.hk. ✆ **852/2268 7000** (852/2268 7888 for reservations). Fax 852/2739 9315. 368 units. HK$980 single; HK$1,080–HK$1,330 double; from HK$1,800 suite. Dormitory bed HK$240. AE, DC, MC, V. MTR: Tsim Sha Tsui. **Amenities:** 2 restaurants, babysitting; badminton; climbing wall; exercise room, Jacuzzi; 2 indoor pools; room service; sauna; 2 squash courts. *In room:* A/C, TV, hair dryer, minibar, Wi-Fi (for a fee).

Central

EXPENSIVE

Four Seasons Hotel Hong Kong ★★★ Just a stone's throw from the Central Ferry Piers, ifc mall, and Hong Kong Station, this gorgeous, 45-story property is a cool urban oasis, buffered from the city's constant bustle and providing a polished service that rises above even Hong Kong's legendary pampering. It has a luxurious spa, outdoor lap and infinity pools with great harbor views, and one of the hottest French restaurants in town. Its rooms are to die for, decorated in either contemporary Western style or a modern take on traditional Chinese design, with either city or harbor views. Spacious marbled bathrooms have two sinks, shower stalls, and deep soaking tubs.

8 Finance St., Central, Hong Kong. www.fourseasons.com/hongkong. ✆ **800/819-5053** in the U.S. and Canada, or 852/3196 8888. Fax 852/3196 8899. 399 units. HK$4,200–HK$5,300 single or double; extra HK$800 single or HK$1,000 standard for executive lounge privileges; from HK$8,800 suite. AE, DC, MC, V. MTR: Central. **Amenities:** 2 restaurants, including Caprice (p. 564); bar; lounge; babysitting; concierge; executive-level rooms; health club and spa w/free tai chi classes; 2 outdoor heated pools w/whirlpool, year-round; room service. *In room:* A/C, TV/DVD/CD, hair dryer, minibar, Wi-Fi (for a fee).

Island Shangri-La Hong Kong ★★★ With Hong Kong Park on one side and the upscale Pacific Place shopping mall on the other, Hong Kong Island's tallest hotel offers the ultimate in extravagance and luxury, rivaling the grand hotels of Europe with its Viennese chandeliers, lush Tai Ping carpets, and artwork throughout. The 17-story atrium, which stretches from the 39th to the 56th floors, features a marvelous 16-story-high Chinese painting, drawn by 40 artists from Beijing and believed to be the largest landscape painting in the world. Elegant, spacious rooms face either Victoria Peak or spectacular Victoria Harbour.

Pacific Place, Supreme Court Rd., Central, Hong Kong. www.shangri-la.com. ✆ **866/565-5050** in the U.S., or 852/2877 3838. Fax 852/2521 8742. 565 units. HK$3,200–HK$3,600 single or double; HK$3,950–HK$4,350 executive floor; from HK$6,500 suite. Children 11 and under stay free in parent's room. AE, DC, MC, V. MTR: Admiralty. **Amenities:** 7 restaurants, including Petrus and café TOO (p. 564 and 565); bar; lounge; babysitting; concierge; executive-level rooms; health club and spa w/free yoga classes; indoor/outdoor Jacuzzis; medical clinic; outdoor heated pool big enough for swimming laps; room service; free shuttle to Central and Wan Chai. *In room:* A/C, TV/DVD, fax/printer/scanner, hair dryer, minibar, Wi-Fi.

Mandarin Oriental ★★★ Opened in 1963 but with a recent overhaul that made it Central's newest yet most familiar property, this hotel remains one of Hong Kong's top hotels. Although updates include a spa with a 1930s Shanghai atmosphere, new dining ventures, and remodeled rooms, many features are back by popular demand, including its retro-gilded lobby and popular watering holes like the Captain's Bar. Gone from the rooms are the small balconies, replaced by comfortable sitting areas perfect for that first morning coffee while you peruse the newspaper and gaze out the window (the choicest rooms face the harbor). And whatever you do, don't miss a stroll past the cake shop; its fantastic chocolate creations are displayed in glass cases like crown jewels.

5 Connaught Rd., Central, Hong Kong. www.mandarinoriental.com. ✆ **800/526-6566** in the U.S. and Canada, or 852/2522 0111. Fax 852/2810 6190. 502 units (some with showers only). HK$4,500–HK$5,800 single or double; from HK$6,500 suite. AE, DC, MC, V. MTR: Central. **Amenities:** 4 restaurants; 3 bars; lounge; babysitting; concierge; health club and spa; indoor pool w/flume jet for a real workout; room service. *In room:* A/C, TV/DVD/CD, hair dryer, minibar, MP3 docking station, Wi-Fi (for a fee).

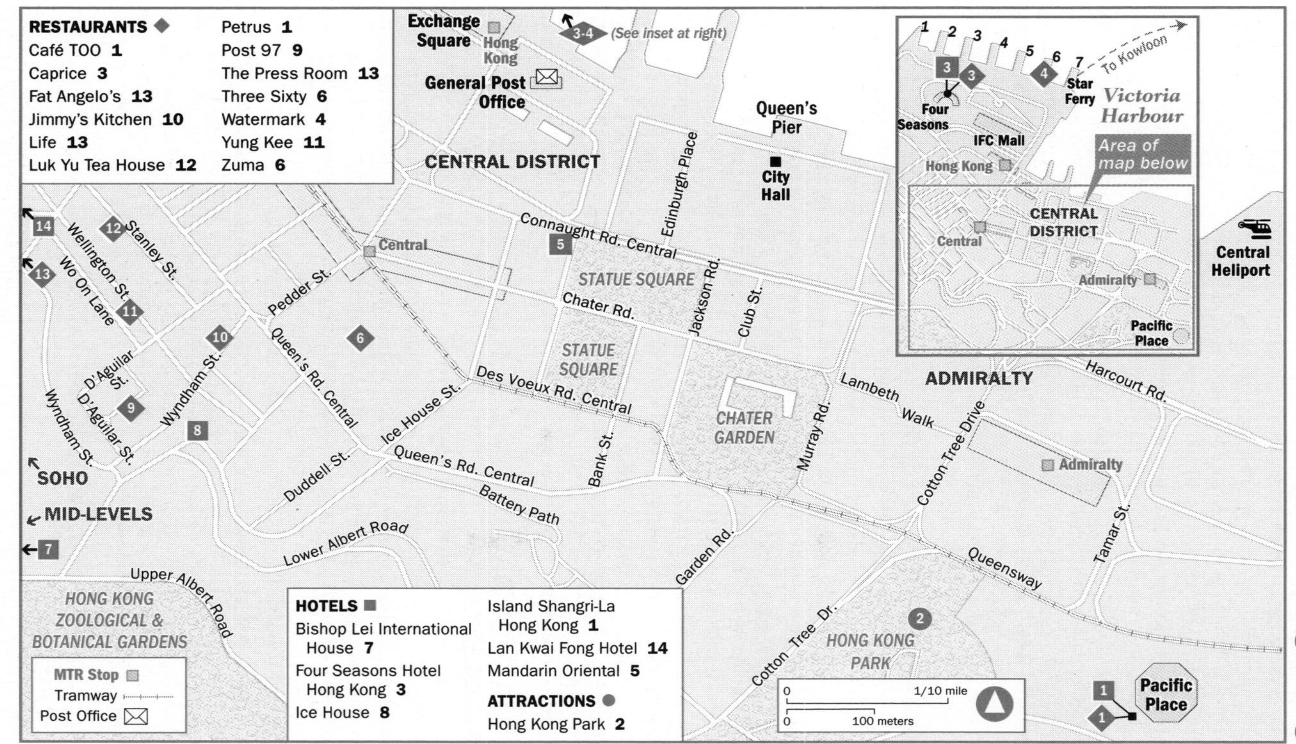
RESTAURANTS
Café TOO 1
Caprice 3
Fat Angelo's 13
Jimmy's Kitchen 10
Life 13
Luk Yu Tea House 12
Petrus 1
Post 97 9
The Press Room 13
Three Sixty 6
Watermark 4
Yung Kee 11
Zuma 6
Exchange Square
Hong Kong
3-4 (See inset at right)
General Post Office
CENTRAL DISTRICT
Queen's Pier
City Hall
1 2 3 4 5 6 7
To Kowloon
Four Seasons
Star Ferry
Victoria Harbour
IFC Mall
Hong Kong
Area of map below
CENTRAL DISTRICT
Central
Admiralty
Pacific Place
Central Heliport
Central
Connaught Rd. Central
Edinburgh Place
STATUE SQUARE
Jackson Rd.
Club St.
Chater Rd.
STATUE SQUARE
Stanley St.
Wellington St.
Wo On Lane
Pedder St.
Queen's Rd. Central
D'Aguilar St.
D'Aguilar St.
Wyndham St.
Wyndham St.
Ice House St.
Des Voeux Rd. Central
CHATER GARDEN
Murray Rd.
Lambeth Walk
ADMIRALTY
Harcourt Rd.
Cotton Tree Drive
Admiralty
Bank St.
Duddell St.
Queen's Rd. Central
Battery Path
SOHO
MID-LEVELS
Lower Albert Road
Garden Rd.
Queensway
Tamar St.
Upper Albert Road
HONG KONG ZOOLOGICAL & BOTANICAL GARDENS
MTR Stop
Tramway
Post Office
HOTELS
Bishop Lei International House 7
Four Seasons Hotel Hong Kong 3
Ice House 8
Island Shangri-La Hong Kong 1
Lan Kwai Fong Hotel 14
Mandarin Oriental 5
ATTRACTIONS
Hong Kong Park 2
Cotton Tree Dr.
HONG KONG PARK
0
1/10 mile
0
100 meters
Pacific Place

MODERATE

Lan Kwai Fong Hotel ★★★ Despite its name, this boutique hotel is actually in the Western District, surrounded by narrow streets with ma-and-pa shops and only minutes from the Graham Street wet market, Hollywood Road with its antique shops, and SoHo with its many ethnic eateries and hole-in-the-wall bars. The hotel's interior is a hip twist on traditional Chinese decor, with red-and-gold-colored rooms sporting quirky touches like Internet cables tucked inside decorative stone turtles and Chinese-style doors leading to, unfortunately, very tiny bathrooms. If you can overlook the fact that this 33-story hotel is a player in the gentrification of what was once a traditional Chinese neighborhood, this is a great place to stay.

3 Kau U Fong, Central, Hong Kong. www.lankwaifonghotel.com.hk. ✆ **852/3650 0000.** Fax 852/3650 0088. 162 units (some bathrooms have showers only). HK$2,400–HK$3,800 single or double; from HK$5,800 suite. AE, DC, MC, V. MTR: Sheung Wan. **Amenities:** Restaurant; lounge; babysitting; exercise room; room service; free shuttle bus to Hong Kong Station every 30 min. *In room:* A/C, TV, hair dryer, minibar, Wi-Fi (for a fee).

INEXPENSIVE

Ice House ★★★ This is an excellent choice if you can get in, and that's a big if due to its small size, excellent location near Lan Kwai Fong, serviced rooms/apartments, reasonable prices, and high demand for its monthly rates. Smart-looking rooms are great homes-away-from home, with queen-size beds, maid service (except Sun and holidays; bed linen is changed once a week), 24-hour security, a dedicated phone line with your own personal number and free local calls, and generous desk space. If you're coming to Hong Kong to work, don't need the services and facilities of a hotel, and don't want to spend a fortune, this is a top pick, but book early. The one drawback: It's a killer walk uphill from Central.

38 Ice House St., Central, Hong Kong. www.icehouse.com.hk. ✆ **852/2836 7333.** Fax 852/2801 0355. 64 units (bathrooms have showers only). HK$1,000–HK$1,800 single or double. Monthly rates available. AE, DC, MC, V. MTR: Central. **Amenities:** Coin-op laundry. *In room:* A/C, TV, hair dryer, Internet, kitchenette.

Mid-Levels

MODERATE

Bishop Lei International House ★★ Located about halfway up Victoria Peak in a residential area favored by expats and abounding in charming restaurants and bars, this hotel makes up for its out-of-the-way location with free shuttle service; a half-dozen city buses stop outside its door, and the Central–Mid-Levels Escalator is nearby. It offers tiny standard rooms (with even tinier bathrooms) that have large windows letting in lots of sunshine but that face inland. If you can, spring for a more expensive room (all twins or suites) with fantastic harbor views.

4 Robinson Rd., Mid-Levels, Hong Kong. www.bishopleihtl.com.hk. ✆ **852/2868 0828.** Fax 852/2868 1551. 224 units (most bathrooms have showers only). HK$1,280 single; HK$1,480–HK$2,080 twin; from HK$2,480 suite. Long-term packages available. 1 child 11 and under stays free in parent's room. AE, DC, MC, V. Bus: 3B, 12, 12M, 23, 23A, or 40 to Robinson Rd. **Amenities:** Coffee shop w/outdoor terrace; babysitting; small exercise room; small outdoor pool; room service; free shuttle bus to Central, Admiralty and Wanchai. *In room:* A/C, TV, hair dryer, minibar, Wi-Fi.

Causeway Bay/Wan Chai

MODERATE

JIA ★★ Hong Kong's hippest (and first) boutique hotel, designed by Philippe Starck, goes out of its way to prove it's no ordinary place of abode, with a staff decked out in chic Shanghai Tang–designed uniforms and stylish rooms bathed in white. Studios and one- and two-bedroom suites are available, complete with kitchens and home entertainment centers. Add a bunch of freebies—like local complimentary telephone calls, Internet access, breakfast, cocktail hour, and access to a local gym and several hot clubs—and it seems well positioned for both business and tourist markets.

1–5 Irving St., Causeway Bay, Hong Kong. www.jiahongkong.com. ✆ **852/3196 9000.** Fax 852/3196 9001. 54 units (bathrooms have showers only). HK$2,500 single or double; from HK$3,500 suite. Monthly rates available. Rates include continental breakfast. AE, DC, MC, V. MTR: Causeway Bay. **Amenities:** Restaurant; lounge; free access to nearby health club; sun deck; room service. *In room:* A/C, TV/DVD/CD, hair dryer, kitchen, Wi-Fi.

Lanson Place Hotel ★★★ Following close on JIA's heels (and just down the street), this stylish boutique hotel caters to long-staying guests with cheerful, contemporary rooms and one- and two-bedroom residences, all with kitchenettes (and a welcome basket of goodies), home theater systems (you can check out DVDs free at reception), and free use of a cell phone during your stay (on a request basis). While in-house facilities are limited, this is a perfect home-away-from-home for weary road warriors, and the staff, which runs operations from sit-down desks, couldn't be nicer.

133 Leighton Rd., Causeway Bay, Hong Kong. www.lansonplace.com. ✆ **852/3477 6888.** Fax 852/3477 6999. 194 units (bathrooms have showers only). HK$2,500–HK$3,800 single or double; from HK$4,800 suite. Weekly/monthly rates available. Children under 12 stay free in parent's room. AE, DC, MC, V. MTR: Causeway Bay. **Amenities:** Bar; babysitting; small gym; free shuttle to Wan Chai and Central. *In room:* A/C, TV/DVD/CD, hair dryer, kitchenette, MP3 docking station, Wi-Fi (for a fee).

INEXPENSIVE

Express by Holiday Inn Causeway Bay Hong Kong ★ Targeting budget business travelers in town for only a night or two, this is a bare-bones, do-it-yourself kind of place, with luggage carts instead of bellboys and even a designated ironing room. That said, it does offer a few perks, such as computers off the lobby with free Internet, and it also houses a China Travel Service office. Its rooms are identical and priced the same (the range below reflects low to peak seasons), but try to get one of the 15 rooms on the highest floors that have partial harbor views between buildings.

33 Sharp St. E., Causeway Bay, Hong Kong. www.expressbyholidayinn.com.cn. ✆ **888/465-4329** in the U.S. and Canada, or 852/3558 6688. Fax 852/3558 6633. 282 units (bathrooms have showers only). HK$1,000–HK$1,500 single or standard. Rates include breakfast buffet. AE, DC, MC, V. MTR: Causeway Bay. **Amenities:** 4 restaurants; access to nearby fitness club (fee charged). *In room:* A/C, TV, fridge, hair dryer, Internet.

Near the Airport

Regal Airport Hotel ★ This is the only hotel at Hong Kong International Airport, a 5-minute walk from the terminal via covered walkway. Guest rooms are large and soundproof, with modern furniture in eye-popping colors of purple, red, or lime green, but there's no mistaking that this is an airport hotel, functional but rather characterless.

9 Cheong Tat Rd., Chek Lap Kok, Hong Kong. www.regalhotel.com. ✆ **800/457-4000** in the U.S. and Canada, or 852/2286 8888. Fax 852/2286 8686. 1,171 units. HK$3,200–HK$4,000 single or double; from HK$4,600 Regal Club. Children under 13 stay free in parent's room (maximum 3 persons per room). AE, DC, MC, V. Airport Express Liner: Hong Kong International Airport. **Amenities:** 5 restaurants; bar; babysitting; concierge; executive-level rooms; health club and spa; indoor and outdoor pools; room service. *In room:* A/C, TV, hair dryer, minibar, Wi-Fi (for a fee).

WHERE TO EAT

With approximately 11,000 restaurants from which to choose, in a few short days you can take a culinary tour of China, dining on Cantonese, Sichuan, Shanghainese, Beijing, Chiu Chow, and other Chinese specialties. Other national cuisines are also popular, including French, Italian, American, Thai, Indian, and Japanese. Avoid dining from 1 to 2pm on weekdays, the traditional lunch hour for office workers.

Kowloon

For Kowloon restaurant locations, see the map on page 555.

EXPENSIVE

Felix ★★★ FUSION Designer Philippe Starck has made sure that Felix is not your ordinary dining experience, beginning with the elevator's wavy walls and continuing inside the restaurant, where two eye-catching zinc cylinders contain cozy bars and two glass facades reveal stunning views of Kowloon and Hong Kong Island. The food, featuring Pacific Rim ingredients brought together in East-meets-West combinations, rarely disappoints. You might start with Dungeness crab cake served with avocado and jalapeño rémoulade, followed by the prawn cracker–crusted sea bass. Bargain hunters can dine before 7pm and opt for a three-course fixed-price dinner for HK$448. Or just come by for a drink, but make sure you're dressed smart casual.

In The Peninsula Hong Kong, Salisbury Rd., Tsim Sha Tsui. ✆ **852/2315 3188.** www.peninsula.com. Reservations required. Main courses HK$320–HK$680; fixed-price dinner HK$788. AE, DC, MC, V. 6pm–1:30am (last order 10:30pm). MTR: Tsim Sha Tsui.

Fook Lam Moon ★★★ CANTONESE Upon entering this restaurant you immediately feel as if you've stepped back a couple of decades. The decor is outdated, and, unless you're a regular, the waiters are indifferent. Yet this remains *the* place to go for exotic dishes, including shark's fin, bird's nest, and abalone. Some Hong Kong old-timers swear this restaurant serves the best Cantonese food in the world, but you can dine more cheaply here on dim sum for lunch. There's another branch in Wan Chai at 35–45 Johnston Rd. (✆ **852/2866 0663;** MTR: Wan Chai), with the same hours.

53–59 Kimberley Rd., Tsim Sha Tsui. ✆ **852/2366 0286.** www.fooklammoon-grp.com. Reservations recommended for dinner. Main dishes (excluding exotic dishes) HK$120–HK$250. AE, DC, MC, V. Mon–Sat 11:30am–3pm; Sun 11am–3pm; daily 6–11pm. MTR: Tsim Sha Tsui.

SPOON by Alain Ducasse ★★★ FRENCH Dinner at this sophisticated venue is more than just a meal—it's an experience. The focal point of the dining room is the ceiling, where 550 handblown Murano glass spoons are lined up like a landing strip, directing one's attention to the open kitchen and to the stunning harbor view just beyond the massive windows. The innovative cuisine, by chef and restaurateur Alain Ducasse, can include classic duck foie gras, pan-seared tuna with satay sauce and vegetables, or beef tenderloin and foie gras cooked in brioche. Or, your entire group may opt for the Sexy Spoon, a tasting menu costing HK$888 for five courses.

In the InterContinental Hong Kong, Salisbury Rd., Tsim Sha Tsui. ✆ **852/2313 2323.** www.hongkong-ic.intercontinental.com. Reservations required. Main courses HK$350–HK$680; Sun lunch HK$558, including champagne and wine. AE, DC, MC, V. Sun noon–2:30pm; daily 6–11:30pm. MTR: Tsim Sha Tsui.

MODERATE

Hutong ★★★ NORTHERN CHINESE This stunning restaurant is about as far from a real *hutong* (ancient Beijing alleyway) as one can get, since it's located on the 28th floor of a strikingly modern high-rise. Still, the restaurant is to be commended for its down-to-earth yet dramatic setting, with red lanterns providing the only splash of color against a dark, muted interior, and windows providing fantastic views of Hong Kong. The cuisine uses new ingredients and combinations to create its own trademark dishes, along with classic north Chinese fare, including drunken raw crab (an appetizer marinated 3 days in Chinese wine), crispy deboned lamb ribs, and crispy soft-shelled crab with Sichuan red chili. Note that there's a minimum charge of HK$300 per person.

1 Peking Rd. (28th floor), Tsim Sha Tsui. ✆ **852/3428 8342.** www.aqua.com.hk. Reservations required for dinner. Main dishes HK$138–HK$468. AE, DC, MC, V. Daily noon–3pm and 6–11pm. MTR: Tsim Sha Tsui.

Spring Deer Restaurant ★ BEIJING This 40-some-year-old restaurant offers excellent Beijing food at reasonable prices. It's nothing fancy yet is usually packed. Best on the menu is its specialty—honey-glazed Peking duck, which costs HK$280. You'll probably have to wait 40 minutes for the duck if you order it during peak time (7:30–9:30pm). Chicken dishes are also excellent, as are the handmade noodles. Most dishes come in small, medium, and large sizes; the small dishes are suitable for two people to share.

42 Mody Rd., Tsim Sha Tsui. ✆ **852/2366 4012.** Reservations recommended. Small dishes HK$65–HK$90. AE, MC, V. 11:30am–3pm and 6–11pm. MTR: Tsim Sha Tsui.

INEXPENSIVE

Fat Angelo's ITALIAN This local chain offers good value with its hearty, American renditions of Italian food, including pastas ranging from traditional spaghetti marinara to fettuccine with salmon and main courses that include rosemary-roasted chicken, grilled salmon with pesto, and eggplant Parmesan, all of which come with salad and homemade bread. The emphasis is on quantity, not quality, though the food isn't bad. And they really pack 'em in; this place is bustling and loud. Also at the Elizabeth House, 250 Gloucester Rd. in Causeway Bay (✆ **852/2574 6263;** MTR: Causeway Bay), Wu Chung House, 213 Queen's Rd. E., Wan Chai (✆ **852/2126 7020**), and 49A-C Elgin St., Central (✆ **852/2973 6808;** MTR: Central), all open noon to midnight.

The Pinnacle (basement), 8 Minden Ave., Tsim Sha Tsui. ✆ **852/2730 4788.** www.fatangelos.com. Reservations recommended. Pastas HK$98–HK$148; main dishes HK$118–HK$238. AE, DC, MC, V. Daily noon–midnight. MTR: Tsim Sha Tsui.

Nomads ★ ASIAN This very popular Mongolian restaurant allows diners to select their own raw ingredients for one-dish meals and pizzas that are then stir-fried by short-order cooks. All-you-can-eat lunches and dinners give choices of vegetables, meats, seafood, sauces, noodles, rice, and spices, spread buffet-style along a counter together with salads and dessert. Sheepskin-draped chairs, rawhide lampshades, animal skins, and tribal weaponry hung on walls transport this restaurant straight into the Mongolia of our fantasies.

55 Kimberley Rd., Tsim Sha Tsui. ✆ **852/2722 0733.** www.igors.com. Lunch buffet HK$68 Mon–Fri, HK$80 Sat–Sun and holidays; dinner buffet HK$178. AE, DC, MC, V. Daily noon–2:30pm and 6:30–10:30pm. MTR: Tsim Sha Tsui.

Serenade Chinese Restaurant ★★ 🎁 CANTONESE This is my top choice in Tsim Sha Tsui for moderately priced dim sum with a view of the harbor. Located up on the first floor of the Hong Kong Cultural Centre next to the Star Ferry (you might have to look for its entrance, it has a comprehensive dim sum menu (only desserts are served from trolleys), including "figurine" dim sum, like the steamed shrimp dumpling in the shape of a fish. My favorite is the deep-fried spring rolls with crushed garlic, which is also beautifully presented and comes with a yummy dipping sauce. Note that on weekdays (excluding public holidays) from 9am to noon and 2 to 4:30pm, dim sum prices are cheaper than those below.

Hong Kong Cultural Centre (1st floor), Restaurant Block, Salisbury Rd., Tsim Sha Tsui. ✆ **852/2722 0932.** Dim sum HK$18–HK$38. AE, DC, MC, V. 9am–4:30pm. MTR: Tsim Sha Tsui.

Central

For Central Hong Kong restaurant locations, see the map on p. 559.

EXPENSIVE

Caprice ★★★ FRENCH Ensconced in the sleek Four Seasons Hotel Hong Kong, this is one of the best places to dine in Hong Kong. Caprice garners high marks for its innovative take on French classics and gorgeous setting affording dramatic views of Victoria Harbour. The menu, orchestrated around the seasons and drawing inspiration from provincial influences throughout France, may include the likes of langoustine ravioli with veal sweetbreads, chanterelle mushrooms, and delicate lobster bisque; Kagoshima beef; or roast Bresse chicken with morel mushrooms.

In the Four Seasons Hotel Hong Kong, 8 Finance St., Central. ✆ **852/3196 8860.** www.fourseasons.com/hongkong. Reservations required. Main courses HK$400–HK$770. AE, DC, MC, V. Daily noon–2:30pm and 6–10:30pm. MTR: Central.

Restaurant Petrus ★★★ 🎁 FRENCH Simply put, the views from this 56th-floor restaurant are breathtaking, probably the best of any hotel restaurant on the Hong Kong side. The restaurant is decorated like a French castle, with the obligatory crystal chandeliers, statues, thick draperies, and murals gracing dome-shaped ceilings. The traditional haute cuisine is spiced sparingly to complement the dishes' natural aroma and flavor, with such intriguing choices as sautéed frog legs and veal sweetbread in a watercress sauce or poached salmon with garlic, black olives, and artichokes.

In the Island Shangri-La (56th floor), Pacific Place, Supreme Court Rd., Central. ✆ **852/2820 8590.** www.shangri-la.com. Reservations recommended. Jacket required for dinner. Main courses HK$360–HK$780; fixed-price lunches HK$328–HK$388. AE, DC, MC, V. Daily noon–3pm and 6:30–11pm. MTR: Admiralty.

Zuma ★★★ JAPANESE Located in the upscale Landmark shopping center, Zuma is a contemporary twist on the casual Japanese *izakaya* style of eating and drinking, in which dishes are shared and ordered in no particular order. A spiraling staircase joins the main dining room and outdoor terrace to the lounge and sake bar (where you should order the Rubabu, a rhubarb-infused sake with vodka and passion fruit). The menu offers contemporary interpretations of authentic Japanese cuisine, like maki rolls (such as salmon, *hamachi,* and sea bass with avocado and sesame-lime sauce); grilled foods (like Hokkaido scallops with grated apple, wasabi, and sweet soy sauce); and signature dishes like miso-marinated black cod wrapped in *hoba* (magnolia) leaf.

Tasting menus are available for HK$870 and HK$1,280, which require a two-person minimum order and must be ordered by the whole table.

The Landmark, Levels 5 & 6, 15 Queen's Rd. Central, Central. ✆ **852/3657 6388.** www.zumarestaurant.com. Reservations recommended. Main dishes HK$180–HK$1,200; fixed-price lunches HK$290–HK$480; Sun brunch HK$428. AE, DC, MC, V. Mon–Sat noon–3pm; Sun 11:30am–3pm; daily 6–11pm. MTR: Central.

MODERATE

cafe TOO ★★★ INTERNATIONAL The most interesting buffet in Hong Kong, cafe TOO features open kitchens and seven "stations" of food presentations spread throughout the restaurant, thereby giving it a theatrical touch. Browse the appetizer and salad table; a cold seafood counter with sushi, fresh oysters, crab, and other delights; and a Chinese section with dim sum and main courses. Other stations serve Western hot entrees, noodles that are prepared to order (and run the gamut from Chinese to Italian), and Asian dishes from Thai curries to Indian tandoori. The dessert table is the crowning glory.

In the Island Shangri-La Hotel, Pacific Place, Supreme Court Rd., Central. ✆ **852/2820 8571.** www.shangri-la.com. Reservations recommended. Lunch buffet HK$298 Mon–Fri, HK$348 Sat–Sun and holidays; dinner buffet HK$438 Mon–Thurs, HK$478 Fri–Sun and holidays. AE, DC, MC, V. Mon–Fri noon–2:30pm; Sat–Sun noon–3pm; Mon–Thurs 6:30–10pm; Fri–Sun 6–11pm. MTR: Admiralty.

Jimmy's Kitchen ★ CONTINENTAL Opened in 1928, this restaurant, a replica of a similar, American-owned restaurant in Shanghai, has an atmosphere reminiscent of an American steakhouse, with white tablecloths, dark-wood paneling, and elevator music. It's popular with older expats for its dependably good European comfort food. An extensive a la carte menu offers salads and soups, steaks, chicken, Indian curries, German fare, and a seafood selection that includes sole, scallops, and the local garoupa. Also at 29 Ashley Rd., Tsim Sha Tsui (✆ **852/2376 0327**), open the same hours.

1 Wyndham St., Central. ✆ **852/2526 5293.** www.jimmys.com. Main courses HK$148–HK$370. AE, DC, MC, V. 11:30am–3pm and 6–11pm. MTR: Central.

Luk Yu Tea House ★★ DIM SUM Luk Yu, first opened in 1933, is the most famous dim sum teahouse remaining in Hong Kong, a wonderful Art Deco–era Cantonese restaurant with ceiling fans, spittoons, individual wooden booths for couples, marble tabletops, and stained-glass windows. It's one of the best places to try Chinese teas like *longjing* (a green tea) or *sui sin* (narcissus or daffodil), but Luk Yu is most famous for its dim sum, served from 7am to 3pm, all listed on an English menu that changes weekly but has included the likes of steamed rice with duck meat wrapped in fresh lotus leaves; deep-fried Chinese ham and chicken meat pie; and jumbo size chicken buns. Although pricey, with an indifferent staff, it's a slice of a bygone era.

24–26 Stanley St., Central. ✆ **852/2523 5464.** Dim sum HK$32–HK$75. MC, V. 7am–5pm. MTR: Central.

Post 97 ★ CONTINENTAL This is one of the old-timers in Lan Kwai Fong, opened in 1982 (its name is a cheeky reference to the handover, which seemed far in the future at the time). Yet it's every bit as popular as it was before all the surrounding competition moved in, due to down-to-earth good food, reasonable prices, cheerful staff, an inviting bar with daily happy hours (3–8pm), and a comfortable, laid-back atmosphere. Catering to businesspeople during lunch and to night revelers in the evening, it offers an all-day/all-night menu that includes breakfast items like eggs Benedict, salads, sandwiches and burgers, pasta, and fish and chips, as well as a weekday salad buffet (HK$115 for the buffet; HK$30 extra to add a main course).

9 Lan Kwai Fong, Central. © **852/2186 1817.** www.ninetysevengroup.com. Main dishes HK$90–HK$208. AE, DC, MC, V. Sun–Thurs 9:30am–1am; Fri–Sat 9:30am–2am. MTR: Central.

The Press Room ★★ FRENCH Occupying a site once held in the 1920s by *Hua Qiao Daily* newspaper, The Press Room is yet more proof of the relentless westward gentrification along Hollywood Road. Still, there's little to reproach in this bustling brasserie that would look right at home in Paris or New York with its wall-to-wall blackboards, split-level dining room, comfortable booths, and open kitchen. Although the emphasis is on French cuisine—with the likes of classic beef bourguignon, as well as a huge selection of oysters from around the world and sinfully delicious French desserts—it also serves Italian bistro food and burgers.

108 Hollywood Rd., Central. © **852/2525 3444.** www.thepressroom.com.hk. Reservations required. Main dishes HK$202–HK$310. AE, DC, MC, V. Mon–Fri noon–11pm; Sat–Sun 10am–11pm. MTR: Central.

Watermark ★★ CONTINENTAL This establishment atop the Central ferry piers, with a soaring ceiling, glass panel walls that can be pushed open, and an outdoor terrace, provides unobstructed sweeping views of the harbor and feels like you're dining alfresco even when you aren't, making it a great choice in any kind of weather. The menu includes such mouthwatering starters as crab cake with pickled cucumber and lime butter, but many simply go with the wonderful seafood platter. Angus beef, aged on the premises, is a house specialty, but other temptations include red emperor (a kind of snapper) with jalapeno salsa, pinto beans, and balsamic dressing and Boston lobster. For those taking the ferries, this place couldn't be more convenient.

Central Ferry Pier 7, Central. © **852/2167 7251.** www.igors.com. Reservations required. Main dishes HK$205–HK$390; fixed-price lunches (Mon–Fri only) HK$148–HK$188; Sun brunch HK$298. AE, DC, MC, V. Mon–Sat noon–2:30pm; Sun 11:30am–3pm; daily 7–10:30pm (last order). MTR: Central.

Yung Kee ★ CANTONESE Popular for decades, Yung Kee started out in 1942 as a street stall selling roast goose. Its specialty is still roast goose with plum sauce, cooked to perfection with tender meat on the inside and crispy skin on the outside and available only for dinner (a small portion for two people costs HK$130). Other specialties include thousand-year-old eggs (eggs preserved in a mixture of lime, clay, salt, and rice straw for several weeks or even months) and any of the fresh seafood, like braised garoupa tail. Dining is on one of the upper three floors, but if all you want is a bowl of congee or takeout, join the office workers who pour in for a quick meal on the informal ground floor.

32–40 Wellington St., Central. © **852/2522 1624.** www.yungkee.com.hk. Main dishes HK$102–HK$180. AE, DC, MC, V. 11am–11:30pm. MTR: Central.

INEXPENSIVE

Life ★ VEGETARIAN Located beside the Central–Mid-Levels Escalator, Life is a godsend to travelers seeking vegetarian and vegan alternatives, as well as those with dietary restrictions (the restaurant will prepare dishes that are free of yeast, gluten, garlic, onion, or wheat). Occupying the second story above a health-foods store and with rooftop dining available in the evening, this down-to-earth venue serves salads, whole-wheat pizzas, quiche, noodles, and daily specials, along with juices, power and protein shakes, teas, and organic wine and beer.

10 Shelley St., Central. ✆ **852/2810 9777.** Main dishes HK$95–HK$110. AE, MC, V. Mon–Fri noon–11pm; Sat–Sun 9am–11pm. MTR: Central.

Three Sixty ★ INTERNATIONAL What's not to like about this health-food store and cafeteria specializing in earth-friendly products and organic foods? Self-service counters offer a wide variety of dishes, including salads, Indian curries, pasta, pizza, sandwiches, wraps, burritos, stir-fries, noodles, and daily specials like chicken roast or lasagna, as well as desserts, gelato, and smoothies. There's ample seating (if you avoid the lunchtime rush), or you can order it to go and have a picnic in nearby Chater Garden.

There's also a large branch in the Elements shopping mall, shop 1090, 1 Austin Rd. W., Kowloon (✆ **852/2196 8066;** MTR: Kowloon), open daily from 8am to 10pm.

The Landmark (4th floor), 15 Queen's Rd., Central. ✆ **852/2111 4880.** www.threesixtyhk.com. Main dishes HK$25–HK$98. AE, DC, MC, V. 8am–9pm. MTR: Central.

Causeway Bay

MODERATE

The Pawn ★★ MODERN BRITISH This 1888 landmark, formerly housing a Chinese pawn shop and other tenants, was converted by local artist and film director Stanley Wong into an "adult playground," with the first floor serving as a bar and the second-floor restaurant staying true to the building's heritage with plank wood flooring, wooden tables, white-washed walls, and balcony seating. Lunch and dinner menus change daily, with starters such as pork belly with green apple, spinach, red onion, and red wine vinaigrette, and main dishes like chargrilled lamb chops with minted mash, pot roast vegetable, and rosemary gravy.

62 Johnston Rd., Wan Chai. ✆ **852/2866 3444.** www.thepawn.com.hk. Main dishes HK$180–HK$220; set lunches (Mon–Fri only) HK$150–HK$190. AE, DC, MC, V. Mon–Fri noon–3pm; Sat–Sun 11am–3pm; daily 6–11pm. MTR: Wan Chai.

INEXPENSIVE

Tsui Wah ★ VARIED CHINESE/INTERNATIONAL This down-home chain of very popular restaurants serves its own version of Hong Kong comfort food and international fare. During peak dining hours you'll probably be asked to share a table. Start with the local favorite milk tea, followed by one of the soups or noodle or fried rice dishes. Or, go for one of the international dishes such as Japanese udon noodles, Russian borscht, Malaysian curry, or even a hot dog. It can be argued that if you haven't been to Tsui Wah, you haven't experienced Hong Kong at all. There are branches everywhere, most with very late hours or open 24 hours. Convenient locations are at 15–19 Wellington St., Central (✆ **852/2525 6338;** MTR: Central); 2 Carnarvon Rd., Tsim Sha Tsui (✆ **852/2366 8250**); and 77–81 Parkes St., Yau Ma Tei (✆ **852/2384 8388;** MTR: Jordan).

20–22 Cannon St., Causeway Bay. ✆ **852/2573 4338.** www.tsuiwahrestaurant.com. Main dishes HK$30–HK$62; set meals HK$68–HK$78. No credit cards. 24 hr. MTR: Wan Chai.

Victoria Peak

MODERATE

The Peak Lookout ★★ INTERNATIONAL Although it's on the Peak, across the street from the Peak Tram terminus, there are only limited views of the South China Sea from The Peak Lookout's terrace. A former tram station, it's a delightful place for a meal, with exposed granite walls, a tall, timber-trussed ceiling, an open fireplace, wooden floors, and a greenhouselike room that extends into the garden. You can also sit outdoors amid the lush growth where you can actually hear birds singing—it's one of the best outdoor dining opportunities in Hong Kong on a glorious day. The menu is eclectic, offering a combination of American, Chinese, Indian, and Southeast Asian dishes, including tandoori chicken tikka, Thai noodles, penne with prawns, grilled steaks and salmon, and curries like Thai green chicken curry with coconut milk.

121 Peak Rd., Victoria Peak. ✆ **852/2849 1000.** www.peaklookout.com.hk. Reservations required for dinner and all weekend meals. Main courses HK$138–HK$328. AE, DC, MC, V. Mon–Thurs 10:30am–11:30pm; Fri 10:30am–1am; Sat 8:30am–1am; Sun 8:30am–11:30pm. Peak Tram.

Aberdeen

MODERATE

Jumbo Kingdom ★ CANTONESE There are many other restaurants that are more authentic and more affordable, but this has been in operation for more than 30 years and attracts a bustling crowd with its claims to be the largest floating restaurant in the world. Simply take the bus to Aberdeen and then board one of the restaurant's own free shuttle boats, which depart every few minutes from Aberdeen Promenade. The floating venue specializes in fresh seafood and changing seasonal dishes, as well as dim sum available from an English menu (from carts on Sun and holidays) until 4pm. On the roof of Jumbo Kingdom is **Top Deck, at the Jumbo** (✆ **852/2553 3331;** www.cafedecogroup.com), an alfresco venue where an open kitchen turns out excellent platters of seafood and international dishes ranging from sushi and Asian curries to pasta, as well as an excellent Sunday seafood brunch, making this a great place to chill.

Aberdeen Harbour, Hong Kong Island. ✆ **852/2553 9111.** www.jumbo.com.hk. Main dishes HK$80–HK$439; dim sum HK$18–HK$48. Table charge HK$10 per person. AE, MC, V. Mon–Sat 11:30am–11:30pm; Sun 7am–11:30pm. Bus: 7 or 70 from Central, 72 or 77 from Causeway Bay, or 973 from Tsim Sha Tsui to Aberdeen, then the restaurant's free shuttle boat.

EXPLORING HONG KONG

Every visitor to Hong Kong should eat dim sum in a typical Cantonese restaurant, ride the Star Ferry across Victoria Harbour, and, if the weather is clear, take the Peak Tram for the glorious views from Victoria Peak.

Victoria Peak

At 552m (1,811 ft.), Victoria Peak is Hong Kong Island's tallest mountain and offers spectacular views (go on a crystal-clear day, since fog—and smog—can greatly curtail vistas). Since the Peak is typically cooler than the sweltering city below, it has always been one of Hong Kong's most exclusive places to live. More than a century ago, the rich reached the Peak via a 3-hour trip in sedan chairs, transported to the top by coolies. In 1888 the **Peak Tram** began operating, cutting the journey to a mere 8 minutes.

The easiest way to reach the Peak Tram Station, located in Central on Garden Road, is to take the no. 15C open-top shuttle bus that operates between the tram terminal and the Star Ferry in Central. Otherwise, the tram terminal is about a 10-minute walk from the MTR Central Station. Trams depart from Peak Tram Station every 10 to 15 minutes between 7am and midnight. Round-trip tickets cost HK$36 for adults and HK$16 for seniors and children.

Upon reaching the Peak, you'll find yourself at the very modern **Peak Tower** (✆ **852/2849 0668;** www.thepeak.com.hk), 396m (1,300 ft.) above sea level. Head straight for the rooftop **Sky Terrace** (admission HK$25 for adults and HK$12 for seniors and children; combination tickets for the tram and Sky Terrace are HK$56 and HK$26, respectively), where you have one of the world's most breathtaking views: the South China Sea, the skyscrapers of Central, the boats plying Victoria Harbour, Kowloon, and the many hills of the New Territories undulating in the background.

The Peak Tower and adjacent Peak Galleria have many shops and restaurants but the best thing to do atop Victoria Peak is to take an hour-long **circular hike** on Lugard Road and Harlech Road, located just a stone's throw from the Peak Tower. Mainly a footpath overhung with banyan trees and passing through lush vegetation (with glimpses of secluded mansions), the road snakes along the cliff side, offering views of Central District below, the harbor, Kowloon, and then Aberdeen and the outlying islands on the other side. This is one of the best walks in Hong Kong; pick up a map of this and other hikes on the Peak at the **Hong Kong Tourism Board Visitor Centre,** located in front of Peak Tower in a 50-year-old tram car, open 9am to 9pm.

Museums

Municipal museums are closed December 25 and 26, January 1, and the first 3 days of Chinese New Year.

Hong Kong Heritage Museum ★★ ☺ Presenting both the history and culture of the New Territories, this museum is probably the best reason to take the MTR to Sha Tin in the New Territories. Come here to learn about the customs, religions, and lifestyles of the early fishermen and settlers and how they have changed over the centuries. See a barge loaded for market, traditional clothing, models of Sha Tin showing its mind-numbing growth since the 1930s, musical instruments, elaborate costumes used in Chinese opera, porcelains, bronzes, jade, and other works of

A Money-Saving Museum Pass

The Museum Pass, available at HKTB for HK$30, is valid for 1 week and allows entry to the Hong Kong Museum of Art, Hong Kong Museum of History, Hong Kong Space Museum, Hong Kong Science Museum, Hong Kong Museum of Coastal Defence, Dr. Sun Yat-sen Museum, and Hong Kong Heritage Museum. Note, however, that admission to all seven museums is free on Wednesdays.

Chinese art dating from the Neolithic period to the 20th century. At the Children's Discovery Gallery, youngsters can practice being archaeologists, wear traditional costumes, and learn about marshes. Plan on spending 2 hours here.

1 Man Lam Rd., Sha Tin. ✆ **852/2180 8188.** http://hk.heritage.museum. Admission HK$10 for adults, HK$5 for children, students, and seniors. Free admission Wed. Mon and Wed–Sat 10am–6pm; Sun and holidays 10am–7pm. MTR: Che Kung Temple (a 5-min. walk) or Sha Tin (a 15-min. walk).

Hong Kong Museum of Art ★★★ Because of its location on the Tsim Sha Tsui waterfront just a 2-minute walk from the Star Ferry terminus, this museum is the most convenient and worthwhile if your time is limited. Feast your eyes on ceramics, bronzes, jade, cloisonné, lacquerware, bamboo carvings, and textiles, as well as paintings, wall hangings, scrolls, and calligraphy dating from the 16th century to the present. The Historical Pictures Gallery provides a visual account of life in Hong Kong, Macau, and Guangzhou in the late 18th and 19th centuries. Another gallery displays contemporary Hong Kong works by local artists. You'll spend at least an hour here, though art aficionados can devote more time by renting audio guides for HK$10.

Hong Kong Cultural Centre Complex, 10 Salisbury Rd., Tsim Sha Tsui. ✆ **852/2721 0116.** www.hk.art.museum. Admission HK$10 adults, HK$5 children, students, and seniors. Free admission Wed. Fri–Wed 10am–6pm (Sat to 8pm). MTR: Tsim Sha Tsui.

Hong Kong Museum of History ★★★ If you visit only one museum in Hong Kong, this should be it. Its permanent exhibit, the Hong Kong Story, is an ambitious attempt to chronicle 6,000 years of history. Through displays that include life-size dioramas, replica fishing boats, reconstructed traditional housing, furniture, clothing, and items from daily life, the museum introduces Hong Kong's ethnic groups, traditional means of livelihood, customs, and beliefs. You can peer inside a fishing junk, see what Kowloon Walled City looked like before it became a park, view the backstage of a Chinese opera, read about the arrival of European traders and the Opium Wars, and study a map showing land reclamation since the 1840s. One of my favorite parts of the museum is a re-created street of old Hong Kong, complete with an original Chinese herbal medicine shop located in Central until 1980 and reconstructed here. There are also 19th- and early-20th-century photographs, poignantly showing how much Hong Kong has changed through the decades. You can easily spend 2 hours here. Audio guides providing commentaries on more than 100 exhibits are available for HK$10.

100 Chatham Rd. S., Tsim Sha Tsui East. **852/2724 9042.** http://hk.history.museum. Admission HK$10 adults, HK$5 children and seniors. Free admission Wed. Mon and Wed–Sat 10am–6pm; Sun and holidays 10am–7pm. MTR: Tsim Sha Tsui (a 20-min. walk from exit B2). Bus: 5 or 5C from Star Ferry bus terminus.

Sam Tung Uk Museum ★★ Located in the New Territories but easily accessible from either Central or Tsim Sha Tsui in about 25 minutes via MTR, this is actually a restored Hakka walled village, built in the 18th century by members of the farming Chan clan. It consists of tiny lanes lined with tiny tile-roofed homes, four houses that have been restored to their original condition, an ancestral hall, two rows of side houses, an exhibition hall depicting Tsuen Wan's history, and an adjacent landscaped garden. The four windowless restored houses are furnished much as they would have been when occupied, with traditional Chinese furniture (including

VIEWS FROM THE 100th floor

It's not as high as Victoria Peak (p. 568), but **sky100,** 393m (1,289 ft.) above sea level, offers spectacular views of Kowloon, Victoria Harbour, and Hong Kong Island from its perch on the 100th floor of Hong Kong's tallest building, the International Commerce Centre at 1 Austin Rd. W. (✆ **852/2613 3888;** www.sky100.com.hk; MTR: Kowloon). Along with its interactive exhibition on the history and culture of Hong Kong, it's open daily from 10am to 10pm. Admission is HK$150 for adults and HK$105 for children, but discounts are offered for online purchase made at least 24 hours in advance.

elegant blackwood furniture). Although as many as 300 clan members once lived here, the village was abandoned in 1980. An 8-minute video describes the village's restoration into a folk museum and the purpose of its many rooms. Today the museum is a tiny oasis in the midst of high-rise housing projects.

2 Kwu Uk Lane, Tsuen Wan. ✆ **852/2411 2001.** http://hk.heritage.museum. Free admission. Wed–Mon 9am–5pm. MTR: Tsuen Wan (a few minutes' walk from exit E).

Temples

Man Mo Temple ★ Hong Kong Island's oldest and most important temple was built in the 1840s and is named after its two principal deities: Man, the god of literature, and Mo, the god of war. Two ornately carved sedan chairs in the temple were once used during festivals to carry the statues of the gods around the neighborhood. But what makes the temple particularly memorable are the giant incense coils hanging from the ceiling, imparting a fragrant, smoky haze—these are purchased by patrons seeking favors such as good health or a successful business deal, and may burn as long as 3 weeks.

Hollywood Rd. and Ladder St., Western District. ✆ **852/2803 2916.** Free admission. 8am–6pm. Bus: 26 from Des Voeux Rd. Central (in front of the HSBC headquarters) to the 2nd stop on Hollywood Rd., across from the temple. Or take the Central–Mid-Levels Escalator to Hollywood Rd. and turn right.

Wong Tai Sin ★★ Located six subway stops northeast of Yau Ma Tei in the far north end of Kowloon Peninsula, Wong Tai Sin is Hong Kong's most popular Daoist temple and attracts worshipers from the Daoist, Buddhism, and Confucianism religions, most of whom come to seek information about their fortunes. Although the temple is less than 100 years old, it adheres to traditional Chinese architectural principles with its red pillars, two-tiered golden roof, blue friezes, yellow latticework, and multicolored carvings. On the temple grounds are halls dedicated to the Buddhist Goddess of Mercy and to Confucius; a clinic with both Western medical services and traditional Chinese herbal treatments; and the Good Wish Garden with ponds, an artificial waterfall, a replica of the famous Nine Dragons relief (the original is in Beijing's Imperial Palace), and circular, square, octagonal, and fan-shaped pavilions.

Wong Tai Sin Estate. ✆ **852/2327 8141.** www.siksikyuen.org.hk. Free admission to temple, though donations of HK$2 is expected for the Good Wish Garden. Temple 7am–5:30pm; garden 9am–4:30pm. MTR: Wong Tai Sin (exit B2) and then a 3-min. walk (follow the signs).

Organized Tours & Cultural Activities

For information and pamphlets on the following tours, stop by HKTB; most hotels also have tour desks.

CITY TOURS For general sightseeing, the **Gray Line** (✆ **852/2368 7111;** www.grayline.com.hk) offers a variety of tours to such locations as Man Mo Temple, Victoria Peak, Aberdeen, Stanley, Po Lin Monastery on Lantau island, and the New Territories, as well as sunset cruises and visits to the horse races. **Splendid Tours & Travel** (✆ **852/2316 2151;** www.splendidtours.com) is another company offering tours, which can also be booked through Hong Kong hotels.

"MEET THE PEOPLE" Through this unique program of free, 1-hour tours, lectures, classes, and seminars, visitors can meet local specialists and gain in-depth knowledge of Hong Kong's traditions. Programs are updated and revised annually; past offerings have covered Cantonese opera, feng shui (geomancy), Chinese tea, Chinese medicine, and *taijiquan,* with something going on virtually every day of the week. Reservations are not necessary. For details on what, when, and where, pick up a *Cultural Kaleidoscope* brochure at HKTB or go to HKTB's website, www.discoverhongkong.com.

Outdoor Pursuits

PARKS & GARDENS

Hong Kong Park ★★ ☺ Stretching some 8 hectares (20 acres) along Supreme Court Road and Cotton Tree Drive in Central, this park features a dancing fountain at its entrance, one of Southeast Asia's largest greenhouses with more than 2,000 rare plant species, an aviary housing 600 exotic birds in a tropical rainforest setting, various gardens, a children's playground, and a viewing platform reached by climbing 105 stairs. The most famous building on the park grounds is the Flagstaff House, the oldest colonial building in Hong Kong and completed in 1846 in Greek Revival style for the commander of the British forces. Today it houses the **Flagstaff House Museum of Tea Ware** (✆ **852/2869 0690;** www.lcsd.gov.hk/hkma), with some 150 items of tea ware shown on a rotating basis, drawn from a 600-piece collection of primarily Chinese origin dating from the 7th century to the present day. The park is open from 6am to 11pm, the greenhouse and aviary are open from 9am to 5pm, and the museum of tea ware is open Wednesday through Monday from 10am to 5pm. Admission is free to everything. Take the MTR to Admiralty Station (exit C1), then follow the signs through Pacific Place and up the escalators.

Nan Lian Garden ★ This beautiful garden was built in the classical style of the Tang Dynasty (A.D. 618–907) using the blueprint of China's Jiangshouju, the only Tang landscape garden remaining with its original layout. Using traditional Chinese landscaping techniques such as "borrowed scenery" (incorporating surrounding scenery, such as a hill or range of mountains, into the overall garden design) and employing artificial hillocks, ornamental rocks, water features, wooden buildings, and trees to create both natural and artificial beauty, the garden is designed to be toured in a one-way circular route, with each step bringing different vistas and scenery. Across the street is the **Chi Lin Nunnery** (✆ **852/2329 8811**), which was reconstructed in the 1990s in the ancient Tang dynasty monastic style without the use of nails.

To reach the garden, open daily from 7am to 9pm, take exit C2 from the Diamond Hill MTR Station, from which it's a 15-minute walk. Admission is free.

A Junk Cruise

The most unique cruise in town is aboard the **Duk Ling,** an authentic Chinese junk built in Macau a half-century ago as a fishing boat. One-hour cruises, costing HK$100, are offered 2 days a week (Thurs and Sat, though days are subject to change; call ahead). I find the cruise interesting not only because Duk Ling is powered by the wind, but also because it sails in the opposite direction from ferries to the outlying islands, providing different vistas of the Hong Kong skyline as it cruises toward North Point and Kai Tak. Pre-registration is required beforehand at the Hong Kong Tourism Board Visitor Centre in Tsim Sha Tsui. For more information or the latest sailing schedule, contact HKTB at ✆ **852/2508 1234** or go to www.discoverhongkong.com.

Yuen Po Street Bird Garden ★★★ ☺ Birds are favorite pets in Chinese households; perhaps you've noticed wooden bird cages hanging outside shops or from apartment balconies, or perhaps you've even seen someone taking his bird for an outing in its cage. To see more of these prized songbirds, visit the fascinating Yuen Po Street Bird Garden, Prince Edward Road West, Mongkok, which consists of a series of Chinese-style moon gates and courtyards lined with stalls selling songbirds, beautifully crafted wood and bamboo cages, live crickets and mealy worms, and tiny porcelain food bowls. Young children love it here. Take the MTR to Prince Edward Road station (exit B1) and walk 10 minutes east on Prince Edward Road West, turning left at the overhead railway onto Yuen Po Street. Admission to the garden is free and it's open from 7am to 8pm.

Ocean Park ★★★ ☺ This combination aquarium and amusement park, situated along a dramatic rocky coastline on Hong Kong Island's southern shore, is divided into two parts, connected by cable cars and a funicular. The most popular residents are the four giant pandas, but there are also red pandas, Chinese alligators, jellyfish, Chinese sturgeon, sharks, rays, and performing dolphins and sea lions. The Atoll Reef, one of the world's largest aquariums, has an observation passageway encircling the aquarium on four levels, enabling you to view the sea life—everything from giant octopi to schools of tropical fish—from various depths. Thrill rides include a roller coaster that turns upside down three times, a 20-story vertical drop in the Abyss, kiddie rides, and, in summer, water slides and attractions.

Aberdeen, Hong Kong Island. ✆ **852/2552 0291.** www.oceanpark.com.hk. Admission HK$250 adults, HK$125 children. 10am–6pm. Bus: Ocean Park Citybus 629 from the Central Ferry Pier no. 7 or Admiralty MTR station directly to park every 10 to 20 min.; or 70 from Exchange Square, 72 from Causeway Bay, or 973 from Tsim Sha Tsui (get off at the 1st stop after the tunnel and then walk 20 min.).

TAI CHI

Taijiquan (shadow boxing), called "tai chi" in the West (and English literature put out by HKTB), is an ancient Chinese regimen designed to balance body and soul and thereby release energy from within. Visitors can join free, 1-hour **lessons** in English, offered by HKTB's "Meet the People" cultural program, every Monday, Wednesday, and Friday at 8am in front of the Hong Kong Museum of Art in the Sculpture Court near the Tsim Sha Tsui waterfront promenade (MTR: Tsim Sha Tsui, Exit E). For more information, stop by or call HKTB (✆ **852/2508 1234**).

HIKING

With 23 country parks—amounting to more than 40% of Hong Kong's space—there are many trails of varying levels of difficulty throughout Hong Kong, including hiking trails, nature trails, and family trails. Serious hikers may want to consider the famous **MacLehose Trail** in the New Territories, which stretches about 100km (62 miles) through eight country parks, while the **Lantau Trail** is a 70km (43-mile) circular trail on **Lantau island** that begins and ends at Mui Wo (also called Silvermine Bay). Easier to reach is the 50km (31-mile) **Hong Kong Trail,** which spans Hong Kong Island's five country parks. The HKTB has trail maps, a hiking and wildlife guidebook called *Exploring Hong Kong Countryside: A Visitor's Companion,* and a nifty booklet called *Discover Hong Kong Nature.* Its website, www.discoverhongkong.com, also lists recommended hikes.

HORSE RACING

If you're here anytime from September to mid-June, join the rest of Hong Kong at the horse races. Introduced by the British more than 165 years ago, horse racing is by far the most popular sporting event in Hong Kong, due to the fact that, aside from the local lottery, racing is the only legal form of gambling in Hong Kong. Winnings are tax-free.

There are two tracks—**Happy Valley** on Hong Kong Island, which you can reach by taking the tram to Happy Valley or the MTR to Causeway Bay; and **Sha Tin** in the New Territories, reached by taking the MTR to Racecourse Station. Races are held Wednesday evenings and some Saturday and Sunday afternoons. The lowest admission price is HK$10, which is for the general public and is standing room only. If you want to watch from the more exclusive Hong Kong Jockey Club members' enclosure, are at least 18 years old, and are a bona fide tourist, you can purchase a temporary member's badge for HK$100 for most races and HK$150 on rare special race days. It's available on a first-come, first-served basis by showing your passport at either the Badge Enquiry Office at the main entrance to the members' private enclosure (at either track), or at designated off-course betting centers like the ones at 10-12 Stanley in Central and 4 Prat Ave. in Tsim Sha Tsui.

You can also see the races by joining an organized tour offered by Gray Line or Splendid Tours (see "Organized Tours & Cultural Activities," above).

SWIMMING

There are numerous public swimming pools, including those at **Kowloon Park,** with admission costing around HK$19 for adults and HK$9 for children and seniors. About 40 **beaches** are free for public use, most with lifeguards on duty April through October, changing rooms, and snack stands or restaurants. On Hong Kong Island, beaches include Big Wave Bay and Shek O on the east coast, and Stanley, Deep Water Bay, South Beach (popular with the gay crowd), and Repulse Bay on the southern coast. There are prettier beaches on the outlying islands, including Hung Shing Ye and Lo So Shing on Lamma, Tung Wan on Cheung Chau, and Cheung Sha on Lantau.

Outlying Islands

An excursion to an outlying island provides not only an opportunity to experience rural Hong Kong but also the chance to view Hong Kong's skyline and harbor by ferry, and very cheaply at that. I recommend either Lantau, famous for its giant outdoor Buddha, monastery serving vegetarian meals, and other attractions, or Cheung Chau, popular with families for its unhurried, small-village atmosphere and beach. Both islands are reached in an hour or less via ferries that depart approximately every hour or so from the Central Ferry Piers, location also of the Star Ferry (pick up a free timetable at HKTB). Tickets range from HK$11 to HK$37 depending on the day (weekdays are cheaper), class (ordinary and deluxe), and boat (regular ferry or more expensive but quicker Fast Ferry). Upper-deck deluxe class entitles you to sit on an open deck out back on some ferries.

In addition to the ferries above, there is also infrequent ferry service from Tsim Sha Tsui's Star Ferry concourse on Saturday afternoon and Sunday. You can also reach Lantau via the Tung Chung MTR Line, with a connecting cable car that delivers passengers directly to the Giant Buddha in just 17 minutes.

LANTAU

Hong Kong's largest island and twice the size of Hong Kong Island, Lantau has a population of 100,000 and is home to Hong Kong's international airport. Luckily, more than half of the mountainous and lush island remains preserved in country parks. For a change of scenery, you might want to arrive at Lantau via the ferry from Central to Silvermine Bay (called *Mui Wo* in Cantonese), then take bus no. 2 to Ngong Ping Plateau. On the return trip, take the Ngong Ping Skyrail cable car to Tung Chung, where you can board the MTR. In any case, you should allow for at least 5 hours for a visit to Lantau.

At the plateau of Ngong Ping, with an elevation of 738m (2,421 ft.), is Lantau's biggest attraction, the **Giant Tian Tan Buddha,** erected in 1993 as the largest seated outdoor bronze Buddha in the world. It's almost 30m (100 ft.) tall and weighs 220 metric tonnes (243 tons); it's reached via 268 steps and offers great views of the surrounding countryside. Admission to the viewing platform is free and it's open from 10am to 5:30pm.

Here, too, is **Ngong Ping Village** (**© 852/2109 9898;** www.np360.com.hk), which contains shops, restaurants, a teahouse, a museum called **Walking with Buddha** that chronicles Siddhartha Gautama's path to enlightenment, and the **Monkey's Tale Theatre,** which presents a computer-animated comical story about a selfish monkey who learns about greed, humility, friendship, and kindness. Ngong Ping Village is open Monday to Friday from 10am to 6pm and Saturday and Sunday from 9am to 6:30pm. Admission to either the museum or theater is HK$36 for adults and HK$18 for children.

For dining, **Po Lin Monastery** (**© 852/2985 4736;** www.plm.org.hk) is famous for its vegetarian meals. Be sure to explore the grounds of the colorful monastery, established near the turn of the 20th century by reclusive Buddhist monks.

Also on Lantau is **Hong Kong Disneyland** (**© 852/1830 830;** www.hongkong disneyland.com), a 126-hectare (311-acre) theme park reached via the Tung Chung MTR line. Open hours vary with the season, with admission priced at HK$350 for adults, HK$250 for children, and HK$170 for seniors.

CHEUNG CHAU

If you have only a few hours to spare and don't want to worry about catching buses and finding your way around, Cheung Chau is your best bet. It's a tiny island (only

2.5 sq. km/1 sq. mile), with more than 25,000 people in its thriving fishing village. There are no cars on the island, making it a delightful place for walking around and exploring. The island is especially popular with Chinese families for its rental bicycles and beach, but my favorite thing to do here is to walk the tiny, narrow lanes of Cheung Chau village.

Inhabited for at least 2,500 years by fisher folk, Cheung Chau still supports a sizable population of fishing families, and fishing (along with tourism) remains the island's main industry. Inhabited junks are moored in the harbor, and the waterfront where the ferry lands, known as the **Praya,** buzzes with activity as vendors sell live fish and vegetables. The village is a fascinating warren of narrow alleyways, food stalls, open markets, and shops selling everything from medicinal herbs to toys.

About a 3-minute walk from the ferry pier is **Pak Tai Temple,** near a playground on Pak She Fourth Street. Built in 1783, it's dedicated to the "Supreme Emperor of the Dark Heaven," long worshiped as a Daoist god of the sea. As you roam the village, you'll pass open-fronted shops selling incense, paper funeral objects such as cars (cremated with the deceased to accompany him or her to the next life), medicinal herbs, jade, rattan, vegetables, rice, sun hats, sunglasses, and beach toys. On the other side of the island (directly opposite from the ferry pier and less than a 10-min. walk away) is **Tung Wan Beach.**

SHOPPING

Shopping is one of the main reasons people come to Hong Kong, and at first glance the city does seem to be one huge department store. Good buys include Chinese antiques, clothing, shoes, jewelry, furniture, carpets, leather goods, luggage, handbags, briefcases, Chinese herbs, watches, toys, and eyeglasses. Electronic goods and cameras are not the bargains they once were, though good deals can be found in recently discontinued models. Hong Kong is a duty-free port, so there is no sales tax.

Best Shopping Areas

Tsim Sha Tsui has the greatest concentration of shops in Hong Kong, particularly along Nathan Road, with its many electronics stores (which should be avoided in favor of the reliable chain Fortress). Be sure to explore its side streets for shops specializing in casual clothing, and luggage. Harbour City, one of the largest malls in the world, stretches along Canton Road.

For upscale shopping, **Central** is where you'll find international designer labels, in boutiques located in the Landmark in the ifc mall beside Hong Kong Station. There's also the upscale Pacific Place at Admiralty. **Causeway Bay** caters more to the local market, with lower prices, small shops selling everything from shoes and clothing to Chinese herbs, department stores, and a large shopping complex called Times Square.

Antiques and curio lovers usually head for **Hollywood Road** and **Cat Street** on Hong Kong Island, where everything from snuff bottles to jade carvings to reproductions is for sale. Finally, one of my favorite places to shop is the touristy but fun **Stanley Market,** on the southern end of Hong Kong Island, where vendors sell business and casual wear, as well as Chinese crafts and products. Another good place for Chinese imports and souvenirs is one of several Chinese **craft emporiums.** Finally, another good stomping ground is **Horizon Plaza,** 2 Lee Wing St., Ap Lei

Buyer Beware

Hong Kong is a buyer-beware market. To be on the safe side, try to make your major purchases at HKTB member stores, which display the HKTB logo (a gold circle with black Chinese calligraphy in the middle and the words "Quality Tourism Services"). Member stores are listed at www.discoverhongkong.com/qts. Still, it's always a good idea to obtain a receipt from the shopkeeper with a description of your purchase, including the brand name, model number, serial number, and price for electronic and photographic equipment. For jewelry and gold watches, there should be a description of the precious stones and the metal content. If you're making a purchase using a credit card, ask for the customer's copy of the credit card slip, and make sure "HK$" appears before the monetary total.

Chau, a huge warehouse with more than a dozen shops selling antiques, as well as outlet designer stores.

Because shopping is such big business in Hong Kong, most stores are open 7 days a week, closing only for 2 or 3 days during the Chinese New Year. Most stores open at 10am, closing at 7:30pm in Central, 9 or 10pm in Tsim Sha Tsui, and 9:30pm in Causeway Bay. Street markets are open every day.

Shopping A to Z

ANTIQUES & COLLECTIBLES

The most famous area for antiques and chinoiserie is around **Hollywood Road** and **Cat Street,** both above the Central District on Hong Kong Island. Hollywood Road twists along for a little more than half a mile, with shops selling original and reproduction Qing and Ming dynasty Chinese furniture, original prints, scrolls, porcelain, clay figurines, silver, and rosewood and blackwood furniture, as well as fakes and curios. Near the western end is Upper Lascar Row, popularly known as Cat Street, where sidewalk vendors sell snuff bottles, reproductions, and other curios. Another good bet is **Horizon Plaza,** 2 Lee Wing St. in Ap Lei Chau, with more than a dozen shops selling antiques (take bus no. M590 from Exchange Square in Central to Ap Lei Chau).

Arch Angel Antiques ★ Established in 1988 by an American and Dutch couple, this is one of Hollywood Road's largest and most reputable shops for Asian antiques and art, including museum-quality ceramics, furniture, Ming dynasty figurines, terra-cotta animals, boxes, and collectibles. In addition to this three-story main shop, nearby galleries (which the owners will show you on request) showcase ancient ceramics, bronze Buddhas, terra-cotta figures, stone sculptures, and contemporary Vietnamese art. Every antique item for sale is accompanied by a detailed certificate of authenticity. The main shop is open daily from 9:30am to 6:30pm. 53–55 Hollywood Rd., Central. ✆ **852/2851 6848.** MTR: Central.

Dragon Culture ★★ All serious fans of Chinese antiques eventually end up here. One of the largest and most knowledgeable purveyors of antiques in Hong Kong, owner Victor Choi began collecting Chinese antiques in the 1970s, traveling throughout China from province to province and to all the major cities. He shares his expertise in three books: *Collecting Chinese Antiquities in Hong Kong* (a must for both the novice and the experienced buyer), *Horses for Eternity* (proceeds from this go to charity), and *Antiquities through the Ages,* all of which you can purchase in his shop. Choi has also given lectures on Chinese antiques in the HKTB's Meet the People program, but make an appointment if you want to meet him specifically. He carries Neolithic pottery, three-color glazed pottery horses from the Tang dynasty, Ming porcelains, bronzes, jade, woodcarvings, snuff bottles, calligraphy, paintings, brush pots, stone carvings, and more, and also guarantees authenticity for all items he sells. He's open Monday through Saturday from 10:30am to 6pm. 231 Hollywood Rd., Sheung Wan. ✆ **852/2545 8098.** www.dragonculture.com.hk. MTR: Sheung Wan. Bus: 26 from Des Voeux Rd. Central (in front of the HSBC headquarters) to the 2nd stop on Hollywood Rd., at Man Mo Temple. Or take the Central–Mid-Levels Escalator to Hollywood Rd. and turn right.

CHINESE CRAFT EMPORIUMS

In addition to the shops listed here, which specialize in traditional and contemporary arts, crafts, souvenirs, and gift items from China, there are souvenir shops at Stanley Market, located in Stanley on the southern end of Hong Kong Island, that carry lacquered boxes, china, embroidered tablecloths, figurines, and other mainland imports. All these items will be much cheaper across the border, of course.

Chinese Arts and Crafts Ltd. In business for more than 50 years, this is the best upscale chain for Chinese arts and crafts and is one of the safest places to purchase jade. You can also buy silk clothing, arts and crafts, antiques, jewelry, watches, carpets, cloisonné, furs, Chinese herbs and medicine, rosewood furniture, chinaware, Chinese teas, and embroidered tablecloths or pillowcases—in short, virtually all the upmarket items produced by China. It's a great place for gifts, though prices are high. Open from 10am to 9:30pm. The shop is located in Star House near the Star Ferry at 3 Salisbury Rd., Tsim Sha Tsui (✆ **852/2735 4061;** www.crcretail.com; MTR: Tsim Sha Tsui). Branches are located in the Asia Standard Tower, 59 Queen's Rd. Central, Central (✆ **852/2901 0338;** MTR: Central); Shop 220 in Pacific Place, 88 Queensway, Central (✆ **852/2523 3933;** MTR: Admiralty); and in the China Resources Building., 26 Harbour Rd., Wan Chai (✆ **852/2827 6667;** MTR: Wan Chai).

Shanghai Tang ★★ 🎁 Step back into 1930s Shanghai at this upscale, two-level store with its gleaming wooden and tiled floors, raised cashier cubicles, and ceiling fans. This is Chinese chic at its best, with neatly stacked rows of updated versions of traditional Chinese clothing ranging from cheongsams and silk pajamas to padded jackets, caps, and shoes—all in bright, contemporary colors and styles. If you're looking for a lime-green or shocking-pink padded jacket, this is the place for you. It's open Monday to Saturday from 10am to 8pm and Sunday from 11am to 7pm. You will also find children's clothing and funky accessories and home furnishings, from silk-covered photo albums and beaded picture frames to funky clutch purses and silver chopsticks. Pedder Building, 12 Pedder St., Central. ✆ **852/2525 7333.** www.shanghaitang.com. MTR: Central.

Yue Hwa Chinese Products ★ Yue Hwa caters to the local market with its household goods, clothing (including traditional wear), shoes, jade jewelry, arts and crafts, china, embroidered linens, furniture, foodstuffs (in the basement), and medicinal products like tiger balm and dried sea horses. Don't miss the fifth floor tea department, where you can sample products before you buy. It's open daily from 10am to 10pm. 301–309 Nathan Rd., Yau Ma Tei, Kowloon. ✆ **852/3511 2222.** www.yuehwa.com. MTR: Jordan.

FASHION

Hong Kong has been a center for the fashion industry ever since the influx of Shanghainese tailors fleeing the 1949 Communist revolution in China. If you're looking for international designer brands and money is no object, the **Landmark,** located on Des Voeux Road Central, Central, is an ultra-chic shopping complex with the highest concentration of international brand names in Hong Kong, including Gucci, Tiffany & Co., Polo/Ralph Lauren, Marc Jacobs, Manolo Blahnik, Sonia Rykiel, Jimmy Choo, Paul Smith, Vivienne Tam, and Dior, as well as British luxury import Harvey Nichols. Other shopping arcades and malls with well-known international designer boutiques include the **Prince's Building,** next to the Mandarin Hotel, **ifc mall** next to Hong Kong Station, and **The Peninsula,** on Salisbury Road in Tsim Sha Tsui.

For trendier designs catering to an upwardly mobile younger crowd, check out the **Joyce** (www.joyce.com) chain, established in the 1970s by Joyce Ma to satisfy Hong Kong women's cravings for European designs. Today her stores carry clothing by Galliano, Vera Wang, Alexander McQueen, Rei Kawakubo (Comme des Garçons), and others on the cutting edge of fashion. You'll find Joyce shops at 18 Queen's Rd. Central, Central District (✆ **852/2810 1120;** MTR: Central); Shop 232 Pacific Place, 88 Queensway, Central (✆ **852/2523 5944;** MTR: Admiralty); and Shop G106 in The Gateway, Canton Rd., Tsim Sha Tsui (✆ **852/2367 8128;** MTR: Tsim Sha Tsui). For bargains, head to the Joyce Warehouse, Horizon Plaza, 2 Lee Wing St., Ap Lei Chau (✆ **852/2814 8313;** bus: M590 from Exchange Square in Central).

FACTORY OUTLETS Hong Kong's factory outlets offer excess stock, overruns, and quality-control rejects. Because these items have been made for the export market, the sizes are Western. Bargains include clothes made of silk, cashmere, cotton, linen, knitwear, and wool. On Hong Kong Island, the best-known building housing factory-outlet showrooms is the **Pedder Building,** 12 Pedder St., Central; Ladies' Market (see below) also serves as an outlet for mainland factories. Otherwise, the best place for one-stop discount shopping is **Citygate,** located at the end of Tung Chung MTR Line on Lantau island (✆ **852/2109 2933;** www.citygateoutlets.com.hk; MTR: Tung Chung). Hong Kong's only outlet mall, it offers discounts of 30% to 70% off international brand names, including Bally, Burberry, Benetton, Esprit, Laura Ashley, Levi's, Rockport, Vivienne Tam, Timberland, Adidas, Nike, and more.

MARKETS

Jade Market Jade is available in all sizes, colors, and prices at this market at the junction of Kansu Street and Battery Street, in two temporary structures in the Yau Ma Tei District. Unless you really know your jade and pearls, you won't want to make any expensive purchases here, but it's fun for inexpensive bangles and other trinkets. It's open from 10am to about 4pm (mornings are best), though some vendors stay until 6pm on busy days like Sunday. The market is located near the Jordan MTR station or less than a 30-minute walk from the Star Ferry.

Ladies' Market Stretching along Tung Choi Street (between Argyle and Dundas sts.) in Mongkok, Kowloon, Ladies' Market specializes in inexpensive women's and children's fashions, shoes, jewelry, sunglasses, watches, handbags (including fake designer bags), and other accessories. Some men's clothing is also sold. Although many of the products are geared more to local tastes, an increase in tourism has brought more fashionable clothing and T-shirts, including overruns and rejects from mainland factories. In any case, the atmosphere is fun and festive, especially at night. The nearest MTR station is Mongkok. Vendors' hours are from 1 to 11pm.

Li Yuen Street East & West These two streets are parallel pedestrian lanes in the heart of Central, very narrow and often congested with human traffic. Stalls are packed with Chinese jackets, handbags, clothes, scarves, sweaters, toys, baby clothes, watches, makeup, umbrellas, needles and thread, knickknacks, and even brassieres. Don't neglect the open-fronted shops behind the stalls. These two streets are located just a couple minutes' walk from the Central MTR station, between Des Voeux Road Central and Queen's Road Central. Vendors' hours are from noon to 7pm.

Stanley Stanley Market is probably the most popular and best-known market in Hong Kong. Located on the southern coast of Hong Kong Island, it's a fun place to buy inexpensive clothing, especially sportswear, cashmere sweaters, silk blouses and dresses, and women's suits. Men's, women's, and children's clothing are available. The inventory changes continuously—one year it seems everyone is selling washable silk; the next year it's Chinese traditional jackets or Gore-Tex coats. The market also has souvenir shops selling paintings, embroidered linen, beaded purses, handicrafts, and other products from mainland China.

To reach Stanley, take bus no. 6, 6A, 6X, or 260 from Central's Exchange Square bus terminal or from Queensway Plaza in front of Pacific Place, or take Minibus no. 40 from Causeway Bay. The bus ride to Stanley takes approximately 30 minutes. From Kowloon, take bus no. 973 from Mody Road in Tsim Sha Tsui East or from Canton Road in Tsim Sha Tsui. Shops are open from about 10am to about 6:30pm.

Temple Street Night Market Temple Street in the Yau Ma Tei district of Kowloon is a nightmarket that comes to life when the sun goes down. It offers T-shirts, jeans, menswear, watches, jewelry, CDs, mobile phones, electronic gadgets, alarm clocks, luggage, and imitation designer watches and handbags. Bargain fiercely, and check the products carefully to make sure they're not faulty or poorly made. The nightmarket is great entertainment, a must during your visit to Hong Kong though the surge of shoppers can be overwhelming. North of Temple Street, near Tin Hau Temple, are fortunetellers and sometimes street performers singing Chinese opera. Although some vendors begin setting up shop at 4pm, the nightmarket is busiest from about 7 until the 10pm closing; it's located near the Jordan MTR station.

HONG KONG AFTER DARK

Hong Kong's nightlife is concentrated in Tsim Sha Tsui, in Central's entertainment areas of Lan Kwai Fong and SoHo, and in Wan Chai. If you're watching your Hong Kong dollars, take advantage of happy hour (happy hours is more like it), when many bars offer two drinks for the price of one or drinks at reduced prices. Furthermore, many pubs, bars, and lounges offer live entertainment, from jazz to Filipino combos, which you can enjoy simply for the price of a beer. With only a couple of exceptions, most nightclubs in Hong Kong are small, simple bars that morph into miniature discos late at night or on weekends, as well as trendy clubs that cater mostly to their in-crowd members but may occasionally allow nonmembers on slow nights (the best plan of action to get into a membership club is to dress smartly, come on a weeknight or early in the evening, and be nice to the doorman). Many clubs are "member" clubs in name only, giving them license to turn away those who don't fit their image. Discos and dance clubs in Hong Kong generally charge more on weekend nights, but the admission price usually includes one or two free drinks. After that, beer and mixed drinks are often priced the same. Bars, whether with DJs or live music, rarely charge cover. Remember, however, that a 10% service charge will be added to your bill.

In addition to the recommendations below, be sure to watch the nightly "Symphony of Lights" show from 8 to 8:18pm, when an impressive laser and light show is projected from more than 40 buildings on both sides of the harbor. The best vantage points? From the Tsim Sha Tsui waterfront and Bauhinia Square in Wan Chai.

To obtain tickets for the Hong Kong Chinese Orchestra, Chinese opera, rock and pop concerts, and other major events, call the **Urban Council Ticketing Office (URBTIX)** at ✆ **852/2734 9009,** or drop by outlets located in City Hall, Low Block, 7 Edinburgh Place in Central, or in the Hong Kong Cultural Centre, 10 Salisbury Rd. in Tsim Sha Tsui. Both are open from 10am to 9:30pm. You can also reserve tickets before arriving in Hong Kong, either by calling the Credit Card Hotline at ✆ **852/2111 5999** or through the website, www.urbtix.hk.

Performing Arts

CHINESE OPERA The most popular regional styles of Chinese opera in Hong Kong are Peking-style opera, with its spectacular costumes, elaborate makeup, and feats of acrobatics and swordsmanship; and the less flamboyant but more readily understood Cantonese-style opera. For visitors, the easiest way to see a Chinese opera is during a festival, such as the Hong Kong Arts Festival, held from about mid-February through early March. Otherwise, Cantonese opera is performed fairly regularly at town halls in the New Territories, as well as in City Hall in Central and at the Hong Kong Cultural Centre in Tsim Sha Tsui. Tickets, ranging from HK$100 to HK$300, usually sell out well in advance, so book before arriving in Hong Kong. Contact HKTB for an updated schedule.

HONG KONG CHINESE ORCHESTRA Established in 1977, the Hong Kong Chinese Orchestra (www.hkco.org) is the world's largest professional Chinese-instrument orchestra, with 80-some musicians performing both new and traditional works using traditional and modern Chinese instruments and combining them with Western and Chinese orchestrations. Performances are held at the Hong Kong Cultural Centre, 10 Salisbury Rd., Tsim Sha Tsui (✆ **852/2734 2009**), and at City Hall, Edinburgh Place, Central District (✆ **852/2921 2840**). Tickets for most concerts are HK$120 to HK$260.

The Bar Scene

KOWLOON

Aqua Spirit ★★★ This glam venue is one of Hong Kong's hottest bars, due in no small part to its unbeatable location on the 30th floor of a Tsim Sha Tsui high-rise, where slanted, soaring windows give an incredible bird's-eye-view of the city. Circular booths shrouded behind strung beads, designer drinks, and a voyeur's dream location on an open mezzanine overlooking a restaurant on the 29th floor make this one of Kowloon's trendiest venues. There's a HK$150 drink minimum, and it's open Sunday to Thursday from 5pm to 2am and Friday and Saturday from 5pm to 3am. 1 Peking Rd., Tsim Sha Tsui. ✆ **852/3427 2288.** MTR: Tsim Sha Tsui.

Bahama Mama's One of many bars lining Knutsford Terrace, this one is decorated in a kitschy Caribbean theme and offers a few tables outside from which to watch the passing parade, as well as a small dance floor. It's open Monday through Thursday from 4pm to 3am, Friday and Saturday from 4pm to 4am, and Sunday from 4pm to 2am. 4–5 Knutsford Terrace, Tsim Sha Tsui. ✆ **852/2368 2121.** MTR: Tsim Sha Tsui.

Delaney's This upmarket Irish pub with a convivial atmosphere gets an extra boost from a Tuesday quiz night with prizes for winners and DJ Thursday and Friday nights, all free of charge, as well as big soccer and rugby events shown on a big screen. An a la carte menu features Irish stew and other national favorites. Happy hour is from 5 to 9pm; regular hours are from 8am to 2am. There's another Delaney's in Wan Chai at 18 Luard Rd. (✆ **852/2804 2880**). 71–77 Peking Rd., Tsim Sha Tsui. ✆ **852/2301 3980.** MTR: Tsim Sha Tsui.

Lobby Lounge This comfortable cocktail lounge has gorgeous, water-level views of Victoria Harbour and Hong Kong Island. You'll fall in love all over again (with Hong Kong, your companion, or both) as you take in one of the world's most famous views (this is a very civilized place for watching the nightly Symphony of Lights laser show) and listen to live music (6pm–12:45am). It's open 7am to 1am. In Hotel Inter-Continental Hong Kong, 18 Salisbury Rd., Tsim Sha Tsui. ✆ **852/2721 1211.** MTR: Tsim Sha Tsui.

CENTRAL DISTRICT

Club 97 ★★ Opened about 30 years ago and still one of Lan Kwai Fong's most revered nightlife establishments, this open-fronted club packs 'em in with a small dance floor and a string of popular weekly events, including Salsa Wednesdays, Thursday Ladies' Night with drink specials, Friday gay happy hour (6–10pm) complete with drag shows, and Sunday reggae night, which draws a huge crowd wishing to chill out before the workweek begins. It's open Monday to Thursday from 6pm to 2am (happy hour 6–9pm), Friday from 6pm to 4am (happy hour 6–10pm), Saturday from 8pm to 4am (happy hour 8–9pm), and Sunday from 8pm to 3am (happy hour 8–9pm). 9 Lan Kwai Fong, Central. ✆ **852/2810 9333.** MTR: Central.

Joyce is Not Here Artists' Bar & Café ★★ This tiny establishment, with a Bohemian atmosphere, attracts artistic intellectuals whose idea of entertainment is more than just drinking beer. Wednesday is poetry reading night, Thursday is jam night, Friday and Saturday feature live music from mostly local talents (string music, classical, blues, vocal jazz, fusion, urban folk, and so forth), and Sunday is movie night with international films. Tuesday nights, photographers and designers can present their work. Across the street is **Peel Fresco Music Lounge** (✆ **852/2540 2046**), by the same owners and with live music (mostly jazz) nightly. Admission is free to both (there's a two-drink minimum). Joyce is open, according to its quirky owners, Tuesday to Friday from 4:33pm and Saturday from Sunday from 1:22pm "until we get tired." 38–44 Peel St., ✆ **852/2851 2999.** www.joycebakerdesign.com. MTR: Central.

Lei Dou ★ Its name translates as "Right Here," which for the longest time seemed like a cruel joke since there was no outdoor sign to alert passersby exactly where right here might be. That's been remedied with a HUGE sign, so there's no mistaking this place as you walk up Lan Kwai Fong. Inside, the decor is old-world-boudoir-meets-edgy-contemporary, with sofas and easy chairs spread through several cozy rooms, palm trees, fanciful decorations, and artwork spotlit on the walls. It's open 5pm to 3am, with happy hour Monday to Friday until 8pm. 20–22 D'Aguilar St., Central. ✆ **852/2525 6628.** MTR: Central.

CAUSEWAY BAY/WAN CHAI

Inn Side Out Causeway Bay isn't known for nightlife, making this bar/American bistro even more of a standout. It's one of the few places selling the local Hong Kong beer, along with an impressive list of mostly Belgian micro beers and free peanuts, and has large patio seating complete with palm trees between its two glass-enclosed bar areas, where big screens show major sporting events. The menu has salads, pizza, burgers, and ribs, making it a good place for a meal too. It's a bit hard to find, behind Sunning Plaza and off Sunning and Hoi Ping roads. It's open Sunday to Thursday from 11:30am to 1am and Friday and Saturday from 11:30am to 1:30am (happy hour 2:30–8:30pm daily). 10 Hysan Ave., Causeway Bay. ✆ **852/2895 2900.** MTR: Wan Chai.

The Wanch ★★★ Established in 1987 and claiming to be Hong Kong's oldest bar in its original state (not relocated or renovated), this small and intimate unpretentious bar is one of Hong Kong's best for live music, offering free live music nightly. With a long history of nurturing local and international talent, it supports all genres of music, from blues and folk to jazz and rock. Monday is jam night, Tuesday is acoustic night, and every other Sunday it's sing-along music. In contrast to many other Wan Chai bars, this is not a pick-up bar, making it a good bet not only for music lovers but also couples and women traveling solo. Live music begins at 9pm Monday through Saturday and 3pm Sunday. Happy hour is until 10pm every day except Sunday. Open Monday through Saturday 5pm to 2am and Sunday 3pm to 2am. 54 Jaffe Rd., Wan Chai. ✆ **852/2861 1621.** www.thewanch.hk. MTR: Wan Chai.

MACAU

Macau was established as a Portuguese colony in 1557, centuries before the British acquired Hong Kong. Just 64km (40 miles) west of Hong Kong, across the Pearl River Estuary, Macau is Lilliputian, only 29.2 sq. km (11.4 sq. miles) in area. Once a sleepy backwater, it has experienced tremendous growth since the turn of the millennium, with massive land reclamation projects, spanking-new boutiques and restaurants, and an explosion of world-class hotels and casinos that have transformed it into Asia's hottest gambling mecca. The number of tourists to Macau—mostly from mainland China—has more than tripled since 1999.

While much has been lost in the flurry of development, Macau is still a unique destination in the world, an intriguing mix of Chinese and Portuguese traditions and culture. On December 20, 1999, Portugal's 400 years of rule came to an end when Macau was handed back to China. Like Hong Kong, Macau is a Special Administrative Region of China, permitted its own internal government and economic system for another 50 years after the Chinese assumed control. As with Hong Kong, no advance visa is required.

Macau has beaches, churches, fortresses, temples, gardens, museums, and fascinating neighborhoods to explore, as well as restaurants serving wonderful Macanese cuisine. What's more, Macau's prices are slightly cheaper than Hong Kong's, particularly for dining.

Arriving

BY PLANE **Macau International Airport** (✆ **853/2886 1111;** http://macau-airport.gov.mo), located on Taipa Island and connected to the mainland by bridge, has international connections to Taipei, Singapore, Kuala Lumpur, Manila, Seoul, Osaka, Tokyo, and Bangkok. It also has flights with Chinese airlines from Hangzhou,

Fuzhou, Kaohsiung, Shanghai, and Xiamen; and flights with Air Macau from Beijing, Hangzhou, Kaohsiung, Nanjing, Nanning, Ningbo, Chengdu, Shanghai, and Xiamen. Several first-class hotels offer complimentary transfers on request. Otherwise, airport bus AP1 travels from the airport to the ferry terminal and Hotel Lisboa; the fare, in Macau pataca currency, is MOP$4.20. A taxi to the Lisboa costs approximately MOP$47. Airport-departure tax is included in the price of plane tickets.

BY BOAT Macau is easily accessible from Hong Kong by **high-speed jetfoil,** with most departures from the **Macau Ferry Terminal,** located just west of the Central District in the Shun Tak Centre, 200 Connaught Rd., on Hong Kong Island. Situated above Sheung Wan MTR station, the terminal houses jetfoil ticket offices, as well as the Macau Government Tourist Office (room 336, on the same floor as boats departing for Macau). Limited service is also available from Kowloon, from the China Hong Kong Terminal on Canton Road, Tsim Sha Tsui.

The fastest, most convenient way to travel to Macau is via a 55-minute ride on jetfoils operated by **TurboJET** (✆ **852/2859 3333** in Hong Kong, or **853/8790 7039** in Macau; www.turbojet.com.hk), with departures from the Macau Ferry Terminal every 15 minutes, 24 hours a day. One-way fares Monday through Friday are HK$236 for super class and HK$134 for economy class; fares on Saturday, Sunday, and holidays are HK$252 in super class and HK$146 in economy. Fares for night service (6:15pm–6am) are HK$267 and HK$168, respectively. Seniors older than 61 and children younger than 12 receive a HK$15 discount. For those who wish to travel in style, with reclinable leather seats and complimentary food and beverages, there are 10 daily Premier Jetfoils to Macau, starting at HK$212 for regular Premier Class and HK$312 for Premier Grand Class.

Tickets can be purchased at the Macau Ferry Terminal on Hong Kong Island, the China Ferry Terminal in Kowloon, and all China Travel Service branches in Hong Kong. You can also book by credit card by calling ✆ **852/2921 6688** or online. Note that passengers are allowed only one hand-carried bag, not to exceed 20 kilograms (44 lb.), with one additional piece checked in 20 minutes prior to departure for a fee ranging from HK$20 to HK$40, depending on weight.

There is also TurboJET Sea Express service directly from Hong Kong International Airport (transfers are made without passing through Hong Kong Customs), with nine sailings daily costing HK$215 for economy class and HK$315 for super class.

In Macau, you'll arrive at the **Macau Ferry Terminal,** on the main peninsula. After going through Customs, stop by the Macau Government Tourist Office for a map and brochures. In the arrivals hall is also a counter for free shuttle buses to major hotels. Otherwise, city bus nos. 3, 3A, and 10 travel from the terminal to Avenida Almeida Ribeiro, the main downtown street, for MOP$2.50.

If your destination is Taipa, Cotai, or Colôane, you can also travel from the Macau Ferry Terminal directly to Taipa via **Cotai Waterjets** (✆ **852/2359 9990** in Hong Kong, **853/2885 0595** in Macau; www.cotaijet.com.mo). Ferries depart every 15 or 30 minutes between 7am and 1am. One-way fares Monday through Friday are HK$236 for super class and HK$134 for economy class; fares on Saturday, Sunday, and holidays are HK$252 and HK$146, respectively. Night sailings (from 6pm) cost more.

To the Mainland

Travel to the mainland (on foot across the border to Zhuhai, by jetfoil to Shenzhen, or by plane) requires a Chinese visa. For all but land crossings, buy visas in Hong Kong (see "Traveling to & from the Mainland" in the Hong Kong section, earlier in

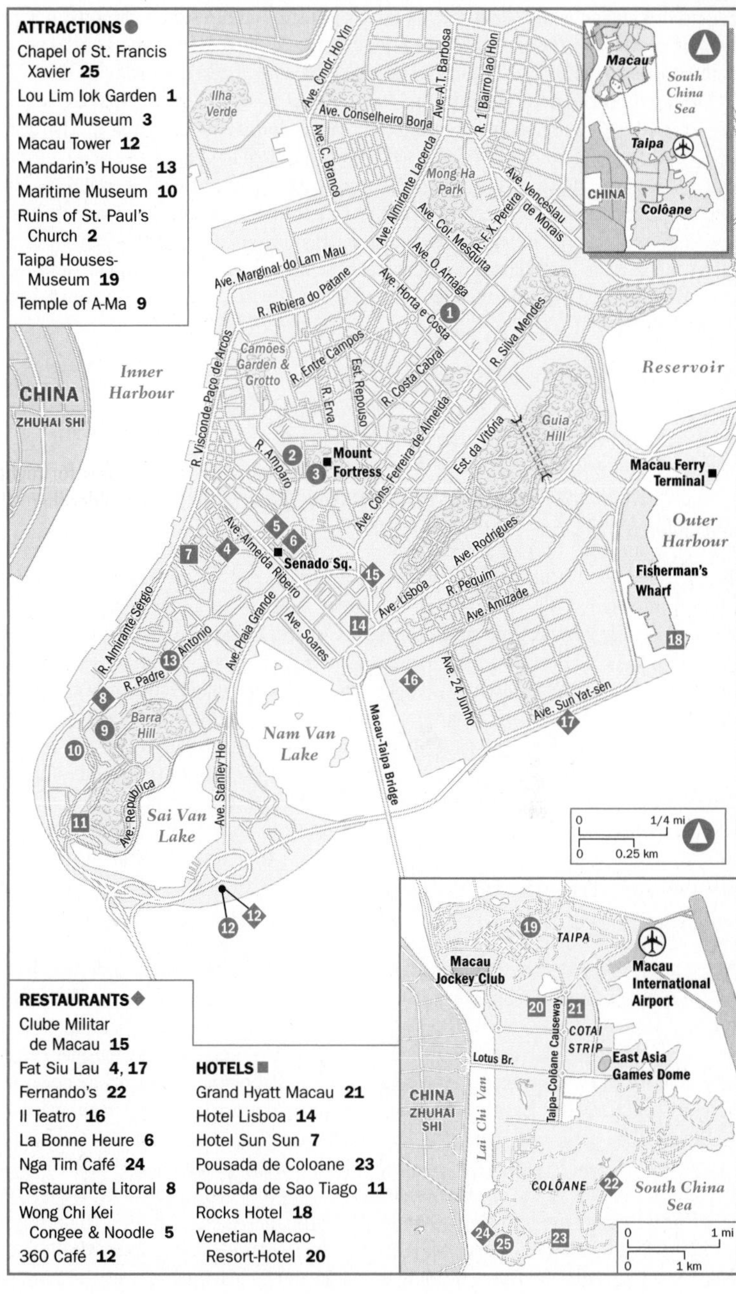
ATTRACTIONS ●
Chapel of St. Francis Xavier 25
Lou Lim Iok Garden 1
Macau Museum 3
Macau Tower 12
Mandarin's House 13
Maritime Museum 10
Ruins of St. Paul's Church 2
Taipa Houses-Museum 19
Temple of A-Ma 9
RESTAURANTS ◆
Clube Militar de Macau 15
Fat Siu Lau 4, 17
Fernando's 22
Il Teatro 16
La Bonne Heure 6
Nga Tim Café 24
Restaurante Litoral 8
Wong Chi Kei Congee & Noodle 5
360 Café 12
HOTELS ■
Grand Hyatt Macau 21
Hotel Lisboa 14
Hotel Sun Sun 7
Pousada de Coloane 23
Pousada de Sao Tiago 11
Rocks Hotel 18
Venetian Macao-Resort-Hotel 20
Ilha Verde
Ave. Cmdr. Ho Yin
Ave. Conselheiro Borja
Ave. A.T. Barbosa
R. 1 Bairro Iao Hon
Ave. C. Branco
Ave. Almirante Lacerda
Mong Ha Park
Ave. Venceslau de Morais
R. F.X. Pereira
Ave. Col. Mesquita
Ave. O. Arriaga
Ave. Marginal do Lam Mau
R. Ribiera do Patane
Ave. Horta e Costa
R. Silva Mendes
Camões Garden & Grotto
R. Entre Campos
Est. Repouso
R. Erva
R. Costa Cabral
Inner Harbour
CHINA
ZHUHAI SHI
R. Visconde Paço de Arcos
Reservoir
Guia Hill
Est. da Vitória
Ave. Cons. Ferreira de Almeida
R. Amparo
Mount Fortress
Macau Ferry Terminal
Outer Harbour
Ave. Almeida Ribeiro
Senado Sq.
Ave. Rodrigues
Ave. Lisboa
R. Pequim
Ave. Amizade
Fisherman's Wharf
R. Almirante Sérgio
Antonio
R. Padre
Ave. Praia Grande
Ave. Soares
Ave. 24 Junho
Ave. Sun Yat-sen
Barra Hill
Nam Van Lake
Macau-Taipa Bridge
Ave. Stanley Ho
Ave. Republica
Sai Van Lake
0 1/4 mi
0 0.25 km
Macau
South China Sea
Taipa
CHINA
Colôane
TAIPA
Macau Jockey Club
Macau International Airport
Taipa-Colôane Causeway
COTAI STRIP
Lotus Br.
East Asia Games Dome
CHINA
ZHUHAI SHI
Lai Chi Van
COLÔANE
South China Sea
0 1 mi
0 1 km

this chapter). The **border crossing** is open from 7am to midnight, but arrive by 11:30pm.

Turbojet operates 1-hour ferries between Macau and Shenzhen Airport Fu Yong Ferry Terminal five times a day (with fares starting at MOP$196), She Kou 10 times daily (starting at MOP$171), and Guangzhou (Nansha) once a day (from MOP$180).

Guangzhou can be reached by bus from Zhuhai Gong Bei bus station, ahead and slightly to the right as you emerge from the Macau/Zhuhai border crossing. There are departures every 15 minutes or so between 8am and 8pm to Guangzhou Station, from where there's a choice of taxi, bus, or metro to take you the 8km (5 miles) to the airport. There are also frequent services to **Shenzhen** and **Kaiping** between 8:30am and 7:30pm. In addition, the Kee Kwan Motor Road Company (✆ **853/2893 3888**) offers bus service from downtown Macau at the end of Av. Almeida Ribeiro and Rua das Lorchas (near the Master Hotel) to major cities in Guangdong Province from 7:15am to 9:30pm.

Visitor Information

Two **Macau Government Tourist Offices (MGTO)** are in Hong Kong—at counter A06 in the arrivals lobby of the International Airport (✆ **852/2769 7970;** www.macautourism.gov.mo), open from 9am to 6pm (closed for lunch 1–2pm); and in room 336 on the third floor of the Macau Ferry Terminal, Shun Tak Centre, in Central (✆ **852/2857 2287**), open 9am to 8pm.

In Macau, you'll find an MGTO at the Macau Ferry Terminal, open from 9am to 10pm; there is also an MGTO at Macau International Airport, open 9am-10pm (closed for lunch 1:30–2:15pm and for dinner 7:30–8:15pm). In town, there's the main office, the **Macau Business Tourism Centre**, Largo do Senado (Senado Sq.), located in the center of town on the main plaza just off Avenida Almeida Ribeiro and open from 9am to 6pm. Other MGTO counters are located at **Fisherman's Wharf,** open from 10am to 1pm and 2 to 6pm; **Guia Fort and Lighthouse,** open from 9am to 1pm and 2:15 to 5:30pm; the **Border Gate** (also called Barrier Gate and serving visitors from the mainland), open from 9:15am to 1pm and 2:30 to 6pm; and the **Taipa Ferry Terminal,** open 9:30am to 1pm and 2:30 to 6:15pm. Be sure to pick up a free city map, brochures on everything from churches to fortresses, and the tourist tabloid *Macau Travel Talk.* For information by telephone, call the **Tourist Hotline** at ✆ **853/2833 3000.**

Getting Around

Macau comprises a small peninsula and Taipa and Colôane, two islands that have merged due to land reclamation (called Cotai) and are linked to the mainland by bridges. The peninsula—referred to simply as Macau and surrounded by an Inner and an Outer Harbour—is where you'll find the city of Macau, as well as the main ferry terminal. Macau's main road is **Avenida Almeida Ribeiro;** about halfway down its length is the attractive **Largo do Senado (Senate Square),** Macau's main plaza.

Because the peninsula is only 9.3 sq. km (about 3½ sq. miles), you can walk most everywhere. If you get tired, jump into a metered **taxi,** which charges MOP$13 at flagfall for the first 1.6km (1 mile), then MOP$1.50 for each subsequent 230m (759 ft.). **Public buses** run from 7am to midnight, with fares costing MOP$3.20 for travel within the Macau Peninsula, MOP$4.20 for travel to Taipa, and MOP$5 to MOP$6.40 to Colôane. Buses heading for Taipa and Colôane make a stop in front of Hotel Lisboa, located on the peninsula near the Macau-Taipa Bridge. MGTO has a free map with bus routes.

Where to Stay

In addition to the rack rates given below (quoted in Hong Kong dollars; be sure to bargain for a better rate, especially in the off season), there's a 10% hotel service charge and a 5% government tax. If you plan on coming during Chinese New Year, Easter, July, August, the two major holidays for mainland Chinese (the so-called Golden Week following May 1 and in autumn for up to 10 days from Oct 1), or late November when the Grand Prix is held, book well in advance.

EXPENSIVE

Pousada de São Tiago ★★ Built around the ruins of the Portuguese Fortress da Barra, which dates from 1629, this delightful small inn on the tip of the peninsula is perfect for travelers looking for a romantic getaway. The entrance is dramatic—a flight of stone stairs leading through a cavelike tunnel that was once part of the fort, with water trickling in small rivulets on one side of the stairs (there is no elevator). Once inside, guests are treated to the hospitality of a Portuguese inn, with a delightful Spanish restaurant with an outdoor terrace shaded by banyan trees, as is the nearby outdoor swimming pool. Rooms, however, all of which are two-room suites, don't live up to expectations (the crocodile-skin-covered desk can only be described as odd), but most have balconies facing the Inner Harbor and all have spalike bathrooms with steam-room showers, Jacuzzi tubs, and bidets.

Avenida da República, Fortaleza de São Tiago da Barra, Macau. www.saotiago.com.mo. ✆ **853/2837 8111.** Fax 853/2855 2170. 12 units. HK$3,000 single or double weekdays, HK$3,600 Sat–Sun. AE, DC, MC, V. Free shuttle bus (on request) or bus 28B from ferry terminal. **Amenities:** Restaurant; lounge; outdoor pool; room service. *In room:* A/C, TV/DVD, hair dryer, minibar, free Wi-Fi.

Venetian Macao-Resort-Hotel ★★ ☺ This is Macau's biggest development, twice as big as its Las Vegas sister property and comprising the second-largest building in the world (be sure to pick up a map at the concierge, because you're going to need it). In addition to the world's largest casino, the property has 300 specialty shops, a dizzying array of dining options (including a 1,000-seat food court), a 15,000-seat arena with big-name acts, a Cirque du Soleil theater, and entertainment for kids, from an 18-hole minigolf course to four outdoor pools, including wave pool and wading pools. Clearly, this is a destination in itself; some guests check in and go nowhere else.

Estrada da Baia de N. Senhora da Esperanca, Cotai Strip, Macau www.venetianmacao.com. ✆ **853/2882 8877.** Fax 853/2882 8822. 3,000 units. HK$5,500 single or double; from HK$8,000 suite. AE, DC, MC, V. Free shuttle bus from both ferry terminals. **Amenities:** 19 restaurants; 2 bars; lounge; 24-hr casino; children's play center; concierge; gym; Jacuzzi; minigolf (fee charged); 4 outdoor pools; room service; spa. *In room:* A/C, TV, fax/scanner/printer, hair dryer, minibar, Wi-Fi (for a fee).

MODERATE

Grand Hyatt Macau ★ ☺ Located in the City of Dreams, an aquatic-themed entertainment resort that rivals the nearby Venetian complex, this property is more down to earth than the Venetian. A rarity in Macau these days, it doesn't have its own casino (though there is one in City of Dreams), but it does offer diversions for adults and children alike, including a 40m (131-ft.) outdoor pool and a toddler pool, and, in City of Dreams: Kid's City with climbers, slides, video games, and other activities; Dragon's Treasure, a 10-minute show about dragon kings in a "bubble" standing theater; and The House of the Dancing Water, a high-powered performance that combines water with acrobats, dancers, and musicians. Large contemporary rooms, decorated with photographs of local heritage sites, provide all the creature comforts and then some, including TV hookups for your iPod, camera, and laptop.

City of Dreams, Estrada do Istmo, Cotai, Macau. www.macau.grand.hyatt.com. ✆ **853/8868 1234.** Fax 853/8867 1234. 791 units. HK$1,788–HK$1,988 single or double; HK$2,188–HK$2,388 club floors; from HK$6,888 suite. Children 12 and under stay free in parents' room. AE, DC, MC, V. Free shuttle bus from both ferry terminals. **Amenities:** 2 restaurants; bar; lounge; free shuttle bus to downtown Macau; concierge; executive-level rooms; fitness center; Kid's City in City of Dreams for kids 12 and under (MOP$90 for 2 hr.); outdoor heated 40-m. pool open year-round and toddler pool; room service; spa. *In room:* A/C, TV, hair dryer, minibar, MP3 docking station; free Wi-Fi.

Hotel Lisboa 🎁 The Lisboa is in a class by itself. Built in 1969, it's a Chinese version of Las Vegas—huge, flashy, and with a bewildering array of facilities that make it almost a city within a city, and its 24-hour casino has long been one of the most popular in Macau. It has countless restaurants, shops, and nighttime diversions, including, you might say, the countless women roaming the shopping complex's halls, hoping for some short-term business from a lucky gambler. Ah, the Lisboa. The rooms are located in an older east wing and a tower that was completed in 1993 (a 49-story sister hotel, the Grand Lisboa, opened across the street in 2007). The tower, which added 14 floors, offers the best—and most expensive—harbor views, including rooms with traditional Chinese architecture and furniture. Otherwise, small standard rooms have some recommendable perks, including Jacuzzi tubs, free in-house movies, and free drinks in the fridge. In short, this is a unique, retro choice in the thick of it. Buses traveling to the outlying islands and other parts of Macau stop right outside the front door, and downtown Macau is only a 5-minute walk away.

2–4 Avenida de Lisboa, Macau. www.hotelisboa.com. ✆ **853/2888 3888.** Fax 853/2888 3838. 927 units. HK$1,850–HK$3,400 single or double; from HK$4,400 suite. Children 12 and under stay free in parent's room. AE, DC, MC, V. Free shuttle bus from Macau Ferry Terminal or bus no. 3, 3A, 10, 10A, 10B, 12, 28A, or 32 from the ferry terminal. **Amenities:** 18 restaurants; bar; lounge; 24-hr casino; room service. *In room:* A/C, TV w/free movies, hair dryer, free Internet, minibar w/free drinks.

Rocks Hotel ★ 🎁 Fisherman's Wharf is pure fantasy, so a Victorian-style boutique hotel doesn't seem out of place here. In fact, because it's located on a spit of land, with water on most sides, it has a breezy, resortlike feel, far from Macau's density just a short walk away. All the rooms take advantage of this location with balconies (the priciest directly face the sea), and, keeping in character, have claw-foot tubs and period furniture. Those searching for a relaxed, convenient 1-night getaway from Hong Kong can find refuge here.

Fisherman's Wharf, Macau. www.rockshotel.com.mo. ✆ **853/2878 2782.** Fax 853/2872 8800. 72 units. HK$1,880–HK$2,580 single or double; from HK$4,080 suite. Children 11 and under stay free in parent's room. AE, DC, MC, V. Free shuttle bus from Macau Ferry Terminal or a 10-min. walk. **Amenities:** Restaurant; lounge; babysitting; small gym; room service. *In room:* A/C, TV, hair dryer, minibar, free Wi-Fi.

INEXPENSIVE

Hotel Sun Sun ★★ 🎁 With a charming location near the Inner Harbour, across from a small square with a fountain and exercise equipment, this Best Western offers nondescript motel-like rooms with tired-looking décor and is often abuzz with tour groups. However, the highest-priced rooms have views of the Inner Harbour with its boat traffic, and executive floor rooms have been redone in modern chic. Although pricey, a beach package is available for HK$550, which provides transportation to Colôane beaches, towels, chairs, and drinks. But what I love most about this hotel is its location in Old Macau, making it highly recommendable despite its modest rooms.

14–16 Praca Ponte E. Horta, Macau. ✆ **800/780-7234** in the U.S. or Canada, or 853/2893 9393. Fax 853/2893 8822. 175 units. HK$1,200–HK$1,650 single or double; HK$1,800 executive floor;

HK$2,680 suite. 1 child 12 and under stays free in parent's room. AE, DC, MC, V. Bus: 3, 3A, 10, or 10A from Macau Ferry Terminal. **Amenities:** Bar; executive-level rooms; room service. *In room:* A/C, TV/DVD, hair dryer, minibar, free Wi-Fi.

Pousada de Colôane ★★ This small, family-owned gem, perched on a hill above Cheoc Van Beach with views of the sea, is ideal for couples and families in search of a reasonably priced isolated retreat. Opened in 1977, it's a relaxing, rather rustic place, with modestly furnished rooms, nothing fancy but all with Portuguese-style furnishings, Jacuzzi bathtubs, two sinks, and balconies facing the sea and popular public beach. There's an outdoor terrace where you can relax over drinks, and the inn's Portuguese restaurant is especially popular for the Sunday lunch buffet offered during peak season. The main drawback is one of access, but buses to Macau pass by frequently; when arriving at Macau Ferry Terminal, you're best off traveling to the hotel by taxi (fares average MOP$115).

Praia de Cheoc Van, Colôane, Macau. www.hotelpcoloane.com.mo. ✆ **853/2888 2143.** Fax 853/2888 2251. 30 units. HK$750–HK$880 single or double. MC, V. Bus: 21A, 25, or 26A from Lisboa Hotel (tell the bus driver you want to get off at the hotel). **Amenities:** Restaurant; bar; lobby computers w/free Internet access; outdoor pool; children's pool. *In room:* A/C, TV, hair dryer, minibar, free Wi-Fi (superior rooms only).

Where to Eat

EXPENSIVE

Il Teatro ★★★ SOUTHERN ITALIAN This restaurant lives up to its name, with theatrics supplied by an open kitchen and dancing fountains in the Wynn Macau's outdoor Performance Lake. Although there are three balcony tables bringing you closer to the choreographed water displays (which includes balls of fire), you'll get more bang for your buck if you book one of the comfy, elegant ringside tables inside. Everything is wonderful, from the handmade pastas and gourmet pizzas to artichoke-crusted black cod or prime beef tenderloin with porcini cannelloni. The dessert sampler is a great choice for those who want it all.

Wynn Macau, Rua Cidade de Sintra, NAPE. ✆ **853/8986 3663.** www.wynnmacau.com. Reservations required. Pizza and pasta MOP$118–MOP$218; main courses MOP$288–MOP$448. AE, DC, MC, V. Tues–Sun 5:30–11:30pm. Bus: 1A, 3, 3A, 8, 10A, 12, 28A, 28C, or 32.

MODERATE

Clube Militar de Macau ★★ MACANESE/PORTUGUESE With its tall ceilings, whirring ceiling fans, arched windows, wood floor, and displays of antique Chinese dishware, this is one of Macau's most atmospheric dining halls. It's located in a striking pink colonial building, built in 1870 for military officers and opened to the public in 1995. It's best to stick to the classics, such as roasted codfish in a crust of olives and herbs, chickpeas puree and emulsion of roasted tomato. The lunch buffet is a downtown favorite, and the list of Portuguese wines is among the best in town.

795 Av. da Praia Grande. ✆ **853/2871 4009.** www.clubemilitardemacau.net. Reservations recommended for lunch. Main courses MOP$123–MOP$198; fixed-price lunch or dinner MOP$128. AE, DC, MC, V. Daily noon–3pm and 7–11pm. Bus: 3, 3A, 8, 9, 10A, 10B, 11, 26A, 28A, 32, or 33.

Fat Siu Lau MACANESE This is Macau's oldest restaurant (dating from 1903). Its three floors of dining have been updated, but its exterior matches all the other storefronts on this revamped street—whitewashed walls and red shutters and doors. Dishes include roast pigeon marinated according to a 109-year-old secret recipe; spicy African chicken; curried crab; and grilled king prawns. Branches are located at the Docks nightlife district, Avenida Dr. Sun Yat-sen (✆ **853/2872 2922**), open daily noon to 3pm and 6 to 11:30pm; and Rua do Regedor 181–185, Taipa Village (✆ **853/2882 5257**), open daily noon to 10:30pm.

64 Rua da Felicidade. ✆ **853/2857 3580.** www.fatsiulau.com.mo. Main courses MOP$85–MOP$180. AE, MC, V. Daily noon–11pm. Bus: 2, 3, 3A, 5, 10, 10A, 11, 18, 21A, 26A, or 33.

Fernando's ★★ PORTUGUESE Although outwardly there is nothing to distinguish it from the other shacks on Hac Sa Beach (it's the brick one closest to the beach, below the vines), Fernando's, with a pavilion out back and an adjacent open-air bar with outdoor seating (a good place to wait; reservations are not accepted), is *the* place to dine on the beach and a destination in itself. The menu is strictly Portuguese and includes Portuguese chorizo, clams, crabs, fried prawns, codfish, *feijoada,* chargrilled chicken, pork ribs, suckling pig, stewed beef, and salads. Only Portuguese wine is served, stocked on a shelf for customer perusal (there is no wine list). It's all very informal, and not for those who demand pristine conditions—there is no air-conditioning, not even in the kitchen.

9 Praia de Hac Sa, Colôane. ✆ **853/2888 2531.** Reservations not accepted. Main courses MOP$80–MOP$180. No credit cards. Daily noon–9:30pm (last order). Bus: 15, 21A, 25, or 26A.

La Bonne Heure ★ FRENCH With the exception of Portuguese restaurants, most of Macau's Western eateries are ensconced in casino/hotel complexes, so it's nice to find an independent establishment centrally located in Old Macau. Near Senado Square, La Bonne Heure offers a cozy ambience and a menu that eschews fancy preparations in favor of simple yet delicious creations, such as crunchy roasted lamb in sesame crust served with mashed potatoes. This hideaway is a great place for a romantic dinner or a relaxed evening with friends.

12AB Travessa de S. Domingos. ✆ **853/2833 1209.** www.labonneheure.com. Reservations recommended. Main courses MOP$98–MOP$298. AE, MC, V. Mon–Sat noon–3pm; Mon–Thurs 6–10pm; Fri–Sat 6–11pm. Bus: 2, 3, 3A, 5, 10, 10A, 11, 18, 21A, 26A, or 33.

Restaurante Litoral ★★ MACANESE Exactly which restaurant serves the most "authentic" Macanese food in town is a hotly contested subject, but this attractive restaurant, with its dark-gleaming woods, whitewashed walls, and stone floor, can certainly lay claim to the title. All the traditional favorites are here, including curry crab; African chicken; feijoada; and *minchi,* a Macanese dish prepared with pork cubes, potatoes, onion, and garlic. Still, Portuguese specialties like codfish baked with potato and garlic, roast Portuguese sausage, and Portuguese green soup are not to be overlooked. Wash it all down with Portuguese wine or beer. The restaurant is located along the covered sidewalk not far from the Maritime Museum and A-Ma Temple.

261A Rua do Almirante Sérgio. ✆ **853/2896 7878.** www.restaurante-litoral.com. Main courses MOP$148–MOP$200. AE, MC, V. Daily noon–3pm and 5:30–10:30pm. Bus: 2, 5, 9, 10, 10A, 11, 18, 21A, or 28B.

360 Cafe INTERNATIONAL This is Macau's most conspicuous restaurant, more than 219m (719 ft.) above reclaimed ground in the soaring Macau Tower. Although there's an observation deck in the tower with an admission of MOP$100, head instead to the tower's revolving restaurant, where for the price of a buffet meal you'll get an equally good view. It takes 1½ hours for a complete spin, giving you ample time to sample the various Portuguese, Southeast Asian, Indian, Chinese, Macanese, and Continental dishes as you soak in the view. Note that there are two sittings for lunch.

In the Macau Tower, Lago Sai Van. ✆ **853/8988 8622.** www.macautower.com.mo. Reservations recommended Sat–Sun. Buffet lunch MOP$198; buffet dinner MOP$288. 11:30am–1pm and 1:30–3pm for lunch, 6:30–10pm for dinner. AE, DC, MC, V. Bus: 18 or 32.

INEXPENSIVE

Nga Tim Cafe ★ CANTONESE/MACANESE/PORTUGUESE This lively, open-air pavilion restaurant is a good place to rub elbows with the locals. It's situated on the tiny main square of Colôane Village, dominated by the charming Chapel of St. Francis Xavier. Its popularity with the locals lends it a festive atmosphere. The food, which combines Chinese and Macanese styles of cooking and ingredients, is in a category all its own, with many dishes not available elsewhere. Try the salt-and-pepper shrimp or baked chicken in a fresh coconut.

8 Rua Caetano, Colôane Village. ✆ **853/2888 2086.** Main courses MOP$48–MOP$128. MC, V. 11:30am–12:30am. Bus: 15, 21, 21A, 25, or 26A.

Wong Chi Kei Congee & Noodle CANTONESE Opening its first shop in mainland China in 1946, this inexpensive eatery on Senado Square has been a Macau mainstay for 40 years. It's a noisy, busy place, with several floors of dining for people pouring in to sample wonton in noodle soup, barbecue duck in noodle soup, fried noodle with shrimp, fried noodle with shredded chicken, and congee. It doesn't get any more local than this.

17 Largo do Seal Senado. ✆ **853/2833 1313.** Main dishes MOP$23–MOP$48. AE, DC, MC, V. 8am–11pm. Bus: 2, 3, 3A, 5, 10, 10A, 11, 18, 21A, 26A, or 33.

Seeing the Sights

Ruins of St. Paul's Church ★★ Macau's most famous structure crowns a hill in the center of the city and is approached by a grand sweep of stairs. However, only its ornate facade and some excavated sites remain. Designed by an Italian Jesuit, it was built in 1602 with the help of Japanese Christians who had fled persecution in Nagasaki. In 1835, the church caught fire during a typhoon and burned to the ground, leaving its now-famous facade, adorned with carvings and statues depicting Christianity in Asia—an intriguing mix of images that includes a Virgin Mary flanked by a peony (representing China) and a chrysanthemum (representing Japan). Beyond the facade is the excavated crypt, where glass-fronted cases hold the bones of 17th-century Christian martyrs from Japan and Vietnam. Here, too, is the tomb of Father Allesandro Valignano, founder of the Church of St. Paul and instrumental in establishing Christianity in Japan. Next to the crypt is the underground Museum of Sacred Art, with religious works of art produced in Macau from the 17th to 20th centuries, including 17th-century oil paintings by exiled Japanese Christian artists, crucifixes of filigree silver, and wooden saints.

Rua de São Paulo. ✆ **853/2835 8444.** Free admission. Grounds 24 hr.; museum daily 9am–6pm. Bus: 2, 3, 3A, 5, 10, 10A, 11, 18, 21A, 26A, or 33 to Senado Sq. (off Av. Almeida Ribeiro) and then a 10-min. walk.

Macau Museum ★★★ A must-see, this very ambitious project beside St. Paul's Church in the bowels of ancient Monte Fortress provides an excellent overview of Macau's history, local traditions, and arts and crafts. Chronological displays start with the beginnings of Macau and the arrival of Portuguese traders and Jesuit missionaries. Particularly interesting is the room comparing Chinese and European civilizations at the time of their encounter in the 16th century, including descriptions of their different writing systems, philosophies, and religions. Other displays deal with the daily life and traditions of old Macau, such as festivals, wedding ceremonies, and industries ranging from fishing to fireworks factories. Displays include paintings and photographs of Macau through the centuries, traditional games and toys, an explanation of Macanese cuisine and architecture, and a re-created Macau street.

Citadel of São Paulo do Monte (St. Paul Monte Fortress). ✆ **853/2835 7911.** www.macaumuseum.gov.mo. Admission MOP$15 adults, MOP$8 seniors, students and children. Tues–Sun 10am–6pm. Located next to St. Paul's Church.

Temple of A-Ma ★★ Macau's oldest temple is situated at the bottom of Barra Hill at the entrance to the Inner Harbour, across from the Maritime Museum. With parts of it more than 600 years old, it's dedicated to A-Ma, goddess of seafarers. The temple was already here when the Portuguese arrived, and they named their city A-Ma-Gao (Bay of A-Ma) after it. The temple contains images of A-Ma and stone carvings of the boat that carried her to Macau, as well as several shrines set on a rocky hillside linked by winding paths through moon gates and affording good views of the Inner Harbour.

Rua de S. Tiago da Barra. Free admission. 6:30am–6pm. Bus: 1, 1A, 2, 5, 6, 7, 9, 10, 10A, 11, 18, 21, 21A, 28B, or 34.

Mandarin's House ★★★ This restored mansion, part of the World Heritage Site's Historic Centre of Macau (p. 593), is a must-see for anyone interested in history or architecture. Constructed around 1860 by the Zheng family, it's a magnificent home, occupying a 4,000 sq. m (43,055 sq. ft.) compound of more than 60 rooms and a series of courtyards. Although it retains the essential characteristics of a traditional Guangdong residence, including an Earth God shrine at the entrance, "moon gates," and plaster ornamentation, it incorporates architectural details from other cultures as well, such as arched doorways and French windows. Not only is a private residence of this scale rare in Macau, but it also remains Macau's largest mansion.

10 Travessa Antonio da Silva. ✆ **853/2896 8820.** www.wh.mo/mandarinhouse. Free admission. Fri–Tues 10am–6pm. Bus: 18 or 28B.

Macau After Dark

Most of Macau's large hotels have casinos offering a wide range of games, including blackjack, baccarat, roulette, boule, "big and small," fan-tan, and slot machines (known, appropriately enough, as "hungry tigers"), designed mostly for the Asian market. If you're interested in seeing the largest casino in the world, head to the casino at **Venetian Macao-Resort-Hotel** on Cotai (✆ **853/2882 8888;** www.venetianmacao.com), a 50,725-sq.-m (546,000-sq.-ft.) space with more than 3,400 slot machines and 800 table games. Nearby in the **City of Dreams** is another casino with 378 tables and more than 1,000 machines (✆ **853/8868 6688;** www.cityofdreamsmacau.com). More centrally located is the **MGM Grand Macau,** Avenida Dr. Sun Yat-sen (✆ **853/8802 8888;** www.mgmgrandmacau.com), with 386 table games and 1,000 slot machines. Nearby, the **Wynn Macau,** Rua Cidade de Sintra (✆ **853/2888 9966;** www.wynnmacau.com), attracts crowds not only to its casinos but also to Performance Lake with its choreographed dancing fountains. Here also is the **Grand Lisboa,** Avenida de Lisboa (✆ **853/2828 3838;** www.grandlisboa.com), the first to add Texas Hold 'em in its casino.

One of the few benefits to have arisen from reclaimed-land development on the Outer Harbour is the **Docks,** a string of sidewalk cafes and bars lining Avenida Dr. Sun Yat-sen near the Kun Iam Statue; they are busiest after 10pm.

Taipa & Colôane Islands

Closest to the mainland, **Taipa** has exploded with new construction in recent years, but it's still worth coming to see **Taipa Village,** a small, traditional community with

EAST meets WEST

The Historic Centre of Macau, a World Heritage Site, celebrates more than 400 years of cultural exchange between the East and the West. Encompassing most of the historic old town, it ensures the preservation of both traditional Chinese architecture and the oldest Western structures on Chinese soil, with forts, temples, churches, mansions, squares, a library, cemetery, and a garden among 25 protected sites. Three of the most famous attractions—A-Ma Temple, the ruins of St. Paul's, and Mandarin's House—are described here, but for a complete list of protected structures and a map, stop by the Macau Government Tourist Office for its *Macau World Heritage* pamphlet. Among my favorites: the Moorish Barracks, Mandarin's House, Leal Senado Building, Senado Square, Lou Kau Mansion, the Protestant Cemetery, and Guia Fortress.

At the other end of the spectrum is another "town," **Fisherman's Wharf** (**© 853/2829 9330;** www.fishermanswharf.com), just a few minutes' walk from the main ferry terminal. With replica Tang dynasty, North American, European, and South African architecture, it contains upscale shops, restaurants, and regularly scheduled street performances and other events, making for an interesting stroll.

narrow lanes; two-story colonial buildings painted in yellows, blues, and greens; and hanging baskets of flowers. There are a number of fine, inexpensive restaurants here, making dining reason enough to come. For sightseeing, don't miss the **Taipa Houses-Museum,** on Avenida da Praia (**© 853/2882 7088**), where five colonial-style houses once belonging to Macanese families in the early 1900s line the banyan-shaded street. Combining both European and Chinese designs and furnishings as a reflection of the families' Eurasian heritage, one of the houses displays a dining and living room, kitchen, and upstairs bedrooms filled with period furniture. A couple of the other former homes contain displays relating to the history of Taipa and traditional regional costumes of Portugal. Hours are Tuesday through Sunday from 10am to 6pm, and admission is MOP$5. Bus nos. 11, 15, 22, 28A, or 33 all go to Taipa Village.

Farther away and connected to Taipa via a huge strip of reclaimed land called Cotai, **Colôane** is less developed than Taipa and is known for its **beaches,** particularly Cheoc Van and Hac Sa, both with lifeguards. To reach them, take bus no. 21A or 26A. Farther along the coast is the laid-back community of **Colôane Village,** with its sweet **Chapel of St. Francis Xavier,** built in 1928. **Cotai** is home to a growing number of hotel, shopping, and casino complexes, including the **Venetian Macao-Resort-Hotel** (**© 853/2882 8888;** www.venetianmacao.com) and **City of Dreams** (**© 853/8868 6688;** www.cityofdreamsmacau.com).

12 THE SOUTHWEST: MOUNTAINS & MINORITIES

by Christopher D. Winnan

"The most interesting part of China, from a geographical and ethnological point of view, is the West—geographically, because its recesses have not yet been thoroughly explored, and ethnologically, because a great part of it is peopled by races which are non-Chinese." In describing the attraction of southwest China for a few iconoclastic foreigners in 1889, British consul Alexander Hosie may as well have been describing the region's appeal today for hundreds of thousands of travelers, both foreign and Chinese. Considerably more explored than in Hosie's day but still retaining large swaths of undiscovered territory, today's splendid southwest is beginning to attract its deserved share of attention and is fast becoming one of China's major tourist destinations.

For starters, this region, encompassing the provinces of **Yunnan** and **Guangxi,** is home to some of China's most spectacular mountain scenery. As the Himalayan mountain range in northwest Yunnan gives way to the Yunnan-Guizhou plateau to the southeast, the scenery changes from the awesome 5,000m-high (16,400-ft.) glacier peaks of the **Jade Dragon Snow Mountain range** to the lower, but no less beautiful, famed limestone hills of eastern Guangxi. Three of Asia's mighty rivers—the Salween, the Mekong, and the Yangzi—cut parallel paths all within 150km (90 miles) of each other in the northwest mountains before they flow their separate ways, creating in their passage some of the most breathtaking gorges and lush river valleys in the country.

Even more appealing is the fact that this region is easily the most ethnically diverse in China. Twenty-six of China's 56 ethnic groups can be found in the southwest, which claims about 45 million of China's 100-million-strong minority population. If geography is destiny, then this inhospitable mountainous terrain, to which many ethnic minorities were historically displaced by earlier expanding Chinese empires, has not only

The Southwest Region

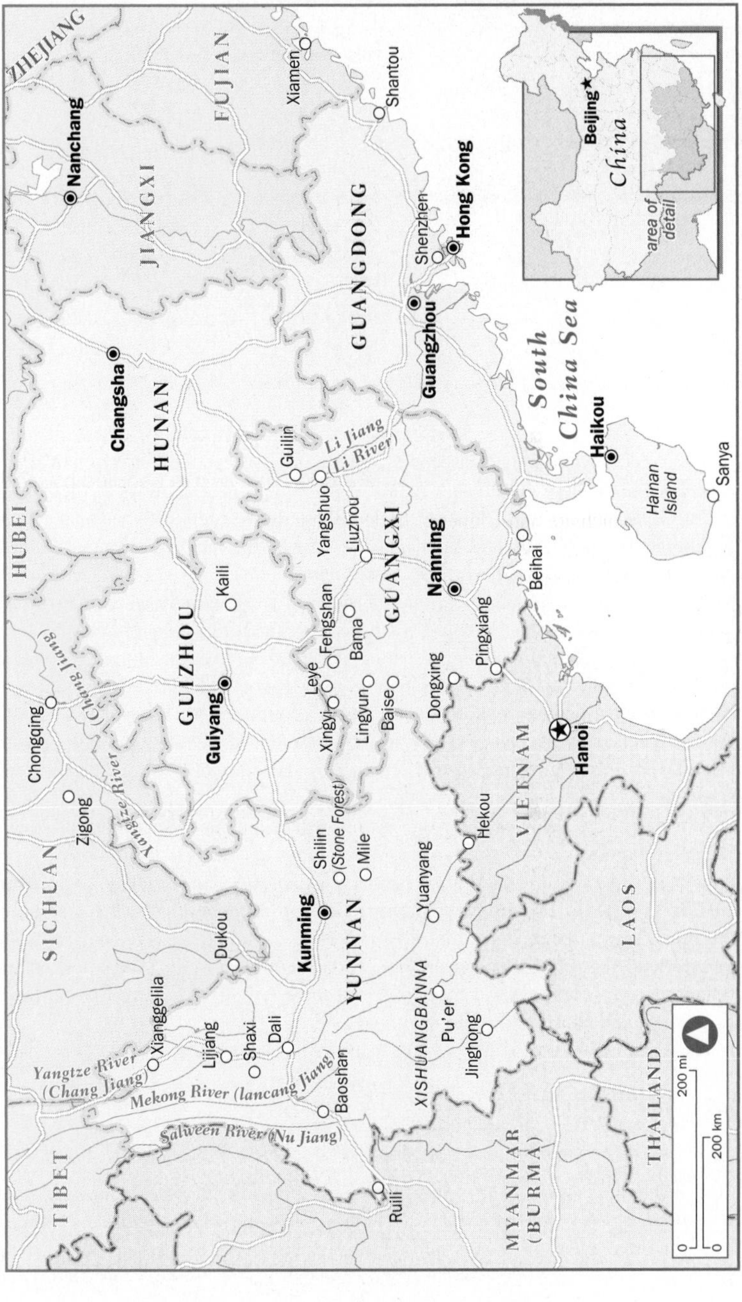

Select Festivals in the Southwest

FESTIVAL	LOCATION	LUNAR CALENDAR	2012	2013
Fireworks Festival (Dong)	Guilin	(Feb 5 fixed in Western calendar)		
Bangbang Festival	Lijiang	15th of 1st	Feb 6	Feb 24
Sanduo (Naxi)	Lijiang	8th of 2nd	Feb 29	Mar 19
Water Splashing (Dai)	Xishuangbanna	(Apr 13–15 fixed in Western calendar)		
Sanyuesan	Dong areas	3rd of 3rd	Mar 24	Apr 12
Sanyue Jie (Bai)	Dali	15th of 3rd	Apr 5	Apr 24
Raosanling (Bai)	Dali	23rd–25th of 4th	June 12-13	June 1-3
Dragon Boat (Miao)	Shidong	25th of 5th	July 13	July 2
Huoba Jie (Bai)	Dali	24th of 6th	Aug 11	Jul 31
Zhuan Shan Jie	Lugu Hu	25th of 7th	Sept 10	Aug 31

***Dates are based on information provided by local tourism sources. However, there are many date fluctuations, especially with festivals like the Miao New Year. Check with the local CITS or other local sources before setting off.*

helped create a vibrant kaleidoscope of peoples, languages, and cultures, but it has helped some of these cultures maintain their unique traditional ways in the face of encroaching modernization. At the same time, shared borders with Sichuan, Tibet, Myanmar (Burma), Laos, and Vietnam have allowed the region to absorb and integrate the colorful and diverse influences of its neighbors.

Historically, this area has undertones of the Wild West, with the minorities replacing the American Indians. Although the massacres and genocide have been going on for hundreds of years, French missionary Father Paul Perry summed up the situation coldly and bluntly in 1871. "The Chinese government is determined to obliterate these aboriginal peoples by a systematic policy of repression." The policy seems to have succeeded, as the indigenous populations are indeed now the minorities, driven relentlessly into these remote mountains by never-ending waves of Chinese colonists.

A traveler can easily spend years in this region and not exhaust its offerings. Between the obvious draws of **Guilin,** which ranks as one of China's top five most popular destinations, the backpacker mecca of **Yangshuo,** and the increasingly popular trifecta of **Dali, Lijiang,** and **Shangri La,** is a legion of other delights awaiting discovery. Travel is a lot less arduous than it used to be and there is no long any need to experience hardship in or to have journey of discovery, unveiling some new names that are touting themselves as destinations of tomorrow such as **Lingyun** and **Leye** in Guangxi and **Shaxi** and **Mile** in Yunnan.

Note: Unless otherwise noted, hours listed for attractions and restaurants are daily.

GUILIN 桂林

Guangxi Province, 500km (310 miles) NW of Hong Kong, 1,675km (1,039 miles) SW of Beijing

One of the most-visited Chinese cities, Guilin is probably the oldest tourist destination in China. Formed more than 200 million years ago when the oceans receded from this area, limestone towers sprout from a patchwork of paddy fields and flowing streams, creating a dreamy, seductive landscape that leaves few souls unstirred. Time

0 1/2 mi
0 0.5 km
HOTELS
Guilin Cairns Hotel 5
(Kai En Si Shang Wu Jiu Dian)
桂林凯恩斯商务酒店
Home Inn 6
(Ru Jia Kuai Jie Jiu Dian)
如家快捷酒店
Royal Garden 1
Sheraton Guilin 3
(Guìlín Dàyǔ Dàfàndiàn)
桂林大宇大饭店
RESTAURANTS
Anyway (Ai Ni Wei) 2
Milton's Place 7
(Li She)
丽舍
Rosemary Café 4
(Mi Dié Xiāng)
迷迭香
Bus Station
Bank
Information
Post Office
Rail Station
Public-Security Visas
Travel Agent
Lúdí Yán
(Reed Flute Cave)
芦笛岩
Taohua (Peach Blossom) River
Shengli Lu
Guìlín North Station
Ludi Lu
Zhongshan Beilu
Beijing
China
GUANGXI
Guìlín
Diécaì Shān
(Folding Brocade Hill)
叠彩山
FULONG ISLE
Fúbō Shān
(Wave-Subduing Hill)
伏波山
Dúxiù Fēng
(Solitary Beauty Peak)
独秀峰
Xinyi Lu
Yiwu Lu
Binjiang Lu
Lijun Lu
Zhèngyáng Pedestrian Street
(Zhèngyáng Bùxíng Jiē)
正阳步行街
Jiefang Lu
Qixia Lu
Liuhe Lu
Rong Hu (Banyan Lake)
Ronghu Nan Lu
Zhongshan Lu
Shanhu Bei Lu
Chuanshan Lu
Qixing Gōngyuán
(Seven Star Park)
七星公园
Cedar Lake
(Shan Hu)
ZIZHOU ISLE
Longyin Lu
Camel Hill
Dong'an Lu
Nanhuan Lu
Xiàngbí Shān
(Elephant Trunk Hill)
象鼻山
Qixing Lu
To Airport
Guìlín Railway Station
Minzhu Lu
Cuizhu Lu
Shanghai Lu
LUOBO ISLE
River
Zhongshan Nan Lu
Xiadong
CHUAN SHAN PARK
Li River
Chongxin Lu
WUJIAREN ISLE

and space meet here to produce a masterpiece of nature's handiwork. The scenery here is so alien that the makers of *Star Wars* decided to film the scenes of Chewbacca's home world Kashyyyk among the karst columns. The Li River cruise from Guilin to Yangshuo remains one of the top river journeys in the world. Unfortunately, the cost of Guilin's overwhelming popularity is a degree of unrelenting exploitation and extortion, audacious even by Chinese standards; foreigners especially are overcharged for everything.

With summer's heat and humidity and winter's low rainfall affecting water levels in the Li River, April, May, September, and October are the best months for cruising. April to August also marks the rainy season, however, so be prepared with rain gear, especially as these past few years have seen summer time flash floods in the area. July can become unbearably hot, and this is the last place on earth that you want to be holed up in your hotel room, clinging to the air conditioner. If possible, avoid national holidays, when the Li River becomes even more congested with tourist boats than usual, and the price of everything doubles at the very least.

Essentials

GETTING THERE From Guilin's airport 28km (17 miles) west of town (located on Nixon Rd. in honor of the U.S. president who visited in 1971), **flights** connect to most of the major cities within China. There are also international flights to Seoul (4 hr.), Bangkok (2 hr.) Kuala Lumpur (3 hr.), Fukuoka (5 hr.), and Hong Kong (1½ hr.). Tickets can be purchased at the CAAC office in **Minhang Dasha** on Shanghai Lu (**© 0773/384-3922**), and also at travel agencies or hotel tour desks. Airport shuttles depart from here every half-hour from 6:30am to 10pm for ¥25 and takes about 40 minutes. Minhang Dasha is only two stops away from the train station and can as easily be walked as being taken the long way round by a taxi. Taxis to the airport cost around ¥80 to ¥120. Many expats simply skip Guilin altogether in preference for a weekend in Yangshuo as the taxi fare is only ¥200 direct from the airport.

Train travel to and from Guilin is very convenient. The city has two railway stations, though the main one used by most travelers is the **Guilin Huochezhan** (**© 0773/383-3124**) in the southern part of town. Trains leave for Beijing (15 hr.), Guangzhou (13 hr.), Shanghai (10 hr.), and Kunming (18 hr.). The route from Guilin to Guangzhou is a flagship journey for overseas tourists and so the staff are handpicked and the carriages are spotless. If you want to try the comforts of a Chinese train, then this is one of the best routes to choose. There is even a "special soft sleeper" class, consisting of just two bunks with their own private bathroom for ¥700. The T5 from Beijing to **Hanoi** stops in Guilin every Monday and Friday and it is best to have a travel agent or your hotel tour desk arrange tickets because they are sometimes difficult to come by. Trains for Baise, in the eastern part of Guangxi, depart every evening just before 5pm. This is not a busy route and tickets can nearly always be purchased right up until departure, giving important access to the towns of Leye, Fengshan, Bama, and Lingyun.

Relax While You Wait

Nearly all bus and train stations have a public water heater, so if you have some packets of coffee or tea on hand, you can enjoy a relaxing cuppa while sitting in the waiting room.

The **Guilin Bus Station** (**Guilin Qichezhan; ✆ 0773/382-2153**), just north of the railway station, is in an appalling condition. One would have expected the road transport hub of China's most popular tourist city to be an architectural and logistical showpiece. In reality, it is dirty and run down, with overcrowded waiting rooms full of tin spittoons, looking out on a snarled-up bus yard. From here large, air-conditioned direct *(zhida)* **buses** go to a vast selection of destinations but are popular only with backpackers and economic migrants on the most extreme budgets. Regular minibuses run to Yangshuo (1 hr.; ¥19) from the bus station and are slightly more comfortable than those outside the railway station. Buses run almost hourly to Liuzhou. (3 hr.; ¥58) There are also long distance buses to Bama once a day at 8.40am but at 8 hours, it is probably better to go via Baise on the train.

GETTING AROUND Guilin is a compact area and is easy to get around by foot or bicycle. **Bikes** can be rented at many hotels, for anywhere from ¥10 to ¥50 per day plus a deposit.

Taxis cost ¥7 for 2km (1¼ miles), then ¥1.60 per kilometer for 2 to 4km (1¼ miles–2½ miles), and then ¥2 beyond. From 11pm onward, this increases to ¥7.80, 2 to 4km (1¼ miles–2½ miles) ¥1.80 per kilometer, exceeding 4km (1¼ miles) ¥2.40 per kilometer. Guilin is unusual that most of its bus stop signs are dual language, which makes it much easier for the international traveler to get around on public transport.

Guilin City 4A scenic area free tourist buses: When tourists travel on 4A scenic spots, as long as they buy the ticket from the appointed ticket sales office, then tourists can travel by the tourist buses for free provided by tourism development company. The tourist buses depart from Seven Stars Park (Qixingyuan) every 15 minutes and stop at each attraction for 3 minutes.

TOURS **CITS** at Binjiang Lu 41 (**✆ 0773/286-1623;** fax 0773/282-7424) has full-day city tours with English-speaking guides for ¥400 per person. The CITS Panda Bus picks up daily from the Fubo, Sheraton, Bravo, and Royal Garden hotels. CITS can also organize Li River cruises for ¥450; day trips to Yangshuo by bus for ¥280 per person; and overnight trips to the massively overrated Longsheng Rice Terraces for ¥550 per person. The small travel agency below Flower's Guest House is used to dealing with the needs of Western travelers and offers some of the best prices in town for arranged trips.

VISITOR INFORMATION For information on hotels and sights, there are at least 10 offices of the **Guilin Tourism Information Service** centers around town, including the train station, with the best English language service at (**✆ 0773**).

[FastFACTS] GUILIN

Banks, Foreign Exchange & ATMs **Bank of China** (Mon–Fri 8am–noon and 3–6pm) is at Shanhu Bei Lu 5. It offers forex and an ATM.

Internet Access Visit the third floor of **Lequn Shouji Cheng** at Zhongshan Zhong Lu 49, corner of Lequn Lu. Internet access is 24 hours, at ¥2 per hour. Dial-up is **✆ 96163.**

Post Office The main post office (8am–8pm) is at Zhongshan Zhong Lu 249.

Visa Extensions The **Gonganju (PSB; ✆ 0773/582-9930;** Mon–Thurs 8:30am–noon and 3–6pm, Fri 8:30–11:30am) is on the east side of the Li River. Take a bus up to Chuan Shan Bridge and then walk left along Longyin Lu for 500m. Extensions take 5 working days.

Exploring Guilin

In the center of town are two of Guilin's main lakes left over from the moat that ringed the city in the Tang dynasty. To the western side of Zhongshan Lu is **Rong Hu (Banyan Lake),** named after an 800-year-old banyan tree on its shore. On the eastern side is **Shan Hu (Cedar Lake),** with its twin pagodas. A **Liang Jiang Si Hu (Two Rivers and Four Lakes) boat tour** offers visitors a chance to tour these lakes together with Gui Hu (Osmanthus Lake), Mulong Hu (Wooden Dragon Lake), and parts of the Li Jiang and Taohua Jiang (Peach Blossom) rivers, all of which are now connected by newly dredged waterways. Day sailings for ¥100 last around 90 minutes, begin at 8am, while the much more impressive evening sailings for ¥149 continue until 10pm, depart from the Jiefang Qiao Matou (pier) on Binjiang Lu near Jiefang Qiao, and from the Zhiyin Tai Matou on the eastern side of Cedar Lake. Buy tickets at hotel tour desks and at Shizi Jie next to the Dashijie Bridge (© **0773/282-2666**).

If you would like to extend your time in China, then we recommend the **Chinese Language Institute,** International Education Center Office 206, 5 Yu Cai Road (© **1364/111-9382;** www.studycli.org), in Guilin as one of the best places in the country to work on your mandarin skills. Run by two American brothers, they offer excellent immersion programs and even offer housing in the local teaching university shared with graduate students, so that you get plenty of opportunities to practice your skills.

MOUNTAINS & CAVES

Duxiu Feng (Solitary Beauty Peak) ★ Tapering to a pavilion-capped peak, this 152m-high (498-ft.) limestone beauty in the middle of town is the most dramatic of Guilin's hills. There are 306 steep stairs winding to the top, where awaiting you is a spectacular panorama of Folding Brocade Hill to the north, Wave Subduing Hill to the east, and Seven Star Crag to the southeast. The hill is actually located on the grounds of the 14th-century former palace *(wangcheng)* of a Ming dynasty prince, occupied today by the Guangxi Normal University. A gallery sells works by local artists at exorbitant prices, but is worth dropping by just in case they are having a painting demonstration for a tour group.

Wangcheng 1. Admission ¥35. Apr–Oct 7am–7pm; Nov–Mar 7:30am–6:30pm. Bus: 1 (Lequn Lu stop); from Zhongshan Lu, take a right onto Xihua Lu for about 150m (490 ft.). The park entrance is on your left.

Nan Xi Gong Yuan (Nan Xi Park) This lesser-known park is just a kilometer away from the train station on the way out to Yangshuo. Nan Xi Hill, with its two adjacent peaks reaches almost 300m and the Longji Pavilion that is situated directly between them is a great lookout point for the southern part of the city. At 500m, the White Dragon Cave is the largest of four separate caverns here and is named after the stalactites that hang down like giant teeth. The White Dragon Bridge is a scaled down reproduction of the famous Zhaojia Bridge that was originally built in the Sui Dynasty. The five airy pavilions that make up its area span a total of 30m. Take a walk down past the side of the now closed Oceanarium and you will find a back entrance to the park with no ticket office. Watch out for locals with slingshots and catapults that hunt birds in the park.

Zhongshan Nan Lu. Admission ¥6 or ¥27 including the cave 6:30am–6:30pm (cave 7am–4pm). Bus: 12 or 99.

Shopping

With generally overinflated prices, Guilin is no place for bargains. Snacks and candies that make nice gifts include *guihua su* (a crisp, sweet osmanthus cracker) and *guihua wangcha* (osmanthus flower tea). **Zhengyang Pedestrian Street** has a plethora of shops and stalls selling everything from teapots and jade to clothing and minority handicrafts and embroidery. The **Guilin Weixiao Tang Shangsha (Guilin Niko Niko Do Co, Ltd.)** at Zhongshan Zhong Lu 187, open from 9am to 10pm, is the largest **department store** in town.

Guilin Wholesale Carving Market ★★ For an afternoon of amazement away from the other tourists, have a stroll among the craftsman up at the Guilin Commercial Carving Market, out past Wa Yao wholesale area. Start off at the large viewing stone gallery (Da Cang Jia) on the corner of Wayao Lu and the South 2nd Ring Road. On a short walk south along Wayao, you'll see life-sized elephants, even larger kirin and tigers that are at least 10m in length, all carved from single logs. Pay a visit to Mr. Tian Yi Tang (22 Qifeng Lu; ✆ **1373/770-5229**), whose small showroom displays a number of smaller but no less impressive pieces. At the rear are dozens of stone warehouses, and while some seem to be little more than stockpiles, others such as the Hua Nan Jing Ti Guan (Wa Yao Lao Dian Chang; ✆ **0773/355-7080**) make the geological collections of major world museums seem inadequate and unimpressive.

Ping Shan Da Cun. Bus: 4 (30 min. from downtown).

Guilin's Darker Days

Although the basement-level CD store of the Xinhua Bookstore on Zhongshan Bei Lu is not particularly well stocked, it does offer an insight into Guilin's past. Check out the heavy steel bomb doors at the entrance, remnants from a paranoid time when every building had such an installation for fear of Soviet attack.

Where to Stay

Most tour groups stay at the **Sheraton,** 15 Binjiang Rd. (✆ **0773/282-5588**), which is still poor value if you are a walk-in guest. Smart travelers know that the **Royal Garden,** 186-1 Linjiang Rd. (✆ **0773/568-8888;** www.glroyalgarden.com), on the opposite side of the river, is much quieter and only half the price. The newly opened **Shangri La,** 111 Huancheng N. Second Rd. (✆ **0773/269 8888**), is a very ugly building and located well out of town. Neither of these big chains can match the atmosphere and secluded location of the HOMA Chateau.

EXPENSIVE

HOMA Chateau (Guilin Xia Duo Jiu Dian) ★★★ If money is not a problem, then a stay at HOMA Chateau is an experience that you won't forget. Located within a huge international sculpture park, the main accommodation is itself a piece of abstract art, and each of the luxury rooms is absolutely unique in its style and decor. Rooms come with their own butler service (each speaking surprisingly good English), and there are workshops for budding artists as well as galleries to peruse and a particularly outstanding world-class spa.

Yuzi Paradise, Dabu Town. www.guilinhoma.com. ✆ **0773/386-9027.** Fax **0773/386-9033.** 64 units. ¥1,200 standard room; ¥2,800 suite. AE, DC, MC, V. Amenities: 3 Restaurants, spa, gift shop, art workshops, cave dining area, gallery. In room: A/C, TV, Internet.

MODERATE

Guilin Cairns Hotel (Kai En Si Shang Wu Jiu Dian) If you are looking for a slightly more luxurious option than the Home Inn, Cairns is located just around the corner from the station and quite close to the airport shuttle drop off. This is a new hotel, built into a floor of an existing apartment building but done so with slightly more opulence than the budget business hotels.

26 Shanghai Rd. ✆ **0773/211-7888.** Fax 0773/211-7888. 64 units. ¥280 standard room; ¥580 suite. Chinese credit cards accepted. Amenities: Restaurant; karaoke. In room: A/C, TV, Internet.

Home Inn (Ru Jia Kuai Jie Jiu Dian) Located directly opposite the train station, this is one of the most convenient hotels in town. Staff are friendly and speak English, while rooms are clean and cheerful, as they are throughout this popular nationwide chain.

64 Shang Zhi Xiang, Zhongshan Nan Lu. www.homeinns.com. ✆ **0773/387-7666.** Fax 0773/387-7555. 64 units. ¥140 standard room; ¥280 suite. Chinese credit cards accepted. Amenities: Restaurant; karaoke. In room: A/C, TV, Internet.

Where to Eat

Guilin's most famous local dish is *Guilin mifen* (Guilin rice noodles), served at practically every street-corner eatery. Order it dry or in broth, with chicken, beef, even the local favorite, horse meat *(marou)*, or plain, then add chives, chili, and pickled sour green beans. Other local favorites, including snake, dog, seafood, and a variety of wild animals sometimes too exotic for foreign tastes, are available in many local restaurants, which usually don't have English menus.

Anyway (Ai Ni Wei) CHINESE FAST FOOD This is a small, unassuming, lunchtime pit stop near the Jiefang Bridge. It has a reasonable selection of Taiwan-style dishes, including a very tasty rice with marinated pork (¥8) and a good choice of soups including a tasty oak mushroom and meat cake soup (¥4) and best of all a clear English menu. The interior is decorated with some interesting, very early photos of what Guilin used to be like in the 1930s.

Jiefang Xi Lu (look for the large soup pot outside). ✆ **0773/281-9985.** Meal for 2 ¥40. No credit cards. 11am–midnight.

Midiexiang (Rosemary Cafe) ★ WESTERN While the usual traveler's fare such as banana pancakes is ubiquitous in Yangshuo, this is one of the few places in Guilin to have a reliable Western menu. Conveniently located near the Sheraton and just off the pedestrian walking street, Rosemary's is a hit with the overseas tourists that stumble across it. The only downside is that that there are only half a dozen tables and it soon fills up with European package tourists enjoying extended breakfasts or sipping ice-cold watermelon juice to escape the summer heat outside.

Yiren Lu 1–1. ✆ **0773/281-0063.** Meal for 2 ¥120. No credit cards. 11am–midnight.

Milton's Place (Li She Coffee) TEA/COFFEE This spot is slightly away from the tourist track and popular with overseas students studying Chinese in Guilin, Milton (the Taiwanese boss) has a nice selection of bread and muffins as well as doing good pizza and pasta dishes. Despite being located on the first floor of a rather anonymous apartment building, Milton has gone to town on the decor with a lounge area that is all French baroque furniture from a modern Chinese perspective. There are richly upholstered banquettes and tables for group seating on the upper level.

Seven Star Gardens. ✆ **0773/267-7992.** Meal for 2 ¥80. No credit cards. 10am–1am.

Spring of Countryside (Du Shi Tian Yuan) TEA/COFFEE The riverside location here is excellent, with a modest selection of set lunches and sandwiches at reasonable prices, including the obligatory Guilin noodles, a variety of fried rice, and even a passable BLT. This is a great place to kick back when you need a break from Guilin's touts and ticket offices. The park in which this place is set is wonderful for strolling. Musicians use the resonance under the bridges, health fanatics jog and play badminton, and couples linger on benches among the trees.

Guihu, Xi Qing Qiao, Xi An. ✆ **0773/285-8188.** Meal for 2 ¥80. No credit cards. 10am–1am.

Guilin After Dark

Acrobatic performances (Meng Huan Xi You) are held nightly at the **Li Jiang Theater (Li Jiang Juyuan),** 38 Binjiang Lu. Performances cost ¥180 and run from 8 to 9:15pm. The **Meng Huan Li Jiang (Meng Huang Ju Chang)** at 95 Qixing Lu charges ¥150 to ¥180 for tickets to its combination ballet acrobatics show that also starts at 8pm. The **Songs of Liu San Jie** showcase local Zhuang minority music and dancing (**Ge Xian Liu San Jie;** Yi Shu Guan, 15 Jiefang Lu), with costs between ¥100 and ¥180. It lasts for 2 hours starting at 8pm, but is only fractionally better than the other two. Tickets for all three shows can be booked on the tourist hot line ✆ **12301** or from hotel concierges and receptions.

A Popular Boat Trip: Li Jiang (Li River; 漓江)

A boat cruise from Guilin to Yangshuo along the 432km (270-mile) Li River is usually sold as the highlight of a Guilin visit, and indeed, the 83km (52-mile) stretch between the two towns affords some of the country's most breathtaking scenery as the river snakes gracefully through tall karst mountains, gigantic bamboo sprays, and picturesque villages—sights that have inspired countless poets and painters for generations. Foreigners, segregated onto "foreigner boats," pay ¥460 to ¥480. Though it may be less comfortable, some travel agencies can arrange tickets priced at around ¥340. If time and convenience are your priorities, then take the cruise by all means. Otherwise, if you plan to spend some time in Yangshuo, consider bypassing the cruise; more beautiful karst scenery can be better toured on foot, by bike, or by boat from Yangshuo.

Currently, river trips for foreigners depart from Zhu Jiang Matou (Zhu Jiang Pier) 24km (15 miles) and a half-hour bus ride south of Guilin at around 8:30am, where you will join 10,000 other tourists, all departing at the same time. The river often turns into an aquatic highway, complete with belching diesel fumes, and blaring horns for 5½ hours straight. On quieter days, the first 1½ hours of the cruise to the town of Yangdi is serene with imaginative names of hills along the way, such as a Woman Yearning for Her Husband's Return, the Eight Immortals, even a Calligraphy Brush. Visual highlights are clustered between **Yangdi** and the picturesque town of **Xingping. Jiuma Hua Shan (Nine Horses Fresco Hill)** is a steep cliff face with shadings and markings said to resemble a fresco of nine horses. A little farther on, **Huangbu Daoying,** a series of karst peaks and their reflections, is the tableau burnished on the back of a Chinese ¥20 note.

Boats arrive in Yangshuo in the early afternoon after 4 or 5 hours of sailing. There's a stop for shopping, after which tour buses transport passengers back to Guilin (1 hr.). Tickets for the cruise can be bought at hotel tour desks or at CITS, and include round-trip transportation to Zhu Jiang Pier, an English-speaking guide, and a Chinese lunch.

Note: See chapter 16 for Chinese translations of key locations listed above.

YANGSHUO 阳朔 ★★

Guangxi Province, 65km (40 miles) S of Guilin

Located at the terminus of the Li River cruise from Guilin, the small town of Yangshuo has long been a mecca for backpackers, but even before that, it was a geomancer's delight, too. Set amid an awesome cluster of limestone pinnacles—a zigzag, serrated skyline superior even to that of Manhattan—Yangshuo is more beautiful, less expensive, and significantly less crowded than Guilin. Some of the most accessible karst scenery in Guangxi can be found just a short bike ride outside town. With its inexpensive hostels and Western-style cafes, some foreigners have been known to stay for months, sometimes even years. Once a sleepy little town, today's Yangshuo is being overtaken by rabbit hutch hotels, endless shops, and hordes of eager tourists. It remains to be seen how long this sleepy little town can retain its charm, so go now.

Essentials

GETTING THERE The nearest **rail** and **air** connections are in Guilin, but tickets can be purchased here from most travel agencies. From the bus station on Pantao Lu, **buses** depart for Guilin (70 min. travel time) but leave at least 2 hr. before your train departs to allow for traffic in Guilin; ¥15 every 10 to 15 minutes from 7:30am to 8pm.

Tip: Ignore the touts that yell out "Guilin" as you approach the station. Instead go into the station and buy a ticket for the official bus, which has much more leg room and is non-stop. Direct sleeper buses with very poor reputations for safety run to Guangzhou and Shenzhen.

Taxis from Guilin (your hotel in Guilin can arrange this) will make the trip in an hour at a cost of around ¥250 to ¥300. If heading straight to Yangshuo, call ahead and your hotel can arrange a taxi for between ¥160 and ¥200.

Getting out of Yangshuo is less convenient. Although there is a fast new road to the airport, there are no direct bus services, so that local taxis can maintain their monopoly on this route. It's certainly not good from an environmental perspective; we hope that this situation will change soon.

GETTING AROUND From the bus station on Pantao Lu, **buses** depart for Xingping (1 hr.; ¥6.50 every 15 min. 6am–7:30pm); for Fuli (20 min.; ¥10 every 15 min. 6am–7:30pm); and for Gaotian (30 min.; ¥10 every 15 min. 6:30am–7pm). Yangshuo's main thoroughfare is the cobblestone pedestrian street **Xi Jie (West St.)**. It runs from Pantao Lu to the Li River boat docks and is where the bulk of travelers' cafes, shops, and basic guest houses are clustered. The town itself is small enough to be traversed by foot in less than an hour. **Bikes** are the best means of getting to outlying sights and are available for rent for ¥10 per day at many Xi Jie cafes and hotels. **Motorcycle taxis,** will offer to take tourists out to Moon Mountain and nearby caves for ¥40, but be sure to agree on all the desired destinations and cost beforehand. Many places now offer electric bikes and motorbikes for rent.

Note: While West Street remains pretty much crime free, not all of the town is so lucky. Groups of pickpockets are familiar sights up around the gas station and some of the newer Chinese hotels, where they employ long thin tweezers to remove valuables while their accomplices distract the victim. Be vigilant.

TOURS & GUIDES Unfortunately in Yangshuo, as in other tourist spots, a tour guide is simply someone who takes you to the most common sights where he can get

Yangshuo 阳朔

HOTELS ■

Jia Yun Hotel (Jiā Yùn Jiǔdiàn) **2**
嘉韵酒店

Magnolia Hotel **3**
(Baí Yù Lǎn Dàjiǔdiàn)
白玉兰酒店

New West Street Hotel
(Xīn Xī Jiē Dàjiǔdiàn) **8**
新西街大酒店

ATTRACTIONS ●

Bīlián Fēng (Green Lotus Peak) **6**
碧莲峰

Yángshuò Park **9**
(Yángshuò Gōngyuán)
阳朔公园

RESTAURANTS ◆

Café China **5**
原始人餐厅

Karst Cafe **4**

Pure Lotus Vegetarian Restaurant **3**
(Àn Xiāng Shū Yíng Sū Caì Guǎn)
暗香疏影蔬菜馆

Rock & Grill **1**

Ryleys Cafe **7**
(N Chong Men Kafei Ba)
N重门咖啡吧

¥ Bank

⊟ Bus Station

ⓘ Information

⊠ Post Office

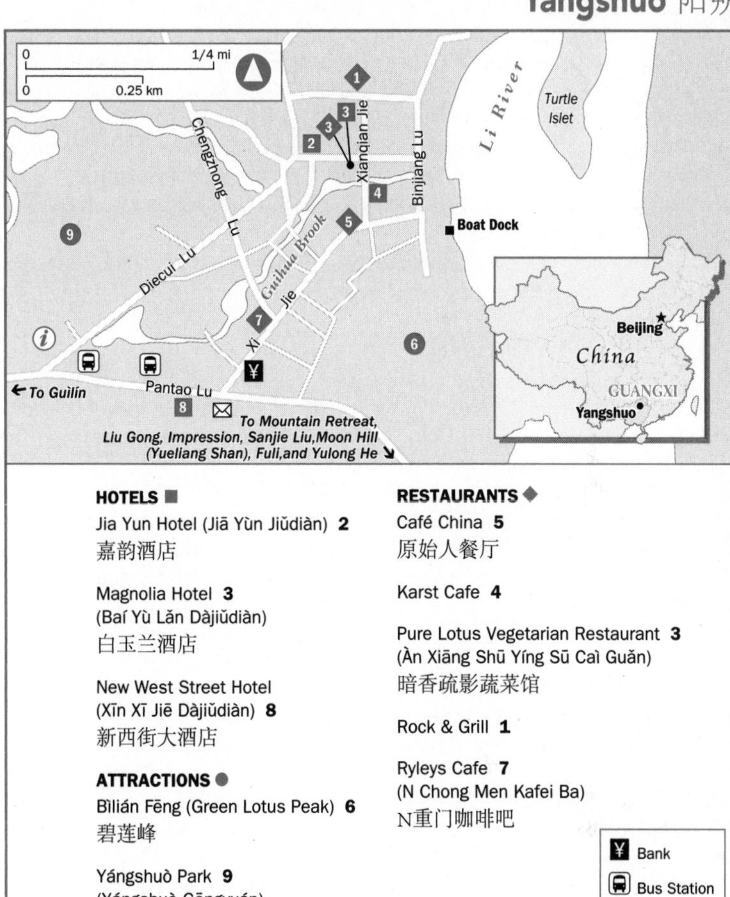

the biggest commissions. Better to save your money and buy a good map, or, rather than take a tour with a stranger you meet on the street, ask your hotel to organize something for you. Be aware that all specialist agents in Yangshuo are now charging a booking fee of ¥50 for train and plane tickets, so plan ahead and arrange to get these yourself.

VISITOR INFORMATION The friendly **Yangshuo Luyou Zixun Fuwu Zhongxin (Yangshuo Tourism Information Service Center)** just south of the bus station on Pantao Lu (② **0773/882-7922**) can answer basic questions on accommodations, local sights, and tours.

[FastFACTS] YANGSHUO

Banks, Foreign Exchange & ATMs The **Bank of China** is located at the beginning of West Street near the KFC. Forex hours are Monday to Friday from 9am to 5pm and this is just one of many 24-hour ATMs in town.

Internet Access Internet access is available at most cafes, and Wi-Fi users should be able to find a few unsecured nodes just about wherever they are in the town.

Post Office The post office (9am–9:30pm) is at Pantao Lu 28 and usually has at least one English speaking staff member.

Visa Extensions The unhelpful Inspector Bing at the Yangshuo PSB office on Chengbei Lu 39 tells foreigners to go to Guilin to renew their visas.

Exploring Yangshuo

The majority of Yangshuo's treasures are located a bike ride out of town. **Xi Jie (West St.),** with its souvenir shops and travelers' cafes, has become a bona fide tourist attraction for Chinese visitors, who completely take over the street starting in the early afternoon when boats from Guilin pull in.

In the southeastern part of town along the western banks of the Li River, the **Shanshui Yuan Park** (¥21; 8:30am–6pm) is home to the impressive karst mountain **Bilian Feng (Green Lotus Peak),** which towers over the town and the harbor. In the western part of town next to the bus station, **Yangshuo Gongyuan** (**Yangshuo Park;** Diecui Lu 22) is now free to all, and can be a good place to escape the heat. You can hike to the top of Xilang Shan for some arresting views of the countryside.

Outdoor Activities

With so many karst hills and caves around the area, Yangshuo has become a little mecca for **rock climbing,** with some 70 climbing circuits. Sun and Jack at **Terratribes** currently organize the best trips (✆ **0773/882-2005;** sun@terratribes.com), at ¥280 for a half day's climbing and ¥500 per person, for a full day. Sun is very well traveled in China, and can organize adventure sports trips well beyond Yangshuo. During the summer months, **Richard Chen** (✆ **1350/783-9490;** richardtour@yahoo.com) organizes some of the best **rafting** and **kayaking** trips on the Li River and on smaller rivers like the Yulong He (Jade Dragon River). Other trips include the wonderfully scenic stretch between Fuli and Puyi (¥200) or even an all-inclusive (that means riverside campfire barbecues and sleeping in tents) 2-day trip from Yangshuo to the islands around Liugong and then on to Pingle (¥500). Those preferring something more sedate can take courses on tai chi, Chinese cooking, Chinese calligraphy, Chinese medicine, or Mandarin at various outfits in town, including the excellent **cooking courses** at Cloud Nine Restaurant at the corner of Chenzhong Road and West Street (✆ **0773/881-3686**).

Shopping

While much of the souvenir junk in Yangshuo can be found at much better prices elsewhere, the two chopsticks stores in town, **Jiu Mu Tang Kuai Zi Fang,** Xi Jie 63 (✆ **0773/886-3000**), and **Quan Yi Kuai Zi Fang,** Xin Xi Jie (✆ **0773/298-1771**), do deserve serious attention. Both shops have a fair selection of travel sticks that are a great investment for the environmentally conscious traveler who does not want to be responsible for deforestation through the daily use of disposable chopsticks. A selection of models is available from ¥10 to ¥100; they also make beautiful gifts for other ecologically minded friends, either at home or on the road.

Where to Stay

Xi Jie, once a backpacker's dream with its cheap hostels and guest houses, has grown steadily but improved little over the last 5 years. While there are always new places opening, often they close quite quickly. We suggest avoiding the larger hotels along Pantao Lu and finding something more on a human scale, just on the outskirts of the town, or better yet, well outside. Some seriously offensive price gouging occurs during holidays and peak periods (summer), when rooms can cost up to four times the usual price.

Magnolia Hotel (Bai Yu Lan Jiu Dian) ★★★ This is one of the newest and definitely the best choice of accommodations in Yangshuo town at the moment. Formerly a run-down student dormitory, the Magnolia has been transformed into a great-value boutique hotel by an Australian entrepreneur with an eye for detail and a knack for getting the best out of local staff. Four floors are built around a bright, spacious atrium, with rooms that are equally bright and outfitted with super-comfortable king-size beds. This is the favorite among organized tour groups. Look out for the owner's great taste in quirky Chinese antiques that are scattered about the place. This is especially true in the impressive new imperial suites.

Diecui Lu 7. www.yangshuomagnolia.com. ✆ **0773/881-9288.** Fax 0773/881-9218. 30 units. ¥260 standard room. Imperial suites¥580. AE, DC, MC, V. In room: A/C, TV, hair dryer.

Mountain Retreat (Yangshuo Shengdi) ★★★ Built by a successful American businessman, this is one of China's true gems and has one of the best locations in the entire province. Rooms are a good size with massive picture windows and balconies to take advantage of views that are both amazing and inspiring. The retreat itself has a Confucian academy feel to it and is especially popular with western visitors and families. Located a good half-hour outside the town by bike but just 10 minutes by taxi, it remains my number-one choice for the ultimate Yangshuo experience.

Wang Gong Shan Jiao in Gaotian, Yangshuo. www.yangshuomountainretreat.com. ✆ **0773/877-7091**. Fax 0773/877-709. 29 units. ¥350 Hill View Twin Room, ¥550 River View Deluxe Twin/King Room (with balcony). MC, V. Amenities: Restaurant; coffee shop; boutique; bike rental; Wi-Fi. In room: A/C.

Where to Eat

Yangshuo abounds with great cafe food, if you choose the right places. The **Karst Cafe ★★**, Xianqian Jie 42 (✆ **0773/882-8482**), hangs onto the title of best pizza in town, with a bacon, egg, and blue cheese creation. At the corner of West Street and Xianqian Jie, **Cafe China's** (✆ **0773/882-7744**) rooftop is one of the best locations in town, with excellent mountain views. Local specialties such as delicious *pijiu yu* (fish cooked in beer and spices) and *baochao tianluo* (Li River snails stuffed with pork) are extremely reliable here, but it might be wise to book a table in advance as this is the number-one choice for Western tour groups. **Rock and Grill,** Xian Qian Jie 2 (✆ **0773/881-9178;** www.yangshuoholiday.net), outside the municipal government building, has an interesting menu of dishes that are a definite step up from the usual cafe fare. Their chef shows a lot of creativity, and their outdoor terrace is a great place to while away the evenings. **Pure Lotus Vegetarian Restaurant**

(An Xiang Su Ying Su Cai Guan), Diecui Lu 7 (✆ **0773/881-9079;** www.yangshuo magnolia.com/purelotus.htm), has a relaxing ambiance. We recommend the almond roll *(shi su xing ren quan),* the taro and egg yolk balls *(li yu dan huang wan),* and the sweet-and-sour eggplant *(tang chu qie gua).* **Ryley's Cafe** (96 West St.; ✆ **0773/888-5368**) has had many previous incarnations on West Street but is still popular for its shepherd's pie and apple crumble. Better than both of these is the latest addition to the menu, beef and taro pie.

Around Yangshuo

See chapter 16 for Chinese translations of key locations.

RIVER TRIPS

There are plenty of opportunities to take shorter and significantly less expensive river trips from the Yangshuo area—check with the travel agencies and backpackers' cafes on Xi Jie for your options. The Li River patrol authorities have a stranglehold on all river traffic, and there are strict laws about the kinds of boats foreigners can ride on (boat licenses can cost up to a million yuan), so stick with the legitimate outfits rather than with the random touts who approach you, no matter how friendly they are.

One of the more popular trips is downriver to the umbrella and fan town of **Fuli** (see below). Another trip is to the town of **Xingping,** about 3 hours upstream from Yangshuo. Official boats make the run in summer for about ¥100 to ¥200 per person. Rather than sail upstream, some tourists prefer to cycle or take a bus to Xingping and catch a boat downstream back to Yangshuo. Some tour operators come up with creative combinations of hiking/river-trip tours, which involve traveling to Xingping by bus or bike, then hiking along the river for part of the way before hopping onto a boat for the rest of the journey.

MOON MOUNTAIN (YUELIANG SHAN; 月亮山)

Named after the crescent shaped opening that cuts straight through this peak, this impressive Karst mountain has 800 steps leading up to the viewing area. The natural arch has more than a dozen of incredibly challenging climbing routes, and watching the acrobatics of these daredevils is almost as impressive as the mountain itself. A bike trip out along the main highway with endless trucks involves riding 8km (5 miles) out to **Moon Mountain (Yueliang Shan)** in the direction of Gaotian. Follow Pantao Lu in the opposite direction from Guilin until the traffic circle, and bear right onto Kangzhan Lu. Once you leave town, you'll be greeted around each bend with unbelievably scenic vistas of karst pinnacles stretching as far as your eyes can see.

Along the road to Moon Mountain are several recently built attractions geared strictly toward Chinese tour groups that can be safely missed. About 6km (4 miles) from Yangshuo, the **Gurong Gongyuan** (¥18; 6am–sunset) has an intriguing 17m-tall (56-ft.), more-than-1,500-year-old banyan tree that looks like a collection of entwined snakes up close and like a giant umbrella from afar. It's easily as old as any American redwood. The whole area is now a bit of a circus, so it is better to view the tree just as easily from atop **Moon Hill,** 1km (⅔ mile) away (¥15; 7am–6pm), so named because of the large moon-shaped arch under its peak. A series of steep steps winds through thick bamboo brush all the way to the top, where there are some marvelous views.

If there's an adventurous spelunker in you waiting to break free, there are several interesting caves around here worth exploring. However, some of these are suitable only for the fit, as none have paved paths and all will require you to get down-and-dirty by crawling through holes and climbing rickety ladders. **Buddha Cave,** where entry now costs a whopping ¥168 (summer 8am–6pm, winter 9am–5pm), and the **Water Cave (Shuiyan)** both have underground pools and rivers on which you can paddle and get that mud bath you've always wanted.

A more civilized alternative is 90 minutes (25km) south at the magnificent **Silver Cave (Yinzi Yan;** www.yinziyan.net ¥68) situated in spectacular parkland about 20km (13 miles) south of Yangshuo. Spectacular underground chambers stretch for more than 2km through 12 separate mountains. Any local agency will arrange tickets and transportation for around ¥120 per person.

Where to Stay

Village Inn Once the busloads of domestic tourists depart, Moon Hill Village becomes a tranquil place at night. The Village Inn has eight individually designed rooms, all with antique furniture, and many with balconies overlooking the pomelo orchard. In addition, the Farmhouse annex at the rear is a restored mud brick building with full mod cons and a genuine Chinese feel. Best of all is the underfloor heating that ensures these are the toastiest rooms in Yangshuo's brutal winter season. The staff are all trained at Mountain Retreat and so service is impeccable. There are plenty of inspiring eco-friendly touches, including Mountain Air brand ceiling fans. In addition there is a very respectable Italian restaurant, Luna, on the top floor.

Yueliang Cun. www.yangshuoguesthouse.com. © **0773/877-8169**. 14 units. ¥390 Farmhouse rooms, ¥400 moonhill view rooms. MC, V. Amenities: Restaurant, bar, Internet. In room: A/C, fan.

XINGPING 兴坪

Surrounded by a jungle of karst pinnacles, the village of Xingping is about 25km (15 miles) upstream of Yangshuo. Regular buses run to Xingping from the Yangshuo bus station, or you can ride your bike here in 3 to 4 hours.

Xingping itself is rather charmless, but it's a good base for an interesting side trip to **Yucun** (literally "Fishing Village"), a tiny, picturesque Ming dynasty village (1506–21) 20 minutes downstream along the Li Rive. Famous visitors to the village have included Sun Yat-sen in 1921 and Bill Clinton in 1998. Full of traditional Ming and Qing dynasty houses with white walls and gray-tiled roofs with upturned eaves, as well as the occasional ancestral hall, the village requires a ¥5 entrance fee. River trips up to Jiuma Hua Shan (Nine Horses Fresco Hill) on the other hand, should be avoided at all costs—it's ¥80 for a deafening 30-minute ride on a look-alike bamboo raft actually made out of sewer pipes, up to a dirty beach with grabby vendors.

DA HE BEI ISLAND 大河背岛

Just across the water from Xingping, but far enough away from the deafening tour boats and tacky new town, this island in the Li River is quiet and relatively undisturbed. It is an especially good choice for lunch, but could also be a useful base to explore, this being some of the most spectacular karst in the area. There are a couple of ¥1 (¥.5 for locals!) ferries that cross the 100m or so of water every few minutes. From there, stroll up the path that cuts through the middle of the island. About half a kilometer inland on the right hand side is the **Greenland Inn,** Lu Zhou Xiao Yuan (© **0773/870-3482**), a great spot for lunch, either up on the balcony out of the midday sun, or down on the lawn if it is a little bit cooler. If the peace and calm of the island tempt you to stay a little longer, then check out **Sui Mo Ju** (© **0773/870-2969;** www.suimoju.com) just next door, which has rooms with awesome views up on the top floors for only ¥100 per night.

YULONG HE (JADE DRAGON RIVER) ★★★

One of the loveliest trips outside Yangshuo, this river is even more beautiful than the River Li. The river's more famous landmarks may be its bridges, in particular the 59m-long (194-ft.) Ming dynasty **Yulong Qiao (Jade Dragon Bridge)** found near the town of **Baisha,** but it's the scenery of small villages nestled at the foot of karst hills surrounded by rice paddies, and a lazy winding river that most visitors remember long after they've left. Many of the travelers' cafes offer full-day tours of the river and surrounding sights, but it's entirely possible to visit on your own. Just pack a picnic, plenty of film or a spare memory card, and rain gear; check your bike's tire pressure; and you're off.

There are several routes by which to explore the river. From Yangshuo, head out toward Moon Hill. Before the bridge crossing the Yulong He, head right, which will eventually take you all the way up to Baisha and the Jade Dragon Bridge. You can return along these back paths, or head back from Baisha on the main Guilin-Yangshuo highway. Or reverse the order and take the highway to Baisha (9km/6 miles of noisy main road from Yangshuo), then cycle back down through the villages. Chances are you'll get lost on some of these paths, which can narrow to the width of your bicycle (so get off and walk carefully or you may end up face first in a rice paddy!), but that's half the fun. Not to worry, the villagers around here are more than happy to set you right, and there are enough paths between the river and the highway that you won't be lost for long.

The full journey to Yulong Qiao may be a bit much for some, especially in the summer when heat stroke and sunburn are serious threats. A less exhausting alternative is to stop off at Mountain Retreat for some lunch and then explore the bridges and side roads from there.

TWO SECRET SPOTS ★★★

While much of Yangshuo is now overcrowded year-round, here are three of my own secret locations, where you can get away from the endless busloads of tourists.

Rent a bike and head out of Yangshuo on the Guilin road until you come to the end of the residential development and the last large electric pylon on the left-hand side. Follow the path down through the village and out past the two disused quarries on either side of the track as you ride farther into the countryside. Just after the large fish farm on the left, cross the stone bridge and follow the path that goes along the left-hand bank of the stream, until you come to another even smaller stone bridge that recrosses the water. On the far side, haul your bikes up over the small stone wall that surrounds the copse on the left, lock them up around a tree, and continue from here on foot. Look for a natural stone staircase that rises up from the woods. It is only a 10-minute climb, but pay attention to the steps themselves as some of them are fragments of an old temple that was torn down here by Red Guards during the Cultural Revolution.

As you emerge into the first of a series of hidden valleys, you will probably hear the bleating of goats. The pint-size Mr. Jiang keeps a herd of around 200 goats up here that sleep in a barn about three times the size of his own shack, which he shares with a couple of scaredy-cat dogs. To the right of the valley are some beautiful stone outcroppings, but if you continue to the left and then skirt around to the right of a sunken forest, it will lead you down through an area of pomelo trees and sinkholes. Continue up the hill until you reach a clump of pine trees that form a natural canopy from which a variety of local birds sing. To the right, the bold can venture into a depression of mold-covered thorn trees, the ideal location for a Japanese slasher movie, but up to the left is a charming boulder-strewn paddock, surrounded on all sides by wonderfully symmetrical karsts. Although the grass is cropped tight like a super-exclusive fairway, this natural pasture has a very urgent sense of growth with nature pushing out in all directions. After a while, despite the beauty, I like to head back to the shade of pine trees for lunch.

Once you are back down with your bicycles, recross the stone bridge and continue along the bank path to the Yangshuo-to-Baisha back road. Take a right onto the tarmac and ride until the road takes a sharp right with a fork off to the left. Follow the fork through two villages and past the Giggling Tree Farm Guest House on the left. By now you should be able to see that you are on the bank of the Yulong River somewhere away to the right. It takes another 15 or 20 minutes to Mountain Retreat (p. 607) where you can stop for a rest and a cold drink, and then continue down the hill and around the bend. The road forks off to the right and fords the river. The recklessly brave can pedal across at any time of year but the more timid might want to remove their shoes and wheel their bikes across. Zigzag quickly through the village on the other side, and then once you are past the large karst on the left, take a sharp right into the grounds of the secondary school. Exit at the left and follow the path, watching out for the cobbles, all the way through the village until you reach the water's edge. This is the **Jin Bao River,** and the weir at the edge of **Feng Huang (Phoenix) Village** is my favorite swimming spot in the area. While 20 bamboo rafts a minute now squeeze down the Yulong River, you'll be lucky if you see more than half a dozen all afternoon here. There are a few sharp stones at the bottom of the weir but after that, the water drops to about 3m (9 ft.) and is ideal for cooling off. Directly below the falls, the current is strong enough that it'll feel like you have your own personal swimming trainer. Best of all, the view upstream is fantastic and apart from a few local farmers and their water buffalo crossing the weir, you'll probably remain undisturbed all afternoon.

Yangshuo After Dark

Every night 2,000 spectators are herded into the purpose-built riverside amphitheater for acclaimed director Zhang Yimou's waterborne spectacular, **"Impression, Sanjie Liu."** The show itself is on such a grand scale, with over 200 bamboo rafts in the water at once and a total production crew of 600, that it can hardly fail to impress. With such a spectacular backdrop as the Li River and the mix of floodlights, singing, and processions, the effect is magical. Tickets start at ¥180 and can be arranged through most hotels. The show starts at 8pm but it's best to get there a half-hour early, leaving time to wander Liu San Jie Park. Bring binoculars or rent them for ¥5; insect repellent is also a good idea. At the bottom of West Street in Yangshuo is an endless succession of boat owners who will take you to an alternative viewing point on the river for ¥30 to ¥60. For more info, visit **www.yxlsj.com**.

While many of the bars on Xianqian Jie seem to be full of Chinese youngsters looking for a bit of holiday romance or "yan yu" in Chinese, an interesting alternative might be the weekly Tuesday trivia team quiz night that is held at **Bar 98** (42, Guihua Lu) along with a delicious Australian style barbecue. **The Alley** (102/103 Guihua Lu; **✆ 1366/786-6922;** www.yangshuo-beer-bar.com) has imported German and Belgian beers, as well as a pool table and foosball. Start off with one of their excellent cocktails, before settling down to a steak or their special beef burger with chips with one free beer for just ¥25. It's a popular haunt with all the local English teachers.

LIUZHOU 柳州

Guangxi Province, 170km (105 miles) SW of Guilin, 732km (454 miles) NW of Guangzhou

While Guilin has always been one of China's most popular tourist destinations, Liuzhou is famous for strikingly different reasons. Historically it has always been well known thanks to the saying, "Born in Suzhou, married in Hangzhou, eat in Guangzhou, and die in Liuzhou," although the quality of its camphor wood coffins is hardly inspiration to visit the place. The clear Liujiang River, like an enormous belt, encircles the downtown area. A panoramic view from atop Yufeng Peak on the southern bank of Liujiang River reveals that the entire city is a gigantic circle, with the mountains, river, and urban architecture forming an enormous three-dimensional painting. It was originally Longcheng (Dragon City) in 742 A.D., but changed into Liuzhou in 1736. In the modern era, Liuzhou has grown into the most important center of heavy industry in all of China, and it is home to many of the biggest brands that you will see on your travels. Liugong excavators, Dongfeng trucks, and GM Wuling Microbuses are all made in Liuzhou. Most people therefore have very low expectations of Liuzhou, but the majority are pleasantly surprised to find a midsize city that retains a strong Cantonese Lingnan authenticity.

Essentials

GETTING THERE Clean express buses from Guilin run every 15 minutes and take between 2 and 2½ hours to reach Liuzhou. These are some of the few coaches around that still have polite uniformed attendants and complimentary drinking water. Expressways link Liuzhou with Nanning to the south. Additionally there are highways linking to Guangzhou and to the port of Beihai in the far south of Guangxi. The **Liuzhou Bus Station** (**Liuzhou Zhongzhan**), just 10 minutes away from the train station is old but well organized. Buses run both by day and by night (sleeper bus). Coaches to Guangzhou and Shenzhen are faster than the train, but infinitely less comfortable.

Train travel to and from Liuzhou is also very convenient. Liuzhou has one of the largest train stations in Southwest China with good connections all over the country. Take note that the soft sleeper waiting room is a good hundred meters to the right of the main station building. There is a railway ticket office (more of a kiosk actually) outside Liuzhou Public Library on San Zhong Road.

Liuzhou has its own airport (Liuzhou Bailian Fe Ji Chang), which is 12km (7.5 miles) south of the city center. Flights are available to Beijing and Shanghai as well as Guangzhou, Chongqing and Chengdu. Airport buses leave for the city regularly and take just 15 minutes. For other cities in China or for Hong Kong and other countries in South East Asia, it is necessary to fly from Guilin or Kunming.

GETTING AROUND **Taxis** start at ¥3, with ¥1.40 added every kilometer, but there is also a ¥2 fuel price surcharge (irrespective of distance) that is not shown on the meter. Motorcycle taxis offer a cheaper alternative but they are technically illegal (the police turn a blind eye most of the time) and the accident rate is high.

Liuzhou has a useful double-decker bus service. Route 201 runs from E'shan Park to Bayi Road, passing the railway station, Yufeng Road, Gong Mao, Centurymart and the north side of the square. Scheduled to run every 6-8 minutes, the route operates between 6:45am and 9:30pm. The fare is the standard ¥1.

TOURS The Guilin branch of China International Travel Service (CITS) has opened an office in Liuzhou. It is at 97 Jiefang Nan Lu, and the phone number is ✆ **0772/287-0280.** There is an English speaker by the name of Stephen Lu, and you can reach him at ✆ **1397/803-4570.**

[Fast FACTS] LIUZHOU

Banks, Foreign Exchange & ATMs **Bank of China** (Mon–Fri 8am–noon and 3–6pm) is on Jiefang North Road. It offers forex and an ATM.

Post Office The Liuzhou Post Bureau is located at 36-8 Wuyi Rd. (✆ **0772/383-3158;** 8am–6pm).

Exploring Liuzhou

Liuzhou is blessed with a plethora of beautiful parks that are all free for visitors. In addition to the sights below, there's an interesting **City Museum** (Liuzhou Bo Wu Guan; 37 Jiefang Bei Lu; ✆ **0772/280-3317;** www.lzbwg.com) that has plenty of local ethnic minority displays, including some incredibly long-barreled hunting rifles. The **Panlong Shan Culture Park** (Panlongshan Wenhua Gong Yuan) is best viewed from the Wenhua Bridge in the evening, when its brightly lit waterfalls are very spectacular, even if the park itself is a bit of a disappointment. The imposing **East Gate Tower** on Shuguang East Road is one of the coolest places in the city during the summer heat.

PUBLIC PARKS

Fish Peak Park (Yu Feng Gongyuan) ★ Yufeng Shan (Fish Peak—allegedly it looks like a jumping fish), next door to Ma'an Shan (Horse Saddle Mountain), has an antique cable car up to the top charging just ¥50 for cable car return ticket (✆ **0772/203-0377**). Notice that while there are more than 50 cable cars, none of them end in the digit 4 as this sounds like death in Chinese and is considered to be very unlucky. The views from the top are spectacular and for ¥20, you can get a panoramic photo that captures the city. Be careful on the steps up here as many are very narrow and steep. Just outside is the Ho Chi Minh Museum, but with labels only in Chinese and Vietnamese it can be safely skipped. You might also want to pass on the Sanjie Rock Cave, with its amateurish figurines on the story of Liu Sanjie—the movie epitomized the love story of a Tang Dynasty songbird, Liu Sanjie and her lover, Ah Niu, which is extremely popular among the Chinese.

Yufeng Road. Free admission. 7am–10pm.

Jianpan Mountain Rare Stone Garden (Qi Shi Yuan) ★★ This is the biggest special viewing stone garden in China and probably the world. Over a thousand pieces are displayed in the Bagui Fantastic Stone Hall and the gardens are filled with very photogenic sculptures in a style known as Chinese historical minimalism. Visitors can also climb the 160m Jianpan Karst Peak for more great views of the city.

Ping Shan Da Dao. ✆ **0772/383-7685.** Free admission. 9am–6pm.

Liuhou Garden (Liuhou Yuan) ★★★ Located in the city center, and built in 1906 to commemorate the Tang Dynasty writer, thinker and statesman, Liu Zongyuan (A.D. 773–819) who was magistrate and later, governor of Liuzhou. He was most famous for working to free women from being bonded slaves. As well as zigzag walkways, quiet pavilions, and moon-shaped bridges, there is also a smaller Chinese private garden with a ¥30 entrance fee. Here among the 300 year old bonsai, the

Guangxi's Bounty

Guangxi Province is a center of fruit production. Throughout the year, you should be able to find cups of freshly squeezed sugar cane juice for just a few RMB. In late spring, the markets are awash with juicy loquats (pipa) and then equally delicious persimmons (shi zi) in the early fall.

bamboo walkways, and the misting waters, you can easily spend the whole day reading, writing, and contemplating. On the entrance facing the museum, there is a small lake where locals enjoy feeding thousands of hungry koi.

Wenhui Road. ✆ **0772/282-4260.** Free admission. 7:30am–9:30pm.

Longtan Park (Longtan Gong Yuan) ★ Located 3km (1.9 miles) south of the city center, this vast park combines karst landform, cultural immersion, and subtropical karst vegetation, including some beautiful acacia lined boulevards. All of the karst peaks including Mirror Hill and Sleeping Tiger Hill are climbable and have some fascinating caves and vantage points. Some of the manmade features are a bit tawdry, though the cave that doubles as a fun fair type house of horrors is good for a giggle.

Longtan Road. Free admission. 7:30am–9:30pm. Bus: 19 terminates at the park gates.

Shopping

Due to Liuzhou's hot and humid climate, most of the shopping malls are located underground. While it is great to get out of the heat, take care as these huge walkways are not featured on maps and it is easy to lose your bearings and emerge completely lost.

Liuzhou Fantastic Stone City (Qi Shi Cheng) ★ While most people have heard of bonsai, far less are familiar with viewing stones. These are natural stones prized for their shape, texture, color or markings, often used as display items and sometimes incorporated in bonsai gardens. They range in size from tiny to enormous and can be extremely valuable, especially in China, Korea, and Japan. Regarded as a world center for viewing stones, Liuzhou has held six International Stone Festivals and there are several fascinating stone markets in town, but this is the largest one. Our favorite gallery here is Gao Jian Shang Shi Hui Sho (✆ **1397/806-7895**), where some beautiful stones with Buddhist designs are tastefully displayed. It's best to keep your hands in your pockets here, as prices can be frightening.

232 Dong Huan Lu. Bus: 4 (30 min. from downtown).

Where to Stay

While there is a spanking new Radisson out in the new CBD to the East of the city, there are many more great value small hotels in the city center.

MODERATE

52 Hotel (Mei Xu Guan) Located right in the downtown at one end of the ladies shopping street, this boutique hotel with its designer rooms is a favorite with younger domestic tourists. Rooms are modern and fashionable and there are at least six different themes going on. The suites are particularly impressive, especially the one with human profile shaped alcoves. The red room features a circular bed and velvet couches, while the valentine room is completely done in shocking pink.

28 Yinshanjie. www.52hotel.me. ✆ **0772/301-0600.** 64 units. ¥180 standard room; ¥380 suite. Chinese credit cards accepted. Amenities: In room: A/C, TV, Internet.

99 Hotel (Ai Er Jiu Jiu Shang Wu Jiu Dian) This small hotel in a converted school building is located on the loveliest stretch of road in the whole city. Lined with huge trees, this is one of the coolest spots in a notoriously sweaty city. Rooms are mediocre but great value at this price. Best of all, this place has the fastest Internet that we experienced in all of China this year.

193 Sanzhong Rd. ✆ **0772/289-2299.** 34 units. ¥110 standard room; ¥280 suite. Chinese credit cards accepted. In room: A/C, TV, Internet.

Where to Eat

For Western visitors, food is where Liuzhou stumbles. There is a real dearth of good restaurants with English menus, but overall this is a minor quibble in a city that otherwise represents such great value. The best choice of bread and cakes is at the **Bakery Maison Cherry** (Mi Song Qi Li, 1, Jin Yu Xiang, off Jiefang South Rd., the curved side pedestrian street that shoots off just north of McDonald's; ✆ **0772/230-8995**) in the main center near the Xinhua Bookstore. There's not much fresh fruit juice around, but you can make do with the large ¥2 cups of mango, coconut, and orange juice that are available at the many branches of **Happybar** (Kai Xin Ba), a local KFC clone that is all over the city.

Bani Coffee (Ba Ning Ka Fei) CHINESE/WESTERN With its huge leather couches and wide selection of "exquisite teas," the 24 hour Bani Coffee is part of the 4-star Jingdu Hotel. It has an English menu, though it's a bit pricey. You may also want to check out the "eat and drink all you can" Peninsula Restaurant buffet on the first floor of the hotel proper, where food ranges from Asia to the west and back again.

Jindu Hotel, 40, Yue Jin Road. ✆ **0772/230-0220.** Meal for 2 ¥40. No credit cards. 11am–midnight.

Lucy Luo (Ming Ren Fan Xi Chang Jiu Ba) ★ CHINESE/WESTERN Almost opposite the Liuzhou Hotel, the exterior has plenty of English signage. The gaudy baroque interior, with waitresses clad in skimpy French maid uniforms, are less impressive, and there were no English menus. Even so, staff are helpful and the food was fairly decent.

72 Wan Tang Road. ✆ **0772/286-3223.** Meal for 2 ¥120. No credit cards. 10am–2am.

BAMA 巴马

Guangxi Province, 410km (317 miles) N of Nanning, 222km (138 miles) SW of Baise

Bama's claim to fame is that out of a population of just over 300,000, it has 73 centenarians, one of the highest ratios in the world. Scores more nonagenarians and octogenarians fill the surrounding villages. Many of these elderly residents attribute the secret of their longevity to the *huo ma you,* a soup made from the oily seeds of the cannabis plant, ironic in a country where this ancient medicinal plant is still vilified as an evil deserving execution. Still, many of these extremely senior citizens, some of them veterans of the Long March, take a dim view of tourists and dislike being stared at like zoo animals, which is why it's best to focus on the amazing scenery of this area. The Panyang River, for example, is a bright aquamarine waterway. Bama has now become a famous brand name for longevity in China and in the last few years, the town has expanded at the speed of light, almost quadrupling in size. For a feel of what the town used to be like, head over to Lingyun. See chapter 16 for Chinese translations of key locations.

Essentials

GETTING THERE The highway to the east is now complete but access to Guilin is still a long and convoluted process changing at Hechi and Liuzhou. A daily direct bus from Bama Bus Station (Bama Qiqezhan; ✆ **0778/242-8867**) to Guilin leaves at 9:20am and costs ¥60.

[FastFACTS] BAMA

Banks, Foreign Exchange & ATMs Stock up with Renminbi before you arrive in Bama as Bank of China does not yet have an office here at the Agricultural Bank, and the Rural Credit Cooperative only operates domestic ATM networks. There are no capabilities for exchanging foreign currency or traveler's checks.

Post Office There is a small post office (9am–6pm) on Shou Xiang Da Dao, the main street.

Visa Extensions The PSB office is at 127 Shou Xiang Da Dao (✆ **0778/621-2088**), but cannot handle visa extensions, and will refer you to the provincial capital.

Exploring Bama

The town has a small **Peoples' Park** on Gong Yuan Lu with a few pagodas dotting karst outcrops, but watch out as the caves have been taken over by beggar squatters. There are far better sights outside of town. The **Longevity Museum** (Bama Chang Shou Bo Wu Guan) is rarely open

Where to Stay

The amount of accommodation has exploded in Bama in the last 2 years but most are unlicensed, family-run guest houses operating in various side streets, with squat toilets and poor facilities. Better to get out of the town and stay in Poyue instead.

Where to Eat

This is currently one of Bama's main problems. Small noodle shops abound, but they are not always so hygienic. On the main square are two local burger copycats, **MKJ** and **Happy Burger.** There is also a small place just behind the Shou Xiang hotel that serves tasty steamed *baozi* on kindergarten-size chairs and tables.

Around Bama

POYUE 坡月 ★★★

It looks like the little village of Poyue might soon become one of the biggest tourist spots in China. Poyue is growing at light-speed and is quickly becoming a center for senior citizen tourists. According to the latest data, citizens over 60 years of age amount to 130 million, 10% of the population, and are increasing at a rate of 3% per year. The longevity reputation of the area combined with the restorative powers on the Pan River is rapidly transforming this one-water-buffalo town into a Chinese Lourdes. Visitors stay for 3 months rather than 3 days, and unlike many of the larger tourist towns, everything that is built is quickly occupied. The water, the air, and even the magnetism of this area are all believed to cure even the most chronic of conditions and so the town has become a mecca for old folks from Beijing looking for a less extreme climate and better natural conditions.

GETTING THERE Poyue is located about half way between Bama and Fengshan. Simply look for the signs for Baimo Dong and there you will find an ever-expanding concrete cluster that was until recently only a tiny village. A slow public bus runs all the way from Bama Bus Station to the entrance of Baimo Dong every 20 minutes for just ¥4.

GETTING AROUND The Internet cafe opposite Poyue School (at the Hou Liao Xian Jiang Tour Services; ✆ **0778/614-0235**) has a couple of **bicycles** to rent (¥25 per day), but walking is currently the preferred mode of transportation in Poyue. The streets are always lined with strolling 60 and 70 year olds, heading off for a swim, or going to collect some mineral water, or simply heading out for a morning constitutional.

BAIMO DONG 百魔洞 ★★★

Despite its malevolent name, the **Cave of One Hundred Demons** (✆ **0778/628-2250**) is what makes Poyue so popular, for it is here that the mineral-laden underground springs emerge into the atmosphere. The cave itself is an enormous beast, opening up like a gaping 200m (656-ft.) rift in the mountainside. An asphalt road leads from the village to the cave, where the entrance is now becoming the center of construction for the area, but beyond the inky blackness lay plenty more surprises. The upper chambers possess some uniquely extraterrestrial formations, while coincidentally the whole area is quickly getting a reputation for UFO sightings. The main area of Baimo Cave is a vast open *tiankeng* that joins three vast cave networks together, two of which are currently open to visitors. What few visitors realize is that the roof of the cave is also home to an isolated Yao village, the only access being through the subterranean river that connects the *tiankeng* to the outside world. The entrance fee is ¥60, and helmets are available but an extra flashlight is more useful, especially if you want to explore the upper chambers, which are currently closed to tour groups but a real lure for the adventurous. Surprisingly, the cave begins with a steep climb of 70m (230 ft.) rather than a sharp descent. Many of the formations are gigantic in proportion and completely alien to anything seen on the outer surface of this planet. Look out for small blind, white cave worms that wriggle around on slowly forming stalagmites. In places the ceiling reaches a height of some 200m (656 ft.), and the silence is as still as an isolation tank, the darkness as black as pitch. Only later, the middle section opens up into a vast *tiankeng* or doline, where the cave collapsed, leaving it open to the elements. The ticket office employees head home at 6pm, so early evening is a great time to bring your own flashlight and do some exploring. There are plenty of safe, solid paths through the darkness, so you can explore without getting into any dangerous situations. Swimmers congregate at the mouth of the cave and stories abound of how the waters have swept away leukemia, diabetes, and a host of other medical complaints. Perhaps beyond the miracle healings and alien sightings, the most amazing experiences in this very strange part of the world are the evening firefly symphonies. By 8pm in the month of June, the surrounding corn fields are lit up with vast oceans of breeding fireflies, creating a light spectacular that even Vegas would struggle to match.

AROUND POYUE ★★★

Heading north out of Poyue on the Fengshan Road, just next to the road construction company offices you will find a **1,000-year-old banyan tree** that is still worshiped as a god by shamanistic locals. Entwining its branches is the thickest, gnarliest grape vine that I have ever seen, easily the same age as the tree and maybe even older. Obviously it is not only the folks here that live to a ripe old age. From here that is a small path up the hillside behind the clumps of bamboo, leading to a back entrance to Baimo Cave and the **isolated Yao Village** of Qingnan. A half an hour climb will bring you to a spectacular top entrance looking down onto the *tiankeng* and you can take an elevated goat track into the village area. The folks here are poorer than most you will meet on your journey so bring biscuits or candies to share around. Feel free to visit Miss Zhang in the makeshift schoolroom, then trek back down the main path into the cave to see what it feels like to live in such splendid isolation every single day.

BAINIAO YAN 百鸟岩 ★★★

Bainiao cave (© **0778/622-1515**) is about halfway between Bama and Poyue. The bus will drop you off just below a small, antique hydro station where you cross the bridge and follow the track on the right-hand side of the river. Boat tours for this spectacular cavern begin at a specially constructed wharf, and are still a very reasonable ¥80 for a 1-hour trip (you may be told that at least four customers are necessary before they can depart—simply play dumb and you can soon get past this minor obstacle rather than sitting around waiting).

The cave itself is one of the most spectacular you'll ever see. There are no psychedelic lights, and a flat-bottomed pontoon with a single oarsman keeps the noise to a minimum. Even the approach is inspiring—a gaping cleft in the rock face. Just inside the mouth are colonies of bats and swallows, but their chirps and squeaks soon fade into the distance, leaving only the rhythmic sound of the oar against its rubber grommets. There are places where the rocks can be seen plunging away into the 20m (66-ft.) inky depths, although this drops as far as 50m (164 ft.) in some parts. Best of all, there are no ripples to disturb the wonderful silence.

Back out on the main drag, head up the hill through the village, until you see a small turn that leads down into a tunnel. The recently constructed main road heads up around the mountains, but walking down through the tunnel leads to a number of wonderful surprises. The first is a scree slope that falls away down to the Panyang River. Follow the road down the side of the ravine and then backtrack along the water buffalo path, which will take you to the point where the rapids plunge into the water cave that you just visited half an hour before.

Back out in the valley is a stone-and-iron suspension bridge that is a perfect gateway for hard-core trekkers wanting to get into the real wealth of this area. Continue alongside the beautiful turquoise waters through a small cluster of houses each with a good selection of Bama ancient residents, and after an hour or so you will reach the main road, where you can flag a bus back to Bama or on to Poyue for Baimo Dong.

Where to Stay & Eat

Just off the main drag, you can find **Longevity Villas** (Yan Nian Shan Zhuang; © **0778/614-0311**), now a pair of rather ugly six-story Chinese houses but with friendly owners and half decent rooms for ¥120, including three fantastic farmer's-style meals per day, served in the communal dining area where it is easy to make friends with some of the resident oldsters. Walk up the road toward Baimo Dong until you reach the big hemp bushes next to the stairs leading up. Hemp in the form of seeds and oil is one of the area's secrets to healthy living and astounding longevity. This is one of the busier places in town so always call first to ensure that there are rooms available. Even so, they are more for long termers, coming with kitchenettes but no towels. Shorter term tourists might prefer the double rooms over at the **Shan Sui Jia Lian Suo Jiu Dian** (✆ **0778/614-0119**), which are more along the lines of a regular hotel, with private bathrooms and lovely views out onto the river. A handful of mom and pop eateries have already sprung up outside the village. Our favorite is the small unnamed place at the back of the market next to the police station, manned by a Shandong aunty with a wide beaming smile. Ayi cooks up a great selection of farmer's-style dinners, focusing especially on vegetables that we Westerners recognize such as onions, potatoes, and carrots.

FENGSHAN 凤山

Guangxi Province, 390km (242 miles) N of Nanning, 1,008km (626 miles) NW of Guangzhou, 216km (134 miles) NE of Baise, 80km (50 miles) N of Bama

The construction boom that swept through the rest of China has only just reached this previously remote part of Guangxi in the last couple of years, but the town is quickly making up for lost time. The population of 20,000 is mostly Zhuang (53%), with the remainder being a scattering of Na Dian Yao, Gao Shan Han (the long established Han Chinese), and the more recent coastal Han Chinese colonists. Keen to improve its reputation as a tourist hot spot, Fengshan hosts a number of interesting annual events. These include the Caving Festival and the Twins Festival in November and December, the Sanyuesan–Zhuang Festival on the 3rd day of the 3rd month in the lunar calendar, and the ghost festival on the 14th day of the 7th lunar month. See chapter 16 for Chinese translations of key locations.

Essentials

GETTING THERE **Baise Tianyang Airport** is located 1½ hours away and currently has only two flights per day, one to Guangzhou and one to Guilin. The airport is 38km (24 miles) from Baise and a ¥15 shuttle bus runs from Baise Qichezhongzhan about 1 hour before each flight. The nearest **train** stations are Baise to the west, Hechi to the east, and Nanning to the south. The **Fengshan Bus Station** (**Fengshan Qichezhan;** ✆ **0778/681-9033**) now has three major routes in and out of Fengshan (up until 2006, there were only rutted roads and mountain tracks for goat herders). To the east, visitors can connect with the mainline railway at Jinchenjiang (previously called Hechi; 4 hr.; ¥55) 8 times per day. The switchbacks just outside of Fengshan as you climb into the karst peaks make this route worthwhile in itself. To the south, the town has direct buses to and from Nanning (7 hr.; ¥120) at 6:10am, 7:50am, 9:20am, 10:40am, 2:10pm, and 3:40pm that also serve Bama, although this road is still regularly prone to landslides. The road west to and from Leye is probably best avoided (6 hr. 30 min.; ¥50) with departures at 7:10am and 12:30pm at the moment. Untopped, it becomes a quagmire in late spring and you may find yourself, as we did, disembarking along with the rest of the passengers, to assist in clearing rockfalls. Until 2013 when the new road is scheduled to be completed, allow a good 6½ hours for this tortuous journey. To reach the airport and train station at Baise, a far better option are express buses that go through Lingyun take 4 hours, cost ¥55, and depart four or five times a day. The most important local route is the minibus to Sanmenhai, which leaves every 30 minutes and costs ¥5.

GETTING AROUND Motorcycle rickshaws *(dian san lun)* are slightly more expensive here than in Leye at ¥3 per trip, although most of the major sights are too far out of town, so local buses and travel agencies are better options. **Taxis** are a relative rarity, but red Xialis do exist and charge ¥4 for most locations in town. More common are the silver micro vans that serve as China's jeepney service. Always agree on a price first and be prepared for criminal overcrowding.

TOURS **FZL Travel Agency (Feng Zhi Lu Lu Xing She)** at 88 Yang Guan Da Dao (✆ **0778/678-8799;** hxf1209@yahoo.cn) and **Qing Nian Travel Agency (Qing Nian Lu Xing She)** at 1st Floor, Fengshan Guest house, opposite the bus station (✆ **0778/681-2222**), are able to arrange trips with English-speaking guides for ¥100 per person. Rather than mess about with local buses and their irregular, unreliable schedules, it is better to let these guys arrange trips to the out of town sights such as Sanmenhai for around ¥50 per person or the Yao Village for ¥150 to ¥260 depending on the quality of lunch.

VISITOR INFORMATION The Chinese language **Tourism Information Hot Line** is at (✆ **0778/681-5399**).

[FastFACTS] FENGSHAN

Banks, Foreign Exchange & ATMs There is no **Bank of China** in Fengshan, only an Agricultural Bank and a Rural Credit Union, neither of which have international ATMs, only those designed for the domestic Unionpay system. Stock up with RMB at larger towns such as Nanning, Baise, and Hechi.

Internet Access Most hotels now have Internet access in their rooms, though in this area it seems to be popular to offer *dian nao fan* (rooms equipped with PCs) for slightly higher prices. Try asking for a standard room and a *wang xien* to avoid any extra costs if you have your laptop with you.

Post Office The main post office (8am–8pm) is on Fengyang Lu.

Visa Extensions These are much more easily arranged at a popular package tour destination such as Guilin, even more so than Nanning, where the authorities ask for proof of funds of at least US$1,000.

Exploring Fengshan

Fengshan is bisected into an old and new town by the Qiaoyin River that flows north out of the city through the enormous Chuang Long Dong (cave). The town is tightly hemmed in on all sides by towering karst peaks.

MOUNTAINS & CAVES

Sanmenhai Water Caves This 40-minute show cave boat ride consists of three huge subterranean lake chambers and their interconnecting passages. In places the water reaches up to 120m (394 ft.) in depth making it a favorite location for international cave divers. Floating across the surface is distinctly less appealing, with a constant stream of other pontoons. There is also a path that leads up into the spectacular Jiangzhou karst valley, with its rock formations, an amazing rock arch bridge, and the longest underground tunnel in the province. The entire valley is around 30km (19 miles) in length, but the villages are well served by minibuses and this is a great opportunity to view this almost pristine area before it becomes a hugely popular attraction.

Poxin Chen, Paoli Xiang. ✆ **0778/695-8292.** Admission ¥80 (¥60 for Fengshan ID holders). 8am–6pm. Bus: Sanmenhai.

Fengshan Museum Set inside the world's fifth largest cavern, this is an imaginative location for a geological museum. Displays are very informative and in surprisingly good English for such a remote location. When big tour groups are in town, the museum organizes minority song and dance shows. These usually start at either 10am or 8pm. Just across the road in the museum car park, local youngsters have set up an impromptu roller skating rink to take advantage of the cool cave conditions. For even more impressive karst, head out of the cavern, where there is a waterfall and a tunnel leading to some of the most spectacular formations that you may ever see, where vertical cliff faces tower above on all sides like looming cathedral walls.

Chuanglong Cavern. Admission ¥68. 8am–6pm

A Local Toast

Impress the locals with your minority language skills. Cheers in the Zhuang dialect is *"gen lou"* and in Yao *"hap diu."*

Shopping in Fengshan

For those wishing to sample the local firewater, **Long Feng Jiu** (Dragon Phoenix alcohol) is made from a selection of local herbs and is popular for toasting.

Where to Stay

MODERATE

Hengsheng Hotel (Hengsheng Da Jiu Dian) This large four-star on the new side of town is the most comfortable choice in Fengshan. The rooms are still in reasonable condition, and just outside is Fengshan Karst Park, where steps lead up into the peaks and make a good spot to begin some hiking.

Xihuan Lu, Yinglong City Plaza. ✆ **0778/681-5988.** Fax 0778/681-3111. 121 units. ¥178 standard room; from ¥358 suite. No credit cards. Amenities: 2 restaurants. In room: A/C, TV, hair dryer, Internet, mini bar

INEXPENSIVE

Fang Xun Hotel (Fang Xun Da Jiu Dian) Another brand new small hotel just opposite the Hengsheng, the Fang Zun has beautiful, inspirational local photography on the walls but the lack of Internet and Western toilets is a little disappointing. Even so, this is still a major step up from other local hotels. It has tastefully decorated private rooms on the first floor. The hotel's restaurant serves an excellent selection of dishes; we especially recommend the tofu triangles *(fan qie qing gua men dofu gan)* and the dog meat (if you dare).

Add. Yangguan Da Dao. ✆ **0778/681-2888.** 30 units. ¥100 standard room. No credit cards. Amenities: Restaurant. In room: A/C, TV, kettle.

Where to Eat

Macros FAST FOOD This cheap and cheerful Western-inspired canteen does a selection of reasonable bento boxes for ¥12 that are a godsend if you have just arrived in town off a 6-hour bus ride and do not want to hunt around. The place is also popular with local youngsters for its burgers and ice cream.

Hongdu Lu. ✆ **0773/282-0470.** No credit cards. 11:20am–2pm and 5:20–9pm.

Yo Yo Canting LOCAL FOOD Popular with visiting cavers and climbers for its hygiene and reasonable prices, the *qing zhen jie* (steamed chicken) is well worth asking for, as is the *wo wo tou,* a strange kind of sunken bread with a vegetable filling.

Yangguan Da Dao ✆ **0773/281-0063.** Meal for 2 ¥80. No credit cards. 11am–midnight.

LEYE 乐业 ★

Guangxi Province, 460km (286 miles) N of Nanning, 165km (102 miles) NE of Baise, 135km (84 miles) N of Fengshan

Leye holds the annual International Mountain Outdoor Sports Challenge in May, when dozens of international teams arrive for a week of cross-country running, climbing, abseiling, mountain biking, and kayaking. Leye must also rank among the most extreme karst terrains in the world, with an amazing 28 tiankeng formations, making it a great alternative for those who feel that Yangshuo has lost its charm. Although it is much more difficult to reach, the rewards are many. In fact, some might describe Leye as being what they imagine Yangshuo may have been 20 years ago, before tourism arrived en masse. Still, this is no pristine wilderness. The Chinese economic miracle has taken its heavy toll even in this remote corner of the country. The town center is a hodgepodge of half-finished cinder-block boxes and yet a few miles away karsts, caves, and clear waters rival anything else in the entire province. Best of all, apart from a few intrepid speleologists, both Western and domestic tourists are still a rarity here. The fact that there is no railway connection or airport means that Leye has not yet been overrun by either Western or Chinese tourists. See chapter 16 for Chinese translations of key locations.

Essentials

GETTING THERE The nearest **train** station is Baise, conveniently located on the recently opened Guangzhou-Kunming rail line, with Guangzhou, Shenzhen, and Hong Kong being a comfortable 18 hours overnight sleeper to the southeast. From Baise, it is only 2 hours on good new roads up to Leye. Express buses leave every 2 hours for ¥28. If you arrive in **Baise** late, then the **Jindu Hotel** (**Jindu Dajiudian;** ✆ **0776/288-1188**) is conveniently located next to the bus station on Chenbei Yi Lu, although the rooms are a bit drab even for ¥140. The new **Leye Bus Station** (**Leye Qichezhan;** ✆ **0776/255-2062**) is now right at the southern edge of town and has buses to Lingyun (2 hr.), Fengshan (6 hr.), and Bama (7 hr.).

GETTING AROUND Leye has an admirable local bus system that is being undermined by an army of motorized trikes that charge a meager ¥2 for any location in town, and yet create terrible noise and air pollution. **Taxis** are all well-worn hand-me-downs from larger provincial centers but are useful for out of town locations such as Huomai Village. The **public bus** to Dashiwei is especially good value being only ¥2 for the 20 minute run up to the Tiankeng Park. The drive up to the park is sometimes even more stunning than the park itself, with huge sinister caves every few 100m (328 ft.).

[Fast FACTS] LEYE

Banks, Foreign Exchange & ATMs There is no Bank of China in Leye, only an Agricultural Bank with no international ATMs, only those designed for the domestic Union-pay system. Stock up with RMB at larger towns such as Nanning, Baise and Hechi.

Internet Access Sanle Lu is quickly becoming littered with local-style Internet cafes charging ¥2 per hour.

Post Office The main post office (8am–8pm) is on the Tongle Lu.

Exploring Leye

Leye Geological Museum ★★★ You'll find this museum impressive for the large amount of detailed information (with English translations) about the local geology. With some of the most extensive dual language displays about karst formations in the region, this is definitely your first stop in exploring the region. The museum is packed with quality information about local flora and fauna, with great pictures and detailed local maps. Just outside there are even more displays, this time focusing more on the surrounding regions, their topography, and minority customs and practices. Best of all, this is the starting point for a number of well-marked hiking routes that form part of the National Trails System.

Tongle Zhong Lu. Free admission. 9am–5pm.

Huomai ★★ Although Huomai claims to be an eco-village, it's going to be many years before the words "eco" and China can be used in the same sentence. Even so, Huomai is genuinely impressive, and one of the best small villages in China.

To get there, take a taxi ¥30 from Leye town center (you can ask at one of the *nongjiale* restaurants in the village for a taxi back down to town). Just 8km (5 miles) from downtown Leye, the village's entrance is marked by a fantastic wooden frame guest house with balconies overlooking the valley. If you'd like to stay overnight, the rooms are simple but acceptable, with a bed, shower, and Western toilet for ¥80 per night. Ornate panels carved by local craftsmen adorn the walls with intriguing images of legend: An outlaw of the marsh slays a tiger with his bare hands and a Sung dynasty physician helps a patient cough up a goldfish.

Next door are a couple of farmhouse restaurants where a full table of hearty local fare costs only ¥20 per person. We like the second of the two best (✆ **138/7766 3302**); make sure that you have a peek into the traditional kitchen to see how the same burning logs that boil the rice also smoke the ham.

Up toward the center of the village is a wall map showing local points of interest. These include a pick-your-own fruit and vegetable patch (walnuts and pomegranates are local specialties) and Feihu cave, which contains a strange rock formation known as the "first trousers in the world." Bring your own flashlight for this one. The brave and the foolhardy can head out to Lost Souls Cavern (Mihu Dong). A resident explained that this cave got its name because so many people went in, but never came out—be warned.

Up past the small village temple, a path leads up the highest peak in the area, a spectacular viewpoint for Huomai's most famous sight, a magnificent sunrise over the clouds and karst peaks. The path back down is equally impressive with a chance to check out the Dacuo Tiankeng, a collapsed cave equally as impressive as any in the

Dashiwei Park Area. The locals here have not been corrupted by mass tourism and are still friendly and outgoing.

Tip: On the way back down to Leye, stop by the cave that was used as a base for the adventure race and clamber across the terraces to a second cave at the right, to the rear. For some bizarre reason, an eerie cloud stretches the full length of this dark and creepy cavern, a strange phenomenon.

MOUNTAINS & CAVES

Dashiwei Tiankeng ★★ A true wonder of geography, Dashiwei Tiankeng is the largest of its kind in the world and yet has only been known to the outside world since 1998. *Tiankeng,* literally "sky pit" in Chinese, refers to the large vertical-sided collapsed caves that have formed over millions of years. This is a giant of a *tiankeng,* 600m (1,968 ft.) from east to west and is 613m (2,011 ft.) deep with unbroken, vertical perimeter walls that cut through three conical hills. The virgin forest at the bottom covers an area of 96,000 sq. m (1,033,335 sq. ft.) and is home to rare species such as the flying squirrel. A long section of downstream river cave lies below the edge of the breakdown pile on the *tiankeng* floor. The park is home to a suite of large *tiankeng* and major cave systems that are only partly explored. The tour bus gives glimpses of rims and walls of the various *tiankeng,* with roadside stops above the degraded Datuo Tiankeng and another at the lip of Maoqi Dong. The bus then drops visitors off to walk around the rim of Dashiwei Tiankeng. The ticket office is refreshingly honest here, warning visitors when cloud conditions make viewing impossible. The paths are lined with blackberries while the sound of cuckoos and cowbells echo away into the distance.

Admission ¥60. 8am–6pm. Bus: Dashiwei bus every 30 min. from Leye bus station.

Buliu River Gorge This huge natural stone arch bridge, the world's largest at 177m (581 ft.) long, and 145m (476 ft.) high, formed by three fallen mountains, stretches over the beautiful Buliu River like an enormous dragon crossing the water. Visitors can raft down the 3½ hour stretch of azure blue waters from Dongla near Moli village at a cost of ¥90 for adults and ¥60 for children. Unfortunately this stunning attraction is still very difficult to reach. The twice daily public bus to Fengshan passes Moli (¥20) but takes nearly 2 hours. Surprisingly this tiny village has its own modern bus station, but it is better to hire a motorbike out to the rafting spots. Better still is to arrange everything including transportation from Leye, where you can expect to pay around ¥200 per person.

Moli Cun, near Xing Hua Zhen. ✆ **0776/792-7899.** 9am–5pm.

Lotus Cave (Luomei Lianhua Dong) A 1,000m (3,280 ft.) tourist cave in a passage just above the level of the Leye field floor, this cave is notable for its many fine, circular shelf stone deposits up to 2m (7 ft.) across that were formed in pools (now drained) around stalagmite stumps (often known as lotus deposits in China or as lily pads in the West) some of which are almost 10m (32 ft.) across and are the largest anywhere in the world.

Tongle Zhong Lu. Admission ¥23. 9am–5pm.

Where to Stay

MODERATE

Tian Yuan Hotel (Tian Yuan Da Jiu Dian) This cavernous new three-star construction seems to be constantly empty, but at least that is keeping the wear and tear down on the rooms. There's not much English out here in the sticks, but the staff are enthusiastic and friendly.

Xingle Lu. ✆ **0776/255-3888.** 250 units. ¥138 standard room. Suite ¥480 No credit cards. Amenities: Restaurant; karaoke. In room: A/C, TV, Internet.

Where to Eat

Guo Guo Wang CHINESE This is a small but friendly eatery just up from the market area, and the same brand that is found down the road in Lingyun. The lack of English menu means that you will have to point at what the other diners are enjoying, but rest assured that the kitchen is clean and the food is tasty.

Tongle Bei Lu. ✆ **0773/792-7792.** Meal for 2 ¥40. No credit cards. 11am–8pm.

LINGYUN 凌云 ★★

Guangxi Province, 100km (62 miles) N of Baise, 180km (111 miles) W of Bama

As an introduction to northwest Guangxi, Lingyun cannot be beaten. At one end of the sheltered valley, the crystal clear river emerges from the water cave and flows all the way through the center of town, a relatively clean and unspoiled place. The karst scenery here humbles even the best that Guilin and Yangshuo have to offer, and as an added bonus, it has not yet been discovered by tourists. If we could only pick one location in Guangxi to visit, it would be Lingyun—just be careful to not tell too many other people about it.

Essentials

GETTING THERE Lingyun is only just over an hour to Baise, where the train station has very convenient connections to Liuzhou and Guilin in the East and Kunming in the West. There are regular buses to and from Fengshan (3 hr., on one of the most spectacular karst routes) as well as daily buses every morning up to Leye (2 hr.). Make sure when you buy your bus tickets that you are getting on a regular scheduled bus with seats (ban che) and not a sleeper bus that is just passing through. Baise has a small airport with a small number of flights to selected domestic cities, but with the rail being so convenient it hardly seems worth bothering with flight hassles.

GETTING AROUND Converted three-wheel motorcycles will take you anywhere within the town for ¥3. For those venturing farther afield, the local buses are a good way to get up close and personal with the local Miao and Zhuang Minorities.

VISITOR INFORMATION Lingyun has large tourist maps posted all over the town, detailing many more locations than I can possibly fit in here. Most of the in-town sites are well signposted and even have English introductions. Unfortunately it's difficult to find a town map to purchase.

[Fast FACTS] LINGYUN

Banks, Foreign Exchange & ATMs The Agricultural Bank, just east of the bus station on 318 Provincial Road has an ATM that can handle international cards but do not expect any currency exchange services.

Post Office There is a small post office (9am–6pm) on San Le Lu, the main street.

Visa Extensions Due to the distinct lack of tourists, these are much better handled back in Guilin or Kunming.

Exploring Lingyun

Lingyun is a very likable little town, with plenty to see, but the real splendor is out in the surrounding karst peaks. Unlike Yangshuo and Guilin, where your perspective is limited mainly to a flat plain from which the peaks thrust up, the mountain roads around Lingyun are perched way up on the high slopes. Heights and distances feel much greater and over every ridge and brow, vast new cauldron valleys are revealed, each one beckoning to be explored.

Where to Stay

There are no backpacker dorms here, but even the most budget minded can afford to splurge on a four-star Mountain Villa when it is only ¥138.

Xiang Yun Bian Jie Hotel (Xiang Yun Bian Jie Jiu Dian) Just overlooking the public park area, this is a new and friendly little guest house that would make a good alternative in the unlikely circumstance that the Mountain Villa (below) is fully booked. Rooms are comfortable, but may seem a little basic.

Wu Ling Road. ✆ **0776/261-6555.** Fax 0776/261-6555. 70 units. ¥100 standard room. No credit cards. In room: A/C, TV, Internet

Yinghui Mountain Villa (Yinghui Shan Zhuang) ★★★ While the building has served cadres and their entourages for the last 20 years, this place was fully refurbished just 2 years ago, so the rooms are lean and there is a feeling of four-star elegance. Rooms are large and airy, even more so when there are so few other guests. The front desk manager May speaks very passable English and the rest of the staff are all extremely pleased to see overseas visitors. To the rear of the hotel, steps lead up into the mountains where you will find pagodas and secluded seating areas. This is one of the best value hotels in China.

28 Yinghui Road. ✆ **0776/761-1110.** Fax 0776/761-1125. 80 units. ¥188 standard room; from ¥388 suite. No credit cards. Amenities: Restaurant; lounge; meeting and conference facilities; room service; souvenir store. In room: A/C, TV, Internet, minibar.

Where to Eat

Don't expect to find banana pancakes and English menus here. Even so, there are plenty of interesting options for the intrepid. For snacks and light meals, do not miss the baozi (steamed buns) store, just opposite the bus station front doors. The delicate fruit flavors go down well, whether you are just arriving or on your way out. Just opposite the west entrance to main market hall, look out for a small dumpling shop that does huge bowls of delicious jiaozi soup for just ¥5. In the evening, try **Guo Guo Wang** next to the Golden Water Bridge (Jin Sui Qiao; ✆ **0776/761-9256**) that is very popular with locals. There are no English menus but you can point at what the other diners are enjoying or perhaps try the Xiang Gu Zhu Ro, which is filling and tasty.

Around Lingyun

The town itself is worth exploring with attractions such as the world's largest teapot (8.18m high, 13.8m in diameter, and weighing 6.8 tons and the Taiping Bridge with its tree root door. The Wen Miao temple seems very ordinary and overpriced at ¥60 and the Samsung Tower is a very dull pagoda. Even so, Lingyun has real charm, so

LINGYUN OFF THE beaten path

The area passed by bus approaching Lingyun from the gritty town of Luo Lou is some of the most spectacular karst scenery in all of China, so you may be keen to experience some of it close up. Get on a Luo Lou bound bus headed back out of town to the Long Zhao turn off in the next valley to the north. From the lobby of the Mountain Villa I had spotted about a bijillion stone steps leading up from the Zhongshan Memorial Hall all the way up to the top of the surrounding peaks, and wanted to use that as my route back into town. The road leading south from the main road to the village of Long Zhao is brand new, and you can still clearly see the star impressions in the rock where TNT has blasted away the limestone leaving beautiful spiders' web designs in the rock. Across vast boulder-littered valleys, ancient terraces support a variety of crops that have fed the locals for many generations, when this region was all but cut off from the outside world. Cross over onto the northern side of the road and you will immediately discover a collection of stone and carved rock pathways that run parallel to the modern tarmac. It's amazing to step back in time and traverse just a section of these ancient routes, and to get a feeling of the struggle and danger involved in just getting to the next village. Jump back on the hardtop for a couple of hundred meters. The road ahead zigzags down the mountain, and to your right is a man-made outcrop allowing the buses to cut through. If you take the first left turn it will take you up into a small hamlet of just half a dozen homes, and from there look for the ancient mule trail that takes you up and over the mountain. Of course it is not so easy that you immediately arrive at the Lingyun gate that you saw from the hotel. This route will take you down steep rock faces into isolated Zhuang villages, and beyond into huge valleys that stretch up, down, and away for mind-boggling distances. Bear right and over a sharp crest you will see the evidence of machine construction, and steps that lead all the way back down to Lingyun. If Lingyun is my find of this edition, then this up and over hike has to be the highlight of the trekking I did this year, and I hope that you enjoy it as much as I did.

take advantage with a stroll around the old town, enjoying the twists and turns of the playful Buliu River.

WATER CAVE 水源洞 ★★★

Shuiyuan Cave, which used to be called Ling Cave during the Qing Dynasty, is located at the foot of Baihua Mountain. It's just a short 1km (.6 mile) stroll away from the center of town. Follow the main road south and then cross the bridge, keeping to the far side of the river that leads up to the cave mouth. There is a small temple inside the cave with a reserved Buddhist monk who claims that there are no tunnels to be explored, but the main attraction is out front. As the calcium rich water emerges from the mouth of the cavern, it forms what we consider to be the best swimming spot in Southeast China. Locals take a dip here on a regular basis, and it is a real pleasure to join them.

KUNMING 昆明 ★

Yunnan Province, 1,200km (744 miles) NW of Hong Kong, 450km (270 miles) SW of Guiyang

As the capital of Yunnan Province, Kunming is known as the "city of eternal spring." Though it was founded over 2,000 years ago, the city did not gain prominence until it became the eastern capital of the Nanzhao Kingdom in the 8th century. By the time the Mongols swept through in 1274, Kunming, or Yachi as it was then known, was enough of a flourishing town to have attracted the attention of Marco Polo, who described it as a "very great and noble" capital city. The city's bloodiest period occurred during the Qing dynasty, with a series of Muslim rebellions. Between 1648 and 1878, more than 12 million Hui and Uighur Muslims were killed in 10 unsuccessful uprisings against the Qing Dynasty. In the late 19th century, foreign influence appeared in the form of the French, who built a narrow-gauge rail line to Vietnam. During World War II, Kunming played an important role as the terminus of a major supply line (the famous Burma Rd.) in the Allies' Asian theater of operations.

Today, Kunming's wide streets, towering office blocks, and giant shopping centers all convey the impression of a modern, 21st-century city. These days, local media often refer to Kunming as Ducheng, loosely meaning "Congestion City," as cars have taken over. Combined with the city's elevation, and the fact that it is enclosed by mountains on three sides, pollution is becoming a very serious problem.

Still, Kunming remains a useful starting point even if its offerings do not match some of Yunnan's other treasures. A subtropical location and high elevation (1,864m/6,213 ft.) give Kunming a temperate climate year-round. Its days are filled with sunshine, making almost any time good for a visit, though the balmy months of September and October are especially fine.

Essentials

GETTING THERE Kunming is connected by daily flights to more than a dozen provincial airports including Dali (30 min.), Lijiang (40 min.), and Zhongdian (1 hr.), as well as 50 domestic routes including Beijing (2½ hr.), Chengdu (1 hr.), Guilin (1½ hr.) and Shanghai (2½ hr.) Tickets can be purchased at the **CAAC/Yunnan Airlines** office at Tuodong Lu 28 (✆ **0871/316-4270** domestic, or 0871/312-1220 international). Tickets can also be purchased at the airport, at CITS and other travel agencies, and at hotel tour desks. On the international front, Yunnan Airlines and several international carriers serve Hong Kong, Bangkok, Chiang Mai, Yangon, Mandalay, Vientiane, Osaka, Singapore, New Delhi, Kolkata, Kathmandu, Siem Reap, Phuket, Phnom Penh, Dacca, and Hanoi. Foreign airline offices include: **Dragonair,** Beijing Lu 157 (✆ 0871/356-2828); **Lao Aviation,** Camellia Hotel, Dongfeng Dong Lu 96 (✆ 0871/316-3000, ext. 5166); **Thai Airways,** Beijing Lu 98, second floor, King World Hotel annex (✆ 0871/351-2269); **Silk Air/Singapore Airlines,** Dongfeng Dong Lu 25 (✆ 0871/315-7125); **Japan Airlines,** Bank Hotel, Qingnian Lu 399, third floor (✆ 0871/315-8111); and **Vietnam Airlines,** Tuodong Lu 80 (✆ 0871/315-7175). **Sanya Travel** usually beats anything online (✆ 0871/351-6888); they accept foreign credit cards (with a 4% fee) and are about 2 blocks up from the train station. The airport is 5km (3 miles) south of city center, a quick ¥30 taxi ride depending on your destination in town. There are no CAAC airport buses, but public bus nos. 52, 67, and 78 also serve the airport at ¥1. This is all soon likely to change when the new Kunming international airport, which is projected to be the third-largest in China, will be located 21km (13) miles northeast of Kunming.

The **Kunming Railway Station** is at the far southern end of Beijing Xi Lu just past the bus station, which you will see on your right. Kunming is well connected by rail to many major Chinese cities, and major investment into the railway network means that all these routes are getting faster all the time. Trains run to Beijing (38 hr.), Shanghai (36 hr.), Guangzhou (26 hr.), Guilin (16 hr.), Chengdu (18 hr.), and Shilin/Stone Forest (90 min.). There are at least four trains a day to Dali and Lijiang, including a day train that is long and laborious, and three huge double-decker sleeper trains in the evening, which leave late in the evening and arrive first thing the next morning (8:40pm–5:06am; 9:43pm–6:15am; 11pm–8am). There is also a small ticket office on Kunshi Lu near the University, the first road on your right as you walk downhill on Jianshe Lu from its intersection with Wenlin Jie. After turning onto Kunshi Lu, walk about 75 to 100m (246 ft.–328 ft.) until you find an alley on the left (south) side of the road. About 15m (49 ft.) into the alley you should find a train ticket office on the left (east) side of the alley. Train fans will be pleased to hear that many new projects are underway in Kunming. A new high-speed rail line will shorten the travel time between Shanghai and Kunming from 37 hours to less than 9 hours. The Dali-Ruili railway will extend the existing line 366km (227 miles) through to China's border with Myanmar by 2015.

Eleven bus stations close to the city center were abruptly closed in 2010, including the long-distance bus stations that have all been relocated outside of the city center, but there are still connecting buses at the otherwise closed **Nanyao Qiche Keyun Zhan** at Beijing Lu 60 (✆ **0871/351-0617**), at the northwest corner of Beijing Lu and Yongping Lu. Numbers 71, 72 and 73 serve the East South and West Bus Stations and cost ¥5 each, leaving every 20 minutes to half an hour. The **West Station,** Chunyu Lu/Yining Lu Intersection (✆ **0871/532-7326**), is most heavily used by foreigners because it serves the northwestern tourist circuit, is commonly known by locals as **Majie bus station** has buses to Xiaguan (Dali New Town; 5 hr.); to Lijiang (9 hr.); to Xianggelila/Zhongdian (12 hr.) although these are all very poor alternatives to the overnight train. The **South Bus Station** (Caiyun Bei Lu; ✆ **0871/736-1722;** www.km-ky.com) serves destinations in southern Yunnan including Pu'er, Xishuangbanna, Yuxi, Jianshui, Yuanyang, and many others. The long distance buses are cheap; however, overnight sleepers can be cold, bumpy, and dirty. Check out the bus before you buy the tickets. It also has international departures to Laos and Vietnam, though these services are not always running. The bus to Laos goes all the way from Kunming to Vientiane, and costs approximately ¥800 and lasts 40 hours if you go all the way. The journey to Vietnam is less arduous. Buses to Hekou, the border city on the Chinese side, leave regularly. Night buses leave Kunming at 8pm from the bus station next to the train station and arrive at Hekou in time to cross the border as soon as it opens. The bus station is just a few blocks from the border crossing. From there, you can take one of the many buses to Hanoi, Sapa, or elsewhere. The new East Bus Station on the Dongsanhuan Hongqiao Flyover (✆ **0871/383-3680**) serves destinations in east and southeast Yunnan, including Shilin, Mile, Luliang, Shizong, and Luoping. This leaves the North and Northwest Bus Stations or Longtou Lu and Puji Lu respectively that cover destinations less popular with tourists. Tickets can be purchased at the stations 7 days before the date of departure, or can be booked online 2 days in advance through the official passenger transit website, which as yet has no English interface.

For the really adventurous, **cycling** into Southern Yunnan from Kunming deserves serious consideration. Not only are there some beautiful back roads, but it is downhill

Kunming 昆明

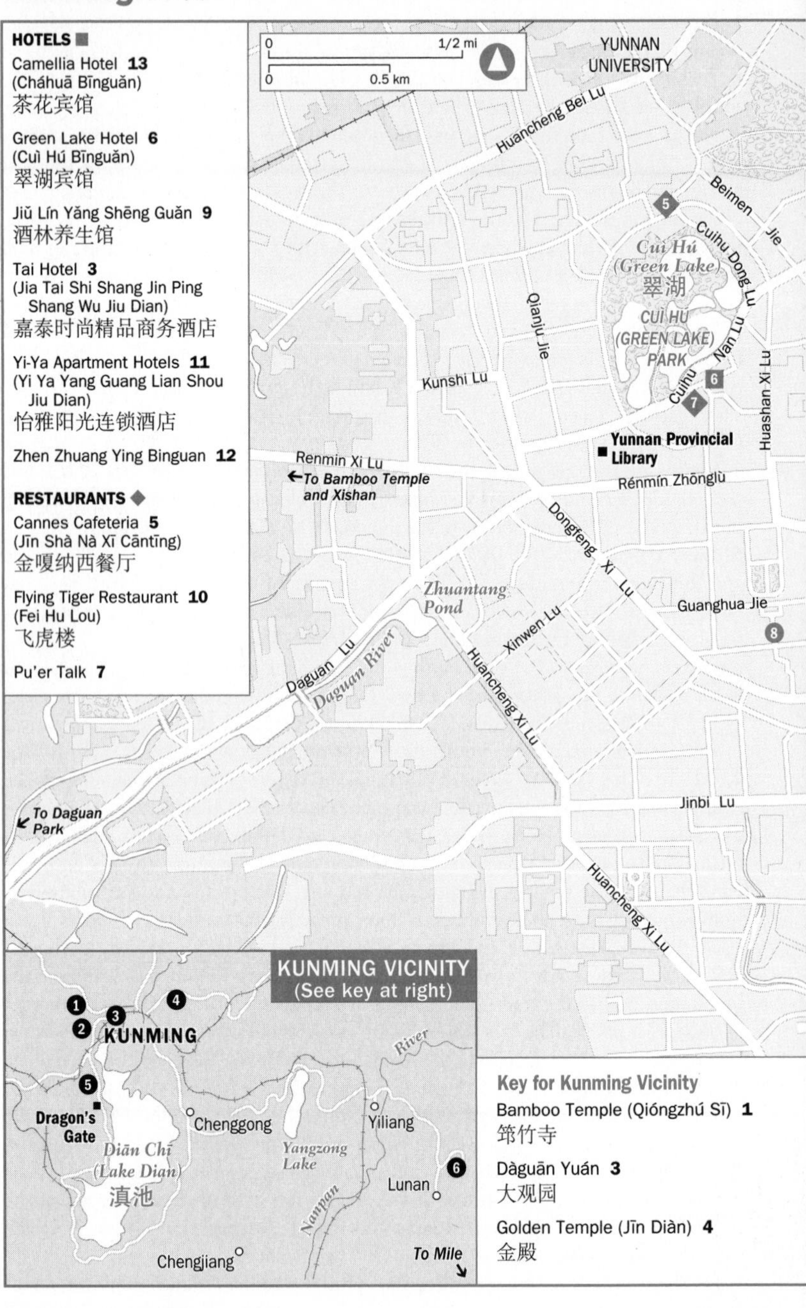
HOTELS
Camellia Hotel 13
(Cháhuā Bīnguǎn)
茶花宾馆
Green Lake Hotel 6
(Cuì Hú Bīnguǎn)
翠湖宾馆
Jiǔ Lín Yǎng Shēng Guǎn 9
酒林养生馆
Tai Hotel 3
(Jia Tai Shi Shang Jin Ping Shang Wu Jiu Dian)
嘉泰时尚精品商务酒店
Yi-Ya Apartment Hotels 11
(Yi Ya Yang Guang Lian Shou Jiu Dian)
怡雅阳光连锁酒店
Zhen Zhuang Ying Binguan 12
RESTAURANTS
Cannes Cafeteria 5
(Jīn Shà Nà Xī Cāntīng)
金嗄纳西餐厅
Flying Tiger Restaurant 10
(Fei Hu Lou)
飞虎楼
Pu'er Talk 7
0 1/2 mi
0 0.5 km
YUNNAN UNIVERSITY
Huancheng Bei Lu
Beimen Jie
Cuihu Dong Lu
Cui Hú (Green Lake)
翠湖
CUI HU (GREEN LAKE) PARK
Cuihu Nan Lu
Qianju Jie
Kunshi Lu
Huashan Xi Lu
Yunnan Provincial Library
Renmin Xi Lu
To Bamboo Temple and Xishan
Rénmín Zhōnglù
Dongfeng Xi Lu
Zhuantang Pond
Guanghua Jie
Xinwen Lu
Daguan Lu
Daguan River
Huancheng Xi Lu
Jinbi Lu
To Daguan Park
Huancheng Xi Lu
KUNMING VICINITY
(See key at right)
KUNMING
River
Dragon's Gate
Chenggong
Yiliang
Diān Chí (Lake Dian)
滇池
Yangzong Lake
Lunan
Nanpan
Chengjiang
To Mile
Key for Kunming Vicinity
Bamboo Temple (Qióngzhú Sī) 1
筇竹寺
Dàguān Yuán 3
大观园
Golden Temple (Jīn Diàn) 4
金殿

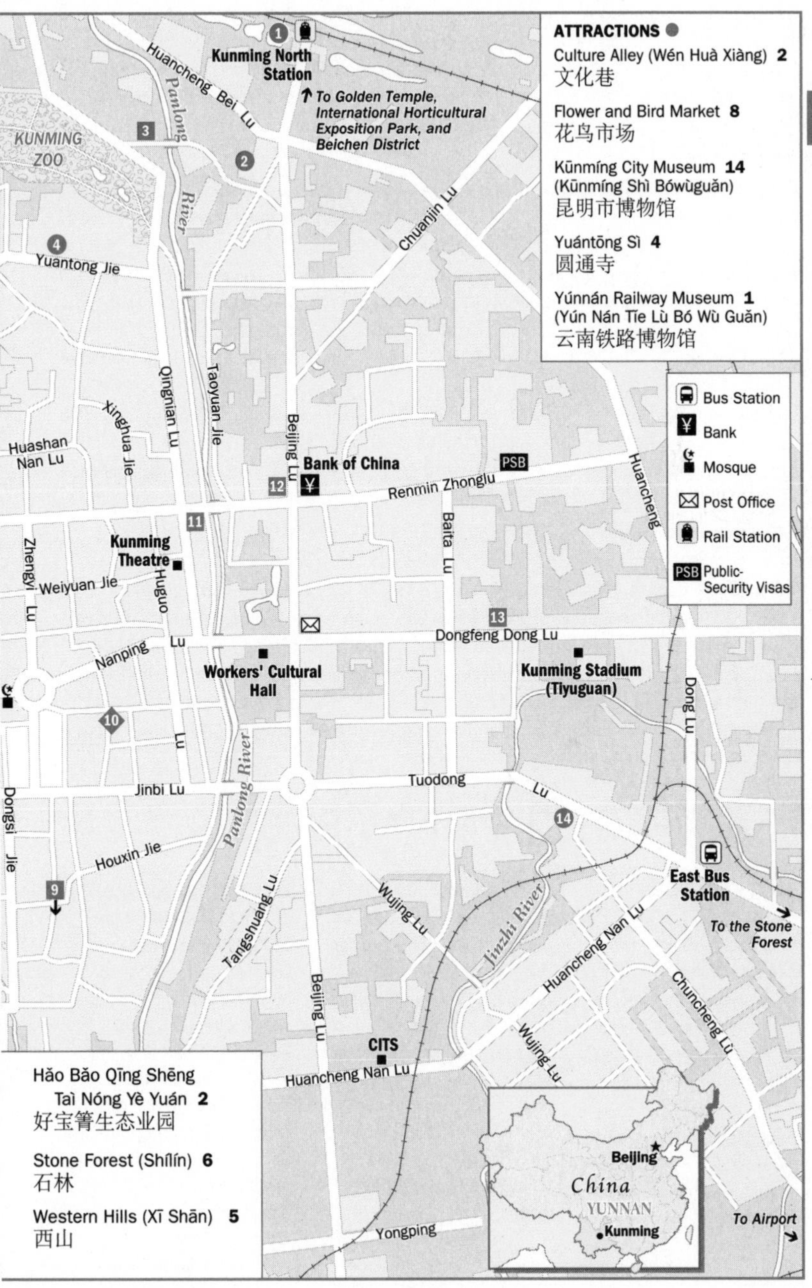

ATTRACTIONS
Culture Alley (Wén Huà Xiàng) 2
文化巷
Flower and Bird Market 8
花鸟市场
Kūnmíng City Museum 14
(Kūnmíng Shì Bówùguǎn)
昆明市博物馆
Yuántōng Sì 4
圆通寺
Yúnnán Railway Museum 1
(Yún Nán Tiě Lù Bó Wù Guǎn)
云南铁路博物馆
Hǎo Bǎo Qīng Shēng Taì Nóng Yè Yuán 2
好宝箐生态业园
Stone Forest (Shílín) 6
石林
Western Hills (Xī Shān) 5
西山
Bus Station
Bank
Mosque
Post Office
Rail Station
PSB Public-Security Visas
Kunming North Station
To Golden Temple, International Horticultural Exposition Park, and Beichen District
Huancheng Bei Lu
Panlong River
KUNMING ZOO
Yuantong Jie
Chuanjin Lu
Taoyuan Jie
Qingnian Lu
Xinghua Jie
Huashan Nan Lu
Beijing Lu
Bank of China
Renmin Zhonglu
Baita Lu
Huancheng
Kunming Theatre
Huguo Lu
Zhengyi Lu
Weiyuan Jie
Nanping
Dongfeng Dong Lu
Workers' Cultural Hall
Kunming Stadium (Tiyuguan)
Dong Lu
Jinbi Lu
Tuodong Lu
Dongsi Jie
Houxin Jie
Tangshuang Lu
Wujing Lu
Jinzhi River
East Bus Station
To the Stone Forest
Huancheng Nan Lu
Chuncheng Lu
CITS
Yongping
To Airport
Beijing
China
YUNNAN
Kunming

all the way. For further inspiration and a day-to-day report from somebody who has already done this, check out www.pratyeka.org/bike/southern-yunnan.html. China has already completed renovations on its 600km (373-mile) segment of the Stilwell Road, upgrading the route to a six-lane expressway that will cut the distance between China and India by 5,000km (3,106 miles). A former World War II supply route, the road is named after U.S. General Joe Stilwell, who oversaw its construction in 1944. The 1,700km (1,000-mile) road once connected Kunming with the city of Ledo in Assam state.

GETTING AROUND Downtown sights can be toured on foot or by bike. If your hotel does not offer bike rental, the Camellia Hotel (96 E. Dongfeng Rd.) rents them for ¥2 an hour or ¥15 for the day. For a choice of mountain bikes for rent, visit **Fattire Fun Mountain Bike Club** at Beimen Jie 1 hao, Qianju Lu 61, off Cui Hu Nan Lu (✆ **0871/530-1755;** owner Xiong Jinwu's e-mail: bear_bike@hotmail.com).

Flag fall for **taxis** is ¥8 for 3km (2 miles) and ¥1.80 per kilometer after that; from 10pm to 6am, flag fall is ¥9.60 for 3km (2 miles). Taxis start at ¥8 and usually have reliable meters.

Bus fares are either ¥1 or ¥2. Unlike other cities in China, buses have special access to the innermost lane rather than the outside lane. This is a very effective innovation and makes buses the fast way to get around the city, especially during rush hour. In addition, most routes now have bilingual stop announcements making travel around the city very easy. A subway system is scheduled to open in late 2012 but for the time being expect lots of road work and plenty of delays.

TOURS **CITS** at Huancheng Nan Lu 285 (✆ **0871/353-5448;** fax 0871/316-9240; www.kmcits.com.cn; Mon–Fri 8:30am–noon and 2–6pm) is often busy juggling international tour groups but can be very helpful with arranging accommodations, ongoing transportation, or customized tours throughout Yunnan for individual travelers. The **Camellia Travel Service** on the ground floor of the Camellia Hotel is the rudest and most unhelpful agency in town and worth avoiding. Yunnan travel service hot-line is ✆ **12301.**

[Fast FACTS] KUNMING

Banks, Foreign Exchange & ATMs The main branch of the **Bank of China** (Mon–Fri 8:30am–noon and 2–5pm) is at Renmin Dong Lu 448. ATMs here accept international cards.

Consulates The **Laos consulate** is in room 120 of the Camellia Hotel at Dongfeng Dong Lu 96 (✆ **0871/317-6623;** Mon–Fri 9–11:30am and 2–4pm). Transit visas (5–7 days) and standard 15-day tourist visas (valid within 2 months of issue) can be issued in 3 working days (ordinary service) or by the next working day (express service). Fees vary from ¥260 to ¥360 for ordinary service and from ¥400 to ¥500 for express service. You cannot currently get a Laos visa at the border. Bring two photos and complete two application forms.

The **Myanmar consulate** is located in Room A504, 5th Floor, Long Yuan Hao Zhai, 166, Wei Yuan Jie (✆ **0871/360-3477;** fax 0871/360-2468; www.mcg-kunming.com/consulate.htm; Mon–Fri 8:30am–noon and 1–2pm). Standard 28-day travel visas costing ¥285 and valid within 3 months of issue can be issued in 3 working days; for same-day service, expect to pay an extra ¥150. This visa is only good for flying into Yangon or Mandalay.

The **Thai consulate** is located on the grounds of

the Kunming Hotel at Dongfeng Dong Lu 50–52 (✆ **0871/316-2033,** ext. 62105; fax 0871/316-6891; Mon–Fri 9am–1:30pm).

The **Vietnamese consulate** is located at 2/F, Jiahua Square Hotel, 157 Beijing Rd. (✆ **0871/352-2669;** fax 0871/351-6667; e-mail: tlsqcm@yahoo.com; Mon–Fri 9am–1:30pm).

The **Cambodian Consulate** is located on the 4th Floor, Kunming Guangfang Hotel, No 172, Xinying Rd. (✆ **0871/331-7320;** fax 0871/331-6220; rcgcamkm@yahoo.com; Mon–Fri 9am–1:30pm).

Internet Access The imposing **Yunnan Provincial Library** on Cui Hu Nan Lu 141 has a large number of machines on the third floor (9am–8pm); ¥1 per hour. Alex in the English language section is also a mine of information on Kunming sightseeing.

Post Office The main post office (8am–8pm) is at Dongfeng Dong Lu 14, and another (9am–8pm) is west of the railway station.

Visa Extensions The visa office is located at counter 57 of the **People's Service Center** of Kunming Municipality (Kunming Shizhengfu Bianmin Zhongxin), Renmin Dong Lu 196 (✆ **0871/319-6540;** Mon–Fri 8:30–11:30am and 1–5:30pm), but things are distinctly more efficient up in Dali.

Exploring Kunming

While Kunming is great for eating, it can be downright dull in terms of sightseeing if you stick to the official sights. Black Dragon Pool is seriously neglected (apart from the Opium War Memorial, which actually took place in distant Guangdong), and much of the Botanical Garden is closed down and in a very sad state.

Cui Hu (Green Lake) ★ Kunming's nicest park is a pleasant retreat from the bustling city, even though it can get quite crowded on weekends. Bridges and pavilions connect the various islands on the lake, and sipping tea at a lakeside teahouse is one of the more pleasant activities in town. The park is home to the Siberian black-headed gulls, which migrate here during the winter.

Cui Hu Nan Lu. Free admission. Bus: 4, 59, 22, 74, 78, 85, or 101.

Yunnan Tie Lu Bowuguan (Yunnan Railway Museum) Well designed and packed with information for the rail history buff, the majority of displays here describe the construction and eventual demise of the French-built narrow-gauge rail network in the province, which at one time led all the way to Hanoi and beyond. Many of the aging photos make clear the hardships and obstacles faced when trying to build 3,422 bridges and tunnels without any of the huge modern extraction tools. The locomotives and carriages (including a very strange Michelin model with pneumatic tires) are kept in an annex just down the road. This is a great spot for travelers who prefer to climb all over the displays rather than simply stand and look.

North Station, Beijing Lu. ✆ **0871/613-8610.** Admission ¥20. Tues–Sun 10am–4pm.

Yuantong Si This unusual temple, the largest and oldest Buddhist shrine in Kunming, combines elements from Mahayana, Hinayana (or Theravada), and Tibetan Buddhism (Lamaism). Originally built between 780 and 807, and rebuilt during the Qing dynasty, the temple is dedicated to the worship of Avalokitesvara (the original male Buddha who was later transfigured into the female Guanyin in Chinese Mahayana Buddhism). In the back of the complex is a Hinayana-style hall with a bronze statue of Sakyamuni donated by the Buddhist Association of Thailand. To the east is an altar hall of the Lama sect.

Yuantong Jie. Admission ¥4. 8am–5pm.

Wenhua Xiang This is Kunming's unintentional version of Khao San Road in Bangkok. Stretching for about 5 blocks up from Yunnan University and then another 3 blocks to the right, this is where college students, expats, local residents, and foreign language teachers get together throughout the day and into the evening. It has everything from French cafes to Indian restaurants, a host of Korean restaurants, an English bookstore, DVD stores, and bars. There's also a host of bakeries, most notably Just Hot at 436 Dongfeng Xi Lu (✆ **0871/5370800**), just around the corner past the cinema.
Wen Ling St. and Wen Hua St.

Outdoor Activities

According to U.S.-based *Golf Digest* magazine, if you're looking for China's best courses, forget Shanghai, Beijing, or Shenzhen—the best golf is in Kunming. Kunming took three of the top six spots on Golf Digest's top 10 in China list. The **Spring City Golf and Lake Resort,** located 48km (29 miles) southeast of Kunming, has a championship 18-hole golf course designed by Jack Nicklaus and another by Robert Trent Jones, Jr.

For something more exciting, **Mike Fougere** (✆ **15825256431;** mike4g_air@yahoo.ca) is a Hang Gliding and Paragliding Association of Canada (HPAC)-certified paragliding instructor based in Kunming. He has been paragliding for more than 10 years and is available—winds permitting—to pilot tandem flights around Kunming at a rate of ¥300 per person (plus transport expenses).

Shopping

The area around Zhengyi Lu and Nanping Lu has turned into Kunming's main shopping district. The **Guwan Cheng** (8:30am–7:30pm) at the southwest corner of Huguo Lu and Nanping Lu has a collection of stores selling antiques, curios, and ceramics. The **Flower and Bird Market** in Jingxing Jie is worth a browse for souvenirs and minor, mostly fake, antiques, but do not expect anything much different from all the other souvenir markets. For something more original, head down Beijing road past the Jinda Hotel and the PLA Headquarters. There are plenty of army surplus shops here that sell everything from fur caps (¥20) to military police ID wallets (¥25), all of which make very unusual gifts. For police gear, try Longjin Jie, which is full of paramilitary supply shops. For even more unusual gifts, the annual Kunming Sex Expo takes place in May at the Yunnan Provincial Science and Technology Hall on Cuihu Xi Lu, across from the southwest corner of Green Lake Park.

Where to Stay

While many overseas visitors continue to stay at the unimpressive Camellia Hotel (Chahua Fandian), there are far better choices if you look a bit further. One interesting option might be the **Zhen Zhuang Ying Binguan** (Beijing Lu 514; ✆ **0871/316-5869**) where the Chinese president and other high-ranking officials stay when in Yunnan, but not much English is spoken.

Green Lake Hotel (Cui Hu Binguan) ★★★ Originally opened by the Hongta tobacco group in 1956, and later run by the Hilton Group, this was Kunming's very first hotel open to foreigners. The location easily surpasses any of the downtown five-stars, and its two new wings make it a very tempting choice. The rooms are very well maintained and luxuriously appointed with huge king-size beds, making this one of the few locally run five-stars that can give the multinationals a run for their money.

South Cui Hu Nan Lu 6. ✆ **0871/515-888.** Fax 0871/515-3286. 302 units. ¥1,180 standard room; from ¥1,380 suite. 35% discounts. AE, DC, MC, V. Amenities: 2 restaurants; teahouse; 24-hr. butler service; concierge; driving range; forex; health club; nightclub; indoor pool; sauna; free shuttle to city center. In room: A/C, satellite TV, DVD player, hair dryer, Internet, minibar

Jia Tai Hotel (Jia Tai Shi Shang Jin Ping Shang Wu Jiu Dian) This brand-new hotel opened in 2011. The rooms are large and attractively furnished. Although the staff do not speak any English, the front desk tries to be as helpful as it can. The location is slightly away from the action, just next to the river, above the Little Sheep restaurant.

122 Gulou Lu, behind Yuantong Temple. www.5091988.com. ✆ **0871/509-1988.** Fax 0871/512-5759. 44 units. ¥160 standard room; from ¥580 suite. In room: A/C, cable TV, Internet.

Yi-Ya Apartment Hotels (Yi Ya Yang Guang Lian Shou Jiu Dian) A small band of local entrepreneurs in Kunming have converted many vacant apartments into very nice guest rooms. While the office is on the sixth floor, the rooms are scattered all the way up to the 14th. Each one is uniquely furnished in the latest Chinese urban styles with huge comfortable beds and loads of amenities. You may have a balcony, a fridge, an automatic mah-jongg table with smoke extractor hood, or a DVD player. Head for Renmin Lu and look for the signs that say AC Enjoy. This huge circular complex has a number of entrances and you should look for door B. In the same building, if the Yi-Ya is full, try the I-Like Hotel (Ai Lai Ke Jiu Dian; ✆ **0871/808-0126**).

Room Number A120, A06th Floor, Aocheng Dasha, 39, Renmin Zhong Lu. www.yi-yasunkm.com. ✆ **0871/361-1555.** 33 units. ¥198 standard room. In room: A/C, TV Internet.

Where to Eat

The most famous Yunnan dish is **"crossing the bridge noodles"** *(guoqiao mixian)*, a hot pot consisting of steaming chicken broth to which you add thinly sliced chicken, pork, fish, other meats, vegetables, mushrooms, and rice noodles, all seasoned with peppers and chilies to taste. The oil on top keeps the simmering food hot enough to scald tongues, so be careful with your first bites! According to legend, the dish was invented over a century ago by the wife of a scholar who discovered that a layer of oil on top of her husband's food could keep it warm all the way from her kitchen across the bridge to a pavilion where he was studying for his imperial examinations, hence the dish's name. Another popular local dish is *qiguo ji* (chicken stewed with medicinal herbs). Along with a pharmacopoeia of allegedly healthful herbs and spices that are often used in many local dishes, Yunnan mushrooms are also valued for their medicinal qualities. Fried goat cheese, Yunnan sweet ham, and Yunnan coffee are some other local favorites.

Cannes Cafeteria (Jin Ga Na Xicanting) ★★ MEDITERRANEAN While this may not be Las Ramblas, Green Lake Park does have a relaxing Latin feel to it

Local Flavors

Just on the other side of the Yuantong Bridge are a number of holes in the wall serving excellent roast duck. The dish is so popular among locals that whole racks of birds are lined up for the oven every single day. Combined with a couple of fresh fruit juices, this makes an excellent choice for lunch.

at times, especially with all the pavement cafes. The owner of Cannes lived in Spain for more than 20 years and his extensive knowledge of the country's cuisine is reflected in the menu. The second floor is a great place to spend a lazy afternoon; the staff is friendly and the prices reasonable.

Cui Hu Bei Lu 78, Green Lake. ✆ **0871/519-9696.** Main courses ¥40–¥150. No credit cards. 11am–midnight.

Flying Tigers Restaurant (Fei Hu Lou) YUNNAN/CANTONESE Located in the old headquarters of the legendary Flying Tigers, this is as much a museum as restaurant, with all its military memorabilia displayed in showcases and along the corridors. Staff model eye-catching olive-drab uniforms, and the shark-mouthed P-40 hanging in the atrium adds the finishing touch. Be sure to inquire whether the new Flying Tigers museum is open yet.

45-48 Xiangyun Jie. ✆ **0871/3169-788.** No credit cards. 11am–9.30pm.

Jiu Ling Yang Sheng Guan ★★ CHINESE This sophisticated venue specializes in medicinal soups and wines. While these can be a little pricey, the food menu is surprisingly reasonable and full of innovation. Apart from favorites such as the barbecued fish (*jiu lin mi zi tian ma fen kao yu;* ¥38), and the wok-fired walnuts, beans, and ginkgoes (*yao shan chao san guo;* ¥28), we were really impressed by the shrimp and cucumber pancake (*xian xia qing gua luo;* ¥28), as well as the potato and ham flatcake (*tie bang yang yu ni;* ¥22). You'll have plenty left to take away for the train ride. For those who can read ancient Chinese characters, the menu is presented on both a bamboo scroll and also on temple shaker sticks (*chou qian*), as well as a picture menu for the rest of us.

Xiba Lu, Opposite Bai Yao Chang (medicine factory). ✆ **0871/419-1570.** Main courses ¥20–¥200. No credit cards. 11am–9:30pm.

Pu'er Talk JUICE/TEA In an interesting twist on the fruit juice stalls that are now popular along the side of the lake, this little place has a different spin on the famous Pu'er tea, now served with a selection of sweet fruit flavors including blueberry, lemon, ginger, and orange.

Cui Hu Nan Lu Zhong Duan. ✆ **0871/516-2526.** No credit cards. 24 hr.

Samoana (Sha Mu An Kafe Wu) WESTERN/PACIFIC ISLANDER Five generations ago, the owner's great-great-grandfather opened the first Chinese restaurant in the western Pacific, and so it only seemed appropriate that he should come and open a Samoan restaurant in China. The Warrior's breakfast is a great way to start the day, but the menu has so much more to choose from. Our faves include the pango pango tropical fruit cocktails and the Hawaiian Mud Pie. Check upstairs for an eccentric collection of vintage English language books for sale.

BeiChen Walkway, Section D, No 2. ✆ **0871/573-9231.** Main courses ¥30–¥80. No credit cards. 9am–7pm. Closed on Sundays.

Wicker Basket (Xing Xiang Kao Wu) BAKERY Probably the best value bakery in China, this is a definite shopping stop if you're about to board a long distance train to another province. As well as employing disabled locals, these guys make the best cookies this side of the Himalayas and at ¥12 for a bag of 10, the prices simply cannot be beaten. Look out for the muffins and the apple pies. Upstairs has a seating area and a full breakfast, lunch, and dinner menu.

BeiChen Walkway, Section D, No 1. ✆ **0871/573-0647.** Main courses ¥20–¥60. No credit cards. Mon–Sat 9am–8pm.

Kunming After Dark

The popular **Camel Bar (Luotuo Jiuba)** at Baita Lu 274 (✆ **0871/337-6255**) serves inexpensive beer and has live music on weekends. The local bar scene thrives at dark but trendy bar **The Hump,** Jinmabiji Square, Jinbi Rd. (✆ **0871/364-4197;** noon–2am or until last customer), has a full bar and posters of American pop and movie stars, and attracts loads of backpackers. For more sophisticated venues, try some of the bars around Green Lake, such as **Uprock** on 267 Xichang Lu (✆ **1580/881-5075**).

Around Kunming

See chapter 16 for Chinese translations of key locations.

Qiongzhu Si (Bamboo Temple) ★ Built in 639 and rebuilt from 1422 to 1428, this temple houses an incredibly vivid tableau of 500 arhats carved between 1883 and 1890 by Sichuanese sculptor Li Guangxiu and his six apprentices, who gave to each arhat a different and incredibly naturalistic facial expression and pose. It is thought that some of these arhats, who range from the emaciated to the pot-bellied, the angry to the contemplative, were carved in the images of the sculptor's contemporaries, friends, and foes. A wildly fantastical element dominates the main hall, where an arhat surfs a wave on the back of a unicorn, while another stretches a 3m (10-ft.) arm upward to pierce the ceiling.

12km (7 miles) northwest of town. Admission ¥40. 7:30am–5pm. Bus: 1 from Nanping Jie and Zhengyi Lu to Huangtu Po; transfer to miandi (van) taxis (¥10) for Qiongzhu Si.

Haobao Jing Organic Farm (Hao Bao Qing Sheng Tai Nong Ye Yuan) Slightly farther out of town is a 96-hectare (237-acre) farm and quasi-resort about 35km (22 miles) northwest of Kunming. In addition to delicious lunches that include produce freshly picked from their fields and organic chickens served to order, the farm has 20 rooms of farm-style accommodation for ¥88 to ¥188. Fresh organic strawberries and cherries are also available in season. Haobao supplies the Parkson and Trust-Mart supermarket chains in Kunming with organic vegetables and recently signed on to supply Wal-Mart supercenters. For English inquiries, contact Kunming-based Angela at Kunming-based Pesticide Eco-Alternatives Center (peac.office@gmail.com) for assistance.

Located at the east end of the Haobaoqing valley, near Tuanjie Village. You will see a large billboard just before the farm, which is located on the left side of the road. ✆ **0871/883-4533.** Free admission.

SHI LIN (STONE FOREST; 石林)

Located 90km (55 miles) southeast of Kunming in the Lunan Yi Autonomous County, Shi Lin is Kunming's most famous attraction—a giant forest of limestone rocks formed 270 million years ago when the ocean receded from this area. Millions of years of tectonic shifts and erosion from wind and rain have resulted in today's maze of sharp-edged fissures and sky-piercing pinnacles, which are punctuated by walkways, ponds, and pavilion lookouts. Fed by subterranean rivers, **Jianfeng Chi** is the only natural body of water in the forest. The reflection of the blue sky, white clouds, and swordlike stone peaks in the pond makes this one of the most photographed

Another, Quieter Stone Forest

About 8km (5 miles) northeast of the Stone Forest is the 300-hectare (741-acre) **Naigu Shilin Black Pine Stone Forest** (¥25), which predates the Stone Forest by about 2 million years. The park is a much quieter option; in fact, we only saw two other Western tourists the entire day that we were there. There are some interesting geological signs in English and the terrain varies from underground karst caves to magnificent black volcanic lookout points. On your own, catch a horse and cart for ¥25 from the main road outside the Stone Forest.

locales in the forest. **Shizi Ting (Lion Pavilion),** the highest point in the Stone Forest, and **Wangfeng Ting (Peak Viewing Pavilion)** offer the best panoramas.

This geological wonder is quite a sight if you've never before seen a petrified forest, but some visitors are more amazed at the immense parking lots and long lines at the ticket offices. It could be the hordes of tourists that tramp through here during the day, for the forest takes on a much more ethereal and mysterious quality only in the evening after the tour groups have left. The Stone Forest can be comfortably navigated in a 2½- to 3-hour loop with plenty of opportunities to get off the trodden path. An English-speaking tour guide can be hired for ¥100 but is not really necessary.

This area is also home to the Sani branch of the Yi minority group. Young Sani men and women (allegedly) in colorful costumes greet all arriving visitors and act as tour guides through the forest, while Sani vendors sell a variety of handicrafts and some very nice batiks. There are also Sani song and dance performances during the day and on most nights at the Minor Stone Forest (Xiao Shi Lin) right next to the Stone Forest. For early risers, the route down through the Sani village bypasses the ticket gates and means free entrance if you arrive before 8am. Otherwise it is ¥175 per person.

Although most people know Shilin as the Stone Forest, in 1998 the central government decided that the nearby City of Lunan should also be renamed to become Shilin City, even though it is a good 7 miles away from this world-famous tourist site. Despite its new name, **Lunan** remains a depressing hole of a city. The ticket price to the official park is now a whopping ¥175 and yet there is precious little to show for it.

MILE ★★

Yunnan Province, 143km (89 miles) SE of Kunming, 137km (85 miles) S of Luoping

While the old downtown of Mile (pronounced mee-luh) itself is dirty and soulless, the new area around the Huquan eco lake is an unexpected saving grace, and makes this little town well worth a visit. The city itself is dominated by the Hong He Corporation not only with their enormous cigarette factory on Hong Yan Lu, but dozens of other industrial plants, offices and worker residential blocks scattered all over the town. Fortunately the eastern new area has been built with an eco focus in mind and it is very attractive. Best of all, Mile is bang in the middle of stone forest country, where bizarre rock formations similar to those at Shilin abound, just waiting to be explored. Of the 23 nationalities that live in this area, the Yi people make up 30% of the total population. Weaving into the grand tapestry of Yi culture are the sub-groups of Yi, including the Axi, the Azhe, the Sanni, the Black Yi, and the White Yi.

Essentials

GETTING THERE The bus ride from Kunming East Station is an impressive 3 hours (¥40) though stone forest landscape. In fact there is a new direct highway being built, so traveling time should be reduced to around 2 hours when you make this spectacular journey. By 2015, the new train line will have cut that down to 30 minutes.

GETTING AROUND Mile abounds with taxis that charge a flat rate of ¥5 for most journeys within the city.

VISITOR INFORMATION There is a useful, but Chinese only map available for ¥5 at the Xinhua bookstore on Ran Weng Lu.

[FastFACTS] MILE

Banks, Foreign Exchange & ATMs **Bank Of China** is situated on Jishan Nan Lu just below the roundabout.

Post Office There is a small post office (9am–6pm) on the West Ring Road.

Visa Extensions The PSB office is at Shijin Street (✆ **0873/612-2420**), but it cannot handle visa extensions and will refer you to the provincial capital.

Exploring Mile

The old town is the usual hodge-podge of ugly city blocks and not really worth the effort of exploring. Despite this, many travelers find that a visit to the local supermarket provides an interesting insight into the locality. **Tian Tian Le Supermarket** on Ran Weng Lu is certainly no exception and unsurprisingly, stocks a huge selection of local wine, even including some interesting pear and blueberry varieties. Our personal top tip is the coconut coffee, which should please any sweet tooth.

The new area of town is just the opposite, built around a 495 acre (and growing) man-made ecological lake preserve, filled with clean clear spring water, and featuring lagoons, sandy beach fronts, and natural hot springs. While small minibuses run throughout the area, it is also very pleasant to walk around the edge of the lake.

Where to Stay

Hui Bing Lou Guest House (Hui Bing Lou Bing Guan) If you must stay in the old town, then this guest house is the most interesting option. Staff are dressed in Qing dynasty period costume and all the rooms feature replica antique furniture. It does not have the authenticity of the Linden Center, but it is much lower priced and good fun for tourists with a sense of humor

8 Jishan Bei Lu. www.mlhbl.com. ✆ **0873/612-2655.** 96 units. ¥100 standard room; from ¥388 suite. No credit cards. In room: A/C, TV, mini bar

Huquan Hotel (Huquan Jiu Dian) ★★★ This showcase resort remains one of the best bargains that you will find in all of China. It consists of four separate complexes, referred rather unimaginatively as A, B, C, and D. Block A is the five-star VIP area, while the others are built to a very attractive four-star standard and loaded with facilities. The whole complex surrounds the lake with all of the rooms having either a water or mountain view. In addition, there are at least 30 hot spring pools scattered over the hillside area, all freely available to guests. (¥60 per day for nonresidents).

Huquan Shen Tai Yuan. ✆ **0873/638-8888.** Fax 0873/638-8666 192 units. ¥350 standard room; ¥400 suite. No credit cards. Amenities: 3 restaurants; bar; concierge; room service, table tennis room, billiard room, gym, KTV, multifunctional halls, lecture rooms, tea room, hot springs, water park, fishing In room: A/C, TV, Internet.

Sui Yuan Hotel (Sui Yuan Bing Guan) If ¥350 for a five-star hotel is still out of your tight budget, then the Sui Yuan is a great alternative. Only 100m (109 yards) from the beach, it is far better value than the competitors that surround it. We really enjoyed the little touches here, like being able to feed the fish in the lobby pond. Best of all, it is just around the corner from Mile Story restaurant (below), with rooms at the rear looking out onto its courtyard garden.

Middle section Wenchuan Lu. ✆ **0873/622-2777.** 70 units. ¥100 standard room; ¥400 suite. No credit cards. In room: TV.

Where to Eat

In addition to Mile Story (below), on Jishan Bei Lu just east of the Hui Bing Lou Guest House is the small but trendy **Sense Restaurant.** This is a good place for lunch with lots of fried rice dishes and fresh fruit juices, but there's unfortunately no English menu. Near the supermarket, the **Jiayuan Bakery** has the best bread and cakes in town, although you might want to avoid the meat floss pancakes. The Huquan hotel (see above) has a number of restaurants with surprisingly good prices, including the **Shuyunjian,** with a wall poster picture menu and relaxing outdoor terraces. After your meal, hidden away on Wang Zhi Lu is an unexpected bar street with at least 20 or so bars that might be worth exploring (as well as some amazing water pipe carving shops).

Mile Story (Yunnan Hong Mile Gu Shi) ★★★ YUNNAN This is possibly the best restaurant in the whole guide, in terms of quality and value. Set in a beautiful garden courtyard, we ate here 3 nights in a row, always had at least four of their impressive dishes, and never paid more than ¥80 on each occasion. The huge picture menu (with English) is a culinary adventure in itself, especially since some things are still lost on translation. Prices range from ¥198 for crocodile stew, all the way down to ¥6 for sour soup with stewed pig brains. In between there is an enormous selection that will satisfy you for multiple visits, including the delicious melon balls in red wine sauce (¥22), deep fried red beans in green tea (¥12), and the unbelievably bourgeois fois gras fried rice (¥28).

Zhong Shan Lu (just around the corner from the Sui Yuan Hotel). ✆ **0873/622-2333.** Main courses ¥18–¥300. No credit cards. 5–11pm.

Around Mile

THE WESTERN ECOLOGICAL VINEYARD

Yunnan Red Chateau (Yunnan Hong Jiu Zhuang) Just on the side of the Kunming–Hekou highway, about 14km (8.7 miles) from Mile are the Yunnan Hong Vineyards. With more than 10,000 acres, this is the largest grape growing and processing base in southern China. In the '90s, the vines were finally identified as an old French species—Rose Honey, which had long disappeared in France. In 1866, an epidemic brought in from America with imported timber caused vineyards throughout France to be stricken by grape phylloxera, which resulted in the total extinction of Rose Honey, or so it was thought. Not only do these vineyards have the highest elevation and

Wine Tips

If you are visiting the winery or Mile Story, look out for the following vintages, which come highly recommended. "French Wild" is a 2003 vintage that retails at ¥198. For a white look out for "Crystal Dry White 99999," a 2006 vintage at ¥140.

lowest latitude in the world (this is the only wine production area above 1,500m), but it also boasts the earliest maturing grapes, the earliest new wine each year, and perhaps most importantly, the best quality sunshine in the world. Unsurprisingly, Yunnan Red has quickly become the largest single wine brand in southwestern China.

Five years ago, the company built a huge French style chateau in which to house its operations. For ¥10 you can have a guided tour (in Chinese) around the factory and the cellars, and a free tasting. The chateau itself is about what you would expect of a Chinese knock-off, and far more interesting is the chapel that they have built on the grounds. Visible from miles away, this replica Christian church does not hold any religious services, but is there so that wealthy Chinese families can enjoy the experience of a western wedding. There is even a handbook with instructions on what's included in a western marriage ceremony.

Dongfeng Town. Take a bus from Mile's old station for ¥6. The chateau is past the hotel and the "grape-seeding base." ✆ **0873/633-1888.** Admission ¥10. 8:30am–6pm.

Mile Temple (Mile Si) Silver Screen Mountain (Yinpin Shan), about 10km (6.2 miles) is a complex of temples is topped off by a 20m (65-ft.) statue of the Maitreya Buddha. The construction is all very recent and not much different from all the other thousands of temples that have sprung up to attract tourists in the last decade. Fortunately, there is a very clear farmers' track into the fields just to the right of the main ticket office, that comes out up near the Kassapa Hall. From here you can explore all the way up to the peak (the catacombs are especially eerie) without paying the extortionate ticket price. There are plenty of paths down the northern side of the mountain, and you can pick up one of the many buses back to Mile at the bottom.

Jin Ping Mountain. ✆ **0873/626-4399.** www.ynmls.com. Admission ¥60. 8:30am–6pm. Bus no 4 or 12 (¥5).

YU HUANG GE PARK (YU HUANG GE GONG YUAN)

In the northwest corner of town is a free entry temple complex with a tall pagoda that provides great views out onto Mile. Even more interesting is the Qinglai school campus directly behind the pagoda, which is one of the most impressive schools that I have ever seen in China. Cool. Modern architecture, plus a huge outdoor swimming lake complete with diving boards, I found this place even more interesting than the temple.

DALI 大理 ★★

Yunnan Province, 392km (243 miles) NW of Kunming, 15km (9 miles) N of Xiaguan, 150km (90 miles) S of Lijiang

The charming town of Dali, traditionally one of the best places in China to tune in, turn on, and drop out for a while, remains a wonderful place to visit. Its small size belies its important place in Yunnan's history: During the Tang dynasty (609–960),

Xiaguan's Market Treats

Most visitors completely ignore Xiaguan, but it has one of the best wet markets in the province on Weishan Road. Where else can you find rich opaque Weishan honey for just ¥20 per large jar? Depending on the season, look out for everything from semi tropical custard apples to high altitude giant snow peaches.

Dali was the capital of the Nanzhao Kingdom, and during the Song dynasty (960–1079), it was the capital of the Dali kingdom. Deserted after Kublai Khan overran Dali in 1252, it was reconstructed during the Ming dynasty (1382). Today's Dali is the capital of the Bai Autonomous Prefecture (although it's run from Xiaguan). Located in a mountain valley at an elevation of 1,948m (6,496 ft.), Dali is sunny year-round, though winter nights can be chilly. The best times to visit are between February and October, when the majority of festivals take place. The **Dali Folk Festival** now includes a rock festival featuring top rock bands from Kunming and Dali in May. The festival coincides with Dali's Third Moon Market, with scores of shops selling food, handicrafts, traditional Chinese medicines, and more (www.dali360.com).

Essentials

GETTING THERE All travelers arriving in Dali whether by plane, train, or bus first arrive in Xiaguan, the new part of Dali. The Dali airport (DLU), also named Dali Huangcaoba Airport, is 13km (8 miles) from Dali City. Dali's transportation hub is **Xiaguan,** 15km (9 miles) to the south. From the Dali Airport, another 15km (9 miles) northeast of Xiaguan, are daily **flights** to Kunming (40 min.) and Xishuangbanna (50 min.). From the airport to Dali is about a 1-hour taxi ride, which will cost up to ¥100. If you need to purchase additional plane tickets, take a taxi into Xiaguan for about ¥40 to ¥50 (or see the buses below) and go to the **Yunnan Airlines** ticket office (✆ **0872/231-5339**), located next to the railway station across from the China Telecom building. There is another outlet in the Cang Shan Fandian at Cang Shan Lu 118. Travel agencies or your hotel in Dali may be able to help you purchase airline tickets, but give them as much advance notice as possible and expect to pay a fee for the service.

From the railway station, bus no. 8 (45 min.; ¥3) runs to the West Gate of the old city in Dali, while bus no. 10 runs into Xiaguan. A taxi to the old town will cost ¥45. Tickets can be purchased at the train station office inside the main bus station on 21 Jianshe Lu, which is open 9am to 6pm. Returning to Kunming, trains depart Xiaguan at 7:26pm (arrive Kunming 5:10am), 8:24pm (arrive Kunming 6:10am), and 10:15 (arrive Kunming 7:10am).

The expressway between Kunming and Xiaguan has brought the 9-hour journey down to just 4 hours. Back in the 1980s, this route took a good 2 days, although for Marco Polo it was nearly 2 weeks. Most Dali-bound buses actually stop in Xiaguan, which has several bus stations, but the main one that travelers will likely use the most is the confusingly named **Dali Qiche Keyun Zhan** (✆ **0872/218-9330**) on Jianshe Lu. From here air-conditioned buses depart for Kunming (5 hr.) every half-hour; for Lijiang (3 hr.); and for Xianggelila/Zhongdian (6 hr.). In Dali, it's best to have a tourist cafe arrange your Dali-Kunming bus for ¥120, as they will take care of sending

Dali 大理

ATTRACTIONS ●

Nan Men Cheng
  Huang Mia **8**

Three Pagodas Park **1**
(Sān Tǎ Sì Gōngyuán)
三塔寺公园

Zhōnghé Temple **10**
中和寺

HOTELS ■

Jim's Tibetan Guest House **9**
(Jí Mú Zàng Shì Jiǔdiàn)
吉姆藏式酒店

Landscape Hotel **3**
(Lán Líng Gé Jiǔdiàn)
兰林阁酒店

Moonshine Inn **2**
(Cāng Yuè Bié Yuàn)
苍岳别院

RESTAURANTS ◆

The Bakery No. 88 **5**

Café de Jack **6**
樱花园

La Stella Pizzeria **4**
新星比萨房

Sweet Tooth **7**

Pagoda

TA Travel Agent

To Xiaguan

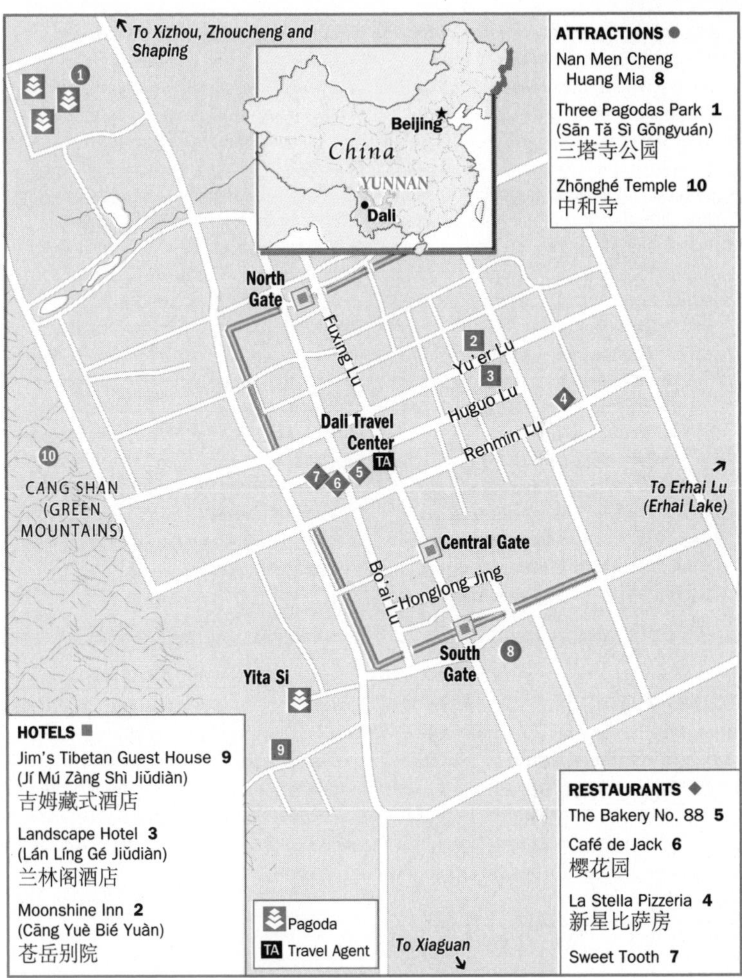

you to Xiaguan for the transfer. There is usually a ¥5 fee for this service. Buses to Lijiang also mostly originate out of Xiaguan. Again, the most hassle-free option is to have a travel agency or cafe book your ticket.

GETTING AROUND   The beauty of Dali is that the old town is so small that it's possible to walk from the North Gate (Bei Men) to the South Gate (Nan Men) in half an hour. To explore farther afield, **bikes** are the best way to get around and can be rented all along Bo'ai Lu for around ¥10 a day. A **taxi** to nearby sights such as the Three Pagoda Park or the Cang Shan chairlift will run between ¥20 and ¥50. Many visitors head for the Hui village of Weishan in the south, but Shaxi valley in the north is a far superior experience.

THE bai

Occupying the Er Hai Lake region for some 3,000 to 4,000 years, the Bai people are among the oldest and the second-largest minority group in Yunnan. Over 80% of the Bai, now numbering close to 1.4 million, live in Dali and the surrounding villages and countryside in what is known as the Bai Autonomous Prefecture. More than most minority groups, the Bai, who've had a long illustrious history throughout the Nanzhao and Dali kingdoms, are one of the best adapted to the Han majority. The Bai—the "white"—revere the color, which is regarded as noble and is the main color of their traditional dress.

The Bai celebrate many festivals, the largest of which is **Sanyue Jie** (Third Month Festival), which had its origins more than 1,000 years ago when Buddhist monks and adherents gathered to celebrate Guanyin's (the Goddess of Mercy) appearance to the Bai. Today's festival, which starts on the 15th day of the third lunar month (usually Apr or early May), has become more secular as the Bai and other minorities from around the area gather in the foothills of Cang Shan (Green Mountains) for 5 days and nights of singing, dancing, wrestling, horse racing, and large-scale trading of everything from Tibetan-made felt hats and silk floss to horses and medicinal herbs. Raosanling, which involves a procession to three nearby temples, is held between the 23rd and the 25th days of the fourth lunar month (usually May). Huoba Jie (the Torch Festival) is held on the 24th day of the sixth lunar month (usually July) and involves the parading of flaming torches through homes and fields. There are also fireworks and dragon boat races.

TOURS & GUIDES Many of the Dali cafes provide a variety of tours, including a **boat trip** on Er Hai Lake that costs ¥50 to ¥100 per person, depending on group size; or **horseback riding** to a mountain monastery or local Bai village for about ¥60 to ¥100 per person. Local English-speaking guides can be hired through cafes for about ¥50 to ¥100 per hour, or around ¥300 per day. The **Dali Travel Center,** next to the Golden Flower Hotel (Huguo Lu 76; ✆ **0872/267-1282**), offers all the above services and also sells bus tickets to local destinations.

[Fast FACTS] DALI

Banks, Foreign Exchange & ATMs The **Bank of China** (Mon–Fri 8am–6pm) is at Fuxing Lu 333. It has a number of ATMs.

Internet Access Many cafes offer Internet access including the **Tibetan Cafe** at Renmin Lu 58.

Post Office The post office (8am–6pm) is at the corner of Fuxing Lu and Huguo Lu. There are two post offices in Dali Old Town. One is on the corner of Fuxing Lu and Yang Ren Jie. The second is about a 600m (1,970-ft.) walk out of the East Gate on the left-hand side.

Visa Extension These are available in Xiaguan at the **Gonganju (PSB),** located at Tianbao Jie 21 (✆ **0872/216-6090;** Mon–Fri 8:30–11am and 2:30–5pm). An extension of the normal tourist visa can be done in 5 working days. To get to the PSB office from Dali old town, take bus no. 8 and get off at the north bus station; walk another 400m (1,312 ft.) and you'll see a building with a large steel Eiffel Tower on top. Here your China visa can be extended twice with few questions asked.

Free Maps

An American company produces excellent free maps for Dali, Yangshuo, and Guilin. Check out their website at **www.trax2.com** for details.

Exploring Dali

Old town Dali, with its 9m-high (30-ft.) battlements, dates from the Ming dynasty (1368–1644), but the current wall was restored and extended only in 1998 as part of a project to gentrify Dali and attract tourists. From the top of the freshly painted **Nan Cheng Men** (**South City Gate;** ¥2; 8am–9pm), are some lovely views of the town and the Cang Shan to the west. You can also walk along the restored city wall to **Xi Men (Western Gate)** and if you climb the stairs at the southwestern corner, you can avoid the small entrance fee.

Dali's charm is that visitors still can see the original residents slowly going about their daily business, as if traveling back in time. Old people move slowly through the main thoroughfares like from a long-gone era, but always responding positively to any attempt we might make to interact with them.

Foreigner Street is a photo-op must for domestic tourists and has expanded rapidly, but if you prefer not to be on display, **Renmin Lu** is a little more laid-back. The **Hong Longjing** is certainly the most photogenic part of the town while those looking for a little solitude might try the west wall, where local and international students practice their tai chi.

San Ta Si Gongyuan (Three Pagodas Park) ✋ About 2km (1¼ miles) northwest of town at the foot of the Cang Shan, Dali's most famous landmark has unfortunately become a massive tourist trap (in 5 years, ticket prices have increased from ¥10 to ¥180). The central pagoda, the statuesque 16-story, 69m-high (226-ft.) **Qianxun Ta,** resembling Xi'an's Small Goose Pagoda, was built first between 824 and 859 and is a hollow square brick structure with graceful eaves. A popular photo op is from a small lake in the northeast corner of the park that captures the reflections of all three pagodas in a stunning tableau. Apart from that one particular vista, the rest of the site is overrated. The monastery itself was destroyed in the Qing dynasty, and what you see today dates only from 1999.

San Ta Gongyuan. Admission ¥180. 8am–7pm.

Nan Men Cheng Huang Miao ★ Just a few hundred yards to the east of South Gate is a small local temple that remains a center of local tradition for the Bai community. During June especially, women from all the local villages make the trek here to celebrate the successful completion of rice planting. Mostly this involves cooking offerings for the temple gods and long chanting sessions. Beyond the haze of incense and camp fire smoke, this is a colorful lively scene that is unknown to most tourists.

Yita Lu., next to Hucheng Stream. Free admission.

Shopping

Dali's growing season is almost never ending and **fruit** here is nothing like you see in the average supermarket. Watch out for peaches so large that they would frighten even Roald Dahl, sweet syrupy figs, and dozens of different apple-pear combinations. Also be on the lookout for dozens of varieties of mushroom.

Hundreds of shops in town sell Dali **marble,** famous for its beautiful cloudlike patterns and anti-corrosive nature; the marble is now even more in demand because the practice of quarrying from the Cang Shan has been officially prohibited. For now, most of it comes in the unfortunate form of cheap tacky ashtrays, but a growing number of sculptors are setting up studios in the area, which could be promising. Other local specialties include **sliced walnut vases and lampshades,** but a block of **Pu'er tea** might be a little wiser. As always, comparison shop before you commit to anything: A piece of batik on Huguo Lu can sometimes cost 10% to 20% more than another along Fuxing Lu (or vice versa). For **batiks,** you can usually get better prices in the wholesale factories and workshops in Zhou Cheng (see below). In stores, it's not uncommon to bargain to half or two-thirds of the asking price.

A **market** visit is highly recommended for a sense of local color. Many of the markets around Dali are scheduled according to the lunar calendar, so check with the local cafes before you set out. Dali itself has a market every 7 days (usually on the 2nd, 9th, 16th, and 23rd days of the lunar month). Once the most popular, the **Shaping market,** held every Monday, has become a bit of a commercialized circus. The town of **Wase** on the eastern shores of Er Hai Lake also has a popular market every 5 days from 9:30am to 4pm. Foodstuffs and produce are the main goods here, as the market still caters to locals instead of tourists. The easiest way to visit is to sign up with a local cafe that will arrange round-trip transportation for around ¥50 per person.

Where to Stay

Accommodations can be scarce during festivals and also in June and July, so be sure to book your hotel ahead of time if you plan to visit then.

Jim's Tibetan Guest House (Ji Mu Zang Shi Jiudian) ★ This is one of the best hotel choices in town. The location, a bit off the beaten track, is more than made up for by the levels of service, interior design, and imagination on the part of the owners (one of the owners is Kampa Tibetan, the other Dutch). Rooms are bright and colorful as well as comfortable, but often booked solid with Western tour groups. This is also a great place to eat. For four people or more, go for the Tibetan smorgasbord at ¥30 per person. We counted at least 16 dishes as well as a delicious dessert. You may want to keep away from Jim's No. 1 Whiskey, a local moonshine whose harshness is disguised by a few local herbs, but would probably be better in a tractor carburetor than in some unwary tourist's stomach.

Yu Xiu Lu Zhong Duan 13, Lu Yu Xiaoqu. www.china-travel.nl. ✆ **0872/267-7824.** Fax 0872/266-1822. 14 units. ¥180 standard room. No credit cards.

Moonshine Guest house (Cang Yue Bie Yuan) ★★ Slightly away from the action, Moonshine is a modern take on traditional Bai architecture. Three floors of elaborate wood carving and attractive stonework come together around a small family courtyard. The top floor offers spectacular views of the Cang Shan. The local family that runs this place is especially charming.

16 Yu Er Xiang, off Yu Er Lu (walk down Yu Er Rd. toward Erhai Lake [east]. About 2 blocks past the Landscape Hotel you will see a small alley on your left. About 46m (150 ft.) down the alley and on your right you will find the Inn.). ✆ **1398/850-7390.** 12 units. ¥100–¥150 standard room. AE, DC, MC, V. In room: TV.

Where to Eat

Baba is sold all around northwest Yunnan, where it mostly consists of a piece of flat rice dough grilled or fried and flavored with salty and spicy seasonings. In Dali, the

munching ON FLOWERS

Visitors cannot help but notice that many of the dishes on display in Dali eateries are colorful local blooms, and while we Westerners may not be used to chowing down on petals and flowers, in Yunnan, this is an integral part of the local cuisine. Here are 10 introductory examples for you to try yourself.

- ***Bai bu juan chao rou:*** White azalea flowers stir-fried with diced pork.
- ***Bai du juan dou fu tang:*** White azalea flower soup with tofu cubes.
- ***Bai du juan yu tou tang:*** White azalea flower soup with sliced taro.
- ***Chao si hua:*** Assorted blooms (honeysuckle, golden osmanthus, and pomegranate petals, for example) stir fried with chilies.
- ***Hai cai hua yu er tang:*** Erhai seaweed flower soup with sliced taro.
- ***Qing chao hua cai hua:*** Stir-fried Erhai seaweed flowers.
- ***San hua chao dan bin:*** Rose petals, jasmine petals, and pineapple broom petals lightly fried into a crispy omelet.
- ***Shi liu hua chao rou:*** Stir-fried pomegranate petals with diced pork.
- ***Xian huang hua chao tian jiao:*** Stir-fried Asiatic lilies and sweet red peppers.
- ***Ye shan ju zhou:*** White azalea flower rice porridge.

Flower vocabulary has even made it into everyday greetings. Among the Bai, for example, attractive ladies are known as golden flowers (jin hua), a lovely alternative to the usual "xiaojie" or "fu yuen" that are commonly used to address waitresses or service staff. Bai men on the other hand, are referred to as "a-peng ge."

dough is stuffed with salted vegetables, sweet sauce, chili sauce, crushed peanuts, and *youtiao* (fried, salty doughnut) and grilled to tender perfection. This "Dali calzone" is one of the most popular breakfast items, often sold on street corners like Huguo Lu and Fuxing Lu. Other typical local dishes include *shaguo yu* (stewed fish casserole) and the Bai specialty, *rushan* (milk fan), a delicious local goat's cheese sliced in thin layers and fried until "rubbery."

The foreigners' cafes clustered along Huguo Lu and Bo'ai Lu serve inexpensive and generally tasty Western, Chinese, Bai, and Tibetan meals. **Cafe de Jack** at Bo'ai Lu 82 (✆ **0872/267-1572**) has recently been refurbished, but as yet the reliability of the menu does not match the new decor. It is mostly standard backpacker fare, with more focus on burgers and pancakes than local Bai cuisine. Tony at **La Stella Pizzeria** at 21 Huguo Lu (✆ **0872/267-9251**) is one of the friendliest guys that you will meet in China, serves excellent pizza, and does a very generous goat's cheese and tomato salad.

Sweet Tooth, at the corner of Renmin Lu and Bo'ai Lu (Mon–Sat 10am–10pm), is wildly popular with foreigners but sees very few domestic customers. Set up by an American entrepreneur to provide jobs for Dali's deaf community, Sweet Tooth's traditional chocolate chip cookies are just what a stressed traveler needs (though their huge slabs of Oreo cheesecake will make you wonder if you are still in China). Even better is **The Bakery No. 88 ★★★**, 52 Bo'ai Lu (✆ **0872/267-9129;** www.bakery88.com). Delicious fresh-baked European breads (try the walnut and potato bread), imported and local cheeses, great juice, and fresh-baked croissants make this a great place for breakfast, lunch, and especially takeaways for the bus.

Around Dali

Please turn to chapter 16 for Chinese translations of key locations.

CANG SHAN (GREEN MOUNTAINS; 苍山)

Running down the west side of Dali, the 42km-long (25-mile) Cang Shan mountain range with its 19 peaks (a number of them permanently snow-covered), 18 streams, and acres of verdant forests, is well worth exploring, even though an army of old men is scattered throughout the mountain area to make sure that tickets have been purchased. The easiest way to ascend the mountain is by chairlift (8:30am–6:30pm), a lovely ride for ¥30 up and¥60 down. It offers some of the loveliest vistas of the old town and the shimmering blue Er Hai Lake in the distance. (From the western gate of the old town, head north until you see the sign for the chairlift; or take a taxi for ¥10.) At the chairlift's upper terminus is **Zhonghe Si,** a not particularly memorable temple. At the upper terminus the sign for the **Highlander Guest House** (www.higherland.com/index2.htm; ✆ **0872/266-1599**) says 100m (328 ft.); what it doesn't say is that it's 100m (328 ft.) straight up. Due to its location, the guest house has superb potential and will one day be a star attraction, but not yet. Until then, expect spartan rooms that could definitely do with a new coat of paint.

Several trails branch out from Zhonghe Si. Hiking options in the Cang Shan range include trips to lakes, waterfalls, mountain peaks, and temples. For those looking for a leisurely hike, the Cloud Pass is an easy choice. The stone path is fairly flat and winds around six mountains, past five waterfalls and three temples. Side trails jut out from the Cloud Pass near the waterfalls and lead upward to clear pools, more waterfalls, and excellent vistas. Stretching about 20km (12 miles), Cloud Pass can also provide a nice workout. With road signs and plenty of other hikers, there is no danger of losing your way.

Another option if you don't have time to make a day of it is the trek through pretty terrain to **Fengyan Dong (Phoenix Cave),** which takes you through the back of Longquan Mountain (about an hour each way). There's also a vigorous 11km (7-mile), 4½- to 5-hour hike to **Gantong Si,** a temple first built in 900 on the southern slope of Yingsheng Peak. The road down the mountain from Gantong Temple will take you back to the main road, from where you can take a taxi or bus no. 4 back to Dali. Another trail leads to the lovely **Qingbi Xi** in the valley between Malong and Shengying peaks. Flowing through three large ponds, this stream eventually empties into Er Hai.

ER HAI HU (ER HAI LAKE; 洱海湖)

East of Dali and north of Xiaguan, Er Hai Hu, named after its resemblance to a human ear *(er),* is one of the seven largest freshwater lakes in China and the second largest in Yunnan after Dian Chi in Kunming. Originating in the Heigu Shan mountains to the northwest and fed partially by the 18 streams of Cang Shan, the lake spans 42km (25 miles) from north to south, and 7km (4 miles) from east to west, and has an average depth of 10m (33 ft.). Many settlements and towns are scattered around the lake, along with some tourist traps on the eastern side. ***Warning:*** Some recent travelers have reported that the lake was unsafe for swimming as it contained

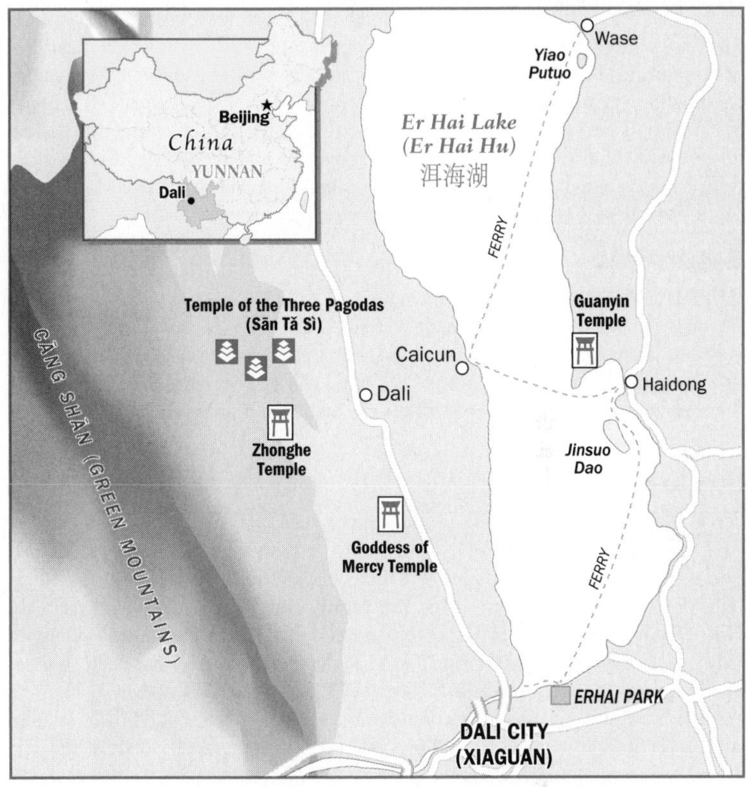

the schistosomiasis (bilharzia) parasite; unfortunately, accurate up-to-date information on the situation is hard to come by.

However, a **boat ride ★** on the lake is an option. Giant tourist boats charge ¥90 to make a 3½- to 4-hour run of the lake from the Taoyuan Matou (dock) in Zhou Cheng to Xiaguan, stopping along the way at **Putuo Dao, Guanyin Ge (Guanyin Pavilion),** and **Jinsuo Dao,** an island full of caves and caverns and inhabited by Bai fishermen. You can also negotiate with smaller private boats, which charge an average of ¥100 to ¥200 for the round-trip; or get a travelers' cafe in town to help you with any special arrangements. Do not be tempted to stay on the other side of the lake. The area around Shuanglang has horrendous roads and poor transportation connections. Even worse, the accommodation in this area is extremely mediocre. **Sky and Sea Lodge** (Dajianpang Village; ✆ **0872/246-1672**) is hidden away in a maze of back alleys and dead ends. **The Lady Four Hotel** (✆ **0872/246-1468**) is the pet project of local celebrity Yang Li Ping, famous for her peacock dance, but with rather dreary lake-view rooms costing a massive ¥680 and rats running around all over the place, this too should be avoided.

XIZHOU 喜州 ★★

Yunnan Province, 315km (196 miles) NW of Kunming, 25km (15 miles) NW of Dali

The town of Xizhou is finally starting to flower. Historically, this was a military fortress of the Nanzhao Kingdom and a temporary palace. Because of its favorable geographical situation, the town thrived prior to 1949 when there were more than 140 nationalist families, collectively known as the "Xizhou Chamber of Commerce," flourishing here. It now showcases incredibly well preserved Bai architecture that feature capacious courtyards and peaceful streets with a calmness and elegance typical in ancient times. See chapter 16 for Chinese translations of key locations.

Essentials

GETTING THERE Buses from the bottom of Yu Er Lu in Dali to Xizhou run every 20 minutes (¥10) and will drop visitors at an attractive residential development that is Xizhou's new face to the outside world. From here you can take a horse and cart directly to the Linden Center at the back of the village or explore some of the other fine examples of architecture here. **Bikes** can be rented from several cafes for around ¥15 a day.

Exploring Xizhou

While Dali started out as a hodgepodge of home-stays and cafes, the Linden Cultural Center (see below) in Xizhou is leading the way in terms of professional restorations. The three most popular examples of Bai architecture for domestic tourists and the "must-sees" on package tours are the **Yan family compound** (Yan Jia Taiyuan), the **Hou family compound** (Hou Jia Taiyuan), and the **Dong's compound** (Dong Jia Taiyuan). Admission ranges from ¥50 to ¥120 depending on what has been arranged by the tour group. Each of these follows the typical Bai design, known as "Sanfang Yizhaobi" (a courtyard with rooms on three sides and a screen wall on the remaining side) and "Sihe Wutianjing" (one big courtyard with four smaller ones at the four corners). According to the tradition of Bai-style architecture, the screen wall should face east in order to make use of the early morning sun and reflect the light into the inner rooms. The Yan's compound, built in the 1920s, lies in the central part of Xizhou. It is made up of five courtyards from north to south, including an independent three-storied Western-style building. Each of the houses puts particular emphasis on designing an elaborate front gate and many offer shows for the tourist trade. An interesting element is the "Sandaocha," a traditional regional tea ceremony consisting of three unique tea flavors. The host begins by presenting a bitter tea that stands for the hardships in life. Then a sweet tea of sesame and walnut symbolic of happiness in life. Finally, a bitter, sweet, and spicy tea symbolic of a more pensive lifestyle.

Behind the Linden Center grow two ancient but vibrant elms that symbolize the prosperity of the area and are known locally as Feng-Shui trees. It is said that one represents the forces of yin while the other represents yang. One grows new branches and leaves while the other is shedding leaves. An even older tree is just to the northeast of the town, which plays host to snow-white bitterns in the autumn months.

About 7km (4 miles) north of Xizhou, the village of **Zhou Cheng** is famous for its **tie-dyed batiks ★**. The minute you step off the bus, you'll be approached by Bai women who will invite you to visit their batik workshops. This is worth considering, as you can often pick up batik tablecloths or shirts for considerably less than you would pay in the shops in Dali—subject to bargaining, of course. There is also a local

market in the center of town; uphill from there, part of the old town is worth exploring. Catch an Eryuan-bound bus from either Dali or Xizhou.

Where to Stay & Eat

The Linden Cultural Center (Xi Lin Yuan) ★★★ 🎁 Described by visitors as "breathtakingly beautiful," this is definitely one of the top three places to stay in all of China. The Center is intended as a sort of cultural retreat, offering classes in traditional Chinese calligraphy and painting, meditation, and sweeping views of Xizhou's rice fields. The Lindens deal Asian antiquities and contemporary Chinese art at their gallery in Wisconsin, and have an impressive selection of their collection on display at the Center. They are already renovating a second complex elsewhere in the village that will be a workshop for local artisans and craftspeople from around the world. For the time being, there is plenty here to keep you occupied. The gardens are especially relaxing, the library is extensive, and the rooms themselves are filled with endless little details that make for a transformative experience. The restaurant here is also your best choice in town.

5, Chengbei. www.lindens.cn. ✆ **0872/245-2988.** Fax 0872/245-3699. 14 units. ¥830 standard room. ¥1,130 family suite. AE, DC, MC, V. Amenities: Restaurant; bar; children's area; entertainment room; gallery; gym; library; meditation room; music room. In room: Hair dryer, heater fans.

Yang Jia Yong Xiang Ju If the Linden Center is slightly out of your price range, a budget option is just next door. This locally run guesthouse has passable rooms that are furnished in a rather ugly style, but has amazing wooden arches in each of the rooms and a main door that will blow you away. If on a tight budget, you might opt to stay here, but spend your days in the library next door or out on the Linden's back patio.

Opposite Wenle Garden. ✆ **0872/245-2361.** 10 units. ¥100 standard room. No credit cards. In room: TV.

SHAXI 沙溪 ★★★

Yunnan Province, 524km (325 miles) NW of Kunming, 132km (82 miles) NW of Dali

Deep in the heart of Shaxi valley, Sideng village square is the only surviving temple way-station along the old tea and horse caravan trail that linked Southern China through the Himalayas, to Nepal and India. Today, around 22,000 people, 80% of them Bai, live in the Shaxi valley, most still working in agriculture. The local government is trying hard to avoid the type of mass tourism found in nearby Dali and Lijiang whose primary beneficiaries are outside entrepreneurs. Lijiang already sees 10 million visitors per year. Shaxi Valley, on the other hand, is lucky if it sees 10,000—making it a firm favorite with overseas visitors interested in conservation and sustainable development. In addition, the locals claim 300 days of sunshine per year, but also four distinct seasons every single day. It will be interesting to see how long this sanctuary lasts, as just last year the school in the middle of the old town was sold to the owner of the Landscape Hotel in Dali for a cool $1,000,000. One can only guess as to what kind of changes that will bring.

Arriving by the right door

When arriving in old town, ask the driver to drop you at the East Gate (Dong Men) by the river, as this is a much better entrance than from the main street.

Essentials

GETTING THERE **Buses** from Dali Old Town to the nearest large town of Jianchuan, are approximately hourly and take about 3½ hours (¥40), although this is often 5 hours plus due to the massive roadworks on this stretch. Buses drop visitors in a small square outside a supermarket in the small village of Diannan from where it is a 40-minute bus ride (¥10) into Shaxi Valley. Buses start from the North Bus Station near the PSB, but you can flag one down outside the South Town Complex near the bottom of Yu Er Lu.

Taxis will take you into the valley for around (¥60). There are buses from Jianchuan to Lijiang (2 hr.; ¥25), but the bus station area of Jianchuan, like most towns is only worth visiting to catch the bus. Accommodation owners in Shaxi can also organize transportation in advance but you can expect to pay at least ¥600 for a private car from Lijiang. Getting back to Dali, I much prefer the bus down to Yangbi, which is far more scenic and much faster that the main road. From Yangbi it is easy to transfer to Xiaguan.

GETTING AROUND Shaxi is a small, less developed valley with few regular taxis. For arriving and departing, arrange transportation through Mr. Wu at the Dragonfly (see below). For visits to the various sights, hiking, biking, or horse riding is the best option.

Shaxi Old Town ★

The Shaxi old town was placed on the watch list of the world's 101 most endangered sites released by the World Monuments Fund (WMF). Not long after, Switzerland Technological University began working to recover the prosperity of the ancient bazaar, as part of the Shaxi rehabilitation project in 2002, hoping to restore the decaying but beautiful Bai houses in a traditional and sustainable way. So far they have completed the open air theater (with a small museum currently housed in the north and south wings), the old **Sideng Market Square,** and the **Ming Dynasty Xingjiao temple,** the only Azhali Buddhism Temple built by the Bai people. Be sure to check out the ceiling of the theater and Kuixing, the god of culture housed on the top floor, so that you can do a comparison with the Dragonfly (see "Dragonfly Homestay," below). The regular Friday market now takes place on the main street, rather than the tiny marketplace. The temple, theater, and surrounding buildings are especially calm first thing in the morning and so if you plan to practice a little tai chi in China, this might well be the best place to try. All of the above are currently free admission.

Around Shaxi ★★★

Shaxi lies just below the forest covered hills of **Shibaoshan ★★**, famous for its Indian-influenced rock hewn sculptures and its Buddhist temples dating from the

Secret Spots

Just a few minutes' walk north of Diannan on the road to Jianchuan is a fascinating collection of traditional brick kilns where you can still see blindfolded buffalo preparing the clay by tromping around in circles. At the back of the complex is a charming old temple that very few visitors even know exist.

HOTELS ■
Laomadian Guest House **2**
(Lǎo mǎ diàn)
老马店

ATTRACTIONS ●
Xingjiao Temple **1**
(Xīng jiào sì)
兴教寺

Taxi Drop-off

Zhao Family
Compound

Benzhu
Temple

North Tibetan Alley

Old Ouyang
Entrance Gate

Parking

Sun's
Gate ■

East Alley

0   65 ft
0   20 m

Sideng Market Square
寺登四方街

East Gate ■

Pingdian Rd.

South Tibetan Alley

South
Gate ■

Hei Hui River

RESTAURANTS ◆
Allen's Cafe **4**
(Allen's kā feī)
咖啡

Old Pagoda Tree Cafe **3**
(Lǎo guái shù kā feī)
老槐树咖啡

Yujin Bridge

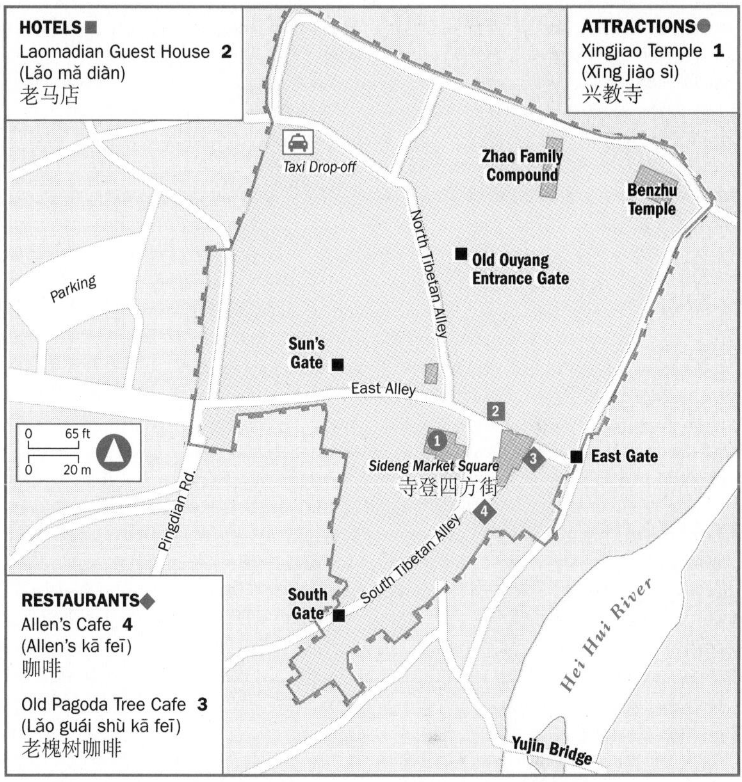

Nanzhao and Dali kingdoms (649–1053). The rich bio diversity of this area meant that Shibao Mountain was designated as the first important National tourist scenic area in China by the State Council as far back as 1982. This ideal hiking territory is our preferred choice over other more famous locations such as Tiger Leaping Gorge and the Meili Snow Mountains. At the **Shizhong Temple,** 139 artfully carved statues of Buddha reside in a total of 16 grottoes. Farther along the valley is the **Baoxiang Temple (Bao Xiang Si)** ★, a hanging temple spectacularly but precariously located on the cliff face. Be warned, the stone steps that ascend to the site are almost as formidable as they appear. In addition, watch out for the colony of 300 or so wild monkeys that live here and make the steep inclines look like child's play. You might even want to take some fruit with you for these guys. We think the best spot in the valley is at the southern extreme, a protected pond known as White Dragon Spring **(Bailongtan).** From Shi'ao (stone turtle) Bridge, head up to the ridge and look for the old pagoda. From there you will be able to see the old growth area of trees that surrounds the spring. You can bike down here, have a picnic lunch on the water's edge, and hike up into the surrounding hills. A more strenuous day trip is out to the small Bai mountain village **Mapingguan,** where a recently restored wind and rain bridge was a popular crossing point on the Tea Horse Road. Simply pottering around

Beware of the Dark

If you are staying in a rural homestay or a small village, make sure that you pack a flashlight so that you can find your way home at night. There is nothing worse than emerging from a local tavern after a few drinks and some good conversation only to find that it is pitch black outside.

the rice fields here is a rewarding experience. There is a timeless nature to this area, unspoiled by tourists.

Where to Stay & Eat

While the old town does have a good selection of guest houses, we personally prefer the peace and quiet of the **Dragonfly Homestay ★★★**, run by Mr. Wu (who speaks impeccable English) and his wife in Duanjiadeng village (✆ **1357/785-1712;** www.teahorse.net; ¥150), a couple of kilometers upstream from the old town. This is one of the most unique Chinese buildings where you may ever have the pleasure to stay. The focus point is the most beautiful four-story community temple that was originally built in 1735. There are chairs and tables on the temple stage, and there may be no better place in all of China to have a coffee and check your e-mail than the second floor of this authentic Qing dynasty temple. Two primary school classrooms have been converted into five cozy guest rooms, each with private porches at the rear. Mr. Wu's wife serves delicious home cooking in the main building. Full spread dinners of half a dozen local dishes cost ¥35 per person, and she can whip up a variety of delicious breakfasts from noodles to pancakes. Best of all, nearly everything is locally produced—even the rice comes from the family's fields just outside the door. In summer you might opt to catch your dinner at one of the local fish farms and bring it back to the Dragonfly for preparation.

Down in the old town, **Lao Ma Dian,** Sideng Jie (✆ **0872/472-2666**), just off the square, has an interesting if somewhat expensive restaurant with good Western food for about ¥60 per person.

LIJIANG 丽江 ★

Yunnan Province, 527km (316 miles) NW of Kunming, 150km (90 miles) NW of Dali

Located in the northwest part of Yunnan Province, this capital of the Lijiang Naxi Autonomous County (pop. 302,000) is home to the Naxi people (who constitute almost 60% of its population) and to a smaller number of Bai, Tibetan, Yi, Mosu, and Han peoples. Though its history dates from the Warring States (475–221 B.C.), its most influential period was when it was governed by Naxi chieftains during the Ming dynasty (1368–1644).

In February 1996, an earthquake hit Lijiang, killing over 300 people, injuring 17,000 more, and destroying 186,000 homes, comprising much of the city. Amazingly, many of the traditional Naxi houses held up quite well, leading the government in its reconstruction process to pour millions of yuan into replacing concrete buildings with traditional wooden Naxi architecture. The World Bank came up with rebuilding funds, and Lijiang was conferred with the ultimate imprimatur (some would say the kiss of death) as a UNESCO World Heritage town in 1999. All this attention plus the

Lijiang 丽江

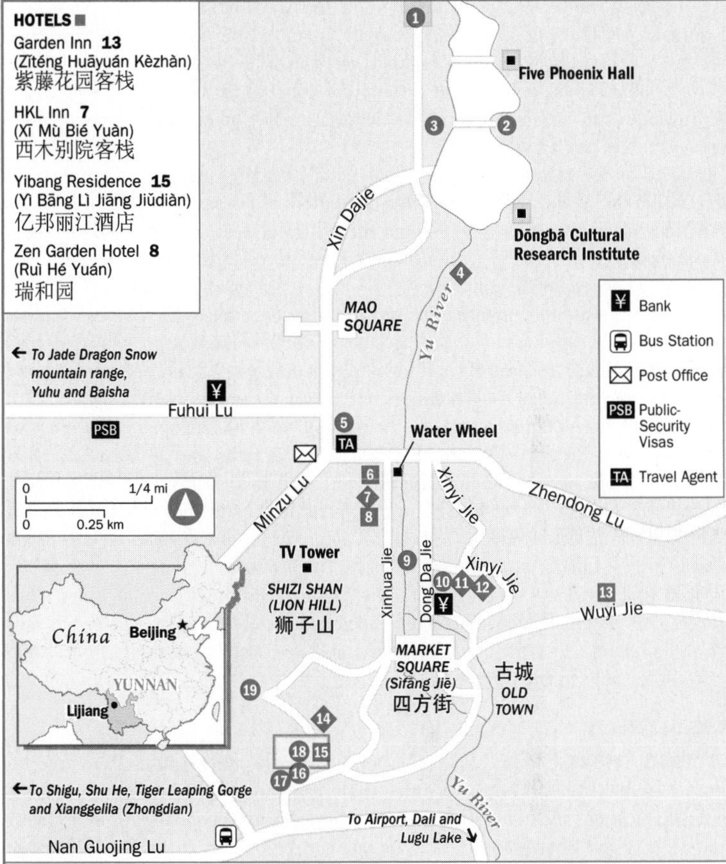

ATTRACTIONS ●

Black Dragon Pool Park **3**
(Heilóng)
黑龙潭公园

Dōngbā Gōng **9**
东巴宫

Dōngbā Wénhuà Bówùguǎn **1**
(Museum of Nàxī Dōngbā Culture)
东巴文化博物馆

Mù's Residence (Mù Fǔ) **18**
木府

The Nature Conservancy's Lijiang Visitor Center **16**
(Dà Zì Rán Bǎo Hù Xié Huì Lì Jiāng Bàn Gōng Shì)
大自然保护

Nàxī Music Academy **10**
(Nàxī Gǔyuè Huì)
纳西古乐会

Red Indian Outdoor Clothing Store **5**
(Yìn Dì'Ān Rén Hù Waì Diàn)
印第安人户外店

Tea-Horse Road Museum **2**
(Chá Mǎ Gǎ Daò Bó Wù Guǎn)
茶马古道博物馆

Tourist Information Center **17**
(Lìjiāg Yoú Kè Zhōng Xīn)
丽江游客中心

Wàngǔ Lóu **19**
万古楼

RESTAURANTS ◆

Dōngbā House **12**
东巴豪斯客栈

Nàxī Fēngwèi Xiǎochī **7**
纳西风味小吃

Nordic Delight Cafe **4**
(Nuòdìkè Kāfeī)
诺蒂克咖啡

N's Kitchen **11**
(èr'Loú Xiaǒ Chú)
二楼小厨

Shùn Shuǐ Loú Cāntīng **14**
顺水楼餐厅

construction of a new airport and hotels has turned it into a major tourist destination. Lijiang's old town, with its cobblestone streets, gurgling streams, and Naxi architecture, thankfully preserves a modicum of traditional ways, but as Han merchants move in to cater to hordes of stampeding tourists, many of the Naxi who still live there (about 6,000 households) are finding their old way of life being challenged. Lijiang's commercialization has emerged as a source of concern for UNESCO, encouraging them to put it on "examination" status (along with five other Chinese sites), which may eventually result in de-listing.

Located on the road to Tibet in a region widely regarded as being one of the most beautiful in the world, Lijiang also offers a plethora of fascinating side trips that can easily take up to a week or more of your time. Lijiang (elev. 2,340m/7,800 ft.) has a pleasant climate year-round with average temperatures in the spring, summer, and fall ranging between 60°F and 80°F (16°C–27°C). Spring and fall are the best times to visit, as the summer months are unbelievably crowded with Chinese tourists, busier even than the big-city shopping areas. Officially there is an ¥80 "Old Town Preservation Ticket" to enter the old town, this is only sporadically enforced. You will however need your ticket to gain entrance to many of the surrounding sights.

Despite its overcommercialization, the ancient town of Lijiang is still a must see on every tourists itinerary. The presence of a huge Pizza Hut and 24-hour KFC (Starbucks will also be here by the time this guide is published) at the very entrance to the old town, should give you an idea of how rampant profiteering has affected this magical little Naxi enclave. Even so, there is still plenty to see and despite the crowds and inflated prices, Lijiang is still well worth a few nights stay.

Most people's first encounter with the Dayan (Old Town) is the water wheel square. This is a great place to hang out and get a taste of Chinese tourism at its most intense. Look out also for the hilariously translated wooden signs that now adorn most of the shops in the new town.

Essentials

GETTING THERE From Lijiang's airport, 28km (17 miles) and a 30-minute taxi ride (around ¥100) southwest of town, there are daily **flights** to a wide range of domestic locations including Kunming (50 min.), Xishuangbanna (30 min.), Guangzhou (3 hr.), and Shanghai (4½ hr.). Tickets can be bought at the **CAAC/Yunnan Airlines** ticket office at Fuhui Lu, Minhang Zhan (✆ **0888/516-1289**). CAAC airport buses (¥20) depart from the office 90 minutes before scheduled departures. There is another CAAC office on the first floor of the Lijiang Dajiudian at Xin Dajie (✆ **0888/518-0280;** 8:30am–6:30pm).

From Lijiang's **long-distance bus station** on Kanzhong Lu (✆ **0888/512-1106**), **buses** run to Xiaguan (5 hr.) every half-hour from 7:00am to 6:30pm. Express buses run to Kunming (8 hr.) but are a long and tedious haul compared to the train. Buses also run to Zhongdian/Xianggelila, passing Qiaotou (3 hr.; ¥65) every hour from 7:30am to 4pm.

Lijiang has a brand new passenger train station near Wenbi Mountain that opened in the summer of 2011 and is a lead toward Shangri-la (ETA 2014) and will handle about 9 million passengers per year. The old station to the east of town has now been relegated to cargo only. By taxi it is about 20 minutes from Lijiang and will cost between ¥30 and ¥40. Bus nos. 4, 16, and 18 all serve the new station. Day trains to Dali take a rapid 80 minutes and there are three or four night trains to Kunming that do the trip in a steady 7 hours overnight. Hard sleepers cost around ¥150 and the number 13 bus goes right past the old town for just ¥1. There is a downtown ticket office (✆ **0888/511-5055;** 8am–5pm) just behind the bank of China on Fuhui Lu.

GETTING AROUND The old town, off-limits to motor traffic, can be comfortably toured on foot. **Taxis** cost ¥6 for 3km (2 miles), then ¥1.60 per kilometer. From midnight to 7am, in-town taxis charge ¥10 per trip. **Bikes** can be rented from several cafes in the old town and also in Mao Square at Ali Baba (✆ **0139/8704-7896**) for around ¥15 a day.

TOURS & GUIDES We recommend Kiwi guide Keith Lyons (✆ **1376/900-1439**) and his lovable collie, Lassie. Keith was here as an NGO just after the quake and knows the area like the back of his hand. Lassie loves hiking and will jump at the chance to take visitors to Haba Snow Mountain or Stone Village. Of course, the area around Lijiang is very accessible for independent travelers too, and so if you just want advice, ask for Linda at the Tourist Information Centre (Yuke Zhong Xing; ✆ **0888/511-9111**) at the White Dragon Cultural Square (Bailong Wenhua Guang Chang) near the South Gate and the TNC.

[FastFACTS] LIJIANG

Banks, Foreign Exchange & ATMs The main branch of the **Bank of China** (Mon–Fri 8:30am–5:30pm) is on Xin Daje south of Fuhui Lu and has an ATM. In the old town, the **Industrial and Commercial Bank of China (ICBC)** across from the post office (Mon–Fri 8:30am–5pm) can exchange cash and traveler's checks.

Internet Access A number of cafes in the old town offer Internet service for ¥2 an hour. One of the most reliable is the **Dongba House Inn,** Xinyi Jie Jishan Xiang 16. Dial-up is ✆ **163.**

Post Office The main post office in new Lijiang (8am–8pm) is on Xin Dajie. A smaller post office (8am–8pm) is in the old town just to the north of Sifang Jie.

Visa Extensions The **Gonganju (PSB)** is located at Taihe Lu (✆ **0888/518-8437;** Mon–Fri 8am–noon and 2:30–5:30pm).

Exploring Lijiang

OLD TOWN ★★

When visitors and travel guide writers gush about Lijiang, they're really referring to its raison d'être, the **old town** *(gucheng)*, built over 800 years ago during the Southern Song dynasty. A delightful maze of twisting cobblestone streets and Naxi-style homes but more and more shops, usually of the souvenir variety, the old town still affords glimpses of traditional Naxi life as residents go about their daily lives despite the staggering crowds and the increasingly commercial tenor of the whole place.

Unlike many ancient towns in China, Lijiang does not have a city wall. It is said that the first ruling family of Lijiang, surnamed Mu, prohibited the building of a wall around the old town because drawing a box around the character of *mu* turned it into the character *kun,* meaning "difficulty," and was therefore not auspicious. What the old town does have, however, is a web of flowing canals fed by the Yuquan springs in today's Black Dragon Pool to the north. These streams often flow into several three-pit **wells** scattered around the old town with designated pits for drinking, washing vegetables, and washing clothes. You can see such a well at the **Baima Long Tan** in the south of town. The **Yican Quan,** for drinking water only, can be found on Mishi

THE naxi

The majority of China's Naxi population, numbering just under 290,000, lives in Yunnan, and of this group, more than half reside in the Lijiang Naxi Autonomous County; the rest reside in Zhongdian, Ninglang, Yongsheng, and Deqin counties to the northwest. Though the Naxi's exact origins are not known, they are thought to be descendants of the ancient nomadic Tibetan Qiang tribes of Qinghai. Driven south by northern invaders, the Naxi have been resident in the Lijiang area for around 1,400 years.

The Naxi believe in a polytheistic religion called *dongba* (meaning "wise man" or "scripture reader"), which is a blend of Tibetan Lamaism, Daoism, and shamanistic beliefs in various gods and spirits in nature. *Dongba* are also Naxi shamans, the most revered figures because they not only act as mediators between the present and the spirit world but are the only ones who can read, write, and interpret the approximately 1,400 pictographic characters that comprise the Naxi script created over 1,000 years ago.

The importance of the shaman notwithstanding, women play a dominant role in Naxi society, which is matrilineal in nature. Inheritance passes from the mother through the youngest daughter, and women control the purse strings, work the fields, and trade at markets. The men traditionally function as child-raisers, gardeners, and musicians. The revival in recent years of traditional Naxi music has helped keep alive an ancient art form that the Naxi have been practicing since before the days of Kublai Khan's invasion of Lijiang in the 13th century. Many of the songs, rarely heard anywhere else and some dating as far back as the Song and Tang dynasties, are played on rare and unusual musical instruments several hundred years old. Dongba music and dance performances are held every evening in the old town, and feature prominently as well in Naxi festivals, including the traditional Sanduo Festival held on the eighth day of the second lunar month to honor the god Sanduo, believed to be the great protector of the Naxi against a whole horde of pestilence and disasters.

Xiang next to the Blue Page Vegetarian Restaurant. The old town used to have several water mills as well, but the only one standing today is a reconstructed **water wheel** at the old town entrance. In the center of town is **Market Square (Sifang Jie),** ringed with shops and restaurants. During the day, Naxi women come here to trade, and on certain evenings, residents will gather here and break into spontaneous circle dances.

From Market Square, a cobblestone path leads uphill along the eastern flanks of **Shizi Shan (Lion Hill),** which separates the old town from the new. This area, known as Huang Shan, is one of the region's oldest neighborhoods and is a lovely place to wander, as it's a relatively tourist-free zone. At the top of the hill is the 33m-tall (108-ft.) **Wangu Lou;** admission is ¥15 and it's open from dawn to dusk. Each meter represents 10,000 of Lijiang's 330,000 people; it is said to be the tallest wooden pagoda in China. Supported by 16 massive 22m-high (72-ft.) pillars made from old local wood, the square pagoda has 13 soaring eaves (representing the 13 peaks of the Jade Dragon Snow Mountain range) and over 2,300 Dongba designs

Lost in Lijiang

If you ever get lost in the old town, just find a stream and walk against the current, as it will invariably lead you back to an entrance of the town.

carved into the structure. There are some stunning **views** ★ of the old town, new town, and majestic Jade Dragon Snow Mountain range from the top.

Anchoring the southern part of the old town is **Mu Fu** (**Mu's Residence;** ¥65; 9am–6pm). The former home of the Naxi ruling family, which ruled Lijiang for 22 generations until 1723, the residence was actually completely destroyed in the Qing dynasty (1644–1911) and, until the earthquake of 1996, the houses of ordinary Naxi stood in the palace's stead. Post-earthquake authorities apparently determined that World Bank rebuilding funds would be better justified by an imperial residence that could attract legions of tourists rather than by banal domestic housing; the result is the sprawling residence you see today. Stepped into the side of Lion Hill are six main halls separated by courtyards said to resemble those of the Forbidden City, including a meeting hall where the clan chiefs met and a library of Dongba writings. From the back of the residence, steps lead up the hill to Wangu Lou.

Heilong Tan Gongyuan (Black Dragon Pool Park) ★ About 1.5km (1 mile) north of the old town, this park, which contains the source of much of the old town's water, also offers Lijiang's most famous photo op: the distant snowcapped Jade Dragon Snow Mountain fronted by the park's Deyue Lou (Moon Embracing Pavilion), and Wukong Qiao (Five Arch Bridge). In the eastern section is the three-story Ming dynasty Wufeng Lou (Five Phoenix Hall), with soaring eaves meant to resemble flying phoenixes. Also here is the Dongba Cultural Research Institute (Dongba Wenhua Yanjiusuo), where you can see experts translating Dongba pictographs. Visitors are usually asked for the Old Town Preservation Ticket. The area is especially attractive just after sunset when the streams and trees are all lit up.

Xin Daje. Free admission. 6:30am–8:30pm.

The Nature Conservancy's Lijiang Visitor Center (Da Zi Ran Bao Hu Xie Hui Lijiang Bang Gong Xi) ★★★ The Nature Conservancy has moved down to the public park just next to the Visitor's Centre at the Bai Ma entrance to the old town. This new location is much larger than before and that means even more beautiful photos of Yunnan and its wildlife. This is the place to find inspiration for further explorations. Especially interesting are Bill Mosely's then and now photos where he compares the shots taken by Joseph Rock nearly 100 years ago and the same locations today. The Nature Conservancy's Lijiang Visitor Center provides an overview of the rich biological and cultural diversity of northwest Yunnan and is intended to arouse visitor's interest and desire to protect the spectacular and unique nature and culture of Northwest Yunnan, guide them to consider environmentally friendly methods of tourism, and encourage their support for related conservation activities. You could stay here all afternoon watching their collection of videos about the area, with everything from local CCTV shows to CNN special reports. This is by far the best site in Lijiang. The Visitor Centre next door has free Internet and some helpful English speaking staff.

White Dragon Cultural Square (Bailong Wenhua Guang Chang). ✆ **0888/515-9916.** Free admission. 8:30am–5:30pm.

The Tea Horse Road Museum (Cha Ma Gu Dao Bo Wu Guan) ★ Up a back alley next to the Black Dragon Pool Car Park, this is a fascinating virtual tour to the ancient Tea Horse Trail. The Naxi artist owner and a team of clever locals have built a full diorama of the entire route on two separate floors. You will certainly recognize many of the models from their real world counterparts such as the Old Square in Shaxi all the way up to the Potala Palace. The models are very well constructed and there are English signs as well as clear audio commentary. The shop has a huge selection of Pu'er tea and some very nice Tibetan handkerchiefs on sale.

44-45 Gu Lu Wu Xia Duan, Heilongtan ✆ **0888/511-5507.** Free admission. 8:30am–5:30pm.

Where to Stay

While Lijiang is attracting its fair share of upscale resorts, none of them can match the charming ambience and coziness of the old town's traditional Naxi guesthouses. The **Crowne Plaza** feels the same as every other five-star resort. During the quieter months, it's like an empty movie set but in winter, this is the top choice if you're looking for warm comfortable rooms. The **Pullman** and **Banyan Tree** are also overrated.

Garden Inn (Zi Teng Hua Yuan Ke Zhan) ★★ At the budget end of the price range, this is currently the most popular haunt for young backpackers, both Chinese and overseas. Dorms start from ¥25 but there are also simple but clean and spacious private rooms for ¥100 to ¥150. The owner English speaking owner May, is a charming Mongolian lass, and her three local staff are as polite and friendly as any of the staff at the five-star resorts. Popular with long term guests, partly because of the genial atmosphere thanks to the smiling and laughing staff. Approach from Jinhong Road near the North Gate Market.

7 Yishang Cun, Wenming Jie, Off Wuyi Jie. mayhostel@gmail.com. ✆ **1510/887-3494.**16 units. ¥120 standard room. No credit cards.

The HKL Inn (Xi Mu Bie Yuan) This is our pick of the mid-range vernacular guest houses. English-speaking Sally is a welcoming hostess and the second floor rooms are especially charming with the beam and tile ceilings and awe inspiring views of Yulong Snow Mountain. The location is easy to get to by taxi, but at the same time right in the heart of the old town. There is no audible noise from the bar street way below. The only drawback is the open plan bathrooms. Approach from Shishan Lu to avoid having to carry your luggage up some steep stone steps.

34 Shuang Shi Duan, Xin Hua Jie. ✆ **0888/511-8838.** 20 units. ¥400 standard room. ¥600 suite. Chinese credit cards. In room: A/C, Internet,

Yibang Residence (Yibang Lijiang Jiu Dian) A large Shanghai real estate company has bought up much of the street behind the Mu palace and turned the sprawling collection of courtyards into upmarket accommodation. Almost every room is unique and prices range from around ¥800 all the way up to the six-person hillside villa with its own outdoor plunge pool for ¥28,000 per night. Ask for Candy, the helpful English-speaking manager and be sure to try the small bakery out front. Approach from the south entrance, rather than the waterwheels.

57 Guangbi Alley, Guangyi St. ✆ **0888/555-1818.** 20 units. ¥800 standard room. ¥1,000 suite. AE, DC, MC, V. In room: A/C, Internet

Zen Garden Hotel (Lion Mountain Yard) The descending internal courtyards, filled with Chinese antiques and soothing waterfalls have made this a top choice in online reviews, and it is obvious to see why. Even so, the rooms themselves are disappointing business style suites that could be found anywhere in the new town. The other downside is the nightly zoo that takes place down on bar street and can be annoyingly repetitive in this place. I personally prefer the HKL just around the corner.

Rui He Yuan 37 Shuang Shi Alley, Xin Hua Street. www.zengardenhotel.com. ✆ **0888/518-9799.** 20 units. ¥400 standard room. ¥600 suite. No credit cards. In room: A/C, Internet

Where to Eat

Old town Lijiang offers plenty of friendly cafes and family-operated restaurants catering to foreign travelers with Western, Chinese, and Naxi food at prices that have recently increased so much they almost match those of the big cities.

He Shi San Wei Shi Wu ★ NAXI This no-frills restaurant serves some of the best local fare in all of Lijiang. Naxi favorites include *jidou chao mifan* (fried rice with soy bean), *Lijiang baba* (a local baked pastry that can be ordered sweet or salty), and *zha rubing* (fried goat cheese).

15 Zhen Xing Xiang, Wuyi Jie. ✆ **0888/511-8603.** Meal for 2 ¥40–¥80. No credit cards. 11am–11pm.

N's Kitchen (Er Lou Xiao Chu) ★ WESTERN This is the number-one choice in Lijiang if you want a break from Chinese food. With its second floor balcony, this is also a great place to hang out, watch the comings and goings on the square below and enjoy the relaxing tunes coming from the flute shop opposite. Norman, the owner, does really good breakfasts, big enough to keep you going on a full day of hiking

2nd Floor, 17 Jishan Alley, Xin Yi Jie. ✆ **0888/512-0060.** Meal for 2 ¥40–¥100. No credit cards. 7:30am–11pm.

Nordic Delight WESTERN There is no better way to start the day than a Viking Breakfast at the Nordic Delight. They also bake the tastiest cookies in town, so it is well worth stocking up before you set off on some of the area's beautiful hikes. For inspiration on other places to visit, they have a great selection of locally produced guidebooks, with plenty of lesser-known sites for you to consider exploring.

On the path from the water wheels to Black Dragon Pool. ✆ **0888/512-6705.** Meal for 2 ¥40–¥120. No credit cards. 9:30am–8:30pm.

Shun Shui Lou Canting NAXI This restaurant has one of the best settings in town, right beside one of the numerous streams. This is another good choice for experimenting with the more bizarre tastes of Naxi food such as *shu wa* (frog-skin fungus) or the numerous types of deep-fried insects that are available here. The English menu is a starting point, but as this place is popular among Cantonese diners, see what everybody else is trying before making your own choices.

Bai Sui Fang, 80, Xinyi Jie. ✆ **0888/512-9029.** Meal for 2 ¥50–¥100. No credit cards. 11:30am–11:30pm.

Savory Needs Sweet

Yunnan goat's cheese always tastes better when dipped in sugar or honey.

Shopping

Down at the southeastern corner of the old town, the **Zhong Yi market** is a refreshingly authentic break from the repetitive souvenir stores near the square. Depending on the season, this is the place to find giant snow peaches, Huaping mangoes, and snow lotus. The little alley that leads off to the car park is where mountain tribe people sell a vast array of exotic mushrooms. Also look out for unusual honeys and heritage varieties of vegetables, such as the red streaked potatoes and imperial purple carrots. To avoid confusion, make your way down to Mu Palace. Face the main gate, and look for the cafes overlooking the stream. Head down the alleyway between, take a right at the Mu Fu Guan Hotel, and then a sharp right by the fruit vendors, into the market itself.

The most reliable option for replacing those worn out hiking boots before you hit the gorge is the **Red Indian Outdoor Clothing Store** (Yin Di An Ren Hu Wai Dian) just around the corner from the water wheels, almost diagonally opposite the Construction Bank on the junction of Minzhu Lu and Fuhui Lu. They have a large range of equipment, sizes to suit even the lankiest of foreigners, and polite staff that are not pushy in the least.

If you are having pastry withdrawal symptoms, head for the Bread Bay, just up near the Bank of China and the train ticket office. This is our favorite Lijiang bakery. This is the place to stock up before heading out for a hike with pizza sandwiches, reasonably priced croissants, and our personal fave, the almond twists.

Lijiang After Dark

Attending a Naxi concert is one of the more popular evening activities in Lijiang. The original Naxi Orchestra at the **Naxi Guyue Hui (Naxi Music Academy)** is led by esteemed Naxi ethnomusicologist Xuan Ke, who delivers witty introductions and explanations to the music and instruments in both English and Chinese but mainly Chinese. Nightly performances are held at the Naxi Concert Hall (Dong Dajie) from 8 to 9:30pm. Purchase tickets for ¥120 to ¥160 ahead of time; performances are frequently sold out. There is also the Zhang Yimou branded extravaganza, **Impression Lijiang** with some 600 actors out at Jade Dragon Mountain. Show time is around noon (the time changes from time to time so check before you go). The ticket is pricey at ¥198 to ¥260, but the show is world class. It's a song and dance about the life on the Tea and Horse Caravan Trail that conveys the feel of those bygone days. A taxi out there will cost ¥90, but it will probably be closer to ¥150 for the return trip. From Red Sun Square, the no. 7 bus is a much cheaper alternative.

Lijiang has a raucous bar street that is well worth avoiding. A huge fight here recently put the entire Chinese Olympic Speed Skating Team and an equal number of security in the local hospital. More sedate options are **Freshnam** (68 Wang Jia Zhuang Xiang, Wuyi Jie; ✆ **1357/838-3745**), a Korean owned bar that is very popular with backpackers from the Mama Naxi guesthouse next door, or the much larger and more Chinese **2146 Bar,** owned by a local who previously spent many years as a musician in London.

Around Lijiang

Please turn to chapter 16 for Chinese translations of key locations.

YUFENG SI 玉峰寺

About 13km (8 miles) northwest of Lijiang at the foot of Jade Dragon Snow Mountain, this small lamasery belonging to the Scarlet Sect of Tibetan Buddhism was first built in 1660. Today it is best known for its *wanduo shancha* (10,000-flower camellia tree). Formed from the merger of two trees planted by monks between 1465 and 1487, the camellia tree is said to bloom 20 times between March and June, bearing a total of 20,000 blossoms! If you're cycling here (2 hr.), follow Xianggelila Da Dao out of town. About 5km (3 miles) past the town of Baisha, take a left at **Yushui Zhai (Jade Water Village),** go past the **Dongba Village,** and continue on to Yufeng Temple.

YU HU (NGULUKO; 玉湖)

Just before the Dongba Village is the turnoff for the village that was Joseph Rock's home in the 1920s and 1930s. The Austrian-born botanist and anthropologist, whose *Ancient Nakhi Kingdom of Southwest China* is the definitive account of Naxi culture and language, is a local legend who lived in Lijiang for 27 years. Following the turn-off—which you can't miss, as large letters proclaim FOLLOW ROCKER'S TRAIL TO SHANGRI-LA (the misspelled name turns out to be an English transliteration of the literal Chinese pronunciation of "Rock," or "Luoke")—take a right at the first fork for about 3km (2 miles), then follow signs directing you to the village where all the houses are built entirely from large stones and rocks. Thanks to the tourist boom, Yuhu now has a huge parking lot for tour buses and locals (who use the area to arrange impromptu dog fights). When foreigners arrive they will break off to demand a village entrance fee. **Joseph Rock's former residence** (**Luoke Guju Chenlieg-uan;** ¥15; 8am–6pm) is a two-story wooden house where Rock lived with his Naxi assistant Li Siyu. Rock's quarters on the second floor contain his original twin bed, his suitcase, a folding table, two chairs, and kerosene lamps. A newly built exhibition hall next to the residence has displays of Rock's gun, clothing, pictographic cards used to help Rock learn the Dongba language, and Rock's own photographs of Naxi funeral ceremonies and festivals. The rest of the museum is disappointing, a bunch of low quality photocopies and some unrelated text books. More impressive is the new wing of the nearby school that shows how modern and Naxi architecture can be cleverly combined.

BAISHA 白沙

Ten kilometers (6 miles) northwest of Lijiang, 1km (½ mile) off the main road to Jade Dragon Snow Mountain, this dusty historic town is most famous these days for its Ming- and Qing-dynasty **temple frescoes,** which were painted by Naxi, Tibetan, Bai, and Han artists and hence incorporate elements of Buddhism, Lamaism, and Daoism. The largest fresco, found on the front wall of the **Dabaoji Palace** (¥30; 7:30am–6pm), is a gorgeous Ming dynasty mural of Buddha preaching to his disciples.

In the street behind the Dabaoji Palace, visitors can also find Baisha's most famous personality, Dr. Ho (He), at his Chinese herbal clinic. Immortalized by travel writer Bruce Chatwin as the "Taoist physician in the Jade-Dragon Mountains of Lijiang," and visited by countless journalists and curious travelers ever since, Dr. Ho can dispense herbs for any ailment and sells his special tea made from homegrown herbs, which has many fans, as seen in the scrapbooks of letters from grateful patients.

YULONG XUESHAN (JADE DRAGON SNOW MOUNTAIN; 玉龙雪山)

This magnificent 35km-long (21-mile) mountain range framing Lijiang has become a very expensive day out. The tallest of the mountain's 13 peaks is the daunting **Shanzi-feng** (**Fan Peak;** elev. 5,596m/18,355 ft.), perennially snowcapped and climbed for the first time only in 1963 by a research team from Beijing. Today's visitors have a number of options for exploring the mountain. All require you to pay a hefty ¥120 entrance fee to the Jade Dragon Snow Mountain Scenic Area, about 30km (20 miles) north of Lijiang. Many tourists visit as part of an organized tour. To get out here on your own, take a bus for Baoshan or Daju. The Lijiang no. 7 bus (¥10) goes from Red Sun Square (Hong Tai Yang Guang Chang) opposite the Mao statue to Jade Dragon Mountain.

The most popular visit is a round-trip cable-car ride for an even more expensive ¥150 from the village just inside the main gate to **Bingchuan Gongyuan (Glacier Park).** If possible, purchase your ticket in town the day before at the Jade Dragon Snow Mountain ticket office at Xianggelila Da Dao and Xiangshan Dong Lu, as ornery ticket attendants at the reception center will sometimes insist you cannot purchase a ticket on the spot. Buses for ¥10 round-trip will transport you the 4km (2½ miles) from the reception center to the cable car terminus. From here it's a two-section ride on a chairlift to the foot of Fan Peak. You can climb a walkway all the way up to 4,480m (14,700 ft.), where visitors are greeted with a stunning view of glaciers and with ice caverns. If you feel any altitude sickness, Chinese vendors will happily sell you an oxygen canister for around ¥30.

About 20 minutes north of the reception center past the Baishui He River, a 10-minute ride on yet another chairlift for ¥120 round-trip and a 30-minute ramble through groves of spruce and pine trees leads you to **Yunshan Ping (Spruce Meadow;** elev. 3,206m/10,515 ft.). During the annual Torch Festival, young Naxi men and women come here to pray for eternal love.

The third cable car, which costs ¥120 round-trip and takes you another 20km (12 miles) north, arrives at **Maoniu Ping (Yak Meadow,** elev. 3,500m/11,480 ft.), the least visited of the three spots. The meadow has grazing yaks, blooming flowers (in spring and summer), and a number of hiking possibilities. One of the more popular routes leads to Xuehua Hu (Snow Flake Lake), which brilliantly captures the crystalline reflection of the surrounding mountains.

HUTIAO XIA (TIGER LEAPING GORGE; 虎跳峡)

One of the most spectacular sights in Lijiang and a must-hike for trekkers, the 30km-long (18-mile) Tiger Leaping Gorge, which sits between the Jade Dragon Snow Mountain of Lijiang and the Haba Snow Mountain of Zhongdian to the north is breathtaking. Reaching a depth of over 3,000m (9,842 ft.), the gorge is divided into upper *(shang hutiao),* middle *(zhong hutiao),* and lower *(xia hutiao)* sections, with two main entrances, one at the town of **Qiaotou** at the upper gorge and the other at the town of **Daju** at the end of the lower gorge (¥50; 8am–7pm). Most hikers now start from Qiaotou, as all foreigners traveling on buses from Lijiang to Daju are required to pay the ¥120 entrance fee to the Jade Dragon Snow Mountain Scenic Area between Lijiang and Daju. For most visitors short on time, the gorge can be visited as a day trip from Lijiang or on the way to Shangri-La. Recently, instead of going all the way to Qiaotou, many private-hire taxis and tour buses like to drop off visitors at a newly constructed parking lot on the south side of the gorge across from the town of Qiaotou. After paying the entrance fee of ¥50, it's a 2.6km (1.5-mile) walk along a wide paved path to the gorge's most famous sight, the **Tiger Leaping Stone (Hutiao Shi),** a large rock in the middle of the raging river that gave the gorge its name. The legend goes that a tiger being chased by a hunter escaped capture by leaping over the river with the help of this rock.

On the north side of the gorge, a new road for buses and cars has been built all the way from Qiaotou to Tiger Leaping Stone, allowing for even more busloads of tourists. Fortunately, few venture farther than this and so you can head up past Walnut Groves and even the water terraces on paved roads.

For trekkers approaching from Qiaotou, there are two paths: the lower path, which is relatively easy and flat, and the higher path, which is longer, more strenuous, and more dangerous because of falling rocks and narrower paths. Check with the travelers' cafes in Lijiang beforehand for the latest hiking conditions. It is possible but not advisable to do the hike in a day. Basic but charming guesthouses along the way, all with hot water and restaurants, make overnighting at the gorge a relatively painless affair. In general, hikers on the high path can overnight at **Nuoyu** village, 6.3km (4 miles) and 2 hours from Qiaotou, or you can stay at **Bendiwan** village, 17km (10 miles) and 4 to 8 hours from Qiaotou, which has several guesthouses, and some of the best views. Some hikers even manage to get to **Walnut Grove (Hetao Yuan),** 23km (14 miles) from Qiaotou and 2 to 4 hours from Bendiwan, in 1 day. However, the middle rapids between Tina's Guesthouse on the lower path and Walnut Grove is one of the prettiest sections of the gorge, so you may want to take your time through there. Guesthouses at Walnut Grove include the very social Sean's Spring Guesthouse (Shanquan Kezhan) with beds for ¥60 to ¥120. From Walnut Grove, you can either hike back to Qiaotou via the 4- to 5-hour lower path, or you can take a taxi back to Qiaotou for ¥30. Another option is to continue on to Daju, a section considerably less scenic that requires crossing the river; the old ferry costs ¥10, the new ferry ¥12.

To get to Qiaotou from Lijiang, take a Zhongdian-bound bus (2½ hr.; ¥33), which runs every half-hour to hour from 7:30am to 3pm, and ask to be let off at Qiaotou. From Qiaotou, the last bus to Lijiang passes at around 6:30pm, while the last bus to Zhongdian passes at around 5pm. The last bus (3 hr.; ¥35) from Daju to Lijiang leaves at 1:30pm. Frequent minibuses, running until 5pm, take 2½ hours and cost ¥35 to get from Daju to Zhongdian.

XIANGGELILA (ZHONGDIAN; 香格里拉)

Yunnan Province, 651km (390 miles) NW of Kunming, 198km (119 miles) NW of Lijiang

To its majority Tibetan residents, the capital of the Diqing Tibetan Autonomous Prefecture, a small town on the road between Lijiang and Tibet, is known as Gyalthang. To the town's smaller Han population, it's still called Zhongdian. To tourist authorities, hotel owners, and tour operators around the country, the town is now the earthly paradise of Xianggelila (that's Shangri-La to you). A rose never had it so difficult, and we'll continue to refer to it as "Zhongdian" in practical information.

Tourist authorities are working hard to build new hotels and roads, but for now this is still a small, dusty town (elev. 3,380m/11,092 ft.) to be visited mostly for its rebuilt Tibetan monastery if you aren't going to make it to Tibet. Uprisings and their immediate repressions had a very negative effect on the town, and it still has that feeling of being a startup project. What was virgin forest has undergone environmental excesses, leaving windswept plains that are bitterly cold outside of the summer.

Shangri-La is divided into two areas: Dukezong Ancient Town and a more modern citylike area. The old town is much calmer than Lijiang, and there are many more English menus and foreign-run guest houses to choose from here.

Note: Turn to chapter 16 for Chinese translations of key locations.

GETTING THERE Diqing Shangri-La Airport (DIG; ✆ **0887/822-9901**) is located about 4km (2.49 miles) southeast of Zhongdian and serves the airlines traveling to Kunming, Lhasa, Guangzhou, and Shanghai. A taxi downtown is about ¥15. The starting price for taxis is ¥5.

The Zhongdian Coach Bus Station is located in Changzheng Middle Road and has buses back to Lijiang every 40 minutes ranging in price from ¥53 to ¥65. There are multiple buses to Deqin, but at the time of writing this road is a construction nightmare and there have been reports of trips taking anywhere from 10 to 17 hours.

Where to Stay & Eat

Zhongdian has an enormous range of accommodation choices ranging from dorm beds for backpackers at **N's Kitchen and Lodge,** 33 Yiruomuland, Beimen St. (✆ **0887/688-6500**), all the way up to the US$1,000-per-night villas out at the Banyan Tree in Ringha. There are two highly rated but slightly pricey Songtsams out by the Sonzanlin Temple, the 75-room **Songtsam Retreat** (www.mgallery.com/gb/hotel-7078-songtsam-retreat-at-shangri-la/index.shtml; ✆ **0887/828-5577**) at the rear of the temple complex that is part of the prestigious McGallery collection, where rooms start at about ¥1,200; and the smaller 23 room **Songstam Hotel** (www.songtsam.com; ✆ **0887/828-8889**) at the foot of the monastery, where rooms standard rooms start at around ¥600.

For most visitors, Zhongdian offers so much local food and yet so little time in which to try it all. Tsampa is the Tibetans' staple food, made from highland barley flour and usually eaten with buttered tea. Pipa, a non-greasy preserved form of pork is a delicacy usually kept for entertaining guests. Then there is yak hot pot, momos, and even suolima (a kind of Tibetan liquor brewed with the highland barley) all waiting to be sampled by the adventurous visitor. Perhaps the most popular chef in town is Bhaskar, who owns **Bhaskar's Kitchen,** Dawa Road (✆ **0887/888-1213**), just opposite the Old Town car park where he serves up a delicious range of Tibetan, Nepali, and Indian cuisine. For authentic ambiance, the badly named **Karma Cafe,** 66 Jinlong St. (✆ **0887/822-4768**), at the back of the old town is one of the best traditional Tibetan house restorations that we have seen in a long time. Apart from the great food, it would be very easy to fantasize that you were back in the glory days of the Lamas in this incredible setting. Right in the middle of town is the **Zangxi Tibet Restaurant,** 9 Chilang Lane (✆ **0887/823-0048**). Most tourists seem to be a little intimidated by this local favorite, but this is the eatery that local officials use when entertaining guests and VIPs. There is a reasonable English menu and if you stuff yourself silly, it doubles as a decent hotel just at the back. **The Shangri-La Yak Cheese Shop,** Mei Xiang Nai Lao 3, Chi Lang Shuo (✆ **1598/759-5185**), produces locally sourced yak cheese (Shangri-La Premier and Geza Gold) with Western methods. While the service leaves a lot to be desired, they do offer accommodation in authentic log herding cabins out at their Langdu creamery about 2 hours out of town.

Kersang's Relay Station (Ge Sang Zang Yi) This is our number-one choice for accommodation in the Old Town area. The property has an all-wooden construction and a quiet location behind what used to be the Arro Khampa Restaurant. The views from the rooms and the terrace are amazing, especially at night when the Old Temple and the giant prayer wheel are completely lit up. It's owned and operated by a Frenchman and his Tibetan wife.

1 Yamenlang Jinlong Street, Old Town; ✆ **1398/878-9193.** 10 units. ¥180 standard en suite room. No credit cards.

Shopping

While there are plenty of interesting Tibetan shopping opps in the new town, it is the old town that has the real charm. Check out the new free museum at the back end of town next to the large square and then explore the hill top temple and giant prayer wheel. **Dropenling Tibetan Handicraft Center** (✆ **1365/891-3323**) is a non-profit Social Enterprise handicraft project selling high-quality, authentic Tibetan handicrafts. There are lots of great items here, including gorgeous hand puppets and crazy headgear. Even more amazing is the **Thanka shop** (Gu Jie Thanka; ✆ **0887/888-1516**) on the old square where the highly detailed mandalas are a perfect gift.

Shangri-La abounds in various herbs, such as saffron and angelica. Saffron is said to have the ability to promote blood circulation and beautify the skin (as well as being great for cooking). Angelica is another local cure-all, as well as Chinese caterpillar fungus (Dongchong-Xiacao in Chinese).

Zhongdian After Dark

As soon as night falls, the dancing begins. Zhongdian is far more energetic that the slow rhythmic plodding that you see in the Naxi circles of Lijiang. Tibetans are much more lively and encourage tourists to join in their giant carousels that often comprise over a thousand people. In the Tibetan folk dance Guozhuang, all join hands, form a circle, and follow the principal dancer. Everybody is encouraged to join in. Look out at the Museum Square, the Old Town Square, and the Sifanglou Plaza in the new town, which all become dance stages at about 7pm.

Around Zhongdian

Songzanlin Monastery is located 5km (3 miles) north of Shangri-La on the number 3 bus. It is a Gelupa Sect (Yellow Hat), first constructed by the fifth Dalai Lama in 1679. In 1958 it housed more than 2000 monks, and then a year later its more than 100 buildings were shelled relentlessly before the PLA forces looted the gilded roof and jewel encrusted statues and methodically destroyed every remaining structure. Rebuilding began in 1982 by a team of returnees from Dharamsala and is an ongoing process. This is the largest monastery in Yunnan, consisting of two main lamaseries, and six colleges, which can house up to 1,500 novices. The main chamber houses a

Shakyamuni Buddha beneath which monks recite the holy scriptures in the eerie glow of yak butter lamps. Admission costs ¥50, and it's open from 9:30am to 6pm.

The horse riding out at Napa Hai Grasslands is rather disappointing. For a more authentic experience, Constantin de Slizewicz (✆ **1589/436-7094;** www.caravane-liotard.com) organizes multi-day horse treks into the reaches of the Himalayan foothills with luxury tents. Prices average at about ¥1,000 per night for this once-in-a-lifetime-experience.

YANGZI & BEYOND

by Lee Wing-sze

13

In addition to shared borders, the landlocked provinces of Sichuan, Hubei, and Hunan and the municipality of Chongqing have in common the world's third-longest river, the Chang Jiang ("Long River," aka Yangzi), whose navigable reaches start in Sichuan, thread through Chongqing, and roughly define the border between Hubei and Hunan. Now China's heartland, this region—home to the Chu, Ba, and Shu cultures—was for centuries a land of exile and colonization for the ruling kingdoms of the North China Plain. The Qin (221–206 B.C.) banished thousands to faraway, inhospitable Shu (present-day Sichuan), and China's most famous martyr, Qu Yuan, was exiled to the southern edges of his own Chu kingdom where he drowned himself in the Miluo River (in present-day northern Hunan).

Five hundred years later, this same swath of central China was the battlefield on which the rulers of Wei, Shu, and Wu contended for complete dominion over China. Many sights along the Yangzi commemorate the heroes of those 60 years of turmoil known simply as the Three Kingdoms Period (220–280). By the 3rd century, Buddhism and Daoism were spreading rapidly through the region, and many of the hundreds of temples that dot the sacred mountains of Sichuan, Hubei, and Hunan were constructed at this time.

The heartbreaking catastrophic earthquake in Sichuan on May 12, 2008, killed over 68,000 people and caused damages to capital city Chengdu and attractions Wolong Nature Reserve and Dujiangyan city. While signs of damages could hardly be found in Chengdu a year after the disaster, the reconstruction of Wolong Nature Reserve is expected to be complete in late 2012, and Dujiangyan is now basically complete. The pandas, which were moved to other panda research centers in Sichuan province, will return to Wolong when it reopens in 2012.

Travelers come to this part of central China to see the Three Gorges—the spectacular 242km (150-mile) channel comprising Qutang, Wu, and Xiling gorges—and with China's equivalent of the New Deal underway, new airports, rail lines, and expressways are opening all the time, making travel to remote areas much less trying.

The Yangzi Region

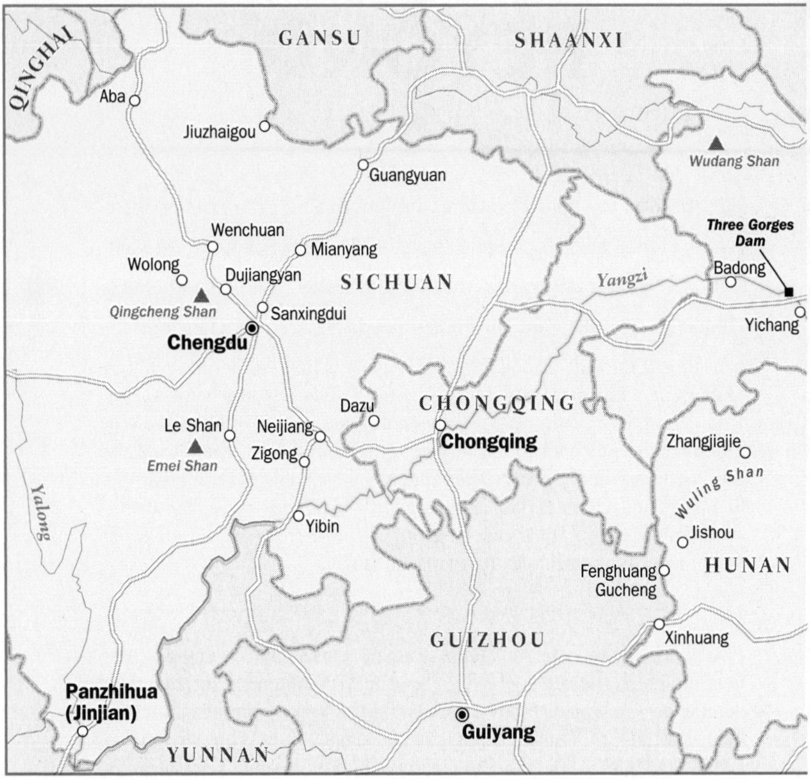

If the Three Gorges are on your itinerary, try to leave yourself a few days on either end to explore Chongqing and Wuhan. And a day trip from Chongqing to the Buddhist grottoes at Dazu is well worth the time. Sichuan is best explored over 2 or 3 weeks. Use Chengdu as a place to leave extra luggage and to return to for a break and some urban sightseeing before going out again. In Hunan, do the same with Changsha.

October and November is the best time to visit Jiuzhaigou and other natural scenic spots in the region. During summer, June to September, it is sweltering and sultry, and rains continually. ***Note:*** Unless otherwise noted, hours listed for attractions and restaurants are daily.

CHENGDU 成都 ★★

Sichuan Province, 504km (313 miles) NW of Chongqing, 842km (523 miles) SW of Xi'an

Ask any Chinese what to do in Sichuan's capital of Chengdu, and 9 times out of 10 they'll tell you to drink tea and eat hot pot, such is the city's reputation as a culinary capital that knows how to take it easy. Indeed, Chengdu's cuisine is irresistible and

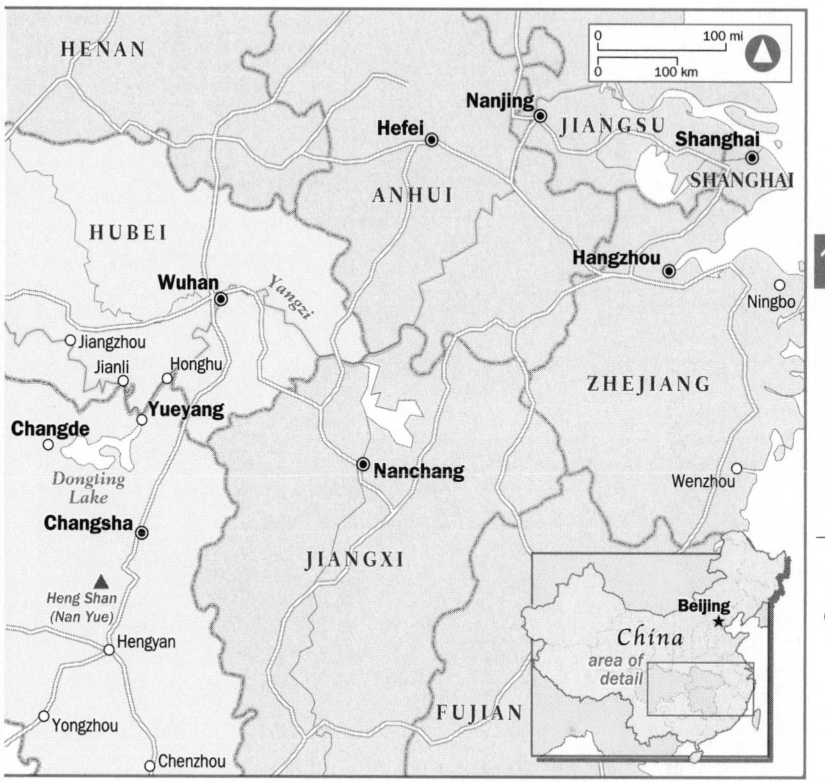

tea drinking is a custom that took hold here 1,300 years ago and never let go. With few genuine ancient sights within the city proper (Du Fu's cottage is only a replica; Wuhou Temple is ho-hum unless you are a huge Three Kingdoms buff), drinking tea may be Chengdu's most durable link to the past. But what Chengdu lacks in ancient sites, it makes up for in charm and atmosphere. Like so many cities in central China, Chengdu has a pretty little river running through it. The narrow Fu He and its southern tributary form a sort of moat around the city, sections of which are lined with attractive restaurants and teahouses. The city is also in the midst of a building boom, but a few old ramshackle warrens and outdoor markets still survive just west of the city square.

Chengdu is the gateway to scenic Jiuzhaigou, the Buddhist mountains of Emei Shan and Le Shan, one of the most important panda breeding centers as well as some lesser-known scenic spots in the west of Sichuan. It's also a traveler's haven and a place to gather information between trips. People are friendly and the pace unrushed. And because Chengdu is one of the few cities with daily flights to Lhasa, many travelers come here to arrange transportation to Tibet.

Chengdu 成都

0 1/2 mi
0 0.5 km

Sānxīng Duī Museum
(Sānxīng Duī Bōwùguǎn)
三星堆博物馆

Panda Research Base/
Giant Panda Breeding Center
(Xióngmāo Jīdì/
Dàxióngmāo Fánzhí Zhōngxīn)
熊猫基地／大熊猫繁殖中心

Jiuyanqiao Bar Street
(Jiǔyǎnqiáo Jiǔbājiē)
九眼桥酒吧街

M Metro station
¥ Bank
Bus Station
Rail Station
Temple
PSB Public-Security Visas
TA Travel Agent

Er Huan Lu Bei
Er Huan Lu Xi
North Railway Station
Renmin Bei Lu
Yi Huan Lu Bei
Jiefang Lu 1
Sha He (Sha River)
Yi Huan Lu Dong
Wenshu Yuan
Wenshu Yuan Jie
Wenwu Lu
Babao Jie
Zhong Lu
Beida Jie
Shuncheng Da Jie
Luomashi
Renmin
Wufu Jie
Kuan/Zhai Xiangzi
Shi Er Qiao Lu
Hongxing Lu
Qingyang Zheng Jie
Tianfu Square
Renmin Xi Lu
Renmin Dong Lu
Bin Long Jie
Mao Statue
Zongfu Lu
Chunxi Lu
Yi Huan Lu Xi
Nan He (Nan River)
Jinjiang Hotel
Renmin Nan Lu
Binjiang Xi Lu
Linjiang Xi Lu
Binjiang Zhong Lu
Linjiang Zhong Lu
Binjiang Dong Lu
Linjiang Dong Lu
Wuhou Ci Da Jie
Wuhou Ci Dong Jie
Huaxiba
Xin Nan Lu
Yi Huan Lu Nan
Wangjiang Lu
Sichuan Stadium
SICHUAN UNIVERSITY
Wangjianglou Gongyuan
Yongfeng Lu
Kehua Bei Lu
Er Huan Lu Dong
Nijiaqiao
Nijia Qiao Lu
Lingshi Guan Lu
Jinxiu Lu
U.S.Consulate
Er Huan Lu Nan
Tongzilin
Tongzi Lin Bei Lu

HOTELS ■

Buddha Zen Hotel **3**
(Yuanheyuan Fodan Kezhan)
圆和圆客栈

Crowne Plaza Chengdu **6**
(Chéngdū Zǒngfǔ Huángguān Jiàrì Jiǔdiàn)
成都总府皇冠假日酒店

Jinli Renjia Kezhan **11**
(Jinli Home Hotel)
锦里人家客栈

Kempinski Chengdu **24**
(Chéngdū Kǎibīnsījī Fàndiàn)
成都凯宾斯基饭店

Shangri-la Chengdu **18**
(Xiānggélǐlā Dàfàndiàn)
香格里拉大饭店

Sheraton Chéngdū Lido **4**
(Tiānfǔ Lìdé Xǐláidēng Fàndiàn)
天府丽都喜来登饭店

Sim's Cozy Garden Hostel **2**
(Chéngdū Lǎochén Qīngnián Lüshè)
成都老沈青年旅舍

Sofitel Wanda Chengdu **14**
(Chengdu Soufeite Wanda Dafandian)
成都索菲特万达大饭店

Sunjoy Inn (Xīnzú Bīnguǎn) **23**
心族宾馆

Traffic Inn (Jiaotong Qingnian Lvshe) **16**
交通青年旅舍

RESTAURANTS ◆

Anchor Bar (An Ba) **15**
岸吧

Bāguó Bùyī **21**
巴国布衣

Càigēn Xiāng **26**
菜根香

Fiesta Thai **17**
(Fēicháng Tái Táigúo Fēngwèi Cāntīng)
非常泰泰国风味餐厅

Grandma's Kitchen **20, 22**
(Zǔmǔ de Chúfáng)
祖母的厨房

Little Bar **27**
(Xiǎojiǔguǔn)
小酒馆

Tandoor Indian Cuisine **23**
(Téngdūěr Yìndù Cāting)
腾都尔印度餐厅

Tanyoto **25**
谭鱼头

Xīzàng Fēngqíng Wū **13**
西藏风情屋

ATTRACTIONS ●

Green Ram Monastery **10**
(Qīngyáng Gōng)
青羊宫

Jinli Ancient Street **12**
(Jǐnlǐ Gǔ Jiē)
锦里古街

Jinsha Site Museum **7**
(Jinsha Yizhi Bówùguǎn)
金沙遗址博物馆

Máo Museum **5**
(Wáng Āntíng Xiǎoxiǎo Zhǎnlǎnguǎn)
王安廷小小展览馆

Sichuan Museum **9**
(Sichuan Bowuyuan)
四川博物院

Sichuan University Museum **19**
(Sìchuān Dàxué Bōwùguǎn)
四川大学博物馆

Songshan Bridge Art City **8**
(Sòngxiān Qíao Yìshù Chéng)
送仙桥艺术城

Wenshu Monastery **1**
(Wénshū Yuàn)
文殊院

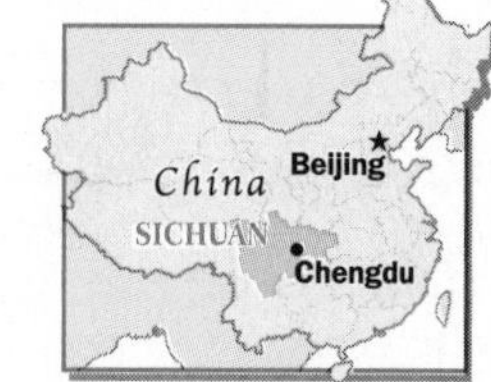

Essentials

GETTING THERE **Shuangliu Airport** is 17km (11 miles) south of Chengdu. Destinations include Beijing (30 flights daily); Guangzhou (20 flights daily); Shenzhen (16 flights daily); Hong Kong (12 flights daily); and Kunming (14 flights daily). Up to 8 to 10 flights daily, from 6am to 3pm, take off for Lhasa. Travelers are no longer required to enter Tibet with a group of five or more, but Tibet Tourism Bureau permits (TTP) are, for the time being, still required. It takes 3 to 7 days to obtain a permit. The price of a one-way flight to Tibet, TTP permit, and airport transfer in Chengdu is from ¥1,500 to ¥3,000. All flights can be booked with any of the several English-speaking travel agents at and near the Traffic Hotel. **Dragonair** has an office in the Sheraton Lido at Renmin Zhong Lu 15, 1 Duan (✆ **028/8676-8828**). The **airport bus,** no. 303, is outside the domestic arrival exit. It takes 30 to 40 minutes to city center and costs ¥10. The airport bus at the China Southwest office on Renmin Nan Lu Er Duan (next to Min Shan Fandian) costs ¥10 and departs every half-hour. Or take bus no. 300 at the North Railway Station. The 22km (14-mile) ride takes 70 minutes and costs ¥6. A **taxi** from the city center to the airport costs ¥60 to ¥75, including a ¥10 toll.

The main **railway station** Northern Chengdu is at the northern end of Renmin Bei Lu, 8km (5 miles) north of the Mao statue in the city center. The ticket office, open 24 hours, is to the right of the main building. Try to purchase tickets at least 2 days in advance. Major destinations include Beijing Xi (fast train; 27 hr. 30 min.; hard sleeper ¥430), Kunming (fast train; 19 hr.; ¥257), Shanghai (36 hr. 30 min.; hard sleeper ¥467), and express train (Dong Che) to Beijing Xi (15 hr. 40 min.; 2nd class ¥430; soft sleeper ¥1,045), Shanghai Hongqiao (15 hr. 30 min.; second class ¥501, soft sleeper ¥1,165), Chongqing Bei (2 hr. 15 min.; second class ¥98, first class ¥117), Dujiangyan (30 to 40 min.; ¥15) and Qingcheng Shan (50 min.; ¥15). The new **Eastern Chengdu Railway Station (Chengdu Nan Huochezhan),** currently the largest and most advanced transportation hub in West China, opened in 2011. The station is a bit far away from city center. Take the metro line 2 (scheduled to open in July 2012) to Chengdu Dong Zhan (Eastern Chengdu Railway Station). Or take bus no. 2 at Northern Chengdu Railway Station; the bus ride takes an hour. Express trains go to Chongqing Bei (2 hr.; second class ¥98, first class ¥117) and high-speed trains to Shanghai will be added.

Xin Nan Men Bus Station (Xin Nan Men Qichezhan), at the corner of Xin Nan Lu and Linjiang Zhong Lu and next to the Traffic Hotel, is clean, efficient, and tourist-friendly (has signs in English). Air-conditioned buses leave from here for Le Shan (2 hr.; ¥43–¥49), Emei Shan (2 hr. 15 min.; ¥43), Jiuzhaigou (8 hr.; ¥144), Dujiangyan (1 hr.; ¥25), and Qingcheng Shan (1 hr. 20 min.; ¥25).

Chadianzi Bus Station (Chadianzi Qiche Keyun Zhan), in the northwest of the Third Ring Road, has air-conditioned buses to Dujiangyan (50 min.; ¥16) and Qingcheng Shan (1 hr. 10 min.; ¥17), Le Shan (3 hr.; ¥47), and Jiuzhaigou (7:20 and 9am; 8 hr.; ¥118).

GETTING AROUND Chengdu's flat terrain and many bike lanes make walking and biking easy, but blocks are long, and crossing the river can require a trek before reaching a bridge. Renmin Road (Renmin Lu) bisects the city on the north-south axis. Its east-west counterpart is less straightforward: At the heart of the city (Tianfu Sq.), Renmin Road West (Renmin Xi Lu) runs west from the square and Renmin Road

East (Renmin Dong Lu) runs east; after a block in either direction, the names change every block or so. Most of Chengdu's avenues have a multitude of names, making a street map essential.

Traffic Hotel (Jiaotong Binguan) at Linjiang Zhong Lu 77 rents **bicycles** for ¥15 per day with a ¥300 deposit. Take bus no. 6, 49, 50, or 55 and get off at the Xin Nan Men stop. City **buses** (¥1; air-conditioned ¥2) serve all parts of the city. Some buses charge ¥1 extra at night. Routes are on city maps. Chengdu has two kinds of **taxis,** the midrange Jetta and Suteng. Taxi rates are ¥8 and ¥9 for the first 2km respectively, then ¥1.90 per kilometer thereafter. From 11pm to 6am the first 2km costs ¥10; after that the fare is ¥2.20 per kilometer.

The first line of the city's underground railway, **Chengdu Metro,** running along Renmin Lu from 6:30am to 10pm, started operating in 2010. It has stops at Tianfu Guangchang, the North Railway Station and the South Railway Station. One single trip costs ¥2 to ¥4. However, the opening of the first line has not really eased the bad traffic in the city. Traffic is still unpleasantly chaotic most of the time, especially during peak hours when some roads are temporarily turned into one-way streets. Another line of the railway is to be completed by late 2012, with stations at Tianfu Guangchang, the Chengdu Nan Railway Station, Jinsha Yizhi, and Chadianzi.

VISITOR INFORMATION Pick up the free monthly English magazine, ***Chengdoo,*** in hotels and Western-style restaurants, or go to www.gochengdoo.com for its listings of local entertainment, dinning, and shopping.

TOURS Chengdu has enough good, English-speaking **independent travel agents** that you needn't bother with CITS and its generally higher rates. The best deals can be found inside and in the vicinity of the Jiaotong Binguan (Traffic Hotel). The **Traffic Travel Service** (inside the hotel) and **Tianfu International Travel Service** at the entrance to the hotel both book air and train tickets and offer a variety of tour packages. For a **private guide,** Mr. Tray Lee is a highly recommended freelance guide. His prices are competitive, his English excellent, and he's always reachable by mobile phone (✆ **0139/8160-5307;** message only 028/8555-4250; fax 028/8556-4952; lee_tray@hotmail.com). His "Sichuan Opera" tour (see "Chengdu After Dark," p. 686) costs ¥180 for admission, a backstage visit, one-way transportation, and an English-speaking guide. Die-hards stay for the whole 4 hours, but that's not required. **BikeChina Adventures** (www.bikechina.com), an American company based in Chengdu, arranges adventure bicycle tours through any part of China.

[FastFACTS] CHENGDU

Banks, Foreign Exchange & ATMs The **Bank of China** (Mon–Fri 9am–5pm), Zhimin Lu 36 near the Traffic Hotel and Xin Nan Men Bus Station, has full foreign-exchange facilities and an ATM. The branch at Renmin Nan Lu opposite the Min Shan Fandian also has an ATM, and is open the same hours.

Consulates The **U.S. Consulate** is at Lingshiguan Lu 4 (✆ **028/8558-3992;** http://chengdu.usembassy-china.org.cn; Mon–Fri 8am–5pm). Take bus no. 76, 77, 79, or 114 to Lingshiguan Lu or take metro to Nijiaqiao Station. The **Singapore Consulate** is on the 31st floor of First City Plaza East Wing, at Shuncheng Da Jie 308 (✆ **028/8652-7222;** Mon–Fri 9am–noon and 1–5pm).

Internet Access Try the **Qilin Wangba,** halfway down the alley off Lingshiguan Lu, and **Reli Wangba,** at Kehuabei Lu 60, are both close to the U.S. Consulate. An Internet cafe is on the second floor above **Xin Nan Men Bus Station** that is surrounded by computer game machines. It also charges ¥2 per hour. Otherwise, you can find Internet cafes around the university, the U.S. Consulate, and the Jiaotong Binguan, most of them are open 24 hours and charge ¥3 to ¥4 per hour. Dial-up is ✆ **163.**

Post Office The Jinjiang Hotel post office (8am–noon and 2–5:30pm) at Renmin Nan Lu 80, 2 Duan, opposite the Min Shan Fandian, is reliable and conveniently located.

Visa Extensions The Exit-Entry Office of the **PSB (Jingwai Renyuan Banzheng Qianzheng Ting)** is at Wenwu Lu 144 (✆ **028/8640-7067;** Mon–Fri 9am–noon and 1–5pm). The entrance is at 391 Shuncheng Dajie. Processing time is officially 5 days, but 3 days seems to be the average, and it's even speedier if you show an ongoing ticket. Take bus no. 55, 62, or 73 from railway stations 16 or 64; get off at the junction of Renmin Zhong Lu and Wenwu Lu and walk east; or take Metro Line 1 to Wenshu Yuan station.

Exploring Chengdu

The best way to enjoy Chengdu is to take long walks or cycle through the city, relax in a few teahouses and hot pot restaurants, and spread your visits to the best sights over a few days—or longer if you're using Chengdu as a base from which to visit out-of-town attractions. Here are some of my favorite strolls:

- Much of Chengdu's Tibetan community lives southeast of the Wuhou Temple, and the area around the Southwest Minority Nationalities College and the Tibetan Hospital is interesting for its bookstores, Tibetan shops, and people. **Wuhou Ci Heng Jie,** in particular, has lots of shops selling Tibetan and minority goods. Have lunch at **Xizang Fengqing Wu** (p. 685).
- Directly to the east of Wuhou Temple is Chengdu's entertainment landscape, **Jinli Gu Jie (Jinli Ancient St.).** This narrow strip of restaurants, bars, and souvenir stores is built in the style of traditional Eastern Sichuan architecture and is surprisingly tastefully done. The walk is as interesting for the architecture as it is for the opportunity to just mingle with middle-class Chinese. The strip is also well worth visiting for its alley of traditional Sichuan street food—an infinitely more hygienic environment than where you'll usually find it.
- To truly experience local people's lifestyle, one of the best ways used to be heading to **Kuan/Zhai Xiangzi (Wide/Narrow Lanes),** located in the west of the city center, which were full of teahouses and traditional Chinese architecture erected back in the Ming and Qing dynasties. However, under a redevelopment plan, most residents were evacuated and old buildings on Zhaixiangzi were demolished. The then-residential area has transformed into another entertainment spot like Jinli Gu Jie, with stylish cafes, tea houses, restaurants, bars, and souvenir stores. But few residential courtyards still remain on Kuan Xiangzi. Locals still love to spend their day on Zhaixiangzi, enjoying a cup of tea, playing cards and mahjong.
- Spend an afternoon or an evening strolling at the **Wangjianglou Park,** located by the Jinjiang River and in the southeast of the city, you will see locals playing mahjong and drinking tea, seniors practicing Chinese yo-yos (*kongzhu*), amateur musicians playing Chinese opera, as well as people offering ear-cleaning (*taoerduo*) and massage services. The calm and relaxing park is a huge bamboo garden, with over a hundred kinds of bamboo.

- It is worth taking an afternoon to wander through the stalls of "antiques," old party propaganda, Chinese handicrafts, and art at the complex, **Songxian Qiao Yishu Cheng (Songshan Bridge Art City),** on Huanhua Bei Lu. While much of what is on offer is indistinguishable from the pap passed off as Chinese culture in every city you are likely to visit, there are enough gems to warrant some of your time. Of particular interest is the **Zhongchuan Shoucang** (**Zhongchuan Collection;** A Qu, second floor no. 53), run by Yang Xiguang, a former cadre selling off his extensive personal collection of Cultural Revolution propaganda. Mr. Yang does not speak English, but the collection more than speaks for itself.

Qingyang Gong (Green Ram Monastery) Directly west of the city center, this Daoist monastery is culturally and historically the most important sight in the city. It's said that at Qingyang Fair (its first incarnation), Lao Zi attained immortality. And it was here that he revealed the *Daode Jing (Classic of the Dao)* to Yin Xi, frontier guardian at the Hangu Pass and last man to see Lao Zi before he left the world of men for Mount Kunlun, gateway to the Western Paradise. Today Qingyang Gong is one of the most active and important Daoist monasteries in China. Among its treasures, of greatest historical significance is a set of rare and elegant pear-wood printing plates of abstracts of scriptures in the Daoist canon. The grounds contain six halls on a central axis, a room for printing Daoist texts that stands to the east, and a room for worshiping Daoist sages that stands to the west. The **Hall of Three Purities (Sanqing Dian)** is the monastery's main building, but the most emblematic has to be the **Bagua Ting (Pavilion of the Eight Trigrams).** This octagonal building sitting on a square pedestal (symbolic of the earth) rises 20m (65 ft.) and has two flounces of upturned roofs covered in yellow, green, and purple ceramic tiles. Between the roofs, each facet of the octagon has at its center a plaque of the eight trigrams set off by a pattern of swastikas, symbolic of the sun or the movement of fire. The 81 carved dragons are said to symbolize the 81 incarnations of Lao Zi, but the number has closer associations with Chinese numerology and the belief in nine as the most "accomplished" of numbers. A bookstore in the **Hunyuan Dian (Hall of Chaotic Origin)** sells souvenirs alongside Mao bookmarks, Daoist study guides, and a fortunetelling manual called "Unlocking the Secrets of the *Book of Changes*." If you buy one of the likenesses of Lao Zi that comes in a cloth envelope and hand it to the Daoist priest behind the counter, he'll burn incense over it to *kaiguang* or "open its light."

Escape the din of the city at the partially covered outdoor **teahouse,** where customers play mahjong and chat with friends (albeit sometimes on cellphones). Next door is a **vegetarian restaurant,** open 9am to 2pm.

Yi Huan Lu Xi, 2 Duan (at Yi Huan Lu and Qingyang Zheng Jie intersection, on the grounds of Wenhua Gongyuan/Cultural Park). Admission ¥5. 8am–5:30pm. Bus: 11, 42, 47, 59, or 302.

Sanxing Dui Bowuguan (Sanxingdui Museum) ★★ This modern, spiral-shaped museum, opened in 1997, houses one of the most remarkable collections of ancient sculpture, masks, and ritual bronzes in China—don't miss it. Discovered in 1986, these otherworldly, artistically sophisticated tomb relics have sparked debate about the origins of the culture that produced them (as far back as the 14th c. B.C.) and its connection, if any, to the later Shu culture. The museum brochure equates the Sanxingdui civilization with the Shu, but some scholars doubt this, and many questions remain unanswered. For example, why is there no mention of this culture in historical records? When and why did the civilization disappear? Why do many of the masks and human busts seem to have been burned and deliberately shattered—quite possibly by the very people who created them?

Still, it's a marvelous collection. Highlights include a delightful ornament-bearing bronze holy tree supported by three kneeling guards and crowned with hawk-beaked birds. The piece most emblematic of the Sanxingdui is a 2.4m (8-ft.) standing bronze figure thought to be a sorcerer. Barefoot and standing on a pedestal of zoomorphic design, the creature has a long forehead, oversize eyes, and ears shaped like butterfly wings. Many of the bronze heads wear masks of pure gold. Also on display is an impressive gold-covered stick believed to be the ritual wand of a shaman. There are photos of the excavation process, English labels and English-speaking guide on duty for ¥120. Give yourself about 2 hours to explore the museum.

Guanghan, 40km (25 miles) north of Chengdu. ✆ **0838/550-0349.** www.sxd.cn. Admission ¥82. 8:30am–6pm. Direct buses (¥13) leave Chengdu Tourist Transportation and Service Center at 8:30am, 1 hr. ride. From Zhaojue Si Qichezhan (Zhaojue Temple bus station) Guanghan, frequent departures throughout the day. Express bus (¥12), 45-min. ride. Bus no. 6 leaves Guanghan for Sanxingdui every 20 min. for ¥2.

Jinsha Yizhi Bowuguan (Jinsha Site Museum) ★ Jinsha Yizhi, northwest of the city center, is another major ancient relic discovered in Sichuan after Sanxingdui. The new museum has two exhibition buildings comprised of the actual excavation site and five display rooms housing large collections of gold wares, bronze, jade, ivory, and stone statues of human portraits and animals, excavated from the site, which was discovered in 2001. Like Sanxingdui, it is believed to be part of the ancient Shu Kingdom 3,000 years ago. Some of the collections are quite similar to that of Sanxingdui. Highlights are the giant ivories, a gold disk with aesthetic carvings of the Sun and Immortal bird, and a 19.6cm-tall (7¾-in.) bronze figurine, which is believed to be a spiritualist. An English-speaking guide charges ¥100 for not more than 10 people.

Jinsha Relics Lu 2 (west of Chengdu city). ✆ **028/8730-3522.** www.jinshasitemuseum.com. Admission ¥80. 8am–6pm. Bus: 7, 14, 82, 96, 311, 401, or 502 to Qingyang Dadao Bei or 163 or 901 to Jinsha Yizhi Lu. Audio guide ¥20, with passport and ¥200 deposit.

Sichuan Bowuyuan (Sichuan Museum) The provincial museum's collection is not as appealing as other museums in the region, but it's a good place to spend a couple of hours if you would like to get some knowledge of the history and culture of Sichuan. The three-story museum houses an exhibition of the development of Tibetan Buddhism in Sichuan on the third floor. It features a collection of Tibetan Buddhism cultural relics, religious instruments, sutra, Tangka (scroll painting) and hundreds of gold-copper statuettes of Tibetan Buddha mainly from Ming (1368–1644) to Qing dynasty (1644–1912). In the Gallery of Sichuan crafts on the same floor, you can find a man-faced jade ornament back in the New Stone age about 4,000 years ago and unearthed in Chongqing's Daxi. Another exhibit introduces the culture and customs of minorities such as Yi, Qiang, and Miao of Sichuan. An art gallery features work of Chinese painter-scholar Zhang Daqian (1899–1983), who hailed from Sichuan and is renowned for his copies of the exquisite Buddhist wall paintings in Dunhuang.

Huanhua Nan Lu 251. ✆ **028/6552-1888** or 6552-1569. www.scmuseum.cn/en. Free admission. Get tickets at the gate by showing passport. Free lockers are available on the left hand side after entering the entrance. Tues–Sun 9am–5pm. Bus: 19, 35, 47, 82, 301, 309A or 407 to Songxianjiao Zhan. English audio guide ¥20 plus passport or ¥200 deposit.

Sichuan Daxue Bowuguan (Sichuan University Museum) Despite the opening of the provincial museum, it's still worth a visit to the Sichuan University's fascinating, well-presented collection, which includes Han and Tang dynasty Buddhist carvings; important Daoist documents, ritual instruments, talisman blocks, and clothing worn by shamans from the Eastern Han dynasty (25–220) to the Qing dynasty (1644–1912); bronzes from Ba and Shu cultures; a shadow puppet theater; and an ethnology collection featuring artifacts from a dozen central China minorities. Rarely are costumes displayed in such a dignified manner and without mannequins.

On the first floor, in the **Hall of Stone Carvings,** look for the exquisite 2m (7-ft.) carved Tang dynasty figure of a **bodhisattva** draped in cloth and jewels. On the second floor are several standouts. In the small room of ancient pottery from the Eastern Han dynasty, look for the life-size **clay dog** with hanging jowls and bulbous nose. The **Tibetan trumpet** made of a human femur can be found in the Exhibition Hall of Tibetan Artifacts. In the Daoist room, don't miss the **stone certificate of purchase** for a piece of subterranean real estate. In the bureaucratic netherworld, these funerary land deeds were taken to the grave as the deceased's proof of ownership of the land in which he or she was buried. Lastly, located in the same room is a circular **jade disk** *(bi)* from the Shang dynasty, symbol of Heaven (thought to be round), which was used in worship and burial (when it was probably placed beneath the corpse's back).

Wangjiang Lu 29 (adjacent to the east gate of Sichuan University). ✆ **028/8541-2451.** Admission ¥30. Mon–Fri 8:30am–5pm. Bus: 19, 35, or 335 to Sichuan Daxue Zhan.

Wang Anting Xiaoxiao Zhanlanguan ★ Informally known as the **Mao Museum,** this very small exhibition hall/apartment is the most eccentric museum you're likely to find in China. The 57,000 badges and Mao pins, along with 2 tons of Mao memorabilia still boxed in the attic, were all collected by the museum's owner, Wang Anting—who said that Mao came to him in a dream instructing him to share his collection with the world. In addition to badges, are busts, buttons, posters, magazines from the 1960s, and photographs from the same era. At the apartment's center, where a dining room table should be, is a large framed sepia-toned portrait of a beatific Mao. In front of it are burning incense and offerings of packages of instant noodles, and usually a plate of pears or a dish of candies. Other photos include one of a decrepit-looking Mao as he shakes the hand of Julie Nixon Eisenhower.

The best day to visit is December 26, when the museum and its small street are packed with people who've come to celebrate Mao's birthday.

Wufu Jie 23, northwest of the Mao statue; facing Mao, walk left (west). Turn right at the big street with a traffic light; pass Jinjiaba (lane with a market); turn at the 2nd left down Ping'an Xiang; the entrance to Wufu Jie is on the right. Free admission; however, the proprietor will encourage donations to support the museum. 9am–5pm.

Wenshu Yuan The best things about this active, Tang-founded Buddhist monastery are neither its gilded statues nor its relatively youthful buildings, but its teahouse filled with people reading, knitting, and just relaxing, and its excellent vegetarian restaurant with tables for two and windows overlooking the gardens. Outside, the street is lined with shops selling incense, paper money, and other Buddhist paraphernalia, and the square has stores selling folk handicrafts, traditional Sichuan snack and street food as well as Confucius religious ornaments. Inside, locals come to worship and burn incense. The 1st and 15th days of the lunar month are the most active. Another day that draws large crowds is the 19th day of the second lunar month, when the monastery celebrates the birthday of China's favorite bodhisattva, Guanyin, Goddess of Mercy. The Huayan Scripture, written in human blood, and the cranial bones of the monk Xuanzang (p. 259) are among the treasures housed at Wenshu. A pleasing and unusual Song fresco of a child worshiping Guanyin can be found near the gold-plated bronze Guanyin.

Wenshu Yuan Jie, just off Renmin Zhong Lu. Admission ¥5. 8am–6pm; restaurant 10:30am–10:30pm. Enter to the right of main entrance. Bus: 16 or 55; Metro: Wenshu Yuan Zhan.

Xiongmao Jidi/Daxiongmao Fanzhi Zhongxin (Panda Research Base/Giant Panda Breeding Center) ★ ☺ This research base, veterinary lab, panda habitat, and zoo is one of the best places to see giant pandas. Since the much more wild and natural Wolong Nature Reserve was damaged by the 2008 earthquake, it is your best option for panda sightings. The stated purpose of the breeding center is to increase the captive population of pandas in order to reintroduce some to the wild. The grounds of the research base, covered with trees, flowers, and 14 species of bamboo, are lovely and, at the very least, provide a pleasant escape from the noise and congestion of Chengdu proper. As you follow pathways through the reserve you may see not only giant pandas but red pandas (closer to a raccoon than a panda), black-necked cranes, and white storks. You might also run into visiting field researchers. Your best chance of seeing pandas is at feeding time, 8:30 to 10am, although a few, mostly those for breeding, are in cages. Ask if any cubs are around—a mother panda with babe in arms is a sight not to be missed. When the temperature is over 79°F (26°C), all the pandas will hide in an air-conditioned room. So, don't expect to see them playing around on the grounds on a hot day. By contributing ¥1,000 to the research base, you can get a chance to hold a baby panda and take photos with it. Allow an hour to get to the base, two to stroll the grounds. Alternately you can take a tour cart for ¥10 and reduce the visit to about 50 minutes; the tour is in Chinese, but at least you go straight to the pandas.

Xiongmao Da Dao, northern suburb, northeast of the zoo. ✆ **028/8351-0033.** www.panda.org.cn. Admission ¥58. 8am–6pm. Bus: 902 outside Traffic Hotel or 107 or 532 from Zhaojue Si Qichezhan (Zhaojue Temple bus station).

Shopping

Chengdu has six **Carrefour (Jialefu)** stores (9am–10pm). Thanks to discounts and a broad selection of Chinese and imported products, shopping here always feels like the day before Christmas—festive, but impossibly crowded. If you abhor body contact with perfect strangers, go elsewhere. If you don't mind it, the most accessible location is at Babao Jie 1 (✆ **028/8626-6789**). Take bus no. 4, 7, or 56 to Babao Jie. **Trust-mart (Haoyouduo Chaoshi),** is located at Daye Lu 39, south of Tianfu Guangchang. Open from 9am to 10pm, it's a grocery store, drug store, and department store in one. Take bus no. 1, 8, 26, or 43 to Daye Lu. The best, most convenient supermarket at which to buy snacks for a long train and coach journey is the huge **Renmin Shangchang (People's Market)** opposite the main railway station. It also has a bakery and a fast-food restaurant that serves a Chinese breakfast. Open 7:30am to 9:30pm. **Chunxi Lu** is the most lively shopping and dining area. It has restaurants of different cuisines from Sichuan to Japanese, Korean, American, and major shopping malls such as Ito Yokado, New Asia Plaza, and Japanese brand Isetan. Take bus no. 58, 81 or 98 to Chunxi Lu Bei Kou.

Where to Stay

EXPENSIVE

Crowne Plaza Hotel Chengdu City Centre (Chengdu Zongfu Huangguan Jiari Jiudian) Compared with other five-star hotels in the city, Crowne Plaza enjoys a more convenient location, a few blocks from the city center and next door to Parkson. After a renovation in 2011, the hotel is equipped with better facilities. Staff is pleasant. Rooms with a single king-size bed are bigger than twins.

Zongfu Jie 31 (4 blocks east of the Mao statue). www.crowneplaza.com. ✆ **800/968-688** or 028/8678-6666. Fax 028/8678-9789. 402 units. ¥800 standard room, without breakfast. 15% service charge. AE, DC, MC, V. Bus: 3, 4, 7, 45, 58, or 98. **Amenities:** 4 restaurants; 2 bars; babysitting; forex; health club; indoor pool; room service; spa and sauna; airline ticketing; Wi-Fi. *In room:* A/C, satellite TV, fridge, hair dryer, Internet, minibar.

Kempinski Chengdu (Chengdu Kaibinsiji Fandian) Located close to the U.S. Consulate area, Kempinski is a good choice in the south of the city. Though its lobby and facilities are not as exquisite as Shangri-la and Sheraton, the light-tone rooms have plush beds. The white bed lamps and the big circular mirror on the wall next to the bed add a stylish touch to the room.

Renmin Nan Lu, 4 Duan, 42. www.kempinski-chengdu.com. ✆ **028/8526-9999.** Fax 028/8512-2666. 483 units. ¥866–¥1,588 standard room. 15% service charge. AE, DC, MC, V. **Amenities:** 2 restaurants; deli; bar; forex; small health club; KTV; indoor pool; room service; spa; tennis court; airline, train, and bus ticketing. *In room:* A/C, satellite TV, fridge, hair dryer, Internet, minibar.

Shangri-la Hotel, Chengdu (Chengdu Xianggelila Dajiudian) ★★ With its excellent service, Shangri-la Chengdu is now the best luxurious choice in the city and is vibrant all day long. Located beside the Jiajiang River, the hotel enjoys a spectacular view of the Hejiang Pavilion and the beautiful garden along the riverside. It has oil paintings by renowned Chengdu and Asian artists such as Guo Wei and Guo Jin, turning the lobby and foyer of the function rooms into a mini gallery. Guest rooms are soothing, decorated with tasteful and sophisticated oriental-style fittings. The large marbled bathrooms have a separate tub and a shower cubicle equipped with a rainforest showerhead. The sizable health club has advanced gym equipment and a large swimming pool. Free broadband Internet is in all rooms and public areas.

Binjiang Dong Lu 9 (near Tianxianqiao Binhe Lu). www.shangri-la.com. ✆ **028/8888-9999.** Fax 028/8888-6666. 593 units. ¥976–¥1,400 standard room. 15% service charge. AE, DC, MC, V. **Amenities:** 3 restaurants; bar; forex; health club; indoor pool; room service; luxurious spa; tennis court; airline, train, and bus ticketing. *In room:* A/C, satellite TV, fridge, hair dryer, minibar, Wi-Fi.

Sheraton Chengdu Lido (Tianfu Lidu Xilaideng Fandian) Located 1km (½ mile) north of the city center, the Sheraton is one of the most attractive luxury hotels in Chengdu. The lobby's fountain and large floral arrangement give this spot a warmer ambience than a standard hotel, and the front desk staff is amiable and efficient. Although the standard rooms aren't spacious, the cozy decor is inviting. Free Wi-Fi access is in all public areas.

Renmin Zhong Lu 1, Duan 15. www.sheraton.com/chengdu. ✆ **028/8676-8999.** Fax 028/8676-8888. 403 units. ¥1,010 standard room, including 1 breakfast. 15% service charge. AE, DC, MC, V. Bus: 16. Minibus: 5 from railway station. **Amenities:** 2 restaurants; 2 bars; forex; health club, Jacuzzi; indoor heated pool; room service; sauna; airline, train, and bus ticketing; Wi-Fi. *In room:* A/C, satellite TV, fridge, hair dryer, Internet, minibar.

Sofitel Wanda Chengdu (Chengdu Soufeite Wanda Dafandian) The French hotel brand is one of the most experienced hotels in the city. Situated at the intersection of Renmin Nan Lu and the Jinjiang River, it is conveniently located within walking distant of the Xin Nan Men Bus Station. The lobby bar with live performances is a fine place to relax after a busy day of sightseeing. The decent-sized rooms are complete with a computer with free Internet access.

Binjiang Zhong Lu 15. www.sofitel.com. © **028/6666-9999.** Fax 028/6666-3333. 262 units. ¥1,104 standard room, including breakfast. 15% service charge. AE, DC, MC, V. **Amenities:** 3 restaurants; bar; babysitting; fitness center, sauna, massage, spa; forex; indoor heated pool; room service; smoke-free floor; airline, train, and bus ticketing; Wi-Fi. *In room:* A/C, satellite TV, fridge, hair dryer, computer with broadband Internet, minibar.

MODERATE

Buddha Zen Hotel (Yuanheyuan Fodan Kezhan) ★ With its Zen decor theme, this hotel at Wenshu Fang, has thoughtful design accents in every corner. Live Chinese music is played in the courtyard and garden during the afternoon. Rooms are furnished with traditional Chinese–style wooden furniture and elegant Sichuan embroidery on the wall. Some rooms have a small balcony. The bathrooms are small and have a shower only, but are clean and well-kept. Deluxe suites feature an ancient Chinese–style canopy bed. The hotel has a vegetarian restaurant serving tasty Chinese–style vegetarian dishes. With such a limited number of rooms, the hotel is always fully booked. Make reservations in advance.

Wenshu Fang B6-6. www.buddhazenhotel.com. © **028/8692-9898** or 8693-1522. Fax 028/8693-1250. 35 units. ¥380–¥468 standard room; ¥630–¥880 suite. No credit cards. **Amenities:** Vegetarian restaurant; tea house; room service; spa. *In room:* A/C, flat-screen TV.

Jinli Home Hotel (Jinli Renjia Kezhan) This Sichuan–themed hotel is one of the new economical choices in Chengdu. It is close to Jinli Gu Jie and Wuhou. Rooms are clean and simple with red decor. Beds are comfy enough, but bathrooms are a bit small, with shower only. Noise from the strip of Chinese restaurants across the street can be heard inside the room, but at an acceptable level.

Jiang Cheng Hua, Daosangshu Jie, Wuhou District. © **028/8559-5111.** Fax 028/8555-5111. 80 units. ¥288 standard room. 20% discount is standard. No credit cards. **Amenities:** Restaurant; room service; airline, train, and bus ticketing. *In room:* A/C, TV.

Sunjoy Inn (Xinzu Binguan) Located just a short walk from the U.S. consulate, this three-star hotel was renovated in 2004. Management and staff pride themselves on continued maintenance of the building and guest rooms. Clean hallway carpets and unstained sinks—rarities in all but the priciest hotels—attest to their sincerity. Guest rooms and bathrooms are medium in size. Furnishings are run-of-the-mill but better maintained than most in this range. The hotel is connected to one of the best non-Chinese restaurants in Chengdu, **Tandoor Indian Cuisine** (p. 685).

Renmin Nan Lu, 4 Duan 34. www.sunjoy-inn.com. © **028/8557-1660.** Fax 028/8554-6598. 189 units. ¥420–¥480 standard room. Rates include breakfast. 20% discount is standard. AE, DC, MC, V. Bus: 16, 19, or 72. Minibus: 5. **Amenities:** 3 restaurants; bar; exercise room; forex; room service; sauna; airline, train, and bus ticketing. *In room:* A/C, TV, fridge, Internet, minibar.

INEXPENSIVE

Sim's Cozy Garden Hostel (Chengdu Lao Shen Qingnian Lushe) The cheapest of Chengdu's budget offerings, Sim's is spartan but clean and a true value. Formerly located on a side street close to Wenshu Temple, the hostel moved to its present location in late 2007, with better facilities and a larger space. The founders are a couple from Singapore and Japan who met in Lhasa and later opened a guesthouse in Chengdu. The hostel has spacious common areas with a big shelf of books and travel information, a 24-hour movie room with an extensive DVD collection, and a garden with tables and chairs—ideal in summer to meet fellow travelers. The staff and the in-house travel agent all speak English and are helpful. In late 2010, it was sold to a new owner, but its quality still remains.

No. 221, North Section 4, First Ring Road. www.gogosc.com. ✆ **028/8197-9337.** Fax 028/8335-5322. ¥70–¥120 single room; ¥160–¥240 twin room; ¥90–¥240 double room; ¥180–¥240 triple room; ¥45/bed in 4-person room en suite. No credit cards. Bus: 27, 28, 34, 60, 308, 412, or 902. **Amenities:** Restaurant; bar; bike rental; Internet bar; 24-hr. movie room; airline and train ticketing; free Wi-Fi, baby bed, and car. *In room:* A/C, TV, DVD player, Internet (in some).

Traffic Hotel (Jiaotong Fandian) Catering to independent travelers and backpackers, this one-star hotel puts Internet access, Tibet travel news, rental bikes, and bag storage at your fingertips. Equally important, room rates range from inexpensive to moderate. The staff is friendly and helpful (most speak some English), and the **Anchor Bar** (see below) is *the* place to meet other like-minded travelers. Although the elevator has a disturbing rattle, rooms are clean and sort of cozy. Limited budget single rooms, with communal bathrooms, are only available for walk-in customers.

Linjiang Zhong Lu 6 (next to the Xin Nan Men Bus Station). www.traffichotelchengdu.cn. ✆ **028/8545-1017.** Fax 028/8544-0977. 134 units. ¥200–¥240 standard room; ¥180 triple with communal shower/toilet; ¥50 single bed with A/C and communal shower/toilet. No credit cards. Bus: 902 or 904. **Amenities:** 2 restaurants; bar; bike rental; airline, train, and bus ticketing. *In room:* A/C, TV, minibar.

Traffic Inn (Jiaotong Qingnian Lvshe) ★ Right next to the Traffic Hotel, this small inn is another good choice for independent travelers and backpackers. The green wooden French doors and wooden furniture set up a relaxing and soothing ambiance in the rooms. Beds are surprisingly comfortable. Rooms on the ground floor have shared shower rooms and toilets (with two Western-style toilets) that are clean and well maintained. Its cafe has an alfresco patio as well as a bean-bed sofa area for travelers to hang out and watch movies. The staff is nice and speaks English.

Linjiang Zhong Lu 6 (next to the Xin Nan Men Bus Station). www.trafficinnhostel.com/en. ✆ **028/8545-0407.** traffic.nihao@gmail.com. 30 units. ¥90–¥110 basic room; ¥160–¥240 standard room; ¥180–¥240 triple en suite; ¥40–¥55 bed in 4-person room; ¥35 bed in 6-person room with A/C and communal shower/toilet. No credit cards. Bus: 15, 16, 28, or 55. **Amenities:** Restaurant; bar; bike rental; airline, train, and bus ticketing. *In room:* A/C, TV, Wi-Fi.

Where to Eat

Anchor Bar (an Ba) HOME-STYLE WESTERN/CHINESE Situated in front of the Traffic Hotel, this cozy little bar is a great place to relax over a cold beer; plus, Internet access is free if you buy a meal here. For the most part, the menu lacks imagination—both in the Chinese and Western offerings—with the exception of an excellent hot Western breakfast. But all is forgiven when you sink into one of the soft, welcoming couches that are a godsend after a day spent pounding city streets. The rest of the decor is Tibetan-inspired with warm, earthy colors. The staff speaks limited English but is a friendly lot and will burn your pictures onto a CD, and let you use the TV to watch a DVD after 8pm.

Linjiang Zhong Lu 6. ✆ **028/8545-4520.** Main courses ¥30–¥50. No credit cards. 9am until the last customer goes home. Book exchange. Bus: 15, 16, 28, or 55.

Baguo Buyi ★ SICHUAN Delicious local fare made with fresh, natural ingredients is served here in artfully rustic surroundings—dried corn stalks and red peppers hang between photographs of farmhouses and peasant life. A spiral wooden staircase wrapped around a large artificial tree leads to second-floor tables with views of the open kitchen. The restaurant is spacious enough to afford for some privacy and service is excellent. House specialties include the gelatinous green turtle stewed with taro *(yuer shao jiayu)*—a regional delicacy, but not to everyone's taste. More reliable would be *huiguo houpi cai* (twice-cooked thick-skinned greens), a leafy green vegetable boiled and stir-fried in a delicious broad bean sauce, and more inspired than its name suggests. Also try *yecai ba* (steamed glutinous rice bread with wild vegetables wrapped in corn husks), and *doufu jiyu* (tofu and golden carp). The tasty sauce, made of tomato, spring onion, chilies, and beans, makes this a particular favorite with locals.

Renmin Nan Lu 20, 4 Duan (near Lingshiguan Lu). ✆ **028/8553-1688.** English menu. Meal for 2 ¥80–¥120. No credit cards. 11:30am–2:30pm and 5–10pm. Bus: 16 or 99.

Caigen Xiang ★ SICHUAN With four outlets and a cooking school, this is one of Chengdu's most popular restaurants. Specializing in dishes made with traditional pickled vegetables *(pao cai)*, the restaurant has won awards for its *paojiao moyu zai* (pickled pepper with baby squid). Two other distinctive dishes are Caigen Xiang spareribs *(Caigen Xiang paigu)*, which fall off the bone and are cooked in a delicious sauce that renders them juicy and tender, and fish with pickled vegetables *(paocai jiayu)*. This is a whole fish served in a red sauce with a variety of fresh and pickled vegetables. You have to deal with the bones, but the fish is delicate and tasty.

Renmin Nan Lu (near corner of Tongzi Lin Bei Lu). ✆ **028/8518-5967.** Picture menu. Meal for 2 ¥150–¥200. No credit cards. 9:30am–9:30pm. Bus: 16 or 99 to Jinxiu Huayuan.

Fiesta Thai (Feichang Tai Taiguo Fengwei Canting) ★ THAI Nestled in next to the Anchor Bar, the food at Fiesta isn't exactly authentic—suffering from the Sichuan tendency to make everything a little hotter than necessary—but the service and environment more than compensate. The polished wooden floor boards and elegantly dressed serving staff add a touch of class, and the high ceilings add a breezy feeling that makes the restaurant a pleasant escape from the summer heat.

Linjiang Zhong Lu 6 (just in front of the Traffic Hotel). ✆ **028/8545-4530.** English menu. Meal for 2 ¥80–¥120. No credit cards. 5–10:30pm. Bus: 15, 16, 28, or 55.

Grandma's Kitchen (Zumu de Chufang) AMERICAN Farm-style chandeliers and wall lamps, straight-back wooden chairs with gingham cushions, and framed photos on the wall give this split-level restaurant an appropriately homey atmosphere—and goes a long way toward explaining how Grandma's is turning itself into a booming franchise with two locations in Chengdu and two in Beijing. The menu might not be entirely familiar—tuna-fish pizza is undoubtedly the result of a recipe confused in the translation—but the rest of the menu, which includes fried chicken, a variety of steaks, and much more, is a prayer answered for any U.S. resident craving a taste of home—as are the homemade pies and desserts. The comfortable atmosphere with small collections of donated English-language paperbacks makes either Grandma's location a perfect place to hole up on a rainy day and write postcards. The other location is Renmin Nan 4 Duan Lu, 22 (✆ **028/8555-3856**).

2/F, Kehua Bei Lu 143. ✆ **028/8524-2835.** Main courses ¥40–¥60. No credit cards. English spoken. Sun–Fri 9:30am–11:30pm; Sat 8:30am–11:30pm. Bus: 55, 110, 49, or 6.

Tandoor Indian Cuisine (Tengduer Yindu Canting) ★ NORTHERN INDIAN Tandoor's Indian chef clearly takes care in buying and preparing ingredients to make authentic dishes from chiefly the north, but also from southern India. The food and service are equally superb. A delicious specialty from Goa is the Portuguese-influenced pork vindaloo. This very hot dish is made with Indian spices, vinegar, and chilies. One of the best northern specialties is *murgh malai* kabob, chunks of chicken marinated in ginger-garlic paste, then mixed with cheese, cream, coriander, chili, cinnamon, and anisette, and cooked in a tandoori oven. Connected to the Xinzu Binguan (Sunjoy Inn), Tandoor is airy and handsome; elegant wooden rafters give it flair, and soft Indian music enhances an already pleasing ambience.

Renmin Nan Lu 34, 4 Duan (directly behind the Xinzu Binguan). ✆ **028/8555-1958.** Meal for 2 ¥100–¥130. AE, DC, MC, V. 11:30am–2pm and 5:30–10pm. Bus: 99 or 16.

Tanyoto ★ HOT POT You'll appreciate this hot pot restaurant as much for its good food as for its warmly lit, inviting dining room. The space is large and airy and affords privacy at every table. Ambience aside, the keys to great hot pot are the broth—here it is rich and flavorful—and the dipping sauce. Ingredients vary, but are likely to include bean sprouts, leeks, a variety of mushrooms, sausages, seafood, organ meats, and/or duck tongues. Fish heads, which may sound exotic, are the signature ingredient of the shop and you get to choose from different kinds of fish heads. They are fresh and go well with the spicy broth. I recommend the *ma la* (hot and numbing) hot pots, but a handful of selections of non-chili broth is also available. *Bin tofu* (frozen tofu), which absorbs the essence of the soup, is a must-have item.

Renmin Nan Lu 4 Duan, 49 (10 min. walk south from Kempinski Hotel). ✆ **028/8522-2266.** Meal for 2 ¥160–¥200. No credit cards. 11am–10pm. Bus: 16, 99, 102, or 118 to Renmin Nan Lu 4 Duan Nan.

Xizang Fengqing Wu TIBETAN Situated in a Tibetan neighborhood and frequented by Tibetans (many Khampas from western Sichuan), this intimate three-room restaurant (with four to six tables in each room) serves top-quality dishes in a warm, cheerful environment. Tibetan music usually plays in the background, and almost any time of day you'll find monks at several of the tables, eating snacks and drinking milk tea. Three great dishes are *jiarong suancai kaobing* (jiarong Tibetan bread stuffed with pickled cabbage and barbecued pork), *maoniu roubao* (yak meat *baozi*), and *suan luobo chao maoniurou* (pickled cabbage with fried yak meat). For a snack, try Tibetan bread with milk tea. A large pot of tea costs ¥15.

Wuhou Ci Dong Jie 3, Fu 2 (look for painting of yak on an ocher-yellow building with Tibetan script in blue, red, orange, and yellow). ✆ **028/8551-0112.** Menu has some English. Meal for 2 ¥80. No credit cards. 8am–10:30pm. Bus: 8 or 21 to Wuhou Ci Hang Jie or 1, 57, 82, 334 335 or 503 to Wuhou Ci.

TEAHOUSES

For the typical Chengdu experience, go to Qingyang Gong or Wenshu Yuan monasteries (see "Exploring Chengdu," earlier in this chapter). For something trendier, Chengdu has upmarket teahouses for the connoisseur or connoisseur-in-training. The best of the bunch is **Guanghe Chalou,** on the river at Linjiang Zhong Lu 16 (✆ **028/8550-1688**). Rattan chairs, palm trees, lots of large potted plants, and blondwood lend a clean, spalike atmosphere to this teahouse. The Chinese/English menu has pages of teas, some medicinal or therapeutic, others special for the locale in which they're grown. Under "Teas for Women" are "Aloe Beauty Face Tea," "Heart

THE ways OF TEA

In the 8th-century *Classic of Tea,* author and tea sage Lu Yu says that there are "nine ways by which man must tax himself when he deals with tea."

1. He must manufacture it.
2. He must develop a sense of selectivity and discrimination about it.
3. He must provide the proper implements.
4. He must prepare the right kind of fire.
5. He must select a suitable water.
6. He must roast the tea to a turn.
7. He must grind it well.
8. He must brew it to its ultimate perfection.
9. He must, finally, drink it.

In modern China, there are still many ways to drink tea, from the highly ritualized, heavy-on-equipage style prescribed by Lu Yu, to the style favored on long-distance trains (toss a pinch of tea leaves into a glass jar with a screw-top and keep adding water and drinking until you reach your destination). The Chengdu way doesn't use a teapot or a glass jar: The typical setting is the riverside, a park, or temple grounds—in an outdoor teahouse with bamboo tables and chairs. Here, patrons sip tea from 3-ounce cups that sit on saucers small enough to rest in the palm of the hand while protecting it from the heat of the cup. A lid keeps the tea hot and can be used to sweep aside tea leaves that rise to the top as you drink. Melon seeds, boiled peanuts, or dried squid are typical snack accompaniments.

Tea," and "Chinese Yew Tea for Lady." A small pot of "Rose Love Things" is ¥48, but my favorite is always Wulong, of which there are many kinds. The best come from the high mountains of Taiwan and Fujian Province. A pot of tea costs ¥38 to ¥68. The teahouse is open from 9am to midnight.

Chengdu After Dark

Unlike many Chinese cities, Chengdu offers a variety of ways to pass the evening. **Sichuan opera** is a favorite for foreign and Chinese tourists alike. Known for its humor and dynamism, an integral part of every performance is *bianlian* or "changing faces." The character is often a villain who changes his face to escape recognition. The reputed record is 14 changes in 24 seconds. Over its 300-year tradition, the trick has changed, but it has always been a closely guarded secret within the operatic community. Traditional stick puppets and flame balancing are also incorporated into the drama. Nightly performances are held at the strictly-for-tourists **Shufeng Yayun** in Wenhua Gongyuan, on 23 Qintai Lu (✆ **028/8611-1025;** 8–9:30pm); the fee is ¥200, ¥260, or ¥320. Take bus no. 35 to Baoyun An or no. 13, 64, 78, 81 or 163 to Tonghui Men.

Lan Kwai Fong, adjacent to Shangri-la, is the latest and hippest dinning, drinking and clubbing spot for the middle-class and the young ones. Inspired by the famous Hong Kong nightlife area, the entire street has a range of Chinese and Western restaurants, cafes, clubs and bars. Another highlight is the **Jiuyanqiao Bar Street,** along the river near the Jiuyanqiao Bridge and across the river from the Shangri-la.

The street is filled with plenty of pubs of different ambience as well as outdoor pubs. It is one of the most popular nightlife spots among locals and the entire street is lively from dusk till dawn. **Kehua Bei Lu,** in the Sichuan University area, has several clubs which are party-goers' favorites. **Kuan/Zhai Xiangzi** also has a list of lounge bars that are well-liked by the white-collar and sophisticated crowd. The **Lotus Palace Bar and Restaurant** (**Lianhua Fudi; ✆ 028/8553-7676;** 3pm–3am), nestled halfway down Jinli Ancient Street, is a popular city bar. The entrance to the bar itself is hidden behind two heavy black doors and walled in by a granite facade in the traditional Sichuan style. The inside of the bar has a complete new look, fusing stylish modern design into the Chinese building, after a massive renovation in 2011. If you go early in the evening, the music is sufficiently loungey and good for enjoying a quiet drink; go later and the music gives way to heavier dance mix enjoyed by Chengdu's young, bright things. It is worth a visit to see how China is trying to reclaim its cultural heritage—without giving into kitsch.

If you are interested to explore the mainland underground music scene, go to **Little Bar (Xiaojiuguan),** Fangxin Jie 87 (**✆ 028/8515-8790;** 5pm until late), on the ground floor of the Hengfeng Yinhang next to the Yongfeng Stereo Bridge. You won't miss the red table and chair hung on the exterior wall next to the glass door. First established by local musician Tang Lei in 1997, the Fangxin bar is the second branch of Little Bar. Despite its poor sound quality, this bar is the most popular stage for local and overseas bands and organizes shows every Friday and Saturday night. You can also find a large variety of mainland underground acts' CDs on a big shelf inside.

EMEI SHAN 峨眉山 ★

Sichuan Province, 143km (89 miles) SW of Chengdu, 36km (22 miles) E of Le Shan

Emei means "lofty eyebrows," but it's also a pun on a poetic expression referring to the delicate brows of a beautiful woman. The mountain was named for two of its high adjacent peaks, whose outlines, according to 6th-century commentary on the "Book of Waterways," did indeed conjure the image of two long, thin, graceful eyebrows. Once richly endowed with both flora and fauna, this sacred Buddhist mountain is still home to 10% of China's plant species; fauna have fared less well. Threatened species include Asiatic black bear, giant salamander (the famous "crying fish," or *wawa yu* in Chinese), gray-hooded parrot bill, and Asiatic golden cat. You'll also bump into monkeys that want a handout, but try to resist—they already suffer from obesity and hypertension. As of 2002, park wardens have put them on a diet.

Come here for scenic hiking and active Buddhist shrines and monasteries (where the monk and nun population was once as threatened as the golden cat but has now returned, albeit in smaller numbers). Nature enthusiasts will delight in the exotic insects and butterflies along the way.

Altitudes on the mountain range from 500 to 3,099m (1,640–10,167 ft.) at the Wanfo Ding summit. Not surprisingly, average yearly temperatures vary significantly from one part of the mountain to another. In the subtropical zone at the bottom, the average is 63°F (17°C); at the summit, 3°C (37°F). Bring layers of clothes. The best months to visit are late August through early October. The busiest months are July and August. Avoid national holidays.

Note: For Chinese translations of establishments in this section, see chapter 16.

A proper visit TO EMEI SHAN

The Chinese say a proper visit to Emei Shan involves at least one of the following:

- Watching the **sunrise** from the summit (which requires staying the night on or near it—the earliest shuttle arrives after sunup).
- Standing in the **Cloud Sea.** Like many a Chinese mountain, Emei is famous for its clouds and mists. The classic experience happens when layers of clouds gather between Jiulao Dong and Xi Xiang Chi (Elephant Bathing Pool). You see the clouds above, climb through them, then look down to see clouds billowing and surging at your feet like the sea. Of course, conditions aren't always right.
- Witnessing **Buddha's Halo.** When the sun shines through misty clouds, and you're standing between the clouds and the sun, you can see your shadow outlined by a halo-shaped rainbow. Optimal time: 2 to 5pm. Optimal place: Sheshen Yan.
- Seeing the **"Strange Lamps" (Guai Deng).** Photos and witnesses are both scarce, but supposedly in the evening when the moon is waning, especially after it has rained and the sky has cleared, those looking down from Sheshen Yan at the layers of mountains in the distance can see thousands of floating orbs of light.

Essentials

GETTING THERE Several **fast trains** run from Chengdu to Emei Shan on the Chengdu-Kunming line. The trip takes 2 to 3 hours and costs ¥24. Minibuses and taxis connect the **Emei Railway Station** (3.2km/2 miles east of town) with the mountain entrance at Baoguo. The fare is ¥16 and it's a 20-minute drive.

Taking the bus to Emei Shan is faster and more direct than the train. In Chengdu, **buses** to Emei Shan depart from Xin Nan Men every 20 minutes; the first leaves at 6:40am. It costs ¥43 and takes 2½ hours. Buses terminate at Baoguo Town, where the mountain trails begin. The Emei Bus Station is connected to Baoguo Si, the monastery at Emei's entrance, by **minibuses** that make the 20-minute, 6.4km (4-mile) drive for ¥10. You can also take one of the public buses leaving every 5 minutes; the fare is ¥2. Buses also run between Emei Shan and Le Shan bus stations every few minutes. Buy your ticket for the half-hour trip inside the terminal for ¥8. Buses unload at Le Shan's north gate. You can also hop on one of the many Le Shan–bound minibuses that wait outside the Emei gate. They don't depart until every seat is taken; the fare is ¥4.

VISITOR INFORMATION The very modern and helpful **Emei Shan Tourist Center (Luren Zhongxin),** near Baoguo Temple (✆ **0833/559-0111**), provides free information and materials about Mount Emei. Guides can be hired here, although you're sure to pay less if you hire one of the many freelance guides (whose English may not be as good) outside Baoguo Temple. For quiet and tranquillity, you may opt to go it alone.

Bilingual maps are sold at the tourist center and at any of the many postcard and book stands near the entrance and along the trail. The map costs ¥5; one side of the map shows Emei Shan, the other Le Shan (see below).

Exploring Emei Shan

Emei Shan (✆ **028/8737-1405;** www.ems517.com; ¥150; ¥90 Dec 15–Jan 14, student discount ¥80; monasteries ¥6–¥10) has two main **hiking routes** to the Jin Ding summit, and two involving bus and/or cable car. Both hiking routes follow the same path from **Baoguo Si** (at the entrance) to **Niuxin Ting.** At Niuxin Ting, they split into a higher and a lower trail, which meet up again at **Xi Xiang Chi,** where they merge into a single path that leads to **Jin Ding Peak.** Since 80km (50 miles) of trails lead to the peak, a combination of hiking, buses, and cable car is recommended.

You can take a **bus** from Baoguo Si to Leidong Ping; from there, take a **cable car** to the top. Buses travel between Baoguo Si and Leidong Ping all day (Golden Weeks 5am–5pm; Nov–Apr 7am–4pm; May–Oct 6:30am–5pm). The trip each way takes 2 hours and costs ¥70. The cable car runs the 500m (1,666-ft.) leg between the last parking lot, at Jieyin Dian (next to Leidong Ping), and Jin Ding (Golden Peak); ¥65 for the ascent, ¥55 descent; 5:30am to 6pm.

Another option is to take the bus as far as **Wannian Cable Car Station (Wannian Chechang).** Begin your trek there or take the 8-minute cable car ride to Wannian Si and start climbing from there. The cable car ride costs ¥65 for the ascent, ¥45 for the descent, from 6:40am to 6pm.

All roads lead to Jin Ding, but the highest peaks are **Qianfo Ding** and **Wanfo Ding.** These can be reached by a **monorail** that runs between Jin Ding and Wanfo Ding. The round-trip takes 20 minutes and costs ¥60; 8am to 6pm.

Note: If you get caught without enough warm clothing, rent a Chinese army jacket for ¥10 at several spots on the mountain, including the Leidong Ping (Leidong parking lot).

Where to Stay

For the most comfort, stay in one of the several full-service hotels near the entrance to Emei Shan. At the summit, the Jin Ding Dajiudian is quite comfortable (see below). Other than that, if you want to overnight on the mountain, be prepared for relatively spartan accommodations. Beginning at Baoguo Si—the first temple you encounter upon entering the Emei Shan scenic area—and continuing to the summit, all the monasteries have guesthouses with rates ranging from ¥20 to ¥160 per night. Accommodations are as basic as the rates suggest: The least expensive have dorm-style rooms for four to six people, limited or no hot water, and a hallway bathroom. In the higher range, expect air-conditioning and limited hot water. Meals can consist of vegetarian, mock-meat dishes or a simple bowl of noodles for around ¥6. Two popular monasteries are **Xianfeng Si** and **Xi Xiang Chi.** Guesthouses at the peak and in the vicinity of the cable-car terminus at Jing Shui offer more comfortable lodging (with TV, air-conditioning, and hot showers) for a bit more—but not all of them accept foreigners. They charge ¥150 to ¥250.

Emei Shan Dafandian (Emei Shan Hotel) ★ This hotel in Emei is fresh and sparkling. Each deluxe standard room is spacious and comfortably furnished with a sofa, chair, and coffee table. Located next to the bus station, the hotel is convenient for late arrivals or early departures, but it's about 8km (5 miles) from Emei Shan. To get to the mountain, catch a bus in front of the station for ¥2 or take a taxi for ¥15 or less.

Baoguo Si (by the Emei Shan Bus Station, 8km/5 miles from Baoguo Si). ✆ **0833/559-5166.** Fax 0833/559-5870. 458 units. ¥420–¥610 standard room. Rates include Chinese breakfast. AE, DC, MC, V. **Amenities:** Restaurant; bar; Internet; room service. *In room:* A/C, TV, fridge/minibar (in some).

Hongzhu Shan Hotel (Hongzhu Shan Binguan) ★★ On park grounds with a lake and surrounded by dense forest, this is the most beautiful place to stay at Emei Shan, and the choice of visiting dignitaries. Several buildings comprise the hotel, but no matter where you stay, you're guaranteed a gorgeous, wooded view. The no. 4 Wing was the villa of the former Chinese Nationalist Party leader Chiang Kai-shek erected in 1935. The premise was listed as a cultural heritage by the Leshan government in 1986. Guest rooms and bathrooms are large, with tastefully appointed furnishings.

Emei Shan Baoguo Si Zuoce (approaching Emei Shan from town, after passing Emei Museum on the right, and just before reaching Baoguo Si, turn left and follow road to end). www.hzshotel.com. ✆ **0833/552-5888.** Fax 0833/552-5666. 510 units. ¥980–¥1,280 standard room. AE, DC, MC, V. **Amenities:** 3 restaurants; 2 bars; forex; health club; room service; smoke-free floors; hot spring; outdoor tennis court and badminton court; airline, train, and bus ticketing. *In room:* A/C, satellite TV, hair dryer, Internet, minibar/fridge.

Jin Ding Dajiudian (Golden Summit Hotel) If you'd like to see the sunrise, this three-star hotel close to the summit is the place to stay. The rooms may be standard issue, but the views are incredible.

Jin Ding (at the Jin Ding summit). ✆ **0833/509-8058.** 100 units. ¥580–¥980 standard room. 20%–30% discounts. No credit cards. **Amenities:** Restaurant; room service. *In room:* A/C, TV, Internet (in some).

Where to Eat

The two restaurants at **Hongzhu Shan Binguan** serve excellent food. The prices are higher than usual, but basic meat and vegetable dishes are still quite reasonable. A number of restaurants sit along the road leading to Baoguo Si. The biggest draw for Western tourists is **Teddy Bear Cafe** (✆ **0833/559-0135**), which serves Chinese and Western dishes and has an English menu. Next door is the Teddy Bear Hotel, whose English-speaking staff is extremely useful in organizing tours and booking tickets.

LE SHAN 乐山

Sichuan Province, 154km (96 miles) SW of Chengdu, 36km (22 miles) W of Emei Shan

The carved stone statue of the Great Buddha (Da Fo) at Le Shan is one of Sichuan's top tourist destinations, but whether it's worth a day in a tight travel schedule is debatable. The thrill of Le Shan is in your first sighting of the Great Buddha. Whether that's from the top looking down, from a boat looking straight up, or from the path of nine switchbacks (Lingyun Zhandao) looking somewhere in between, the moment it dawns on you that the large, gracefully curved, stone wall (for example) that you're looking at is actually the lobe of a colossal ear, and that the ear is only a small slice of a well-proportioned giant—that moment is thrilling. But after you've marveled at the Great Buddha from all the various angles, what's left to explore is not much more than an overcrowded theme park.

The town of Le Shan is not without charm, but with a 2,300-year history and situated as it is at a confluence of rivers, it should offer much more than it does. Mass demolition and reconstruction have rendered it indistinguishable (except for its pretty waterways) from a thousand others undergoing the same process. I suggest you skip the town and go directly to the mountain. Le Shan is best done as a day trip from Chengdu or as a stopover on the way to Emei Shan from Chengdu. Two to 3 hours is plenty of time to enjoy it. Admission to the mountain is ¥90 and includes the Great Buddha, Wuyou Temple (Wuyou Si), and Mahaoya Tomb (Mahaoya Mu). It's open from 7:30am to 7:30pm, May through September; and from 8am to 6pm, October through April. ***Note:*** For Chinese translations of establishments in this section, see chapter 16.

Essentials

GETTING THERE Air-conditioned **buses** depart for Le Shan from Chengdu's Xin Nan Men Bus Station every 20 minutes from 7am to 7pm for ¥43 to ¥49; the ride takes 2 hours. They arrive at the Le Shan Xiao Ba Lu Bus Station. Return buses for Chengdu leave from the bus station every half-hour or so. The last bus returning to Chengdu from the entrance leaves between 5:30 and 6pm (whenever it fills up). Buses run between Emei Shan and Le Shan bus stations every few minutes for ¥8. On the return leg to Chengdu, be aware of which bus station you are being taken to. **Taxi** fare between Emei and Le Shan is about ¥60.

GETTING AROUND Buses arrive in the Le Shan Xiao Ba Lu Zhan. From the bus stop, you can take a taxi (¥15), or take bus no. 3 or 13 (¥1) to the Great Buddha. What should be a 10-minute drive stretches to a half-hour as the bus driver trawls for passengers along a circuitous route. The bus unloads at Le Shan's north gate. It's a 7-minute walk to the park entrance, or you can hitch a motorcycle lift for a few yuan. Pedicabs are an option that will shave time off the journey between the bus stop and Le Shan scenic area; they charge ¥8 to ¥10. By taxi from the bus stop to the Le Shan scenic area, expect to pay ¥12 to ¥15. A round-trip **tour boat** or **motorboat** from the north gate to Wuyou Temple costs ¥70 and allows time for photos of the Great Buddha. **Ferries** run between the Le Shan City dock and both Lingyun Shan and Wuyou Si for ¥5; the last boat leaves Le Shan at 6pm.

At the entrance to Le Shan scenic area, vendors sell **maps** of the mountain for ¥5. Small stands near the head of the Great Buddha also sell maps. One side of this bilingual map shows Le Shan; the other shows Emei Shan.

Exploring Le Shan

On foot from the entrance, it's a 10-minute walk along a stone path to the Great Buddha. When the road forks into two staircases, take the staircase to the right. This leads around the side of the mountain looking back at the town. It also affords a panoramic view of the three converging rivers, the Min Jiang, the Dadu He (Chang Jiang), and the Qingyi Jiang. The path leads to a terrace and souvenir area beside and around the back of the Buddha's head. From here you can look into his ear and over his shoulder. For a variety of views of Da Fo, descend the zigzag staircase called **Jiuqu Zhandao (Path of Nine Switchbacks)** by the statue's right side. This leads to a large viewing platform that puts visitors at toe level.

DA FO (THE GREAT BUDDHA) ★ At 71m (233 ft.) tall, Le Shan's Da Fo—hewn out of a mountain—is similar in size, subject, and artistic medium to the recently demolished Bamiyan Buddhas in the Hindu Kush. Carved some 500 years later, between 713 and 803, Da Fo is one of the world's largest stone sculptures of Buddha. It was the inspiration of the Buddhist monk Hai Tong, abbot of Lingyun Monastery, who hoped that a giant Maitreya Buddha (Future Buddha) overlooking the water might subdue floods and violent currents. In 1996 it was added to UNESCO's World Heritage List, and large-scale repairs started in 2001: The Buddha's head, shoulders, and torso were cleaned up and repaired and a cement coating (added in modern times) was removed. The 10-month next stage was completed in 2002. Repairs were made to the statue's ingenious, hidden drainage system that slowed, but could not stop, erosion; and cracks as deep as 4m (13 ft.) in the base of the Buddha were filled in. For an idea of how massive this statue is: Each eye is 3m (11 ft.) long; each ear, 7m (23 ft.); and his middle finger is 8m (27 ft.) long. His head is covered with 1,021 buns of coiled hair, carved out of tapered stone blocks that fit into his head like pegs in a cribbage board.

WUYOU SHAN After viewing the Great Buddha, there isn't a lot more to do, except stroll the park grounds and enjoy the views. To reach the adjacent southern hill, Wuyou Shan, cross the **Haoshang Da Qiao** footbridge on the south side of the Great Buddha. The plain, six-hall monastery by the same name, built in the Tang dynasty and rebuilt many times since, sits atop the hill. The Luohan Tang contains an army of terra-cotta arhats, each in a different pose. Most impressive is the view of the rivers from the top of the complex.

Where to Stay & Eat

The best stays in Le Shan were once within the park itself, but they have all since closed down. A nice alternative is the **Xiandao Dajiudian (Xiandao Hotel),** Wulong Ba 2 (✆ **0833/230-1755;** fax 0833/2301352), a 2-minute walk to the back entrance of the park. Out of the city on Dao Long Island, it is surrounded by waterways and greenery. Although the rooms can be a little damp, it makes for a pleasant escape from the dust of Le Shan itself. Standard rooms cost ¥280, but management is open to negotiation. The most comfortable place to stay in downtown Le Shan is the **Jia Zhou Binguan,** Baita Jie 19 (✆ **0833/213-9888;** fax 0833/213-3233). It's a three-star hotel with basic modern rooms for ¥360 (up to 50% discount) and a restaurant. A number of good small restaurants are also in the vicinity of this hotel. **Yang's,** at Baita Jie 49 (✆ **0833/211-2046**), is inexpensive, with Chinese and Western food and an English menu. Proprietor Richard Yang has a wealth of local knowledge and personal anecdotes. A vegetarian restaurant specializing in faux meat dishes is on Wuyou Shan behind Daxiong Temple.

DUJIANGYAN 都江堰 & QINGCHENG SHAN 青城山 ★

Sichuan Province, 55km (34 miles) NW of Chengdu, 16km (10 miles) SW of Dujiangyan

The over 2,200-year-old irrigation infrastructure of Dujiangyan made Sichuan the most productive agricultural region in China. Built in 256 B.C. during the Warring States Period to tackle the yearly flooding problem of the Minjiang River, the irrigation system, which is still in use today, has advanced and ingenious engineering that amazes scientists to this day, and is a UNESCO World Heritage Site.

Designed by Qin governor Li Bing, who was later worshipped as a deity for his immense contributions to the local livelihoods, the system, without a dam, comprises three major constructions, Yuzui (Fish Mouth Levee)—a watershed divides the river into inner and outer streams, Feishayan (Flying Sand Weir)—a spillway diverting the sand and stones of the inner river into the outer river, and Baopingkou (Bottle-neck Channel)—bringing water into the inner river and controlling the intake water amount. Visitors usually stop by and spend an hour or two to admire its infrastructure before heading to Qingcheng Shan. Admission to the site is ¥90 for adults and ¥45 for children and students. Combo ticket to both Dujianyan and Qingcheng Shan is ¥160 and allows multiple entries in 2 days. Spend at least 3 hours in the site.

As a convenient subalpine getaway, Qingcheng Shan is better than all the other mountains in this chapter. It offers solitary climbing on stone steps and wooden paths through dense forests of pine, fir, and cypress. Along the way are caves, ponds, a pedestrian bridge, ancient ginkgoes, and 16 Daoist and Buddhist monasteries housing statues dating from as far back as the 6th century.

More important (though it may have slim bearing on the travel plans of most Westerners), Mount Qingcheng is considered the birthplace of China's only indigenous religion, Daoism—that is, "organized" Daoism, which gelled a half century after Lao Zi. It was to this mountainous part of western Sichuan (the Shu Kingdom) that the pilgrim Zhang Daoling came to cultivate the *Dao*. Some years later, in A.D. 142, the deified Lao Zi appeared at Heming Shan (just south of Qingcheng) and made Zhang the first Celestial Master. Zhang went on to establish 24 peasant communities throughout Shu, whose customs included confession and the regular payment of 5 pecks of rice to a communal grain reserve.

Less awe-inspiring than other World Heritage mountains, Qingcheng Shan nevertheless makes an invigorating day trip from Chengdu. If you wish to stay longer, you'll find lodging in monasteries and inns on the mountain. Escape crowds and high guesthouse rates by coming midweek. Summer is considered the best time to visit, but it's also the busiest, as Chengdu residents flee the city heat.

Compared with the situation in Qingcheng front mountain, the damages from the 2008 earthquake to Qingcheng rear mountain is more obvious and severe, with several large-scale landslides. The rear mountain was closed for over 2 years for facilities reconstruction and re-opened in 2011. Admission is ¥20. In Dujiangyan, a minor fracture of the Yuzui is also reported. Fortunately, the damage doesn't affect the major structure of the system.

Essentials

GETTING THERE **Express trains** leave from Chengdu to Dujianyan and Qingcheng Shan from 6:35am to 7:44pm daily, fare is ¥15. The ride to Dujianyan is about 30 to 40 min.; to Qingcheng Shan is 40 to 50 min. At Dujianyan Railway Station, take bus no. 4 (¥1 or ¥2 air-conditioned) to the terminus that is the main entrance of Dujianyan. From Qingcheng Shan Railway Station, take bus no. 101 (¥2) to the main gate. **Buses** depart Chengdu's Xin Nan Men Bus Station for Dujiangyan and Qingcheng Shan frequently from 8:40am to noon (1 hr.; ¥30); they run in the afternoon as well but are more sporadic. Return buses leave every 30 minutes from 3 to 5pm, from Qingcheng's main entrance. From Dujiangyan are buses to Qingcheng Shan. Buses make the 16km (10-mile) trip between Dujiangyan and Qingcheng Qian Shan every half-hour from 6:20am to 5:30pm for ¥4.50; to Qingcheng rare mountain for ¥10.

GETTING AROUND The hike to the 1,260m (4,133-ft.) summit is less strenuous than the Emei trail, but it includes a few short, steep sections. At a leisurely pace, Shangqing Gong can be reached in about 2 hours. It's possible to cut that time in half by taking the ferry across Yuecheng Hu and from there a cable car, upgraded in 2011, to just below Shangqing Gong. Passage is ¥30 one-way; ¥50 round-trip. The cable car stops at 5:30pm. It's a fun way to go, but you sacrifice seeing the sights. Admission is ¥90.

Exploring Qingcheng Shan: Suggested Route (3–4 hr.)

From the entrance, follow the main trail, keeping to the left. Pass **Yile Wo (Nest of Pleasures);** continue to **Tianshi Dong (Celestial Master Cave).** This is the core site of Qingcheng Shan. The six surrounding peaks were to act as natural inner and outer walls that would protect the area from the world of men. A temple first built in 730 now stands in the spot where Zhang Daoling is supposed to have built a hut for himself. It's said that he planted the **ancient ginkgo tree** that grows here—which would make it about 1,700 years old. Continue on to **Zushi Dian (Hall of the Celestial Master Founder**) and **Chaoyang Dong (Facing the Dawn Cave).** The narrow section of path between these two sights passes through beautiful dark forest and thick undergrowth. Continue on the path; after veering right and passing a couple of viewing pavilions, it leads to **Shangqing Gong (Temple of Highest Clarity).** First built in the 4th century, the present building is considerably newer. The tearoom here also sells snacks. From here to the summit at **Laojun Ge (Lord Lao Pavilion)** is a short but steep climb.

Return Hike: Coming back down the mountain, the road forks at Shangqing Gong. The left trail leads to the cable car. The ride down takes you to the small **Yuecheng Hu (Moon Wall Lake).** From here, boats ferry people across for ¥5. If you don't take the cable car, it's only about a half-hour walk through pine forest to the lake.

Where to Stay & Eat

If you've come to watch the sunrise, you'll need to spend the night on the mountain. Tianshi Dong and Shangqing Gong both have basic but clean lodgings for ¥40 to ¥100, depending on the season. These monasteries also serve vegetarian meals. The **Lingyun Shanzhuang (Lingyun Mountain Inn)** near the top cable-car station has lodgings and a restaurant.

JIUZHAIGOU 九寨沟 ★★★ & HUANGLONG 黄龙

Sichuan Province, 450km (280 miles) N of Chengdu, 102km (63 miles) NE of Songpan

Photographs of this World Heritage nature site look retouched. The lakes are too "jewel-like," the pools too "limpid," the fall colors too "flaming." Surprisingly, the brochures aren't lying; they aren't even exaggerating. For sheer scenic beauty and variety, Jiuzhaigou has it all: dense forest, green meadow, rivers, rapids, ribbon lakes in various shades of blue and green, chalky shoals, and waterfalls of every kind—long and narrow, short and wide, terraced, rushing, and cascading. Of cultural interest are

Carry Cash

Be sure to carry Chinese currency. Only the five-star hotels accept credit cards. None accept traveler's checks, and only a few change U.S. dollars.

the six remaining Tibetan villages of the original nine from which this valley gets its name. Some 1,000 Tibetans, of 130 families, live within the site. And to facilitate sightseeing, so-called "green buses" run along special highways within the valley delivering passengers to all scenic spots. Another aid to tourism is a network of raised plank paths and wooden pavilions that afford visitors a proximity to natural wonders that would otherwise be unapproachable.

Jiuzhaigou (Valley of Nine Villages) gets three stars for its scenery—few places on earth have a prettier landscape. The park is swarmed by tourists during peak seasons especially in October and November. But you can still find some solitude along the plank paths as the majority of tourists stay on the bus except for a few photo-taking forays. After the Wenchuan earthquake in 2008, massive efforts and resources were allocated to rebuild the affected towns, villages as well as roads in Wenchuan. Therefore, the road condition via Wenchuan to Jiuzhaigou has drastically improved and the bus ride to the picturesque site from Chengdu has shortened to about 8½ hours. Two days spent inside the reserve are absolutely worth it. Jiuzhaigou can be seen in 1 day, but 2 days is optimal.

The best time to go is October and November, when all the lakes are filled with jewel-like water, the leaves change colors, and before the weather cools down significantly. Even at the height of summer, have a jacket on hand for rain and sudden temperature drops. To avoid crowds and get the best hotel discounts, come midweek. The scenery during winter, especially in February, is also captivating as everything is covered by snow and the spectacular waterfalls are turned into giant ice pillars. You can indulge in the breathtaking snow wonderland without the disturbance from the crowds during this low season time. Busy times are Chinese New Year, Labor Day week (first week of May), and National Day week (first week of Oct). Some four-star and budget hotels close between December and March. ***Note:*** For Chinese translations of establishments listed in this section, see chapter 16.

Essentials

GETTING THERE The **Jiuhuang Airport,** just northeast of Jiuzhaigou, has greatly increased the park's accessibility, putting the park within striking distance of tourists from all neighboring provinces. From April to November, flights arrive from Chengdu, Chongqing, Beijing, and Shanghai. During December to March, there are only flights from Chengdu. The single-trip ticket of the 45-minute flight from Chengdu is about ¥880 to ¥1,250. From the airport, you can take a bus to Jiuzhaigou (1 hr. 30 min.; ¥40). A taxi between the airport and Jiuzhaigou costs ¥200.

Several air-conditioned **buses** (¥144) depart Chengdu between 7 and 8:30am from the Xin Nan Men Bus Station and arrive approximately 8½ hours later at the Jiuzhaigou Long-Distance Bus Station (Jiuzhaigou Changtu Qiche Keyun Zhan) behind the Jiutong Binguan—leaving you the evening to check into a hotel and have dinner. Four return buses leave at 6:20am, 7am, 8am, and 1pm. Buy tickets at least a day in advance. Buses also leave Chengdu from the less convenient Chadianzi Keyun Zhan west of the city center, dropping passengers near the Jiuzhaigou entrance for ¥118 (7:20am and 9am; 8 hr.).

Though the route from Chengdu to Jiuzhaigou has become much more pleasant, you may still get stuck on the road for a couple of hours during bad and snowy weather.

GETTING AROUND Jiuzhaigou's five designated scenic zones run along a Y-shaped route. Over 200 **shuttle buses** travel the 58km (36-mile) route from 7am until 6pm. The best sights and most of the plank paths are along the right branch, so if you haven't time to trace the entire route, go to the right first. If you're tempted to walk the full length, bear in mind that the distance from the entrance to the last scenic spot on this route—Yuanshi Senlin (Primeval Forest)—is about 32km (20 miles). For the best views, take the bus to the end and walk back. You can reboard at bus stops along the way. Very useful bilingual **tourist maps** are available for ¥5 at the **Tourist's Center (Youke Zhongxin)** near the ticket office.

Exploring the Valleys

With 2 days, using a combination of shuttle bus and walking, you can see all five scenic zones. For a more relaxed pace or extended walking, add a third day. Of the scenic zones, the two with the highest concentration of natural wonders are **Shuzheng Jingqu** and **Rize Jingqu.** Each zone covers several miles and has wooden planks or stone paths that lead the visitor right up to waterfalls, across shoals, or to the edge of turquoise waters. These can be done in a day if that's all you have, or they can be spread over 2 days, leaving half of each day for wandering in the less-visited areas beyond **Panda Lake (Xiongmao Hai)** to the right or beyond **Wucai Hai (Five-Color Pool)** to the left. Admission to Jiuzhaigou, which is open from 7am to 6pm, is April to mid-November ¥220, for 1 day only, and mid-November to March ¥80 per person, for 2 days. The shuttle bus costs ¥90; from mid-November to March ¥80.

HUANGLONG 黄龙

If you are visiting Jiuzhaigou between July and November, it is would be nice to spare 1 more day and make a day-trip to Huanglong (Yellow Dragon), 88km (55 miles) south of Jiuzhaigou. Listed as a natural world heritage by the UNESCO in 1992, this scenic site, surrounded by dense and primitive forests, has a different beauty compared to the more well-known Jiuzhaigou. Its extensive colorful jade plateslike and crystal clear water-filled travertine ponds create a unique terraced and surreal landscape. The huge limestone slopes covered by a thin layer of flowing water radiates and emits golden rays under the sun.

If you prefer to hike all the way, after entering through the main gate, take the right path at the first fork (300m from the main gate) and avoid all the scenic spots on your way up. The 3.6km (2.2-mile) wooden plank path takes you about 2 hours to reach the highest spot and the main attraction **Wucai Chi (Multi-Coloured Pond),** the largest cluster of travertine ponds in the site that nestle at 3,569m (11,709 ft.) above sea level. However, many people find the steep trek too challenging due to the effects of high altitude. Otherwise, take the cable car (¥80 uphill; ¥40 downhill; 8am–5pm) to the upper station, after a short and easy walk, you can overlook the snow mountain ridge and the Xuebao Peak, a huge valley and the lush highland forest at **Wanglong**

Ping (Dragon Viewing Platform). Another 1-hour walk will lead you to Huanglong Gu Si (Huanglong Ancient Temple), built in the Ming Dynasty. Right behind the temple is the **Wucai Chi.** The circular wooden plank allows you to appreciate the terraced jade-green ponds from various angles and distances. On your way downhill, after passing Huanglong Zhong Si (Huanglong Middle Temple), take the right path at Jiexian Qiao (Immortal Waiting Bridge). This zigzag path leads you to all scenic spots including the second largest travertine ponds, **Zheng Yan Chi (Beauty-Competing Pond);** Suo Luo Ying Cai Chi (Rhododendron Pond), Ming Jing Dao Ying Chi (Mirror Pool), Pen Jing Chi (Bonsai Pond); the golden sand beachlike platform, **Jin Sha Pu Di (Golden Sand on Earth);** Xi Shen Dong (Body Washing Cave), Lian Tai Fei Pu (Lotus Platform Waterfall), Lian Yan Chi; the site's highest waterfall **Fei Pu Liu Hui (Marvellous Flying Waterfall);** and Ying Bin Cai Chi (Guest Greeting Pond). Admission is ¥200 and ¥150 for students.

Buses to Huanglong depart from Jiuzhaigou Changtu Qiche Keyun Zhan at 7 and 7:30am daily. The 2½-hr. bus ride costs ¥40. They return to Jiuzhaigou at 3 and 3:30pm respectively, giving you 5 hours to explore the site. Buy return tickets on the bus when you are on the way to Huanglong in the morning. A round-trip **taxi** to Huanglong from Jiuzhaigou costs ¥380 to ¥400. You can also ask the driver to wait for you at the gate and take you directly to the airport after visiting Huanglong, if you are taking a late flight. It costs ¥380 to ¥400.

Though a few stalls sell water, drinks, snacks, and instant bowl noodles inside the park, they are expensive and have very limited selections. Bring your own lunch.

Where to Stay

For now, officials who say that tourists may not stay inside the park seem to be winning their battle with villagers who offer basic beds for around ¥50, and simple meals for ¥10 to ¥25. Rooms are basic with limited hot water, but some are in Tibetan style with brightly painted tables and window frames. Inquire at the Zharu Si and at villages on the west side of the main road. You'll probably be asked to arrive after 6pm and leave before 7am, to avoid problems with officials.

Most visitors stay in one of the many hotels lining the 11km (7-mile) stretch of road outside Jiuzhai Gou Goukou (Jiuzhai Gou Entrance), identified on the map as Zhangzha Town.

EXPENSIVE

Sheraton Jiuzhaigou Resort (Jiuzhaigou Xilaideng Dajiudian) ★ This huge complex is the first international five-star hotel in Jiuzhaigou and remains one of the best and offers the most comfortable stay in the area. The rooms are elegantly appointed and infused with a Tibetan quality, all the more notable considering the Chinese propensity for reducing minority cultures into kitsch. The bathrooms, with shower and bathtub, are compact yet clean. The hotel has restaurants that serve appetizing food and amenities such as an indoor swimming pool and sauna. The grounds include a 500-seat theater with revolving stage for nightly Tibetan and minority ethnic song and dance performances. The hotel started its upgrading project in late 2011 to enlarge each room and update the in-room facilities.

Jiuzhai Gou Scenic Area (1.5km/1 mile from entrance to Jiuzhai Gou). www.sheraton.com/jiuzhaigou. ✆ **0837/773-9988.** Fax 0837/773-9666. 482 units. ¥3,000–¥3,200 standard room. Rates include breakfast. 20%–60% discount. No discount during October and November. 15% service charge. AE, DC, MC, V. **Amenities:** 3 restaurants; deli; bar; clinic; concierge; limited forex; gym; indoor pool; room service; sauna; smoke-free rooms; spa; theater; airline, train, and bus ticketing. *In room:* A/C, satellite TV, fridge, hair dryer, minibar.

MODERATE

Grand Jiu Zhai Gou Hotel (Jiuzhaigou Xingyu Guoji Dajiudian) This four-star hotel has a few Tibetan touches, but for the most part, the rooms, lobby, and restaurants hold no surprises. Bathrooms have 24-hour hot water but shower only. Discounted prices are reasonable, and staff is friendly and professional. For the comfort of a pricier hotel (but without some of the five-star luxuries), this hotel serves well.

Jiuzhai Gou Scenic Area (under 1.5km/1 mile from entrance to Jiuzhai Gou). www.scxingyu.com. ✆ **0837/776-6888.** Fax 0837/773-9773. 194 units. ¥1,480 standard room. Rates include breakfast. 20%–50% discounts. 15% service charge. No credit cards. **Amenities:** Restaurant; bar; Internet bar; massage; room service; theater; airline, train, and bus ticketing. *In room:* A/C, TV, fridge (in some).

Qian He International Hotel (Qian He Guoji Dajiudian) After a renovation in 2011, this hotel is now one of the best and most comfortable choices. White crane paintings and Tibetan and Qiang ornamentations adorn this four-star hotel. Rooms are inviting and well-appointed with clean good-sized bathrooms. Staff is friendly. The restaurant only serves Chinese food.

Jiuzhai Gou Scenic Area (under 1.5km/1 mile from entrance to Jiuzhai Gou). www.jzqhhotel.com.cn. ✆ **0837/773-9188.** Fax 0837/773-9266. 251 units. ¥708–¥1,280 standard room. ¥1,008–¥1,680 suite. Rates include breakfast. 20%–40% discounts. 15% service charge. No credit cards. **Amenities:** Restaurant; Internet bar; KTV; massage; room service; sauna; airline, train, and bus ticketing. *In room:* A/C, TV, fridge.

INEXPENSIVE

Many budget accommodations and three-star hotels are clustered in Pengfeng Cun (Pengfeng Village), a kilometer west of the entrance. They offer simple rooms with limited hours of hot water and air-conditioning. A standard room costs ¥200 to ¥400 in peak season. Up to 50% discount is available at other times of the year. Make reservations early if you are visiting in October. Cao Gen Renjia (www.gogojz.com; ✆ **0837/776-4922 or 776-4926;** 7jzg@163.com) and Ziyou Qingnian Lvshe (✆ **0837/776-4617 or 776-4985;** 57jzg@163.com) have basic rooms with small bathroom with shower only. Staff speak competent English.

Where to Eat

Except for hotel restaurants, you don't have lots of dining choices. For inexpensive (but still overpriced) local food, try one of the several identical *huoguo* (hot pot) restaurants on the main street of Zhangzha Town. Another option is to pay ¥160 for dinner and a performance of Qiang and Tibetan folk entertainment, which includes dancing, singing, and audience participation. Tibetan-style barbecued mutton, Tibetan tea, and a ritual welcoming liqueur are included in the ticket price. The **Gesangla Art Troupe (Gesangla Yishu Tuan)** performs nightly at 7:30pm at Jiuxin Shanzhuang (Jiuxin Mountain Villa), on the hotel strip 1km (½ mile) east of the Jiuzhaigou entrance. For information, call ✆ **0837/773-9588.**

A snack bar selling kabobs, watermelon juice, pearl milk tea (a Taiwanese-style drink made of tea, milk, and sago palm starch), and tofu on a stick is outside the Jiuzhai Gou entrance, next to the tourist center. Snacks are also sold inside the reserve, but they've overpriced and not very good.

CHONGQING 重庆

Chongqing Municipality, 334km (208 miles) SE of Chengdu, 1,346km (836 miles) S of Xi'an, 1,000km (620 miles) upstream of Three Gorges Dam

Since Chongqing became the fourth city, after Beijing, Tianjin, and Shanghai, to achieve the status of municipality in 1997, it has undergone a radical face-lift and economic boost. With summers so hot it's been dubbed one of China's Three Furnaces, and streets so steep that no one rides a bike, weather and terrain were once its chief claims to fame. Now, this cliff-side city overlooking the confluence of the Chang and Jialing rivers has much to boast about. Chongqing is the biggest metropolitan area in the world (surpassing Tokyo); it's got the world's biggest dam site downriver; and it's in the midst of building the world's tallest skyscraper (the Chongqing Tower).

As recently as the 19th century, Chongqing was a remote walled city. Even after the steam engine eased passage through the Three Gorges, few Easterners had any reason or desire to make the trip. That all changed in 1938, when Hankou fell to the Japanese and downriver residents made a mass exodus up the Chang Jiang (Yangzi River). Chongqing became China's last wartime capital, and after withstanding 3 years of Japanese bombing, the city never looked back. Very few of the old ramshackle neighborhoods rebuilt after the war have survived "urban improvement," and except for an old prison complex and a few small museums and memorials, you'll find little evidence of earlier eras.

Most travelers come to Chongqing because it's the first or last stop on a Three Gorges cruise. Levels of sulfur dioxide and suspended air particles used to be so high that visitors couldn't wait to leave. As the city implements pollution control programs, that seems to be gradually changing. Chongqing's pleasures are modest, but there's enough here to make a 2- or 3-day stay enjoyable. The city is also just a 2-hour bus ride from the Buddhist Grottoes at Dazu.

Essentials

GETTING THERE **Jiangbei Airport** is 25km (15 miles) north of Chongqing, and 30 minutes by taxi (around ¥67). It offers daily domestic service to Beijing, Chengdu, Guilin, Hong Kong, Kunming, Shanghai, and Xi'an; it offers service to Lhasa twice a week. International destinations include Tokyo, Seoul, Bangkok, and Düsseldorf. The Minhang (CAAC) **airport shuttle bus** (**© 023/6386-5824**) leaves every half-hour from 6am to 9pm from Shangqing Si, Yuzhong District, for ¥16. Domestic and international air tickets are also on sale here from 7:30am to 6:30pm. **Dragonair** has offices in the Metropolis Building (Daduhui Shangsha), Zourong Lu 68 (**© 023/6372-9900**).

The **Main Railway Station** and **Long-Distance Bus Station** are next to each other on Nanqu Lu, near the Yangzi River. **Trains** from Shanghai and Beijing take approximately 28 and 25 hours, respectively. Express trains from Chongqing Bei Zhan (Chongqing North) to Chengdu take between 2 and 2½ hours, costing ¥98 for a second-class seat and ¥117 for first class.

Since the launching of the express trains, **buses** to Chengdu became a less preferred option. Luxury **buses** with a uniformed attendant and bathroom onboard connect Chongqing to Chengdu; the 4-hour trip costs ¥88. The bus makes two stops in Chongqing: the first, at Chenjia Ping, for those going to the wharf; the second, at the Long-Distance Bus Station. As you exit, ignore the throng of private drivers vying to overcharge you. Walk across the parking lot to the taxi queue in front of the railway station. Insist on using the meter. The ride to any of the major hotels is ¥20 to ¥30.

Large Volvo and Mercedes buses leave the Long-Distance Bus Station for Chengdu every half-hour throughout the day for ¥88. Buses to Le Shan leave from the Caiyuan Ba Qiche Keyun Zhan (Caiyuan Ba Bus Station) every 30 to 60 minutes from 7am to 6pm for ¥111. (For Yangzi River travel, see the section "Middle Reaches of the Chang Jiang" in this chapter.)

GETTING AROUND **Taxi** rates during day time are ¥8 for 3km (2 miles), then ¥1.80 per kilometer thereafter. At night, from 10pm to 7am, cabs charge ¥8.90 for the first 3km (2 miles), then ¥2.25 per kilometer afterwards. In addition to the 10 bridges that span the Jialing and Yangzi rivers is one **cable car** line, leaving from Xinhua Lu to cross the Yangzi; it costs ¥2. The Jialing Cable Car, from Cangbai Lu to cross the Jialing, ceased operating in early 2011. **Buses/trolleys** serve all parts of the city. Rides with air-conditioning are ¥2 to ¥3; rides without are ¥1 to ¥1.50. Cable cars and some buses/trolleys have attendants. The **light rail** has one line running from Yuzhong District center (Jiao Chang Kou) to the Jialing River side, to Jiulongpo District, and ending at Dadukou District's Xinshancun. Fare is ¥2 to ¥5; from 6:30am to 10:30pm. The first line of the **underground railway** launched in 2011, connects Chaotianmen and Shapingba, and costs ¥2 to ¥6.

VISITOR INFORMATION **CITS** is located near the People's Square (Renmin Guangchang). This branch, at Zaozi Lanya Zheng Jie 120, second floor (✆ **023/6385-0693;** fax 023/6385-0196; citscq@cta.cq.cn.), is particularly helpful.

[Fast FACTS] CHONGQING

Banks, Foreign Exchange & ATMs The main branch of **Bank of China** (Mon–Fri 9am–noon and 2–5:30pm), north of Liberation Monument on the north side of Minzu Lu, has full foreign-exchange services and an ATM. The branch cater-cornered from Harbour Plaza Hotel, Zourong Lu at Bayi Lu, has a 24-hour ATM and offers foreign-exchange service, although limited to cash and U.S. dollar traveler's checks.

Consulates Both the Canadian and United Kingdom consulates are in the Metropolitan Plaza building (Daduhui Shangsha) on Wuyi Lu. The **Canadian Consulate** (✆ 023-6373-8007; chonq@international.gc.ca), in suite 1705, is open Monday to Friday from 9am-noon and 1-5pm. The **United Kingdom Consulate** (✆ 023/6369-1500; consular.chongqing@fco.gov.uk), at Suite 2801, is open Monday to Friday from 9am-noon and 1:30-3:30pm. Take bus no. 306, 402, 413, or 601 to the Jiefang Bei stop. From there, walk southeast on Zourong Lu to Wuyi Lu. Metropolitan Plaza is next to the Harbour Plaza Hotel.

Internet Access The area around Liberation Monument has lots of Internet bars, including **Reader's Club (Duzhe Julebu),** open 24 hours on the third floor of the Xinhua Bookstore at Minsheng Lu 181 (opposite Nuren Guangchang; ✆ **023/6371-6367**). Rates are ¥4 per hour; less with membership card. Coffee and tea are served. Enter from Xinhua Shudian or from the side door of the adjacent bank. Dial-up is ✆ **163.**

Post Office The main post office is near Jiefang Bei (Liberation Monument), at Minquan Lu 3.

Visa Extensions The **Exit and Entry Section, Yuzhong District Subbureau of Chongqing Municipal Bureau of Public Security (Churujing Guanli Ju)** processes visa extensions in 5 working days. Located at Heping Lu 211 (✆ **023/6373-5599** or 023/6384-9400; Mon–Fri 9–11:30am and 2–5pm), it's inside the District Administrative Service Center. Take bus no. 109, 114, 476 or 601 to the Qixing Gang bus station at Zhongshan Yi Lu, walk south to Heping Lu and turn left.

Chongqing 重庆

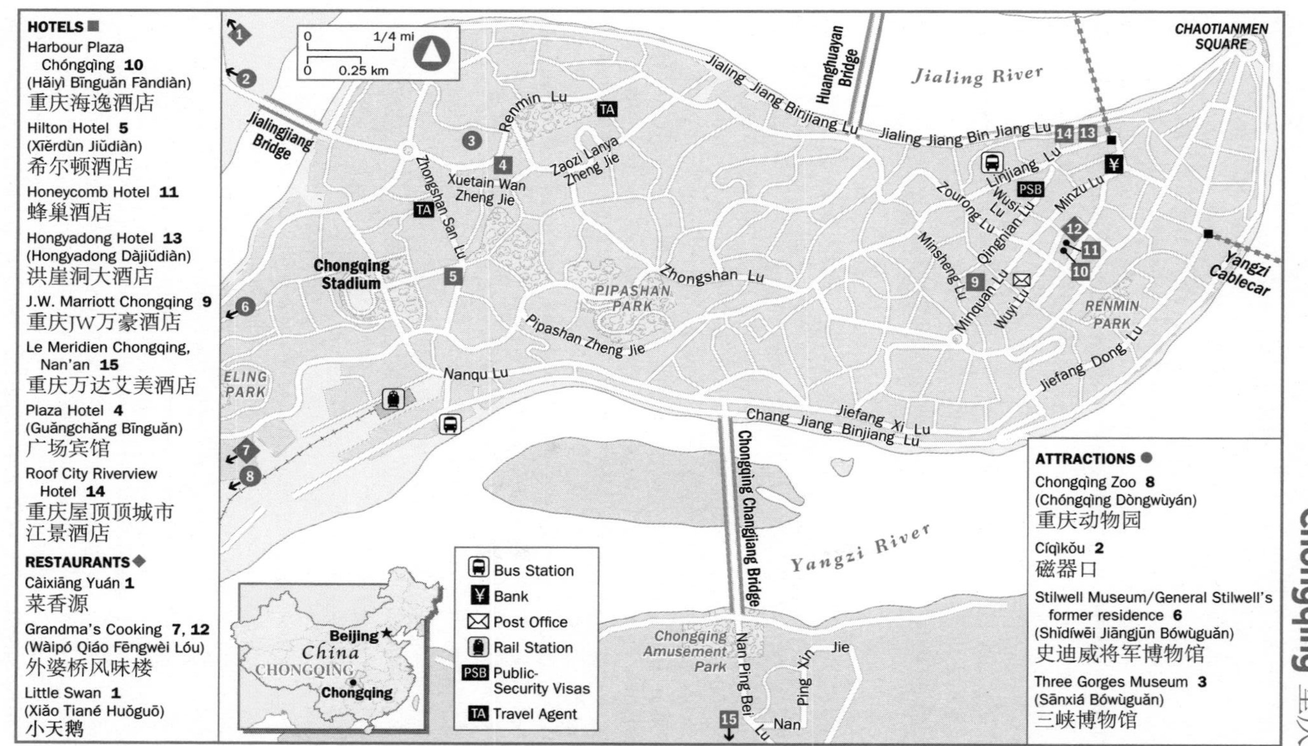

HOTELS
Harbour Plaza Chóngqìng 10
(Hǎiyì Bīnguǎn Fàndiàn)
重庆海逸酒店
Hilton Hotel 5
(Xīěrdùn Jiǔdiàn)
希尔顿酒店
Honeycomb Hotel 11
蜂巢酒店
Hongyadong Hotel 13
(Hongyadong Dàjiǔdiàn)
洪崖洞大酒店
J.W. Marriott Chongqing 9
重庆JW万豪酒店
Le Meridien Chongqing, Nan'an 15
重庆万达艾美酒店
Plaza Hotel 4
(Guǎngchǎng Bīnguǎn)
广场宾馆
Roof City Riverview Hotel 14
重庆屋顶顶城市
江景酒店
RESTAURANTS
Càixiāng Yuán 1
菜香源
Grandma's Cooking 7, 12
(Wàipó Qiáo Fēngwèi Lóu)
外婆桥风味楼
Little Swan 1
(Xiǎo Tiané Huǒguō)
小天鹅
ATTRACTIONS
Chongqìng Zoo 8
(Chóngqìng Dòngwùyán)
重庆动物园
Cíqìkǒu 2
磁器口
Stilwell Museum/General Stilwell's former residence 6
(Shǐdíwēi Jiāngjūn Bówùguǎn)
史迪威将军博物馆
Three Gorges Museum 3
(Sānxiá Bówùguǎn)
三峡博物馆
Bus Station
Bank
Post Office
Rail Station
PSB Public-Security Visas
TA Travel Agent
0 1/4 mi
0 0.25 km
CHAOTIANMEN SQUARE
Jialing River
Yangzi River
Yangzi Cablecar
Huanghuayan Bridge
Jialingjiang Bridge
Chongqìng Changjiang Bridge
Jialing Jiang Binjiang Lu
Jialing Jiang Bin Jiang Lu
Linjiang Lu
Minzu Lu
Wusi Lu
Qingnian Lu
Zourong Lu
Minsheng Lu
Minquan Lu
Wuyi Lu
Jiefang Dong Lu
Jiefang Xi Lu
Chang Jiang Binjiang Lu
Zhongshan Lu
Zhongshan San Lu
Renmin Lu
Zaozi Lanya Zheng Jie
Xuetain Wan Zheng Jie
Pipashan Zheng Jie
Nanqu Lu
Chongqing Stadium
PIPASHAN PARK
RENMIN PARK
ELING PARK
Chongqing Amusement Park
Nan Ping Bei Lu
Nan Ping Xin Jie
China
Beijing
CHONGQING
Chongqing

Exploring Chongqing

Baigong Guan/SACO Standing in a lovely setting with trees, shrubs, stone walkways, and a babbling brook, Baigong Guan was originally a Sichuan warlord's *pied-à-terre,* but it was taken over by the notoriously brutal Dai Li—head of the Nationalist (KMT) secret police and guerrilla forces—and turned into a prison in 1939. Two years later, the U.S. spy agency SACO (Sino-American Cooperation Organization), which trained secret agents for the KMT, housed its servicemen here. It reverted to a prison in 1945, and it was here that the KMT slaughtered several hundred Communists and dissidents before retreating to Taiwan in 1949. The incident is known as the Bloodbath of 11/27, and many locals still come here to pay homage on that date.

The wooden prison buildings are open to visitors. Photos of prisoners are displayed on the walls with poems and excerpts from letters—some in English translation—reflecting the political idealism of an earlier age.

Shapingba Qu (3.2km/2 miles west of Hongyan Cun). Free admission. Tues–Sun 8:30am–5pm. Bus: 210 from Caiyuanba to Baigong Guan.

Chongqing Zoo (Chongqing Dongwuyuan) If you're going to Chengdu and have time to visit the panda breeding center, then don't bother with the Chongqing Zoo. But if this is your only chance to see pandas, consider spending part of a morning at the giant panda and red panda enclosures. To get to the red pandas, go to the left of the English introduction board and down the stairs. The outdoor enclosure has a half-dozen extremely active small red pandas. The zoo has also brought in new animals including antelope, giraffe, and elephant in recent years.

Tip: The best chance of seeing pandas is during feeding—between 8:30 and 10:30am. If the pandas aren't out, poke your head in the office behind the English introduction board and ask the zoo warden if he'll feed them. Sometimes that's all it takes.

Jiulong Po Qu, Xijiao Yi Cun 1, in city's southeast quadrant. ✆ **023/6842-2285.** Admission ¥20. Zoo summer 6:30am–9pm; winter 7am–9pm. Panda enclosures 8:30–10:30am and 3:30–4:30pm. Light rail or bus: 463 from Jiefangbei to Dongwuyuan.

Ciqikou ★ This small neighborhood with cobblestone streets in the Shaping District is popular with travelers who have a few days in Chongqing; however, it has somewhat turned into a theme park. The two main streets—lined with modest eastern Sichuan–style buildings—form a T from the entrance. Shops on the first street sell paintings, batik clothing, and other items geared mainly for tourists.

At the top of the T, a right turn leads to the wharf. Along the way are several teahouses and restaurants. One teahouse, Qingdai Minju, has a nice courtyard just off the main thoroughfare where you can enjoy performances on traditional Chinese instruments. Farther along at Lingyun Minyue in another tearoom, a small ensemble of musicians gathers most days to play traditional music.

Take the light rail to Daiping Station, then take bus no. 467 on Daiping Zheng Jie for Ciqikou.

Sanxia Bowuguan (Three Gorges Museum) ★ While the museum itself lacks a certain charisma, several items in this museum make the trip worthwhile. First is its lovely collection of Tang and Song heads carved out of stone. Most are of Buddha, Guanyin, and various bodhisattvas, but what distinguishes them are their human rather than heavenly miens. A fine collection of terra-cotta sculptures from an Eastern Han tomb is also on display. Discovered in Chongqing north of the Yangzi, they are small, whimsical figurines of musicians, dancers, singers, and storytellers—a lively group to spend eternity with. The museum also boasts collections that stretch as far as the Shang dynasty (ca. 1600–1045 B.C.). Of particular interest are the paulownia-wood "boat coffins" of the ancient Ba culture.

Renmin Lu, north side of the People's Sq. (Renmin Guangchang). Free admission. 8:30am–5pm. Closed Mon. Bus: 129, 215, 22, 111, 103, or 104. Light rail to Zengjiayan.

Stilwell Museum/Former Residence of General Stilwell (Shidiwei Jiangjun Jiuju) After Pearl Harbor, President Roosevelt sent Gen. Joseph Stilwell (1883–1946) to Chongqing as commander in chief of Allied forces in the China-Burma-India theater of the war. Unfortunately, "Vinegar Joe" and the KMT general he was supposed to advise—Chiang Kai-shek—had rather different agendas, not to mention temperaments, and in 1944, at Chiang's urging, Stilwell was relieved of his post. Nonetheless, his contribution to the Burma Road campaign was significant—reason enough for the local government to continue to maintain a museum honoring him. His disdain for Chiang must also have endeared him to the party. The museum, housed in Stilwell's Chongqing residence, has a collection of newspaper clippings, photographs, letters, and Stilwell's personal belongings. A video tells the Chinese version of Stilwell's tour of duty and includes rare clips. Explanations are in English and Chinese. The Stilwell and Flying Tiger T-shirts sold here make unique gifts.

Jialing Xin Lu 63. ✆ **023/6360-9515.** Admission ¥5. 9am–5pm. Light rail or Bus: 104, 215, or 261 to Liziba stop.

Shopping

Carrefour Supermarket (Jialefu Chaoshi) is inside the Xin Chongqing Building. It's open from 9am to 10:30pm; take bus no. 111 or 166 to the Xiao Shizi stop. The supermarket is crammed with customers because you can get anything here—and cheaply. **KFC** is inside the same building. A **Watson** drugstore is on the first floor of Metropolitan Plaza (Daduhui Guangchang), next to the Harbour Plaza on Wuyi Lu, 1 block southeast of Jiefang Bei. This seven-floor indoor mall has restaurants, upscale and international clothing stores, and even an ice-skating rink on the sixth floor.

Where to Stay

EXPENSIVE

Harbour Plaza Chongqing (Haiyi Fandian) This five-star luxury hotel has a convenient downtown location (next to deluxe shopping on the city's pedestrian mall) cater-cornered to a 24-hour ATM. The new, enlarged reception area is open and airy. Guest rooms are decorated in rich blues and golds, and most have views of the cityscape. Bathrooms are spacious and most have separate tub and shower. Though less glamorous than the Marriott, the Harbour Plaza still meets international standards in every way.

Wuyi Lu (at Zourong Lu, 1 block southeast of Liberation Monument). www.harbour-plaza.com/hpcq. ✆ **023/6370-0888.** Fax 023/6370-0778. 388 units. ¥658–¥1,016 standard room; ¥1,158–¥1,516 suite. 15% service charge. AE, DC, MC, V. Bus: 306, 402, 413, or 601 to Jiefang Bei. **Amenities:** 2 restaurants; 4 bars; executive floors; forex; health club; indoor pool; room service; airline and train ticketing. *In room:* A/C, TV w/satellite channels, IDD phone, fridge, hair dryer, minibar.

Hilton Chongqing (Xierdun Jiudian) ★ ☺ This five-star hotel is one of Chongqing's finest, and highly recommended. Views are of the rivers and the Datianwan Sport Stadium; rooms are soothing, attractively decorated with tasteful touches such as an artsy Chinese calligraphy wall scroll and bamboo shape bed lamp. Beds are plush and comfy. The diamond-shaped marble bathroom has a large tub, separate shower, and Crabtree & Evelyn toiletries. The hotel is well located near the business district and less than 3km (2 miles) from the railway station. It's also a short, interesting walk from Pipa Shan Gongyuan and the City Museum.

Zhongshan San Lu 139 (near Datianwan Sport Stadium). www.hilton.com. ✆ **800/820-0600** or 023/8903-9999. Fax 023/8903-8700. 435 units. ¥577–¥884 standard room; ¥1,077–¥1,735 suite. 15% service charge. AE, DC, MC, V. Bus: 224, 368, 402, 411, or 605 to Liang Lukou stop. **Amenities:** 3 restaurants, bar; forex; health club; indoor pool; room service; sauna; spa; airline, train, and bus ticketing. *In room:* A/C, satellite TV, fridge, hair dryer, Internet, minibar.

JW Marriott Chongqing (Chongqing JW Wanhao Jiudian) This hotel is near the commercial area Jiefang Bei. With a high-ceilinged lobby flanked by two sweeping staircases, palm trees, a steakhouse overlooking the rivers, and a Japanese restaurant with traditional architecture and decor, the Marriott is one of the best choices in town. Rooms were renovated and expanded in 2008 and now have better in-room facilities such as flatscreen TVs, separate bathroom, and shower. A DVD player is provided upon request.

Qingnian Lu 77 (corner of Qingnian Lu and Minsheng Lu), Yuzhong. www.marriott.com. ✆ **023/6388-8888.** Fax 023/6399-9999. 452 units. ¥750–¥1,100 standard room; ¥1,500–¥2,300 suite. 15% service charge. AE, DC, MC, V. **Amenities:** 4 restaurants; deli; lounge; bar; 24-hr. health club; indoor pool; room service; airline, train, cruise, and bus ticketing; Wi-Fi. *In room:* A/C, HD TV w/ satellite channels, DVD player, fridge, hair dryer, Internet, minibar.

Le Meridien Chongqing, Nan'an (Chongqing Wanda Aimei Jiudian) The brand-name hotel, renowned for its chic design, is located in the commercial area of mainland property group Wanda in the newly developed Nan'an district. The exceptionally high-ceiling lobby and the wall comprised of columns of red bottles in the lobby lounge is impressive and contemporary. The roomy guestrooms feature stylish red and grey fixtures and modern Oriental touches. The bed is against an artsy wall inspired by the map of Chongqing. The huge bathrooms have separate shower and tub. However, minor defects can be spotted in bathrooms, such as slow-to-drain bathtubs, as well as in different public areas of the hotel, such as discoloration in the public bathroom tiles.

Jiangnan Dadao 10, Nan'an District (light rail to Zengjiayan). www.lemeridien.com/chongqing nanan. ✆ **023/8638-8888.** Fax 023/8638-6666. 319 units. ¥830–¥930 standard room. Rates include breakfast. 15% service charge. AE, DC, MC, V. **Amenities:** 3 restaurants; bar; forex; fitness center; indoor pool; room service; sauna; airline, train, and bus ticketing. *In room:* A/C, satellite TV, iPod dock, fridge, hair dryer, Internet, minibar.

MODERATE

Hongyadong Hotel This four-star hotel sits beside the Jialing River and is part of the traditional Chinese–style Hongyadong complex of shopping malls, restaurants, and bars. Some of the guest rooms overlook the river and Jiangbei District. The entire hotel is decorated with classy wooden furniture, modern Chinese–style decor, and Chinese paintings. The bathrooms and furniture in rooms with river view are a bit worn-out, probably due to a higher occupancy rate. Rooms without the river view are kept in a better shape, but the bathrooms have showers only. The staff speak English.

Cangbai Lu 56, Yuzhong District. ✆ **023/6399-2888.** Fax 023/6399-2999. 176 units. ¥338–¥518 standard room; ¥518–¥988 suite. Rates include breakfast. AE, DC, MC, V. **Amenities:** 3 restaurants; bar; room service; sauna; airline, train, and bus ticketing. *In room:* A/C, TV, fridge, Internet, minibar.

Roof City Riverview Hotel (Wudingding Chengshi Jiangjin Jiudian) All the 40 rooms of this hotel established in 2011 enjoy a pleasant view of the Jialing river. Rooms with small balconies where you can sit back and relax to watch the sunset cost a bit more. Expressionist oil paintings add a bit of character to the guest rooms. Bathroom is small yet clean, with shower only. Though the hotel has only one restaurant and no extra facilities, it guarantees a comfortable stay. As this hotel is part of the Hongyadong commercial complex, you have access to restaurants and pubs within minutes.

Jiangbin Lu 88, Yuzhong District. ✆ **023/6303-6699.** Fax 023/6303-6662. 40 units. ¥338–¥398 standard room. ¥398–¥468 suite. Rates include breakfast. No credit cards. **Amenities:** Restaurant. *In room:* A/C, TV, fridge, Internet, minibar.

INEXPENSIVE

Guangchang Binguan (Plaza Hotel) Located opposite Renmin Guangchang, this midsize three-star hotel is a particularly good value for three people traveling together, even without the hefty discounts that are standard. Room decor and furnishings are standard and forgettable, but the staff, outfitted in crisp uniforms, is warm and welcoming, despite (or perhaps, due to) the fact that few foreigners have discovered this hotel. The two standard room types are slightly bigger "A" rooms with slightly higher bathroom ceilings, and standard and perfectly acceptable "B" rooms. The difference isn't enough to warrant the additional cost for an "A" room. The location is within walking distance of the Municipal Museum, People's Square, People's Auditorium, and CITS.

Xuetianwan Zheng Jie 2. ✆ **023/6355-8989.** Fax 023/6355-9000. 129 units. ¥240–¥430 standard room. AE, DC, MC, V. Bus: 103, 162, 181, or 261. **Amenities:** 2 restaurants; bar; forex; room service; airline, train, and bus ticketing. *In room:* A/C, TV, hair dryer, minibar/fridge.

Honeycomb Hotel (Fengchao Jiudian) Newly opened in early 2011, this small business hotel only has 42 rooms. It is situated right in the commercial Yuzhong district and within walking distance of Jiefang Bei. Rooms facing the street are larger and have better lighting, but can be noisy during the day or when there are outdoor activities at the shopping mall across the road. The compact bathrooms only have a shower, but are simple and clean.

Zhonghua Lu 168, Yuzhong District. ✆ **023/8690-5588** or 8690-5599. honeycombhotel@163.com. 40 units. ¥258–¥298 double room; ¥248–¥298 single room. No credit cards. *In room:* A/C, TV, fridge, Internet, minibar.

Where to Eat

One of the dishes most identified with Sichuan cooking (though it may have come from Mongolia) is hot pot or *huoguo* (fire pot). It is so popular here that street stalls and small restaurants serving this dish line a block of Wuyi Lu street. Hot pot restaurants are recognizable by their dining tables, the centers of which have a cooking pot with boiling broth and hot oil. Diners add meat, fish, sprouts, scallions, and any other ingredients they like to the pot. Once the submerged meat or vegetables are cooked, diners pluck pieces out with chopsticks and eat them plain or with a spicy dipping sauce. By tradition in both Sichuan and Inner Mongolia, locals favor organ meats, intestines, brains, and chicken feet for this poor-man's stew, but these days, in restaurants, choices abound. Like the best meals, the best hot pots use ingredients that combine a variety of tastes, textures, shapes, and colors.

Near Liberation Monument is a **McDonald's** on the corner of Zourong Lu and Wuyi Lu, cater-cornered from Harbour Plaza, and a **KFC** on Minquan Lu at Jiefang Bei. **Starbucks** and **Subway** can be found at Hongyadong and Jiefang Bei.

Caixiang Yuan ★ SICHUAN Very popular with locals, this place serves traditional and nouveau Sichuan. Strange-flavored duck *(guaiwei Yazi)*, with its perfect blend of salty, sweet, tingling, hot, sour, savory, and fragrant flavors, is a favorite here, and for good reason.

Building C-4 Jiazhou Huayuan (Jiazhou Garden in Yubei District). ✆ **023/6762-9325.** Meal for 2 ¥50–¥70. No credit cards. 11:30am–2:30pm and 5:30–10pm. Bus: 465 or 602 to Jiazhou Huayuan.

Waipo Qiao Jiucai Zuofang (Grandmother's Cooking) SICHUAN This extremely popular restaurant, now with nine locations, is more evidence that nostalgia is selling well in China. One manager, lumping over 500 years together, defined the cuisine as "Ming-Qing," and a real *waipo* (grandmother), dressed in simple garb, greets customers. The larger restaurant, in the Metropolitan Plaza, has a separate hot pot dining room next door that does an equally rousing business. Three of the best entrees in the main restaurant are *tieban shao zhi yinxueyu* (silver snow fish cooked on an iron plate), serves six; the slightly hot *qingjiao bao ziji* (baby chicken quick-fried with green pepper); and *guoba roupian* (pork with bamboo shoots over crispy rice). Faintly sweet corn cakes *(yumi bing)* complement the latter two dishes well.

Zourong Lu 68, Daduhui Guangchang 7 lou (7/F, Metropolitan Plaza, near Jiefang Bei and next to Harbour Plaza Hotel). ✆ **023/6383-5988.** Reservations accepted. English menu. Meal for 2 ¥100. No credit cards. 11:40am–2pm and 5.30–9pm. Bus: 306, 413, or 601 to Jiefang Bei.

Xiao Tian'e Huoguo (Cygnet) ★ HOT POT One of the most popular hot pot restaurants in Sichuan and beyond is a chain of 126 stores, the first of which opened over 20 years ago in Chongqing. Cygnet continues to be one of the best in town. This restaurant gives patrons a choice of hot or mild broth, and its buffet table of ingredients allows non-Mandarin speakers more control than usual over what goes into the pot. You can find another store on the fourth floor of Hongyadong (see above; ✆ **023/6399-2888**).

Jianxin Bei Lu 78, inside Cygnet Hotel (Xiao Tian'e Binguan). ✆ **023/6785-5328.** Meal for 2 ¥100–¥150. No credit cards. 11am–10pm. Bus: 181, 411, 601, or 902 to Haiguan.

Chongqing After Dark

Nightlife in Chongqing starts after 9pm. The most popular clubs and bars are clustered around Jiaochangkou and Bayi Lu Kou. **Babyface** (✆ **023/6311-1198**) and **N0.88 Bar** (✆ **023/6372-1088**), both on Bayi Lu, are two of the hottest spots for the young. The former plays hip-hop and has rapper playing live after 10:30pm; the latter has pulsating live pop music by Chinese singers every night.

DAZU 大足 ★★

Chongqing Municipality, 83km (52 miles) W of Chongqing, 251km (156 miles) SE of Chengdu

Among the most impressive and affecting artistic monuments that have survived through the ages are the extensive Buddhist cave paintings, sculptures, and carvings of Datong, Luoyang, Dunhuang, and Dazu. Of the four sites, **Dazu's stone carvings,** executed between 892 and 1249, are among the subtlest and most sophisticated, and worth going out of your way to see.

An unusual aspect of Dazu is that in addition to Buddhist images, it contains Daoist and Confucian statues and themes—not only in separate areas but, in rare instances, in the same cave. Initiated outside the monastic establishment, the Dazu carvings also commemorate historical figures as well as the project's benefactors, including commoners, warriors, monks, and nuns. In addition to what these carvings reveal about artistic advances made from the late Tang to the late Song, the garments and ornaments, along with garden and architectural settings, shed much light on everyday life in ancient China.

Of the six largest sites scattered around the county seat of Dazu, two are most worth a visit—**Bei Shan,** completed in the late Tang dynasty (618–907); and **Baoding Shan,** started and completed in the Song dynasty (960–1279). If you have time or interest for only one, make it Baoding Shan.

Essentials

GETTING THERE **Buses** leave Chongqing for Dazu from the Caiyuanba Long-Distance Bus Station (next to the railway station) every 20 minutes. The earliest bus is at 7am; the last return bus is scheduled to leave at 8pm. It's best to be at the Dazu bus station by 5pm for the return trip to Chongqing. The 2½-hour drive from Chongqing to Dazu Xian Bus Station costs ¥46 or ¥53. From the Dazu Bus Station, catch a **minibus** for Baoding Shan. Buses depart every half-hour and cost ¥4.50 each way. Buses also depart from the small bus station in the north part of town for ¥4.50. A **taxi** from Dazu Xian to Baoding Shan is about ¥30.

Taking the **train** to Dazu is slow and requires first going to Youting; from Youting, transfer to a bus going to the bus station. From the station, transfer to another bus to the grottoes. Whether coming from Chengdu or Chongqing, the bus is considerably faster and more convenient.

TOURS & GUIDES Guided trips to Baoding Shan can be arranged at Chongqing **CITS,** Zaozi Lanya Zheng Jie 120, second floor (**✆ 023/6385-0693;** fax 023/6385-0196; citscq@cta.cq.cn). The ¥1,300 fee for one or two people includes admission to Baoding and Bei Shan, a guide, transportation, and lunch. Alternately, English-language books give brief explanations of the more important carvings.

[FastFACTS] DAZU

Dazu has no useful services for visitors. Exchange money before you leave Chongqing.

Exploring Dazu

Baoding Shan ★★ Carvings of the cliff-side grottoes known as Da Fo Wan (Big Buddha Cove) were initiated and directed by Zhao Zhifeng, a self-styled Buddhist monk whose brand of Esoteric Buddhism incorporated current religious ideas and popular beliefs. Beginning in 1178 with the construction of Shengshou Temple at Xiao Fo Wan (Little Buddha Cove)—just north of Da Fo Wan—the Baoding Shan project continued for 71 years, possibly halted by the Mongol offensive in Sichuan. If Zhao lived that long (he'd have been 90) it would explain the unity of design and absence of repetition that mark Baoding Shan. The carvings are a series of instructive and cautionary scriptural stories arranged in order around a U-shaped cove with interludes of inscriptions and caves devoted to Buddhist deities. At the bottom curve of the U is a massive carving of a reclining **Sakyamuni Buddha** as he enters Nirvana (no. 11). It is just one of the many imposing sculptures at Baoding Shan. Others that should be noted include the stories of **parental devotion** (no. 15) and **Sakyamuni's filial piety** (no. 17). Local guides usually say these attest to the merging of Confucianism and Buddhism during the Song. But scholars see their inclusion as either a concession to Confucianism—when you want government endorsement, there's no point alienating folks—or, possibly, an answer to it from Buddhist scriptures. (In the parental devotion story, look for the nursing boy at the far right wearing the same split pants Chinese toddlers still wear today instead of diapers.) The gruesome **Hell of Knee-Chopping** (no. 20) captures the many faces of drunkenness (none flattering) without crossing the line into kitsch. These carvings are first and foremost works of art. The last story in the cove (no. 30) depicts the taming of a water buffalo and is meant to be a metaphor for taming the mind in meditation. One of the most accomplished carvings in this cove is no. 8, the **Thousand-Arm Avalokitesvara** (aka Guanyin), said to be the only Thousand-Arm Avalokitesvara that really has a thousand arms (1,007, actually). Remarkably, each of its hands is in a different pose. Expect to spend 1½ to 2 hours if you're exploring on your own, another hour if you've hired a guide.

Tip: The greatest obstacle to enjoying these caves is the crowds. The best time to visit Baoding Shan is at noon, when they go to lunch. Go to Bei Shan (below) anytime—tours usually skip it.

15km (9 miles) northeast of the town of Longgang Zhen (often called Dazu Xian). It's about ½ km (¼ mile) from the drop-off point (where the restaurants and souvenir stands are) to the entrance. Mini-trolley shuttle between parking lot and entrance ¥3. A private pay bathroom is by the parking lot (5 mao) and another, cleaner restroom halfway to the entrance. No restrooms inside. Admission ¥120. Combination ticket for Baoding Shan and Bei Shan ¥170. 8:30am–6pm.

Bei Shan ★ The problem with visiting Bei Shan after Baoding Shan is that it's a bit of a letdown. If you visit it first, though, you risk being glutted before properly feasting on the best. That said, Fo Wan (Buddha Cove), the cove at the top of Bei Shan, offers a fine series of religious and commemorative carvings, if somewhat less dazzling than the Song carvings. In 892, Wei Junjing, a military commander and imperial envoy, began carving Buddha images in what, at that time, was his encampment atop Bei Shan. That started a 250-year trend that resulted in the completion of nearly 10,000 statues scattered over the county by the end of the Song dynasty. Highlights of Bei Shan include the story of **Amitabha Buddha and his Pure Land** in Cave 245, which contains exquisite carved heads that look remarkably alive. Another is the statue of the **Bodhisattva Manjusri** in the largest cave at Fo Wan (no. 136). He appears high-minded and lofty, but it's the touch of self-satisfaction in his expression that captures his humanity and sets this statue apart.

2km (1¼ miles) north of the town of Longgang Zhen (often called Dazu Xian). Admission ¥90. 8:30am–6pm. A taxi from Dazu Xian to Bei Shan is about ¥10.

Where to Stay

Ramada Plaza Chongqing West (Chongqing Huadi Wangchao Huameida Guangchang Jiudian) This is the first full-fledged and the finest hotel in the town. Rooms are spacious and comfortable, equipped with large flat-screen TVs. Attentive details in the rooms include sensors turning on the lights automatically once you enter the room and laser alarm clocks projecting the time on the wall in the dark. The spotless bathroom has a shower cubicle with a rainforest showerhead and a separate tub. Next to the main building are two luxurious villas—one Chinese style and another western style—featuring swanky fixtures and facilities.

Wuxing Lu 386, Longgang Zhen, Dazu County. www.ramada.com. ✆ **023/8522-6666.** Fax 023/8522-7777. 243 units. ¥438–¥468 standard room. ¥898–¥998 suite. ¥5,888 villa. Rates include breakfast. No credit cards. **Amenities:** 2 restaurants; bar; fitness center; outdoor pool (summer only); room service; spa; tennis courts; airline, train, and bus ticketing. *In room:* A/C, satellite TV, hair dryer, Internet, minibar.

Where to Eat

The tourist town of Baoding Shan outside the entrance gate has a number of small restaurants, noodle shops, and kabob stands serving good, simple dishes at inflated (but still inexpensive) prices. It's usually the Qingdao or imported beer that hikes the bill up; unless you ask for local, that's what you'll get.

MIDDLE REACHES OF THE CHANG JIANG 长江 ★

The Three Gorges Dam (Sanxia Ba; 三峡坝)

The dream of constructing an enormous dam to harness and utilize the power of the Chang Jiang (Yangzi River) originally belonged to Sun Yat-sen in the early 1920s, but every Chinese leader since—including Mao and Deng Xiaoping—has shared it. The appeal of this massive project to premiers and presidents may have more to do with classical Chinese flood myths than engineering logic. The most enduring is the story of Yu, who was born out of the belly of his father's corpse. Through superhuman feats of repositioning mountains and changing the courses of rivers, Yu quelled the great flood of the world and restored natural order. Selfless and moral, his efforts left his body half-withered, yet he went on to found the (semimythical) Xia dynasty (ca. 21st–16th c. B.C.). There are also historical models of men who tamed rivers: Shu governor Li Bing supervised ancient China's largest irrigation project (256 B.C.) and is still admired for it; and the Sui Yangdi emperor (reigned 604–617) completed the building of the Grand Canal linking the north and south. Latest to see himself in the role of a new Yu out to suppress floods is the former premier Li Peng (best remembered for suppressing the student democracy movement), who pushed approval of the dam through the National People's Congress in 1992, and with whom the dam is most identified, though he no longer holds office.

The massive project was finished in 2009, but whether it ensures Li's fame or infamy is yet to be seen. It broke so many records in terms of size, manpower utilized in its construction, volume of building materials (including 10 million lb. of cement), and projected energy output (equal to "10 nuclear power stations"), that there is no real precedent by which to assess the short-term, let alone long-term, effects. But that hasn't stopped pundits (and nonpundits) from trying.

The chief aims of the dam are flood control, power generation, safer navigation, and increased river shipping, but critics of the project cite more than a few concerns, such as the resettlement of one million to two million people; the destruction of wildlife habitats, archaeological sites, and historical relics; and the environmental threat of trapped sewage and industrial waste.

DAM EFFECTS ALONG THE THREE GORGES ROUTE

Following are the effects the 175m (574-ft.) water level has on sites along the Three Gorges route:

- The residents of Fengdu were moved to the new city built across the river on higher ground. The mountain and kitsch, ghoulish temple complex with its sculptures of bug-eyed demons and "scenes of hell" remains.
- A tall weir has been built surrounding the town of Shibao Zhai. The intriguing old town and temples inside are preserved.
- Zhangfei Temple was moved to higher ground across the river. The temple commemorates the upright Shu warrior who was beheaded by two dastardly commanders in his own army. The bulk of the temple and its collection were destroyed during the Cultural Revolution. What stands is the restored building.
- Baidi Cheng (White Emperor City) is half submerged and became an island. A new bridge was built to connect to the city. Trackers' paths carved into the cliffs of Qutang Gorge are submerged.
- Three-quarters of Wan Xian is inundated. The last quarter, renovated and developed, has become the new downtown.
- Fuling (site of ancient royal tombs of the Ba Kingdom and the port town of 150,000 people that is the setting of *River Town,* Peter Hessler's fine personal account) is inundated. Excavation of the tombs has been completed.
- The building of the underwater viewing chamber for the ancient stone carvings at White Crane Ridge has been completed but only open to public sporadically. The official opening of museum had yet to be announced at press time.
- The Daning and Shennong gorges are slightly diminished, but naturally not enough to stop tours. Boats are able to venture farther into these narrow gorges and provide a closer look at the ancient hanging coffins—among them a cluster of 24.
- The western part of Xiling Gorge is submerged.
- The population of Badong was moved upstream to the opposite side of the river. Landslide-prevention projects veil the nearby slopes.

TO CRUISE OR NOT TO CRUISE

Debate rages around the question of whether the **Three Gorges cruise** is the thrill of a lifetime or an overrated, overpriced yawn. Members of tour groups invariably rave about their luxury trip. The boats are plusher than they expected; the cabins roomier; the food better. If the scenery comes as a bit of a letdown—well, they weren't expecting *A Single Pebble.* And if the excursions aren't all they're cracked up to be, at least they're short. Perhaps one reason tour members find their Three Gorges cruise so delightful is that it puts a halt to the mania of touring for a few days.

While it's true that other parts of China have better scenery, prettiness isn't everything. The best part of these cruises is watching life on the river as it is today—in flux. A new city springs up on high, and a few hundred yards below it, the old city sits like a sloughed-off shell. If you choose to take an excursion, as most do, see "The Top Excursions," below, for the very best.

If you'd like to take the excursion but can't afford the steep cruise prices, cheaper tourist ferries also make the trip. Some boats sail all the way to Shanghai, but unless

THE RIVER BY any other NAME

The name "Yangtze" is troublesome. English dictionaries usually give it two or three accepted pronunciations and an equal number of ways to spell it: Yangtze, Yangtse, Yangzi. The irony of it is that Chinese almost never use that name. As far back as the Zhou dynasty (1045 B.C.–246 B.C.), China's longest river was simply called Jiang, meaning "River." ("He," also meaning "River," was used to refer to the Yellow River, China's other great waterway.) Sometime in the 3rd century, Chinese started calling it the Chang Jiang (meaning "Long River"), and that's what it's called today. Theories abound on how the name Yangzi came about. Some say it came from Cantonese; others that it was a Western invention. In fact, in the 6th century the name Yangzi Jiang started showing up in poetry to refer to a short stretch of the river near Yangzhou. By the 19th century the name was applied to the whole river; and for a time, under the Republic, Yangzi Jiang was even the official name. But it returned to Chang Jiang under the People's Republic, and is the river's proper name.

you're fanatical about river travel, limit your journey to the stretch between Chongqing and Yichang. From there eastward, the river widens and the scenery becomes decidedly prosaic, and train, bus, or plane is preferable.

The best times to go are September and October. In terms of weather, May, early June, and early November can be lovely, when rains and mist form a picturesque scenery resembling a composition in Chinese ink. Summer is the rainy season, and winter is usually dry but quite cold. Fewer ships sail off season, and schedules are less reliable.

CRUISING INDUSTRY DAMMED?

The Gorges are still worth a visit after all. As the river now becomes much wider and less dangerous, more cruise lines are adding the Three Gorges to their cruise roster, more and larger riverboats are now cruising along the river. After the completion of the dam in 2009 and total water level gain of 90m (295 ft.), the peaks towering above the river are not as high, nor is the bottom of the ravine as narrow. The ghost towns that now dot the banks of the Yangzi, evacuated in anticipation of the rising water level, make for a novel if unintended tourist curiosity, but the majesty of the Gorges themselves has definitely been compromised.

THE CRUISE LINES

The following liners have the best English-speaking guides and the best ships. And after years of experience with foreign passengers, most have removed from their itineraries excursions that require a thorough familiarity with characters and events of the Three Kingdoms in order to enjoy them. Take advantage of off-season rates, book and buy in China, compare prices, bargain, and ask what the excursions are. The prices quoted here are rack rates, but 50% discounts are standard even during high season.

The cruising high seasons are April, May, September, and October. Shoulder seasons are late March, June, July, August, November, and early December. Some cruise ships offer specials in December, January, February, and March.

Orient Royal Cruises Until the appearance of Viking River Cruises (below), Orient's *East King* and *Yangzi Explore* were arguably the plushest ships on the Yangzi—built to five-star standards and tied with the *Yellow Crane* (see Presidential Cruises, below) for the best food. Their cruise directors, both from the Philippines, do a superior job of attending to passenger needs and special requests, and their Chinese river guides deliver expert commentary in well-spoken English. Standard cabins have twin beds, a desk, and small fridge. Orient Royal offers 4-day route from Chongqing to Yichang and 5-day, from Yichang to Chongqing.

Orient Royal Cruise, Wuhan office. Xinhua Lu 316, 14th floor, E Zuo (Block E), Liangyou bldg. ✆ **027/8576-9988.** Fax 027/8576-6688. East King 96 cabins. ¥2,270–¥3,620. Yangzi Explore 62 cabins. ¥6,500–¥9,250. All prices are per person based on double occupancy, standard cabin, including shore excursions. AE, DC, MC, V. **Amenities:** Restaurant; 2 bars; fitness center; library; room service. *In room:* A/C, TV, hair dryer, minibar/fridge.

Presidential Cruises The cruises, run by a China's Wuhan Yangtze Cruise, have six boats, imaginatively named the *President Prime,* M/V *President No. 1,* M/V *President No. 2,* and so on. The *President Prime,* launched in 2011, is built to five-star standard and surpasses the other President cruises in luxury. Its spacious cabins have European-style facilities. It's well-staffed with an English-speaking crew. While the no. 2 *(Yellow Crane)* lacks the slick promotion of Victoria and Orient Royal, the ship itself serves better food and very nearly meets five-star standards. Standard rooms are comparable in size and furnishing to those in Victoria Cruises' fleet. The cruise travels between Chongqing and Yichang (4 days downriver, 5 days upriver).

Xima Zhang Jie 88, Hangyang, Wuhan (behind Holiday Inn Riverside Wuhan). www.yzpresidentcruise.com. ✆ **027/8471-1412** or 8471-3429. Fax 027/8471-7415. yzpresidentcruise@yzpresidentcruise.com. 102 cabins. (Yellow Crane) ¥2,900–¥3,300 per person, standard cabin. ¥5,800–¥6,400 per person, business cabin. Check website for rates of other boats. AE, DC, MC, V. **Amenities:** 2 restaurants; bar; exercise room; reading room. *In room:* A/C, satellite TV, hair dryer on request.

Victoria Cruises Based in New York, this is one of the few Western-managed lines. In 2009, the cruise liner launched its new riverboat *Jenna.* With 189 cabins, *Jenna* is the largest riverboat on the Yangzi at press time and one of the most luxurious choices on the river. With the launching of the new cruise, Victoria now has seven fleets cruising on the Yangzi. Some of their old fleets were recently renovated or rebuilt. Their first-rate cruises have some of the best English-speaking and knowledgeable cruise directors and river guides. The on-board talks and activities, such as tai chi and mahjong classes, are interesting and fun. The crew are friendly and helpful while the kitchens provide tasty food. Standard cabins have twin beds and writing desk, but are slightly smaller than Orient Royal's *East King* and *East Queen.*

Victoria offers two routes: between Chongqing and Yichang (downriver 4 days, upriver 5 days); and between Chongqing and Shanghai (downriver 7 days, upriver 9 days).

57–08 39th Ave., Woodside, NY 11377. www.victoriacruises.com. ✆ **800/348-8084** or 212/818-1680. Fax 212/818-9889. 99–189 cabins. Cruise between Chongqing and Yichang: $980–$1,180 per person, standard cabin; $1,590–$2,560 per person suite. Shore excursion $90 per person. Cruise between Chongqing and Shanghai: $1,610 per person, standard cabin; $2,350–$3,850 per person suite. Shore excursion $240 per person. Fuel surcharge $240 per person. AE, DC, MC, V. **Amenities:** Restaurant; bar; acupuncture; exercise room; forex; Internet; massage; reading room. *In room:* A/C, TV, hair dryer.

Viking River Cruises Not only the most recent cruise line to start plying the Three Gorges, Viking's *Viking Emerald* comfortably float above the competition as the top way to see the river. Effortlessly five-star, every room is spacious and tastefully appointed with blond woods. The food is excellent and plentiful—to the extent that it sometimes feels as though you are living from meal to meal—and the staff has a working grasp of English and are extremely friendly. Viking cruises are mainly sold as part of package tours visiting China's other key tourist meccas: Xi'an, Beijing, Tibet, Shanghai and Suzhou. Prices vary according to package, time of year, and type of cabin you choose, so check the website for current rates.

5700 Canoga Ave., Suite 200, Woodland Hills, CA 91367. www.vikingrivercruises.com. ✆ **800/304-9616.** 128 cabins. Check website for current rates. AE, DC, MC, V. **Amenities:** Restaurant; 2 bars; exercise room; Internet; sauna. *In room:* A/C, closed-circuit/satellite TV, fridge, hair dryer, minibar.

THE TOP EXCURSIONS

One of the best excursions is to **Shi Bao Zhai (Stone Treasure Fortress).** Admission is ¥80. This square-edged **red pagoda** built in the 18th century hugs the cliff and is an elegant vision from the river. The climb up its 12 narrow staircases is only difficult when other tour groups are pressing from behind or blocking the way in front. Since the descent is down a back staircase, just let them all go ahead. Inside, look for the two "magic" holes. The first is the **Hole of the Greedy Monk.** As the story goes, when monks lived in the tower, the hole spouted just enough rice for their daily rations. One monk, thinking he'd like rations to sell in the market, tried to make the hole bigger. His avarice shut the source for good. Of the second hole, it is said that if you drop a duck down it **(Duck Tossing Hole),** within seconds you'll see the duck floating far below on the river.

Close to the top of the pagoda, if you peek under the **arched bridge** (which is meant to be crossed in three steps or less), you'll get a good look at a *wawa yu*—the **giant Chinese salamander** that supposedly cries like a baby. This one has been here for years—how it survives is a mystery.

For impressive scenery, the half-day trip up the **small gorges of Daning River** (near Wushan) is the best of the excursions. Cruise passengers board a ferry passing through the **Longmen Gorge, Bawu Gorge,** and **Dicui Gorge** and then to **Madu River,** which is named the **Xiao Xiao Sanxia.** From there, you get off to climb into "peapod" boats rowed and pulled upstream by trackers. Each boat has a guide whose English isn't always up to the task, but he/she makes up for it by singing a Tujia minority song for the group during the return trip. If the trackers are in the mood, one or two will join in. The scenery on this narrow stream is probably closer to what most travelers expect of the Three Gorges. **Towering cliffs** rise on either bank, and the water is crystal clear. On rare occasions, passengers catch sight of **monkeys** along the cliffs. The trackers used to go only far enough to glimpse the first **hanging coffin,** but now that the water level has risen, they may continue farther (though time is a factor, too).

Whether or not you have any interest in engineering or construction, the sheer immensity of the **Three Gorges Dam Site** (¥105) at **San Dou Ping** makes this worth a visit. Not only is it a unique photo opportunity, its monumental size lends it the visual (if not yet the historical) power of the Great Wall or Xi'an's Terra-Cotta Warriors. The luxury cruise ships usually include it on their itineraries, while local tourist ferries don't. Before booking, make sure it's included. Its absence from the itinerary is reason enough to look elsewhere.

LOWER-COST CRUISE ALTERNATIVES: LOCAL PASSENGER BOATS & TOURIST FERRIES

Yangzi River supercheap **passenger boats** depart from Wuhan (for upriver trips) and from Chongqing (for downriver trips) year-round, but their facilities are foul, and so is the food. Their raison d'être is transport, not tourism, so they make no effort to go through the gorges in the light of day, and naturally there are no tourist excursions.

Numerous Chinese **tourist ferries** operate on the Yangzi, some of them with quite comfortable cabins and facilities. Management and staff are not used to foreign travelers and they rarely speak English, but the price, even for first class, is considerably less than the price on a luxury ship. These boats will invariably only take you as far as Yichang. The remaining leg on to Wuhan is best accomplished on the air-conditioned buses that travel the recently completed freeway that connects the two cities; in fact, the option to sail to Wuhan is becoming less available. Fourth-class passage from **Chongqing to Yichang** starts at ¥249 and isn't much better than ferry accommodations—a bunk in an eight-person dorm with a filthy toilet down the hall. Prices for first-class passage (two-bed cabin with private shower/toilet), excluding meals and excursions, start at ¥1,042 per person. Since you can pay on board or at the site for excursions, make sure they're *not* included in your ticket price, giving you more flexibility. Typically, excursions are to Fengdu, Shi Bao Zhai, and the Little Three Gorges, but these ships do not stop at the Three Gorges Dam construction site. Tickets can be booked in Chongqing inside the Navigation Office Building at Chaotian Men near the Chaotian Men Hotel, but you probably won't find an English-speaker. Beware of so-called "government-run tour agencies" along the wharf; they are likely to charge much higher fees than the actual ticket cost. And be sure to ask which pier your boat will depart from.

In this instance, the better way to book is through **China International Travel Service (CITS)** in Wuhan, Taibei Yi Lu 26, seventh floor, Xiao Nan Hu Building (✆ **027/8578-4100;** fax 027/8578-4089; citswuh@public.wh.hb.cn). In Chongqing, CITS is at Zaozi Lanya Zheng Jie 120 (✆ **023/6385-0693;** fax 023/6385-0196; citscq@cta.cq.cn). The booking fee of ¥50 is worth every cent. The agents in the international division of both these offices are unusually well-informed and helpful, and speak excellent English.

WUHAN 武汉

Hubei Province, 1,125km (699 miles) W of Shanghai, 1,354km (841 miles) E of Chongqing, 1,047km (650 miles) SE of Xi'an

Wuhan is primarily an industrial and business center. Were it not for the fact that many of the Three Gorges tours traditionally begin or terminate in Wuhan, few Western tourists would ever make it here. However, trisected by the Yangzi River and its longest tributary, the Hanshui, and dotted with a hundred-plus lakes and scores of parks, this city of 4.8 million urban residents is an agreeable place to spend a couple of days. Wuhan is also the gateway to the Daoist mountain Wudang Shan. Three districts—Wuchang, Hanyang, and Hankou—which used to be separate cities, comprise present-day Wuhan. Avoid summers when the city inevitably lives up to its reputation as one of China's Three Furnaces.

Essentials

GETTING THERE **Tianhe International Airport** is 26km (16 miles) northwest of Wuhan. Destinations include Beijing (15 flights daily); Guangzhou (at least 7

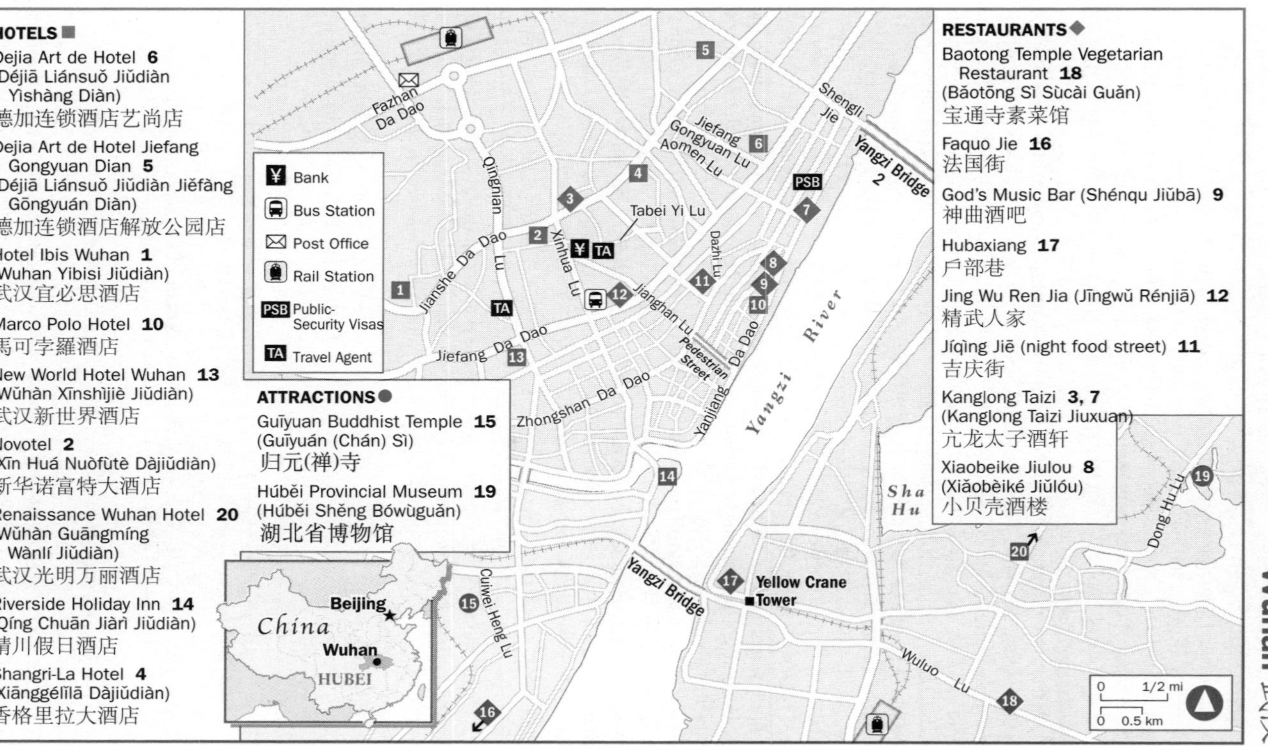
HOTELS
Dejia Art de Hotel 6
(Déjiā Liánsuǒ Jiǔdiàn Yìshàng Diàn)
德加连锁酒店艺尚店
Dejia Art de Hotel Jiefang Gongyuan Dian 5
(Déjiā Liánsuǒ Jiǔdiàn Jiěfàng Gōngyuán Diàn)
德加连锁酒店解放公园店
Hotel Ibis Wuhan 1
(Wuhan Yibisi Jiǔdiàn)
武汉宜必思酒店
Marco Polo Hotel 10
馬可孛羅酒店
New World Hotel Wuhan 13
(Wǔhàn Xīnshìjiè Jiǔdiàn)
武汉新世界酒店
Novotel 2
(Xīn Huá Nuòfùtè Dàjiǔdiàn)
新华诺富特大酒店
Renaissance Wuhan Hotel 20
(Wǔhàn Guāngmíng Wànlí Jiǔdiàn)
武汉光明万丽酒店
Riverside Holiday Inn 14
(Qíng Chuān Jiàrì Jiǔdiàn)
晴川假日酒店
Shangri-La Hotel 4
(Xiānggélǐlā Dàjiǔdiàn)
香格里拉大酒店
Bank
Bus Station
Post Office
Rail Station
PSB Public-Security Visas
TA Travel Agent
ATTRACTIONS
Guīyuan Buddhist Temple 15
(Guīyuán (Chán) Sì)
归元(禅)寺
Húběi Provincial Museum 19
(Húběi Shěng Bówùguǎn)
湖北省博物馆
RESTAURANTS
Baotong Temple Vegetarian Restaurant 18
(Bǎotōng Sì Sùcài Guǎn)
宝通寺素菜馆
Faquo Jie 16
法国街
God's Music Bar (Shénqu Jiǔbā) 9
神曲酒吧
Hubaxiang 17
戸部巷
Jing Wu Ren Jia (Jīngwǔ Rénjiā) 12
精武人家
Jíqìng Jiē (night food street) 11
吉庆街
Kanglong Taizi 3, 7
(Kanglong Taizi Jiuxuan)
亢龙太子酒轩
Xiaobeike Jiulou 8
(Xiǎobèiké Jiǔlóu)
小贝壳酒楼
Fazhan Da Dao
Qingnian Lu
Jianshe Da Dao
Xinhua Lu
Tabei Yi Lu
Jiefang Gongyuan Lu
Aomen Lu
Shengli Jie
Yangzi Bridge 2
Dazhi Lu
Jianghan Lu
Pedestrian Street
Da Dao
Yanjiang
Jiefang Da Dao
Zhongshan Da Dao
Yangzi River
Yangzi Bridge
Yellow Crane Tower
Cuiwei Heng Lu
Sha Hu
Dong Hu Lu
Wuluo Lu
China
Beijing
Wuhan
HUBEI
0 1/2 mi
0 0.5 km

Wuhan 武汉

flights daily); Hong Kong (2 flights daily); Shanghai (11 flights daily); Chengdu (8 flights daily); Chongqing (7 flights daily); Xian (5 flights daily); and Seoul (5–6 flights weekly).

An **airport bus** between the airport and Hankou (¥16), Hanyang (¥21), and Wuchang (¥31) departs when full; board near the airport entrance. The trip takes 1 hour and the bus stops at Hangkong Lu, The Yangtze Plaza, and terminates at Fujiapo Bus Station. A **taxi** to Hankou should be ¥50 to ¥70, plus a ¥15 toll. Stand in the taxi line and use the meter. Ignore independent drivers who will offer to drive you for hundreds of yuan.

Wuhan has three major **railway stations, Wuhan Huochezhan** (mostly high-speed trains), **Hankou Huochezhan** (mostly northbound), and **Wuchang Huochezhan** (mostly southbound). High speed trains leave Wuhan Station for Changsha Nan (1 hr. 30 min.; ¥165 or 2 hr. ¥110); Guangzhou Nan (4 hr.; ¥490); express trains to Shanghai Hongqiao (4 hr. 40 min., ¥500; or 5 hr. 40 min., ¥417). D-series trains from Wuchang Station to Shanghai (5½ hr.; ¥280), express trains for Changsha (3½ hr.; ¥54 hard seat) and Yueyang (2½ hr.; ¥33 hard seat); Beijing (Z38; 10 hr.; ¥429 soft sleeper; Z12; 10 hr.; ¥281 hard sleeper only); Guangzhou (T15, T225, T97; 10 hr. 30 min.; hard sleeper ¥257); and Shanghai (Z25/28; 9 hr. 30 min.; hard sleeper ¥274). Major connections with Hankou Station are fewer: Shanghai (4 hr. 40 min.; ¥274); Beijing (9 hr.; ¥281); and Chongqing North (15 hr.; hard sleeper ¥254).

Tickets can be booked 20 days in advance at the respective stations. Hotels and CITS will book tickets for a ¥5 fee.

The two main **long-distance bus stations** are the **Hankou Changtu Qichezhan** on Jiefang Da Dao at the Youyi Lu intersection (mostly northbound), and the **Wuchang Changtu Qichezhan,** northeast of the railway station on Wuluo Lu (mostly southbound). Buses for Shanghai leave from both stations (12 hr.; ¥307). It's best to buy tickets a day in advance.

GETTING AROUND Standard **taxi** rates are ¥6 for the first 2km (4 miles), then ¥1.40 for each additional kilometer up to 7km. Above 7km (4⅓ miles), the rate is ¥2.10 per kilometer. Newer taxis charge ¥8 for the first 2km; ¥1.60 per kilometer up to 7km and ¥2.14 per km thereafter. A ¥1 fuel surcharge is added to each ride.

Buses without air-conditioning charge ¥1 and ¥2 with air-conditioning go to all parts of the city.

A **light rail** line is currently exclusive to Hankou but is being extended to Wuchang. It runs along the old rail line on Jing-Han Da Dao, making stops every kilometer. It is operational between 6:30am and 9:30pm, and tickets cost ¥1.50 to ¥5.

[Fast FACTS] WUHAN

Banks, Foreign Exchange & ATMs A large **Bank of China** is just off the pedestrian street at Zhongshan Da Dao 593 (at the junction with Jianghan Lu; look for a stately old European concession building near the overhead walkway) and it has an ATM out the front. Foreign exchange is Monday through Friday from 8:30am to noon and 1:30 to 5pm. An ATM can also be found at the HSBC on the ground floor of New World Trade Centre.

Consulates The **U.S. Consulate** is at New World International Trade Tower 1, Jianshe Dadao 568 (✆ **027/8555-7791;** http://wuhan.usembassy-china.org.cn; Mon–Fri 9am–6pm; closed on American and Chinese holidays).

Internet Access Several Internet cafes are on Jianghan Street, charging ¥3 to ¥4 per hour. Dial-up is ✆ **163.**

Post Office A useful post office is at the west side of the railway station opposite the city bus terminal. There's another one on Jianghan Da Dao Pedestrian Street, no. 134, which is open from 8:30am to 5pm.

Tours **China International Travel Service (CITS)** is exceptionally helpful and straightforward about prices. They book flights, train rides, and cruises, and arrange guided tours. CITS is located at Zhongshan Da Dao 909, near the intersection with Yiyuan Lu (✆ **027/8277-3071**).

Visa Extensions Applications are available at the **PSB Exit-Entry Administration Department (Gonganju Churujing Guanli)** at Zhang Zizhong Lu 306 (✆ **027/8539-5333**), open Monday through Friday from 8:30am to noon and 2:30 to 5:30pm and Saturday 9am to 4pm. The process takes 3 working days.

Exploring Wuhan

Guiyuan (Chan) Si (Guiyuan Buddhist Temple) Best known for its hall of 500 gilded *luohan* (enlightened disciples), each in a different posture and having distinct features, this temple was founded in the mid–17th century by the monk Bai Guang. The present buildings date from the late Qing dynasty to the beginning of the Republican era (1911–49), but the *luohan* were sculpted between 1822 and 1831. Men proceed to the left and women to the right, counting one *luohan* until the number equals their age. They note the number that designates that statue and, on their way out, for ¥3, they buy the corresponding "*luohan* card," which tells their fortune. In the sutra library at the far end of the complex is a pretty jade Buddha with Indian influence that dates from the Northern Wei dynasty (4th–5th c.).

Cuiwei Heng Lu 20. ✆ **027/8243-5212.** Admission ¥20. 8am–5pm. Bus: 401 is the only bus that can enter the narrow Cuiwei Heng Lu, but buses 6 and 528 run along Yingwu Da Dao, which intersects Cuiwei Heng Lu. From this intersection, it's a short walk to Guiyuan.

Hubei Sheng Bowuguan (Hubei Provincial Museum) ★★ "When the Master was in Qi he heard the Shao [ceremonial music] and for 3 months was oblivious to the taste of food. He marveled, 'I never expected music to do this to me'" (from *The Analects,* Confucius).

Since no musical notations survive from the time of Confucius (ca. 551–479 B.C.), there's no way of knowing what the music he refers to above sounded like, but thanks to the excavation in 1978 of the intact tomb of Marquis Yi of Zeng (d. ca. 433 B.C.), visitors to this museum can see some of the actual instruments on which the music was played. In addition to an ensemble of ancient musical instruments, the tomb included coffins, gold and jade decorative items, weapons, and impressive bronze- and lacquerware from China's Warring States period (474–221 B.C.). The centerpiece of the exhibition is a huge set of 65 bronze chime bells, said to be the heaviest and possibly oldest extant musical instrument in the world. Inscriptions on the bells and hooks that hold them constitute the earliest known work on musicology. To give visitors an idea of how the bells were played and how their pentatonic scale sounded, musicians give an excellent 20-minute performance on classical instruments, which include replicas of the bronze bells. Two performances are scheduled at 11am and 4pm each day. Two newer halls feature Bronze Age artifacts and additional items from the Warring States period.

Wuchang, Donghu Lu 156. ✆ **027/8679-4127.** www.hubeimuseum.net. Free admission. Tues–Sun 9am–5pm (no admission after 3pm). Bus: 14, 402, or 578. Audio tour rent ¥20 for 3 hr., ¥40 for a day. Deposit ¥200 and show passport.

Shopping & Strolling

The 1km (½-mile) stretch of **Jianghan Street** (btw. Jianghan Da Dao and the wharf) is lined up with trendy shops. The street is a popular place to stroll, especially on hot summer evenings. If you walk south from Jianghan Street to the wharf, you'll get to the Customs Building and the former **foreign concession** area of Hankou, which under the Treaty of Tianjin was forced open to British trade in 1859. The dozen or so remaining buildings in the European style of the 1920s and 1930s are spread along the wharf on **Yanjiang Da Dao** (a left turn off the pedestrian street). A number of the buildings (which include the Russian police station, the former German and U.S. consulates, several banks, businesses, and living quarters) are identified by signs in English. In efforts to entice foreign investors, Wuhan's mayor has invited overseas businesses to set up offices in these historical buildings.

During the cherry blossom season from March to April, hundreds of thousands of locals and tourists swarm into the **Wuhan University campus,** in Wuchang's Luojia Shan, where a thousand Japanese Cherry grow. The hundred-year-old university is also regarded as the most beautiful campus in China for its classic and charming architecture. Take bus no. 519 and 608 to Luojia Shan.

The **Xin Shijie Baihuo Shangchang (New World Department Store)** on Jianshe Da Dao (around the corner from Novotel Hotel) has a large supermarket on the basement level. Each of the three districts of Wuhan has a Carrefour. The one in Hankou is on Wusheng Lu.

Where to Stay

EXPENSIVE

Marco Polo Wuhan (Wuhan Makeboluo Jiudian) ★★ Among all the luxurious choices in Wuhan, this hotel enjoys the best riverfront view and provides the most capacious rooms. Rooms are inviting and stylish, equipped with large flat-screen TVs, plush beds, and decorated with horse paintings. A wardrobe is inside the sizable bathroom, which overlooks the Yinjiang Dadao and the riverside park. The fitness center features the most up-to-date equipment, including two advanced and effective stretching machines. The indoor pool has a whirlpool by the window with a panorama of the Yangzi River.

Yanjiang Dadao 159, Jiangan. www.marcopolohotels.com. ✆ **027/8277-8888.** Fax 027/8277-8866. 370 units. ¥1,277 standard room. Rates include breakfast. 20%–40% discount available; 15% service charge. AE, DC, MC, V. **Amenities:** 3 restaurants; lounge; babysitting; concierge; executive floor; forex; health club; indoor pool; room service; sauna; smoke-free floor; airline, train, and bus ticketing. *In room:* A/C, satellite TV, fridge, hair dryer, minibar, Wi-Fi.

New World Hotel Wuhan (Wuhan Xinshijie Jiudian) ★ The New World is now one of the finest hotels in the city. Standard rooms are comfy with a young and stylish design. Glass and wooden panels form a circular partition to separate the bathroom and bedroom, adding an interesting and harmonious touch to the light wood-colored room. Bathrooms are spacious, with separate shower and bath tub. Spend the afternoon at the outdoor pool in the hot summer days before heading out to indulge in the city's vibrant nightlife.

Jiefang Dadao 630, Hankou. www.newworldhotels.com. ✆ **027/8380-8888.** Fax 027/8380-8889. 327 units. ¥713–¥773 standard room. Rates include breakfast. 20%–40% discount available; 15% service charge. AE, DC, MC, V. Amenities: 2 restaurants; lounge; babysitting; concierge; executive floor; forex; health club; outdoor pool; room service; sauna; tennis court; airline, train, and bus ticketing; Wi-Fi in public area. *In room:* A/C, satellite TV, adapters, fridge, hair dryer, Internet, minibar.

Renaissance Wuhan Hotel (Wuhan Guangming Wanli Jiudian) ★ Despite being a bit distant from the commercial areas, Renaissance is the most luxurious choice in Wuchang. The entire design of the hotel is inspired by the surrounded-by-water city. The element of water is embraced subtly in different corners, including a pond in the lobby. Rooms are dignified and furnished with sumptuous beds. The bathrooms, with separate shower and tub, have pleasing mosaic wall tiles on the mirror wall and in the shower cubicle. Some of the rooms overlook Sha Lake. The fitness center and indoor pool are open around the clock. Staff are friendly and helpful; service is one of the best in the city.

Xudong Dadao 98, Wuchang. www.marriott.com. ✆ **027/8662-1388.** Fax 027/8662-1288. 278 units. ¥738 standard room. Rates include breakfast. 15% service charge. AE, DC, MC, V. **Amenities:** 2 restaurants; bar; concierge; executive floor; forex; health club; indoor pool; room service; sauna; tennis court; airline, train, and bus ticketing; Wi-Fi in public area. *In room:* A/C, satellite TV, fridge, hair dryer, minibar, Wi-Fi.

Shangri-La Hotel (Xianggelila Dafandian) ★★ The most established international hotel in the city, Shangri-la offers the best service in the city. This hotel has undergone a massive facelift to offer guests better facilities and environment. The facade, lobby, and restaurants changed completely after the renovation, and rooms are appointed with new facilities such as flat-screen TV and new fixtures. Guest rooms are decently sized, comfortable, and attractive with Chinese paintings.

Jianshe Da Dao 700, Hankou. www.shangri-la.com. ✆ **027/8580-6868.** Fax 027/8577-6868. 448 units. ¥888–¥968 standard room. Rates do not include breakfast. 15% service charge. AE, DC, MC, V. **Amenities:** 3 restaurants; 2 bars; babysitting; executive floor; forex; health club; indoor pool; room service; sauna; tennis court; airline, train, and bus ticketing. *In room:* A/C, satellite TV, LCD TV, fridge, hair dryer, Internet, minibar.

MODERATE

Holiday Inn Riverside Wuhan (Qingchuan Jiari Jiudian) Perched on the west bank of the Yangzi River across from the Yellow Crane Tower—emblem of Wuhan—this four-star hotel has one of the best views in the city. The rooms themselves are immaculate and comfortably appointed even if the decor isn't inspired. Some rooms overlook the Yellow Crane Tower and all rooms have comparable river views. One possible disadvantage of the Riverside's location is that it's across the Han River from Hankou; but the actual distance to the city center is only about 4km (2½ miles).

Ximachang Jie 88 (next to Qingchuan Pavilion), Wuhan. www.hirw.com. ✆ **027/8471-6688.** Fax 027/8471-1808. 305 units. ¥598 standard room. Rates do not include breakfast. 15% service charge. AE, DC, MC, V. **Amenities:** 3 restaurants; bar; deli; concierge; exercise room; forex; golf driving net; KTV; reflexology center; room service; sauna; tennis court; airline, train, and bus ticketing. *In room:* A/C, satellite TV, fax (in some), fridge, hair dryer, Internet, minibar.

Novotel Xinhua Wuhan (Xinhua Nuofute Dafandian) This French joint-venture (part of the Accor group) distinguishes itself from the pack of four-star hotels with its European touch—the look is smart and streamlined. In the guest rooms, cone-shaped bed lamps are set against blondwood. Though standard rooms are on the small side, they still feel light and airy. The smallish bathrooms are made to feel roomier by an elegant black marble counter big enough to accommodate a travel case and toiletries. Novotel's central location between the concession area and the Hankou railway station is convenient for both shopping and sightseeing.

Jianshe Da Dao 558 (next to New World Department Store Xin Shijie Baihuo). www.novotel.com. ✆ **027/8555-1188.** Fax 027/8555-1177. 303 units. ¥350–¥510 standard room. 15% service charge. AE, DC, MC, V. Bus: 509 from railway station. **Amenities:** 3 restaurants; 2 bars; deli; executive floors; forex; health club; Jacuzzi; indoor pool; room service; sauna. *In room:* A/C, satellite TV, fax (in some executive rooms), fridge, hair dryer, minibar, Wi-Fi.

INEXPENSIVE

Hotel Ibis Wuhan (Wuhan Yibisi Jiudian) This relaxing hotel—part of the French franchise—opened in Wuhan in 2006 and is a great budget choice. Rooms are clean and cozy, though standard. Staff are helpful and friendly.

Jianshe Da Dao 539, Hankou. www.ibishotel.com. ✆ **027/8362-3188.** Fax 027/8368-3177. 243 units. ¥179 standard room. AE, DC, MC, V. **Amenities:** Restaurant; bar; Wi-Fi. *In room:* A/C, TV, Internet.

Dejia Art de Hotel (Dejia Liansuo Jiudian Yishang Dian) This themed hotel, with a rainbow-colored facade, offers value and a novel lodging experience in Wuhan thanks to its art features. Replica paintings by impressionist masters, such as Pablo Picasso and Joan Miró, are the hotel's main decorations. Women's rooms are compact but femininely designed with a wine-red wall and bed screen. A standard room is larger and comfortably furnished. Bathrooms have shower only. The local hotel group also has another site located near Jiefang Gongyuan.

Jianshe Da Dao 975, Hankou (across Wuhan Evening Post). www.dejiahotel.com. ✆ **027/8226-0888.** Fax 027/8226-0800. 93 units. ¥188 women's room; ¥180–¥210 standard room. No credit cards. **Amenities:** Restaurant. *In room:* A/C, TV, Internet.

Where to Eat

If you're after a meal that's *not* Chinese, the coffee shop at the Shangri-la hotel serves the best **Western buffet breakfast** in town. Western chains are all concentrated on the same intersection on Jianghan Lu, 1 block northwest of the overhead walkway at the Zhongshan Da Dao intersection. **K11,** alongside the New World Hotel, has a handful of fast food outlets, cafes, and western restaurants. **Faguo Jie (French St.)** is a street full of Western restaurants, coffee shops, and pubs opened by foreigners living in Wuhan; take bus no. 202, 204, 205, or 208. For some local flavor, go to **Hubuxiang** (bus no. 542 to Simenkou), the "Breakfast Street." Stalls sell local street food such as *reganmian* (Wuhan-style dry noodles), a wide range of *baozi* (steam buns), and pastry. If you like spicy food and are adventurous enough, you must try Wuhan's famous snack spot, **Jing Wu Ren Jia,** located on the Jingwu Road of Hankou (bus no. 522 to Xinhua Lu); you won't miss the red signs and neon lights of this franchise's original shop. It's open 24 hours. Be warned that it's so spicy that it will bring you to tears.

Baotong Si Sucai Guan (Baotong Temple Vegetarian Restaurant) ★ BUDDHIST VEGETARIAN Almost as popular with nonvegetarians, this restaurant prepares *zhaicai* (Buddhist cuisine) in the temple tradition, specializing in faux meat, fish, and fowl dishes. A delicious appetizer is *wuxiang niurou* (faux beef with blended spices). Made from *doufu pi* (the top, most nutritious layer of the tofu), this cold dish is served with hot sesame oil and soy sauce. Another *doufu pi* main dish is *hongshao fuzhu* (braised *doufu pi* rolls with bamboo shoots and green pepper). Two dishes that don't pretend to be anything else are *quanjiafu* (several kinds of mushroom sautéed with dates) and sautéed *youmaicai,* which is a dark-green leafy vegetable similar to spinach. Both dishes are delicate and tasty.

Wuluo Lu no. 289 (next to the temple entrance). No phone. Meal for 2 ¥100. No credit cards. 9am–8pm. Bus: 18, 25, 518, 519, 577, or 710 to Hong Shan Gongyuan stop.

Jiqing Jie (Night Food Street) HUBEI This street used to be a crowded area of outdoor restaurants, making it an evening of dining and enjoying roving singers, musicians, sketch artists, flower sellers, photographers, and shoe shiners. However, the place has been overwhelmingly commercialized and some of the restaurants charge tourists unreasonably, which earned the area a bad reputation. Since then, fewer people go here. All the restaurants on this street serve similar fare and mainly seafood, which is generally satisfying. Like Sichuan cuisine, Hubei dishes incorporate a lot of pepper—but not all the dishes are fiery.

Jiqing Jie starting from Dazhi Jie. Meal for 2 ¥60–¥100. No credit cards. From 6:30pm until everyone goes home; liveliest time is after 10pm.

Kanglong Taizi ★ CHINESE This franchise, with five locations, makes for one of Wuhan's more popular dinning places. Nearly always packed, the restaurants don't claim to offer any particular type of Chinese cuisine, although Hunan and Hubei dishes feature prominently. The food is generally good and the place is clean. It features new and seasonal dishes from time to time. In any case, the picture menu will help you order. Also at Hankou, Yanjiang Da Dao 226 (✆ **027/8271-2228**).

Jianshe Dadao 735, Hankou. ✆ **027/8576-8666.** Picture menu. Meal for 2 ¥80–¥120. No credit cards. 10am–10pm.

Xiaobeike Jiulou HUBEI This restaurant, housed in a historic European-style building, serves tasty Hubei home-style food for a good value. Xiaobeike is popular among locals and it's always hard to get a table during dinner hours. Try *tangcu paigu* (sweet and sour ribs), it is one of the most highly rated dishes of the restaurant. *Liangban maodou* (green soybeans salad) mixes green soybeans with garlic, chili, vinegar, and soy sauce. The mildly spicy cold dish stimulates your taste buds as well as your appetite. End your meal with desert *huanxi tuo* (sweet deep-fried glutinous rice ball). The crispy surface and soft glutinous rice and red bean paste inside create a nice contrast.

Dongting Jie 129, Hankou (intersection of Cai'e Lu and Dongting Jie, near Yuehan Pier). ✆ **027/8284-4071** or 027/8283-2846. Picture menu. Meal for 2 ¥80–¥100. No credit cards. 10:30am–9pm. Bus no. 38, 45, or 579 to Yuehan Matou.

Wuhan After Dark

Along the Yanjiang Da Dao are loads of bars and clubs. **SOHO,** at Nanjing Lu intersection (✆ **027/5223-3668**), and **CASH,** Shanghai Lu 19 (✆ **132/6066-9282**), are two of the most popular ones. **Take Five,** located next to the Zhong Binguan on

Xinhua Xiao Lu, features great live jazz from 9pm every night. **God's Music Bar** (Shenqu; ✆ **027/8284-2865**), at Chezhan Lu 25, was originally a church during the foreign concessions in the 1800s. The owner, a renowned interior designer in the city, carefully retained the original fixtures and features of the Gothic building when he transformed it into a bar back in 1997 and created some ancient Greek mythical oil paintings as decorations. A local band plays Chinese pop music at the bar from 9pm to midnight. It is nice to have a drink at the outdoor area during spring and early summer nights. Check out **VOX** in Wuchang, at Luxiang Lumo Lu Caojiawan Chezhan Guoguang Daxia (✆ **027/5076-1020;** bus no. 59, 709, or 401), for local underground music and shows during weekends.

WUDANG SHAN 武当山

Hubei Province, 500km (311 miles) NW of Wuhan

In the hierarchy of sacred Daoist mountains, Wudang is number one because of its association with the popular god Zhenwu (Perfected Warrior). In the 7th century, a cult developed around him, and his popularity continued to grow for the next 7 centuries. By the Ming dynasty, Zhenwu was considered the 82nd transformation of Lao Zi, and even supplanted the deified Lao Zi as the most important of the Daoist gods. Visitors to Wudang have the Perfected Warrior to thank for many of the monasteries and temples that still stand on the mountain. It was in his honor that the Yongle emperor ordered a massive building campaign on Wudang Shan in 1412. Several of the extant buildings date back to that time.

Unlike Emei Shan, Qingcheng Shan, and Nan Yue Heng Shan, Wudang receives relatively few tourists, and it has preserved its temples and its Daoist tradition more successfully than the less-remote mountains. The price of preservation for the traveler is a longer journey and less-comfortable lodging. However, the mountain's rugged peaks covered in old-growth forest, along with its ancient monasteries—some built to fit the contours of the cliffs, others to mirror them—are well worth the sacrifice.

Another name associated with these mountains is Zhang Sanfeng, the Daoist Immortal credited with inventing the discipline of *taijiquan* in the late 14th century. Though less well known overseas, Wudang's "internal" form of *wushu* (martial arts) is as highly regarded as Shaolin Temple's "external" form (p. 343). Students come from all parts of China to study at the many martial arts schools in town and on the mountain. The famous swords used in the Wudang style are for sale everywhere.

The best times to visit are April through June and September through October, when the leaves turn as red as the gorgeous temple walls.

Note: For Chinese translations of establishments in this section, see chapter 16.

Essentials

GETTING THERE Direct **train** service from Wuchang to Wudang Shan has stopped operating since the completion of the express rail between Hankou (Wuhan) and Shiyan in October 2009. A D-series express train to Shiyan departs at Hankou at 9am (3 hr.; second class ¥152, first class ¥183). The return train from Shiyan for Hankou leaves at 12:13pm.

From Shiyan, take the **express tour bus** at Argyle Shiji Baiqiang Grand International Hotel (Shiji Baiqiang Yage Gouji Dajiudian), at Beijing Bei Lu 78, to Wudang Shan. The 30-minute ride takes you directly to the Wudang Shan entrance.

Exploring the Mountain

The entrance to the mountain is less than a mile east of Wudang Shan Town. **Tour vans** pick up passengers outside the railway station and drop them at the entrance of the mountain (¥2).

Buy tickets at the tourist service center located at the end of Wudang Jinjie, a street filled with shops selling souvenirs and Wudang swords. Admission to the scenic area is ¥210; the fee includes admission to the mountain, transportation from the entrance to main temples, and entrance to all but **Jin Dian** and **Zixiao Gong,** which charge an extra ¥20 and ¥15 respectively.

At the tourist service center, you can just get on the **tour buses** to different scenic spots in the mountain. A **cable car,** which starts at Qiongtai, goes to Taihe Gong (near the peak). The 15-minute trip costs ¥80 up, ¥70 down, ¥150 round-trip. The peak can also be reached **on foot** in 2½ hours up stone stairs. The views along the 12km (7 miles) trail are magnificent. Save energy for the final very steep leg to the peak. The round-trip by **sedan chair** is ¥120.

Best preserved from the Ming dynasty building boom is Wudang Shan's **Zixiao Gong (Purple Mist Palace),** located on **Zhanqi Peak** (below the cliff Taizi Yan). This large, still very active monastery was built in 1413. Its striking red halls often bustle with priests and pilgrims. You may also come upon a *taijiquan* class practicing on one of the open terraces. Famous among its relics is a series of statues of Zhenwu at various stages of his life.

The most dramatic of the existing temples, **Nanyan Gong (Southern Cliff Palace),** is built into the side of a sheer cliff, recalling Northern Heng Shan's Xuankong Si—another Daoist temple that seems to defy gravity (p. 211). From Zixiao Gong, follow the trail up the mountain (southwest) to Wuya Ling (about 2.5km/1½ miles); Nanyan is just after Nantian Men. **Jin Dian (Golden Hall),** which sits on **Tianzhu Feng,** highest of Wudang's 72 peaks (1,612m/1 mile high), is part of the 15th-century **Taihe Gong (Palace of Supreme Harmony)** complex. Its two-tiered roof, covered in gilded bronze, is, naturally, best viewed on a clear day when it sparkles. To reach Jin Dian from Nanyan Gong, continue up the path to Huanglong Dong (Yellow Dragon Cave). From here, both ascending paths lead to the Golden Hall. The steeper route is to the right through the three "Heaven Gates."

Where to Stay & Eat

The best two places to stay are on the mountain near Tianzhu Peak. **Taihe Gong** offers very basic accommodations in their **Jinding Guibin Zhaodaishi** (✆ **0719/568-7155**). The cost of ¥200 each person includes a room with twin beds, shared bathroom, and limited hot water. This is where you stay if you want to see the sunrise on the peak. The **Jingui Jiudian** (✆ **0719/568-9198**) just down the hill from the Wuya Ling parking lot is basic and satisfactory, and costs ¥280 for a standard room, with discounts of up to 40% available. None of the hotels in Wudang Shan have the charm, views, or quiet of the mountain. The **Wudang Shan Qiongtai Binguan**

(© **0719/852-9991**), which is just adjacent to the cable car station at Qiongtai, is the most comfortable and cleanest. Furniture and bedspreads are standard, and the bathroom is small with shower only. A Chinese restaurant is on the premises. The price of a standard room ranges from ¥260 to ¥280 on normal days and ¥500 to ¥550 on holidays.

CHANGSHA 长沙

Hunan Province, 1,419km (882 miles) SE of Chongqing, 707km (440 miles) N of Guangzhou

Changsha is another hazy, congested, modern Chinese city hurrying to divest itself of any architectural trace of its past. But it is the capital of Hunan Province and gateway to one of the Five Sacred Mountains of Daoism and the gorgeous scenic area of the World Heritage Site, Wulingyuan, better known as Zhangjiejia. It is also home to one of the most exciting tomb collections in China—the Mawang Dui, which dates from the Western Han dynasty and one of the major academies in Ancient China. The city itself is most often associated with Mao Zedong and the model worker Lei Feng. As the city's underground is under construction, traffic could give you a headache, especially in peak hours.

Essentials

GETTING THERE The **Changsha Huanghua Airport** is 34km (21 miles) east of town. Destinations include Beijing (12 or more flights daily); Guangzhou (4–5 flights daily); Shenzhen (7 flights daily); Hong Kong (2 flights daily); Kunming (10 flights daily); Chengdu (6 or more flights daily); Shanghai (14 flights daily); Xi'an (over 7 flights daily); Zhangjiajie (1 daily); Lijiang (1 daily); Taipei (8 flights weekly); and Seoul (at least 1 daily). An **airport shuttle** from Minhang Dajiudian (Civil Aviation Hotel) at Wuyi Da Dao 5 (300m/984 ft. west of Changsha Railway Station; © **0731/417-0288**) takes about 30 minutes and costs ¥17; it departs the hotel every 20 minutes from 6am to 10pm. A taxi to the airport from city center is around ¥100. **Changsha Huochezhan (Changsha Railway Station)** is at the east end of Wuyi Da Dao. The city is on the Beijing-Guangzhou railway line. Major connections include Beijing Xi (13 hr.; hard sleeper ¥345); Guangzhou (7 hr.; hard sleeper ¥183); Shanghai (D106/107; 7 hr. 30 min.; ¥274); and Wuchang (3 hr.; ¥108). **Changsha Nan Huochezhan (Changsha South Railway Station)** is one of the stops of the Gotei (high-speed railway) running through Wuhan and Shenzhen Bei (Shenzhen North). The ride only takes 1½ hours to Wuhan and 2½ hours to Guangzhou, and is ¥175 and ¥333 respectively. Changsha has three main **bus stations: Qiche Nan Zhan (South Station), Qiche Dong Zhan (East Station),** and **Qiche Xi Zhan (West Station).** Buses to Nan Yue Heng Shan, Shao Shan, Xiamen, and Guilin leave from the South Station. Buses to Hankou (Wuhan), Guangzhou, and Nanjing leave from the East Station. Buses to Zhangjiajie, Fenghuang, Shao Shan and Yichang leave from the West Station.

GETTING AROUND Air-conditioned **public buses** cost ¥2 to ¥3; non-air-conditioned buses cost ¥1. Standard **taxi** rates are ¥6 for the first 2km (1¼ miles) and ¥1.80 per kilometer thereafter; from 9pm to 5am, the rates are ¥7 for the first 2km and ¥2.16 per kilometer thereafter.

Changsha 长沙

Xiang River Bridge 2
China
Beijing
HUNAN
Changsha
Xiang River
Xiang River Bridge 1
To West Bus Station
To East Bus Station
To South Bus Station
Ying Pan Lu
Ying Pan Dong Lu
Zhong Shan Lu
Bayi Lu
Wuyi Dadao
Jiefang Lu
Jiefang Zhong Lu
Jiefang Dong Lu
Renmin Zhong Lu
Yingpan Lu
Huangxing Zhong Lu
PEDESTRIAN STREET
Furong Bei Lu
Furong Zhong Lu
Furong Nan Lu
Dongfeng Lu
Chaoyang Lu
Shaoshan Bei Lu
Shaoshan Zhong Lu
Shaoshan Nan Lu
Chezhan Lu
Zhong Bei Lu
Lao Dong Xi Lu
LaoDong Dong Lu
RESTAURANTS
City Pub 12
(Chéngshì Jiǔbā)
城市酒吧
Feast Hunan Flavours 2
(Húnán Fēngwèi Cāntīng)
湖南风味餐厅
Grand Sun City Hotel 12
(Shénnóng Dàjiǔdiàn)
神农大酒店
Teppanyaki Xiang 11
57度湘
HOTELS
Crown Plaza Hotel City Centre Changsha 4
(Chángshā Huángguān Jiàrì Jiǔdiàn)
长沙皇冠假日酒店
Days Hotel & Suites Changsha City Centre 7
长沙小天鹅戴斯酒店
Dolten International Hotel 9
(Tōngchéng Guójì Dàjiǔdiàn)
通程国际大酒店
Huatian Hotel 8
(Huátiān Dàjiǔdiàn)
华天大酒店
Jinjiang Inn Wuyi Square 6
锦江之星五一广场店
Sheraton Changsha Hotel 2
(Chángshā Yùndá Xīláidēng Jiǔdiàn)
长沙运达喜来登酒店
Wonder's Hotel 3
(Wàndài Dàjiǔdiàn)
万代大酒店
Wyndham Grand Plaza Royale Furongguo Changsha 10
长沙芙蓉国温德姆至尊豪廷大酒店
ATTRACTIONS
Húnán Provincial Museum 1
(Húnán Shěng Bówùguǎn)
湖南省博物馆
Léi Fēng Memorial 5
(Léi Fēng Jìniànguǎn)
雷锋纪念馆
Máo Zédōng's Former Residence 13
(Máo Zédōng Tóngzhì Gùjū)
毛泽东同志故居
Sháo Shān 13
韶山
Yuelu Academy 5
岳麓书院
Bank
Museum
Post Office
Rail Station
Travel Agent
0 1/2 mi
0 0.5 km

[Fast FACTS] CHANGSHA

Banks, Foreign Exchange & ATMs The main **Bank of China** is at Furong Lu 593, near Ba Yi Qiao (8-1 Bridge) and opposite Carrefour. It has full foreign exchange services Monday through Friday from 8:30am to noon and 2 to 5pm, and an ATM. It also gives cash advances on credit cards. An **ATM** is in the lobby of Huatian Dajiudian.

Internet Access Internet cafes are fairly prolific along the stretch of Zhongshan Lu, near the corner of Huangguang Lu, conveniently located to most of the hotels listed in this section. Alternately Shan Nan Lu, near Hunan University, has inexpensive Internet cafes on every block, but getting there requires crossing the Xiang River. Dial-up is © **163,** 165, or 169.

Post Office The main post office is on the east side of the pedestrian block of Huangxing Lu. Another is just north of the railway on Chezhan Zhong Lu. It's open from 8am to noon and 2:30 to 5:30pm.

Exploring Changsha

Hunan Lei Feng Jinianguan (Lei Feng Memorial of Hunan) Those looking for a trace of Mao's China will find it here. The selfless soldier whose only ambition was to be "a little screw that would never rust in the revolutionary machinery" ended up getting a whole memorial to himself, not to mention the Lei Feng Hospital, the Lei Feng Hotel, and the big statue that flanks the street to the museum. Unfortunately, there are no English signs in this monument to a past era, but much of the collection is self-explanatory. It includes propaganda posters that trace the life of Lei Feng and his family members, some obviously retouched photographs, and a number of Lei Feng's personal effects. Give yourself about 45 minutes to an hour here.

Lei Feng Zhen 9, across Xiang River, about 8km (5 miles) beyond the West Bus Station. © **0731/8810-7959.** Free admission. 8am–5:30pm. Bus: 315 from West Bus Station to terminus.

Hunan Sheng Bowuguan (Hunan Provincial Museum) ★★ Between 1972 and 1974, the family plot of the chancellor to the prince of Changsha (which was in the Chu Kingdom) was excavated at **Mawang Dui** in the eastern suburbs of Changsha. Of the three tombs—one each for the husband, wife, and son—only wife Xin Zhui's tomb was left undisturbed. Inside her tomb and her son's tomb (the chancellor's was looted) were thousands of funeral objects and hitherto lost classics copied on silk. Among them are the earliest known text of the Zhou *Book of Changes* and two important versions of the *Daode Jing (The Laozi)*. But the bulk of the manuscripts concern the quest for immortality through meditation, exercises, sexual practices, drugs, and alchemy. These rare records attesting to one family's search for the Dao are invaluable for what they reveal about the actual practice of religion in the early Han dynasty.

Perhaps the most astonishing object discovered in the tombs was the well-preserved corpse of Xin Zhui herself—who, after all, did achieve immortality of a kind. At the time of her death, she was 50 years old, stood 1.5m (5 ft.) tall, and weighed 75 pounds. She suffered from a variety of illnesses and ailments that included tuberculosis, hardening of the arteries, and lead poisoning; and her death was probably from a heart attack induced by an acute episode of gallstones. Reading her litany of ailments and looking at the intact corpse, it would appear that 50 years of life took a far greater toll on her body than did 2,100 years of death.

The new wing hosts the temporary exhibitions. Free English guides are now available if you book 3 days in advance; call ✆ **0731/8451-5566.**

Dongfeng Lu 50. ✆ **0731/8451-4630.** www.hnmuseum.com. Free admission. 9am–5pm. Show passport to get ticket at the box office on the left hand side of the main gate from 8:30am–4pm. Closed Mon. Bus: 113 or 303.

Yuelu Shuyuan (Yuelu Academy) This institution has over a thousand years of history and was one of the four major academies in ancient China, alongside Shigu Shuyuan in Hengyang, Bailudong Shuyuan in Jiangxi, and Yingtian Shuyuan in Henan. Shuyuan was a kind of independent educational institution, first appeared back in Tang Dynasty, where scholars mingled and discussed academic and cultural topics. Founded in the year of 976, during the Northern Song Dynasty, Yuelu Shuyuan turned into today's Hunan University in 1926. The building, comprised of several lecture halls, lush gardens and pavilions, are mostly renovated or rebuilt in the Qing Dynasty. The school was the cradle of many famous scholars throughout the centuries and Mao Zedong also stayed in a small room in the academy for a couple of years during his mid-20s when he founded the revolutionary group Xinmin Institute. Limited written English is on site, but its website has detailed descriptions.

Yuelu Shan. ✆ **0731/882-2316.** www.dm.hnu.cn. Admission ¥30. 7:30am–6pm (May 1–Oct 31); 8am to 5:30pm (Nov 1–Apr 30). Guided tours are available from 9–10am and 3–4pm. Bus: 113 or 303.

SHAO SHAN 韶山

In 1893, Mao Zedong was born in this village 98km (60 miles) south of Changsha. Beginning with the frenzied early years of the Cultural Revolution (1966–76) and continuing into the early 1990s, Shao Shan was a mecca of sorts to millions of Chinese who made the pilgrimage here for reasons that changed over the years—from revolutionary zeal to coercion to, finally, nostalgia. As 2011 marked the 90th anniversary of the Communist Party of China founded by Mao, crowds have increased significantly since then, especially on holidays and on Mao's birthday, December 26. The sights include the house Mao grew up in, a memorial exhibition, the Mao's personal items exhibition, the Mao Library, and the family ancestral home, but the latter two will be of little interest without knowledge of written Chinese. This is an easy day trip from Changsha.

Mao Zedong Tongzhi Guju (Comrade Mao Zedong's Former Residence) Best of the two main sights, Mao's former home doesn't look that different from some of the present farmhouses in Hunan and Sichuan. The spartan but attractive brick buildings with curved wooden shingles have signs in Chinese and English that identify each room and contain a variety of intriguing implements, such as a large wok in the kitchen, grain-milling bowls, and equipment for hulling rice. Photos of Mao's family grace the walls. The barn is part of the house, and the bedroom of Mao's brother, Zetan, is right next to the pig pen. Give yourself 45 minutes to see the house and stroll the bucolic grounds.

Free admission. Queue up outside the site. 8:30am–5pm. Buses between Changsha South Station (Nan Zhan) and Shao Shan leave both places every half-hour 8am–5pm for ¥26; the ride takes 1 hr. 20 min. The ride from Shao Shan Bus Station to Mao's old home is 6km (3¾ miles). By motorcycle the trip costs ¥5; by bus ¥2.50.

Mao Zedong Tongzhi Jinianguan (The Memorial Hall of Mao Zedong) This museum, opened in 1964, glorifies the whole life story of Mao, portraying how he grew into a communist follower and a leader of the nation from the day he was

MAO'S roots

Mao's father was a poor peasant compelled out of poverty to join the army. Years later he returned to Shao Shan with ambitions of bettering his lot. When Mao was born, his father owned 15 hectares (37 acres) of land and was a "middle peasant." By the time Mao was a teenager, his father had 22 hectares (55 acres) and the status of "rich peasant." Mao spent his childhood in Shao Shan working in his father's rice paddies and, from age 8, studying the Confucian *Analects* and *The Five Classics*—meaning the most modern of his textbooks (the *Analects*) was from the 3rd century B.C.

In his interviews with Edgar Snow, Mao described a strict upbringing by a father he perceived as oppressive. What isn't often mentioned is that his mother was a devout Buddhist who raised her children in the religion. It wasn't until Mao broadened his reading that he lost his religious faith. Though Mao's family never went hungry, it was in Shao Shan that he witnessed famine and the oppression of the poor. He claimed that such incidents and a natural rebelliousness inclined him toward revolution.

born. Books he read and articles and books he published in his early years are on display. But the descriptions are mostly in Chinese only and some displays lack maintenance (surprisingly).

Free admission. ✆ **0732/8568-5347.** 9am–5pm. Closed Mon. Show passport to get ticket from 9am–4pm. From Mao's former residence, follow the path past the souvenir stands; to the left is the gravesite of Mao's parents; turn right and walk through long, narrow, dark tunnel.

Mao Zedong Yiwu Guan (The Relic Hall of Mao Zedong) This museum is the latest establishment in Shao Shan to dignify "Mao Yeye" (Grandpapa Mao)—the way Chinese people call Mao today. Housing a collection of over 800 items used by Mao during his life, it is undoubtedly the highlight of visiting Shao Shan. It offers an interesting insight into the idiosyncrasies of the Great Helmsman, such as the bed that permanently slants to one side. About 300 pieces of vinyl and tapes of Chinese and foreign opera and music collected by Mao are displayed in the hall on the second floor.

Just right next to Mao Zedong Tongzhi Jinianguan. Free admission. ✆ **0732/8568-5347.** 9am–5pm. Closed Mon. Show passport to get ticket from 9am–4pm.

Where to Stay

EXPENSIVE

Crown Plaza Hotel City Centre Changsha (Changsha Huangguan Jiari Jiudian) Its convenient location situated near the Wuyi Guangchang used to be the advantage of Crown Plaza. However, since the city is building its underground transportation system, the hotel is deeply affected by the surrounding construction sites. Rooms are decent-size and soothing, equipped with LCD TV and dark-wood bed panel. The marble bathrooms are roomy and stylish with separate shower cubicle and bath tub. The Wuyi Lu and Huangxing Zhong Lu commercial area is in walking distance.

Wuyi Da Dao 868. www.crowneplaza-changsha.com. ✆ **0731/8288-8888.** Fax 0731/8282-8888. 431 units. ¥1,400–¥1,500 standard room. 40%–60% discount is standard. AE, DC, MC, V. **Amenities:** 3 restaurants; ATM; concierge; forex; health club; indoor children's playground; indoor pool; room service; sauna; tennis court. *In room:* A/C, satellite TV, fridge, hair dryer, Internet, minibar.

Huatian Dajiudian This hotel used to be Changsha's biggest and most luxurious. It's also one of the most expensive, but with the 40% to 50% discounts that are standard here, the rates become reasonable. Rooms in the VIP Tower are luxurious while those in the Huatian Tower are compact but cheaper. Conformity usually defines hotel design in China, but the bold-colored fresco behind the reception counter of this hotel sets a tone of originality that carries throughout. For example, on the way to the elevator, guests cross a glass bridge that spans a pond full of goldfish. The guest rooms, too, have original touches. Bathroom sinks look like elegant glass bowls. In plusher rooms, a walk-in closet connects with both the bathroom and the bedroom.

Jiefang Dong Lu 300. www.huatian-hotel.com. ✆ **0731/8444-2888.** Fax 0731/8444-2270. 700 units. ¥999 standard room in Huatian Tower; ¥1,288 standard room in VIP Tower. Rates do not include breakfast. 40%–50% discount is standard. AE, DC, MC, V. **Amenities:** 4 restaurants; food court; bar; ATM; forex; health club; KTV; indoor pool; room service; sauna; tennis court; airline, train, and bus ticketing. *In room:* A/C, satellite TV, fridge, hair dryer, Internet, minibar.

Sheraton Changsha Hotel (Changsha Yunda Xilaideng Jiudian) ★ This is the first five-star international and the swankiest hotel in Changsha. The stylish light wall in the lobby changes color with the time and weather of the day. Compared with Crown Plaza, Sheraton is more opulent. Rooms are capacious and comfortable with plush beds. The marble bathrooms are roomy but plain, with separate rainforest shower and tub. Service is satisfying and the dining facilities are some of the best in city.

Furong Zhong Lu 478, Section 1. www.sheraton.com/changsha. ✆ **0731/8488-8888.** Fax 0731/8488-8889. 384 units. ¥1,408–¥1,488 standard room; ¥2,060–¥2,288 suite. Rates include breakfast and 15% service charge. AE, DC, MC, V. **Amenities:** 4 restaurants; bar; tea house; room service; concierge; forex; fitness center; indoor pool; spa; airline, train, and bus ticketing; Wi-Fi. *In room:* A/C, LCD TV w/pay movies, fridge, hair dryer, Internet, minibar.

Wyndham Grand Plaza Royale Furongguo Changsha (Changsha Furongguo Haoting Jiudian) The opening of this hotel adds another luxury option in Changsha. Service is up to standard. The properly sized rooms have a round ceiling and are fitted with brown-colored classic European–style furniture. Marble bathrooms are large, with separate shower and a large tub.

Furong Middle Road 106, 2nd Section. www.plazaroyale-hotel.com/changsha-home.html. ✆ **0731/8868-8888.** Fax 0731/8868-8889. 316 units. ¥964–¥1,034 standard room. Rates include breakfast. 15% service charge. AE, DC, MC, V. **Amenities:** 2 restaurants; bar; teahouse; gym, indoor pool; room service; smoke-free floors; table tennis room; airline, train, and bus ticketing. *In room:* A/C, satellite TV, fridge, hair dryer, Internet, minibar.

MODERATE

Days Hotel & Suites Changsha City Centre (Changsha Xiaotiane Daisi Jiudian) Launched in late 2010, this hotel's rooms and bathrooms are small, but it has everything you need. To compensate for its small room size, the hotel offers customers flexible check-out time. Customers can check out at any time in 24 hours after they checked in. Rooms on the lower floors are in light wooden color, while rooms on the higher executive floors are in darker brown. Black and white lamps in the rooms create a nice contrast. Sunshine rooms have panoramic windows, making it a great spot to appreciate the city's firework show at 8pm every Saturday. The hotel is conveniently located across the Furong Plaza and one of the major stations of the city's future underground system.

Wuyi Dadao 648. www.csdaysinn.com. ✆ **0731/8989-9999.** Fax 0731/8441-0400. 238 units. ¥498 standard room; ¥520 sunshine rooms. Rates include breakfast. 35%–50% discount is standard. 15%

service charge. AE, DC, MC, V. **Amenities:** 2 restaurants; bar; forex; room service; spa; airline, train, and bus ticketing. *In room:* A/C, TV w/pay movies, fridge, hair dryer, Internet, minibar.

Dolten Hotel Changsha (Tongcheng Guoji Dajiudian) This hotel used to compete with the Huatian for the title of Changsha's plushest. The guest rooms are spacious, the bedspreads and furnishings are tasteful. Service is efficient and this staff is friendly and professional—nothing is missing here. But there's nothing extra, either. The Dolten is a standard five-star hotel, and for that it can be counted on.

Shao Shan Bei Lu 159. www.dolton-hotel.com. ✆ **0731/8416-8888.** Fax 0731/8416-9999. 450 units. ¥918–¥1,118 standard room; ¥1,380–¥1,680 suite. Rates include breakfast. 35%–50% discount is standard. 15% service charge. AE, DC, MC, V. Bus: 7 or 139 from railway. **Amenities:** 3 restaurants; bar; teahouse; bowling alley; cigar bar; forex; gym, indoor pool; room service; airline, train, and bus ticketing. *In room:* A/C, satellite TV, fridge, hair dryer, Internet, minibar.

Wandai Dajiudian (Wonder Hotel) This four-star hotel occupies floors 7 to 15 in an office building. Guest rooms frame the indoor garden plaza, but the best views are on the east side, overlooking Wuyi Square, and on the west side, facing the river. Each standard room is clean and comfortable, with a Japanese-inspired wooden screen between the bed and the living area that gives the illusion of two rooms.

Huangxing Zhong Lu 87 (at Wuyi Da Dao; reception on 7th floor). ✆ **0731/8488-2333.** Fax 0731/8488-2111. 310 units. ¥528–¥588 standard room. Rates include breakfast. 40% discount is standard. AE, DC, MC, V. Bus: 132 from railway to Wuyi Guangchang stop. **Amenities:** 2 restaurants; bar; exercise room; limited forex; KTV; room service; airline, train, and bus ticketing. *In room:* A/C, TV, hair dryer.

INEXPENSIVE

Jinjiang Inn Wuyi Square (Jinjiang Zhixing Wuyi Guangchang Dian) Close to the Wuyi commercial area, this hotel is a good budget option. Rooms are clean, decent size, and plainly furnished in a soothing off-white tone. Bathrooms have shower only.

Wuyi Dadao 775. www.jinjianginns.com. ✆ **0731/8822-1888.** 139 units. ¥169 single room; ¥189 standard room. Rates do not include breakfast. No credit cards. **Amenities:** Restaurant; smoke-free rooms; airline, bus and train ticketing. *In room:* A/C, TV, Internet.

Where to Eat

Feast Hunan Flavours ★ HUNAN This fine restaurant on the third floor of the Sheraton Changsha Hotel serves delicious and beautifully presented Hunan dishes. The executive chef, a Hunan native with over 2 decades of cooking experience overseas and in different mainland Chinese cities, has modified the unbearably spicy and strong-flavored Hunan fare into less oily and mild-spicy dishes approved by foreigners. One of the delicacies is steamed pork with pickled chili. The pork melts in the mouth and the spicy flavor is just right. Steamed river fish with preserved salted brown bean and stir fried rice with soy sauce in Hunan style are also recommended.

Furong Zhong Lu 478, Section 1 (Sheraton Changsha Hotel), 3rd floor. ✆ **0731/8488-8888.** Meal for 2 ¥150–¥200. English picture menu. AE, DC, MC, V. 11am–1am.

Teppanyaki Xiang (Wushiqi Du Xiang) ★ HUNAN Before digging in, the eye-catching and stylish white facade and chic interior decor of this Hunan restaurant is appealing enough to whet your appetite. Inspired by the Japanese cooking style teppanyaki, the restaurant has made the foreign cooking method its own to create innovative and toothsome Hunan dishes. Teppanyaki stations are set up on each floor of the two-story joint. Try *yuzhituadan* (steamed egg with roe), a signature dish that almost every customer orders for the way it's presented: The chef adds water to a heated iron plate, creating a big puff of steam to cook the egg. *Mitofu* (rice curd) and *daixia* (shrimp with garlic) have that authentic Hunan taste—spicy and strong. Watch the friendly chefs making the dishes, while savoring your freshly cooked meal.

Furong Zhong Lu 195, Section 2. ✆ **0731/8877-5757.** Meal for 2 ¥80–¥150. Picture menu. No credit cards. 11am–10pm.

Changsha After Dark

The Huangxing Zhong Lu and Jiefeng Xi Lu commercial area transforms into a **night market** after 10pm every night. Stalls sell downmarket clothes, accessories, bits and pieces on both sides of the streets. Make a visit and feel the vivid street ambience before spending your night in the **lively pubs** on Jiefeng Xi Lu or Taiping Jie.

NAN YUE HENG SHAN 南岳衡山

Hunan Province, 137km (85 miles) S of Changsha

"Those who mix medicines, who are avoiding political turmoil, or who seek quietude in order to practice the Way, have always gone into the mountains."

—from The Master Who Embraces Simplicity, Ge Hong (283–343)

Located on the southwestern bank of the Xiang River in the middle of Hunan Province, Nan Yue Heng Shan—known locally as Nan Yue (Southern Mountain) or Heng Shan—is one of the five sacred peaks (symbolizing the four directions and the center) of Daoism. It was believed that these peaks were supernatural channels connecting heaven and earth. For Daoists, mountains were the sites where *qi* (cosmic energy) was at its most refined; herbs and minerals—the ingredients of health and longevity elixirs—were found on mountains; and it was on mountains and in mountain caverns that seekers were most likely to find transcendent beings.

As far back as the 6th century, Nan Yue was also a place of Buddhist worship; and it is the birthplace of the Nan Yue school of Southern Chan (Zen) Buddhism, which got its start here in the 8th century.

Late summer and fall are the best times to visit. Locals warn visitors to resist the temptation of shortcuts on overgrown and little-used paths, where you're likely to encounter snakes.

Essentials

GETTING THERE Direct **buses** (Iveco or Turbo) depart from Changsha's South Bus Station every half-hour from 6:30am to 6pm for the 2¼-hour drive; the fare is ¥38 to ¥45. Buses leave the station when they're full. Return buses leave every 20 minutes from the same drop-off point in the town of Nan Yue. If you take an early bus, it is possible to make this a day trip. You'll have time to enjoy the mountain and its temples if you combine hiking with cable car, bus, or motorcycle taxi. **High-speed trains *(gaotei)*** connect Changsha and Heng Shan Xi Railway Station (West Heng Shan Station). The 30-minute ride costs ¥66. From there, buses for Paifang (the memorial archway) charge ¥5. **Trains** also run between Changsha and Heng Shan Railway Station, but the trip takes 1 hr. 40 min., plus another 30 to 40 minutes from the railway station to the town of Nan Yue.

GETTING AROUND The bus from Changsha drops passengers off at the west end of town. To get to the mountain, walk east on the same road (Hengshan Lu) to the memorial archway on Zhurong Lu. Inside the archway, **minibuses** take passengers to the entrance for free. If the bus is slow to fill up, you can pay a bit more to be taxied there alone. Price is negotiable, but ¥5 is about right. The distance is 1.5km (just under a mile). The **mountain park entrance** is at the north end of the village. Admission is ¥101, covering entrance to all the sites and temples on the mountain and tour buses to major sites between the park entrance and below **Nantian Men.** The mile-long cable cars that operate from Banshan Ting (the midway point) to Nantian Men charge ¥70. The footpath from **Nantian Men** to the top is 3.1km (2 miles) long and takes about 1½ hours to walk at a comfortable but steady clip.

Exploring Nan Yue

The best preserved and most famous of the mountain temples is **Nan Yue Da Miao** at the southern foot of the town, outside the mountain park. Originally built in the Tang dynasty (618–907), it was destroyed by fire a number of times. The present temple dates to the Qing dynasty (1644–1911). The main hall is noteworthy for its double roof supported by 72 columns representing the inevitable 72 peaks of Nan Yue. Admission to the temple is ¥40.

Halfway up the mountain, past the cable car entrance, is the Daoist monastery **Xuandu Guan.** Here, worshipers light firecrackers, kowtow in front of the white marble statues of three Daoist Celestial Masters, or cast their fortunes by throwing two halves of a wooden oval on the ground. Eleven Daoist priests live in this monastery. Lodging is available for up to 3 days here. There is also a vegetarian restaurant.

Daoist and Buddhist monasteries and temples are scattered over the mountain. Most are small and worth a peek, but they don't need lots of time. **Zhurong Hall** is at Nan Yue's highest peak, **Zhurong Feng** (1,290m/4,232 ft.), where the views are magnificent.

Where to Stay & Eat

To better preserve the natural environment of the mountain, the authority has ordered that buildings and inns that don't blend in with the landscape be torn down. Approximately 80% of buildings were torn down. But lodging can still be found at the summit near Zhurong Dian and midway up the mountain just above the bus parking lot, in the vicinity of the cable car. The best accommodations on the mountain are at the **Caifu Mountain Villa** (**Caifu Shanzhuang; © 0734/566-2628**), at Bai Shan Ting, built in 2000 and renovated in 2008. To date, its primary claim to fame is that Jiang Zemin stayed here while visiting the mountain in 2003. The unimaginatively furnished standard rooms go for ¥380, but it does offer the most comfortable stay on the mountain by far.

Near Zhurong Feng, **Zhurong Feng Shanzhuang** (**© 0734/566-3178**) provides standard rooms with communal bathroom for ¥220. Rooms are without character and basically clean. You can try to bargain with the hotel to get a better price.

In the summertime, you can stay in the guesthouse of **Shangfeng Si (Shangfeng Monastery)** near the peak for ¥40 a bed, including breakfast and dinner.

On the mountain are some small restaurants in different spots. Since there are no English menus, you may have to go to the kitchen and point to your order. Settle on a price in advance or you may end up getting the most expensive dish on the menu—or the largest serving. On average, each dish should cost about ¥25 to ¥40. In town, Deng Shan Lu, running from the memorial archway through the center of town, has lots of restaurants serving local food.

WULINGYUAN 武陵源 & ZHANGJIAJIE 张家界 ★★

Hunan Province, 269km (167 miles) NW of Changsha, 480km (298 miles) SW of Wuhan

Wulingyuan's landscape might well have inspired the shamanistic poems of the classic collection *Songs of Chu*. Unlike most famous sights in China, the area remained remote and little visited until relatively late. To the ancients, that part of northwestern Hunan (at the southern periphery of the Chu Kingdom) was an inhospitable wilderness—mountainous terrain populated by wild animals. And unlike the sacred Buddhist and Daoist mountains, it did not draw pilgrims.

But that's all changed. Wulingyuan Scenic and Historic Interest Area (also called Zhangjiajie) became China's first National Forest Park in 1983, and in 1992, its core zone was inscribed as a World Heritage Site. Prior to that, whatever damage humans inadvertently spared this wild region over the centuries, they undid in a few decades of poaching, land clearing, tree felling, and polluting. Despite that, the natural beauty of the region—dominated by quartzite sandstone peaks and pillars—remains stunning and unusual; and opportunities to see rare plants and insects in this dense, subtropical forest still abound. What's more, restrictions on construction and pollution, as well as a total fire ban, are just a few of the measures now in place to protect this singular environment.

Essentials

GETTING THERE Changsha is the gateway city to Zhangjiajie. **Bus** has become the most convenient way to travel between the two spots with the completion of the expressway. Buses depart at the **Changsha Xi Qiche Zhan (Changsha West Bus Station)** for Zhangjiajie every hour. The 4-hour ride costs ¥114.

Hehua Airport is 5km (3 miles) from Zhangjiajie City (formerly called Dayong) and 37km (23 miles) from Zhangjiajie National Forest Park. It has flights connecting with many major cities in China, including Beijing, Shanghai, Guangzhou, Changsha, and Wuhan. It also has air service from Hong Kong. If you arrive by plane, there's no reason to bother with charmless Zhangjiajie City (Zhangjiajie Shi). Go directly to **Wulingyuan,** which is just outside the national park entrance. By taxi, it's ¥70.

The **Zhangjiajie Railway Station** is 8km (5 miles) southeast of town. A fast train T8308/T8309 departs from Changsha for Zhangjiajie at 8:30am every morning. The train ride takes 4½ hr. and costs ¥55 (hard seat). An overnight train K9031/K9034 leaves Changsha at 10:20pm and arrives in Zhangjiajie the next morning at 9:25am. Hard and soft sleepers cost ¥183 and ¥276 respectively. The railway station is 29km (18 miles) south of Zhangjiajie Village, which is at the main park entrance, and 34km (21 miles) south of Wulingyuan, and both are the best places to find lodging. As you exit the station, taxi drivers, porters, and kids selling maps will pounce, but just keep walking. A bus from the railway station to Zhangjiajie Village departs from the square when it's full (an hour-plus wait sometimes). An alternative is taking bus no. 6 for ¥1 at the middle of the railway square to Baihuo Dalou, walk west to Renmin Lu, then turn left and walk straight 5 minutes to the bus station in town. From there, catch one of the many buses for the 1-hour trip to Wulingyuan; the fare is ¥11. To National Forest Park, the buses charge ¥9; to Tianzi Shan, ¥16. Or you can take a taxi directly to Zhangjiajie Village or Wulingyuan for about ¥60 or ¥70. As you exit, go to the **taxi stand** at the left end of the railway square. Taxi rates are ¥4 for 3km (1¼ miles), then ¥1 per kilometer. After 10km (6 miles), add 50% per kilometer.

GETTING AROUND Vehicular and hiking paths provide access to some 240 designated scenic spots within Wulingyuan. The scenic area comprises the three adjoining parklands of **Zhangjiajie National Forest Park** to the south, **Tianzi Shan Natural Reserve** to the north, and **Suoxiyu Natural Reserve** to the east. **Huangshi Zhai Cable cars** for ¥50 one-way and ¥96 round-trip lead to viewing platforms from Huangshi Zhai in the Zhangjiajie forest area. **Bailong Tianti (Bailong Tourist Lift),** which runs 356m (1,068 ft.) vertically, connects Suoxiyu and Yuanjiajie, and costs ¥56. Tianzi Shan Cable cars cost ¥52, which takes you from Tianzi Shan if you don't want to walk downhill.

Once you're inside the park, free buses will take you between designated stops, allowing you the freedom to alternate between walking and taking a ride.

In terms of lodging and proximity to the most sights, **Zhangjiajie Village** and **Wulingyuan** make the best base. Zhangjiaji village has one main street, Jinbian Da Dao, with hotels and leads to the park entrance. As you approach the park, you'll see a small street to the left; it leads to the Xiangdian Mountain Villa and a few restaurants and Internet cafes. In Wulingyuan, hotels, restaurants, supermarkets, and stores selling souvenirs are everywhere.

TOURS For most of the sightseeing within the park, there's no need for a guide. But you must join a tour to go river rafting. This can be organized by **Zhangjiajie National Forest Park Travel Service,** conveniently located and much more customer-oriented than the CITS branches in either Zhangjiajie City or Village. Their office is in Zhangjiajie City and they are willing to either meet you at the train, or come out to the park (✆ **0744/822-7088;** fax 0744/822-8488).

Freelance guides near the park entrance charge considerably less than the travel agencies, but you need to bargain. Generally the asking price for an English-speaking guide starts at ¥100 a day. Be sure the person has a guide's license; otherwise, you'll have to pay their entry fee.

HIKING Exploring the mountain means following stone paths through spectacular forests of bamboo, oak, and pine to scenic spots that afford breathtaking views. Since every tour group takes these paths, you won't be alone, but the crowds can be part of the fun. For solitude, take the less-traveled paths, where the setting and scenery can be as dramatic as the popular sights. Admission is ¥248, good for 2 days.

[Fast FACTS] ZHANGJIAJIE

Internet Access Zhangjiajie Village has several Internet cafes on the side street near the park. Turn left off the main street just before the park. The cafes usually charge ¥2 per hour. Dial-up is ✆ **163.**

Top Spots in the Three Parklands

ZHANGJIAJIE NATIONAL FOREST PARK To reach **Huangshi Zhai,** at the first fork after the entrance to the park, take the left road; hike 2 hours to this former mountain stronghold that is 1,080m (4,542 ft.) high and affords a panoramic view of forested peaks and jagged sandstone pillars. A cable car also goes to the plateau (see "Getting Around," above).

Yuanjiajie, located on the north of the park, is another scenic spot that shouldn't be missed. Head to the right path of the park, where the **Jinbian Si (Golden Whip Stream)** starts. Follow the path; after passing Zicao Tan (Zicao Pool), a small road goes up to Yuanjiajie. The hike, all staircases, takes another 2½ hours, and leads you to **Houhuayuan (Back Garden)** and **Mihuntai (Enchanting Terrace)** of Yuanjiajie. Or you can walk farther to **Shui Rao Si Men (Stream Winding Around Four Gates)** of Suoxiyu. From there, take a bus to the **Bailong Tianti.** During the 2-minute journey, you can enjoy the magnificent panoramic view of hundreds of sandstone pillars. After that, take a bus from Bailong Tianti to Mihuntai. The huge quartz sandstone mountain has breathtaking landscapes of sandstone pillars. Keep walking west along the path to the **Tianxia Diyi Jiao (Greatest Natural Bridge)**, a 50m-long (164-ft.) natural arch.

IN TIANZI SHAN NATURAL RESERVE Located just southeast of the cable car platform at Tianzi Shan, **Yubi Feng (Imperial Writing Brush Peaks), Tianzi Ge (Tianzi Pavilion),** the circuit path in **Helong Gongyuan (Helong Park)** and **Dianjiantai (Arranging Battles Platform)** are the most famous spots for their imposing views of forested peaks and jutting sandstone pillars. To go downhill, either take a bus outside Helong Gongyuan to Tianzi Shan Cable Car Upper Station, or take the path behind Tianzi Ge. The walk takes about 2½ hours to **Shili Gallery.**

IN SUOXIYU NATURAL RESERVE A boat ride on the lovely, clear **Baofeng Hu (Baofeng Lake)** surrounded by lush forest is included in the admission fee of ¥74.

The colored lights that illuminate famous Chinese caves are an acquired taste, but they shouldn't get in the way of appreciating the 11km-long (7-mile) **Huanglong Dong (Huanglong Cave)** that contains spectacular calcite deposits as well as a waterfall 50m (164 ft.) high. Entrance is ¥80. Taxi to the site costs ¥30.

TIANMEN SHAN 天门山

Other than the Wulingyuan scenic zone, Tianmen Shan (Tianmen Mountain), 8km (5 miles) from Zhangjiajie downtown, has huge quartzite sandstone peaks and a giant natural sandstone arch, offering astonishing scenery different from in Wulingyuan. It's worth visiting if you are going to spend one more day in Zhangjiajie.

Regarded as the number one miraculous mountain in Western Hunan for its unique landscape comprised of **Tianmen Dong (Tianmen Cave),** which literally means "Gate to Heaven" in Chinese, and **Gaoshan Huayuan (Garden in the Air),** a small plateau covered by a lush forest.

Named as Songliang Mountain before the Three Kingdoms period, the steep cliff face of the mountain collapsed and formed a 130m-high (426-ft.) and 30m-wide (98-ft.) "cave," or a natural bridge, in the year of 263. Since then, the mountain has been named as Tianmen.

The 7,455m (24,458-ft.) cableway, **Tianmen Shan Suodao (Tianmen Mountain Cable Car),** operates from 8am to 5:40pm, takes you straight to the upper station and the **Gaoshan Huayuan** at the attitude of 1,500m (4,921 ft.). Along the 40-minute ride, the bonsai-like landscapes formed by numerous hillocks and mountains are incredibly fascinating and thrilling. At Gaoshan Huayuan, take the west route and the stunning mountainous landscape along the **Ghost-valley Plank Road (Guigu Zhandao),** which is built on the over 1,400m-high (4,593-ft.) steep cliff, is breathtaking. If you can successfully avoid the tour groups, you can enjoy the serenity and a wonderful stroll as if you are walking in the sky. A **sightseeing cable car,** which starts at Yingtao Wan (Cherry Bay), goes to **Yunmeng Xian Ding (Yunmeng Fairy Summit)** at the highest peak (1,519m/4,983 ft.). On a clear day, a panorama of the 16 peaks of Tianmen Shan, Wulingyuan and Zhangjiajie City come into view at the summit. The trip costs ¥23 one-way, and ¥39 round-trip. Or you can climb up stone stairs to reach the peak in 45 minutes to an hour.

Tour buses wait at the midway station and take you to Tianmen Dong via Tongtian Da Dao (Heaven-Linking Ave.), a driveway with 99 turns. A fascinating graphical picture formed by the serpentine turns can be seen when you are about to reach the terminus. From there, you climb up 100 stairs to go to the bottom of Tianmen Dong.

Take circular bus line no. 10, charging ¥1, to Tianmen Shan Suodao Zhan (Tianmen Mountain Cable Car Station). By taxi, it costs about ¥6 to ¥8 from Zhangjiajie downtown and ¥5 from Zhangjiajie train station. Admission to the mountain is ¥258 and includes the round-trip cable car ride and tour bus between the midway station to Tianmen Cave; the sightseeing cable car to Yunmeng Xian Ding (Yunmeng Fairy Summit) is not included.

Where to Stay

Hotels in Wulingyuan and Zhangjiajie Village are more attractive and close to the park. Staying at the guesthouses with simple lodging provided by locals inside the park is another good option. **Yuanjiajie Qingnian Lvshe (Yuanjiajie Youth Hostel; ✆ 0744/820-0448)**, at Wangqiaotai in Yuanjiajie, has clean rooms with basic bathroom facilities. Standard rooms cost ¥150. Its kitchen makes tasty fried rice. **Bailong Xianju Kezhan** (www.bailongxianju.com; ✆ **0139/744-0129**), located 200m (650 ft.) west of the Bailong Tianti Upper Station, offers air-conditioned rooms with hot shower. Standard room are ¥128.

Hotel Pullman Zhangjiajie (Zhangjiajie Jingwu Boerman Jiudian) ★ Since its inception in 2007, this five-star resort has been the most comfortable hotel in Wulingyuan. It is conveniently located and close to most of the scenic spot entrances. The staff provides standard service but does not speak much English. As different rooms provide different views and have different settings (some big beds are made up of two double beds instead of one king-size bed), be specific of your preference and ask for more details when you make your booking.

Huajuan Lu, 2km (1¼ miles) from the Wulingyuan scenic spot entrance. www.pullmanhotels.com. ✆ **0744/888-8888.** Fax 0744/566-9888. 482 units. ¥900–¥1,300 standard room. Rates include breakfast. 15% service charge. AE, DC, MC, V. **Amenities:** 3 restaurants; bar; teahouse; limited forex; gym; indoor and outdoor pools; spa. *In room:* A/C, TV, fridge, hair dryer, Internet, minibar.

Pipa Xi Binguan This hotel and the Xiangdian Mountain Villa are the best in Zhangjiajie Village. The majority of guests are with tour groups, and on holidays it's full. Rooms are clean but unadorned, and most have picture windows overlooking gardens and/or mountains. Some standard rooms have balconies. From the hotel, it's a 10-minute walk along the main street (Jinbian Da Dao) to the park entrance. Whether you call first or just turn up, do negotiate for a substantial discount.

Jinbian Da Dao, Zhangjiajie Village. www.pipaxi-hotel.com. ✆ **0744/571-8888.** Fax 0744/571-2257. 180 units. ¥580–¥680 standard room. Rates include breakfast. 20% discounts. AE, DC, MC, V. **Amenities:** Restaurant; limited forex; room service. *In room:* A/C, TV, fridge, hair dryer, Internet, minibar.

Xiangdian Gouji Jiudian (Xiangdian International Hotel) ★ Visiting dignitaries usually stay at the Pipa Xi Hotel (above), but that should change now that this hotel has upgraded to four stars. After a renovation in 2008, rooms are even more pleasant with better furnishings and tasteful decorations. Bathrooms combine tub and shower in a small, spotless space. The beautifully landscaped grounds include lawns, a pond, and a pagoda; classical Chinese music plays faintly in the background—all to a wonderful effect. Many of the rooms have close-up views of the mountains.

As you approach the Zhangjiajie National Forest Park on Jinbian Dajie, turn left on the small lane just before you reach the park. The hotel is about 300m (984 ft.) ahead. www.xiangdianhotel.com.cn. ✆ **0744/571-2999.** Fax 0744/571-2266. 156 units. ¥980 standard room. ¥3,880 suite. Rates include breakfast. 20%–30% discounts. AE, DC, MC, V. **Amenities:** 3 restaurants; bowling alley; limited forex; health center; KTV; sauna. *In room:* A/C, TV, fridge, hair dryer, Internet, minibar.

Where to Eat

Zhangjiajie City and Village, Tianzi Shan, and Suoxiyu all have inexpensive restaurants featuring spicy Hunan dishes, but the food is not outstanding, nor are English-language menus available. One of the popular dishes in Zhangjiajie is *sanxiaguo.* It is a special local cuisine similar to hot pot but without broth. All the ingredients, including meat or organs, and vegetables, are cooked together with chili and garlic in a small wok. Try *hetao ruo* (a kind of pork) and *ganbian changzi* (sausage). **Hushifu Sanxiangao** and **Junge Changzi Guan** are two of the best sanxiangao restaurants. Take buses no. 5, 7 or 10 to Fengwan Lukou and Libin Xiaoxue, respectively. A meal for two costs between ¥40 to ¥60; both open from 11am to 9pm. They're always packed during lunch and dinner.

Small restaurants serving Tujia dishes can be found all along the main street of Zhangjiajie Village. Tujia cuisine specializes in fresh game (such as rabbit and various guinea pig– and weasel-like animals), reptiles (including poisonous snakes), crayfish, eel, and crab, so if you're feeling adventurous, point to the creature that interests you, and they'll cook it for you. Settle on a price, first, though; these dishes can be expensive. The hotels have restaurants that are more accessible to foreign travelers, but the food is mediocre.

FENGHUANG GUCHENG 凤凰古城

Hunan Province, 700km (435 miles) W of Changsha, 211km (131 miles) SW of Zhangjiajie

With over 300 years of history, Fenghuang Gucheng (Fenghuang Ancient Town), also known as Phoenix Ancient Town, is one of the best-preserved historical villages in China and was listed as a World Heritage site in 2008. Settled in the far west of the Hunan Province, the ancient town was built at the foot of mountains and along the Tuojiang River, following the natural flow of water like the Yunnan ancient town Lijiang. The Diaojiao Lou (traditional Chinese gabled wooden houses built on stilts), the river and the mountains form the incredibly charming and picturesque landscape.

Fenghuang got its present name in the Qing Dynasty. Tujia and Miao minorities inhabited the ancient town for hundreds of years and most of them still live in the way their ancestors used to centuries ago.

The ancient town was also the home of the respected modern Chinese author Shen Congwen (1902–88). His former residence, a courtyard house on Zhongyin Jie, is now a **museum** housing the author's authentic writings, photos, and possessions. Admission is ¥20. For tourist information, call ✆ **0743/322-3315.**

Essentials

GETTING THERE **Tongren Airport** is 31km (19 miles) from Fenghuang Ancient Town. It has flights connecting with Guyang, Chongqing, Shenzhen, and Guangzhou.

Two direct **buses** depart from Zhangjiajie Ke (Zhangjiajie Long Distance Bus Station) to Fenghuang at 8:30am, 2:30, and 4:30pm. The ride takes 4 hours and costs ¥65. Buses from Changsha to Fenghuang (6 hr.; ¥120) depart at 9am, 10:40am, 3:20, and 5:20pm. Buses won't take you directly to the ancient town, you have to take a taxi to Hongqiao when you get off, it costs ¥4 to ¥5.

From Zhangjiajie, the less convenient way is to take the **train** to Jishou (2 hr.; ¥11 hard seat), then change to a busto Fenghuang (1 hr. 30 min.; ¥17).

Exploring Fenghuang Gucheng

Hongqiao (Rainbow Bridge), built in the Ming Dynasty over 600 years ago, is the ancient town's most well-known tourist spot. Strolling along the riverside and the narrow streets paved by flagstones early in the morning (before 7am) is one of the best ways to admire the real beauty of the ancient town. You see locals start their day by doing laundry, working out along the river, and old Miao women dressed in traditional blue outfits carrying goods in bamboo baskets on their backs to the market. It is fun and thrilling to cross the river through the stepping stones, **Tiaoyan (Leaping Stones),** and the narrow primitive bridge near the Beimen Matou (North Gate Pier). **Gucheng Qiangcheng (the Ancient Town Wall),** is located south of the river, between the North and East Gate. To see the **Diaojiao Lou** on both sides of the river and Hongqiao up close, small rowboats take tourists from Beimen Matou downstream. It costs ¥20 per person. At night, the ancient town is vibrant, sometimes too noisy, with pubs concentrating on Laoyingshao Jie, between the Hongqiao and Tiaoyan section.

However, since being listed as a World Heritage site, the ancient city has transformed into something more like a theme park and the mother river has been getting more polluted. It could be overwhelmingly and unpleasantly crowded from Friday evening to Sunday noon. To truly experience its beauty, avoid going there during these days as well as Chinese public holidays.

Where to Stay

Plenty of guesthouses and inns operated by locals provide basic lodging in the ancient town. Most of them have two beds and a spartan bathroom and cost about ¥80 a room. Rooms with better facilities and at better locations along the riverside can cost up to ¥300. Bargain with the guesthouses to get a better price. **Phoenix Jiangtian Holiday Village** (**Fenghuang Jiangtian Luyou Dujiacun;** www.fhjt-hotel.com; ✆ **0743-326-1998;** fax 0743/326-1288.), on Hongqiao Lu, is the only full-fledged four-star hotel in the ancient town. Rooms are clean and without much character and don't have river views. Standard rooms are ¥258. Turn left at the north end of Hongqiao and walk for about 50m (164 ft.) to the hotel. **Yifeng Renjia Binguan,** at

Xiangxi Zhi Chuang Hebian E-2-111, Hongqiao Lu (✆ **0743/642-9300** or 326-1266; fax 0743/326-1666), has standard rooms that enjoy a charming view of Tuojiang and cost ¥380. They are not large but have traditional Chinese–style wooden windows overlooking the river. It can be quite noisy as the hotel is at one of the busiest spots in the ancient town.

Where to Eat

Restaurants are everywhere inside the ancient town, offering Chinese food, noodles, and Western food. A number of small cafes are on Laoyingshao Jie. Western fare is comparatively pricey at about ¥80 to ¥120 for a meal for two. You can get a bowl of Chinese noodles for ¥5 to ¥7. Handmade ***jiangtang*** (ginger candy) is a famous snack of the ancient town. When the weather is good, candy makers twist and pull the soft ginger candy hanging on a giant hook outside the shops. A small pack of crispy ginger candy, with heavy or light ginger flavors, is ¥2 to ¥3. **Zhang Shi Jiangtang Laozihao** at Zhongyin Jie 12, near Sheng Congwen Residence, is one of the four most renowned ginger candy shops in the town.

Plenty of pubs are lined along the river. Most of them get swarming after 9pm and stay open until late.

THE TIBETAN WORLD

by Simon Foster

Less than half of the world's Tibetans reside in the Tibetan Autonomous Region (TAR), established in 1965. Tibetans form the majority in large regions of neighboring Nepal, India, Sikkim, and Bhutan, as well as in the adjacent provinces of **Qinghai, Gansu, Sichuan,** and **Yunnan.** Disagreement over where Tibet begins and ends is an ongoing stumbling block in negotiations between the Tibetan government-in-exile, based in Dharamsala (India), and the Chinese government.

14

For this guide, **Qinghai** has been included, as it is part of the Tibetan plateau, and most of its area—which covers much of **Amdo** (northern Tibet) and **Kham** (eastern Tibet)—is culturally and ethnically Tibetan. In many ways a better destination than the TAR, it has yet to be overwhelmed by Han migration, and restrictions on both locals and travelers are less onerous.

Tibet may be the "roof of the world," but it became that only recently, when the Indian subcontinent collided with the Eurasian landmass 35 million years ago. Prior to that, the Himalayas formed the seabed of the Tethys Sea. Mollusks are still found throughout the region.

Tibet is dominated by the vast, dry Tibetan plateau, a region roughly the size of western Europe, with an average elevation of 4,700m (15,400 ft.). Ringed by vast mountain ranges, such as the **Kunlun range** to the north and the **Himalayas** to the south, the plateau's west side features high plains, and the north is dominated by the deserts of the **Changtang** and the **Tsaidam Basin.** China's great rivers—the Yellow River and the Yangzi—rise in the east, carving out steep gorges. The greatest diversity in landscape, vegetation, and wildlife is found in the broad and fertile valleys of the Himalayas, but most of the border regions are closed to individual travel.

Most Tibetans still look back to the "heroic age" (7th–9th c.) of their history, when their armies dominated the Silk Routes and much of western China, assimilating the culture and technology of these regions. At the same time, Buddhism was introduced to Tibet from northern India. With the disappearance of Buddhism from India around the 13th century, Tibet became the new bearer of a complex faith, which combined a strict monastic code with tantric Buddhism (with a strong emphasis on ritual). It is often characterized as "complete Buddhism."

Tibet

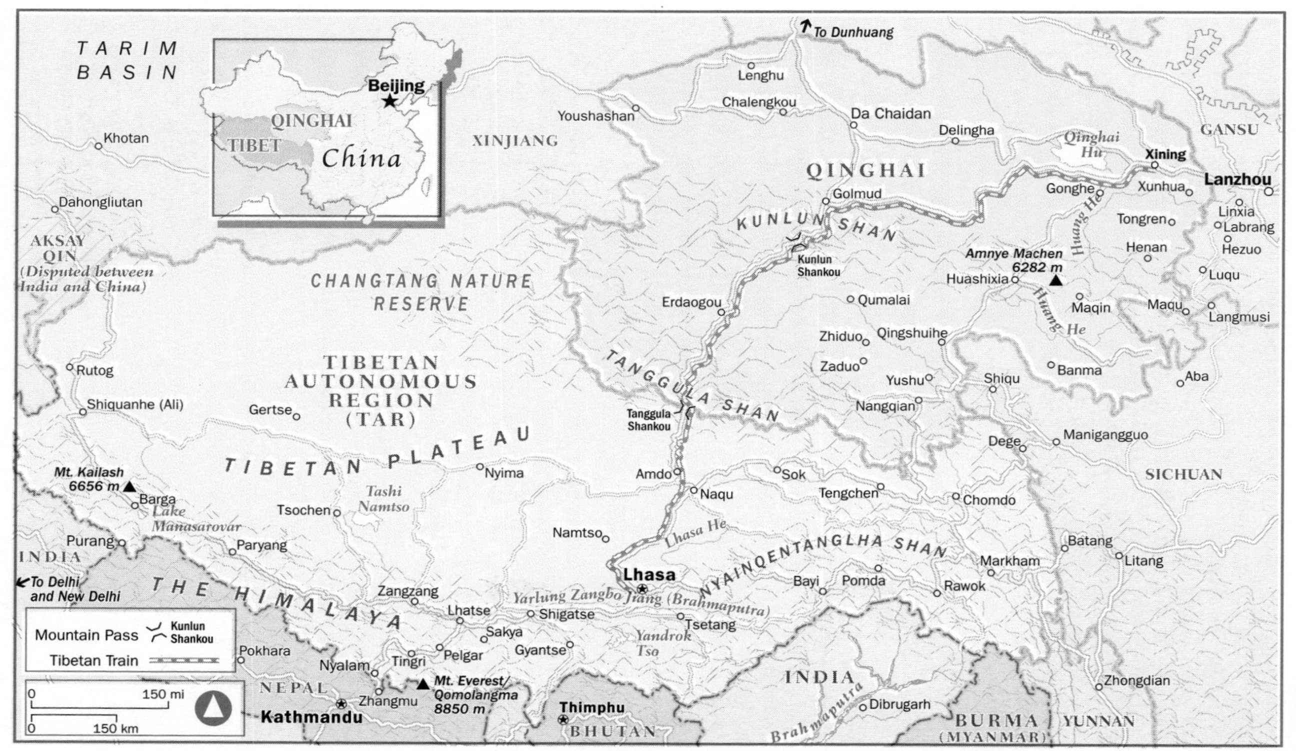

TARIM BASIN
Beijing
QINGHAI
TIBET
China
XINJIANG
GANSU
QINGHAI
SICHUAN
YUNNAN
AKSAY QIN (Disputed between India and China)
CHANGTANG NATURE RESERVE
TIBETAN AUTONOMOUS REGION (TAR)
TIBETAN PLATEAU
KUNLUN SHAN
TANGGULA SHAN
NYAINQENTANGLHA SHAN
THE HIMALAYA
INDIA
NEPAL
BHUTAN
BURMA (MYANMAR)
To Dunhuang
To Delhi and New Delhi
Khotan
Dahongliutan
Rutog
Shiquanhe (Ali)
Mt. Kailash 6656 m
Barga
Lake Manasarovar
Purang
Paryang
Pokhara
Kathmandu
Zhangmu
Nyalam
Tingri
Mt. Everest/ Qomolangma 8850 m
Pelgar
Sakya
Lhatse
Zangzang
Gyantse
Shigatse
Yarlung Zangbo Jiang (Brahmaputra)
Yandrok Tso
Tsetang
Lhasa
Lhasa He
Thimphu
Tsochen
Tashi Namtso
Gertse
Nyima
Namtso
Amdo
Naqu
Tanggula Shankou
Erdaogou
Kunlun Shankou
Youshashan
Lenghu
Chalengkou
Da Chaidan
Delingha
Golmud
Qinghai Hu
Xining
Lanzhou
Gonghe
Xunhua
Huang He
Linxia
Labrang
Tongren
Henan
Hezuo
Luqu
Amnye Machen 6282 m
Huashixia
Maqin
Maqu
Langmusi
Qumalai
Zhiduo
Qingshuihe
Zaduo
Yushu
Nangqian
Shiqu
Banma
Aba
Dege
Manigangguo
Sok
Tengchen
Chomdo
Bayi
Pomda
Rawok
Markham
Batang
Litang
Zhongdian
Dibrugarh
Brahmaputra
Mountain Pass
Kunlun Shankou
Tibetan Train
0 150 mi
0 150 km

The Tibetans went on to convert an entire people—the Mongols—despite being weakened by civil war and fighting between different schools of Tibetan Buddhism.

Just as China was often characterized as "closed" until it was "opened" by the West, the idea of Tibet as an inherently inward-looking Shangri-la is a long-standing myth. Isolationism was encouraged by the Manchu rulers from the 18th century onward, with some success. Regents backed by the Manchus held sway over young Dalai Lamas who often died mysteriously before they were old enough to rule.

Dalai Lama XIII (1876–1934) tried to reverse the policy of isolation, but encountered resistance from the conservative monastic hierarchy. Troubled by the destruction of Mongolia by Russian Communists during the 1920s, he prophesied, "The officers of the state, ecclesiastical and secular, will find their lands seized and their other property confiscated, and they themselves forced to serve their enemies, or wander about the country as beggars do. All beings will be sunk in great hardship and in overpowering fear."

In 1951, Chinese Communist armies entered Lhasa, and the prophecy began to unfold. A revolt against Chinese rule rose in Kham (eastern Tibet) 5 years later, and Dalai Lama XIV (b. 1935) fled for India in March 1959, soon after the **Great Prayer (Monlam)** was celebrated in Lhasa. Tibet's darkest hour was the Cultural Revolution (1966–76), known to the Tibetans as the time when "the sky fell to earth." Monks and nuns were tortured, executed, and imprisoned. Monasteries were looted and razed, and a vast body of Tibetan art was lost. Adding to the pain is the fact that many Tibetans, either willingly or coerced, participated in the destruction.

A revival of Tibetan culture and religion throughout the 1980s was checked after pro-independence protests, led by monks from **Drepung Monastery,** resulted in the declaration of martial law in March 1989, signed by chief of the local Communist Party Hu Jintao, now president of China. Tensions remained throughout the 1990s. More recently the situation appeared to be relaxing and dialogue between the Dalai Lama and the Chinese government seemed more promising for a time, but tensions were heightened immeasurably by the protests, and then riots, which broke out all over the Tibetan world in the run up to the 2008 Olympics. While the PRC insists that the riots were

Dealing with Altitude Sickness

It's likely that you'll suffer from a headache and shortness of breath upon your arrival in Tibet—they are both common signs of altitude sickness. Other visitors have complained of sleeplessness, fatigue, and even vomiting. So take it easy and let yourself get acclimatized to the altitude during your first days in Tibet, certainly before you venture to any higher altitudes. Altitude sickness pills called Diamox (acetazolamide) can also help; they can be taken a few hours before your arrival in Tibet. In Lhasa, you can pick up a Chinese medicine alternative called Hongjingtian at the local pharmacies. Oxygen canisters are available for around ¥20 in Lhasa outdoors shops, or (more expensively) in many hotels. Many hotels also have a doctor on call.

Most visitors to Tibet get through the trip with just a few minor symptoms, and cases of altitude sickness typically go away after a couple of days. There are a few danger signs, however, such as a deep liquidlike cough accompanied by a fever, that you should watch out for that may indicate your case is more serious. For more information, go to **www.highaltitudemedicine.ie**.

> **Signage in Tibet**
>
> In Tibet you'll see a mix of signs in Chinese, Tibetan, and English. Where there are no Chinese characters for a name, then the name and sign is generally written in English and Tibetan.

orchestrated by the Dalai Lama, he counters that these peaceful protests were the actions of a discontented people. Armed Chinese soldiers patrolling the streets are now an unfortunate part of everyday life in Lhasa.

The completion of the rail line to Tibet in 2006 has made Lhasa more accessible than ever, but increased restrictions make visiting the TAR troublesome for individual foreign travelers. Following the 2008 Tibet protests, restrictions have tightened dramatically. While Han Chinese arrive by the trainload, foreign visitors are required to pre-book a tour with guide and driver to secure a **Tibet Travel Permit (TTP).** In order to travel outside Lhasa, an **Aliens Travel permit** is also required, and for Mount Kailash you'll need yet another (military) permit. While the TAR is undeniably worth visiting, these restrictions and greater numbers of tourists make a visit to the "other Tibet" in Gansu, Qinghai, Sichuan, and Yunnan all the more appealing.

Aside from the difficulties of actually getting here, travel in Tibet should not be taken lightly. There are wide variations in temperature throughout the day, and many visitors experience altitude sickness (see box below), particularly those who fly directly to Lhasa. The northern and western regions of Tibet are cold and arid, with an annual average temperature of about 32°F (0°C), while southern and eastern regions are warmer and wetter. Peak season runs from May to mid-October. Winter in Lhasa is cozy, but transport to elsewhere in Tibet can be difficult to arrange. The last half of this chapter, from the section on Shigatse onward, covers towns on the Friendship Highway, a loose way of describing the road built from Lhasa, passing near the Himalayas and Mt. Everest, to the Nepali border. In spite of increasing restrictions on travel, the trip remains popular with foreign travelers. ***Note:*** Unless otherwise noted, hours listed for attractions and restaurants are daily.

XINING 西宁

232km (144 miles) W of Lanzhou, 781km (484 miles) E of Golmud. Altitude: 2,300m (7,544 ft.)

Once a key trading post on the southern Silk Route, Xining is perched on the northern edge of the Tibetan plateau and has a sizable Muslim population. Tibetan and Mongol monks and pilgrims may still be spied, drawn by **Kumbum (Ta'er Si)** ★ monastery to the south. A recent boom in the economy from the discovery of oil reserves and the city's attempt to market itself as a "summer resort" with its cooler-than-average temperatures has increased the supply of hotels and amenities the city has to offer. Still, there's little of interest in the city itself, but it's a useful base for exploring the **Amdo** and **Kham** regions to the south, or arranging a trip to Lhasa and the Tibetan Autonomous Republic.

Essentials

GETTING THERE The **airport** is 29km (18 miles) east of Xining. An airport bus runs to the **CAAC** ticket office, Bayi Lu 32 (✆ **0971/813-3333**). The bus trip from the airport takes 40 minutes and costs ¥23. From the bus drop-off point, take bus no. 28 from Bayi Lu to the railway and bus stations. Another ticket office is at the Wusi Dajie Shoupiao Chu (✆ **0971/612-2555**). Daily flights go to Beijing, Shanghai,

Chengdu, Guangzhou, Xi'an, and Golmud. To support the Qinghai-Tibet train, direct flights to Lhasa have been suspended indefinitely, although flights via Chengdu or Xi'an (with a mandatory overnight stay) are available.

The main **railway station** at the north end of town was being given a complete overhaul at the time of writing. Until completion in 2013 services depart from **Xining West**, a giant makeshift hangar, 20- to 30-minute taxi ride west of town. Taxis congregate outside the station, charging ¥10 per person into town, or ¥40 for the whole car, although it's only ¥20 on the meter. Regular trains connect with Lanzhou (2–3 hr.). Trains also connect with Beijing (T152; 24 hr.) at 11:56am; Chengdu (K1060; 25 hr.) at 9:15am; Shanghai (T166; 25 hr.) at 10:27am; and Yinchuan (K916; 12 hr.) at 7:15pm. All Lhasa trains pass through Xining and one train daily (K9801; 24 hr.) at 3:02pm starts in Xining. However, while it's easy to get tickets heading east, if you're planning on heading from Xining (or Golmud) to Lhasa, be prepared to spend a couple of days in town or book your tickets in advance through an agent; it's far easier to get a ticket coming down from Lhasa than for the journey up. The problem in Qinghai is that the bulk of the tickets are snapped up by local hoods the moment they become available. These tickets are then sold to well-connected travel agents to provide tickets for the army of baseball cap–clad Chinese tourists you'll see in Lhasa. Soft-sleeper tickets are nigh on impossible to get hold of, but you may have more luck with hard-sleeper. And of course, before you even consider how you're going to try and secure a berth, you'll need to get your hands on a Tibet Travel Permit (TTP; see "Permit Purgatory," p. 757). The easiest way to proceed for both permits and tickets is to make your arrangements through a reliable local agent; **Snowlion Tours** (see "Tours & Guides," p. 761) is recommended.

All ticket offices, including those at the station, sell tickets up to 10 days in advance for regular tickets, 2 days in advance for Tibet tickets. The easiest place to buy tickets is from the **Huoche Shoupiao Chu** (7:30am–6:30pm) on the second floor at Wusi Dajie 70-4 (✆ **0971/615-5203**). A ¥5 commission is charged.

The **Long-Distance Bus Station** (✆ **0971/711-2094**) is just south of the railway station. Buses service Lanzhou (3 hr.; ¥58) every half-hour between 7:20am and 6:30pm; Tongren (4 hr.; ¥33) hourly between 7:30am and 5pm; Linxia (6 hr.; ¥48); Liujia Xia (5 hr.; ¥33) at 10:30am and 11:30am; Hezuo (6 hr.; ¥56) at 7:45am; Xia He (¥77; 6 hr.); Golmud sleeper service (12 hr.; ¥153) at 5pm and 6pm; Tianshui (9 hr.; ¥84) at 6pm; Dunhuang (18 hr.; ¥208) at 2pm; Maqin (12 hr.; ¥135) is served by four regular buses daily plus an express service at 10:30am (¥152); Banma (14 hr.; ¥166 sleeper) at 4pm; Yushu (17 hr.) is served by sleeper buses (¥175) at 12:30pm, 3:30pm, and 6pm and a regular bus (not recommended) at 2:30pm (¥141). For Nangqian there's one bus a day at 4:30pm (20 hr.; ¥220).

GETTING AROUND Santana and Xiali **taxis** cost ¥6 for 3km (2 miles), ¥1.30 per kilometer thereafter. From 10pm to 6am they charge ¥1.50 per kilometer. **Buses** require you to pop ¥1 in a box. Bus no. 1 runs from the railway station to the main intersection *(da shizi)*, passing the Bank of China. Bus no. 9 departs from opposite the railway station, passing the railway ticket office, and Casa Mia.

TOURS & GUIDES Xining has several branches of **CITS.** A reasonably competent branch is on the first floor of Xining Dasha (✆ **0971/814-9254**). Get far more reliable info and service from the refreshingly professional **Snowlion Tours** (✆ **0971/816-3350;** www.snowliontours.com), based at Room 1212 on the 12th floor of the Chenglin Dasha at Dong Dajie 7. Snowlion operates tours through the region, and budget trips to the TAR (including permits and train tickets). Tashi

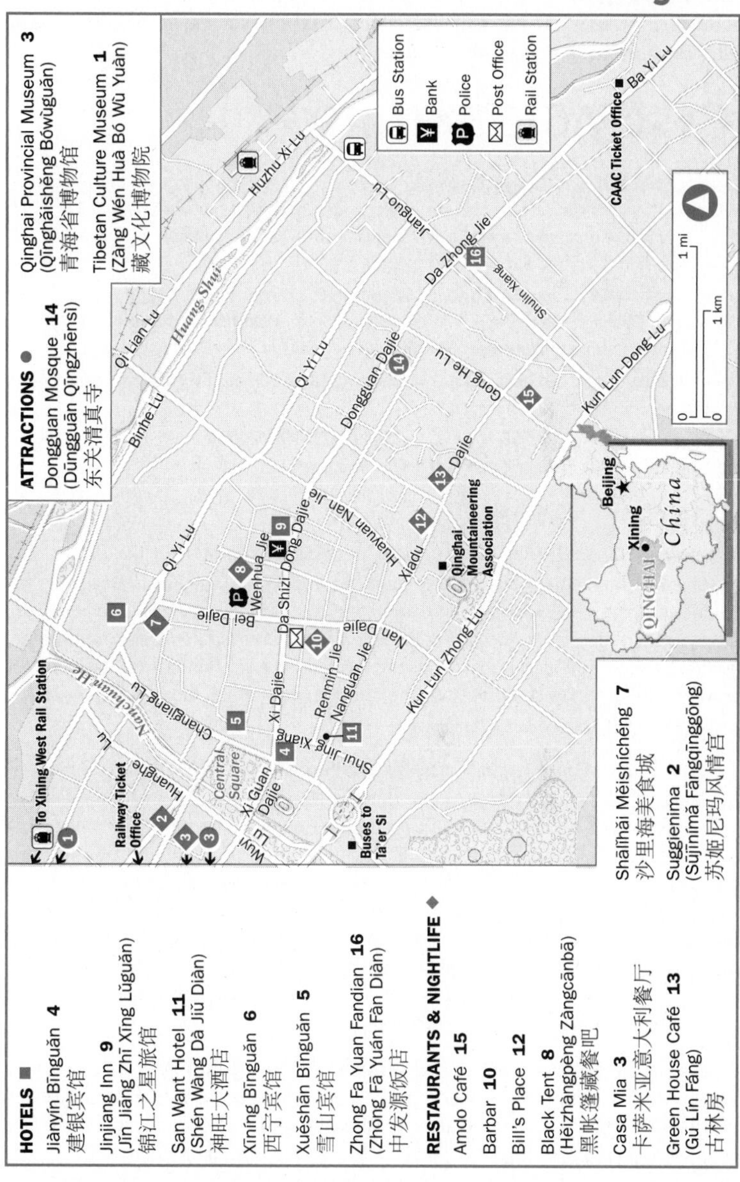

Phuntsok of **Wind Horse Adventure Tours,** Nan Dajie 19 (✆ **0971/613-1358** or 139/9712-4471; www.windhorseadventuretours.com), can also arrange customized trekking trips in Qinghai and the surrounding areas. He's a former monk who lived in India for 10 years, speaks great English, and is a great resource for any questions about Tibet and Qinghai. For mountaineering expeditions, **Qinghai Mountaineering Association,** Tiyu Xiang 7 (© **0971/823-8877;** www.qma.org.cn; May to mid-Oct 8am–noon and 2:30–6pm; closed winter weekends), should be your first port of call. Take bus no. 33 to Nan Men Tiyuchang.

[Fast FACTS] XINING

Banks, Foreign Exchange & ATMs Xining is overrun with branches of the **Bank of China.** Traveler's checks and cash may be changed and most branches have ATMs which accept foreign credit cards. Convenient branches can be found on Bei Dajie and Xi Dajie (Mon–Fri 9am–5pm; Sat–Sun 10am–4pm).

Internet Access There's a 24-hour *wangba* which charges ¥3 per hour on the 3rd floor of **Chenglin Dasha** at Dong Dajie 7. In the west of town, **Wangchong Julebu** is at Shengli Lu 25. Near the station, **Liuxingyu Wangba** is downstairs at Zhan Dong Xiang 9.

Post Office The main post office is on the southwest corner of the main crossroads at Da Shizi (second floor; 8:30am–6pm).

Visa Extensions The **PSB** at Bei Dajie 35 (© **0971/825-1758;** Mon–Fri 8:30–11:30am and 2:30–5:30pm) will arrange visa extensions in 3 days.

Exploring Xining

Dongguan Qingzhensi (Dongguan Mosque) Located in the center of a bustling Muslim district, this is where some of Qinghai's 800,000 Muslims gather for the call to prayer. The buildings here aren't much to look at, but if you come during prayer times, you'll get an interesting glimpse into the lives of Chinese Muslims. During other times, elderly men sit in the square and gossip. Behind the mosque is a crowded produce market and next to the mosque are stores selling Muslim wares.

On Dongguan Dajie. Admission ¥25. 8am–6pm.

Qinghai Sheng Bowuguan (Qinghai Province Museum) If you're interested in Tibetan culture specifically then give this museum a miss and head for the Tibetan Culture Museum, but for those short on time (or money), the provincial museum is worth a quick visit. Its collection of relics includes Mongolian pottery, Tibetan *mani* stones (stones carved with religious script and images), *thangkas,* and carpets, along with Qing dynasty carved wooden and bronze religious icons. English descriptions are fine but hardly insightful. To find the museum head for the grand-museum looking building in Xining Guangchang, leave your bag on the ground floor and then walk through the cut-price clothes stands and Tibetan stores and up the stairs.

Xining Guangchang. Free admission. 9am–4:30pm.

Tibetan Culture Museum (Zang Wenhua Bowuguan) ★★ Housed in a huge modern Tibetan style edifice, this new museum on the northern outskirts of town offers a tantalizing introduction to Tibetan culture. The big name draw is the world's longest *thangka,* an incredibly detailed piece 618m (more than ⅓ mile) long, which took a team of more than 300 artists 4 years to finish. The work, unveiled in 1997, was carried out in nearby Tongren (p. 751), and details the history of Tibet in beautifully ornate scenes, which, it is said, need 6 to 8 hours for even a cursory glance. Like the rest of the museum, display is state-of-the art and the *thangka* guides you though the story along its snakelike course. The site was previously known as the Tibetan Medicine Museum, and the huge collection of medicine *thangkas* on the ground floor are as detailed as they are fascinating: There are treatises on urinalysis, embryology, and two *thangkas* full of death omens. If you've hired a guide (or speak Chinese) you can also avail of a Tibetan medical consultation in the basement. Other sections to look out for are the traditional dress collection in the basement which include incredibly elaborate hairpieces from around the Tibetan world. English introductions aren't always easy to read, and there is more than a touch of spin to the history (Tibet was "ushered into a new era after liberation"), but this museum is a must for anyone with the slightest interest in Tibetan culture. Allow at least 2 hours.

Northern suburbs. ✆ **0971/531-6970.** Admission ¥60. English guide fee ¥100 for 90 min. Summer 9am–6pm (5pm in winter). Bus no.1 or 34.

Around Xining

Kumbum (Ta'er Si) ★ Jesuit missionary Emmanuel Huc, who visited in 1860, recorded, "On either side of the ravine, and up the edges of the mountains, rise, in amphitheatrical form, the white dwellings of the Lamas, each with its little white terrace and wall of enclosure, adorned only by cleanliness, while here and there tower far above them the Buddhist temples, with their gilt roofs glittering with a thousand colours and surrounded by elegant peristyles. . . ."

One of the six largest **Geluk (Yellow Hat)** monasteries, Kumbum was established in 1560 to mark the birthplace of **Tsongkapa (Zongkaba),** founder of the Geluk School (p. 771). The image of Tsongkapa is easily recognized by his pointed cap with long earflaps. Guides charging ¥50 cluster around the entrance, but as there are English signs, a guide is not essential. Facing away from the ticket office, a path leads up the hill from the left side of a row of eight white *chorten* (Tibetan stupas). Keep your ticket: It will be punched by bored monks lounging around the major temples. Shrill guides, huge Chinese tour groups, and glassed-in relics lend Kumbum the feel of a museum, but Han visitors are more respectful than in the past.

The most striking building is **Serdong Chenmo (Da Jinwa Dian) ★**, at the heart of the complex, with its aquamarine tiles. The original structure is said to have been built by Tsongkapa's mother, around a sandalwood tree that sprouted from Tsongkapa's fertile placenta. The **Butter Sculpture Exhibition (Suyouhua Zhanlanguan),** farther up the slope, is popular with the locals. These sculptures were once only made for festivals, after which they would be destroyed.

Festivals are held the 8th to the 15th of the first **(Monlam)** and fourth **(Saka Dawa)** lunar months, as well as the 3rd to 8th of the sixth lunar month, and the 20th to the 26th of the ninth lunar month, which celebrates **Tsongkapa's birthday.** Call ahead to check exact dates. Religious dancing, mass chanting, and "sunning the Buddha" can be seen, as well as crowds of Tibetans who, in missionary Huc's day, "sang till they were fairly out of breath; they danced; they pushed each other about; they tumbled head over heels: and shouted till one might have thought that they had all gone crazy." Current festivals may be tamer.

✆ **0971/223-2357.** Admission ¥80. 8:30am–5:30pm. Buses (28km/17 miles; 1 hr.; ¥7) have their destination marked as HUANGZHONG, and depart after 6am from south of Kunlun Qiao (bus 3 from station). The last bus returns at 7:30pm. A round-trip taxi ride from the leagues of drivers waiting at the bus stop should only cost ¥50, but if you hail a regular cab they'll charge ¥80 to ¥100, including a couple of hours waiting time.

TSONGKAPA: TIBET'S first catholic?

While many portray **Tsongkapa** as a reformer or even a revolutionary, in the history of Tibetan Buddhism he was actually a conservative who appealed to existing (but neglected) monastic precepts. Drawing on his prodigious knowledge of the Mahayana Buddhist canon, Tsongkapa emphasized monastic discipline, insisting on abstinence from sex and intoxicants. The Jesuit missionary Emmanuel Huc believed he saw a touch of Catholicism about the man, and hypothesized that "a premature death did not permit the Catholic missionary to complete the religious education of his disciple [Tsongkapa], who himself, when afterwards he became an apostle, merely applied himself . . . to the introduction of a new Buddhist liturgy."

Qinghai Hu (Lake Kokonor) Large, high, salty, and stunningly blue, the lake that gave Qinghai (Blue Sea) Province its name provides an ornithological spectacle in April and early July, and wild vistas year-round. Over 100,000 birds migrate from the Indian Ocean to feed on spawn of Lake Kokonor's one variety of fish, the slow-growing scaly carp *(huangyu)*, which swims up the Buka He each spring. The fattened birds crowd onto tiny **Niao Dao (Bird Island),** actually a peninsula situated on the northwest side of the lake. Tibetans consider this island as the plug for the lake. In 2005, a bird flu scare closed down the lake for several weeks, when hundreds of migratory birds were found dead near the shore.

Most hotels in Xining offer tours to Lake Kokonor, starting from ¥100. Be clear about what your tour includes. To come independently you can take a morning bus (3 hr.; ¥29) from the long-distance station. Snowlion Tours can organize overnight trips to the lake which stop at Ta'er Si en-route and drive via the 4,400m (14,436 ft.) La Ji Shan pass; for a car holding 4 people the cost is ¥600. Bird-watchers should head for **Niao Dao Binguan** (✆ **0970/865-5098**) on Bird Island, which has basic rooms for ¥300 to ¥350.

Admission to Bird Island Sanctuary ¥100 plus ¥25 for the electric car from the entrance. 8:30am–5:30pm.

Shopping

Food supplies can be picked up from the **supermarket** in the basement of the shopping center on the northeast corner of the Xi Dajie and Changjiang Lu intersection. Near the Provincial Museum and Casa Mia, tiny **Europe Chocolate** at 4-14 Wusi Dajie is worth a visit for those craving imported chocolate or beer. For local Amdo crafts, **Amdo Café ★** at 19 Ledu Lu (✆ **0971/821-3127;** www.amdocraft.com) is recommended; a good range of handicrafts including bags, belts, and purses are on sale, all of which are made by Amdo women in Qinghai, and the profits go to support local Tibetan communities. One of Qinghai's special exports is caterpillar fungus, called *dongchongxiacao,* mainly sourced around Yushu, which can be soaked in vodka like a worm in tequila or brewed with soup. You can purchase the fungus at the stores to the right of the gate of **Xining Binguan,** with prices ranging from ¥50 to ¥100 per gram.

Where to Stay

For a city of its size, Xining has a wide choice of hotels. A 20% to 30% discount is standard at most establishments.

VERY EXPENSIVE

San Want Hotel (Shenwang Dajiudian) ★ Opened in 2008 and part of the sophisticated Taiwanese chain, the well-located San Want is Xining's most luxurious choice, and is popular with business travelers. Give the pokier economic rooms a miss, and choose a standard or deluxe, both of which feature huge beds, tasteful muted decor and all mod cons, plus deep tubs in the bathrooms. Service is competent

Changjiang Lu 79. www.sanwant.com. ✆ **0971/820-1111.** 253 units. ¥1,670 to ¥1,800 standard room; from ¥3,000 suite. Rates include breakfast. Up to 75% discount. AE, DC, MC, V. **Amenities:** 2 restaurants; cafe; conference center. *In room:* A/C, satellite TV, fridge, Internet, minibar.

EXPENSIVE

Jianyin Binguan This hotel, owned by the China Construction Bank, used to be one of the few places in town that allowed foreign tourists, and in spite of increased competition its central location and recent renovations still make it a decent choice. Once the tallest building in town, the Jianyin is now overshadowed by a building across the street. The comfortable rooms feature pleasant decor, large beds, and good bathrooms. A revolving restaurant on the 28th floor with Western food is popular with Chinese businessmen and tourists.

Xi Dajie 55. ✆ **0971/826-1888.** Fax 0971/826-1551. 115 units. ¥668 standard room; from ¥768 suite. Up to 55% discount. AE, DC, MC, V. **Amenities:** 2 restaurants; conference center; travel agent. *In room:* A/C, TV, fridge, Internet, minibar.

Zhong Fa Yuan Fandian ★ In an interesting part of town close to the Dongguan Mosque, the Zhong Fa Yuan's discounts make it a good deal for the quality of the rooms. Staff are keen to please and standard (1) rooms are spacious and homey, with tubs and good amenities. Standard (2) rooms are smaller, but have the same facilities.

Shuilin Xiang 1. ✆ **0971/711-1888.** 138 units. ¥628 standard room 1, ¥588 standard room 2. 40-50% discount. AE, DC, MC, V. **Amenities:** 2 restaurants; conference center. *In room:* AC, TV, fridge, hair dryer, Internet.

MODERATE

Xining Binguan ★ On pleasant grounds away from the city traffic, this hotel has better-than-average service for a three-star, state-owned hotel. The Soviet-style architecture adds character, and the high ceilings and recent room renovations make for an enjoyable stay. Furnishings in the rooms match the dark, albeit fake, redwood floors; the bathrooms are spotless. The single rooms, while somewhat cramped, feature a larger-than-average twin bed and are ideal if you're traveling alone.

Qiyi Lu 348. ✆ **0971/846-3333.** 315 units. ¥320 single room; ¥420 standard room; from ¥1,080 suite. 40%–50% discount possible. AE, DC, MC, V. **Amenities:** 4 restaurants; concierge. *In room:* A/C, TV, Internet (¥2 per hour).

INEXPENSIVE

Jinjiang Inn ★ The Jinjiang chain trumps again with comfy beds, good showers, and clean modern amenities in a variety of different sized rooms. Service is friendly and the location, on Dong Dajie a few minutes walk from Da Shizi, is also good. Breakfast in the canteen costs ¥15.

Yima Jie ✆ **0971/492-5666.** www.jinjianginns.com. 82 units. ¥169 standard room. No credit cards. **Amenities:** Restaurant. *In room:* A/C, TV, Internet.

Where to Eat

Xining's dining scene has always been diverse and more and more small cafes and Tibetan ventures are opening all the time. One such new establishment is **Amdo Café** on Ledu Lu; while the sandwiches aren't great, the coffee is good value and the handicrafts on sale are all produced by Amdo women in Qinghai and profits benefit local Tibetan communities. In the summer months, one of the most popular things to do at night is to eat on one of Xining's renowned **"eat streets."** The biggest one is on **Daxin Jie,** where touts sell everything from barbecued fish to fried dumplings. ***Warning:*** This isn't the most hygienic environment; make sure you use your own chopsticks. As well as the Western options listed below, there's the usual array of **KFCs, Dicos,** and an **Origus** pizza, all of which can be found at the junction of Changjiang Lu and Xi Dajie.

Black Tent NEPALESE/TIBETAN When it opened a few years ago, Black Tent was an instant hit with both Tibetans and Xining's foreign community. The restaurant has since moved locations, but has retained the same relaxed ambience, friendly (but erratic) service, and decent Nepalese and Tibetan fare. The yak *momos,* vegetable curries and lassis are all tasty.

3rd floor, Wenmiao Guangchang, Wenhua Jie. ✆ **139/972-24192.** Meal for 2 less than ¥70 to ¥100. English menu. No credit cards. 9am–10pm.

Casa Mia (Kasa Miya Yidali Canting) ★ WESTERN If you've been on the yak butter road for too long and are in need of some Western sustenance, this is your best bet. Casa Mia's chef, formerly of Beijing, serves up first-rate home-made pastas and wood-fired pizzas, along with excellent hamburgers and there's also a decent wine-list to accompany your meal. The atmosphere in the warm and cozy space is relaxed, but more restaurant than cafe. Next door, Boronia, used to be the expat's top choice, but these days it is far surpassed by Casa Mia.

Wusi Xi Da Jie 10-4. ✆ **0971/631-1272.** Meal for 2 ¥100 plus. AE, DC, MC, V. English menu. Wi-Fi. 9am–11pm (lunch 11am–2:30pm, dinner 5–11pm; food all day on weekends).

Greenhouse Café (Guilinfang Kafei) ★ WESTERN Owned by a friendly expat family who previously worked for NGOs in the region, Greenhouse has got it all exactly right. A cozy wooden interior, great food, and excellent coffee have made it a favorite with locals and travelers alike. It's worth coming here for the sandwiches alone, where you get the pick of focaccia or wrap bread, a variety of spreads including hummus, herbed cream cheese, or vinaigrette, imported cheeses, and a host of vegetables. There's also free WiFi.

Xiadu Dajie 222-22. ✆ **0971/820-2710.** Sandwiches ¥20; pizzas ¥28; coffees ¥15–¥30. No credit cards. 8am–10:30pm.

Shalihai Meishicheng ★ MUSLIM Recently spruced-up Shalihai feels much more upscale these days, but the food is equally as good and keeps the customers trooping through the doors. The *chao mianpian,* small pieces of noodles stir-fried with green squash, beef, and peppers, is a steal at ¥6 a bowl and incredibly satisfying—kind of like a spicy Chinese version of pasta primavera (with meat). After 6pm, the chefs fire up the front grill to serve *yangrouchuan* (lamb skewers).

Bei Dajie 4. ✆ **0971/823-4444.** Meal for 2 ¥40–¥100. No credit cards. 11:30am–12:30am. Bus: 102, 35, 14, or 15.

Suggienima (Sujinima Fangqinggong) ★ TIBETAN This atmospheric restaurant serves a host of tasty Tibetan specialties including momos and yak steak, and also does a decent curry. The dimly lit interior is beautifully decked out with Tibetan furnishings, and there's live Tibetan music from 7:30pm onward.

Huanghe Lu. ✆ **0971/610-2282.** Meal for 2 from ¥60. No credit cards. 10am–11pm.

Xining After Dark

Wenmiao Guangchang houses several floors of bars, clubs, and restaurants, or for a quieter drink you could wander along Xiadu Dajie and pick a place that strikes you—**Bill's Place,** just along the road from Greenhouse Café, has a range of cocktails and some great photos from around the region for sale. Other options are relaxed and comfortable **BarBar,** at Nan Dajie 46-2 (✆ **0971/823-5488**), a 5-minute walk south of Da Shizi, or **Soho,** behind the Sports Center on Ximen (✆ **0971/822-3299;** 7pm–2:30am), which features R&B most nights. Another popular nighttime activity is a visit to a Tibetan ***nangma,*** a variety show with singing and dancing. One of the most popular *nangmas,* for both Tibetan and Han Chinese, is in the basement of Donghu Binguan out by East Lake (Donghu). The entertainment runs nightly from 9:30pm.

TONGREN (REBKONG; 同仁)

181km (112 miles) S of Xining, 107km (66 miles) NW of Xiahe. Altitude: 2,400m (4,872 ft.)

Tongren is at the center of a major revival in Tibetan art, particularly in sculpture and the painting of appliquéd *thangkas* (silk paintings). Although viewed by both Lhasa and Beijing as being on the periphery of the Tibetan world, a number of monks were arrested here during the 2008 protests and historically locals remember their crucial role in the Sino-Tibetan peace treaty signed in 822. The treaty is still marked by the **Lurol Festival,** held in the middle of the sixth lunar month. With fertility dances and body piercing, it has a pagan feel. Monks are *not* allowed to attend. The major **Buddhist festival** is held from the 5th to the 12th days of the first lunar month, with debates, religious dancing, and the unveiling of large *thangkas* moving between the main temples of **Sengeshong Gompa, Gomar Gompa,** and **Rongpo Gompa.** The town itself is drab; nearly all the sites of interest are located several miles north. ***Note:*** For Chinese translations of establishments listed in this section, turn to chapter 16.

Essentials

GETTING THERE The **Tongren Bus Station** (✆ **0973/872-2014**) connects Tongren with Xining (hourly; 4 hr.; ¥31) between 7:20am and 4pm; with Lanzhou (5 hr.; ¥60) at 6:50am; with Xia He (4 hr.; ¥24) at 8am; and with Linxia (3 hr.; ¥37) at 8am. Uphill from the bus station is a large roundabout. To the right is Zhongshan Lu, the main street, which runs west to Xiaqiong Lu.

TOURS & GUIDES The **Rebgong Cultural Center** at Fengwu Zhonglu 217 (✆ **0973/879-7139;** rebgonglibrary@yahoo.com) is the town's community center. The center features a library of Tibetan, Chinese, and English books, and can help arrange art classes. Sherab (✆ **139/0973-4619**), a friend of the director's, is a jolly ex-monk who knows everyone in town and can act as an English-speaking tour guide.

[Fast FACTS] TONGREN

Banks, Foreign Exchange & ATMs None available.

Internet Access Immediately east of the entrance to the Telecom Hotel is the non-smoking Huangnan Dianxin Fengongsi Wangba (✆ 0973/872-4196; 8am–midnight), which charges ¥3 per hour.

Post Office The main post office (Mon–Fri 8:30am–5:30pm; Sat–Sun 10am–4pm) is located on Xiaqiong Zhong Lu, next to the junction with Zhongshan Lu.

Exploring the Region

The main Geluk monastery of the region, **Rongpo Gompa** (**Longwu Si;** ¥50), is to the south of town. But the most popular outing for those interested in Tibetan art is a visit to the villages of **Shang Wutun (Upper Wutun)** and **Xia Wutun (Lower Wutun),** 6.4km (4 miles) north of Tongren. The villages are filled with monks and laypeople turning out masses of Buddhist art for temples as far away as western Tibet; each village charges a ¥30 admission. The monks from **Sengeshong Yagotsang** (✆ **0973/872-9227;** ¥10) in the upper village are exceptionally friendly and happy to show their work. *Thangkas* can be purchased for ¥200 to tens of thousands, depending on the size of the piece, how intricately drawn the artwork is, and how much gold paint is used. Don't be afraid to bargain, even if you are buying from a monk!

Minivans charging ¥2 depart when full for **Shang Wutun** and **Xia Wutun** from the roundabout near the Tongren bus station, or hail a three-wheeler for ¥8. You can hire a taxi to make the round-trip for around ¥20. Directly across the river (Longwu He) is **Gomar Gompa** (**Guomari Si;** ¥10), marked by a spectacular five-tiered chorten (stupa). The climb to the top of the 38m (125-ft.) structure is a nervy one, as the ledges get narrower closer to the apex. The reward is a spectacular view down the valley. The monks are Tu, not Tibetan—even those fluent in the Amdo dialect won't understand a word they say.

Where to Stay

Tongren doesn't have much choice in the way of accommodation, but things have improved with the opening of the **Regong Binguan** (✆ **0973/593-6666**) across the bridge from town. This friendly hotel has cheaper standard rooms (¥200) and more expensive Tibetan style rooms (¥320), all of which have modern amenities including free cabled Internet connection. In town the best option is the **Dianxin Binguan** (Telecom Hotel) at Zhongshan Lu 38 (✆ **0973/872-6888;** ¥189 standard twin), which has clean, simple, functionally furnished rooms with blue bathrooms, and refreshingly efficient service. Over the road the **Huangnan Binguan** (✆ **0973/872-2293;** ¥90–¥130) is a last resort and offers shabby rooms in the older front wing and newer rooms in the back.

Where to Eat

There are a handful of Tibetan restaurants in Tongren, but the ambience doesn't get better than at the **Homeland of Rebkong Artist Restaurant (Regong Yishuke)** ★ (✆ **0973/872-7666**), just west of the Huangnan Binguan. Monks and Tibetan government officials stroll in to sip yak butter tea and eat *momos* (yak dumplings). Try the *chao yangrou* (stir-fried mutton), the *tsampa* (barley flour mixed with yak butter, tea, and sugar), and the *renshenguo mifan* (ginseng rice). It's also a good place to relax with a cup of tea or a beer.

Tongren After Dark

Weekend nights, the most happening place in town is **Meinaxia,** Xiaqiong Zhong Lu 37, a Tibetan *nangma,* or nightclub. Entering via a fire escape on the side of the building feels like going to a club on New York's Lower East Side. Inside, young men in black sleeveless T-shirts take over the dance floor, grooving to a Chinese version of Backstreet Boys only to be edged out by couples (straight and gay) slow dancing to sappy love songs.

YUSHU earthquake

Five hundred miles southwest of Xining, the Khampa town of **Yushu** was slowly making its way onto the itineraries of intrepid travelers, aided by the opening of an airport in 2009. Travelers came to this rough and ready town for its authentic Tibetan culture, monasteries, *mani* stones, breathtaking scenery, and the horse festival. On April 14, 2010 a warning tremor struck around 4am, and then a few hours later the **main 7.1 quake** literally shook the town apart. Buildings collapsed, infrastructure and monasteries were damaged and thousands of people were killed and injured. The official death toll was reported at 2,698, but many believe this figure could be 10 times higher. The extreme conditions and isolation of the town have made the recovery all the more difficult, and while Yushu has been designated as a tourism development zone to help regenerate the economy, at the time of writing it was still tent city, with an estimated 60,000 to 70,000 people living under canvas throughout the prefecture. Tourism can certainly play a crucial role in the town's recovery, but for the time being visitors are advised to stay away. For this reason we have removed Yushu from this edition of the book. Check out **www.kekexili.typepad.com** for the latest. If you want to help, you can make online donations at **www.yushuearthquakerelief.com**.

MAQIN (DAWU; 玛卿)

552km (342 miles) S of Xining, 525km (326 miles) NW of Aba. Altitude: 3,700m (12,136 ft.)

Few capital cities are one-street towns, but **Maqin,** the capital of Golok Tibetan Autonomous Prefecture, is just that. Efforts to "settle" nomads are rarely successful (p. 754), and the town has a Wild West ambience. Nomads wander around for a few hours, and then amble out again. North of town is a picturesque **Mani temple,** choked with *tar-choks* (prayer flags), and the bustling **market** to the left of the bus station is worth a look. But the main reason to come here is to visit **Amnye Machen,** Amdo's holiest mountain. ***Warning:*** Maqin is one of the coldest towns in Qinghai—and Qinghai is a cold place. ***Note:*** For Chinese translations of selected establishments listed in this section, turn to chapter 16.

Essentials

GETTING THERE Compared to the trek out to Tibet's other renowned holy mountain, Kailash, getting to Amnye Machen is straightforward. The **bus** from Xining (8 hr.; ¥85) passes **Lajia Si,** a charming Geluk monastery on the upper reaches of the Yellow River en-route to Maqin's **bus station** at Tuanjie Lu 137. Facing out from the bus station, you are on Tuanjie Lu. As major streets go, that's it. The direction to your left is roughly north. Buses and minibuses run to Thelma and Chawo from Amnye Machen, but Jeeps are quicker; either way you'll need to pay the ¥50 environmental protection fee to walk the circuit.

TOURS & GUIDES Permits and trips to Amnye Machen are best arranged through **Snowlion Tours** or the **Qinghai Mountaineering Association** in Xining.

THE panchen lama's LETTER

The Great Leap Forward (1959–61) killed an estimated 30 million Chinese, but the horror of Qinghai was unparalleled. The leftist policies of the city's radical governor, Gao Feng, are said to have wiped out up to half the population. Starvation claimed most lives, while the PLA's policy of "fighting the rebellion on a broad front" *(pingpan kuoda)* saw countless monks and nuns murdered. The Panchen Lama, viewed as a puppet of Beijing, was sent to Qinghai on a fact-finding mission in 1962. Upon his return, he penned a 70,000-word tract—*The Panchen Lama's Letter*—which implied genocide: "The population of [greater] Tibet has been seriously reduced. . . . It poses a grave danger to the very existence of the Tibetan race and could even push the Tibetans to the last breath." Mao was enraged, the "puppet" was put under house arrest, and he was only rehabilitated by the Party in 1988. Ending nomadism, of which Marxism takes a dim view, is still official government policy.

[Fast FACTS] MAQIN

Banks, Foreign Exchange & ATMs None are available.

Internet Access Hong Niu Wangba is across the road, just north of the bus station, on the second floor of a music shop (10am–10pm; ¥4 per hour).

Post Office The main post office (Mon–Fri 9:30am–5:30pm; Sat–Sun 10:30am–4:30pm) is a 5-minute walk north of the bus station.

Where to Stay & Eat

Choices are thin on the ground in Maqin, with the best choices being the **Xueshan Binguan** (✆ **0975/838-2142**) and the **Dianxin Binguan** (Telecom Hotel; ✆ **0975/838-6208**), both of which have rooms with bathrooms for ¥120 to ¥150, and neither of which are worth writing home about.

For food, there are plenty of Sichuan canteens on Tuanjie Lu, and you'll also find stores here to stock up on supplies if you're heading out to the mountain.

A Nearby Holy Mountain

About 86km (53 miles) from Maqin stands **Amnye Machen (Magi Gantry)** ★★★. In 1929, American botanist Joseph Rock incorrectly measured its height at over 9,000m (30,000 ft.), making it (for a while) the world's highest peak. It actually comes in well short, at 6,282m (20,605 ft.), but it was unconquered until 1981 (partly because an earlier Chinese expedition climbed the wrong peak). One of the first Western visitors was the French adventurer Gerard, who was impressed by "a prodigious and resplendent mass of snow and ice, which strikes any man, however accustomed to mountains, with admiration and astonishment." The protector deity who resides in the mountain, **Machen Parma,** is popular with Bonpos (followers of the Bon faith) and is also revered by Buddhists.

Many pilgrims start the trek from **Santiago (Thelma Chemo),** where the road meets the pilgrimage circuit. Farther down the motor road is **Baita (Chowan),** the traditional starting point for the trek where yaks or horses (and drivers) may be hired from ¥100 per day. The full circuit is a hefty 132km (82 miles), and there is no way of retracing your steps without incurring the wrath of Machen Parma! It is possible to walk only part of the loop by starting farther around the mountain and many travelers choose a 4-day circuit, rather than the complete 8-day *kora*. Alternatively, riding on horseback should take no more than 5 days. The atmosphere of the *kora* is pious and social. Entire villages or families make the trip, coming from all corners of the Tibetan world for a pilgrimage that is equal to Kailash in significance. The scenery is unsurpassed.

The easiest way to make arrangements is through **Snowlion Tours** or **Qinghai Mountaineering Association** in Xining, which will cost US$60 to US$80 per day including tent, sleeping bag, food, and guide. You should take a spare pair of light shoes or sandals for the numerous stream crossings, and if you choose to do the walk independently a sturdy water filter would also be good idea—there is a lot of glacial silt in the streams. Most pilgrims abstain from meat during the *kora*—a real sacrifice for the meat-loving Tibetans. June through September are the best months, after the deadly cold of winter.

GOLMUD (GE'ERMU; 格尔木)

1,165km (722 miles) N of Lhasa, 781km (484 miles) W of Xining, 524km (325 miles) S of Dunhuang. Altitude: 3,000m (9,840 ft.)

Unless you're heading to Lhasa from the southern Silk Route, there is no reason to visit Golmud, isolated out in the wild and gloomy landscape of the **Tsaidam Basin.** Golmud used to be the only option for the overland journey to Lhasa, but these days you have the preferable option of passing straight through the town on the new Qinghai-Tibet rail line. ***Note:*** For Chinese translations of selected establishments listed in this section, turn to chapter 16.

Essentials

GETTING THERE The **airport** is 20km (12 miles) west of Golmud. Taxis charge around ¥20 for the journey into town. You can buy air tickets at the **CAAC** office at Chaidamu Zhong Lu 4 (✆ **0979/842-3333**). Daily flights head to Xining and Xi'an. All Lhasa **trains** (14 hr.) pass through Golmud, and although it has a relatively small sleeper ticket allocation you should be able to get a berth within a couple of days, and seat tickets are readily available. Heading east to Xining (9 hr.) or Lanzhou (12 hr.), tickets in all classes are readily available. The **Golmud Bus Station** (✆ **0979/845-3688**) is directly opposite the train station, with buses to Dunhuang (8 hr.; ¥101 lower berth, ¥99 upper berth) at 9am and 6pm; and to Xining (12 hr.; ¥125) at 5pm and 7pm. To Lhasa the train is an infinitely preferable means of transport, but if you want to do it the old-fashioned way there is one daily bus for Lhasa (¥240; 18 hr.) from the **Tibet Bus Station** on Yanqiao Lu.

GETTING AROUND **Taxis** charge ¥5 to ¥6. **Buses** cost ¥1, paid to the conductor. Bus no. 2 runs from the railway station to the center of town.

[FastFACTS] GOLMUD

Banks, Foreign Exchange & ATMs The **Bank of China,** Chaidamu Lu 19 (Mon–Fri 8:30am–6:30pm; Sat–Sun 9:30am–4pm), changes cash and traveler's checks and has an ATM.

Internet Access **Ai wo ba** (9am–midnight) is above a grocery store, on the corner of Xi Shichang San Lu and Zhanqian Er Lu.

Post Office The main post office (8:30am–5pm) is on the northeast corner of Kunlun Lu and Chaidamu Lu.

Travel Permits If you want to buy a ticket to Lhasa and don't have a permit you'll need to visit **CITS** (✆ **0979/849-5123**) in the Ge'ermu Binguan. Offices are open Monday to Friday 8:30am to noon and 2:30 to 6pm.

Visa Extensions The **PSB** at Chaidamu Dong Lu (✆ **0979/844-2511;** Mon–Fri, 8:30am–noon and 2:30–6pm) grants 1-month extensions in 2 days.

Where to Stay

Accommodation options have improved (a little) in Golmud, and foreigners are no longer required to stay at the overpriced **Ge'ermu Binguan** (✆ **0979/842-4288;** ¥340 standard room).

Wei'ershi Dajiudian Tucked in a quiet location between town and railway station, this two-star hotel has clean and comfortable furnished rooms; service is efficient and unobtrusive. The deluxe rooms have Internet access.

Jiangyuan Nan Lu 16. ✆ **0979/843-1208.** Fax 0979/842-4888. 50 units. ¥120 standard room; ¥140 deluxe room; ¥260 suite. Rates include breakfast. No credit cards. **Amenities:** Concierge. *In room:* TV, Internet (deluxe rooms only).

Youzheng Binguan (Post Hotel) This is a clean and friendly three-star establishment. Rooms vary in size; a larger room is worth paying more for. The friendly travel agency provides free information.

Yingbin Lu (directly opposite railway station). ✆ **0979/845-7000.** 59 units (51 with shower only). ¥80 bed in a shared room; ¥160–¥180 standard room. No credit cards. **Amenities:** Restaurant; concierge. *In room:* TV.

Where to Eat

Liuyi Shou HOTPOT If you don't speak Chinese, a waiter will lead you straight to the kitchen, where you can select all the meat and vegetables you want. A *yuanyang huoguo* (yin-yang hot pot consisting of both a spicy and a non-spicy broth) is then brought to your table so you can do the cooking yourself. As an added bonus, you get a bib to protect your shirt from any unforeseen splashes of spicy soup.

Chaidamu Lu 59. ✆ **0979/841-5333.** Meal for 2 ¥50–¥80. No credit cards. 10am–10:30pm.

LHASA (LASA; 拉萨)

1,165km (722 miles) S of Golmud, 278km (172 miles) E of Shigatse. Altitude: 3,600m (11,808 ft.)

The religious and political heart of the Tibetan world, Lhasa sits on the north bank of the Kyi Chu, surrounded by colossal mountain ranges to the north and south. The first hint that you are entering the traditional capital of Tibet is the red and white palaces of the **Potala ★★**, home to Tibet's spiritual and temporal leaders, the Dalai Lamas, since the 17th century. Most Western visitors, however, are disillusioned to find a Chinese city. The Dalai Lama, the other enduring symbol of Tibetan purity and mystery, fled the grounds of his summer residence, the **Norbulingka,** over 50 years ago.

The effects of martial law, declared in March 1989, are still felt in Lhasa, particularly in the nearby Geluk monasteries of **Drepung ★** and **Sera.** Hu Yaobang, general secretary of the CCP during the early 1980s, compared Chinese policies and attitudes in Tibet to colonialism, and this feeling is still hard to shake. Nowhere is the grip of Chinese rule tighter, all the more so since the Olympic demonstrations, and now in the run-up to the 60 year anniversary of the "peaceful liberation" of Tibet. Since the 1980s, waves of Han migration from poor neighboring provinces have made Tibetans a minority in their own capital and the opening of the Qinghai-Tibet rail line has only exacerbated the situation. Ironically, Hu Yaobang's policy of opening Tibet to migration and trade led to this influx of Han migrants, which most Tibetans consider the most odious aspect of Chinese rule.

All Tibetan Buddhists aim to visit Lhasa at least once in their lives, drawn by the sacred **Jokhang Temple ★★★**, which forms the heart of the Tibetan quarter. It is

permit PURGATORY

As well as the problem of actually getting a train ticket to Lhasa, there has always been the inconvenience of getting the relevant permits to visit the TAR. Permit restrictions, a subject long shrouded in mystery, appeared to be relaxing and, in recent years, independent foreign travelers have found themselves able to visit the TAR as individuals rather than part of a mandatory group (which most visitors then abandoned as soon as they reached Lhasa). But restrictions have always been subject to change at short notice, and following the 2008 demonstrations, controls are tighter than ever. Foreign visitors are sometimes completely banned from entering Tibet (most recently in July 2011), and currently travelers are required to visit as part of an organized tour through a licensed agent. Agencies in Beijing, Shanghai, Chengdu, Chongqing, Guangzhou, Lanzhou, Xining, and Golmud can arrange tours and permits. To buy a plane, train, or bus ticket to Lhasa and then to visit the surrounding monasteries and the secondary city of Shigatse, a **Tibet Travel Permit (TTP)** is required. In the past individual travelers could obtain these permits from Tibet Tourism Bureaus in major cities around China, but currently all permits are issued in Lhasa and must be arranged through the licensed agent through which you book your tour. Permits take a week to process so either forward your passport and visa details to your agency in advance, or be prepared to spend a few days at your start point. The cost of the permit is included in the tour price. You may receive the actual permit, but more likely you will get a photocopy; either way the guide who meets you in Lhasa will have an original. It's worth making a few copies of your permit as it is likely to be checked frequently (and sometimes taken) on your journey to the TAR. In Lhasa itself you are nominally required to visit sights with your guide; however, this is easily avoided. Once outside of Lhasa though, you will certainly need to be accompanied by a guide and driver.

For travel beyond Lhasa and Shigatse an **Alien Travel Permit (ATP)** and a guide, vehicle, and driver are all required. Foreigners aren't allowed to travel on public transport anywhere outside of Lhasa, and to this end, most bus details have been omitted from this edition. These tours and permits can be arranged in advance or once in Lhasa. The situation becomes yet more complex if you wish to travel to sensitive regions such as Kailash, for which a **Military Permit** (¥100) is required.

As always there are stories of those who slip through the net, but the exceptions are far fewer than those who get turned back (and fined). There is hope that the regulations will relax again, but this seems unlikely in the near future.

Lhasa 拉萨

HOTELS ■

Dhod Gu Hotel (Dūngù Bīnguǎn) **13**
敦固宾馆

Four Points Sheraton **25**
(Fu Peng Xīlaidēng Jiǔdian)
拉萨福朋喜来登酒店

House of Shambhala (Xiāng Bā Lā Fǔ) **12**
香巴拉府

Kyichu Hotel (Jíqī Fàndiàn) **17**
吉曲饭店

Oh Dan Guesthouse (Oudān Bīnguǎn) **10**
欧丹宾馆

Shambhala Palace **23**
(Xiāng Bā Lā Gōng)
香巴拉宫

St. Regis **24**
(Ruì Jí Dù Jià Jiǔ Diàn)
瑞吉度假酒店

Yak Hotel (Yǎkè Bīnguǎn) **16**
亚宾馆

RESTAURANTS & NIGHTLIFE ◆

Alu Cang Restaurant **18**
(A'uócāng Cāntīng)
阿罗仓餐厅

Dunya Bar & Restaurant **11**
(Dūnya Jiǔbā)
敦亚酒吧

Ganglamedo **14**
(Wǎng Lā Mei Duǒ)
冈拉梅朵

Hao Wai Xuan **15**
好外宣

Holy Land Vegetarian Restaurant **8**
(Gāoyuán Hóngshū Càiguǎn)
圣地素餐馆

Makye Ame (Mǎjí A'mǐ) **22**
玛吉阿米

Niúwěi **6**
牛尾

Snowland Restaurant **20**
(Xuěyù Cāntīng)
雪域餐厅

Summit Café **9, 19**

ATTRACTIONS ●

Drepung Monastery (Zhébàng Sì) **1**
哲蚌寺

Himalaya Hotel **26**

Jokhang Temple **21**
(Dàzhāo Sì)
大昭寺

Nechung Monastery (Nǎiqióng Sì) **2**
乃琼寺

Norbulingka (Luóbùlínkǎ) **3**
罗布林卡

Potala Palace (Bùdálā Gōng) **5**
布达拉宫

Sera Monastery (Sèlā Sì) **7**
色拉寺

Tibet Museum (Xīzàng Bówùguǎn) **4**
西藏博物馆

recommended that you stay and spend most of your time exploring this captivating neighborhood, also known as the **Barkhor District.**

Essentials

GETTING THERE Aside from the problems of securing a travel permit (see the "Permit Purgatory" box) getting to Lhasa is now far more straightforward since the opening of the railway, and there are flights from various major cities throughout China. Those arriving overland or by air from Kathmandu can obtain a standard 1-month tourist (L) visa and a TTP permit only by joining a group tour through a travel agency. Two good choices are **Royal Mt. Trekking,** P.O. Box 10798, Durbar Marg, Katmandu

(✆ **977-1/424-1452;** fax 977-1/424-5318; www.royal-mt-trekking.com); and **Green Hill Tours & Treks,** P.O. Box 5072, Kathmandu (✆ **977-1/442-2467;** fax 977-1/441-9985; www.greenhill-tours.com).

Gongkar Airport is 97km (60 miles) southeast of Lhasa. Buses (1 hr.; ¥25) connect the airport with the **CAAC** ticket office in Lhasa at Niangre Lu 1 (✆ **0891/683-3446;** 9am–12:30pm and 3–6pm). The buses depart from the courtyard behind the office every half-hour. Alternatively, a taxi to the airport should cost ¥150. A new airport road was just completed and should reduce the journey time to 30 to 40 minutes. There are daily flights to Beijing, Chengdu, Chongqing, and Xi'an. Flights from Chengdu connect to most destinations in China. There are also flights to Zhongdian and international flights to Katmandu on Tuesdays, Thursdays, Saturdays, and Sundays. You will need to show your passport to purchase tickets from the CAAC.

The new **rail station** is 10km (6 miles) southwest of town, reached by an equally new stretch of road. Chances are you will be met by the agency through which you booked your trip, but if not taxis charge ¥2 to ¥30, or you can take public bus nos. 2, 16 or 98 into town for ¥1. At the station you'll find ticket offices, left luggage, and shopping opportunities aplenty, if you like paying over the odds for tack. There are direct trains for Beijing (T28; 1:45pm; 43 hr.), Chengdu (T24; 12:45pm; 44 hr.),

RAILWAY on the roof OF THE WORLD

China's (and the world's) highest and most ambitious railway link opened to great fanfare on July 1, 2006. The rail line took 6 years to build and passes through some of the harshest, most inhospitable, and beautiful landscapes on the planet. Most of the 1,142km (709-mile) track lies at an altitude above 4,000m (13,123 ft.), and the highest pass is a staggering 5,072m (16,636 ft.). The line also claims another record: the highest rail tunnel in the world at 4,905m (16,088 ft.). Oxygen is pumped into all carriages and additional supplies are available for those who are really suffering. Aside from these special features, the trains are much like any other you'll travel on in China, albeit more modern (all soft sleeper berths have TVs).

While such altitude may seem like a scary prospect, taking the train actually offers the opportunity to acclimatize more easily than flying directly to Lhasa at 3,600m (11,808 ft.). Critics are quick to point out the environmental and social impact of the rail line, which passes through pristine habitats and is currently bringing at least 3,000 visitors to Lhasa every day (during the summer). Indeed, Tibetan culture in Lhasa is being further diluted day by day, and the TAR's minerals are efficiently being converted into cash, all of which makes visiting the Tibetan world outside of the TAR a more appealing proposition. However, most Han visitors limit themselves to taking the train up to Lhasa and flying out a few days later, leaving the rest of the TAR relatively unaffected (although the rail line is due to reach Shigatse by 2012 and ultimately is planned to stretch all the way to Nepal). If you ask most Tibetans how they feel about the rail line, the answers also include something about the increased wealth brought by tourists, and the ease of travel that it affords, meaning students can return home for the holidays and businessmen can bolster profits by saving on airfares. Also, in spite of all the hoo-ha about the environment, the railway is infinitely preferable to the emissions caused by aircraft. Whatever you think of the rail line, it's here to stay and the trip is one of the most incredible journeys China has to offer.

Chongqing (T224; 11:15am; 46 hr.), Shanghai (T166; 11:25am; 48 hr.), Guangzhou (T266; 12:05pm; 55 hr.), and Xi'an (T166; 33 hr.), all of which pass through Golmud (14 hr.), Xining (23 hr.), and Lanzhou (27 hr.). There's also a specific train for Golmud, Xining, and Lanzhou (K918; 8:20am).

The old **bus station** (© **0891/682-4469**) is at the south end of town, while a new terminal near the university serves similar destinations, although they are both equally obsolete to foreign travelers with the current restrictions on independent travel in the TAR.

GETTING AROUND **Taxis** within town are ¥10 for most journeys. **Buses** (with conductors) charging ¥1 are plentiful. Cycle rickshaws are a fun way to get around and should charge ¥5 for a 10-minute journey.

TOURS & GUIDES Most visitors arrive in Lhasa with a tour pre-arranged, but if you have just booked a Lhasa tour and want to extend your trip out into other parts of the TAR beyond Shigatse, you'll probably have to organize the tour through your original agent. To travel to other parts of the TAR (beyond Lhasa, Sera, Drepung, and Shigatse) you require an Alien Travel Permit (ATP), a tour guide, vehicle, and driver. Restrictions are very tight at the moment (see "Permit Purgatory," p. 757), but even if they relax, they tend to increase around certain dates, particularly the Monlam Festival (sometime mid-Jan to mid-Feb), the Saka Dawa Festival (sometime mid-May to mid-June), and the Dalai Lama's birthday on July 6. If you're planning an extensive trip and have limited time you should organize your tour well before you arrive.

Experienced and recommended operators include **Tibet Lhasa Travel Agency,** located in the Sunlight Hotel at 27 Linju Lu (© **0891/633-7237;** fax 0891/634-8925; www.tibetlhasatravel.com); **Tibet Highland Tours,** who have offices in the Banak Shol Hotel courtyard at Beijing Dong Lu 8, and also just inside the gate of the Shangbala Hotel on Zhang Yiyuan Lu (© **0891/691-2080;** fax 0891/671-5646; www.tibethighlandtours.com); and **Shigatse Travels,** located inside the Yak Hotel (© **0891/633-0489;** fax 0891/633-0482; www.shigatsetravels.com), although they focus on larger groups rather than individual travelers. For off-the-beaten-track trips **Tibet Wind Horse Adventure** (© **0891/683-3009;** www.windhorsetibet.com) offers a range of options, but specializes in white-water rafting tours. Longer tours are best arranged a few months in advance but they also operate half-day and day tours, which can be put together at shorter notice. Their main office is at B32 Shenzheng Huayuan, Sera Lu, but they have a branch on Zang Yiyuan Lu. To explore this high altitude by bicycle, **Grasshopper Adventures** (www.grasshopperadventures.com), run cycling trips from Lhasa to Katmandu, but these are best arranged well ahead of your trip.

If you only have time to visit Lhasa, then the cheapest 5-day trips start from about ¥1,700 including permit and guide but nothing else. Outside of the capital, the most popular trip in the TAR is the 5- to 8-day tour from Lhasa to Zhangmu on the Nepali border. This trip should cost around ¥7,000 to ¥8,000, A more arduous, but incredibly beautiful trip is to Kailash (p. 784), and costs for this 15 to 21 day trip start at ¥17,000. Prices for both tours include a Land Cruiser that will comfortably seat three passengers, four at a push (plus the driver and guide), a guide, and Alien Travel Permits (ATP, plus a Military Permit for Kailash) for all passengers; meals, accommodations and entry fees are extra. If you're looking to share a ride with other passengers, check out the bulletin-board postings at hotels and cafes. Be sure to clearly establish the itinerary stating where you will visit and how long the trip will last; make a deposit and try to negotiate withholding the balance (ideally 25%) until your tour is completed—some travelers have been left stranded. Also be sure to check out the vehicle before you embark on your trip—you may even want to take the car and driver on a test drive on the streets of Lhasa to see how the car performs before agreeing to embark into the wilderness. Once you do arrive at your destination, and if you're happy with the service, tip your guide and driver at least ¥100 per person. Gifts of music cassettes and un-needed winter gear are also highly appreciated.

Those planning mountaineering expeditions must obtain permits from the **Tibetan Mountaineering Association** (✆ **0891/633-3720;** yang_735@yahoo.com.cn; Mon–Fri 9am–1pm and 3:30–6pm), housed in a building immediately north of the Himalaya Hotel. Staff are friendly, but getting permits can be an onerous procedure.

[Fast FACTS] LHASA

Banks, Foreign Exchange & ATMs The main branch of the **Bank of China,** west of the Potala Palace at Linkuo Xi Lu 28, accepts traveler's checks and credit cards at counters 7 and 9. There are two international ATMs here. Hours are weekdays from 9am to 6pm. There are several other branches of the bank throughout town, including one on the northeast side of town, at Najin Lu 188 and another just west of the Banak Shol Hotel on Beijing Dong Lu. Hours are the same for all branches.

Consulates North of the Norbulingka Palace, the **Nepalese Consulate-General** at Luobulinka Bei Lu 13 (✆ **0891/683-0609**) is open weekdays 10am to noon for visas. You'll need a passport photo and ¥280 for a 30-day visa processed in 2 days. Non-Chinese nationals can also arrange visas at the border (Zhangmu) for the same fee.

Internet Access The **Summit Cafe** has branches in the courtyard of the Shangbala Hotel on Zang Yiyuan Lu and another opposite Niuwei on Linkuo Bei Lu and offers comfortable broadband access for ¥16 per hour, or free Wi-Fi if you have your own laptop. Many hotels and guesthouses also offer Internet access, but if you want a genuine Internet cafe, the 24-hr **Yingdayuan Wangba,** next to the Bank of China on Beijing Dong Lu, charges ¥3 per hour, but requires a deposit of ¥10 and they will need to see your passport.

Post Office The main post office is at Beijing Dong Lu 33. Summer hours are from 9am to 8pm; winter hours are from 9:30am to 6:30pm. A counter toward the far left designated INTERNATIONAL BUSINESS is efficient.

Visa Extensions You can't miss the imposing **PSB** on Linkuo Bei Lu (✆ **0891/632-4528**) where visa officers spit out the term "individual traveler" as through it's a disfiguring and contagious affliction. They might offer extensions of up to a week if there's less than 3 days on your visa, but any longer and they'll refer you to a travel agent. Hours are weekdays from 9am to 12:30pm and 3:30 to 6pm.

Exploring Lhasa

Drepung Monastery (Zhebang Si) ★ Founded in 1416 by Tsongkapa's disciple Jamyang Choeje, Drepung was once Tibet's largest and most influential monastery, with over 10,000 monks, a number which now stands at a paltry 700. The seat of the Dalai Lamas before the "Great Fifth" Dalai Lama built the Potala Palace, many of its buildings survived the Cultural Revolution, but the order now pays a price for its prominent role in the pro-independence demonstrations of 1987. On September 27, 1987, about 20 Drepung monks unfurled banners and the Tibetan flag, and marched around the Barkhor before being arrested in front of the TAR Government HQ. This politicization of the monks is remarkable, as they were once loyal to their college first, and country second. Monks at Loseling College fought *against* Tibetan independence after the fall of the Qing. The effects of a program of political indoctrination undertaken in 1996 are still felt. A PSB compound sits below the monastery, and "cadre monks" keep a close eye on day-to-day activities.

A circuit of the monastery begins with **Ganden Podrang (Ganden Palace),** and continues on to **Tsokchen (Assembly Hall), Ngakpa Tratsang (College of Tantric Studies), Jamyang Drubpuk** (Jamyang Choeje's **meditation cave,** attached to the east wall of the Assembly Hall), **Loseling Tratsang (College of Dialectics),** and **Tashi Gomang Tratsang.** The pilgrimage trail continues southeast down to the shadowy and enthralling **Nechung Monastery (Naiqiong Si) ★**, home of the Nechung Oracle, who is consulted by the Dalai Lama on important matters of state. Separate admission to Nechung is ¥10.

To the left (west) of Drepung's Assembly Hall is the **kitchen,** where butter tea is prepared in huge wooden vats. Make much-needed donations to the monastery here. With the passing of the charismatic teacher Gen Lamrim in 1997, Drepung lost a major source of income. This master's lectures once drew devotees from all over the Tibetan world. The first floor of the **Assembly Hall ★★** holds a striking statue of Dalai Lama XIII, magnificently lit by filtered sunshine and pungent yak butter lamps. The tombs of Dalai Lamas II, III and IV are also now on display. Readings of the scriptures are often held at midday; it is hoped that you will be able to enjoy the spectacle of novices tumbling over one another in the race to fetch tea from the kitchen for their elders. Also popular with pilgrims is a chapel to the north of the second floor, which houses a mirror said to cure the facial diseases of those who gaze into it. The most revered image is a 15m-tall (49-ft.) statue of the 8-year-old **Maitreya Buddha,** designed by Tsongkapa and housed in the northwest section of the building, usually viewed from the third floor. You will be offered holy water: Cup your right hand above your left, take a quick sip, and splash the rest on your head.

Note that at the time of writing the monastery was undergoing extensive renovations and only the Assembly Hall was open to visitors. Work should be completed in 2012.

✆ **0891/686-3149.** Admission ¥50. 9am–4:30pm. You'll need to travel with your guide to enter the monastery, but in case this changes bus no. 25 covers the route (10km/6¼ miles; 30 min.; ¥1). Taxis charge ¥20 each way.

Jokhang Temple (Dazhao Si) ★★★ This is Tibet's spiritual heart, and from 8am pilgrims line up to enter the Jokhang, waiting for the rooms to be unlocked, in order that they can rub their foreheads furiously against the sacred images within. From 9:30am a gate to the right of the main entrance admits tourists, giving an opportunity to view the ancient statuary and woodwork, although if you want a chance to explore the interior without the bustle it's worth coming in the afternoon.

Don't miss the image of **Palden Lhamo ★** on the third floor. The fierce protector of both Lhasa and the Dalai Lama, she is said to have murdered her own child to bring her husband and king to his senses and put an end to his endless military campaigns. Note the exquisite **deer and wheel motifs** on the roof. Both symbols allude to Sakyamuni's first sermon, "Turning the Wheel of the Doctrine," delivered in the deer park at Sarnath in Varanasi, India. Sakyamuni was initially reluctant to expound his teachings, believing they would be incomprehensible to most, but the god Brahma intervened. The deer and the wheel hark back to a time when believers respectfully avoided depicting the Buddha. A bodhi tree and a solitary footprint were also common symbols.

The most revered object in Tibet is **Jowo Rinpoche ★★★**, a 1.5m (5-ft.) image of the young Buddha, which originated in India and was brought with Princess Wencheng as dowry. Many credit her with selecting the temple's location according to the principles of geomancy (*feng shui*). Without the bustle of the morning crowd it's also possible to take the time to appreciate the ancient Newari door frames, columns, and finials (7th and 8th c.). Note the more recent *yab-yum* images of sexual union in a chapel to the south. Many mistakenly believe tantric practice has no place in the "reformed" Geluk School, but Tsongkapa simply restated the principle that only advanced practitioners should engage in tantric sex.

✆ **0891/633-6858.** Admission ¥85. 9:30am–4:30pm.

Norbulingka (Luobulinka) Whatever traits the various manifestations of the Dalai Lama share, architectural taste is not one of them. The manicured gardens of the summer residence are pleasant—especially on weekends when locals gather for picnics—but the buildings, added by the VII (who chose the site for its medicinal springs), VIII, XIII, and XIV incarnations, do not sit well together. The most interesting is **Takten Podrang,** commissioned by Dalai Lama XIV in 1954, 5 years before he fled to India. As at the Potala Palace, the lack of luxuries is striking, but the rooms give a distinctly human insight to the Dalai Lama, particularly the grubby bathtub, full of financial offerings. On the second floor is a fascinating **mural ★** depicting the history of Tibet, from the legendary union of a wild ogre with a monkey (an emanation of Avalokitesvara), to the final frame of the young Dalai and Panchen Lamas meeting with Mao Zedong and Zhou Enlai.

✆ **0891/682-6274.** Admission ¥60. 9am–5pm.

Potala Palace (Budala Gong) ★★ Commissioned by Dalai Lama V (17th c.), the Potala was built around the fortress of King Songtsen Gampo, which had stood on **Mount Mapori** for a millennium. "Potala" refers to a mountain in south India, the abode of Tibet's patron deity, Avalokitesvara (Chenresik). Both the ancient kings and the Dalai Lamas are said to be manifestations of this bodhisattva, feminized in the Chinese Buddhist pantheon as Guanyin, the goddess of mercy. A monastery, a palace, and a prison, it symbolizes the fusion of secular and religious power in Tibet. Early Tibetan temples, such as Samye Monastery, followed the Indian practice of modest locations, allowing temples to adhere to a mandala design. The Great Fifth, the last significant Dalai Lama before Dalai Lama XIII, was fond of imposing hilltop locations, making adherence to the mandala pattern impossible. Tibetologist Giuseppe Tucci saw the Potala as an "outgrowth of the rock underlying it, as irregular and whimsical as nature's work," and it was not a simple project. **Podrang Marpo (Red Palace)** was completed under the regent Desi Sangye Gyatso, 15 years after the then–Dalai Lama's death in 1682, and involved over 8,000 workers and artisans.

Visitors can enter the palace via the south or east entrance, and then proceed up the central staircase up to the **Eastern Courtyard (Deyang Shar).** Buildings are denoted numerically. You first reach the **Eastern Apartments** of the Dalai Lama XIV (3). Portraits of Dalai Lamas XIV and XIII once hung above the entrance, but they were removed in 1996. Inside the entrance is a splendid mural of Wutai Shan in northeast China, the earthly Pure Land of Manjusri, a bodhisattva who symbolizes wisdom. The simplicity of the present Dalai Lama's personal chambers, with prayer beads still resting by the bed, is moving, particularly for those who have met His Holiness. You next enter the **Red Palace,** the spiritual center and home to the remains of most of the Dalai Lamas (notable exceptions include Dalai Lama VI, who was fonder of wenches than worship and was eventually chased into exile by the Mongols). The throne room of Dalai Lama VII, **Sasum Lhakang** (6), contains an exquisite silver statue of Avalokitesvara and an inscription on the north wall, dated 1722, wishing that the Chinese emperor would reign for 10,000 years. The Kangxi emperor died in 1722. The most sacred chapel is **Phakpa Lhakang ★** (10), part of the original 7th-century palace and housing a "self-arising" image of Avalokitesvara. Even Chinese visitors are awed. As Tucci observed in the 1950s, "The crowds of pilgrims daily ascending the stairs of the Potala were a tangible proof of devotion. Rich or poor, dignitaries or peasants, they kneeled before each image: faith and ecstasy could be read on their faces. Holding copper pitchers full of clarified butter, they went to feed the temple lamps."

A meditation cave, **Chogyel Drupuk** (17), contains an image of Songtsen Gampo, with his Nepali and Chinese wives; it dates from the 7th or 8th century. The Dalai Lama V's death was kept secret for 12 years; his reliquary stupa is the most magnificent structure in the palace, with over 3,000 kilograms (6,600 lb.) of gold, encrusted in jewels, and disappearing into the darkness of **Serdung Lhakang** (21).

The Potala is firmly entrenched on Lhasa's must-see list, but it's hardly the most stalwart of structures, which has led authorities to limit the number of visitors per day to 2,500. Sounds like a lot, but if you come during one of the major Chinese holidays you'll struggle to get a ticket. Plans to build a museum housing the Potala's greatest treasures below the building and cease visits to the palace itself are as yet unsubstantiated. In the meanwhile in order to further protect the palace, guided visits have been limited to 1-hour from the time that you ascend the wooden staircase by Deyang Shar. Guides can be fined ¥200 if their charges are even a minute late. To get the most from your visit either visit alone, or clock out with the guide and then head back in alone. Note that even if you come alone your guide will need to arrange your tickets the day before.

Warning: Visits to the Potala are best made *after* you are accustomed to the altitude.

Beijing Zhong Lu. ✆ **0891/683-4362.** Admission ¥100. Your guide will need your passport to make a reservation 24 hr. in advance; at the ticket counter you will be assigned a time to return for entry, and you should get there in plenty of time as security checks can take a while. Admission to relics museum and roof additional ¥10 each. 9am–4pm entry.

Sera Monastery (Sela Si) This major Geluk monastery was founded in the early 15th century by Sakya Yeshe, a disciple of Tsongkapa. A pilgrimage circuit of the complex passes the colleges **Sera Me Tratsang, Ngakpa Tratsang,** and **Sera Je Tratsang** before reaching **Tsokchen,** the huge assembly hall (ca. 18th c.), which houses an image of Sakya Yeshe. The path continues up to **Sera Utse,** a hermitage that predates the monastery, a stiff 1½-hour hike up the mountain. Most visitors are drawn to Sera by the lively **debates ★★★** held in the Sera Je Tratsang Courtyard Monday to Friday from 3 to 5pm.

Debates provide an opportunity for monks to demonstrate their scholarship and rise through the ranks. A prodigious body of religious literature must be digested before a monk can become a useful sophist. Visitors usually are struck by the physicality of the debates, with one monk sitting down, biding his time, while the other launches a verbal and physical attack. One monk noted that they were instructed that "the foot must come down so strongly that the door of hell may be broken open; and that the hands must make so great a noise that the voice of knowledge may frighten the devils all the world over."

✆ **0891/638-3639.** Admission ¥50. 9am–5pm. You'll need to travel with your guide to enter the monastery, but in case this changes, bus nos. 16, 17, and 20 run to the monastery. Taxis charge ¥10 each way.

Tibet Museum (Xizang Bowuguan) ★ While not as well-displayed or curated as other new provincial museums in China, the wonderful Tibetan *thangkas,* statuary, masks and jewelry make a visit worthwhile. The museum traces Tibet's history through the ages, starting with pre-history, moving through the dynastic period, reminding visitors at every available opportunity of the inalienable historical links with China. Nowhere is this more evident than the Jade and Pottery exhibition rooms on the third floor, which are by far the best-curated part of the museum: Whilst the pieces on display are undoubtedly exquisite, the fact that they were donated by China to Tibet through the ages is used to justify the current status quo. Insights aside, the highlights of the museum are the well-preserved *thangkas,* the extensive collection of Buddhist statuary, and the operatic masks, all of which are on the second floor. The ancient Tibetan texts, which include scripts penned in gold and silver, and a Tibetan form of short-hand, are also worth seeking out, as are the somewhat gruesome looking medical instruments.

Minzhu Lu. ✆ **0891/683-5244.** Admission Free. ¥20 English audio guide. Tues-Sun 10am–6pm.

Shopping

There are plenty of supermarkets to be found along Beijing Dong Lu, including **Baiyi Chaoshi** opposite the post office and **HY Mart,** a few minutes walk farther east. If you're heading out into the wilds and haven't got the necessary kit, Lhasa has lots of outdoor stores, but don't believe the brand names you'll see in many of these places. For genuine outdoor gear, head for **Toread** at Beijing Zhong Lu 182, opposite HY Mart.

Tibetan art is seeing something of a renaissance and *thangka* shops seem to be all over Lhasa now, although many sell items of questionable quality produced over the border in Kathmandu. If quality and authenticity are important to you, it's worth heading into a shop where you can see the craftsmen at work, painting the tiny details onto the Tibetan scroll that is used for meditation. Prices can range from several dollars to several thousand. The **Ancient Art Reconstruction Company** (✆ **0891/632-2860**) in the building opposite Lhasa Villages Handicrafts (see below) is recommended for *thangkas.* If you're interested to see artisans at work, Lhasa Villages Handicrafts also operates walking tours (¥20–¥40) of the old city which last a couple of hours and take in four to six workshops.

Jatson School (Caiquan Fuli Teshu Xuexiao) ☺ 🎁 By shopping here, you are helping Tibet's handicrafts tradition to survive, and giving poor, orphaned, and disabled children a shot at life. They don't receive a *fen* from the government, so your support is valued. Shopping doesn't have to be a guilty pleasure. The store, tucked away to the right of the entrance, sells traditional Tibetan clothing, paper, incense, mandala *thangkas,* yak-hide boots, dolls, door hangings, and more. Prices are more than fair, and you'll probably want to give more (or you can donate online). The quality of work is astounding, and as nearly everything is made on-site, you can watch how it's done. Store hours are Monday through Saturday from 8:30am to 5:30pm.

Chumi Lu. ✆ **0/139-0891-1214.** www.jatsontibet.org.

Khawachen Carpet and Wool Handicraft Co. Ltd (Kawajian Ditan He Yangmao Gongyipin Youxian Gongsi) The hardy sheep of the Changtang produce wool ideal for carpet making. Unfortunately, most new Tibetan carpets or

Han-inspired rugs use frightening themes or colors. This U.S.-Tibetan joint venture in the west of town gets it right: rich but tasteful shades woven into delightful traditional patterns. (See the designs at www.innerasiarugs.com.) You'll be able to pick them up a lot cheaper here than from the US headquarters or the Lufthansa Center in Beijing. Carpets can be custom made, but you'll need to allow 22 weeks for an average-size carpet. You're free to inspect the entire process from dyeing and drying to weaving and cutting. Unlike Lhasa's main Han-run factory (where 14-hr. shifts are common), conditions here are excellent. Credit cards are accepted, and shipping can be arranged. Hours are Monday to Saturday from 9am to 1pm and 3 to 7pm.

Jinzhu Xi Lu 102. ✆ **0891/686-3257.**

Lhasa Villages Handicrafts ★ The original name Dropenling (which means "giving back for the betterment of all mankind" in Tibetan) sounded better, but this store, tucked away near the Muslim quarter, is still a gem, giving all its profits back to the Tibetan artisans who make the handicrafts. The aim of the store, and wider project, is to enable Tibetan artisans to compete with the Nepalese, whose goods have flooded Tibetan markets in recent years. The emphasis here though, is on quality—from fine-woven rugs to handbags and jewelry. Rugs start from ¥800 up to ¥1,800, plus shipping, but make a cozy addition to any home. The store's goods have inspired pirates to make knockoffs for sale on the pilgrim's circuit of Jokhang, but they aren't of the same quality.

Chak Tsal Gang Lu. 11 (about a 10-min. walk from Jokhang Monastery, near Lhasa Mosque. Look for the sign off the Barkhor near Makye Amye and then follow the lane to the mosque). ✆ **0891/636-0558.** www.tibetcraft.com. AE, DC, MC, V. 9:30am–8pm.

Where to Stay

Lhasa's high-end hotel scene has heated up immeasurably with the opening of the St. Regis, and a Shangri-La is also on the way. The Lhasa Hotel was undergoing extensive renovations at the time of writing, but looks set to re-open in grand style by 2012. More and more boutique options are also opening their doors, including a new venture from the Red Capital group south of House of Shambhala (see below). Decent choices also exist for those on a budget, many of which are to be found in the narrow lanes of the old city. From December to March, Lhasa sees very few tourists, and most hoteliers halve their prices.

VERY EXPENSIVE

Four Points Sheraton Previously Lhasa's most luxurious accommodation (now superseded by its Starwood partner around the corner, the St. Regis) the Four Points remains a solid, if anodyne option. Its location in the far south of town is hardly convenient and finding the low-key entrance to the hotel is something of a challenge, and once inside the subtlety continues. Rooms are light and modern and feature blond-wood furniture and attractive bathrooms with showers.

Bo Linka Lu 10. www.fourpoints.com/lhasa. ✆ **0891/634-8888.** 102 units. ¥1,080 standard room; from ¥3,188 suite. 50% discount in winter. AE, DC, MC, V. **Amenities:** Restaurant. *In room:* A/C, satellite TV, fridge, hair dryer, Internet, minibar.

St. Regis (Ruiji Dujia Jiudian) ★★ A huge new development taking up almost a whole city block, the St. Regis somehow manages to gracefully combine modern luxury with Tibetan styling. Electric buggies ferry guests from the imposing main entrance along bamboo-lined walkways to the various villa blocks. Rooms are tastefully understated and feature thick chocolate carpets, Tibetan photo collections, huge beds, and enormous bathrooms. Suites are super-sized and some have views of the Potala. The serene hotel spa has a gold tinted pool and offers excellent (but pricey) massage.

Jiangsu Lu 22. www.stregis.com/lhasaresort. ✆ **0891/680-8888.** 162 units. ¥2,300 standard room; from ¥6,274 suite. Discount available in winter. AE, DC, MC, V. **Amenities:** 3 restaurants; bar; butler service; spa; travel agency. *In room:* A/C, satellite TV, DVD player, CD player with MP3 dock, fridge, hair dryer, Internet, minibar.

EXPENSIVE

House of Shambhala (Xiangbala Fu) ★★ Brainchild of author, filmmaker, and boutique hotelier Laurence Brahm, this excellent addition to the Red Capital rostrum offers you the opportunity to stay inside a stunningly restored Tibetan courtyard house. House of Shambhala's unmarked heavy wooden door is tricky to find, but this is unquestionably the most stylish address in Lhasa. The three grades of room (small, medium, and large) all feature the same bold colors, meticulous attention to detail, and antique Tibetan furnishings. Bathrooms are set in solid stone and have reliable hot water showers and locally produced toiletries. If you have the cash, splurge on suite 204, with its fine beam carving, a veiled bed platform, and at least 8 cushions. The rooftop restaurant enjoys good views and the food is pretty decent. The spa next door is relaxation defined. A 10-minute walk south of here the Red Capital group has opened another boutique property, **Shambhala Palace (Xiangbala Gong) ★**, with equally as attractive rooms.

Jiri Er Xiang 7. www.shambhalaserai.com. ✆ **0891/632-6533.** 9 units in House of Shambhala, 18 rooms in Palace of Shambhala. ¥675–¥1,015 small to large standard room. Up to 50% discount at Palace of Shambhala. AE, DC, MC, V. **Amenities:** Restaurant; bar; health club; room service; spa. *In room:* Hair dryer, heater, Internet (Wi-Fi at House of Shambhala).

MODERATE

Dhod Gu Hotel ★ A Nepalese-owned venture, this hotel gets rave reviews from American tourists. It's conveniently located in the Tibetan quarter, the staff speaks English, and the rooms are comfortable. Furnished with a sensory overload of tasteful Tibetan decorations, each room is uniquely designed, and some have views of the Potala (add ¥80), although lighting could be better. Bathrooms, though a bit worn, are squeaky-clean.

Xialasu Lu 19. www.dhodgu-hotel.com. ✆ **0891/632-2555.** Fax 0891/632-3555. 63 units. ¥450 standard room. 20% discount. AE, DC, MC, V. **Amenities:** 2 restaurants; bakery; doctor on call; forex. *In room:* A/C, TV.

Kyichu Hotel (Jiqu Fandian) ★ Located in the Tibetan quarter, the Kyichu combines Western comfort with a welcoming Tibetan atmosphere. Rooms in the south wing opened in 2001; overlooking the lawn cafe, these bright midsize rooms have clean wooden floors, simple furnishings, and spotless bathrooms with deep tubs. Downsides are that the solar-heated hot water can be unreliable. The restaurant on the first floor prepares a decent buffet breakfast for ¥30.

Beijing Dong Lu 149. www.kyichuhotel.com. ✆ **0891/633-1347.** Fax 0891/633-5728. 52 units (22 with shower only). ¥320 standard room. AE, DC, MC, V. **Amenities:** Restaurant; concierge. *In room:* TV, Internet.

Yak Hotel (Yake Binguan) Popular with tour groups and individual travelers, this hotel is several notches up from some of the decrepit guesthouses that line Beijing Dong Lu, but then so are the prices. Standard rooms are comfortable and tasteful, but the smaller standard B rooms offer the best deal, and still feature Tibetan decor. The Yak is considered a hub for tourists to gather and share information. Next door is the ever-popular Dunya restaurant and Shigatse Travels is also on the property. Reserve ahead of time.

Beijing Dong Lu 100. ✆ **0891/632-3496.** 129 units. ¥650 standard room; ¥480 standard A room; ¥380 standard B room; ¥200 common room. Discounts of 20-40%. No credit cards. **Amenities:** Restaurant; travel agent. *In room:* A/C, TV, Internet (¥5 per hour).

INEXPENSIVE

Oh Dan Guesthouse (Oudan Binguan) Tucked away on a street that runs past Ramonche Monastery just north of Beijing Dong Lu, this guesthouse offers clean and fresh rooms and bathrooms with touches of Tibetan decor. Rooms at the back are quieter. It's near the Barkhor, but its location on a typical Tibetan street is so far devoid of the trappings of backpacker development. New ownership from Kham seems to be doing ok, but the rooftop and its stunning view of the Potala Palace remains undeveloped. Farther up the street the same owners have a budget property with very basic but clean dorms housed in a beautiful traditional style exterior.

Xiaozhao Si Lu 15. ✆ **0891/634-4999.** 28 units. ¥368 standard room; ¥258 standard room without bathroom. Up to 60% discount. No credit cards. **Amenities:** Restaurant; travel agent. *In room:* TV.

Where to Eat

Lhasa's dining options are ever more diverse and present everything from excellent Tibetan to decent Chinese and Western fare. If you can't face any of the above at 3,600m (11,808 ft.), there are branches of the Chinese burger joint **Dicos,** one of which is opposite the Jokhang. For a fine cup of coffee or *chai* and a good cake selection while you surf the Net, **The Summit Café** (8am–10pm) has branches in the courtyard of the **Shambhala Hotel ★** on Zang Yiyuan Lu and another opposite Niuwei on Linkuo Bei Lu. Most of the places listed below have English menus.

Alu Cang Restaurant (A'luocang Canting) ★ TIBETAN On the western edge of the Tibetan quarter, this restaurant is a longtime favorite with locals, who appreciate its unpretentious style and hearty cuisine. The second floor is packed at most hours. The English menu is unreliable, with beef and lamb often translated as yak. Specialties include radish with yak meat (lamb) and fried mutton spareribs. The simple curry rice (¥8) is an excellent choice for those on the run.

Duosenge Lu 21–32. ✆ **0891/633-8826.** Meal for 2 ¥30–¥70. No credit cards. 9am–11pm.

Dunya Restaurant and Bar ★ WESTERN Located on the east side of the Yak Hotel, Dunya serves decent if uninspired Western and Tibetan cuisine enhanced by a lively atmosphere replete with happily singing staff. The menu offers pizza, pasta, burgers and a range of Asian dishes, from Indonesian noodles to vegetable dumplings. The convivial bar and terrace upstairs, open late, is a favorite with Lhasa's expat community, and the kitchen is supposedly one of the cleanest in town.

Beijing Dong Lu 100. ✆ **0891/633-3374.** www.dunyarestaurant.com. Reservations recommended. English menu. Main courses ¥25–¥55. No credit cards. Apr–Oct 8am–10:30pm; bar noon–midnight.

Ganglamedo TIBETAN/WESTERN This clean, cozy restaurant has a limited range of Western and Tibetan dishes, along with some innovative dishes such as Tintinnabulation which consists of deep fried meat balls with yoghurt and potato chunks. There's also a good choice of pricey coffees (¥20–¥48) and imported beers and wines (¥135–¥560 per bottle). Staff is friendly and walls are adorned with local paintings.

Beijing Dong Lu 127. ✆ **0891/633-3657.** www.ganglamedo.com. Meal for 2 ¥60–¥100+. No credit cards. 11am–midnight.

Hao Wai Xuan ★ SICHUAN Most of Lhasa's best Chinese restaurants are located in the gaudy bathroom-tiled part of town, but why make the effort when you can get delicious Sichuanese food right next to Barkhor Square? Popular with Tibetan pilgrims and backpackers, this unassuming joint with plastic chairs and grubby tables serves spicy, juicy dumplings in soup and a good twice-cooked pork. The steamed buns with pork *(baozi)* deserve a special mention.

Zang Yiyuan Lu 9. ✆ **0891/671-1719.** English menu. Meal for 2 ¥30–¥80. No credit cards. 7am–11pm.

Holy Land Vegetarian Restaurant ★★ VEGETARIAN/SICHUAN This simple restaurant may be owned by a local monk, but the culinary delights within are far from frugal and attract pilgrims and locals alike. Waitresses greet you with a light tea and a watermelon slice, and then the gluttony begins. Fake meats tend to creep some people out, but the wheat gluten and tofu replicas of chicken, sausage, and even intestines, are more delicious than the real thing. Try the *gongbao jiding* (kung pao chicken), *qingchao maodou* (beans with soy beef), and *songren yumi* (pine nuts, carrots, and sweet corn). If you prefer less spicy dishes, let the kitchen know. The surprising array of juice combinations on offer includes kiwi and orange.

Linkuo Bei Lu Waibanshang Pingfang 10. ✆ **0891/636-3851.** Meal for 2 ¥60–¥80. No credit cards. 9am–10pm.

Makye Ame (Maji A'mi) ★ NEPALI/TIBETAN On the southeast corner of the Barkhor circuit stands Lhasa's most enchanting eatery, Makye Ame, which can be translated as Holy Mother. This may be the first Tibetan chain restaurant—they have two outlets in Beijing and another in Kunming. If it's chilly, take a seat on the second floor, with its comfy sofas and relaxing Tibetan folk music. On a sunny day, soak up the spectacle of the *kora* (circuit) from the third-floor balcony. There's a shiny new menu, but the trusted dishes are the same and along with meaty favorites such as mutton sausages and Amdo Yak momos, there are many excellent vegetarian choices; try the vegetable curry set with chapati.

Bajiao Jie Dongnan Jiao. ✆ **0891/632-8608.** English menu. Main courses ¥18–¥93. No credit cards. 9:30am–12:30am.

Snowland Restaurant ★ INTERNATIONAL/TIBETAN Tibetan restaurant meets New York diner seems an unlikely combo, but Snowland manages to feel just like that and is frequented by Tibetan elites and international travelers alike. The variety of options, from Japanese teriyaki to Indian curries, is at least decent if not pretty good. The yak pepper steak, croquettelike potato momos, nan, dumplings, and crêpes suzette are all recommended.

Zang Yiyuan Lu (near Barkhor Sq.). ✆ **0891/633-7323.** English menu. Meal for 2 ¥100. No credit cards. 9am–11pm.

Lhasa After Dark

The **theater** at the Himalaya Hotel on Linkou Dong Lu has nightly performances at 6:30pm by the acclaimed Tibet Shol Opera Troupe. Tickets cost ¥180 (including dinner) and performances are viewed from low seats in this ornately decorated and intimate theater. Many hotels and travel agencies can arrange tickets, or you can call ✆ **0891/632-1111.**

Niuwei at Linkou Bei Lu 13 (**© 0891/655-8383**) remains one of the hottest *nangma* (Tibetan nightclub) in town. Join Tibetans downing beers and groove to Tibetan singers on a stage with a picture backdrop of the Potala Palace. Get here by 10pm to ensure good seats; to find Niuwei head through the red arch off Linkou Bei Lu and enter through the doors beneath the Budweiser sign. Another new *nangma* to try is **Kunga Amala Nangma** on the 4th floor at Yutuo Lu 30, which is owned by Tibetan pop star Kunga Phuntsok. For more of a regular drink, new bars are springing up all over Lhasa, but the best ones are to be found in the Tibetan quarter. The **Dunya** restaurant and bar (see above; open until midnight) is a hub for expats, and the surrounding streets hold plenty of smaller, more intimate bars.

Around Lhasa

Chimpu Caves (Qingpu Shandong) The Chimpu retreat caves gave monks relief from constant study, but were also crucial in maintaining Buddhist traditions during periods of persecution, and in transmitting teachings before formal monasteries were established. A warren of caves set in a lush U-shaped valley, Chimpu has some of the most sacred pilgrimage destinations in Tibet, including the cave where Guru Rinpoche first instructed his Tibetan disciples. Below is **Guruta Rock,** where Guru Rinpoche displayed his yogic prowess by leaving an enormous footprint. Above and to the left is the **meditation cave of Vairocana,** where the master translator dwelt for 12 years, eating the naked rock and thus solving the twin dilemmas of food and shelter. Grains and beans are appreciated as gifts by less-gifted retreatants; to understand why, imagine subsisting on *tsampa* for a year.

Northeast of Samye Monastery (which you'll need an ATP to get to). Free admission. The walk takes 4 hr.

Ganden Monastery (Gandan Si) Shelled by the Chinese army during the peaceful liberation of Tibet and further damaged during the Cultural Revolution, the most significant monastery of the **Geluk School** is slowly undergoing a revival, and has been extensively renovated in recent years. The importance of the monastery means it is a major pilgrimage center, and police observe the scene from a new station at the start of the *lingkhor.*

Dramatically perched on a mountain east of Lhasa, to the south of the Kyi Chu, Ganden was built in 1409 by **Tsongkapa.** Drawing on support from monks of the older schools, as well as laypeople, the school rapidly expanded, with disciples opening Drepung and Sera monasteries in 1416 and 1419 respectively. Mongol support during the 17th century eventually assured their status as the preeminent school of Tibetan Buddhism, and more than 3,000 monks lived here prior to 1950.

The **Meditation Hall (Ngachokhang) ★**, to the right (east) of the path beyond the bus stop, is atmospheric. Tsongkapa instructed his first disciples here. Chanting and the creation of *torma* (butter sculptures) take place throughout the day. Inside, to the left, is one of several dark and gruesome protector deity shrines that are off-limits to women. Other notable buildings are the **Assembly Hall,** behind and to the right of a prominent white chorten, where a jolly monk is likely to thwack you on the head with the shoes and hat of Tsongkapa. On the opposite side of a courtyard is a printing house, and above it stands **Tsongkapa's Reliquary (Serdung Lhakang),** which was devastated during the Cultural Revolution. Tsongkapa's tooth remains. Pilgrims waste little time in undertaking a spectacular ***lingkhor*** **(pilgrimage**

circuit) ★★. Allow at least an hour—you are above 4,000m (13,120 ft.). For the fit and acclimatized, the peak to the west offers spectacular views of the lush surrounding countryside.

✆ **0891/614-2077.** Admission ¥45. You'll need to travel with your guide to enter the monastery, but in case this changes there are buses for Ganden from west of Barkhor Sq. at 6:30am and 7am (45km/28 miles; 2 hr.; ¥25 round-trip). Buses return at 2pm.

Samye Monastery (Sangye Si) ★★ About 39km (24 miles) west of Tsetang, on the northern banks of the **Yarlung Tsangpo (Brahmaputra River),** stands Tibet's first monastery (late 8th c.), famous for its striking mandala design and as the site of the "Great Debate" (792–94) between the Indian Mahayanists and Chan (Japanese: Zen) Buddhists from China. This intriguing and protracted religious debate, held in the **Western Temple (Jampa Ling),** ended in victory for the Mahayanists. A predictable result, as Tibet was at war with China on several fronts. Chinese records claim that they won the theological battle, but the numerous Chinese monks and translators were nonetheless expelled from Tibet, and Mahayanist orthodoxy was established. Although Samye has been razed several times, the mandala symmetry is intact. The main temple, **Samye Utse,** symbolizes Mount Meru, the center of the universe, surrounded by the four temples of the continents, the eight temples of each subcontinent, and the sun (south, ruined) and moon (north) temples. The best view is from **Hepo-Ri** to the east of Samye, where Padmasambhava (Guru Rinpoche) is said to have subdued the local demons, making the site safe for construction. The secular support of King Trisong Detsen, who proclaimed Buddhism the state religion in 779, was perhaps more crucial.

Samye Utse demonstrates the classic principles of Tibetan architecture. A solid barnlike first floor tapers to refined and intricate upper tiers. To the left of the entrance is an original 5m-tall (16-ft.) obelisk that proclaims Buddhism to be the state religion and urges future generations to obey Buddhist law and support the temple. Many of the murals on the first and second floors are original.

Basic dorm beds (¥35) and twins (¥150) are available at the **Samye Monastery Guesthouse** (**✆ 0891/736-2761**) and the **East Friendship Hotel** (¥25 dorm bed). English menus and adequate fare are offered at both.

Admission ¥45. You'll need an ATP and to travel with your guide to enter the monastery. 8am–5:30pm

A Trip to a Nearby Lake

Namtso Lake ★ The crystal-blue waters surrounded by snowcapped mountains are stunning and make a nice change from the (relatively) bustling pace of Lhasa, although the lake's popularity has recently led to something of a building spree. You can visit Namtso as a day trip through most agents in town for around ¥150, or you can give the lake its due and stay overnight. Better still, rent a Land Cruiser for a night or two (¥1,500–¥2,000). Jeeps can take up to four travelers. It's a 4- or 5-hour journey from Lhasa, and at an altitude of 4,700m (15,416 ft.), you should definitely acclimatize in Lhasa for a few days before attempting the journey here. Admission to the lake is ¥80; save your ticket, it may be checked during your stay.

You can stay in mock nomad tents or metal cabins at the lake for around ¥120 per room. Basic meals are available for around ¥25 at most of the accommodation options.

SHIGATSE (RIKAZE; 日喀则)

278km (172 miles) W of Lhasa, 91km (56 miles) NW of Gyantse. Altitude: 3,900m (12,792 ft.)

Set to the south of the confluence of the Brahmaputra River and the Nyang Chu, the second-largest town in Tibet is considerably smaller than Lhasa, its ancient rival for political power. For a period between the 16th and 17th centuries, **Shigatse** was the capital of Tibet, and even after the capital shifted to Lhasa, it maintained influence both as the center of the **Tsang region** and as the home of the **Panchen Lama,** who traditionally resides in **Tashilhunpo Monastery.** Chinese-style development has taken over much of the town, and this will only increase when the train line reaches here in 2012, but the area around the monastery still bustles with pilgrims. ***Note:*** For Chinese translations of selected establishments listed in this section, turn to chapter 16.

Essentials

GETTING THERE At the time of writing a Tibet Travel Permit and a guide, vehicle, and driver were required for travel to anywhere in the TAR (see "Permit Purgatory," p. 757), Shigatse included. Landcruisers used to make the journey to Lhasa in around 3 hours, but since a bus crash in 2006 which killed 26 tourists on this road, police speed checkpoints mean that the journey now takes 5 hours. Destinations beyond Shigatse require an ATP, which guides can arrange here or in Lhasa. Foreigners are unable to travel on local buses, but in case the situation changes the **bus station** is on Shanghai Lu (✆ **0892/882-2903**), near the junction with Zhufeng Lu.

[Fast FACTS] SHIGATSE

Banks, Foreign Exchange & ATMs Cash and traveler's checks may be changed at the **Bank of China,** on Zhufeng Lu, by the intersection with Shandong Lu. Hours are weekdays 9:30am to 6pm and weekends 10:30am to 4:30pm and there are 24-hourATMs here.

Internet Access 24-hr. **Xinkong Wangba** is opposite the Shigatse Hotel on Shanghai Zhong Lu, and charges ¥3 to ¥5 per hour.

Post Office The main post office is at Zhufeng Xi Lu 12 (summer 9:30am–6:30pm and winter 10am–6:30pm).

Visa Extensions The **PSB** on Qingdao Lu (✆ **0892/882-2056**) is open from 9:30am–12:30pm and 3:30–6:30pm summer and 10am–1pm and 3:30–6:30pm winter. This is also where your guide will have to go to arrange your Alien Travel Permit.

Exploring Shigatse

When Tibetologist Giuseppe Tucci visited, he found the ***dzong*** (fortress) in the north of town (a model for the Potala) to be "huge and dreary," but he needn't have worried. A few years later, PLA artillery did a thorough job. The government then waited until the completion of the railway to make amends and reconstruct the *dzong*. As yet, there's nothing inside.

Tashilhunpo Monastery (Zhashilunbu Si) ★ This vast monastery of the **Geluk School** was established by the first Dalai Lama in 1447. The monastery gained standing when Panchen Lama IV, head abbot of Tashilhunpo and teacher of

WHERE IS THE panchen lama?

In 1995, the world was stunned to learn that China's Marxist leaders were authorities on Tibetan Buddhism. Shortly after the Panchen Lama's death in 1989, then-premier Li Peng declared that "outsiders" would not be allowed "to meddle with the selection process." It was clear Beijing wanted to minimize the Dalai Lama's role in the selection of the child who will eventually become the teacher of the next Dalai Lama. The list of candidates was leaked to Dharamsala and the Dalai Lama announced his choice in May, catching the Chinese authorities by surprise. Predictably, the 6-year-old candidate disappeared a month later and has not been seen since. Gyaltsen Norbu, the "official" Panchen Lama XI, was chosen in a clandestine ceremony held in the **Jokhang** in November 1995, and recently made his first public appearance at **Tashilhunpo Monastery.** Tibet's religious leaders, with a few brave exceptions, recognize Gyaltsen as the Panchen Lama. But Beijing wasn't the only side playing politics with a young boy's life. As one of the few levelheaded commentators on this tragedy noted, "The two protagonists in the dispute were clearly swayed by their eagerness to use the issue to gain maximum propaganda value." Norbu's public appearance at the 2006 World Buddhist Forum in Hangzhou was intended to cement the puppet Panchen's status, and his short speech (to an international audience) focused on the need for ethnic Chinese unity and patriotism. Neither the Dalai Lama nor the Karmapa Lama was invited to the forum. In March 2009 Norbu attended a government symposium to celebrate 50 years since Tibetan "liberation." The location of the real Panchen Lama remains a mystery.

Dalai Lama V, was accepted as the personification of Amitabha Buddha, the Buddha of Longevity, thus becoming the "number-two" lama in Tibet. The Mongols, Han, and British have exploited this division to good effect. Due to the size of the complex, start early in the morning, as all the temples are locked at midday.

The pilgrimage circuit begins at **Jamkhang Chenmo,** at the west end of the complex, which houses a massive 26m (85-ft.) Maitreya (ca. 1914), a mass of gold around a wood and metal core. It was built by hand; around 900 artisans dedicated 4 years of their lives to it. But from an artistic perspective, Tashilhunpo is mediocre. As Tucci noted, "Everything was new and garish here. The collected composure of the primitives had been succeeded by baroque pomposity." Some composure remains in the gorgeous murals of Tsongkapa and his disciples that surround the reliquary stupa of Panchen Lama IV **(Kundung Lhakhang),** in the narrow cobblestone paths, and in the Assembly Hall, erected around an ancient sky-burial slab. The adjacent courtyard, with its striking flagpole, is the heart of the temple and the focus of religious dances. Admission ¥55. 9am–noon and 3:30–6:30pm.

Shopping

Shigatse bazaar stands in the shadow of the newly reconstructed *dzong,* and aside from catering to the tourists, it has changed little. Khampa and Hui vendors hawk large knives, wooden tea bowls, prayer wheels, "bronze" statues, "ancient" coins, Tibetan medicine, incense from Calcutta, and cowboy hats and boots. A good selection of handmade carpets can be found at **Gang-Gyen Carpet Factory** on Zhufeng Lu near the intersection with Buxing Jie (✆ **0892/882-6192;** 9am–7pm). Proceeds go to local Tibetan communities and monks. The best-stocked supermarkets are **Sifang Chaoshi** (9:30am–10:30pm), and **Shanghai Square Supermarket** (9am–11pm), beneath the Dicos, both on Zhufeng Lu. For outdoors gear, head for **Toread** (9:30am–9:30pm) near the Shigatse Hotel on Shanghai Lu.

Where to Stay

Manasarovar Hotel (Shenhu Jiudian) ★ Owned by the same group as the Yak Hotel in Lhasa, the Manasarovar is tidy and well run. Staff is foreigner-friendly but more competent at dealing with groups than individuals. The slightly worn rooms are spacious and comfortably furnished and have big bathrooms, but that still doesn't make them worth the asking price.

Qingdao Dong Lu 20. www.hotelmanasarovartibet.com. ✆ **0892/883-2085.** Fax 0892/882-8111. 74 units. ¥1,080 standard room. Up to 70% discount. No credit cards. **Amenities:** 2 restaurants; cafe; concierge. *In room:* A/C, TV, Internet.

Shigatse Hotel (Shigatse Fandian) ★ Following renovations, Shigatse's first hotel remains a contender for the best place in town and offers friendly staff, good facilities, and a decent choice of rooms. Standard rooms are bright and clean, but the Tibetan rooms have the same facilities, cost the same, and are decorated with *thangkas,* Tibetan furniture, and attractive photographs, which makes them preferable.

Shanghai Zhong Lu 13. ✆ **0892/880-0336.** Fax 0892/882-1900. 143 units. ¥580 standard and Tibetan room; ¥1,880 suite. 30% discount. No credit cards. **Amenities:** 2 restaurants, bar. *In room:* TV, fridge, Internet.

Tenzin Hotel (Dan Zeng Binguan) ★ Guides don't like this place and will try and discourage you from staying here, but if you're on a budget this is one of the best deals in town. Standard rooms are nicely decorated with Tibetan furnishings, but bizarrely all of the pictures are askew. The bathrooms are clean and hot water is reliable. Common rooms without bathrooms and dorms are nothing special but fine for the money.

Bang Jia Ling 8. ✆ **0892/882-2018.** 40 units. ¥280 standard room with bathroom; ¥180 shared room without bathroom; ¥35 dorm bed. Up to 45% discount on rooms (not dorms). No credit cards. *In room:* TV.

Wuzi Dajiudian (Wutse Hotel) Located in a quiet Tibetan residential area to the southeast, this three-star hotel, run by the owners of the Wutse Hotel in Gyantse, has decent and spacious rooms. The bathrooms are small but fine, although the hot water takes a while to warm up. The competent, English-speaking staff works long hours.

Heilongjiang Zhong Lu. ✆ **0892/883-8999.** 60 units. ¥650 standard room. Up to 70% discount. No credit cards. **Amenities:** Restaurant; concierge. *In room:* TV, minibar.

Where to Eat

Laoyou Leyuan (Old Friend Hotel) ★ NOODLES Near the arch which marks the start of the pedestrian street *(buxing jie)* that leads to the Tashilhunpo, this unassuming noodle shop run by a family from Sichuan province might be a bit hard to spot, but it's worth the effort. With little decor to speak of—just plastic blue-and-white chairs and tables that are fixed to the ground—and no menu, there's little to look at other than the food. But that seems to suit the diners just fine—just specify what you'd like: *mian tiao* (noodles with pork), *baozi* (steamed buns with pork), or *jiaozi* (dumplings in soup). Noodles and dumplings can be prepared spicy *(la)* or not *(bula)*, with vinegar *(cu)* or without *(buyao cu)*.

Buxing Jie. ✆ **0892/851-0531.** Meal for 2 ¥20. No credit cards. 9am–9:30pm.

Songtsen Tibetan Restaurant TIBETAN/NEPALI/WESTERN This is a popular spot for travelers, so you're likely to end up here. The traditional decor is cozy and the food is fine, but it's nothing to write home about. There's an extensive bar which is popular in the evenings.

Buxing Jie. ✆ **0892/883-2469.** Meal for 2 ¥60–¥90. No credit cards. 8:30am–10pm.

Tashi Restaurant (Zhaxi Zhangcan) NEPALI/WESTERN Another friendly branch of this deservedly popular Nepali chain, Tashi serves up the same assortment of sandwiches, *momos,* curries, and lassis as its counterparts in Lhasa and Gyantse.

Buxing Jie. Meal for 2 from ¥60. No credit cards. 8am–10pm.

Yak Head Restaurant (Niutou Zangcan) TIBETAN You'd think a picture menu would help in most restaurants, but in this restaurant's case, it does more to hinder the ordering process with its obscenely blurry photos tucked neatly into an album. But no worries, a plucky waitress will do her best to explain what each photo is in broken English. Try the potato dumplings, the *renshenguo* (fried ginseng), or if you're feeling particularly adventurous, the goat head for a mere ¥35. The ambience can't be beat—a series of comfy rooms which feel like living rooms for the monks, pilgrims, and youths who hang out and watch TV at all hours of the day.

Buxing Jie. ✆ **0892/883-7186.** Picture menu. Meal for 2 ¥30–¥60. No credit cards. 12:30pm–midnight.

Shigatse After Dark

If you haven't had a chance to hit a *nangma* yet in Tibet, Shigatse gives you an opportunity with **Huaiyu Minzu Biaoyi Zhongxin,** on Shanghai Lu just south of Zhufeng Lu. A lively performance with dancers dressed in yak costumes leaping on stage to techno-Tibetan music begins at 11pm and continues to the small hours.

GYANTSE (JIANGZI; 酱孜) ★★★

67km (42 miles) SE of Shigatse, 255km (158 miles) SW of Lhasa. Altitude: 4,040m (13,255 ft.)

Presided over by the spectacular **Gyantse Dzong,** and once the third-largest town in Tibet, **Gyantse** ★★ is the only substantial settlement in the TAR to retain its vernacular architecture of sturdy two- and three-story farmhouses. Offering a rare and beautiful glimpse of Tibetan rural life, Gyantse should not be missed by any visitor to the TAR. Historically, it was a trading town for goods from Nepal, Sikkim, and Bhutan, and the closure of the border at Dromo (Yadong) has saved Gyantse from the ravages of development and Han colonization. Many of Tibet's current generation of political leaders hail from Gyantse.

Essentials

GETTING THERE At the time of writing, the only way for foreigners to get to Gyantse was in a private vehicle with a guide. The journey from Lhasa via stunning **Yam Drok Lake** (4488m/14,724ft.) takes about 6 hours. Just after the lake you can break for a meal in the small town of Namgartse. Getting to and from Shigatse, the journey is 2 hours.

[Fast FACTS] GYANTSE

Banks, Foreign Exchange & ATMs None available.

Internet Access The fastest connection is at the 24-hr. Damuzhi Wangba, just across the road and east a little from the Gyantse Hotel. They charge ¥8 per hour.

Post Office The main post office (9:30am–noon and 3:30–6pm) is on Weiguo Lu, a few minutes walk east from the intersection with Yingxiong Lu.

Exploring Gyantse

Gyantse Dzong (Jiangzi Zong Shan) ★ Towering above the settlement, this awesome fortress (ca. 13th c.) immediately catches your eye as you approach Gyantse. It's a short, steep hike up, but views of Pelkhor Choede, the ancient alleyways, and the jagged surrounding peaks are breathtaking. The meager contents of the "museum" have now dwindled to an alarming collection of mannequins, and, unless you ask to see the dusty old caption boards hidden in the back, U.K. visitors are spared most of the anti-British sentiments formerly expressed in the museum; the only one remaining on show states "the place of jump in cliff against that British hero martyrs."

Admission ¥30. 9am–5pm.

Pelkhor Choede (Baiju Si) Although these days it is home to only 80 monks, the once-mighty temple complex of Gyantse (ca. 1418) still houses three different orders under the one roof. Following recent renovations the monastery stands resplendent and all shrines are open to visitors, although the requirement to pay a new photography charge for each different shrine is a little frustrating.

The nine-story **Kumbum ★★★**, the largest chorten in Tibet, towers to a height of 42m (140 ft.). The first five floors are four-sided, while the upper floors are circular, forming a huge three-dimensional mandala. Kumbum means "the hundred thousand images," and while the actual number of Buddhist images is around one-third of that estimate, even the most dedicated pilgrim won't have time to properly inspect all the chapels. They house the finest art preserved in Tibet. Vibrant color and a lively, naturalistic style characterize the murals, while the broad faces of the statues point to Chinese influence. The mandalas of the upper levels are exquisite. Bring a flashlight. To the right (east) is the bizarre **Neten Lhakhang,** decorated in Chinese style with leaping tigers and dragons, floating clouds, and pagodas, representing Manjusri's Pure Land in Wutai Shan.

Admission ¥40. Photography ¥10 per shrine. 9am–6pm.

Shopping

Gyantse is famous for its carpets and there are plenty of shops around town, although you'll have to sift through hundreds of garish designs to find anything tasteful. If you're in need of more warm weather apparel then **Outside Outdoor Sports** on the eastern side of Yingxiong Lu has a decent selection of genuine and not-so-genuine gear. To stock up on snacks there's a small supermarket, **Baccarat Shopping Mall,** on Shanghai Xi Lu, just west of the intersection with Yingxiong Lu.

Where to Stay

Gyantse Hotel (Jiangzi Fandian) ★ It's not saying too much, but this hotel offers Gyantse's best accommodations. There are bland, conventional rooms or

Tibetan twins outfitted with colorful furniture and *thangkas* on the walls—opt for the latter. Bathrooms in either style are shiny and welcoming and include amenities like a hair dryer and a magnifying mirror, which you won't find elsewhere in town.

Shanghai Dong Lu 2. ✆ **0892/817-2222.** Fax 0892/817-2366. 146 units. ¥360 standard or Tibetan-style room. 25% discounts possible. No credit cards. **Amenities:** 2 restaurants; cafe; bike rental. *In room:* Satellite TV, hair dryer.

Jian Zang Fandian Just south of the Wutse Hotel, this small, orderly guesthouse was opened in 2001 by a genial Tibetan doctor, Jian Zang. Recent extensions have brought extra rooms which are clean and comfortable, if obviously pre-fab. And, as the doctor is keen to stress, the beds are bigger than those at the Gyantse Hotel.

Yingxiong Lu 14. ✆ **0892/817-3720.** Fax 0892/817-3910. jianzanghotel@yahoo.com.cn. 40 units. ¥380 standard room; ¥50 dorm bed. Up to 30% discount. No credit cards. **Amenities:** Restaurant, doctor on call. *In room:* Satellite TV.

Where to Eat

Gyantse Kitchen (Jiangzi Chufang) NEPALI/WESTERN This recent addition to Gyantse's dining scene offers the usual range of Nepali, Tibetan, and Western dishes; friendly service; and a homey atmosphere.

Shanghai Zhong Lu, just east of the intersection with Yingxiong Lu. ✆ **0892-817-6777.** Meal for 2 ¥60–¥100. No credit cards. 7am–midnight.

Tashi (Zhaxi Zangcan) ★ NEPALI/WESTERN Located at the northern end of Yingxiong Lu, this is the furthest branch west of a Lhasa-based chain and is the nicest place to eat in town. The clean and spacious restaurant is decorated in traditional style and serves a good range of Chinese, Tibetan, Indian, Nepali, and Western dishes. If the restaurant is quiet, ask the friendly chef to show off and prepare something off the menu. Chicken Whitehouse, crumbed chicken breast stuffed with lamb mince, mushroom, ginger, and garlic, is his specialty. On the menu, the yak sizzler and fresh flavored lassis are recommended. There's Nepali music in the evenings.

Yingxiong Lu, second floor, just north of Wutse Hotel. ✆ **0892/817-2793.** Meal for 2 ¥60–¥120. No credit cards. 7:30am–10pm. Closed Dec 1–Feb 1.

Zhuang Yuan Restaurant ★ CHINESE Mr. and Mrs. Zhuang are originally from Sichuan and serve up a range of their home favorites here on the Tibetan plateau. Dishes to try include *gongbao jiding* (chicken with peanuts), *gulou rou* (sweet and sour pork), and for dessert, *basi pinguo* (apples in caramelized sugar). Prices are aimed at foreigners, but the friendly service and tasty food will soon make you forget about that.

Yingxiong Nan Lu. ✆ **1367/802-0792.** Meal for 2 ¥80. No credit cards. 7am–10pm.

SAKYA (SAJIA; 萨迦)

150km (93 miles) SW of Shigatse, 55km (34 miles) SE of Lhatse. Altitude: 4,200m (13,776 ft.)

This remote Tibetan township has one of the best-preserved monasteries in the TAR, and is the home of the **Sakya** school of Buddhism. Founded by Konchok Gyalpo in 1073, it is similar to the Kagyu order in being heavily influenced by Indian Tantric Buddhism, but it differs in that its lineage is hereditary, passed down through the **Khon family.** In 1247, Kodan Khan offered the head lama, Sakya Pandita, absolute power to rule over Tibet, in exchange for submission to Mongol rule. Mindful of the fate of the Xixia Kingdom to the north of Tibet, annihilated 20 years previously by the hordes of Genghis Khan, Sakya Pandita readily agreed. At this point, theocratic rule in Tibet was born, and the concept of "priest and patron," was developed. Marco Polo noted that the magical powers of the Sakya lamas were highly regarded, and it is said they won over Kublai Khan when they triumphed in a battle of supernatural powers with Daoists and Nestorian Christians. You wonder what Sakyamuni would have made of this. He once reprimanded a follower who levitated above a crowd, likening him to a prostitute showing herself for a few coins. While the influence of Sakya faded with the Mongols, they produced stunning religious paintings during the 15th and 16th centuries, and the monastery houses some remarkable statuary.

GETTING THERE Land Cruisers make the trip from Lhatse, 50km (31 miles) away, in around an hour; a trip from Shigatse, 130km (81 miles) away, takes 2 or 3 hours.

GETTING AROUND There are no street addresses in the simple town of Sakya, but everything is within a 10-minute walk of the monastery.

A 13th-Century Monastery

Sakya Monastery (Sajia Si) ★★ The massive 35m (115-ft.) windowless gray walls of **Lhakhang Chenmo** tower above the village and fields on the southern bank of the Trum Chu. Completed in 1274, this monastery fort was largely funded by Kublai Khan, and unlike the older temples of north Sakya, it survived the Cultural Revolution. Little was left standing on the north side of the river, although a **nunnery** to the northeast is being revived.

Unlike the rich and confusing pantheon seen in most Geluk temples, most images in the **Assembly Hall (Dukhang) ★★** are of the historical Buddha, Sakyamuni. You'll need a flashlight to see the exquisite statuary and murals. Look for a striking 11th-century image of the **"speaking" Buddha,** third from the left on the back wall, with its cheeky grin. Other great works include an image of the bodhisattva **Manjushri,** second from the right on the back wall, leaning gently to one side, suggesting a sympathetic ear to believers. Walk around the monastery's walls, which offer fantastic views of the surrounding areas. Three hundred twenty monks remain, but they're a young, friendly bunch. They may show you the monastery's greatest treasure—a white **conch shell,** said to have housed a very early incarnation of Sakyamuni. Mountains of white *kata* (silk cloths) give away its location.

✆ **0892/824-2181.** Admission ¥45. 9:30am–4pm.

Where to Stay

Sakya Family Hotel (Luwa Sajia Binguan) Easy to spot by its traditional pink exterior, this cozy guesthouse is run by a friendly Tibetan family, and has great atmosphere and basic budget twin rooms. Shared toilets are of the pit variety and there are no showers, but if you can do without the amenities, choose this place over the Sakya Manasarovar Hotel and the shabby guesthouses in town.

✆ **0892/824-2156.** 20 beds. ¥60 per bed. No credit cards. *In room:* TV, no phone.

Sakya Manasarovar Hotel (Shenhu Sajia Binguan) As you push out farther into the hinterlands of Tibet, modern amenities like hot water and flush toilets become harder to find. In theory this hotel has those things, but it is poorly run and feels neglected. Rooms are blandly clean and spacious, but carpets are shabby and bathrooms gloomy. For the budget conscious, there are several dorm rooms; the fewer beds in the room the more they cost.

✆ **0892/824-2555.** 32 units. ¥280 standard room; ¥50 dorm bed. 15% discount. No credit cards. **Amenities:** Restaurant, Internet (¥15 per hour). *In room:* TV, no phone.

Where to Eat

In between the monastery and the Sakya Manasarovar Hotel, the **Sakya Farmer's Taste Restaurant** (**Sajia Nongmin Meishi Ting;** ✆ **0892/824-2221**) is a cozy, local restaurant and bar. Friendly staff offer simple Chinese and Tibetan dishes such as Rice with Potatoes and Yak Meat (¥12). Other options include the **Sakya Monastery Restaurant** (✆ **0892-824-2988**), or for something marginally more formal, the **Sakya Manasarovar Hotel.**

LHATSE (LAZI; 拉孜)

148km (92 miles) W of Shigatse, 325km (202 miles) NE of Zhangmu. Altitude: 4,000m (13,120 ft.)

The Friendship Highway now bypasses the small town of **Lhatse** by a few miles, but it remains the jumping-off point for trips to **Mount Kailash** (p. 784) and **Ali.** Though there's nothing much to see here, the Tibetan end of town is attractive, and the town can be used as an overnight stop between Lhasa and the Nepali border.

Essentials

GETTING THERE Traveling by Land Cruiser, the journey from Shigatse takes a couple of hours. The journey to Xin Dingri, 90km (56 miles) away, takes around an hour.

[Fast FACTS] LHATSE

Banks, Foreign Exchange & ATMs None available.

Internet Access None available

Post Office The post office is located east of the intersection, on the south side.

Where to Stay

Shanghai Hotel (Shanghai Binguan) The grand white edifice of Lhatse's newest hotel sits incongruously in the center of this small farming town. Service is indifferent, but rooms are as clean and comfortable as you'll find in this part of the world.

Main Intersection. ✆ **0892/832-3678.** www.lazihotel.com. 44 units. ¥380 standard room; ¥658 suite. Up to 50% discount. No credit cards. **Amenities:** Restaurant. *In room:* TV.

Tibetan Farmer's Adventure Hotel (Nongmin Yule Luguan) A 5-minute walk east of the main intersection on the north side of the highway, this friendly Tibetan-run place is fly-infested, but offers great atmosphere—the owner Loede may even play a little *danye* melody for you. Set around a sunny courtyard, the small rooms are homey and have wash-stands, but no bathroom. The snug restaurant serves decent yak-fried noodles and other simple dishes.

Zhongni Lu 8. ✆ **0892/832-2333.** 38 units. ¥70 twin without bathroom; ¥80 triple. No credit cards. **Amenities:** Restaurant. *In room:* TV, no phone.

Where to Eat

For Chinese food, try the **Shanghai Hotel,** or for Tibetan and Nepali, next door you'll find **Lhatse Kitchen** (**Lazi Chufang;** ✆ **0892/832-2858**), owned by Loede from the Farmer's Adventure Hotel. The restaurant is warm and the staff friendly and a range of set meals are on offer.

XIN DINGRI (NEW TINGRI; 新定日)

228km (141 miles) SW of Shigatse, 255km (158 miles) NE of Zhangmu. Altitude: 4,000m (13,120 ft.)

Confusingly, there are at least two towns known as **Dingri.** 7km (4¼ miles) before the county capital town of **Shelkar, Xin Dingri (New Tingri),** is a decent place to break your journey, while **Dingri,** or **Lao Dingri (Old Tingri),** the other base for treks in the Everest region, lies 60km (37 miles) farther to the west. Pick up your ticket for the **Qomolangma Nature Reserve** (see "Everest Trekking," p. 782) at the Qomolangma Service Center (10:30am–6:30pm) in Xin Dingri, opposite the Snowlands Hotel.

GETTING THERE By Land Cruiser, the journey from Shigatse takes around 3 hours. On the hour's drive from Lhatse to Xin Dingri, you'll drive past the Gyantsola Pass at 5,200m (17,056 ft.), a great place for your first view of the Himalayas.

VISITOR INFORMATION The **Qomolangma Service Center** offers information and tickets.

Where to Stay & Eat

Qomolangma Hotel (Zhufeng Binguan) Just around the corner from the Snowlands, this hotel aims to be a little grander but its rooms are inferior and more expensive. If you need more than one room, the deluxe rooms with an attached shared sitting room are worth considering.

✆ **0892/826-2775.** 80 units. ¥368 standard room; ¥560 deluxe room. Up to 30% discount. No credit cards. **Amenities:** Restaurant; bar. *In room:* A/C, TV.

Snowlands Hotel (Xueyu Fandian) ★ Located opposite the ticket office, the Snowlands has recently added some comfy twin rooms which come with thick carpets, small bathtubs and, the real bonus, lots of hot water. Basic older rooms without bathrooms are also available. The staff is very gracious and helpful and the cozy attached restaurants (new and old) have English menus and great food; the fried potatoes and yak with green peppers were both excellent.

✆ **0/138-8902-2848.** 25 units. ¥250 standard room; ¥80 common room without bathroom; ¥30 dorm bed. 20% discount on standard rooms. No credit cards. **Amenities:** 2 restaurants. *In room:* TV, no phone.

LAO DINGRI (OLD TINGRI; 老定日)

289km (179 miles) SW of Shigatse, 184km (114 miles) NE of Zhangmu. Altitude: 4,300m (14,104 ft.)

An impoverished settlement with a breathtaking view of the world's highest peaks, **Old Tingri** is the favored starting point for those wishing to walk to **Everest Base Camp,** and a common overnight stop between Kathmandu and Lhasa. A row of white-tiled houses and shops to the east of town represents the Han section of the settlement. Good views of Everest may be gained from the ruins of the late-18th-century **Tingri Dzong,** spread across a hill south of town.

Where to Stay & Eat

Be forewarned: Most of the guesthouses in Old Tingri are very basic, so keep your expectations low on the cleanliness, plumbing, and electricity fronts. On the very

EVEREST trekking

The trek out to **Everest Base Camp** follows two main routes—from **Xin Dingri** via the wretchedly poor village of Chay, and from **Lao Dingri** via Lungjiang. The former route (113km/70 miles) is usually traveled by 4WD in 3 hours along a much-improved road. The latter is a tough 3- to 4-day journey, and the path is hard to follow in places. Gary McCue's *Trekking in Tibet* is a reliable guide for this route and for other hikes in the Qomolangma Nature Preserve. At ¥400 per jeep plus another ¥180 per person (plus the guide which passengers must also pay for), the permit price matches the steepness of the mountain. Tickets can be purchased at Xin Dingri and Lao Dingri. There are also basic rooms at **Rongbuk Monastery** (¥80) and a new(ish) guesthouse (✆ **0892/890-6404**) next door which charges a ridiculous ¥300 for its simple rooms without bathrooms. The best place to experience the mountain is to spend the night in a black tent at **Base Camp** (¥40 per person) at an elevation of 5,150m (16,890 ft.). Make sure you get your guide to reserve places in advance as the encampment can quickly fill up. The highest post office in the world can also be found here, and charges ¥5 for a stamp, or ¥50 to stamp your passport. The "real" Base Camp with real expeditions and mountaineers is 4km (2½ miles) farther on; there are buses which cost ¥25 round-trip or you can walk it in around an hour although even a simple stroll can be challenging above 5,000m (16,404 ft.).

The exact height of Mount Everest is still a fiercely contended subject, and varies from 8,844 to 8,848m (29,015–29,029 ft.), depending on whether the icecap is included. Although the mountain is still growing, its icecap looks set to continue shrinking, which will doubtless keep the protagonists busy over the coming years. However, a few yards are invisible to the naked eye and on a clear day it presents an astounding vista. Insistence on the use of Qomolangma (Zhumulangma) rather than Mount Everest to label the world's highest peak would have pleased Sir George Everest, who staunchly believed in using local place-names.

eastern edge of town, the **Xuebao Fandian** (**Everest Snow Leopard Hotel;** ✆ **0892/826-2711**) offers the best accommodations in town, but it's still nothing special and prices are steep (¥280 standard room; ¥180 common room). Regular rooms have worn carpets and there's only electricity and hot water in the evenings. Of the other options in town, the **Tingri Snowland Hotel** (✆ **152/0802-7313**) on the very western edge is the most popular with guides and has very simple, but clean and attractive rooms (¥30 per person) set around a dusty parking lot. The restaurant here is also decent. In the town center the **Lhasa Hotel** (**Lhasa Fandian;** ✆ **0892/826-2703**) has similarly small, simple, and attractive rooms (¥80) without facilities, and a cozy restaurant which serves a good veg curry. Other eating options include a host of Sichuan places on the south side of the road in the center of town. For snacks and supplies, **Friends and Supermarkets** on the north side of the road is a well-ordered convenience store—but Lao Dingri is a long way from anywhere, so don't expect anything to be cheap.

ZHANGMU (DRAM; 樟木)

473km (293 miles) SW of Shigatse. Altitude: 1,900m (6,232 ft.)

The Friendship Highway drops 1,400m (4,600 ft.) during the treacherous 38km (24 miles) of road between Nyalam and Zhangmu. The arid Tibetan plateau gives way to lush greenery, waterfalls, and deliciously damp air and, as border towns go it's really rather pleasant. Nepalis complain about the cold, but you'll be shedding layers if you've arrived from Lhasa. A tiny collection of wooden houses before the border opened in 1980, Zhangmu is now one of the wealthiest towns in Tibet, due to licit and illicit trade in gold, clothing, and footwear. Zhangmu stretches for several miles through a series of switchbacks toward the border. Buildings are referred to in this section as though you are facing downhill.

Essentials

GETTING THERE The 180km (112 miles) road from Lao Dingri to Zhangmu is currently in fairly good condition, and should take about 5 hours in a Land Cruiser. At present, arriving overland from Nepal involves arranging a "group visa" and travel permits through a travel agency in Katmandu (p. 759).

The border is open from 9:30am to noon and 3:30pm to 5:30pm, with a time difference of 2¼ hours. If you've hired a vehicle from Lhasa, many drivers are not allowed to take you the extra 8km (5 miles) to Nepali Customs, but taxis and minibuses (¥10 per person) wait beyond the immigration building.

GETTING AROUND **Taxis** are ¥10 for short journeys.

[Fast FACTS] ZHANGMU

Banks, Foreign Exchange & ATMs The **Bank of China** (Mon–Sat 9:30am–1pm and 3–6:30pm) is toward the top of the hill on the right-hand side (as you head downhill). They accept traveler's checks, but not credit cards. There is no ATM.

Internet Access The **Internet Bar** just downhill from the Post Office charges ¥10 per hour. It's open from 10am to 3am.

Post Office The main post office (Mon–Fri 10am–1pm and 3:30–7pm) is located toward the middle of town on the right-hand side (as you head downhill).

Visa Extensions As you approach the border, the **PSB** (✆ **0892/874-3133;** Mon–Fri 9:30am–12:30pm and 3:30–5:30pm) is on the left-hand side in a large, white-tiled building. As the border is in sight, you're unlikely to need to extend your visa.

Where to Stay & Eat

Zhangmu is an expensive place to stay and there are few good options, although many rooms enjoy fine views over the gorge. The best choice is two-star **Zhangmu Binguan** (✆ **0892/874-2221**), on the right-hand side just before the border. Rooms have wooden floors, good views, and clean bathrooms (with hot water 7:30–10am and 7pm–midnight). Standard rooms go for ¥300 to ¥380 depending on your bargaining prowess, while simple rooms without bathrooms cost ¥100. Another decent but overpriced choice is the **Caiyuan Binguan** (✆ **0892/874-5888;** ¥420), a 5-minute

WILD CHINA: mount kailash & LAKE MANASAROVAR

Worshiped by the followers of no less than four religions—Tibetan Buddhists, Bonpos, Hindus, and Jains—**Mount Kailash (Gangdise)** draws pilgrims from the Tibetan world and beyond. For Tibetan Buddhists, it is Mount Meru, the center of the universe, and many aim to circumambulate the mountain 108 times, thus attaining Buddhahood in this lifetime. For Hindu pilgrims, who are allowed to cross the border at **Purang (Pulan),** it is the abode of Shiva, one of the three supreme gods. The beauty of the 6,714m (22,028-ft.) peak, jutting up from the surrounding arid plain, is astounding, and the sight of **Lake Manasarovar** under a full moon is enough to have even the most cynical visitor believing in supernatural possibilities.

The **Saka Dawa Festival,** the traditional pilgrimage holiday held from late May to early June, is the most spectacular time to visit, but access (even for prebooked tours) is often restricted during this festival. Regardless, try to time your visit to coincide with the full moon.

To reach Kailash, Western visitors need a guide, vehicle, driver, and a military permit (¥100, which will be arranged by the agency). Short tours, from either Lhasa or Katmandu, last 15 days and cost from ¥15,000. More extensive tours of the region run for 21 days and cost about ¥17,000. Costs can be split between four travelers. **Tibet Lhasa Travel Agency** and **Tibet Highland Tours** in Lhasa can arrange a variety of trip options. The trip is not feasible from November to mid-April.

Accommodations along the route are usually ¥50 per bed. Even basic amenities, such as hot showers, are usually unavailable. Dishes at restaurants tend to cost more than they would in Lhasa, so figure that you'll spend around ¥100 per day on food, unless you're okay with instant noodles.

The traditional gateway to the mountain is the village of **Darchen (Dajin),** which sits on the southern edge of the pilgrimage circuit, although you can't see the mountain from here. Admission to the Kailash area is ¥200, collected at a

walk uphill from the Zhangmu Binguan. Standard rooms are similar to those at the Zhangmu, but make sure to ask for a room with a view as they cost the same as those without. If you're not willing to spend that much on a standard room, then the **Sherpa Hotel** (✆ **0/135-1898-5853;** ¥120 small standard room with bathroom; ¥80 standard room without bathroom), in between the Zhangmu and the Caiyuan, has cleanish rooms with hot showers and many rooms have views.

Zhangmu has plenty of dining options. The friendly **Himalaya Restaurant,** next to the Zhangmu Binguan (✆ **0892/874-3068**) is pricey, but does good Nepali set meals as well as tasty sandwiches and a delicious mushroom soup and is a nice place to relax before or after a trip to Nepal. The owners are from Gansu and also offer decent exchange for Chinese yuan, Nepalese rupees, and American dollars. A meal for two is about ¥80 to ¥100. Across the road the **Base Camp Bar** (✆ **0892/874-2882**) is owned by a local climber who has summited Everest and accordingly the place is decked out from floor to ceiling with climbing gear. The menu spans the usual range of Chinese, Tibetan, Nepali, and Western, and the coffee is the best in town. Finally if you want checkpoint at the entrance to town. Guides must register guests with the PSB in Darchen upon arrival. Accommodations range in price from ¥60 to ¥80 for a dorm bed, and popular places include the Yak Hotel and the Darchen Guesthouse. At the **Gangdisi Binguan** private standard rooms and triples with decent bathrooms go for ¥240 and ¥300 respectively. Outside the eastern entrance of the Gangdisi Binguan is the **Lhasa Restaurant,** run by a charming retired teacher from Tsetang.

Most people take 3 days to complete the 53km (33-mile) circuit. Buddhists undertake the journey in a clockwise direction, while a handful of Bonpos walk counterclockwise. Stick with the majority. Waterproof hiking boots (or a change of shoes) are a must, as there are numerous small river crossings. Bring plenty of food, as you'll only find instant noodles and a few other snacks for sale on the circuit. Even if you intend to hire a yak and driver at ¥120 to ¥150 per day, you should be very fit, as the trek is above 4,500m (14,760 ft.), rising to over 5,600m (18,370 ft.) on the second day. Another option is to hire a horse for ¥120 per day.

Hor Qu (Huo'er Qu), 39km (24 miles) southeast of Darchen, is the most common jumping-off point for **Lake Manasarovar** (4,560m/14,957 ft.). Here you can enjoy unparalleled views of the Himalayas across turquoise waters which freeze over in winter, visit monasteries carved from the naked rock of the lakeshore, and even attempt the 90km (56-mile) circuit of the lake. **Chiu Gompa,** 35km (22 miles) south of Darchen and 8km (5 miles) south of the main road, has a few unmarked guesthouses that will rent you a bed for ¥40. A wash in the bathhouse that has unlimited hot-springs water costs ¥60. Entrance to the Chiu Monastery is free, and its setting, on a crag facing Lake Manasarovar, is the perfect place to relax and enjoy the view. If you go to Chiu Gompa, bring food from Darchen or Hor Qu. The **Indian Pilgrims Ashram** by the lakeshore, where you can spend the night for ¥100, serves a few minimal dishes like egg-fried rice.

some genuine Sichuan spice, **Lhasa Restaurant** (**Lhasa Canting; ✆ 0892/874-2436**) next to the Post Office, serves all the usual favorites including *gongbao jiding* (spicy chicken with peanuts) and *yuxiang rousi* (fish-flavored pork).

PLANNING YOUR TRIP TO CHINA

15

Travel in China isn't as hard as you may think: If you can manage Paris without speaking French, you can manage Beijing without Mandarin. China's international visitor arrivals have rocketed from a mere 300,000 back in 1978 to an impressive 56 million in 2010, making it the world's third most visited country. Tens of thousands of visitors travel in China independently each year, making their arrangements as they go, with nothing more than a guidebook and a phrase book to help them. You can certainly arrange various levels of assistance, either upon arrival or from home, but you can also travel just as freely as you would elsewhere, perhaps using agents to get your tickets, and picking up the odd day tour.

But whether you plan to travel at random, with a preplanned, prebooked route, or with a fully escorted tour, reading this chapter carefully will not only assist you in avoiding common pitfalls, but will enhance your time in the Middle Kingdom.

GETTING THERE

By Plane

Flying remains the easiest, and most popular, way to arrive in China. Beijing **(PEK),** Shanghai **(PVG),** and Hong Kong **(HKG)** are the major international hubs to choose from, and are all served by a wide range of international and domestic carriers. Guangzhou's new Baiyun Airport **(CAN)** is also connected to an increasing number of cities around the world, and prices can be considerably lower than to nearby Hong Kong. You should select your hub airport according to where you want to travel, and consider flying into one and out of another if that fits your itinerary and you can get a reasonable fare.

Note that there is no departure tax on either domestic or international flights and that all taxes and fees are usually included in ticket prices.

FROM NORTH AMERICA Among North American airlines, **Air Canada, Delta Airlines,** and **United Airlines** fly to Beijing and Shanghai. **Japan Airlines** flies via Tokyo to Beijing and Shanghai, but also to Guangzhou, Dalian, and Qingdao. **All Nippon Airways** also flies via Tokyo to Beijing, Dalian, Qingdao, Shanghai, Shenyang, and Xiamen.

Korean Air flies via Seoul to Beijing, Shanghai, Guangzhou, Qingdao, Shenyang, and Tianjin; and **Asiana Airlines** flies via Seoul to Beijing, Changchun, Chengdu, Chongqing, Guangzhou, Guilin, Harbin, Nanjing, Shanghai, Xi'an, and Yantai.

Hong Kong is served by **Air Canada, American Airlines, Continental Airlines, Delta Airlines, US Airways,** and **United Airlines,** as well as Hong Kong's **Cathay Pacific Airlines,** Hong Kong's main international carrier, which is effortlessly superior to North American airlines in service standards, and should be the first choice for direct flights where available. Indirect routes are offered by **China Airlines, Eva Airways, All Nippon Airways, Japan Airlines, Asiana Airlines,** and **Korean Air.**

FROM THE UNITED KINGDOM **British Airways** flies to Beijing, Shanghai, and Hong Kong, **Virgin Atlantic Airways** flies to Shanghai and Hong Kong, and **China Eastern** flights head to Shanghai. **Cathay Pacific** also flies directly to Hong Kong. Fares with **KLM** Royal Dutch Airlines via Amsterdam, with **Lufthansa** via Frankfurt, and with **Finnair** via Helsinki, can often be considerably cheaper. Fares with eastern European airlines such as **Tarom Romanian Air Transport** via Bucharest, and with **Aeroflot** via Moscow, or with Asian airlines such as **Jet Airways** via Mumbai, **Malaysia Airlines** via Kuala Lumpur, or **Singapore Airlines** via Singapore, can be cheaper still. There are even more creative route possibilities via the Persian Gulf States.

FROM AUSTRALIA & NEW ZEALAND There's not much choice to the mainland from down under, although Sydney is served by **Air China** to Beijing, Shanghai, and Guangzhou. **Qantas** flies to Shanghai and Hong Kong and **Air New Zealand** offers Hong Kong flights. There are possible indirect routes with **Philippine Airlines** via Manila, and with **Garuda Indonesia** via Jakarta. Hong Kong's **Cathay Pacific Airlines** flies directly from Sydney, Melbourne, Perth, Brisbane, and Auckland.

FROM ASIA As well as the flag carriers of various countries throughout Asia, China is also served by several budget Asian airlines including **Air Asia, Cebu Pacific, Jet Star,** and **Tiger Airways.**

By Train

From Hung Hom station in Kowloon (Hong Kong), expresses run directly to Guangzhou, Beijing, and Shanghai (see **www.it3.mtr.com.hk** for schedules and fares). From Almaty in Kazakhstan trains go to Ürümqi in Xinjiang. From Moscow trains to China travel via Ulaan Baatar in Mongolia to Beijing, and via a more easterly route directly to Harbin in China's northeast and down to Beijing. Rail service is available between Beijing and Pyongyang in North Korea, and to Hanoi in Vietnam from Beijing, Kunming, and Nanning. See **www.seat61.com** for advice on all of these international train routes.

By Car & Bus

Whilst driving your own vehicle into China is theoretically possible, it is a complicated business only worth undertaking for serious road enthusiasts (see "Getting Around: By Car," later in this chapter, p. 792).

In the northwest, **bus services** from both Sost in Pakistan and Osh in Kyrgyzstan connect to Kashgar, and run between Almaty in Kazakhstan and Ürümqi. In the south, buses run between Vientiane in Laos and Kunming, and between Hanoi in

Vietnam and Nanning in Guangxi. Hong Kong and Macau are both still considered international border crossings and buses connect to various points on the mainland from both territories.

By Boat

Few travelers arrive by ship, but it is still an option, and as well as ferries from Japan and South Korea to China's eastern seaboard, cruise liners stop off at Hong Kong, Xingang (for Beijing), and Shanghai. Cruises last from a fortnight to months, but generally only spend a few days in dock. Cruise companies which run to China include **Cunard** (www.cunard.com), **P&O** (www.pocruises.com), **Princess** (www.princess.com), **Seabourn** (www.seabourrn.com), and **Star** (www.starcruises.com).

GETTING AROUND

The first thing to do upon arrival at any Chinese destination is to buy a **map** for ¥3 to ¥6. Even though few of these are bilingual, and many are inaccurate, they're useful for navigation. Your hotel staff can mark on them where you want to go, and you can show the characters to the taxi driver or bus conductor. Although building numbers are given in this book, they're of little use for directions. Everyone navigates by street names and landmarks.

By Plane

As Chinese businesses and individuals have more disposable income, air travel is becoming increasingly popular. To this end, China plans to build nearly 100 new airports in the next 10 years, costing an estimated US$64 billion. Even now, it is possible to fly to most of the destinations in this book, or if not, to take a flight to within a few hours' drive. However, this isn't good for the environment, and where possible you should try and use the efficient and extensive rail network.

Booking domestic flights before you arrive in China is advisable if you will be traveling during peak season, or have limited time; however, on most routes there is generally an oversupply of flights and booking a ticket a few days before your journey is easily arranged. If you do choose to book tickets before you travel there are a number of good online booking sites including **http://ticket.9588.com**, which often has discounts of up to 50%.

While you can buy tickets between any two destinations from any Civil Aviation Administration of China (CAAC) office, you'll usually get a much better price from agents in the town from which you plan to depart. Prices are always better from agents than from the airline, even if they are next door to each other, and you can and should bargain for a lower price, and shop around. No agent with an online terminal connected to the Chinese domestic aviation system charges a booking fee. Agents sitting in four- and five-star hotels will not offer you the discounts they could, however. You need to look out in the street away from your hotel. You usually *cannot* get a refund on an unused ticket from anywhere except the agent where you bought it. Note that heading to or from the mainland Hong Kong and Macau are treated *as international flights,* with prices to match.

By Train

The train is still the best way to travel in China for many reasons. Railway journeys tend to be more scenic than endless highways, trains are more comfortable than even the best buses, and they also afford you the chance to wander around on longer journeys. Train stations tend to be located much closer to city centers than airports, and you also avoid the tedious airport waits. Though in backwater areas slow trains can be primitive, intercity trains are usually air-conditioned and mostly kept very clean. On sleeper services it is possible to avoid the cost of a hotel night, while still being able to spread out and relax. Do not underestimate the advantage of being able to lie down as you travel. No matter how long the journeys are, I have never seen a fellow passenger suffer from motion sickness, an affliction that is all too common on buses.

Even on a short trip, taking at least one train journey during your time in China is recommended to get a real flavor for the country, and with China's booming economy and rapidly advancing infrastructure, sometimes the train lines are attractions in their own right: The world's highest train line runs to Lhasa and the world's first commercial maglev (magnetic levitation) line speeds from Shanghai to Pudong airport. In 2011 the high-speed Beijing to Shanghai line opened, whisking visitors between the two cities in just under 5 hours. A further 16,000 kilometers of high-speed track are set to be laid in the next decade, which will give China more than the rest of the world combined! However, many locals balk at prices, and a high-speed rail crash in Wenzhou in July 2011 left 32 dead and many more injured, which has shed further doubt on China's ambitious high-speed rail program.

SEAT CLASSES Given China's size, most (non high-speed) intercity services are overnight (or sometimes over 2 nights), so sleeper accommodations are the most common. The best choice is **soft sleeper** *(ruan wo)*, consisting of four beds in a lockable compartment, the two upper berths slightly cheaper than the lower ones. Compartments have a volume control for the PA system and berths have individual reading lights. Modern trains (including all Lhasa trains) have individual TVs for each berth. **Hard sleeper** *(yiing wo)* has couchettes, separated into groups of six by partitions, but open to the corridor. Berths are provided in columns of three and are cheaper as they get farther from the floor. The top berth has very little headroom and can be uncomfortably cramped for foreigners, although it offers the most privacy. While the bottom berth is the most spacious, it also becomes public seating for the middle and upper berths during daylight hours. Lights go off at about 10pm and come on again at 6am. Thermoses of boiled water are in each compartment and group of berths, refilled either by the attendants or by you from a boiler at the end of each car. Bring your own cup or get one of the clear plastic tea flasks that many Chinese carry and are widely available in supermarkets. Bed linens are provided in both classes.

More modern trains have a mixture of Western (usually at the end of the soft sleeper carriage) and Chinese squat toilets. Washbasins are found at the end of each carriage, and except on the highest-quality trains, there's cold water only (and this may sometimes run out). A tiny handful of trains have deluxe soft sleeper *(gaoji ruan wo)*, with two berths in a compartment (Kowloon-Shanghai and Kowloon-Beijing, for instance), and in the case of some trains on the Beijing-to-Shanghai run, these compartments have private bathrooms.

Almost all trains also have a **hard seat** class *(yiing zuo)*, which on many major routes is now far from hard, although not the way to spend the night. **Soft seat** *(ruan zuo)* appears on daytime expresses only, is less crowded, and is now often in two-deck form, giving excellent views from the upper level.

TYPES OF TRAINS Where possible, choose a train with a C, D, G, Z, T or K prefix. **C, D,** and **G** trains are new, high-speed intercity services with all the latest amenities. **Z** (*zhida*) trains are the next level down, but still fast and very comfortable, while **T** (*tekuaai*) are the expresses, and still come with high levels of accommodations and service. Staff in all of these classes may be uniformed and coiffed like flight attendants, willing and helpful. **K** trains (*kuaaisu*—"quick speed") are more common, and nearly as good. Occasionally **Y** trains (*luyou,* services for tourists) and **L** trains (*linshi,* temporary additional services, particularly at Spring Festival), can be found. The remaining services with no letter prefixes vary widely in quality across the country, from accommodations as good as that on K trains but at slower speeds, to doddering rolling stock on winding, out-of-the-way lines and with cockroaches and mice for company (no extra charge).

TIMETABLES A national railway timetable can be found for sale at stations in larger cities, updated twice a year, and some regional bureaus produce their own, or smaller summaries of the most important trains. All are in Chinese only, and most are so poorly organized that they are initially incomprehensible even to most Chinese. Rail enthusiast Duncan Peattie produces an annual **English translation** of the national timetable. At $20 for the PDF format (or $40 for an A4), it is a very useful addition to the reference selection of independent travelers. If you don't need this much information then his free Quick Reference Guide may suffice. All can be downloaded from **www.chinatt.org**. For individual train enquiries **www.travelchina guide.com** is also a useful resource.

Timetables for a particular station are posted in its ticket office, and can be read by comparing the characters for a destination given in this book with what's on the wall. The best trains between selected locations are also given in this book, but be aware that train numbers (and times) are subject to change.

TICKETS Rail ticket prices are fixed by a complicated formula involving a tiny sum per kilometer, and supplements for air-conditioning, speed, and higher classes of berth (soft sleepers are typically a third more expensive than hard sleepers). Prices, samples of which are given throughout this book, are not open to negotiation. In my experience, hard sleeper berths are quite acceptable for short overnight trips of 12 hours or so. For longer journeys of 24 hours or more, I usually spend the extra for a soft sleeper.

Ticket offices always have a separate entrance from the main railway station entrance. In a few larger cities, there are separate offices for VIPs and foreign guests, or just for booking sleepers. Payment is only in cash. Depending on the route, bookings can be made between 5 days and 20 days in advance.

Most seats on an individual train are sold at its point of departure, with only limited allocations kept for intermediate stops depending on their size and importance. Thus your best choice of train is generally one that is setting off from where you are. With the exception of public holidays, tickets are seldom difficult to obtain, but you may not get the exact train, class or berth you want. If you can only obtain a hard sleeper (or seat) ticket but want a soft sleeper, you can attempt to upgrade on the train. A desk for this purpose is in the middle of the train.

Buying tickets at the station is generally a straightforward, if time-consuming business; to skip the queues look out for in-town *shoupiaochu* (ticket offices; listed where available) where tickets can be bought for a ¥5 commission. Otherwise book through a travel agent and expect to pay ¥30 to ¥50 commission, which may include free delivery to your hotel. Agents within hotels often try to charge more. It's best to give agents a choice of trains and berth. You pay upfront, but the exact ticket price, printed clearly on the ticket, will depend on the train and berth obtained. Advance booking from overseas is possible through CITS and some other agents at large markups, and so are not advised. Contact your local China National Tourist Office to find agents (see "Visitor Information," in "Fast Facts," later in this chapter) if you must. In **Hong Kong,** you can buy tickets for intercity trains departing Hung Hom online at **www.it3.mtr.com.hk**. **China Travel Service** also sells tickets for these trains commission free, and tickets for a selection of trains between other Chinese cities for a reasonable markup. Avoid using online agents, either Hong Kong or mainland based, as they charge up to *70% more* than they should.

You'll need your ticket to get to the platform, which will only open a few minutes before the train's arrival (if you buy a soft sleeper ticket, you may be able to use the VIP *guii bin* waiting room, but some stations now charge to enter these facilities, regardless of the ticket you have). On the train, the attendant will swap your ticket for a token with your berth number. Shortly before arrival, she will return to re-exchange it (you never miss your stop in China). Keep the ticket ready, as it will be checked again as you leave the station.

REFRESHMENTS Attendants push carts with soft drinks, beer, mineral water, and instant-noodle packages through all classes at regular intervals. Separate carts bring through *kuaai can* (fast food) in cardboard boxes. This is usually dreadful, and costs ¥15. Licensed carts on platforms often sell freshly cooked local dishes, which are slightly better, and they also offer fresh fruit in season. All overnight trains have dining cars, but the food is usually overpriced and not that tasty. It's best to bring a supply of what pleases you, bought in convenience stores, supermarkets, and bakeries.

COMFORT & SAFETY Berths aren't that big (approximately .6m×2m/2 ft.×6 ft. 4 in.), but they are reasonably comfortable (particularly soft sleeper). However, while some people (notably Chinese snorers) find the gentle (and sometimes not so gentle) motion of the train sends them to sleep, others struggle to get a decent night's rest. Earplugs are a good idea, although sleeping pills may be the only solution for insomniacs.

In the hundreds of overnight Chinese rail journeys I've made, I have never had anything stolen. Take sensible precautions as you would anywhere, and keep vital items (passport/money, and so on) close to you, but there is certainly no need for paranoia.

By Bus

China's highway system, nonexistent 20 years ago, is growing rapidly, and journey times by road between many cities have been dramatically cut to the point where on some routes, buses are now faster than trains. Although many buses are fairly battered, in some areas they offer a remarkable level of luxury—particularly on the east coast, where there are the funds to pay for a higher quality of travel. Some buses even have on-board toilets (although they may not work) and free bottled water.

Many bus stations now offer a variety of services. At the top end are *kongtiao* (air-conditioned) *gaosu* (high-speed, usually meaning that toll expressways are used) *haohua* (luxury) buses, on which smoking is usually forbidden and that rule is largely enforced, at least in urban areas. These tickets are usually easy to obtain at the bus station, and prices are clearly displayed and written on the ticket. There are no extra charges for baggage, which in smaller and older buses is typically piled up on the cover over the engine next to the driver. During public holidays, if you have to get to your destination by a certain time, or if you're heading somewhere remote, then it might be worth booking your ticket a day in advance, but generally speaking if you just turn up you'll be on your way in under half an hour.

Buses usually depart punctually, pause at a checking station where the number of passengers is compared with the number of tickets sold in advance, then dither while empty seats are filled with groups waiting at the roadside who bargain for a lower fare.

A few rough and ready rural journeys are a great way to meet the locals and get a flavor for the country, but you may quickly tire of these: Many of the rural population are unused to travel and get sick very quickly, and although sick bags are provided, people still tend to puke on the floor, down their trouser leg, or lean across you so that they can vomit out of the window. Some coach companies have started handing out complimentary travel sickness pills, but rather than reassure you this will probably mean that this particular trip is going to be a long and unpleasant one.

Sleeper buses, although cheaper, should generally be avoided when an overnight train is an alternative. Usually they have three rows of two-tier berths, which are extremely narrow and do not recline fully. Sleeper buses are also a favorite haunt for pickpockets.

By Car & Taxi

Foreigners are now allowed to drive in China providing they hold a Chinese driving license. These can be obtained at the Vehicle Administration Offices at Beijing and Shanghai international airports. Temporary 3-month licenses are easiest (but most expensive) to obtain, requiring only your passport (with visa and latest entry stamp) and foreign driving license. Once you have the license you can hire a vehicle through **Avis** (www.avis.com) or **Hertz** (www.hertz.com) at either airport. For enthusiasts looking for a real driving expedition, contact **Nature Adventure Voyage Off-road** (NAVO; www.china-driving.com), who have many years experience organizing self-drive trips in China, and can arrange for you to drive your own car or a local hire vehicle. Whether off-road in the wild hinterlands or on road in cities, driving in China is not to be undertaken lightly and can be very challenging, and to the uninitiated, downright scary. The best advice for drivers in China is to expect the unexpected. **Hong Kong** and **Macau** offer more regulated driving conditions, but are so small that there's simply no point in renting a car and facing navigational and parking difficulties, when plentiful, well-regulated taxis are available.

All larger mainland hotels have transport departments, but book a vehicle from a five-star Beijing hotel to take you to the Eastern Qing Tombs, for instance, and you may be asked for ¥1,200. Walk outside and flag down a taxi (not those waiting outside), and you can achieve the same thing for a quarter of the price. Branches of CITS and other travel agencies will also be happy to arrange cars for you, but again at a hugely marked-up price.

Despite the language barrier, bargaining with taxi drivers is more straightforward than you might expect. Most areas have far more taxis than there is business, and half- and full-day hires are very welcome. Start flagging down cabs the day before you want to travel, and negotiate an all-in price, using characters from this book (for your destination), those written down for you by your hotel receptionist (times, pickup point, and other details), and a pen and paper (or calculator) to bargain prices. Avoid giving an exact kilometer distance, since if you overrun it (and with China's poor road signage and the drivers' lack of experience outside their own town centers, you may well get lost), there will be attempts to renegotiate. For the same reason, it's best to avoid being precise to the minute about a return time, but note that especially in big

TIPS FOR taking taxis AROUND TOWN

1. ***Never*** go with a driver who approaches you at an airport. Leave the building and head for the stand. As they are everywhere else in the world, airport taxis are the most likely to cause trouble, but drivers who approach you are often *hei che*—illegal and meterless "black cabs."
2. Cabs waiting for business outside major tourist sights, especially those with drivers who call out to foreigners, should generally be avoided, as should cabs whose drivers ask you where you want to go even before you get in. Always flag down a passing cab, and 9 times in 10 the precautions listed here will be unnecessary.
3. If you're staying in an upmarket hotel, do not go with taxis called by the doorman or waiting in line outside. Even at some famous hotels, drivers pay kickbacks to the doormen to allow them to join the line on the forecourt. Some cabs are merely waiting because many guests, Chinese and foreign alike, will be out-of-town people who can be easily misled. Instead, just walk out of the hotel and flag down a passing cab for yourself. Take the hotel's business card to show to a taxi driver when you want to get back. This said, better hotels often give you a piece of paper with the taxi registration number on it as you board or alight, so that you can complain if something goes wrong or retrieve items mistakenly left in the cab.
4. Look to see if the supervision card, usually with a photo of the driver and a telephone number, is prominently displayed. If it isn't, you may have problems and you should choose another cab.
5. Can you clearly see the meter? If it's recessed behind the gear stick, partly hidden by the artfully folded face cloth on top, choose another cab.
6. Always make sure you see the meter reset. If you didn't actually see the flag pushed down, which shouldn't happen until you actually move off, then you may end up paying for the time the cab was in the line.
7. Have a map with you and look as if you know where you are going (even if you don't).
8. Rates per kilometer are usually clearly posted on the side of the cab. They vary widely from place to place, as well as by vehicle type. Flagfall, not usually more than ¥10, includes a few kilometers; then the standard kilometer rate begins. But in most towns, after a few more kilometers, the rate jumps by 50% if the driver has pushed a button on the front of the meter. This is for one-way trips out of town, and the button usually should not be pushed, but it often is.
9. Pay what's on the meter, and don't tip—the driver will insist on giving change (although in some cities they will round up or down to the nearest yuan). Always ask for a receipt. Should you leave something in a cab, there's a remarkably high success rate at getting even valuable items back if the number on the receipt is called, and the details on it provided.

cities drivers sometimes have to be back in time to hand the car to the man who will drive it through the night. Be prepared to pay road tolls, and ensure that the driver gets lunch. If you find a driver who is pleasant and helpful, take his mobile phone number and employ him on subsequent days and for any airport trips.

VISAS

Mainland China

All visitors to mainland China must acquire a **visa** in advance. Long-term visas are generally not granted at the border. Visitors to mainland China must have a valid **passport** with at least 6 months' validity and two blank pages remaining. Visa applications typically take 3 to 5 working days to process, although this can be sped up to as little as 1 day if you apply in person and pay an additional fee. "L" (tourist) visas are valid for 30 days. Double and multiple entry tourist visas are also available at some consulates.

You should apply to your nearest consulate. It varies, but typically your visit must *begin* within 3 months of the date of issue. Note that although postal addresses are given below, some consulates (including all those in the U.S. and Canada) will only accept applications in person, and applications by post or courier must go through an agent, with further fees to be paid. Telephone numbers are given, but many systems are automated, and getting a human to speak to can be next to impossible; faxes and e-mail rarely get a reply.

Applying for a visa requires completion of an application form that can be downloaded from many consular websites or acquired by mail. Temporary restrictions may be placed, sometimes for years at a time, on areas where there is unrest, and a further permit may be required. This is currently the case with Tibet where travelers are required to book a tour with guide and driver to secure a permit. For details of Tibet permits, see chapter 14. Do not mention Tibet or Xinjiang on your visa application, or it may be turned down.

One passport photograph is required per applicant and some consulates indicate that sight of an airline ticket or itinerary is required, or that you give proof of sufficient funds, or that you must be traveling with a group, while they happily carry on business with individuals who have none of this supporting documentation. Such statements provide a face-saving excuse for refusing a visa should there be unrest or political difficulties, or should Tibet or Xinjiang appear on the application.

The visa fees quoted below by country are the current rates for *nationals of that country,* and can change at any time. U.S. citizens applying for a double-entry visa in the U.K., for instance, are charged more than British citizens. Regulations may also vary. In addition to the visa fees quoted, there may be supplementary fees for postage, and higher fees can often be paid for speedier service. Payment must always be in cash or by money order.

Once you're inside China, visas can usually be extended for a maximum of 30 days at the Aliens Entry-Exit department of the **Public Security Bureau (PSB)** in most major towns and cities. First extensions are usually granted easily, but second time and beyond you may be refused, and have to leave the country and re-enter. Again visa extension processing times and requirements vary from place to place, and while some PSBs will issue an extension on the spot, others will take up to 5 working days to process. A passport photo, completed application form (available at the PSB), and the hotel receipt for that night are usually required, and some PSBs will only grant an extension if you have less than a week (or sometimes only 3 days) left on your current visa. See individual PSB listings for details. Extension costs also vary, but typically U.S. citizens pay ¥940, U.K. citizens ¥469, Canadians, Australians and new Zealanders ¥160. If you have trouble getting an extension, local agencies can sometimes help, although they will charge a hefty fee.

AUSTRALIA Single-entry visas are A$40; double-entry A$60. Add A$50 per package dealt with by mail or courier, and a prepaid return envelope. Go to **au.china-embassy.org** for more information.

CANADA Single-entry visas are C$50; double-entry C$75. Visit **ca.china-embassy.org** for an application form. Applications must be delivered and collected by hand, or sent via a visa agency.

NEW ZEALAND Single-entry visas are NZ$140; double-entry NZ$210. Add NZ$15 per package dealt with by mail or courier, and a prepaid return envelope. Go to **www.chinaembassy.org.nz** for more information.

THE UNITED KINGDOM Single-entry visas are £30; double-entry £45. There's a supplementary charge for each package dealt with by mail. Visit **www.chinese-embassy.org.uk** for an application.

THE UNITED STATES Single-entry and double-entry visas are $140. Visit **www.china-embassy.org**, which has links to all U.S. consular sites and a downloadable application form. Applications must be delivered and collected by hand, or sent via a visa agency.

ELSEWHERE A complete list of all Chinese embassies and consulates can be found at the Chinese foreign ministry's website: **www.fmprc.gov.cn/eng** (or various mirror sites around the world). Click on "The Ministry" and then "Missions Overseas."

BUYING VISAS IN COUNTRIES BORDERING CHINA

Note that the Chinese Consulate in Katmandu, Nepal, will not issue visas to individual travelers wanting to enter Tibet overland, or they may stamp the visa to prohibit overland entry via the Friendship Highway. The consulate in Bishkek, Kyrgyzstan, will usually refuse visas to those not holding a fax or telex from a Chinese state-registered travel agency, or they will stamp the visa to prohibit overland entry via the Torugart Pass. Obtaining visas at the consulate in Almaty can also sometimes be difficult for non-residents of Kazakhstan.

BUYING VISAS IN HONG KONG

The easiest place to apply for a mainland visa is Hong Kong, where there are several options. Single-entry tourist "L" visas valid for 30 days are easily obtainable, as is the double-entry version. Multiple-entry "F" visas are also easy to obtain via visa agents and without the letter of invitation required to obtain them at home. Single-entry "L" visas bought through Hong Kong agents typically cost HK$300, double-entry costs HK$400, and "F" (business) visas are HK$400 and HK$500 respectively. Expect fees of twice this for British citizens and up to four times as much for U.S. citizens. See chapter 11, "Hong Kong," for recommendations.

ENTERING CHINA FROM HONG KONG & MACAU

It is possible to buy a HK$160 5-day permit from the visa office on the second floor of the Chinese side of the Lo Wu border crossing from Hong Kong to Shenzhen, but this is valid for travel in the Shenzhen Special Economic Zone *only.* Similar short-term travel permits can also be arranged at Guangzhou East station if you arrive by direct express railway from Hong Kong, and on the mainland side of the crossing from Macau to Zhuhai. All of these permits are three times the price for U.K. passport holders, and are *not* available to U.S. citizens. See chapter 11 for more details.

Hong Kong & Macau Visas

U.S., Canadian, Australian, and New Zealand citizens, and those of most other developed nations, are granted 90-day stays free on arrival in **Hong Kong.** British citizens are granted 180 days. In theory, proof of sufficient funds and an onward ticket may be demanded, but this request is almost unheard of. On arrival in **Macau** U.S., Canadian, Australian, and New Zealand citizens are granted 30-day stays free on arrival. British and most other E.U. nationals can stay up to 90 days without a visa. For both territories passports should be valid for 1 month longer than the planned return date.

MONEY & COSTS

THE VALUE OF CHINESE RENMINBI VS. OTHER POPULAR CURRENCIES

RMB	Aus$	Can$	Euro (€)	NZ$	UK£	US$
1	A$0.14	C$0.15	€0.11	NZ$0.19	£0.1	$0.15

Frommer's lists exact prices in the local currency. The currency conversions provided were correct at press time. However, rates fluctuate, so before departing consult a currency exchange website such as **www.oanda.com/currency/converter** to check up-to-the-minute rates.

It's always advisable to bring money in a variety of forms on a vacation: a mix of cash and credit cards.

Currency

MAINLAND CHINA

For most destinations it's usually a good idea to exchange at least some money before you leave home so you can avoid the less-favorable rates you'll get at airport currency-exchange desks. **Mainland China** is different. **Yuan,** also known as **RMB** (**Renminbi,** or "People's Money"), are not easily obtainable overseas, and rates are generally worse when they can be found.

There is no legal private money-changing in mainland China, and rates are fixed to be the same at all outlets nationwide on a daily basis. So change at the airport when you arrive, and then at branches of the Bank of China, or at desks administered by the bank in your hotel or at major department stores in larger cities. If you find a shop offering to change your money at other than a formal Bank of China exchange counter, they are doing so illegally, and you open yourself to shenanigans with rates and fake bills, which are fairly common. Even the meanest hole-in-the-wall restaurant has an ultraviolet note tester. *Do not deal with black-market money-changers.*

Hotel exchange desks are open very long hours 7 days a week, but will often only change money for their guests. **Bank hours** vary from province to province, so be sure to check. See "Banks, Foreign Exchange & ATMs," in the "Fast Facts" section of each destination.

In a bid to avert a trade war with the U.S., China allowed a 2% appreciation of the yuan in 2005. From this point the yuan was pegged to a basket of currencies and this "crawling peg" held until the global financial crisis in 2008 when the Chinese currency

WHAT THINGS COST IN CHINA (RMB)

Taxi from the airport to downtown [Beijing]	100.00
Double room, moderate	300.00
Double room, inexpensive	180.00
Chinese meal for two, moderate	50.00
Bottle of beer in restaurant	5.00–10.00
Small bottle of water	1.50
Good cup of coffee	15.00–30.00
Admission to most museums	Free
Admission to most scenic areas	100.00–200.00

was once again tied solely to the dollar. In 2011 there was discussion of returning to the crawling peg and another similar percentage appreciation, but in the eyes of many Western economists this will still leave the yuan substantially undervalued.

There are notes for ¥100, ¥50, ¥20, ¥10, ¥5, ¥2, and ¥1, which also appears as a coin. The word *yuan* is rarely spoken, and sums are usually referred to as *kuai qian,* "pieces of money," usually shortened to just *kuai. San kuai* is ¥3. Notes carry Arabic numerals as well as numbers in Chinese characters, so there's no fear of confusion. The next unit down, the *jiao* (¥.10), is spoken of as the *mao.* There are notes of a smaller size for ¥.50, ¥.20, and ¥.10, as well as coins for these values. The smallest and almost worthless unit is the *fen* (both written and spoken) or cent and when you change money you may be given tiny notes or lightweight coins for ¥.05, ¥.02, and ¥.01, but this is the only time you'll see them except in the bowls of beggars or donation boxes in temples. The most useful note is the ¥10, so keep a good stock. Street stalls, small stores, and taxis are often not happy with ¥100 notes.

Keep receipts when you exchange money, and you can **reconvert** excess yuan into hard currency when you leave China, although sometimes not more than half the total sum for which you can produce receipts, and sometimes these receipts must be not more than 3 months old.

HONG KONG & MACAU

In **Hong Kong** the currency is the **Hong Kong dollar** (HK$), whose notes are issued by a variety of banks, although all coins look the same. It is pegged to the U.S. dollar at around HK$7.80 to US$1. Keep foreign exchange to a minimum at the airport (use the ATMs at departures level) or at other points of entry. Do not change in hotels or banks, but with money-changers, and choose money-changers away from the main streets for a significantly better rate. Banks have limited weekend hours, but money-changers are open every day.

Macau's official currency is the **pataca** (MOP$), pegged to the Hong Kong dollar (and thus to the U.S. dollar) at a rate of MOP$103 to HK$100—about MOP$8 to US$1. Hong Kong dollars are accepted everywhere, including both coins and notes (even on buses), but at par. If you arrive in Macau from Hong Kong for a short stay, there's little point in changing money beforehand.

ATMs

Unfortunately, while there are many ATMs in China, some won't accept foreign cards, and those that do tend to have a maximum limit of between ¥1,000 and ¥2,500 per transaction, but often allow a second transaction the same day. Check the back of your ATM card for the logos of the **Cirrus, Maestro, MasterCard, Visa,** and **American Express;** as long as your card has one of them it should work in **Bank of China ATMs** around the country. Beijing and Shanghai are both fairly well served, and have additional Citibank and HSBC machines, which take just about any card ever invented. Thus it is possible, as long as you plan ahead, to travel in China relying on ATMs—just be sure to replenish your supplies of cash before they run out, and have a couple of hundred U.S. dollars in cash as a backup. In **Hong Kong** and **Macau** there are ATMs everywhere that are friendly to foreign cards.

Note: Many banks impose a fee every time you use a card at another bank's ATM, and that fee can be higher for international transactions than for domestic ones. In addition, the bank from which you withdraw cash may charge its own fee. For international withdrawal fees, ask your bank.

Banks that are members of the **Global ATM Alliance** charge no transaction fees for cash withdrawals at other Alliance member ATMs; these include Bank of America, Scotiabank, Barclays, Deutsche Bank, and BNP Paribas. Alternatively, British citizens can obtain a **Caxton FX Card (www.caxtonfx.com),** which allows holders to withdraw money overseas without paying any bank charges, and to load more cash from other accounts by phone or online. Not only does this save money, it also means that if your card is stolen, only the amount loaded can be withdrawn.

Traveler's Checks

Traveler's checks are only accepted at selected branches of the Bank of China, at foreign exchange desks in hotels, at international gateways, and at some department stores in the largest cities. In the most popular destinations, checks in any hard currency and from any major company are welcome, but elsewhere, currencies of the larger economies are preferred, and hotels may direct all check-holders to the local head office of the Bank of China. U.S. dollars cash, in contrast, may be exchanged at most branches of almost any Chinese bank, so even if you plan to bring checks, having a few U.S. dollars cash (in good condition) for emergencies is a good idea. Checks attract a marginally better exchange rate than cash, but the .75% commission makes the result slightly worse (worse still if you paid commission when buying them). Occasionally, if the signature you write in front of the teller varies from the one you made when you bought the check, it may be rejected. In **Hong Kong** and **Macau,** checks are accepted at banks and money-changers in the usual way.

Credit Cards

Upscale hotels, restaurants, and some large tourist-oriented shops usually accept the full gamut of cards (American Express, Diners Club, MasterCard, and Visa), but outside of these places their use is limited. Although Visa and MasterCard signs abound, in many cases only the Chinese versions of the cards are accepted.

You can also obtain cash advances on your MasterCard, Visa, Diners Club, or Amex card from major branches of the Bank of China, with a minimum withdrawal of ¥1,200 and 4% commission, plus whatever your card issuer charges—a very expensive way to withdraw cash, and for emergencies only. If you do plan to use your card while in China, it's a good idea to call your card issuer and let it know in advance.

All major credit cards are widely accepted in **Hong Kong** and **Macau.**

Emergency Cash

American Express also runs an **emergency check cashing system,** which allows you to use one of your own checks or a counter check (more expensive) to draw money in the currency of your choice from selected banks. This works well in major cities but it can cause confusion in less-visited spots, and the rules on withdrawal limits vary according to the country in which your card was issued. Consult American Express for a list of participating banks before you leave home.

If you're stuck in a province where banks are closed on weekends, you can have money wired from **Western Union** (✆ **800/325-6000;** www.westernunion.com) to many post offices and branches of the Agricultural Bank of China across China. You must present valid ID to pick up the cash at the Western Union office. In most countries, you can pick up a money transfer even if you don't have valid identification, as long as you can answer a test question provided by the sender. This should work in Hong Kong but might cause difficulties in mainland China. Let the sender know in advance that you don't have ID.

TIPS ON ACCOMMODATIONS

When China reopened its doors to tourists in the early 1980s, hotel choices were very limited for foreigners, but these days there are increasingly more options, and the only thing that is thin on the ground is character. At the upper end of the scale, **international chains** are keen to get their slice of the Chinese pie and are opening new joint venture hotels around the country. In the major cities you'll find the gamut of international chains, including Best Western, Crowne Plaza, Grand Hyatt, Harbor Plaza, Hilton, Holiday Inn, Kempinski, Marco Polo, Marriott, Ramada, St. Regis, Shangri-La, Sheraton, and Sofitel, among others. In most joint venture hotels the buildings are Chinese-owned, and the foreign part of the venture is the management company, which provides senior management and trains the staff, tries to ensure conformity with their standards, does worldwide marketing, and generally provides up to 90% of what you'd expect from the same brand at home. **Chinese-owned chains** are also improving and expanding, however while the exterior appearances of domestic and international five-stars may be similar, if you have the choice, go for the latter, as while prices will be comparable, service is almost always better. Unfortunately, such large operations also have **large carbon footprints,** and often put very little back into the local economies. It is therefore wise to remember that every time you open your wallet, you are voting either yes or no for the environment. **Budget choices** are more limited, in part because hotels require licenses to receive foreign guests, and many cheapies don't have these. Saving the day, though, are a new breed of **business chain hotels** such as Jinjiang Inn and 7-Days Inn, which are sweeping the nation, and offer inexpensive (usually under ¥220) functional, modern rooms, often with good locations near the city center.

In general, Chinese hotels receive almost no maintenance once they open. There are "five-star" hotels in Beijing that have gone a decade without proper redecoration or refurbishment. Foreign managements force the issue with building owners, but it's rare elsewhere that standards are maintained. Thus **the best choice is almost always the newest**—teething troubles aside, most things will work, staff will be eager to please (if not quite sure how), rooms will be spotless, and rates will be easily bargained down, since few hotels spend any money on advertising their existence.

HOTEL AMENITIES The international chain hotels will feature all of the facilities you'd expect around the world, but the **Chinese star-rating system** itself is virtually meaningless. Five-star ratings are awarded from Beijing authorities, but four-star and lower depend upon provincial concerns. In some areas a four-star hotel must have a pool, in others a bowling alley, and in others a tennis court. The Jacuzzi may have more rings than a sequoia, the bowling alley be permanently out of order, and the tennis court be used for barbecues, but the hotel will retain its four stars, as long as it banquets the inspectors adequately. This said, most three-star places and above will have a functioning business center, restaurant, laundry facilities, and maybe a travel desk. In theory, all hotels approved to take foreign guests should also have at least one English-speaking staff member, but they often fail to materialize. Salons, massage rooms, nightclubs, and karaoke rooms are often merely bases for other kinds of illegal entertainment (for men). You may receive unexpected **phone calls.** If you are female, the phone may be put down without anything being said, as it may be if you are male and answer in English. But if the caller persists and is female, and you hear the word *anmo* (massage), then what is being offered probably needs no further explanation, but a massage is only the beginning. Unplug the phone when you go to sleep.

TYPES OF ROOMS Ordinary Chinese hotels usually speak of a *biaozhun jian,* or **standard room,** which means a room with twin beds, occasionally with a double bed, and with a private bathroom. Often double beds have only recently been installed in a few rooms, which are now referred to as *danren jian* or single rooms. Nevertheless, two people can stay there, and the price may be lower than that of a twin room. In older hotels, genuine single rooms are available, and in many hotels below four-star level there are triple rooms and quads, which can also serve as dorms shared with strangers. Children 12 and under can stay for free in their parent's room. Hotels will add an extra bed to your room for a small charge, which you can negotiate.

Almost all rooms in China have the following: a telephone; air-conditioning, which is either central with a wall-mounted control, or individual to the room with a remote control, and which may double as a heater; a television, usually with no English channels except CCTV 9 (to which no buttons may be tuned) and possibly an in-house movie channel using pirated DVDs; and a thermos of boiled water or a kettle to boil your own, usually with cups and free bags of green tea. In a cupboard somewhere there will be a quilt. Between the beds (most rooms still have twin beds) will be an array of switches, which may or may not actually control what they say they control. In the bathroom there are free soap and shampoo, and in better hotels a shower cap, and toothbrush/toothpaste package (but bring your own).

International hotels regularly describe their standard accommodations as deluxe, and, along with the facilities listed above, in the room you should expect to find a fridge, maybe a minibar, a hairdryer, satellite TV, and either broadband or Wi-Fi (often for a fee).

CHECKING IN & CHECKING OUT Foreign **credit cards** are increasingly accepted in three-star hotels upwards, but never rely on this. Most hotels accepting foreigners have foreign exchange facilities on the premises, although some may send you elsewhere to exchange checks. Almost all require **payment in advance,** plus a deposit *(yajin),* which is refundable when you leave. Keep your deposit receipt as you will need to show it on check out in order to collect your money.

To **check in,** you'll need your passport and you'll have to complete a registration form (which will usually be in English). Always inspect the room before checking in. You'll be asked how many nights you want to stay, and you should always say just one, because if you say four, you'll be asked for the 4 nights' fee in advance (plus a deposit), and because it may turn out that the hot water isn't hot enough, the karaoke rooms are over your head, or a building site behind the hotel starts work at 8am sharp. Once you've tried 1 night, you can pay for more.

When you **check out,** the floor staff will be called to make sure you haven't broken or stolen anything (there is usually a list in each room detailing the costs of every item within); this may not happen speedily, so allow a little extra time.

Saving on Your Hotel Room

The **rack rate** is the maximum rate that a hotel charges for a room. In China these rates are nothing more than the first bid in a bargaining discussion, designed to keep the final price you will actually pay as high as possible. You'll almost never pay more than 90%, usually not more than 70%, frequently not more than 50%, and sometimes as little as 30% of this first asking price. Guidelines on discounts are given for each city. Avoid booking through Chinese hotel agencies and websites specializing in Chinese hotels. The discounts they offer are precisely what you can get for yourself, and you can in fact beat them because you won't be paying their markup. Many of these have no allocations at all, and simply jump on the phone to book a room as soon as they hear from you. Here are some tips to lower the cost of your room:

- **Do not book ahead.** Just show up and bargain. In China this applies as much to the top-class joint-venture names as to all the others. The best price is available over the counter, as long as there's room. For most of the year, across China, there are far more rooms than customers at every level. For ordinary Chinese hotels you may well pay double by booking ahead, and there's no guarantee your reservation will be honored if the hotel fills up or if someone else arrives before you, cash in hand.
- **Bargain hard and smart.** If the hotel isn't coming down in price as much as you'd like, tell them you don't need breakfast, or ask about any cheaper rooms, which may well end up being the same as all of the rest of the rooms, but just gives staff the opportunity to lower their "last" price without losing face.
- **If you need to reserve in advance, dial any central booking number.** Contrary to popular wisdom, as the better hotels manage their rates with increasing care, the central booking number is likely to have a rate as good as or better than the rate you can get by calling the hotel directly, and the call is usually toll-free.

In Hong Kong & Macau

Hong Kong in particular is well stocked with hotels that regularly make their way onto lists of the world's best, while Macau's booming casino scene has given rise to an expanding array of big name properties. Service is second to none, and they are worth flying halfway around the world to stay in. Little of what's said about mainland hotels above applies.

ONLINE TRAVELER'S toolbox

- **ATM Locator: www.visa.com** for locations of VISA and PLUS locations worldwide; or **MasterCard ATM Locator** (www.mastercard.com), for locations of Cirrus, Maestro and MasterCard ATMs worldwide.
- **Chinese Language: Google Translate** (http://translate.google.com) is an incredible translation tool with written and spoken forms available. **www.mandarintools.com** has dictionaries for Mac and Windows, facilities for finding yourself a Chinese name, Chinese calendars for conversion between the solar and lunar calendars, and more. **www.zhongwen.com** has an online dictionary with look-up of English and Chinese and explanations of Chinese etymology using a system of family trees.
- **General Travel Information:** As well as the tourist office websites listed under "Visitor Information" in Fast Facts sections for each relevant city, town or region: **www.travelchinaguide.com** is organized by only one Chinese tour company but has an active and informative community section and up-to-date train schedules; **Wikitravel.org** (http://wikitravel.org/en/China) is a project to create a free, complete, up-to-date, and reliable worldwide travel guide, so far with over 25,000 destination guides and other articles written and edited by Wikitravelers from around the globe, and growing all the time. **Virtualtourist** (www.virtualtourist.com/travel/Asia/China/TravelGuide-China.html) is an advertising-supported alternative to Wikitravel, but with some 30,000 traveler's tips for China alone, still a very useful resource.
- **Hotel & Travel Booking: Ctrip** (www.english.ctrip.com) is one of the better Chinese hotel and flight booking sites and this one also has a great deal of useful travel information in English. **eLong** (www.elong.net) offers excellent prices on domestic and international tickets which can be booked online or by phone. **Ticket9588** (http://ticket.9588.com) is an easy to use online domestic flight booking site with regular discounts.
- **Travel Warnings:** See **http://travel.state.gov** for the U.S., **www.fco.gov.uk** for the U.K., **www.voyage.gc.ca** for Canada, **www.smarttraveller.gov.au** for Australia, and **www.safetravel.govt.nz** for New Zealand.
- **Universal Currency Converter: www.oanda.com/currency/converter** has the latest exchange rates of any currency against the yuan, HK$, and MOP$.
- **Weather in China: Weatherbase** (www.weatherbase.com) gives month-by-month averages for temperature and rainfall in individual cities in China. **Intellicast** (www.intellicast.com), **Weather.com** (www.weather.com), and **Wunderground** (www.wunderground.com) give weather forecasts for cities around the world.

HEALTH

Plan well ahead. While a trip to Hong Kong or Macau can be made with little extra protection, a trip to mainland China, depending on its duration and time spent outside larger cities, may require a few new inoculations, especially if you haven't traveled much in the less-developed world before. Some of these are expensive, some need multiple shots separated by a month or two, and some should not be given at the same time. So start work on this 3 or 4 months before your trip. Note that family doctors are rarely up to date with vaccination requirements, so when looking for advice at home, contact a specialist travel clinic.

For the latest information on infectious diseases and travel risks, and particularly on the constantly changing situation with malaria and respiratory viruses, consult the **World Health Organization** (www.who.int) and the **Centers for Disease Control** (www.cdc.gov). Look in particular for the latest information on respiratory viruses such as SARS, bird flu, and A(H1N1), which may continue long after the media has become bored with reporting it.

To begin with, your standard inoculations, typically for **polio, diphtheria,** and **tetanus,** should be up-to-date. You may also need inoculations against **typhoid fever, meningococcal meningitis, cholera, hepatitis A and B,** and **Japanese B encephalitis.** If you will be arriving in mainland China from a country with **yellow fever,** you may be asked for proof of vaccination, although border health inspections are cursory at best. See also advice on **malarial prophylactics,** below. Tuberculosis is making a resurgence in many parts of the country and due to the explosive growth of the canine population, **rabies** is also on the rise again, although the risks in tourist areas are minimal.

General Availability of Health Care

Advanced facilities staffed by foreign doctors are available in Beijing, Shanghai, Guangzhou and, best of all, Hong Kong; these are listed as appropriate in this book and can also be found in local expat magazines. If you need to go to a Chinese hospital outside of these places, try and head to the biggest hospital in a large town. Foreigners who do end up in provincial facilities often get special treatment, but you may not consider it special enough.

Contact the **International Association for Medical Assistance to Travelers (IAMAT; ✆ 716/754-4883,** or 416/652-0137 in Canada; www.iamat.org) for tips on travel and health concerns in the countries you're visiting, and for lists of local, English-speaking doctors. The United States **Centers for Disease Control and Prevention** (**✆ 800/232-4636;** www.cdc.gov) provides up-to-date information on health hazards by region or country and offers tips on food safety. **Travel Health Online (www.tripprep.com),** sponsored by a consortium of travel medicine practitioners, may also offer helpful advice on traveling abroad. You can find listings of reliable medical clinics overseas at the **International Society of Travel Medicine (www.istm.org).**

Common Ailments

Far fewer travelers get sick in China than India, Egypt, or a host of other tourist destinations in less-developed countries. However, if you're here for a while, there is of course a chance you'll fall ill somewhere along the way.

RESPIRATORY ILLNESSES A billion Chinese spitting, pollution, and the contrast in temperature and humidity between freezing dry air-conditioning and sweltering summer heat, makes a **respiratory tract infection** the most likely illness to affect you in China. If you're lucky a sore throat might be the worst of it, but cold- or flulike symptoms are also a possibility. A good range of local products can be used to treat respiratory infections (Golden Throat can stop your throat from getting too sore), but if you have a fever, are in serious discomfort, or the illness hasn't improved after 48 hours, see a doctor.

STOMACH UPSETS In many less-developed countries around the world stomach upsets are the most likely cause of illness for visitors, but, in China, where fresh food is cooked at high-temperatures, this is less of a worry. That isn't to say that it never happens and you should forego basic personal hygiene, but don't let worrying about what you eat dominate your trip to China. Keep your hands frequently washed and away from your mouth. Choose busy restaurants, with a high turnover, and only eat freshly cooked hot food, and fruit you can peel yourself. Drink only boiled or bottled water and use the same to brush your teeth. *Never* drink from the tap.

MALARIA Mosquito-born **malaria** is present in parts of China's deep south, but unless you are going to be spending a lot of time out in the jungle during the wet season, it isn't a serious risk. If you will be visiting malarial regions for extended periods then it's worth considering prophylactic drugs. There are various prophylactics available, but you should ensure that the type you take is effective against the strains to be found in your destination. Often these drugs need to be taken up to a week before you arrive in the malarial zone, and for up to a month after you leave, and some (notoriously Lariam) can have unpleasant side effects. Also bear in mind that even if you take anti-malarial prophylactics, if you are bitten by an Anopheles mosquito carrying the virus, chances are you will still get malaria; the drugs simply buy you a little time to get to a hospital (although they can also mask the symptoms, making it more difficult to diagnose).

OTHER RISKS If you visit Tibet, you may be at risk from **altitude sickness,** usually marked by throbbing headache, loss of appetite, shortness of breath, overwhelming lethargy, and paradoxically, difficulty sleeping. Other than retreating to a lower altitude, avoiding alcohol, and drinking plenty of water, many find a drug called Diamox (acetazolamide) to be effective. Locally, Hongjingtian is a widely available over-the-counter substitute. See the box, "Dealing with Altitude Sickness," on p. 742 for more.

Standard precautions should be taken against exposure to **strong summer sun,** its brightness often dimmed by pollution but its power to burn undiminished.

As people have more money, time, and enjoy more social liberties, there has been something of a sexual revolution in China. This has led to the spread of **sexually transmitted diseases** (including **AIDS**) and, in spite of educational attempts by the government, knowledge about the subject among the general populace remains limited. In short, you should not undertake intimate activities without protection. Condoms are widely available, and are often to be found (either free or for sale) in hotel rooms. Where possible use Western brands which can be purchased in bigger cities.

Pre-Trip Preparation

No matter how good your pre-trip health is, it's worth taking a basic first aid kit and a selection of your preferred over-the-counter medicines with you. If you have a chronic illness, ask your doctor to write a summary of the condition before you leave in case a problem develops while you are away. Pack prescription medications in your carry-on luggage, and leave them in their original containers, with pharmacy labels—otherwise, they might not make it through airport security. Also take note of the generic name of your prescription medicines, in case a local pharmacist is unfamiliar with the brand name. For glasses (or contact lens) wearers, it's also worth taking a copy of your prescription with you, which will enable you to replace them if they get lost or broken, and will also allow you to take advantage of cheap opticians and buy a spare pair. You should also make sure you have some form of medical insurance, ideally a policy that includes emergency evacuation. If you're ever hospitalized more than 150 miles from home, **MedjetAssist** (✆ **800/527-7478;** www.medjet assistance.com) will pick you up and fly you to the hospital of your choice virtually anywhere in the world in a medically equipped and staffed aircraft 24 hours day, 7 days a week. Annual memberships are $250 individual, $385 family; you can also purchase short-term memberships.

What to Do If You Get Sick Away from Home

For accidents and emergencies, head directly to the **nearest large hospital,** ideally one in a big city. For minor ailments and illnesses your first contact should be with your hotel reception. Many **major hotels have doctors on staff** who will treat minor problems, and who will be aware of the best place to send foreigners for further treatment. If the doctor gives you medicine, make sure you ask what each tablet is for as there is a tendency to prescribe a veritable candy-store of different colored tablets and a complicated schedule of when to take them, but some of them might just be multi-vitamins.

For coughs, colds, and minor stomach upsets, local pharmacies generally stock a wide range of **over-the-counter medications** (including many that are prescription only in the West), but you should make sure you understand the possible side-effects before taking anything, and ideally consult a doctor.

FAST FACTS: CHINA

Area Codes See "Telephones," later in Fast Facts, for international codes and individual destinations for local area codes.

Business Hours Offices are generally open from 9am to 6pm but are closed Saturday and Sunday. Most shops, sights, restaurants, and transport systems offer the same service 7 days a week. Shops are typically open at least from 8am to 8pm. Bank opening hours vary widely (see the "Fast Facts" sections for individual destinations). In **Hong Kong** and **Macau,** most offices are open Monday through Friday from 9am to 5pm, with lunch hour from 1 to 2pm; Saturday business hours are generally 9am to 1pm. Most Hong Kong and Macau shops are open 7 days a week, from 10am to at least 7pm.

Car Rental Self-drive rental options are limited in China and driving is not recommended. See "Getting Around" earlier in this chapter, p. 788.

Cellphones See "Mobile Phones," later in this section.

Crime See "Safety," later in this section.

Customs Generally, you can bring into China anything for personal use that you plan to take away with you when you leave, with the usual exceptions of firearms and drugs, or plant materials, animals, and foods from diseased areas. Other prohibitions include "printed matter, magnetic media, films, or photographs which are deemed to be detrimental to the political, economic, cultural and moral interests of China," as the regulations put it. Large quantities of religious literature, overtly political materials, or books on Tibet might cause you difficulties (having a pile of pictures of the Dalai Lama certainly will, if discovered), but in general, small amounts of personal reading matter in non-Chinese languages won't get a second glance. There are no problems with cameras or video recorders, GPS equipment, laptops, or any other standard electronic equipment. Customs officers are for the most part easygoing, and foreign visitors are very rarely searched. Customs declaration forms have now vanished from all major points of entry, but if you are importing or exporting more than US$5,000, or RMB20,000 in cash, theoretically you should declare it. Chinese currency is anyway best obtained within China (or in Hong Kong), and is of little use once you leave. An official seal must be attached to any item created between 1795 and 1949 that is taken out of China; older items cannot be exported. But in fact you are highly unlikely to find any genuine antiques, so this is a moot point (and if the antiques dealer is genuine, then he'll know all about how to get the seal). There are no such prohibitions on exporting items from Hong Kong, where you can find reliable dealers with authentic pieces and a willingness to allow thermo-luminescence testing to prove it. Cheap DVDs on sale in China are extremely tempting, especially compared to the prices at home, but if discovered on arrival in your home country these may be confiscated. More importantly, you should be aware that the producers of these discs are often the same gangsters who smuggle undocumented migrants in containers and sell females into sexual slavery; don't give them your money.

Disabled Travelers Although China has a large number of people with disabilities, provisions for the disabled are limited, and this can make travel difficult. As the economy booms, many cities resemble building sites, and uneven paving, unavoidable steps, and heavy traffic are all hindrances. Therefore it is easiest to travel in a specialist group or with those who are fully familiar with giving you whatever assistance you may need. **Tour Beijing** (www.tour-beijing.com/disability_travel) has a good reputation. In theory, some major hotels in the largest cities have wheelchair-accessible rooms, but they are often not properly executed—the door to the bathroom may be wider, or the bathroom suite lower, but not both, and other switches and controls may be out of reach. In spite of what the brochure or website says, you should call to confirm what is actually available. **Hong Kong** has far better facilities for travelers with disabilities, which are listed online at **www.accessguide.hk**.

Discrimination In general foreigners receive better treatment in China than the Chinese give one another, but there are also some ingrained cultural stereotypes: Darker skinned travelers may have a harder time than lighter skinned travelers whilst those of Asian descent might find they can get into tourist sites more cheaply, and be allowed to stay in a wider range of hotels (especially if they can speak a bit of Chinese), but on the other hand, might be treated as poorly as a local by officialdom. As a country closed for so long to outside influences, the **Chinese are fascinated by *"laowai"*** (old outsiders) and their long noses, round eyes, and strange hair. In remote spots, and conversely at major attractions that draw tourists from around the country, you may quickly find yourself the center of attention. Being stared at and having your photo taken with your newfound friends can get old fast, but it's important to remember that many Chinese come from foreigner-free towns and may only have seen a *laowai* on TV up until this point, so meeting you is an event to be commemorated and discussed for weeks to come. Some foreign visitors even grow to love this "fame," and as more and more Chinese learn English, you might even get some conversation; if not, a quick smile and a *"ni hao"* usually leaves everyone happy. Of course there are times when you really want this attention (at a hotel reception or police station, for example) and everyone seems to ignore you, or worse still, just laughs at your requests. Laughing often hides embarrassment at not knowing how to deal with a foreigner, and you should refrain from getting angry or shouting; frustrating as it may be, persisting calmly is the way forward.

Doctors See "Health", earlier in this chapter, p. 803.

Drinking Laws China has very liberal drinking laws and alcohol is widely available. Theoretically you need to be over 18 to purchase alcohol, but this is seldom enforced. Alcohol can be bought in any convenience store, supermarket, restaurant, bar, hotel, or club, 7 days a week, and may be drunk anywhere you feel like drinking it. If the shop is open 24 hours, then the alcohol is available 24 hours, too. Closing times for bars and clubs vary according to demand, but typically it's all over by 3am. In **Hong Kong,** liquor laws largely follow the U.K. model; restaurants, bars, and clubs must obtain licenses to sell alcohol for consumption on the premises, and shops must have licenses to sell it for consumption off the premises. In either case, licenses prohibit sale of alcohol to persons under 18. The same holds true for Macau. Licensing hours vary from area to area. In 2011 drunk driving (specified at over 0.08% blood-alcohol) was made a criminal offence, with occasional checkpoints in cities.

Driving Rules See "Getting Around," earlier in this chapter, p. 788.

Electricity The electricity used in all parts of China is 220 volts, alternating current (AC), 50 cycles. Most devices from North America, therefore, cannot be used without a transformer. If you have 110V devices your hotel may be able to supply a voltage converter. The most common outlet takes the North American two-flat-pin plug (but not the three-pin version, or those with one pin broader than the other). You may also come across outlets for the three-flat-pin (two pins at an angle) variety used in Australia and, less frequently the two-round-pin plugs common in Europe. Some hotel rooms have outlets designed to take all three plugs. Adapters with two or three flat pins are available inexpensively in department stores, and good hotels can often provide them free of charge. China is quite sophisticated in this area, and one can easily buy a power strip that has the requisite plug to go into a Chinese wall outlet and eight universal outlets that will accept any type of plug used in the world. Shaver sockets are common in bathrooms of hotels from three stars upward. In **Hong Kong** and **Macau,** the British-style three-chunky-pin plugs are standard, although Macau also has round-pin varieties.

Embassies & Consulates Most countries maintain embassies in Beijing and consulates in Hong Kong. Australia also has consulates in Guangzhou and Shanghai; Canada and the U.K. in Chongqing, Guangzhou, and Shanghai; New Zealand in Shanghai; and the U.S. in Chengdu, Guangzhou, and Shanghai. See the relevant chapters for further information.

Emergencies ✆ **110** for the police, ✆ **119** for fire, or ✆ **120** for ambulance, although the three are soon to be merged into a super-emergency number, ✆ **110.** Some English may be spoken but it's best to have a Chinese speaker make the call if possible. In **Hong Kong** and **Macau** dial ✆ **999** for police, fire, or ambulance.

Family Travel Travel with children is increasingly popular, and family-oriented China is a great place to take the kids. Children must have their own passport and visa, but parents will be pleased to know that many travel expenses are discounted for kids: Children under 1.4m (4 ft. 7 in.) get 25% discounted tickets on sleeper trains, those under 11 travel half-price on planes, and many attractions also offer reduced rates.

When planning a trip with children it is important to think carefully about the balance of activities. As well as taking in the sights you want to see, you should also ensure that there are plenty of fun things for the kids to do, and that hotels and restaurants are as kid-friendly as possible (look for the "Kids" icon throughout the book). Your biggest challenges will be the long journeys between destinations (certainly if you travel by land) and the lack of familiar foods (unless your children have been brought up with Chinese food).

A few companies organize family trips to China, including: **Pacific Delight World Tours** (www.pacificdelighttours.com) and **Rascals in Paradise** (www.rascalsinparadise.com). Pacific runs tours that take in the Three Gorges and the Chengdu Panda Breeding Research Center, while San Francisco–based Rascals offers 14-day tours stretching from Beijing all the way down to Yangshuo.

Health See "Health", earlier in this chapter, p. 803.

Insurance For China, purchase travel insurance with air ambulance or scheduled airline repatriation built in. Be clear on the terms and conditions—is repatriation limited to life-threatening illnesses, for instance? If you do end up in hospital in China, you may face a substantial bill, and you will not be allowed to leave until you pay it *in cash*. For insurance payouts, you'll need to claim the expense when you return home, so make sure you have adequate proof of payment.

For further information on traveler's insurance, trip cancelation insurance, and medical insurance while traveling, please visit www.frommers.com/planning/.

Internet & Wi-Fi Despite highly publicized clamp-downs on Internet cafés, monitoring of traffic, and blocking of websites, China remains one of the easiest countries in the world in which to get online. Almost any hotel with a business center, right down to Chinese government–rated two-star level, offers expensive Internet access, and every town has a few Internet cafes *(wangba)*, with rates typically ¥2 to ¥5 per hour, many open 24 hours a day. Locations of cafes are given for most cities in this guide, but they come and go very rapidly. Keep your eyes open for the *wangba* characters given in chapter 16, "The Chinese Language." In **Hong Kong** many coffee bars have a free terminal or two.

Thanks to ADSL (Asymmetric Digital Subscriber Lines) many progressive bars and guesthouses are now offering free Internet on the mainland, too. Note that some Internet bars are often noisy and smoky places crammed full of teenage online gamers; you will usually find that the local library is a much cleaner, often cheaper alternative.

See the "Online Travelers Toolbox", earlier in this chapter (p. 802) for useful websites. Note that many media websites and those with financial information or any data whatsoever on China that disagrees with the party line are blocked from mainland China, as are some search engines. These days you may also be asked to show your passport before being able to surf the net.

Many hotels in Chinese cities (and tourist destinations) offer **in-room broadband Internet access.** This is often free, and you simply need to ask reception for a cable *(wangxin)*, but sometimes it is chargeable. Typical charges range from ¥10 per day in budget places, to ¥80 or more in five-star hotels. Most of the time you'll connect automatically, but on occasion you might need to input the IP address and password the hotel will provide you with. Some hotels also have **Wi-Fi** in the lobby, and maybe in the rooms; if you plan to use this, check that you get a decent signal as soon as you check in, and if it's weak, ask to change rooms. Finally, as a last resort, there's free, **anonymous dial-up access** across most of China, although this is slow, and seldom used these days.

Mainland China uses the standard U.S.-style RJ11 telephone jack also used as the port for laptops worldwide—that is, if you have a laptop that still has a phone jack. Cables with RJ11 jacks at both ends can be picked up for around $2 in department stores and electrical shops without difficulty. In **Hong Kong** and **Macau,** however, phone connections are often to U.K. standards, although in better hotels an RJ11 socket is provided. Standard electrical voltage across China is 220v, 50Hz, which most laptops can deal with, but North American users in particular should check. For power socket information, see "Electricity," above, p. 807.

Language English is widely spoken in Hong Kong, fairly common in Macau, and rare in the mainland, although this is changing. There will often be someone who speaks a little English at your hotel and you can ask that person to help you with phone calls and bookings, but for the bulk of the population "Hello" is where it starts and ends. No need to despair though, as charades, pointing, a sense of humor, and some pre-trip practice will all go a long way. Common courtesy aside, the two most common situations when you'll need some Chinese are getting around and dining, and to this end the names of hotels, attractions and recommended dishes are listed in Chinese and pinyin (Romanization of Chinese characters) at the back of this book. Those who choose to invest some time in learning a little Mandarin before their trip will find their efforts appreciated by locals (and maybe replied to with a torrent of unintelligible Chinese). Recommended phrasebooks include the Periplus ***Essential Mandarin Chinese Phrasebook,*** and **Google Translate** can also go a long way, or for those who want to get deeper beneath the surface of China, Mandarin classes are widely available in bigger cities.

Legal Aid If you get on the wrong side of the law in China, contact your consulate immediately.

LGBT Travelers In 2001 legislation was relaxed to the tune that homosexuality is no longer considered as a mental disorder in China. This was seen as a tacit declaration that homosexuality had been legalized and while much of China is still in denial, there is now a growing gay scene. Big cities, particularly Beijing, Shanghai, and Hong Kong, have gay bars, clubs, saunas, and massage parlors. For more information check out **www.utopia-asia.com**, publisher of the ***Utopia Guide to China,*** which has details of the gay scene in 50 of the country's cities.

Mail Sending mail from China is remarkably reliable, although sending it to private addresses within China is not. Take the mail to post offices rather than using mailboxes. Some larger hotels have postal services on-site. It helps if mail has its country of destination written in characters (which hotel staff can help with), but this is not essential. Letters and cards written in red ink will occasionally be rejected. Overseas mail: **postcards** ¥4.50, **letters under 10g** ¥5.40, **letters under 20g** ¥6.50. EMS (**express parcels** under 500g): to the U.S.: ¥180 to ¥240; to Europe ¥220 to ¥280; to Australia ¥160 to ¥210. **Normal parcels** up to 1 kilogram (2¼ lb.): to the **U.S.** by air ¥102, by sea ¥20 to ¥84; to the **U.K.** by air ¥142, by sea ¥22 to ¥108; to **Australia** by air ¥135, by sea ¥15 to ¥89. Letters and parcels can be registered for a small extra charge. Registration forms and Customs declaration forms are in Chinese and English. The post offices of **Hong Kong** and **Macau** are reliable, but both have their own stamps and rates.

Medical Requirements See "Health" earlier in this chapter, p. 803.

Mobile Phones All Europeans, most Australians, and many North Americans use GSM (Global System for Mobiles) cellphones. But while everyone else can take a regular GSM phone to China, North Americans (particularly U.S. wireless customers) operate on a different frequency, and need to have a more expensive tri-band model. International roaming charges can also be horrendously expensive, so it's far cheaper to buy a "pay as you go" **SIM card** on arrival in China. These are available at airports and train stations, and you can buy top-up cards from the service provider shops, as well as some news kiosks and post offices in larger cities. **China Mobile** tends to have the best coverage, but there are plenty of other options, including China Unicom. SIM cards generally cost around ¥100 and include a limited amount of talk-time. Getting the shop that you buy the SIM from to install and activate it makes life easier. If you're going to be traveling extensively around the country, bear in mind that calls will be cheapest in the "home zone" where you bought the SIM card, so if you have any choice about it, buy the SIM where you will be spending most of your time (or where you expect to make and receive the most calls). If your phone doesn't work in China (or if you don't want to risk losing your expensive phone while away), **buying a local cellphone** is a good option; the cheapest models are available for under ¥200, although they are unlikely to work in North America on your return.

Renting a phone is another alternative, although this is expensive, and best done from home, since such services are not widely available in China. That way you can give out your new number, and make sure the phone works. You'll usually pay $40 to $50 per week, plus air-time fees of at least $1 a minute. In the U.S., two good rental companies are **InTouch USA** (www.intouchglobal.com) and **RoadPost** (✆ **888/290-1616** or 905/272-4934; www.roadpost.com).

Money See Money & Costs earlier in this chapter, p. 796.

Multi-cultural Travelers See "Discrimination", earlier in Fast Facts.

Newspapers & Magazines Sino-foreign joint-venture hotels in the bigger cities have a selection of foreign newspapers and magazines available, but these are otherwise not on sale. The content of the English-language government propaganda sheet ***China Daily*** has improved in recent years, and it is often available free at hotels, and an English version of the **People's Daily** is available online at www.english.peopledaily.com.cn. Cities with larger populations support a number of self-censoring entertainment magazines with accurate entertainment listings, restaurant reviews, and local healthcare details. A vast range of English publications is easily available in **Hong Kong** and **Macau,** as well as local newspapers such as the ***South China Morning Post.***

Packing Whilst there are a few important items to remember, generally speaking, the less you pack the better, especially if you're planning to take a lot of public transport during your trip. Most items can be purchased easily (and more cheaply) in China than at home, and if you decide to take the items back with you then they'll become mementos of your trip. Of course China is a big country with a diverse climate range and so what you take will also depend on where you're going and when. By and large everywhere (except for the Himalayas) gets hot in the summer, and everywhere (except Hainan) gets cold in the winter, so pack accordingly. Taking clothes you can layer will give you the greatest flexibility, and a **raincoat, hat, and good sunglasses** can come in handy any time of year. Aside from **money, tickets, insurance, and passport** (and photocopies or electronic copies of the latter four), and the usual items you'd take on any trip, a few things that can be useful or difficult to get in China are as follows: business cards; photos of home; specific medicines; travel bathplug; and for women, moisturizer (it is difficult to purchase creams without whitener in China) and tampons (expensive and not always available).

Passports All visitors to China need a passport. Allow plenty of time before your trip to apply for a passport; processing normally takes 3 weeks but can take longer during busy periods (especially spring). And keep in mind that if you need a passport in a hurry, you'll pay a higher processing fee.

Australia **Australian Passport Information Service** (✆ **131-232,** or visit www.passports.gov.au).

Canada **Passport Office,** Department of Foreign Affairs and International Trade, Ottawa, ON K1A 0G3 (✆ **800/567-6868;** www.ppt.gc.ca).

Ireland **Passport Office,** Setanta Centre, Molesworth Street, Dublin 2 (✆ **01/671-1633;** www.foreignaffairs.gov.ie).

New Zealand **Passports Office,** Department of Internal Affairs, 47 Boulcott Street, Wellington, 6011 (✆ **0800/225-050** in New Zealand or 04/474-8100; www.passports.govt.nz).

United Kingdom Visit your nearest passport office, major post office, or travel agency or contact the **Identity and Passport Service (IPS),** 89 Eccleston Sq., London, SW1V 1PN (✆ **0300/222-0000;** www.ips.gov.uk).

United States To find your regional passport office, check the **U.S. State Department** website (http://travel.state.gov/passport) or call the **National Passport Information Center** (✆ **877/487-2778**) for automated information.

Police Known to foreigners as the **PSB** (**Public Security Bureau;** *gong'an ju*), although these represent only one of several different types of officer in mainland China, the police *(jingcha)* are best avoided unless absolutely necessary. If you must see them for some reason, then approach your hotel for assistance first, and visit the PSB offices listed in this guide as dealing with visa extensions, since these are the most likely branches to have an English-speaker. In **Hong Kong** and **Macau,** however, you can usually ask policemen for directions and expect them to be generally helpful.

Safety China was long touted as one of Asia's safest destinations, but this is changing. Physical violence is still virtually unheard of, but petty theft and scams are definitely on the rise. Be cautious about theft in the same places as anywhere else in the world—crowded markets, popular tourist sights, bus and railway stations, and airports. Take standard precautions against pickpockets (distribute your valuables around your person, wear a money belt inside your clothes, and avoid obvious displays of wealth). If you are a victim of theft, make a police report (go to the same addresses given for visa extensions in each city, where you are most likely to find an English-speaking policeman). But don't necessarily expect sympathy or action. The main purpose is to get a theft report to give to your insurers for compensation.

Visitors should be aware of various **scams** in areas of high tourist traffic, and be wary of Chinese who approach and speak in English: "Hello, friend! Welcome to China!" or similar. Those who want to practice their English and who suggest moving to some local haunt may leave you with a bill that has two zeros more on it than it should. Fake "art students" who approach you with a story about raising funds for a show overseas are another pest. In fact they are merely enticing you into a shop where you will be lied to extravagantly about the authenticity and true cost of various paintings, which you will then be pressured into buying.

While there have been minor terrorist attacks and general **unrest** in the Muslim northwest of the country, and anti-Han sentiment is rising in many peripheral regions (notably Tibet, Xinjiang, and Inner Mongolia), this seldom involves or relates to foreign tourists. Nevertheless, check government travel advisories for current conditions before traveling to these regions (see "Online Travelers Toolbox," p. 802 for details).

Senior Travel While Chinese seniors receive discounted admissions to many attractions these rarely apply to foreigners (although it's always worth having ID and asking). Some familiar foreign brand-name hotels may offer senior rates if you book in advance, although you'll usually beat those prices simply by showing up in person, if there are rooms available.

Smoking New laws passed in 2011, which deem smoking illegal in all enclosed public places, have thus far had little effect. Although over a million Chinese die each year from smoking related diseases, the health implications of smoking are not widely publicized, and the Chinese government remains the world's biggest cigarette manufacturer. On trains, smokers are generally sent to the spaces between the cars, but they won't bother to do so if no one protests.

Student Travel Education is highly esteemed in China and students are well-received and often eligible for discounts at attractions, providing they have a valid **ISIC** (International Student Identity Card; www.isic.org).

Taxes In **mainland China,** occasional taxes are added to hotel bills, but these are minor and usually included in the room rate. Service charges appear mostly in joint-venture hotels, and range from 10% to 15%. Many Chinese hotels list service charges in their literature, but few have the nerve to add them to room rates unless the hotel is very full. However, restaurants may add the service charge. There is no departure tax for domestic and international flights. There are also lesser taxes for international ferry departures at some ports. In **Hong Kong,** better hotels will add a 10% service charge and a 3% government tax to your bill. Better restaurants and bars will automatically add a 10% service charge. In **Macau,** better hotels charge 10% for service as well as a 5% tax. Marine departure taxes are included in ticket prices. Transit passengers who continue their journey within 24 hours of arrival are exempted from passenger tax.

Telephones To call China, Hong Kong, or Macau:

1. Dial the international access code (**011** in the U.S. and Canada, **00** in the U.K., Ireland, and New Zealand, or **0011** from Australia).
2. Dial the country code: **86** for China, **852** for Hong Kong, **853** for Macau.
3. For China, dial the city code, omitting the leading zero, and then the number. Hong Kong and Macau have no city codes, so after the country code, simply dial the remainder of the number.

To call within China: For calls within the same city, omit the city code, which always begins with a zero when used (**010** for Beijing, **020** for Guangzhou, and so on). All hotel phones have direct dialing, and most have international dialing. Hotels are only allowed to add a service charge of up to 15% to the cost of the call, and even long-distance rates within China are relatively low. To use a public telephone you'll need an **IC (Integrated Circuit) card** *(aaisei ka)*, available in values from ¥20. You can buy them at post offices, convenience stores, street stalls, or wherever you can make out the letters "IC" among the Chinese characters. A local call is typically ¥.22 for 3 minutes. Phones show you the value remaining on the card when you insert it, and count down as you talk.

To call within Hong Kong: In Hong Kong, local calls made from homes, offices, shops, and other establishments are free, so don't feel shy about asking to use the phone. From hotel lobbies and public phone booths, a local call costs HK$1 for each 5 minutes; from hotel rooms, about HK$4 to HK$5. **To call within Macau:** Local calls from private phones are free, and from call boxes cost MOP$1.

To make international calls: From mainland China or Macau, first dial **00** and then the country code (U.S. or Canada **1,** U.K. **44,** Ireland **353,** Australia **61,** New Zealand **64**). Next, dial the area or city code, omitting any leading zero, and then the number. For example, if you want to call the British Embassy in Washington, D.C., you would dial ✆ 00-1-202/588-7800. Forget taking access numbers for your local phone company with you—you can call internationally for a fraction of the cost by using an **IP (Internet Protocol) card,** *aaipii ka,* purchased from department stores and other establishments—wherever you see the letters "IP." Instructions for use are on the back, but you simply dial the access number given, choose English from the menu, and follow the instructions to dial in the number behind a scratch-off panel. Depending on where you call, ¥50 can give you around half an hour of talking, but you should bargain to pay less than the face value of the card—sometimes as little as ¥70 for a ¥100 card from street vendors. From a public phone, you'll need an IC card (see above) to make the local call. In **emergencies,** dial **108** to negotiate a **collect call,** but again, in most towns you'll need help from a Mandarin speaker.

From **Hong Kong** dial **001, 0080,** or **009,** depending on which of several competing phone companies you are using. Follow with the country code and continue as for calling from China or Macau. It's much cheaper to use one of several competing phone cards, such as *Talk Talk,* which come in HK$50 and HK$100 denominations and are available at HKTB information offices and convenience stores.

For directory assistance: In mainland China dial ✆ **114** which should have an English speaker in Beijing and Shanghai. If you want other cities, dial the city code followed by 114—a long-distance call. In Hong Kong dial ✆ **1081.** In Macau dial ✆ **181** for domestic numbers, and ✆ **101** for international ones.

For operator assistance: If you need operator assistance in making a call, just ask for help at your hotel. In Hong Kong dial ✆ **1010** for domestic assistance, **10013** for international assistance.

Toll-free numbers: Numbers beginning with **800** within China are toll-free, but not accessible from all cellphone networks. Calling a toll-free number abroad from China is a full-tariff international call, as is calling one in Hong Kong from mainland China, or vice versa. For **400** numbers callers will only pay the cost of the local access call.

Time

The whole of China is on Beijing time, which means that in the far northwest of the country sundown may not be until 11pm, causing the locals to use their own local "Xinjiang time", 2 hours behind Beijing time. Beijing time is 8 hours ahead of GMT (and therefore of London), 13 hours ahead of New York, 14 hours ahead of Chicago, and 16 hours ahead of Los Angeles. There's no daylight saving time (summertime), so subtract 1 hour in the summer. For help with time translations, and more, download our convenient Travel Tools app for your mobile device. Go to www.frommers.com/go/mobile/ and click on the Travel Tools icon.

Tipping

In **mainland China,** tipping is not expected and will likely be refused if offered. The Chinese do not tip, but those involved in the tourist trade are familiar with tipping and are unlikely to refuse it. If you are on an escorted tour, your leader may collect a kitty to be distributed as appropriate.

In **Hong Kong** and **Macau,** even though restaurants and bars will automatically add a 10% service charge to your bill, you're still expected to leave small change for the waiter, up to a few US dollars in the very best restaurants. You're also expected to tip taxi drivers, bellhops, barbers, and beauticians. For taxi drivers, simply round up your bill to the nearest HK$1 or add a HK$1 tip. Tip people who cut your hair 5% or 10%, and give bellhops HK$10 to HK$20, depending on the number of your bags. If you use a public restroom that has an attendant, you may be expected to leave a small gratuity—HK$2 should be enough.

Toilets Street-level public toilets in China are common, many detectable by the nose before they are seen. There's often an entrance fee of ¥.20 to ¥.50, but not necessarily running water. Toilet paper isn't provided but can often be purchased from an attendant at the entrance. In many cases you merely squat over a trough. So, use the standard Western equipment in your hotel room, in department stores and malls, and in branches of foreign fast-food chains. In Hong Kong and Macau, facilities are far more hygienic.

VAT See "Taxes" above.

Visas See "Visas" earlier in this chapter, p. 794.

Visitor Information **China National Tourist Offices** (www.cnto.org):

In the United States New York office: 370 Lexington Ave., Suite 912, Empire State Building, New York, NY 10017 (✆ **212/760-8218;** fax 212/760-8809; ny@cnto.org). California office: 550 North Brand Blvd., Suite 910, Glendale, CA 91203 (✆ **818/545-7507;** fax 818/545-7506; la@cnto.org).

In Canada 480 University Ave., Suite 806, Toronto, ON M5G 1V2 (✆ **416/599-6636;** fax 416/599-6382; www.tourismchina-ca.com).

In the U.K. 4 Glentworth St., London NW1 5PG (✆ **020/7935-9787;** fax 020/7487-5842; london@cnta.gov.cn).

In Australia 19F, 44 Market St., Sydney, NSW 2000 (✆ **02/9299-4057;** fax 02/9290-1958; sydney@cnta.gov.cn).

Hong Kong Tourism Board (www.discoverhongkong.com):

In the U.S. New York office: 370 Lexington Ave., Suite 1812, New York, NY 10017 (✆ **212/421-3382;** fax 212/421-8428; nycwwo@hktb.com). California office: 5670 Wilshire Blvd., Suite 1230, Los Angeles, CA 90024-3915 (✆ **323/938-4582;** fax 323/938-4583; laxwo@hktb.com).

In Canada 9 Temperance St., Toronto, ON M5H 1Y6 (✆ **416/366-2389;** fax 416/366-1098; yyzwwo@hktb.com).

In the U.K. 6F, Mutual House, 70 Conduit St., London W1S 2GF (✆ **020/7432-7700;** fax 020/7432-7701; lonwwo@hktb.com).

In Australia Level 4, Hong Kong House, 80 Druitt St., Sydney, NSW 2000 (✆ **02/9283-3083;** fax 02/9283-3383; sydwwo@hktb.com).

Macau Government Tourism Office (www.macautourism.gov.mo):

In the U.S. New York office: 501 Fifth Ave., Suite 1101, New York, NY 10017 (✆ **646/277-0690;** fax 646/366-8170; macau@myriadmarketing.com). California office: 1334 Parkview Ave., Ste. 300, Manhattan Beach, CA 90266 (✆ **310/545-3464;** fax 310/545-3464; macau@myriadmarketing.com).

In the U.K. 11 Parkshot House, 5 Kew Rd., Richmond, Surrey, TW9 2PR (✆ **020/8334-8325;** fax 020/8334-8100; macau@humewhitehead.co.uk).

In Australia Level 11, 99 Bathurst St., Sydney, NSW 2000 (✆ **02/9264-1488;** fax 02/9267-7717; macau@worldtradetravel.com).

In New Zealand Level 10, 120 Albert St., P.O. Box 6247, Auckland (✆ **09/308-5206;** fax 09/308-5207; macau@aviationandtourism.co.nz).

Water Tap water in mainland China is not drinkable, and should not even be used for brushing your teeth. Use bottled water, widely available on every street, and provided for free in all the better hotels. Tap water is drinkable in Hong Kong, but bottled water tastes better.

Wi-Fi See "Internet & Wi-Fi," earlier in this section.

Women Travelers When compared with many other countries, travel for women in China throws up few more problems than it does for men. You may well be stared at, but this is not the intimidating ogle faced in some countries. In the northwest more care is advised, and as with anywhere you'd be wise to take a few basic precautions, such as avoiding unlit areas late at night. In urban China, dress for women is fairly relaxed, but in rural areas conservative clothing is advised. Sanitary pads are widely available, although tampons are harder to come by outside of the big cities.

16 THE CHINESE LANGUAGE

Chinese is not as difficult a language to learn as it may first appear to be—at least not once you've decided what kind of Chinese to learn. There are six major languages called Chinese. Speakers of each are unintelligible to speakers of the others, and there are, in addition, a host of dialects. The Chinese you are likely to hear spoken in your local Chinatown, in your local Chinese restaurant, or used by your friends of Chinese descent when they speak to their parents, is more than likely to be Cantonese, which is the version of Chinese used in Hong Kong and in much of southern China. But the official national language of China is **Mandarin** (**Pǔtōnghuà**—"common speech"), sometimes called Modern Standard Chinese, and viewed in mainland China as the language of administration, of the classics, and of the educated. While throughout much of mainland China people speak their own local flavor of Chinese for everyday communication, they've all been educated in Mandarin, which in general terms is the language of Beijing and the north. Mandarin is less well known in Hong Kong and Macau, but is also spoken in Taiwan and Singapore, and among growing communities of recent immigrants to North America and Europe.

Chinese grammar is considerably more straightforward than that of English or other European languages, even Spanish or Italian. There are no genders, so there is no need to remember long lists of endings for adjectives and to make them agree, with variations according to case. There are no equivalents for the definite and indefinite articles ("the," "a," "an"), so there is no need to make those agree either. Singular and plural nouns are the same. Best of all, verbs cannot be declined. The verb "to be" is *shì*. The same sound also covers "am," "are," "is," "was," "will be," and so on, since there are also no tenses. Instead of past, present, and future, Chinese is more concerned with whether an action is continuing or has been completed, and with the order in which events take place. To make matters of time clear, Chinese depends on simple expressions such as "yesterday," "before," "originally," "next year," and the like. "Tomorrow I go New York," is clear enough, as is "Yesterday I go New York." It's a little more complicated than these brief notes can suggest, but not much.

There are a few sounds in Mandarin that are not used in English (see the rough pronunciation guide below), but the main difficulty for foreigners lies in tones. Most sounds in Mandarin begin with a consonant and end in a vowel (or -n, or -ng), which leaves the language with very few distinct noises compared to English. Originally, one sound equaled one idea and one word. Even now, each of these monosyllables is represented by a single character, but often words have been made by putting two characters together, sometimes both of the same meaning, thus reinforcing one another. The solution to this phonetic poverty is to multiply the available sounds by making them tonal—speaking them at different pitches, thereby giving them different meanings. *Mā* spoken on a high level tone (first tone) offers a set of possible meanings different to those of *má* spoken with a rising tone (second tone), *mǎ* with a dipping then rising tone (third tone), or *mà* with an abruptly falling tone (fourth tone). There's also a different meaning for the neutral, toneless *ma*.

Cantonese has *eight* tones plus the neutral, but its grammatical structure is largely the same as Mandarin, as is that of all versions of Chinese. Even Chinese people who can barely understand each other's speech can at least write to each other, since written forms are similar. Mainland China, with the aim of increasing literacy (or perhaps of distancing the supposedly now thoroughly modern and socialist population from its Confucian heritage), instituted a ham-fisted simplification program in the 1950s, which reduced some characters originally taking 14 strokes of the brush, for instance, to as few as three strokes. Hong Kong, separated from the mainland and under British control until 1997, went its own way, kept the original full-form characters, and invented lots of new ones, too. Nevertheless, many characters remain the same, and some of the simplified forms are merely familiar shorthand for the full-form ones. But however many different meanings for each tone of *ma* there may be, for each meaning there's a different character. This makes the written form a far more successful communication medium than the spoken one, which leads to misunderstandings even between native speakers, who can often be seen sketching characters on their palms during conversation to confirm which one is meant.

The thought of learning 3,000 to 5,000 individual characters (at least 2,500 are needed to read a newspaper) also daunts many beginners. But look carefully at the ones below, and you'll notice many common elements. In fact, a rather limited number of smaller shapes are combined in different ways, much as we combine letters to make words. Admittedly, the characters only offer general hints as to their pronunciation, and that's often misleading—the system is not a phonetic one, so each new Mandarin word has to be learned as both a sound and a shape (or a group of them). But soon it's the similarities among the characters, not their differences, that begin to bother the student. For help with navigation to sights, simply point to the characters below. When leaving your hotel, take one of its cards with you, and show it to the taxi driver when you want to return. At the end of section 2 is a limited list of useful words and phrases, which is best supplemented with a proper phrase book, such as *Frommer's Chinese Phrasefinder & Dictionary.*

A GUIDE TO PĪNYĪN PRONUNCIATION

Letters in pīnyīn mostly have the values any English speaker would expect, with the following exceptions:

c ts as in bits
q ch as in chin, but much harder and more forward, made with tongue and teeth
r has no true equivalent in English, but the *r* of *r*eed is close, although the tip of the tongue should be near the top of the mouth, and the teeth together

x also has no true equivalent, but is nearest to the *sh* of *sh*eep, although the tongue should be parallel to the roof of the mouth and the teeth together
zh is a soft j, like the *dge* in ju*dge*

The vowels are pronounced roughly as follows:

a as f*a*ther
e as in *e*rr (*leng* is pronounced as English "lung")
i is pronounced *ee* after most consonants, but after c, ch, r, s, sh, z, and zh is a buzz at the front of the mouth behind the closed teeth
o as in s*o*ng
u as in t*oo*
ü is the purer, lips-pursed u of French t*u* and German *ü*. Confusingly, u after j, x, q, and y is always ü, but in these cases the accent over "ü" does not appear.
ai sounds like *eye*
ao as in *ou*ch
ei as in h*ay*
ia as in *ya*k
ian sounds like *yen*
iang sounds like *yang*
iu sounds like *you*
ou as in t*oe*
ua as in g*ua*va
ui sounds like *way*
uo sounds like *or,* but is more abrupt

Note that when two or more third-tone "ˇ" sounds follow one another, they should all, except the last, be pronounced as second-tone "ˊ."

MANDARIN BARE ESSENTIALS

GREETINGS & INTRODUCTIONS

English	Pinyin	Chinese
Hello	Nǐ hǎo	你好
How are you?	Nǐ hǎo ma?	你好吗?
Fine. And you?	Wǒ hěn hǎo. Nǐ ne?	我很好,你呢?
I'm not too well/things aren't going well	Bù hǎo	不好
What is your name? (very polite)	Nín guì xìng?	您贵姓?
My (family) name is . . .	Wǒ xìng	我姓......
I'm known as (family, then given name)	Wǒ jiào.......	我叫......
I'm [American]	Wǒ shì [Měiguó] rén	我是美国人
[Australian]	[Àodàlìyà]	澳大利亚
[British]	[Yīngguó]	英国
[Canadian]	[Jiānádà]	加拿大
[Irish]	[Àiěrlán]	爱尔兰
[New Zealander]	[Xīnxīlán]	新西兰

English	Pinyin	Chinese
I'm from [America]	Wǒ shì cóng [Měiguó] lái de	我是从美国来的
Excuse me/I'm sorry	Duìbùqǐ	对不起
I don't understand	Wǒ tīng bù dǒng	我听不懂
Thank you	Xièxie nǐ	谢谢你
Correct (yes)	Duì	对
Not correct	Bú duì	不对
No, I don't want	Wǒ bú yào	我不要
Not acceptable	Bù xíng	不行

BASIC QUESTIONS & PROBLEMS

English	Pinyin	Chinese
Excuse me/I'd like to ask	Qǐng wènyíxià	请问一下
Where is . . . ?	......zài nǎr?	......在哪儿?
How much is . . . ?	......duōshǎo qián?	......多少钱?
. . . this one?	Zhèi/Zhè ge......	这个......
. . . that one?	Nèi/Nà ge......	那个......
Do you have . . . ?	Nǐ yǒu méi yǒu......?	你有没有......?
What time does/is . . . ?	......jǐ diǎn?	......几点?
What time is it now?	Xiànzài jǐ diǎn?	现在几点?
When is . . . ?	......shénme shíhou?	......什么时候?
Why?	Wèishénme?	为什么?
Who?	Shéi?	谁?
Is that okay?	Xíng bù xíng?	行不行?
I'm feeling ill	Wǒ shēng bìng le	我生病了

NUMBERS

Note that more complicated forms of numbers are often used on official documents and receipts to prevent fraud—see how easily 1 can be changed to 2, 3, or even 10. Familiar Arabic numerals appear on bank notes, most signs, taxi meters, and other places. Be particularly careful with *4* and *10,* which sound very alike in many regions—hold up fingers to make sure. Note, too, that *yī,* meaning "one," tends to change its tone all the time depending on what it precedes. Don't worry about this—once you've started talking about money, almost any kind of squeak for "one" will do. Finally note that "two" alters when being used with expressions of quantity.

English	Pinyin	Chinese
0	líng	零
1	yī	一
2	èr	二
2 (of them)	liǎng ge	两个
3	sān	三
4	sì	四
5	wǔ	五
6	liù	六

English	Pinyin	Chinese
7	qī	七
8	bā	八
9	jiǔ	九
10	shí	十
11	shí yī	十一
12	shí èr	十二
21	èr shí yī	二十一
22	èr shí èr	二十二
51	wǔ shí yī	五十一
100	yì bǎi	一百
101	yì bǎi líng yī	一百零一
110	yì bǎi yī (shí)	一百一（十）
111	yì bǎi yī shí yī	一百一十一
1,000	yì qiān	一千
1,500	yì qiān wǔ (bǎi)	一千五百
5,678	wǔ qiān liù bǎi qī shí bāi	五千六百七十八
10,000	yí wàn	一万

MONEY

The word *yuan* (¥) is rarely spoken, nor is *jiao*, the written form for 1/10th of a *yuan*, equivalent to 10 *fen* (there are 100 *fen* in a *yuan*). Instead, the Chinese speak of "pieces of money," *kuai qian*, usually abbreviated just to *kuai*, and they speak of *mao* for 1/10th of a *kuai*. *Fen* have been overtaken by inflation and are almost useless. Often all zeros after the last whole number are simply omitted, along with *kuai qian*, which is taken as read, especially in direct reply to the question *duoshao qian*—"How much?"

English	Pinyin	Chinese
¥.30	sān máo qián	三毛钱
¥1	yí kuài qián	一块钱
¥2	liǎng kuài qián	两块钱
¥5.05	wǔ kuài líng wǔ fēn	五块零五分
¥5.50	wǔ kuài wǔ	五块五
¥550	wǔ bǎi wǔ shí kuài	五百五十块
¥5,500	wǔ qiān wǔ bǎi kuài	五千五百块
Small change	língqián	零钱

BANKING & SHOPPING

English	Pinyin	Chinese
I want to change money (foreign exchange)	Wǒ xiǎng huàn qián	我想换钱
credit card	Xìnyòngkǎ	信用卡
traveler's check	lǚxíng zhīpiào	旅行支票
department store	bǎihuò shāngdiàn	百货商店
or	gòuwù zhōngxīn	购物中心
convenience store	xiǎomàibù	小卖部/便利店

English	Pinyin	Chinese
market	shìchǎng	市场
supermarket		超市
shopping mall	gòuwù zhōngxīn	购物中心
May I have a look?	Wǒ Kànyíxia, hǎo ma?	我看一下, 好吗?
I want to buy . . .	Wǒ xiǎng mǎi......	我想买......
How many do you want?	Nǐ yào jǐ ge?	你要几个?
Two of them	liǎng ge	两个
Three of them	sān ge	三个
1 kilo	yì gōngjīn	一公斤
Half a kilo	yì jīn	一斤
or	bàn gōngjīn	半公斤
1m	yì mǐ	一米
Too expensive!	Tài guì le!	太贵了
Do you have change?	Yǒu língqián ma?	有零钱吗?

TIME

English	Pinyin	Chinese
morning	shàngwǔ	上午
afternoon	xiàwǔ	下午
evening	wǎnshang	晚上
8:20am	shàngwǔ bā diǎn èr shí fēn	上午八点二十分
9:30am	shàngwǔ jiǔ diǎn bàn	上午九点半
noon	zhōngwǔ	中午
4:15pm	xiàwǔ sì diǎn yí kè	下午四点一刻
midnight	wǔ yè	午夜
1 hour	yí ge xiǎoshí	一个小时
8 hours	bā ge xiǎoshí	八个小时
today	jīntiān	今天
yesterday	zuótiān	昨天
tomorrow	míngtiān	明天
Monday	Xīngqī yī	星期一
Tuesday	Xīngqī èr	星期二
Wednesday	Xīngqī sān	星期三
Thursday	Xīngqī sì	星期四
Friday	Xīngqī wǔ	星期五
Saturday	Xīngqī liù	星期六
Sunday	Xīngqī tiān	星期天

TRANSPORT & TRAVEL

English	Pinyin	Chinese
I want to go to . . .	Wǒ xiǎng qù......	我想去......
plane	fēijī	飞机
train	huǒchē	火车
bus	gōnggòng qìchē	公共汽车

English	Pinyin	Chinese
long-distance bus	chángtú qìchē	长途汽车
taxi	chūzū chē	出租车
airport	jīchǎng	机场
stop or station (bus or train)	zhàn	站
(plane/train/bus) ticket	piào	票
luxury (bus, hotel rooms)	háohuá	豪华
high-speed (buses, expressways)	gāosù	高速
air-conditioned	kōngtiáo	空调
When's the last bus?	Mòbānchē jīdiǎn kāi?	末班车几点开?

NAVIGATION

English	Pinyin	Chinese
north	Běi	北
south	Nán	南
east	Dōng	东
west	Xī	西
Turn left	zuǒ guǎi	左拐
Turn right	yòu guǎi	右拐
Go straight on	yìzhí zǒu	一直走
crossroads	shízì lùkǒu	十字路口
10km	shí gōnglǐ	十公里
I'm lost	Wǒ diū le	我丢了

HOTEL

English	Pinyin	Chinese
How many days?	Zhù jǐ tiān?	住几天?
standard room (twin or double with private bathroom)	biāozhǔn jiān	标准间
passport	hùzhào	护照
deposit	yājīn	押金
I want to check out	Wǒ tuì fáng	我退房

RESTAURANT

English	Pinyin	Chinese
How many people?	Jǐ wèi?	几位?
waiter/waitress	fúwùyuán	服务员
menu	càidān	菜单
I'm vegetarian	Wǒ shì chī sù de	我是吃素的
Do you have . . . ?	Yǒu méi yǒu......?	有没有......?
Please bring a portion of . . .	Qǐng lái yí fènr......	请来一份儿......
beer	píjiǔ	啤酒
mineral water	kuàngquán shuǐ	矿泉水
Bill, please	jiézhàng	结帐

SIGNS

Here's a list of common signs and notices to help you identify what you are looking for, from restaurants to condiments, and to help you choose the right door at the public restroom. These are the simplified characters in everyday use in China, but note that it's increasingly fashionable for larger businesses, and those with a long history, to use more complicated traditional characters, so not all may match what's below. Hong Kong and Macau also use traditional characters, and sometimes use different terms altogether, especially for modern inventions. Also, very old restaurants and temples across China tend to write their signs from right to left.

English	Pinyin	Chinese
hotel	bīnguǎn	宾馆
	dàjiǔdiàn	大酒店
	jiǔdiàn	酒店
	fàndiàn	饭店
restaurant	fànguǎn	饭馆
	jiǔdiàn	酒店
	jiǔjiā	酒家
bar	jiǔbā	酒吧
Internet bar	wǎngbā	网吧
cafe	kāfēiguǎn	咖啡馆
teahouse	cháguǎn	茶馆
department store	bǎihuò shāngdiàn	百货商店
or	gòuwù zhōngxīn	购物中心
market	shìchǎng	市场
bookstore	shūdiàn	书店
police (Public Security Bureau)	gōng'ānjú	公安局
Bank of China	Zhōngguó Yínháng	中国银行
public telephone	gōngyòng diànhuà	公用电话
public restroom	gōngyòng cèsuǒ	公用厕所
male	nán	男
female	nǚ	女
entrance	rùkǒu	入口
exit	chūkǒu	出口
bus stop/station	qìchē zhàn	汽车站
long-distance bus station	chángtú qìchē zhàn	长途汽车站
luxury	háohuá	豪华
using highway	gāosù	高速公路
railway station	huǒchēzhàn	火车站
hard seat	yìng zuò	硬座
soft seat	ruǎn zuò	软座
hard sleeper	yìng wò	硬卧
soft sleeper	ruǎn wò	软卧
direct (through) train	zhídá	直达
express train	tèkuài	特快

English	Pinyin	Chinese
metro/subway station	dìtiězhàn	地铁站
airport	jīchǎng	机场
dock/wharf	mǎtóu	码头
passenger terminal (bus, boat, and so on)	kèyùn zhàn	客运站
up/get on	shàng	上
down/get off	xià	下
ticket hall	shòupiào tīng	售票厅
ticket office	shòupiào chù	售票处
left-luggage office	xíngli jìcún chù	行李寄存处
temple	sì	寺
or	miào	庙
museum	bówùguǎn	博物馆
memorial hall	jìniànguǎn	纪念馆
park	gōngyuán	公园
hospital	yīyuàn	医院
clinic	zhěnsuǒ	诊所
pharmacy	yàofáng/yàodiàn	药房/药店
travel agency	lǚxíngshè	旅行社

SELECTED DESTINATIONS BY CITY

Following are some translations for destinations not covered in maps in this book, organized by chapter, then by city (per location within the chapter). Just point to the characters when asking a cabdriver to take you to the specific destination.

Beijing 北京 & Hebei 河北 (chapter 4)

SIDE TRIPS FROM BEIJING

Cháng Líng	长陵
Dìng Líng	定陵
Jiètái Sì	戒台寺
Jīnshānlǐng	金山岭
Shén Dào (Spirit Way)	神道
Shi San Ling	十三陵
Tánzhè Sì	潭柘寺

SHANHAIGUAN 山海关

Attractions

Jiǎo Shān	角山
Lǎo Lóng Tóu	老龙头
Mèngjiāngnǚ Miào	孟姜女庙
Tiānxià Dìyī Guān	天下第一关
Wáng Jiā Dàyuàn	王家大院

Restaurants

Sì Tiáo Bāoziguǎn	四条包子馆

SHIJIAZHUANG 石家庄

Attractions

Bǎilín Sì	柏林寺
Cāngyán Shān	苍岩山
Zhàozhōu Qiáo	赵州桥
Zhèngdìng	正定

Hotels & Restaurants

Héběi Shìjì Dàfàndiàn (Héběi Century Hotel)	河北世纪大饭店
Huìwén Jiǔdiàn	汇文酒店
Quánjùdé	全聚德
Shāo'ézǎi	烧鹅仔
Shìmào Guǎngchǎng Jiǔdiàn (World Trade Plaza Hotel)	世贸广场酒店

The Northeast (chapter 5)

SHENYANG 沈阳

Outside Shenyang

Qiānshān	千山

DANDONG 丹东

Outside Dandong

Five Dragon Mountain (Wǔlóngshān)	五龙山
Tiger Mountain Great Wall (Hǔshān Chángchén)	虎山长城

DALIAN 大连

Attractions

Bàngchuí Dǎo	棒棰岛
Discoveryland (Fāxiàn Wángguó)	发现王国
Èrlíngsān Gāodì 203	高地
Fu Jia Zhuang Beach (Fùjiāzhuāng Hǎibīn Yùchǎng)	傅家庄海滨浴场
Jīnshí Tān	金石滩
Lǎohǔ Tān Hǎiyáng Gōngyuán	老虎滩海洋公园
Lǎohǔ Tān	老虎滩
Lǚshùn	旅顺
Shuǐshī Yíng	水师营
Sun Asia Ocean World (Shèngyà Hǎiyáng Shìjiè)	圣亚海洋世界
Xīnghǎi Gōngyuán	星海公园

YANBIAN 延边

Attractions

Fángchuān	防川
Yanji	延吉

Hotels & Restaurants

Dazhou Jiǔdiàn (Dazhou Hotel)	大洲酒店
Home Inn (Rújiā)	如家
Jīndálái Fàndiàn	金达莱饭店
Mozhate Kuaicandian	莫扎特快餐店
Yánbiān Dàyǔ Fàndiàn (Yánbiān International Hotel)	延边国际饭店

CHANGBAI SHAN 长白山

Attractions

Běi Pō (North Shore)	北坡
Dìxià Sēnlín (Underground Forest)	地下森林
Jinjiang Canyon	锦江峡谷
Měirén Sōng Sēnlín (Sylvan Pine Forest)	美人松森林
Sōngjiāng Hé	松江河
Tiān Chí (Heavenly Lake) Èrdào Bái Hé (Bái Hé for short)	二道白河
Wēnquán Yù	温泉峪
Xī Pō Shān Mén (West Slope Mountain Gate)	西坡山门
Xiao Tian Chi	小天池

Hotels & Restaurants

Chángbái Shān Dàyǔ Fàndiàn (Chángbái Shān Daewoo)	长白山大宇饭店
Chángbái Shān Guójì Bīnguǎn (Chángbái Shān International Hotel)	长白山国际宾馆
Chángbái Shān Lánjǐng Dàisī Jiǔdiàn	长白山蓝景戴斯酒店
Fúbǎi Bīnguǎn	福柏宾馆
Horizon Resort & Spa Changbai Mountain	长白山天域度假酒店
Jin Shui He International	金水鹤国际酒店
Landscape Hotel & Resorts	蓝景温泉度假酒店
Xìndá Bīnguǎn	信达宾馆
Yùndòngyúan Cūn (Athlete's Village)	运动员村

HARBIN 哈尔滨

Attractions

St. Sophia Church (Shèngsuǒfēiyà Dàjiàotángdàn)	圣索菲亚大教堂
Unit 731 Museum (Qīnhuá Rìjūn Dì Qīsānyī Bùduì Yízhǐ)	侵華日軍第731部队遗址

WU DA LINACHI 五大连池

Attractions

Bīngdòng	冰洞
Lǎohēi Shǎn	老黑山
Nánquán	南泉
Shíhǎi	石海

Hotels

Wu Da Lianchi Worker's Sanatorium (Wǔdàliánchí Gōngrén Liáoyǎngyuàn)	五大连池工人疗养院

MANZHOULI 满洲里

Attractions

Dálài Hú (Hūlún Hú)	呼伦湖
Eluosi Taowa Guangchang (Russian Matryoshka Dolls Plaza)	俄罗斯套娃广场
Guó Mén (Sino-Russian Border Crossing)	国门
Hūlúnbèi'ěr Cǎoyuán (Hulun Buir Grasslands)	呼伦贝尔草原
Nánèrdàojiē	南二道街
Zālàinuòěr	扎赉诺尔

Hotels & Restaurants

Beijiaerhu Xīcāntīng	贝加尔湖西餐厅
Dàmòfáng (Délifrance)	大磨坊
Duolisi Yishu Jiudian	满洲里多利斯艺术酒店
Jiayi Jǐudiàn (Home 1 Hotel)	家易时尚酒店
Mǎnzhōulǐ Yǒuyì Bīnguǎn (Friendship Hotel)	满洲里友谊宾馆
Mengxiangyuan Huǒguō	蒙祥原火锅
Shangri-la Hotel	满洲里香格里拉大酒店
Weiduoliya Jiudian	满洲里维多利亚酒店
Xīnmǎnyuán Xīcāntīng	新满园西餐厅

Along the Yellow River (chapter 6)

DATONG 大同

Attractions

Hanging Temple (Xuán Kōng Sì)	悬空寺
Ying Xian Wooden Pagoda (Yìng Xiàn M ù Tǎ)	应县木塔
Yungang Caves (Yúngǎng Shíkū)	云冈石窟

HOHHOT 呼和浩特

Attractions

Traveler's Holiday Village (Lǚyóu Dùjiàcūn)	旅游度假村

YINCHUAN 银川

Attractions

108 Dagobas (Qīngtóngxiá Yībǎilíngbā Tǎ)	青铜峡一百零八塔
Na Family Mosque (Najiāhù Qīngzhēnsì)	纳家户清真寺
Sea Treasure Pagoda (Hǎibǎo Tǎ)	海宝塔
Western Xia Tombs (Xī Xià Wáng Líng)	西夏王陵

YAN'AN 延安

Attractions

Bǎotǎ (Baǒ Pagoda)	宝塔
Fènghuáng Shān (Phoenix Hill)	凤凰山
Gémìng Jìniànguǎn (Revolutionary Memorial Hall/Museum)	革命纪念馆
Wángjiāpíng Gémìng Jiùzhǐ (Former Revolutionary Headquarters at Wángjiāpíng)	王家坪革命旧址
Yángjiālǐng Jiùzhǐ (Yángjiālǐng Revolutionary Headquarters)	杨家岭旧址

Hotels & Restaurants

Jīnróng Bīnguǎn	金融宾馆
Tianzi Shangwu Jiudian (Tiān Zǐ Shāng Wù Jiǔ Diàn)	天子商务酒店
Wúqǐ Dàjiǔdiàn	吴起大酒店
Yán'ān Bīnguǎn	延安宾馆
Yàshèng Dàjiǔdiàn	亚圣大酒店
Yínhǎi Guójì Dàjiǔdiàn	银海国际大酒店

PINGYAO 平遥

Attractions

Bǎi Chuān Tōng	百川通
Chénghuáng Miào, Cáishén Miào	城隍庙, 财神庙
Gǔ Chéngqiáng (Ancient City Wall)	古城墙
Léi Lǚ Tài Gùjū	雷履泰故居
Qiáo Jiā Dàyuàn	乔家大院
Rìshēng Chāng	日升昌
Shì Lóu (Market Building)	市楼
Shuānglín Sì	双林寺
Wáng Jiā Dàyuàn (Wáng Family Courtyard)	王家大院
Xiànyá Shǔ (or Yámen)	县衙署, 衙门
Zàojūn Miào	灶君庙
Zhangbi Ancient Castle (Zhāngbì Gúbǎo)	张壁古堡
Zhènguó Sì	镇国寺

Hotels

Déjū Yuán	德居源
Kylin Grand Hotel (Shān Xī Píng Yáo Qí Lín Gé Dà Fàn Diàn)	山西平遥麒麟阁大饭店
Tiān Yuán Kuí	天元奎

WUTAI SHAN 五台山

Attractions

Dàilóu Peak	黛螺顶
Fóguāng Sì	佛光寺
Lóngquán Sì	龙泉寺
Nán Shān Sì	南山寺
Nánchán Sì	南禅寺
Tǎyuàn Sì	塔院寺
Wǔtái Shān Lǚ yóu Chē Chūzū (Wǔtái Shān Tour Taxi Ticket Office)	五台山旅游车出租
Xiǎntōng Sì	显通寺

Hotels & Restaurants

Cháoyáng Bīnguǎn	朝阳宾馆
Fúrén Jū Jiǔlóu	福仁居酒楼
Jīnjiè Shānzhuāng	金界山庄
Jīnjiè Sífǔ	金界食府
Jìngxīn Zhāi	精心斋
Qīxiángé Bīnguǎn	栖贤阁宾馆

Xīnjīnglún Guōjì Jiǔdian	新京伦汇宾楼
Yīzhaň Míngdēng Quánsùzhāi	一盏明灯全素斋
Yínhǎi Shānzhuāng	银海山庄

The Silk Routes (chapter 7)

XI'AN 西安

Around Xi'an

Banpo Neolithic Village (Bànpō Bówùgǔan)	半坡博物馆
Chen Lu	陈炉镇
Emperor Jingdi's Mausoleum (Hàn Yānglīng)	汉阳陵
Terra-Cotta Warriors (Bīngmǎyǒng)	兵马俑

TIANSHUI 天水

Attractions

Fuxi Miao (Fúxī Miào)	伏羲庙
Màijī Shān Shíkū	麦积山石窟
Yuquan Guan (Yùquán Guàn)	玉泉观

Hotels & Restaurants

Hualian Fandian (Huálián Fàndiàn)	华睐饭店
La Fu (Là Fù Chuàn Xiāng Guǎn)	辣馥串香馆
Maiji Dajiudian (Màijī Dàjiǔdiàn)	麦积大酒店
Mingyuan Dajiudian (Míngyuǎn Dàjiǔdiàn)	名远大酒店
Niu Dawan (Niú Dàwǎn)	牛大碗
Pei Feng Beef Noodles (Peì Fēng Niú Ròu Diàn)	沛锋牛肉面
Shengan Coffee (Shèngān Dāfēi)	圣安咖啡
Tian Xi Xiaochidian (Tiān Xī Xiǎochīdiàn)	天西小吃店
Tianshui Dajiudian (Tiānshuǐ Dàjiǔdiàn)	天水大酒店
Tianshui Fandian (Tiānshuǐ Fàndiàn)	天水饭店
Zhiwuyuan Zhaodaisuo (Zhíwùyuán Zhāodàisuǒ)	植物园招待所

HEZUO 合作

Attractions

Milarepa Tower (Jiǔcéng Fógé)	九层佛阁

Hotels & Restaurants

Jiāotōng Bīnguǎn	交通宾馆
Xiangbala Dajiudian (Xiangbala Dàjiǔdiàn)	香巴拉大酒店

XIA HE (LABRANG) 夏河

Attractions

Ba Jiao (Bājiǎo)	八角
Drockar Gompa (Báishíyá Sì)	白石崖寺
Ganjia (Gānjiā)	甘加
Labrang Monastery (Lābùléng Sì)	拉卜楞寺
Sāngkē	桑科
Tseway Gompa (Zuǒhǎ Sì)	佐海寺

Hotels & Restaurants

Labuleng Civil Aviation Hotel (Lā Bú Lèng Mín Háng Dà Jiŭ Diàn)	拉卜楞民航大酒店
Overseas Tibetan Hotel (Huáqiáo Fàndiàn)	华侨饭店
Tara Guesthouse (Zhuómă Lŭshè)	卓玛旅社

LANGMU SI (TAKTSANG LHAMO) 郎木寺

Attractions

Flower Cap Mountain (Huā Gaì Shān)	花盖山
Kirti Gompa (Nàmó Sì)	那摩寺
Sertri Gompa (Saìchi Sì)	塞赤寺

Hotels & Restaurants

Langmu Si Binguan (Lángmù Sì Bīnguăn)	郎木寺宾馆
Langmu Si Dajiudian (Láng Mù Sì Dàjiŭdiàn)	郎木寺大酒店
Sana Hotel (Sànà Bīnguăn)	萨娜宾馆

DUNHUANG 敦煌

Attractions

Han Changcheng (Hàn Chángchéng)	汉长城
He Cangcheng (Hé Cāngchéng)	河仓城
Yùmén Guān (Jade Gate)	玉门关

ÜRÜMQI (WULUMUQI) 乌鲁木齐

Attractions

Báiyáng Gōu (White Poplar Gully)	白杨沟
Tiān Chí (Heavenly Lake)	天池

KUQA (KUCHE) 库车

Attractions

Kèzī'ĕr Qiān Fó Dòng (Kizil Thousand Buddha Caves)	克孜尔千佛洞
Kùchē Dà Sì (Kuqa Grand Mosque)	库车大寺
Sūbāshí Gŭchéng (Jarakol Temple)	苏巴什古城
Tianshan Gorge (Tiānshān Dàxiágŭ)	天山大峡谷
Xīngqīwŭ Dàshìchăng (Friday Bazaar)	星期五大市场

Hotels & Restaurants

Kùchē Fàndiàn	库车饭店
Qiūcí Bīnguăn	龟兹宾馆
Wūqià Guŏyuán Cāntīng (Uqa Bhag Resturant)	乌恰果园餐厅
Wúmăi'ĕrhóng Mĕishí Chéng (Omarjan Muhammed Food City)	吴买尔洪美食城

KASHGAR (KASHI) 喀什

Around Kashgar

Shipton's Arch (Tushuk Tash; Tiān Mén)	天洞
Tomb of Mohammed Kashgari (Abāke Huòjiā Mázhā)	阿巴克霍加麻扎

TASHKURGAN 塔什库尔干

Attractions

Kālā Hú (Black Lake)	喀拉湖
National Culture and Arts Center (Guójiā Wénhua Yìshù Zhōngxīn)	国家文化艺术中心
Tashkurgan Fort (Shítou Chéng)	石头城

Hotels & Restaurants

Chongqing Chen Jia Fu (Chòng Qìng Quán Jiā Fú)	重庆全家福
Pamir Hotel (Pàmǐěr Bīnguǎn)	帕米尔宾馆
Stone City Hotel (Shí Toóu Chéng Bīn Guǎn)	石头城宾馆
Tǎxiàn Huángguān Dàjiǔdiàn (Crown Inn)	塔县皇冠大酒店
Traffic Hotel (Jiāotōng Bīnguǎn)	交通宾馆
Wūshì Lǎo Huímín Cāntīng	乌市老回民餐厅
Yangguan Meishi (Yángguān Měishí)	阳光美食

KHOTAN (HETIAN) 和田

Attractions

Dìtǎn Chǎng (Carpet Factory)	地毯厂
Gōngyì Měishù Yǒuxiàn Gōngsī (Jade Factory)	工艺美术有限公司
Sīsāng Yánjiūsuǒ (Silk and Mulberry Research Center)	丝桑研究所
Xīngqītiān Dàshìchǎng (Sunday Market)	星期天大市场

Hotels & Restaurants

Gāoyáng Kǎoròu Kuàicāndiàn	羔羊烤肉快餐店
Hétián Bīnguǎn (Hotan Hotel)	和田宾馆
Marco Dream Café (Má Kě Yì Zhàn)	马可驿站
Marwar (Jīn Gōng Fēng Wèi Cān Tīng)	金宫风味餐厅
Wēnzhōu Dàjiǔdiàn (Wēnzhōu Hotel)	温州大酒店
Wéilìmài Hànbǎo (Wéilìmài Burger)	维利麦汉堡
Zhèjiāng Dàjiǔdiàn (Zhèjiāng Hotel)	浙江大酒店

YINING 伊宁

Attractions

Jingyuan Si (Jìngyuǎn Sì)	靖远寺
Qapqal Xibo Autonomous County (Chábù Chá'ěr Xiàn)	察布查尔县

Hotels & Restaurants

Naren Canting (Nàrén Cāntīng)	纳仁餐厅
Soviet Consulate (Éluósī Lǐngshì Guǎn)	俄罗斯领事馆
Yili Binguan (Yīlí Bīnguǎn)	伊犁宾馆
Yili Xinjiang Dajiudian (Yīlí Xīnjiāng Dàjiǔdiàn)	伊犁 新疆大酒店
Yilite Dajiudian (Yīlítè Dàjiǔdiàn)	伊力特大酒店
Youli Gongshi Shan (Yǒu Lì Gōng Shí Shàn)	友丽宫食膳

Eastern Central China (chapter 8)

DENGFENG 登封 & SONG SHAN 嵩山

Attractions

Guólǚ Dàlóu	国旅大楼
Jùnjí Féng	峻极峰
Sānhuáng Xínggōng (Sānhuáng Palace)	三皇行宫
Shàolín Sì (Shàolín Monastery)	少林寺
Shàolín Sì Tǎgōu Wǔshù Xuéxiào (Shàolín Monastery Wǔshù Institute at Tǎgōu)	少林寺塔沟武术学校
Shàolín Wǔshù Guǎn (Martial Arts Training Center)	少林武术馆
Shàoshì Shān	少室山
Sōng Shān Diào Qiáo	嵩山吊桥
Sōngyáng Suǒdào	嵩阳索道
Sōngyuè Tǎ (Sōngyuè Pagoda)	嵩岳塔
Tàishì Shān	太室山
Zhōngyuè Miào	中岳庙

Hotels & Restaurants

Fēngyuán Dàjiǔdiàn	丰源大酒店
Fúyuán Nóng Jiā Lè	福园农家乐
Jīnguàn Miànbāo Xīdiǎn Fáng	京冠面包西点坊
Shàolín Guójì Dàjiǔdiàn (Shàolín International Hotel)	少林国际大酒店
Xiāngjī Wáng	香鸡王
Zēn International Hotel (Hé Nán Guó Jì Chán Jū Fàn Diàn)	河南国际禅居饭店

LUOYANG 洛阳

Attractions

Báimǎ Sì (White Horse Temple)	白马寺
Gǔmù Bówùgǔan (Ancient Han Tombs)	古墓博物馆
Lóngmén Shíkū (Dragon Gate Grottoes)	龙门石窟
Luòyáng Bówùguǎn (Luoyang Museum)	洛阳博物馆
Wángchéng Gōngyuán	王城公园

Hotels & Restaurants

Bǎo Húlu	宝葫芦
Huáyáng Guǎngchǎng Guójì Dàjiǔdiàn (Huáyáng Plaza Hotel)	华阳广场国际大酒店
Luòyáng Mǔdān Dàjiǔdiàn (Luòyáng Peony Hotel)	洛阳牡丹大酒店
Míngyuàn Dàjiǔdiàn (Míngyuàn Hotel)	明苑大酒店
Mǔdān Chéng Bīnguǎn (Peony Plaza)	牡丹城宾馆
Xīn Yǒuyì Bīnguǎn (New Friendship Hotel)	新友谊宾馆

JI'NAN 济南

Attractions

Bàotū Quán (Bàotū Spring)	趵突泉
Dà Míng Hú Gōngyuán (Dà Míng Hú Park)	大明湖公园

Hotels & Restaurants

Guì Dū Dàjiǔdiàn	贵都大酒店
Guìhé Huángguān Jiǔdiàn (Crowne Plaza Guìhé Jì'nán)	贵和皇冠假日酒店
Jingya (Jìngyǎ Dà Jiǔdiàn)	静雅大酒店
Lǎo Hángzhōu Jiǔ Wǎn Bàn	老杭州九碗拌
Lángdū International Hotel (Lóngdū Guójì Fàndiàn)	龙都国际大酒店
Suǒfēitè Yínzuò Dàfàndiàn (Sofitel Silver Plaza Jì'nán)	索菲特银座大饭店
Yínzuò Quánchéng Dàjiǔdiàn (Silver Plaza Quán Chéng Hotel)	银座泉城大酒店

QUFU 曲阜

Attractions

Kǒng Fǔ (Confucian Mansion)	孔府
Kǒng Lín (Confucian Forest & Cemetery)	孔林
Kǒng Miào (Confucius Temple)	孔庙
Kǒngzǐ Yánjīuyuàn (Confucius Academy)	孔子研究院
Shào Hào Lín (Tomb of Emperor Shào Hào)	少昊林

Hotels & Restaurants

Kǒng Fǔ Dàjiǔdiàn	孔府大酒店
Quèlǐ Bīnshè (Quèlǐ Hotel)	阙里宾舍
Yù Lóng Dàjiǔdiàn (Yù Lóng Hotel)	裕隆大酒店

WUXI 无锡

Attractions

Huì shān Clay Figurine Factory	惠山泥人厂
Tài Hú (Lake Tài)	太湖
Xīhuì Gōngyuán	锡惠公园
Yuántóuzhǔ (Turtle Head Isle)	鼋头渚

Hotels & Restaurants

Húbīn Fàndiàn	湖滨饭店
Sān Fēng Jiǔjiā	三丰酒家
Tài Hú Fàndiàn	太湖饭店
Wángxìng Jì	王兴记
Wúxī Kǎoyā Guǎn (Wúxī Roast Duck Restaurant)	无锡烤鸭馆
Wúxī Xīnshìjiè Wànyí Jiǔdiàn (New World Courtyard Wúxī)	无锡新万怡酒店
Xīláidēng Dàfàndiàn (Grand Park Hotel Wúxī)	无锡君乐酒店

YIXING 宜兴

Attractions

Shànjuǎn Dòng	扇卷洞
Shěng Qìchēzhàn (Yíxīng Bus Station)	宜兴汽车站
Yíxīng Táocí Bówùguǎn	宜兴陶瓷博物馆
Zhānggōng Dòng	张公洞

Hotels

Yíxīng Guójì Fàndiàn (Yíxīng International Hotel)	宜兴国际饭店

QINGDAO 青岛

Attractions

Láo Shān	崂山

ZIBO 淄博

Attractions

Línzī Zhōngguó Gǔchē Bówùguǎn (Lí Museum of Chinese Ancient Chariots)	临淄中国古车博 物馆
Xūn Mǎ Kēng (Ancient Horse Relics Museum)	殉马坑
Zībó Zhōngguó Táocí Guǎn	淄博中国陶瓷馆

Hotels & Restaurants

Zībó Bīnguǎn	淄博宾馆
Zībó Fàndiàn	淄博饭店

HEFEI 合肥

Attractions

Ānhuī Shěng Bówùguǎn (Ānhuī Provincial Museum)	安徽省博物馆
Bāo Gōng Mù Yuán (Lord Bāo's Tomb)	包公墓园
Bāo Hé Gōngyuán	包河公园
Lǐ Hóngzhāng Gùjū	李鸿章故居
Shāngyè Bùxíngjiē	商业步行街
Xiāoyáojīn Gōngyuán	逍遥津公园

Hotels & Restaurants

24 Xiǎoshí Miàn (Noodles in Chopsticks)	24小时面
Héféi Gǔjǐng Jiàrì Jiǔdiàn (Holiday Inn Héféi)	合肥古井假日酒店
Héféi Nuòfùtè Qíyún Shānzhuāng (Qiyun Hotel)	合肥徽商齐云山庄
Jīn Mǎn Lóu Huāyuán Jiǔdū	金满楼花园酒都
Lǎo Xiè Lóngxiā	老谢龙虾
Grand Park Hotel Héféi (Héféi Suǒfēitè Míngzhū Guójì Jiǔdiàn)	合肥明珠国际大 酒店

TUNXI 屯溪

Attractions

Bǎolún Gé (Bǎolún Hall)	宝纶阁
Chéngkǎn	呈坎
Dòushān Jiē	斗山街
Hóng Cūn	宏村
Huīzhōu District	徽州区
Lǎo Jiē (Old Street)	老街
Nánpíng	南屏
Qiánkǒu	潜口
Shè Xiàn	歙县
Tángyuè Páifang Qún (Tángyuè Memorial Arches)	棠樾牌坊群
Xīdì	西递
Xǔguó Shífáng (Xúgúo Stone Archway)	许国石坊
Yī Xiàn	黟县

Hotels & Restaurants

Huáng Shān Guójì Dàjiǔdiàn (Huáng Shān International Hotel)	黄山国际大酒店
Huáng Shān Guómài Dàjiǔdiàn	黄山国脉大酒店
Huáng Shān Huāxī Fàndiàn	黄山花溪饭店
Jiànguó Shāngwù Jiǔdiàn (Jiànguó Garden Hotel)	建国商务酒店
Lǎo Jiē Dìyī Lóu	老街第一楼
Xiang Ming Hotel (Xiāng Míng Jiǔdiàn)	香茗酒店

Shanghai (chapter 9; 上海)

SUZHOU 苏州

Attractions

Hǔ Qiū Shān (Tiger Hill)	虎丘山
Liú Yuán (Lingering Garden)	留园
Pán Mén (Pán Gate)	盘门
Ruìguāng Tǎ	瑞光塔
Shīzi Lín Yuán (Forest of Lions Garden)	狮子林园
Sūzhōu Sīchóu Bówùguǎn (Sūzhōu Silk Museum)	苏州丝绸博物馆
Wǎng Shī Yuán (Master of the Nets Garden)	网师园
Wúmén Qiáo	无门桥
Zhuō Zhèng Yuán (Humble Administrator's Garden)	拙政园

Hotels & Restaurants

Scholars Inn (Shūxiāng Méndì Shāngwù Jiǔdiàn)	书香门第商务酒店
Shangri-La Hotel Suzhou (Sūzhōu Xiānggélǐlā Dàjiǔdiàn)	苏州香格里拉大 酒店
Sōng Hè Lóu (Pine and Crane Restaurant)	松鹤楼
Sofitel Suzhou (Sūzhōu Xúanmiào Suǒfēitè Dàjiǔdiàn)	苏州玄妙索菲特大酒店
Sūzhōu Wúgōng Xǐláidēng Dàjiǔdiàn (Sheraton Sūzhōu Hotel & Towers) (renamed Pan Pacific Suzhou)	泛太平洋苏州酒店

HANGZHOU 杭州

Attractions

Bái Dī (Bái Causeway)	白堤
Duàn Qiáo (Broken Bridge)	断桥
Fēilái Fēng (Peak That Flew from Afar)	飞来峰
Gūshān Dǎo (Solitary Island)	孤山岛
Léi Fēng Tǎ (Léi Fēng Pagoda)	雷峰塔
Língyǐn Sì (Língyǐn Temple)	灵隐寺
Lóngjǐng Wēnchá (Dragon Well Tea Village)	龙井温茶
Sān Tán Yìn Yuè (Three Pools Mirroring The Moon)	三潭印月
Sū Dī (Sū Causeway)	苏堤
Xiǎo Yíng Zhōu (Island of Small Seas)	小瀛洲
Zhèjiāng Bówùguǎn (Zhèjiāng Provincial Museum)	浙江博物馆
Zhōngguó Cháyè Bówùguǎn (Chinese Tea Museum)	中国茶叶博物馆
Zhōngguó Sīchóu Bówùguǎn (China Silk Museum)	中国丝绸博物馆

Hotels & Restaurants

Hángzhōu Suǒfēitè Xīhú Dàjiǔdiàn (Sofitel Westlake Hángzhou)	杭州索菲特西湖大酒店
Hángzhōu Xiānggélǐlā Fàndiàn (Shangri-La Hotel Hángzhōu)	杭州香格里拉饭店
Hyatt Regency Hangzhou (Kǎiyuè Dàjiǔdiàn)	凯悦大酒店
Jiexin Century Hotel (Jiéxīn Shìjì Jiǔdiàn)	杰欣世纪酒店
Lóu Wài Lóu	楼外楼
Xī Hú Tiāndì (West Lake Heaven and Earth)	西湖天地

TONGLI 同里

Attractions

Chángqìng (Glory) Qiáo	常庆桥
Chóngběn Táng	崇本堂
Jiāyīn Táng	嘉荫堂
Jílì (Luck) Qiáo	吉利桥
Tàipíng Qiáo (Peace Bridge)	太平桥
Tuìsī Yuán (Retreat and Reflection Garden)	退思园

Restaurants

Míngqīng Jiē	明清街
Nányuán Cháshè	南园茶社

The Southeast (chapter 10)

ANJI 安吉

Attractions

Cháng Lóng Bǎi Bù (Hidden Dragon Falls)	藏龙百瀑
Dà Kāng Jiā Jù Gōng Cháng (Dà Kāng Furniture Factory)	大康家具工厂
Dà Zhú Haǐ (Big Bamboo Sea)	大竹海
Tiān Huāng Píng Diàn Zhàn (Tiān Huāng Píng Hydro Electric Facility)	天荒坪电站
Tiān Zhú Zhuāng (Tiānzhúzhuāng Bamboo Fiber Company)	天竹庄
Zhú Bó Yuǎn (Bamboo Museum and Gardens)	竹博园
Zhú Yè Chéng (Bamboo Charcoal Factory)	竹业城

Hotels & Restaurants

Gāo Shān Rén Jiā Kè Zhàn (Mountain Clan Guesthouse)	高山人家客栈
Líng Fēng Jíng Qū (Líng Fēng Scenic Spot)	灵峰景区
Xiāng Yì Dù Jià Cūn (Sunny Land Resort)	香溢度假村
Xiàng Yí Jīn Yè Dàjiǔdiàn (Golden Leaf Hotel)	香溢金叶大酒店
Zhū Gé Kǎo Yú	诸葛烤鱼

MOGANSHAN 莫干山

Attractions

Jiàn Chí (Sword Forging Pool)	剑池
Qīng Liáng Tíng (Qīng Liáng Pavillion)	清凉亭

Hotels & Restaurants

Bái Yún Jiǔ Diàn (Baǐ Yún Hotel)	莫干山白云酒店
Mògànshān Zhuāng (Mògànshān Castle)	莫干山庄

Naked Retreats in mountain area known as 395.	村
Sōng Liáng Shān Zhuāng (Mògànshān Lodge)	松粮山庄

WUYI SHAN 武夷山

Attractions

Dà Hóng Pào	大红袍
Dà Wáng Fēng	大王峰
Shǔn Lián Dòng (Water Curtain Cave)	水帘洞
Shuǐ Guāng Dù	水光渡
Táo Yuán Dòng (Eagle's Rock Cave)	桃源洞
Tīan Xīng Yǒng Lè (Ever Happy Temple)	天兴永乐
Tiānyóu Shān	天游山
Xīng Cūn	星村
Xiān Fáng Jiè Mǎ Tóu (Babboo Raft Dock)	仙凡界码头
Yù Nǔ Fēng (Jade Beauty Peak)	玉女峰

Hotels & Restaurants

Bǎodǎo Dàjiǔdiàn (Bǎodǎo Hotel)	宝岛大酒店
Fǎ Tíng Jiē Dài Chù (Court Administration)	法庭接待处
Hoù Niǎo Jiā (Migrant's Home)	候鸟家
Jià Rì Huā Yuán Jiǔdiàn (Wuyishan Holiday Hotel)	假日花园商务酒店
Wǔyí Gōng	武夷宫
Wǔyí Shānzhuāng (Wǔyí Mountain Villa)	武夷山庄

QUANGZHOU 泉州

Attractions

Mǐnnán Jiàn Zhú Dà Guān Yuán (Cài Family Residence)	闽南建筑大观园
Quán Zhoū Guó Jì Jū Lè Bù (Quán Zhoū International Club)	泉州国际俱乐部
Shān Xiá Chì Hú Gōng Yè Qū (Shān Xiá Industrial Zone)	山霞镇赤湖工业区

Chongwu 崇武

Háo Xiáng Shí Yè (Háo Xiáng Stone Factory)	豪翔石业
Huá Fēng Shèn Shí Yè (Huá Fēng Shèn Stone Factory)	华峰盛石业
Shì Xīng Shí Yè (Shì Xīng Stone Factory)	世兴石业

Towns

Guān Qiáo	官桥

XIAMEN 厦门

Attractions

Fù yù Lóu	富裕楼
Hóng Lóu (The Red Chamber)	红楼
Huán xīng Lóu	环兴楼
Húkēng	湖坑
Ke Lai Deng Hotel (Kè lái dēng jiǔ diàn)	客来登酒店
Kuí jù Lóu	奎聚楼
Lóngyán	龙岩
Rú shēng Lóu	如升楼

Tóng Ān Yǐng Shì Chéng (Tóng Ān Film City)	同安影视城
Xīng Hé Bīn Guǎn	星河宾馆
Yongding	永定
Zhèn chéng Lóu	振成楼

JINGDE ZHEN 景德镇

Attractions

Guān Yáo Bó Wù Guǎn (Imperial Porcelain Museum)	官窑博物馆
Jīng Chāng Lì Chí Mào Dà Shà	金昌利瓷贸大厦
Sān Bǎo Shuǐduì (Water-powered Hammers)	三宝水碓
Shang Ping Studio (Shāng pín gōng zuò shì)	尚品工作室
Tán Qíng Xuān Zhì	檀情轩制
Táocí Wénhuà Bólánqū (Pottery Culture Exhibition)	景德镇陶瓷文化博 览区

Hotels & Restaurants

Bīn Jiāng Bīn Guǎn (Bīn Jiāng Hotel)	滨江宾馆
Dí Oū Kā Feī (Dio Coffee)	迪欧咖啡
Kaī Mén Zǐ Dàjiǔdiàn (Kaī Mén Zǐ Hotel)	开门子大酒店
Sān Bǎo Táo Yì Yán Xiū Yuàn (Sānbǎo Ceramic Art Institute)	三宝陶艺研修院
Shèng Shān Jiǔ Diàn (Holy Mountain Hotel)	圣山酒店
Yī Lóng Dàjiǔdiàn (Yī Lóng Restaurant)	伊龙大酒店

GUANGZHOU 广州

Kaiping 开平

Cháo Jiāng Chūn Jiǔdiàn	潮江春酒店
Chì Kān	赤坎
Dong Xi Cun	洞溪村
Fēng Zé Yuán Jiǔ Lóu	丰泽园酒楼
Jínjiànglí	锦江里
Kaī Xuán Mén Jiǔdiàn (Triumphal Arch Hotel)	凯旋门酒店
Lì Yuǎn (Li Garden)	立园
Mǎ Jiàng Lóng	马降龙
Nán Xīng Lí	南兴里
Nán Xīng Xié Lóu	南兴斜楼
Ruishi Lóu	瑞石楼
Sān Mén Lǐ	三门里
Shèngfēng Lóu	盛丰楼
Shì Jì Zhī Zhoū Cān Tīng (Ship of the Century)	世纪之舟餐厅
Weǐ Gǎng Jiǔdiàn (Weigang Hotel)	维港酒店
Zì Lì Cūn	自力村

SHENZEN 深圳

Attractions

Luó Hú Shāngyè Chéng (Luó Hú Commercial City)	罗湖商业城
Minsk World (Míngsīkè Hángmǔ Shìjiè)	明思克航母世界

Hotels & Restaurants

Dà Huī Láng Cān Tīng (Big Gray Wolf)	大灰狼餐厅
Dān Guì Xuān	丹桂轩
Luó Hú Kuài Jié Jià Rì Jiǔdiàn (Holiday Inn Express)	罗湖快捷假日酒店
Qiáo Chéng Lǔ Yóu Guó Jì Qīng Niān Lǔ Shè	侨城旅友国际青年旅舍
Shenzhen Number One Production Team (Hé nán lǎo jiā)	河南老家

The Southwest: Mountains & Minorities (chapter 12)

GUILIN 桂林

Attractions

Nán Xī Gōng Yuán	南溪公园
Wá Yáo Lǎo Diàn Chǎng (Guìlín Wholesale Carving Market)	瓦窑老电厂

LI JIANG 漓江

Huángbù Dǎoyǐng	黄布倒影
Jiǔmǎ Huàshān (Nine Horses Fresco Hill)	九马画山
Yáng Dī	杨堤
Zhújiāng Pier	竹江码头

YANGSHUO 阳朔

Around Yangshuo

Báishā	白沙
Buddha Cave	菩萨洞
Dà Hé Beì Dǎo (Da He Bei Island)	大河背岛
Fèng Huáng Cūn (Phoenix Village)	凤凰村
Fúlì	福利
Gǔróng Gōngyuán (Banyan Tree Park)	古榕公园
Jīn Bǎo Hé (Jīn Bǎo River)	金宝河
Lóng Toú Shān Mǎ Toú	龙头山码头
Moon Hill (Yuè liàng shān)	月亮山
Shuǐyán (Water Cave)	水岩
Xīngpíng	兴坪
Yángshuò Shèngdì (Mountain Retreat)	阳朔胜地
Yínzi Yán (Silver Cave)	银子岩
Yú Cūn (Fishing Village)	渔村
Yùlóng Hé (Yulong River)	遇龙河
Yùlóng Qiáo (Jade Dragon Bridge)	遇龙桥

BAMA 巴马

Attractions

Ba Ma Chang Shou Bó Wù Guǎn	巴马长寿博物馆

Hotels & Restaurants

Shèng Dì Dàjiǔdiàn	圣地大酒店
Shoù Xiāng Dàjiǔdiàn (Long Life Hotel)	寿乡大酒店

Poyue 坡月

Baǐ Mó Dòng (Baǐ Mó Cavern)	百魔洞
Feng Yuan Bīnguǎn	逢源宾馆
Yán Nián Shān Zhuāng (Yán Nián Shān Zhuāng Guesthouse)	延年山庄

Around Poyue

Baǐ Niǎo Yán (Baǐ Niǎo Water Cave)	百鸟岩
Lóng Mén Āo (Dragon Gate)	龙门凹
Qíng nán	勤兰

FENGSHAN 凤山

Attractions

Chuān Lóng Dòng	穿龙洞
Fèng Shān Bó Wù Guǎn (Fengshan Museum)	凤山博物馆
Hóu Shān (Monkey Mountain)	猴山
Sān Mén Hǎi	三门海
Yuān Yāng Dòng	鸳鸯洞

Hotels & Restaurants

Fáng Xùn Da Jiǔdiàn (Fang Xun Inn)	防汛大酒店
Héng Shēng Dà Jiǔdiàn (Heng Sheng Hotel)	恒升大酒店
Yǒu Yǒu Càn Tìng (Yoyo Restaurant)	友友餐厅

LEYE 乐业

Attractions

Bù Liǔ Hé	布柳河
Dà Shí Wéi Tiān Kēng (Dashiwei Tiankeng)	大石围天坑
Huǒ Maì Cūn (Huo Mai Village)	火卖村
Lè Yè Bó Wù Guǎn (Leye Museum)	乐业博物馆

Hotels & Restaurants

Guó Fáng Pé i Xùn Zhōng Xīn Dà Pǎi Dàng	国防培训中心大 排档
Jīn Yuán Guó Jì Da Jiǔdiàn	金源国际大酒店
Lè Yè Bīnguǎn	乐业宾馆
Liǔ Luó Piāo Xiāng	柳螺飘香

KUNMING 昆明

Around Kunming

Chéng Gòng Cūn	呈贡村
Dà Dié Shuǐ Feī Lóng Pù	大叠水飞龙瀑
Dà Guān Loú (Grand View Tower)	大观楼
Dà Guān Yuán	大观园
Huá Tíng Sì (Huá Tíng Temple)	华亭寺
Naì Gǔ Shí Lín (Black Pine Stone Forest)	乃古石林
Niè Ěr Zhī Mù (Niè Ěr's Grave)	聂耳之墓
Sān Qīng Gé	三清阁
Taì Huá Sì (Taì Huá Temple)	太华寺
Xī Shān (Western Hills)	西山

Xīngyà Fēngqíng Garden (Xīngyà Fēngqíng dà jiǔ diàn)	兴亚风情大酒店
Zhōng Loú (Bell Tower)	钟楼

DALI 大理

Around Dali

Cāng Shān (Green Mountains)	苍山
Ěr Hăl (Ěr Hăi Lake)	洱海湖
Fèngyǎn Dòng (Phoenix Cave)	凤眼洞
Gǎntōng Sì (GǎntōngTemple)	感通寺
Gāo Dì (Highlander Guesthouse)	高地客栈
Guānyīn Gé (Guānyīn Pavilion)	观音阁
Jīnsuō Dǎo (Jīnsuō Island)	金梭岛
Pǔtuó Dǎo (Pǔtuó Island)	普陀岛
Qīngbì Xī (Qīngbì Stream)	清碧溪
Wāsè	挖色
Zhōnghé Sì (Zhōnghé Temple)	中和寺

XIZHOU 喜州

Xǐ Lín Yuàn (The Linden Cultural Center)	喜林苑
Yáng Jiā Yǒng Xiáng Jū	杨家永祥居
Zhōu Chéng	周城

SHAXI 沙溪

Around Shaxi

Bǎo xiàng sì (Baoxiang Temple)	宝相寺
Mǎ píng gùan	马平关
Shí Bǎo Shān (Shibao Mountain)	石宝山
Shí Zhōng Sì (Shizhong Temple)	石钟寺
Xiàngtú	象图

Hotels

Sì Lián Duàn Jiā Tún (Dragonfly Homestay)	四联段家屯

LIJIANG 丽江

Around Lijiang

Báishā	白沙
Bīngchuān Gōngyuán (Glacier Park)	冰川公园
Dabaoji Palace (Dà bǎo jī gōng)	大宝积宫
Dongba Village (Dōng bā cūn)	东巴村
Lāshìhaǐ	拉市海
Máoniú Píng (Yak Meadow)	牦牛坪
Qiáo toú	桥头
Tiger Leaping Gorge (Hǔ Tiào Xiá)	虎跳峡
Wenhai Ecolodge (Wén haǐ)	文海
Yù Hú (Nguluko)	玉湖
Yù shuí zhài	玉水寨
Yùfēng Sì (Yùfēng Temple)	玉峰寺

Yùlóng Xuěshān (Jade Dragon Snow Mountain)	玉龙雪山
Yúnshān Píng (Spruce Meadow)	云杉坪

XIANGGELILA (ZHONGDIAN) 香格里拉

Attractions

Ganden Sumtseling Gompa (Sōngzànlín Sì)	松赞林寺
Gǔ Chéng (Old town)	古城
Old Town Scripture Chamber (Gǔchéng Zàngjīng Táng)	古城藏经堂

Hotels & Restaurants

Ā Ruò Kāng Bā (Arro Khampa Restaurant)	阿若康巴
Pí Jiàng Chéng Lǎo Kè Zhàn (Cobbler's Hill Inn)	皮匠城老客栈
Puppet Restaurant (Mù oú xī cān tīng)	木偶西餐厅
Tiānjiè Shénchuān Dàjiǔdiàn (Paradise Hotel)	天界神川大酒店
Tibet Café	西藏咖啡馆

Around Zhongdian

Báishuǐ Tái (White Water Terraces)	白水台
Bìtǎ Hǎi (Bìtǎ Lake)	碧塔海

Yangzi & Beyond (chapter 13)

EMEI SHAN 峨眉山

Attractions

Bàoguó Sì	报国寺
Fúhǔ Sì	伏虎寺
Hóngchūn Píng	洪椿坪
Jīn Dǐng (Golden Peak)	金顶
Jiēyǐn Diàn (Jiēyǐn Hall)	接引殿
Jiǔlǎo Dòng (Jiǔlǎo Cave)	九老洞
Léidòng Píng (Léidòng Terrace)	雷洞坪
Lǚrén Zhōngxīn (Tourist Center)	旅人中心
Niúxīn Tíng (Niúxīn Pavilion)	牛心亭
Qīngyīn Gé	清音阁
Qiānfó Dǐng (Qiānfó Peak)	千佛顶
Shèshēn Yán (Shèshēn Cliff)	摄身岩
Wànfó Dǐng (Wànfó Peak)	万佛顶
Wànnián Chēchǎng (Wànnián Cable Car Station)	万年车场
Wànnián Sì (Wànnián Monastery)	万年寺
Xǐ Xiàng Chí (Elephant Bathing Pool)	洗象池
Xiānfēng Sì (Xiānfēng Monastery)	先峰寺

Hotels & Restaurants

Éméi Shān Fàndiàn	峨眉山饭店
Hóngzhū Shān Bīnguǎn	红珠山宾馆
Jīn Dǐng Dàjiǔdiàn (Golden Summit Hotel)	金顶大酒店

LE SHAN 乐山

Attractions

Dà Fó (Great Buddha)	大佛
Jiǔqǔ Zhàndào (Path of Nine Switchbacks)	九曲栈道
Wūyóu Shān (Wūyóu Mountain)	乌尤山

Hotels & Restaurants

Jiā Zhōu Bīnguǎn	嘉州宾馆
Xiāndǎo Dàjiǔdiàn (Xiandao Hotel)	仙岛大酒店
Yángshì	杨氏

DUJIANGYAN 都江堰 & QINGCHENG SHAN 青城山

Attractions

Cháoyáng Dòng (Facing the Dawn Cave)	朝阳洞
Lǎojūn Gé (Lord Lao Pavilion)	老君阁
Shàng Qīng Gōng (Temple of Highest Clarity)	上清宫
Tiānshī Dòng (Celestial Master Cave)	天师洞
Yílè Wō (Nest of Pleasures)	怡乐窝
Yuèchéng Hú (Moon Wall Lake)	月城湖
Zǔshī Diàn (Hall of the Celestial Master Founder)	祖师殿

Hotels

Língyún Shānzhuāng (Lingyun Mountain Inn)	淩云山庄

JIUZHAIGOU 九寨沟

Attractions

Panda Lake (Xióngmāo Hǎi)	熊猫海
Rìzé Jǐngqū	日则景区
Shùzhēng Jǐngqū	树正景区
Wǔcǎi Hǎi (Five-color Pool)	五彩海

Hotels & Restaurants

Cao Gen Renjia	草根人家
Sheraton Jiuzhaigou Resort (Jiǔzhàigōu Xǐláidēng Dàjiǔdiàn)	九寨沟喜来登大 酒店
Pengfeng Cun (Pengfeng Village)	彭丰村
Qian He International Hotel (Qian He Guoji Dajiudian)	千鹤国际大酒店
Xīngyǔ Guójì Dàjiǔdiàn (Xīngyǔ International Hotel)	星宇国际大酒店
Ziyou Qingnian Lvshe	自游青年旅舍

HUANGLONG 黄龙

Wanglong Platform	望龙坪
Multi-colored Pond	五彩池
Huanglong Ancient Temple	黄龙古寺
Immortal Waiting Bridge	接仙桥
Beauty-competing Pond	争艳池
Golden Sand on Earth	金沙铺地

Body Washing Cave	洗身洞
Lotus Platform Waterfall	莲台飛瀑
Guest Greeting Pond	迎宾彩池

CHONGQING 重庆

Attractions

Baigong Guan/SACO (Báigōngguǎn)	白公馆

DAZU 大足

Attractions

Bǎodǐg Shān	宝顶山
Běi Shān	北山

Hotels

Ramada Plaza Chongqing West	重庆华地王朝华美达广场酒店

SANXIA BA 三峡坝

Attractions

Daning River (Dàníng Hé)	大宁河
Shíbǎo Zhài (Stone Treasure Fortress)	石宝寨
Three Gorges Dam Site (Sānxiá Dàbà)	三峡大坝
Xiǎo Xiǎo Sānxiá	小小三峡

WUDANG SHAN 武当山

Attractions

Jīndiàn (Golden Hall)	金殿
Nányán Gōng (Southern Cliff Palace)	南岩宫
Tàihé Gōng (Palace of Supreme Harmony)	太和宫
Tiānzhù Fēng	天柱峰
Zhanqi Peak (Zhǎnqí Fēng)	展旗峰
Zǐxiāo Gōng (Purple Mist Palace)	紫霄宫

Hotels

Jīn Dǐng Guìbīn Jiēdàishì	金顶贵宾接待室
Jīnguì Jiǔdiàn	金贵酒店
Wǔdāngshān Jǐngtái Bīnguǎn	武当山璟台宾馆

NAN YUE HENG SHAN 南岳衡山

Attractions

Nán Yuè Dàmiào	南岳大庙
Xuándōu Guān	玄都观
Zhurong Hall (Zhùróng Diàn)	祝融殿
Zhùróng Fēng	祝融峰

Hotels

Caifu Mountain Villa (Cáifù Shānzhuāng)	财富山庄
Shàngfēng Sì (Shangfeng Monastery)	上封寺
Zhùróng Fēng Shānzhuāng	祝融峰山庄

WULING YUAN 武陵源/ZHANG JIA JIE 张家界

Attractions

Bǎofēng Hú	宝峰湖
Bailong Tianti (Bailong Tourist Lift)	百龙天梯
Gāoshān Huāyuán (Garden in the Air)	高山花园
Ghost-valley Plank Road (Guǐgǔ Zhàndào)	鬼谷栈道
Huánglóng Dòng (Huánglóng Cave)	黄龙洞
Huángshí Zhài	黄石寨
Jinbian Si (Golden Whip Stream)	金鞭溪
Mihuntai (the Platform of Lost Mind)	迷云台
Shui Rao Xi Men (Stream Winding Around Four Gates)	水绕四门
Sightseeing cable car (Shāndǐng Guānguāng Lǎnchē)	山顶观光缆车
Suǒ Xī Yù Nature Reserve	索溪峪自然保护区
Tiānmén Dòng (Tianmen Cave)	天门洞
Tiānmén Shān Suǒdào (Tianmen Mountain Cable Car)	天门山索道
Tiānmén Shān	天门山
Tiānzǐ Gé	天子阁
Tiānzǐ Shān Nature Reserve	天子山自然保护区
Yīngtáo Wān	樱桃湾
Yuanjiajie	袁家界
Yùbǐ Fēng	御笔锋
Yúnmèng Xiāndǐng (Yumeng Fairy Summit)	云梦仙顶

Hotels & Restaurants

Bailong Xianju Kezhan	张家界白龙仙居客栈
Hotel Pullman Zhangjiajie (Zhangjiajie Jingwu Boerman Jiudian)	张家界京武铂尔曼 酒店
Hushifu Sanxiaguo	胡师傅三下锅
Pípa Xī Bīnguǎn	琵琶溪宾馆
Xiānglóng Guójì Dàjiǔdiàn (Dragon International Hotel)	湘龙国际大酒店
Yuanjiajie Qingnian Lvshe (Yuanjiajie Youth Hostel)	袁家界青年旅舍
Zhangjiajie Samantha Resort & Spa (Zhangjiajie Sheng Mei Da Dujia Jiudian)	盛美达(张家界)度假酒店

FENGHUANG GUCHENG 凤凰古城

Attractions

Diàojiǎo Lóu	吊脚楼
Gǔchéngqiáng Chéngmén (the Ancient Town Wall)	古城墙城门
Hóngqiáo (Rainbow Bridge)	虹桥
Tiàoyán (Leaping Stones)	跳岩

Hotels & Restaurants

Phoenix Jiangtian Holiday Village (Fènghuáng Jiāngtiān Lǚyóu Dùjiàcūn)	凤凰江天旅游度假村
Yìfēng Rénjiā Bīnguǎn	益丰人家宾馆
Zhāngshì Jiāngtáng Lǎozìhào	张氏姜糖老字号

The Tibetan World (chapter 14)

XINING 西宁

Attractions

Kumbum (Tă'ĕr Sì)	塔尔寺
Qīnghăi Hú (Lake Kokonor)	青海湖

TONGREN (REBKONG) 同仁

Attractions

Gomar Gompa (Guōmárì Sì)	郭麻日寺
Rongpo Gompa (Lóngwù Sì)	隆务寺
Shàng Wútún Sì (Upper Wutun)	上吾屯寺
Xià Wútún Sì (Lower Wutun)	下吾屯寺

Hotels & Restaurants

Diànxìn Bīnguăn (Telecom Hotel)	电信宾馆
Homeland of Rebkong Artist Restaurant (Règòng Yìréngè)	热贡艺人阁
Huángnán Bīnguăn	黄南宾馆
Regong Binguan (Règòng Bīnguăn)	热贡宾馆

MAQIN (DAWU) 玛卿

Hotels & Restaurants

Dianxin Binguan (Diànxìn Bīnguăn)	电信宾馆
Xueshan Binguan (Xuĕshān Bīnguăn)	雪山宾馆

GOLMUD (GE'ERMU) 格尔木

Hotels & Restaurants

Gé'ĕrmù Bīnguăn	格尔木宾馆
Liúyi Shŏu	留一手
Wēi'ĕrshì Dàjiŭdiàn	威尔士大酒店
Yóuzhèng Bīnguăn (Post Hotel)	邮政宾馆

LHASA (LASA) 拉萨

Attractions

Ganden Monastery (Gāndān Sì)	甘丹寺
Namtso Lake (Nàmùcuò)	纳木措
Samye Monastery (Sāngyē Sì)	丧耶寺

SHIGATSE (RIKAZE) 日喀则

Attractions

Jímào Shìchăng (Shigatse Bazaar)	集贸市场
Zhāshílúnbù Sì (Tashilhunpo Monastery)	扎什伦布寺

Hotels & Restaurants

Huáiyù Mínzú Biăoyì Zhōngxīn	怀玉民族表艺中心
Lăoyŏu Lèyuán	老友乐园
Niútóu Zàngcān (Yak Head Restaurant)	牛头藏餐
Shénhú Jiŭdiàn (Hotel Manasarovar)	神湖酒店

Shigatse Hotel (Xīzang` Rì Kè Zé Fan`dian`)	西藏日喀则饭店
Songtsen Tibetan Restaurant (Xī Gé Zī Bùxing`jiē Sonḡ Zan` Cañtinḡ)	喜格孜步行街松赞餐厅
Tashi Restaurant (Zháxī Cāntīng)	扎西餐厅
Tenzin Hotel (Dàn Zēng Bīnguǎn)	旦增宾馆
Wūzī Dàjiǔdiàn (Wutse Hotel)	乌孜大酒店

GYANTSE (JIANGZI) 江孜

Attractions

Gyantse Dzong (Jiāngzī Gúbǎo)	江孜古堡
Pelkhor Choede (Báijū Sì)	白居寺

Hotels & Restaurants

Gyantse Hotel (Jiàngzì Fàndiàn)	江孜饭店
Gyantse Kitchen (Jianḡ Zī Chúfang´)	江孜厨房
Jiàn Zàng Fàndiàn	建藏饭店
Tashi's (Zháxī Cāntīng)	扎西餐厅
Zhuang Yuan Restaurant (Zhuāng Yuán Cāntīng)	庄园餐厅

SAKYA (SAJIA) 萨迦

Attractions

Sakya Monastery (Sàjiā Sì)	萨迦寺

Hotels & Restaurants

Sakya Family Hotel (Sàjiā Luwa Lǔguǎn)	萨迦鲁娃旅馆
Sakya Farmer's Taste Restaurant (Sà Jiā Nong´mińMeǐshítinḡ)	萨迦农民美食厅
Sakya Manasarovar Hotel (Shénhú Sàjiā Bīnguǎn)	神湖萨迦宾馆
Sakya Monastery Restaurant (Sàjiā Sì Cāntīng)	萨迦寺餐厅

LHATSE (LAZI) 拉孜

Hotels & Restaurants

Lhatse Kitchen (Xīzang` Lāzī Dàchúfang´)	西藏拉孜大厨房
Shanghai Hotel (Shànghǎi Biñguañ)	上海大酒店
Tibetan Farmer's Adventure Hotel (Nóngmín Yúlè Lǔguǎn)	农民娱乐旅馆

XIN DINGRI (NEW TINGRI) 新定日

Hotels & Restaurants

Snowlands Hotel (Xuěyu Fàndiàn)	雪域饭店
Qomolongma Hotel (Xīzang` Ding` Mu Zhūfenḡ Biñguañ)	西藏定目珠峰宾馆

LAO DINGRI (OLD TINGRI) 老定日

Hotels & Restaurants

Caiyuan Binguan (Caí Yuań Biñguañ)	财缘宾馆
Everest Snow Leopard Hotel (Xuěbào Fàndiàn)	
Lhasa Hotel (Lhāsà Fàndiàn)	拉萨饭店
Lhasa Restaurant (Lāsà Cañtinḡ)	拉萨餐厅
Tingri Snowland Hotel (Ding` Rì Xuě Cheng` Fan`dian`)	定日雪城饭店

ZHANGMU (DRAM) 樟木

Hotels & Restaurants

Caiyuan Binguan (Caí Yuań Biñguań)	财缘宾馆
Himalaya Restaurant (Xĭmălāyăshān Cāntīng)	喜马拉雅山餐厅
Lhasa Restaurant (Lāsà Cañtinĝ)	拉萨餐厅
Zhangmu Binguan (Zhāngmù Bīnguăn)	樟木宾馆

MOUNT KAILASH & LAKE MANASAROVAR 冈底斯山及玛旁雍错

Attractions

Darchen (Dajin) Tă'ěrqīn	塔尔钦
Gangdise (Mount Kailash) Gāngren Bózhāi Fēng	冈仁波齐峰

THE CHINESE MENU

17

One of the best things about any visit to China is the food, at least for the independent traveler. Tour groups are often treated to a relentless series of cheap, bland dishes designed to cause no complaints (aside from about their blandness), and to keep the costs down for the Chinese operator, so do everything you can to escape and order some of the local specialties we've described for you in each chapter. Here are some of them again, listed alphabetically under the cities in which they are mentioned, and with characters you can show your waiter or waitress (but check back to the review first, as some of the dishes are unique to certain restaurants). Widely available Chinese standards are together at the top, so check there if the recommended dish isn't listed under its city heading.

Outside Hong Kong, big hotels, and expat cafes, few restaurants have English menus. If, near your five-star hotel, you see restaurants with signs saying ENGLISH MENU, there's a fair chance you are going to be cheated with double prices, and you should eat elsewhere (unless it's an obvious backpacker hangout).

Menus generally open with *liang cai* (cold dishes). For hygiene reasons in mainland China, except in top-class Sino-foreign joint-venture restaurants, you are strongly advised to avoid these cold dishes, especially if you're on a short trip. The restaurant's specialties also come early in the menu, often easily spotted by their significantly higher prices, and if you dither, the waitress will recommend them, saying, "I hear this one's good." Waitresses always recommend ¥180 dishes, never ¥18 ones. Occasionally, some of these may be made from creatures you would regard as pets or zoo creatures (or best in the wild), may be made from parts you consider inedible, or may contain an odd material like swallow saliva (the main ingredient of bird's nest soup, a rather bland and uninteresting Cantonese delicacy).

Main dishes come next, various meats and fish before vegetables and *doufu* (tofu), and drinks at the end. Desserts are rare, although Guangdong (Cantonese) food has absorbed the tradition of eating something sweet at the end of the meal from across the border in Hong Kong, where all restaurants have something to offer, if only fruit.

Soup is usually eaten last, although dishes arrive in a rather haphazard order. Outside Guangdong Province, Hong Kong, and Macau, rice usually arrives toward the end, and if you want it with your meal you must ask (point at the characters for rice, below, when the first dish arrives).

There is no tipping. Service charges do not exist outside of major hotels, and there are no cover charges or taxes. If you are asked what tea you would like, then you are going to receive something above average and will be charged. Some varieties of tea may cost more than the meal itself.

Most Chinese food is not designed to be eaten solo, but if you do find yourself on your own, ask for small portions *(xiao pan)*.

xiǎo pán **small portion** 小盘

These are usually about 70% the size of a full dish and about 70% the price, but they enable you to sample the menu properly without too much waste.

POPULAR DISHES & SNACKS

Pinyin	English	Chinese
bābǎo zhōu	rice porridge with nuts and berries	八宝粥
bāozi	stuffed steamed buns	包子
bīngqílín	ice cream	冰淇淋
chǎofàn	fried rice	炒饭
chǎomiàn	fried noodles	炒面
cōng bào niúròu	quick-fried beef and onions	宫保牛肉
diǎnxin	dim sum (snacks)	点心
gānbiān sìjìdòu	sautéed string beans	干煸四季豆
gōngbào jīdīng	spicy diced chicken with cashews	宫保爆鸡丁
guōtiē	fried dumplings/pot stickers	锅贴
hóngshāo fǔzhú	braised tofu	红烧腐竹
hóngshāo huángyú	braised yellow fish	红烧黄鱼
huíguō ròu	twice-cooked pork	回锅肉
huǒguō	hot pot	火锅
jiǎozi	dumplings/Chinese ravioli	饺子
jīngjiàng ròusī	shredded pork in soy sauce	京酱肉丝
mápó dòufu	spicy tofu with chopped meat	麻婆豆腐
miàntiáo	noodles	面条
mǐfàn	rice	米饭
mù xū ròu	sliced pork with fungus (mushu pork)	木须肉
niúròu miàn	beef noodles	牛肉面
ròu chuàn	kabobs	肉串
sānxiān	"three flavors" (usually prawn, mushroom, pork)	三鲜
shuǐjiǎo	boiled dumplings	水饺
suānlà báicài	hot-and-sour cabbage	酸辣白菜
suānlà tāng	hot-and-sour soup	酸辣汤
sù shíjǐn	mixed vegetables	素什锦
tángcù lǐji	sweet-and-sour pork tenderloin	糖醋里脊
tǔdòu dùn niúròu	stewed beef and potato	土豆炖牛肉
xīhóngshì chǎo jīdàn	tomatoes with eggs	西红柿炒柿炒鸡蛋
yóutiáo	fried salty doughnut	油条
yúxiāng qiézi	eggplant in garlic sauce	鱼香茄子
yúxiāng ròusī	shredded pork in garlic sauce	鱼香肉丝
zhēngjiǎo	steamed dumplings	蒸饺
zhōu	rice porridge	粥

THE HOT POT MENU

Huǒguō	Types of Hot Pot	锅底种类
Pinyin	**English**	**Chinese**
yuānyang huǒguō	half spicy, half regular soup	鸳鸯火锅
qīngtāng huǒguō	chicken soup hot pot	清汤火锅
hóngwèi huǒguō	only spicy hot pot	红味火锅
yútóu huǒguō	fish head soup	鱼头火锅

Shūcaì lèi	Vegetables	蔬菜类
tǔdoù	potato	土豆
dòufu	tofu	豆腐
dòufu pí	tofu skin	豆腐皮
dòng dòufu	cold tofu	冻豆腐
dōngguā	Chinese melon	冬瓜
qīngsǔn	lettuce shoots	青笋
bái luób	fresh white radish	白罗卜
ǒupiàn	sliced lotus	藕片
fěnsī	glass noodles	粉丝
huángdòuyá	bean sprouts	黄豆芽
bōcaì	green spinach	菠菜
xiāngcaì	caraway seeds	香菜
dōngsǔn	bamboo shoots	冬笋
mùěr	black agaric mushroom	木耳
pínggū	flat mushrooms	平菇
jīnzhēngū	noodle mushrooms	金针菇
xiānggū	straw mushrooms	香菇
niángāo	Chinese rice cake	年糕

Roù leì	Meats	肉类
zhūròu piàn	sliced pork	猪肉片
niúròu piàn	sliced beef	牛肉片
jīròu piàn	sliced chicken	鸡肉片
féi niú	fatty hot pot beef	肥牛
féi yáng	lamb	肥羊
huǒtuǐ	ham	火腿
niúròu wán	beef balls	牛肉丸
ròu wánzi	meatballs	肉丸子
xiajiao	shrimp dumplings	虾饺
dànjiǎo	egg dumplings	蛋饺
ānchun dàn	quail's eggs	鹌鹑蛋
yā cháng	duck's intestines	鸭肠
yā xuě	duck's blood	鸭血
yú tóu	fish head	鱼头
shànyú piàn	sliced eel	鳝鱼片
níqiu	loach	泥鳅
zhū nǎo	pig brains	猪脑

Haǐxiān	**Seafood**	海鲜
Pinyin	**English**	**Chinese**
xiā	shrimp	虾
yú piàn	sliced fish	鱼片
yú wán	fish balls	鱼丸
mòyú piàn	black carp strips	墨鱼片
yóuyú piàn	fish strips	鱿鱼片

Tiáoliào	**Seasoning**	可选调料
làjiāo jiàng	chili hot sauce	辣椒酱
làyóu	chili oil	辣油
là	spicy	辣
búlà	not spicy	不辣
xiāngyóu	sesame oil	香油
huāshēng jiàng	peanut paste	花生酱
shāchá jiàng	barbecue sauce	沙茶酱
zhīma jiàng	sesame paste	芝麻酱
dà suàn	garlic	大蒜
xiāngcài	cilantro	香菜
cù	vinegar	醋
búyào cù	without	不要醋
jiàngyóu	soy sauce	酱油

Miscellaneous

xiǎo wǎn	small bowl	小碗
dà wǎn	large bowl	大碗
píjiǔ	beer	啤酒
kāfēi	coffee	咖啡
kuàngquán shuǐ	mineral water	矿泉水
cháshuǐ	tea	茶水

Useful Phrases

Wǒ shì chī sù de	I'm vegetarian	我是吃素的
Yǒu méi yǒu . . . ?	Do you have . . . ?	有没有……?
Qǐng lái yí fènr . . .	Please bring a portion of . . .	请来一份……
Qǐng lái yī bēi bīng píjiǔ!	May I have a cold beer, please?	请来一杯冰啤酒!
Qǐng bù fàng wèijīng	Don't add MSG.	请不放味精
Wǒ chībǎo le	I'm full.	我吃饱了
Jiézhàng	Bill, please.	结帐

POPULAR DISHES BY DESTINATION

ANJI 安吉

là wèi bù gū niǎo	spicy fried cuckoo	辣味布谷鸟
ròu sháo tǔ dòu	meat and potato stew	肉烧土豆

Pinyin	English	Chinese
shā bǐng	savory unleavened breads	沙饼
sheng si zhu pi	Ānjí bamboo science beer	圣氏竹啤
shān xìng rén	hickory nuts	山杏仁
hóng shǔ gān	dried sweet potatoes	红薯干
qí yì guǒ	dried sliced kiwis	奇异果
shān hé táo	walnuts	山核桃

BAMA 巴马

Pinyin	English	Chinese
huǒ mǎ yóu	cannabis oil soup	火麻油

BEIJING 北京

Pinyin	English	Chinese
dòu zhī	fermented bean purée	豆汁
gōngbào jīdīng	diced chicken with peanuts and hot peppers	宫保鸡丁
huángjiǔ	"yellow" rice wine	黄酒
má dòufu	mashed soy bean	麻豆腐
mápó dòufu	spicy tofu with chopped meat	麻婆豆腐
mìzhì lúyú	whole fish deep fried and broiled, with onions and sauce	蜜汁鲈鱼
suāncài tǔdòu	vinegared potato slices	酸菜土豆
zhá xiāngjiāo	deep fried banana	炸香蕉
zhájiàng miàn	wheat noodles with black bean mince	炸酱面
guòqiáo mǐxiàn	crossing-the-bridge noodles	过桥米线
kǎo yángròu	roast mutton	烤羊肉
lǎogānmā shāo jī	spicy diced chicken with bamboo and ginger	老干妈烧鸡
málà lóngxiā	spicy crayfish	麻辣龙虾
qiáomiàn māo ěrduo	"cat's ear" buckwheat pasta with chopped meat	荞面猫耳朵
yì bǎ zhuā	fried wheat cakes	一把抓
yóutiáo niúròu	sliced beef with fried dough in savory sauce	油条牛肉
zhāngchá yā	crispy smoked duck with plum sauce	樟茶鸭

CHANGCHUN 长春

Pinyin	English	Chinese
dà páigu	big ribs	大排
jiājīdùnzhēnmó	tender pieces of chicken stewed with mushrooms in a dark savory sauce	家鸡炖榛蘑
kou shui ji	chicken with special sauce	口水鸡

CHANGSHA 长沙

Pinyin	English	Chinese
hóng zǎozi	red dates	红枣子
língjiǎo	water chestnuts	菱角
mǐtāng sīguā	rice soup with silk gourd	米面汤丝瓜
qiàng qíncài xiàguǒ	baby celery and pearl onions sautéed with macadamia nuts	炝芹菜夏果
qīngjiāo qiézi	eggplant sautéed with green pepper	青椒茄子

CHENGDE 承德

Pinyin	English	Chinese
cōng shāo yězhū ròu	wild boar cooked with onions	葱烧野猪肉
lù ròu chǎo zhēnmó	venison stir-fried with hazel mushrooms	鹿肉炒榛蘑

Pinyin	English	Chinese
Qiánlóng shuǐjiǎo	jiǎozi dumplings	乾隆水饺
lúròu dàcōng shǔijiǎo	dumplings with donkey meat and onions	驴肉大葱水饺
què cháo shān jī piàn	"Sparrow's nest" pheasant slices	雀巢山鸡片
zhēn mó shānjī dīng	nuggets of pheasant with local mushrooms	榛磨山鸡丁

CHENGDU 成都

Pinyin	English	Chinese
báitāng lǔ	plain broth	白汤卤
Càigēn Xiāng páigu	Càigēn Xiāng spareribs	菜鸽鲜排骨
cuìpí shàngsù	crispy vegetarian duck	脆皮上蔬
dòufu jìyú	tofu and golden carp	豆腐鲫鱼
huíguō hòupícài	twice-cooked thick-skinned greens	回锅厚皮菜
Jiāróng suāncài kǎo bǐng	Jiāróng bread stuffed with cabbage and barbecued pork	荚绒酸菜烤饼
máoniú ròubāo	yak meat bāozi	牦牛肉包
pào cài	pickled vegetables	泡菜
pàocài jiāyú	fish with pickled vegetables	泡菜加鱼
pàojiāo mòyúzǎi	pickled pepper with baby squid	泡椒墨鱼仔
suān luóbo chǎo máoniúròu	pickled cabbage with fried yak meat	酸萝卜炒卜炒牦牛肉
yěcài bā	steamed rice bread with wild vegetable wrapped in corn husks	野菜粑
yùer shāo jiǎyú	green turtle stewed with taro	芋艿烧甲鱼

CHONGQING 重庆

Pinyin	English	Chinese
guàiwèi yāzi	special flavored duck	怪味鸭子
guōbā ròupiàn	pork with bamboo shoots over crispy rice	锅巴肉片
qīngjiāo bào zǐjī	baby chicken quick-fried with green pepper	青椒包子鸡
tiěbǎn shāo zhī yínxuěyú	silver snow fish cooked on an iron plate	铁板烧汁银雪鱼
yùmǐ bǐng	corn cakes	玉米饼

DALI 大理

Pinyin	English	Chinese
ěr kuài	stuffed rice dough	饵块
mùguā jī	fried chicken Bái-style	木瓜鸡
rǔshàn	fried goat cheese	乳扇
shāguō yú	stewed fish casserole	砂锅鱼
shuǐzhǔ ròupiàn	pork and vegetable in spicy broth	水煮肉片

DALIAN 大连

Pinyin	English	Chinese
shíguō bànfàn	stone pot rice	石锅拌饭
dòufu tang	spicy tofu soup	豆腐汤
dàgǔtou	big ribs	大骨头
qīngtāngdàgǔbàng	big bone soup	清汤大骨棒
yánchénghuánghuāyú	salt-dried yellow fish	蒸咸黄花鱼
bōcàibànmáoxiǎn	spinach with mussels	菠菜拌毛蚬
nóngtāng zhūdǔwáwacài	pig stomach cabbage soup	浓汤猪肚娃娃菜
bāyúshuǐjiǎo	fish dumplings	巴鱼水饺

DANDONG 丹东

Pinyin	English	Chinese
lǎncài hǔpíjiāo	pork-stuffed bell peppers in black bean sauce	榄菜糊皮椒
huǒguō	hot pot	火锅
lěngmiàn	cold noodles	冷面
shíguō bànfàn	stone pot rice	石锅拌饭
shēngbàn niúròu	raw beef	生拌牛肉
xiānglà gǒuròu	spicy dog meat	香辣狗肉

DATONG 大同

Pinyin	English	Chinese
chǎo lāmiàn	fried wheat noodles	炒拉面
shāo qiézi	stewed eggplant	烧茄子
sōng yùmǐ	corn cooked with pine nuts	松玉米

DUNHUANG 敦煌

Pinyin	English	Chinese
lǘròu huángmiàn	donkey meat with yellow noodles	驴肉黄面
sāngshèn jiǔ	mulberry wine	桑椹酒
xìngpíshuǐ	dried apricot juice	杏皮水
yángpái	lamb chops	羊排

GOLMUD (GE'RRMU) 格尔木

Pinyin	English	Chinese
huángmèn yángròu	lamb stew	黄焖羊肉
xiānggū càixīn	mushrooms and Chinese greens	香菇菜心
xiāngsū jī	crispy chicken	香酥鸡

GUANGZHOU 广州

Pinyin	English	Chinese
báizzhuó héxiā	Cantonese-style shrimp	白灼河虾
huādiāo zhù jī	chicken cooked in yellow wine	花雕煮鸡
liǔlián xuěgāo	durian ice cream	榴莲雪糕
jiǔhuáng ròusī	sliced pork with yellow chives	韭黄肉丝
mǎtí xiè	horseshoe crab	马碲蟹
qīngzhēng huāxiè	steamed crab	清蒸花蟹
tángcù sūròu	sweet-and-sour pork	糖醋酥肉
yóu zhá chòu dòufu	fried stinky tofu	油炸臭豆腐
wǔ shé bāo lǎo jī	boiled five snakes and old chicken in soup	五蛇煲老鸡
xiān xiā jī dàn cháng	egg and prawns steamed pancake	鲜虾鸡蛋肠
yoú tiáo	fried bread sticks	油条
zhoū	congee	粥

GUILIN 桂林

Pinyin	English	Chinese
dāndān miàn	noodles in spicy peanut sauce	担担面
Guìlín mǐfěn	Guìlín rice noodles	桂林米粉
mǎròu	horse meat	马肉
shāncūn làròu zhēng yúpiàn	steamed taro with smoked meat	山村腊肉蒸肉鱼片
shāncūn tǔjī	free-range chicken	山村土鸡
shuǐzhǔ niúròu	beef and vegetables in a chili sauce	水煮牛肉
tángcù cuìpí yú	crispy sweet-and-sour fish	糖醋脆皮鱼
záliáng zhútǒng fàn	bamboo cooked rice	杂粮竹桶饭

HANGZHOU 杭州

Pinyin	English	Chinese
Dōngpō ròu	a soy sauce pork dish named after the poet	东坡肉
Hángzhōu jiàohuà jī	"beggar' s chicken"—baked in clay	杭州叫花鸡
lóngjǐng xiārén	shelled shrimp sprinkled with lóngjǐng tea	井井虾仁

HARBIN 哈尔滨

dàlièbā	Russian-style crusty bread	打猎粑
dànhuáng jūnánguā	fried crepes with vegetables and egg	蛋黄超卷南瓜
hóngcháng	Russian-style red sausage	红肠
huǒguō	hot pot	火锅
jiācháng tǔdòuní	garlic mashed potatoes	家常豆泥
jiànggǔ	pork ribs	酱骨
pá yángròu tiáo	thinly sliced lamb in soy-garlic sauce	扒羊肉条
sānxiān shuǐjiǎo	three-flavor dumplings/ravioli	三鲜水饺
sōngrén y ù mǐ shuǐjiǎo	boiled corn and pine-nut dumplings	松仁玉米水饺
yīpǐn jūntāng	four-mushroom soup	一品菌汤

HEFEI 合肥

dāndān miàn	spicy noodles with meat sauce	担担面
lóngxiā yī tiáo lù	lobster street	龙虾一条路
lóngxiā	Chinese-style crayfish	龙虾

HOHHOT (HUHEHAOTE) 呼和浩特

chǎo fěn	millet granules	炒粉
chǎo miàn	fried noodles	炒面
dùndun	husked-wheat pancakes	钝钝
guǒtiáo	crisp fried dough	锅条
guōzǎi	stew	锅杂
guōzǎi suāncài yáng zásu ì	pickled vegetables and sheep organ stew	锅杂酸菜羊
jiācháng dòufu	home-style tofu	家常豆腐
lā miàn	pulled noodles	拉面
liángfěn	cold translucent noodles with sauce	凉粉
nǎichá	milk tea	奶茶
nǎi pízi	milk skin	奶皮子
shénxiān báicài tāng	Immortals' cabbage soup	神仙白菜汤
shǒubā ròu	mutton eaten with hands	手扒肉
sù hézi	fried vegetable pie	素盒子
suāncài ròu chǎo fěn	wheat noodles with shredded pork	酸菜肉炒粉
tèsè kǎo rǔniú	barbecued marinated veal	特色烤乳牛
wō bǐng	corn cakes	窝饼
wōwo	husked wheat pasta in steamer	窝窝

HUANG SHAN 黄山

huángshān èrdōng	stir-fried winter mushrooms and bamboo shoots	黄山二冬

JIAYU GUAN 嘉峪关

Pinyin	English	Chinese
fùguì niúròu	roast beef on sesame toast	富贵牛肉
Jiāngnán qiánjiāng ròu	lightly battered chicken in sweet-and-sour sauce	江南钱江肉
kǎo yángpái	grilled rack of lamb	烤羊排
xīqīng bǎihé chǎo xiān yóu	squid with celery, field mushroom, and lotus	西芹百合炒鲜鱿
yángpái	lamb chops	羊排
yángròu chuàn	lamb skewers	羊肉串

JILIN 吉林

Pinyin	English	Chinese
liū ròuduàn	deep-fried pork strips with green pepper	熘肉段
shǒusī yángròu	hand-torn mutton with soy-garlic sauce	手撕羊肉
dà bàn shuǐ lāpí	cold mung-bean flour noodles with cilantro, peanuts, pork, and cucumbers with a spicy sesame sauce	大拌水拉皮
zhēn bù tóng tánròu	pieces of fatty pork braised in a homemade beer-based sauce	真不同坛肉

JI'NAN 济南

Pinyin	English	Chinese
mǎ pópo mèn shuāngsǔn	steamed bamboo and asparagus	马婆婆焖双笋
shāguō	casserole	砂锅
zhuābǐng	flaky fried pastry	抓饼
yóuxuán	bun with spring onions	油旋

JINGDE ZHEN 景德镇

Pinyin	English	Chinese
sāngná niúròu	"sauna" beef	桑拿牛肉
jǐnggāng lǎobiǎo sǔn	peppery bamboo shoots with dried tofu	井岗老表笋

KAIFENG 开封

Pinyin	English	Chinese
huāshēng gāo	peanut cake	花生糕
wǔxiāng shāobǐng	five-spice roasted bread	五香烧饼
xiǎolóng bāo	dumplings filled with pork and broth	小笼包
xìngrén chá	almond tea	杏仁茶
yángròu chuàn	spicy lamb kabob	羊肉串
zhīma duōwèi tāng	sesame soup	芝麻多味汤

KASHGAR (KASHI) 喀什

Pinyin	English	Chinese
bāchǔ mógu	field mushrooms steamed with bok choy, ginger, and garlic	巴楚蘑菇
bàn sān sī	pepper, onion, carrot, and cucumber noodle salad	拌三丝
chǎokǎo ròu	beef stir-fry	炒烤肉
gānbiān tóngzǐjī	dry-fried spring chicken	干煸童子鸡
lāmiàn	"pulled" noodles	拉面
lǔ gēzi	whole pigeon soup	卤鸽子
wánzimiàn	beef ball noodles	丸子面
zhuā fàn	pilaf	抓饭

KUNMING 昆明

Pinyin	English	Chinese
cuìpí rúyì yú	crispy vegetarian fish in a sweet-and-sour sauce	脆皮如意鱼
cuìpí yā	crispy fried vegetarian duck	脆皮鸭
guòqiáo mǐxiàn	crossing-the-bridge noodles	过桥米线
hóngshāo niúròu miàn	spicy beef noodles	红烧牛肉面
hóngshāo shīziqiú	vegetarian mushroom ball	红烧狮子头
hùnhé chǎo	fried mixed vegetables	混合炒
huǒshāo gānbā	barbecued dried beef	火烧干巴
jīnbì yān huóxiā	spicy prawn sashimi	金碧眼活虾
qìguō jī	steamed chicken	汽锅鸡
shāo ya ī	baked duck	烧鸭
shànyú miàn	noodles with eel	鳝鱼面
sūpí guànguàn jī	chicken soup with puff pastry	酥皮罐罐鸡
yēzi qìguō jī	coconut chicken	椰子气锅鸡
yìndù gāli jī miàn	curry chicken noodles	印度咖喱鸡面
zhēng lǎo nánguā	steamed pumpkin	蒸老南瓜
zhútǒng ròu	pork cooked in bamboo	竹桶肉
jiǔ lín mì zhì tián má fěn kǎo yú	barbecued fish	酒淋米纸甜麻粉烤鱼
yào shàn chǎo sān guǒ	wok fired walnuts, beans, and ginkgoes	药膳炒三果
xiān xiā qīng guā luò	shrimp and cucumber pancake	鲜虾青瓜烙
tie ban yang yu ni	potato and ham flatcake	铁板洋芋泥

KUQA (KUCHE) 库车

Pinyin	English	Chinese
dàpán jī	big-plate chicken	大盘鸡
gānzhá niúròu tiáo	spicy beef strips	干炸牛肉条
lǎohǔ cài	spicy salad	老虎菜
tángbàn huángguā	sweet cucumber	糖拌黄瓜

LANZHOU 兰州

Pinyin	English	Chinese
báobǐng yángròu	deep-fried lamb and green pepper pancake	薄饼羊肉
kǎo yángtuǐ	roast leg of lamb with walnuts	烤羊腿
měnggǔ yángpái	Mongolian lamb	蒙古羊排
niúròu miàn	beef noodles	牛肉面
sùshí jīnjú bǎihé	sweet vegetarian lilies	素食金橘百合
shǒuzhuā ròu	meat to be eaten by hand	手抓肉

LEYE 乐业

Pinyin	English	Chinese
luó sī fěng	snail noodles	螺丝粉
shū cài dòu fǔ pái gǔ tāng	spare ribs and tofu soup	蔬菜豆腐排骨汤
dāng dì yě cài	wild local vegetables	当地野菜

LHASA (LASA) 拉萨

Pinyin	English	Chinese
bāozi	steamed buns with pork	包子
cháng xiāngsī	sliced soy-pork sausages	长相思

Pinyin	English	Chinese
gānbiān sùcháng	soy-pork slices with green pepper	干煸素肠
gōngbào jīdīng	kung pao chicken	宫爆鸡丁
ròusī miàntiáo	noodles with pork	肉丝面条
qīngchǎo máodòu	beans with soy beef	清炒毛豆
sōngrén yùmǐ	pine nuts, carrots, and sweet corn	松仁玉米

LHATSE (LAZI) 拉孜

Zāchá fěnsī bāo	vermicelli clay pot	咂茶粉丝煲
niúròu chǎofàn	beef-fried rice	牛肉炒饭
shǐyóu jī	salty chicken	豉油鸡

LI JIANG 丽江

fēngwèi cān	special Nàxī meal	风味菜
guòqiáo mǐxiàn	crossing-the-bridge noodles	过桥米线
jīdòu chǎo mǐfàn	fried rice with soy bean	鸡豆炒米饭
kǎoyú	barbecue fish	烤鱼
Lì Jiāng bābā	Lìjiāng baked pastry	丽江粑粑
Lì Jiāng dàguōcài	vegetables in broth	丽江大锅菜
Nàxī sāndiéshuǐ	Nàxī 36-dish special	纳西三叠水
qìguō jī	stewed chicken	汽锅鸡
shùwā	frog skin fungus	树蛙
zhá rǔbǐng	fried goat cheese	炸乳饼

LINHAI 临海

huáng ní luó	snails	黄泥螺
zuì xiè	crab claws	醉蟹
wǔ gǔ fēng dēng	farmer's plate	五谷丰登
lǎo yā zhǔ shuǐ jiǎo	jiaozi soup with duck bamboo and ginseng	老鸭煮水饺
liáng chá	sweet tea	凉茶

LUOYANG 洛阳

Luòyáng Shuǐxí	Luòyáng water banquet	洛阳水席
mìzhī tǔdòu	sweet-potato fries in syrup	蜜汁土豆
tángcù lǐji	sweet-and-sour fish	糖醋里脊
zhájiàngmiàn	noodles with bean sauce	炸酱面
zhēnyāncài	ham, radish, mushroom, and egg soup	珍腌菜

MANZHOULI 满洲里

qīngshuǐ guōdǐ	vegetarian hot pot	清水锅底
sānxiān fàn	three-flavor rice	三鲜饭
shuàn yángròu	mutton hot pot	涮羊肉
sūbā tāng	Russian-style creamy tomato soup	苏巴汤

NANJING 南京

pánsī yú	sweet-and-sour deep-fried fish tail filets	盘丝鱼
shuǐjīng xiārén	sautéed shrimp	水晶虾仁
tiānmùhú yútóu	white fish head soup	天目湖鱼头
yāxuě fěnsī	duck-blood vermicelli	鸭血粉丝

PINGYAO 平遥

Pinyin	English	Chinese
jiàohuà jī	beggar's chicken	叫花鸡
lǎolao yóumiàn	husked oat pasta	姥姥油面
māo ěrduo	cats' ears pasta	猫耳朵
tǔdòu shāo niúròu	corned beef with potatoes	土豆烧牛肉
xiāngsū jī	crispy aromatic chicken	香酥鸡
yóuzhá gāo	crispy puff with date and red bean paste	油炸糕

QINGDAO 青岛

Pinyin	English	Chinese
gōngzhǔ yú	princess fish cooked in oil and steamed	公主鱼
jīngjiàng ròusī	shredded pork Peking-style	京酱肉丝
shāo èrdōng	sautéed mushrooms with garden asparagus	烧二冬
sōngshǔ guìyú	deep-fried sweet-and-sour fish	松鼠桂鱼
suànxiāng gǔ	fried pork chop with garlic	蒜香排骨
tiěbǎn hélí kǎo dàn	iron plate clams with scrambled eggs	铁板河蜊烤蛋
xiāng sū jī	fragrant chicken	香酥鸡
yóubā gǔfǎ zhēng qiézi	steamed eggplant	油粑古法蒸茄子
yóubào hǎiluó	fried sea snails	油爆海螺

QUANZHOU 泉州

Pinyin	English	Chinese
niúpái	beefsteak	牛排
sùshí	vegetarian food	素食
Xiàmén hǎilì jiān	Xiàmén-style baby oysters	厦门海蛎煎
rì shì sù cì shēn	vegetarian sushi	日式素刺身
baǐ huā zhà liàng sù xi qiǎn	deep-fried crab claws with minced vegetarian "squid"	百花炸嚷素蟹钳
guì huā sù wú paí	vegetarian "spareribs" with sweet osmanthus sauce	桂花素五排
gān sī liǔ liǎn sū	durian pastries	干丝榴莲酥

QUFU 曲阜

Pinyin	English	Chinese
dàizi shàngcháo	stewed pork, chicken, chestnuts, and ginseng	带子上朝
shīlǐ yínxìng	sweet ginkgo	诗意银杏
shénxiān yāzi	Immortals duck	神仙鸭子
yángguān sāndié	chicken, vegetables, and egg folded together	阳关三碟

SAKYA 萨迦

Pinyin	English	Chinese
gōngbào jīdīng	spicy chicken with cashews	宫爆鸡丁
māpó dòufu	spicy tofu with chopped meat	麻婆豆腐
yúxiāng qiézi	eggplant in garlic sauce	鱼香茄子

SHANGHAI 上海

Pinyin	English	Chinese
báopí yángròu juǎn	minced lamb wrapped in pancakes	薄皮羊肉卷
gānbiān tǔdòu bā	fried potato pancake	干煸土豆粑
huǒyán niúròu	beef with red and green peppers	火焰牛肉
kǎo quányáng	roast lamb	烤全羊

Pinyin	English	Chinese
kǎo yángròu	barbecued lamb skewers	烤羊肉
lǎohǔ cài	Xīnjiāng salad	老虎菜
shīzi tóu	lion's head meatballs	狮子头
shuǐjīng xiārén	stir-fried shrimp	水晶虾仁
suān jiāngdòu làròu	sour long beans with chilies and bacon	酸豇豆辣肉
cōngyóu bǐng	scallion pancakes	葱油饼
dāndān miàn	noodles in spicy peanut sauce	担担面
dàzhá xiè	hairy crab	大闸蟹
duòjiāo yútóu	fish head steamed with red chili	剁椒鱼头
gānguōjī guōzi	chicken in chili pot	干锅鸡锅子
hóngshāo ròu	braised pork	红烧肉
hóngshāo huángyú	braised yellow croaker	红烧黄鱼
hóngshāo jiāo bái	soy-braised wild rice stems	红烧茭白
huíguō ròu	twice-cooked pork	回锅肉
huíguōròu jiābǐng	twice-cooked lamb wrapped in pancakes	回火锅肉夹饼
làzi jīdīng	spicy chicken nuggets	辣子鸡丁
méigān cài shāo ròu	braised pork with preserved mustard greens	梅干菜烧肉
mízhī huǒfǎng	pork and taro in candied sauce	蜜汁火舫
Nánxiáng xiǎolóng bāo	Nánxiáng crabmeat and pork dumplings	南翔小笼包
pídàn dòufu	tofu with "thousand year" eggs	皮蛋豆腐
qīngzhēng dòuní	creamy mashed beans	青蒸豆泥
qícài dōngsǔn	winter shoots with local greens	荠菜冬笋
sānsī méimao sū	pork, bamboo, and mushroom-stuffed crisp	三丝眉毛酥
shuǐzhǔ yú	fish slices and vegetables in spicy broth	水煮鱼
sōngshǔ lúyú	sweet-and-sour fried perch	松鼠鲈鱼
suān dòujiǎo ròuní	diced sour beans with minced pork	酸豆肉泥
sùjī	vegetarian "chicken"	素鸡
sùyā	vegetarian "duck"	素鸭
xiǎolóng bāo	pork-stuffed steamed bread dumplings	小笼包
zīrán páigǔ	cumin ribs	孜然排骨

SHENYANG 沈阳

Pinyin	English	Chinese
biānxiàn sānxiān jiǎozi	boiled shrimp, egg, and Chinese chive dumplings	煸馅三鲜饺子
chuántǒng shāomài	steamed dumplings with beef and ginger	传统烧卖
jiǎozi	dumplings/Chinese ravioli	饺子
shāomài	steamed open-top dumplings	烧卖
yùcuì shāomài	jade green steamed open-top dumplings	玉翠烧卖
zhūròu báicài jiǎozi	boiled pork-and-cabbage dumplings	猪肉白菜饺子

SHIGATSE (RIKAZE) 日喀则

Pinyin	English	Chinese
chǎo buōcài	stir-fried spinach	炒菠菜
chǎo miànpiàn	stir-fried noodle pieces	炒面片
gāli tǔdòu	curry potatoes	咖喱土豆
tāng jiǎo	dumplings/ravioli in soup	汤饺
máoniú tóu	yak's head	牦牛头
qīngjiāo niúròu	green peppers and beef	青椒牛肉

Pinyin	English	Chinese
rénshēnguǒ	fried ginseng	人参果
tiěbǎn niúròu	iron plate beef	铁板牛肉
tǔdòu jiǎozi	potato dumplings/ravioli	土豆饺子

SUZHOU 苏州

Pinyin	English	Chinese
gūsū lǔyā	marinated duck	姑苏卤鸭
huángmèn hémàn	braised river eel	黄焖海鳗
sōngshǔ guìyú	sweet-and-sour deep-fried fish	松鼠桂鱼
zuìjī	drunken chicken	醉鸡

TAIYUAN 太原

Pinyin	English	Chinese
cù	vinegar	醋太原
cuōjiāner	twisted points pasta	搓尖儿
guòyóuròu	pork "passed through oil"	过油肉
liángfěn	potato starch noodle	凉粉
māo ěrduō	cat's ears pasta	猫耳朵
tóunǎo	mutton soup	头脑
xiǎobǐng	flat bread	小削饼

TIANSHUI 天水

Pinyin	English	Chinese
chǎo miàn	stir-fried noodles	炒面
niúròu miàn	beef noodles	牛肉面
shāguō jīkuài	chicken clay pot	砂锅鸡块

TONGLI 里

Pinyin	English	Chinese
mín bǐng	sweet glutinous rice pastry	闵饼
xiǎo xūnyú	smoked fish	小硝熏鱼
zhuàngyuán tí	braised pigs' trotters	状元蹄

TONGREN 同仁

Pinyin	English	Chinese
chǎo miànpiàn	stir-fried noodle pieces with squash, beef, and onions	炒面片
chǎo yángròu	stir-fried mutton	炒羊肉
qīngtāng miànpiàn	noodle pieces in soup	清汤面片
rénshēnguǒ mǐfàn	ginseng rice	人参果米饭

TUNXI 屯溪

Pinyin	English	Chinese
chòu dòufu	stinky tofu	臭豆腐
huángshān sùwèi yuán	stir-fried mountain vegetables, tofu, and herbs	黄山素味园
wǔcǎi shànsī	stir-fried eel with peppers, mushrooms, and bamboo shoots	五彩鳝丝
Yángzhōu chǎofàn	Yángzhōu fried rice	扬州炒饭

TURPAN (TULUFAN) 吐鲁番

Pinyin	English	Chinese
kǎo bāozi	samosa	烤包子
sāngshèn jiǔ	mulberry wine	桑椹酒

ÜRÜMQI (WULUMUQI) 乌鲁木齐

Pinyin	English	Chinese
bàobīng	ice frosty	爆冰
hóngshāo ròu	braised pork	红烧肉

WENZHOU 温州

Pinyin	English	Chinese
wāròu mángguǒ chǎofàn	stir-fried rice with mango and frogs' legs	蛙肉芒果 炒饭
niúpái mùguā zhī	steak set with papaya sauce	牛排木瓜汁
qíyì guǒ jiā níngméngzhī	kiwi and lemon juice	奇异果加柠檬汁
yángtiáozhī	star fruit juice	杨桃汁
mùguāzhī	papaya fruit juice	木瓜汁

WUHAN 武汉

Pinyin	English	Chinese
dànbái shāo gǔpái	pork ribs braised in egg white	蛋白烧骨排
dòufu pí	tofu skin	豆腐皮
Fáng Xiàn huāgū	flowering mushrooms from Fáng County	房县花菇
miànwō	rice bread	面窝
qiān biān méi	deep-fried fermented tofu	千煎霉豆腐
quánjiāfú	mushrooms sautéed with dates	全家福
shuǐguǒ xiāngfàn	sticky rice with watermelon, pineapple, and melon	水锅香饭
wǔxiāng niúròu	faux beef with blended spices	五香牛肉
yóumàicài	sautéed Chinese lettuce stalk	油麦菜
Reganmian	Wuhan-style dry noodles	热干面
Baozi	steamed buns	包子
Jing Wu Ren Jia	duck neck	精武人家鸭脖子

WUTAI SHAN 五台山

Pinyin	English	Chinese
báiguǒ nánguā bāo	ginkgo nut with pumpkin	白果南瓜煲
huākāi xiànfó	mock ham with braised tofu	花开献佛
jǐnshàng tiānhuā	yuxiang shredded "pork"	锦上天花
lǎncài ròumò sìjìdòu	olive leaf fried with string beans	榄菜肉末四季豆
luóhànzhāi	mixed vegetables fried with bean-starch noodles	罗汉斋
sùpái	deep-fried "meat" in brown sauce	素排
tiěbǎn hēijiāo níupái	grilled "steak" with black pepper sauce	铁板黑椒牛排
xǐqì yángyáng	"chicken" cubes fried with dried red peppers	喜气洋洋

WUXI 无锡

Pinyin	English	Chinese
miànjīn	fried balls of flour shredded and stir-fried with meat and vegetables	面筋
páigǔ	Chinese-style baby back ribs	排骨
Tàihú yínyú	deep-fried Lake Tài fish	太湖银鱼
Wúxī xiǎolóng	Wúxī dumplings	无锡小笼
xièfěn xiǎolóng	crabmeat and pork dumplings	蟹粉小笼
xiānròu húntun	pork wontons	虾肉馄饨

WULING YUAN/ZHANG JIA JIE 张家界

Pinyin	English	Chinese
hetao ruo	pork	核桃肉
ganbian changzi	sausage	干煸肠子

WUYI SHAN 武夷山

yóuzhá	pan-fried street snacks	油炸
nánguā bǐng	pumpkin cake	南瓜饼
qié zhī zhá xiāngjiāo	fried banana with tomato sauce	茄汁炸香蕉
yě qīng cài chǎo xiǎo mù ěr	wild celery fried with baby tree ears	野青菜炒小木耳
mēn huáng jiǎo yú	baked yellow horn fish	闷黄角鱼
shān yào gēng	yam consommé	山药羹

XIAMEN 厦门

san wen zhi shi juan	golden dragon roll (salmon roll with cheese)	三文芝士卷
màn yú zhà xiā juǎn	green dragon roll (eel, cucumber, and avocado)	鳗鱼炸虾卷
zhà xue gao	deep-fried ice cream	炸雪糕
biánshí	Xiamen-style mini wonton soup	扁食
bàn miàn	Xiamen-style noodles with peanut sauce	拌面
dāngguī miànjīn tāng	Chinese angelica and gluten soup	当归面筋汤
gāli xiān yóu	curried squid	咖喱鲜鱿
hǎilì jiān	pan-fried oysters	海哈蛎煎
huáng zé hé	peanut soup	黄则和
luóhàn zhāi	stew of pine nuts, cabbage, cucumber, corn, mushrooms, and fresh cilantro	罗汉斋
lúsǔn dòufu tāng	asparagus and tofu soup	芦笋豆腐汤
wāng jì xiànbǐng	small pastries stuffed with a variety of sweet fillings	王记馅饼
xiāng ní cáng zhēn	vegetables mashed into a paste	香泥藏珍

XI'AN 西安

bābǎo tián xīfàn	eight-treasure sweet rice porridge	八宝甜稀饭
bìlǜ zá shuāng gū	bok choy with mushrooms	碧绿杂双菇
fěnzhēng yángròu	lamb between two steamed buns 粉蒸羊肉	
guàntāng bāozi	specialty buns	灌汤包子
hóngshāo niúwěi	stewed oxtail	红烧牛尾
ròu jiā mó	shredded pork in a bun	肉夹馍
shǎn nán xiāngyù bǐng	sweet-potato pancake	陕南香芋饼
suāntāng shuǐjiǎo	lamb dumplings	酸汤水饺
wōtóu	corn bun	窝头
xiǎochī	small snacks	小吃
yángròu pàomó	lamb soup with torn pieces of bun	羊肉泡馍
yōuzhì	local bun	优质

XINING 西宁

Pinyin	English	Chinese
chǎo miànpiàn	noodles stir-fried with green squash, beef, and peppers	炒面片
kǎo dàbǐng	roasted scones	烤大饼
liángpí	cold noodles with chili tofu	凉皮
yángròuchuàn	lamb skewers	羊肉串

YAN'AN 延安

Pinyin	English	Chinese
chǎomiàn hélè	pressed buckwheat noodles with vinaigrette dressing	炒面何勒
dāoxiāo miàn	dāoxiāo noodles	刀削面
huángmó	sweet steamed millet cake	黄馍
kǔcài tǔdòu	mashed potatoes with wild vegetables	苦菜土豆
mǐjiǔ	millet wine	米酒
niúròu liángfěn	bean-starched noodles fried with beef	牛肉凉粉
yángròu pàomó	mutton soup	羊肉泡馍
yóu mómo	fried doughnut made of millet	油馍馍
you gao	pan-fried sticky rice cake	油糕

YANBIAN 延边

Pinyin	English	Chinese
lěngmiàn	cold noodles in vinegar broth	冷面

YANDANGSHAN 雁荡山

Pinyin	English	Chinese
shē zú wū mǐ fàn	sweet sticky black rice in a basket	畲族乌米饭
suān jiǎo	bats wing nuts	酸角
píng gū chǎo huáng huā cài	toadstools and chrysanthemum flowers	平菇炒黄花菜
shān sháo chaǒ ròu shī	mountain peonies fried with meat	山芍炒肉丝
máofēng cha	máofēng tea	毛峰茶

YANGSHUO 阳朔

Pinyin	English	Chinese
bàochǎo tiánluó	Li River snails stuffed with pork	爆炒田螺
dàocáo zá ròu	Yao-style braised pork wrapped in rice stalks	稻草杂肉
hóngshǔ téng	sweet-potato shoots	红薯藤
luósī fěn	spicy snail noodles	螺丝粉
píjiǔ yú	fish cooked in beer and spices	啤酒鱼
shí sū xìng rén quǎn	almond roll	时蔬杏仁卷
lì yú dàn huáng wán	taro and egg yolk balls	荔芋蛋黄丸
táng chù qíe guā	sweet-and-sour eggplant	糖醋茄瓜

YANGZHOU 扬州

Pinyin	English	Chinese
bāozi	steamed buns	包子
jiǎozi	dumplings/Chinese ravioli	饺子

YANJI 延吉

Pinyin	English	Chinese
lěngmiàn	cold noodles in vinegar broth	冷面
shíguō bànfàn	stone pot rice	石锅拌饭
dòufu tang	spicy tofu soup	豆腐汤

YINCHUAN 银川

Pinyin	English	Chinese
guàntāng bāozi	unleavened bāozi	灌汤包子
hézi	savory pies	盒子
liángfěn	potato starch noodle	凉粉
suānlà tǔdòu sī	shredded potatoes	酸辣土豆丝
bābǎozhōu	eight treasures soup	八宝粥

YINING 伊宁

Pinyin	English	Chinese
dàpán jī	whole chicken with vegetables and noodles	大盘鸡
géwǎsī	kvass liquor	格瓦斯
náng bāo ròu	lamb and vegetable stew on a wheat pancake	馕包肉
nàrén	roast horse meat noodle salad	纳仁
tǔdòu sī	fried potato strips	土豆丝
yībǎzhuā	samosa with three fingerprints in each bun	一把抓
yóu tǎzi	steamed dumplings	油塔子
zhīma ròunáng	sesame bread and lamb casserole	芝麻肉馕

ZHENGZHOU 郑州

Pinyin	English	Chinese
bāsù shíjǐn	mushrooms, seasonal greens, and bamboo shoots	八素什锦
guōtiē dòufu	tofu casserole	锅贴豆腐
tèyōu huìmiàn	house specialty noodles	特优烩面
xiāngmá shāobǐng jiā niúròu	beef sandwiched between steamed buns	香麻烧饼夹牛肉

Index

C

D

H

I

J

K

L

M

N

O

P

Q

R

T

Y

Z